Sixth Edition

CRIMINAL PROCEDURE

CONSTITUTION AND SOCIETY

Marvin Zalman

Wayne State University

Prentice Hall

Boston   Columbus   Indianapolis   New York   San Francisco   Upper Saddle River
Amsterdam   Cape Town   Dubai   London   Madrid   Milan   Munich   Paris   Montreal
Toronto   Delhi   Mexico City   Sao Paulo   Sydney   Hong Kong   Seoul   Singapore   Taipei   Tokyo

Editor in Chief: Vernon Anthony
Acquisitions Editor: Eric Krassow
Editorial Assistant: Lynda Cramer
Director of Marketing: David Gesell
Marketing Manager: Adam Kloza
Senior Marketing Coordinator: Alicia Wozniak
Marketing Assistant: Les Roberts
Senior Managing Editor: JoEllen Gohr
Project Manager: Jessica H. Sykes
Senior Operations Supervisor: Pat Tonneman
Operations Specialist: Deidra Skahill

Art Director: Jayne Conte
Cover Art: Mollica Design
Media Director: Michelle Churma
Lead Media Project Manager: Karen Bretz
Full-Service Project Management: Sowmyaa Narayani/
  Madhavi Prakashkumar
Composition: S4 Carlisle Publishing Services
Printer/Binder: Edwards Brothers
Cover Printer: Lehigh/Phoenix Color/Hagerstown
Text Font: 10/12 Times

Library of Congress Cataloging-in-Publication Data
Zalman, Marvin.
  Criminal procedure : constitution and society / Marvin Zalman.—6th ed.
    p. cm.
  Includes bibliographical references and index.
  ISBN 978-0-13-245761-3 (alk. paper)
  1. Criminal procedure—United States. 2. Criminal investigation—United
States. 3. Civil rights—United States. I. Title.
  KF9619.Z35 2010
  345.73′05—dc22

                                                         2009053938

10 9 8 7 6 5 4 3 2 1

Prentice Hall
is an imprint of

www.pearsonhighered.com

ISBN 10:   0-13-245761-X
ISBN 13: 978-0-13-245761-3

To Greta

CONTENTS

PREFACE

Criminal procedure is a dramatic subject. Each case tells a story of conflict that pits society's vital need for communal peace and order, which make life livable, against the right of each individual to be free from unreasonable invasions of privacy and freedom by officers of the state. Criminal procedure is also a technical subject. It encompasses many legal rules and doctrines, not all of which are perfectly logical. The drama of criminal procedure may be conveyed by a book that explores one important case, such as *Gideon's Trumpet*, Anthony Lewis's classic story of Earl Clarence Gideon's fight for the right to counsel—a fight that took his case to the U.S. Supreme Court. Simply studying dramatic cases, however, limits the student's exposure to many important topics.

The heart of American law lies in the cases of appellate courts. Textbooks about legal subjects present the subject matter either in a casebook format or in a textbook format. Each has its advantages. *Criminal Procedure: Constitution and Society* is an effort to present the best of both methods, with additional features that are uniquely tailored to social science students in criminal justice, criminology, sociology, and political science. The unique features of this text will make the study of criminal procedure a comprehensive educational experience.

This text is designed to do three things: (1) provide essential information about the law of constitutional criminal procedure for students of criminal justice; (2) present Supreme Court cases in a format that is sufficiently substantial so as to provide the benefits of the casebook method, while adding study aids that make the cases more comprehensible to undergraduate students; and (3) provide materials that help students appreciate criminal procedure in its social, political, and historical contexts.

NEW TO THIS EDITION

Substantial changes have been made to the sixth edition. In addition to reviewing the Supreme Court's continuous series of cases, new sections have been added and in some chapters I have changed the order of sections to make the subjects flow more smoothly.

- Seventy new citations to Supreme Court decisions have been added; some are new cases, and some are older cases cited to provide a better understanding of doctrines.
- Twenty-five important new Supreme Court cases that were decided since the fifth edition was published are discussed, including the middle school strip search case (*Safford School v. Redding*), the automobile search-incident case modifying *Belton* (*Arizona v. Gant*), the reliance on a police computer exclusionary rule case (*Herring v. United States*), the frisk without reasonable suspicion to stop case (*Arizona v. Johnson*), the case overruling *Michigan v. Jackson's Massiah–Edwards* protection (*Montejo v. Louisiana*), the domestic violence Confrontation Clause case (*Giles v. California*), the *McNabb–Mallory* safe harbor case (*Corley v. United States*), the counsel attaches at initial appearance case (*Rothgery v. Gillespie County*), the forensic science Confrontation Clause case (*Melendez-Diaz v. Massachusetts*), the pro-se defense standards case (*Indiana v. Edwards*), and the high-speed chase videocam case (*Scott v. Harris*).
- Care has been taken to keep the length of the text the same as the fifth edition.
- The "time of terror sections" located in nine chapters in the fifth edition have been removed. Instead, an overview of the lessons and dangers to civil liberties posed by the global war on terror are discussed in a new Law in Society section in Chapter 1. This section discusses the four historic cases in which the Supreme Court held fast to the Constitution against public pressure and a theory of an imperial presidency advanced by the Bush administration: *Hamdi v. Rumsfeld* (2004), *Rasul v. Bush* (2004), *Hamdan v. Rumsfeld* (2006), and *Boumediene v. Bush* (2008).
- Chapter 1 has been reorganized to collect sections directly related to the law in a section on Legal Foundations, and revisions to earlier sections are retained in The Context of Criminal Procedure section. Substantial revisions were made to the subsection on Race and Criminal Procedure.

- In Chapter 2 *Mapp v. Ohio* is discussed as text, not as a case with comments and a new Case and Comments, *Herring v. United States*, is included.
- Chapter 2 has been substantially reordered. The chapter begins with a section renamed "Remedies for Constitutional Violations" and expands and updates a discussion of pattern and practice suits. This reordering provides a foundation for and consolidates the discussion of the exclusionary rule. A new subsection on Immunity from Lawsuits has been added to the section on Remedies.
- Chapter 3 includes a new section on "knock and talk," an expanded treatment of curtilage, and the "consent once-removed" case of *Pearson v. Callahan* (2009).
- Chapter 4 includes discussions of two important new Supreme Court cases: the high-speed chase videocam case (*Scott v. Harris*) and the frisk without reasonable suspicion to stop case (*Arizona v. Johnson*), as well as *Virginia v. Moore* (2008) (an arrest based on probable cause that violates state law is constitutional and evidence from a search incident is admissible) and *Los Angeles v. Rettele* (2007) (per curiam, brief detention following discovery of erroneous arrest is reasonable). The chapter also includes an updated and expanded section on station-house strip searches following traffic arrests.
- Chapter 5 includes four new Supreme Court cases: *Safford Unified School District v. Redding* (2009) (strip search of middle school girl unconstitutional under special needs doctrine); *U.S. v. Flores-Montano* (2004) (removal of gas tank reasonable as part of a border search); *Arizona v. Gant* (2009) (*Belton* modified; search of car incident to arrest of immobilized driver reasonable only where police arrested on probable cause of contraband; cannot search where arrest for driving offense); *Brendlin v. California* (2007) (when police stop a vehicle they seize all passengers; passenger can challenge legality of automobile search). The section on Controlling People in a Stopped Automobile was transferred from Chapter 4. The section on fire searches was moved to a new location. A new definition is included for the emergency aid doctrine.
- Chapter 6 includes six new right to counsel cases, involving four areas: (1) the right to counsel: *United States v. Gonzalez-Lopez* (2006) (erroneous depravation of retained counsel); *Harbison v. Bell* (2009) (counsel at clemency hearing); (2) when counsel attaches: *Rothgery v. Gillespie County* (2008); (3) self-representation: *Indiana v. Edwards* (2008); and (4) effective assistance: *Knowles v. Mirzayance* (2009); *Florida v. Nixon* (2004). Substantial changes were made to the section on pro-se representation.
- Chapter 7 includes an addition to the *McNabb–Mallory* section on the "time test" to incorporate *Corley v. U.S.* (2009), which has upheld the six-hour "safe harbor" within which federal confessions are presumed voluntary.
- The Chapter 7 section on the aftermath of *Massiah and Brewer v. Williams* has been completely rewritten following a reanalysis of cases. They are now discussed in chronological order to demonstrate the effect of new appointments and an ideological realignment of the Court. Four post-*Massiah* cases have been added to complete the analysis: *Texas v. Cobb* (2001), *Fellers v. U.S.* (2005), *Kansas v. Ventris* (2009), and *Montejo v. Louisiana* (2009).
- An entirely new section on Discovery was added to Chapter 10. In addition to covering the Jencks Act and the landmark case of *Brady v. Maryland* (1963), the section discusses cases that interpret the *Brady* limited discovery of prosecution evidence rule: *Giglio v. United States* (1972), *United States v. Agurs* (1976), *United States v. Bagley* (1985), *Kyles v. Whitely* (1995), *Strickler v. Greene* (1999), and *Banks v. Dretke* (2004). The section also discusses discovery of the defendant's evidence: *Williams v. Florida* (1970).
- Chapter 10 changed the Case and Comments treatment of *United States v. Armstrong* (1996) to text. The chapter shortened the coverage of the grand jury and preliminary examination, and took material on prosecutorial misconduct previously in Chapter 11 and placed it in the Law in Society section.
- A new subsection "The Appearance of Fairness" at the trial has been added to Chapter 11, concerning issues such as a defendant in restraints and spectators wearing buttons with the picture of the victim: *Carey v. Musladin*, (2006), *Deck v. Missouri* (2005), *Estelle v. Williams* (1976), *Estes v. Texas* (1965), *Holbrook v. Flynn* (1986), and *Taylor v. Kentucky* (1978).
- Major changes and additions were made to the discussion of the Sixth Amendment Confrontation Clause. Child sex-abuse cases on face-to-face confrontation were reanalyzed and more relevant facts were presented to raise the issue of miscarriages of justice.

- Another major change to the Confrontation Clause section was the addition of new materials explaining the Supreme Court's huge change in dropping the "indicia of reliability" rule of *Ohio v. Roberts* (1980), which tended to allow the introduction of hearsay, in favor of the rule more strictly requiring cross-examination of witnesses and testimonial evidence, announced in *Crawford v. Washington* (2004), and its follow-up cases of *Davis v. Washington* (2006) and the blockbuster case of *Giles v. California* (2008). These cases have made it more difficult domestic violence cases.

- Another case with tremendous potential effects in trials is discussed in the Confrontation Clause section: *Melendez-Diaz v. Massachusetts* (2009), which requires that examiners who prepare forensic science reports be subjected to cross-examination when called by the defense.

- *District Attorney's Office v. Osborne* (2009) (no due process access to DNA evidence) was added to the section on Due Process and Access to Evidence, Chapter 11.

- In addition to significant changes, I have re-read the entire text and have improved the writing for clarity and brevity where possible.

- Every Legal Puzzle in each chapter is new. Attention was paid to select puzzle cases from among different states and different federal circuits.

- The biographical sketches of Chief Justice Roberts and Associate Justice Alito have been entirely revised to take into account their votes and written opinions after their first years of service on the Supreme Court.

THE BASIC TEXT

The longest portion of this book presents and explains the core knowledge of constitutional criminal procedure. The topics covered are those of greatest interest to criminal justice students. For example, four chapters are devoted to the Fourth Amendment: the exclusionary rule (Chapter 2); the search warrant and essential Fourth Amendment doctrines, such as plain view (Chapter 3); arrest and *Terry* stops (Chapter 4); and warrantless searches (Chapter 5). The text is up to date, including discussions of cases decided in June 2009. The chapters are divided into coherent subtopics, giving instructors the flexibility to cover a general area but omit specific topics within it as they see fit.

Throughout the text I attempt to show that, in most areas of criminal procedure, there is an ongoing dialogue between justices adhering to the Due Process Model and those whose decisions better reflect the Crime Control Model. The late Professor Herbert Packer's great organizing paradigm provides a convenient way for students to grasp the overall subject matter and each case. Thus both the text and the Case and Comments explicate these conflicting approaches.

The purpose of education, of course, is not the rote memorization of rules but *understanding*. To this end, the text not only includes statements of rules but also describes the case facts out of which the rules emerged and the often conflicting views of the justices who decided the case. The relevant historic, social, and political factors that have influenced the decision are frequently provided. On occasion where a subject is overly complex (e.g., the incorporation doctrine in Chapter 1 or the automobile search doctrine in Chapter 5), I help students thread their way through the maze by providing an overview of the subject in the form of a list. I have not, however, avoided presenting students with challenging theoretical materials in this text. For example, Chapter 2 includes materials on theories of the exclusionary rule that present students with recent philosophical discussions about the justification for the rule. Instructors who want to challenge students are invited to cover this section, but it can be omitted without undermining a student's basic understanding of the topic.

The introductory chapter gives students a broad picture of the context of constitutional criminal procedure. It presents basic information about law and courts that students may have studied in other courses. Chapter 1 helps students see that study of criminal procedure is part of a liberal arts education. Criminal procedure can be a gateway to the study of history, politics, political theory, judicial biography, human rights, and important societal currents, for all of these influence criminal procedure.

An appendix to Chapter 1, on reading and briefing cases, is designed to sharpen the students' skills. Most students find that their reading comprehension and writing skills improve with the study of law, better preparing them for professional careers in criminal justice.

CASE AND COMMENTS

Case and Comments are a major feature of this book. Reading Supreme Court cases is difficult for first-year law students, let alone undergraduates. The cases selected for the "Case and Comments" features are the most important ones that criminal procedure instructors emphasize. They have been carefully edited to provide not just brief snippets of the cases but a fair amount of the actual reasoning of the justices in their own words. To ensure complete understanding, in most of these cases relevant portions of the dissenting opinions have been added. This helps students understand the law as a dialectical process.

To help students read and understand the cases, I have added comments, which are identified by bracketed letters keyed to the text. These critical tools help students read the case on their own. These comments achieve several goals. They (1) point out the meaning or importance of technical legal words; (2) highlight disagreements between opposing justices; (3) point out logical weaknesses and clever arguments; (4) ask pointed questions about the case; (5) highlight underlying value judgments in an opinion; and (6) indicate how the case advances or violates the doctrine of *stare decisis*.

"LAW IN SOCIETY" SECTIONS

These sections at the end of each chapter show the "law in action." Statements of legal rights often convey the idea that they are fully effective. Unfortunately, there is a gap between the ideals of law and the reality of its application. Some sections, such as the accounts of police perjury, racial profiling, and prosecutorial misconduct, show criminal justice personnel at their worst. The unmet promise of equal justice (Chapter 6) shows that our society is not willing to pay for justice for indigents. Of course, most police don't commit perjury, most lawyers and prosecutors do their jobs competently, most judges do not buckle under political pressure, and most people found guilty of crimes *are* guilty. But this is not always the case. It is important for students to ponder the gap between constitutional ideals and courthouse reality. Several "Law in Society" sections rely on social science research to indicate the complexity of the criminal process and to demonstrate that simple statements or beliefs do not capture the full reality of the exclusionary rule, the use of mandatory arrest for domestic violence, or the belief that eyewitnesses who are positive are therefore accurate. In these sections, we see that innocent people confess to crimes they did not commit, despite having been read their *Miranda* warnings, and we see the dark side of undercover policing. Information from news sources and from social science research expands our knowledge of the social reality of law and criminal justice.

BIOGRAPHIES OF SUPREME COURT JUSTICES

Beginning students often fail to appreciate the extent to which constitutional law is the product of the particular men and women who sit on the nation's highest court. Knowing the predilections of the justices helps students better understand the cases. The brief biographical sketches following each chapter highlight the contribution of the justices to criminal procedure and describe their general approach to the law. One reference work is given for each justice so that an interested student can follow up to learn more about the life and work of that justice.

LEGAL PUZZLES

At the conclusion of each chapter, recent cases from lower federal and state courts, covering some of the subjects discussed in the chapter, are presented in the form of "puzzles." They indicate how the courts apply Supreme Court rulings. The answer to the first puzzle in each chapter is given in the text, and additional "answers" are provided to instructors. Working through the puzzles is a very useful way to study and to understand this subject. They may also generate in-class discussions, in part because some court solutions to the legal questions are unexpected. The puzzles give students insight into the fact that the application of legal precedent is not mechanical but requires lower courts to do a good deal of weighing and analyzing to resolve issues. All of the legal puzzles in this edition are new.

SUGGESTED READINGS AND WEB SITES

A few books and Web sites are listed at the end of each chapter. They allow students to explore the issues discussed in the chapter in greater depth.

KEY TERMS AND GLOSSARY

At the beginning of each chapter, students are alerted to key terms that appear in **bold type** within the chapter. Each term is defined in the Glossary, which the instructor can use as a pedagogical tool. A student who knows these key terms will have a good grasp of the content of the text.

EXCERPTS OF THE U.S. CONSTITUTION

Appendix A includes selected portions of the Constitution. This may be used by the student and instructor as a handy reference, and it may be used as a teaching tool, with certain provisions as required reading.

SUMMARY INFORMATION ABOUT SELECTED SUPREME COURT JUSTICES

A one-line summary of the typical voting style of each justice is given in a table in Appendix B. This "scorecard" information provides a valuable tip about each judge's orientation.

SUPPLEMENTS

Supplements include an Instructor's Manual with Test Bank. To access supplementary materials online, instructors need to request an instructor access code. Go to www.pearsonhighered.com/irc, where you can register for an instructor access code. Within 48 hours after registering, you will receive a confirming e-mail, including an instructor access code. Once you have received your code, go to the site and log on for full instructions on downloading the materials you wish to use.

ACKNOWLEDGMENTS

The preparation of this book was made much easier and the resulting text greatly improved thanks to the helpful criticism of colleagues in many institutions, including Barry Langford, Columbia College, Columbia, MO; Kay Henricksen, MacMurray College, Jacksonville, IL; and Jane Younglove, California State Univeristy, Stanislaus, Turlock, CA.

I also owe a great debt to colleagues who reviewed the first and second editions of this text. They include Andrew C. Blanar, John C. Conway, Jerry Dowling, Micheal Falvo, Zoltan Ferency (deceased), Robert A. Harvie, W. Richard Janikowski, Paul A. Mastriacovo, William Michalek, Andrew A. Mickle, Robert R. Reinertsen, Cliff Roberson, Cathryn Jo Rosen, Martha J. Sullivan, Donald H. Wallace, John T. Whitehead, Wayne L. Wolf, and Benjamin S. Wright. Also, several students were more than helpful in providing research assistance for earlier editions: Joyce Andries, Garth J. Milazzo, and Michael J. Vasich.

The editorial staff at Pearson/Prentice Hall has been fantastically supportive and helpful at every turn in making a large job move along very smoothly. Many thanks to Eric Krassow, Jessica Sykes, Adam Kloza, and Sowmyaa Narayani.

The love and support of Greta, Amy, and Seth have made everything possible, including this book.

ABOUT THE AUTHOR

Marvin Zalman began his career in criminal justice education in northern Nigeria. He and his wife, Greta, then recent graduates of Brooklyn Law School, were inspired by President John F. Kennedy's challenge to young Americans: "Ask not what your country can do for you; ask what you can do for your country." As Peace Corps volunteers from 1967 to 1969, they taught at the Faculty of Law at Ahmadu Bello University, in the city of Zaria. Zalman taught classes on criminal law and criminal procedure, beginning a lifetime of study of these subjects. He authored a casebook on northern Nigerian criminal procedure and conducted a study of sentencing patterns in local criminal courts.

Upon returning to the United States, he began formal studies in a then new field of scholarship, at the School of Criminal Justice at the State University of New York at Albany, from which he earned his Ph.D. From 1971 to 1980, he taught at the School of Criminal Justice at Michigan State University and then moved to Wayne State University in Detroit, where he served as chair of the Criminal Justice Department for several years. From 1978 to 1980, Professor Zalman was the executive director of sentencing guideline development projects for the state of Michigan and in 1984 for the state of New York. He has published research and scholarship in the areas of criminal sentencing, criminal procedure, domestic violence, prisoners' rights, assisted suicide, democracy and criminal justice, and wrongful conviction. He teaches classes on criminal justice policy, criminal law, the judicial process, wrongful conviction, and criminal procedure.

Professor Zalman believes passionately that constitutional criminal procedure is the most important course that criminal justice students can take because it deals with individual liberty. His parents fled to the safety of America during World War II; he owes his life to the power and decency of the United States, as embodied in its constitutional values. The message he wishes to convey is that every day, each police officer, defense lawyer, prosecutor, probation officer, and judge who does his or her job properly keeps the promise of liberty alive.

CHAPTER 1

The Meaning of Criminal Procedure

The Constitution of the United States was ordained, it is true, by descendants of Englishmen, who inherited the traditions of English law and history; but it was made for an undefined and expanding future, and for a people gathered and to be gathered from many nations and of many tongues.

—JUSTICE STANLEY MATTHEWS, *Hurtado v. California,* 110 U.S. 516, 530–31 (1884)

CHAPTER OUTLINE

KEY TERMS

adequate and independent
   state grounds
affirm
brief
Burger Court
case law
certiorari, writ of
checks and balances
common law
constitutionalism
court of general jurisdiction
court of limited jurisdiction
Crime Control Model
dictum

due process approach
Due Process Model
ex post facto law
federalism
fundamental rights test
habeas corpus, writ of
hierarchy of constitutional
   rights
holding
human rights
incorporation doctrine
incorporation plus
judicial craftsmanship
judicial restraint

judicial review
jurisdiction
law
legal reasoning
liberty
opinion
order
overrule
police state
precedent
private law
procedural law
public law
Rehnquist Court

remand
remedial law
reverse
rule application
rule making
Rule of Law
selective incorporation
"shocks the conscience" test
stare decisis
substantive law
Supremacy Clause
total incorporation
Warren Court

ORDER AND LIBERTY

Criminal Procedure and the Constitution

A group smashes in the door of a home at 4:00 A.M. They brandish automatic weapons, scream at residents, subdue them with threats and restraints, trash the house, and leave with some household goods and a resident in tow. This could be a violent gang home invasion and kidnapping. Or it could be a lawful search and seizure and arrest by police. The physical action is similar but the motivation is vastly different. What separates the illegality of the gang break-in from lawful police action is not just the motives of the two groups but the methods by which state officers act. Any job-related action by a government officer, whether an FBI agent or local police officer, whether a prosecutor or judge, whether a code enforcement officer or public school teacher, which forces a person to stop or invades an area of personal privacy, whether a backpack, car, or house, involves the Constitution. More specifically, it involves constitutional rules designed by the Framers to limit what state officers can do to individuals in the name of public safety. If the intrusions of state officers are not justified and authorized by law, their actions are illegal, and they undermine the constitutional foundations of American government.

The Constitution was written in 1787, ratified in 1788, and established the second government for the United States of America that went into effect in 1789. Two years later, ten amendments were added to the Constitution, known collectively as the Bill of Rights (some limit the Bill of Rights to the first eight amendments). Central to the study of criminal procedure are the Fourth, Fifth, Sixth, and Eighth Amendments, and the Fourteenth Amendment, ratified shortly after the Civil War in 1868. Equally important are decisions of the U.S. Supreme Court interpreting the constitutional text. For the most part, the study of constitutional criminal procedure is the study of the Supreme Court's **opinions** that interpret the Constitution.

The Preamble to the Constitution lists, in the broadest generalities, the functions of a constitution and a government. The first five apply to any government. The last announces the ideology on which American government is founded. The first function is to establish a government of the United States—in this case one that was "more perfect" than the government under the Articles of Confederation (1781–1789), and the specifics of which are included in the body of the Constitution. It is a "union" or a federation of states, but also a separate government in its own right. The second and third functions—to "establish Justice" and "ensure domestic Tranquility"—are central purposes of the criminal justice system, although justice and tranquility are also achieved by civil courts, and by civil as well a punitive laws. The fourth function, providing national defense, is vital to any nation, and the fifth, "promoting the general Welfare," is a shorthand phrase for the array of ever-changing issues about which a government must legislate and deal with. The last purpose of the Constitution makes it clear that the central purpose of American government is the liberty of its citizens.

Order, Liberty, and the Two Models of Criminal Justice

In paleolithic and ancient societies group solidarity was unquestioned and modern notions of individualism were unknown. Group norms were often imposed in brutal ways, softened a bit by the development of ethically oriented religions and philosophies around the world during the "axial age" in about the first millennium B.C.E.[1] Liberty was not highly prized, except among a small group of nobles. Another great shift in human history, the emergence of the political concept of self-rule, began in the seventeenth century and is still under way today. Going by various labels—including democracy, republicanism, liberalism, and constitutionalism—the American variant "stood for the primacy of the individual."[2] Modern government and political theory includes the "loyal opposition," the idea that dissent can be valuable, and an understanding that unlimited state power, even when exercised for beneficent ends, is extremely dangerous to individual freedom. Individual liberty has unleashed enormous intellectual, spiritual, and productive powers, although not without costs.[3] The United States was the first state founded explicitly on Enlightenment-era ideals of individual liberty and balanced government. This background is relevant to criminal procedure, the branch of American constitutional law concerned with the state's power to maintain an orderly society and the rights of citizens and residents to live in freedom from undue government interference with their liberty. Unlike in earlier periods, American government under the Constitution must "secure the Blessings of Liberty" while simultaneously "insur[ing] domestic Tranquility."

The primary purpose of criminal procedure is therefore to maintain the proper *balance* between **order** and **liberty,** which are continuously in tension. Social order is maintained by the criminal justice apparatus—police, prosecution, courts, and corrections—employing two million people and authorized to use awesome powers against individuals and organizations. These include the power to arrest and detain people; to break into homes and offices; to search purses, backpacks, and computer files; to use electronic means to listen in on conversations and obtain electronic communications; and to put people through a bewildering and expensive court process. If the process results in a conviction, the state is authorized to execute, imprison, or fine the defendant, and to control the lives of offenders placed on probation and parole in ways not consistent with individual liberty.

A system of such enormous power is necessary to deal with high levels of crime.[4] Violent crime takes the lives and destroys the safety of tens of thousands of people annually, while property and white-collar crimes deprive millions more of their wealth and sense of security. Without effective crime control, the lives of many more would be at risk, undermining the normal functioning of society. A society without order does not enjoy liberty—it endures license. The obverse of license is the repressive "order" of dictatorships or authoritarian governments. While nothing like the brutal control over individuals that marked Saddam Hussein's Baathist dictatorship in Iraq, or the stifling repression of dissenters in contemporary China is close to American criminal justice, unfortunately, abuses do occur.[5] Every society, including advanced democracies, must continuously curb the dangers of corruption, abuse of power, and excessive use of force that inevitably arise when criminal justice powers are placed in the hands of human beings.

A classic exposition of the order–liberty continuum in the context of constitutional criminal procedure is Herbert Packer's "two models of the criminal process"[6] Rather than using the political theory terms of liberty and order, Packer examined the competing values in our constitutional order through models. A model, like a map, is an *abstraction* of reality that allows us to better understand the practices and rules of criminal procedure. Packer calls these the **Due Process Model** and the **Crime Control Model.** Both models reflect *necessary* and desired constitutional values in our society, and so co-exist in continuous tension.

These models tend to reflect the ideological predilections held by Supreme Court justices along with most people in society. Packer starts by noting that both conservatives and liberals share common values about the justice system. Shared values include the **Rule of Law:** conservatives and liberals agree that a person can only be arrested and prosecuted for violating a law that is "on the books." No one wants police to be able to stop people at will. Included under the Rule of Law is the constitutional prohibition against **ex post facto laws;** neither the states nor the federal government may criminalize people for behavior that was legal when committed (U.S. Const. art. I.§, § 9 ¶ 3, and § 10 ¶ 1). Such powers are dictatorial, and dangerous to liberty. Another shared belief is the idea and reality that police and prosecutors have a *duty to enforce* the criminal law and cannot ignore violations of law. Liberals want effective law enforcement as much as conservatives. A third shared understanding, "is the assumption that there are *limits to the powers of government* to investigate and apprehend persons suspected of committing crimes." Conservatives do not want the government's justice system "running amok" any more than liberals. Finally, there is a shared belief "that the alleged criminal is not merely an object to be acted upon, but an independent entity" who deserves his or her day in court and may demand a *trial* and other *procedural safeguards*. This last assumption of the adversary system is central to the Due Process Model and is de-emphasized but not entirely eliminated by the Crime Control Model. Within these broad areas of agreement, liberal adherents to the Due Process Model and conservative supporters of the Crime Control Model tend to see the world of criminal justice differently.

The Crime Control Model emphasizes that "the *repression of criminal conduct* is by far the most important function to be performed by the criminal process" because public safety is essential to personal freedom. To be effective, the criminal justice system must *efficiently* process those who have been lawfully apprehended. There is a premium on speed and finality. Speed "depends on informality and uniformity" (for example, plea bargaining); "*finality* depends on minimizing the occasional challenge" (for example, limiting the right to appeal). The administrative and routine functioning of criminal justice is stressed, almost viewing the system as a *conveyor belt*. Supporters of the Crime Control Model hold a presumption of guilt—an assumption that police and prosecutors are *accurate* in arresting and prosecuting suspects. Because they are confident that the investigative process identifies the right suspects, the pretrial stages, trials, and appeals can be relatively perfunctory; any restrictions on the police investigative stages are to be resisted.

"If the Crime Control Model resembles an assembly line," Packer says, "the Due Process Model looks very much like an obstacle course." Supporters of this model do not assume that police fact-finding is accurate; they assume that the criminal justice system is prone to error. They therefore insist "on *formal, adjudicative, adversary* fact-finding processes in which the factual case against the accused is publicly heard by an impartial tribunal and is evaluated only after the accused has had a full opportunity to discredit the case against him." Even after a full trial, the fear of an erroneous conviction generates a desire for many avenues of appeal. "The demand for finality is thus very low in the Due Process Model," Packer says. This model demands the "prevention and *elimination of mistakes* to the extent possible; the Crime Control Model accepts the probability of mistakes up to the level at which they interfere with the goal of repressing crime." For the Due Process Model, the "aim of the process is at least as much to protect the factually innocent as it is to convict the factually guilty." The Due Process Model is highly suspicious of those who wield power and is ideologically driven by the "primacy of the individual and the complementary concept of limitation on official power."

The Due Process Model emphasizes *legal guilt*, whereas the Crime Control Model stresses *factual guilt*. The legal guilt concept pervades the formal legal and trial process—no matter how "factually" guilty a person is, conviction and punishment are not allowed unless all legal requirements are met: a court with **jurisdiction;** a prosecution within the time set by the statute of limitations; and an offender who is lawfully responsible (for example, not insane). The "quixotic" *presumption of innocence* plays a special role. The presumption of innocence is *not* the opposite of the presumption of guilt, but is a *normative* principle that insists that the defendant be treated *as if* he or she were innocent, no matter how apparent the factual guilt. To this end, the prosecutor must prove a case beyond a reasonable doubt, and the jury verdict must be unanimous. The *equality of treatment* of all suspects is an important Due Process Model attribute. Finally, it includes the strong belief that serious procedural errors invalidate convictions. This last point is the one over which many of the most bitter disputes in constitutional criminal procedure have arisen.

The Dangers of Injustice

Every case reaching the Supreme Court involves not only issues of law and state power but also questions of justice and injustice. This does not mean that every defendant has a good case; it is unwise to romanticize defendants. As Justice Felix Frankfurter said, "It is a fair summary of history to say that the safeguards of liberty have frequently been forged in controversies involving not very nice people."[7] Nevertheless, several famous defendants, such as the Scottsboro boys, Earl Clarence Gideon, and Dr. Sam Sheppard, were innocent of the crimes for which they were convicted.[8] It is important to keep in mind that rights are fundamental and must be available to everyone, not just reserved for "actually innocent" defendants, since they cannot always be detected in advance.

Every chapter in this book details abuses of power and errors in the justice system. Many of the "Law in Society" sections focus on the negative—on negligence, abuses, and even crimes committed by criminal justice officials. It goes without saying that most police officers, prosecutors, defense attorneys, and judges act competently and professionally and often perform their work courageously and selflessly. Nevertheless, the burden of constitutional criminal procedure is to unflinchingly confront the negligent and malignant aspects of criminal justice.

Because the text focuses on police practices, it uncovers numerous police-generated abuses that undermine defendants' constitutional rights. Police perjury, for example, can cloak widespread Fourth Amendment violations. Police end-run games around *Miranda* rules can, in effect, overrule the Supreme Court's decisions. Overzealous police officers can unintentionally push defendants into giving false confessions. Errors or falsehoods in search warrant affidavits undermine personal privacy and security. Sloppy police work exacerbates problems of mistaken eyewitness identification, leading to the conviction of innocent people. The "blue wall of silence" makes it more difficult to ensure professionalism and lawful behavior in criminal justice practice.

Other actors must behave properly to ensure that the criminal justice system lives up to its constitutional ideals. Prosecutorial misconduct occurs with regularity and can negate the very rationale of the adversary system. The same effect is produced by inadequate, poorly prepared, and overworked defense lawyers. The history of American justice is replete with trials that were mockeries, with judges unable or unwilling to conduct the proceedings in a manner that guarantees fairness.[9] Judges must remain vigilant to ensure evenhanded trials.

A lesson of the long struggle to ensure the Rule of Law and a civilized justice system is the need to treat suspects and defendants fairly. An unfair or incompetent system leads to the conviction of the innocent. The conviction of "actually innocent" people has been a concern of the common law since the middle ages, as reflected in the maxim, "Better ten guilty go free than one innocent convicted." The maxim is supported by the high level of evidence needed to convict: proof beyond a reasonable doubt. The large number of wrongful convictions revealed since DNA testing became feasible in the early 1990s makes clear the inadequacies of criminal procedure law to prevent injustice.

The Innocence Project has confirmed 243 DNA exonerations as of October 2009.[10] An independent study counted 340 DNA and non-DNA exonerations between 1988 and 2003, and it is plausible that *thousands* are wrongly convicted each year.[11] The causes for wrongful convictions include mistaken eyewitness identification and poor lineup procedures, police "tunnel vision" on the first suspect, interrogation methods that elicit false confessions, pressure for convictions in high-profile cases, jailhouse snitches who lie to get favorable treatment, overzealous prosecutors, incompetent or dishonest forensic investigators, "junk science" (e.g., hair evidence), incompetent defense lawyers, and legal and constitutional rules that act as roadblocks to the truth.[12]

The world of criminal justice is just beginning to grapple with the complex of problems that produces wrongful convictions. Late in 2004 Congress passed the Innocence Protection Act, which increased compensation for wrongly convicted federal prisoners and provided funds for post-conviction DNA testing.[13] Although growing concerns about wrongful conviction involve the entire criminal justice system, they include some special concerns of criminal procedure. This text pays special attention to wrongful conviction in the chapters on the right to counsel (Chapter 6), interrogations and confessions (Chapter 7), identification and lineups (Chapter 8), the pretrial process (Chapter 10), and the trial process (Chapter 11).

Criminal Justice and Alternate Justice Systems

Criminal procedure law is one way to control the formal, adult, felony criminal justice "system." Other justice systems co-exist with the criminal justice system to maintain, ideally, a healthy and functioning civilization, which is the ultimate goal of criminal justice.

THE SOCIAL SYSTEM   All formal or quasi-formal justice systems are parts of our larger, complex, modern society, with its various work, educational, recreational, social, and private routines. Society provides the matrix of ideas of proper action, of right and wrong, and of justice, that are normative foundations of formal justice systems. This "law and society" subject is not formally addressed in this text, although the links between criminal procedure and social norms are occasionally mentioned. Social norms and ideologies are in part produced by national cultures. The culture of a nation-state—centered on a single "nation" with a long history, distinct language, core religion, and sense of "ethnicity"—produces a distinct national culture with deeply etched norms. The United States, however, is an *immigrant society* rather than a nation-state, with norms and values that are more difficult to pin down, especially as immigrants re-interpret the "American dream" in the context of their experiences. Nevertheless there is a distinctively American outlook, with its own bounded set of paradoxes, sometimes called "American exceptionalism." One result is that the Constitution, a legal document, has played a larger role in American culture than is the case in nation-states.[14]

THE CIVIL LAW SYSTEM   All the criminal justice systems listed in this section, which seem large when considered in isolation, are small change compared to the informal and formal civil justice system. The majority of lawyers will never step foot in a criminal court, and spend entire careers advising, negotiating, and litigating about divorces, businesses, nonprofit organizations, taxes, employment, injuries, schools, land ownership and use, wills and estates, and on and on. Alongside lawyers and courts, arbitrators, mediators, case-evaluators, and a host of other dispute resolvers exist, within and between organizations and in communities, to deal with the disputational side of human beings. The civil law and dispute resolution systems work at the largest and smallest levels, from the largest corporations, economy-wide labor-management issues, and social conflicts with national scope, down to struggles within families and between neighbors. The civil justice system probably does more to maintain a just and functioning society for most people than the criminal justice system, however necessary it is.

THE CRIMINAL JUSTICE SYSTEM   The criminal justice system includes government agencies as well as private individuals such as jurors, bail bond agents, and private defense lawyers. The major agencies—police, prosecution, and corrections—are parts of the *executive* branch of government. The *judicial* branch of government, which adjudicates civil and criminal cases, ensures fair procedures. *Legislatures* also play a central role by enacting criminal law, prescribing sentencing guidelines and structures, and setting budgets for the primary agencies of criminal justice. Knowledge of criminal justice practices (e.g., police discretion) allows a better appreciation of criminal procedure.

Formal criminal procedure law covers six stages of practice by police, prosecutors, defense attorneys, trial judges, and appellate courts. These are (1) police investigation, interrogation, search, and arrest; (2) the pretrial process, including the decision to grant bail, grand jury operations, preliminary examination of the charges, and pretrial motions; (3) formal charging by the prosecutor; (4) adjudication—the determination of guilt or innocence by a jury or a bench trial or by the plea negotiation process; (5) sentencing—imposing punishment on the convicted, a judicial decision in which probation officers, prosecutors, defense attorneys, and sometimes victims play roles; and (6) appellate review by higher courts.[15] This book concentrates on the first stage of the criminal process—police activities that touch on individuals' rights and liberties—and also includes information on the pretrial process, charging, and adjudication. Sentencing and correctional law, including prisoners' rights, are distinct areas of law that are not covered in this text. The last stage of the criminal process, appellate review, is where most of the constitutional rights of suspects are formed. This text does not discuss highly technical appellate issues but emphasizes the substance of Supreme Court cases that shape constitutional criminal procedure.

Based on knowledge of human history and human nature, the Framers' fears about government tyranny were at their highest when they put the enormous punitive powers of the state into the hands of those people who operate the justice system. Consequently, they erected many rules of law to limit the power of criminal justice officials, and to make them permanent, embedded them in the Constitution. James Madison, the prime drafter of the Bill of Rights, announced to Congress that judges would be the special guardians of those rights.

THE MISDEMEANOR AND TRAFFIC JUSTICE SYSTEMS   The formal rules of law reviewed in this text apply to misdemeanors as well as felonies, but the focus is on felony-level crimes. At a few points the text mentions the applicability of constitutional protections to misdemeanants. In reality the quasi-criminal traffic justice system operates more like an administrative system, albeit one operated by police officers, prosecutors, and courts. And in actual practice, misdemeanors are often handled in informal ways that approach "assembly-line justice" by courts, ways that often fall below what that is required by law. This does not mean that spending a weekend or six months in jail is a trivial matter.[16] This text, nevertheless, cannot explore this important subject in depth.

THE JUVENILE LAW AND JUSTICE SYSTEMS   For more than a century, American states have treated minors, a large proportion of people who get into trouble, through a separate legal system. The insights that led to the creation of the first juvenile court in the United States in 1899 are if anything confirmed by the most up-to-date neurological research that shows that teens are still in states of physiological development that require that children and teens be handled by an alternate justice system. This large and important subject is discussed in available textbooks and is taught as a separate course in most criminal justice programs. It is only touched on in various places in this text.[17]

THE SHADOW CRIMINAL JUSTICE SYSTEM   In June 2009 the Supreme Court ruled that a strip search of a middle-school girl was unconstitutional (*Safford Unified School District v. Redding*, 2009). The intersection of criminal law and civil institutions like schools comes under the Fourth Amendment through the "special needs beyond the need for normal law enforcement" doctrine. Although this doctrine occupies a small corner of constitutional criminal procedure, legal sociologist Jonathan Simon has described how resort to police and criminal justice mechanisms, *governing thorough crime*, has crept into a host of institutions, even including the family, to deal with unruly behavior that was once handled informally.[18] Americans now take it in stride that thousands of police are present even in middle-class and quite "safe" public high schools,[19] suggesting an unhealthy social trend of the over-criminalization of American culture and society.

THE IMMIGRATION JUSTICE SYSTEM   According to a government official, in 2008 at least "304,000 immigrant criminals [were] behind bars nationwide" awaiting deportation, up from 167,000 in 2007.[20] They are held in "a rapidly growing conglomeration of county jails, federal centers and privately run prisons across the country where problems of detainee mistreatment have been persistent and widespread." After a two-and-a-halfyear delay, a federal court in June 2009 ordered the Obama administration to grant or deny a legal "petition asking for detention rules."[21] Among the problems in recent American immigration detention has been the lack of medical care that has led to a number of unnecessary deaths.[22] Homeland Security secretary Janet Napolitano has ordered a comprehensive review of detention practices.[23]

At the same time, "the nation's immigration courts [are] seriously overburdened." The government hired only four new immigration judges to assist the 234 active immigration judges between 2006 and 2009. A study based on government statistics "found that the shortage of judges had contributed to a 19 percent increase in the backlog of cases since 2006 and a 23 percent increase in the time it takes to resolve them." An immigration judge described it as "a system at its breaking point." The crisis in the immigration courts was brought on by the Bush administration hiring thousands of new immigration agents and stepping up raids in factories and communities. "Many thousands of immigrants have been affected by the delays because the authorities have started to hold many more of them in detention while the immigrants challenge deportation orders or seek political asylum through the courts." There were 186,342 immigration court cases pending at the end of the 2008 fiscal year.[24]

A July 2009 legal clinic report, based on data obtained through Freedom of Information Act lawsuits, confirmed a pattern of unconstitutional home raids by Immigration and Customs Enforcement (ICE) agents, conducted between 2006 and 2009, that had been noted in numerous news accounts and in vocal concerns raised by lawmakers and local law enforcement chiefs.[25] The report identified four kinds of illegal action by ICE agents: (1) illegally entering homes without legal authority, (2) illegally seizing "non-target individuals" during home raid operations; (3) illegally searching homes without legal authority; and (4) illegally seizing individuals based solely on racial or ethnic appearance or on limited English proficiency. These mostly predawn raids were authorized only by administrative and not judicial warrants; as a result, agents were supposed to obtain consent from occupants before entering but frequently just broke in. An odd feature of the raids is that only one-third of the persons arrested were "targeted" as dangerous or suspected of terrorism, while two-thirds were non-dangerous people held on immigration status violations. What could account for this sharp rise in seemingly out-of-control behavior in "home raids [displaying] a lack of law enforcement professionalism and a kind of cowboy mentality that . . . contribute[d] to the apparent lack of attention to the governing constitutional norms"? The most persuasive reason seems to be that in 2006, ICE made dramatic changes in its enforcement strategy "that collectively set the stage for the Bush Administration's widely publicized campaign of immigration home raids." Teams of seven agents, who preciously had annual arrest quotas of 125 illegal aliens, 75 percent of whom were "dangerous," had their quotas increased to 1,000 per year. "Overnight, [the teams] were expected to become eight times more efficient. Simultaneously, the new 2006 quota system eliminated the requirement that 75 percent of the arrests needed to be "criminal aliens." As a result, these teams, after breaking into homes, illegally questioned residents and illegally targeted persons on racial characteristics. The report found that suppression motions and civil lawsuits had almost no effect on this widespread pattern of unconstitutional behavior. The Obama administration had eliminated some of the worst aspects of these rules in early 2009. To prevent violations, the Cardozo Immigration Justice clinic recommended such reforms, among others, as obtaining judicial warrants for home raids, obtaining high-level clearance, limiting them to obtaining dangerous aliens who cannot be found in public, and videotaping raids.

The immigration justice system has grown into a substantial sub-justice system, with rules and procedures that threaten constitutional values while undermining effective local law enforcement based on trust with and gaining information from the local community.

THE TERRORISM JUSTICE SYSTEM   One of the most persistent and worrisome of pubic topics debated since the terror attack of September 11, 2001, has been the treatment of detainees extracted from the Iraq and Afghanistan wars, and how the fear of foreign terrorism may be distorting police priorities and the civil rights of ordinary American citizens. A discussion of the topic is found in the Law in Society section of this chapter.

The alternate juvenile, misdemeanant, immigration, and terrorism justice systems offer fewer procedural and constitutional protections to individuals than are provided by the felony criminal justice system, which is formally controlled by the full panoply of rights under the Due Process Clause and the Bill of Rights. As governments seek to control costs and tend to be sure of themselves, the danger to individuals' liberties is that a kind of "blowback" will lead police and prosecutors to adopt the methods of these alternate justice systems in ways that will permanently cripple civil rights in the felony criminal justice system.

LEGAL FOUNDATIONS

Constitutional criminal procedure involves a good deal of specialized knowledge about the structure, operations, and relationships of courts in the context of American federal government, a fairly sophisticated understanding of how law is classified and created, and an appreciation of special constitutional rules and developments that make the cases understandable. Further, a grasp of criminal procedure's legal foundation only makes sense in relation to information provided in other sections of this chapter. None of this is particularly simple, but as the information provided in this chapter reappears continuously in subsequent chapters, it must be readily at hand.

Law

Collectively, **law** is a body of written rules issued by legitimate government authorities, designed to guide and control individuals and institutions. There are different forms and sources of law; the most important are (1) statutes or legislation and (2) rules created by appellate courts, called **case law** or **common law** (explained in following paragraphs). Other forms of law include executive orders of the president or state governors, administrative agency regulations, ordinances passed by local units of government, and court rules detailing court procedures. Government officials can enforce case law and statutes.

These sources exist in a hierarchical order: a statute, issuing from the legislature (elected by the sovereign people) can modify or eliminate court-made law (created by appointed judges, or elected judges who are not directly accountable to the electorate). Constitutional case law is the major exception to this rule. The Constitution of the United States and the state constitutions are special kinds of statutes. The U.S. Constitution was ratified not by an ordinary session of Congress, but by special ratifying conventions in the states, and so it represents the will of the people as a whole. Because of this, under the authoritative ruling of *Marbury v. Madison* (1803) and under unbroken government practice and tradition, the Supreme Court has come to have the final word on the interpretation of the Constitution, with the power to overrule laws passed by Congress or state legislatures, provisions of state constitutions, and actions by executive officers including the president of the United States, when they are found to conflict with the meaning of the Constitution.

The only direct way for the federal and state governments to override a constitutional interpretation issued by the Supreme Court (constitutional case law) is by formally amending the Constitution by procedures specified in Article V, which requires a proposed amendment passed by two-thirds of the House of Representatives and two-thirds of the Senate (or by a convention called by two-thirds of the state legislatures) and ratified by three-fourths of the state legislatures. The Constitution has been amended only twenty-seven times in two and a quarter centuries, and only a few of those amendments directly overturned Supreme Court cases. A clear example of the Supreme Court's constitutional power is *Dickerson v. U.S.* (2000) (discussed in Chapter 7), which held that a 1968 Act of Congress passed to overrule *Miranda v. Arizona* (1966) was unconstitutional: "We hold that *Miranda*, being a constitutional decision of this Court, may not be in effect overruled by an Act of Congress, and we decline to overrule *Miranda* ourselves" The Supreme Court has enormous power to determine the meaning and content of constitutional law and thus to impose rules of conduct on police, prosecutors, judges, and other officials. In a real sense, the Constitution means what the Supreme Court says it means. Law, then, is not only the words of the rules, but the power that the rules give to courts and government officials to enforce the rules.

CLASSIFICATIONS OF LAW   Law is classified first by its *applicability*. **Private law** concerns disputes between private individuals, groups, and corporations, while **public law** involves government power and arises from disputes between government departments or between private people or groups and government agencies. Law is also classified by its specific *subject matter*. Private law covers such subjects as contracts, property, torts (the law of injuries), commercial law, copyright, sports law, civil procedure, and the like. Public law includes constitutional law, administrative law, tax law, substantive criminal law, and criminal procedure.

Law is classified by its three *functions*. **Substantive law** establishes and defines rights, powers, and obligations. Major areas of substantive private law, for example, establish contractual obligations, property rights, and the freedom from intentional or negligent harm. Substantive criminal law defines crimes such as homicide and theft and defenses such as insanity. **Procedural law** prescribes methods of enforcing substantive rights that are breached and includes rules of jurisdiction, the serving of legal process (e.g., a summons), and rules that guide the conduct of a trial. Rules of criminal procedure include court rules, state and federal statutes, and rules of constitutional law. **Remedial law** determines the actual benefits or "remedies" obtained by a successful party to a lawsuit. Civil remedies include (1) *legal* remedies or money damages to compensate loss and may include punitive damages and (2) *equitable* remedies (i.e., injunctions or specific performance to rectify a violation of rights). Criminal law "remedies" are the lawful punishments that may be inflicted on convicted criminals.[26] Chapter 2 focuses on remedies for constitutional violations and the Fourth Amendment exclusionary rule.

The label "criminal *procedure*" can be misleading because although this branch of law includes genuinely procedural rules it is important for its substantive law. Constitutional criminal procedure is better classified as a branch of civil liberties law. It regulates the relationship between the individual and the state during trials (U.S. Const. amends. V and VI), protects against unlawful arrest and search and seizure (U.S. Const. amend. IV), does not allow compelled confessions (U.S. Const. amends. V and XIV), and provides many other protections against unlawful government conduct when a person's life, liberty or property is at stake.

The Court System

In the American constitutional framework, courts of law constitute a separate branch of government. They exist not only to decide legal disputes but also to provide **checks and balances** against the risk that the "political branches" of government (the executive and legislative branches) will violate the rights of individuals for improper political or corrupt purposes.

COURT STRUCTURE   Courts are *hierarchical*—ranked by authority into appellate and trial courts. Every state and the federal government have supreme courts and trial courts; the federal government and most states also have intermediate courts of appeal. The basic function of trial courts is **rule application**—deciding individual cases in accord with the law. Trial courts decide issues of fact and resolve issues of law that apply to a case. They also encourage pleas in criminal cases. Many states have different levels of trial courts. Lower-tier **courts of limited jurisdiction** (often called *district* or *municipal courts*) decide misdemeanors and oversee the pretrial stages of felony cases. Felony cases are decided in **courts of general jurisdiction** (called *superior courts* in most states, but also known as *circuit* or *district courts*). Trial judges can oversee juries, which decide issues of fact under rules of law and evidence specified by the judge. Juries, incidentally, are not part of the judicial branch but are "the people." If a jury trial is waived, a judge sits as the trier of facts and law in a *bench* or *waiver* trial.

Appellate courts are "above" (or "superior to") trial courts in the court hierarchy. The basic function of appellate courts is **rule making**—that is, making law (legal precedents) by a process of legal interpretation. Every state and the United States has a supreme court, which are the final arbiters of issues of law that may be appealed by losing parties in civil lawsuits or criminal cases. Most states and the United States also have established intermediate courts of appeal, which became necessary as the volume of legal appeals grew too large to be handled by supreme courts. Issues of fact are typically not appealable. This text focuses on constitutional rule making by the U.S. Supreme Court.

APPELLATE COURT PROCESS   A basic understanding of the appellate process is important because almost every case in this text is a Supreme Court decision. Every state gives convicted defendants a statutory right to appeal their convictions to intermediate appellate courts, although defendants who plead guilty may have limited rights. Formally, there is no right to appeal in the federal Constitution. Appeals to state supreme courts, or appeals beyond the first appeal are discretionary and require permission from the appellate court to proceed.

Appeals as of right or discretionary appeals have to be initiated by the party, by a filing that asserts that specific legal rights were violated during the trial. Claimed violations of law, the most typical basis for appeals, are decided by appellate courts de novo—that is, the appellate court is not bound by the lower court decision. Issues of fact, which are less commonly appealed, may be reversed only for "clear error." This is because juries or trial judges who actually saw witnesses testify are in a better position than appellate judges to decide what happened. Appeals based on actors' discretion are decided on the "abuse of discretion" standard.[27]

Unlike trials, in which witnesses are sworn in and testify, appellate courts decide cases based only on legal arguments presented by the lawyers. The arguments are presented in formal written essays called **briefs** and may also be presented in relatively short oral arguments before the court.

> The appeal begins when the party losing the case in the trial court, the "appellant," files a notice of appeal, usually a month or two after the trial court decision. Then within a few months the appellant files the trial court record in the appellate court. The record, often bulky, consists of the papers filed in the trial court along with a transcript of the trial testimony. Next the appellant and the opposing party, the "appellee," file briefs that argue for their respective positions. The briefs are usually followed by short oral presentations to the judge. Finally, the judges decide the case and issue a written opinion.[28]

Appeals to the U.S. Supreme Court are discretionary; the Supreme Court hears only those cases that it wishes to decide based on policy reasons that do not have to be announced. The appellate process in the Supreme Court is taken under a writ with a Latin title that originated in English procedure: a **writ of certiorari.** Appellants in Supreme Court cases are known as *petitioners*, and appellees are called *respondents*.

Appellate courts issue specific decisions in an appeal, in reference to the decision in the last court from which an appeal was taken. For example, before a case reaches the U.S. Supreme Court, there may have been a trial verdict, an appeal in the state court of appeals, a decision of the state supreme court, a decision by a federal district court on a federal **writ of habeas corpus**, followed by a decision by a federal court of appeals. In such a case, the Supreme Court will **affirm** or **reverse** the decision of the federal court of appeals—the court just "below" the Supreme Court. If the appeal involves several legal issues, the Supreme Court may affirm in part and reverse in part. The Supreme Court usually does not apply its decision directly to the parties. Instead, it usually **remands** the case, sending it back to the lower court to handle the details of applying its decision. An appellate court can **overrule** its own prior **precedent** when it finds that its prior decision was incorrect, was unsound, or has become obsolete, and can replace it with a different ruling.

Although the Supreme Court's decision (e.g., "Judgment below affirmed") is exceedingly terse, the important part of the case is the Court's opinion, which is usually a lengthy essay written for the benefit of lawyers and judges in a formal style, which purports to explain the reasons behind the Court's decision. We study these opinions to understand the Court's reasoning.

Federalism

A police officer makes a lawful arrest. Under which law does the officer operate? In a unitary nation like France or England, the arrest is made under the nation's laws. The United States, however, is a federated nation (as are Canada, Germany, and Mexico) with a national government and state governments. An officer making a lawful arrest in Augusta, Maine, must therefore comply with both Maine law and applicable U.S. law.

This complicated arrangement is the result of **federalism**—the legal and power relationship between the national government and the state governments. Federalism is a very important topic in American criminal procedure because up until the mid-twentieth century, state and local criminal justice officials were guided exclusively by state law. In the twentieth century, the Supreme Court began to apply the Bill of Rights to state officials, and this movement created modern constitutional criminal procedure. The story of how this happened and its effects are detailed later in this chapter in the section on the **incorporation doctrine**. This section provides information necessary for understanding "incorporation."

The Constitution's Framers understood that some level of friction (as well as cooperation) would exist between the national and state governments and between the states. They provided rules in the Constitution to create a nation in which the limited sovereignty of the states would be respected but in which the federal government would have certain exclusive powers. Foreign affairs and the war-making power are examples of exclusive federal authority.[29] The Constitution also established numerous rules to ensure a unified nation rather than competing states. These include a federally controlled postal system and federal oversight of interstate and foreign commerce in Article I. Article IV includes rules to make a federal nation work smoothly: the prohibition of a state's giving favorable treatment to its own citizens over the residents of other states ("privileges and immunities"), the requirement that states appropriately apply the laws or court judgments of another state ("full faith and credit"), the extradition of felons, federal control over territories, and the like.[30] Finally, the Constitution requires federal and state governments to adhere to a political philosophy of liberal republicanism. The Preamble to the Constitution emphasizes that the purpose of American government is to "secure the Blessings of Liberty to ourselves and our Posterity." The national government guarantees to every state a "republican form of government"—in Abraham Lincoln's words, a "government of the people, by the people, for the people."[31] State and federal governments are prohibited from passing ex post facto laws or bills of attainder, which undermine political liberty; nor may they create "titles of Nobility" that would create a class of Americans other than citizens.[32]

To understand how federalism works in the criminal procedure context, we must consider the topics of jurisdiction, the Supremacy Clause, the special role of the U.S. Supreme Court, *stare decisis*, and adequate and independent state grounds. Each state is a limited sovereign within the national framework. Each has a constitution that establishes a "republican form of government." The structures of state governments are quite similar, including a chief executive or governor, a legislature, and a state court system with a supreme court and trial courts. With some small variations, the legal systems of each state are comparable and parallel to the federal legal system. Each state legislature makes laws for the benefit of its people, and each has its own bill of rights to guarantee the rights of its citizens and residents.

American federalism recognizes areas of exclusive federal control, areas of exclusive state action, and many areas of concurrent jurisdiction where the federal and state governments can work together. For example, in the last forty years Congress has passed federal criminal laws that overlap substantially with state criminal laws, allowing either federal or state law enforcement agencies to investigate and either federal or state courts to try cases under their respective laws.[33]

JURISDICTION   Jurisdiction, or lawful power, is both the lawful authority of a government to exercise its powers in its territory and the authority of a court to decide cases brought before it. The jurisdiction of the U.S. government is granted by, *and limited by*, the Constitution. The jurisdiction of federal courts, including the Supreme Court, is granted in Article III of the Constitution, which explicitly grants to Congress the power to expand or contract the jurisdiction of federal courts. States are recognized in the Constitution as subordinate sovereignties, not as administrative arms or subdivisions of the national government. Thus, in *Printz v. U.S.* (1997), the Supreme Court held that Congress could not require local sheriffs to enforce the background check portions of the Brady Handgun Violence Prevention Act and the portion of the Brady Bill requiring such action was held to be unconstitutional. States do, however come under the Constitution's jurisdiction in specific ways.[34] Every government officer, state and federal, swears to uphold the U.S. Constitution.[35] As a formal matter, the federal government, which was established by the Constitution, is a government of limited powers. In the legislative realm, state legislatures have *plenary*, or general, powers to pass laws for the good of their residents, whereas the U.S. Congress can only pass laws on topics listed in Article I, section 8 of the Constitution.

Courts can decide cases only if they have lawful jurisdiction to do so. State courts derive their jurisdiction from state constitutions and statutes. Federal court jurisdiction is conferred by Article III of the Constitution and by congressional statutes. The Constitution and Congress grant jurisdiction to the Supreme Court and other federal courts only over *federal questions*—issues that arise under the U.S. Constitution, federal statutes, or treaties made between the United States and a foreign nation. As a result, the Supreme Court can review almost all decisions of lower federal courts.[36] On the other hand, the Supreme Court has *no jurisdiction over matters of state law*. Cases based exclusively on provisions of state constitutions, state legislation, or rules of state common law can be decided only by state courts. The U.S. Supreme Court can review a case from the highest tribunal of a state only if it concerns a federal question.

In constitutional criminal procedure, a federal question arises in a state court when a criminal defendant claims that an action taken by a local or state officer or court violated a right protected by the Fourteenth Amendment or elements of the Bill of Rights that have been applied to the states. Under the Fourteenth Amendment, "No State shall . . . deprive any person of life, liberty, or property, without due process of law." (The discussion of the incorporation doctrine in a later section will explain how the interpretation of this provision allowed federal courts to impose the Bill of Rights on local and state officers and courts in criminal appeals.) Therefore, federal issues can arise out of state criminal justice and be appealed to federal courts and the U.S. Supreme Court. This can occur in collateral criminal appeals under federal habeas corpus, or in federal civil rights suits against municipalities or local or state officers claiming violations of their federal constitutional rights. The civil rights law (42 U.S.C. § 1983) was passed in 1871 under the authority of the Fourteenth Amendment (discussed in Chapter 2).

THE SUPREMACY CLAUSE   State judges can decide issues under the U.S. Constitution in state trials when defendants claim that their federal constitutional rights have been infringed by state officers. When a state court interprets the U.S. Constitution, its ruling can be appealed to a federal court. It is logical that the final determination of the meaning of the Constitution be vested in the Supreme Court. This understanding is confirmed by the **Supremacy Clause** of the Constitution.

Article III of the U.S. Constitution (the "judicial article"), which confers jurisdiction on the Supreme Court, does not directly give that Court the jurisdiction to hear federal questions that arise in state courts. Nevertheless, this power was asserted by the Supreme Court in the early Republic and is inherent in the Supremacy Clause (Article VI, paragraph 2).[37] The clause says that where there is a direct conflict between a state and federal law (i.e., where a state law blocks the application of a valid federal law, or where compliance with both a federal and a state law is impossible), the federal law and the interpretation of the federal courts control. The Supremacy Clause ensures that the United States will be a united nation; otherwise, if every state could decide the meaning of the U.S. Constitution in its own way, constitutional law would not be uniform.

The Supremacy Clause

This Constitution, and the Laws of the United States which shall be made in Pursuance thereof; and all Treaties made, or which shall be made, under the Authority of the United States, shall be the supreme Law of the Land; and the Judges in every State shall be bound thereby, any Thing in the Constitution or Laws of any State to the Contrary notwithstanding.

Source: U.S. Constitution, Article VI, paragraph 2.

The Special Role of the Supreme Court

The Supreme Court and its work lies at the heart of criminal procedure. Two things about the Court and its work should be kept in mind. First, the Court is, in a special way, a political institution, and second, the Court is a special guardian of civil liberties in our system of government.

In what ways is the Court political and in what ways is it not? The Supreme Court, as an appellate court, hears cases brought to it by litigants and ostensibly decides by analyzing legal principles and always reviews prior precedent. Although it sometimes makes sweeping rulings, for the most part its cases build doctrines one small issue at a time. Procedurally, it does not act like a legislature; it is not pressured or educated by lobbyists, and there is no committee structure to investigate specialized topics. Yet, despite public ignorance and politicians' hypocrisy, the Supreme Court is indeed political in special ways. Another way to say this is that the Supreme Court *makes* law and policy. This is so because most important social and domestic issues in the United States are enacted into law and can often be litigated on constitutional grounds. This gives the Court—with its power of **judicial review** to overrule unconstitutional acts, or statutory interpretation to decide on the meaning of a law—a form of "negative" power by preventing government action. Related to this, by the time a case reaches the Court, easy decisions have been resolved and the Court is usually confronted with decisions than can reasonably be decided in different ways. This is made easier in constitutional adjudication because many of the Constitution's provisions are broad principles that allow for interpretive "play in the joints" rather than narrow rules with only one obvious meaning. As a result, in most important decisions, the ideology, life experience, and judicial philosophy of the justice become the most important factor that propels a judge to decide, more or less, in consistent patterns. This is why in criminal procedure some justices *tend* to vote in favor of the prosecution (Crime Control Model), others in favor of the defense (Due Process Model), and others, "moderates," tend to be less predictable.

There are elements of the Supreme Court's judicial *process* that makes it somewhat political. Although the Court is not subjected to lobbying, its cases are often of great importance to interest groups, and such groups can submit amicus curiae briefs that bring the ideas and knowledge of various interest groups to bear. On the positive side, these briefs are available to the public so that anyone can see the formal ideas that are presented to the Court prior to a decision. In this way, the Court's process allows a broader public to participate.

As a Court, the high tribunal cannot decide to take up an issue; it has to wait for a case to come before it for decision. However, the Court has a sophisticated audience of lawyers who understand various signals and will steer cases to the Court or try to avoid bringing cases to favor their positions. This helps the Court to make the policies that a majority wishes to make.

We are used to thinking of constitutional interpretation as "belonging" to the courts. Nevertheless, the president and Congress often justify their actions by citing the Constitution. The courts, however, have final say about the meaning of the Constitution. A state supreme court is the final authority on the meaning of a state constitution, and the U.S. Supreme Court has the last say on the meaning of the U.S. Constitution, giving it great power in shaping criminal procedure. This principle was reaffirmed recently in the titanic struggle to constrain the Bush administration's unprecedented assertion of unlimited power to detain persons under Article II commander-in-chief power. In four landmark cases culminating in *Boumediene v. Bush* (2008) the Court ruled that neither Congress nor the president could strip it of its constitutional powers to consider habeas corpus petitions, barring a proper congressional suspension of the writ (see Law in Society section, this chapter).

From the beginning of the Republic, the Framers believed that courts play an essential role in protecting individual liberty. James Madison's 1789 speech to the House of Representatives proposing the Bill of Rights said that by placing rights "into the constitution, independent tribunals of justice will consider themselves in a peculiar manner the guardians of those rights; they will be an impenetrable bulwark against every assumption of power in the legislative or executive; they will be naturally led to resist every encroachment upon rights expressly stipulated for in the constitution by the declaration of rights."[38]

ADEQUATE AND INDEPENDENT STATE GROUNDS   Prior to the incorporation of the Bill of Rights in the 1960s (discussed later in this chapter), federal criminal procedure rules tended to favor defendants more than state rules. One goal of incorporation was to apply the Constitution equally to state and federal law enforcement and courts. After 1972, the U.S. Supreme Court began to water down individual rights and rule more favorably toward the prosecution. This resulted in a reaction by a minority of state courts, regarding specific criminal procedure issues, granting *more* rights to defendants under their own state constitutions.

This is consistent with the federal structure of the United States. Justice Brennan, who championed defendants' rights, noted that "no State is precluded by [U.S. Supreme Court] decision[s] from adhering to higher standards under state law. Each State has power to impose higher standards governing police practices under state law than is required by the Federal Constitution" (*Michigan v. Mosley*, 1975, Brennan, J. dissenting). This basic element of American federalism was confirmed by the Court: each state has the "sovereign right to adopt in its own Constitution individual liberties more expansive than those conferred by the Federal Constitution" (*Prune Yard Shopping Center v. Robins*,1980).

There is, therefore, a "federal constitutional floor" established by Supreme Court interpretations of the Due Process Clause and Bill of Rights provisions. A state must afford suspects and defendants at least this level of basic rights. Because states are quasi-sovereign, state law operates independently of federal jurisdiction if no federal issue arises. Thus, a state court deciding that the *state* constitution entitles defendants to greater rights than guaranteed by the federal constitution creates the "state constitutional ceiling."

A state supreme court might interpret its constitution differently from the U. S. Supreme Court's interpretation of a Bill of Rights provision for a number of reasons. The wording of a state's constitution might grant greater or different individual freedoms or might put them in positive rather than negative form. A state's constitutional history might show that its Framers intended to award greater liberties. Early state legislation might have more broadly defined the meaning of rights later written into a state bill of rights. Local traditions might lead to heightened definitions of state rights, or distinctive local popular attitudes might lead a state supreme court to interpret a state constitutional provision as more favorable to liberty.[39]

The Supreme Court ruled in *Michigan v. Long* (1983) that when a state court discusses state *and* federal law in its opinion, it will not disturb the state court ruling only if it is based on **adequate and independent state grounds.** A state court could guarantee that its ruling would be honored if its opinion included a "plain statement" that the federal cases are discussed only for the purpose of guidance and not as the basis of the state court's decision. To some commentators, *Long* created a wedge that allows prosecutors an opportunity to have a conservative U.S. Supreme Court overturn more liberal state court opinions and "reflects the Supreme Court's animosity to expansion of individual rights."[40] In *Arizona v. Evans* (1995), Justice Ginsburg, joined by Justice Stevens, forcefully attacked the *Long* doctrine because experience had shown that the "plain statement" rule was not working and that it "interferes prematurely with state-court endeavors to explore different solutions to new problems facing modern society."

THE CONTEXT OF CRIMINAL PROCEDURE

Criminal procedure is not a "closed system" of Supreme Court cases and statutes cut off from the larger society. Criminal procedure law links criminal justice practice to a host of social, cultural, political and legal contexts that are felt by the justices who decide cases. A brief introduction to some of the more salient contexts provides a glimpse of the richness and complexity of criminal procedure. As a branch of constitutional law, the study of criminal procedure requires a basic understanding of American history, values, and society, including an appreciation of race relations—subjects that influence all Americans but that come to bear with intensity when justices make decisions that will shape American life. Further, knowledge of English and American constitutional history, political theory, and human rights enhances our understanding of criminal procedure. This section briefly reviews these contextual areas, and commends their further study.

POLITICAL THEORY   Law is not a self-referential "closed system" of rules. To be fully understood and to be legitimate, law must rest on fundamental beliefs held by the people. For example, criminal laws against murder, rape, robbery, and arson are uncontested because of the powerful underlying value that we place on life, personal autonomy, and the safe enjoyment of the home. On the other hand, laws criminalizing the recreational use of marijuana are controversial because they pit the fears of negative health effects and flouting the law against beliefs in personal autonomy in acts that do not directly harm others.

Similarly, criminal procedure law—and the rights it ensures—draws full meaning and importance from its underlying political theories and values. Individual *liberty* is the central American political philosophy.[41] It was deemed an "unalienable right" in the Declaration of Independence (1776). The Preamble to the Constitution (1789) declares that a basic purpose of government is to "secure the Blessings of Liberty to ourselves and our Posterity." To operate effectively, however, law enforcement officers must deprive people of liberty. The Framers' study of history taught them that rulers had used the state's monopoly of force to unjustly deprive people of liberty, thus leading to tyranny. Because "policing is a metaphor for state power [and] the capacity to use force is the defining characteristic of the police,"[42] the criminal justice system both protects and threatens the basis of American political life.

Criminal procedure law is designed to ensure that individual liberty will not be violated without good cause. Most important, the exercise of power by executive branch officers that interfere with liberty is subject to review by the judicial branch. Searches of persons and places, including electronic eavesdropping, must be authorized by judicial warrants. Persons arrested without a warrant must be brought before a magistrate within forty-eight hours or less to ensure that the police had probable cause for arrest. Illegal detention may be questioned by a court under a writ of habeas corpus. People who are charged with crimes are presumed to be innocent and are, for the most part, entitled to bail.

The Fourth Amendment also protects the value of *personal privacy*. The Supreme Court was strongly criticized in 1928 when it held that wiretapping is not a search and does not violate Fourth Amendment rights (*Olmstead v. United States*, 1928).[43] Such an obvious invasion of privacy did not sit well with the American people. In 1968, Congress passed a law bringing electronic eavesdropping within the Fourth Amendment, supporting reasonable law enforcement use of eavesdropping, but requiring judicial warrants to limit and control it.[44] Where Supreme Court rulings have undermined privacy, Congress has in some cases passed laws to ensure the privacy of personal records, bank records, and the like. Some of these protections were weakened by the USA PATRIOT Act.[45] A troubling example is the "sneak and peek" warrant that allows officers to enter homes surreptitiously to look around without notifying the homeowner for a lengthy period. Such warrants have become routine since 2001, not to investigate suspected terrorists, but for ordinary crimes.[46] This is an example of rights against government intrusion withering away in times of hysteria over public safety.

Equality is another hard-won political value in American life that is supported by criminal procedure rules.[47] Before the landmark case of *Gideon v. Wainwright* (1963), poor defendants often went to trial or pled guilty without having a lawyer. Today, depending on the circumstances, the state may also have to pay for an expert witness (*Ake v. Oklahoma*, 1985). These decisions reflect the value of equal treatment before the law, which demands that both rich and poor have a fair trial. This guaranteed right is often undermined, however, by the limited resources provided for indigent defense, which has reached a crisis level (see Law in Society section, Chapter 6). This crisis is a powerful reminder that rights must exist in practice, and not just on paper, to be effective, and that fundamental rights are always subject to attack or erosion. The fact that the right to counsel rests on the fundamental principle of equality is why the lack of material support for indigent counsel is such a troubling issue and arouses efforts to correct the injustice.

Political philosophies such as liberty, privacy, and equality, dearly held in the United States and other Western democracies, rest on two essential legal and political institutions: **constitutionalism** and the Rule of Law. Broadly speaking, a nation's constitution is its rules and stable arrangements for the exercise of government power. Constitutionalism is essentially the ideal that government balances the interests of all its members and is not "captured" by and used for the benefit of one faction. It has roots in Roman ideals of a state's political structure:[48] "For more than two thousand years there has been a remarkably wide and stable consensus that government ought to be carried on within publicly known and enforceable restraints."[49] The modern concept of constitutionalism includes two ideas: limited government and the Rule of Law—"that governments exist only to serve specified ends and properly function only according to specified rules."[50] Constitutionalism implies balanced government and is antithetical to absolutism or tyranny.

The Rule of Law is neither a rule nor a law, but instead a concept of political and legal theory that holds that the government and its officers are not above the law and that the government conducts its business in accord with established legal norms and procedures. In enforcing the law, the government may not exceed its legal authority. The Rule of Law stands in contrast to arbitrary rule and applies to all branches of government. The president, for example, may be subjected to a civil lawsuit while in office (*United States v. Nixon*, 1974; *Clinton v. Jones*, 1997). Legislation is declared void by courts if found to be unconstitutional, and Supreme Court justices' constitutional rulings can be reversed only by constitutional amendment or by a later Court that interprets the Constitution differently.[51]

Constitutional criminal procedure advances constitutionalism and the Rule of Law primarily when the courts prevent governmental abuses of power. Every trial conducted under due process is an example of the need for the government to accede to the judicial branch in enforcing the law; today, the government routinely operates under the law. Civil lawsuits against police officers also manifest the Rule of Law. In our democracy, abuses by law enforcement can also be checked by legislative action and by chief executives. A good example was an executive order by President George W. Bush banning racial profiling in federal law enforcement, with certain exceptions for terrorism investigations.[52] The constitutional ban on ex post facto laws is a classic example of the Rule of Law because conviction under a retroactive law is conviction under no law at all. The same is true when the Supreme Court banned vague criminal laws (*Papachristou v. City of Jacksonville*, 1972).[53]

The courts, as guardians of constitutional liberties, play a central role in maintaining the Rule of Law and constitutionalism. But the courts cannot maintain freedom if the people are not willing to fight for their rights. To a significant degree, the Rule of Law lies in "supporting institutions, procedures, and values."[54] Traditions of liberty, real political competition between the party in power and the "loyal opposition," a spirit of tolerance, the existence of interest groups who will fight vigorously in the political realm to enforce their rights, the absence of an oligarchy (an extremely lopsided distribution of wealth), a measure of political and economic stability, a vigorous political press, a literate and aware citizenry—all play a role in maintaining the Rule of Law. In this kind of society, courts can more effectively ensure that the Rule of Law continues.

HISTORY   In several places, this text refers to English and American legal, constitutional, and political history. Legal history is more than an aid to understanding constitutional law—it is an integral part of the reasoning process used by constitutional lawyers to argue cases and by judges to justify their opinions. For example, in *Printz v. United States* (1997), the Supreme Court declared unconstitutional the requirement in the federal Brady Handgun Violence Prevention Act that required local law enforcement officers to participate in background checks of prospective handgun purchasers. Justice Antonin Scalia noted that the decision turned in large part on the Court's reading of legal history: "Because there is no constitutional text speaking to this precise question, the answer to the [sheriff's] challenge must be sought in historical understanding and practice, in the structure of the Constitution, and in the jurisprudence of this Court."

The historical references in the text are not included for ornamentation but to provide information essential to understanding the Court's decision. A few definitions and basic points are included here to clarify the text. References in the text to "the common law" can be confusing because the term is used as a synonym for *case law* or *judge-made law* and is also used to describe the long period in English history, from the twelfth century to the eighteenth century, when the bulk of English law was developed by the courts rather than by statutes of Parliament. The term also refers to the body of law developed in this period.

Many of the great rights essential to American freedom and enshrined in the Constitution were products of the English common law period. The concept of *due process* has its roots in the provision of the Magna Carta (1215) that no free man would be deprived of life, property, or liberty but according to the law of the land. The mode of *trial by jury* emerged at that time and was the hallmark of the common law justice system. The *writ of habeas corpus*, which is protected by the Constitution, emerged in the fifteenth century. The *privilege against self-incrimination* became a standard of individual rights during the seventeenth century, a period of civil war that led to the victory of Parliament and the development of the constitutional monarchy. The use of *judicial warrants* to justify entry into homes to search for stolen goods is an English practice that became solidified into a constitutional principle at the time of the American Revolution. The colonists praised these "British liberties," and when the original thirteen colonies declared their independence, each adopted the common law of England as their model.

Additional protections that make a jury trial fair were rooted in common law developments: the right to subpoena witnesses, the right to be notified of charges, the rule against double jeopardy, the right to be confronted with accusing witnesses, the right to an impartial and local jury, and the right to have trials open to the public. The independence of the courts is critical to individual liberty. The Constitution gives federal judges life tenure and does not allow their pay to be cut specifically to ensure that judges would not be subservient to the legislative or executive branches. This concept was first developed by English statute in 1702, after the autocratic monarchy had been replaced with a balanced, constitutional system of government. Only the right to counsel in criminal cases came to be seen as essential to fair trials in America before being universally adopted in England.[55]

The creation of the Constitution in 1789 and the Bill of Rights in 1791 reflected the dominant concern of the governing class in the early Republic for the survival of the United States as a nation. The premise of those who framed, ratified, and implemented these foundational documents was that only a united nation with a strong government would survive against external rivals and internal jealousies. A strong government was created, but it was restrained by deliberately fashioned checks and balances and constitutional guarantes of liberty. These ensure that elected officials would not misuse their power. It is not an accident that the Constitution protects a free political culture by placing limits on the state's criminal justice apparatus.

The Civil War (1861–1865) was as much a constitutional as a national crisis. In the Reconstruction period following the war, the Constitution was reframed, in Lincoln's words, to shape a "new nation" that was not only "conceived in Liberty" but also "dedicated to the proposition that all men are created equal."[56] The three "Reconstruction Amendments" did this by abolishing slavery, establishing national citizenship, and guaranteeing the vote to former slaves in the Thirteenth (1865), Fourteenth (1868), and Fifteenth (1870) amendments, respectively. Section 1 of the Fourteenth Amendment is discussed frequently in the text and is a foundation of modern criminal procedure. Under it, "All persons born or naturalized in the United States, and subject to the jurisdiction thereof, are citizens of the United States and of the State wherein they reside." This overruled the Supreme Court's decision in the *Dred Scott* case (1857) that barred persons of African ancestry from obtaining U.S. citizenship. The next sentence extended three rights to citizens as against the states: the "privileges or immunities of citizens," due process, and "the equal protection of the laws." Over the next century, the Fourteenth Amendment's Due Process Clause became the vehicle used by the Supreme Court to ensure that basic liberties were extended to state residents or citizens. Note the terms of the clause: "nor shall any State deprive any person of life, liberty, or property, without due process of law." If a state deprives a citizen or resident of "due process," that person has recourse to the federal courts for protection. The process by which this occurred is fleshed out later in this chapter.

RACE AND CRIMINAL PROCEDURE   Racism and other forms of prejudice have infected American law enforcement, judging, and corrections from slavery through the Jim Crow and civil rights eras to the present time, when racial profiling is a hot-button item even after the election of the first African-American president.[57] Although studying the effects of racism is important in every criminal justice subject, there is an organic link between race and criminal procedure that is summed up in the title of an article by Professor Michael Klarman: *The Racial Origins of Modern Criminal Procedure.*[58] The next section of this text explores how the Bill of Rights, originally applicable only to the federal government, was extended by the Supreme Court to cover the states. This was made possible by protecting the basic civil and political rights of then newly freed blacks in the "Civil War Amendments" to the Constitution. Most important was the Fourteenth Amendment (1868), which prevented *states* from depriving citizens of life, liberty or property without the due process of law.[59] The promise of equality faded and died in the late nineteenth century with the rise of "Jim Crow" segregation, economic oppression, and the political exclusion of African Americans.[60] This oppression was enforced by brutal policing and indifferent courts in the South, including lynching and Ku Klux Klan terrorism.

The foundation of modern criminal procedure, paving the way to incorporation, was established by several landmark cases. Common to each was that they concerned African-American defendants subject to the worst abuses of southern justice in the period between the world wars: *Moore v. Dempsey* (1923) regarding mob-justice, *Powell v. Alabama* (1932) and inadequate legal defense in capital cases, *Norris v. Alabama* (1935) concerning the exclusions of blacks from southern juries, and *Brown v. Mississippi* (1936) exposing the torture of African Americans to obtain confessions.[61] Professor Klarman explains why the Court issued advanced civil rights rulings in criminal justice while in other rulings upholding segregation and the disenfranchisement of blacks. Prior to 1914 the defendants in these cases would likely have been lynched. By the early 1920s the National Association for the Advancement of Colored People (NAACP) had engaged in a vigorous lobbying campaign for a federal statute to outlaw lynching. Although the law never passed, the campaign raised the consciousness of the nation. In fact, the House of Representatives passed anti-lynching legislation, only to have it blocked by a southern and western plurality in the Senate. These cases became cause célèbres as interest groups provided the funding to mount effective cases. Also, the defendants in these cases were clearly or likely innocent. Most important, the South was out of step with the rest of the nation on criminal justice, operating on a different criminal justice paradigm. "For the southern courts, the simple fact that these defendants enjoyed the formalities of a criminal trial, rather than being lynched, represented a significant advance over what likely would have transpired in the pre-World War I era."[62] The immediate effect of these decisions on actual practices of criminal justice in the South was negligible, but Professor Klarman argues that they had a significant effect in mobilizing the efforts and raising the morale of African Americans that was to pay dividends in the civil rights era.[63] It is also clear, when looking at the doctrinal development of constitutional criminal procedure law, that these cases laid a foundation for incorporation and the expansion of federal court oversight of criminal justice through its criminal procedure rulings.

Violent opposition to the civil rights movement in the 1950s and 1960s made it clear to the Supreme Court that the racial equality required by the Constitution and epitomized by *Brown v. Board of Education* (1954) was threatened by a "lawless" criminal justice system.[64] This understanding links three of the great themes, or "agenda items," of the Warren Court. In a lecture, retired Supreme Court justice Arthur J. Goldberg outlined these themes:

> To me, the major accomplishments of the Court during the fifteen years in which Earl Warren was Chief Justice were a translation of our society's proclaimed belief in racial equality into some measure of legal reality, the beginning of a profound change in the mechanics of our political democracy and the revolution in criminal justice, both state and federal.[65]

Even if the cases themselves often avoided explicit mention of the fact that the defendant was African American (as in *Terry v. Ohio*, 1968), the concern that racism may generate unfair verdicts was a factor in many rulings of the 1960s (*Mapp v. Ohio*, 1961; *Miranda v. Arizona*, 1966; *Duncan v. Louisiana*, 1968). It is perhaps no simple coincidence that the Supreme Court since 1972 has neither eradicated nor extended defendants' rights, coinciding with an era of fitful progress in the economic and social equality of minorities in a changing America, and the end of using criminal justice to overtly enforce racial suppression while the remnants of discrimination linger on.[66]

JUDICIAL IDEOLOGY AND EXPERIENCES   Law is a human and a political product. Supreme Court decisions, in particular, are not the mechanical application of preexisting legal rules to fact patterns, but depend in a large measure on the justices' ideological orientations, life experiences, and judicial philosophies. This is controversial to many Americans. In 2009, Supreme Court nominee Sonia Sotomayor had to "assure senators that she believes a judge's job 'is not to make law' but 'to apply the law,'"[67] after being attacked by Republican senators for past statements hinting at the reality that law reflects a judge's values. Given the political theater that Supreme

Court nomination hearings have become, she retreated to making "motherhood and apple pie" statements that none could publicly disagree with. Harvard Law Professor Alan Dershowitz reflected the common knowledge of all legal scholars and social scientists who study the Supreme Court: "Senators pretend to be outraged that a judge might be influenced by her background; and a nominee pretends she misspoke. Every practicing lawyer knows that these external factors matter—and matter a great deal."[68]

The reason is, first, that every Supreme Court decision concerns important issues of legal or constitutional policy. Second, most cases that reach the Supreme Court rarely can plausibly be decided in different ways, each of which is reasonable. Third, in constitutional adjudication, the rules are often broad generalities, such as "due process," that reflect aspirations rather than unambiguous rules like the Article II requirement that the president must be thirty-five years old (U.S. Const. Art II, sec. 1, ¶ 5). Fourth, justices, like all people, have predilections, such as having a "conservative" (Crime Control Model—favoring the prosecution) or a "liberal" (Due Process Model—favoring the defense) orientation to criminal procedure issues. Decisions that reflect these views simply seem "natural" or "right" to the justice.

Justices tend to vote in more or less predictable ways, not according to some party line, but in response to the facts and issues in a case and to existing precedent. Yet, there is an apparent tendency for justices to decide cases in ways that fit their considered judicial viewpoints. Some justices are more predictably liberal or conservative than others, while others are "moderates" who might decide cases less predictably in favor of the prosecution or the defense. The Appendix to this text includes a table, "Summary Information about Selected Supreme Court Justices," that lists the positions of individual justices.

Justices are not perfectly predictable. Their typical patterns of decision may shift in light of views held about a particular legal rule or of prior experiences. Or, views about *stare decisis* or about judicial activism or restraint may generate unexpected decisions. Conservative justices who opposed the incorporation of the Bill of Rights to the states in the 1960s accused the liberal justices of violating judicial restraint and "making law." Today, many conservative decisions are quite "activist." The influence of justices in getting other justices to join their opinions can depend on the depth of their legal analysis, their willingness to modify majority opinions to accommodate the views of other justices, and on the quality of their writing, which is called **judicial craftsmanship.** Well-crafted opinions have the greatest potential to shape the body of law and to leave a lasting legal legacy.

POLITICS   Connected to the fact that law is a human product is the reality that constitutional law cannot be entirely separated from politics—the contest for goods and values in the public sphere. The justices are not legislators and do not respond to lobbyists, although they tend to vote in ways consistent with the broad perspectives of the presidents who nominated them. The most direct political input into the Court comes not after a justice is appointed but before, in the appointment process, when presidents and senators prefer to appoint and vote for justices who reflect their political and ideological perspectives.

Crime and criminal justice became major national political issues in the 1960s. In 1968 the Republican presidential candidate, Richard Nixon, politicized constitutional criminal procedure by attacking the Supreme Court. He claimed that its 1966 *Miranda* ruling was responsible for increasing crime rates and led to rioting in inner cities and antiwar demonstrations by college students. Nixon accused the Supreme Court of having "gone too far in weakening the peace forces as against the criminal forces in this country."[69]

As president, Nixon appointed justices who were expected to take a "hard line" on criminal justice issues. From 1969 to 2006, Republican presidents have appointed thirteen Supreme Court justices, and Democratic presidents only two. These appointees have generally favored the Crime Control Model, demonstrating the link between political considerations and the general trend of how justices vote on cases.

Subsequent chapters focusing on the development of search and seizure law, the right to counsel, confessions, and lineups display a general trend of *shifts* in criminal procedure doctrines from a "conservative," pro-prosecution phase before the 1950s and 1960s, to a "liberal" phase under the **Warren Court** (1953–1969), then back to a more conservative phase under the **Burger Court** (1969–1986), the **Rehnquist Court** (1986–2005) and the Roberts Court (2005–present). Although characterizing an era, a Court, or a justice as "conservative" or "liberal" over-generalizes and misses important nuances, the historic pattern of conservative-to-liberal-to-conservative helps the reader understand the otherwise bewildering twists and turns in constitutional criminal procedure that result from the Court's general political-ideological orientation.

HUMAN RIGHTS   Although this text focuses on U.S. law, it is worth noting that most of the constitutional liberties found in the Bill of Rights are **human rights** under international law and enshrined in the UN Universal Declaration of Human Rights (UDHR) (1948).[70] The UDHR was deemed necessary after the Nuremberg War Crimes Trials publicized Nazi crimes against humanity committed during World War II.[71] Rights are claims created by law and enforced by courts. Human rights are a special class of rights held by a person simply by virtue of being human. They are moral rights of the highest order, grounded in human equality and moral dignity. They should be made legally binding in national, regional, or international law. They include the rights to a speedy and public trial, to subpoena and examine witnesses, and to a lawyer. Due process rights such as notice of charges, the presumption of innocence, and the right to be present at one's trial are counted as human rights. An independent and impartial judge is a human right and is made effective by the lifetime tenure provision of Article III of the U.S. Constitution.

The UDHR lists criminal procedure rights that are essential to a civilized society. Article 5 states that "No one shall be subjected to torture or to cruel, inhuman or degrading treatment or punishment," which is borrowed from the Eighth Amendment prohibition on cruel and unusual punishment. Article 9 states that "no one shall be subjected to arbitrary arrest, detention or exile," a right that is in essence part of the Fourth Amendment. One right not included as a human right is trial by jury, which is unique to the common law system and is not typically used in other civilized nations.[72]

It is gratifying to know that many American constitutional rights are recognized as human rights by the world community. In much of the world human rights are embedded in international charters, and enforced by regional and international courts of justice.[73] These rights appeal to a sense of justice that transcends local cultures. They are central to other rights because democratic politics and human dignity cannot exist when governments use their police to crush all political opposition. A criminal justice system that adheres to human rights principles of criminal procedure ensures a democratic form of government bound by restraint and decency, which, in turn, helps ensure its legitimacy.[74] The danger that some of this was lost in the "global war on terror (GWOT)" is discussed in the Law in Society Section in this chapter.

LAW AND SOCIETY   The primary focus of this text is on legal content and analysis, but placing criminal procedure issues in a law and society context improves understanding of the legal rules and their effects on practice. Law in Society sections at the end of each chapter highlight social forces that changed legal doctrines (e.g., domestic violence concerns), social science findings (e.g., exclusionary rule research), or the fairness of criminal justice practices (e.g., racial profiling, prosecutorial misconduct, and police perjury). The sections that highlight abuses do not mean that abuses are the norm and are not meant to condemn the entire criminal justice system. The great majority of police officers, prosecutors, defense attorneys, and judges act professionally, competently, and within the law. Complacency, however, is never wise when considering liberties, and systemic abuses must be studied if they are to be corrected. Lon Fuller's classic study of the Rule of Law notes that the greatest way in which law fails is by a lack of congruence between the law as written and the law as practiced.[75] It is too much to expect perfection; but too great a gap between professed constitutional liberties and actual practice breeds cynicism and demoralization and may bring about the collapse of our system, as Justice Louis Brandeis warned in his 1928 dissent in *Olmstead v. United States:* "In a government of laws, existence of the government will be imperiled if it fails to observe the law scrupulously." (See the biographical sketch of Justice Brandeis for the quotation.)

INCORPORATING THE BILL OF RIGHTS

The underlying rule is that the Bill of Rights in the U.S. Constitution protects people's rights only against acts of the federal government, *not* against acts of state or local governments. State citizens and residents can look to their state constitutions for protection of their rights. The U.S. Supreme Court, however, modified this rule in a series of cases under the selective incorporation doctrine. As a result most, but not all, of the Bill of Rights applies not only against the federal government but against state legislatures, courts, and executive branch officers, including local police officers. (References to "state" officials in this text include state and local officers, as distinguished from federal officers.) The story of incorporation stretches from the founding to the present day, when citizens question whether the Supreme Court's 2008 declaration that people have a personal right to possess firearms in the District of Columbia will be extended to the states. Incorporation is not a dry, technical issue. The story of incorporation is the story of the slow and difficult growth (and recession) of liberty, and the growth of America as a unified society, exposing its fault lines.

The term *incorporation* indicates that the mechanism by which specific Bill of Rights provisions (e.g., the Sixth Amendment right to a public trial) are applied to state officers is through the Due Process Clause of the Fourteenth Amendment. To use an awkward metaphor, it is as if the Due Process Clause, which applies directly to the states, were a "container" into which Bill of Rights provisions are poured.

At the outset of the Republic, under the Constitution's federal government structure, the Bill of Rights was held to *not* apply to the states. When the Fourteenth Amendment was ratified in 1868, some proponents in Congress believed that establishing the "dual citizenship" of Americans (as state and U.S. citizens) meant that the Bill of Rights would automatically protect citizens against unconstitutional actions by local and state officials. This, however, did not occur and indeed was resisted by the Supreme Court for a century. When most of the criminal procedure provisions of the Bill of Rights were finally incorporated in the 1960s by the liberal Warren Court, its decisions generated an intense political debate. This debate, part of a larger contest over the meaning of the Constitution in such areas as abortion, affirmative action, flag burning and free speech, voting rights, property rights, and the like, polarized constitutional law to a greater extent than had been the case since the days of the struggle over the constitutionality of President Franklin D. Roosevelt's New Deal legislation in the 1930s. After 1972, the composition of the Court became far more conservative. Although the Burger, Rehnquist, and Roberts courts did not dismantle incorporation, they did whittle down the extent to which provisions of the Bill of Rights protect individuals in a host of rulings. These cases are the main subject of this text.

This section explores the process by which the Supreme Court resisted incorporation. The major reason for resistance was the tug of *federalism*—the belief that the federal courts should not interfere in state matters. When incorporation occurred in the 1960s, it indicated that the nation had become more unified about the rights of its citizens, a result that was set in motion by the Civil War and its legal and constitutional outcome. It is worth noting that "substantive" criminal procedure rights became more meaningful because of the incorporation process.[76]

Before the Civil War

Before the Civil War, the Supreme Court held that the Bill of Rights applied only to the federal government and not to the states, despite the fact that the Constitution itself does apply to the states. Article I, section 10, for example, prohibits the states from many actions. Nevertheless, in Chief Justice John Marshall's last constitutional opinion, *Barron v. Baltimore* (1833), the Supreme Court held that the Bill of Rights did not apply to the states. Barron's waterfront land was taken by Baltimore for public use. He felt Maryland did not pay him enough money and sued in federal court, arguing that the state violated his right to just compensation under the Fifth Amendment. The Supreme Court rejected his claim, saying that Barron simply had no case in the federal courts under the Bill of Rights, primarily because the Framers had intended the Bill of Rights to restrict only the federal government, not state or local governments:

> The Constitution was ordained and established by the people of the United States for themselves, for their government, and not for the Government of the individual States. Each State established a Constitution for itself, and, in that Constitution, provided such limitations and restrictions on the powers of its particular government as its judgment dictated. (*Barron v. Baltimore*, 1833)

Although not all Americans accepted the *Barron* ruling, it was the law of the land, and there was no way to change it without amending the Constitution.[77]

The Growth of Federal Judicial Power

At the founding of the nation, most observers, including some justices, felt that the Supreme Court would play a small role in the nation's governance. Under the Court's third chief justice, John Marshall, the Court became a powerful political institution. Because the Court *is* a powerful institution, its modern rulings on criminal procedure, on topics such as the right to counsel, confessions, and search and seizure, help to shape our national policy on fundamental rights.

The Court's authority rests on three major powers that, while not explicitly conferred in the text of the Constitution, are implicit in constitutional history and were confirmed in authoritative decisions authored by Chief Justice Marshall. The first is the power of judicial review—the power to declare acts of Congress unconstitutional when they conflict with the Court's interpretation of the Constitution. This power was asserted in *Marbury v. Madison* (1803):

> Certainly all those who have framed written constitutions contemplate them as forming the fundamental and paramount law of the nation, and consequently the theory of every such government must be, that an act of the legislature, repugnant to the Constitution, is void. . . .
>
> It is emphatically the province and duty of the judicial department to say what the law is. Those who apply the rule to particular cases, must of necessity expound and interpret that rule. If two laws conflict with each other, the courts must decide on the operation of each. . . . (*Marbury v. Madison*, 1803)

Marbury continues to be controversial, but there is no questioning the judicial review power of the U.S. Supreme Court.[78]

The Court's second great power is its ability to declare a *state* ruling, statute, or constitutional provision void because it conflicts with the U.S. Constitution. This is axiomatic under the Supremacy Clause (U.S. Const. art. VI, cl. 2). The Court's power, however, was directly challenged by the Supreme Court of Virginia at a time when the large states were very powerful and the reach of the federal government's authority was not entirely spelled out. In *Fletcher v. Peck* (1810), the Court ruled a state law unconstitutional because it conflicted with the Contract Clause (U.S. Const. art. I, § 10), which prohibits a state from "impairing the Obligation of Contracts." *Fletcher*'s constitutional significance lay in Marshall's opinion, which

> declared categorically that the states could not be viewed as a single, unconnected sovereign power, on whom no other restrictions are imposed than those found in its own constitution. On the contrary, it is a member of the Union, and "that Union has a constitution the supremacy of which all acknowledge, and which imposes limits to the legislatures of the several states, which none claim a right to pass."[79]

The third great power of the Supreme Court is to take jurisdiction over any state case that interprets federal law, including the Constitution, whether in a civil or in a criminal case. This gives the Supreme Court *final say* over the meaning of the Constitution. The Virginia Supreme Court again tried to shield its rulings over the application of federal laws in Virginia from federal Supreme Court review. In *Martin v. Hunter's Lessee* (1816) and *Cohens v. Virginia* (1821), the U.S. Supreme Court held that the Virginia Supreme Court could not hold federal civil and criminal statutes unconstitutional.

Together, these cases helped establish the United States as a "real country" and not a loose federation of fully sovereign states. They confirmed the Supreme Court's authority as the final arbiter of cases arising under the Constitution. They made state governments and state courts responsible under the Constitution to uphold national law. Under Chief Justice Marshall, the Court became a legitimate wielder of power because "the Justices were able to elevate their decisions above the plane of partisan politics, to transform political issues into legal ones, and thereby to increase the political power of the Court."[80] This power, established in the early Republic, allowed the Court to play a central role in the fight to apply the Bill of Rights to the states a century and a half later.

Dred Scott and the Fourteenth Amendment

The infamous *Dred Scott* case, *Scott v. Sandford* (1857), ruled that the "Missouri Compromise" of 1820, which drew an East–West line between free states to the north and slave states to the south, was unconstitutional. In the course of its ruling, it also held that whether or not a state granted freedom and even state citizenship to Americans of African descent, such persons could not be U.S. citizens. This case inflamed political passions and probably hastened the Civil War. The ruling, part of the nation's constitutional law, could not be eradicated by simple legislation. The Thirteenth Amendment (1866), abolishing slavery after the Union victory in the Civil War, did not entirely clarify the civil status of ex-slaves; they were "free," but were they citizens invested with political as well as social and economic rights? The first sentence of the Fourteenth Amendment (1868) was designed to overrule *Scott v. Sandford:* "All persons born or naturalized in the United States and subject to the jurisdiction thereof, are citizens of the United States and of the State wherein they reside."

Having established *national citizenship* in all state citizens, the Fourteenth Amendment went on to confer three rights that national citizens could assert against the states: "the privileges or immunities of citizens of the United States," due process of law, and the "equal protection of the laws." These were vague and open-ended provisions. Did the Framers intend the amendment to "incorporate" the Bill of Rights into the privileges of national citizenship and overrule *Barron v. Baltimore* (1833), as the first sentence of the amendment had overturned *Dred Scott* (1857)? Statements by the amendment's leading proponents, Representative John A. Bingham and Senator Jacob M. Howard, made in the House and Senate during the debate concerning the Fourteenth Amendment, supported this intent. Nevertheless, for a century this interpretation was refused.[81] An early sign in the opposite direction, however, was found in the *Slaughterhouse Cases* (1873). That case declared that a common employment, such as butchering, is *not* a privilege and immunity of federal citizenship and thus is beyond the protection of federal courts against a monopoly that prevented some butchers from operating in certain places. As a result, the Supreme Court permanently made the Privileges or Immunities Clause a dead letter.[82] Could the Bill of Rights be applied to the states through the Due Process Clause?

The Anti-incorporation Cases, 1884–1908

The *Slaughterhouse Cases* aborted the idea that the Privileges or Immunities Clause would be used to inaugurate **total incorporation** of the Bill of Rights. In a series of criminal appeals brought before the Supreme Court from state convictions, lawyers argued that specific provisions of the Bill of Rights of the U.S. Constitution should be held to apply to the states under the Due Process Clause of the Fourteenth Amendment. The Supreme Court consistently refused to adopt this position in each of these cases from 1884 to 1908, with one exception.

In these cases, Justice John M. Harlan was the lone voice whose dissents consistently argued for the application of the Bill of Rights to the states. He contributed to the debate by ending the focus on the Framers' original intent and asserting the idea that due process was a *fundamental* right whose lineage went back to Magna Carta (1215). He argued that a state could not pretend to have a civilized system of government under constitutional requirements if it were allowed to violate the fundamental due process rights of its citizens.

In *Hurtado v. California* (1884), the first of these cases, a defendant convicted of murder argued that the use of a prosecutor's information instead of a grand jury's decision to indict him, as required in federal prosecutions under the Fifth Amendment, was unconstitutional. The majority held that using the information to formally charge the defendant did not violate his Fourteenth Amendment due process rights. Justice Harlan's dissenting opinion reviewed centuries of common law history to argue that common law institutions, including the grand jury, were essential to the political rights cherished by Americans. The majority opinion agreed with this concept as a general matter but concluded that the grand jury was not a fundamental guarantee of liberty and therefore not a component of due process. Note the language used by the majority:

> In the Fourteenth Amendment, by parity of reason, it refers to that law of the land in each State, which derives its authority from the inherent and reserved powers of the State, exerted *within the limits of those fundamental principles of liberty and justice which lie at the base of all our civil and political institutions. . . .* (*Hurtado v. California* [1884], emphasis added)

This phrasing in effect adopted what came to be called the **fundamental rights test,** which became the ultimate criterion of incorporation and gained clarity as it was applied in specific cases. It meant, in theory, that the Supreme Court would not uphold every state criminal procedure rule. Laws or government practices that are blatantly arbitrary or discriminatory would violate due process, even though established by the democratic process, for they would constitute the "despotism of the many, of the majority."[83] To the *Hurtado* majority, an information issued by an elected prosecutor was not unfair and did not undermine "fundamental principles of liberty and justice which lie at the base of all our civil and political institutions." In short, the grand jury is not a "fundamental" right. This is still the law.

Following *Hurtado,* the Court refused to incorporate a variety of other rights, finding that none of them were fundamental rights essential to the civil and political liberty of Americans. One case held that a state eight-person felony jury did not violate due process although federal felony juries had to be composed of twelve, the traditional common law number, under Article III and the Sixth Amendment (*Maxwell v. Dow*, 1900). The last major nonincorporation case of this era, *Twining v. New Jersey* (1908), held that the Fifth Amendment privilege against self-incrimination was not incorporated into the Fourteenth Amendment. The state trial judge informed members of the jury that when deciding guilt or innocence they could take into consideration a defendant's refusal to testify on his own behalf. In federal courts, such an instruction from a judge violated a defendant's Fifth Amendment absolute right to remain silent at trial. Although jurors are likely to wonder why the defendant did not take the stand, they are instructed that the defendant has an absolute right to not testify under the Fifth Amendment. But if the judge adds that they can still take the defendant's silence into account, the jury will be prone to take such statement as a green light to presume that the defendant has something to hide and is guilty.

The only case in this era that effected an incorporation was *Chicago, Burlington and Quincy Railroad Company v. Chicago* (1897). The Court ruled that compensation paid by the state of Illinois for land taken from a railroad company for street improvements was inadequate and a violation of federal due process standards under the Fourteenth Amendment. This case did not mention or overrule *Barron v. Baltimore* (1833). Holding that the Due Process Clause required the states to grant just compensation, the Court appeared to "incorporate" the Fifth Amendment's Just Compensation Clause. A double standard clearly applied. Property rights were deemed so fundamental to the American polity that state violations of the Just Compensation Clause violated the constitutional rights of property owners. Liberty rights, however, were not offended by state rules of criminal procedure that afforded state criminal defendants fewer protections than did federal rules under the Bill of Rights.

Federalism was an underlying reason for the reluctance to apply the Bill of Rights to the states. The Court made clear it was protecting states' rights, warning that incorporation "diminishes the authority of the State, so necessary to the perpetuity of our dual form of government, and changes its relation to its people and to the Union" (*Twining v. New Jersey*, 1908). The Court also feared that the federal judiciary, few in number and hampered by the jurisdictional limits of the time, did not have the capacity to enforce civil rights on recalcitrant states. In the final analysis, it was just too big a change in the federal–state relationship at the time for the majority of Supreme Court justices to accept.

Nevertheless, the fundamental rights language and reasoning of the cases denying incorporation, initiated by Justice Harlan, opened the door to "selective" incorporation in the 1960s. If a later Supreme Court viewed a provision of the Bill of Rights as fundamental, the state would be obligated to abide by such an interpretation of the Due Process Clause.

The next two steps in the incorporation story helped pave the way, although neither step directly involved incorporation. These steps were the adoption of the "due process approach" and the incorporation of First Amendment rights.

Adopting the Due Process Approach

In this text, the **due process approach** is defined as a ruling by the U.S. Supreme Court that an action of a state criminal justice officer violates the Due Process Clause of the Fourteenth Amendment without violating a specific provision of the Bill of Rights. This is so even if there is a parallel between the action held unconstitutional under due process and a specific Bill of Rights provision.

In 1923, the Supreme Court held, for the first time in a criminal appeal from a state, that state court procedures violated a defendant's Fourteenth Amendment due process rights. Five African Americans were sentenced to death after a murder trial that, although perfect in form, was dominated by a bloodthirsty Arkansas lynch mob just outside the courthouse, screaming for death (*Moore v. Dempsey*, 1923).[84] A similar case had come before the Court in 1915, the notorious *Leo Frank* case in which an Atlanta mob's anti-Semitic chants and threats of lynching (later carried out) could be heard by the jury.[85] The Supreme Court in *Frank v. Mangum* (1915) held that a state prisoner could not use a federal writ of habeas corpus to challenge "mere errors" in his trial. Justice Oliver Wendell Holmes Jr. strenuously dissented in *Frank*, arguing, "Mob law does not become due process of law by securing the assent of a terrorized jury. We are not speaking of mere disorder, or mere irregularities in procedure, but of a case where the processes of justice are actually subverted." Despite the hideous injustices surrounding Leo Frank's trial, the majority of the Court could see no violation of due process.

In the next eight years, four members of the Court retired and were replaced, setting the stage for a different decision.[86] Justice Holmes, now writing for the Court's majority, held that federal habeas corpus applied:

> It certainly is true that mere mistakes of law in the course of a trial are not to be corrected in that way. But if the case is that the whole proceeding is a mask—that counsel, jury and judge were swept to the fatal end by an irresistible wave of public passion, and that the State Courts failed to correct the wrong—neither perfection in the machinery for correction nor the possibility that the trial court and counsel saw no other way of avoiding an immediate outbreak of the mob can prevent this Court from securing to the petitioners their constitutional rights. (*Moore v. Dempsey*, p. 91)

The effect of *Moore v. Dempsey* was that a federal district judge could upset the verdict of a local jury, which had been upheld by a state supreme court, if the federal judge found that the conviction violated the defendant's Fourteenth Amendment right to not be deprived of life, liberty, or property without due process of law. This was a revolutionary change in theory and in judicial attitude, even if it fit the text and logic of the Fourteenth Amendment. *Moore v. Dempsey* breached the wall of federal judicial noninterference in state criminal justice. In the next fifteen years, the Court would slowly begin to use this newfound authority to correct gross injustices in a handful of significant cases, typically featuring appalling examples of racism.

The first was *Powell v. Alabama* (1932), the notorious "Scottsboro Case." The Court held that due process was violated because the defendants were not allowed time to prepare a defense and, under the circumstances, were not afforded adequate legal counsel. The Scottsboro defendants were retried, found guilty, and on further appeal, the Supreme Court held that their trial was unfair because African Americans were systematically excluded from Alabama grand juries (*Norris v. Alabama*, 1935). In 1936, the Court ruled that a confession obtained by torture violated due process (*Brown v. Mississippi*, 1936). This trickle of cases became a stream in the 1940s and a river by the 1950s. The Court had, by that time, given state criminal justice a place on its annual dockets. Without the increased attention to criminal cases on the Court's growing civil rights agenda, it is unlikely that the Court would have eventually incorporated the criminal provisions of the Bill of Rights.

Incorporating First Amendment Civil Liberties

Before the Court again considered incorporating criminal procedure provisions in the Bill of Rights, a momentous shift occurred in American constitutional liberties. By the 1930s, the Supreme Court, for the first time, struck down state laws that violated First Amendment rights by reading them into the Fourteenth Amendment, despite the amendment's text, which began, "Congress shall make no law . . ." The free speech cases arose out of (1) state "criminal syndicalism" prosecutions for advocating violence against the government, designed to suppress left-wing political parties, and (2) World War I–era laws making it criminal to advocate resistance to the military draft.

In dictum in *Gitlow v. New York* (1925), Justice Edward T. Sanford assumed that "freedom of speech and of the press. . . are among the fundamental personal rights and liberties, protected by the Due Process Clause of the Fourteenth Amendment from impairment by the States." In *Fiske v. Kansas* (1927), the Court overturned the conviction of a person who simply carried a radical labor manifesto on his person, stating that the Kansas Criminal Syndicalism Law infringed on due process but without mentioning First Amendment free speech. Finally, *Stromberg v. California* (1931) overturned a California law making it a crime to display a red flag as an emblem of opposition to organized government. Chief Justice Charles Evans Hughes's opinion ruled that First Amendment free speech was "embraced by" Fourteenth Amendment liberty; the state law therefore violated the First and the Fourteenth amendments. *Near v. Minnesota* (1931) followed, in which the Court struck down a state law that allowed a judge, acting without a jury, to stop publication of a newspaper article deemed "malicious, scandalous, and defamatory." *Near* prohibited censorship and "prior restraint" of publications and explicitly stated that the freedom of press is included in Fourteenth Amendment due process and that prior restraint strikes at the core of the First Amendment. And in January 1937, a unanimous Court ruled in *DeJonge v. Oregon* that making it a crime to participate in a peaceful political rally violated the First Amendment right of peaceful assembly via the Due Process Clause. Together, these cases clearly "incorporated" First Amendment rights.

In the First Amendment cases, the Court applied the *fundamental rights* test that the Court had developed during the nonincorporation era. On the next occasions when the Court faced challenges to state criminal prosecutions under the Fifth or Sixth Amendment, the constitutional landscape was vastly different, because the Court had incorporated several provisions of the First Amendment. Did the incorporation of First Amendment rights (with the free exercise of religion to soon follow) mean that the Court would be obliged to incorporate rights into the criminal procedure amendments as well?

Resistance to Incorporation and Growing Support, 1937–1960

The great weight of anti-incorporation precedents in criminal cases still had a hold on the Court. In 1937, an important eight-to-one decision by Justice Benjamin Cardozo in *Palko v. Connecticut* held that the Double Jeopardy Clause of the Fifth Amendment was not a fundamental right and therefore was not incorporated into Fourteenth Amendment due process. The defendant had been convicted once for the murder of a police officer during a robbery and sentenced to life imprisonment. Under existing state law, the prosecution appealed on the ground of trial errors. On retrial, Palko was again found guilty and sentenced to *death*. He argued to the Supreme Court that a retrial after an appeal by the prosecutor violated the double jeopardy guarantee. Also, because the first jury had implicitly acquitted him of first-degree murder, he argued that the retrial on that charge was double jeopardy.[87] The Court held that the Fifth Amendment double jeopardy guarantee did not apply against the states, despite the fact that a federal prosecution would violate double jeopardy on the facts of this case.

Why were First Amendment rights incorporated but not Fifth Amendment rights? Justice Cardozo drew a distinction between *fundamental* rights and *formal* rights. Freedoms of speech and press were "so rooted in the traditions and conscience of our people as to be ranked as fundamental" and thus included in due process liberty, he wrote. Criminal procedure rights were merely "formal" and not a part of due process liberty. To be fundamental, a right had to be essential to justice and to the American system of political liberty. The First Amendment cases blocked the operation of state laws out of the "belief that neither liberty nor justice would exist if [these rights] were sacrificed. . . . This is true, for illustration, of freedom of thought, and speech. Of that freedom one may say that it is the matrix, the indispensable condition, of nearly every other form of freedom" (*Palko v. Connecticut*, 1937).

First Amendment rights are fundamental, then, because political freedom rests on the free exchange of political ideas and the ability of citizens to address the government in protest. On the other hand, to Cardozo the criminal procedure provisions in the Bill of Rights were not "of the very essence of a scheme of ordered liberty." He indicated that many democracies had criminal procedure rules that did not afford procedures such as trial by jury, and that Palko's case was not the same as the state trying him many times to get a conviction. The *Palko* doctrine held sway for a quarter of a century before the Court began to incorporate most of the criminal procedure rights in the Bill of Rights into the Fourteenth Amendment Due Process Clause.

Justice Hugo Black's dissenting opinion in *Adamson v. California* (1947), however, marked a turning point that eventually led to incorporation. The case dealt with the same issue as *Twining v. New Jersey* (1908)—whether a judge's comment on a defendant's failure to testify violated his Fifth Amendment rights as incorporated by the Due Process Clause. Again the Court held that it did not. A defendant in Adamson's position, with a prior criminal record, faced a dilemma: If he testified, the prosecutor could bring out the existence of prior convictions to impeach his testimony. If he did not testify, the prosecutor could not introduce his prior convictions. If Adamson had been tried in federal court, the judge would not have been allowed to comment. Applying the Bill of Rights to the states would make the administration of justice in the United States more uniform and would afford greater constitutional protection to individuals.

The majority opinion essentially rested upon precedent. Justice Felix Frankfurter wrote a strong concurring opinion. He was a political liberal but also a judicial conservative and a supporter of **judicial restraint;** his concurrence made him the champion of the Court's anti-incorporation faction. He challenged Justice Black's "total incorporation" idea by stressing that the Court could employ the due process approach to overturn atrocious state action. Justice Black's opinion, based on solid research, powerfully supported the position that the original intent of the Framers of the Fourteenth Amendment was to incorporate the Bill of Rights. This argument placed incorporation of the Bill of Rights on the "constitutional agenda," as three other liberal justices—William O. Douglas, Frank Murphy, and Wiley Rutledge—agreed that the Bill of Rights should be incorporated. With four votes in favor, the chance that incorporation would become the law of the land was in reach of realization.

Justice Black, as much a "constitutional fundamentalist" as a liberal, argued for "total incorporation" in his *Adamson* dissent. There are at least two problems with a Supreme Court decision in one case to apply all of the twenty-six provisions of the Bill of Rights to the states via the Fourteenth Amendment. The first is that no case can come before the Court raising such an issue. A defendant's case gets to the Court by arguing that a *specific* right has been violated. Second, a case that incorporates a provision of the Bill of Rights involves an intense study of the history and jurisprudence of the right and of its impact on criminal justice practice. To do this for each of the twenty-six rights embedded in the first eight amendments is simply beyond the Court's capacity in a single case and would violate norms of the judicial process.

Instead, the incorporation process proposed in these cases, and that indeed occurred in the 1960s, was **selective incorporation,** the decision in a single case that a *specific* right in the Bill of Rights is included in the concept of Fourteenth Amendment due process "liberty" because the particular right is fundamental to the system of "ordered liberty." Any infringement by a state undermines "those fundamental principles of liberty and justice which lie at the base of all our civil and political institutions" (*Twining v. New Jersey*, 1908).

The next incorporation case demonstrated the cleavages between Justice Black and his more liberal colleagues. Sheriff's deputies in *Wolf v. Colorado* (1949) entered a doctor's office without a warrant and seized patient files. In a federal prosecution, such a blatant violation of the Fourth Amendment would have invoked the exclusionary rule, established in 1914 in *Weeks v. United States*, to exclude the use of these records at trial. The issue was whether the exclusionary rule applied to the states. (This issue is covered in greater depth in Chapter 2.)

The majority in *Wolf* held, under the *Palko* standard, that it did not. In an adroit majority opinion, Justice Frankfurter held that the substance of the Fourth Amendment is a fundamental right and therefore incorporated into the Due Process Clause. However, the exclusionary rule was characterized as a remedy, and the Court declined to incorporate it. Justice Black, the champion of incorporation, concurred. As a "constitutional fundamentalist," he was stymied by the fact that the text of the Fourth Amendment does not include the exclusionary rule, and therefore it could not be applied to the states as a constitutional rule. He believed, however, that the exclusionary rule was appropriately applied to the federal courts under the Supreme Court's supervisory authority. Justices Murphy, Rutledge, and Douglas dissented; they believed that exclusion was the only real "remedy" because the police virtually never lost civil suits brought against them in state courts: A right without a remedy is not a true right.

A further division between Justice Black and the rest of the Court was seen in his growing and partial opposition to the due process approach. Justices who opposed incorporation took the position that the due process approach, initiated with *Moore v. Dempsey* (1923) and that had been used more frequently in cases examining confessions taken by local police officers, was sufficient to protect the rights of Americans against the excesses of state and local criminal justice officers. The three liberal justices who followed Justice Black's incorporation lead (Douglas, Murphy, and Rutledge) nevertheless went beyond total incorporation to espouse **incorporation plus**—that is, incorporation of the Bill of Rights *plus* the due process approach where appropriate. Justice Black opposed the due process approach because he saw the use of discretionary power by the justices as a harbinger of *judicial tyranny* and a violation of the limited constitutional powers of judges to decide cases. His position was designed not only to limit state and local government, but also to limit the discretion of federal judges. Justice Murphy, in a separate dissenting opinion in *Adamson*, stated, "Occasions may arise where a proceeding falls so far short of conforming to fundamental standards of procedure as to warrant constitutional condemnation in terms of a lack of due process despite the absence of a specific provision in the Bill of Rights."

The Court next applied the due process approach in a case that created the **"shocks the conscience" test.** In *Rochin v. California* (1952), police broke into the home of a suspected drug seller, invaded his bedroom, scuffled with him after seeing him swallow pills, and dragged him off to a hospital where he was forced to swallow an emetic to vomit up evidence. Justice Frankfurter, writing for the Court, threw out the evidence by relying on a subjective Fourteenth Amendment due process standard: "[T]he proceedings by which this conviction was obtained do more than offend some fastidious squeamishness or private sentimentalism about combating crime too energetically. This is action that shocks the conscience." These police activities "are methods too close to the rack and the screw to permit of constitutional differentiation." The phrase *shocks the conscience* created a label for the Court's due process rule in search and seizure cases: the *shocks the conscience* test. Justice Black concurred but argued instead that such acts compelled a defendant to be a witness against himself, suggesting that the Fifth Amendment prohibition against self-incrimination, which should be incorporated, applied to tangible as well as to testimonial evidence.

The *Rochin* test was criticized as too vague. What shocked the conscience of appellate judges was too capricious a standard to give guidance to police officers or trial judges. It gave the Court sweeping power to inject its likes and dislikes into the Constitution. This criticism was borne out by *Irvine v. California* (1954). Some justices were clearly shocked by FBI electronic eavesdropping of the bedroom of a married suspect for over a month. Justice Frankfurter characterized it as "repulsive." Still, the majority upheld the introduction of the wiretap evidence, did not incorporate the Fourth Amendment exclusionary rule, and limited *Rochin* to acts of physical violence.

The Court signaled its growing concern with civil liberties in search and seizure by overturning the "silver platter" doctrine in *Elkins v. United States* (1960). State police officers obtained evidence of crime by means of an illegal search and seizure of the defendant's home. The evidence was suppressed by a state court. Afterward, the state officers left the evidence (illegal telephone wiretapping equipment) in the safe-deposit box of a local bank, where federal agents obtained it and used the evidence as the basis of a federal prosecution. The Supreme Court held that the federal exclusionary rule applied even though the federal officers did not directly engage in the illegal search and seizure. This practice undermined state efforts to exclude illegally seized evidence by encouraging federal officers "tacitly to encourage state officers in the disregard of constitutionally protected freedom." Justice Potter Stewart's majority opinion was quite favorable to the exclusionary rule, signaling the coming era of incorporation.

The Due Process Revolution, 1961–1969

By 1962, the Supreme Court's membership had changed to include five pro-incorporation liberals: Justices Black and Douglas (Roosevelt appointees), Chief Justice Earl Warren and Justice William Brennan (Eisenhower appointees), and Justice Arthur Goldberg, appointed in 1962 by President John F. Kennedy. But even before this shift, the Court opened the floodgate of incorporation cases with *Mapp v. Ohio* (1961) (reviewed in the next chapter), which held that the Fourth Amendment exclusionary rule applied to eliminate illegally seized evidence from state as well as federal trials.

After *Mapp*, virtually every year during the 1960s brought the incorporation of an additional Bill of Rights provision into Fourteenth Amendment due process. (See Table 1–1.) The Eighth Amendment Cruel and Unusual Punishment Clause was applied to the states in 1962. A state law criminalized narcotics addiction, but the Court viewed addiction as a disease and held in *Robinson v. California* (1962) that the conviction and punishment of a person for a status such as a disease were constitutionally forbidden cruel and unusual punishment. *Robinson* opened the door for the Supreme Court to consider state death penalty cases in *Furman v. Georgia* (1972) and *Gregg v. Georgia* (1976). In 1962, however, *Robinson* did not attract much popular attention.

The next incorporation case, *Gideon v. Wainwright* (1963), was widely publicized and quite popular. It incorporated the right to counsel in an opinion authored by Justice Black, who

TABLE 1–1   Rights Enumerated in Amendments I–VIII of the Bill of Rights

Rights Enumerated	Selective Incorporation	
	Date	Case
Amendment I		
Freedom of speech	1925	*Gitlow v. New York*
	1927	*Fiske v. Kansas*
	1931	*Stromberg v. California*
Freedom of press	1931	*Near v. Minnesota*
Freedom to peaceably assemble	1937	*DeJong v. Oregon*
Free exercise of religion	1940	*Cantwell v. Connecticut*
Establishment of religion	1947	*Everson v. Board of Education*
Amendment II		
Militia/right to bear arms	Open	[*Dist. Colum. v. Heller*, 2008]
Amendment III		
No quartering soldiers	NI	
Amendment IV		
No unreasonable search and seizure	1949	*Wolf v. Colorado* (basic right)
Exclusionary rule	1961	*Mapp v. Ohio* (exclusionary rule)
Amendment V		
Grand jury	NI	[*Hurtado v. California*, 1884]
No double jeopardy	1969	*Benton v. Maryland*
Due process	NA	(14 Amdt. DPC applies)
No self-incrimination	1964	*Malloy v. Hogan*
Just compensation for taking private property	1897	*Chicago, Burlington & Quincy Railroad Co. v. Chicago*
Amendment VI		
Speedy trial	1967	*Klopfer v. North Carolina*
Public trial	1948	*In re Oliver*
Impartial jury	1966	*Parker v. Gladden*
Jury trial	1968	*Duncan v. Louisiana*
Vicinage and venue	NI	[implied in due process]
Notice	NI	[implied in due process]
Confrontation	1965	*Pointer v. Texas*
Compulsory process	1967	*Washington v. Texas*
Counsel	1963	*Gideon v. Wainwright*
Amendment VII		
Jury trial in civil case	NI	[*Walker v. Sauvinet*, 1875]
Amendment VIII		
No excessive bail	[implied]	[*Schilb v. Kuebel*, 1971]
No excessive fine	NI	
No cruel or unusual punishment	1962	*Robinson v. California*

NI, not incorporated.

had argued for its incorporation in a dissent twenty-one years earlier. Over half the states provided counsel for indigent defendants by 1963. The decision appealed to the American sense of fair play: Once a defendant is haled into court, he should have the same basic "equipment" to fight his fight as does the prosecutor. Congress acted to ensure that counsel would be available for indigents in federal cases, and many local bar associations and courts willingly developed systems to provide counsel. There were no dissents in *Gideon*, although some justices argued that the decision should be based on the due process approach rather than incorporation.

The right against self-incrimination, the point of contention in *Twining v. New Jersey* (1908) and *Adamson v. California* (1947), was incorporated and *Twining* was overruled in 1964 in *Malloy v. Hogan* and *Murphy v. Waterfront Commission of New York Harbor*. *Malloy* was a five-to-four decision bringing the Fifth Amendment right against self-incrimination into the Fourteenth Amendment by allowing a witness to refuse to answer questions before a state investigatory body under the Fifth Amendment. *Murphy* unanimously held that a state witness was protected from self-incrimination in federal courts and a federal witness was protected from self-incrimination in state courts. The specific issue in *Adamson* (1947)—whether a judge could comment on a defendant's failure to testify in a state trial—was in effect overruled in *Griffin v. California* (1965).

Other cases incorporating Bill of Rights provisions came in quick succession: *Pointer v. Texas* (1965)—Sixth Amendment Confrontation Clause; *Parker v. Gladden* (1966)—Sixth Amendment right to an impartial jury; *Washington v. Texas* (1967)—Sixth Amendment right to subpoena witnesses under the Compulsory Process Clause; *Klopfer v. North Carolina* (1967)—Sixth Amendment right to a speedy trial; and *Benton v. Maryland* (1969)—Fifth Amendment protection against double jeopardy, overruling *Palko v. Connecticut* (1937).

The Court incorporated the Sixth Amendment right to trial by jury in *Duncan v. Louisiana* (1968). Was a jury trial required for a crime carrying a maximum penalty of two years' imprisonment? To answer this, Justice Byron White analyzed the trend of the incorporation cases and concluded that the standard of what constituted a fundamental right, worthy of incorporation into the Due Process Clause and made applicable against the state, had shifted considerably since the 1937 *Palko* case:

> Earlier the Court can be seen as having asked, when inquiring into whether some particular procedural safeguard was required of a State, if a civilized system could be imagined that would not accord the particular protection. . . . The recent cases, on the other hand, have proceeded upon the valid assumption that state criminal processes are not imaginary and theoretical schemes but *actual systems bearing virtually every characteristic of the common-law system* that has been developing contemporaneously in England and this country. The question thus is whether given *this kind of system* a particular procedure is fundamental—whether, that is, a procedure is necessary to an Anglo-American regime of ordered liberty. (*Duncan v. Louisiana*, 1968, emphasis added)

By the late 1960s, it appeared that the effect of incorporation rulings was to make state rules of constitutional criminal procedure identical to the federal rules. However, several important decisions made it clear that this was not always the case. The basic reason is that the Court did not hold that the Bill of Rights applied *directly* to the states.[88] To this extent, *Barron v. Baltimore* (1833) still had a residual effect. Incorporation meant that a state procedure that came within the general scope of a Bill of Rights provision but did not afford rights that had been granted to federal defendants under the specific provision was held to violate the Due Process Clause of the Fourteenth Amendment. The ruling then applied the interpretation that had been applied to federal defendants. But the intermediate step of incorporation—going *through* the Fourteenth Amendment—gave the Court some "wiggle room" in a few cases decided after 1970 to hold that the precise impact of the federal rule would not apply to the states.

The Sixth Amendment, for example, guarantees federal defendants a jury trial in all crimes. The Court, nevertheless, upheld state laws that eliminated jury trials for crimes punishable by six months or less of imprisonment, calling them "petty crimes." In *Baldwin v. New York* (1970), the Court drew the line of "petty crimes" at six months and struck down a New York law that allowed the crowded New York court system to deprive defendants of a jury trial for crimes carrying penalties of up to one year of imprisonment. In a case decided the same day, *Williams v. Florida* (1970), federal and state standards for rights diverged for the first time. The Supreme Court held that the common law twelve-person jury was not constitutionally mandated by the Sixth Amendment, upholding a state felony conviction by a six-person jury.

Justice Harlan, who opposed the incorporation doctrine, noted that flexibility could have been introduced into constitutional criminal procedure by adhering to the due process case-by-case approach of *Palko*, *Adamson*, and *Rochin*. Now, he argued, rights guaranteed to federal defendants were being diluted in order to impose Bill of Rights protections on the states. The Court was softening the clear meaning and requirements of the Bill of Rights in federal cases.

The Court continued this trend in jury cases. State felony convictions based on less than unanimous jury verdicts were upheld in *Johnson v. Louisiana* (1972) and *Apodaca v. Oregon* (1972), creating the risk that plurality juries would be far less deliberative than unanimous juries. The Court may have felt that it went far enough with these jury cases, and in *Ballew v. Georgia* (1978), it held that a five-person jury violated the constitutional guarantee of a jury.

At present, a few rights in the First through Eighth Amendments have not been incorporated into the Fourteenth Amendment. These include indictment by grand jury, no excessive bail, jury trial in civil cases, the quartering of soldiers, and the right to bear arms as part of a militia. Reflecting on the rights excluded as a result of the selective incorporation approach, a leading commentator suggests that "perhaps it is just as well that they remain unincorporated."[89] In recent years a huge pro-gun lobbying campaign and reconsideration by scholars led the Supreme Court to rule (5–4), in *District of Columbia v. Heller* (2008), that the Second Amendment guarantees a personal right to own guns for personal protection in the home, subject to reasonable regulation. *Heller* will probably be followed by other federal cases seeking to clarify its specific decision. But *Heller* applied only to federal jurisdictions. A footnote in Justice Scalia's majority opinion pointed out that *Heller* did not incorporate the Second Amendment. Nineteenth-century precedents relied on as the basis to not incorporate the right to possess firearms, "did not engage in the sort of Fourteenth Amendment inquiry required by our later cases" (*District of Columbia v. Heller*, 2008). This suggests two things. First, it provides the pro-gun majority on the Court an avenue to incorporate the Second Amendment by asserting that it is a fundamental right. Given the majority's general language in *Heller*, it is reasonable to predict that the Court will incorporate the Second Amendment. As of August 2009, at least two Circuit Courts of Appeal have scrupulously followed precedent and refused to apply to Second Amendment to state regulations, reasoning that "the Court of Appeals should follow the case which directly controls, leaving to the Supreme Court the prerogative of overruling its own decisions."[90] A panel of the Ninth Circuit found that firearms possession is a fundamental right and incorporated, but the entire circuit court set the decision for rehearing en banc, casting doubt on its effect.[91] Judge Easterbrook's clear opinion in the Seventh Circuit held that under Supreme Court precedent only the Supreme Court has the prerogative to overrule its own precedents. It has told lower courts that they do not have the license to go their own ways and anticipate what the Supreme Court might decide under a new case. To do so "undermines the uniformity of national law but also may compel the Justices to grant certiorari before they think the question ripe for decision."[92]

Second, the tenor of the case shows how deeply the general idea of incorporation has penetrated the constitutional culture. Even a conservative Supreme Court that restricts the extent of rights has jettisoned the reasoning of conservative justices in the 1960s who opposed incorporation on federalism grounds.

The due process revolution therefore *nationalized* criminal justice by opening the door to federal court intervention of local and state agencies and courts, making criminal procedure somewhat more uniform. The due process revolution was in sync with the Warren Court's other major agenda items: eradicating legal racial segregation, providing "one person, one vote," and protecting First Amendment rights. Together, all of these advances were designed to ensure the equal participation of all citizens in the political life of the nation. The due process revolution and the other parts of the Court's agenda generated enormous antagonism toward the Supreme Court and its liberal chief justice, Earl Warren, on the part of conservative politicians and many in law enforcement. Since 1970, the Supreme Court, with a more conservative membership under Chief Justices Warren Burger and William Rehnquist, and now Chief Justice John Roberts, has limited the expansion of pro-defendant criminal procedure rights but has not overruled incorporation. Most Americans, while having mixed views of defendants' rights, nevertheless have come to accept the nationalization of the Bill of Rights.

The Counterrevolution

With historic regularity, revolutions produce counterrevolutions. The Warren Court had severe political critics, and a reaction to its rulings began in the early 1970s. Between 1969 and 1996, twelve new justices were appointed to the Court, four by President Richard M. Nixon, one by President Gerald R. Ford, three by President Ronald Reagan, two by President George H. W. Bush, and two by President Bill Clinton. The appointment of ten new justices by conservative Republicans and two by a "new," or middle-of-the-road, Democrat definitely swung the ideological makeup of the Court to the right. This section provides an overview of the shift from liberal to more-or-less conservative rulings in the period since the due process revolution. This overview is a prelude to most of the cases analyzed in this text.

THE COUNTERREVOLUTION THAT WASN'T: THE BURGER COURT (1969–1986)   President Nixon's appointment of four justices led many to believe that the selective incorporation of the Bill of Rights would be overturned.[93] These fears were abetted by Chief Justice Burger's attack on the *Miranda* doctrine and the *Mapp* exclusionary rule in his early cases.[94] The Burger Court did not, however, execute a reactionary return to the preincorporation era. Instead, it held the line against the expansion of rights. "In place of the expected counterrevolution, the Burger Court waged a prolonged and rather bloody campaign of guerilla warfare. It typically left the facade of Warren Court decisions standing while it attacked these decisions from the sides and underneath."[95] For example, the *Miranda* rule stands after more than thirty years of conservative criticism, but a "public safety" exception allows prewarning questions (*New York v. Quarles*, 1984), and a defendant may subsequently be questioned after having exercised *Miranda* rights by requesting the right to remain silent (*Michigan v. Mosley*, 1975). And although the *Mapp v. Ohio* (1961) exclusionary rule was not overruled, an exception was created that allowed the introduction of evidence based on a defective search warrant if the officer relied on it in "good faith" (*United States v. Leon*, 1984).

The Burger Court was not uniformly pro-prosecution and did extend defendants' rights on several occasions. For example, it established a warrant requirement for entry of a house to make a felony arrest (*Payton v. New York*, 1980), and it declared random automobile stops to check driver licenses to be a Fourth Amendment violation (*Delaware v. Prouse*, 1979).

One measure of the success of a Supreme Court's "agenda" over the period of a chief justice's tenure is whether the Court provides a coherent conceptual foundation for its decisions. In general, scholars have found the Burger Court to be lacking a coherent set of guiding principles by which decisions can be measured. Professor Charles Whitebread, examining the lack of doctrinal consistency, has suggested five ways in which the Burger Court approached criminal procedure cases that account for its generally conservative rulings, while not going to the point of rolling back the Warren Court's Bill of Rights incorporation revolution.

First, the Court emphasized the Crime Control Model of the criminal process and was "eager to accommodate what it perceived as legitimate needs of effective law enforcement" rather than taking an evenhanded approach.[96] Second, the Court established a **hierarchy of constitutional rights**. The Sixth Amendment rights concerned with the integrity of the trial and the truth-finding process are protected more strictly than are Fifth Amendment self-incrimination issues, which in turn are given more protection than Fourth Amendment rights concerning search and seizure. Third, this hierarchy is connected with a concern for the factual guilt or innocence of the party whose case is before the Supreme Court. Whitebread believes that this concern distorted the Supreme Court's overriding duty to develop sound and principled general rules for the guidance of the entire court system.

A fourth aspect of the Court's approach was a "jurisprudential preference for case-by-case analysis rather than announcing its decisions in criminal cases in rules."[97] Whitebread sees this as the most dangerous characteristic of the Court's approach. This attribute fails to give lower courts and police clear-cut rules by which to guide their actions. Whitebread correctly predicted a spate of future cases generated by a need to determine how the narrow distinctions established by the Court are to be applied in specific instances. Fifth, the Court fostered the "new federalism" that partially closed the door to federal courts for state defendants, thus transferring significant power over criminal procedure to the state courts. For example, the Court applied a cost-benefit analysis in *Stone v. Powell* (1976) and ruled that Fourth Amendment claims, once raised and decided in state courts, could not be heard again on federal habeas corpus when the state provided a full and fair hearing. The narrowing of federal habeas corpus jurisdiction reversed a hallmark of the Warren Court: opening the door of the federal courts to state defendants in *Fay v. Noia* (1963). The reimposition of procedural barriers indicated an attitude of wishing to return to an era when federal protection of constitutional rights was minimal.

THE COUNTERREVOLUTION THAT WAS: THE REHNQUIST AND ROBERTS COURTS (1986–PRESENT)   It now seems clear that with a few exceptions, the Supreme Court from the mid-1980s to the present has taken a far more conservative stance than the Burger Court. Mary Weddington and W. Richard Janikowski write about the "counter-revolution that is."[98] The counterrevolution can be seen in search and seizure decisions. Although a few Rehnquist Court rulings have upheld traditional Fourth Amendment rights, these have had little practical effect on law enforcement. For example, the Court ruled that the common law "knock and announce" procedure is required by the Fourth Amendment. This ruling has little practical effect, for the "Amendment's flexible requirement of reasonableness should not be read to mandate a rigid rule of announcement that ignores countervailing law enforcement interests" (*Wilson v. Arkansas*, 1995). On the other hand, rulings that acknowledge drug courier profiles as a basis to stop individuals (*United States v. Sokolow*, 1989), that authorize "bus sweeps" for drugs (*Florida v. Bostick*, 1991), that allow searches based on anonymous telephone tips (*Alabama v. White*, 1990), that uphold the "protective sweep" of homes during an arrest (*Maryland v. Buie*, 1990), that permit "plain feel" pat-downs (*Minnesota v. Dickerson*, 1993), that license electronic eavesdropping without minimization procedures (*United States v. Ojeda Rios*, 1990), that sanction arrests in violation of international law (*United States v. Alvarez-Machain*, 1992), that treat a police chase as not being a "search and seizure" (*California v. Hodari D.*, 1991), and that favor full searches of containers in automobiles without warrants (*California v. Acevedo*, 1991) have all substantially unshackled police from serious Fourth Amendment limitations. Many see this diminution of rights as giving political support to an uncontrolled war on drugs and as condoning modern racism.

As for the highly controversial law of confessions, John Decker writes, "The Burger and Rehnquist Courts have more recently reflected a degree of apparent discomfort with the principles of *Miranda*, for the great majority of the opinions interpreting *Miranda* decided since the Warren Court period have not vigorously followed its lead."[99] For example, the use of undercover agents in a jail setting is allowed. While *Miranda* on its face prohibits custodial interrogation without Fifth Amendment warnings, the Court held that because a jailed suspect who speaks to an officer posing as a fellow inmate is not compelled, no warnings need be given (*Illinois v. Perkins*, 1990). The Court has also supported an aggressive campaign by federal prosecutors to disallow effective opposing defense attorneys (*Wheat v. United States*, 1988), claiming there would be a conflict of interest, and has allowed money paid to defense attorneys by drug defendants to be forfeited (*United States v. Monsanto*, 1989; *Caplin & Drysdale v. United States*, 1989).

More telling than specific conservative rulings is the Rehnquist Court's tampering with underlying doctrines. In *Arizona v. Fulminante* (1991), a majority overturned a long-standing precedent and ruled that a coerced confession could be deemed "harmless error." Thus if police coerce a confession and a court, in error, allows such a constitutionally invalid confession to be heard by a jury, a conviction based on the coerced confession can be upheld. The Court was explicit in directing that the central purpose of a trial is to decide questions of guilt or innocence; the introduction of unconstitutional evidence is of lesser importance. Perhaps the most dramatic example of the Rehnquist Court as an activist-conservative Court, interested more in achieving the "right" result than in upholding basic principles, is *Payne v. Tennessee* (1991), which allowed victim impact statements at death penalty hearings. What has shocked commentators is that *Payne* overruled two precedents that were only four years old and that Chief Justice Rehnquist openly stated that precedent is not important where earlier cases were decided by close votes (*Booth v. Maryland*, 1987; *South Carolina v. Gathers*, 1989). He believed "that *stare decisis* 'is not an inexorable command' but instead a 'principle of policy.'. . . *Stare decisis* principles are at their weakest point in 'constitutional cases,' he said, because correction through legislative initiative is virtually impossible."[100] He went on to say that precedent is more important in property and contract rights than in procedural and evidentiary cases. Justice Thurgood Marshall, dissenting, noted that under the majority's theory, the Court's rulings cannot be considered "impersonal reasoned judgements" and that "[p]ower, not reason, is the new currency of this Court's decisionmaking." This was a polite way of saying that the majority opinion was lawless.

The Rehnquist Court has extended the work of the Burger Court in closing the door to federal and collateral appeals. *Brecht v. Abrahamson* (1993) made it more difficult for defendants to challenge errors on habeas corpus review of constitutional error than on direct appeal. Justice Rehnquist "explained that the beyond-reasonable-doubt standard had become too costly for the government."[101] These decisions display a Court that has become hostile to the claims of defendants. What is curious, and even brilliant, is that the Court has shifted virtually every rule and underlying doctrine in favor of the state while at the same time maintaining the facade of the essential right. Thus the *Mapp* exclusionary rule exists and the *Miranda* warnings are still required, but these general rules are shot through with exceptions.

These trends continue into the Roberts' Court era. A characteristic has been the reduction of the application of the Fourth Amendment exclusionary rule, meaning that defendants cannot seek that remedy to challenge illegal police searches and seizures. In *Hudson v. Michigan* (2006) the Court ruled that even though violations of the knock-and-announce rule are constitutional violations, the rule is designed to protect life and limb and not restrict the seizure of evidence, so the exclusionary rule does not apply. And in *Herring v. United States* (2009) the exclusionary rule was held not applicable to illegal search and seizures when police rely on erroneous information about nonexistent outstanding arrest warrants in police computers. Some commentators believe that such rulings pave the way to the Court overruling the exclusionary rule.[102]

LAW IN SOCIETY

Terrorism, Justice, and Liberty

The Constitution's role in criminal justice, effectuated through criminal procedure law, is, in the most general terms, to maintain a balance between order and liberty. The twentieth century tragically produced too many examples of nations with total order and almost no liberty. Nazi Germany (1933–1945) and Stalinist Russia (1922–1953) were the largest and best documented examples, but numerous state tyrannies with torture apparatuses have existed since the middle of the last century in countries like Greece (1967–1974), Argentina (1974–1986), Zaire (now the Democratic Republic of the Congo) under Mobuto Sese Seko (1971–1997), and others. These countries lacked functioning democracies and are aptly labeled **police states**. Fewer examples of total anarchy exist, but in Lebanon from 1975 to 1987, parts of West Africa (Liberia and Sierra Leone, late 1980s to about 2003), Somalia in East Africa for the last twenty years, and central Africa where wars have sporadically erupted between Congo, Rwanda, and Burundi, warlords have flourished, children were drafted into rag-tag armies, millions have died violently, and outrages like mass rape and chopping off peoples' limbs have been common. The lack of order is as hideous in its own way as life in a police state.

The United States has experienced riots, examples of sustained lawlessness (e.g., Kansas shortly before the Civil War; western territories in the late nineteenth century), and a major Civil War (1861–1865), but has been free from the kind of anarchy resulting from a collapse of official order that makes meaningful personal liberty impossible. Instead, the threats to liberty in America have more often resulted from excessive government power. The worst experience, of course, was the existence of constitutionally authorized slavery, followed by a century of Jim Crow repression, which was sustained by totalitarian regimes over chattel slaves to 1865, and highly repressive authoritarian regimes thereafter. It says something about the ideals of liberty that America overcame the enormous pressure of economic advantage, deep-seated prejudice, and inertia to begin to move beyond this dark heritage. This section explores a different source of threats to liberty, connected to the state's criminal justice apparatus, which in the past has in fact submerged personal liberty and today has the potential to bring large numbers of citizens and residents under excessive and unconstitutional government control.

Justice and Liberty in Times of National Crisis

From the first decade of our nation's existence to the present, foreign wars have excited partisan passions, unleashing very real attacks on civil liberties. In times of war the national emergency concentrates necessary extra power in the hands of the government. In almost every American conflict, war was accompanied by war hysteria, very rarely justified, which led to the misuse of the government's concentrated power to imprison innocent and even loyal citizens. In most cases, the cessation of foreign hostilities has eliminated the assault on liberty, but the twentieth-century "national-security state" and a seemingly endless global war on terror (GWOT) has left us with structures that carry the risk of permanently curtailed civil liberties.

In the 1790s undeclared naval wars by Britain and France were carried out against the fledgling United States in the Atlantic Ocean. The pro-English, Federalist-controlled Congress passed the Alien and Sedition Laws, fanned by political paranoia and aimed at mythical fears that pro-French political rivals in the new Republican Party, led by Thomas Jefferson, would overthrow the government. These laws, clear First Amendment violations, made it a crime to disparage the government. A number of political prosecutions, convictions, and imprisonments resulted. The worst of these laws were repealed when the crisis ebbed, but they left a residue—the paranoid use of criminal justice in times of crisis.[103]

Perhaps the most justified use of extra-legal imprisonments during a war was carried out when President Abraham Lincoln suspended the writ of habeas corpus in thousands of cases during the Civil War. Congress validated his exercise of the Suspension Clause. Many detainees were indeed southern sympathizers and collaborators. Although historians have granted the necessity and even the restraint of these acts, the Supreme Court repudiated this unilateral presidential power after the war ended by ruling that detained citizens could not be tried and convicted by military tribunals while civilian courts were functioning (*Ex Parte Milligan*, 1866).[104]

World War I spawned patriotic enthusiasm and a revival of paranoid fears, combined with virulent ethnic hatreds and class antagonisms that had been brewing for decades. In 1917 Congress passed an Espionage Act (also known as the Sedition Act) that, among other things, criminalized willfully obstructing military recruitment. The Supreme Court upheld the convictions of Socialists who peacefully printed and distributed pamphlets arguing against the war (*Schenck v. U.S.*, 1919), and the imprisonment of Eugene Debs, longtime head of the Socialist Party who ran for president from federal prison in 1920 and won almost a million write-in votes. These prosecutions clearly stifled free speech. In reaction, the American Civil Liberties Union (ACLU) was formed, and in a series of landmark cases, the Supreme Court strengthened First Amendment freedoms, limiting the ability of government to stifle unpopular political expression, and incorporated First Amendment provisions.[105] In the turmoil following World War I, a fear of Bolsheviks, a deadly Wall Street bombing, and assassination threats led to the "Palmer raids" in which thousands of people around the country, mostly leftist or pro-labor, were rounded up without warrants or probable cause by federal authorities for interrogation and deportation. The raids were organized by J. Edgar Hoover, who was then a special assistant to Attorney General A. Mitchell Palmer.[106] While this hysteria faded in the prosperity of the 1920s, it showed once again that American society was inherently prone to paranoid overreaction in times of national crisis. Worse was to come.

It is widely known that more than a hundred thousand Japanese Americans were interned in concentration camps for the duration of World War II in a tragic overreaction to the Japanese attack on Pearl Harbor. This horrible injustice, which has been acknowledged by the U.S. government in later years with reparations, was spurred by a combination of war fears that spies lurked among the Japanese-American population, venomous racism, and openly acknowledged greed as the interned citizens and residents were forced to sell their lands and goods at fire-sale prices.[107] Even the Supreme Court could not withstand the pressures of the moment and upheld the internment in a shameful ruling (*Korematsu v. United States*, 1944). Also during World War II, President Franklin D. Roosevelt authorized wiretapping and eavesdropping for the protection of national security, a necessary expansion of power that led to later abuses that were curbed by the Foreign Intelligence Surveillance Act (FISA).[108]

The Supreme Court finally curtailed excessive presidential wartime power in *Youngstown Sheet & Tube v. Sawyer* (1952). President Harry S. Truman nationalized the steel industry by an executive order during the Korean War in order to break a strike that threatened war production. The Supreme Court swiftly ruled that this was an unconstitutional extension of the president's war powers. Justice Jackson's authoritative concurring opinion in *Youngstown Sheet & Tube* has been important in assessing claimed presidential powers in the GWOT. Presidential power under Article II of the Constitution varies in strength; it is most powerful when the president acts with a congressional authorization, weakest when the president acts against a congressional declaration, and uncertain when the Congress is silent on an issue. Because Congress refused to authorize the seizure, it was declared unconstitutional.[109] The Supreme Court evaded deciding whether the war in Vietnam (1963–1975), which was not directly voted on by Congress, was constitutional. It issued mixed rulings regarding civil liberties issues arising out of that war, upholding the publication of the "Pentagon Papers" under the First Amendment (*New York Times Co. v. United States*, 1971), but refusing to declare that military files on thousands of civilians, including Congress persons, activist political organizations, and U.S. Army surveillance of peaceful political activity were a First Amendment violations (*Laird v. Tatum*, 1972). The protests against the Vietnam War in the 1960s and early 1970s produced repressive political crimes and political trials (such as the Anti-Riot Act of 1968 and the infamous Chicago 7 trial of antiwar activists). This carried over into the wiretapping abuses of the Nixon administration and led to the president's resignation under threat of impeachment.[110] While the post-1960s era generated a permanent national consensus that reduced earlier racial antagonisms, spawned a gender equality movement (also necessitated by economic pressures), and supported personal liberties, it also confirmed a deep ideological national divide, with a portion of the nation attributing the military defeats of Korea and Vietnam to perverse liberals unwilling to wage just war to the bitter end, and ready for mobilization in the next national war crisis.

The longest and most severe threat to civil liberty was the rise of the "national security state" for at least half of the twentieth century in an effort to thwart the real threats of fascism, Nazism, and expansionist Soviet communism under Stalin. Fascism and the Axis Powers were defeated both by military victories in World War II and by postwar assistance that painstakingly built democratic regimes in Japan, Germany, and Italy. The long struggle to contain communist global expansion warped American politics and justice in the 1950s with political trials, loyalty oaths, and communist witch hunts (which missed the real Soviet spies). Artists were blacklisted, people lost jobs without really knowing why, local police departments formed "red squads" for snooping on citizens, CIA operatives spied on Americans within the country, and the FBI wiretapped Martin Luther King Jr. and other civil rights leaders—all of which led to a climate of political fear in which the FBI equated a belief in racial equality or other liberal opinions with support for communism.[111]

After these emergency periods passed, repressive laws were typically repealed or declared unconstitutional, and curbs were even placed on excessive law enforcement behavior. Nevertheless, a huge and permanent national security apparatus was created, which may be necessary in a dangerous world, but with the ready capacity to snoop on every house, telephone and computer in America, and the ability, if mobilized, to monitor, harrass, and detain thousands of citizens, as is now being done to illegal and many legal immigrants. All that would be needed to unleash such terrible and unconstitutional powers would be a government that believed that such action was necessary backed up by a plurality of public opinion. In fact, the United states came very close to such a pass in the first decade of the twenty-first century.

The Global War on Terror and the Threat to Liberty

Almost a decade after the September 11, 2001, terrorist attacks on the United States by radical jihadists that took almost three thousand lives, analysts perceive that the so-called "global war on terror" (GWOT) was used as an excuse to draw the United States into a military quagmire in Iraq. The U.S. is slowly drawing down its role in Iraq while the Obama administration is increasing America's war effort in Afghanistan, from whence the militant Islamist terrorists originated. For a number of years the GWOT fueled support for the Bush administration's Iraq policy, but over time the costs of the Iraq war and its negligible connection to terrorism soured the American electorate, which voted for a cautious policy of withdrawal from Iraq and military containment in Afghanistan in the elections of 2006 and 2008.

Perhaps the most incendiary aspect of the Bush administration's GWOT, which may continue in a less virulent form in the Obama administration, was the way in which it violated international law and treaties in the treatment of captured fighters and detainees, including the authorization of torture at the highest levels of government, and has unlawfully spied on Americans. This large and varied topic is relevant to criminal justice because the penetration of homeland security concerns and mechanisms into local law enforcement poses direct threats to liberty; the attractiveness of "effective" extra-constitutional measures has begun to degrade legal protections to "the Blessings of Liberty."

The rationale for extra-legal measures in the GWOT begins with the war metaphor for the anti-terror campaign, as opposed to viewing terrorism as partly a criminal justice issue. The war metaphor, oddly enough, makes it difficult to think of and act on more effective counterterrorism strategies.[112] In our polity, the *criminal model* includes the full panoply of constitutional rights and protections, and limitations on government power, in comparison to alternate systems of justice detailed previously in this chapter. The *war model*, in contrast, allows the government to act with far fewer legal constraints because its goal is not deterrence and punishment but prevention.[113] Under this "new 'paradigm of prevention' . . . prosecutors [have used] every tool at their disposal to investigate, observe and detain potential terrorists before they strike."[114] In times of war, civil liberties are curtailed. The press is more circumspect; military censorship is necessary; certain areas are off limits; freedom of movement is curtailed; and intelligence agencies are given a freer hand to probe civilian secrets. This had happened in the United States by 2006, as a guest scholar at a prestigious think tank labeled Bush administration efforts as "an *extralegal* terrorism war" that was conducted without "making proper legal provisions for . . . practices" such as domestic spying, indefinite detentions, and "conducting tough interrogations"[115]

If, as *The 9/11 Commission Report*[116] makes clear, the jihadist enemies of modern, secular states in the global economy are grounded in extremist views of Islam and in social and economic malaise, it would seem that classic counterinsurgency tactics that rely heavily on police techniques of monitoring, infiltration, interdiction, and prosecution, along with the judicious use of the military and material support for civilians not involved in terrorism, is the way to successfully counter terrorism.[117] It is, after all, patient, meticulous police work in Britain and elsewhere that identified and thwarted the 2006 plot by a small group of criminal terrorists to destroy airliners with explosives disguised as carry-on liquids.[118] The understanding that law enforcement is a key to fighting terrorism is reflected in the Anti-Terrorism Advisory Councils. These councils, involving federal, state, and local governments and the private sector, were set up by the Justice Department to coordinate antiterrorism training and action.[119] The bulk of their activity focuses on police and prosecution.

Detainees: The Court's Finest Hour

The Supreme Court during World War II did not muster the will to support constitutional liberty in the face of a massive war effort, deep prejudice, and executive action. The GWOT's threat to liberty arose in detainee cases. This time the Court was able to muster a majority that balanced the genuine needs of the government against excessive threats to liberty and the writ of habeas corpus posed by the government's acts.

The Afghanistan war brought a large number of detainees within American control. Some were Taliban fighters captured on the battlefield and some were al Qaeda members. Others turned over locals to U.S. forces that included al Qaeda members, but also entirely innocent civilians who were kidnapped for profit.[120] Few were dressed in standard military uniforms or organized into military units of a regular state's army. These detainees were clearly not classic prisoners of war under the Geneva Conventions, to which the United States is a signatory. The State Department's legal advisor noted that the "restraints and sanctions" of the Geneva Conventions still "apply to both lawful and unlawful belligerents."[121]

Secret Justice Department legal memoranda to the contrary advised President Bush that as commander-in-chief of the armed forces, he had *unilateral* authority to detain *anyone* thought to be a terrorist, whether arrested in the territorial United States or captured on a foreign battlefield. Such persons could be secretly detained *indefinitely* without recourse to legal process. The Geneva Conventions were deemed "obsolete."[122] These lawyers "contended . . . that the president wasn't bound by laws prohibiting torture and that government agents who might torture prisoners at his direction couldn't be prosecuted by the Justice Department."[123] They also argued that pain-inflicting methods of interrogation did not constitute torture. This argument "elaborated the Bush administration's view that the president has virtually unlimited power to wage war as he sees fit, and neither Congress, the courts nor international law can interfere." The *Wall Street Journal* called this "an exceptional argument."[124] These arguments clearly violated international and American law.

Acting on this advice, "President Bush signed a secret order granting new powers to the CIA and authorized the CIA to set up a series of secret detention facilities outside the United States, and to question those held in them with unprecedented harshness."[125] This led to acts of torture committed by U.S. personnel and the attempt to confine detainees *indefinitely* without any review of their status under the laws of war that had been codified in the Uniform Code of Military Justice (UCMJ).[126] Detainees were held in military bases in Afghanistan and other countries and some were transferred to a newly constructed prison at the Guantanamo Bay naval base which was under complete U.S. control.

Defense lawyers working for corporate law firms and civil liberties groups, with great difficulty, began to represent individual detainees. The claim of inherent power to detain persons indefinitely under a "unitary executive" set up an historic legal confrontation between the executive and judicial branches. The result thus far has been four landmark Supreme Court decisions that have fundamentally reasserted the Rule of Law and constitutional balance in the American governmental system even in a time of war and terrorism.

The most recent and most important case, **Boumediene v. Bush** (2008), has summarized the monumental constitutional struggle. Shortly after the 9/11 attacks Congress authorized President Bush to use "all necessary and appropriate force" against those who perpetrated the attacks. In **Hamdi v. Rumsfeld** (2004) the Supreme Court held that this authorization gave the president authority to detain combatants. Because Hamdi was an American citizen he was transferred from Guantanamo to the continental United States. Hamdi claimed he was not a combatant. The Circuit Court ruled that Hamdi had no right to challenge the authority of the president, under his Article II powers as commander-in-chief of the armed forces, to indefinitely detain an alleged combatant for the duration of the GWOT. The Supreme Court reversed, and eight of the justices ruled, on varying grounds, that Hamdi could not be held indefinitely without some kind of due process hearing. Yaser Hamdi, incidentally, was released from custody in October 2004 and transferred to Saudi Arabia.[127]

The Bush administration has also claimed that detainees held at Guantanamo have no right to petition courts under habeas corpus, because Guantanamo is under the *de jure* sovereignty of Cuba. The Supreme Court has twice rejected this argument. In **Rasul v. Bush** (2004) it held (6–3) that federal courts have jurisdiction to consider challenges to the legality of the detention of foreign nationals captured during hostilities abroad and incarcerated at Guantanamo Bay, because "the writ of habeas corpus has served as a means of reviewing the legality of Executive detention" and because the writ "does not act upon the prisoner who seeks relief, but upon the person who holds him in what is alleged to be unlawful custody." The Court in *Boumediene* added, in dealing directly with the constitutional right to habeas and not just with the habeas law enacted by Congress, "that the United States, by virtue of its complete jurisdiction and control over the base, maintains *de facto* sovereignty over this territory." After examining the prior case law minutely, the Court concluded that the government's argument would make it "possible for the political branches to govern without legal constraint. Our basic charter cannot be contracted away like this."

While appeals from detainees were pending, Congress passed the Detainee Treatment Act of 2005 (DTA), which stripped statutory habeas corpus jurisdiction from federal courts over Guantanamo cases and gave the Court of Appeals for the District of Columbia Circuit "exclusive" jurisdiction to review detainee status decisions. The Supreme Court in **Hamdan v. Rumsfeld** (2006) held that (1) military commissions set up by the Bush administration to try detainees were illegal because they were not established by Congress and did not comply with the Uniform Code of Military Justice of the Geneva Conventions, and (2) the DTA did not apply to pending cases like Hamdan's. The military commissions allowed hearsay obtained by coercion and verdicts by a two-thirds vote. (Hamdan, incidentally, was finally tried and convicted by a military tribunal, for supporting terrorism as a low-level driver for Osama bin Laden, sentenced to five and a half years, given credit for five years of time served, and was sent back to Yemen and released after completing his sentence.[128])

After *Hamdan*, Congress established military commissions in an act that again stripped the Courts of hearing habeas corpus appeals. In *Boumediene v. Bush* (2009) the Supreme Court (5–4) held that the act of Congress was not an adequate substitute for a habeas corpus petition. More significantly, it firmly held that the *constitutional* habeas provision, known as the Suspension Clause (U.S. Const. art. I., §9, cl.2), "has full effect at Guantanamo Bay." And even more important was the basis of Justice Kennedy's majority opinion. *Boumediene* intimately linked the writ of habeas corpus to the very structure of the Constitution's separation of powers: "This design serves not only to make Government accountable but also to secure individual liberty." Because "the Framers considered the writ a vital instrument for the protection of individual liberty," it follows that the "separation-of-powers doctrine, and the history that influenced its design, . . . must inform the reach and purpose of the Suspension Clause." Thus, unless Congress declares the kind of emergency (that existed during the Civil War) that suspends habeas corpus, Congress cannot water -down the effective powers of a habeas court and cannot "switch the Constitution on or off at will."

Blowback

What is the likelihood that GWOT techniques will seriously erode the liberties of Americans? It is possible to create exaggerated fears. For example, the worst case of the routine, prolonged and truly hideous use of torture on scores of suspects to obtain confessions (several were innocent and sentenced to death), occurred for almost two decades in Chicago's Area 2 precinct in the 1970s and 1980s. The leader of the effort was the precinct's commander, Jon Burge. Burge apparently learned torture techniques in 1969 while serving as an MP in the Ninth Military Police Company of the Ninth Infantry Division in a U.S. facility in the Dong Tam Delta of Vietnam, which held over 1,500 Viet Cong POWs. Despite this sickening case, it seems that no other Vietnam veterans brought torture home to domestic law enforcement. It therefore seems an overreaction for one commentator to warn that when "troops do pull out of Iraq, tens of thousands of them will take up jobs in domestic law enforcement" and will enforce a religious profiling in an America "where warrantless searches are the norm, where racial or religious profiling is part of protocol, and where secret detentions are accepted."[129]

Without hyper-exaggerated fears, there is still much to worry about. Chapter 3 explains how a rarely used pre-9/11 technique of delaying notice of search warrants (called "sneak and peek") has expanded in ordinary law enforcement following its inclusion in the USA PATRIOT Act. A creepy example of this practice was recalled by Brandon Mayfield, a lawyer and American Muslim who was wrongly targeted as a terrorist. Mayfield, his wife, and children would come back to their modest home and find obvious signs that someone was repeatedly entering: window blinds adjusted higher than anyone could reach, oversized footprints in the living room's plush white carpet, a locked deadbolt that the Mayfields never used, and digital clocks and the VCR blinking as if someone had tripped the breaker.[130]

Another concern is the expanded use of the military in domestic law enforcement. Some scholars and libertarian commentators have worried about the excessive use of para-military SWAT teams to enforce the law.[131] In this light, it has been unnerving to learn that Vice President Dick Cheney and other top administration officials, consisting of the same lawyers who said that acts resembling torture were legal when authorized by the president, "argued that a president had the power to use the military on domestic soil to sweep up the terrorism suspects, who came to be known as the Lackawanna Six, and declare them enemy combatants." This use of the military appears to violate the Posse Comitatus Act of 1878.[132]

The largest concern is with the potential for domestic spying. In the 1960s Congress authorized law enforcement electronic eavesdropping under very strict warrant procedures.[133] In 1978 Congress closed a loophole and brought national security eavesdropping under a special warrant procedure, with a Foreign Intelligence Surveillance Court (FISC) consisting of specially selected federal district judges. Between 1979 and 2001 there were 14,036 applications for FISA surveillances or searches, and all but one of these requests were granted.[134] It seems that the eavesdropping was not being misused for partisan political advantage by the various administrations, nor to trample on First Amendment rights. After 9/11, 2001, the Bush administration authorized the National Security Agency (NSA) to monitor thousands of telephone calls and international e-mails where one party was not in the United States and the other was, without FISA warrants. The government claimed that the process was too cumbersome, although the FISA law allowed warrantless surveillance during emergencies, with after-the-fact warrants. The NSA was engaged in "data mining," which picked up a huge number of messages from locations maintained by private telecommunications companies, screened them via supercomputers for those with tell-tale words, and had FBI agents follow up with investigations.[135] An expert called this a classic fishing expedition.[136] "President Bush characterized the eavesdropping program as a 'vital tool' against terrorism; Vice President Dick Cheney said it has saved 'thousands of lives.'"[137] The bitter irony is that the FBI has complained that virtually all of the "steady stream of telephone numbers, e-mail addresses and names" sent to the FBI by the NSA just after the 9/11 attacks, which grew to a flood and required "hundreds of agents to check out thousands of tips a month," led to dead ends or to innocent Americans.[138] Indeed, a report on this matter authorized by Congress and released in mid-2009, "produced by the inspectors general of five federal agencies, found that other intelligence tools used in assessing security threats posed by terrorists provided more timely and detailed information" than warrantless eavesdropping.[139] There are signs that the NSA has continued warrantless domestic surveillance, and it is unclear whether the Obama administration has been sufficiently effective in curbing abuses, although it "said it had taken comprehensive steps to bring the security agency into compliance with the law."[140]

The latest concern for personal liberty stemming form the GWOT is the development of Seventy-two fusion centers as part of an Information Sharing Environment (ISE) in the United States.[141] These have been in the works for four years and are strongly supported by Homeland

Security Secretary Janet Napolitano. The impetus behind fusion centers is to build a total, interlocking database designed to identify potential terrorists. The sources of data are truly staggering. Most fusions centers subscribe to private information-broker services that keep billions of records about millions of Americans, including unlisted cellphone numbers, insurance claims, driver's license photographs, credit reports, car-rental databases, real estate records, currency transactions, corporate charters, utility records, personal locations, associates, relatives, firearms licenses, and a Federal Trade Commission database with information about hundreds of thousands of identity-theft reports. Maryland authorities rely on a little-known data broker called Entersect, which claims it maintains 12 billion records on about 98 percent of Americans. This private data is combined with a host of government files, including criminal justice information and traffic tickets. Some fusion centers claim access to top-secret CIA data. If even one fusion center has access to CIA data, it will be accessible by others.

To these massive data sets, police in dozens of cities enter information on "terror tip sheets" in a Suspicious Activity Reporting (SAR) initiative. Patrol officers enter activities that seem "out of place," such as someone buying police or firefighter uniforms, taking pictures of a power plant, or espousing extremist views. By 2014 the plan is for fusion centers to have in place a standardized system of codes for suspicious behaviors to be used by the 800,000 officers in the 18,000 state, local, and tribal law enforcement agencies.

The centers use law enforcement analysts and sophisticated computer systems to compile, or fuse, disparate tips and clues and pass along the refined information to other agencies. The approach is justified on the claim that terrorists typically have their targets under surveillance before an attack, conducting dry runs of their operations to note guard schedules, to gauge how emergency personnel react to false alarms or abandoned packages and to seek out security weaknesses. In essence, the operations of the fusion centers will involve channeling all the data collected into the computer system of a centralized security agency and the application of data mining to the reports and databases to identify suspicious individuals.

What is also impressive, or of concern depending on one's perspective, is the level of cooperation between local law enforcement, federal law enforcement, intelligence agencies, homeland security, and the military. At present the fusion centers are organized by the states and differ in size and focus. Sizeable federal grants have supported their development.

Needless to say, fusion centers have raised civil liberties concerns. One is that the SAR system may open the door to racial and religious profiling. In September 2007, a twenty-four-year-old Muslim-American journalism student at Syracuse University was stopped by a Veterans Affairs (VA) police officer in New York for taking photographs of flags in front of a VA building as part of a class assignment. The student was taken into an office for questioning, and the images were deleted from her camera before she was released.

Related to this, the SAR reporting authority is so overbroad as to give law enforcement officers justification to harass practically anyone they choose, and to collect personal information and to pass it along to the intelligence community as suspicious.

Another problem is that the SAR system may be illegal. After the scandals raised by "Red Squads" during the cold war, the federal government adopted a prevision of the code of Federal Regulations that bars law enforcement agencies from compiling dossiers on people not involved in wrongdoing. Even if names of "suspects" are not included, the data-mining capabilities of the Information Sharing Environment (ISE) are so powerful that with a few items, innocent individuals can be picked out.

There is also a concern that involving local police in a mission to seek out terrorists will lead to First Amendment violations of privacy and protected activities. The North Central Texas Fusion System bulletin stated that it is "imperative for law enforcement officers to report" the activities of lobbying groups, Muslim civil rights organizations, and anti-war protest groups in their areas. Maryland State Police used undercover officers to spy on non-violent peace activists and anti-death-penalty activists for fourteen months. Some of the reactions of police are absurd. A fifty-four-year-old female artist and fine arts professor at the University of Washington was stopped by Washington State Police for taking photographs of electrical power lines as part of an art project. She was searched, handcuffed, and placed in the back of a police car for almost half an hour before being released.

Another concern is that fusion centers have grown without much oversight and may not be accountable to the public through the legislature. Jim Dempsey, vice president for public policy at the Center for Democracy and Technology, a nonpartisan watchdog group in the District of

Columbia, said that "Congress and the state legislatures need to get a handle over what is going on at all these fusion centers."

If the goal is to identify terrorists, there is a threat to their effectiveness if poor intelligence, in the words of Mike German, a former FBI special agent and ACLU counsel, pollutes the information bloodstream of the fusion centers.

It is worth noting that the national model for fusion centers requires them to have and submit a privacy policy, guided by a federal matrix, to the Departments of Justice and Homeland Security for approval. ACLU lawyers have met with police and federal officials to try to work out tougher safeguards on vetting information that goes into the reports, police training, and privacy and civil liberties protections. A grand lesson of constitutional government is that the state is typically more effective when it is transparent and acts in ways that do not threaten civil liberties. The cooperation between civil liberties lawyers and those responsible for fusion centers suggests that, despite current problems and the awesome power in a central national data base, this lesson is in play in contemporary criminal justice and national security circles.

Summary

Criminal procedure is a branch of constitutional law that pits public safety against the guarantee of liberty. This tension is resolved by the U.S. Supreme Court, which balances the need for public order against the need for liberty. The poles of the tension between order and liberty are also represented by the Crime Control Model, which stresses finality, and the Due Process Model, which stresses the overriding need to avoid miscarriages of justice. These orientations influence the direction of the Court's decisions. A major concern of criminal procedure is that innocent people can be found guilty of crimes. Criminal procedure erects many legal protections for people charged with felonies, but alternate justice systems, with different and less protective legal regimes also exist within society. These include the civil, misdemeanor, juvenile, immigration, and terrorism justice systems.

The legal foundation of criminal procedure includes understanding the definition, classification, and functions of legal rules. Functions include substantive law, which creates rights and obligations; procedural law, which directs officers, lawyers, and judges about how to carry out their functions; and remedial law, which determines what benefits or remedies can be won by parties who prevail in lawsuits. Criminal procedure is procedural law in guiding the conduct of criminal justice personnel, but simultaneously substantive because it creates constitutional rights of suspects and defendants.

The legal foundation includes the jurisdiction and hierarchy of courts. Appellate courts resolve issues of law; they do not retry the facts of a case. The U.S. Supreme Court decides only federal issues, but when it does, its rulings under the Constitution are superior to federal legislation and to state law (including state constitutions). State high courts can decide criminal procedure issues exclusively under their own state constitutions. When they base decisions on adequate and independent state grounds, state supreme courts can grant parties a greater level of individual rights than that granted by the U.S. Supreme Court under the federal Constitution.

Knowledge of the context of criminal procedure provides a better understanding of the subject than can be gleaned only by reading Supreme Court decisions. The context includes such topics as political theory (e.g., liberty, equality), constitutional history, politics, judicial ideology and experiences, and human rights. Knowledge of the relationship between race and the development of constitutional rights is especially important.

The incorporation doctrine is the idea that the Bill of Rights applies as a limitation against state law and state and local officers. Before the Civil War, the Supreme Court ruled that the Bill of Rights applied only to the federal government. Under the Due Process Clause of the Fourteenth Amendment, a state cannot infringe upon the rights of a person, who is both a state and a federal citizen, to due process and equal protection. Congress and the federal courts have the power to enforce the Fourteenth Amendment. During the century after 1868, the argument was made that specific provisions of the Bill of Rights are also guarantees of due process. The Court accepted this concept in the 1960s, and in that decade incorporated most of the criminal procedure rights in the Bill of Rights, thus requiring that states abide by those rights. The federal courts, in addition to finding that a state law or practice violated a right inherent in the Bill of Rights, may also find that a state practice violated Fourteenth Amendment due process if such a practice is fundamentally unfair, as determined by examining all of the facts and circumstances of the case.

Since the due process revolution of the 1960s, the Supreme Court has become quite conservative in its criminal procedure rulings. The Burger Court (1969–1986), in accord with the temper of the times that combined political conservatism with individualism, maintained the incorporation of rights but limited the expansion of most rights and created several exceptions. The Rehnquist Court (1986–2005) and the Roberts Court (2005–present) accelerated this trend.

Further Reading

Context

Benjamin N. Cardozo, *The Nature of the Judicial Process* (New Haven: Yale University Press, 1921).

Charles Rembar, *The Law of the Land: The Evolution of Our Legal System* (New York: Touchstone, 1981).

Bernard Schwartz, *A History of the Supreme Court* (New York: Oxford University Press, 1993).

Incorporation

Akhil Reed Amar, *The Constitution and Criminal Procedure: First Principles* (New Haven: Yale University Press, 1997).

Michael Kent Curtis, *No State Shall Abridge: The Fourteenth Amendment and the Bill of Rights* (Durham: University of North Carolina Press, 1986).

Leonard W. Levy, *Original Intent and the Framers' Constitution* (New York: Macmillan, 1988).

Useful Web Sites

U.S. Supreme Court

http://www.supremecourtus.gov/

Includes PDF versions of the latest cases and information about the Supreme Court and individual justices.

Cornell Law School, Legal Information Institute (LII)

http://www.law.cornell.edu/

Another source of Supreme Court opinions. For a useful document, click on "Introduction to Basic Legal Citation."

End Notes

1. Karen Armstrong, *The Great Transformation: The Beginning of Our Religious Traditions* (New York: Knopf, 2006).

2. David Fromkin, *The Way of the World: From the Dawn of Civilizations to the Eve of the Twenty-First Century* (New York: Knopf, 1998), 157. Forms of constitutionalism existed in the ancient and medieval polities: Charles Howard McIlwain, *Constitutionalism, Ancient and Modern* (Ithaca, N.Y.: Cornell Univ. Press, 1947).

3. John Ralston Saul, *Voltaire's Bastards: The Dictatorship of Reason in the West* (New York: Vintage Books, 1993).

4. U.S. Bureau of Justice Statistics, "Criminal Victimization, Summary Findings," http://www.ojp.usdoj.gov/bjs/cvictgen .htm (accessed June 23, 2006). In 2004, U.S. residents age twelve or older experienced approximately 24 million crimes, according to findings from the National Crime Victimization Survey: 18.6 million were property crimes and 5.2 million were crimes of violence.

5. See Kanan Makiya (Samiral-Khalil), *Republic of Fear: The Inside Story of Saddam's Iraq* (New York: Pantheon Books, 1990); Editorial, "20 Years after Tiananmen, Chinese Democracy Flags. . . ," *USA Today*, June 4, 2009.

6. Herbert L. Packer, *The Limits of the Criminal Sanction* (Stanford, Calif: Stanford University Press, 1968).

7. *United States v. Rabinowitz*, 339 U.S. 56, 69 (1950) (Frankfurter, J., dissenting).

8. James Goodman, *Stories of Scottsboro* (New York: Pantheon, 1994); Anthony Lewis, *Gideon's Trumpet* (New York: Vintage Books, 1964); and James Neff, *The Wrong Man: The Final Verdict on the Dr. Sam Sheppard Murder Case* (New York: Random House, 2001).

9. Paul Averich, *The Haymarket Tragedy* (Princeton, N.J.: Princeton University Press, 1984); and Felix Frankfurter, *The Case of Sacco and Vanzetti* (Boston: Little, Brown, 1927).

10. The Innocence Project, http://www.innocenceproject.org/ (accessed July 26, 2009).

11. Samuel R. Gross et al., "Exonerations in the United States, 1989 through 2003," *Journal of Criminal Law and Criminology* 95 (2005): 523–60; Marvin Zalman, Brad Smith and Angie Kiger, "Officials' Estimates of the Incidence of 'Actual Innocence' Convictions," *Justice Quarterly* 25 (2008): 72–100.

12. Jim Dwyer, Barry Scheck, and Peter Neufeld, *Actual Innocence* (New York: New American Library, 2003); and *Arizona v. Youngblood* (1988).

13. Michael E. Kleinert, "Note: Improving the Quality of Justice: The Innocence Protection Act of 2004 Ensures Post-conviction DNA Testing, Better Legal Representation, and Increased Compensation for the Wrongfully Imprisoned," *Brandeis Law Journal* 44 (2006): 491–508.

14. Seymour Martin Lipset, *American Exceptionalism: A Double-edged Sword* (New York: W.W. Norton, 1996); Michael Walzer, *On Toleration* (New Haven: Yale University Press, 1977).

15. Barton L. Ingraham, *The Structure of Criminal Procedure: Laws and Practice of France, the Soviet Union, China, and the United States* (New York: Greenwood Press, 1987), 22–25.

16. Malcolm Feeley, *The Process Is the Punishment: Handling Cases in a Lower Criminal Court* (New York: Russell Sage Foundation, 1979).

17. Franklin E. Zimring, *American Juvenile Justice* (New York: Oxford University Press, 2005).

18. Jonathan Simon, *Governing Through Crime: How the War on Crime Transformed American Democracy and Created a Culture of Fear* (Oxford; New York: Oxford University Press, 2007).

19. Editorial, "The Principal's Office First," *New York Times*, Jan. 5, 2009, reporting that 17,000 police officers patrol school hallways nationwide.

20. Julia Preston, "304,000 Inmates Eligible for Deportation, Official Says," *New York Times*, March 28, 2008.

21. Nina Bernstein, "Homeland Security Is Ordered to Respond to Petition on Immigration Jails," *New York Times*, June 27, 2009; Editorial, "Justice Ignored," *New York Times*, July 6, 2009.

22. Nina Bernstein, "Another Jail Death, and Mounting Questions" *New York Times*, Jan. 28, 2009; Nina Bernstein, "Piecing Together a Life That U.S. Immigration Refused to See," *New York Times*, July 6, 2009.

23. Bernstein, "Homeland Security."

24. Julia Preston, "Study Finds Immigration Courtrooms Backlogged," *New York Times*, June 18, 2009.

25. Bess Chiu, Lynly Egyes, Peter L. Markowitz, and Jaya Vasandani, *Constitution on Ice: A Report on Immigration Home Raid Operations* (New York: Cardozo Immigration Justice Clinic, 2009.

26. Stanley Kinyon, *Introduction to Law Study and Law Examination in a Nutshell* (St. Paul: West, 1971), 8–17.

27. Yale Kamisar et al., *Modern Criminal Procedure, 12th ed.* (St. Paul: Thompson West, 2008), 1531, citing *Pierce v. Underwood*, 487 U.S. 552, 557 (1988).

28. Bureau of Justice Statistics, *The Growth of Appeals, 1973–83 Trends* (Washington, D.C.: Bureau of Justice Statistics, 1985).

29. Congress has power to make war (art. I, § 8, cl. 8), raise an army and maintain a navy (art. I, § 8, cl. 9 and 10), punish piracy on the high seas (art. I, § 8, cl. 10), and organize militias, allowing some state authority (art. I, § 8, cl. 16). The president is commander-in-chief of the armed forces (art. II, § 2, cl. 1).

30. Postal (art. I, § 8, cl. 7); commerce (art. I, § 8, cl. 3); equal privileges and immunities (art. IV, § 2, cl. 1); full faith and credit (art. IV, § 1); extradition (art. IV, § 2, cl. 2); and territories (art. IV, § 3, cl. 2). No new state can be carved out of an existing state or by combining states without the consent of both state legislatures and Congress (art. IV, § 3, cl. 1).

31. U.S. Const. art. IV, § 4 (republican form of government); and Abraham Lincoln, *The Gettysburg Address* (1863) (Hay Draft), Library of Congress Web site: http://www.loc.gov/exhibits/gadd/gatr2.html (accessed July 30, 2009).

32. U.S. Const. art. I, § 9, cl. 3 and 8; § 10, cl. 1.

33. Nancy E. Marion and Willard O. Oliver, *The Public Policy of Crime and Criminal Justice* (Upper Saddle River, NJ: Pearson/Prentice Hall, 2006), 150–54; John S. Baker Jr., "State Police Powers and the Federalization of Local Crime," *Temple Law Review* 72 (1999): 673–713.

34. The original thirteen states agreed to be bound by relevant portions of the Constitution, and new states may be admitted to the Union only under art. IV, § 3.

35. U.S. Const. art. VI, cl. 3.

36. A federal court can hear state law issues under Article III's diversity jurisdiction (the parties reside in different states) or under "pendent jurisdiction" in which the court hears a case with federal and state issues. Federal courts decide the state law issues in accord with state precedents. The Supreme Court has no jurisdiction to decide a case based exclusively on state grounds, so it cannot take appeals in such cases from lower federal courts.

37. Bernard Schwartz, *A History of the Supreme Court* (New York: Oxford University Press, 1993), 43–45.

38. Helen E. Veit, Kenneth R. Bowling, and Charlene Bangs Bickford, eds., *Creating the Bill of Rights: The Documentary Record from the First Federal Congress* (Baltimore: Johns Hopkins University Press, 1991), 83–84.

39. See the opinion of New Jersey Supreme Court Justice Handler in *State v. Hunt* (1982).

40. Kermit L. Hall, ed., *The Oxford Companion to the Supreme Court of the United States* (New York: Oxford University Press, 1992), 545.

41. Michael Kammen, *Spheres of Liberty: Changing Perceptions of Liberty in American Culture* (Madison: University of Wisconsin Press, 1986).

42. Candace McCoy, "The Cop's World: Modern Policing and the Difficulty of Legitimizing the Use of Force," *Human Rights Quarterly* 8 (1986): 270–93.

43. Walter F. Murphy, *Wiretapping on Trial: A Case Study in the Judicial Process* (New York: Random House, 1967).

44. Yale Kamisar et al., *Modern Criminal Procedure*, 10th ed. (St. Paul: West Group, 2002), 348–87.

45. Patricia Mell, "Big Brother at the Door: Balancing National Security with Privacy under the USA PATRIOT Act," *Denver University Law Review* 80 (2002): 374–427.

46. Nathan H. Seltzer, "Still Sneaking and Peeking," *Criminal Law Bulletin* 42 (2006): 289–307.

47. J. R. Pole, *The Pursuit of Equality in American History* (Berkeley: University of California Press, 1978).

48. For a readable account of Rome's greatest exponent of constitutionalism and the decline of that ideal, see Anthony Everitt, *Cicero: The Life and Times of Rome's Greatest Politician* (New York: Random House, 2003).

49. Glenn Tinder, *Political Thinking: The Perennial Questions*, 4th ed. (Boston: Little, Brown, 1986), 117.

50. Gordon J. Schochet, "Constitutionalism, Liberalism, and the Study of Politics," in J. Roland Pennock and John W. Chapman, eds., *Constitutionalism* (New York: New York University Press, 1979), 1.

51. Compare Raoul Berger, *Government by Judiciary* (Cambridge, Mass.: Harvard University Press, 1977), with R. Dworkin, "Political Judges and the Rule of Law," in *A Matter of Principle* (Cambridge, Mass.: Harvard University Press, 1985), 9–32.

52. Eric Lichtblau, "Bush Issues Racial Profiling Ban but Exempts Security Inquiries," *New York Times*, June 18, 2003.

53. Marvin Zalman et al., "Michigan's Assisted Suicide Three Ring Circus," *Ohio Northern University Law Review* 23 (1997): 863–968.

54. Jerome Hall, *General Principles of Criminal Law*, 2nd ed. (Indianapolis: Bobbs-Merrill, 1961), 27.

55. Charles Rembar, *The Law of the Land: The Evolution of Our Legal System* (New York: Touchstone, 1981).

56. Abraham Lincoln, Gettysburg Address (Hay Draft), Library of Congress Web site: http://www.loc.gov/exhibits/gadd/gatr2.html (accessed August 3, 2003).

57. Patrik Jonsson, "Police and Blacks: Old Tensions Slow to Heal," *Christian Science Monitor*, July 23, 2009 (commenting on the national furor over President Obama's comment on the arrest of a black Harvard professor in his home for disorderly conduct).

58. Michael Klarman, "The Racial Origins of Modern Criminal Procedure," *Michigan Law Review* 99(2000): 48–97.

59. Earl M. Maltz, *Civil Rights, The Constitution, and Congress, 1863–1869* (Lawrence: University of Kansas Press, 1990); and William E. Nelson, *The Fourteenth Amendment: From Political Principle to Judicial Doctrine* (Cambridge, Mass.: Harvard University Press, 1998).

60. August Meier and Elliott Rudwick, *From Plantation to Ghetto*, 3rd ed. (New York: Hill and Wang, 1976).

61. Richard C. Cortner, *A Mob Intent on Death: The NAACP and the Arkansas Riot Case* (Middletown, Conn.: Wesleyan

University Press, 1988); and James Goodman, *Stories of Scottsboro* (New York: Pantheon, 1994).

62. Klarman, "Racial Origins," 49.

63. Klarman, "Racial Origins," 88–97.

64. Richard Kluger, *Simple Justice* (New York: Andre Deutsch, 1977), 748–78.

65. Arthur J. Goldberg, *Equal Justice: The Warren Era of the Supreme Court* (New York: Farrar, Straus, and Giroux, 1971), 5–6.

66. Randall Kennedy, *Race, Crime and the Law* (New York: Pantheon, 1997); Michael Tonry, *Malign Neglect—Race, Crime and Punishment in America* (New York: Oxford University Press, 1995); and Jamie Fellner and Marc Mauer, *Losing the Vote: The Impact of Felony Disenfranchisement Laws in the United States* (Washington, D.C. and New York: Sentencing Project; Human Rights Watch, 1998).

67. Peter Baker and Neil A. Lewis, "Sotomayor Vows 'Fidelity to the Law' as Hearings Start," *New York Times*, July 14, 2009.

68. The Editors, "The Sotomayor Hearings: A Waste of Time?" *New York Times*, July 15, 2009.

69. Fred P. Graham, *The Due Process Revolution: The Warren Court's Impact on Criminal Law* (New York: Hayden, 1970), 15. Also see Louis M. Kohlmeier Jr., *"God Save This Honorable Court!"* (New York: Charles Scribner's Sons, 1972), 79; and Willard M. Oliver, *The Law and Order Presidency* (Upper Saddle River, N.J.: Prentice-Hall, 2003), 70–76.

70. Mary Ann Glendon, *A World Made New: Eleanor Roosevelt and the Universal Declaration of Human Rights* (New York: Random House, 2001); one author simply uses "human rights" as a term for constitutional rights: Michael J. Perry, *The Constitution, The Courts, and Human Rights* (New Haven, Conn.: Yale University Press, 1982).

71. Ann Tusa and John Tusa, *The Nuremberg Trials* (New York: McGraw-Hill, 1983); and Telford Taylor, *The Anatomy of the Nuremberg Trials* (Boston: Little, Brown, 1992).

72. See Richard J. Terrill, *World Criminal Justice Systems: A Survey*, 5th ed. (Cincinnati: Anderson, 2003); and Bron McKillop, "Anatomy of a French Murder Case," *American Journal of Comparative Law* 45 (1997): 527–83. Some nations use juries, but they do not have the same power of juries in the United States to render verdicts without the direct supervision and vote of judges. For recent exceptions, see Stephen C. Thaman, "Europe's New Jury Systems: The Cases of Spain and Russia," *Law and Contemporary Problems* 62 (1999): 233–59.

73. See M. Cherif Bassiouni, ed., *The Protection of Human Rights in the Administration of Criminal Justice: A Compendium of United Nations Norms and Standards* (Irvington-on-Hudson, N.Y.: Transnational, 1994). Reports such as Amnesty International, *Amnesty International Report 2006: The State of the World's Human Rights* (2006), give information on the status of human rights at a given point in time.

74. "Of course, procedural justice must contribute to the common goal of all governments, which is to further the freedom of each member of society and to secure the liberty of all.. . . Thus, criminal investigations and proceedings full of blind revenge and abhorrent to the spirit of the law are detested in western democratic societies." Wilfried Bottke, "'Rule of Law' or 'Due Process' as a Common Feature of Criminal Process in Western Democratic Societies," *University of Pittsburgh Law Review* 51 (1990): 419–61, 439.

75. Lon Fuller, *The Morality of Law*, rev. ed. (New Haven, Conn.: Yale University Press, 1969).

76. For a readable review of the scholarship on incorporation, see Henry J. Abraham, *Freedom and the Court: Civil Rights and Civil Liberties in the United States*, 4th ed. (New York: Oxford University Press, 1982), 28–91.

77. Akhil Reed Amar, *The Bill of Rights: Creation and Reconstruction* (New Haven, Conn.: Yale University Press, 1998), 145–62 (discussing the existence of "contrarians" who believed that the Bill of Rights should apply to state and local government).

78. See Robert Lowry Clinton, *Marbury v. Madison and Judicial Review* (Lawrence: University of Kansas Press, 1989); Wallace Mendelson, *Supreme Court Statecraft: The Rule of Law and Men* (Ames: Iowa State University Press, 1985), 207–62; and Raoul Berger, *Congress v. the Supreme Court* (New York: Bantam, 1969).

79. Bernard Schwartz, *A History of the Supreme Court* (New York: Oxford University Press, 1993), 43, citing *Fletcher v. Peck* at 136.

80. G. Edward White, *The Marshall Court and Cultural Change*, abridged ed. (New York: Oxford University Press, 1991), 197.

81. Michael Kent Curtis, *No State Shall Abridge: The Fourteenth Amendment and the Bill of Rights* (Durham, N.C.: Duke University Press, 1986), 129: The "weight of the evidence from the Thirty-ninth Congress supports the conclusion that the Fourteenth Amendment was designed to require the states to respect all guarantees of the Bill of Rights." See also Amar, *The Bill of Rights*.

82. David A. J. Richards, *Conscience and the Constitution: History, Theory, and Law of the Reconstruction Amendments* (Princeton, N.J.: Princeton University Press, 1993), makes a convincing argument for the idea of total incorporation based on the Privileges or Immunities Clause.

83. For an excellent history of the case, see Richard C. Cortner, *The Supreme Court and the Second Bill of Rights: The Fourteenth Amendment and the Nationalization of Civil Liberties* (Madison: University of Wisconsin Press, 1981), 12–24.

84. Cortner, *A Mob Intent on Death*.

85. Leonard Dinnerstein, *The Leo Frank Case* (University of Georgia Press, 1987); and Liva Baker, *The Justice from Beacon Hill* (New York: HarperCollins, 1991).

86. Professor Klarman disagrees with this analysis; see Klarman, "Racial Origins," 59–60. He failed to note that Butler, although conservative, joined the majority in *Moore*, and was the lone dissenter in *Palko*, indicating that he had a "sense of injustice."

87. Cortner, *The Supreme Court and the Second Bill of Rights*, 126–39.

88. For an argument that such a theory is feasible, see Amar, *The Bill of Rights*.

89. Abraham, *Freedom and the Court*, 90.

90. *Maloney v. Cuomo*, 554 F.3d 56, 59 (2d Cir. 2009)(internal quotations omitted);

91. *Nordyke v. King*, 563 F.3d 439 (9th Cir. 2009) held the Second Amendment applies to the states (but upheld a regulation). The full Ninth Circuit set the case for en banc review: *Nordyke v. King*, No. 07-15763, En Banc Order (9th Cir. July 29, 2009), John Schwartz, "Appeals Court Sets Rehearing on Ruling That Eased Gun Restrictions," *New York Times*, July 31, 2009.

92. *National Rifle Ass'n. v. City of Chicago*, 567 F.3d 856 (7th Cir. 2009).

93. See, for example, Leonard Levy, *Against the Law: The Nixon Court and Criminal Justice* (New York: Harper & Row, 1974).

94. *Bivens v. Six Unknown Named Agents* (1971); *Harris v. New York* (1971); and see M. Braswell and J. Scheb II, "Conservative Pragmatism versus Liberal Principles: Warren E. Burger on the Suppression of Evidence, 1956–86," *Creighton Law Review* 20 (1987): 789–831.

95. Albert Alschuler, "Failed Pragmatism: Reflections on the Burger Court," *Harvard Law Review* 100 (1987): 1436–56, 1442.

96. C. Whitebread, "The Burger Court's Counter-revolution in Criminal Procedure: The Recent Criminal Decisions of the United States Supreme Court," *Washburn Law Journal* 24 (1985): 471–98.

97. Whitebread, "The Burger Court's Counter-revolution," 472.

98. Mary Margaret Weddington and W. Richard Janikowski, "The Rehnquist Court: The Counter-revolution That Wasn't. Part II: The Counter-revolution That Is," *Criminal Justice Review* 21, no. 2 (1997): 231–50.

99. John F. Decker, *Revolution to the Right: Criminal Procedure Jurisprudence during the Burger-Rehnquist Court Era* (New York: Garland, 1992), 65.

100. Decker, *Revolution*, 112.

101. Weddington and Janikowski, "The Counter-revolution That Is."

102. David A. Moran, "The End of the Exclusionary Rule, among Other Things: The Roberts Court Takes on the Fourth Amendment," 2005–06 *Cato Supreme Court Review* (2006): 283–309.

103. David McCullough, *John Adams* (New York: Simon and Schuster, 2001); James F. Simon, *What Kind of Nation? Thomas Jefferson, John Marshall, and the Epic Struggle to Create a United States* (New York: Simon and Schuster, 2002); "Sedition Act of 1798," in Kermit L. Hall, ed., *The Oxford Companion to the Supreme Court of the United States* (New York; Oxford University Press, 1992), 764–65.

104. Mark E. Neely Jr., *The Fate of Liberty: Abraham Lincoln and Civil Liberties* (New York: Oxford University Press, 1991).

105. Richard Pollenberg, *Fighting Faiths: The Abrams Case, the Supreme Court, and Free Speech* (New York: Viking, 1987).

106. Roberta Strauss Feuerlicht, *America's Reign of Terror: World War I, the Red Scare, and the Palmer Raids* (New York: Random House, 1971).

107. Peter H. Irons, *Justice at War* (New York: Oxford University Press, 1983); and

108. Victor S. Navasky, *Kennedy Justice* (New York: Atheneum, 1971).

109. Alan F. Westin, *The Anatomy of a Constitutional Law Case: Youngstown Sheet and Tube Co. v. Sawyer: The Steel Seizure Decision* (New York: Macmillan, 1958).

110. M. Zalman, "The Federal Anti-Riot Act and Political Crime: The Need for Criminal Law Theory," *Villanova Law Review* 20 (1975): 897–937; and Stanley I. Kutler, *The Wars of Watergate* (New York: Knopf, 1990).

111. Stanley I. Kutler, *The American Inquisition: Justice and Injustice in the Cold War* (New York: Hill and Wang, 1982); Frank Donner, *Protectors of Privilege: Red Squads and Police Repression in Urban America* (Berkeley: University of California Press, 1990); David Wise, *The American Police State* (New York: Random House, 1976); and James MacGregor Burns and Stewart Burns, *A People's Charter: The Pursuit of Rights in America* (New York: Alfred Knopf, 1991).

112. Philip B. Heyman, *Terrorism, Freedom, and Security: Winning without War* (Cambridge, Mass.: MIT Press, 2003).

113. See George C. Harris, "Book Review: Terrorism and the Constitution: Sacrificing Civil Liberties in the Name of National Security," *Cornell International Law Journal* 36 (2003): 135–50 (review of David Cole and James X. Dempsey, *Terrorism and the Constitution: Sacrificing Civil Liberties in the Name of National Security*, 2nd ed. [New York: New Press, 2002]).

114. Mark Hamblett, "Terrorism Cases Put Judges Front and Center in Terror Cases," *New York Law Journal*, July 7, 2003, 1.

115. Jonathan Rauch, "Comment: Unwinding Bush," *The Atlantic*, October 2006 (emphasis added).

116. National Commission on Terrorist Attacks upon the United States, *The 9/11 Commission Report*, authorized ed. (New York: Norton, n.d.), 48–53.

117. Ricks, *Fiasco*, 250–51, 264–67, 418–21.

118. McClatchy-Tribune News Service, editorials on failed terror plot: *Monitor* (McAllen, Texas), August 11, 2006; Alan Cowell and Dexter Filkins, "Terror Plot Foiled; Airports Quickly Clamp Down," *New York Times*, August 11, 2006.

119. The Department of Justice's Terrorism Task Forces: Evaluation and Inspections Report I-2005–007 (Office of the Inspector General, June 2005), http://www.usdoj.gov/oig/reports/plus/e0507/index.htm (accessed September 17, 2006).

120. Margot Williams et al., "Voices Baffled, Brash, and Irate in Guantanamo," *New York Times*, March 6, 2006.

121. William H. Taft, IV, "The Law of Armed Conflict after 9/11: Some Salient Features," *Yale Journal of International Law* 28(2003): 317–323, 320–21.

122. Jordan J. Paust, "Executive Plans and Authorizations to Violate International Law Concerning Treatment and Interrogation of Detainees," *Columbia Journal of Transnational Law* 43 (2005): 811–863.

123. Jess Bravin, "Pentagon Report Set Framework for Use of Torture—Security or Legal Factors Could Trump Restrictions, Memo to Rumsfeld Argued," *Wall Street Journal*, June 7, 2004.

124. Bravin, "Pentagon Report."

125. Paust, "Executive Plans," 836 (internal quotation marks omitted).

126. Craig S. Smith and Souad Mekhennet, "Algerian Tells of Dark Odyssey in U.S. Hands," *New York Times*, July 7, 2006.

127. Abigail D. Lauer, "Note: The Easy Way Out?: The Yaser Hamdi Release Agreement and the United States' Treatment of the Citizen Enemy Combatant Dilemma," *Cornell Law Review* 91 (2006): 927–954.

128. W. Glaberson, "A Conviction, but a System Still on Trial," *New York Times*, Aug 10, 2008; Reuters, "Yemen Releases Former bin Laden Driver from Jail," *New York Times*, Jan 12, 2009.

129. Raj Dhanasekaran, "When Rotten Apples Return: How the Posse Comitatus Act of 1878 Can Deter Domestic Law Enforcement Authorities from Using Military Interrogation Techniques on Civilians," *Connecticut Public Interest Law Journal* 5(2006): 233–62, 239–40, 261.

130. Joseph Rose, "Lawyer's Family Victim of 'Sneak and Peak' Searches," *The Oregonian*, May 25, 2004; Eric Lichtblau, *Bush's Law: The Remaking of American Justice* (New York; Pantheon Books, 2008), 65–73.

131. Peter B. Kraska, ed., *Militarizing the American Criminal Justice System: The Changing Roles of the Armed Forces and the Police* (Boston: Northeastern University Press, 2001); Radley Balko, *Overkill: The Rise of Paramilitary Police Raids in America* (Cato Institute White Paper, July 17, 2006),

http://www.cato.org/pub_display.php?pub_id=6476 (accessd August 2, 2009).

132. Mark Mazzetti and David Johnston, "Bush Weighed Using Military in Arrests," *New York Times*, July 25, 2009.

133. C. Whitebread and C. Slobogin, *Criminal Procedure*, 4th ed. (New York: Foundation Press, 2000), 326–359 (Technological Surveillance).

134. Gerald H. Robinson, "We're Listening! Electronic Eavesdropping, FISA, and the Secret Court," *Willamette Law Review* 36 (2000): 51–81; Lichtblau, *bush's Law* 164–67.

135. James Risen and Eric Lichtblau, "Bush Lets U.S. Spy on Callers without Courts," *New York Times*, Dec. 16. 2005; Eric Lichtblau and James Risen, "Spy Agency Mined Vast Data Trove, Officials Report," *New York Times*, Dec. 24, 2005; "AT&T and Domestic Spying," *New York Times*, April 17, 2006.

136. James Bamford, "The Agency That Could Be Big Brother," *New York Times*, Dec. 25, 2005.

137. Lowell Bergman et al., "Spy Agency Data after Sept. 11 Led F.B.I. to Dead Ends," *New York Times*, Jan. 17, 2006.

138. Ibid.

139. Eric Lichtblau and James Risen, "U.S. Wiretapping of Limited Value, Officials Report," *New York Times*, July 11, 2009.

140. James Risen and Eric Lichtblau "Extent of E-Mail Surveillance Renews Concerns in Congress," *New York Times*, June 17, 2009; see Editorial, "The Eavesdropping Continues," *New York Times*, June 18, 2009.

141. The information on fusion centers has been obtained form the following sources: Mike German and Jay Stanley, "ACLU Report, Fusion Center Update," July 2008; Robert O'Harrow Jr., "Centers Tap into Personal Databases; State Groups Were Formed after 9/11," *Washington Post*, April 2, 2008; ACLU Press Release, "Fusion Center Encourages Improper Investigations of Lobbying Groups and Anti-War Activists," http://www.aclu.org/privacy/gen/38835prs20090225.html (accessed February 25, 2009); Eric Schmitt, "Surveillance Effort Draws Civil Liberties Concern" *New York Times*, April 29, 2009; Spencer Ackerman, "ACLUs German Reacts to Napolitano's Embrace of Fusion Centers," Washington Independent, Newstex Web Blogs, July 29, 2009; Spencer S. Hsu, "Napolitano Seeks New Recruit in Terror Fight: You; Strategy Shift Stresses Greater Collaboration," *Washington Post,* July 30, 2009; Thomas McNamara, "Beyond ISE Implementation: Exploring the Way Forward for Information Sharing"; Testimony to House Homeland Security Subcommittee on Intelligence, Information Sharing and Terrorism Risk Assessment Hearing, Congressional Documents and Publications, July 30, 2009; Joseph Fuentes, Superintendent, New Jersey State Police, "Beyond ISE Implementation: Exploring the Way Forward for Information Sharing"; Testimony to House Homeland Security Subcommittee on Intelligence, Information Sharing and Terrorism Risk Assessment Hearing; Congressional Documents and Publications, July 30, 2009.

How to Read and Brief Cases

Reading and understanding Supreme Court opinions is a necessary skill in a constitutional law course. A Supreme Court case is likely to include concurring and dissenting opinions, authored by individual justices, as well as the Court's majority opinion, authored by one justice who speaks for the other justices who join the majority. The opinions are not written in hypertechnical language and so can be understood with a bit of practice. The challenge for beginning students is grasping the formal and polished usage in Supreme Court opinions, sorting out the major components of the opinion. Most important is understanding the decision and the reasoning by which the Court arrived at the decision. In this book, cases presented in the Case and Comments are accompanied by side comments that are like color commentary in a sports broadcast. The comments help readers by defining technical terms, highlighting conflicts between the justices, noting interesting reasoning strategies, and asking questions about values inherent in the case. The **legal reasoning** of Supreme Court opinions is embedded in a system of precedent.

NOTES ON LEGAL PRECEDENT

An appellate decision is precedent—a rule of case law (the holding) that binds lower courts within the court's jurisdiction (e.g., the state for a state supreme court, the circuit for a federal Court of Appeals, or the nation for the U.S. Supreme Court). A lower court decision that does not follow precedent can be *reversed* on appeal. Precedent is also called *authority*. A supreme court will generally follow its own precedent. American law, however, is dynamic, and many Supreme Court cases *overrule* prior precedent. For example, the landmark case of *Gideon v. Wainwright* (1963), which held that an indigent defendant has a right to government-paid counsel in all state felony trials, overruled the prior precedent of *Betts v. Brady* (1942), which had stood for two decades (see Chapter 6). The overruling of prior precedent is infrequent and tends to produce policy discussions in the Court's opinions.

A more subtle process of modifying earlier case decisions is by *distinguishing* earlier precedent. Distinguishing prior precedent requires you to know the difference between a court's **holding** and its decision. A *decision* is the simple rule issued by the Court. It includes, first, whether the decision of the court that follows is affirmed or reversed, indicating which party "won" the case. The decision, or the judgment of the Court, also includes the specific legal rule for which the case stands. The Court's holding is more complex. The holding is the essential legal principle that is derived from a full reading of the Court's opinion, which is based on the facts that are essential to the Court's decision.

The result of every case can be reduced to an abstract statement of a legal principle. Unfortunately, the usage to describe this is not precise. It might be called the "rule" or the "principle" or the "decision" or the "holding" of a case. But for purposes of briefing a case, the *holding* is the principle or *rule* in light of the *facts* of the case.

Law is dynamic. A court that decides a case and writes an opinion does not fix the rule for all time. A later case can widen or narrow the impact of a prior precedent by the way in which it follows or distinguishes the prior case. In *Rochin v. California* (1952),

for example, evidence was excluded because it "shocked the conscience" and thus violated due process. Police entered Rochin's home without a warrant and took him to a hospital where he was subjected to "stomach pumping" that forced him to vomit up swallowed illicit drugs. Two years later, in *Irvine v. California* (1954), the Court ruled that evidence of conversations obtained by placing a listening device in the bedroom of a married couple for twenty days did not "shock the conscience." The evidence was admitted. *Irvine* did not follow the *Rochin* decision (i.e., it was not bound by *Rochin*) because it distinguished that case on its facts, even though the *Irvine* majority excoriated the police action: "Few police measures have come to our attention that more flagrantly, deliberately, and persistently violated the fundamental principle declared by the Fourth Amendment as a restriction on the Federal Government." Justice Frankfurter, the *author* of the *Rochin* opinion, felt that the police did shock the conscience and that the evidence should be excluded under the Due Process Clause. The majority of the Court, however, disagreed and distinguished the earlier case because there was an element of *violence* in *Rochin* not present in *Irvine*. If the majority of the justices felt that listening in on intimate conversations without a warrant shocked their consciences, they could have expanded the *Rochin* rule to add to the shocks-the-conscience category those intrusions not involving physical coercion but intruding on privacy.

A supreme court might modify an earlier precedent for a number of reasons including the trend of earlier decisions, and novel conditions such as the use of new technologies that intrude on privacy. Another reason is that the Court's composition has changed and the new justices have different policy perspectives. This has clearly been the case in constitutional criminal procedure, as the U.S. Supreme Court's policy orientation shifted from conservative before the 1960s, to liberal in that decade, and back to conservative again in the following years. In any event, the process of constitutional decision making is quite complex, supremely important to the United States, and requires substantial effort to fully comprehend.

THE COMPONENTS OF AN OPINION

The first case and comment in the text, *United States v. Leon*, is found in Chapter 2 on page 80. The first line is the case title. The "*v.*" stands for "versus": The appeal is an adversary contest or fight between two parties seeking victory. The battle is conducted with words and with legal ideas. The United States is the *petitioner*—the party that lost the case in the court from which the case was appealed. Leon is the *respondent*—the party that is responding to the petitioner. In state appellate cases, the terms *appellant* and *appellee* may be used instead.

The citation is in the next line. It tells readers where they can find the original printed source of the excerpted case: volume 468 of the United States Reports (the official reporter published by the U.S. Government Printing Office), beginning at page 897; volume 104 of the Supreme Court Reports (published by the West Group) at page 3405 (published by the West Group, St. Paul); and volume 82, page 677 of the United States Reports, Lawyer's Edition, Second

Series (published by the Lexis Corporation). Next, the name of the justice who wrote the majority opinion appears. This opinion is usually the majority opinion, but on rare occasions where a clear majority cannot be mustered, it is the plurality opinion. Not every opinion is authored. *Per curiam* opinions are issued by the Court without indicating an author. Most *per curiam* opinions are brief, straightforward opinions in relatively minor cases. The name of the justice is followed by the body of the majority opinion, followed by concurring and dissenting opinions, listed in order of the seniority of the justices. The majority opinion ends with a line indicating the decision (e.g., "Reversed and Remanded"), not always printed in this text.

The opinion is the essay written by the justice explaining the decision; it includes the holding and the reasons given by the Court for its decision. The reasoning process of an opinion may be complex or simple, eloquent or plain, convincing or vapid, based on narrow legal precedent or on grand principles. Some opinions of Supreme Court justices are classics of American political rhetoric. A majority opinion is not the author's lone effort but has been agreed to by the justices who "sign on" to it. Often, the opinion's reasoning is a matter of compromise, as each of the justices who votes for it makes suggestions as to the proper legal basis for the decision. A statement in the opinion that is not necessary for the decision or the holding is called **dictum** (or *obiter dictum*). Dicta, which can be several paragraphs in length, do not have weight as precedent.

An appellate case may include more than the court's opinion. In addition, some judges may author *concurring* opinions, in which they join the decision or "judgment" of the court but do so for different reasons. A justice who disagrees with the decision "dissents." A dissenting judge need not explain the dissent in a separate opinion, but it is now typical for dissenting justices of the U.S. Supreme Court to do so. Throughout American constitutional history, many doctrines of constitutional law have been overruled by later courts. When this has happened, the later Court often looks to a dissenting opinion in an earlier case. Thus a dissenting justice writes for the future, in the hope that in a later era his or her dissenting view will be adopted.

BRIEFING A CASE

A Supreme Court opinion includes some or all of the following elements:

- The prior history of the case in the lower courts.
- The facts of the case.
- The legal/constitutional issue or issues that the Court is called on to decide.
- The statute or administrative rule that is relevant to the case.
- Prior precedent.
- The "holding," or legal rule in the case as applied to the case facts.
- The reasoning that is essential to the resolution of the case.
- Other nonessential information, known as *obiter dictum*.
- The decision or judgment (e.g., reversed, affirmed, remanded).

Justices need not write these parts of the opinion in any particular order or fashion, although they are usually presented in the order listed.

Students should make notes (called briefs) of each case to help etch the case in memory and to provide a study aid. It is advised that you read the entire case once without taking notes, though underlining or highlighting may be helpful. After this first reading, write the title, the page number in the text, the year of the decision, the justice who authored the opinion, and enough of the prior history of the case so it is clear how the case got to the Court. This mechanical information is not the essence of the case and should be kept short.

There is no one way to brief a case. Use the method that works best for you. Use abbreviations and short phrases, as long as you will be able to understand them later when studying for a test. Once you have successfully thought through the case and understand the opinion, complete the process by writing out—*in your own words*—the most important parts of the case: the decision, the facts essential for the holding, the legal issue, the essence of the reasoning used to resolve the issues, and the holding. The Supreme Court sometimes explicitly states the issue; at other times, one has to read the entire case carefully to understand the actual issue. Once you have read the case through one time, you will know which party won the case and will have an idea of the issue and how it was resolved.

Stating the legal issue or issues in the case with precision is the key to fully comprehending the Court's reasoning. The Court often announces the issue, but at times it is only a formal issue and not the real issue. In a sense, you have to understand the entire case to accurately ascertain the issue. If you think the Court's statement of the issue is accurate, do not copy it; instead, restate it in your own words.

The Court's reasoning, which it uses to resolve the issue, may include analyses of relevant statutes or prior decisions (precedent) and appeals to history, logic, and social policy. For example, in some criminal procedure cases, the justices will to some degree argue that the convenience of the police in enforcing the law is a factor in the decision. In cases arising from state courts, the Court will often raise the issue of federalism. It can be difficult to determine which parts of the opinion contain essential reasoning and which contain statements that are not essential.

The holding of the case is a concise statement of the decision and the facts on which the decision was based. The holding is different from an abstract rule of law and from the decision. The holding is especially important because the precedent of a case is based on the holding rather than on an abstract statement of the law. The concept of the holding is related to the role of courts, for it prevents appellate courts from usurping the legislative function. A court's primary function is to decide cases, and legal rules are formulated in the context of the case's specific facts. Since only the holding is precedent, courts cannot (or should not) issue broad rules that go beyond the facts of the case. In this way, case law builds incrementally, one case after another, based on unfolding experience. A legal doctrine is ascertained by following a "line" of case holdings on an issue. Learning how to trace the development of case law into doctrines is an important legal skill. Appellate courts often try to clarify a ruling by explicitly stating in a case, "We hold. . ." Look for this when reading cases. The holding is more comprehensive than the decision of a case, but it is important to know who won. Students sometimes get so involved in the reasoning of the Court that they forget the outcome. It is useful to indicate "who won" the case in your brief.

Your brief is a practical thing. It should not be longer than a page or two. When preparing for tests, writing a brief once is a more efficient use of your time than rereading a case multiple times, as long as the brief is the product of your thinking about and understanding the case.

JUSTICES OF THE SUPREME COURT

The Precursor Justices: Harlan I, Holmes, Brandeis, and Cardozo

The "precursor" justices of the U.S. Supreme Court include some of the greatest who have sat on the Court. They occupied seats on the Court from 1877 (Harlan) to 1939 (Brandeis) and for the most part decided cases in areas other than criminal procedure. However, each did make an important contribution to constitutional criminal procedure, especially in framing positions concerning the incorporation of the criminal justice provisions of the Bill of Rights into the Due Process Clause of the Fourteenth Amendment.

Justice John Marshall Harlan I forcefully advocated the total incorporation of the Bill of Rights into the Fourteenth Amendment, thereby anticipating the revival of this doctrine by Justice Hugo Black and its eventual adoption, albeit in its "selective" form, during the 1960s. Justices Oliver Wendell Holmes Jr. and Louis Brandeis contributed to incorporation indirectly. First, they championed First Amendment freedom of speech as fundamental to American democracy. At first dissenting against the violation of free speech by state laws, they ultimately convinced the other justices that state laws that violate free speech are unconstitutional. This amounted to the incorporation of key provisions of the First Amendment and so "breached the wall" of the nonincorporation position. This foundation for incorporation was blocked by Justice Benjamin Cardozo, who built an intellectually strong argument against incorporation in the *Palko* (1938) case. That is, he defined First Amendment rights as fundamental and therefore as a part of due process. Fourth, Fifth, and Sixth Amendment rights, however, were defined as "formal" and not worthy of incorporation.

A profound principle of federalism, with enormous practical implications, was at play. Incorporation would undoubtedly bring the federal courts into the running of state criminal justice, and from the creation of the Republic criminal justice had been left entirely to the states. On this point, incorporation was also assisted by an important ruling, *Moore v. Dempsey* (1923) championed by Justice Holmes. It held that a fundamentally unfair state trial violated the Due Process Clause of the Fourteenth Amendment, which prohibits any state from depriving a person of life, liberty, or property without due process of law. Thus, well before the incorporation doctrine became a matter of constitutional law in the 1960s, the door to federal court interference into state criminal justice had been opened.

John M. Harlan I

Kentucky, 1833–1911

Republican

Appointed by Rutherford B. Hayes

Years of Service: 1877–1911

Collection of the Supreme Court of the United States. Photographer: Mathew Brady.

Life and Career.   Harlan was the son of a prominent Kentucky attorney and of a slaveholding family. An 1850 graduate of Centre College, he studied law in his father's office. After admission to the bar in 1853, he practiced law and was politically active. During the Civil War, he fought on the Union side. In 1864, he was elected attorney general of Kentucky as a Democrat and opposed the Thirteenth Amendment. He later underwent an extreme change of views, becoming a radical Republican and an ardent supporter of African-American civil rights.

Harlan ran unsuccessfully for Kentucky governor in 1871 and 1875. At the 1876 Republican nominating convention, he swung the Kentucky delegation to Rutherford B. Hayes and was rewarded with a nomination to the Supreme Court the following year.

Contribution to Criminal Procedure.   Harlan's great contribution to criminal procedure was to champion the incorporation of the Bill of Rights into the Fourteenth Amendment in order to make the federally guaranteed rights apply against state and local officers. He never succeeded in convincing the Court to incorporate any right other than the Just Compensation Clause of the Fifth Amendment, but his efforts paved the way for the due process revolution of the 1960s.

The importance of Harlan's dissents in *Hurtado v. California* (1884), *Twining v. New Jersey* (1908), and other cases concerning the rights of state criminal defendants under the Fifth, Sixth, and Eighth Amendments was not simply that he championed incorporation. As a "great dissenter," his forceful opinions required the majority to formulate reasoned arguments in response to his position that the post–Civil War Reconstruction amendments fundamentally changed the nature of American federalism. To his mind, these rights were essential to citizenship. The majority opinions in these cases were forced to agree that if a state were to violate the fundamental rights of a citizen, this would violate due process. Although the Court at that time did not view the criminal procedure rights as fundamental, a later Supreme Court used the "fundamental rights" formulation to selectively incorporate most of the Bill of Rights.

Signature Opinion.   Dissenting opinion in *Hurtado v. California* (1884). Harlan argued that the grand jury provision of the Fifth Amendment was violated by charging a person with a felony by a prosecutor's information rather than a grand jury indictment.

Assessment.   In economic matters, Harlan opposed state economic regulations and favored laissez-faire pro-capitalist doctrines; on the other hand, he was a nationalist and so supported federal regulation, such as the Sherman Anti-Trust Act, against great economic concentration. He is best known for his lone dissent in *Plessy v. Furguson* (1896), arguing against the "separate but equal" interpretation of the Equal Protection Clause that upheld the state segregation laws. Harlan, arguing that the very intent of the law was to perpetuate inequality, castigated the majority for joining Louisiana in a charade. He wrote that "there is in this country no superior, dominant, ruling class of citizens. There is no caste here. Our Constitution is color-blind, and neither knows nor tolerates classes among citizens. . . . The destinies of the two races, in this country, are indissolubly together, and the interests of both require that the common government of all shall not permit the seeds of race hate to be planted under the sanction of the law." The Great Dissenter discerned with more accuracy than his brethren the true nature of the American polity and its ideals.

Further Reading

Tinsley E. Yarbrough, *Judicial Enigma: The First Harlan* (New York: Oxford University Press, 1995).

Oliver Wendell Holmes Jr.

Massachusetts, 1841–1935
Republican
Appointed by Theodore Roosevelt
Years of Service: 1902–1932

Collection of the Supreme
Court of the United States.
Photographer: Harris and
Ewing.

Life and Career.   Holmes was born in Boston to an established "Boston Brahmin" family, but not one of great wealth. His father was a professor of medicine at Harvard and a famous essayist. Holmes attended Harvard College in 1857. His family was devoted to the Union cause, and Holmes entered military service soon after the Civil War broke out. He was seriously wounded three times during his three years of service. He rose to the rank of captain and mustered out in the summer of 1864. His war experiences led him to see life as a struggle.

His great ambition was to become famous through his philosophical writings, but he entered the law in order to make a living. Nevertheless, while practicing law he pursued legal scholarship, editing the *American Law Review* and studying the old English cases of the common law. This resulted in a series of lectures and a book, *The Common Law* (1881), a seminal work of legal scholarship that did indeed make him famous. The book delved into the tangled web of old cases and demonstrated that there were coherent utilitarian reasons for seemingly irrational rules of law. The magisterial opening phrase of *The Common Law* sounded the theme of the pathbreaking philosophy of legal realism: "The life of the law has not been logic; it has been experience. The felt necessities of the time, the prevalent moral and political theories, intuitions of public policy, avowed or unconscious, even the prejudices which judges share with their fellow men, have a good deal more to do than the syllogism in determining the rules by which men should be governed."

After a brief appointment to the Harvard law faculty, he accepted an appointment to the Massachusetts Supreme Judicial Court (1883–1902), on which he served with distinction before his appointment to the U.S. Supreme Court.

Contribution to Criminal Procedure.   The Supreme Court heard few criminal procedure cases in his era, and so Holmes had little opportunity to write extensively on these issues. He took a conservative stance in an early Eighth Amendment case, viewing the Cruel and Unusual Punishment Clause as static; he advanced modern Fourth Amendment law in the *Weeks* (1914) and *Silverthorne* (1920) cases by voting for and writing in favor of the exclusionary rule. His adherence to the Rule of Law was displayed in his dissent in the *Olmstead* (1928) wiretapping case. Although not as eloquent as Brandeis who also dissented in that case, he stated bluntly that the government should not be above the law, even at some cost to public safety. "We have to choose, and for my part I think it is a less evil that some criminals should escape than that the government should play an ignoble part."

Signature Opinion.   *Moore v. Dempsey* (1923). This was a monumentally important case. In *Frank v. Mangum* (1915), Holmes had failed to convince the Court that a sham trial violates due process. When the Court's composition changed, Holmes's views became law. The importance of *Moore* was that the Supreme Court for the first time reversed a state criminal decision as a violation of due process. This opened the door to federal court intrusion into state criminal procedure, making criminal justice more civilized and uniform throughout the nation.

Assessment.   Holmes was one of the great Supreme Court justices, perhaps second only to Chief Justice John Marshall (1801–1835). He also stands as one of the greatest shapers of the English and American common law in its eight-hundred-year history.

Holmes's accomplishments on the Supreme Court include (along with Brandeis) the creation of modern First Amendment law enshrining free speech as a foundation of democracy, for free government is not possible unless all ideas are allowed to compete in the "marketplace of ideas."

Further Reading

Liva Baker, *The Justice from Beacon Hill: The Life and Times of Oliver Wendell Holmes* (New York: HarperCollins, 1991).

Louis Dembitz Brandeis

Massachusetts, 1856–1941
Republican
Appointed by Woodrow Wilson
Years of Service: 1916–1939

Collection of the Supreme
Court of the United States.
Photographer: Harris and
Ewing.

Life and Career.   Brandeis was born in Louisville, Kentucky, to a German Jewish family that sided with the Union during the Civil War. He entered Harvard Law School shortly before his nineteenth birthday, supported himself as a tutor, earned the highest grades, and spent a third year at Harvard as an instructor and graduate student. Attracted by Boston's liberal and intellectual atmosphere, he entered law practice there with his classmate Samuel Warren. They built a thriving practice representing midsize businesses. Brandeis developed a tremendous reputation as a thorough attorney whose success was built on a deep study of the law.

Brandeis became wealthy practicing law, but he gave it up to represent the interests of laborers struggling for economic security and protection of health and safety on the job. As an unpaid mediator and attorney in labor disputes, he became a renowned defender of workers' rights in the early twentieth century. In his victory before the conservative Supreme Court in *Muller v. Oregon* (1908), which upheld a state law limiting the working hours of female laundry employees, Brandeis used an innovative written argument (or "brief") consisting of ninety-six pages of social, economic, and health facts about the damaging effects of long working hours and only ten pages with the usual legal arguments. Since that time, this form of presentation has been known as a "Brandeis brief."

As a leading progressive who opposed monopolies, he drew the animosity of the propertied classes but also became a key advisor to President Woodrow Wilson, who nominated him to the Supreme Court. He was appointed after a long and acrimonious confirmation debate in the Senate based mainly on his "radicalism" but also supported to some degree by anti-Semitism.

Contribution to Criminal Procedure.   Brandeis supported the federal exclusionary rule and the extension of federal due process against the states in important cases like *Moore v. Dempsey* (1923), *Powell v. Alabama* (1932)—counsel, and *Brown v. Mississippi* (1936)—confessions.

Signature Opinion.   Dissent in *Olmstead v. United States* (1928). Federal agents violated a state criminal law against wiretapping. The issue was whether this was a search and seizure and, if so, whether the illegally seized wiretap evidence should be excluded. Brandeis's dissent is a classic statement of the Rule of Law:

> Decency, security, and liberty alike demand that government officials shall be subjected to the same rules of conduct that are commands to the citizen. In a government of laws, existence of the government will be imperiled if it fails to observe the law scrupulously. Our government is the potent, the omnipresent teacher. For good or for ill, it teaches the whole people by its example. Crime is contagious. If the government becomes a lawbreaker, it breeds contempt for law; it invites every man to become a law unto himself; it invites anarchy. To declare that in the administration of the criminal law the end justifies the means—to declare that the government may commit crimes in order to secure the conviction of a private criminal—would bring terrible retribution. Against that pernicious doctrine this court should resolutely set its face.

Assessment.   The dissents of Brandeis and Holmes in First Amendment cases ultimately persuaded the Court to hold that free speech and free press rights were so fundamental that the states could not abridge them. This incorporation of First Amendment rights helped open the door to the later incorporation of criminal procedure rights. His work in this and many other areas ranks him as one of the greatest justices.

Further Reading

Philippa Strum, *Louis D. Brandeis: Justice for the People* (New York: Schocken, 1984).

Collection of the Supreme
Court of the United States.
Photographer: Harris and
Ewing.

Benjamin Nathan Cardozo

New York, 1870–1938
Democrat
Appointed by Herbert Hoover
Years of Service: 1932–1938

Life and Career.   Cardozo, born into a distinguished New York family of Sephardic Jews who emigrated to America in the mid-eighteenth century, was a brilliant student and a noted lawyer, in practice with his older brother for twenty years. Despite his personality (described as gentle, courteous, lonely, ascetic, and saintly) and his apparent lack of political involvement, his reputation as a practitioner led to a judicial appointment to New York's highest court, the Court of Appeals, on which he served from 1913 to 1932.

Cardozo's outstanding reputation as a person and a judge led to an unparalleled national clamor for his appointment as the most worthy replacement for Justice Holmes. Thus, despite the facts that he was nominally of the wrong political party, that two justices from New York (Harlan Fiske Stone and Charles Evans Hughes) already sat on the Court, and that a Jewish justice (Brandeis) occupied another seat, President Hoover named Cardozo to the Court.

Contribution to Criminal Procedure.   Cardozo was a conservative judge in criminal matters and had opposed the exclusionary rule as a judge on the New York Court of Appeals.

Signature Opinion.   *Palko v. Connecticut* (1938). The Supreme Court had from 1925 to 1933 incorporated several First Amendment rights; it seemed likely that the Court would next incorporate criminal procedure rights. Palko, found guilty of murder and sentenced to prison, was retried after the prosecutor appealed under state law, was again found guilty, and was sentenced to death. He argued that this second conviction violated the Fifth Amendment Double Jeopardy Clause, which should apply to the states via due process. Cardozo's majority opinion held that the Connecticut law did not violate due process or incorporate the Double Jeopardy Clause. This was achieved by distinguishing between "fundamental" First Amendment rights and "formal" Fifth Amendment rights:

> The line of division may seem to be wavering and broken if there is a hasty catalogue of the cases on the one side and the other. Reflection and analysis will induce a different view. There emerges the perception of a rationalizing principle which gives to discrete instances a

proper order and coherence. The right to trial by jury and the immunity from prosecution except as the result of an indictment may have value and importance. Even so, they are not of the very essence of a scheme of ordered liberty. To abolish them is not to violate a 'principle of justice so rooted in the traditions and conscience of our people as to be ranked as fundamental.' ...

We reach a different plane of social and moral values when we pass to the privileges and immunities that have been taken over from the earlier articles of the Federal Bill of Rights and brought within the Fourteenth Amendment by a process of absorption. These in their origin were effective against the federal government alone. If the Fourteenth Amendment has absorbed them, the process of absorption has had its source in the belief that neither liberty nor justice would exist if they were sacrificed. . . . This is true, for illustration, of freedom of thought and speech. Of that freedom one may say that it is the matrix, the indispensable condition, of nearly every form of freedom.

The conservative *Palko* rationale retarded the advance of the incorporation doctrine for another quarter century.

Assessment.   Cardozo's reputation as a great common law judge is based mainly on his work on the New York Court of Appeals. His opinions were masterpieces of judicial craft that precisely analyzed basic principles of law; his decisions were neither immobilized by precedent nor excessively experimental. His fame was enhanced by his lectures and books (especially *The Nature of the Judicial Function*, 1921), which dissected the work of the appellate judge with such penetrating candor as to add a new chapter to the philosophy of judicial realism. His Supreme Court opinions were marked by total mastery over the subject matter at hand, a graceful and fluid writing style, and a penetrating intelligence. On the Court for only five and a half terms, he mainly supported the New Deal in economic cases and had a mixed record in civil rights cases.

Further Reading

Andrew L. Kaufman, *Cardozo* (Cambridge, Mass.: Harvard University Press, 1998).

CHAPTER **2**

Constitutional Remedies, the Fourth Amendment, and the Exclusionary Rule

We have to choose, and for my part I think it a less evil that some criminals should escape than that the Government should play an ignoble part.

—JUSTICE OLIVER WENDELL HOLMES, JR., DISSENTING IN *Olmstead v. United States*, 277 U.S. 438, 470 (1928)

CHAPTER OUTLINE

KEY TERMS

attenuation
balancing test
Bivens suit
contempt of court
contraband
damages
derivative evidence
disgorgement
exclusionary rule

"fruits of the poisonous tree" doctrine
general-reasonableness construction
general warrant
independent source
inevitable discovery
injunction
originalism

particularity requirement
pattern and practice suit
property theory
Reasonableness Clause
reparation
Section 1983 suit
"silver platter" doctrine
sovereign immunity
standing

target theory
tort
trespass
Warrant Clause
warrant-preference construction
writs of assistance

REMEDIES FOR CONSTITUTIONAL VIOLATIONS

REMEDIES AND THE RULE OF LAW   Law is a practical undertaking, although based on ideals of fairness, rationality, and regularity. As noted in Chapter 1, people and institutions pursue legal cases in order to correct alleged wrongs. Courts provide a forum to fairly adjudicate whether the allegations are true. If plaintiffs or prosecutors prevail, they seek remedies such as winning money damage awards, obtaining injunctions to prevent ongoing illegal practices, or imposing punishment on convicted defendants. This practical business is the embodiment of the second purpose of the Constitution set out in its Preamble—to "establish Justice." Chief Justice John Marshall understood that a stable, successful, and just country could not exist without a reliable, impartial, and independent justice system, which was confirmed by the Court's action in *Marbury v. Madison* (1803) of declaring an act of Congress unconstitutional. And in a just country founded on the principle of liberty, as announced in the Preamble, the justice system has to be impartial not only between private litigants but between the citizen and the state. Thus Chief Justice Marshall recognized that the Rule of Law requires that where the government is proven to have violated the law, a private citizen can go to court and can obtain a legal remedy for that violation. The necessity of legal remedies is therefore embedded in the Constitution. *Marbury v. Madison* (1803), the foundation of federal judicial power, stated

> The very essence of civil liberty certainly consists in the right of every individual to claim the protection of the laws, whenever he receives an injury.
>
> * * *
>
> The government of the United States has been emphatically termed a government of laws, and not of men. It will certainly cease to deserve this high appellation if the laws furnish no remedy for the violation of a vested right.

"According to *Marbury*'s ideal," asserts Professor Cornelia Pillard, "legal rights are not mere precatory or aspirational statements, but remediable claims, redressable in courts, for violations of law."[1] Legal remedies reflect the legitimacy of the government's constitutional promise to do justice (U.S. Const., Preamble). To put it bluntly, constitutional rights become meaningless platitudes unless officers and the state are held accountable and are made to pay if and when their acts trample on the rights of individuals. Without effective legal remedies, the Rule of Law ceases to exist.

REMEDIES AND THE EXCLUSIONARY RULE   The focus of this chapter is on one of the most highly contested issues in criminal procedure: the Fourth Amendment **exclusionary rule**. The contest is ideological and theoretical. Liberal proponents of the 'Due Process Model' seek to expand the scope of the rule and view it as a constitutional right. Conservative proponents of the 'Crime Control Model' seek to limit its scope and view it only as a device to protect Fourth Amendment values. But in order to understand the exclusionary rule, it is first necessary to briefly review the legal remedies for constitutional violations in general.

What legal remedy does a person have if the government violates his or her constitutional rights? There is no doubt that federal or state *civil lawsuits* against police and municipalities for money damages are personal legal remedies. Beyond civil lawsuits the answer becomes more tenuous. *Injunctions* are civil remedies where courts can order specific compliance to remedy an ongoing wrong. They are rare in criminal procedure, but when an injunction has been obtained against police action for widespread Fourth Amendment violations, the benefit is more for the public than for an individual. The *criminal prosecution* of police officers who egregiously violate rights can be viewed as a public remedy for past violations, even though individuals who have been victimized are not compensated. This chapter also includes a discussion of '*administrative measures*'. These are clearly not legal remedies. Nevertheless, many discussions of the exclusionary rule correctly surmise that it would be far better if constitutional violations never occur because police agencies train and supervise personnel to adhere to the Constitution; to round out an understanding of measures that seek to correct legal wrongs, a brief discussion of administrative measures is helpful.

Is the exclusionary rule a real remedy? Can the prosecution rely on evidence that was obtained by breaking the law or violating the Constitution? Can such evidence be used to convict the defendant? Or used in some other way to benefit the state? A major argument in favor of incorporating the exclusionary rule and applying it against the states in *Wolf v. Colorado* (1949) and *Mapp v. Ohio* (1961) was that other remedies, such as civil lawsuits, were rarely effective and so were of little use in gaining police compliance with the Constitution. It was felt that excluding illegally obtained evidence was the only way of legally remedying Fourth Amendment violations. Because of changed legal and social conditions in the last half century, it appears that civil lawsuits and administrative measures have a better chance of modifying police behavior. In *Hudson v. Michigan* (2006), Justice Scalia gave the "increasing professionalism of police forces, including a new emphasis on internal police discipline," as a reason to deny the application of the exclusionary rule to violations of the Fourth Amendment "knock and announce" rule. These views give support to the view that the exclusionary rule ought to be partly reduced in scope if not eliminated as a legal remedy.

This policy approach indirectly confronts the question about whether the rule is a real remedy, a debate that has proceeded on two tracks. A utilitarian track focuses on the effectiveness of the exclusionary rule as a *deterrent* to unconstitutional police action in comparison to other remedies and considers empirical questions as to the "costs" of the exclusionary rule (discussed later in this chapter). The other track involves philosophical questions about the meaning of legal remedies, the status of the exclusionary rule as a constitutional doctrine, whether the rule is constitutionally required, and the extent to which the rule can be manipulated. To provide a foundation to understand the theories of the exclusionary rule later in this chapter, the next section describes a theory of remedies that is relevant to the exclusionary rule debate.

A Theory of Remedies

Exclusionary rule opponents argue that it is not a legal remedy at all. In answer to the critics and as a prelude to the concluding sections, consider Professor William Heffernan's analysis. Unlike most commentators who discuss remedies as a unitary concept, Heffernan demonstrates that there are three types and goals of remedies. *First-party remedies* aim at **reparation**, to restore the injured party to the position he or she occupied before the injury occurred. *Second-party remedies* have the goal of **disgorgement**, to place the wrongdoer (the second party) in no better position than the one he or she occupied prior to the wrongful conduct. *Third-party remedies* aim at deterring future wrongdoing, to the benefit of the general public—that is, "plac[ing] the public in a better position than it would be in if deterrence were not undertaken."[2] In practice, these types and goals of remedies may overlap in a single case and may be mutually supportive or at odds with one another. All three rationales have been used by the Supreme Court to support the exclusionary rule.

The Fourth Amendment protects three distinct rights—liberty, property, and privacy—not just privacy alone. It is true, as conservative justices have said, that once a suspect's privacy rights have been breached by a wrongful search and seizure, it is irreversible. The privacy violation by an illegal search and seizure "is *fully accomplished* by the original search" (*United States v. Calandra*, 1974, opinion of Powell, J., emphasis added). In this view, the only true remedy for a completed violation of privacy rights is reparation, a first-party remedy, via a civil lawsuit for money damages against the officer. However, if the state exploits the privacy violation by also violating a defendant's property or liberty interests, these are ongoing violations that can be repaired by returning the property or freeing the defendant. When the various interests protected by the Fourth Amendment, especially liberty, are considered, the exclusionary rule can be considered as much a true legal remedy as a lawsuit for money. While the invasion of privacy may have been "fully accomplished" at the time police illegally entered a premises, the invasion of the suspect's liberty interests continues during the prosecution, and the exclusionary rule provides a familiar remedy that courts are competent to administer.

The reparation remedy of monetary damages does not exhaust the range of available remedies. Note, by analogy, that a person harmed by a convicted criminal can sue the criminal in a civil suit. Nor does the existence of civil actions against police for Fourth Amendment violations undermine the legitimacy of the additional remedial goals of disgorgement and deterrence. In civil lawsuits for **injunctions** or specific performance, for example, disgorgement may be ordered where possible to prevent one who violated a person's rights from benefiting from the wrong. In the section "Exclusionary Rule Theories," we return to this idea to demonstrate that a disgorgement theory of the exclusionary rule is not only plausible, but is embedded in the Fourth

Amendment. Also by way of example, punitive damages may be paid to an injured party in a civil suit above what is needed to compensate for actual losses, specifically to deter the wrong-doer from doing the acts in the future—that is, to protect the public. Although the Supreme Court now rests the exclusionary rule solely on the deterrence rationale, it has so hedged in the rule that it is reasonable to ask whether the Supreme Court is "soft" on civil liberties.

Civil Lawsuits for Money Damages

The king's officers who invaded the homes of John Wilkes and his associates in the 1760s were sued in English common law courts, found liable for trespass, and ordered to pay substantial sums for violating the rights of British subjects. The colonials challenging writs of assistance were, in effect, seeking injunctions to prevent the Crown from issuing general search warrants. (These cases are discussed in detail in the introduction to the exclusionary rule, in following sections.) When the Bill of Rights was ratified, the Framers likely assumed that violations of privacy by the government would lead to lawsuits, which in turn would embarrass the government into preventing further abuses. As dissenting justices in *Wolf v. Colorado* and the majority in *Mapp v. Ohio* noted, however, police officers were almost never held responsible for violating individuals' Fourth Amendment rights. *Mapp* was predicated in part on the belief that *Weeks's* exclusionary rule was the best way of deterring police breach of rights. More recently, exclusionary rule critics have argued that alternate remedies are preferable.

STATE COMMON LAW TORT SUITS   These exist in every state and are lineal descendants of the English common law suits for trespass. A person whose dwelling was invaded by another who entered without right—whether a burglar, a civilian entering without criminal intent, or a police officer entering without a warrant or probable cause—can sue the intruder for the intentional tort of trespass and related property damage. Such lawsuits can be brought against local, state or federal law enforcement officers who violate a dweller's privacy. Symbolically, such suits put officers' violations of fundamental constitutional rights on the same plane as a civil privacy violations. As a practical matter, juries may be less willing to hold police officers liable, even though their powers to enter and search, and the fright and humiliation to residents where no criminal evidence was found, might be greater.

Private lawsuits against government units or agents were at one time blocked by the common law doctrine of **sovereign immunity** that was inherited from England. States have lifted sovereign immunity in part, but actual rules differ in different states. In a Florida case, for example, a sheriff's deputy gratuitously beat a suspect in handcuffs during a booking procedure, and the injured person sued the deputy and the Volusia County Sheriff's Department. Under Florida law, the deputy could be held liable for a civil battery if he acted within the scope of his employment. The department could be liable only if the deputy's acts exceeded the scope of his employment. Florida law was structured so that either the agency could be held liable or the deputy, but not both.[3]

SECTION 1983 SUITS: STATE OFFICERS IN FEDERAL COURTS   Most civil rights lawsuits against municipal police officers are conducted in federal court under the Civil Rights Act of 1871, which is found in Title 42 *United States Code,* section 1983, and consequently are commonly known as **Section 1983 suits**. This right of action in federal courts against state and local officers was created by Congress after the Civil War, under the authority of the Fourteenth Amendment, in order to counteract Ku Klux Klan terrorism against African Americans. Such a lawsuit is based on a violation of a person's federal statutory or constitutional rights by someone "acting under the color of state law" or custom.

The law was not much used for a century. After the Supreme Court held in **Monroe v. Pape** (1961) that a Section 1983 claim could be based on a Fourth Amendment violation, thousands of Section 1983 suits proliferated. In *Monroe,* Chicago police officers entered the plaintiff's home at night without a warrant, rousted his family, and arrested and detained him for ten hours without probable cause before he was released. The history and wording of Section 1983 prevent lawsuits against state governments. In 1978, the Court reexamined the statute's history and extended Section 1983 lawsuits to cases against municipal and county governments, but not against the quasi-sovereign states (*Monell v. Department of Social Services,* 1978). This made civil lawsuits against police more attractive to plaintiffs, because cities and counties have "deeper pockets" (i.e., greater funds) than do individual officers. Municipal liability under *Monell* does not automatically flow from the fact that officers are employees, a doctrine known in the common law of torts as *respondeat superior*. Rather, for municipalities to be held liable for the errors of police officers in violating rights or in the use of excessive force under Section 1983, plaintiffs must prove that the municipality was deficient in its supervision or training of officers.

A study of hundreds of Section 1983 appeals decided between 1989 and 1993 found that 58 percent were for excessive force, false arrest, and illegal search and seizure. Plaintiffs suing the police won 24 percent of the illegal search and seizure cases. The police prevailed in 44 percent of these cases, and in 32 percent, the case was remanded for further findings. This study indicated that this form of civil lawsuit is not rare, that plaintiffs who sue law enforcement for rights violations have an opportunity to gain redress, but that a strong legal and factual case is needed to prevail.[4]

BIVENS SUITS: FEDERAL CONSTITUTIONAL TORT   In *Bivens v. Six Unknown Named Agents* (1971), the Supreme Court held, for the first time, that a federal constitutional **tort** remedy exists for violations of constitutional rights by *federal* agents. Prior to *Bivens*, a person whose rights were violated by federal officers could only sue for common law trespass in state courts (see above). The Civil Rights Act of 1871 (creating Section 1983 suits) created a distinct remedy for instances where *local* officers violated the *constitutional* rights of people, but no such remedy existed where *federal* officers violated constitutional rights.

Webster Bivens was arrested at home by federal narcotics agents who searched his Brooklyn apartment "from stem to stern" and was strip-searched at booking. He was never prosecuted, so exclusion of evidence was a meaningless remedy. Because it was unlikely that he would again be arrested, an injunction suit made no sense. This made a civil lawsuit for money damages the only logical remedy for the wrongs done to him. His suit for damages based on an illegal arrest and search and seizure, however, was thrown out of federal court because no such cause of action existed in federal law. If Bivens sued in state court, the federal government might have tried to *remove* the case to federal court, where it would be *dismissed* on jurisdictional grounds. This created a catch-22 that made it impossible for people to ever sue federal agents who violated their rights. A federal tort remedy was therefore of real practical as well as symbolic importance.

The Supreme Court agreed with Bivens, saying that the fundamental rule that there must be a legal remedy for every legal wrong outweighed the doctrine of sovereign immunity that had previously blocked the creation of a federal constitutional tort. The Court noted that the constitutional interests in a federal suit were more serious than a trespass suit under state law, especially after *Katz v. United States* (1967) created the "expectation of privacy" doctrine, wherein the Fourth Amendment was held to be based on constitutional interests and not simply on property rights that are vindicated by the law of civil trespass. These federal lawsuits are known as *Bivens* **suits**.

STATE CONSTITUTIONAL TORTS: STATE OFFICERS IN STATE COURT   In addition to shoehorning a constitutional violation into the shape of a common law tort, some state supreme courts, following the federal example, have established distinct state constitutional torts: a direct cause of action for damages for violation of a state constitutional right against a government or individual defendants. Unlike a state common law tort, which is designed to vindicate personal interests, a constitutional tort "reinforces the moral accountability of the state and vindicates the reliance interest of the people;...[it] holds the government responsible as an agent of the people."[5]

By 1998, twenty-one states had recognized an implied cause of action for state constitutional violations. Three additional states had indicated that they would do so under certain narrow circumstances. A private cause of action has been recognized in a twenty-fifth state by federal courts, and four states have enacted statutes that authorize causes of action for violation of state constitutional rights. Seven states have specifically rejected state constitutional causes of action.[6] For example, the New York Court of Appeals, that state's highest court, established a constitutional tort based on a violation of the New York constitution's search and seizure clause. In that case, state police and local law enforcement officials embarked on a five-day "street sweep" in which every nonwhite male found in and around the city of Oneonta was stopped and interrogated for a reported crime.[7]

In addition to these standard avenues of redress, lawyers may seek other remedies that exist in state or federal common law. A startling example, in a ruling by a Reagan-appointed federal trial judge, allowed the Los Angeles Police Department to be sued in August 2000 under the RICO (Racketeer Influenced and Corrupt Organizations) Act for the notorious Ramparts Division scandal. The scandal involved many police officers systematically arresting at least one hundred innocent people, planting incriminating evidence on them, giving perjured testimony, improperly using immigration officials in making arrests, and physically assaulting people without cause. The RICO law was first established to attack organized crime families but has been extended to other organizations that use illegal means to further their goals and interfere with interstate commerce. The benefit to the plaintiffs in the suit is that the RICO statute of limitations is ten years, and it allows triple damages. The potential damages to Los Angeles were put at $100 million.[8] Plaintiffs have not been successful in these cases, however, because a private RICO suit requires a showing of injury to business or property.[9]

Immunity from Civil Lawsuits

There are several kinds of legal immunity. Prosecutors acting under statutes can grant individuals immunity from criminal prosecution in order to obtain their testimony by overcoming the privilege against self-incrimination. Privileges to not testify granted to spouses, clergy, lawyers, and other professionals are forms of immunity. The doctrine of sovereign immunity prevents any lawsuits against the federal or state governments, unless they agree to waive such immunity, as occurred in the Federal Tort Claims Act and *Bivens* (1971). Each kind of immunity is justified by different reasons.

This section examines *governmental tort immunity from civil lawsuits* against those who perform *public functions*. Governmental immunity may be *absolute* or *qualified*. Immunity from suit, whether absolute or qualified, is not just a defense but requires a *dismissal* of a suit on a motion for summary judgment. This saves the public official from the time-consuming pretrial discovery process, depositions, document review, and conferences about litigation strategy. A successful claim of immunity prevents a plaintiff from getting a court to consider a violation of rights in the first place. Because of this, trial courts must "resolve immunity questions at the earliest possible stage in litigation" (*Hunter v. Bryant*, 1991, cited in *Saucier v. Katz*, 2001).

Absolute immunity has been granted to the president of the United States and close counselors (*Nixon v. Fitzgerald*, 1982), federal and state legislators (*Eastland v. U.S. Servicemen's Fund*, 1975; *Tenney v. Brandhove*, 1951), judges (*Stump v. Sparkman*, 1978), and prosecutors (*Imbler v. Pachtman*, 1976)—in the exercise of their *official* duties.[10] Absolute immunity is given for the *acts* performed and not for the *official*. Trial witnesses also receive absolute immunity form lawsuits, even if they may be prosecuted for perjury (*Briscoe v. LaHue*, 1983). A prosecutor's official actions, protected by absolute immunity, include supervision, training, and information system management (*Van de Kamp v. Goldstein*, 2009). A prosecutor, however, does not enjoy absolute immunity for such actions as conducting a press conference (*Buckley v. Fitzsimmons*,1993) or testifying at a preliminary hearing about the facts in a certification for probable cause, because that is not the function of an advocate (*Kalina v. Fletcher*, 1997).

The policy underlying absolute immunity is that the "public interest requires that persons occupying such important positions . . . should speak and act freely and fearlessly in the discharge of their important official functions" (*Gregoire v. Biddle*, U.S. Court of Appeals, 2d Circuit, 1949).[11] It is a very hard policy because it applies even if the officer in fact acted out of real malice. As the great federal judge Learned Hand explained, the policy is a balance of evils:

> It does indeed go without saying that an official, who is in fact guilty of using his powers to vent his spleen upon others, or for any other personal motive not connected with the public good, should not escape liability for the injuries he may so cause; and, if it were possible in practice to confine such complaints to the guilty, it would be monstrous to deny recovery. The justification for doing so is that it is impossible to know whether the claim is well founded until the case has been tried, and that to submit all officials, the innocent as well as the guilty, to the burden of a trial and to the inevitable danger of its outcome, would dampen the ardor of all but the most resolute, or the most irresponsible, in the unflinching discharge of their duties. Again and again the public interest calls for action which may turn out to be

founded on a mistake, in the face of which an official may later find himself hard put to it to satisfy a jury of his good faith. There must indeed be means of punishing public officers who have been truant to their duties; but that is quite another matter from exposing such as have been honestly mistaken to suit by anyone who has suffered from their errors. As is so often the case, the answer must be found in a balance between the evils inevitable in either alternative. . . . [I]t has been thought in the end better to leave unredressed the wrongs done by dishonest officers than to subject those who try to do their duty to the constant dread of retaliation. (*Gregoire v. Biddle*, 177 F.2d 579, 581 [1949])

A similar form of governmental immunity—qualified immunity—holds "that government officials performing discretionary functions, generally are shielded from liability for civil damages insofar as their conduct does not violate clearly established statutory or constitutional rights of which a reasonable person would have known" (*Harlow v. Fitzgerald*, 1982). When a police officer is sued for violating the Fourth Amendment rights of a person stopped, arrested, or searched and the officer claims qualified immunity, the judge on a pretrial motion must determine (1) if the officer violated a constitutional rule and (2) if the rule was clearly established. The "clearly established" rule is designed to give officers fair warning that their actions are illegal.

For example, in *Hope v. Pelzer* (2002), Alabama prison guards disciplined Larry Hope by handcuffing him to a "hitching post" while in leg irons, shirtless, and under a hot sun, for approximately seven hours, during which he was given water only once or twice and was given no bathroom breaks. The lower court found that while this action clearly violated the Eighth Amendment prohibition on cruel and unusual punishment, it was not clearly established. The Supreme Court reversed. Although the Eleventh Circuit did not have a prior case with the precise facts of *Hope*, the contours of cruel and unusual punishment law established in earlier cases were sufficiently clear, banning "unnecessarily and wantonly inflicted pain." The violation of Hope's rights were so obvious that the prison guards had fair notice that it was unconstitutional.

In *Saucier v. Katz* (2001) the Court ruled that lower courts deciding qualified immunity claims must first determine whether a constitutional right was violated and only then determine whether it was clearly established, for the purpose of deciding constitutional questions and preventing "constitutional stagnation." This was reversed in *Pearson v. Callahan* (2009), which found that "consent-once-removed" could be based on consent extended to an undercover informant (see Chapter 3). In *Pearson* the circuit court assumed that the right was clearly established in the circuit but would not be upheld by the Supreme Court and refused to extend qualified immunity. The Supreme Court held that the *Saucier* ordering was too rigid, created inefficiency, and again allowed lower courts to tackle the qualified immunity prongs in the order that was most efficient for disposing the issue. *Saucier* did make it clear, however, that in civil claims based on the Fourth Amendment, courts look to the objective reasonableness of the actions of police officers (*Graham v. Connor*, 1989; see Chapter 4, "Use of Force" section). As a result, "qualified immunity can apply in the event the *mistaken belief* was reasonable" (*Saucier v. Katz*, 2001, emphasis added). Therefore, as is the case in probable cause errors, qualified immunity protects an officer from a lawsuit even if the police action in question in fact violates the Fourth Amendment, as long as the officer's action was objectively reasonable.

Injunctions

Injunctions are not common remedies for Fourth Amendment violations. An injunction is a judicial order that either (1) commands a defendant to perform a particular act, (2) prohibits specified activity, or (3) orders a defendant to cease wrongful activity. Injunctions may be granted by a court where plaintiffs can prove that rights violations are persistent and repeated and that an injunction is the only effective remedy. Injunctions are enforced by the judicial power of **contempt of court**, which can include fines or jail for disobedience.

A prohibitory injunction was issued by a lower federal court and upheld on appeal by the Fourth Circuit in *Lankford v. Gelston* (1966) against a local police department that had been conducting a "dragnet" type search. Police officers searching for the killers of fellow police officers had, over a three-week period, entered three hundred houses based on anonymous tips and without legal justification. Because there were no arrests, the exclusionary rule could not be used to deter the officers; police activity was flagrant and persistent. Under these circumstances, the injunction was justified.[12]

The Supreme Court, however, has struck down federal injunctions against local police departments. In **Rizzo v. Goode** (1976), the Court reversed a federal injunction against the Philadelphia Police Department's cumbersome procedural process for investigating citizens' complaints about the use of excessive force. The Court reasoned that complainants had failed to demonstrate that the existing policy resulted in routine and persistent patterns of excessive force and civil rights violations. It did so despite the fact that the District Court heard a "staggering amount of evidence, including 250 witnesses over a 21-day period," who testified to widespread police abuses.[13] In **Los Angeles v. Lyons** (1983), the Court also struck down an injunction against the Los Angeles Police Department that prohibited the use of chokeholds, which were not specifically prohibited or authorized by departmental regulations. "At the time *Lyons* was decided, the chokehold had caused the deaths of over a dozen persons; by 1991, twenty-seven people had died as a result of this restraint technique. The Court dismissed the suit, holding that in order to have standing to sue for an injunction, the plaintiff must show that he is likely to be a future victim of that same technique."[14]

These cases demonstrate that courts generally, and the Supreme Court specifically, are not the best avenues to initiate systemic reform. It is noteworthy that effective federal oversight of police misconduct is now beginning to occur under congressionally authorized pattern and practices lawsuits (discussed in following sections).

Criminal Prosecution

STATE PROSECUTIONS   Criminal prosecutions of police officers for acts committed in the line of duty are rare and are limited to egregious cases, typically involving the death of a suspect.[15] It is difficult to obtain such a conviction if the defense attorney convinces the jury that the officer acted reasonably to enforce the law or if the victim suffered little or no personal injury. A notable example was the acquittal in February 2000 of four New York City Street Crime Unit police officers of the murder of Amadou Diallo, an African immigrant who was shot nineteen times as he reached for his wallet. The late James Fyfe, an expert who more often testified against police, concluded that the facts showed that the officers, who believed Diallo had a gun, had acted properly. A juror said the prosecution had not proved that the officers acted criminally.[16]

Notorious prosecutions of police officers often capture headlines. Memorable cases include the trial and first acquittal of Los Angeles police officers for beating Rodney King, a speeding motorist, which was videotaped and played to a national audience.[17] In Detroit, police officers were convicted and imprisoned for the beating death of Malice Green.[18] Three white suburban Pittsburgh police officers were acquitted of manslaughter in the asphyxiation death of an African-American motorist, Jonny Gammage.[19] In 2005, a New York City police officer who shot an immigrant during a warehouse chase was found guilty of criminally negligent homicide by a judge after a jury deadlocked on more serious charges. It was the first conviction of an onduty New York officer since a civil rights conviction in 1998 for killing a civilian in a chokehold.[20]

Such prosecutions are proper responses to specific cases but have no impact on systemic errors or abuse unless they spark reforms. In the aftermath of the Louima case, which involved the sexual brutalization of Haitian immigrant Abner Louima by New York City police officers, for example, the city bowed to pressure and agreed to federal monitoring of the way in which officers accused of abuse are investigated and disciplined.[21]

FEDERAL PROSECUTIONS OF LOCAL POLICE OFFICERS   A federal civil rights law originally enacted in 1866 authorizes federal prosecution of local officers who, acting under color of local law or custom, deprive a person of rights under the Constitution (18 U.S.C. § 242). A conviction requires an intent to deprive a person of a specific constitutional right (*United States v. Screws*, 1945). In recent decades, federal prosecutors have become more active in investigating and prosecuting crimes by local police. Federal civil rights prosecutions have included several high-profile cases, such as the second trial of the police officers involved in the Rodney King beating and the trial of officers involved in the brutalization of Haitian immigrant Abner Louima. If the sexual torture inflicted on Louima was perpetrated by a private person, all bystanders would justly be horrified. But the additional concern in a civil rights violation was captured by the words of the federal judge who sentenced the police officer to thirty years' imprisonment: "Short of intentional murder, one cannot imagine a more barbarous misuse of power than [officer] Volpe's."[22] Misuse of power undermines trust in the government, makes people—especially the poor and dispossessed—skeptical of protection by the criminal justice system, and leads to the suspicion that honest police officers are actual or potential rights violators.

Administrative Measures

Ideally, violations of constitutional rights should rarely, if ever, occur. External legal sanction, such as the exclusionary rule or civil suits, may control police behavior to some extent, but such sanctions are reactions to past violations. They encourage future compliance through punishment, which has had limited effectiveness. (See the "Law in Society" section in this chapter.) Police officers are most likely to obey constitutional mandates like the Fourth Amendment when support and rewards for doing so come from within their departments. William Bratton, the innovative former New York City police commissioner, made obedience to the Constitution a key goal for the NYPD.[23] Nonjudicial and administrative methods, therefore, are essential to encourage police to adhere to the Rule of Law.

Many methods have been suggested for making police officers more understanding of the people they police and more mindful of their rights: community policing, civilian review boards,[24] police ombudsman programs,[25] accreditation of police departments,[26] civilianizing many roles in police departments,[27] tightening rules on the use of lethal force,[28] cultural diversity and sensitivity training,[29] higher standards for police recruits,[30] training in Asian martial arts,[31] and similar improvements. Better academy and in-service training in constitutional law is important. Professor Slobogin has proposed replacing the exclusionary rule with a legal–administrative procedure in which a judge would hear defendants' complaints of privacy violations. If the judge found that a violation had occurred, he or she would require the officer personally to pay liquidated damages of between 1 and 5 percent of the officer's salary unless the violation was in good faith, in which case the police department would be financially responsible. In addition, class actions and injunctions would be available remedies.[32] This proposal may prove less than fully effective because the qualified immunity doctrine would protect officers from liability where it is not apparent that a suspect's rights have been violated. A more promising alternative approach was enacted by Congress: the pattern and practice review.

PATTERN AND PRACTICE REVIEW   A 1994 federal law brought the weight of the Department of Justice (DOJ) to bear to create nonjudicial solutions to police violations of constitutional rights. Title 42 U.S.C. §14141 prohibits governmental authorities from engaging in a "pattern or practice of conduct by law enforcement officials" that deprives persons of constitutional rights. When the attorney general has reasonable cause to believe that a violation has occurred, the Justice Department is authorized to sue for equitable and declaratory relief "to eliminate the pattern or practice." DOJ monitoring is not triggered by isolated incidents of unlawful acts but by conditions where unlawful acts have virtually become "standard operating procedure."[33] This law is the best method available to get police agencies and officers to follow the Constitution, although lasting reform will depend on a willingness of the U.S Attorney General to use the law and on effecting real changes in police agency culture.

According to leading police scholar Samuel Walker, **pattern and practice suits** are an important new way of thinking about policing that focuses on *organizational* and *management* problems as causes of police misconduct. Instead of relying on the discredited "rotten apple" theory of police misconduct, which faults individual officers, pattern and practice suits respond to a new consensus—the "rotten barrel" theory.[34] The new model offers organizational strategies to improve policing.

In 1999, two police departments (Pittsburgh, Pennsylvania, and Steubenville, Ohio) entered the first pattern and practice consent decrees for excessive force, improper searches and seizures, and false arrest. Since that beginning, other major departments, including Cincinnati, Detroit, Los Angeles, and the New Jersey State Police, were investigated and have entered into monitoring processes designed to improve critical police performance.[35] By 2007 "21 investigations have reached some kind of formal outcome"[36] Pattern and practice suit outcomes "fall into three categories: consent decrees, Memoranda of Agreement ('MOA'), and Investigative Findings Letters."[37] Consent decrees and MOAs involve the appointment of monitors and impose requirements that police agencies reform the pattern of practices that led to widespread constitutional violations.

Investigative Findings Letters are far more limited in scope, typically focusing on one issue or a narrow range of issues; they are advisory only, and no Independent Monitor is appointed to oversee implementation. Implementation of the recommendations contained in an Investigatory Finding Letter is entirely voluntary. Under the Bush Administration, the Special Litigation Section made greater use of Letters rather than consent decrees or MOAs, and to a large extent the investigation of law enforcement agencies virtually ceased.[38]

The initiation of a civil rights investigation of Maricopa County (Phoenix) Sheriff Joe Arpaio for "patterns or practices of discriminatory police practices and unconstitutional searches and seizures" by the DOJ may revive use of Section 14140 in the Obama administration. This pattern and practice investigation appears to be the first that is related to immigration enforcement.[39] It seems significant that in 2000, Eric Holder, now the Attorney General, was one of the Justice Department lawyers "most responsible for forcing L.A. officials to sign a consent decree requiring reforms to end the LAPD's 'pattern and practice' of violating people's civil rights."[40]

Most Section 14141 settlements impose requirements in three areas: police "training; the receipt and investigation of referrals and complaints concerning improper police behavior; and the development and maintenance of an early warning system."[41] Early intervention systems are deemed one of the most important new management tools for monitoring officer performance,[42] because instead of waiting for misconduct to become egregious and then reacting punitively, they proactively monitor officer behavior and seek to correct the behavior of officers who accumulate a disproportionate number of complaints.[43]

A few evaluations of complete pattern and practice suits have suggested success in some departments in reducing inappropriate police behavior. A successful conclusion in Pittsburgh shows that "a pattern or practice suit can be an effective instrument for enhancing police accountability." Success, however, depends on leadership by the chief, having a meaningful implementation plan, and a process that in fact changes the culture of a department away from one that tolerates misconduct.[44] There is also a concern with sustaining positive changes where they had occurred. For example, after the successful implementation of a consent decree in Pittsburgh, the city cut 22 percent of its officers in a budget crisis, and a new mayor elected with the support of the police union that opposed the pattern and pracice suit fired the police chief who had successfully implemented it.[45] Despite these caveats, the pattern and practice suit remains the most promising vehicle for ensuring that police departments adhere to constitutional standards in law enforcement. Indeed, Walker and Macdonald recommend expanding the model by having the federal law adopted by states to allow pattern and practice suits under state Attorneys General.[46]

Although some jurists and scholars have argued that the remedies and administrative measures described in this section are so effective that they can replace the exclusionary rule, a safer course suggests that the entire spectrum of remedies, including the exclusionary rule, is necessary to ensure that police comply with fundamental constitutional law and values.

THE FOURTH AMENDMENT

COMMON LAW ORIGIN   The old English saying that "a man's home is his castle" at first applied to protection against private intrusion, but from the 1600s onward came to mean legal protection of landowners against "promiscuous searches" by *government* officers[47] This reflected the spread of the political and individual liberty in the eighteenth century, and came to a head in two famous British legal cases decided in the 1760s that influenced the Constitution's framers. The first, the Writs of Assistance Case, was decided in colonial Massachusetts in 1761. Colonials protested against the issuance of **writs of assistance**, a type of **general warrant** authorizing a Crown official "to command the assistance" of a peace officer or a nearby person to execute the writ. These were used to enforce hated revenue laws imposed on the colonies and passed by Parliament, and even to "impress" (i.e., kidnap) "able bodied men for service in the royal navy."[48] General warrants were issued by judicial or nonjudicial government officials, did not require probable cause for a search, and "allowed officers to search wherever they wanted and to seize whatever they wanted, with few exceptions."[49] By the 1760s public opinion had turned against such warrants and searches, although British authorities continued to issue them.

A customs officer in Massachusetts, petitioning for a new writ of assistance in 1761, was opposed by leading Boston merchants who challenged the legality of the application before the colony's high court. James Otis, a leading attorney who represented the merchants, offered a learned and passionate argument: The law authorizing the writs of assistance "is against the fundamental principles of English law" and is therefore unconstitutional and void. John Adams, a young attorney and future president of the United States, was deeply impressed by Otis's argument. In 1776, as a delegate to the Continental Congress and as a signer of the Declaration of Independence, Adams reflected that the movement for American independence began with the writs of assistance dispute. The Boston merchants lost their case, but the suit implanted the idea of challenging the state. As the unpopular writs continued to be used to generate revenue under Parliament's Townshend Act (1767), they became a major source of friction that ultimately led to the Revolutionary War and overthrow of English control and the establishment of a republic that embodied the political ideals of the Enlightenment era and the Rule of Law.[50]

The second legal precedent arose from civil lawsuits against Crown officers following the political persecution of John Wilkes (1725–1797)—a British agitator, journalist, member of Parliament, and a critic of King George III—by the Crown. In 1763 Wilkes published a newsletter sharply critical of the royal government. The government retaliated by charging him with seditious libel, a serious political crime. An English secretary of state issued general warrants to officers to search for the newsletter and other writings. "Crown agents enforcing the warrants had unfettered discretion to search, seize, and arrest anyone as they pleased. They ransacked printer's shops and houses, and arrested forty-nine persons, including Wilkes, his printer, publisher, and bookseller. The officers seized his private papers for incriminating evidence after a thorough search; thousands of pages and scores of books belonging to persons associated with him were also seized."[51]

Wilkes and colleagues charged in civil lawsuits that these general searches were illegal. The courts upheld Wilkes and his allies, finding that the searches were not authorized by law and were excessive. As a legal *remedy*, officers of the Crown could be sued, even though the king, as sovereign, was personally immune from lawsuit. "[T]he government paid a total of about 100,000 pounds in costs and judgments" in all of the lawsuits arising out of the Wilkes affair, an enormous sum at the time.[52] The most important case was ***Entick v. Carrington*** (1765).[53] Lord Camden, chief justice of the Court of Common Pleas, demolished every government argument supporting the legality of the warrants. He ruled that (1) general warrants were not authorized by act of Parliament or by case law; (2) that general warrants to search for papers were not like specific search warrants for stolen goods; and (3) that although the government had issued such warrants since the Glorious Revolution of 1688, that fact does not make the warrants legal "simply through long usage" or the previous silence of the courts. The court firmly rejected the blatantly political argument (4) that the needs of the state took precedence over individual rights: "Political policy is not an argument in a court of law."[54] Lord Camden stressed that the case was of constitutional importance—it upheld the liberal "social contract" political theory, which stressed that a primary function of government is to protect the property of individuals.

These cases laid the foundation of the Fourth Amendment. Illegal searches and seizures and general warrants violated core principles for which the revolutionaries fought for independence: privacy of the home, individual liberty, and the Rule of Law above the executive power of the state. As the American states wrote new constitutions in the years during and after the Revolutionary War (1776–1781), they included prohibitions on general warrants.[55] This reflected the evolving common law that had in effect outlawed general warrants in *Entick* and culminated in the Fourth Amendment. Tellingly, when Representative James Madison presented his draft of the Bill of Rights to the First Congress in 1789, what came to be the Fourth Amendment, with the novel phrase "unreasonable search and seizure," drew heavily on the Massachusetts provision, written by none other than John Adams, the young lawyer present in 1761 in the Boston courtroom where James Otis inveighed against writs of assistance, and now vice president of the United States.

The Fourth Amendment was silent about *remedies* for search and seizure violations. As will be explained shortly, the conditions of the time made it seem unlikely that violations would be common. The precedent of *Entick v. Carrington* was that government searches of private property by officers without a warrant or with defective warrants or general warrants were illegal. A person whose privacy rights under the Fourth Amendment were violated could sue government officers and recover **damages**. Although a rule had emerged in English and American common law courts at that time excluding coerced confessions, there was no common law rule excluding the use of illegally seized evidence from a criminal trial.

FOURTH AMENDMENT STRUCTURE   The Fourth Amendment reads:

> The right of the people to be secure in their persons, houses, papers, and effects, against unreasonable searches and seizures, shall not be violated, and no Warrants shall issue, but upon probable cause, supported by Oath or affirmation, and particularly describing the place to be searched, and the persons or things to be seized. (U.S. Const. amend. IV)

The Fourth Amendment did not simply outlaw "general warrants" in specific terms, although that was its original motivation. The modern interpretation, stated in many cases, is that the amendment contains two clauses: the **Reasonableness Clause** and the **Warrant Clause**. Under this construction, the ultimate test of constitutionality of any search or seizure is whether it is *reasonable*. Not all searches have to be authorized by a judicial warrant. If a search or arrest warrant is required, then it must meet the **particularity requirements** stated in the Warrant Clause.

Conservative and liberal justices and scholars strongly disagree about the relative importance of the Warrant Clause. Conservative jurists apply a **general-reasonableness construction** that establishes a **balancing test** to determine if search and seizures are proper without a warrant; this comes close to saying that search warrants are not actually required by the Fourth Amendment. This construction has gained ground in recent decades and allows the Court to give police greater leeway to search and seize without prior judicial authorization.

The more traditional **warrant-preference construction**, favored by liberal jurists, holds that *warrantless* searches and seizures are *presumptively unreasonable*. A narrow group of search warrant exceptions, which goes back to the common law, is allowed under this interpretation: entries in *hot pursuit*, the search of *mobile vehicles*, and a "search *incident to arrest*" (the search of a person who has just been arrested). All modern legal thinkers, whether favoring the general-reasonableness or the warrant-preference approach, agree on this two-clause way of understanding the Fourth Amendment.[56] Indeed, until the recent findings of historians, they believed that the Framers intended this two-clause construction.[57] More recent studies conclude that the original intent of the Fourth Amendment's Framers and ratifiers was to prevent Congress from authorizing general warrants and to ban judges from issuing them—nothing more.[58] This interpretation threatens the more conservative view but is unlikely to overthrow the Court-established two-clause interpretation.

This seemingly arcane historical debate offers a lesson on constitutional interpretation. The idea that the Fourth Amendment has two discrete clauses, not easily inferred from its obscure text, is a modern invention. Pressing needs of modern law enforcement to allow a variety of *warrantless* arrests are so great that modern commentators have "read back" the two-clause understanding of the Fourth Amendment to color their perceptions of the Framers' intent. Why were the Framers *not* concerned about warrantless searches by police officers? The answer is simple. As Professor Thomas Davies notes, there were no police officers in 1791—at least not in the modern sense. Constables were few, were viewed as untrustworthy, and had no discretion to make warrantless arrests or probable cause searches in the late colonial era or at the time of the framing.[59] Like any citizen, a constable could lawfully arrest or search only if the arrestee in fact committed the crime or if **contraband** was actually found. The constable could *not* act on suspicion or probable cause, as police officers now do; if the constable was wrong, he would be sued for false imprisonment or **trespass**. Thus, misconduct by an officer was seen not as official misconduct, but as personal wrongdoing. The government therefore never committed a wrongful arrest or search, and officers who made arrests or conducted searches almost always did so under the authorization of a *warrant*. "[F]raming-era common law never permitted a warrantless officer to justify an arrest or search according to any standard as loose or flexible as 'reasonableness.'"[60] There was, consequently, no proactive policing at this time and no need to justify warrantless searches under the Fourth Amendment.

The needs of modern society eroded the original understanding and its tight rein on official discretion. The Supreme Court began to erect modern Fourth Amendment law in the late nineteenth and early twentieth centuries, when municipal police forces first became routine. The Court recognized police discretion, but shifted its locus of control from the warrant to the exclusionary rule. Organized police departments are so actively involved in performing warrant-less arrests, stops, and searches that any Court that took Fourth Amendment values seriously would inevitably attempt to provide reasonable controls. Virtually none of the hundreds of Supreme Court Fourth Amendment cases deal with issues of general warrants. Indeed, the Supreme Court seems to have authorized, even required, general warrants for administrative searches (e.g., *Camara v. Municipal Court,* 1967, discussed in Chapter 3).

The historical debate is relevant because the Supreme Court (or at least some of its justices) purports to base its jurisdiction and the legitimacy of its decisions on being true to "the intent of the Framers." If the justices are mistaken regarding the intent of the Fourth Amendment, the body of law they have created comes into question. Worse still, the Framers' intent that constables have absolutely no authority to act "reasonably" when interfering with a person's liberty or privacy, and must instead be strictly controlled by judicial warrant, threatens the constitutionality of modern law enforcement. Much depends on the philosophy of judging held by members of the Court. Ironically, it is Justices Antonin Scalia and Clarence Thomas who most vociferously claim that their decisions are guided by the original intent of the Framers who would seem most likely to be swayed by Davies's "authentic" reading of the Fourth Amendment; this, however, would conflict with their conservative crime control policy orientation. In fact, in most major cases the justices are guided by societal needs, whether or not they openly admit it, and have not been distracted by recent historical interpretation.[61]

Two points need be emphasized. First, some changes to Fourth Amendment doctrines may occur if the "authentic" understanding of the amendment is accepted, making it important to understand the underlying reasons for doctrines rather than simply memorizing the rules. Second, however, the large body of constitutional law is kept fairly stable by the operation of stare decisis, and it is unlikely that there will be a wholesale revolution in Fourth Amendment law. For that reason, the text presents the standard two-clause understanding of Fourth Amendment law, based primarily on the analysis of Supreme Court decisions.

THE FOURTH AMENDMENT EXCLUSIONARY RULE

Development of the Exclusionary Rule, 1886–1921

Court challenges against government misconduct became possible only with the advent of constitutional monarchies and republics in the Age of Enlightenment that recognized individual liberties. In the common law, as represented by *Entick v. Carrington* (1765), criminal defendants could not exclude physical evidence that was seized during illegal searches from their trials, even though an exclusionary rule for coerced confessions originated at this time. This lack of a common law exclusionary rule is reflected in the Fourth Amendment's text, which offers no remedy for illegal search and seizures committed by the state. Nevertheless, the Supreme Court established an exclusionary rule by constitutional interpretation, as it has done in many other areas. Few Fourth Amendment cases were decided by the Supreme Court in the nineteenth and early twentieth centuries, but these cases were sensitive to the Fourth Amendment's civil liberty values. *Ex Parte Jackson* (1878), for example, stated in dictum that postal authorities could not open sealed letters sent through the mails without a warrant. Although in the major case of **Boyd v. United States** (1886) the Supreme Court did suppress the use of evidence obtained illegally by federal customs authorities, it did not establish a clear Fourth Amendment exclusionary rule.

Boyd was an odd case. There was no actual search and seizure; instead, a subpoena was issued to E. A. Boyd & Co. to turn over an invoice on cases of imported glass to determine whether proper customs taxes had been paid (penalties included forfeiture, imprisonment, and fine). If the invoice was not produced, a court could presume it proved the defendant's guilt. Boyd challenged the subpoena and the Supreme Court agreed that the law authorizing the order was unconstitutional and void under the Fourth Amendment *and* the Fifth Amendment privilege against self-incrimination together. "In this regard the Fourth and Fifth Amendments run almost into each other." The Court reasoned that the Fourth Amendment could be violated even though an actual, physical search had not taken place, as long as the government intruded on the defendant's "indefeasible right of personal security, personal liberty and private property," which was the real concern of the amendment. This is no longer good law: a subpoena does not violate the Fourth Amendment. However, by conflating the Fourth and Fifth Amendments, *Boyd* implied that the Fifth Amendment exclusionary rule (see Chapter 7) applied to the Fourth Amendment as well. In fact, *Boyd* did not establish a stand-alone Fourth Amendment exclusionary rule. But its rhetoric, drawing on the lessons of *Entick v. Carrington* and extolling "the sanctity of a man's home and the privacies of life," placed the Court firmly in the position envisioned by the Founders as in James Madison's speech to Congress in 1789, introducing the adoption of the Bill of Rights: to act as an "independent tribunal of justice" and a "guardian" and "impenetrable bulwark against every assumption of power in the legislative or executive" branches, to uphold the "great rights of mankind."[62]

The Supreme Court moved hesitantly toward the exclusionary rule. It affirmed the traditional rule in *Adams v. New York* (1904), saying that "courts do not stop to inquire as to the means by which the evidence was obtained." Allowing the introduction of illegally seized evidence while maintaining the *Boyd* exclusionary rule suggested that the Court felt exclusion required some element of self-incrimination. This changed radically in **Weeks v. United States** (1914), which adopted a straightforward Fourth Amendment exclusionary rule not tied to the Fifth Amendment privilege against self-incrimination. Fremont Weeks was arrested by local police without a warrant at his place of work; at the same time, a U.S. marshal entered Weeks's home without a warrant and "carried away certain letters and envelopes found in the drawer of a chiffonier." Weeks's demand for the return of incriminating papers before trial was denied. He was convicted in federal court for using the mails to transport lottery tickets. The Supreme Court held that all evidence seized without warrant violated the Fourth Amendment and had to be returned; it could not be used against the defendant to prove his guilt. Its language was expansive, protective of individual privacy, and made exclusion a *constitutional* rule:

> The effect of the Fourth Amendment is to put the courts of the United States and Federal officials, in the exercise of their power and authority, under limitations and restraints as to the exercise of such power and authority, and to forever secure the people, their persons, houses, papers and effects against all unreasonable searches and seizures under the guise of law. This protection reaches all alike, whether accused of crime or not, and the duty of giving to it force and effect is obligatory upon all entrusted under our Federal system with the enforcement of the laws. The tendency of those who execute the criminal laws of the country to obtain conviction by means of unlawful seizures and enforced confessions, . . . should find no sanction in the judgments of the courts which are charged at all times with the support of the Constitution and to which people of all conditions have a right to appeal for the maintenance of such fundamental rights. (*Weeks v. United States*, 1914)

The exclusionary rule was limited to *federal* law enforcement only. *Weeks* firmly tied the remedy of exclusion to the constitutional right, making it a part of the Constitution. A deterrence rationale was also hinted at: "If letters and private documents can . . . be seized and held and used in evidence against a citizen accused of an offense [as in this case], the protection of the Fourth Amendment declaring his right to be secure against such searches and seizures is of no value, and, so far as those thus placed are concerned, might as well be stricken from the Constitution."

The *constitutional basis* of the exclusionary rule was confirmed and strengthened in Justice Oliver Wendell Holmes's opinion in **Silverthorne Lumber Co. v. United States** (1920). Frederick W. Silverthorne and his father were indicted for a federal crime and arrested at home while federal agents entered their business offices without a warrant and took business documents. The district court agreed with the defendants' contention that their Fourth Amendment rights were violated and, on their demand, ordered the documents returned. Before complying, the government *photographed* the documents and *used* these copies to get a subpoena for the originals. Silverthorne refused to comply with the subpoena. The district court found that the documents had originally been seized illegally but nevertheless ordered Silverthorne to comply with the subpoena. Silverthorne refused, the company was fined, and he was ordered jailed until he turned over the original documents.

The Supreme Court reversed the lower court's judgment. In Holmes's words, to allow the government to seize evidence in violation of the Fourth Amendment, and then use the knowledge gained by that wrong to obtain the evidence "legally," "reduces the Fourth Amendment to a form of words." Therefore, "[t]he essence of a provision forbidding the acquisition of evidence in a certain way is that not merely evidence so acquired shall not be used before the Court but that it shall not be used at all." This is the crux of one exclusionary rule theory that will be addressed later in this chapter: The government cannot profit from its illegal action. As Professor William Heffernan notes, this "no use" rule was fully rights-based and went further than the scope of the exclusionary rule established in 1974, which allows illegally obtained evidence to be used in a variety of legal arenas (see "Undermining the Exclusionary Rule" section).[63]

Holmes added an important exception to the exclusionary rule: "Of course this does not mean that the facts thus obtained become sacred and inaccessible. If knowledge of them is gained from an **independent source** they may be proved like any others, but the knowledge gained by the Government's own wrong cannot be used by it in the way proposed." These rules later became known as the **"fruits of the poisonous tree" doctrine** and the 'independent source exception'. The rationale is that government violation of a defendant's Fourth Amendment rights does not lead to a windfall in the guise of the dismissal of the case. The government can use other evidence to convict, if that evidence is obtained by legal means.

Gouled v. United States (1921) filled out the law on the development of the exclusionary rule. It first held that the Fourth Amendment is as much violated by a "fraudulent" entry into a home or business office as by a forcible entry. In this case, a government investigator who happened to know Gouled, a fraud suspect, pretended to make a friendly call on Gouled at his business office. While Gouled was out of the room, the investigator furtively took incriminating papers. The Court ruled that the admission of these papers violated the Fifth Amendment privilege against self-incrimination, thus continuing to conflate the Fourth and Fifth Amendments when papers that communicated a person's state of mind were in question.

In this case, search warrants were issued to seize *papers* that were not the direct fruits of crime but were only *evidence of* Gouled's fraudulent conspiracy. The Court elevated a common law rule, known as the "mere evidence rule," part of the Fourth Amendment exclusionary rule, by holding that these papers could not be admitted into evidence. The theory was that property that was not itself a part of the crime (as opposed to items such as stolen goods, the document on which a fraud was based, weapons, or burglar's tools used to commit a crime) could not be seized. The mere evidence rule demonstrates that the Court saw Fourth Amendment rights as essentially resting on *property rights*. The government simply could not seize evidence (other than contraband) owned by the suspect, even temporarily and even though it could be used to prove the suspect's guilt. The Court eventually dropped this rule in *Warden v. Hayden* (1967), one of a series of cases that shifted the conceptual basis of the Fourth Amendment from a property to a functional basis.

State Action Doctrine

In general, the Constitution protects people from the excessive action of *government* officers that threaten individual liberties and the Rule of Law. By analogy, the criminal law protects people from criminal harms committed by *private* persons and institutions; an ordinary crime is *not* a constitutional violation. As a result, the Fourth Amendment and the exclusionary rule apply only to evidence illegally seized by the government. When a private party turns over evidence to a prosecutor, courts follow the common law rule and do not ask about the source of the incriminating evidence, even if obtained by a civil trespass or a burglary (*Burdeau v. McDowell,* 1921). In legal terms, the Fourth Amendment applies only when there is *state action*. State, or government, action also exists when a private person acts as a *proxy for* or at the direction of the police. Evidence illegally seized by a private person acting as a proxy for the government is not admissible. Although this is the law, the Constitution does prohibit some private action, such as the holding of slaves (U.S. Const. Amd., XIII). The state action doctrine was injected into the law in the Civil Rights Cases (1883) as part of a strategy to prevent the expansion of the civil rights of African Americans.[64] In general, the state action doctrine favors the prosecution.

The initial seizure by a private party does not mean that a police agent can proceed without obtaining a warrant. When a private individual turns suspicious items over to police, they may subject the items to only *minimal investigation* before requesting a search warrant. In ***Walter v. United States*** (1980), a box with pornographic videos was mistakenly sent to a company, which turned it over to the FBI. Without obtaining a warrant, agents screened all of the films to determine their content. This screening was held to be state action, and the evidence was inadmissible because it constituted an investigation into an area of privacy. The labels on the outside of the film boxes created probable cause of the films' content, and a further search had to be authorized by a search warrant. To the contrary, in ***United States v. Jacobsen*** (1984), Federal Express employees opened a suspiciously wrapped package, discovered white powder, and turned it over to federal Drug Enforcement Administration (DEA) agents. The agents chemically "field tested" the powder and found it to be cocaine. The action by the FedEx employees was not state action. The warrantless examination by DEA agents was held proper because it was not a *significant expansion* of the earlier private search. The agents later obtained a warrant and the evidence was admissible.

The state action doctrine applies to searches conducted by *any* government officer, not just by police officers acting for law enforcement purposes. Searches by public school teachers, public hospital supervisors, probation officers, municipal building inspectors, Occupational Safety and Health Administration (OSHA) inspectors, federal mine-safety investigators, municipal fire department investigators, and customs agents must adhere to Fourth Amendment rules. Illegal search and seizures by these personnel require the exclusion of evidence. This branch of search and seizure law comes under the "special needs beyond normal law enforcement" doctrine, with lower standards for valid searches (see Chapter 5).

PRIVATE SECURITY PERSONNEL   Is a detention or search by a private security agent state action? The issue arises in federal civil lawsuits (under 42 U.S.C. § 1983, discussed earlier in this chapter) alleging that security personnel have violated a person's civil rights while acting "under color of state law." The Supreme Court has not decided this issue (*Flagg Bros. v. Brooks*, 1978). Lower federal courts have ruled that private police *are* state actors "when the state *delegates a public function* to a private entity."[65]

Privately employed railroad policemen who brutally beat vagrant trespassers, and private security personnel at a Chicago hospital who detained a person, were held liable under the federal civil rights lawsuit as "state actors." The reason is that legislation gave them the powers of regular police officers. They were known as "special police officers," were licensed by the city, underwent background checks, wore "suitable badges" issued by the superintendent of police, and conformed to police officer regulations.[66]

On the other hand, security guards at a private mall who exercised no "police powers" were held not to be state actors.[67] Similarly, a private security guard hired by a Chicago public housing agency who shot a person in the groin was not a state actor. The housing authority did have a private police force with police powers, but this guard was a contract person and not part of the private police force. Although the guard was in uniform and armed, he was assigned specifically to guard lobbies and had no authority to act outside the lobby of the assigned building.

A grandmother was arrested by security guards in a Detroit casino for taking a token worth five cents from the tray of an abandoned slot machine. She was banned from the casino and ejected forthwith. In a federal civil suit against the casino, the district court held that the security personnel acted under "the color of state law." Under Michigan law, an employer may either maintain *private security guards* in order to protect its property or may employ *private security police*. The casino's licensed private security *police* met state training requirements and, when working on the employer's property, had the same authority to arrest a person without a warrant as a municipal police officer. Private guards, on the contrary, did not come under state action because they only had the same right as private business owners to protect their property; at most they could temporarily detain an individual clearly stealing something.[68] In this case, the officers detained the grandmother, displayed handcuffs, photographed her, obtained personal information, including her Social Security number, and banned her from the casino for six months.

The enormous growth of the private security industry has led some to question the general rule that arrests and searches by private security agents are not state action. Critics would extend the Fourth Amendment exclusionary rule to unreasonable searches and seizures committed by private security personnel.[69] For others, the issue is not clear-cut, and the state action doctrine is a poor way of ascertaining the liability of security personnel. Meanwhile, the issue has become more urgent with the expansion of the private police role in protecting the nation against terrorism.[70]

"Fruits of the Poisonous Tree" Doctrine—Derivative Evidence

Silverthorne v. United States (1920) added a necessary corollary to the exclusionary rule: Secondary or addition evidence (the "fruits") *derived from* evidence obtained in illegal search and seizure (the "poisonous tree") is not admissible. Were such **derivative evidence** admissible, police officers could violate Fourth Amendment rights with impunity and then, after the original evidence is excluded, use information gained from the illegality to get a "legal" search warrant.

The derivative evidence rule reflects the axiom that under the Fourth Amendment, *justification* for searches must be provided *prior to* the search. Retroactive justification turns the amendment into a sham. An example is the *per curiam* decision of **Smith v. Ohio** (1990).[71] Two plainclothes police officers, without a warrant and without probable cause or reasonable suspicion, stopped Smith while he was exiting a convenience store carrying a brown paper grocery bag marked with the store's logo. The officers identified themselves, and Smith put the sack on the hood of his car. Smith did not answer a question about the bag's content and tried to push an officer's hand away as he opened the bag. Drug paraphernalia was found. Smith was arrested. His conviction was reversed by the Supreme Court. The search was not justified on any Fourth Amendment ground—neither as a self-protective *Terry* stop, nor as abandoned property. There could be no search *incident* to arrest—indeed, in *Smith,* the arrest occurred *after* the search. The obvious point is that the police simply cannot search whatever they choose and then make a "legal" arrest or seizure if their hunch or baseless action turns up contraband. If they could, the Fourth Amendment would be worthless. The exclusionary rule is essential to prevent this or the police could take their chances and search people who would not be likely to sue or win lawsuits against the police.

The *Silverthorne* derivative evidence rule is called the "fruits of the poisonous tree" doctrine in a metaphor penned by Justice Felix Frankfurter in *Nardone v. United States* (1939): What is excluded is not only the illegally seized evidence (the "poisonous tree"), but also other evidence *derived from* the illegally seized evidence (the "fruits"). Allowing the use of derivative evidence would create a rule "inconsistent with ethical standards and destructive of personal liberty." The Court in *Nardone* excluded not only the *exact words* overheard in a wiretap that violated a federal statute but also *any information derived* from the overheard conversations.

Silverthorne and *Nardone* recognize, however, that the exclusionary rule, including the exclusion of derivative evidence, is not a windfall to the defendant—it does not lead to an automatic dismissal of charges or to a prohibition on the use of other, properly obtained, evidence. The Supreme Court has recognized three *exceptions* to derivative evidence exclusion: (1) evidence obtained from an independent source, (2) **inevitable discovery**, and (3) **attenuation**. One case noted that the inevitable discovery exception is an extrapolation of the independent source exception (*Murray v. United States,* 1988).

INDEPENDENT SOURCE EXCEPTION   The Supreme Court has allowed illegally seized evidence when the evidence was obtained in a constitutional manner that was entirely unconnected to the illegality—that is, from an independent source. In **Segura v. United States** (1984), a group of police officers illegally entered Segura's apartment and saw incriminating evidence in plain view. A search warrant was later obtained based on information developed before the illegal entry took place. The Supreme Court excluded the evidence in plain view during the illegal search but allowed use of evidence obtained under the search warrant because it was independent of the illegal entry. In **Murray v. United States** (1988), police illegally entered a warehouse and saw suspicious bales believed to contain marijuana. This illegal entry was not mentioned in an affidavit for a search warrant. Nevertheless, the Court allowed the use of evidence obtained under the warrant because it was lawfully issued on the basis of *other* competent evidence.

INEVITABLE DISCOVERY EXCEPTION   Illegally seized evidence is admissible if it would have been inevitably discovered independently of the unconstitutional action. *Brewer v. Williams* (1977, known as *Williams I*) held that evidence of a murdered girl's body was excluded because it was discovered based on an unconstitutional interrogation (a so-called Christian burial speech; see Chapter 7). On retrial, Williams's confession was excluded, but the location of the dead girl's body was introduced into evidence. In **Nix v. Williams** (1984, known as *Williams II*), the Supreme Court held that this evidence was properly introduced because a search party was within two and a half miles of the body when it was found. Members of the search party were instructed to look into culverts (where the body was placed) and would have covered the area where the body was located. Thus the body would inevitably have been found, whether or not the defendant divulged its location to the police.

The motivations of the police who improperly took the confession were irrelevant to the Fourth Amendment issue.

ATTENUATION EXCEPTION   Evidence derived from an illegal or unconstitutional source is admissible when, for some reason, the link between the initial illegality and the evidence sought to be introduced has become so *weak* or *tenuous* that the "fruits" have become "untainted." In *Nardone,* Justice Frankfurter wrote: "Sophisticated argument may prove a causal connection between information obtained through illicit wiretapping and the Government's proof. As a matter of good sense, however, such connection may have become so attenuated as to dissipate the taint."

Wong Sun v. United States (1963) explicates the attenuation doctrine. Six or seven narcotics officers illegally entered the San Francisco apartment of James Wah Toy behind his laundry shop at 6 A.M., looking for drugs. They rousted the inhabitants and questioned Toy. No drugs were found, but Toy named some people whom the agents questioned about drug dealing, including Wong Sun. The Supreme Court excluded from evidence an incriminating statement made by Toy as well as confessions and drugs obtained from a person questioned immediately after the raid on Toy's apartment because this evidence was *derived from* the illegal entry into Toy's apartment (i.e., "fruit of the poisonous tree"). Wong Sun was arrested but then released; a few days later, he returned *voluntarily* and made an incriminating statement. The Court held that this voluntary statement was admissible because the connection between the arrest and the statement had "become so attenuated as to dissipate the taint." The test for determining whether attenuation exists is this: "whether, granting establishment of the primary illegality, the evidence to which instant objection is made has been come at by exploitation of that illegality or instead by means sufficiently distinguishable to be purged of the primary taint."

Attenuation issues arise when a "proper," *Mirandized*, confession is made after an illegal arrest. The fact that *Miranda* warnings are given does not automatically break the link between the illegal arrest and a resulting confession, nor does the passage of *two hours* between the illegal arrest and the confession attenuate the illegality (*Brown v. Illinois,* 1975). To make *Miranda* warnings a "cure-all" for illegal police action would encourage illegal arrests and would dilute the effectiveness of the *Miranda* exclusionary rule. Likewise, a *six-hour* delay between an illegal arrest and a confession, followed by a ten-minute meeting between the defendant and friends, did not attenuate the initial illegality despite three *Miranda* warnings (*Taylor v. Alabama,* 1982).

On the contrary, a confession following an illegal arrest was allowed into evidence in *New York v. Harris* (1990). Police illegally arrested Harris at his home without a warrant, read *Miranda* warnings, and obtained a confession in the house. Taken to the police station, Harris again was read his rights, signed a waiver form, and confessed. The first confession was suppressed as the fruit of an illegal police action: entry into the home without a warrant when no exigency existed (*Payton v. New York,* 1980). But the Court held the station house confession to be admissible. The Court ruled that because Harris was legally in custody because an illegal arrest does not deprive the court of jurisdiction to try the suspect. Therefore "the statement, while *the product* of an arrest and being in custody, was *not the fruit* of the fact that the arrest was made in the house rather than somewhere else" (*New York v. Harris,* emphasis added). The Court did not apply attenuation analysis but rather saw the case as a straightforward example of evidence not being the "fruit," or actual result of, a prior illegal police action. The 5–4 decision in *Harris* may be explained by the hostility of a growing conservative majority on the Court toward the exclusionary rule. The majority, however, *distinguished* the facts of *Harris* from those of *Brown* and *Taylor* because in *Harris,* the police had *probable cause* to arrest the defendant, unlike the earlier cases. The opinion said that excluding the first confession vindicated the rule that made in-home arrests without a warrant unconstitutional, but as for allowing the second confession, "it does not follow from the emphasis on the exclusionary rule's deterrent value that 'anything which deters illegal searches is thereby commanded by the Fourth Amendment'" (*New York v. Harris,* 1990).

Determining whether the original illegality has become attenuated is not found by applying mechanical rules. It depends on whether, considering the *totality* of the circumstances, the questioned evidence in the case would have been discovered had not the original violation taken place. If the subsequent evidence is considered to be *independent* of the original "tainted" search and seizure, then it can be used against the defendant in court. In *United States v. Ceccolini* (1978), a police officer, without any design to investigate gambling, discovered betting slips in the defendant's flower shop by improperly looking into an envelope with cash sticking out located behind the customer counter. Ceccolini denied that gambling occurred in his place of business to a grand jury, but was convicted of perjury after an employee testified about illegal gambling at his shop. The Court of Appeals, ruling that the employee's statement was the fruit of the officer's original unconstitutional search, excluded the testimony. The Supreme Court reversed. The link between the search and the witness's testimony had become so attenuated that the testimony could no longer be considered to be caused by the officer's unconstitutional act. The Court relied on a variety of facts: Federal officials previously had the shop under suspicion and observation; several months passed between the officer's telling the FBI about the slips and the initial questioning of the employee; the witness was in no way coerced or induced to testify, but did so for honorable motives; the betting slips were not used in the questioning of the witness; and the officer had no intent to investigate gambling. In this case, the Court also felt that the deterrent effect on police misconduct of excluding the evidence would be very limited.

The Movement to Incorporate the Exclusionary Rule, 1949–1963

Shortly after *Adamson v. California* (1947), the Supreme Court considered incorporating the Fourth Amendment *and* its exclusionary rule into the Fourteenth Amendment, making them applicable to the states. (See Chapter 1.) In **Wolf v. Colorado** (1949), authorities in Denver received "definite information" that Dr. Wolf had performed an abortion. Sheriff's deputies under the district attorney's instruction "went to the office of Wolf without a warrant and took him into custody and there they took possession of . . . his day books of 1944 and 1943 up to the time of the arrest. They were records of patients who consulted him professionally." The records were introduced in evidence and used to convict Dr. Wolf, who received a twelve- to eighteen-month prison sentence. The Colorado Supreme Court held the evidence admissible, although the search was illegal.[72] Had this been a federal search, it would have violated the Fourth Amendment, and the evidence would have been ruled inadmissible under the *Weeks* exclusionary rule. The Fourth Amendment, however, did not bind local or state police and courts at that time. The U.S. Supreme Court held, in an opinion by Justice Frankfurter, that (1) the Fourth Amendment *is* "incorporated" but (2) the exclusionary rule is *not* "incorporated." That is, "in a prosecution in a State court for a State crime the Fourteenth Amendment does not forbid the admission of evidence obtained by an unreasonable search and seizure" (*Wolf v. Colorado,* 1949). As to the first holding, Justice Frankfurter dismissed the idea of "total incorporation" as one that had consistently been rejected by the Supreme Court in many cases. Turning to "selective incorporation" under the Due Process Clause, Justice Frankfurter noted that due process encompasses rights that are basic to a free society. As a free society advances, so may its rights. To this conservative justice, therefore, the Constitution is a living document whose meaning evolves with society, instead of being immutable and unchangeable:

> The security of one's privacy against arbitrary intrusion by the police—which is at the core of the Fourth Amendment—is basic to a free society. It is therefore implicit in "the concept of ordered liberty" and as such enforceable against the States through the Due Process Clause. The knock at the door, whether by day or by night, as a prelude to a search, without authority of law but solely on the authority of the police, did not need the commentary of recent history to be condemned as inconsistent with the conception of human rights enshrined in the history and the basic constitutional documents of English-speaking peoples.
>
> Accordingly, we have no hesitation in saying that were a State affirmatively to sanction such police incursion into privacy it would run counter to the guaranty of the Fourteenth Amendment. (*Wolf v. Colorado,* 1949)

This elegant language, interspersed among paragraphs that disparage the incorporation doctrine, incorporates the *substance* of the Fourth Amendment; that is, it forbids the states from creating rules that violate the Fourth Amendment. However, the Court's majority refused to impose the exclusionary rule on the states via incorporation:

> But the ways of enforcing such a basic right raise questions of a different order. How such arbitrary conduct should be checked, what remedies against it should be afforded, the means by which the right should be made effective, are all questions that are not to be so dogmatically answered as to preclude the varying solutions

which spring from an allowable range of judgment on issues not susceptible of quantitative solution.

> In *Weeks v. United States,* this Court held that in a federal prosecution the Fourth Amendment barred the use of evidence secured through an illegal search and seizure. This ruling was made for the first time in 1914. It was not derived from the explicit requirements of the Fourth Amendment; it was not based on legislation expressing Congressional policy in the enforcement of the Constitution. The decision was a matter of judicial implication. Since then it has been frequently applied and we stoutly adhere to it. But the immediate question is whether the basic right to protection against arbitrary intrusion by the police demands the exclusion of logically relevant evidence obtained by an unreasonable search and seizure because, in a federal prosecution for a federal crime, it would be excluded. As a matter of inherent reason, one would suppose this to be an issue as to which men with complete devotion to the protection of the right of privacy might give different answers. When we find that in fact most of the English-speaking world does not regard as vital to such protection the exclusion of evidence thus obtained, we must hesitate to treat this remedy as an essential ingredient of the right. The contrariety of views of the States is particularly impressive in view of the careful reconsideration which they have given the problem in the light of the *Weeks* decision. (*Wolf v. Colorado,* 1949)

Justice Frankfurter emphasized that the basic Fourth Amendment right, now applicable against state as well as federal encroachment, was protected by the "remedies" of civil lawsuits in all states, whether or not they had adopted their own exclusionary rules. As of 1949, sixteen states had adopted the *Weeks* exclusionary doctrine as a matter of local law, while thirty-one had rejected it.

Justice Black, the leading proponent of incorporation, surprisingly joined the majority because he felt that "the federal exclusionary rule is not a command of the Fourth Amendment but is a judicially created rule of evidence which Congress might negate"—that is, it is not a constitutional requirement. He managed to combine judicial *activism* with **originalism**—a seemingly incongruous combination. He agreed that the Due Process Clause incorporated the Fourth Amendment's substance as a fundamental right. Limiting the *Weeks* exclusionary rule only to *federal* law enforcement, because it was absent from the Fourth Amendment's *text*, necessarily meant that the majority viewed the exclusionary rule as based on the Court's supervisory power and *not* as a constitutional rule. Whether or not inconsistent, Black's position in *Wolf* would later create an anomaly in *Mapp v. Ohio* (1961) that he would have to explain away when he changed his position.

Three liberal justices, William O. Douglas, Frank Murphy, and Wiley Rutledge, dissented in *Wolf,* arguing for incorporating the exclusionary rule. They argued that civil lawsuits and criminal prosecutions against police and prosecutors are virtually never successful, especially if the person claiming an unconstitutional search has a criminal record. For all practical purposes, without exclusion the Fourth Amendment was a right without a remedy. Justice Murphy noted that police are carefully trained in the law of search and seizure in states with the exclusionary rule, whereas the subject was virtually ignored in states without it. "The conclusion is inescapable that but one remedy exists to deter violations of the search and seizure clause. That is the rule which excludes illegally obtained evidence" (*Wolf v. Colorado,* 1949).

Three years after *Wolf,* the Supreme Court in **Rochin v. California** (1952) did suppress evidence obtained in a state search and seizure, not via *Weeks*'s Fourth Amendment exclusionary rule, but under the more flexible due process rule of the Fourteenth Amendment. Los Angeles police officers, believing that Rochin was dealing drugs, invaded his home without a warrant, went up the stairs, and forced open a door to his bedroom.

> Inside they found [Rochin] sitting partly dressed on the side of the bed, upon which his wife was lying. On a "night stand" beside the bed the deputies spied two capsules. When asked "Whose stuff is this?" Rochin seized the capsules and put them in his mouth. A struggle ensued, in the course of which the three officers "jumped upon him" and attempted to extract the capsules. The force they applied proved unavailing against Rochin's resistance. He was handcuffed and taken to a hospital. At the direction of one of the officers a doctor forced an emetic solution through a tube into

Rochin's stomach against his will. This "stomach pumping" produced vomiting. In the vomited matter were found two capsules which proved to contain morphine. (*Rochin v. California,* 1952)

The justices unanimously agreed that the evidence obtained by this outrageous police action was inadmissible, but for different reasons. Justice Frankfurter's majority opinion avoided the *Weeks* automatic exclusionary rule. It relied instead on a due process exclusionary rule where the totality of the circumstances "shocked the conscience" of the appellate court. To him, the "shocks the conscience" test was an objective standard that would guide lower courts. Justice Douglas concurred in the decision but strongly disagreed with the 'shocks the conscience' test. As with any due process test that rests on the "totality of the circumstances," the application of the rule could differ from one judge to another. As he saw it, unlike the "unequivocal, definite and workable rule of evidence" of the *Weeks* exclusionary rule, the rule fashioned in *Rochin* "turn[s] not on the Constitution but on the idiosyncrasies of the judges who sit here" (*Rochin v. California,* 1952).

Justice Douglas's criticism was proven true in **Irvine v. California** (1954). Local police, suspecting Irvine of illegal bookmaking, secretly entered his home and, without a judicial search warrant, wired the house for sound, including the bedroom. The police listened in on the private conversations of Irvine and his wife for weeks and testified to what they heard at Irvine's trial. The overheard conversations were used to convict Irvine. Justice Robert Jackson's majority opinion stated, "Few police measures have come to our attention that more flagrantly, deliberately, and persistently violated the fundamental principle declared by the Fourth Amendment" (*Irvine v. California,* 1954). Despite this, the Supreme Court upheld the use of this evidence. The *Weeks* exclusionary rule did not apply to the states, and the majority refused to apply the *Rochin* "shocks the conscience" test because the facts of *Rochin* included the element of *coercion* not found in the *Irvine* case. This was too much for Justice Frankfurter, who dissented on the grounds that *Rochin* did apply, arguing fruitlessly that "a State cannot resort to methods that offend civilized standards of decency and fairness." The subjectivity of the 'shocks the conscience' test was exposed when the majority in *Irvine* did not find such a flagrant violation of Fourth Amendment privacy to "shock the conscience." In a spirited dissent, Justice Douglas called again for incorporating the exclusionary rule, saying, "The search and seizure conducted in this case smack of the police state, not the free America the Bill of Rights envisaged."

As the 1950s wore on, more states adopted the exclusionary rule by court action, most notably the California Supreme Court.[73] The tide in favor of reversing *Weeks* was "halting but seemingly inexorable."[74] A harbinger of the exclusionary rule was the Court's abolition of the **"silver platter" doctrine**. Soon after *Weeks* (1914), local and federal police began to practice end-runs around the exclusionary rule. If state or local police seized evidence of a federal crime by an illegal search and seizure, the evidence was admissible in a federal trial as long as the federal officers did not participate in the illegal search. This, of course, put a premium on "pious perjury," or winking at the truth.

The Supreme Court signaled its unhappiness with this in **Rea v. United States** (1956). The Court exercised its supervisory authority to prevent a federal narcotics agent, who illegally seized marijuana that was excluded from a federal prosecution, from testifying about the marijuana in a *state* prosecution. This eliminated a federal-to-state "silver platter" (or "reverse silver platter") delivery of tainted evidence. In **Elkins v. United States** (1960), the Supreme Court put an end to the state-to-federal transfer of illegally seized evidence, bringing the behavior of local police under the federal exclusionary rule. Justice Potter Stewart, writing for the majority (5–4), noted that *Wolf v. Colorado's* (1949) holding that *substantive* Fourth Amendment rights applied against the states eroded the basis of the silver platter doctrine. The four dissenting justices complained that the Court was interfering with states' rights. In reply, Justice Stewart wrote, "The very essence of a healthy federalism depends upon the avoidance of needless conflict between federal and state courts." Thus, in states with state exclusionary rules, the 'silver platter' doctrine undermined *state* policy. *Elkins* was decided not on constitutional grounds but on "the Court's supervisory power over the administration of criminal justice in the federal courts." Nevertheless, Justice Stewart's strong defense of the exclusionary rule, and its grounding in "the imperative of judicial integrity" foreshadowed the decision in *Mapp v. Ohio* (1961) and its basis as a constitutional rule.

Incorporating the Exclusionary Rule: *Mapp v. Ohio*

The due process revolution of the 1960s, which incorporated a host of rights (see Chapter 1), was initiated by *Mapp v. Ohio* (1961). Although the movement is associated with a five-justice liberal majority of the Warren Court sitting from 1962 to 1969, the *Mapp* opinion was authored by Justice Tom Clark, who more often than not voted for the prosecution.

Dollree Mapp, an independent-minded African-American woman, was thirty-three years old in 1957. She had left an abusive husband and owned a house in the Shaker Heights neighborhood of Cleveland, Ohio, where she took in boarders. She had many friends in the professional prizefighting community and in illegal numbers gambling. The house of Don King (later a well-known boxing promoter), an acquaintance of Ms. Mapp, was bombed in May 1957. King told police he believed the bombers were involved in the Cleveland numbers racket. Days after the bombing an anonymous tip informed police that a suspect, Virgil Ogletree, was at Ms. Mapp's house. Police showed up at 1:30 p.m. and spotted Ogletree's car. Mapp refused the entry of police detectives into her home. The police waited. Mapp caller her lawyer, who told her that they could enter only if they had a search warrant. A standoff continued until 4:30 p.m. Just as Mapp's lawyer arrived at the house, police forced their way in through the front door. The lawyer asked if they had a warrant but never got a satisfactory answer. He tried to enter the house but was kept out by the police. Inside the house, an officer waved a paper as if it were a warrant. Mapp grabbed it and "put it down the front of her dress." An officer retrieved it after a scuffle with Mapp. For the next hour Mapp was handcuffed while the police searched every nook and cranny of her house. Ogletree was found and arrested in the apartment of Minerva Lockheart, a renter. In the basement a trunk was found with "policy paraphernalia" and books thought to be obscene that belonged to a former tenant, Morris Jones. Nevertheless, Mapp was arrested and later convicted for possession of obscene literature. A search warrant was never obtained. Her case got to the Supreme Court as a First Amendment obscenity issue. By a narrow majority, however, the Court decided to treat it as a Fourth Amendment case.[75] The Ohio courts acknowledged that the books were unlawfully seized during an unlawful search of her home but still allowed the evidence to be used, relying on *Wolf v. Colorado.*

The majority opinion in *Mapp v. Ohio* (1961) overruled that portion of *Wolf* holding that the *Weeks* exclusionary rule applied only to federal prosecutions and not to the states. Under *Wolf,* the exclusionary rule was necessarily created by the Court's supervisory authority over federal law enforcement, and was not in itself a fundamental right under the Due Process Clause that would have made it a constitutional rule binding on the states under an "incorporated Fourth Amendment." Justice Clark's majority opinion changed this. "We hold that all evidence obtained by searches and seizures in violation of the Constitution is, *by that same authority*, inadmissible in a state court" (*Mapp*, emphasis added). The Fourth Amendment exclusionary rule was now incorporated into the Due Process Clause, applicable to state prosecutions as "part and parcel" of the Fourth Amendment. Considering that the language of *Weeks* grounded the exclusionary rule in the Constitution, *Mapp* could be viewed as returning the rule to its proper constitutional status after being demoted by a Court too unsure about incorporation in 1949.

This however, is not the end of the story. A scant thirteen years after *Mapp,* a changed and conservative Court went back to viewing the exclusionary rule not as a constitutional rule or a private right of a defendant but as a device to "deter future unlawful police conduct and thereby effectuate the guarantee of the Fourth Amendment against unreasonable searches and seizures" (*U.S. v. Calandra*, 1974). *Calandra* began a train of cases the have continued, until *Herring v. United States* (2009), to whittle away the scope and effectiveness of the exclusionary rule. Thus, a student who looks to the Supreme Court as a rock of doctrinal stability ought to consider that from 1914 to 1949 the Court, under *Weeks,* saw the exclusionary rule as a constitutional requirement. Yet, from 1949 to 1961, under *Wolf,* the exclusionary rule lost its constitutional status. Its constitutional status was regained in *Mapp v. Ohio,* and the rule was "part and parcel" of the Fourth Amendment from 1961 to 1974. Yet in 1974 to the present, the Court's majority has treated the exclusionary rule as essentially nonconstitutional, but constitutional enough for federal courts to apply it to the states in flagrant cases. As late as 2009, almost a century after *Weeks,* the Court split 5–4 over its view of the exclusionary rule in *Herring.*

To return to *Mapp,* the Court supplied a number of reasons for incorporating the Fourth Amendment exclusionary rule. First, it viewed *Weeks* (1914) as resting firmly on *constitutional* grounds: "the Court in that case clearly stated that use of the seized evidence involved 'a denial of the constitutional rights of the accused,'" and "the plain and unequivocal language of *Weeks*—and its later paraphrase in *Wolf*—to the effect that the *Weeks* rule is of constitutional origin, remains entirely undisturbed." Next, the *Mapp* majority agreed with the conclusion of *Weeks* and the concerns of liberal justices from the 1940s onward that the exclusionary rule was the only way to effectively protect individuals' Fourth Amendment rights. Third, it took the position, grounded in *Boyd*, that when interpreting the Bill of Rights and other individual liberties, it "is the duty of courts to be watchful for the constitutional rights of the citizen, and against any stealthy encroachments thereon." Fourth, it suggested that the holding of *Wolf*, incorporating the substance of the Fourth Amendment, weakened the nonapplicability of the exclusionary rule. Fifth, it noted a shifting trend in the states that undermined the factual basis of *Wolf*: Prior to *Wolf* in 1949 "almost two-thirds of the States were opposed to the use of the exclusionary rule" but more than half of the states adopted the rule by state legislative or judicial decision. Sixth, the discarding of the silver platter doctrine weakened opposition for the exclusionary rule and put the states and the federal government on an equal footing, which strengthened a "healthy federalism" and federal–state law enforcement cooperation. Finally, the decision rested on the Rule of Law and the nonutilitarian role of courts as guardians of liberty:

> There are those who say, as did Justice (then Judge) Cardozo, that under our constitutional exclusionary doctrine "the criminal is to go free because the constable has blundered." *People v. Defore,* [N.Y. Court of Appeals, 1926]. In some cases this will undoubtedly be the result. But, as was said in *Elkins*, "there is another consideration—the imperative of judicial integrity." The criminal goes free, if he must, but it is the law that sets him free. Nothing can destroy a government more quickly than its failure to observe its own laws, or worse, its disregard of the charter of its own existence. (*Mapp v. Ohio*, 1961)

A curious feature of the majority ruling was its awkward reliance, in part, on the idea in *Boyd* (1886) that the exclusionary rule was based in part on the Fifth Amendment privilege against self-incrimination, which is an exclusionary rule. This was done essentially to garner Justice Black's concurrence. Black, a leader of incorporation, had nevertheless joined the majority in *Wolf* (1949) based on his textualist philosophy that the exclusionary rule was not a constitutional rule because it was not included in the amendment's text. He explained his switch in *Mapp* by saying he was "still not persuaded that the Fourth Amendment, standing alone, would be enough to bar the introduction into evidence" of items seized "in violation of its commands." Upon "reflection," he concluded "that when the Fourth Amendment's ban against unreasonable searches and seizures is considered together with the Fifth Amendment's ban against compelled self-incrimination, a constitutional basis emerges which not only justifies but actually requires the exclusionary rule." Thus, a majority for partially overruling *Wolf* was achieved. It could be argued that only a plurality supported a stand-alone Fourth Amendment exclusionary rule in *Mapp*, rendering the rule shaky, although in later cases clear majorities upheld the rule (*One 1958 Plymouth Sedan v. Pennsylvania*, 1965). Justice Stewart expressed no opinion on the search and seizure issue; he would have reversed the conviction on First Amendment grounds.

Justice Harlan dissented, joined by justices Frankfurter and Whitaker, based first on a complaint that *stare decisis* was not followed by overruling the fairly recent decision of *Wolf*. His main argument was opposed to incorporation in general—on the idea that the Bill of Rights' criminal provisions did not apply to the states. Even if *Wolf* did incorporate the substance of the Fourth Amendment, it did not follow that every rule created and applied to federal courts under the amendment necessarily applied to the states under the Due Process Clause, through which an amendment is incorporated. The dissent emphasized federalism, and the freedom of the states, as "sovereign judicial systems," to establish their own rules of criminal procedure. The dissenters did not see the use of illegally seized evidence as "going to the heart of our concepts of fairness in judicial procedure."

Two years after *Mapp,* in **Ker v. California** (1963), the Court fully "federalized" the exclusionary rule, saying that the "standard of reasonableness is the same under the Fourth and Fourteenth Amendments." Essentially, state courts would have to abide by the U.S. Supreme Court's exclusionary rule interpretations. The Court noted that it had no supervisory authority over the states, only the jurisdiction to interpret the Constitution. The majority opinion said that

Mapp "implied no total obliteration of state laws relating to arrests and searches in favor of federal law. *Mapp* sounded no death knell for our federalism." On the other hand, "Findings of reasonableness, of course, are respected only insofar as consistent with federal constitutional guarantees." In practice, this meant that state search and seizure law had to conform to minimum constitutional standards as determined by the Supreme Court, but under the adequate and independent state grounds concept, a state could expand a suspect's rights in a search and seizure case. (See Chapter 1.)

In 1965, the Supreme Court held, in ***Linkletter v. Walker,*** that the exclusionary rule was not retroactive to state cases decided prior to *Mapp;* its effect was prospective only. Applying the Court's pragmatic approach to determining if a constitutional rule should be applied retroactively, the seven-to-two majority opinion stated that "*Mapp* had as its prime purpose the enforcement of the Fourth Amendment through the inclusion of the exclusionary rule within its rights. This, it was found, was the *only effective deterrent to lawless police action.* Indeed, all of the cases since *Wolf* requiring the exclusion of illegal evidence have been based on the necessity for an effective *deterrent* to illegal police action. . . . We cannot say that this purpose would be advanced by making the rule retrospective" (*Linkletter v. Walker,* 1965, emphasis added). At the time of this decision, the majority probably felt that the exclusionary rule was relatively secure. But these words in the *Linkletter* case became highly significant in the 1970s, when the theory of the exclusionary rule was reconsidered by a more conservative Court with a view to eliminating or weakening the rule.

The Warren Court's positive approach to the exclusionary rule was underscored by applying it to the *civil forfeiture* of an automobile that state liquor control officers stopped and searched because it was "low in the rear, quite low." Upon inspection, the officers found thirty-one cases of liquor. In ***One 1958 Plymouth Sedan v. Pennsylvania*** (1965), the Court agreed with the state trial judge's finding that the stop was made without probable cause. In applying the exclusionary rule, the Court noted that forfeitures are quasi-criminal procedures in which the penalty is often more onerous than a criminal sentence.

The exclusionary rule was subjected to judicial and political criticism during the remaining years of the Warren Court (to 1969). In fact, liberal Warren Court decisions regarding criminal suspects became a major issue in the 1968 presidential campaign. After his election, President Richard M. Nixon nominated justices who were hostile to these decisions. (See Chapter 1.) Within a decade of *Mapp,* a "counterrevolution" to erode the exclusionary rule was begun by a Supreme Court that had become more conservative.

Undermining the Exclusionary Rule

After 1972, the Court's new conservative majority had a guarded, if not outrightly hostile, attitude toward the exclusionary rule. Chief Justice Warren Burger, dissenting in *Bivens v. Six Unknown Agents* (1971), called for its overruling and stated that the only foundation for the rule was the deterrence of police illegality. The Court has never overruled the exclusionary rule, but it has limited its application since 1974. ***United States v. Calandra*** (1974) was the first case to limit the exclusionary rule. A six-justice majority held that a grand jury question could be based on information obtained from an unconstitutional search resulting from a defective search warrant. Justice Lewis Powell's majority opinion set the foundation for the Court's later exclusionary rule decisions. These reasons upended the constitutional foundation of the exclusionary rule established in *Weeks* and *Mapp.*

The heart of the majority's reasoning in *Calandra* is that the "purpose of the exclusionary rule is not to redress the injury to the privacy of the search victim. . . . Instead, the rule's prime purpose is to *deter future unlawful police conduct* and thereby effectuate the guarantee of the Fourth Amendment against unreasonable searches and seizures" (*United States v. Calandra,* 1974, emphasis added). The logic of this reasoning is that the government has already "ruptured [the] privacy of the victims' homes and effects, [which] cannot be restored. Reparation comes too late" (*Calandra,* quoting *Linkletter v. Walker,* 1965). An important consequence is that in deciding how and when to apply the exclusionary rule, the Court has to balance the needs of law enforcement against individual rights. The Court emphasized that grand juries have broad powers to investigate crimes that are necessary to effective law enforcement. Applying the exclusionary rule to grand jury proceedings would turn them into protracted "preliminary trials" while adding little deterrence to police. Illegally seized evidence could still not be admitted at trial.

Justice William Brennan, dissenting, held a very different view of the exclusionary rule. Although deterrence was one reason for the exclusionary rule, the Court's primary goal was "to fashion an enforcement tool to give content and meaning to the Fourth Amendment's guarantees" (*Calandra,* 1974, Brennan, J., dissenting). A "vital function of the rule [is] to insure that the judiciary avoid even the slightest appearance of sanctioning illegal government conduct," he wrote. Otherwise, judges become "accomplices in the willful disobedience of a Constitution they are sworn to uphold" and undermine popular trust in the government (*Calandra,* quoting *Elkins v. United States,* 1960).

In **Stone v. Powell** (1976), the Supreme Court held that challenges to illegal searches from state courts under federal habeas corpus were no longer allowed if state courts already provided a full and fair opportunity to litigate a Fourth Amendment claim. Justice Powell stressed that the exclusionary rule was a judicially created means of enforcing Fourth Amendment rights by deterring police misconduct, rather than a right itself. He denied that the rule was based on "the imperative of judicial integrity." He criticized the rule, noting that it "deflects the truthfinding process and often frees the guilty." The Burger and Rehnquist Courts, by not limiting federal habeas corpus review of other constitutional guarantees, created a hierarchy of constitutional rights, with Fourth Amendment rights held in lower esteem than Fifth or Sixth Amendment rights.

Chief Justice Burger, who had earlier called for overruling the exclusionary rule, came to accept it but in a weakened form. He stated that "the exclusionary rule has been operative long enough to demonstrate its flaws. The time has come to modify its reach, even if it is retained for a small and limited category of cases" (*Stone v. Powell,* 1976, concurring). A majority of the Court may have felt constrained by *stare decisis* and uneasy with dismantling an important protection of a fundamental constitutional right. Chief Justice Burger thus shifted toward limiting the exclusionary rule rather than eliminating it.[76]

Calandra and *Stone* set the foundation of constitutional reasoning on which the Court weakened the exclusionary rule. It held, in a series of cases, that the exclusionary rule does *not* apply to various procedures. These include the Internal Revenue Service in a *civil tax proceeding* (**United States v. Janis,** 1976) and Immigration and Naturalization Service *deportation* hearings (**I.N.S. v. Lopez-Mendoza,** 1984) (an illegal immigrant can be deported even though he was illegally arrested). *Lopez-Mendoza* did "leave the door open for suppression in cases of 'egregious' or 'widespread' constitutional violations. Subsequently, lower courts and the Board of Immigration Appeals (BIA) have recognized that egregious constitutional violations do warrant suppression in removal proceedings." Despite this finding, a 2009 report on home raids by Immigration and Customs Enforcement (ICE) agents finds that sporadic suppression has not been effective in preventing widespread illegal entries and arrests.[77] These rulings undercut the viability of *One 1958 Plymouth Sedan* (1965), although that decision was never overruled and has been reaffirmed in later civil forfeiture cases. The Court also declined to apply the exclusionary rule to parole revocation in **Pennsylvania Board of Probation and Parole v. Scott** (1998). Parole officers, without a warrant, entered the home of a parolee whom they believed possessed weapons in violation of parole conditions. The state courts ruled that the warrantless search of a parolee's home violated the Fourth Amendment because "illegal searches would be undeterred when officers know that the subjects of their searches are parolees and that illegally obtained evidence can be introduced at parole hearings." The Supreme Court reversed the lower court in an opinion by Justice Clarence Thomas that referred to the exclusionary rule as a "grudgingly taken medicant" (*Scott,* 1998). He reviewed the Court's approach to the exclusionary rule in cases since *Calandra* and noted that the rule now applies only in criminal trials, and even there with some exceptions. Justice John Paul Stevens, writing for four dissenting justices in *Scott,* endorsed the view made by Justice Stewart in a journal article: The "rule *is* constitutionally required, not as a 'right' explicitly incorporated in the fourth amendment's prohibitions, but as a remedy necessary to ensure that those prohibitions are observed in fact."[78] Justice David Souter, in dissent, noted that parole revocation proceedings often serve the same function as criminal trials.

The Supreme Court also held that illegally obtained evidence can be used to *impeach* the credibility of a defendant who testifies—that is, to show that the defendant's testimony is contradicted by the illegally seized evidence. This exception to the exclusionary rule was first recognized in **Walder v. United States** (1954), where a prosecutor was allowed to introduce heroin seized in an illegal search to undermine the credibility of the defendant's testimony that he never possessed drugs. An impeachment exception has also been recognized in confessions law (*Harris v. New York,* 1971; *Oregon v. Hass,* 1975; see Chapter 7). In **United States v. Havens** (1980), the Supreme Court allowed the introduction of illegally seized drugs that were found in

Havens's specially constructed T-shirt, when on proper cross-examination Havens denied any connection to the shirt, which was designed to conceal drugs. The decision was based on the importance of getting at the truth in criminal trials and not allowing a constitutional shield to be "perverted into a license to use perjury."

The Supreme Court drew the line to this exception in ***James v. Illinois*** (1990). In this case, the defendant was arrested without probable cause. During this illegal detention, he made a statement indicating that he tried to change his appearance on the day after a killing. The statement itself was inadmissible under the exclusionary rule. A defense witness testified that James's appearance was the same after the killing as before, although several prosecution witnesses testified that his appearance had changed. The prosecutor then introduced James's illegally obtained statement to impeach the defense witness. The Supreme Court ruled that this was improper. The impeachment exception to the exclusionary rule is limited to the defendant's testimony and not that of other witnesses. The Court reasoned that a witness will be more constrained by the risk of a perjury conviction than a defendant. Allowing the impeachment exception to expand to witnesses would give the prosecutor leverage to discourage honest defense witnesses from telling the truth. Thus the majority in *James* felt that expanding the impeachment exception would not clearly advance the truth-seeking value of a trial. In an opinion that bucked the trend of cases undermining the exclusionary rule, the *James* opinion reasserted that the exclusionary rule was essential to giving Fourth Amendment protections real effectiveness. Expanding the exception "would significantly weaken the exclusionary rule's deterrent effect on police misconduct."

The phenomenon of a line of cases weakening a major ruling is familiar in constitutional law. The Court often speaks of a rule having been "eroded" by a series of inconsistent cases, often preceding the overruling of the precedent. Although this has not happened to the *Weeks–Mapp* exclusionary rule, the law as it now stands has been permanently weakened. Most recently, the Court ruled in ***Hudson v. Michigan*** (2006) that evidence seized in a drug raid on a house was admissible after police, although armed with a warrant, did not obey the constitutionally required "knock and announce" rule (discussed in Chapter 3). Michigan courts found that waiting only three to five seconds before entering a home before executing a warrant to search for drugs and guns violated the Fourth Amendment, a finding not disputed by the Supreme Court. Justice Scalia's majority opinion stated that a Fourth Amendment violation is a necessary but not a sufficient reason for exclusion. He reasoned that the "knock and announce" rule protected such values as the lives, safety, and dignity of inhabitants and the protection of property, but not the "interest in preventing the government from seeing or taking evidence described in a warrant." Since the warrant was properly issued, this opinion used the reasoning of the "fruits of the poisonous tree" cases and argued that since the government could have lawfully obtained the drug evidence, the exclusionary rule did not apply. The majority also said that even if it were true that "without suppression there will be no deterrence of knock-and-announce violations at all," it would make no difference because there are "many forms of police misconduct that are similarly 'undeterred'" where civil lawsuits are available. Justice Stephen Breyer, writing for four dissenting justices, said that because the Supreme Court has ruled that the "knock and announce" rule is part of the Fourth Amendment (*Wilson v. Arkansas,* 1995), a search made in violation of the rule is unreasonable and illegal. The exclusionary rule therefore applies as a matter of "elementary logic." There are many reported cases of "knock and announce" violations and no cases showing that victims of such government misconduct "have collected more than nominal damages" in civil suits. "The upshot is that the need for deterrence—the critical factor driving this Court's Fourth Amendment cases for close to a century—argues with at least comparable strength for evidentiary exclusion here." He further argued that relying on the reasoning from the derivative evidence (fruits of the poisonous tree) cases was misplaced. Even if evidence was seized improperly, the government cannot avoid suppression of evidence by showing that it *could have* been properly seized.

The next two sections on the good faith exceptions and on the doctrine of standing analyze the further weakening of the exclusionary rule.

Good Faith Reliance Exceptions

The Supreme Court's strongest attack on the exclusionary rule allowed illegally seized evidence to be introduced into the trial to prove the defendant's guilt, unlike *Calandra* and similar cases that allowed tainted evidence only in peripheral proceedings. The "good faith exception" theory reasoned that allowing tainted evidence in the "case in chief" would not undermine the exclusionary rule's deterrent effect. These cases consolidated the Court's view that the rule is "only" a judicially created remedy designed to deter police from violating Fourth Amendment rights while modifying the original theory of the exclusionary rule.

The good faith exception in *United States v. Leon* (1984) was presaged by **Michigan v. DeFillippo** (1979). Evidence was allowed of illegal drugs, obtained in a search incident to an arrest made in good faith reliance on a local *ordinance* allowing police to demand personal identification of a reasonably stopped person, even though on appeal state courts held the ordinance to be unconstitutional. The stage was set for a major reassessment and limitation of the exclusionary rule in *United States v. Leon.*

Read Case and Comments:
United States v. Leon

In **Massachusetts v. Sheppard** (1984), a companion case to *Leon,* a police officer filed a homicide search warrant affidavit on a form for controlled substances searches because it was Sunday, the courts were closed, and the officer could not find the proper form. Although the officer and the magistrate modified the form, the search warrant erroneously authorized a search for controlled substances and did not incorporate the affidavit. (See Chapter 3.) The officers executing the warrant searched Sheppard's residence for items listed in the affidavit but not in the warrant. Incriminating evidence was found and entered into the trial. The Supreme Court held that the police objectively relied in good faith on a defective warrant. In this instance, the good faith reliance exception avoided an unreasonable conclusion. Indeed, Justice Stevens, who concurred in the decision, felt that the warrant and affidavit were quite specific and that the magistrate and the police officers were fully aware of their contents. Thus he believed there was no Fourth Amendment defect and that the majority manufactured one in order to expand the good faith exception.

Leon was followed by **Illinois v. Krull** (1987), which held (5–4) that the exclusionary rule does not apply where the police violate a person's rights in good faith reliance on a *statute.* Chicago police officers, acting under an Illinois regulatory statute, searched cars and records of an automobile wrecking yard without a search warrant. The statute was declared unconstitutional by a federal court. On appeal, the Supreme Court, applying the reasoning of *Leon,* found that because similar regulatory search schemes had been held constitutional in the past, the officers relied on the statute in good faith. Justice Sandra Day O'Connor, who joined the majority in *Leon,* dissented, joined by Justices Brennan, Marshall, and Stevens. Noting that the Fourth Amendment was originally designed to constrain the legislature, she minced no words: "Legislatures have, upon occasion, failed to adhere to the requirements of the Fourth Amendment." She argued that a legislature could be deterred by applying the exclusionary rule in a case like this one. "Providing legislatures a grace period during which the police may freely perform unreasonable searches in order to convict those who might otherwise escape provides a positive incentive to promulgate unconstitutional laws." Justice O'Connor's experience as a leader of the Arizona Senate provided the insight that legislators sometimes intentionally pass laws for political gain that violate individual rights.

Arizona v. Evans (1995) is more disturbing. Evans was stopped by a Phoenix police officer for driving the wrong way on a one-way street. A computer check indicated an outstanding misdemeanor warrant. He was arrested and marijuana was discovered. However, the arrest warrant against Evans had actuality been *quashed* seventeen days prior to his arrest. An error in the *court clerk*'s office resulted in the information not being conveyed to the sheriff's office to remove the arrest notation from the law enforcement computer database. The Arizona Supreme Court excluded the evidence because there was no legal basis for the arrest and the "application of the exclusionary rule would 'hopefully serve to improve the efficiency of those who keep records in our criminal justice system.'"

The state appealed, and the Supreme Court reversed. Chief Justice William Rehnquist, writing for the Court, held that the exclusionary rule did not apply. The Court noted that the rule is designed to deter unconstitutional police activity, and not errors made by judges or personnel in judicial bureaucracies. It reasoned that there is no reason to believe that the exclusionary rule will deter errors by court clerks. Unlike police who are "zealous" in their desire to "get" suspects, court clerks "have no stake in the outcome of particular criminal prosecutions."

This reasoning seems as wrongheaded as the application of the exclusionary rule in *Sheppard.* Justice O'Connor apparently recognized this in her concurring opinion, which expressed concern that widespread computer errors might undermine individual rights. Justice Stevens dissented on the grounds that the Fourth Amendment's text and history have the more majestic goal of protecting individual privacy and liberty from encroachment from any part of

CASE AND COMMENTS

United States v. Leon

468 U.S. 897, 104 S.Ct. 3405, 82 L.Ed.2d 677 (1984)

JUSTICE WHITE delivered the opinion of the Court.

    This case presents the question whether the Fourth Amendment exclusionary rule should be modified so as not to bar the use in the prosecution's case in chief of evidence obtained by officers acting in reasonable reliance on a search warrant issued by a detached and neutral magistrate but ultimately found to be unsupported by probable cause. **[a]** To resolve this question, we must consider once again the tension between the sometimes competing goals of, on the one hand, deterring official misconduct and removing inducements to unreasonable invasions of privacy and, on the other, establishing procedures under which criminal defendants are "acquitted or convicted on the basis of all the evidence which exposes the truth." * * *

I

[Local police obtained a "facially valid" search warrant from a state judge based on information from a confidential informant "of unproven reliability." A stakeout revealed suspected drug dealing at a house, and a car parked outside belonged to Leon, a previously convicted drug dealer. A search warrant affidavit was prepared by an experienced drug enforcement officer and reviewed by several assistant prosecutors. A warrant was issued by a state judge. The warrant was executed, and drugs were found. On this evidence, Leon and others were indicted in a federal district court for drug dealing. They moved to suppress evidence and challenged the constitutionality of the search warrant. The federal judge overturned the warrant and suppressed the evidence because the informant's reliability was not established and probable cause of drug sales was therefore not independently established. (This rule is covered in Chapter 3 under "Probable Cause and the Fourth Amendment.") The court stated that the case was a close one and that the officers acted on the warrant in the good faith belief that it was based on probable cause, even though probable cause was not established. The federal court of appeals upheld the district court. The case is decided on the understanding that the search warrant was not valid under the Fourth Amendment and that, in effect, the search violated Leon's Fourth Amendment rights.]

    We have concluded that, in the Fourth Amendment context, the exclusionary rule can be modified somewhat without jeopardizing its ability to perform its intended functions. **[b]** Accordingly, we reverse the judgment of the Court of Appeals.

II

Language in opinions of this Court * * * has sometimes implied that the exclusionary rule is a necessary corollary of the Fourth Amendment, * * * [or] the conjunction of the Fourth and Fifth Amendments. [*Mapp v. Ohio*] **[c]** * * * These implications need not detain us long. The Fifth Amendment theory has not withstood critical analysis or the test of time, * * * and the Fourth Amendment "has never been interpreted to proscribe the introduction of illegally seized evidence in all proceedings or against all persons." * * *

A

The Fourth Amendment contains no provision expressly precluding the use of evidence obtained in violation of its commands, and * * * the use of [unlawfully seized evidence] "work[s] no new Fourth Amendment wrong." * * * The wrong condemned by the Amendment is "fully accomplished" by the unlawful search or seizure itself, * * * and the exclusionary rule is neither intended nor able to "cure the invasion of the defendant's rights which he has already suffered." The rule thus operates as "a judicially created remedy designed to safeguard Fourth Amendment rights generally through its deterrent effect, rather than a personal constitutional right of the party aggrieved." * * *

    Whether the exclusionary sanction is appropriately imposed in a particular case is "an issue separate from the question whether the Fourth Amendment rights of the party seeking to invoke the rule were violated by police conduct." * * * **[d]** Only the former question is currently before us, and it must be resolved by weighing the costs and benefits of preventing the use in the prosecution's case-in-chief of inherently trustworthy tangible evidence obtained in reliance on a search warrant issued by a detached and neutral magistrate that ultimately is found to be defective.

    The substantial social costs exacted by the exclusionary rule for the vindication of Fourth Amendment rights have long been a source of concern. **[e]** * * * "[U]nbending application of the

---

[a] Justice White states the issue and establishes a "judicial methodology"—the "balancing test"—to resolve the issue. This choice helps produce his desired outcome. Is anything left out of the "competing goals"?

[b] This conclusion is like a structural engineer constructing a bridge without using materials that maximize safety. Does this kind of cost/benefit analysis have a place in civil rights law?

[c] Justice White's phrasing dismisses the *Mapp* holding that the exclusionary rule is a *constitutional* rule. The Fifth Amendment theory, used in *Mapp* to gain Justice Black's vote, linked the Fourth Amendment to a clear-cut exclusionary rule in the Fifth Amendment. By relying on post-*Mapp* cases, Justice White, a long-standing critic of *Mapp,* is now able to use precedents he helped create to weaken its effect.

[d] In criminal law, a crime definition is incomplete without the penalty provision—the public's remedy is part of the right. Is the Fourth Amendment a true right without a remedy? Is the exclusionary rule a true remedy? (See the section on remedies in this chapter.)

exclusionary sanction to enforce ideals of governmental rectitude would impede unacceptably the truth-finding functions of judge and jury." * * * Particularly when law enforcement officers have acted in objective good faith or their transgressions have been minor, the magnitude of the benefit conferred on such guilty defendants offends basic concepts of the criminal justice system. * * * Indiscriminate application of the exclusionary rule, therefore, may well "generat[e] disrespect for the law and administration of justice." * * * Accordingly, "[a]s with any remedial device, the application of the rule has been restricted to those areas where its remedial objectives are thought most efficaciously served." * * *

B

[This section reviews cases in which the Court has "demoted" the exclusionary rule, including *Stone v. Powell* (1976); *United States v. Calandra* (1974); and *United States v. Janis* (1976), among others.] **[f]**

III

A

* * *

* * * To the extent that proponents of exclusion rely on its behavioral effects on judges and magistrates, * * * their reliance is misplaced. **[g]** First, the exclusionary rule is designed to deter police misconduct rather than to punish the errors of judges and magistrates. Second, there exists no evidence suggesting that judges and magistrates are inclined to ignore or subvert the Fourth Amendment or that lawlessness among these actors requires application of the extreme sanction of exclusion.

* * *

[M]ost important, we discern no basis, and are offered none, for believing that exclusion of evidence seized pursuant to a warrant will have a significant deterrent effect on the issuing judge or magistrate. **[h]** * * * [A]s neutral judicial officers, they have no stake in the outcome of particular criminal prosecutions. * * * Imposition of the exclusionary sanction is not necessary meaningfully to inform judicial officers of their errors. * * *

B

If exclusion of evidence obtained pursuant to a subsequently invalidated warrant is to have any deterrent effect, therefore, it must alter the behavior of individual law enforcement officers or the policies of their departments. One could argue that applying the exclusionary rule in cases where the police failed to demonstrate probable cause in the warrant application deters future inadequate presentations or "magistrate shopping" and thus promotes the ends of the Fourth Amendment. Suppressing evidence obtained pursuant to a technically defective warrant supported by probable cause also might encourage officers to scrutinize more closely the form of the warrant and to point out suspected judicial errors. **[i]** We find such arguments speculative and conclude that suppression of evidence obtained pursuant to a warrant should be ordered only on a case-by-case basis and only in those unusual cases in which exclusion will further the purposes of the exclusionary rule.

We have frequently questioned whether the exclusionary rule can have any deterrent effect when the offending officers acted in the objectively reasonable belief that their conduct did not violate the Fourth Amendment. "No empirical researcher, proponent or opponent of the rule, has yet been able to establish with any assurance whether the rule has a deterrent effect. * * *" But even assuming that the rule effectively deters some police misconduct and provides incentives for the law enforcement profession as a whole to conduct itself in accord with the Fourth Amendment, it cannot be expected, and should not be applied, to deter objectively reasonable law enforcement activity.

* * *

This is particularly true, we believe, when an officer acting with objective good faith has obtained a search warrant from a judge or magistrate and acted within its scope. In most such cases, there is no police illegality and thus nothing to deter. * * * **[j]**

C

* * *

Suppression * * * remains an appropriate remedy if the magistrate or judge in issuing a warrant was misled by information in an affidavit that the affiant knew was false or would have known was false except for his reckless disregard of the truth. * * * The exception we recognize today will also not apply in cases where the issuing magistrate wholly abandoned his judicial role. * * * Nor would an officer manifest objective good faith in relying on a warrant based on an affidavit "so lacking in indicia of probable cause as to render official belief in its existence entirely unreasonable." * * * **[k]** Finally, depending on the circumstances of the particular case, a warrant may be so facially deficient—*i.e.*, in failing to

[e] The exclusionary rule is "put on the defensive" by stressing its costs, limits, and status as a "mere" remedy. The social costs of the exclusionary rule are still open to debate. Note how the "imperative of judicial integrity" of liberal justices becomes the "ideal of governmental rectitude" to conservative justices; the phrases convey different meanings.

[f] The text has reviewed these cases, showing the exclusionary rule's erosion. Precedent is "ammunition" used by justices to get the desired result.

[g] The Bill of Rights protects individual rights against violations by *all* branches of government. Not applying the exclusionary rule to judges' errors supports the interpretation that it is not constitutionally based.

[h] Judges have immunity from lawsuit for errors made on the bench, but are subject to reversal on appeal to correct their errors and deter them from not following precedent. Are not magistrates concerned if their warrants are overturned as illegal?

[i] Does Justice White select his assumptions? He brushes aside the educative function of the law—the idea that over time the exclusionary rule will educate police officers to follow the amendment. (See the "Law in Society" section on the effects of the exclusionary rule.)

[j] What does Justice White imply by "no police illegality"? Leon's Fourth Amendment rights *have* been violated. If the officer is not civilly liable and there is no exclusion, what is the value of Leon's rights?

[k] The good faith reliance-on-the-warrant exception is not a blank check to the police. Several examples that apply the exclusionary rule are given here. This cautions police to get warrants where possible. It might have been simpler for the Court to issue a bright line rule requiring warrants.

[l] Justice Blackmun's concurrence says that the Court *may* reverse its rule in *Leon if* the police misuse it with pretext searches. Isn't the Court supposed to establish firm rules of law? Is he being honest about the law's flexibility or is he fooling himself?

particularize the place to be searched or the things to be seized—that the executing officers cannot reasonably presume it to be valid. * * *

* * *

JUSTICE BLACKMUN, concurring.

* * *

* * * [T]he Court has narrowed the scope of the exclusionary rule because of an empirical judgment that the rule has little appreciable effect in cases where officers act in objectively reasonable reliance on search warrants. * * * **[l]**

What must be stressed, however, is that any empirical judgment about the effect of the exclusionary rule in a particular class of cases necessarily is a provisional one. By their very nature, the assumptions on which we proceed today cannot be cast in stone. To the contrary, they now will be tested in the real world of state and federal law enforcement, and this Court will attend to the results. If it should emerge from experience that, contrary to our expectations, the good-faith exception to the exclusionary rule results in a material change in police compliance with the Fourth Amendment, we shall have to reconsider what we have undertaken here. The logic of a decision that rests on untested predictions about police conduct demands no less.

* * *

JUSTICE BRENNAN, with whom JUSTICE MARSHALL joins, dissenting.

Ten years ago in *United States v. Calandra* (1974), I expressed the fear that the Court's decision "may signal that a majority of my colleagues have positioned themselves to reopen the door [to evidence secured by official lawlessness] still further and abandon altogether the exclusionary rule in search-and-seizure cases" (dissenting opinion). **[m]** Since then, in case after case, I have witnessed the Court's gradual but determined strangulation of the rule. It now appears that the Court's victory over the Fourth Amendment is complete. * * *

[m] This strong language may be discounted as a tactic, but it *is* a way of reaching beyond the majority to stir a wider audience and future generations in the hope that a different Court might overturn this decision.

* * *

The majority ignores the fundamental constitutional importance of what is at stake here. * * * [W]hat the Framers understood [in 1791] remains true today—that the task of combating crime and convicting the guilty will in every era seem of such critical and pressing concern that we may be lured by the temptations of expediency into forsaking our commitment to protecting individual liberty and privacy. It was for that very reason that the Framers of the Bill of Rights insisted that law enforcement efforts be permanently and unambiguously restricted in order to preserve personal freedoms. * * * **[n]** [T]he sometimes unpopular task of ensuring that the government's enforcement efforts remain within the strict boundaries fixed by the Fourth Amendment was entrusted to the courts. * * * If those independent tribunals lose their resolve, however, as the Court has done today, and give way to the seductive call of expediency, the vital guarantees of the Fourth Amendment are reduced to nothing more than a "form of words." * * *

[n] Justice Brennan accuses the majority of "selling out" the constitutional rights of citizens because fear of crime was a popular political issue to the presidents who appointed them. Do you agree?

I

* * *

A

[JUSTICE BRENNAN restated the majority argument here: The exclusionary rule is a mere judicial remedy designed to deter police illegality; the constitutional wrong is complete when the police invade a person's constitutionally protected privacy; and thus there is no constitutional violation if unconstitutionally seized evidence is admitted into evidence.]

Such a reading appears plausible, because * * * the Fourth Amendment makes no express provision for the exclusion of evidence secured in violation of its commands. * * * [M]any of the Constitution's most vital imperatives are stated in general terms and the task of giving meaning to these precepts is therefore left to subsequent judicial decision making in the context of concrete cases. **[o]** The nature of our Constitution, as CHIEF JUSTICE MARSHALL long ago explained, "requires that only its great outlines should be marked, its important objects designated, and the minor ingredients which compose those objects be deduced from the nature of the objects themselves." * * *

[o] This point might better apply to a more open-textured right such as "due process" than to the more narrowly focused Fourth Amendment.

A more direct answer may be supplied by recognizing that the Amendment, like other provisions of the Bill of Rights, restrains the power of the government as a whole; it does not specify only a particular agency and exempt all others. The judiciary is responsible, no less than the executive, for ensuring that constitutional rights are respected.

* * * Once that connection between the evidence-gathering role of the police and the evidence-admitting function of the courts is acknowledged, the plausibility of the Court's interpretation becomes more suspect. * * * The Amendment therefore must be read to condemn not only the initial unconstitutional invasion of privacy—which is done, after all, for the purpose of securing evidence—but also the subsequent use of any evidence so obtained.

The Court evades this principle by drawing an artificial line between the constitutional rights and responsibilities that are engaged by actions of the police and those that are engaged when a defendant appears before the courts. **[p]** According to the Court, the substantive protections of the Fourth Amendment are wholly exhausted at the moment when police unlawfully invade an individual's privacy and thus no substantive force remains to those protections at the time of trial when the government seeks to use evidence obtained by the police.

I submit that such a crabbed reading of the Fourth Amendment * * * rests ultimately on an impoverished understanding of judicial responsibility in our constitutional scheme. For my part, "[t]he right of the people to be secure in their persons, houses, papers, and effects, against unreasonable searches and seizures" comprises a personal right to exclude all evidence secured by means of unreasonable searches and seizures. The right to be free from the initial invasion of privacy and the right of exclusion are coordinate components of the central embracing right to be free from unreasonable searches and seizures.

* * *

B

* * *

* * * [T]he Court since *Calandra* has gradually pressed the deterrence rationale for the rule back to center stage. * * * [JUSTICE BRENNAN then reviewed the cost-benefit analysis utilized by the majority.] * * *

* * * To the extent empirical data are available regarding the general costs and benefits of the exclusionary rule, it has shown, on the one hand, as the Court acknowledges today, that the costs are not as substantial as critics have asserted in the past, * * * and, on the other hand, that while the exclusionary rule may well have certain deterrent effects, it is extremely difficult to determine with any degree of precision whether the incidence of unlawful conduct by police is now lower than it was prior to *Mapp.* * * * The Court has sought to turn this uncertainty to its advantage by casting the burden of proof upon proponents of the rule. * * *

* * * [B]y basing the rule solely on the deterrence rationale, the Court has robbed the rule of legitimacy. A doctrine that is explained as if it were an empirical proposition but for which there is only limited empirical support is both inherently unstable and an easy mark for critics. **[q]** The extent of this Court's fidelity to Fourth Amendment requirements, however, should not turn on such statistical uncertainties. * * * Rather than seeking to give effect to the liberties secured by the Fourth Amendment through guesswork about deterrence, the Court should restore to its proper place the principle framed 70 years ago in *Weeks* that an individual whose privacy has been invaded in violation of the Fourth Amendment has a right grounded in that Amendment to prevent the government from subsequently making use of any evidence so obtained.

* * *

[p] Do you agree that the line between Fourth Amendment rights and the exclusionary rule is artificial—that is, that the two should be inseparable? All legal doctrines involve line drawing. Do you think Justice Brennan provides a better rationale for the exclusionary rule as a constitutional right?

[q] This is a strong point. Should basic rights depend on measured effectiveness? If so, could a tyrant fail to uphold rights and then demand that they be abolished because they don't "work"? Does this critique properly apply to a "remedy"?

the government. *Arizona v. Evans* (1995) shows that rights can be lost from the negligent maintenance of modern technology as they can from more direct state action.

It is important to note that there is no free-floating "good faith exception" that allows police officers to enter homes or other areas in which people have an expectation of privacy because they reasonably feel they have probable cause. The Supreme Court has not approved an exclusionary rule exception for using illegally obtained evidence based on a police officer's good faith observations leading to a warrantless stop, arrest, or search. Each good faith exception is tied to the officer's *objective reliance* on the decision of a magistrate, a statute, or official records. According to Professors Charles Whitebread and Christopher Slobogin, the Court has deliberately avoided the issue of a general good faith exception.[79] There may indeed be instances when police arrest or search without probable cause but do so in objective good faith. Nevertheless, the inherent human subjectivity that tends to make every person a "biased judge" about his or her own actions would make such an exception a more risky proposition for individual rights than allowing the use of unconstitutional evidence obtained by the officer's good faith reliance on the judgment of the legislature or a judge. It seems that allowing officers to dispense with warrants on their own evaluation would destroy the Warrant Clause and seriously damage Fourth Amendment protections.

The Supreme Court reminded police that they are *personally liable* in civil lawsuits to those whose houses they enter if they rely on *obviously defective* search warrants. ***Groh v. Ramirez*** (2004) held (5–4) that a search warrant failing to list *any* of the items to be seized is plainly unconstitutional. Joseph Ramirez was not prosecuted after a search of his ranch, and he sued Special Agent Jeff Groh, of the Bureau of Alcohol, Tobacco, and Firearms (ATF), for violating his Fourth Amendment rights. The Supreme Court ruled that Agent Groh could not claim qualified immunity from the lawsuit because it was clear to a reasonably competent officer that his conduct was unreasonable. The Court, in *Groh,* quoted *Leon:* "[D]epending on the circumstances of the particular case, a warrant may be so facially deficient—*i.e.,* in failing to particularize the place to be searched or the things to be seized—that the executing officers cannot reasonably presume it to be valid." A law enforcement officer is not absolved from personal responsibility to read a warrant carefully and be sure it is constitutional on its face before executing it merely because a magistrate has issued the warrant. (The case is discussed in Chapter 3.)

Groh was an example of a civil sanction applying against a police officer who flagrantly but objectively violated the Fourth Amendment. *Herring v. United States* (2009) shows the Roberts Court continuing the trend of the Burger and Rehnquist Courts in narrowing the scope of the exclusionary rule wherever possible. *Herring* provides a clear jurisprudential divide between the five majority and four dissenting justices, and illuminates their different views on the theories that underlie the exclusionary rule. Review *Herring* after reading the following sections on the theories of remedies and the theories of the exclusionary rule. *Herring* demonstrates that these theories are not abstractions, but dynamic principles that reflect the justices' deep-seated values.

Read Case and Comments: *Herring v. United States*

CASE AND COMMENTS

Herring v. United States

555 U.S. ___, 129 S. Ct. 695; 172 L. Ed. 2d 496 (2009)

CHIEF JUSTICE ROBERTS delivered the opinion of the Court.

The Fourth Amendment forbids "unreasonable searches and seizures," and this usually requires the police to have probable cause or a warrant before making an arrest. What if an officer reasonably believes there is an outstanding arrest warrant, but that belief turns out to be wrong because of a negligent book keeping error by another police employee? **[a]** The parties here agree that the ensuing arrest is still a violation of the Fourth Amendment, but dispute whether contraband found during a search incident to that arrest must be excluded in a later prosecution.

Our cases establish that such suppression is not an automatic consequence of a Fourth Amendment violation. Instead, the question turns on the culpability of the police and the potential of exclusion to deter wrongful police conduct. **[b]** Here the error was the result of isolated negligence attenuated from the arrest. We hold that in these circumstances the jury should not be barred from considering all the evidence.

I

. . . Investigator Mark Anderson learned that Bennie Dean Herring had driven to the Coffee County Sheriff's Department to retrieve something from his impounded truck. Herring was no stranger to law enforcement, and Anderson asked the county's warrant clerk, Sandy Pope, to check for any outstanding warrants for Herring's arrest. When she found none, Anderson asked Pope to check with Sharon Morgan, her counterpart in neighboring Dale County. After checking Dale County's computer database, Morgan replied that there was an active arrest warrant for Herring's failure to appear on a felony charge. Pope relayed the information to Anderson and asked Morgan to fax over a copy of the warrant as confirmation. Anderson and a deputy followed Herring as he left the impound lot, pulled him over, and arrested him. **[c]** A search incident to the arrest revealed methamphetamine in Herring's pocket, and a pistol (which as a felon he could not possess) in his vehicle.

There had, however, been a mistake about the warrant. * * * [The physical warrant was not in the Dale County Sheriff's files.] Normally when a warrant is recalled the court clerk's office or a judge's chambers calls Morgan, who enters the information in the sheriff's computer database and disposes of the physical copy. **[d]** For whatever reason, the information about the recall of the warrant for Herring did not appear in the database. Morgan immediately called Pope to alert her to the mixup, and Pope contacted Anderson over a secure radio. This all unfolded in 10 to 15 minutes, but Herring had already been arrested and found with the gun and drugs, just a few hundred yards from the sheriff's office.

---

[a] The Chief Justice is noted for his down-to-earth "conversational" writing style. His reference to a "negligent bookkeeping error" seems designed to diminish the rights at stake.

[b] As he does later in his opinion, the Chief Justice holds to the view that the only purpose of the exclusionary rule is to deter police misconduct. This is in clear contrast to the dissent, which emphasized other rationales.

[c] Anderson targeted a person rather than a crime episode. Police in fact treat some people as always potentially guilty and may harass them. This can apply to those who have been rehabilitated—such as in the case of Calvin Johnson, a rehabilitated ex-burglary offender who was targeted by police and spent fifteen years in prison for a rape he did not commit.[80]

[d] It seems obvious that any such subjective and personal data system, even operated by normally competent and well-meaning personnel, is prone to error, as happened here, especially in the often hectic atmosphere of police agencies. See dissenting opinion at Part III A.

[Herring, indicted for illegal gun and drug possession, moved to suppress the illegally seized evidence. The federal district court and the Eleventh Circuit Court of Appeals allowed the use of the illegally seized evidence because (1) the Dale County Sheriff Department's error was negligent and not deliberate, and (2) the arresting officers relied, in good-faith, on an objective belief that the warrant was still outstanding.]

* * * We now affirm the Eleventh Circuit's judgment.

II

[The case could have been treated as a mistake about probable cause, which would not have violated the Fourth Amendment]. For purposes of deciding this case, however, we accept the parties' assumption that there was a Fourth Amendment violation. The issue is whether the exclusionary rule should be applied.

A

The Fourth Amendment * * * "contains no provision expressly precluding the use of evidence obtained in violation of its commands." **[e]** Nonetheless, our decisions establish an exclusionary rule that, when applicable, forbids the use of improperly obtained evidence at trial. See, *e.g., Weeks v. United States* (1914). We have stated that this judicially created rule is "designed to safeguard Fourth Amendment rights generally through its deterrent effect." *United States v. Calandra* (1974).

[The error in the *Dale* County Sheriff's Office counts against the search made by *Coffee* County officers, even though they did nothing improper. The Eleventh Circuit] court also concluded that this error was negligent, but did not find it to be reckless or deliberate. That fact is crucial to our holding that this error is not enough by itself to require "the extreme sanction of exclusion."

B

1. The fact that a Fourth Amendment violation occurred * * * does not necessarily mean that the exclusionary rule applies. Indeed, exclusion "has always been our last resort, not our first impulse," *Hudson v. Michigan* (2006), and our precedents establish important principles that constrain application of the exclusionary rule.

First, the exclusionary rule is not an individual right and applies only where it "'result[s] in appreciable deterrence.'" We have repeatedly rejected the argument that exclusion is a necessary consequence of a Fourth Amendment violation. **[f]** [citing *U.S. v. Leon* (1984); *Arizona v. Evans* (1995); and *Pennsy. Bd. of Prob'n and Parole v. Scott* (1998).] Instead we have focused on the efficacy of the rule in deterring Fourth Amendment violations in the future.

In addition, the benefits of deterrence must outweigh the costs. "We have never suggested that the exclusionary rule must apply in every circumstance in which it might provide marginal deterrence." * * * The principal cost of applying the rule is, of course, letting guilty and possibly dangerous defendants go free—something that "offends basic concepts of the criminal justice system." *Leon.* "[T]he rule's costly toll upon truth-seeking and law enforcement objectives presents a high obstacle for those urging [its] application." **[g]**

These principles are reflected in the holding of *Leon*: When police act under a warrant that is invalid for lack of probable cause, the exclusionary rule does not apply if the police acted "in objectively reasonable reliance" on the subsequently invalidated search warrant. We (perhaps confusingly) called this objectively reasonable reliance "good faith." In a companion case, *Massachusetts v. Sheppard (1984),* we held that the exclusionary rule did not apply when a warrant was invalid because a judge forgot to make "clerical corrections" to it. **[h]**

* * * [I]n *Evans,* we applied this good-faith rule to police who reasonably relied on mistaken information in a court's database that an arrest warrant was outstanding. * * * *Evans* left unresolved "whether the evidence should be suppressed if police personnel were responsible for the error,"an issue not argued by the State in that case, but one that we now confront. **[i]**

2. The extent to which the exclusionary rule is justified by these deterrence principles varies with the culpability of the law enforcement conduct. As we said in *Leon*, "an assessment of the flagrancy of the police misconduct constitutes an important step in the calculus" of applying the exclusionary rule. * * *

* * * [Police behavior that led to suppression in *Weeks, Silverthorne Lumber Co. v. U. S.* (1920), and *Mapp v. Ohio* (1961) was egregious]. And in fact since *Leon*, we have never applied the rule to exclude evidence obtained in violation of the Fourth Amendment, where the police conduct was no more intentional or culpable than this. **[j]**

3. To trigger the exclusionary rule, police conduct must be sufficiently deliberate that exclusion can meaningfully deter it, and sufficiently culpable that such deterrence is worth the price paid by the justice system. As laid out in our cases, the exclusionary rule serves to deter deliberate, reckless, or grossly negligent conduct, or in some circumstances recurring or systemic negligence. The error in this case does not rise to that level. **[k]**

---

[e] This simple review emphasizes the diminished status of the exclusionary rule initiated by the Burger Court, and refers to the creation of the exclusionary rule almost as a passing matter.

[f] This paragraph makes it crystal clear that the majority does not view the exclusionary rule to be a constitutional right.

[g] This emphasis on costs paves the way to another case that whittles down the scope of the exclusionary rule's effect.

[h] The Chief Justice's attention to the label, suggesting that the "good faith" rule is better called the "objectively reasonable reliance" rule, hints that the majority does not wish to create a free-floating good faith exception that immunizes all ""good faith" police action that violates the Fourth Amendment, only those where the officer relies on a warrant or other legal authorization.

[i] The Supreme Court often leaves issues that are suggested by a ruling unanswered, to be decided after the issues are decided in lower courts. This avoids premature and possibly erroneous rulings.

[j] The Court, at this point and in the next section, establishes *flagrant* police misconduct—that is, a deliberate attempt to circumvent the Fourth Amendment—as an element of the exclusionary rule. This is a significant change in the law.

[k] The fact that a person's rights under the Constitution have been violated is no longer a good enough reason, standing alone, to trigger the exclusionary rule.

* * *

The pertinent analysis of deterrence and culpability is objective, not an "inquiry into the subjective awareness of arresting officers." * * *

4. We do not suggest that all recordkeeping errors by the police are immune from the exclusionary rule. In this case, however, the conduct at issue was not so objectively culpable as to require exclusion. * * *

If the police have been shown to be reckless in maintaining a warrant system, or to have knowingly made false entries to lay the groundwork for future false arrests, exclusion would certainly be justified under our cases should such misconduct cause a Fourth Amendment violation. * * * Petitioner's fears that our decision will cause police departments to deliberately keep their officers ignorant, are thus unfounded.

* * * In a case where systemic errors were demonstrated, it might be reckless for officers to rely on an unreliable warrant system. * * * But there is no evidence that errors in Dale County's system are routine or widespread. * * *

* * *

* * * [W]e conclude that when police mistakes are the result of negligence such as that described here, rather than systemic error or reckless disregard of constitutional requirements, any marginal deterrence does not "pay its way." In such a case, the criminal should not "go free because the constable has blundered." [citation omitted].

JUSTICE GINSBURG, with whom JUSTICE STEVENS, JUSTICE SOUTER, AND JUSTICE BREYER join, dissenting.

[The sheriff's deputies violated Herring's Fourth Amendment rights.] The exclusionary rule provides redress for Fourth Amendment violations by placing the government in the position it would have been in had there been no unconstitutional arrest and search. **[l]** The rule thus strongly encourages police compliance with the Fourth Amendment in the future. The Court, however, holds the rule inapplicable because careless recordkeeping by the police—not flagrant or deliberate misconduct—accounts for Herring's arrest.

I would not so constrict the domain of the exclusionary rule and would hold the rule dispositive of this case: "[I]f courts are to have any power to discourage [police] error of [the kind here at issue], it must be through the application of the exclusionary rule." [Although the police found] methamphetamine in Herring's pocket and a pistol in his truck, . . . the "most serious impact" of the Court's holding will be on innocent persons "wrongfully arrested based on erroneous information [carelessly maintained] in a computer data base."

I

[In a footnote, Justice Ginsburg took a bleaker view of the police computer error "It is not altogether clear how 'isolated' the error was in this case. When the Dale County Sheriff's Department warrant clerk was first asked: '[H]ow many times have you had or has Dale County had problems, any problems with communicating about warrants,' she responded: 'Several times.'"]

II

A

* * * As the Court recounts, * * * deterrence of police improprieties could be "sufficiently accomplished" by confining the rule to "evidence obtained by flagrant or deliberate violation of rights."

B

Others have described "a more majestic conception" of the Fourth Amendment and its adjunct, the exclusionary rule. *Evans* (Stevens, J., dissenting). Protective of the fundamental "right of the people to be secure in their persons, houses, papers, and effects," the Amendment "is a constraint on the power of the sovereign, not merely on some of its agents." . . . I share that vision of the Amendment.

The exclusionary rule is "a remedy necessary to ensure that" the Fourth Amendment's prohibitions "are observed in fact." . . . The rule's service as an essential auxiliary to the Amendment earlier inclined the Court to hold the two inseparable. See *Whiteley v. Warden,* (1971). Cf. *Olmstead v. United States,* (1928) (Holmes, J., dissenting); (Brandeis, J., dissenting). **[m]**

Beyond doubt, a main objective of the rule "is to deter—to compel respect for the constitutional guaranty in the only effectively available way—by removing the incentive to disregard it." *Elkins v. United States* (1960). But the rule also serves other important purposes: It "enabl[es] the judiciary to avoid the taint of partnership in official lawlessness," and it "assur[es] the people—all potential victims of unlawful government conduct—that the government would not profit from its lawless behavior, thus minimizing the risk of seriously undermining popular trust in government." * * * **[n]**

[l] Justice Ginsburg makes two points: (1) the exclusionary rule *requires* all unconstitutionally seized evidence to be excluded; and (2) the *disgorgement theory* is a fundamental basis of the exclusionary rule (see later discussion, this chapter).

[m] The dissent adheres to the position of *Weeks* and *Mapp* that the exclusionary rule is a fundamental right—part and parcel of the Fourth Amendment. Two of the greatest justices, Holmes and Brandeis, are cited as supporters of this interpretation.

[n] Again, the dissent asserts that deterrence is not the only rationale for the exclusionary rule. By affirming the judicial integrity and disgorgement theories, the dissent provides the foundation for the position that the exclusionary rule is a constitutional right.

The exclusionary rule, it bears emphasis, is often the only remedy effective to redress a Fourth Amendment violation. * * * Civil liability will not lie for "the vast majority of [F]ourth [A]mendment violations—the frequent infringements motivated by commendable zeal, not condemnable malice." * * * Criminal prosecutions or administrative sanctions against the offending officers and injunctive relief against widespread violations are an even farther cry. **[o]**

[o] The functional impotence of other remedies was a reason why the exclusionary rule was adopted in the first place.

III

The Court maintains that Herring's case is one in which the exclusionary rule could have scant deterrent effect and therefore would not "pay its way." I disagree.

A

* * * "[T]he risk of exclusion of evidence encourages policymakers and systems managers to monitor the performance of the systems they install and the personnel employed to operate those systems." [citation omitted]

Consider the potential impact of a decision applying the exclusionary rule in this case. * * * [T]here is no electronic connection between the warrant database of the Dale County Sheriff's Department and that of the County Circuit Clerk's office. * * * When a warrant is recalled, one of the "many different people that have access to th[e] warrants," must find the hard copy of the warrant in the "two or three different places" where the department houses warrants, return it to the Clerk's office, and manually update the Department's database. The record reflects no routine practice of checking the database for accuracy, and the failure to remove the entry for Herring's warrant was not discovered until Investigator Anderson sought to pursue Herring five months later. Is it not altogether obvious that the Department could take further precautions to ensure the integrity of its database? **[p]** The Sheriff's Department "is in a position to remedy the situation and might well do so if the exclusionary rule is there to remove the incentive to do otherwise." * * *

[p] This point seems unarguable. One could argue, however, that installing a modern, integrated electronic system would more routinely protect rights than the operation of the exclusionary rule. The answer depends on the state of recordkeeping systems in the more than 3,000 sheriff's offices and almost 13,000 local police departments in the nation.

B

Is the potential deterrence here worth the costs it imposes? In light of the paramount importance of accurate recordkeeping in law enforcement, I would answer yes, and next explain why, as I see it, Herring's motion presents a particularly strong case for suppression.

Electronic databases form the nervous system of contemporary criminal justice operations. In recent years, their breadth and influence have dramatically expanded. Police today can access databases that include not only the updated National Crime Information Center (NCIC), but also terrorist watchlists, the Federal Government's employee eligibility system, and various commercial databases. Moreover, States are actively expanding information sharing between jurisdictions. As a result, law enforcement has an increasing supply of information within its easy electronic reach.

The risk of error stemming from these databases is not slim. Herring's *amici* **[q]** warn that law enforcement databases are insufficiently monitored and often out of date. Government reports describe, for example, flaws in NCIC databases, terrorist watchlist databases, and databases associated with the Federal Government's employment eligibility verification system.

Inaccuracies in expansive, interconnected collections of electronic information raise grave concerns for individual liberty. **[r]** "The offense to the dignity of the citizen who is arrested, handcuffed, and searched on a public street simply because some bureaucrat has failed to maintain an accurate computer data base" is evocative of the use of general warrants that so outraged the authors of our Bill of Rights.

[q] In addition to the briefs (written arguments) submitted to the Court by the petitioner and respondent, briefs are submitted by "friends of the Court." In Latin these are known as *amicus curiae* briefs (*plural, amici curiae*).

[r] The dissent cites powerful evidence that the poor state of various American law enforcement databases puts a large number of innocent people at risk of "good faith" police harassment because of database errors. See Amici Curiae brief by the Electronic Privacy Information Center (EPIC), supported by conservative and liberal organizations.

C

The Court assures that "exclusion would certainly be justified" if "the police have been shown to be reckless in maintaining a warrant system, or to have knowingly made false entries to lay the groundwork for future false arrests." This concession provides little comfort.

[(1) A civil lawsuit in a case like the present one would fail because officers are protected by immunity from lawsuit, and it would be close to impossible to identify the employee who created the data error. (2) Without the exclusionary rule police forces do not possess sufficient incentives to maintain up-to-date records. (3) Poor defendants have difficulty proving even good cases, and relying on civil lawsuits places a burden on the police systems that have to answer discovery motions. (4) The rule of *Herring* that requires proof of *deliberate* police misconduct runs counter to the Fourth Amendment doctrine that only *objective* factors that do not involve analysis of the officer's intention may be relied on in civil suits.]

* * *

[JUSTICE BREYER, in a separate dissent joined by JUSTICE STEVENS, agreed with JUSTICE GINSBURG but added that *Arizona v. Evans* (1995) held that recordkeeping errors made by a *court* clerk, as opposed to a police clerk, do not trigger the exclusionary rule because the exclusionary rule was designed to deter *police* misconduct. Chief Justice Roberts, in a footnote, disputed that this reason was dispositive of the decision in *Evans*.]

* * *

Standing

To have **standing** to sue, a party must have a real stake in a legal controversy to bring a lawsuit. In federal cases, standing is predicated on Article III of the Constitution, which confers jurisdiction on federal courts only in "cases or controversies." A "stranger" to a controversy, who does not have a real legal claim, is not allowed to file a case or to pursue an issue in a court case. As applied to Fourth Amendment issues, rules of standing *weaken* the exclusionary rule because they prevent defendants from challenging the legality by which the evidence is obtained, unless they have standing.

The search and seizure standing doctrine grew out of the older concept that Fourth Amendment rights are based on property rights: One had to have some level of property interest in a place or thing to assert a claim that it was illegally searched or seized. Standing was first limited to owners, renters, or others with a legal connection to a place, such as a hotel guest. House guests did not have standing. Suspects charged with possessory crimes (e.g., drugs) or crimes where possessing an item proved guilt (e.g., burglar's tools) had standing only by claiming possession of the seized item, which was an admission of guilt.

Jones v. United States (1960) eased standing rules. Police entered an apartment with a warrant, discovered drugs inside, and charged Jones with possession. Jones did not rent the apartment, but the owner gave him a key to the place and allowed him to sleep and keep some clothing there. The Supreme Court held that a defendant who is "legitimately on the premises" and has some connection to the place has standing to raise a Fourth Amendment challenge. Jones therefore did not have to assert ownership of the drugs to claim that the search warrant was unconstitutional. In *Jones,* the Court rejected technical property law classifications as the basis of standing.

The *Jones* opinion used broad language that suggested the **target theory** of standing: that *anyone* charged with a crime based on evidence obtained in a search and seizure (except burglars or trespassers) could challenge the legality of the seizure. The Court, however, *rejected* the target theory and retained the standing requirement in ***Alderman v. United States*** (1969). *Alderman* held that "Fourth Amendment rights are personal rights which, like some other constitutional rights, may not be vicariously asserted." In *Alderman,* conversations made by co-defendants that did not include Alderman were picked up by electronic eavesdropping. The Court ruled that *Alderman's* Fourth Amendment right to privacy was not violated by eavesdropping on the conversations of *others.*

The Court has continued to uphold standing and the specific rule of *Jones*. In fact, a person without a key has standing to challenge an apartment entry as long as there is enough of a connection to create an expectation of privacy. *Minnesota v. Olson* (1990) affirmed a state court ruling holding that a defendant who was an *overnight guest* had standing to challenge the introduction of evidence taken from the apartment. Olson had indefinite permission to stay and had the right to allow or deny visitors entry. "To hold that an overnight guest has a legitimate expectation of privacy in his host's home merely recognizes the everyday expectations of privacy that we all share. . . . From the overnight guest's perspective, he seeks shelter precisely because it provides him with privacy, a place where he and his possessions will not be disturbed by anyone but his host and those his host allows inside" (*Minnesota v. Olson,* 1990).

Business occupants of an apartment, to the contrary, generally do not have standing. In ***Minnesota v. Carter*** (1998), police entered an apartment on a tip that illicit drug business was being conducted there and found two men bagging cocaine. They were from out of town and "had come to the apartment for the sole purpose of packaging the cocaine. [They] had never been to the apartment before and were only in the apartment for approximately 2 1/2 hours. In return for the use of the apartment, [they] had given [the renter] one-eighth of an ounce of the cocaine." On these facts, the Court held that the defendants had no standing to challenge the constitutionality of the police search. The majority noted that the apartment was not the dealers' home and that they had less connection to the apartment than an employee has in his or her private office. The Court characterized the facts of this case as "between" the expectation of privacy of the apartment dweller in *Olson* and a case where someone who is "legitimately on the premises" has no standing. Factors that negated standing included "the purely commercial nature of the transaction engaged in here, the relatively short period of time on the premises, and the lack of any previous connection between respondents and the householder" (*Minnesota v. Carter*, 1998). Justice Ginsburg dissented, arguing that the decision undermines the security of short-term guests and that anyone whom a homeowner or renter invites "into her home to share in a common endeavor, whether it be for conversation, to engage in leisure activities, or for business purposes licit or illicit, . . . should share his host's shelter against unreasonable searches and seizures."

These holdings reflect the impact of *Katz v. United States,* which created the "expectation of privacy" doctrine in 1967. (See Chapter 3.) The idea that a person, under *Katz,* has a subjective and objective expectation of privacy in a premises where a search took place would tend to expand Fourth Amendment standing. The Supreme Court, however, has not applied *Katz* consistently, as seen in **Rakas v. Illinois** (1978). A police officer on a routine patrol stopped an automobile fitting the description of a getaway car used in a robbery and ordered the four occupants to exit. Two officers searched the vehicle's interior and found a box of rifle shells in the locked glove compartment and a sawed-off rifle under the front passenger seat. The woman who owned the car was the driver. The issue was whether Rakas, as a passenger, had standing to claim that the automobile search was unconstitutional in a prosecution in which the shells and rifle were entered into evidence against him. Rakas did not claim ownership or possession of the gun and shells. He argued that he had standing because he was legitimately in the car.

The Supreme Court, refusing to expand the *Jones* rule, and even narrowing it, held that Rakas did not have standing. Justice Rehnquist, writing for a five-justice majority, said that the concept of standing added little to the analysis of the case. The real issue was whether the search violated the defendant's personal Fourth Amendment rights, which had to be determined by examining the facts of the case. The *Rakas* majority stated that the phrase "legitimately on the premises" is too broad and would extend standing too far. Instead, a court must examine the defendant's connection with the premises. A casual visitor to an apartment, for example, has no standing to challenge a search, while an overnight guest does have standing. By analogy, the Court ruled that a passenger in a car does not have enough of a connection to challenge the seizure of a weapon that he claimed not to own.

Justice Byron White dissented. He felt that *Katz*'s "expectation of privacy" doctrine clarified the focus of Fourth Amendment analysis as being on the defendant's privacy right, uncoupled from ownership. Because Rakas was legitimately in the car, he had as much a privacy interest against an improper police search as did the driver. The flaw in the majority opinion was that "[t]he distinctions the Court would draw are based on relationships between private parties, but the Fourth Amendment is concerned with the relationship of one of those parties to the government" (*Rakas v. Illinois,* 1978, White, J., dissenting). The dissent noted that "the ruling today undercuts the force of the exclusionary rule in the one area in which its use is most certainly justified—the deterrence of bad-faith violations of the Fourth Amendment." The *Rakas* holding tempts police to engage in questionable automobile searches in which there is a passenger, in the hope that the passenger would not have standing to challenge an illegal search.

The extremes to which police may go when unconstrained by the exclusionary rule is seen in **United States v. Payner** (1980). Jack Payner was convicted of income tax fraud on the basis of information illegally seized from the briefcase of Michael Wolstencroft, the vice president of a Bahamian bank. Richard Jaffe, an Internal Revenue Service (IRS) special agent, hired Norman Casper, a private investigator, to study the bank. Casper struck up a friendship with Wolstencroft and introduced him to Sybol Kennedy, also a private investigator. On a business trip to Miami, Wolstencroft went to Kennedy's apartment, and the two went out to dinner. Wolstencroft left his briefcase in the apartment. Using a key supplied by Kennedy, Casper delivered the briefcase to Jaffe, who had four hundred bank documents photographed. A "lookout" observed Kennedy and Wolstencroft at dinner to ensure that the "briefcase caper" would not be discovered. Because the seizure violated only *Wolstencroft's* privacy, *Payner* had no standing to attack the legality of the seizure, even though the evidence was used against him.

Justice Powell, in his majority opinion, wrote, "No court should condone the unconstitutional and possibly criminal behavior of those who planned and executed this 'briefcase caper'"

(*United States v. Payner,* 1980). The majority nevertheless upheld the use of the evidence, noting that the Court had to weigh the benefits of the exclusionary rule "against the considerable harm that would flow from indiscriminate application of an exclusionary rule." Justice Marshall, dissenting, commented that the Court's "holding effectively turns the standing rules created by this Court for assertions of Fourth Amendment violations into a sword to be used by the Government to permit it deliberately to invade one person's Fourth Amendment rights in order to obtain evidence against another person." The dissent made sense because the lower courts found that the IRS "affirmatively counsel[ed] its agents that the Fourth Amendment standing limitation permits them to purposefully conduct an unconstitutional search and seizure of one individual in order to obtain evidence against third parties, who are the real targets of the governmental intrusion, and that the IRS agents in this case acted, and will act in the future, according to that counsel."

Professor Heffernan points out that the Supreme Court's restrictive standing rule is in conflict with its theory that the only purpose of the exclusionary rule is to deter police illegality. If the Court were more serious about deterrence, it would allow a broader scope for challenging possibly illegal searches.[81] It seems clear that the Burger and Rehnquist Courts' restrictive standing doctrine is tied to their distaste for the exclusionary rule, a distaste that continues into the Roberts Court (*Hudson v. Michigan,* 2006).

Exclusionary Rule Theories

The Supreme Court's development and interpretation of the exclusionary rule from 1886 to 2009 has been conflicted. The justices perennially divide over whether it is a truly constitutional rule, a real remedy, and a personal right, or whether it just an instrument to deter especially bad police violations of privacy. The Court has not recently threatened to abolish the exclusionary rule, but the open hostility to the rule by the Court's conservative majority, calling it a "grudgingly taken mendicant" (*Pa. Board v. Scott,* 1998), has added many exceptions and limited it to deliberate and flagrant violations of the Constitution (*Herring v. U.S.,* 2009). At base, the difference between opponents and proponents of the exclusionary rule reflects the ideological divide separating 'Due Process Model' justices from 'Crime Control Model' justices. Their differences have been reflected in (1) their view as to whether the exclusionary rule is a constitutional rule, and (2) the theories propounded to explain the exclusionary rule.

IS THE EXCLUSIONARY RULE A CONSTITUTIONAL RULE?   Regarding the constitutional stature of the rule, to simplify to some extent, it was noted earlier that from 1914 to 1949 the Court, under *Weeks*, applied the exclusionary rule to federal courts as a constitutional requirement. Yet, from 1949 to 1961, under *Wolf*, the Court's majority—while extending the prohibition on unreasonable searches and seizures to the states as a substantive constitutional rule—held that the exclusionary rule did not apply to the states because it was only a device to enforce the Fourth Amendment among federal officers. This changed in 1961, when the rule's constitutional status was regained in *Mapp v. Ohio*, and the rule was seen as "part and parcel" of the Fourth Amendment, equally applicable to federal and state law enforcement. The pendulum swung again in 1974, when, under *Calandra* and fortified by *Leon* (1984), the Court's majority treated the exclusionary rule as essentially non-constitutional, but constitutional enough for federal courts to apply it to the states in flagrant cases. As late as 2009, almost a century after *Weeks*, the Court split 5–4 over its view of the nature of the exclusionary rule in *Herring*.

Several reasons are given for viewing the rule as a non-constitutional device to protect the Fourth Amendment prohibition on unreasonable searches and seizures. (1) The rule is not included in the text of the Fourth Amendment and there was no a common law exclusionary rule in 1791. (2) When police violate the Fourth Amendment, the invasion of a person's privacy is "fully accomplished" and cannot be repaired by excluding the evidence in court. (3) *Mapp* (1961) was held not to be retroactive in *Linkletter v. Walker* (1965) because "all of the cases since *Wolf* requiring the exclusion of illegal evidence have been based on the necessity for an effective deterrent to illegal police action. We cannot say that this purpose would be advanced by making the rule retrospective" (*Linkletter v. Walker,* 1965). (4) In *Walder v. U.S.* (1954), the Court held that the *Weeks* exclusionary rule did not prevent the government from alluding to illegally seized drugs on cross-examination to *impeach* the defendant's testimony (he denied on direct examination ever having drugs in his possession). Any exception to a Supreme Court ruling under a provision of the Bill of Rights proves that the right is not constitutional.[82] (5) *Elkins v. United States*

(1960), in eliminating the silver platter doctrine, stated that the purpose of the exclusionary rule "is to deter—to compel respect for the constitutional guaranty in the only effectively available way—by removing the incentive to disregard it." The deterrence rationale is thus the rule's primary goal. (6) Crime control should be seen as the higher goal whenever possible: "The pertinent general principle, responding to the deepest needs of society, is that society is entitled to every man's evidence. As the underlying aim of judicial inquiry is ascertainable truth, everything rationally related to ascertaining the truth is presumptively admissible" (*Elkins v. U.S.*, 1960, Frankfurter, J., dissenting). (7) The exclusionary rule encourages police perjury. While very few rogue police officers manufacture or plant evidence on innocent suspects, many officers apparently "shade the truth" when testifying in court, especially in possession cases. (See the "Law in Society" section in Chapter 3.) This undermines a sense of fairness in the courts, but makes police cynical because they learn that they can reduce the effectiveness of the exclusionary rule by their own success in undermining it.[83]

A number of arguments support the view that the rule is constitutional. (1) If it is not a constitutional rule, the federal courts have no jurisdiction under Article III to impose it on the states, and yet they do.[84] (2) The fact that the text of the Fourth Amendment does not mention exclusion is not an impediment because the Court has established rights in the Constitution by interpretation, including the due process privacy right that has voided state laws that banned contraceptive devices or advice to married couples or that prohibited the abortion of a fetus. Under the theory of the Constitution as a living document, the Court has expanded its civil liberties protection over time. (3) The "fully accomplished" argument fails to understand that an illegal search and seizure violates not only privacy rights but property and liberty rights as well, which can be remedied by the return of noncontraband and the exclusion of evidence. (4) As for retroactivity, the Court said in *Linkletter* that it no longer adhered to the English common law rule that a court only declares what the law is and that an unconstitutional law or rule was totally void; the Court is free to make its rulings retroactive depending upon circumstances. Other reasons for not making *Mapp* retroactive were "interests in the administration of justice and the integrity of the judicial process . . . To make the rule of *Mapp* retrospective would tax the administration of justice to the utmost." The Court concluded: "All that we decide today is that though the error complained of *might be fundamental* it is not of the nature requiring us to overturn all final convictions based upon it." (*Linkletter v. Walker*, 1965, emphasis added). (5) The use of illegally seized evidence to impeach a defendant (*Walder v. U.S.*, 1954) does create an exclusionary rule exception, but modern constitutional law upholds exception to constitutional rules (e.g., *Dickerson v. U.S.*, 2000, holding that *Miranda* warnings are constitutional, see Chapter 7). (6) *Elkins* (1960) relied not only upon the deterrence rationale for the exclusionary rule but also on the rule of law: "But there is another consideration—the imperative of judicial integrity."

It can be seen that those who wish to strengthen *or* diminish the exclusionary rule have an armory of arguments on which to rely. We now turn to a number of exclusionary rule theories propounded to justify the existence of the rule, and to help determine whether it is of constitutional stature. It is worth reexamining *Herring v. United States* (2009) to notice that the five "conservative" justices relied exclusively on the deterrence theory to justify a narrow rule, while the four "liberal" justices relied on deterrence and a number of non-utilitarian rules to support a constitutional rule with broader scope.

FIFTH AMENDMENT THEORY   *Boyd v. United States* (1886) excluded evidence on the idea that the "Fourth and Fifth Amendments run almost into each other," basing the exclusion of seized evidence on the Fifth Amendment exclusion of "compelled" evidence. Several cases relied on *Boyd*'s Fourth + Fifth formula (*Gouled v. United States*, 1921), and Justice Black's crucial fifth vote in *Mapp* was based on this theory. It made some sense because letters or documents were seized in many early exclusionary rule cases, including *Weeks*. Nevertheless, the Court discarded the theory in *Andresen v. Maryland* (1976), which held that *seizing* business records under a warrant did not violate the Fifth Amendment self-incrimination clause. Justice White, in *Leon* (1984), buried the Fifth Amendment theory, stating that it "has not withstood critical analysis or the test of time."[85] The idea that a search *compels* the disclosure of evidence would virtually make prosecutions based on seized evidence impossible, because "the Fifth Amendment excludes all compelled testimony, whether or not it was obtained by police who had probable cause."[86] This could not have been contemplated by the Fourth Amendment's Framers.

PROPERTY THEORY   *Weeks* (1914), *Silverthorne* (1920), and other cases seemed to rest on the idea that a defendant has a greater property right over evidence illegally seized than the state does. Several inconsistencies undermine the **property theory** as a basis for the exclusionary rule. A successful defendant, for example, will not have contraband returned, even if the evidence is suppressed.[87] Under existing forfeiture laws, all sorts of "innocent" items used in the commission of a crime may be forfeited. In theory, the "expectation of privacy" doctrine of *Katz v. United States* (1967) abolished the property basis of Fourth Amendment jurisprudence. (See Chapter 3.) Thus, for example, a "seizure" of conversations by electronic eavesdropping violates Fourth Amendment privacy even if there is no trespass to property. The *Katz* doctrine was confirmed and strengthened by *Warden v. Hayden* (1967), which abolished the "mere evidence" rule. After *Warden,* police could lawfully seize any property relevant to a criminal investigation, not just contraband, loot, or instruments used to commit the crime, and they could hold "mere property" until the case was completed. The *Katz* doctrine balances law enforcement needs against individual privacy and property rights. As will be seen later in this text, however, the Court in some cases has implicitly relied on the value of property, especially private homes, in applying the rule.

DUE PROCESS THEORY   Both Professors Slobogin and Heffernan recall that a rights-based exclusionary rule exists under the "shocks the conscience" test of *Rochin v. California* (1952).[88] This test has not been advanced as a basis of a Fourth Amendment exclusionary rule. It might be viewed as a "back-up" test, somewhat analogous to the due process exclusionary rule for coerced confessions that continues to exist after *Miranda v. Arizona* (1966) (see Chapter 7). An open question arises under *Herring v. United States* (2009). *Herring* ruled that the exclusionary rule operates where police act in "reckless disregard of constitutional requirements." If this rule comes to be the same as the 'shocks the conscience' test, it could be argued, either that *Herring* overruled *Weeks* (1914) and *Mapp* (1961) *sub silentio*, or that such an effect requires an exclusionary rule for Fourth Amendment violations that creates greater protection.

THE IMPERATIVE OF JUDICIAL INTEGRITY/RULE OF LAW   In *Weeks* (1914) and *Mapp* (1961), the Court justified the rule as one *required* by the Constitution and enforceable against violations by federal and (later) state legislatures, executive agencies (i.e., the police), and courts. In *Elkins v. United States* (1960), which banned the 'silver platter' doctrine, Justice Potter Stewart reasoned that *Wolf v. Colorado* (1949), by incorporating the Fourth Amendment's substantive ban on illegal search and seizures into the Due Process Clause, undermined its other ruling that the exclusionary rule did not apply to the states. This was so because while the exclusionary rule rested in part on deterring police illegality, "there is another consideration—the imperative of judicial integrity" (*Elkins,* 1960). In other words, courts undermine the Rule of Law if they allow illegally seized evidence to be admitted in trials. This a nonutilitarian rationale, with several aspects. *First*, it enables "the judiciary to avoid the taint of partnership in official lawlessness," no small matter in a branch of government destined by the Founders to be the *guardian of civil rights and liberties* (*Calandra,* 1974, Brennan, J., dissenting). *Second*, it is an "enforcement tool [that] give[s] content and meaning to the Fourth Amendment's guarantees" (ibid.). In other words, it serves a similar function as the penalty portion of a criminal statute, which, by prescribing a sanction for wrongful conduct, gives moral substance to the rule, whatever its effectiveness. *Third*, the imperative also assures "the people—all potential victims of unlawful government conduct—that the government would not profit from its lawless behavior" (ibid.). This is the disgorgement rationale, discussed in the section on theories of remedies. As nonutilitarian and ethical foundations, the imperative of judicial integrity implies that courts must *never* allow evidence seized in violation of the Constitution to be used. As Justice Holmes wrote in *Silverthorne* (1920), "The essence of a provision forbidding the acquisition of evidence in a certain way is that not merely evidence so acquired shall not be used before the Court but that it shall not be used at all."

DETERRENCE THEORY   All cases that developed and rely on the exclusionary rule, including *Weeks* (1914) and *Mapp* (1961), rest on the theory that the exclusion of evidence deters the government from violating constitutional rights. The big divide between "liberal" and "conservative" justices is whether deterrence is the *only* theoretical support. The current Supreme Court's majority, since *Calandra* (1974), has made deterrence the *only* basis for the exclusionary rule.

Where deterrence is thought to be minimal, therefore, the rule has not been held applicable.[89] Because deterrence is a utilitarian rationale, its legitimacy turns largely on whether it is effective, a subject of debate that is the focus of the "Law in Society" section in this chapter.

STATUS QUO ANTE THEORY   The exclusionary rule returns the parties to where they would have been had the Constitution been followed. This is a commonsense and ethical rationale. It also explains the inevitable discovery exception to the 'fruits of the poisonous tree' doctrine: Because the police would have legally obtained the evidence in any event, they should not be placed in a difficult position because an unconstitutional search occurred. Prof. Slobogin claims that the theory is inadequate because it does not result in the return of contraband, but this is no answer to the underlying logic that this would not have been an issue if the Constitution had been obeyed. His objection that the rule cannot restore the "ruptured privacy" of the person subjected to an illegal search and seizure misses the multiple values protected by the amendment. Slobogin also objects that the status quo ante does not allow introduction of evidence where the police *could have* lawfully obtained the evidence. This idea is the basis of the "inevitable discovery" exception to the derivative use corollary (i.e., 'fruits of the poisonous tree') to the exclusionary rule. Professor Slobogin pushes this argument too far because it is always possible to conjure up some way in which police *might have* properly obtained evidence—such reasoning makes any compliance rule impossible.[90]

The *per curiam* decision of *Smith v. Ohio* (1990), enforcing the rule against retrospective justification, was discussed earlier in the section on the 'fruits of the poisonous tree' doctrine. The rule is simplicity itself. Police cannot search without any legal justification and then argue that the search is proper *if* they find incriminating evidence. The Fourth Amendment, which protects individual privacy, liberty, and property, *requires* that government officers have justification *before* they search or seize. This rule is so basic that it is rarely discussed, but it embodies all of the justifications of the exclusionary rule: deterrence, status quo ante, and judicial integrity.

According to Prof. Heffernan, the internal logic of the Fourth Amendment against retroactive justification *requires* the "remedy" of *exclusion* even if the Framers did not consider exclusion, because without the exclusionary rule the amendment "collapses on itself."[91] The government cannot insist on holding on to illegally seized evidence in order to determine if it discloses incriminating information, for that would allow seizures *before* probable cause is obtained. "Absent exclusion, all personal property is held on a probationary basis: government agents can seize personal property at will, inspect it, and return it only if it is found not to provide evidence of a crime."[92] The internal logic of the Fourth Amendment cannot allow this kind of retroactive legitimation. If the exclusionary rule were totally eliminated, police could choose to violate Fourth Amendment rights in specific cases they deem important and be willing to pay the price in a tort action if it came to that. Thus Heffernan believes that Justice Holmes and the Court had it right in *Silverthorne* (1920). Whatever the Framers thought about exclusion as a remedy, the Court in *Weeks* and *Silverthorne* intuited correctly that the exclusionary principle "emerges from an analysis of the internal logic of the Amendment itself."[93]

This is so even if exclusion does not repair the violation of first-party privacy interests and extracts a heavy cost to the public whose third-party interest in deterrence is offset by an interest in convicting the guilty. Nevertheless, the liberty-protecting function of the Constitution coalesces with and is required by the second-party remedy of disgorgement via exclusion that is required by the logic of the Fourth Amendment.

LAW IN SOCIETY

Debating the Exclusionary Rule

Inherent Limits of Deterrence

The dislike of the exclusionary rule is also connected to the belief that the exclusionary rule is a completely ineffective deterrent to police illegality. This argument seems logical because (1) the impact of exclusion is directly felt by the prosecutor rather than the officer, (2) police know and count on the fact that the rule is rarely applied, (3) judges are reluctant to find a Fourth Amendment violation when they know that evidence points to guilt (hindsight biasing),[94] (4) negative sanctioning for improper searches occurs indirectly via prosecutors' complaints to police administrators, which are relayed down the chain of command, and (5) negative sanctioning for illegal searches is offset by the praise and recognition that officers receive for making good arrests.[95] Aside from logical arguments that downplay deterrence, it is important in forming a sound policy to examine the empirical evidence about the "costs" and the deterrent effect or "benefits" of the exclusionary rule.

Costs and Benefits of the Exclusionary Rule

Since 1974, the Supreme Court has confronted two empirical issues concerning the exclusionary rule: its deterrent effect and its costs in lost convictions. Both issues have been used in arguments for and against the rule, such that studies and findings have been examined with partisan intensity. In the course of examining these empirical questions, the Supreme Court has used and, on occasion, mis-used social science data. This section reviews some of the findings on these sensitive issues.

To understand human behavior, social scientists first attempt to measure behavior accurately, systematically, and with quantitative precision to the greatest extent possible. Statistical tests are applied to data to determine the extent to which the collected data (a sample) reflect actual behavior (the universe). These rigorous attempts to quantify knowledge contrast with the human tendency to generalize—that is, to make overly broad conclusions about human behavior based on a small number of personal experiences or on the basis of a few secondhand stories.

The Deterrent Effect of the Exclusionary Rule

United States v. Calandra (1974) "adopted the view that the primary rationale for the federal exclusionary rule is the factual premise that suppression of illegally seized evidence will deter the police from conducting illegal searches."[96] Only a few studies of the exclusionary rule had been published by 1974. The most prominent, by Dallin Oaks, appeared to show that the exclusionary rule had no effect on police behavior in several cities.[97] Oaks's data did not conclusively show whether the exclusionary rule deterred police misconduct. Rather, his stated personal opinion was that the rule failed to deter and should be abolished. According to Thomas Davies, "the Oaks study has probably established something of a record for being widely cited as empirical support for a finding it did not really claim to make."[98]

Proponents of the exclusionary rule were fearful that the Supreme Court would use a finding of no deterrence to abolish the rule. For example, in his *Bivens* dissent, Chief Justice Burger stated: "If an effective alternative remedy is available, concern for official observance of the law does not require adherence to the exclusionary rule." This would be especially troublesome if the Court made constitutional law based on flawed research. Indeed, Oaks's research conclusion, if not his data, was flawed in that he believed the exclusionary rule failed simply because Fourth Amendment violations continued to occur after the *Mapp* decision. This was a conceptual failure: The more appropriate question was whether the number and rates of such violations increased, decreased, or remained level after *Mapp*. Oaks failed to make these comparisons.[99]

In *United States v. Janis* (1976), a careful and exhaustive review of the deterrence research in Justice Harry Blackmun's majority opinion finally put to bed the deterrence issue. The issue in *Janis* was whether the exclusionary rule would be extended to federal IRS civil tax assessment hearings to exclude illegally seized evidence. A strong finding about the deterrent effect could sway the Court to extend the rule or to abolish it. Justice Blackmun's honest review of the research literature concluded that there is no conclusive evidence that the rule has or does not have a deterrent effect: "The final conclusion is clear. No empirical researcher, proponent or opponent of the rule, has yet been able to establish with any assurance whether the rule has a deterrent effect even in the situations in which it is now applied" (*Janis*, fn. 22). The way in which the Court applied this equivocal and correct empirical conclusion is interesting. Justice Blackmun said that even if the exclusionary rule has a strong deterrent effect, "the additional marginal deterrence provided" by -extending the rule to federal civil tax proceedings "surely does not outweigh the *cost to society* of extending the rule to that situation" (*Janis*, pp. 453–54, emphasis added). The majority in *Janis* clearly did not want to extend the exclusionary rule, and so its analysis had a "heads I win, tails you lose" quality, switching the focus of inquiry from deterrence to the costs of the exclusionary rule.

Nevertheless, the Court's conclusion in *Janis* in regard to the empirical research is supported by Davies's most thorough review of the issue.[100] The problem is not so much that of poor research designs, but of the special difficulty of defining and studying legal deterrence. According to Davies, "It is quite unlikely that there will be any rigorous measurement of the rule's specific deterrent effect in terms of how often illegal searches have been prevented."[101] This problem arose partly because the research community paid little attention to the exclusionary rule when criminal justice research made it clear that the rule was a minor factor in the total disposition of cases. Thus studies on the effectiveness of deterrence and on its "costs" were left to policy-relevant studies that framed the issue narrowly.[102]

The Educative Effect of the Exclusionary Rule

Another empirical question is whether the exclusionary rule has had a broad educative effect. Proponents have not been able to establish this by rigorous empirical research, but there is some anecdotal evidence suggesting that because of the rule, police are now trained in the law, police and prosecutors seriously discuss search and seizure rules, and the police community generally takes the Fourth Amendment more seriously than it did before *Mapp*.[103] A study comparing drug, weapons, and gambling arrests in nineteen cities before and after *Mapp* appears to indicate that *Mapp* had a decided effect in six cities, an intermediate effect in three cities, and no effect in ten cities.[104] This suggests that "*Mapp*'s impact largely has been mediated by differentials in attitudes and styles among police and civic leaders . . . . [T]he police are likely to behave differently in a city where the chief almost openly encourages evasion of a Supreme Court decision than in one where the chief insists on obedience."[105]

This is supported by the observational study of police by law professor Richard Uviller, who noted that honest police officers bring to their work an "innate sense of limits" that prevails "over the broad license allowed by law" in many situations.[106] Too often the "legal focus" portrays police as overly aggressive, overly zealous, and guided only by a crime control mentality. Uviller's closely observed police officers displayed common sense, decency, and a real desire to operate within the limits of the law, even if they were not always precisely correct about the operative rules. This perspective suggests that over the long run, police behavior actually will become more law-abiding. One may also speculate that as Court decisions become more favorable to the police, it will be easier for officers to obey the rules of constitutional criminal procedure. A more cynical possibility may be that successful evasion of the exclusionary rule is a factor in police acquiescence to the rule. All these factors may be at play simultaneously. In any event, to bring police behavior into line with constitutional norms requires practical training for police officers. Where the law does place limits on what the police may do, departments are well advised to include some training into the reasons for these limits.

Costs of the Exclusionary Rule

The Court, in its anti-exclusionary-rule mood, tended to emphasize the costs of lost convictions in broad terms. Justice White's concurrence in *Illinois v. Gates* (1983) is an example of the poor review of social science studies. For example, White's broad conclusion—"We will never know how many guilty defendants go free as a result of the rule's operation"[107]—is wrong. To make matters worse, he quoted a misleading National Institute of Justice (NIJ) study that reported that "prosecutors rejected approximately 30 percent of all felony drug arrests because of search and seizure problems."[108] As we shall see, this was a gross exaggeration of the costs of the exclusionary rule.

Unlike deterrence, which is inherently difficult to measure, lost cases can be more precisely measured. Because the total number of arrests and the number of cases dismissed owing to search and seizure errors can be obtained from prosecution and court records, the proportion of "lost cases" can be calculated. Several research studies are in general agreement that the "costs" of the exclusionary rule are not great. In almost all instances, the percentage of cases dropped because of search and seizure problems is less than 1 percent:

1. *Forst, Lucianovic, and Cox* (1977).   In Washington, D.C., prosecutors rejected 168 out of 17,534 arrests (1 percent) for all kinds of due process problems, including search and seizure violations.[109]
2. *Brosi* (1979).   Prosecutors declined to issue complaints for all types of due process errors in 1 percent of the cases in Washington, D.C.; 2 percent in Cobb County, Georgia; 2 percent in Salt Lake City; 4 percent in Los Angeles; and 9 percent in New Orleans.[110]
3. *Forst et al.* (1977 and 1982).   Due process violations led to dismissals in less than 1 percent of arrests in six cities, 2 percent in Los Angeles, and 6 percent in New Orleans.[111]
4. *General Accounting Office* (1979).   Prosecutors declined to accept 46 percent of all cases; 6.6 percent of the declined cases were rejected for legal violations overall, and 0.4 percent of all cases were declined because of illegal searches.[112]

5. *Nardulli* (1983). A review of 7,500 cases in nine counties in three states found that motions to suppress physical evidence were filed in fewer than 5 percent of the cases and were successful in 0.69 percent of the cases, and motions to suppress illegal confessions or identifications were filed in 2 percent of the cases and were successful in 4 percent of these. Some defendants were convicted even after the evidence was suppressed. In the entire sample, 46 out of 7,500 cases were lost (less than 0.6 percent) because of the three exclusionary rules combined.[113]

6. *Feeney et al.* (1983). Nine out of 885 nonconvictions (1 percent) were lost due to illegal searches; since about half of the arrests resulted in nonconvictions, 0.5 percent of the cases in Jacksonville and San Diego were lost because of the exclusionary rule.[114]

7. *Uchida and Bynum* (1991). In seven cities, 1.4 percent of all defendants (19 out of 1,355) in cases based on search warrants were granted motions to suppress.[115]

Despite the virtually unanimous conclusion that about 1 percent or less of cases are lost because of the rule, Justice White claimed in *Gates* that 30 percent of the cases were lost due to excluded evidence. He based this on a federal study of California case processing and repeated the figure put forward in the solicitor general's brief. Davies notes that the NIJ study was seriously flawed and that the 30 percent figure is grossly misleading. First, the NIJ study showed that 4.8 percent of all rejected felony cases are lost because of search and seizure problems. This in no way indicates the cost of the exclusionary rule; it instead shows that among those cases *that prosecutors rejected*, 4.8 percent were lost due to the exclusionary rule. This is meaningless because the percentage calculated in this way can change dramatically depending on changes in the other reasons for dismissals. When the NIJ data of lost cases are calculated against a base figure of total arrests, those lost due to the exclusionary rule drop to about 0.8 percent, more in line with the other studies. As for the 30 percent figure, it was drawn from a sample of 150 drug cases from two local prosecutors' offices in Los Angeles, which was not at all representative: As Davies indicates, between 1978 and 1982, California prosecutors rejected 2.4 percent of felony drug arrests because of illegal searches.

Further, the studies show that the number of cases rejected on Fourth Amendment grounds in serious violent felonies is lower, about 0.2 percent of all arrests, and somewhat higher for drug offenses. Davies makes the point that many such rejected arrests in drug cases may not be those of carefully planned raids, but rather are arrests on suspicion where drugs are found and the probable cause basis is very weak to begin with. Thus, unlike the inconclusive result of the exclusionary rule's deterrent effect, research findings of its costs firmly show that fewer than 1 percent of arrests are lost because of the exclusionary rule. In half of these lost cases, convictions are still obtained because of other evidence.

Do these findings mean that the costs are low? This is a normative issue. The figures show that the exclusionary rule is not subverting law enforcement efforts. Yet its effect may still be unacceptably high to some. "Indeed, some critics have taken the position that *even one lost arrest* is an excessive cost."[116] Thus when Justice White had to confront this new evidence, he stated that "the small percentages with which [the researchers] deal mask a large absolute number of felons who are released because the cases against them were based in part on illegal searches or seizures" (*United States v. Leon,* 1984, fn. 6). Of course, in a country with a population of 300 million, virtually any small percentage will generate large numbers. I would tend to agree with Uchida and Bynum "that the exclusionary rule, though seldom invoked, serves as an incentive for many police officers to follow the limits imposed by the Fourth Amendment as defined in their jurisdictions."[117] Thus the exclusionary rule debate presents an interesting case history of the use and misuse of social science data in the judicial decision-making process.

The Effectiveness of Tort Remedies

Another aspect of the exclusionary rule debate is the effectiveness of tort suits against the police. The evidence is generally that they do not provide strong control over police misbehavior, including police brutality. Empirical studies of *Bivens* suits, for example, disclose that they virtually never lead to findings of police officer liability.

Government figures reflect that out of approximately 12,000 *Bivens* claims filed between 1971 and 1985, *Bivens* plaintiffs actually obtained a judgment that was not reversed on appeal in only four cases. While similar figures have not been systematically kept since 1985, recoveries from both settlements and litigated judgments continue to be extraordinarily rare. According to one estimate, plaintiffs obtain a judgment awarding them damages in a fraction of 1 percent of *Bivens* cases and obtain a monetary settlement in less than 1 percent of such cases. The low rate of successful claims indicates that, notwithstanding *Bivens*, federal constitutional violations are almost never remedied by damages. The low success rate of these claims also reflects that the courts are processing a tremendous amount of *Bivens* litigation. When analyzed by traditional measures of a claim's "success"—whether damages were obtained through settlement or court order—*Bivens* litigation is fruitless and wasteful because it does not provide the remedies contemplated by the decision, and it burdens litigants and the judicial system.[118]

While recovery in other kinds of tort cases against the police does exist, such recovery is hard to obtain, and monetary claims are low. In a study based on telephone interviews with civil rights attorneys in southern California, a variety of reasons were given for the lack of success:[119]

- Civil rights attorneys are unwilling to take weak cases.
- Witnesses with past criminal records are not credible to jurors.
- Police have a qualified immunity defense for acts done in good faith.
- Municipalities provide the costs of defense and pay for any settlement in cases won by plaintiffs.
- It is more difficult for plaintiffs to discover facts in the hands of defendants in these cases compared to other civil litigation.
- Defendants can tie up plaintiffs, who tend to have limited resources, with interlocutory appeals in Section 1983 suits.
- The "blue curtain" of silence makes police witnesses very reluctant to testify.
- Police perjury is rampant. (See the "Law in Society" section in Chapter 3.)
- Jurors almost always believe the police.

As a result, the likely deterrent effect of lawsuits on police brutality is very low. Commissions on police brutality report that many cases of abuse are committed by officers who are repeat offenders, indicating that departments do a poor job of sanctioning officers with a history of excessive violence. Many cities in the last decade have paid millions of dollars in tort damages for police brutality, and the numbers do not appear to have substantially diminished. Although there seems to be a slight, growing public interest in police brutality currently, there is virtually no political pressure for police departments to abide by the Constitution.[120] As Professor Bradley Canon noted in his study of police departments that follow warrant procedure, much depends on the attitudes of the police chief. "The chief and higher-ranking supervisors establish the tone and culture within a police department. If the upper ranks do not enforce violations of department policy, there will be no curb on officers' misconduct out on the street."[121] Chiefs who are concerned with the legal conduct of their officers can affect policy and action by the selection of field training officers, by their own disciplinary decisions, by the emphasis given to legal issues in academy and in-service training, and by having records of tort cases become part of an officer's file and be taken into account in promotions.[122] All such measures should not lead to demoralization or overdeterrence that causes police officers to shy away from performing their difficult jobs effectively. But there are examples, such as William Bratton's tenure as New York City police commissioner, demonstrating that, to paraphrase Justice Tom Clark, there is no war between effective policing and law-abiding policing.

Summary

Legal remedies against the government for constitutional violations are indispensable to the Rule of Law and constitutionalism. The theory of remedies includes three types: first-party remedies—reparations—that restore the injured party to the position occupied before the injury occurred. Second-party remedies—disgorgement—that place the wrongdoer (the second party) in no better position than the one occupied prior to the wrongful conduct. Third-party remedies—deterring future wrongdoing—that benefit the general public, putting it in a better position than if no deterrence were undertaken.

Aside from the exclusionary rule, individuals whose Fourth Amendment rights have been violated have other potential sources of relief. These include lawsuits against the police officer or the department. The different types of tort lawsuits include state common law tort suits, state constitutional torts wherein state officers are sued in state courts, Section 1983 civil rights suits against state and local officers and municipalities (but not state governments) in federal courts, and *Bivens* suits against federal officers in federal courts. Judges and prosecutors enjoy absolute immunity against lawsuits for acts performed in the ocurse of their duties. Police officers enjoy qualified immunity for performing discretionary functions if their conduct does not violate clearly established rights which a reasonable person would have known existed.

For violations likely to persist against specific individuals, injunctions that prohibit the illegal police activity from recurring are available, but the Supreme Court generally disfavors injunctions. Federal and state criminal prosecutions may also be brought against police officers, but they are typically reserved for the most egregious violations involving unnecessary violence. Police departments can improve their record of abiding by the law by adopting better recruitment, training, and supervision procedures and by other administrative measures. Congress passed 42 U.S.C. § 14141 in 1994, allowing the Department of Justice to bring suits against police departments to correct violations by means such as improved hiring, training, and complaint procedures where a pattern or practice of conduct by law enforcement officials that deprives people of constitutional rights has been proven.

The Fourth Amendment is grounded in the English common law rule of home privacy against government invasion, which was established shortly before the framing of the Constitution (1787) in the *Writs of Assistance* case and the *Wilkes* cases. They held that general warrants are illegal and that a victim of a general warrant could sue the government for damages.

Fourth Amendment interpretation can follow either general reasonableness (conservative) or warrant-and-exception (liberal) approaches. The Fourth Amendment was intended to eliminate the government's use of general search warrants. In the founding era, police had no power to conduct warrantless arrests or searches based on probable cause; a warrant was required. Nevertheless, modern constitutional interpretation authorizes warrantless arrests and searches upon probable cause under the general-reasonableness construction of the Fourth Amendment. The warrant-preference construction holds that warrants are required except in hot pursuit, vehicle searches, and search incident to arrest.

The Fourth Amendment exclusionary rule states that illegally seized evidence may not be introduced into evidence in a trial. It was established in *Weeks v. United States* and *Silverthorne Lumber Co. v. United States*, based on the Constitution, that illegally seized evidence shall not be used at all. The rule applies only to government officers, not to illegal searches by private individuals. Evidence derived from illegally seized materials cannot be introduced into evidence ('fruits of the poisonous tree' doctrine). However, illegally obtained evidence of a crime may be introduced if it is obtained from an independent source, by inevitable discovery, or because the link between the primary illegality and the evidence seized has become attenuated.

The Supreme Court incorporated the exclusionary rule (extended it to the states) in *Mapp v. Ohio* after having refused to do so in *Wolf v. Colorado* and *Rochin v. California*. In the latter case, the Court excluded evidence that was seized by methods that "shocked the conscience." This was a due process, "totality of the circumstances" test, and criticism of its subjectivity was a factor in the *Mapp* decision. The basis of *Mapp* was that the exclusionary rule is required by the Fourth Amendment and that exclusion is the best deterrent of police misbehavior.

After *Mapp,* a more conservative Supreme Court eroded the exclusionary rule. It upheld the use of illegally seized evidence as a basis of a grand jury question in *United States v. Calandra,* which modified the theoretical basis of the exclusionary rule. It became viewed as a judicially created remedy designed to safeguard Fourth Amendment rights generally through its deterrent effect on future unlawful police conduct, rather than a personal constitutional right of the aggrieved party. This concept was expanded by *United States v. Leon,* which allowed the introduction of illegally seized evidence for the proof of guilt where the evidence was obtained by police officers in the "good faith" reliance on a statute or search warrant. It also held that the exclusionary rule does not apply to unconstitutional acts committed by the judiciary. A ruling that evidence is admissible where police execute a search without complying with the knock and announce rule, a constitutional requirement, exemplifies the Court's distaste for the exclusionary rule (*Hudson v. Michigan*). In *Herring v. United States* the Supreme Court held that the exclusionary rule does not apply to an illegal search based on an officer's good faith reliance on errors in police computers.

To challenge evidence taken in violation of the Fourth Amendment, a party must have standing—that is, the party must have suffered a personal invasion of privacy rights rather than suffered harm because of the invasion of the privacy rights of another person. In *Rakas v. Illinois,* the Court held that a passenger of an automobile does not have such a personal right. A personal interest to raise a Fourth Amendment challenge does not depend on the defendant's strict property right but on his or her level of interest in a place; thus overnight guests in an apartment have standing, but guests invited into an apartment for business purposes do not have standing.

Fourth Amendment law has been confused because there are overlapping and conflicting theories of the exclusionary rule. These include the idea that the rule is required by the Constitution; that it is only a judicially created rule designed to deter police from violating individuals' rights; that it is based on the Fifth Amendment privilege against self-incrimination; that it is based on property rights; that it is based on returning the parties to their original position; that, once breached, privacy rights can never be repaired; and that violations of privacy interests involve property or liberty violations that should be repaired under a theory of disgorgement. Each of these theories has at least one weakness. Thus there is some level of policy choice open to jurists in deciding how to justify the exclusionary rule. The most philosophically coherent view is that the exclusionary rule is a Fourth Amendment requirement; otherwise, the government could justify illegal searches retroactively, subject only to tort remedies, which causes the amendment to collapse.

Legal Puzzles

HOW HAVE COURTS DECIDED THESE CASES?

Qualified Immunity

2-1. During the night and early morning of June 24–25, Albert Sheldon and his girlfriend Dora Williams attended a party in Ambler, Alaska, and consumed alcohol. They left the party and walked around the village, fighting and yelling at each other. At about 6:00 a.m., friends went to Ambler's Village Police Officer (VPO) Bryan Jones, asking him to restrain Sheldon.

VPO Jones, wearing his police uniform and equipment, recorded the encounter. He tried but failed to subdue Sheldon by orders, threats, pepper spray, and striking Sheldon on his hands and the back of his knees with his police baton. VPO Jones then struck Sheldon on the back of his head with the baton, non-fatally according to a medical expert. Sheldon continued to hold on to the handlebars of a four-wheeler. VPO Jones then put Sheldon in a "bear hug," wrapping his arms over Sheldon's arms and shoving him, performing a "take-down." The two men fell. Sheldon was unable to use his arms, and he struck his head on the ground when he landed underneath Jones. Within an hour Sheldon was dead, caused by the blow to his head from hitting the ground while in VPO Jones's bear hug and take-down.

In a civil lawsuit, was the officer's "bear hug and "take-down" maneuver entitled to qualified immunity?

Held. YES

2. In *Saucier v. Katz* (2001), the U.S. Supreme Court emphasized that deciding whether an officer is eligible for qualified immunity depends not merely on whether an officer's actions were objectively reasonable, but also on whether the officer might have reasonably believed that his actions were reasonable. Was a reasonable officer "on notice" that his particular use of force would be unlawful? Or could he have reasonably believed that his actions were legal? This test recognizes that there may be behavior that is objectively unreasonable but that nonetheless an officer might have reasonably believed was reasonable. If so, then the officer should be entitled to qualified immunity for his behavior.

If VPO Jones had "fair notice" that a bear hug and take-down were unlawful, and if there is a factual disagreement over whether he used excessive force, then the case should go to trial. The legal standard in Alaska statutes—that a police officer making an arrest may not use any restraint that is not necessary and proper for the arrest or detention of a person—is too general to give officers notice that specific actions taken in specific circumstances may or may not be reasonable. There is only one federal case that suggests that a bear hug and take-down may be reasonable, which is not sufficient to establish clear law that says that a bear hug and a take-down are excessive uses of force when applied to an intoxicated and assaultive arrestee.

However, if Jones's use of a bear hug was so egregious, so excessive, that he should have known it was unlawful, then the nature of the act gave sufficient warning that a bear hug and a take-down were excessive means to restrain someone. One should not let the lack of explicit law in an area be a substitute for the reasonable officer's common sense.

Although the events in this case resulted in tragedy, Jones's conduct was not shocking. He did not do anything we can now, on reflection, say that he should have known at the time was excessive and unlawful. Cognizant of the reality that officers must often make quick judgments that might have unanticipated consequences, we must resist the urge to second guess those actions when things turn out badly. Jones, in acting as he did, could have reasonably believed that his actions were not excessive. Jones is entitled to immunity.

Sheldon v. City of Amber, 178 P.3d 459 (Alaska Supreme Court 2008)

State Action or Private Action?

2-2. Rowley was taken into police custody on an unrelated matter. He asked his parents to take care of the things in the bed of his pickup truck, parked in front of his parents' home. Rowley's father, concerned about possible weather damage to the heavy items in the bed of the truck, moved it inside the garage. While in the cab of the truck, his father saw a syringe and a porcelain cup both containing an unknown substance in an open cubby hole under the dashboard. Father took these items into the house and showed them to his wife. Mother then searched the bags that were in the back of Rowley's truck and found a digital scale. Father contacted a sheriff's officer, whom Father knew, and informed him of what he and Mother had found in their son's truck. Father followed Officer's instructions and returned the items to where they had been found. When the officer arrived at Father's home, Father invited him into the garage and Officer retrieved the evidence in question from Rowley's truck. The substances were later tested and determined to be methamphetamine.

Did Father's obedience to Officer's order constitute state action, making Officer's seizure of the syringe and cup without a warrant unconstitutional?
Holding available from instructor

Exclusionary Rule

2-3. Tamika Smith, driving a rental car, was stopped driving west on I-94 between Detroit and Chicago for speeding. Her two small children and Todd Fletcher were passengers. Drivers' licenses were checked; Smith's had been suspended; Fletcher's was valid, but he was a person of "officer safety caution" based on previous arrests for cocaine possession and weapons offenses. The trooper searched the trunk of the rental car *without consent* and discovered $180,975 in cash in a backpack. Smith was cited for speeding and driving on a suspended license but with no crimes. Neither she nor Fletcher could provide a good explanation for possession such a large sum of cash.

State law requires the forfeiture of money when the state can prove on a preponderance of evidence that the money was intended to buy drugs. In a civil forfeiture proceeding by the state, the prosecutor admitted the search and seizure of the cash violated the Fourth Amendment. The cash itself was not introduced in evidence but the prosecutor presented evidence to show that Smith was a drug courier and that the $180,975 seized by the trooper had been intended for the purchase of illegal drugs.

Was the civil forfeiture invalid because the state introduced evidence about illegally seized cash?
Holding available from instructor.

Standing

2-4. Darold Jorlantin was charged with driving under the influence. An officer answered a possible gang fight report at a gas station. People pointed to a departing van, saying that individuals inside the van wanted to fight. The officer went to the van, observed the driver and multiple passengers inside, and directed the driver to stop. The officer smelled the odor of an alcoholic beverage emanating from the driver's side of the van, and he saw a nearly empty bottle of brandy on the floor of the driver's side of the van. The driver's eyes were bloodshot and watery, and he stated that he had consumed "a little bit" of alcohol. The driver failed to perform satisfactorily on roadside sobriety tests and was arrested.

Jorlantin made a pretrial motion to suppress the arresting officer's observations on the grounds that the officer lacked reasonable suspicion to stop the van and lacked probable cause to arrest him, thus violating the Fourth Amendment. In his testimony at the suppression hearing, the officer did not expressly identify Jorlantin in the courtroom as the van's driver. No evidence was introduced that Jorlantin was a passenger, and not the driver, of the van.

Does Jorlantin have standing to challenge the stop and arrest on Fourth Amendment grounds?
Holding available from instructor.

Further Reading

Richard C. Cortner, *The Supreme Court and the Second Bill of Rights: The Fourteenth Amendment and the Nationalization of Civil Liberties* (Madison: University of Wisconsin Press, 1981).

J. David Hirschel, *Fourth Amendment Rights* (Lexington, Mass.: Lexington Books, 1979).

H. Richard Uviller, *The Tilted Playing Field: Is Criminal Justice Unfair?* (New Haven, Conn.: Yale University Press, 1999).

Useful Web Site

National Criminal Justice Reference Service

http://www.ncjrs.gov/index.html

Essential information for everyone interested in criminal justice. Includes reports from the National Institute of Justice, the Bureau of Justice Statistics, and the Office of Juvenile Justice and Delinquency Prevention. Provides links for courts, crime, justice, law enforcement, and other topics.

End Notes

1. Cornelia T. L. Pillard, "Taking Fiction Seriously: The Strange Results of Public Officials' Individual Liability under *Bivens*," *Georgetown Law Journal* 88 (1999): 65–105, 69.
2. William C. Heffernan, "Foreword: The Fourth Amendment Exclusionary Rule as a Constitutional Remedy," *Georgetown Law Journal* 88, no. 5 (2000): 799–878, 806.
3. *McGhee v. Volusia County*, 679 So.2d 729 (Fla. 1996).
4. Kathryn Scarborough and Craig Hemmens, "Section 1983 Suits against Law Enforcement in the Circuit Courts of Appeal," *Thomas Jefferson Law Review* 21 (1999): 1–21.
5. T. Hunter Jefferson, "Note: Constitutional Wrongs and Common Law Principles: The Case for the Recognition of State Constitutional Tort Actions against State Governments," *Vanderbilt Law Review* 50 (1997): 1525–76, 1549–50.
6. Gail Donoghue and Jonathan I. Edelstein, "Life after *Brown*: The Future of State Constitutional Tort Actions in New York," *New York Law School Law Review* 42 (1998): 447–556, 447, n. 2.
7. *Brown v. New York*, 89 N.Y.2d 172, 674 N.E.2d 1129, 652 N.Y.S.2d 223, 75 A.L.R. 5th 769 (1996).
8. Henry Weinstein, "Judge OKs Use of Racketeering Law in Rampart Suits; Scandal: LAPD Can Be Sued as a Criminal Enterprise, He Rules. The Decision Could Triple the City's Financial Liability for Mistreatment of Citizens, Experts Say," *Los Angeles Times*, August 29, 2000, A1; and David Rosenzweig, "L.A. Seeks to Appeal Racketeering Ruling; Rampart: The City Asks Judge's Permission to Challenge His Decision That the LAPD Can Be Sued under RICO Law," *Los Angeles Times*, August 31, 2000, B3.
9. *Diaz v. Gates*, 354 F.3d 1169 (9th Cir. 2004).
10. Paul W. Hughes, "Not a Failed Experiment: *Wilson-Saucier* Sequencing and the Articulation of Constitutional Rights," *University of Colorado Law Review* 80 (2009): 401–30.
11. *Gregoire v. Biddle*, 177 F.2d 579 (1949).
12. *Lankford v. Gelston*, 364 F.2d 197 (4th Cir. 1966).
13. Samuel Walker, *The New World of Police Accountability* (Thousand Oaks, Calif.: Sage, 2005), 34 (internal quotation marks ignored).
14. Alison L. Patton, "Note: The Endless Cycle of Abuse: Why 42 U.S.C. § 1983 Is Ineffective in Deterring Police Brutality," *Hastings Law Journal* 44 (1993): 753–808, 766–67.
15. P. Applebome and R. Suro, "Texas Slaying: A Tale of Two Counties," *New York Times*, May 11, 1990. In 1990, a local jury in Tyler, Texas, convicted three white police officers of the killing of Loyal Garner Jr., an African-American man with no prior criminal history, while he was held in jail for alleged drunk driving.
16. Jan Hoffman, "Police Reformer Draws on His Experience," *New York Times*, February 24, 2000; Somini Sengupta, "The Diallo Case: The Jurors; 2 Jurors Defend Diallo Acquittal," *New York Times*, February 27, 2000; and Winnie Hu, "The Diallo Case: The Deliberations; When Case Was Weighed,

Prosecution Was Wanting, Juror Says," *New York Times*, February 28, 2000.

17. M. Zalman and M. Gates, "Rethinking Venue in Light of the 'Rodney King' Case: An Interest Analysis," *Cleveland State Law Review* 41, no. 2 (1993): 215–77.

18. J. Wilson, "Ex-Cops Get Prison, Budzyn, Nevers Are Remorseful over Death," *Detroit Free Press*, October 13, 1993.

19. Robyn Meredith, "Jurors Acquit White Officer in the Death of Black Driver," *New York Times*, November 14, 1996.

20. Anemona Hartocollis, "Officer Guilty of Negligence in '03 Killing," *New York Times*, October 22, 2005.

21. William K. Rashbaum, "A Reversal on Oversight of the Police," *New York Times*, July 7, 2000.

22. Joseph P. Fried, "Volpe Sentenced to a 30-Year Term in Louima Torture," *New York Times*, December 14, 1999.

23. William Bratton and Peter Knobler, *Turnaround: How America's Top Cop Reversed the Crime Epidemic* (New York: Random House, 1998), 241–44.

24. Samuel Walker, *Police Accountability: The Role of Citizen Oversight* (Belmont, Calif: Wadsworth, 2001).

25. Suggested in Whitebread and Slobogin, *Criminal Procedure*, 65.

26. Jerome H. Skolnick and James J. Fyfe, *Above the Law: Police and the Excessive Use of Force* (New York: Free Press, 1993), 243–45.

27. Skolnick and Fyfe, *Above the Law*, 255–57.

28. D. Johnston, "Reno Tightening Rules on Use of Lethal Force by Federal Agents," *New York Times*, October 18, 1995.

29. M. Newman, "Training for Trust; A Course for Police Recruits Examines How They Judge and Are Judged," *Pittsburgh Post-Gazette*, April 10, 1996.

30. Editorial, "Higher Standards for Police Recruits," *New York Times*, November 28, 1995.

31. J. McKinnon, "Police Add Japanese Martial Art to Skills," *Pittsburgh Post-Gazette*, January 23, 1996.

32. Christopher Slobogin, "Why Liberals Should Chuck the Exclusionary Rule," *University of Illinois Law Review* 1999 (1999): 363–446, 405–6.

33. See generally, Walker, *The New World of Police Accountability*; Debra Livingston, "Police Reform and the Department of Justice: An Essay on Accountability," *Buffalo Criminal Law Review* 2 (1999): 815–57; Samuel Walker and Morgan Macdonald, "An Alternative Remedy for Police Misconduct: A Model State 'Pattern or Practice' Statute," *George Mason University Civil Rights Law Journal* 19 (2009): 479–552.

34. Walker & Macdonald, 484.

35. M. L. Elrick and Ben Schmitt, "U.S. Plans to Oversee Detroit Cops; Costly Changes May Be Required," *Detroit Free Press*, June 11, 2003; David Shepardson and Darren A. Nichols, "Detroit Cop Reform Launched; Federal Watchdog Takes over Today, Says Five-Year Oversight Plan Will Top $6 Million," *Detroit News*, July 23, 2003; and Eugene Kim, "Note: Vindicating Civil Rights under 42 U.S.C. 14141: Guidance from Procedures in Complex Litigation," *Hastings Constitutional Law Quarterly* 29 (2002): 767–805.

36. Walker and Macdonald, 502.

37. Ibid.

38. Walker and Macdonald, 503.

39. Daniel González, "Feds investigate Arpaio," *Arizona Republic* (Phoenix), March 11, 2009.

40. Tim Rutten, "Change Has Come to the LAPD Too," *Los Angeles Times*, January 21, 2009.

41. Livingston, "Police Reform," 826.

42. Walker and Macdonald, 508.

43. Livingston, "Police Reform," 846–48.

44. Walker and Macdonald, 527–30.

45. Walker and Macdonald, 533–34.

46. Walker and Macdonald, 536–51.

47. William J. Cuddihy, "The Fourth Amendment: Origins and Meaning, 602–1791" (unpublished doctoral dissertation, Claremont Graduate School, 1990), c.

48. Levy, *Original Intent*, 224.

49. Leonard W. Levy, *Original Intent and the Framers' Constitution* (New York: Macmillan, 1988), 226.

50. Levy, *Original Intent*, 222–29; and Catherine Drinker Bowen, *John Adams and the American Revolution* (New York: Grosset and Dunlap, 1950), 208–19. See also Cuddihy, "Fourth Amendment," 757–825; and M. H. Smith, *The Writs of Assistance Case* (Berkeley: University of California Press, 1978).

51. Levy, *Original Intent*, 229.

52. Levy, *Original Intent*, 231.

53. 95 Eng. Rep. 807. See C. Stephenson and F. Marcham, *Sources of English Constitutional History* (New York: Harper, 1937), 705–10.

54. C. R. Lovell, *English Constitutional and Legal History* (New York: Oxford University Press, 1962), 454.

55. Cuddihy, "Fourth Amendment," 1231–1358; and Thomas Y. Davies, "Recovering the Original Fourth Amendment," *Michigan Law Review* 98, no. 3 (1999): 547–750 , 668–93.

56. Davies, "Recovering the Original Fourth Amendment," 557–60.

57. Akhil Reed Amar, *The Constitution and Criminal Procedure: First Principles* (New Haven, Conn.: Yale University Press, 1997), 1–45. Professor Amar's scholarship is refuted in detail by Professor Davies, "Recovering the Original Fourth Amendment."

58. Gerard V. Bradley, "The Constitutional Theory of the Fourth Amendment," *DePaul Law Review* 38, no. 4 (1989): 817–72; and Davies, "Recovering the Original Fourth Amendment."

59. Davies, "Recovering the Original Fourth Amendment," 577.

60. Davies, "Recovering the Original Fourth Amendment," 578, 620–29, 632–34, 660–64.

61. *Planned Parenthood v. Casey* (1992); and *Dickerson v. United States* (2000).

62. Bernard Schwartz, *The Great Rights of Mankind: A History of the American Bill of Rights* (Madison, Wis.: Madison House, 1992) 162–68.

63. Heffernan, "Foreword," 812.

64. Beermann, Jack M., "The Supreme Common Law Court of the United States," *Boston University Public Interest Law Journal* 18 (2008): 119–170, 134.

65. *Payton v. Rush*, 184 F.3d 623, 628 (7th Cir. 1999) (emphasis added).

66. *Payton v Rush*, 184 F.3d at 624; *United States v. Hoffman*, 498 F.2d 879, 881–82 (7th Cir. 1974).

67. *Payton v. Rush*, 184 F.3d at 628, citing district court cases.

68. *Romanski v. Detroit Entertainment, L.L.C.*, 265 F. Supp.2d 835 (E.D. Mich. 2003).

69. John M. Burkoff, "Not So Private Searches and the Constitution," *Cornell Law Review* 66 (1981): 627; and Lynn M. Gagel, "Comment: Stealthy Encroachments upon the Fourth Amendment: Constitutional Constraints and Their Applicability to the Long Arm of Ohio's Private Security Forces," *University of Cincinnati Law Review* 63 (1995): 1807–50.

70. David A. Sklansky, "The Private Police," *UCLA Law Review* 46 (1999): 1165–1287; and Elizabeth E. Joh, "Conceptualizing the Private Police," *Utah Law Review* (2005): 573–617.

71. The case was brought to my attention by Heffernan, "Foreword," 838–40.

72. *Wolf v. People*, 117 Colo. 279, 187 P.2d 926 (1947).

73. *People v. Cahan*, 44 Cal.2d 434, 282 P.2d 905 (1955).

74. *Elkins v. United States* (1960), 218.

75. Carolyn N. Long, Mapp v. Ohio: *Guarding against Unreasonable Searches and Seizures* (Lawrence: University Press of Kansas, 2006).

76. Justice Burger's thinking is examined in M. Braswell and J. Scheb II, "Conservative Pragmatism versus Liberal Principles: Warren E. Burger on the Suppression of Evidence, 1956–86," *Creighton Law Review* 20 (1987): 789–831.

77. Bess Chiu, Lynly Egyes, Peter L. Markowitz, and Jaya Vasandani (2009). *Constitution on Ice: A Report on Immigration Home Raid Operations* (New York: Cardozo Immigration Justice Clinic).

78. Potter Stewart, "The Road to *Mapp v. Ohio* and Beyond: The Origins, Development and Future of the Exclusionary Rule in Search-and-Seizure Cases," *Columbia Law Review* 83 (1983): 1365–1404, 1389.

79. Charles H. Whitebread and Christopher Slobogin, *Criminal Procedure: An Analysis of Cases and Concepts*, 4th ed. (New York: Foundation Press, 2000), 33–34.

80. Innocence Project, http://www.innocenceproject.org/Content/186.php (accessed July 16, 2009); Calvin C., Johnson, Jr., with Greg Hampikian, *Exit to Freedom* (Athens: University of Georgia Press, 2003).

81. Heffernan, "Foreword," 859.

82. Slobogin, "Why Liberals Should Chuck the Exclusionary Rule," 435–36.

83. Slobogin, "Why Liberals Should Chuck the Exclusionary Rule," 376, n. 40.

84. Lawrence Crocker, "Can the Exclusionary Rule Be Saved?" *Journal of Criminal Law and Criminology* 84 (1993): 310–51, 329. Crocker provides a refined explanation of why *U.S. v. Payner* (1980) necessarily implied a Fourth Amendment basis for the exclusionary rule, despite the fact that Justice Scalia suggested that *Weeks* (1914) was an exercise of the Court's supervisory authority in *United States v. Williams* (1992); see Crocker, 328–31.

85. See Slobogin, "Why Liberals Should Chuck the Exclusionary Rule," 425–27.

86. Slobogin, "Why Liberals Should Chuck the Exclusionary Rule," 427.

87. Federal Rules of Criminal Procedure 41(e). Heffernan notes that several lower courts in the 1920s did return contraband, but the issue never reached the Supreme Court ("Foreword," 813).

88. Slobogin, "Why Liberals Should Chuck the Exclusionary Rule," 436–41; Heffernan, "Foreword," 815–17.

89. Slobogin, "Why Liberals Should Chuck the Exclusionary Rule," citing *U.S. v. Havens* (1980) and *U.S. v. Janis* (1976).

90. Slobogin, "Why Liberals Should Chuck the Exclusionary Rule," 430–33.

91. Heffernan, "Foreword," 832–40, 848–60, quote at 840.

92. Heffernan, "Foreword," 837.

93. Heffernan, "Foreword," 838.

94. Slobogin, "Why Liberals Should Chuck the Exclusionary Rule," 372–76.

95. Slobogin, "Why Liberals Should Chuck the Exclusionary Rule," 378–79.

96. Thomas Davies, "A Hard Look at What We Know (and Still Need to Learn) about the 'Costs' of the Exclusionary Rule: The NIJ Study and Other Studies of 'Lost' Arrests," *American Bar Foundation Research Journal* 1983 (1983): 611–90, 626.

97. Dallin Oaks, "Studying the Exclusionary Rule in Search and Seizure," *University of Chicago Law Review* 37 (1970): 665.

98. Davies, "A Hard Look," 628.

99. This criticism is raised by Donald Horowitz, who is generally not an advocate of an activist judiciary. See D. Horowitz, *The Courts and Social Policy* (Washington, D.C.: Brookings Institution, 1977), 224–25.

100. Davies, "A Hard Look."

101. Davies, "A Hard Look," 619.

102. For example, D. Oaks, "Studying the Exclusionary Rule in Search and Seizure," *University of Chicago Law Review* 37 (1970): 665; and J. Spiotto, "Search and Seizure: An Empirical Study of the Exclusionary Rule and Its Alternatives," *Journal of Legal Studies* 2 (1973): 243. These were sharply criticized by Davies, "A Hard Look," 627–28.

103. Davies, "A Hard Look," 630.

104. Bradley C. Canon, "Testing the Effectiveness of Civil Liberties Policies at the State and Federal Levels: The Case of the Exclusionary Rule," *American Politics Quarterly* 5, no. 1 (1977): 57–82.

105. Canon, "Testing the Effectiveness," 71.

106. H. R. Uviller, *Tempered Zeal* (Chicago: Contemporary Books, 1988), 131.

107. *Illinois v. Gates* (1983), 257.

108. National Institute of Justice, *The Effects of the Exclusionary Rule: A Study in California* (Washington, D.C.: U.S. Dept. of Justice, 1982).

109. B. Forst, J. Lucianovic, and S. Cox, *What Happens after Arrest: A Court Perspective of Police Operations in the District of Columbia* (Washington, D.C.: U.S. Dept. of Justice, Law Enforcement Assistance Administration, 1977).

110. K. Brosi, *A Cross City Comparison of Felony Case Processing* (Washington, D.C.: U.S. Dept. of Justice, Law Enforcement Assistance Administration, 1979).

111. B. Forst et al., *Arrest Convictability as a Measure of Police Performance* (Washington, D.C.: U.S. Dept. of Justice, National Institute of Justice, 1982).

112. Report of the Comptroller General of the United States, *Impact of the Exclusionary Rule on Federal Criminal Prosecutions* (Washington, D.C.: U.S. General Accounting Office, 1979).

113. P. Nardulli, "The Societal Cost of the Exclusionary Rule: An Empirical Assessment," *American Bar Foundation Research Journal* 1983 (1983): 585–609.

114. F. Feeney, F. Dill, and A. Weir, *Arrests without Conviction: How Often They Occur and Why* (Washington, D.C.: U.S. Dept. of Justice, National Institute of Justice, 1983).

115. Craig D. Uchida and Timothy S. Bynum, "Search Warrants, Motions to Suppress and 'Lost Cases': The Effects of the Exclusionary Rule in Seven Jurisdictions," *Journal of Criminal Law and Criminology* 81, no. 4 (1991): 1034–66.

116. Davies, "A Hard Look," 679 (emphasis in original).

117. Uchida and Bynum, 1065, quoting from R. Van Duizend, L. Sutton, and C. Carter, *The Search Warrant Process: Preconceptions, Perceptions, and Practices* (National Center for State Courts, 1985), 106.

118. Pillard, "Taking Fiction Seriously," 65–105, 69, 66 (footnotes excluded).

119. Patton, "The Endless Cycle," 753–808, 755–67. See John L. Burris, *Black vs. Blue* (New York: St. Martin's Press, 1999).

120. Patton, "The Endless Cycle," 767–79.

121. Canon, "Testing the Effectiveness,"

122. Patton, "The Endless Cycle," 780–90, drawing heavily on the Christopher Commission Report, issued after the Los Angeles riots following the Rodney King beating case.

JUSTICES OF THE SUPREME COURT

The Adversaries: Black and Frankfurter

It is ironic that two New Deal liberals appointed by President Franklin Roosevelt came to be bitter foes on the Supreme Court. For many years, Justices Hugo Black and Felix Frankfurter clashed over vital issues, including the incorporation of the Bill of Rights, the extent to which speech could be regulated by the government, and whether the Supreme Court should intervene to equalize the voting representation of electoral districts. In the 1940s and 1950s, Justice Frankfurter usually had the upper hand as the intellectual leader of the conservative wing of the Court. But over time, Black's dogged pursuit of a more liberal agenda bore fruit, preventing Frankfurter from imposing his views on the entire Court.

Both justices championed democracy, yet each took a different approach to modern government and the Court's role in it. Their disagreements, based on deeply held philosophies of judging, became a matter of personal antagonism. On the question of incorporation, Justice Black was motivated by a strong belief that the Supreme Court must adhere as closely as possible to the strict meaning of the Constitution and should not use the Due Process Clause to insert its notion of what is "reasonable" into constitutional law. He recalled that a conservative Supreme Court had done this very thing prior to the New Deal, and he understood that unfettered power allowed courts to be as unjust as the legislative or executive branches. Out of this emerged the idea that the Supreme Court had to apply the Bill of Rights totally and literally to the states. Justice Frankfurter, although a great proponent of the philosophy of judicial restraint, came to opposite conclusions. He believed not only that the justices ought to fill out the contours of the Due Process Clause in order to achieve fundamental fairness in criminal procedure, but also that the Fourteenth Amendment was not intended to incorporate the Bill of Rights.

Hugo LaFayette Black

Alabama, 1886–1971

Democrat

Appointed by Franklin Delano Roosevelt

Years of Service: 1937–1971

Life and Career.　The son of a country storekeeper, Black received a law degree from the University of Alabama. He practiced law in Birmingham, representing poor people, white and black, in civil cases against large corporations and in criminal matters. He also served terms as a district attorney and as a city judge, where he tried to mitigate the harsh treatment of poor people. Active in politics, he was elected to the U.S. Senate in 1926 as a populist. He was a key supporter of President Roosevelt's New Deal program, backed the "court-packing" legislation to increase the size of the Supreme Court, and was Roosevelt's first choice to fill a vacancy on the Court.

Collection of the Supreme Court of the United States. Photographer: Harris and Ewing.

Contribution to Criminal Procedure.　Justice Black was the chief architect of modern constitutional criminal procedure. His foremost contribution was to champion the incorporation doctrine, picking up the mantle of the first Justice Harlan and ultimately getting the Court to agree in the 1960s that the criminal provisions of the Bill of Rights should apply to the states as a matter of Fourteenth Amendment due process. He also wrote powerful opinions against coerced confessions and took the lead in formulating the doctrine that an attorney was an absolute requirement in all criminal cases.

Signature Opinion.　*Gideon v. Wainwright* (1963). In 1942, Justice Black dissented in *Betts v. Brady*, which held that a state felony trial in which an indigent had to defend himself or herself was fair under the Due Process Clause. He strongly believed that a fair trial is impossible without a defense attorney and that if a person cannot afford a lawyer, the government must provide one without cost. Prior to *Betts*, he wrote the majority opinion in *Johnson v. Zerbst* (1938), which held that in a federal felony prosecution, the assistance of counsel is essential unless the defendant knowingly and intelligently waives counsel. His persistence in pursuing this goal succeeded in *Gideon*, where the Court incorporated the Sixth Amendment right to counsel into the Fourteenth Amendment, thus requiring the states to provide counsel for indigent defendants.

Assessment.　Justice Black is widely recognized as one of the greatest justices, an intellectual leader of the Warren Court, and the single greatest influence on the development of modern constitutional criminal procedure. In other constitutional areas, he led the Court, along with Justice Douglas, toward an "absolutist" vision of First Amendment free speech, and he spearheaded the move to require states to reapportion voting districts to equalize the voting power of voters in different districts.

Although many of the positions he supported defined a "liberal" policy agenda, he was not as liberal in judicial philosophy as were other Roosevelt appointees, such as Justices Douglas, Murphy, and Rutledge. Rather, his judicial philosophy may be better described as "strict constructionist" or "constitutional fundamentalist." He believed that the Court should strictly adhere to the terms of the Constitution, which he tended to define rather narrowly.

Thus even in the incorporation area, he maintained an independent stance. He did not vote for the incorporation of the Fourth Amendment exclusionary rule in *Wolf v. Colorado* (1949) because the rule was not stated explicitly in the Constitution. He later developed the perspective that the exclusionary rule could be incorporated only if it were seen as also protecting Fifth Amendment values against self-incrimination.

Further Reading

Gerald T. Dunne, *Hugo Black and the Judicial Revolution* (New York: Simon and Schuster, 1977).

Felix Frankfurter

Massachusetts, 1882–1965

Independent

Appointed by Franklin Delano Roosevelt

Years of Service: 1939–1962

Collection of the Supreme
Court of the United States.
Photographer: Pach
Brothers Studio.

Life and Career.   Frankfurter emigrated to America with his family from Vienna at the age of twelve and grew up in the Lower East Side Jewish ghetto in New York City. He graduated from the City College of New York and attended Harvard Law School, becoming editor of the *Harvard Law Review* on the basis of his top grades. After graduating in 1906, he worked in a large law firm for a while but soon chose a public service career. As a protégé of Henry L. Stimson, a leading Progressive, he went to Washington in 1911 when Stimson became secretary of war, forming an intellectual circle of young lawyers who befriended Justice Holmes.

In 1914, Frankfurter was appointed to the Harvard Law School faculty, a position he held until his appointment to the Court. During his tenure, he became a nationally known liberal activist who served as a labor mediator during World War I, attended the Paris Peace Conference in 1919, represented Zionist interests, cofounded the American Civil Liberties Union, contributed to the *New Republic* magazine, spoke out for the convicted anarchists Sacco and Vanzetti, and provided free counsel for the National Consumers' League. His coauthored book, *The Labor Injunction*, attacked the federal courts for stifling the labor movement. He was the codirector in 1921 of the groundbreaking Cleveland Crime Survey, a multidisciplinary social scientific study of the administration of justice. He appeared frequently before the Supreme Court on behalf of unions and other progressive causes.

As a Harvard professor, he developed a following among his students as a result of his passion for academic excellence and his zeal for public service. He had a close rapport with several Supreme Court justices and selected law clerks from among his students for Justices Oliver Wendell Holmes and Louis Brandeis. During the New Deal, he became an important advisor to President Roosevelt and placed many of his former students in important administrative and policy-shaping positions, thus enhancing his influence.

Contribution to Criminal Procedure.   Justice Frankfurter's liberal policy temperament clashed with his philosophy of judicial restraint. As a result, his positions in criminal procedure were inconsistent but must generally be counted as conservative. For example, he staunchly opposed the total incorporation of the Bill of Rights championed by Justice Black and favored by the liberal wing of the Court; he voted for the rule that a judge's comment on a defendant's silence does not undermine the privilege against self-incrimination; he opposed the extension of the right to counsel to all defendants in state cases; and he characterized the Fourth Amendment exclusionary rule as a mere remedy and not a constitutional rule. Nevertheless, he was sharply critical of abuses of power by the police, and when interpreting the flexible Due Process Clause, he ruled in favor of defendants in cases involving coerced confessions and search and seizures that "shocked the conscience." In the entrapment area, he favored the objective test.

Signature Opinion.   *Rochin v. California* (1952). The "stomach pump" case perfectly expressed Justice Frankfurter's judicial philosophy of restraint and respect for the authority of the states, except where the actions of local police or state courts have so grossly violated a person's right to fair treatment that a judge could exercise judgment to deem the actions as violations of due process. In these instances, Frankfurter's standard was that due process is violated where police action "shocks the conscience." He trusted the wisdom of courts to determine what shocks the conscience, and he somehow believed that such judgment would be objective and not simply private notions of what is acceptable. Justices Black and Douglas dissented in *Rochin*, arguing that this vague standard gave judges too much power.

Assessment.   Justice Frankfurter was a giant of American constitutional law as a scholar, a public servant, and a justice. He was expected to be a leading liberal on the Court, but his judicial philosophy of restraint overcame his liberal instincts. As the Court's agenda swung from economic issues to civil liberties, he failed to sense the direction of the country and the Court's special role as a guardian of liberty. Thus he adopted cramped positions in many free speech cases and ruled against finding that seriously imbalanced state electoral districts violated the Equal Protection Clause. In supporting the school desegregation case, Frankfurter played a leading liberal role, but thereafter he took a more cautious approach than did other justices. His conservative views were generally repudiated by the liberal Warren Court, although some of his rulings, including the shocks the conscience test, have been relied on by today's far more conservative Court.

Further Reading

Melvin I. Urofsky, *Felix Frankfurter: Judicial Restraint and Individual Liberties* (Boston: Twayne, 1991).

CHAPTER 3

Essential Fourth Amendment Doctrines

Power is a heady thing; and history shows that the police acting on their own cannot be trusted. And so the Constitution requires a magistrate to pass on the desires of the police before they violate the privacy of the home.

—JUSTICE WILLIAM O. DOUGLAS, *McDonald v. United States*, 335 U.S. 451, 456 (1948)

CHAPTER OUTLINE

KEY TERMS

anticipatory warrant
beeper
consent search
constitutionally protected
    area
controlled delivery
curtilage
enhancement device

exigency
ex parte
expectation of privacy
industrial curtilage
inventory and return
"knock and announce" rule
magistrate
media ride-along

neutral and detached
    magistrate
no-knock warrant
open fields
plain feel rule
plain view
plurality opinion
probable cause

reasonable suspicion
secret informant
"sneak and peek" warrant
telephonic warrant
thermal imaging
two-pronged test
undercover agent

This chapter presents five basic areas of Fourth Amendment law: (1) the search warrant, (2) the **'expectation of privacy'** doctrine, (3) probable cause, (4) the plain view doctrine, and (5) consent searches. Although in practice most searches are conducted without a warrant (i.e., are "warrantless"), the Fourth Amendment presumes that judicial search warrants are essential for preserving the privacy protections of the people. The expectation of privacy doctrine, established in 1967, is now the theoretical backbone of Fourth Amendment analysis. **Probable cause,** the level of evidence required by the Constitution before government agents can invade individual privacy, is the required basis for arrests and searches and seizures. Plain view is a concept that helps us understand when the Fourth Amendment applies and when it does not. Individuals may voluntarily waive their Fourth Amendment protections, making the consent doctrine a highly practical aspect of police work, by eliminating the need for police to follow Fourth Amendment strictures.

THE SEARCH WARRANT

Search Warrant Values: A Neutral and Detached Magistrate

A prime function of the Constitution is to protect individuals' liberty and rights from excessive government and law enforcement control. Requiring *executive branch* officers to get permission from *judicial* officers, via search warrants, is a principal method of keeping the government under control.

> The presence of a search warrant serves a high function. Absent some grave emergency, the Fourth Amendment has interposed a **magistrate** between the citizen and the police. This was done not to shield criminals nor to make the home a safe haven for illegal activities. It was done so that an objective mind might weigh the need to invade that privacy in order to enforce the law. The right of privacy was deemed too precious to entrust to the discretion of those whose job is the detection of crime and the arrest of criminals. (*McDonald v. United States,* 1948)

These values are embodied in the Fourth Amendment's traditional *'warrant-preference construction'* (see Chapter 2), under which search and seizures are presumed unreasonable unless authorized by a judicial warrant, except for a few well-established exceptions.

The Supreme Court has expressed a *preference* for search warrants and has encouraged police use of warrants by easing strict probable cause requirements for warrants in close cases. The issue in **United States v. Ventresca** (1965), for example, was whether hearsay was sufficient to establish probable cause and support a warrant to search a house for an illegal liquor distillery. The Court made clear it would lean in favor of upholding searches in *close cases*, where warrants are obtained: "A grudging or negative attitude by reviewing courts toward warrants will tend to discourage police officers from submitting their evidence to a judicial officer before acting." Of course, this does not mean that a magistrate must automatically grant a warrant simply on request (*Ventresca*).

Three factors support the search warrant preference: the long *history* of warrant use, the Fourth Amendment's *text*, and the *values* that underlie the amendment. The values protected are highly prized by Americans: personal autonomy, privacy, security, and freedom. The amendment protects these values via *procedures* that place the decision whether to invade a person's liberties for law enforcement purposes in the hands of *judges*. The rationale was best expressed by Justice Robert Jackson:

> The point of the Fourth Amendment, which often is not grasped by zealous officers, is not that it denies law enforcement the support of the usual inferences which reasonable men draw from evidence. Its protection consists in requiring that those inferences be drawn by a **neutral and detached magistrate** instead of being judged by the officer engaged in the often competitive enterprise of ferreting out crime. Any assumption that evidence sufficient to support a magistrate's disinterested determination to issue a search warrant will justify the officers in making a search without a warrant would reduce the Amendment to a nullity and leave the people's homes secure only in the discretion of police officers. (*Johnson v. United States,* 1948)

In *Johnson*, an experienced federal narcotics officer standing in a hotel corridor smelled burning opium coming from behind a closed door. He demanded entry into the hotel room and found one person inside in possession of opium. The Court noted, "At the time entry was demanded the officers were possessed of evidence which a magistrate might have found to be probable cause for issuing a search warrant." The evidence was nevertheless *excluded* because the officer invaded Anne Johnson's room without first submitting his evidence to the judgment of a judicial officer.

Judges are not given priority in ascertaining probable cause because of any belief of greater intelligence or expertise than police officers, or simply because warrant use is traditional. The policy is wrapped up in Justice Jackson's memorable phrase "a neutral and detached magistrate." The point is that the magistrate is part of the judicial branch, *detached* from "the government" (i.e., the executive branch) and therefore not part of the apparatus that seeks to prosecute the suspect. Further, the judge is *neutral* in the case. The officer is a partisan who is "engaged in the often competitive enterprise of ferreting out crime." Because the officer is a partisan, he or she is prone to judge a case in his or her own favor and thus find that probable cause exists. This does not mean that the officer is dishonest; but human nature is such that a partisan almost always sees things his or her way. The judge is formally neutral—an arbiter between the police and prosecution on the one side, and the defendant on the other. It is because the magistrate is neutral that he or she is more likely to exercise balanced judgment.

The Supreme Court has decided several revealing cases that determined whether the actions of magistrates or other government officers rose to the standards of a "neutral and detached magistrate." In *Coolidge v. New Hampshire* (1971), the state attorney general, an executive branch officer, personally took charge of a murder investigation. An archaic statute made him a justice of the peace, and as such, he issued a search warrant to *himself*! Over the dissents of three justices, who viewed this action as "harmless error," the Supreme Court ruled that it violated the fundamental Fourth Amendment premise that warrants must issue from a neutral and detached magistrate. Although the statute called the attorney general a "justice of the peace," in fact he was not a "detached" judicial officer but was the chief investigator and *prosecutor* in the case.

Shadwick v. City of Tampa (1972) shows that a formal title is less important than the actual situation of the officer issuing a warrant. Here, law and practice allowed a municipal *court clerk* to issue *arrest* warrants for municipal ordinance violations. This was upheld because the clerk met two tests: (1) he was *capable* of determining whether probable cause existed as to ordinance violations, such as impaired driving or breach of the peace, and (2) he was neutral and detached—he was not under the authority of the prosecutor or police but worked in the *judicial* branch, subject to the supervision of the municipal court judge. Thus, under limited circumstances, a valid warrant can be issued by a person who is not a lawyer or a judge.

A magistrate is *not* neutral or detached if he receives a *fee*, even a small one, for each warrant that is issued, instead of a salary. In *Connally v. Georgia* (1977), the magistrate received five dollars for each search warrant issued but nothing if a warrant was denied. The *possibility* of personal financial gain is sufficient to violate a suspect's due process and Fourth Amendment rights, whatever the magistrate's subjective disposition. In addition, a magistrate's *actions* can cause the loss of neutrality in a specific case. This occurred in *Lo-Ji Sales, Inc. v. New York* (1979). An overly helpful town justice, rather than simply issuing a search warrant for the seizure of films from an adult bookstore, joined police officers and prosecutors on a six-hour raid of the store, determining *at the scene* whether there was probable cause to seize various materials. In determining that the warrant was improper, a unanimous Court said, "The Town Justice did not manifest that neutrality and detachment demanded of a judicial officer when presented with a warrant application for a search and seizure." This loss of "detachment" was not, according to the Court, a matter of subjective intent but was inferred from the *objective* fact that the town justice "allowed himself to become a member, if not the leader, of the search party which was essentially a police operation." Yet despite the objective nature of the rule, it is easy to imagine that a judge who works too closely with the prosecutors will subjectively come to see himself as a member of the "prosecution team" rather than as a neutral and detached magistrate in a subjective sense.

The neutral and detached magistrate principle led the Supreme Court to invalidate a portion of the 1968 electronic eavesdropping law that allowed the *president* of the United States to *authorize* electronic eavesdropping for a "national security" purpose without a warrant (*United States v. United States District Court,* 1972). The Court ruled that even if the president was exempt from the particular procedural requirements of the rest of the electronic eavesdropping statute, he was still required to seek "judicial approval prior to initiation of a search or surveillance" under the Fourth Amendment. The Court reasoned that dangers to free speech and political liberty are too great in national security cases to entrust exclusively to the executive branch, and that national security would not be compromised by requiring the president to seek prior judicial approval for electronic eavesdropping. Since 1978, under the Foreign Intelligence Surveillance Act (FISA), warrants for electronic eavesdropping for national security purposes are issued by a special court drawn for each case from among sitting federal judges.[1] This formerly obscure function came under great scrutiny after national security electronic eavesdropping was massively abused by the Bush administration in the 2000s.[2]

There are costs to the warrant process. Obtaining a search warrant from a judge is *less efficient* than allowing police to decide for themselves to enter a home on their assessment of probable cause. This may add a cost to *public safety*—a cost that the Framers felt was necessary to maintain liberty, exhibiting a consciousness of the Due Process Model. Skeptics question whether the warrant practice, in fact, adds that much protection. In high-publicity cases, public pressure can cause a magistrate to blunder. This happened when Judge Kathleen Kennedy-Powell ruled that Los Angeles Police detectives Mark Fuhrman and Philip Vannatter were justified in vaulting over the wall of O. J. Simpson's estate in the early morning hours of June 13, 1994, without a search warrant because they claimed that they feared for his safety.[3] This was a patently weak reason because ex-husbands are typically prime suspects in spouse killings, and Fuhrman had been called to the Simpson residence earlier to investigate a wife beating. As lawyer–novelist Scott Turow noted, "If veteran police detectives did not arrive at the gate of Mr. Simpson's home thinking he might have committed these murders, then they should have been fired."[4] Ironically, Judge Kennedy-Powell's case-saving ruling backfired. When Fuhrman's perjurious, racist statements later came out, the jury might have also questioned his truthfulness about the entry and search of Simpson's home and grounds.

To add to the skepticism, there is some concern that magistrates tend to *rubber-stamp* warrant requests. Despite all this, the late Professor Richard Uviller, after observing police for a year, reflected on the value of search warrants:

> It's easy to say that the whole routine is a sham: magistrates are not actually neutral or detached but just as closely associated with the prosecution as the cops; they don't really read the affidavits, many of those exercising the authority would not know the difference between probable cause and potato chips, much less the complexities of the law regarding the reliability of third-party informants who supply the hearsay on which the cop's belief may be founded.
>
> However much truth there may be in such assertions, it has always seemed to me that the real values of the search warrant procedure are: (1) It makes the officer pause in his pursuit and reflect on whether he has a good reason to go into someone's private space; (2) it requires him to make a record of his reasons, recording what he knows about the case before he makes the move; and (3) his recorded reasons stand immutably for review by a knowledgeable judge after the fact, at trial, and again on appeal, if the search is challenged. In the enforced hesitation, recorded articulation, and prospect of true review, the objectives of the Fourth Amendment are well served.[5]

These comments remind us that the warrant procedure still requires police and prosecutors to fairly evaluate the facts and make their own probable cause decisions before applying for a warrant.

Obtaining a Search Warrant

The Fourth Amendment states that "no Warrants shall issue, but upon probable cause, supported by Oath or affirmation." To obtain a search warrant, law enforcement officers must (1) *present a written affidavit* to a magistrate requesting that a warrant be issued (see the example), (2) *swear under oath* that the information in the affidavit is truthful, and (3) convince the magistrate that the information they have sworn to *establishes probable cause* to believe that the warrant is justified. The magistrate should question the officer requesting the warrant about the circumstances of the case and must be personally satisfied that the evidence constitutes probable cause. The oath signifies that the officer takes responsibility for the facts alleged.[6]

The affidavit, or sworn statement, is presented to the court at an *ex parte* hearing—that is, a hearing with only one party present. Such a procedure would normally violate due process but is allowed out of necessity and is hemmed in with other safeguards, such as the **inventory and return,** which requires the officer to report on the execution of the warrant. The magistrate usually questions only the affiant but may require additional witnesses to testify before being satisfied that there is sufficient evidence to issue a warrant. The law enforcement agency applying for a warrant should keep all evidence and records of its application; if the warrant is challenged, the loss of such information would weigh heavily against the agency. Also, if a jurisdiction allows the agency to make a new warrant application to a different magistrate if an initial request is turned down, then the evidence submitted in the first application must be submitted in the second application.

The *classes of evidence* that may be searched and seized under a warrant are spelled out in the Federal Rules of Criminal Procedure: "A warrant may be issued for any of the following (1) *evidence* of a crime; (2) *contraband*, fruits of crime, or other items illegally possessed; (3) *property* designed for use, intended for use, or used in committing a crime; or (4) a *person* to be arrested or a person who is unlawfully restrained." (F.R.C.P. Rule 41(c), 2006, emphasis added).

The typical affidavit and warrant for a search need not be lengthy; they are often only one or two pages long. It is essential that the affidavit provide sufficient information to establish probable cause and that the warrant give clear directions to the executing officers. In some jurisdictions, a warrant is issued without attaching the affidavit; in others, the warrant incorporates the affidavit. This is the practice in Detroit, Michigan, which supplied the sample warrant and affidavit (with names and identifying information changed) as an example of what is required to establish probable cause.

TELEPHONIC WARRANTS   With laptop computers in police cars and officers armed with smart phones and personal digital assistants (PDAs), it is now possible for officers to obtain search warrants from the field in less than an hour, regardless of the distance from the crime site to the courthouse.[7] California first enacted legislation to allow **telephonic warrants** in 1970, and nineteen states and the federal government now authorize oral search warrants.[8]

Under F.R.C.P. Rule 41(d)(3), a federal magistrate may issue a warrant "based on information communicated by telephone or other appropriate means, including facsimile transmission." The officer requesting the warrant is placed under oath and a record of the conversation providing the warrant information is made, signed by the magistrate, and filed with the court clerk.

Example of a Warrant and Affidavit

State of Michigan

Search Warrant and Affidavit

County of Wayne

TO THE SHERIFF OR ANY PEACE OFFICER OF SAID COUNTY: Wayne; Police Officer Phillip Melon.

Affiant, having subscribed and sworn to an affidavit for a Search Warrant, and I having under oath examined affiant, am satisfied that probable cause exists.

THEREFORE, IN THE NAME OF THE PEOPLE OF THE STATE OF MICHIGAN, I command that you search the following described place:

18793 Colorado, a one story brick building, bearing the name O'Grady's Collision, located in the City of Detroit, County of Wayne, State of Michigan, and to seize, secure, tabulate and make return according to law the following property and things:

1. A 1984 Chevrolet Nova, Blue, VIN#1FABPO758EW236587, bearing license plate #241-LUS
2. Any stolen vehicles or parts of stolen vehicles
3. Any and all other vehicles belonging to Stephen Switzerland and Warren Switzerland
4. Any repair orders, estimates or other paperwork relating to the repair of vehicles.

The following facts are sworn to by affiant in support of the issuance of this Warrant:

Affiant is a member of the Detroit Police Department, assigned to the Commercial Auto Theft Section. Affiant on January 19, 1988 and January 20, 1988 executed search warrants on this location and seized a stolen vehicle, a 1984 Chevrolet, 241-LUS. Affiant while conducting an investigation in regards to this stolen vehicle discovered that the vehicle had been falsely reported stolen in order to collect the insurance monies from Mackinac Insurance Company. On March 24, 1988, a warrant for Attempted OMUFP 0/100 (Obtaining Money under False Pretenses over $100) was obtained against Irwin Schmidlopp (Owner of the 1984 Chevrolet Nova) and for Stephen Switzerland (Owner of O'Grady's Collision). During the investigation it was discovered that persons would obtain insurance through the Mackinac Agency for vehicles that they did not own and then a claim would be submitted to the insurance company and an adjuster would arrive at O'Grady's Collision (an unlicensed motor vehicle repair facility). The insurance company would then issue a check to O'Grady's Collision and the insured party for the repair of this vehicle. One vehicle, a 1985 Oldsmobile, was repaired at least three times by O'Grady's listing three different owners when in fact, none of these alleged owners ever owned the vehicle or got into an accident with this 1985 Oldsmobile. All three checks were co-issued to O'Grady's Collision and all three checks, totaling about $15,000.00, were cashed by Stephen Switzerland through his account at First of America. Affiant on March 29, 1988, observed the 1984 Chevrolet, belonging to defendant, Irwin Schmidlopp, still inside this location. Affiant believes that estimates and bills and receipts will be found inside this location to show further schemes and frauds committed by these suspects to defraud the insurance companies.

Phillip Melon
Affiant

Subscribed and sworn to before me and issued under my hand this 30th day of *March, 1988*
Approved:

John Carter   **Jane Ellis**

Assistant Prosecuting Attorney   Judge of 36th District Court,
                                                                Wayne County, Michigan, and a Magistrate *P91234*

It appears that little use is made of telephonic warrants in the United States. "While law enforcement eagerly uses the latest technology to catch criminals, it rarely uses that technology to comply with the command of the Constitution requiring search warrants."[9] Detective Mark Fuhrman stated on cross-examination in the notorious O. J. Simpson trial that he never used telephonic warrants.[10] Failure to use telephonic warrants is especially serious because widespread use of the subjective exigent circumstances exception "is arguably the greatest threat to the continued viability of the warrant requirement"[11] Although a few courts in the 1980s excluded searches because police did not seek telephonic warrants, few do so today. Police will have no incentive to use telephonic warrants until defense attorneys press this issue in appropriate cases.

Particularity

The Fourth Amendment requires that a warrant "particularly describ[e] the place to be searched, and the persons or things to be seized." This is a substantive and not merely a formal rule. An officer making an affidavit, for example, must investigate and accurately describe the place to be searched in addition to providing a street number, because a mistake might render a search illegal. Police, planning a drug raid at a house located at the corner of Short and Adkinson Streets, incorrectly listed the place as "325 Adkinson Street" on the warrant when in fact it was 325 Short Street. The affidavit, however, described the house as a single residence with silver siding and red trim on the south side of the street. Despite the street number error, the search was held to be valid because the description met the particularity requirement. The "test for determining the sufficiency of the description of the place to be searched is whether [it] is described with sufficient particularity as to enable the executing officer to locate and identify the premises with reasonable effort, and whether there is any reasonable probability that another premise might be mistakenly searched."[12]

The Supreme Court confirmed that "reasonable" mistakes in a warrant do not violate the Fourth Amendment. In ***Maryland v. Garrison*** (1987), police obtained "a warrant to search the person of Lawrence McWebb and 'the premises known as 2036 Park Avenue third floor Apartment.'" Diligent police investigation did not reveal that there was another apartment on the third floor. When executing the warrant, police officers encountered McWebb downstairs and required him to walk up to the third floor. He opened the only apartment door, which led to a vestibule. Garrison was standing there, and doors to both Garrison's and McWebb's apartments were open. The police did not know at that time that there were two apartments. They entered Garrison's apartment and seized drugs in plain view. As soon as they were told that it was not McWebb's apartment, they left. Because the police could not have reasonably known that there were two apartments on the third floor, the Supreme Court ruled that their mistake did not invalidate an otherwise valid warrant and the seizure of drugs in Garrison's apartment. "[S]ufficient probability, not certainty, is the touchstone of reasonableness under the Fourth Amendment."

The goal of the "things to be seized" particularity requirement is that "nothing is left to the discretion of the officer executing the warrant" (*Marron v. United States*, 1927). Nonetheless, reasonable latitude is allowed. If police investigation shows that heroin is being sold from a particular location, the warrant can specify that police search for and seize "a quantity of drugs." It is important that the police investigate the situation to the greatest extent feasible and make a good faith effort to know in advance what is likely to be discovered in the place to be searched. The plain view doctrine (discussed later in this chapter) necessarily creates an expansion of what items the police may lawfully seize from a premises. Executing a valid search warrant is one of the ways in which police are legitimately in a premises; once legitimately in a place, they may seize all contraband in plain view, even if it is unrelated to the object of the search warrant.

In ***Groh v. Ramirez*** (2004), "a concerned citizen informed [Bureau of Alcohol, Tobacco and Firearms (ATF) agent Groh] that on a number of visits to [the Ramirez] ranch the visitor had seen a large stock of weaponry, including an automatic rifle, grenades, a grenade launcher, and a rocket launcher." Based on this hearsay, agent Groh prepared and signed a warrant application to search for "any automatic firearms or parts to automatic weapons, destructive devices to include but not limited to grenades, grenade launchers, rocket launchers, and any and all receipts pertaining to the purchase or manufacture of automatic weapons or explosive devices or launchers." The application was supported by a detailed affidavit and a warrant form that Agent Groh filled out. A federal magistrate signed the warrant, even though it completely "failed to identify any of the items that [Groh] intended to seize." In the place on the form "that called for a description of the 'person or property' to be seized, [Groh] typed a description of respondents' two-story blue house rather than the alleged stockpile of firearms." When he executed the warrant, only Mrs. Ramirez was home. Agent Groh apparently told her that he was looking for "an explosive device in a box."

The Supreme Court held that by failing to particularly describe the things to be seized, the warrant violated the Fourth Amendment. Despite the absence of *any* description of the things to be seized, the warrant would have been found constitutional *if* a detailed affidavit were attached or if it cross-referenced a supporting application or affidavit that accompanied the warrant. The fact that the magistrate *believed* there was probable cause to support the warrant does not cure this defect. Groh argued that the *search itself was reasonable*, and because of this, the warrant's defect should be *overlooked*. The Court rejected this: "Even though [Groh] acted with restraint in conducting the search, 'the inescapable fact is that this restraint was imposed by the agents themselves, not by a judicial officer'" (*Groh v. Ramirez*, 2004, citing *Katz v. United States*, 1967). Groh also argued that he "orally described" what he was searching for to Mrs. Ramirez, thus giving her actual notice. But the Supreme Court ruled that her version, that the agents were looking for explosives in a box, had to be believed. The problem with police officers' giving *verbal descriptions* of what they are authorized to seize is that verbal descriptions can be open-ended and vague, leaving the householder no basis to argue that a search may be going *too far*. Searches based on verbal descriptions in effect become *general searches*.

The Intersection of the First, Fourth, and Fifth Amendments

Defendants in some cases have argued that the search and seizure of documents had violated not only the Fourth Amendment but also the First and the Fifth Amendments. Searches that tread on the First Amendment are closely scrutinized because free speech is a highly valued liberty. In **Stanford v. Texas** (1965), a warrant authorized police to search Stanford's San Antonio home to seize "books, records, pamphlets, cards, receipts, lists, memoranda, pictures, recordings and other written instruments concerning the. . .operations of the Communist Party of Texas." In actions eerily reminiscent of *Entick v. Carrington* (1765), officers spent almost five hours in Stanford's home, taking more than a thousand books from his small business and his personal library, including books written by "Karl Marx, Jean Paul Sartre, Theodore Draper, Fidel Castro, Earl Browder, Pope John XXIII, and MR. JUSTICE HUGO L. BLACK." Many of Stanford's private documents and papers, "including his marriage certificate, his personal insurance policies, his household bills and receipts, and files of his personal correspondence," were seized. Ironically, no "records of the Communist Party" or any "party lists and dues payments" were found. This was a general warrant. It violated the Fourth and Fourteenth Amendments. When the things to be seized are books "and the basis of their seizure is the ideas which they contain," the First Amendment is implicated and particularity must "be accorded the most scrupulous exactitude." Noting the historic continuity between this case and the earliest days of the American republic, Justice Potter Stewart concluded by stating that "the Fourth and Fourteenth amendments guarantee to John Stanford that no official of the State shall ransack his home and seize his books and papers under the unbridled authority of a general warrant—no less than the law 200 years ago shielded John Entick from the messengers of the King."

A search warrant supported by probable cause was issued in *Andresen v. Maryland* (1976) for the seizure of business records and employees' notes in Andresen's law office related to a real estate fraud that he was alleged to have committed. Andresen challenged the introduction of these records on the ground that "the seizure of these business records, and their admission into evidence at his trial, compelled [him] to testify against himself in violation of the Fifth Amendment." The trend of modern cases is that the Fifth Amendment does not protect business records; the state does not violate a person's privilege against self-incrimination by obtaining business records by subpoena. A search warrant did not require Andresen to do or say anything and so had no element of self-incrimination. Papers could be seized like any other property as long as there was probable cause that the papers were contraband or evidence of crime. Neither the seizure of the papers nor their introduction into evidence at a trial violated the Fifth Amendment.

In *Zurcher v. Stanford Daily* (1978), a violent demonstration led to assaults on police officers. The police could not identify most perpetrators but knew that photographs of the incident were taken by the student-run *Stanford Daily* newspaper. The police obtained and executed a search warrant to seize photographs of the demonstrators. A civil suit challenged the use of a search warrant. The *Stanford Daily* argued that the police had to use a subpoena *duces tecum* instead of a warrant because it sought evidence from a third party (the newspaper) and not from the suspect, and because the First Amendment Free Press Clause requires a process that allows a newspaper to voluntarily turn over the relevant documents to prevent the police from rummaging through all of the newspaper's files.

The Court dismissed both arguments. As to the "third-party" search issue, the Court held that the "critical element in a reasonable search is not that the owner of the property is suspected of crime but that there is reasonable cause to believe that the specific 'things' to be searched for and seized are located on the property to which entry is sought." The state's interest in enforcing the criminal law and recovering evidence is the same whether the evidence is in the premises of the suspect or a third person. Allowing a third party the option and the time to decide whether to obey a subpoena would make criminal investigations more cumbersome and could undermine effective prosecution in many cases.

Arguments that police had to proceed via a subpoena when searching newspaper offices included: (1) searches would disrupt the timely publication of the news, (2) confidential sources would dry up, (3) reporters would not record and preserve their recollections for future use, (4) news processing and dissemination would be chilled by the fear that searches would disclose editorial deliberations, and (5) the press would resort to self-censorship to conceal information of potential interest to the police. The Court discounted these fears as speculative; if abuses arose, they could be dealt with in later cases. The warrant in this case was narrowly tailored to specific kinds of items that would not implicate confidential sources or interfere with editorial decisions. The Court declined to "reinterpret the Amendment to impose a general constitutional barrier against warrants to search newspaper premises."

Justice Stewart, joined by Justice Thurgood Marshall, dissented on the grounds that "police searches of newspaper offices burden the freedom of the press." Barring exigencies, "a subpoena would afford the newspaper itself an opportunity to locate whatever material might be requested and produce it." Unlike the majority's dismissal of the newspaper's arguments, Justice Stewart cited cases of intrusive police searches of news offices and felt that the ransacking of news offices, the drying up of information sources, and "unannounced police searches of newspaper offices will significantly burden the constitutionally protected function of the press to gather news and report it to the public."

Anticipatory Warrants and Controlled Deliveries

Courts since the 1980s have issued **anticipatory warrants** to police, typically involving **controlled deliveries** of contraband. This useful law enforcement tool was recognized by the Federal Rules of Criminal Procedure in 1991.[13] The Supreme Court upheld the constitutionality of anticipatory search warrants in *United States v. Grubbs* (2006). Grubbs purchased a child pornography videotape from a Web site run by an undercover postal inspector. In such cases, there may be additional child pornography on the premises. Postal inspectors applied for a warrant to search Grubbs's house. The affidavit stated that the warrant would *not* be executed *until* a person received the package and physically took it into the home. This "triggering condition" was not stated in the search warrant, which did include a description of the house and of the items to be seized. The warrant was issued; two days later, the videotape was delivered. Grubbs's wife signed for it and took the unopened package into the house. Grubbs was later detained as he left the house and the search commenced. A half hour into the search he was given a copy of the warrant but not the affidavit. Grubbs argued that the search violated the Particularity Clause because the warrant did not include the triggering condition.

The Court unanimously held that anticipatory warrants are constitutional. "An anticipatory warrant is a warrant based upon an affidavit showing probable cause that at some future time (but not presently) certain evidence of crime will be located at a specified place" (*Grubbs*, 2006, internal quote marks deleted).

> Most anticipatory warrants subject their execution to some condition precedent other than the mere passage of time—a so-called "triggering condition." . . . If the government were to execute an anticipatory warrant before the triggering condition occurred, there would be no reason to believe the item described in the warrant could be found at the searched location; by definition, the triggering condition which establishes probable cause has not yet been satisfied when the warrant is issued. (*United States v. Grubbs*, 2006)

The Court noted that in a sense all search warrants are "anticipatory" because a warrant requires "the magistrate to determine (1) that it is *now probable* that (2) contraband, evidence of a crime, or a fugitive *will be* on the described premises (3) when the warrant is executed" (*United States v. Grubbs*). An anticipatory warrant complies with the Fourth Amendment when the magistrate is given probable cause to believe that the triggering condition will occur and that if the triggering condition occurs "there is a fair probability that contraband or evidence of a crime will be found in a particular place" (*United States v. Grubbs*). As for Grubbs's specific challenge, the Court noted that the Fourth Amendment does not require a warrant to include information about the *method or conditions of execution*; it only requires the warrant to state the particular place to be searched and the persons or things to be seized. The Court also did not credit Grubbs's argument that a warrant has to be presented to the homeowner *before* the search commences.

Anticipatory warrants encourage the use of search warrants over warrantless searches based on exigent circumstances, especially in drug-related crimes.[14] Controlled deliveries in drug cases often arise when police become aware that illicit drugs are in transit. Police then *delay* the movement of the goods long enough to obtain a warrant and follow the package to its destination. Probable cause is established by a reasonable seizure made by customs or mail officials establishing that the goods are contraband. At that point, law enforcement agents will have probable cause to arrest the recipient of the package and to search the package.

This, however, does not give agents probable cause to search the place to which the suspected package was delivered because it is not certain that other contraband is in the place.[15] Therefore, the scope of the search following the controlled delivery depends on the extent of the information that the police have *before* they initiate the search. To be sure that officers do not write affidavits for anticipatory searches that are subterfuges for officers to enter and to "create" plain view, "affidavits in support of such warrants should demonstrate probable cause to believe additional evidence is on the premises and should specify the nature of that additional evidence."[16]

When the final destination of the contraband is not previously known, it may be impossible to meet the Fourth Amendment requirement that the place to be searched be particularly described. In that case, several courts have stated that the police should have as little discretion in determining the place, or the "ultimate location," as possible.[17]

Controlled deliveries create extra hazards of unconstitutional searches. Therefore, police who request and magistrates who issue anticipatory warrants have to be especially careful about (1) the basis for probable cause, (2) the degree of certainty that a seizable item will be delivered to a specified location, (3) the specificity of the place to be searched, and (4) the appropriate scope of the warrant.[18]

Challenging a Search Warrant Affidavit

Police officers who lie on search warrant affidavits, or glide around the truth, subvert the integrity of the warrant system. Prior to **_Franks v. Delaware_** (1978), a defendant could not directly challenge an invalid search warrant before trial. In *Franks*, the Court held (7–2) that a defendant is entitled to a hearing to challenge a warrant if he can show that police injected lies into an affidavit. Two detectives swore in an affidavit that they contacted Jerome Franks's coworkers about relevant evidence of an alleged rape and "did have personal conversation with both these people." After the warrant was executed, the defense attorney requested a hearing in order to call Franks's coworkers to testify that they never spoke personally to the detectives and that "although they might have talked to another police officer, any information given by them to that officer was 'somewhat different' from what was recited in the affidavit." The Delaware courts denied the hearing. The United States Supreme Court reversed.

Franks v. Delaware requires that a defendant first make a *substantial preliminary showing* that the police made a false statement on the search warrant affidavit, either *knowingly* and intentionally or with *reckless disregard for the truth*. If this is shown the Fourth Amendment requires a hearing. At the hearing, the defendant must establish falsehoods by a *preponderance* of the evidence. If the defendant prevails, the magistrate then sets aside the false statements and decides whether probable cause still exists to support the warrant. If not, the warrant is voided, and the fruits of the search are excluded to the same extent as if probable cause was lacking on the face of the affidavit. This exacting standard precludes frequent challenges to affidavits.

Several arguments were raised against *ever* allowing a hearing to challenge an affidavit, including the weak ones that police are deterred from lying by swearing an oath and by the fear of perjury prosecutions. It was also argued that allowing a post-warrant challenge somehow diminished the authority of the magistrate who issued the warrant and that the magistrate could screen out lies on affidavits at the *ex parte* warrant application. This makes little sense, as a magistrate does not have the means to expose police perjury in a brief and often perfunctory *ex parte* session to review the affidavit. More substantial objections were that an additional hearing was collateral to the truth, wasted time and resources, and weakened finality. Justice Blackmun's majority opinion noted that the need to make a preliminary showing would prevent frivolous challenges, and such hearings do not undermine the truth-finding aspects of the criminal case. The dissenters were upset that this provided an area where the *exclusionary rule* would operate, but the majority believed that the exclusionary rule should be applied to evidence obtained by means of police perjury and that a "flat ban on impeachment of veracity could denude the probable-cause requirement of all real meaning" (*Franks v. Delaware*, 1978).

Executing a Search Warrant: Knock and Announce

Search warrants can become *stale*. If not executed quickly, the probable cause that supported the warrant may disappear if the evidence is moved, destroyed, or loses its character as contraband. Therefore, F.R.C.P. Rule 41(e)(2)(A) states: "The warrant must command the officer to execute the warrant within a specified time no longer than 10 days." Similar rules exist in every state.

Because nighttime searches create a greater intrusion on privacy and raise the risk of greater violence born of confusion, the federal rules specify: "The warrant must command the officer to execute the warrant during the daytime, unless the judge for good cause expressly authorizes execution at another time" (F.R.C.P. 41(e)(2)(B)). Some states leave the decision of whether to conduct nighttime searches to the discretion of law enforcement officers.

The common law rule that officers must announce their presence before entering and state that they have a warrant—the **"knock and announce" rule**—is designed to (1) reduce the potential for violent confrontations, (2) protect individual privacy by minimizing the chance of forced entry into the dwelling of the wrong person, and (3) prevent a physical invasion of privacy by giving the occupant time to voluntarily admit the officers.[19] However, when officers have reason to believe, based on specific facts, that prior announcement of entry would produce immediate violence or an attempt to destroy all the evidence, they may dispense with the announcement.[20] Although this is a well-litigated area, the Supreme Court only recently decided the constitutional status of the knock and announce rule.

Petitioner Sharlene Wilson, in ***Wilson v. Arkansas*** (1995), made a series of narcotics sales to a police informant at the home that she shared with Bryson Jacobs. At one sale, Wilson produced a semiautomatic pistol, waved it in the informant's face, and threatened to kill her if she turned out to be working for the police. Based on information supplied by the informant, police obtained a warrant, which included a knock-and-announce provision, to search the house and to arrest Wilson and Jacobs. The affidavits stated that Jacobs had previously been convicted of arson and firebombing.

> The search was conducted later that afternoon. Police officers found the main door to petitioner's home open. While opening an unlocked screen door and entering the residence, they identified themselves as police officers and stated that they had a warrant. Once inside the home, the officers seized marijuana, methamphetamine, valium, narcotics paraphernalia, a gun, and ammunition. They also found petitioner in the bathroom, flushing marijuana down the toilet. Petitioner and Jacobs were arrested and charged with delivery of marijuana, delivery of methamphetamine, possession of drug paraphernalia, and possession of marijuana. (*Wilson v. Arkansas*, 1995)

The Arkansas Supreme Court upheld the search and seizure and specifically found that the Fourth Amendment does *not* include a rule that police must knock and announce. A unanimous U.S. Supreme Court reversed that decision.

Because there is no "knock and announce" rule in the Fourth Amendment's *text*, the state argued that it is not a constitutional rule. The opinion of "originalist" Justice Clarence Thomas took a different tack: "In evaluating the scope of this right, we have looked to the traditional protections against unreasonable searches and seizures afforded by the common law at the time of the framing." The Court will engraft an English common law rule onto the Fourth Amendment so long as it existed *prior to* the adoption of the Constitution. This was justified by arguing that the general-reasonableness construction of the Fourth Amendment (see Chapter 2) requires that searches be reasonable, and what was reasonable to the Framers is determined by knowing late-eighteenth-century common law rules. Also significant was the fact that most new states, shortly after July 4, 1776, passed "reception" statutes making the English common law the law of the state up until independence. Justice Thomas cited a noted seventeenth-century case, *Semayne's Case* (1603), and several prominent English commentators to establish that "[a]t the time of the framing, the common law of search and seizure recognized a law enforcement officer's authority to break open the doors of a dwelling, but generally indicated that he first ought to announce his presence and authority." Furthermore, the "common-law knock-and-announce principle was woven quickly into the fabric of early American law." In all, the Court's opinion surmised that the Framers thought that the "knock and announce" rule was part of the "reasonableness" analysis of the Fourth Amendment.

The Court did not rule on the constitutionality of the actual search in this case. It did note that *exceptions* to the "knock and announce" rule existed when:

- A threat of physical violence exists.
- A suspect escapes from an officer and retreats to his or her dwelling.
- A demand to open the door is refused.
- There is reason to believe that evidence would likely be destroyed if advance notice were given.

The case was remanded to the Arkansas courts to determine if any exception existed to uphold the search and seizure in this case.

In fact, *Wilson v. Arkansas* does not create an impediment to unannounced entry when justified by an exception. The Supreme Court has insisted, nevertheless, that the circumstances allowing a constitutional unannounced search must be justified in *each* case. In ***Richards v. Wisconsin*** (1997), the magistrate *denied* a police request for a **no-knock warrant**. Police tried to enter a suspected drug dealer's hotel room with a ruse, but Richards spotted a uniformed officer and slammed the door shut. The officers waited two or three seconds before breaking in the door and identified themselves *after* they entered. Richards was caught escaping through a window, and cash and cocaine hidden in the room were seized. Although the police did not "knock and announce" *before* entering as required by law, the trial court allowed the introduction of the evidence because drugs are easily disposable. The Wisconsin Supreme Court, affirming, held that when police officers execute a warrant to search for drugs, the circumstances *automatically* raise exigent circumstances. This in effect held that police *never* have to knock and announce in a drug case. The United States Supreme Court unanimously *reversed*. A blanket no-knock exception has two flaws: (1) some drug search warrants might be executed at a house where the occupants, at the time of the search, were not involved in the drug trade; and (2) such an exception would soon negate the rule, because it would be extended to all other crimes. The *Richards* Court also specified *reasonable suspicion*—a very low standard—as the evidentiary standard to support the no-knock warrant exception.

United States v. Ramirez (1998) confirmed that police officers are not held to a higher standard than "reasonable suspicion" when the *execution* of a no-knock warrant results in *damage to property*. A reliable confidential informant told federal agents that a dangerous prisoner, who escaped from an Oregon county jail where he was held while testifying in a case, was hiding in the home of Hernan Ramirez. A 'no-knock' warrant was obtained to search Ramirez's home for the prisoner.

> In the early morning of November 5, approximately 45 officers gathered to execute the warrant. The officers set up a portable loud speaker system and began announcing that they had a search warrant. Simultaneously, they broke a single window in the garage and pointed a gun through the opening, hoping thereby to dissuade any of the occupants from rushing to the weapons the officers believed might be in the garage.

Ramirez, awakened by this, thought his house was being burglarized and took his pistol and fired it into the garage ceiling. He dropped the gun when he realized the besiegers were police officers. Ramirez was indicted for being a felon in possession of firearms. The federal district court granted his motion to suppress evidence regarding the weapon possession; it found that the Fourth Amendment had been violated because there were "insufficient exigent circumstances" to justify the police officer's destruction of property in their execution of the warrant. The Ninth Circuit Court of Appeals affirmed, holding that property destruction accompanying a no-knock entry required more than a "mild" **exigency**. The Supreme Court unanimously *reversed*. It held that there is not a higher standard for a no-knock entry when property damage occurs as part of the entry. While noting that excessive property damage created during an entry could amount to a Fourth Amendment violation, the breaking of a single pane of glass in this case was reasonable.

The standard by which to evaluate the constitutionality of the *delay* between announcing police presence and breaking into a home was established in ***United States v. Banks*** (2003): the test is whether the entry is *reasonable* under all of the facts and circumstances of the case. In the *Banks* case, the police executed a warrant to search for cocaine during the daytime, when people are up and about. They loudly announced their presence. Under these circumstances, the Court ruled that it was reasonable to force open the door after waiting for *fifteen to twenty seconds* with no answer. The test was *not* the time it would take a person *to get to the door*, but the time a person needed *to destroy contraband*. A "prudent dealer" was likely to keep cocaine "near a commode or kitchen sink" and would have the opportunity to get rid of the illegal drugs within a short period of time. "Police seeking a stolen piano may be able to spend more time to make sure they really need the battering ram" (*United States v. Banks*, 2003).

As discussed in Chapter 2, the Supreme Court held (5–4) in ***Hudson v. Michigan*** (2006) that violations of the "knock and announce" rule, which *are* Fourth Amendment violations, do *not* result in *excluding* the evidence seized. In reaching this conclusion, the majority offered several comments about the "knock and announce" rule that *diminished* its stature. The rule has many exigency exceptions that are put into operation if the police or magistrate merely have reasonable suspicion of their existence. Further, the rule is somewhat vague, depending on the facts and circumstances of the situation to determine whether the delay between announcing police presence and forced entry was reasonable. To cap it off, while the "knock and announce" rule is designed to protect life and limb, property, and elements of privacy and dignity, "[w]hat the knock-and-announce rule has never protected . . . is one's interest in preventing the government from seeing or taking evidence described in a warrant. Since the interests that *were* violated in this case have nothing to do with the seizure of the evidence, the exclusionary rule is inapplicable" (*Hudson v. Michigan*, 2006, emphasis in original). The majority and the dissenters differed as to whether eliminating exclusionary rule protection will undermine the rule. The effects of *Hudson* remain to be seen, although with no effective remedy it is logical to believe that the "knock and announce" rule will not be followed in the most typical kinds of drug busts.

Inventory and Delayed Notice, "Sneak and Peek" Warrants

Federal rules require that a copy of the search warrant be given to the property owner or left at the premises after execution (F.R.C.P. Rule 41(f)(3)). An officer present at the search must prepare and verify a detailed written inventory of the property seized in the presence of another (F.R.C.P. Rule 41(f)(2)). The officer must return the warrant and the inventory to the judge who issued the warrant, and the judge in turn must give a copy of the inventory to the person from whom the property was taken and to the warrant's applicant (F.R.C.P. Rule 41(f)(4)). These practices ensure the *regularity* of the search warrant process, provide *notice* to suspects that the state has intruded on their privacy, and protect police officers from charges of theft.

A significant exception to the rule of immediate notice is the relatively novel *"sneak and peek"* or *covert-entry* warrant. Beginning in 1984, federal agents in a few drug cases requested warrants to enter a premises, observe the premises and perhaps take photographs, and leave the premises undisturbed. The few federal appeals courts that decided cases where **"sneak and peek" warrants** were issued have held that covert entry under a warrant is a search and that information gained about the area of privacy is a seizure. The courts held that although "sneak and peek" warrants violated the Federal Rules of Criminal Procedure, which required immediate notice, they did *not* necessarily violate the Fourth Amendment. The 1968 federal wiretap law, for example, was held to allow covert entry into places to place the listening devices without immediate notice. *Dalia v. United States* (1979) ruled that the Fourth Amendment or the eavesdropping statute did not require a separate warrant to authorize a covert entry to install the listening device. Covert entries are constitutional as long as they are made pursuant to a *warrant*. The cases make it clear that to be constitutional, "sneak and peek" warrants must provide notice of the entry to the defendants within a reasonable time, which usually means within a week.[21]

Legislative authorization for "sneak and peek" warrants in all cases, not just terrorism investigations, was established by the USA PATRIOT Act in 2001. The law now allows *delay* in the notice of a warrant execution *if* the issuing court finds that immediate notification may have adverse results such as endangering the life or physical safety of an individual, flight from prosecution, destruction or tampering with evidence, intimidation of potential witnesses, or something else that seriously jeopardizes an investigation or unduly delays a trial. Notice of the search can also be delayed if the warrant prohibits the seizure of any tangible property. A "sneak and peek" warrant must provide "notice within a reasonable period not to exceed 30 days after the date of its execution, or on a later date certain if the facts of the case justify a longer period of delay" (18 U.S.C. §§ 3103a, 2705).[22]

Author Robert Duncan, who favors surreptitious or covert-entry warrants as necessary law enforcement tools in a dangerous age, nevertheless is concerned that the new law is too broad and has suggested modifications. First, requesting agents should provide more information than is needed for an ordinary search warrant, similar to that required for electronic eavesdropping warrants (e.g., showing that other law enforcement techniques have failed to provide needed information). The time limit for notice should be reduced to seven days, and there should be limits on the number of times extensions can be requested. Finally, covert-entry warrants should be limited to crimes that involve "well-planned, well-organized, and in-depth criminal behavior," including terrorism, racketeering, and gang-related activity.[23]

Notice—formally alerting individuals that the government will or has acted against their interests—is a fundamental part of the due process "timely notice and fair hearing" formula, stretching back in our law to Magna Carta (1215). Secret arrest, secret search, secret interrogation, secret trial, and secret detention are the very definition of lawless government. Being able to spy on someone's constitutionally protected private areas should raise profound concerns about "Big Brother" government.[24] One innovation that has allowed greater intrusion with delayed notice has been electronic eavesdropping. There is no disagreement that electronic eavesdropping is a necessary law enforcement tool in serious conspiracy, white-collar crime, organized crime, bribery, and terrorism cases. But the 1968 electronic eavesdropping law (and subsequent additions) has been carefully hedged in with substantial checks to ensure that this potentially coercive tool will not be abused by government officials for partisan or corrupt purposes.

The problem, in the years after the 9/11 attacks, is that the public and even members of Congress may be kept in the dark by the administration about the scope of "sneak and peek" warrants. According to the *Los Angeles Times*, "FBI agents are [using] 'sneak and peek' warrants on a wider scale, entering hundreds of homes clandestinely to gather intelligence and copy files and computer drives . . . without notification. And they have conducted surveillance on antiwar, religious, civil rights and environmental groups, including Greenpeace and the American-Arab Anti-Discrimination Committee."[25] This politicized use of the government's law enforcement powers is reminiscent of the Watergate abuses that brought down the Nixon administration in the 1970s.[26] In a time of war, ordinary political differences become magnified, and opponents come to be seen as traitors. Prosecutions in such times of crisis can be motivated by these deep emotions, even if the actual charges are not for treason.[27]

Even if fears about the politicized use of "sneak and peek" warrants are exaggerated, a highly intrusive law enforcement technique has been slipped into the law with virtually no discussion—and it can be used in ordinary criminal investigations, not just terror-related cases.[28] The "sneak and peek" provision was in the Justice Department's grab bag of desired powers, just waiting for the right opportunity to be enacted.[29] Another concern is that state and local law enforcement authorities are likely to lobby for such powers, and the potential exists for "sneak and peek" searches to become a regular feature of investigations of low-level drug possession and other crimes that occur with regularity.

Deadly Errors

The importance of police honesty and accuracy in the search warrant process cannot be overstated. In September 1999, four Denver SWAT officers were sent to execute a no-knock warrant at 3738 High Street, a two-story home. It was the wrong house. While executing the warrant, the officers who broke in killed forty-five-year-old Mexican migrant laborer Ismael Mena, father of nine, who raised a gun as the police entered his bedroom. Officer Joseph Bini, who swore out the affidavit, however, was charged with perjury for "'unlawfully and knowingly' lying on a search warrant affidavit." He swore in his affidavit that "he *personally* observed an informant make his or her way on foot to the house" at 3738 High Street. Based on his affidavit, an assistant district attorney and a county judge signed off on the warrant. In fact, the drug deal took place at 3742 High Street, a single-story home. Bini dropped the informant off four blocks from the house. The district attorney believed "[the informant] attempted to determine the address by counting the houses down the alley and up the front on this particular block. He apparently miscounted the houses and wrote the address down wrong."

As a result, a man died, Denver paid Mena's family $400,000 to settle legal claims, and the police chief was fired. Officer Bini pleaded guilty to misdemeanor charges, and the SWAT team was officially exonerated in the shooting after a close examination of their responses. Denver adopted several reforms: Police have only three days instead of ten days to serve no-knock warrants, more training is provided, and experienced police supervisors evaluate and approve no-knock raids. Denver's mayor said that "the public can expect to see a decrease in the number of no-knock raids" as a result of the tighter guidelines. But it took an unnecessary death to achieve that result.[30] Unfortunately, the overuse of paramilitary police raids by SWAT teams in America, estimated at forty thousand per year, has led to many cases like that of Ismael Mena.[31]

REVOLUTIONIZING THE FOURTH AMENDMENT

For many years, Fourth Amendment law was tied to property concepts, especially the idea that a search and seizure involved a physical trespass onto a person's **constitutionally protected area**. This concept was based on traditional practice and on the Fourth Amendment's words, protecting "persons, houses, papers, and effects" from unreasonable search and seizure. This thinking created problems when, in *Olmstead v. United States* (1928), the Supreme Court held that wiretapping did not constitute a search and seizure. This decision withdrew constitutional protection from a vital area of privacy and caused many to realize that the Fourth Amendment protected vital interests and not simply property. The Court finally overruled *Olmstead* in 1967, but to do so it had to establish an entirely new "expectation of privacy" doctrine because protecting intangible privacy rights was not compatible with the older "constitutionally protected area" doctrine.

Modernizing Search and Seizure Law

In 1967 and 1968, the Supreme Court "revolutionized" Fourth Amendment law in four cases that upset established doctrines and opened the door for a more flexible mode of search and seizure interpretation. The first of these cases, *Katz v. United States* (1967), was the centerpiece of this revolution. It broke the law of search and seizure away from its traditional mooring in property law. In its stead, issues were now to be decided more explicitly on balancing of the interests deemed central to the Fourth Amendment: the need for effective law enforcement versus the protection of privacy and liberty rooted in the expectation of privacy.

Katz was followed by **Warden v. Hayden** (1967), the second case in this series, which abolished the "mere evidence" rule of *Gouled v. United States* (1921). (See Chapter 2.) *Gouled* held that only the fruits of a crime, contraband, or the instrumentality used to commit the crime could be seized by police. So-called *mere evidence* that did not fit these categories could not be seized by police to be used in evidence. In *Warden v. Hayden*, police seized clothing that could be used to identify an alleged robber during a lawful search of Hayden's house. The Supreme Court held that seizing the clothing was proper, and it could be held by the state for the duration of the prosecution to be used as evidence that a man wearing similar clothing was the perpetrator. The mere evidence rule (1) did not serve a defendant's legitimate privacy interest; (2) was based on outmoded property concepts; and (3) hampered the legitimate law enforcement interests of the state. The new rule better balanced the competing interests.

Next came **Camara v. Municipal Court** (1967) and its companion case, *See v. City of Seattle* (1967), which appeared to expand Fourth Amendment rights of individuals by requiring a warrant for administrative searches that did not directly enforce the criminal law. Under a 1959 case, *Frank v. Maryland*, the Supreme Court held that the search of a house or a business place, conducted by an *administrative officer* for the purpose of enforcing administrative regulations rather than the state's penal code, was simply not a search protected by the Fourth Amendment. In *Camara*, the Court rethought the issue and held that the Fourth Amendment text applied to an intrusion by any government officer into "areas" protected by the expectation of privacy. Entry by health, fire, or housing inspectors, for purposes of enforcing regulations, was now covered by the Fourth Amendment.

This, however, created a dilemma. Most administrative inspection programs are based not on particularized probable cause of a safety hazard in a particular home or business, but on bureaucratic assessments that houses or businesses in an entire neighborhood should be entered and inspected. Requiring a municipality to get particularized probable cause for each house in the neighborhood would be too burdensome, and the inspection program would fail. The Court solved the problem by authorizing less-specific administrative warrants based on general area in-spections. Information about such general conditions as the age of buildings in a subdivision or statistical information about the number of fires in a neighborhood would support such warrants. Probable cause was "defined down," so to speak. This solution created a new and more flexible way of thinking about the Fourth Amendment. *Camara* thus opened the door to the general-reasonableness construction of the Fourth Amendment. (See Chapter 2.) The Court reasoned that the Fourth Amendment text does not absolutely require search warrants, and at minimum requires that all search and seizures be reasonable. Under this newer, flexible reasoning, the Supreme Court upheld general or "area" warrants, the very thing that the generation of 1776 found abominable. This relaxed mode of interpretation was later used to allow greater govern-ment intrusion into areas of privacy by non-law-enforcement officers under the special needs doctrine. (See Chapter 5.)

The last case in this series, ***Terry v. Ohio*** (1968), for the first time in American constitu-tional history, upheld temporary but forcible stops of individuals even though the police officer did not have probable cause to believe that the person committed a crime, the only evidentiary standard found in the Fourth Amendment's text. A state deprivation of liberty could now be based on a lesser standard of evidence that came to be known as **reasonable suspicion**. (*Terry* is covered in Chapter 5.) The decision in *Terry* depended on the new mode of Fourth Amendment reasoning: balancing of interests between the state and the individual, flexibility, and reliance on the Reasonableness Clause.

These four revolutionary decisions were not inherently liberal or conservative. Two of them, *Warden* and *Terry*, explicitly expanded the state's powers, while *Katz* and *Camara* formal-ly expanded the rights of individuals. In their larger effects, the cases were "liberal" in that they brought a larger measure of police work under constitutional oversight, but they were "conserva-tive" in permitting a flexible approach that made it easier for the Court to water down traditional Fourth Amendment standards. It is ironic that the liberal Warren Court laid a foundation for flex-ible interpretation—an approach that was resisted by relatively "conservative" justices like John M. Harlan II. The flexible approach was then adapted by the politically conservative Burger and Rehnquist Courts to make new law and expand the powers of the state against the individual.

Creating the "Expectation of Privacy" Doctrine

This section takes a closer look at the decision and reasoning in ***Katz v. United States*** (1967). Modern conditions generate problems that require novel legal thinking. Electronic communica-tion by telegraph, telephone, and wireless communication—unknown to the Framers in 1791—led to invasions of privacy by police that did not have the appearance of a traditional search and seizure, with the police pounding at the door and physically searching the home. In 1928, the Supreme Court thus ruled in *Olmstead v. United States*, by a five-to-four decision, that wiretap-ping did *not* constitute a search because there was no physical trespass into the house and no tangible evidence was taken. This ruling was deeply disturbing because wiretapping and elec-tronic eavesdropping by the government are an obvious intrusion into the lives and privacy of in-dividuals, and privacy is at the core of the Fourth Amendment. A powerful dissent by Justice Louis Brandeis reflected the decision's unpopularity. (See the biographical sketch of Brandeis following Chapter 1.) A federal statute soon placed some controls on telephone wiretapping.[32] The federal law, incidentally, did not cover "bugging"—electronic eavesdropping by means of a wireless listening device—which was not as well known and not then seen as being within the purview of the federal government's jurisdiction over interstate communications.[33]

Over the next few years, the Court grappled with the question of electronic eavesdropping. The application of traditional, property-based Fourth Amendment concepts produced weirdly in-consistent results. ***Goldman v. United States*** (1942), for example, held that placing an electronic listening device against a wall of a house was not a trespass and therefore, under *Olmstead*, was not a search and seizure under the Fourth Amendment. Evidence so obtained could be used against the defendant. Dissatisfied with the notion of leaving individuals open to government spying, the Court in ***Silverman v. United States*** (1961) held that when a microphone was driven into a wall, rather than placed up against it, there was a physical trespass and it was thus a search and seizure subject to the rules of the Fourth Amendment. In this case, the evidence seized by the eavesdropping was not admissible. These contradictory decisions were inherently unstable. The Supreme Court, nevertheless, was not eager to clear up this doctrinal mess.

The Court was chiefly concerned that a case squarely holding electronic eavesdropping to be a search and seizure within the purview of the Fourth Amendment could entirely outlaw bugging and wiretapping. The reason is that a bug or wiretap is an inherently general search that picks up all conversations—of nonsuspected people who happen to call or be in the place being bugged, as well as the suspect. It was difficult to see how a warrant for an electronic eavesdropping device could ever square with the Fourth Amendment's particularity requirement. The justices in the 1940s and 1950s included former prosecutors, senators, and attorneys general who were familiar with how government worked. They knew that electronic eavesdropping was a useful law enforcement tool and that it was often impossible to obtain evidence of organized crime, white-collar crime, and government fraud and bribery without bugs and taps. On the other hand, they were well versed in the dangers of unchecked government electronic spying. As became later known to the general public, the FBI under its long-time director J. Edgar Hoover, often with the compliance of presidents, spied on members of Congress and a significant number of citizens. At least one Supreme Court justice believed that he was the subject of FBI taps.[34] The dilemma confronting the Court, seemingly insoluble until the late 1960s, was how to allow but to tame electronic eavesdropping.

The answer to this dilemma emerged in the 1960s. Under established doctrine, no statutory or Fourth Amendment rights (including the expectation of privacy) are violated when a person's voice is secretly recorded while voluntarily talking to an interceptor. A person who says things in a conversation to another lives with the risk that the false friend will reveal any confidences to others, including the authorities (*Hoffa v. United States*, 1966; *Lewis v. United States*, 1966). This is the case even if the false friend is speaking on a telephone and a police officer is listening on an extension line (*Rathbun v. United States*, 1957) or secretly wearing a listening device (*On Lee v. United States*, 1952; *Lopez v. United States*, 1963). In short, a law enforcement officer or agent need not obtain a judicial warrant to "wear a wire."[35] Despite this firm rule, to be on the safe side, government investigators in **Osborn v. United States** (1966) had Vick, a private cooperating undercover agent, make a written statement under oath that he had been hired by Osborn, an attorney, to bribe a juror in a prosecution of national labor leader James R. Hoffa. The statement was taken to two federal district judges who authorized Vick to wear an electronic recorder when next speaking to Osborn about the bribery. This practice was upheld by the Court in *Osborn*, although not made mandatory. The following year, in *Katz*, the Supreme Court praised the practice of seeking a warrant for a narrow and precise electronic search—for capturing a conversation that would not draw in innocent speakers.

Shortly before deciding *Katz*, the Supreme Court struck down New York's electronic eavesdropping law as too broad in **Berger v. New York** (1967). Objectionable features of the New York law included the fact that it "lays down no requirement for particularity in the warrant as to what specific crime has been or is being committed," that a warrant is granted for sixty days of uninterrupted listening, that the statute failed to describe the conversations sought with specific particularity, that once incriminating conversations were recorded the eavesdropping did not have to cease, that extensions of the initial sixty-day listening period could be obtained without new reasons, and that no return was required, so that a person who was tapped or bugged would not know of it. *Osborn* and *Berger* were the extreme ends of electronic eavesdropping—one extremely precise and narrow, and the other overly broad.

The facts in *Katz* were simple. Federal agents suspected that Charles Katz, a "bookie," was transmitting betting information across state lines by telephone in violation of federal law. Katz was observed making calls from the same telephone booth at about the same time every day in Los Angeles. For a week, FBI agents placed a microphone on the top of the telephone booth and activated it only when Katz used the booth to make calls, recording incriminating conversations. Katz appealed his conviction on the ground that the electronic eavesdropping violated his Fourth Amendment rights. The government argued that this case was the same as *Goldman* in that no physical intrusion into a constitutionally protected area, and so no Fourth Amendment violation, had occurred.

The Supreme Court overruled *Olmstead* and *Goldman* and replaced the concept that the Fourth Amendment applies in "constitutionally protected areas" with a memorable phrase in Justice Potter Stewart's majority opinion: "For *the Fourth Amendment protects people, not places.* What a person knowingly exposes to the public, even in his own home or office, is not a subject of Fourth Amendment protection. But what he seeks to preserve as private, even in an area accessible to the public, may be constitutionally protected" (*Katz v. United States*, 1967, emphasis added). It did not matter that Katz was visible to the eye in the phone booth.

But what he sought to exclude when he entered the booth was not the intruding eye—it was the uninvited ear. He did not shed his right to do so simply because he made his calls from a place where he might be seen. . . . One who occupies it, shuts the door behind him, and pays the toll that permits him to place a call is surely entitled to assume that the words he utters into the mouthpiece will not be broadcast to the world. To read the Constitution more narrowly is to ignore the vital role that the public telephone has come to play in private communication. (*Katz*, 1967)

The Court made it clear that property interests do not determine the scope of Fourth Amendment protections. It held that "[t]he Government's activities in electronically listening to and recording the petitioner's words violated the privacy upon which he justifiably relied while using the telephone booth and thus constituted a 'search and seizure' within the meaning of the Fourth Amendment" (*Katz*, 1967).

The government's search and seizure of Katz's conversations violated the Fourth Amendment because the agents did not seek a warrant. The Court took special pains to note that the search was very narrow in that it seemed to be based on probable cause and was conducted in such a way as to obtain only Katz's words at a time and place likely to involve his suspected criminal activity. The Court noted that a magistrate probably could have issued a warrant. No matter how strong the probable cause, the *actual issuance* of the warrant is critical; failing to obtain one rendered the search unconstitutional.

The Katz doctrine is a product not only of the majority opinion but of that decision plus the heart of Justice Harlan's concurrence. "My understanding of the rule that has emerged from prior decisions is that there is a twofold requirement, first that a person have exhibited an actual (subjective) expectation of privacy and, second, that the expectation be one that society is prepared to recognize as 'reasonable'" (*Katz v. United States*, 1967, Harlan, J., concurring). This **two-pronged test** means that there is a *subjective* (personal) and an *objective* (societal) component of the expectation of privacy. The objective component prevents defendants from making outlandish or unacceptable claims of Fourth Amendment privacy.

Justice Hugo Black was the lone dissenter. He argued that although electronics were unknown in 1791, eavesdropping was a familiar practice, and the Framers could have protected private conversations if they so wished. He instead adhered to the notion of *Olmstead*, that the Fourth Amendment indeed did refer to and protect the seizure of tangible items. By this narrow adherence to the words of the Fourth Amendment, Justice Black solidified his standing as a "constitutional fundamentalist" rather than a "judicial liberal."

Applying the "Expectation of Privacy" Doctrine

Despite the new mode of expectation of privacy Fourth Amendment analysis introduced by *Katz*, the Supreme Court continues to decide some cases under the "constitutionally protected area" idea, which affords greater protection to the home than other places. In Fourth Amendment standing cases, for example, the Court has resisted the logic of *Katz*. Justice Byron White, dissenting in *Rakas v. Illinois* (1978), noted that

> [t]he Court today holds that the Fourth Amendment protects property, not people, and specifically that a legitimate occupant of an automobile may not invoke the exclusionary rule and challenge a search of that vehicle unless he happens to own or have a possessory interest in it. . . . The majority's conclusion has no support in the Court's controlling decisions, in the logic of the Fourth Amendment, or in common sense.

In such cases, the conservative Court seems to be motivated more to limit suspects' rights than to create a coherent body of Fourth Amendment law. One might almost say that the *Katz* doctrine is used by the Court to resolve Fourth Amendment issues except when it does not.

EXPECTATION OF PRIVACY IN ONE'S BODY   Obtaining physical evidence from within a person's body raises Fourth Amendment questions that are answered by examining the severity of the intrusion and the law enforcement interests. Factors include the risk to a person's safety or health in the procedure, the extent of control used on the body, and the effect on the suspect's dignity. Forced surgery to remove a bullet lodged in a robbery suspect was held to violate his

Fourth Amendment rights because the expectation of privacy in one's bodily integrity is great (***Winston v. Lee,*** 1985). On the other hand, taking blood in a medical setting by medical personnel to determine a driver's blood alcohol level after a fatal accident has been upheld as constitutional: It presents virtually no health risk and is so routine as to involve minimal interference with Fourth Amendment dignity interests (***Schmerber v. California,*** 1966). Lower courts have also perceived a greater privacy interest in bodily integrity in cases involving body cavity searches and strip searches. (See Chapter 4.)

A person's observable physical characteristics, such as one's facial description, voice, or handwriting, are not "seized" if someone testifies to them at a trial or if a person's description is taken by police in an investigation (***Holt v. United States,*** 1910; *United States v. Dionisio*, 1973; *United States v. Mara*, 1973). Requiring a person to participate in a lineup does not violate that person's Fourth or Fifth Amendment rights (*United States v. Wade*, 1967).

The Supreme Court has held that urine collection and testing to ascertain the presence of drugs in a person's body intrudes upon expectations of privacy that society has long recognized as reasonable. "There are few activities in our society more personal or private than the passing of urine. Most people describe it by euphemisms if they talk about it at all. It is a function traditionally performed without public observation; indeed, its performance in public is generally prohibited by law as well as social custom." The Court noted that the expectation of privacy is not only rooted in the traditional dictates of modesty but also in the fact that the chemical analysis of urine, like that of blood, can reveal a host of medical facts about a person. Although urine testing by state agencies in order to detect drugs or alcohol is protected by the Fourth Amendment, the collection is allowed under certain conditions (***Skinner v. Railway Labor Executives' Association,*** 1989). (See Chapter 5.) In contrast, private business is not restricted in this practice by the Fourth Amendment because there is no state action.

MAINTAINING PROPERTY INTERESTS AFTER KATZ   The Fourth Amendment continues to protect property interests. In ***Soldal v. Cook County*** (1992), a mobile home park evicted Soldal and his mobile home from its property and utilities. The park's owner requested that sheriff's deputies stand by in the event that the eviction might lead to violence. The park's employees, not acting in accordance with local statutes, pushed Soldal's trailer into a road, causing major property damage. There was no invasion of Soldal's privacy, because the employees never entered Soldal's trailer, but his property was damaged. The officers did not physically assist in the eviction, but the Supreme Court held that their presence established state action. (See Chapter 2.) Soldal sued the sheriff's department under 42 U.S.C. §1983, claiming that his Fourth Amendment rights were violated. The government argued that without a *Katz*-like violation of privacy rights, there was no Fourth Amendment wrong. This argument was firmly rejected: *Katz* protects both privacy and property rights. According to Justice White, although there was no search, there was a seizure—a "meaningful interference with an individual's possessory interests in that property." Because "[w]hat matters is the intrusion on the people's security from governmental interference," this case fell within the Fourth Amendment, allowing Soldal's lawsuit to go forward.

EXPECTATION OF PRIVACY IN DWELLINGS   "At the risk of belaboring the obvious, private residences are places in which the individual normally expects privacy free of governmental intrusion not authorized by a warrant, and that expectation is plainly one that society is prepared to recognize as justifiable" (*United States v. Karo*, 1984). The Supreme Court often leans in favor of a defendant's home rights for this reason. In *Payton v. New York* (1980) (see Chapter 4), for example, the Court ruled that an arrest warrant must be obtained in order to forcibly enter a home to arrest a person. The "physical entry of the home is the chief evil against which the wording of the Fourth Amendment is directed" (*Payton*, citing *United States v. United States District Court*, 1972). The protection of the home applies to apartments, offices, garages, and temporary dwellings, such as hotel rooms. This has been confirmed in cases where the Court has denied landlords and hotel keepers the right to consent to police searches of tenants' rooms (*Chapman v. California*, 1967; *Stoner v. California*, 1964). The protection of home privacy was a key reason for the Court's modification of the hot pursuit doctrine to disallow warrantless home entry for relatively minor offenses (*Welsh v. Wisconsin*, 1984; see Chapter 5).

Even a conservative Court has scrupulously upheld the Fourth Amendment protections of the warrant and probable cause when the core area of the home is involved. A person has no expectation of privacy in his or her public movements, and thus no warrant was required when police placed an electronic **beeper** in a drum containing chloroform to monitor a suspected drug manufacturer route along public streets (*U.S. v. Knotts*, 1983). On the other hand, a suspect's Fourth Amendment rights were violated when, without a warrant, agents used a beeper to trace the movement of a drum *inside* the suspect's home. "The beeper tells the agent that a particular article is actually located at a particular time in the private residence and is in the possession of the person or persons whose residence is being watched. Even if visual surveillance has revealed that the article to which the beeper is attached has entered the house, the later monitoring not only verifies the officers' observations but also establishes that the article remains on the premises" (*United States v. Karo*, 1984).

There is no Fourth Amendment protection of real estate as such, called **open fields** in *Hester v. United States* (1924) and *Oliver v. United States* (1984). The Supreme Court has taken the common law concept of the **curtilage**—the area immediately surrounding a house—and has given it constitutional protection (*Oliver v. United States* 1984; *United States, v. Dunn*, 1987). Still, the Court has strained to not apply the curtilage idea to police observations of backyards from low-flying fixed-wing airplanes and helicopters (*California v. Ciraolo*, 1986; *Florida v. Riley*, 1989).

PERSONS UNDER CORRECTIONAL JURISDICTION   The one dwelling not clothed with Fourth Amendment protection is a prison cell, no matter how strong a prisoner's subjective sense of privacy in it. A "prison shares none of the attributes of privacy of a home." Although prisoners retain constitutional rights that do not conflict with legitimate prison objectives (rights such as freedom of religion and protection from cruel and unusual punishment), "society is not prepared to recognize as legitimate any subjective expectation of privacy that a prisoner might have in his prison cell; . . . the Fourth Amendment proscription against unreasonable searches and seizures does not apply within the confines of the prison cell." As a result, prison authorities are allowed under the Constitution to make random shakedown searches of prisoners' cells. There are limits to the practice if it is intended only to harass prisoners (*Hudson v. Palmer*, 1984).

Similarly, the Court, over a strong dissent, allowed a probation officer to enter a probationer's home without a warrant and on less than probable cause (*Griffin v. Wisconsin,* 1987). The Court said that a "probationer's home, like anyone else's, is protected by the Fourth Amendment's requirement that searches be 'reasonable.'" On the other hand, in Wisconsin all probationers fall under a regulation that permits any probation officer to search a probationer's home without a warrant as long as his or her supervisor approves and as long as there are "reasonable grounds" to believe that contraband is present. The Supreme Court upheld the regulation on the ground that probation supervision is a "special need beyond the normal need for law enforcement"—a Fourth Amendment doctrine that permits warrantless searches on less than probable cause. (See Chapter 5.) *Griffin* implied that a probationer's status imposes a lower expectation of privacy at home than that of an unconvicted person. It was the last case in this group based on the special needs doctrine, which upholds standardless searches that are not designed to promote law enforcement.

Probationers' home privacy rights were further diminished in **United States v. Knights** (2001). A California probationer signed a probation order acknowledging as a condition of probation that he would "submit his . . . person, property, place of residence, vehicle, personal effects, to search at anytime, with or without a search warrant, warrant of arrest or reasonable cause by any probation officer or law enforcement officer." Knights's apartment was searched by a police officer who investigated an arson and had reasonable suspicion but not probable cause that evidence of the crime was in the apartment. The officer did not obtain a search warrant because he knew of Knights's probation condition. Incriminating evidence was found in a search of Knights's home and was used to convict him of a new crime. Knights argued that a warrantless search was permissible only for the special needs purpose of enforcing probation regulations and not for the investigation of new crimes. In rejecting this position, the Court noted that "'the very assumption of the institution of probation' is that the probationer 'is more likely than the ordinary citizen to violate the law.'"

The major difference between the privacy expectation in a prison cell and in a probationer's home is the level of cause required before probation or police officers can enter without a warrant. A few years before *Knights*, the Supreme Court held, in **Pennsylvania Board of Probation and Parole v. Scott** (1998), that the exclusionary rule does not apply to exclude evidence from a parole revocation hearing, where a parole officer illegally entered the home that a parolee shared with his mother, without consent, a warrant, or authorization "by any state statutory or regulatory framework ensuring the reasonableness of searches by parole officers." This clearly implies that a parolee has a lesser expectation of privacy in a home than a free citizen does, although the Supreme Court did not analyze the case under *Katz*.

In a six-to-three decision, the Court held in ***Samson v. California*** (2006) that a state can, by statute, obliterate virtually all of the Fourth Amendment rights of a parolee. Donald Samson was walking down the street with a woman and a child. A police officer who knew that Samson was a parolee verified that there were no outstanding warrants against him. The officer nevertheless searched Samson and found drugs. A California law, probably the only one like it in the United States, required a parolee to consent to warrantless and standardless searches at any time. The majority found the condition to be reasonable and upheld the search because a parolee's status is essentially like that of a prisoner and because of the high recidivism rates of California parolees.

MEDIA RIDE-ALONGS   *Wilson v. Layne* (1999) held it to be "a violation of the Fourth Amendment for police to bring members of the media or other third parties into a home during the execution of a warrant when the presence of the third parties in the home was not in aid of the execution of the warrant." A proper arrest warrant, supported by probable cause, was issued to U.S. Marshals to enter a Rockville, Maryland, home to arrest Dominic Wilson, a dangerous fugitive. Unbeknownst to the police, it was the home of Wilson's parents. The arrest warrant was executed at 6:45 a.m., much to the surprise of Wilson's parents. After discovering that Dominic was not at the house, the arrest team departed. The team "was accompanied by a reporter and a photographer from the *Washington Post*, who had been invited by the Marshals to accompany them on their mission as part of a Marshal's Service ride-along policy." The photographer took numerous photographs but published none. The reporters did, however, observe a scuffle and the handcuffing of Mr. Wilson, who was wearing briefs. They did not assist in executing the warrant. The Wilsons brought a civil lawsuit for money damages against the Marshal's Service for violating their Fourth Amendment right of privacy by bringing reporters into their home.

The government tried to justify the **media ride-along** by arguing that (1) media presence promotes accurate reporting and crime fighting, (2) the presence of third parties minimizes police abuses and protects the suspects, and (3) the police should be allowed to determine whether these law enforcement interests are advanced by the ride-along. The Court was unpersuaded by these reasons. These factors, even if reasonable, promote general interests and are not sufficient to overcome the specific constitutional right held by the Wilsons.

The Court did not refer to *Katz* or to the expectation of privacy in *Wilson;* instead, it emphasized "the importance of the right of residential privacy at the core of the Fourth Amendment," a "centuries-old principle of respect for the privacy of the home." Beyond this, the Court did not reason except to say, "Were such generalized 'law enforcement objectives' themselves sufficient to trump the Fourth Amendment, the protections guaranteed by that Amendment's text would be significantly watered down." *Wilson* shows a trend of recent cases that emphasize the expectation of privacy in the home but do not apply the *Katz* doctrine to the fullest extent in other areas of law enforcement.

EXPECTATION OF PRIVACY IN AUTOMOBILES   There is a lesser expectation of privacy in an automobile than in a home (*California v. Carney*, 1985). The Supreme Court has found that at common law, mobile vehicles could be stopped without a warrant and has generally extended this exception into the Fourth Amendment "automobile exception" (*Carroll v. United States*, 1925). Yet the Court has applied the "expectation of privacy" doctrine to the stopping of automobiles by law enforcement officers, on the ground that stopping an automobile is a seizure that can cause annoyance or fright. A warrantless stop of a vehicle, therefore, must be justified by reasonable suspicion or probable cause of a traffic violation or crime (*United States v. Brignoni-Ponce*, 1975; *Delaware v. Prouse*, 1979). To the contrary, a stop at a fixed checkpoint does not produce the same level of anxiety as being stopped by a roving patrol, and so the expectation of privacy is less and the stop need not be justified by particularized suspicion (*United States v. Martinez-Fuerte*, 1976; *Michigan Department of State Police v. Sitz*, 1990).

EXPECTATION OF PRIVACY IN PROPERTY AND EFFECTS   In ***United States v. Chadwick*** (1977), the Supreme Court held that a footlocker is protected by a subjective and objective expectation of privacy. Police had probable cause to believe that a footlocker contained marijuana, had arrested its possessor, and had the luggage in custody. Opening the footlocker violated Chadwick's Fourth Amendment rights, and the evidence was suppressed. The police should have sought a search warrant from a magistrate.

The Court has further extended the expectation of privacy to soft baggage that was squeezed by a Border Patrol agent. A bus traveling from California to Arkansas stopped at a Border Patrol checkpoint in Texas, and the agent boarded the bus to check the immigration status of its passengers. After reaching the back of the bus, having satisfied himself that the passengers were lawfully in the United States, the agent began walking toward the front. Along the way, he squeezed the soft luggage that passengers had placed in the overhead storage space above the seats. He squeezed a green canvas bag belonging to passenger Steven Dewayne Bond and noticed that it contained a "brick-like" object later identified as methamphetamine. The Supreme Court held that this physical examination was a search. Bond exhibited an actual expectation of privacy by using an opaque bag and placing that bag directly above his seat. The agent's manipulation of the bag went beyond that tolerated by society:

> When a bus passenger places a bag in an overhead bin, he expects that other passengers or bus employees may move it for one reason or another. Thus, a bus passenger clearly expects that his bag may be handled. He does not expect that other passengers or bus employees will, as a matter of course, feel the bag in an exploratory manner. But this is exactly what the agent did here. We therefore hold that the agent's physical manipulation of petitioner's bag violated the Fourth Amendment. (**Bond v. United States,** 2000)

On the other hand, the Court has come close to stating that a person has no expectation of privacy in the odor of drugs emanating from a piece of luggage in a public area if detected by a trained drug-sniffing canine (*United States v. Place*, 1983; *Illinois v. Caballes*, 2005). There is no expectation of privacy in abandoned property such as trash left in opaque plastic bags at the curb. It may be seized and searched without a warrant. The general public does not believe that a person expects trash to be kept private because the bags can be opened by children playing, by animals, or by scavengers (**California v. Greenwood,** 1988). The same result occurs under the older property theory: Once people abandon property, they lose all control over it.

EXPECTATION OF PRIVACY IN BUSINESS RECORDS AND COMMERCIAL PROPERTY   The Court has held that by depositing money in banks, people expose financial information in bank records to strangers such as bank employees and thus lose an expectation of privacy. As a result, Congress may require that large cash or other transactions be reported to federal agencies without showing particularized suspicion. One's banking records can be subpoenaed by the government under the Bank Secrecy Act (*California Bankers Association v. Shultz*, 1974; *United States v. Miller*, 1976).

The Court has held that business records are not protected by the Fifth Amendment privilege against compelled self-incrimination and thus are subject to seizure under the Fourth Amendment with a proper search warrant (*Andresen v. Maryland,* 1976). Business premises, however, are protected by the Fourth Amendment (*Hale v. Henkel,* 1906; *See v. City of Seattle,* 1967). If commercial property such as a retail store is open to the public, a police agent may enter the premises and observe or purchase suspected items, and such an entry and purchase is not a search and seizure (*Maryland v. Macon,* 1985). Although warrants are required for commercial health or safety inspections under the *Camara–See* doctrine, they require a lesser standard of evidence than the traditional probable cause standard (*Marshall v. Barlow's, Inc.,* 1978). Some commercial properties are subject to warrantless inspections, although retaining expectations of privacy, because of the nature of the business or the special risks that the business creates (e.g., mining) (*Donovan v. Dewey,* 1981).

Undercover Agents and the Fourth Amendment

In **Gouled v. United States** (1921), U.S. Army investigators sent a "secret agent" into Gouled's office, not by means of a trespass or burglary, but by false pretenses. The Court held that a physical seizure of papers in these circumstances violated Gouled's Fourth Amendment rights. The question not answered was whether gaining entry by false pretenses invalidated the use of *statements* made in confidence by the suspect to the **undercover agent**. The Supreme Court resolved the issue in two cases decided on the same day in 1966. There is no Fourth Amendment right of privacy against "inviting" a person who is a secret government agent into the home.

Lewis v. United States (1966) dealt with the common situation of a narcotics agent being invited into a home to conclude an illicit drug transaction after having misrepresented his intentions. The Fourth Amendment was not violated because Lewis had converted his home "into a commercial center to which outsiders are invited for purposes of transacting unlawful business." Whether one applies the older property theory or the *Katz* "expectation of privacy" concept of Fourth Amendment rights, there is no constitutional violation in this scenario. The Court warned that entry gained by invitation did not give the undercover investigator the right to conduct a general search of the premises. In *Lewis,* the Court also expressed its concern for the practical needs of law enforcement:

> Were we to hold the deceptions of the agent in this case constitutionally prohibited, we would come near to a rule that the use of undercover agents in any manner is virtually unconstitutional *per se*. Such a rule would, for example, severely hamper the Government in ferreting out those organized criminal activities that are characterized by covert dealings with victims who either cannot or do not protest. A prime example is provided by the narcotics traffic. (*Lewis v. United States,* footnote omitted)

In *Hoffa v. United States* (1966), national Teamsters Union president James Hoffa was convicted of bribing jurors in an earlier trial. Evidence of the jury tampering was offered by Edward Partin, a Teamsters Union official who was in trouble with the law and who was present in Hoffa's hotel apartment during the earlier trial. He had assisted Hoffa while simultaneously reporting on the jury tampering to federal agents. Partin went to Hoffa's apartment as a government agent; in return for his spying, state and federal criminal charges against him were dropped, and Partin's wife was paid $1,200 out of government funds. Hoffa argued that Partin's entry into the apartment violated his Fourth Amendment right to privacy and was an illegal "search" for verbal evidence. The Court agreed that Hoffa had a Fourth Amendment right to privacy in the hotel apartment and that entry could have been made both by a trespass and, as in *Gouled,* by trickery. What Hoffa relied on was the protection offered by the place. Thus if Partin had opened a desk drawer or a filing cabinet and had stolen incriminating evidence, this would have intruded into Hoffa's constitutionally protected area. The same result would occur by applying the *Katz* expectation of privacy analysis. However,

> [i]t is obvious that [Hoffa] was not relying on the security of his hotel suite when he made the incriminating statements to Partin or in Partin's presence. Partin did not enter the suite by force or by stealth. He was not a surreptitious eavesdropper. Partin was in the suite by invitation, and every conversation which he heard was either directed to him or knowingly carried on in his presence. The petitioner, in a word, was not relying on the security of the hotel room; he was relying upon his misplaced confidence that Partin would not reveal his wrongdoing. . . .
>
> Neither this Court nor any member of it has ever expressed the view that the Fourth Amendment protects a wrongdoer's misplaced belief that a person to whom he voluntarily confides his wrongdoing will not reveal it. (*Hoffa v. United States,* 1966)

The Fourth Amendment does not protect a person against false friends.

A related question is whether there is any Fourth Amendment protection when a "false friend" wears a concealed microphone on his body to transmit and/or record incriminating conversations. The Supreme Court has consistently ruled that this practice is not prohibited by the Fourth Amendment. When a person "invites" an undercover agent to speak with him or her voluntarily, the effect of the recording device is to improve the accuracy of the agent's testimony against the defendant. The Court has so held, both before and after *Katz,* and the federal electronic eavesdropping law has confirmed this rule as a matter of federal law.[36]

PROBABLE CAUSE AND THE FOURTH AMENDMENT

The Fourth Amendment states that warrants must be issued on probable cause, a standard that is the evidentiary touchstone of all Fourth Amendment action, including arrests, warrantless searches, and both search and arrest warrants. Until *Terry v. Ohio* (1968), a forcible police interference with liberty, property, or privacy on less than probable cause violated the Fourth Amendment. *Terry's* flexible interpretation, first applied to field interrogation, introduced the lower evidentiary standard of reasonable suspicion. This section explores the meaning and contours of probable cause.

The Concept of Evidence Sufficiency

Liberty is a fundamental precept of American political life. This means that a person's liberty interests—freedom of movement, privacy, and property—must not be stopped or interfered with by the government unless the government can first show a need to interfere that is justified by law. In Fourth Amendment terms, a police officer must have evidence to support a stop, arrest, or search *before* the search takes place. The best way for a police agent to do this is to obtain a warrant. If a warrantless stop, arrest, or search is challenged, the officer must convince a court that he or she had a sufficient level of evidence to lawfully interfere with the defendant's liberty interests. In other areas where the criminal justice or legal process interferes with liberty, different levels of evidence sufficiency are required. The concept of evidence sufficiency is therefore a latent part of due process and helps to ensure fundamental fairness.

Defining Probable Cause

Probable cause, defined as "known facts that could lead a reasonably prudent person to draw conclusions about unknown facts," is a standard of evidence that triggers and justifies government interference with liberty. It is also referred to as *reasonable cause*. Because the evidence standard of stops under *Terry v. Ohio* is commonly known as *reasonable suspicion*, it is important to use these technical terms precisely. *Evidence* is any kind of proof offered to establish the existence of a fact. Evidence may be (a) the testimony of a witness as to what was heard, seen, smelled, tasted, or felt; or (b) physical items such as documents, drugs, or weapons. Physical evidence is sometimes called *real evidence*.

Probable cause is one of several standards of evidence that trigger and justify intrusive governmental action. Table 3–1 displays a hierarchy of evidentiary standards. These standards pertain to the sufficiency or weight of evidence rather than to its admissibility. In general, the greater the impact of a legal action on an individual, the more stringent is the evidentiary standard.

Probable cause is the evidentiary standard for a wide variety of police and legal decisions in the pretrial criminal process: arrest, search and seizure, a magistrate's authorizing a charge after an initial hearing, a magistrate's bind-over decision after a preliminary hearing, and the formal charging of a criminal defendant by a prosecutor's information or by an indictment by a grand jury's voting a "true bill" against a suspect. (In some states, the grand jury or bind-over decision might be subjected to the slightly more rigorous "prima facie case" standard.) Probable cause to arrest a person consists of facts that would lead a prudent person to believe that a crime has been committed and that the suspect has committed it. Probable cause to search a place and seize evidence consists of facts that would lead a prudent person to believe that "seizable" items (i.e., contraband, the fruits of a crime, instrumentalities used to commit a crime, or evidence of criminality) are or soon will be located at a particular place.

There is a fine line between probable cause and reasonable suspicion. *Terry* (1967) did not use the term *reasonable suspicion* but upheld a temporary "stop"—a lesser intrusion than an arrest—where an officer believed that "criminal activity is afoot" based on articulable facts, taken together with logical inferences from those facts. A mere hunch does not support reasonable suspicion. (Reasonable suspicion will be explored at greater length in Chapter 4.)

Probable cause is not only a lower "weight" of evidence than that needed for civil or criminal verdicts, but it also relies on less stringent rules guiding the admissibility of evidence. Thus probable cause may be established on the basis of hearsay evidence; it is up to the magistrate to weigh the hearsay to determine whether it is plausible and genuine on the one hand, or farfetched or even fabricated on the other.

TABLE 3–1 Standards of Evidence Sufficiency

STANDARD	MEANING	LEGAL CONSEQUENCE
Proof beyond a reasonable doubt	No actual and substantial doubt must be present; not a vague apprehension or imaginary doubt; not absolute certainty	Conviction of guilt in a criminal trial
Clear and convincing evidence	Higher than a preponderance of evidence; need not be conclusive	Hold a person without bail under preventive detention; involuntary civil commitment; establish civil fraud; prove a gift
Preponderance of the evidence	Evidence reasonably tending to prove the essential facts in a case; the greater weight of the evidence	Verdict for the plaintiff in a civil litigation
Prima facie case	Evidence good and sufficient on its face to prove a fact or group of facts	Evidence that makes out the plaintiff's or prosecutor's case at trial and is strong enough to prevent a directed verdict for the defendant; in some jurisdictions, a prima facie case is required as the basis for indictment instead of probable cause
Substantial evidence on the whole record	Such evidence that a reasonable mind might accept as adequate to support a conclusion	Judicial review upholding administrative agency action
Probable cause	Known facts that would lead a reasonably prudent person to draw a conclusion about unknown facts	Lawful arrest; reasonable search and seizure; judicial determination to hold a suspect after an initial inquiry; bind-over by magistrate after preliminary examination; prosecutor's information; indictment after grand jury deliberations
Reasonable suspicion	Facts that would lead an experienced police officer to believe that a crime has been, is, or is about to be committed	Stop, pat-down search of outer clothing, and brief questioning of a person
None or "mere" suspicion	Whimsy; randomness; mere suspicion	Observation and surveillance of a person by police or government agent that do not amount to harassment or otherwise unduly interfere with the reasonable expectation of privacy

Probable Cause Based on Informers' Tips

An officer/affiant seeking a search warrant swears to the magistrate that the information presented is true. Where the officer affirms that he or she saw things or smelled odors (common in drug cases) that would lead a prudent person to believe that contraband is located at a specific place, the magistrate can directly question the officer to be sure of the accuracy of the evidence. Likewise, information given to an officer or magistrate by a victim of a crime is usually considered to be honest and accurate.

However, much criminal activity—including bribery by government officials, white-collar crime, organized crime, and illicit drug trading—is conducted in secret. Officers or blameless victims cannot get access to the criminal behavior. Often, the only way for law enforcement agencies to detect and prosecute such crimes is by using undercover agents to infiltrate the worlds of drug trafficking, organized crime, and white-collar crime. These **secret informants** are themselves often involved in criminal activity. Professors Robert Reinertsen and Robert Bronson note, "Informants are generally unsavory types, engaged in marginal activities that involve betrayal of others. Nonetheless, despite their negative image, informants play such a large and important role in law enforcement efforts that they cannot be ignored."[37] The common terms *'snitch'*, *'fink'*, and *'stool pigeon'* attest to the negative image and reality of informants. They rarely aid the police out of altruistic motives. More likely, they are being paid, given a promise of prosecutorial leniency, or even rewarded with illicit drugs.

Law enforcement agencies are caught in a dilemma. Knowing the risk of receiving unreliable information when using criminal informants, agencies establish policies regarding informants' recruitment, control, and payment. The proper use of informants depends in large measure on the honesty and mature judgment of the law enforcement officers who control them and good management practices.[38]

Despite internal law enforcement controls, informants have an incentive to lie and have sent many innocent people to prison.[39] The question facing the judicial system is whether it can take steps to ensure that the threat to justice from lying informants is minimized. One solution would be to have the police bring informers before the magistrate so that instead of accepting hearsay, the magistrate can examine the informant personally. The Supreme Court refused to take this path. In ***Rovario v. United States*** (1957), the Court held that the identity of an informant must be made available at the trial, but prior to trial, law enforcement agencies are allowed to keep the identity of informants secret. (See the biographical sketch of Justice Harold Burton following Chapter 4.) There is a legitimate fear that bringing the informant to the courthouse and having the identity made known to judges and other court personnel would undermine the integrity and success of investigations. It is also not the role of the judicial branch to exercise administrative oversight of the executive branch.

Still, magistrates play an important role in screening out fabrications by secret informants, who are often unreliable. Magistrates therefore have good reason to examine affidavits based on the hearsay of confidential sources with special care. In a series of decisions beginning in 1933, the Court has struggled with the question of whether hearsay supplied by "snitches" had established probable cause under the Fourth Amendment or had to be excluded.

In ***Nathanson v. United States*** (1933), the Court excluded liquor seized from a private home based on a warrant that "went upon a mere affirmation of suspicion and belief without any statement of adequate supporting facts." A magistrate cannot "properly issue a warrant to search a private dwelling unless he can find probable cause therefore from facts or circumstances presented to him under oath or affirmation. Mere affirmance of belief or suspicion is not enough." Another way of stating the rule of *Nathanson* is that a magistrate cannot issue a warrant on the mere say-so of the officer.

Nathanson was supported in ***Aguilar v. Texas*** (1964). The search warrant application from police officers simply stated that "[a]ffiants have received reliable information from a credible person and do believe" that drugs are located in Aguilar's home. Here, the hearsay basis of the officers' suspicions were more clearly stated than in *Nathanson*. The Court reaffirmed that "an affidavit may be based on hearsay information and need not reflect the direct personal observations of the affiant." Nevertheless, "the magistrate must be informed of some of the *underlying circumstances* from which the informant concluded that the narcotics were where he claimed they were, and some of the underlying circumstances from which the officer concluded that the informant, whose identity need not be disclosed, was '*credible*' or his information '*reliable.*'" (*Aguilar v. Texas*, emphasis added). Again, the Supreme Court ruled that a magistrate's warrant is fatally flawed under the Fourth Amendment if the magistrate simply takes the police officer's word that an informant is reliable or credible and that the contraband is where the officer says it is. This rule is a necessary corollary to the "detached and neutral magistrate" doctrine. If a warrant is issued simply on an officer's say-so, the magistrate becomes a rubber stamp for the executive branch and fails to uphold his or her duty under the Constitution.

Justice Harlan, a conservative jurist, concurred in *Aguilar*. Justice Tom Clark's dissent, joined by Justices Black and Stewart, argued that the officers' statement that they "received reliable information from a credible person" was sufficient to provide probable cause.

The rule of *Aguilar* was confirmed and strengthened in ***Spinelli v. United States*** (1969). William Spinelli was being investigated by the FBI for bookmaking in St. Louis. A search warrant was obtained to enter an apartment for evidence of an illegal gambling establishment. The affidavit, when reduced to its essential information, contained four facts: (1) that for four of the five days he was followed, Spinelli crossed into Missouri from Illinois at about noon, went to the same apartment house at about 4:00 p.m., and was seen to enter a particular apartment; (2) that there were two telephones in the apartment listed under another's name; (3) that Spinelli had a reputation as a bookmaker and gambler among law enforcement agents, including the affiant; and (4) that a "confidential reliable informant" told the FBI agent that Spinelli was operating a gambling operation with the telephones in the apartment. Evidence seized in the apartment was used to convict Spinelli of interstate travel in aid of racketeering, specifically, of illegal bookmaking.

Justice Harlan's majority opinion held that this affidavit did not provide probable cause and that the evidence seized had to be excluded. He quickly tossed out the first three items in the affidavit as essentially not supportive of probable cause. There is simply no reason why traveling from one city to another every day would lead anyone to suspect the traveler of being a bookie. The existence of two telephones in the apartment, described as a "petty luxury," was also not deemed at all suspicious.

The third item, Spinelli's reputation, was dismissed: "[T]he allegation that Spinelli was 'known' to the affiant and to other federal and local law enforcement officers as a gambler is but a bald and unilluminating assertion of suspicion that is entitled to no weight in appraising the magistrate's decision." Justice Harlan cited *Nathanson* for this point, although *Nathanson* does not discuss reputation evidence. Reputation evidence is hearsay, and hearsay is proper evidence in a search warrant affidavit. It would appear that the Court, almost instinctively, understood that hearsay about an individual can be entirely baseless and scurrilous and indeed could even be manufactured by the government. Although it may be useful as a starting point for investigation, the reliance on a person's reputation as a matter of Fourth Amendment law could lead to gross injustices.

This, then, left the statement about the "confidential reliable informant" as the sole basis for the warrant. The prosecution argued that the innocent facts in the affidavit corroborated the informant's tip, "thereby entitling it to more weight." The Court disagreed, saying that "the *'totality of circumstances'* approach . . . paints with too broad a brush." Instead of a "totality" approach, Justice Harlan, refining the elements of the *Aguilar* case, provided "a more precise analysis" by which the affidavit's statements regarding a secret informant had to stand on its own. He stated the rules of *Aguilar* that could be reduced to two tests:

> [W]e first consider the weight to be given the informer's tip when it is considered apart from the rest of the affidavit. It is clear that a Commissioner could not credit it without abdicating his constitutional function. Though the affiant swore that his confidant was "reliable," he offered the magistrate no reason in support of this conclusion. Perhaps even more important is the fact that *Aguilar*'s other test has not been satisfied. The tip does not contain a sufficient statement of the underlying circumstances from which the informer concluded that Spinelli was running a bookmaking operation. We are not told how the FBI's source received his information—it is not alleged that the informant personally observed Spinelli at work or that he had ever placed a bet with him. Moreover, if the informant came by the information indirectly, he did not explain why his sources were reliable. . . . In the absence of a statement detailing the manner in which the information was gathered, it is especially important that the tip describe the accused's criminal activity in sufficient detail that the magistrate may know that he is relying on something more substantial than a casual rumor circulating in the underworld or an accusation based merely on an individual's general reputation. (*Spinelli v. United States,* 1969)

The *Aguilar–Spinelli* two-pronged test to obtaining a warrant based on an informer's hearsay includes (1) a veracity, or truthfulness, prong—showing that the informant is truthful because he was used successfully in the past or because the tip is so strong that it is inherently believable; and (2) a basis-of-knowledge prong—showing that the facts were obtained by the informant in a manner that is sufficiently reliable to establish probable cause. The facts that support the prongs must be strong enough to convince the magistrate making an independent determination that the informant had a real basis for knowing about the criminal activity. The facts would also give the magistrate a basis for ascertaining whether they support probable cause.

The dissenters in *Spinelli,* Justices Black, Fortas, and Stewart, felt that the four elements found wanting by the majority constituted probable cause. Justice Abe Fortas referred to the length of the affidavit to indicate that it was not simply conclusory. But he did not adequately respond to Justice Harlan's analysis that cut through the lengthy verbiage of the affidavit to reduce it to its essential elements. Justice White concurred in the holding of *Spinelli,* but he expressed concern that it did not fully comport with that of *Draper v. United States* (1959), on which the Court relied.

Justice Harlan, in *Spinelli,* demonstrated how a magistrate should critically evaluate information presented in an affidavit by drawing on the 1959 case of **Draper v. United States.** In that case, a paid informer named Hereford told Bureau of Narcotics agents that Draper would travel from Chicago to Denver on a train on one of two days with three ounces of heroin. Hereford precisely described what Draper looked like and told the agents that Draper would be carrying "a tan zipper bag," that he habitually "walked real fast," and that he would be wearing a light-colored raincoat, brown slacks, and black shoes. Agents waited at the incoming trains from Chicago in the Denver station and saw a man fitting the exact description given by Hereford. The man, who turned out to be Draper, was found to be carrying heroin and was arrested. The Supreme Court held that the agents had probable cause to arrest and search Draper, based on the hearsay description of the informant, Hereford. Although Hereford did not provide information to show how he obtained his information about Draper, the "basis of knowledge" prong of the *Aguilar–Spinelli* rule was inferred. The Supreme Court upheld the seizure and search in *Draper* because the highly detailed facts were verified by the agent (except for the possession of heroin) before making the arrest. *Draper,* therefore, stands for the proposition that the police can strengthen any weaknesses in the information provided by the informant by gathering corroborating information.

Conservative Revisions

A task of the Supreme Court, to lay down clear rules for the guidance of lower court judges and government officers, seems to have been fulfilled in *Spinelli* when the Court clarified a line of informers' tip decisions, beginning with *Nathanson v. United States* (1933), with relatively clear procedural guides for resolving probable cause issues. *Spinelli* exemplified the Warren Court's penchant for establishing structured rules. This changed with the advent of the Burger Court, as conservative activism replaced liberal activism.

Professor Charles Whitebread described the five elements of the Burger Court's criminal procedure jurisprudence (see Chapter 1):[40]

- A crime control orientation.
- A hierarchy of constitutional values, with Sixth Amendment trial rights on a higher plane than Fourth Amendment rights.
- A preference for case-by-case analysis rather than establishing general rules.
- A tendency to uphold the prosecution side if the Court believes in the defendant's factual guilt.
- The denial of federal jurisdiction from state cases.

These tendencies were clearly at work in *Illinois v. Gates,* which upset the *Aguilar–Spinelli* rule after fourteen years, during which there was little criticism of the two-pronged test.

Read Case and Comments: *Illinois v. Gates*

It is interesting that the nine justices in *Illinois v. Gates* came up with four different analyses of whether the facts established probable cause:

1. The majority (Chief Justice Warren Burger and Justices William Rehnquist, Harry Blackmun, Lewis Powell, and Sandra Day O'Connor) found probable cause to exist under the new totality-of-the-circumstances test.
2. Justice White, concurring, found that probable cause existed under the *Aguilar–Spinelli* two-pronged test.
3. Justices William Brennan and Thurgood Marshall, dissenting, found that the anonymous letter plus the corroboration did not amount to probable cause under either test.
4. Justice John Paul Stevens, dissenting, found no probable cause because at the time when the magistrate issued the warrant, he did not know that the Gateses had driven twenty-two hours nonstop from West Palm Beach to Bloomingdale, a suspicious activity in light of the anonymous letter. The anonymous letter predicted that Sue Gates would fly back to Illinois while Lance drove. This discrepancy undermined probable cause because (1) the couple's willingness to leave their house unattended suggested that it did not contain drugs, and (2) their activity was not as unusual as if they had left separately.

CASE AND COMMENTS

Illinois v. Gates

462 U.S. 213, 103 S.Ct. 2317, 76 L.Ed.2d 527 (1983)

JUSTICE REHNQUIST delivered the opinion of the Court.

Respondents Lance and Susan Gates were indicted for violation of state drug laws after police officers, executing a search warrant, discovered marihuana and other contraband in their automobile and home. * * * The Illinois Supreme Court * * * held that the affidavit submitted in support of the State's application for a warrant to search the Gateses' property was inadequate under this Court's decisions in *Aguilar v. Texas,* 378 U.S. 108 (1964) and *Spinelli v. United States* [this volume] (1969).

We granted certiorari to consider the application of the Fourth Amendment to a magistrate's issuance of a search warrant on the basis of a partially corroborated anonymous informant's tip. * * *

II

* * * On May 3, 1978, the Bloomingdale Police Department received by mail an anonymous handwritten letter which read as follows: **[a]**

> "This letter is to inform you that you have a couple in your town who strictly make their living on selling drugs. They are Sue and Lance Gates, they live on Greenway, off Bloomingdale Rd. in the condominiums. Most of their buys are done in Florida. Sue his wife drives their car to Florida, where she leaves it to be loaded up with drugs, then Lance flys [*sic*] down and drives it back. Sue flys back after she drops the car off in Florida. May 3 she is driving down there again and Lance will be flying down in a few days to drive it back. At the time Lance drives the car back he has the trunk loaded with over $100,000.00 in drugs. Presently they have over $100,000.00 worth of drugs in their basement.
>
> "They brag about the fact they never have to work, and make their entire living on pushers.
>
> "I guarantee if you watch them carefully you will make a big catch. They are friends with some big drugs dealers, who visit their house often.
>
> "Lance & Susan Gates
>
> "Greenway
>
> "in Condominiums"

The letter was referred by the Chief of Police * * * to Detective Mader, who decided to pursue the tip. Mader learned * * * that an Illinois driver's license had been issued to one Lance Gates, residing at a stated address in Bloomingdale. He contacted a confidential informant, whose examination of certain financial records revealed a more recent address for the Gateses, and he also learned from a police officer assigned to O'Hare Airport that "L. Gates" had made a reservation on Eastern Airlines Flight 245 to West Palm Beach, Fla., scheduled to depart from Chicago on May 5 at 4:15 P.M.

Mader then made arrangements with an agent of the Drug Enforcement Administration for surveillance of the May 5 Eastern Airlines flight. The agent later reported to Mader that Gates had boarded the flight, and that federal agents in Florida had observed him arrive in West Palm Beach and take a taxi to the nearby Holiday Inn. They also reported that Gates went to a room registered to one Susan Gates and that, at 7 o'clock A.M. the next morning, Gates and an unidentified woman left the motel in a Mercury bearing Illinois license plates and drove northbound on an interstate highway frequently used by travelers to the Chicago area. In addition, the DEA agent informed Mader that the license plate number on the Mercury was registered to a Hornet station wagon owned by Gates. The agent also advised Mader that the driving time between West Palm Beach and Bloomingdale was approximately 22 to 24 hours. **[b]**

Mader signed an affidavit setting forth the foregoing facts, and submitted it to a judge of the Circuit Court of Du Page County, together with a copy of the anonymous letter. The judge of that court thereupon issued a search warrant for the Gateses' residence and for their automobile. The judge, in deciding to issue the warrant, could have determined that the *modus operandi* of the Gateses had been substantially corroborated. As the anonymous letter predicted, Lance Gates had flown from Chicago to West Palm Beach late in the afternoon of May 5th, had checked into a hotel room registered in the name of his wife, and, at 7 o'clock A.M. the following morning, had headed north, accompanied by an unidentified woman, out of West Palm Beach on an interstate highway used by travelers from South Florida to Chicago in an automobile bearing a license plate issued to him. **[c]**

At 5:15 A.M. on March 7, only 36 hours after he had flown out of Chicago, Lance Gates, and his wife, returned to their home in Bloomingdale, driving the car in which they had left West Palm Beach some 22 hours earlier. The Bloomingdale police were awaiting them, searched the trunk of the Mercury,

[a] What motivates such an anonymous letter? Motives like envy or revenge could enhance its reliability; on the other hand, a false, incriminating letter could be written as a prank or as a means to harass someone. The police and the magistrate did not rely exclusively on the letter to initiate the search.

[b] Can you think of any legitimate explanations for this travel plan? Is the couple's travel consistent only with a criminal conspiracy? If there is a legitimate explanation, does it negate probable cause to search?

[c] Are the level and type of specificity in the letter similar to, or different from, that given by Hereford in *Draper?* Although the travel plans stated in the letter were mostly corroborated, does that dissolve doubts about the fact that Officer Mader had no idea who wrote the letter?

and uncovered approximately 350 pounds of marihuana. A search of the Gateses' home revealed marihuana, weapons, and other contraband. * * *

The Illinois Supreme Court concluded—and we are inclined to agree—that, standing alone, the anonymous letter * * * would not provide the basis for a magistrate's determination that there was probable cause to believe contraband would be found in the Gateses' car and home. **[d]** The letter provides virtually nothing from which one might conclude that its author is either honest or his information reliable; likewise, the letter gives absolutely no indication of the basis for the writer's predictions regarding the Gateses' criminal activities. Something more was required.

* * *

[The evidence was suppressed by the Illinois courts. They all held that probable cause was not made out under the *Aguilar–Spinelli* test.]

* * * The Illinois Supreme Court, like some others, apparently understood *Spinelli* as requiring that the anonymous letter satisfy each of two independent requirements before it could be relied on. * * * According to this view, the letter, as supplemented by Mader's affidavit, first had to adequately reveal the "basis of knowledge" of the letterwriter—the particular means by which he came by the information given in his report. Second, it had to provide facts sufficiently establishing either the "veracity" of the affiant's informant, or, alternatively, the "reliability" of the informant's report in this particular case.

The Illinois court * * * found that the test had not been satisfied. First, the "veracity" prong was not satisfied because, "[t]here was simply no basis [for] conclud[ing] that the anonymous person [who wrote the letter to the Bloomingdale Police Department] was credible." * * * The court indicated that corroboration by police of details contained in the letter might never satisfy the "veracity" prong, and in any event, could not do so if, as in the present case, only "innocent" details are corroborated. * * * **[e]** In addition, the letter gave no indication of the basis of its writer's knowledge of the Gateses' activities: [it] * * * failed to provide sufficient detail to permit such an inference. Thus, it concluded that no showing of probable cause had been made.

We agree with the Illinois Supreme Court that an informant's "veracity," "reliability," and "basis of knowledge" are all highly relevant in determining the value of his report. We do not agree, however, that these elements should be understood as entirely separate and independent requirements to be rigidly exacted in every case, which the opinion of the Supreme Court of Illinois would imply. Rather, as detailed below, they should be understood simply as closely intertwined issues that may usefully illuminate the commonsense, practical question whether there is "probable cause" to believe that contraband or evidence is located in a particular place.

III

This totality-of-the-circumstances approach is far more consistent with our prior treatment of probable cause than is any rigid demand that specific "tests" be satisfied by every informant's tip. **[f]** Perhaps the central teaching of our decisions bearing on the probable-cause standard is that it is a "practical, nontechnical conception." * * * "In dealing with probable cause, * * * as the very name implies, we deal with probabilities. These are not technical; they are the factual and practical considerations of everyday life on which reasonable and prudent men, not legal technicians, act." * * *

* * * [P]robable cause is a fluid concept—turning on the assessment of probabilities in particular factual contexts—not readily, or even usefully, reduced to a neat set of legal rules. * * * "Informants' tips, like all other clues and evidence coming to a policeman on the scene, may vary greatly in their value and reliability." Rigid legal rules are ill-suited to an area of such diversity. "One simple rule will not cover every situation." * * *

Moreover, the two-pronged test directs analysis into two largely independent channels—the informant's "veracity" or "reliability" and his "basis of knowledge." **[g]** There are persuasive arguments against according these two elements such independent status. Instead, they are better understood as relevant considerations in the totality-of-the-circumstances analysis that traditionally has guided probable-cause determinations: a deficiency in one may be compensated for, in determining the overall reliability of a tip, by a strong showing as to the other, or by some other indicia of reliability. * * *

[Justice Rehnquist suggests that an unusually reliable informant should be believed when on occasion he fails to state the basis of knowledge regarding a prediction of crime.] * * *

* * *

We also have recognized that affidavits "are normally drafted by nonlawyers in the midst and haste of a criminal investigation. Technical requirements of elaborate specificity once exacted under common law pleadings have no proper place in this area." * * * Likewise, search and arrest warrants long have been issued by persons who are neither lawyers nor judges, and who certainly do not remain abreast of each judicial refinement of the nature of "probable cause." * * * **[h]** The rigorous inquiry into the *Spinelli* prongs and the complex superstructure of evidentiary and analytical rules that some have seen implicit in our *Spinelli* decision, cannot be reconciled with the fact that many warrants are—quite properly,—issued

---

[d] The Court is wary of information from anonymous tips—yet it does not close the door on the use of such information.

[e] Did the close match between the couple's travels and the letter establish the veracity of the anonymous letter writer? If so, was it veracity regarding the couple's travel patterns or veracity as to their drug dealing?

[f] "Totality of the circumstances" was proposed to the Court by the government in *Spinelli* but rejected by the Court at that time. What factors caused the Court to shift gears?

[g] Justice Harlan, a noted conservative, said in *Spinelli* that a weakness in one prong should not be made up in another: Even a "reliable" informant may, at times, obtain information from a weak hearsay source.

[h] This analysis is belied by a recent article that shows that police agencies prefer the two-prong rule, reviewed at the conclusion of this case. Is Justice Rehnquist setting his sights too low regarding the mental capabilities of lay magistrates and police officers?

on the basis of nontechnical, common-sense judgments of laymen applying a standard less demanding than those used in more formal legal proceedings. Likewise, given the informal, often hurried context in which it must be applied, the "built-in subtleties," * * * of the "two-pronged test" are particularly unlikely to assist magistrates in determining probable cause.

* * *

[Justice Rehnquist urged that courts not review the facts of magistrates' probable cause decisions but pay them great deference. He also argued that if courts continue to scrutinize affidavits according to the two-prong test, police will stop using warrants and will turn more to warrantless searches.]

Finally, the direction taken by decisions following *Spinelli* poorly serves "[t]he most basic function of any government": "to provide for the security of the individual and of his property." * * * **[i]** If, as the Illinois Supreme Court apparently thought, that test must be rigorously applied in every case, anonymous tips would be of greatly diminished value in police work. * * *

* * * [W]e conclude that it is wiser to abandon the "two-pronged test" established by our decisions in *Aguilar* and *Spinelli.* In its place we reaffirm the totality-of-the-circumstances analysis that traditionally has informed probable-cause determinations. * * *

* * *

JUSTICE BRENNAN's dissent also suggests that "[w]ords such as 'practical,' 'nontechnical,' and 'common sense,' as used in the Court's opinion, are but code words for an overly permissive attitude towards police practices in derogation of the rights secured by the Fourth Amendment." * * * **[j]** [N]o one doubts that "under our Constitution only measures consistent with the Fourth Amendment may be employed by government to cure [the horrors of drug trafficking];" * * * but this agreement does not advance the inquiry as to which measures are, and which measures are not, consistent with the Fourth Amendment. "Fidelity" to the commands of the Constitution suggests balanced judgment rather than exhortation. The highest "fidelity" is not achieved by the judge who instinctively goes furthest in upholding even the most bizarre claim of individual constitutional rights, any more than it is achieved by a judge who instinctively goes furthest in accepting the most restrictive claims of governmental authorities. The task of this Court, as of other courts, is to "hold the balance true," and we think we have done that in this case.

IV

Our decisions applying the totality-of-the-circumstances analysis outlined above have consistently recognized the value of corroboration of details of an informant's tip by independent police work. * * *

* * *

The showing of probable cause in the present case was * * * compelling. * * * **[k]** Even standing alone, the facts obtained through the independent investigation of Mader and the DEA at least suggested that the Gateses were involved in drug trafficking. In addition to being a popular vacation site, Florida is well known as a source of narcotics and other illegal drugs. * * * Lance Gates' flight to Palm Beach, his brief, overnight stay in a motel, and apparent immediate return north to Chicago in the family car, conveniently awaiting him in West Palm Beach, is as suggestive of a prearranged drug run, as it is of an ordinary vacation trip.

In addition, the judge could rely on the anonymous letter, which had been corroborated in major part by Mader's efforts. * * *

Finally, the anonymous letter contained a range of details relating not just to easily obtained facts and conditions existing at the time of the tip, but to future actions of third parties ordinarily not easily predicted. The letterwriter's accurate information as to the travel plans of each of the Gateses was of a character likely obtained only from the Gateses themselves, or from someone familiar with their not entirely ordinary travel plans. If the informant had access to accurate information of this type a magistrate could properly conclude that it was not unlikely that he also had access to reliable information of the Gateses' alleged illegal activities. Of course, the Gateses' travel plans might have been learned from a talkative neighbor or travel agent; under the "two-pronged test" developed from *Spinelli,* the character of the details in the anonymous letter might well not permit a sufficiently clear inference regarding the letterwriter's "basis of knowledge." But, as discussed previously, * * * probable cause does not demand the certainty we associate with formal trials. It is enough that there was a fair probability that the writer of the anonymous letter had obtained his entire story either from the Gateses or someone they trusted. And corroboration of major portions of the letter's predictions provides just this probability. It is apparent, therefore, that the judge issuing the warrant had a "substantial basis for * * * conclud[ing]" that probable cause to search the Gateses' home and car existed. The judgment of the Supreme Court of Illinois therefore must be

Reversed.

JUSTICE BRENNAN, with whom JUSTICE MARSHALL joins, dissenting.

* * *

[i] Is this a "constitutional" reason or a "policy" reason? Can such a division be neatly made? Does this seem result oriented?

[j] Justice Brennan, a result-oriented liberal, argues in his dissent that Justice Rehnquist's opinion is result oriented. In reply, Justice Rehnquist makes the valid point that different justices (and different people) genuinely view constitutional rules differently.

[k] Do you agree with Justice Rehnquist that this evidence is "compelling," or is it a close call? When deciding to intrude into a person's home and car, should magistrates lean toward restraint? If the warrant were not issued in this case, how much additional investigation would the Bloomingdale Police Department have to do after the couple's return to make a stronger case for probable cause? Given the Court's allowance of a corroborated anonymous letter as the basis of probable cause, does this create a risk that a dishonest police officer will be tempted to have an "anonymous" letter submitted in a

I

* * *

Until today the Court has never squarely addressed the application of the *Aguilar* and *Spinelli* standards to tips from anonymous informants. Both *Aguilar* and *Spinelli* dealt with tips from informants known at least to the police. * * * And surely there is even more reason to subject anonymous informants' tips to the tests established by *Aguilar* and *Spinelli.* By definition nothing is known about an anonymous informant's identity, honesty, or reliability. * * *

To suggest that anonymous informants' tips are subject to the tests established by *Aguilar* and *Spinelli* is not to suggest that they can never provide a basis for a finding of probable cause. [I] It is conceivable that police corroboration of the details of the tip might establish the reliability of the informant under *Aguilar*'s veracity prong, as refined in *Spinelli,* and that the details in the tip might be sufficient to qualify under the "self-verifying detail" test established by *Spinelli* as a means of satisfying *Aguilar*'s basis of knowledge prong. The *Aguilar* and *Spinelli* tests must be applied to anonymous informants' tips, however, if we are to continue to ensure that findings of probable cause, and attendant intrusions, are based on information provided by an honest or credible person who has acquired the information in a reliable way. * * *

II

* * *

* * * But of particular concern to all Americans must be that the Court gives virtually no consideration to the value of insuring that findings of probable cause are based on information that a magistrate can reasonably say has been obtained in a reliable way by an honest or credible person. I share JUSTICE WHITE's fear that the Court's rejection of Aguilar and Spinelli and its adoption of a new totality-of-the-circumstances test, * * * "may foretell an evisceration of the probable-cause standard. * * *" * * *

> **[I]** What sort of fact would verify the basis of knowledge in an anonymous tip? Perhaps a verifiable reference to criminal activity that would not be known to an average person? If it would be impossible for a magistrate to rely on an anonymous tip, would the proper law enforcement response be to get additional corroboration in order to establish independent probable cause?

Gates is a constitutionally important decision that significantly shifted the criminal procedure balance in favor of the state, a result that has been criticized by some legal commentators.[41] An interesting study published in 2000, examining the practices of six Atlanta-area police academies, shows that the departments train their officers in the *Aguilar–Spinelli* two-pronged test rather than the open-ended *Gates* totality test. Two reasons were given by the training officers: (1) they felt that prosecutors and courts were likely to demand adherence to the two-pronged or a similar test, and (2) "almost all of the instructors stated that they did not believe a majority of their recruits could master the intricacies of an open-ended standard such as the *Gates* standard."[42] This is contrary to the main reason given by Justice Rehnquist for the majority opinion, and it is not the first time that police practice did not agree with legal speculation.

PLAIN VIEW AND RELATED DOCTRINES

Plain view is a useful doctrine for police officers. It allows seizures of evidence without a warrant when the police are already lawfully in a place or have made a lawful search. This section also examines the related "open fields" doctrine, curtilage, and the use of enhancement devices.

Plain View

The simple idea that a police officer can seize contraband lying about in a public place is so obvious that it has rarely been litigated. In **Cardwell v. Lewis** (1974), the Court articulated the principle that there is no Fourth Amendment privacy interest in material or possessions that are exposed to public scrutiny. In this case, a car owned by a murder suspect was in a public parking lot; the police scraped a bit of paint from a fender to be used as evidence. The court found no constitutional violation: "[W]here probable cause exists, a warrantless examination of the exterior of a car is not unreasonable under the Fourth and Fourteenth Amendments."

It is a different matter for police to seize material from inside a place that is protected by the Fourth Amendment. Professors Whitebread and Slobogin assert, correctly, that a police officer who saw marijuana through a house window while standing on a sidewalk could not enter and seize the evidence, although in a factual sense it was in "plain view."[43] As the Supreme Court stated in *Agnello v. United States* (1925): "Belief, however well-founded, that an article sought is concealed in a dwelling house furnishes no justification for a search of that place without a warrant." In such a case, the officer has to obtain a warrant to enter lawfully.

PRIOR JUSTIFIED SEARCH   The basic rules of plain view were established in ***Coolidge v. New Hampshire*** (1971). Justice Stewart, writing for a plurality, made clear the ancillary, or "piggyback," nature of the doctrine:

> What the "plain view" cases have in common is that the police officer in each of them had a *prior justification* for an intrusion. . . . The doctrine serves to supplement the prior justification—whether it be a warrant for another object, hot pursuit, search incident to lawful arrest, or some other legitimate reason for being present unconnected with a search directed against the accused—and permits the warrantless seizure. (*Coolidge v. New Hampshire,* emphasis added)

Under *Katz,* a plain view seizure of property is justified on the ground that there is no reasonable expectation of privacy in items that are contraband or the clear evidence of crime; police have a legitimate interest, not blocked by the Fourth Amendment, to take such items.

Nevertheless, it must be stressed that the first rule of plain view is that there must be a lawful intrusion. In *Coolidge,* Justice Stewart noted,

> But it is important to keep in mind that, in the vast majority of cases, *any* evidence seized by the police will be in plain view, at least at the moment of seizure. The problem with the "plain view" doctrine has been to identify the circumstances in which plain view has legal significance rather than being simply the normal concomitant of any search, legal or illegal. (*Coolidge v. New Hampshire,* 1971, emphasis in original)

Police cannot "create" plain view by taking advantage of an illegal search. Justice Stewart put it this way: "[P]lain view alone is never enough to justify the warrantless seizure of evidence." It would destroy Fourth Amendment protections to allow the police to search at will, or without a warrant where a warrant is otherwise required, and to rationalize a seizure because an unearthed item is seen to be contraband or evidence of criminality.

IMMEDIATELY APPARENT   *Coolidge* established a second rule of plain view—the "immediately apparent" rule. The police in *Coolidge* conducted a warrantless search of an automobile suspected to contain fiber evidence and sought to justify it because the car itself was "in plain view." The car was obviously in plain view, but the vacuumed microscopic particles certainly were not. Justice Stewart said, "Of course, the extension of the original justification is legitimate only when it is *immediately apparent* to the police that they have evidence before them; the 'plain view' doctrine may not be used to extend a general exploratory search from one object to another until something incriminating at last emerges." The rule that the evidence in plain view must be immediately apparent as contraband is another way of saying that *probable cause* must exist to secure the evidence at the moment of seizure.

As with all probable cause decisions, absolute certainty is not required. For example, in *Texas v. Brown* (1983), a police officer looked into an automobile at night with a flashlight at a routine traffic license checkpoint and saw an opaque, green party balloon knotted about one-half inch from the tip. The Supreme Court ruled that he had probable cause to believe that the balloon contained illegal drugs because it was known that this was a common way for drug dealers to carry their wares. The Court thus allowed the police some leeway for making an inference in determining whether it was immediately apparent that drugs were in the car.

Read Case and Comments: *Arizona v. Hicks*

It is interesting to note that in *Coolidge* a plurality of four justices adopted a rule—that plain view searches must be "inadvertent" or unintentional—which was later dropped in ***Horton v. California*** (1990). If police seek to subvert the plain view doctrine by deliberately "creating" plain view they will necessarily violate the rule that the police must be in a public area or a place where they have a right to be or violate the immediately apparent rule. In *Horton* a police warrant affidavit particularly described guns used to commit a robbery and the robbery proceeds as things to be seized. The warrant, however, only mentioned the robbery proceeds. When the warrant was executed, the robbery proceeds were not in Horton's home but the distinctive weapons (an Uzi machine gun, a .38-caliber revolver, and a stun gun) were. The detective, knowing that the guns tied Horton to the robbery, seized them as evidence.

Because the detective knew about the guns, they were not seized inadvertently. Nevertheless, the officer was properly in Horton's house under the warrant and did not exceed the scope of the search allowed by the warrant. Therefore the inadvertence rule did not create any additional privacy protection and could frustrate legitimate law enforcement. Justice Brennan, dissenting, expressed concern that eliminating the inadvertence rule would lead to a larger number of pretext searches. Because the Court has since ruled that a pretextual auto stop is not unconstitutional as long as an officer has a valid basis to search or make an arrest, this argument has taken on greater urgency.[44]

PLAIN FEEL   Plain view is not limited to matters viewed by eyesight, but applies to evidence known to any of the senses. In ***Minnesota v. Dickerson*** (1993), police lawfully stopped Dickerson outside a known drug house when his overall behavior created a reasonable suspicion that he carried drugs. An officer, following *Terry* (1968), patted down the outside of Dickerson's jacket to check for weapons. He testified, "I felt a lump, a small lump, in the front pocket. I examined it with my fingers and it slid and it felt to be a lump of crack cocaine in cellophane." The officer then retrieved a small plastic bag with crack cocaine from Dickerson's pocket.

Dickerson raised two plain view issues. First, must the police *visually observe* an item for it to be in plain view? The Court answered that plain "view" applies to any seizable item apparent to *any of the senses*:

> To this Court there is no distinction as to which sensory perception the officer uses to conclude that the material is contraband. An experienced officer may rely upon his sense of smell in DWI stops or in recognizing the smell of burning marijuana in an automobile. The sound of a shotgun being racked would clearly support certain reactions by an officer. The sense of touch, grounded in experience and training, is as reliable as perceptions drawn from other senses. "Plain feel," therefore, is no different than plain view and will equally support the seizure here. (*Minnesota v. Dickerson*, 1993, quoting trial judge)

Two arguments to the contrary were raised by the Minnesota Supreme Court to reject the so-called **plain feel rule**: (1) that the sense of touch is inherently less immediate and less reliable than the sense of sight and (2) that the sense of touch is far more intrusive into personal privacy. The U.S. Supreme Court disagreed; the facts in *Terry v. Ohio* (1968) itself relied on the sense of touch—the pat-down search—to establish probable cause to arrest for gun possession.

Dickerson had to resolve a second issue: whether what the officer felt was *immediately apparent* as crack cocaine. Justice White's close examination of the facts led him to conclude that the officer "overstepped the bounds" of the limited search authorized by *Terry* because he continued to explore Dickerson's outer pocket after determining that it contained no weapon. The *Terry* rule overlapped with the immediacy/probable cause rule: "If . . . the police lack probable cause to believe that an object in plain view is contraband without conducting some further search of the object—*i.e.*, if 'its incriminating character [is not] "immediately apparent,"' . . . the plain-view doctrine cannot justify its seizure" (*Dickerson*, 1983) Here, because the officer had to slide the object in the pocket around, it was not immediately apparent as contraband and was not admissible as evidence in a trial.

Curtilage and Open Fields

The Fourth Amendment protects the privacy, liberty, and property interests of "persons, houses, papers, and effects, against unreasonable searches and seizures." Is a "house" limited to the precise structure of residence? If so, can police roam at will around the yard of a suburban house, as they can on streets? Or does a "house" include surrounding property? If it does include some property around the house, does it include all of the real estate around a house, even extending for miles? Do these issues apply to apartments in multi-occupant dwellings? Can police roam the entrance areas, stairways, and halls of apartment houses, perhaps with drug-sniffing dogs? It should be obvious from these questions that genuine home privacy requires some "breathing room" around the precise boundary of living quarters.

CASE AND COMMENTS

Arizona v. Hicks

480 U.S. 321, 107 S.Ct. 1149, 94 L.Ed.2d 347 (1987)

Justice SCALIA delivered the opinion of the Court.

In *Coolidge v. New Hampshire* (1971), we said that in certain circumstances a warrantless seizure by police of an item that comes within plain view during their lawful search of a private area may be reasonable under the Fourth Amendment. * * * [The issue] in the present case [is] whether this "plain view" doctrine may be invoked when the police have less than probable cause to believe that the item in question is evidence of a crime or is contraband.

I

[Police entered an apartment without a warrant to search for a person who shot a bullet through the floor, injuring a man in the apartment below.] **[a]** They found and seized three weapons, including a sawed-off rifle. * * *

One of the policemen, Officer Nelson, noticed two sets of expensive stereo components, which seemed out of place in the squalid and otherwise ill-appointed four room apartment. Suspecting that they were stolen, he read and recorded their serial numbers—moving some of the components, including a Bang and Olufsen turntable, in order to do so—which he then reported by phone to his headquarters. On being advised that the turntable had been taken in an armed robbery, he seized it immediately. It was later determined that some of the other serial numbers matched those on other stereo equipment taken in the same armed robbery, and a warrant was obtained and executed to seize that equipment as well. Respondent was subsequently indicted for the robbery.

[On a suppression motion, the state trial court and court of appeals held that the view of the serial numbers was an additional search unrelated to the exigency of the search for the shooter. These holdings implied rejection of the idea that the actions were justified by the plain view doctrine. The evidence was suppressed, and the state appealed.]

II

* * * We agree that the mere recording of the serial numbers did not constitute a seizure. * * * In and of itself * * * it did not "meaningfully interfere" with respondent's possessory interest in either the serial number or the equipment, and therefore did not amount to a seizure. * * *

Officer Nelson's moving of the equipment, however, did constitute a "search" separate and apart from the search for the shooter, victims, and weapons that was the lawful objective of his entry into the apartment. Merely inspecting those parts of the turntable that came into view during the latter search would not have constituted an independent search, because it would have produced no additional invasion of respondent's privacy interest. **[b]** But taking action, unrelated to the objectives of the authorized intrusion, which exposed to view concealed portions of the apartment or its contents, did produce a new invasion of respondent's privacy unjustified by the exigent circumstance that validated the entry. This is why * * * the "distinction between 'looking' at a suspicious object in plain view and 'moving' it even a few inches" is much more than trivial for purposes of the Fourth Amendment. It matters not that the search uncovered nothing of any great personal value to the respondent—serial numbers rather than (what might conceivably have been hidden behind or under the equipment) letters or photographs. A search is a search, even if it happens to disclose nothing but the bottom of a turntable.

III

The remaining question is whether the search was "reasonable" under the Fourth Amendment.

* * * [W]e reject, at the outset, the * * * position * * * that because the officers' action directed to the stereo equipment was unrelated to the justification for their entry into respondent's apartment, it was *ipso facto* unreasonable. **[c]** That lack of relationship *always* exists with regard to action validated under the "plain view" doctrine; where action is taken for the purpose of justifying entry, invocation of the doctrine is superfluous. * * *

We turn, then, to application of the doctrine to the facts of this case. "It is well established that under certain circumstances the police may *seize* evidence in plain view without a warrant," *Coolidge v. New Hampshire* * * * (*plurality opinion*) (emphasis added). Those circumstances include situations "[w]here the initial intrusion that brings the police within plain view of such [evidence] is supported . . . by one of the recognized exceptions to the warrant requirement. * * * It would be absurd to say that an object could lawfully be seized and taken from the premises, but could not be moved for closer examination." It is clear, therefore, that the search here was valid if the "plain view" doctrine would have sustained a seizure of the equipment.

[a] The three standard exigency exceptions to the warrant requirement are hot pursuit, automobile search, and search incident to arrest. The lawfulness of the entry in *Hicks* demonstrates that a general exigency (emergency) category exists. Police have a *community caretaking* function and may enter premises without warrants when reasonable to save lives or prevent serious injury.

[b] This paragraph implies that the plain view rule simply recognizes commonsense reality. If Officer Nelson saw obvious contraband—for example, drugs—sitting on a table in the apartment, it would be silly to hold that the officer could not act on that information. On the other hand, allowing Officer Nelson, lawfully in the apartment for the limited purpose of looking for the shooter, to expand that search into another could provide incentives for pretext searches of homes.

[c] The defendant argued that the police could seize only items in plain view that related to the shooting; such an argument would destroy the practical value of the plain view doctrine and would not adhere to its logic. Note that both the defense and the prosecution make extreme arguments to the Court in this case.

[d] Why should the turntable be in "plain view" if Officer Nelson had probable cause to believe it was stolen but not if he had reasonable suspicion?

[e] The *practical* justification for the plain view rule is couched in terms of assisting police. The theoretical justification is not discussed in depth. Does the rule have practical justification that benefits the defendant?

[f] The examples in this paragraph are applications of the *Terry* "stop and frisk" doctrine. This simply does not apply to the facts of *Hicks*.

[g] To the dissent, lifting the stereo is not a search but a "cursory inspection." But the majority fears that to allow police to rummage in a home beyond their lawful purpose, to *create* plain view, opens a theoretical rift in the plain view doctrine that can have negative practical consequences.

[h] Is Justice Scalia's opinion "conservative" or "liberal"? what do you make of a "liberal" decision by a "conservative" justice?

[i] Justice O'Connor seeks to create a new rule: a "cursory inspection" plain view seizure.

[j] Do you think that a "cursory examination" doctrine based on reasonable suspicion would prevent police from engaging in "exploratory rummaging"? If this rule existed, do you think that Officer Nelson would have limited his exploration only to moving the turntable?

There is no doubt it would have done so if Officer Nelson had probable cause to believe that the equipment was stolen. [d] The State conceded, however, that he had only a "reasonable suspicion," by which it means something less than probable cause. * * *

We now hold that probable cause is required. To say otherwise would be to cut the "plain view" doctrine loose from its theoretical and practical moorings. The theory of that doctrine consists of extending to nonpublic places such as the home, where searches and seizures without a warrant are presumptively unreasonable, the police's longstanding authority to make warrantless seizures in public places of such objects as weapons and contraband. And the practical justification for that extension is the desirability of sparing police, whose viewing of the object in the course of a lawful search is as legitimate as it would have been in a public place, the inconvenience and the risk—to themselves or to preservation of the evidence—of going to obtain a warrant. [e] Dispensing with the need for a warrant is worlds apart from permitting a lesser standard of *cause* for the seizure than a warrant would require, *i.e.*, the standard of probable cause. No reason is apparent why an object should routinely be seizable on lesser grounds, during an unrelated search and seizure, than would have been needed to obtain a warrant for that same object if it had been known to be on the premises.

We do not say, of course, that a seizure can never be justified on less than probable cause. [f] We have held that it can—where, for example, the seizure is minimally intrusive and operational necessities render it the only practicable means of detecting certain types of crime. See, *e.g., United States v. Cortez (1981)* (investigative detention of vehicle suspected to be transporting illegal aliens);* * * *United States v. Place, (1983)* (dictum) (seizure of suspected drug dealer's luggage at airport to permit exposure to specially trained dog). No special operational necessities are relied on here, however—but rather the mere fact that the items in question came lawfully within the officer's plain view. That alone cannot supplant the requirement of probable cause.

The same considerations preclude us from holding that, even though probable cause would have been necessary for a *seizure*, the *search* of objects in plain view that occurred here could be sustained on lesser grounds. A dwelling-place search, no less than a dwelling-place seizure, requires probable cause, and there is no reason in theory or practicality why application of the "plain view" doctrine would supplant that requirement. * * * [g] [T]o treat searches more liberally would especially erode the plurality's warning in *Coolidge* that "the 'plain view' doctrine may not be used to extend a general exploratory search from one object to another until something incriminating at last emerges." * * * In short, whether legal authority to move the equipment could be found only as an inevitable concomitant of the authority to seize it, or also as a consequence of some independent power to search certain objects in plain view, probable cause to believe the equipment was stolen was required. [h]

* * *

For the reasons stated, the judgment of the Court of Appeals of Arizona is *Affirmed*.

JUSTICE O'CONNOR, with whom THE CHIEF JUSTICE and JUSTICE POWELL join, dissenting.

The Court today gives the right answer to the wrong question. The Court asks whether the police must have probable cause before either seizing an object in plain view or conducting a full-blown search of that object, and concludes that they must. I agree. In my view, however, this case presents a different question: whether police must have probable cause before conducting a cursory inspection of an item in plain view. [i] Because I conclude that such an inspection is reasonable if the police are aware of facts or circumstances that justify a reasonable suspicion that the item is evidence of a crime, I would reverse the judgment of the Arizona Court of Appeals, and therefore dissent.

[A *Coolidge* requirement is that for evidence to be within the "plain view" exception,] it must be "immediately apparent" to the police that the items they observe may be evidence of a crime, contraband, or otherwise subject to seizure.

* * *

The purpose of the "immediately apparent" requirement is to prevent "general exploratory rummaging in a person's belongings." If an officer could indiscriminately search every item in plain view, a search justified by a limited purpose—such as exigent circumstances—could be used to eviscerate the protections of the Fourth Amendment. * * *

* * *

* * * When a police officer makes a cursory inspection of a suspicious item in plain view in order to determine whether it is indeed evidence of a crime, there is no "exploratory rummaging." Only those items that the police officer "reasonably suspects" as evidence of a crime may be inspected, and perhaps more importantly, the scope of such an inspection is quite limited. [j] In short, if police officers have a reasonable, articulable suspicion that an object they come across during the course of a lawful search is evidence of crime, in my view they may make a cursory examination of the object to verify their suspicion. If the officers wish to go beyond such a cursory examination of the object, however, they must have probable cause. This distinction between a full-blown search and seizure of an item and a mere inspection of the item * * * [is] based on their relative intrusiveness. * * *

* * *

The answers to these questions depend on how the courts have defined the extent of the curtilage, which does extend Fourth Amendment protection to some area around a dwelling, and what is referred to as "open fields," which do not come under the protection of the amendment. As a result, police do not need a warrant to go onto open fields, and any contraband found there may be seized in plain view. Put another way, government intrusions in open fields are not "searches" in the constitutional sense.

CURTILAGE   In *Oliver v. United States* (1984), the Supreme Court noted that "[a]t common law, the curtilage is the area to which extends the intimate activity associated with the 'sanctity of a man's home and the privacies of life,'. . . and therefore has been considered part of the home itself for Fourth Amendment purposes. Thus, courts have extended Fourth Amendment protection to the curtilage; and they have defined the curtilage, as did the common law, by reference to the factors that determine whether an individual reasonably may expect that an area immediately adjacent to the home will remain private."

More precisely, the curtilage includes the area under the eaves of the main house; small structures near the main house such as a shed, smokehouse, or garage; and the area around a house. The yard of a typical suburban home is a curtilage; the wall around O. J. Simpson's Brentwood estate (the scene of one of the most notorious police investigations of the twentieth century) described its curtilage, and before Detective Mark Fuhrman could enter, he should have had a search warrant or a valid warrant exception. Courts have, depending on specific facts, included chicken coops and backyards, and have differed over whether driveways are to be included.[45]

In *United States v. Dunn* (1987), Drug Enforcement Administration (DEA) agents, without a warrant, went onto Dunn's land to see if they could detect evidence of illegal amphetamine manufacture. Dunn's house was a half mile from a public road on a 198-acre ranch that was completely encircled by a perimeter fence. Two barns were located about fifty yards from the residence. The property contained several interior fences, constructed mainly of posts and multiple strands of barbed wire. The house and a small greenhouse were surrounded by a fence. One barn was enclosed by a wooden fence. The DEA agents crossed the perimeter fence and one interior fence. Standing approximately midway between the residence and the barns, they smelled what was believed to be the odor of phenylacetic acid coming from the direction of the barns. They then crossed another barbed wire fence and a wooden fence to get to the large barn. They walked under the barn's overhang and, using a flashlight, peered into the barn. "They observed what the DEA agent thought to be a phenylacetone laboratory. The officers did not enter the barn. At this point the officers departed from respondent's property." A warrant was issued on the basis of facts obtained by police observations of the barn (*United States v. Dunn*, 1987).

The Court ruled that the barn was not within the curtilage and that the police officers violated no Fourth Amendment expectation of privacy when they went up to the barn and observed an illegal drug factory inside. To decide whether property outside the dwelling fell in the protected curtilage or unprotected "open fields," the Court examined four factors: "the *proximity* of the area claimed to be curtilage to the home, whether the area is included within an *enclosure* surrounding the home, the nature of the *uses* to which the area is put, and the *steps taken* by the resident to *protect* the area from observation by people passing by" (*U.S. v. Dunn*, 1987, emphasis added). An astute commentary has noted that in the lower courts "the curtilage doctrine is far from consistently applied" and this is so in part "because the curtilage doctrine arose historically in the context of rural areas, in cases involving evidence seized from large tracts of land, which was the context in which the open fields/curtilage distinction was particularly relevant."[46] Perhaps as a result of this rural mind-set, while the Supreme Court has extended the Fourth Amendment protection of the home to places like hotel rooms, "courts have also generally ended this protection at the inside door of an individual apartment or motel room, largely on the basis of the *Dunn* factors," although there are some exceptions.[47] Furthermore, where curtilage protection is in conflict with the ruling that there is no constitutional protection in "abandoned" trash, courts have generally upheld "the increasingly routine law enforcement practice of trespassing within the cartilage of a residence to make a warrantless seizure of garbage prior to its collection by the regular trash collectors."[48] The limited protection that courts have extended to the curtilage in recent years has allowed police to extend and often abuse their powers to use dog-sniffing canines, the "talk and knock" technique (discussed in a following section), and the community caretaking function to conduct warrantless entries and searches of premises.

OPEN FIELDS "Conversely, the common law implies, as we reaffirm today, that no expectation of privacy legitimately attaches to open fields" (*Oliver v. United States,* 1984). The rule was first stated tersely by Justice Oliver Wendell Holmes Jr. in *Hester v. United States* (1924): The "special protection accorded by the Fourth Amendment to the people in their 'persons, houses, papers, and effects,' is not extended to the open fields. The distinction between the latter and the house is as old as the common law." After *Katz,* the question arose as to whether this distinction still stood under a modernized, nonproperty interpretation of the Fourth Amendment, or whether expectation of privacy analysis would extend Fourth Amendment protection to so-called open fields.

Oliver v. United States (1984) consolidated two cases. The essential facts were that police officers, without warrants or consent, went into the lands owned by defendants and discovered marijuana patches. The privately owned fields were posted with "No Trespassing" signs. One site was highly secluded, over a mile from the defendant's house, and a gate to the fields was locked. To reach the other site, officers had to walk a path between the defendant's house and a neighbor's house. In one case, the lower court upheld the search; in the other, the evidence was suppressed. The Supreme Court found that both searches passed constitutional muster.

Justice Powell's majority opinion provided several reasons for upholding the "open fields" rule. First, the explicit language of the Fourth Amendment "is not extended to the open fields." Second, open fields are not "effects" within the meaning of the Fourth Amendment. Significantly, a first draft of the Fourth Amendment included a protection of "other property" along with persons, houses, and papers. The change in wording confirms the idea that "effects" refers to personal property. Third, the majority felt there was no expectation of privacy in open fields that society is prepared to recognize as reasonable—in other words, *Katz* had not changed the "open fields" rule. Open land is put to uses, such as the cultivation of crops, that are not the kinds of intimate activities that occur in homes and have historically called for strong privacy protection.

Fourth, "as a practical matter these lands usually are accessible to the public and the police in ways that a home, an office, or commercial structure would not be." Rural land may be fenced and posted with "No Trespassing" signs, but these do not effectively keep hikers or hunters off the land. They certainly do not provide the same kind of psychological barrier that apartment and house doors and windows provide. Also, "the public and police lawfully may survey lands from the air." Fifth, the common law distinction between open fields and the curtilage supports the idea that the Framers did not intend to extend Fourth Amendment protection to open fields. Sixth, a defendant's property interest, such as ownership or leaseholding, that is violated by police committing a trespass to land, no longer decides the case under *Katz.* "The existence of a property right is but one element in determining whether expectations of privacy are legitimate."

The Court also provided practical reasons for supporting the "open fields" doctrine. An argument was made that in each case where police trespass on real estate and discover contraband, the courts should conduct a factual inquiry to discover whether the land and its uses come within the "open fields" rule. The Court rejected this. Under a case-by-case approach, "police officers would have to guess before every search whether landowners had erected fences sufficiently high, posted a sufficient number of warning signs, or located contraband in an area sufficiently secluded to establish a right of privacy. The lawfulness of a search would turn on '[a] highly sophisticated set of rules, qualified by all sorts of ifs, ands, and buts and requiring the drawing of subtle nuances and hairline distinctions. . . .'" A bright-line rule better serves law enforcement and ensures that constitutional rights will uniformly be enforced.

Justice Marshall, joined by Justices Brennan and Stevens, wrote a spirited dissent. He felt, first, that provisions that "identify a fundamental human liberty" should "be shielded forever from government intrusion" and so should be interpreted in an expansive manner "to lend them meanings that ensure that the liberties the Framers sought to protect are not undermined by the changing activities of government officials." Next, he argued that if, as the majority believed, the Fourth Amendment offered no protection to real property, then the protection extended to the curtilage is inconsistent. Again, the objective expectation of privacy is seen in laws that allow the prosecution of trespassers. Posting and fencing are clear ways in which owners announce their expectation of privacy, and they are understood by all. Finally, the dissent disagreed with the majority that the uses to which property owners put lands are not the sort of activities that society deems worthy of privacy:

> The uses to which a place is put are highly relevant to the assessment of a privacy interest asserted therein. . . . If, in light of our shared sensibilities, those activities are of a kind in which people should be able to engage without fear of intrusion by private persons or government officials, we extend the protection of the Fourth Amendment to the space in question, even in the absence of any entitlement derived from positive law. . . .
>
> Privately owned woods and fields that are not exposed to public view regularly are employed in a variety of ways that society acknowledges deserve privacy. Many landowners like to take solitary walks on their property, confident that they will not be confronted in their rambles by strangers or policemen. Others conduct agricultural businesses on their property. Some landowners use their secluded spaces to meet lovers, others to gather together with fellow worshippers, still others to engage in sustained creative endeavor. Private land is sometimes used as a refuge for wildlife, where flora and fauna are protected from human intervention of any kind. Our respect for the freedom of landowners to use their posted "open fields" in ways such as these partially explains the seriousness with which the positive law regards deliberate invasions of such spaces, . . . and substantially reinforces the landowners' contention that their expectations of privacy are "reasonable." (*Oliver v. United States*)

The curtilage concept expands the Fourth Amendment definition of a house to a certain "reasonable" amount of land around a house. This gives the constitutional protections of the Fourth Amendment some "breathing room" and prevents the "open fields" exception from allowing police to tightly surround a house or creep up to windows to peer in or eavesdrop.

Airspace

If the curtilage is open to view, police may observe it from a public vantage point such as a road. What they may not do as a general rule is physically invade the curtilage itself to encroach on the zone of privacy that one expects to have around a dwelling. In several cases that the Framers surely could not have contemplated, the Supreme Court considered the extent to which the curtilage protection applied to airspace above premises.

The *Katz* doctrine provided no protection against the warrantless aerial surveillance by police of a backyard where marijuana was growing. The Court in ***California v. Ciraolo*** (1986) upheld the police action, saying that the defendant's expectation of privacy in his backyard was not one that society was prepared to honor. The owner surrounded his backyard, which also contained a swimming pool, with a six-foot outer fence and a ten-foot inner fence. Police could not observe the backyard to confirm an anonymous tip that Ciraolo was growing marijuana, so they hired a private *airplane* and buzzed the suburban backyard to gather visual evidence with the naked eye from about one thousand feet. The Court reasoned that the yard was *exposed to the public* because it was subject to the gaze of passengers in commercial airplane flights. The search was held to fit the "open fields" category. Justice Powell rebuked the Court, in a stinging dissent, for failing to uphold its role as a guardian of rights by allowing a "stealthy encroachment" on rights by the remote intrusion of commercial overflights. He believed that the curtilage protected against the use of a private airplane to peer down into Ciraolo's backyard, pool and all.

On the same day, the Court, in ***Dow Chemical v. United States*** (1986), upheld an aerial search of two thousand acres of commercial property by an airplane equipped with a sophisticated camera that could magnify its pictures to detect pipes a half-inch thick from twelve hundred feet. Even if the government officers could not, under the Fourth Amendment, physically go onto the commercial complex, the warrantless overflight was held not to be a search and seizure. *Dow Chemical* upheld the concept of an **industrial curtilage** but, as in *Ciraolo,* held that it did not protect property from aerial surveillance while using ordinary camera resolution.

The Court continued this approach in ***Florida v. Riley*** (1989). A four-justice plurality upheld the surveillance of a partially covered greenhouse in a residential backyard from a *helicopter* hovering four hundred feet above the ground. Justice White reasoned that this flight did not violate any law or regulation, and any member of the public with a helicopter could have legally hovered above Riley's property and observed the contents of the greenhouse. This reasoning was not satisfactory to Justice O'Connor, who concurred only in the judgment. She thought that the Court relied too heavily on police compliance with Federal Aviation Administration (FAA) regulations and suggested that if lower overflights were sufficiently rare, even if they were in FAA compliance, in such a case, the householder would have a reasonable expectation of privacy. Justice Brennan dissented (joined by Justices Marshall and Stevens), arguing that by not taking into account the difficulty and lengths to which the police must go in making an "open fields" aerial search, the Court was ignoring the "the very essence of *Katz*."

In these cases, areas that are within the curtilage and nominally protected by the Fourth Amendment were, in fact, opened up to warrantless police surveillance under reasoning that stretched the traditional categories of open fields, thus narrowing curtilage protection. The fact that conservative justices such as Lewis Powell and Sandra Day O'Connor were bothered by the decisions shows the malleability of constitutional concepts and suggests that the Court's decisions are at times influenced by result-oriented jurisprudence.

Enhancement Devices

Is an item in plain view if it is detected, or its contraband nature is disclosed, by the use of an **enhancement device?** Logically, if the police have to resort to technology to determine whether evidence is incriminating, then it is not immediately apparent as such. If so, a judicial warrant based on probable cause is required to use the technology. This logic seemed to be at work in *Coolidge v. New Hampshire* (1971), where evidence obtained by the warrantless vacuuming of a car for fiber evidence was deemed inadmissible. Similarly, in *Katz* and other surreptitious electronic eavesdropping cases, private conversations that are obtained via enhancement devices that amplify the aural sense are protected by the Fourth Amendment. Such information is within the individual's zone of constitutionally protected privacy.

The Supreme Court's cases on the use of "beepers" provide a baseline of analysis. Beepers are radio transmitters, usually battery-operated, that emit periodic signals. They allow agents to trace the movement of an object in which the beeper is surreptitiously placed. As noted previously, the Court ruled that there is no constitutional impediment to the government's using beepers to enhance the senses (e.g., visual observation) if the device does not infringe on an expectation of privacy. In **United States v. Knotts** (1983), agents placed a beeper in a five-gallon can of chloroform and tracked its movement in an automobile driven on public streets. A person has no reasonable expectation of privacy in his movements from one place to another, and so the use of the beeper was held not to constitute a search. In **United States v. Karo** (1984), however, the Court ruled that detecting motion with the use of beepers inside a person's house equated to a search and required a prior warrant. The beeper was the equivalent of an agent secretly entering a house to verify that a drum of ether is inside, a clear Fourth Amendment violation. Justice White expressed the policy that "[i]ndiscriminate monitoring of property that has been withdrawn from public view would present far too serious a threat to privacy interests in the home to escape entirely some sort of Fourth Amendment oversight." For this kind of in-house tracking to be constitutional, a warrant must be obtained.

Some uses of enhancement devices pose no constitutional problems. In **Texas v. Brown** (1983), the Court said that it was "beyond dispute" that an officer "shining his flashlight to illuminate the interior of [a] car trenched upon no right secured . . . by the Fourth Amendment." Citing *United States v. Lee* (1927), the Court also found no constitutional objection to "the use of a marine glass or a field glass. It is not prohibited by the Constitution." Flashlights and field glasses are in such common use that allowing their use may be explained by the fact that they are common devices used everyday in ordinary situations. However, the Court has also found no Fourth Amendment impediment to more high-tech devices. In *Dow Chemical* (1986), the Court upheld a warrantless aerial surveillance of a two-thousand-acre chemical manufacturing facility, heavily secured against entry on the ground but partially exposed to visual observation from the air, by agents of the Environmental Protection Agency, to check emissions from the facility's power plant. The "EPA employed a commercial aerial photographer, using a standard floor-mounted, precision aerial-mapping camera, to take photographs of the facility from altitudes of 12,000, 3,000, and 1,200 feet." In upholding this level of surveillance as not protected by the Fourth Amendment, the Court noted, "The photographs at issue in this case are essentially like those commonly used in mapmaking. Any person with an airplane and an aerial camera could readily duplicate them." With the end of the Cold War, "spy satellites" are now commercially available and have been used by "mining companies, mapmakers, geologists, city planners, ecologists, farmers, hydrologists, road makers, journalists, land managers, disaster-relief officials and others seeking to monitor the planet's changing face. The global market in such imagery is expected to reach as high as $5 billion by 2004."[49] The implications are that there are virtually no limits to aerial surveillance by the police for law enforcement purposes.[50]

Read Case and Comments: *Kyllo v. United States*

The Supreme Court has recently acted to exert some judicial control over the use of **thermal imaging** and has attempted to establish rules to guide the use of advanced information-gathering technology.

CONSENT SEARCHES

"The consent-based procedure is the bread and butter of the criminal justice system."[51] While precise figures are not available, "there is no dispute that [consent] searches affect tens of thousands, if not hundreds of thousands of people every year."[52] In one city, an estimated 92 percent of searches were **consent searches**.[53] Most consent searches occur in the course of traffic enforcement and automobile stops, and they play a significant role in racial profiling.[54] (See the "Law in Society" section in Chapter 5.) "Moreover, even if there is probable cause to search, obtaining a warrant may be time consuming or inconvenient. 'A consent search allows an officer to bypass paperwork and the need to locate a magistrate who can issue a warrant.'"[55] To an astonishing degree, criminal suspects plead guilty, confess to crime, allow police into their homes, and meekly submit to arrests rather than go to jury trial, stay mum, refuse to allow police entry without a warrant, and forcibly resist arrest. In these scenarios, suspects give up their constitutional rights to trial, self-incrimination, and privacy, which are guaranteed by the Sixth, Fifth, and Fourth Amendments. Defendants are allowed to give up these rights under proper conditions, although other fundamental rights, like prohibitions on cruel and unusual punishment or slavery or the guaranty of due process, cannot be voluntarily set aside.

Police favor consent searches and stops because they eliminate questions about a suspect's constitutional rights. "[B]ecause consent searches require no degree of suspicion on the officer's part, they allow an officer to pursue inarticulable hunches in detecting crime."[56] A person may have an absolute constitutional right to refuse to stop or to open the door to his or her home or automobile trunk when requested to do so by a police officer. But if the person consents, it matters not that the officer had no reasonable suspicion to stop or no warrant to enter. Once voluntarily allowed in, the officer is lawfully in the premises; if contraband is observed in plain view, it may be seized and the possessor arrested for possession. "[A] search authorized by consent is *wholly* valid."[57]

Voluntariness Requirement

The basic requirement of a valid consent search is that consent must be given voluntarily. A consent search obtained by threats or force will be voided by the courts. The test of voluntariness is the totality of circumstances, which courts routinely apply to determine whether an arrested person voluntarily consented to searches of cars, houses, or other protected areas. A consent obtained within minutes of a *routine* arrest, for example, will be upheld, while an arrest made by four officers with *guns drawn* will negate the voluntariness of consent to search.[58] This seems incongruous because an arrested person is by definition *in custody* of the police and "forcibly" detained. The incongruity is reflected in the holding in *Schneckloth v. Bustamonte* (1973), the Supreme Court's leading consent search decision, which defines voluntary consent as when the "subject of a search is *not in custody*" (emphasis added). Courts nevertheless continue to uphold most consents to search given by suspects under arrest.[59]

The burden of proof is on the government to prove consent: "When a prosecutor seeks to rely upon consent to justify the lawfulness of a search, he has the burden of proving that the consent was, in fact, freely and voluntarily given. This burden cannot be discharged by showing no more than acquiescence to a claim of lawful authority" (*Bumper v. North Carolina,* 1968). The following examples help to define voluntariness.

CASE AND COMMENTS

Kyllo v. United States

533 U.S. 27, 121 S. Ct. 2038, 150 L. Ed. 2d 94 (2001)

JUSTICE SCALIA delivered the opinion of the Court.

This case presents the question whether the use of a thermal-imaging device aimed at a private home from a public street to detect relative amounts of heat within the home constitutes a "search" within the meaning of the Fourth Amendment. **[a]**

[a] After reading the entire case, do you think that the case and its rule apply only to thermal-imaging technology or to all sense-enhancing technology?

I

[U.S. Department of Interior Agent Elliott suspected] that marijuana was being grown in the home belonging to * * * Danny Kyllo, part of a triplex * * * in Florence, Oregon. Indoor marijuana growth typically requires high-intensity lamps. In order to determine whether an amount of heat was emanating from petitioner's home consistent with the use of such lamps, at 3:20 A.M., * * * Agent Elliott and Dan Haas used an Agema Thermovision 210 thermal imager to scan the triplex. Thermal imagers detect infrared radiation, which virtually all objects emit but which is not visible to the naked eye. The imager converts radiation into images based on relative warmth—black is cool, white is hot, shades of gray connote relative differences; in that respect, it operates somewhat like a video camera showing heat images. The scan of Kyllo's home took only a few minutes and was performed from the passenger seat of Agent Elliott's vehicle across the street from the front of the house and also from the street in back of the house. The scan showed that the roof over the garage and a side wall of petitioner's home were relatively hot compared to the rest of the home and substantially warmer than neighboring homes in the triplex. Agent Elliott concluded that petitioner was using halide lights to grow marijuana in his house, which indeed he was. Based on tips from informants, utility bills, and the thermal imaging, a Federal Magistrate Judge issued a warrant authorizing a search of petitioner's home, and the agents found an indoor growing operation involving more than 100 plants. * * *

[Kyllo was indicted and pled conditionally guilty. On appeal, the Court of Appeals upheld the conviction: Kyllo had shown no subjective expectation of privacy because he had made no attempt to conceal the heat escaping from his home, and even if he had, there was no objectively reasonable expectation of privacy because the imager "did not expose any intimate details of Kyllo's life," only "amorphous 'hot spots' on the roof and exterior wall."]

II

* * * With few exceptions, the question whether a warrantless search of a home is reasonable and hence constitutional must be answered no. * * *

On the other hand, the antecedent question of whether or not a Fourth Amendment "search" has occurred is not so simple under our precedent. **[b]** The permissibility of ordinary visual surveillance of a home used to be clear because, well into the 20th century, our Fourth Amendment jurisprudence was tied to common-law trespass. * * * Visual surveillance was unquestionably lawful . . . As we observed * * * "the Fourth Amendment protection of the home has never been extended to require law enforcement officers to shield their eyes when passing by a home on public thoroughfares." **[c]**

* * * [W]e have held that visual observation is no "search" at all. * * * In assessing when a search is not a search, we have applied somewhat in reverse the principle first enunciated in *Katz* (1967).* * *

The present case involves officers on a public street engaged in more than naked-eye surveillance of a home. We have previously reserved judgment as to how much technological enhancement of ordinary perception from such a vantage point, if any, is too much. While we upheld enhanced aerial photography of an industrial complex in *Dow Chemical*, we noted that we found "it important that this is *not* an area immediately adjacent to a private home, where privacy expectations are most heightened." * * *

[b] Does Agent Elliott's thermal scan fit your idea of a search? Do you think what constitutes a search can be determined by an "objective" test, or should the definition of a search depend on the policy issues and values involved?

[c] Would it make sense to require a search warrant every time investigators "stake out" a house to see who enters and leaves?

III

It would be foolish to contend that the degree of privacy secured to citizens by the Fourth Amendment has been entirely unaffected by the advance of technology. For example, * * * the technology enabling human flight has exposed to public view (and hence, we have said, to official observation) uncovered portions of the house and its curtilage that once were private. * * * The question we confront today is what limits there are upon this power of technology to shrink the realm of guaranteed privacy.

* * * While it may be difficult to refine *Katz* when the search of areas such as telephone booths, automobiles, or even the curtilage and uncovered portions of residences are at issue, in the case of the search of the interior of homes—the prototypical and hence most commonly litigated

area of protected privacy—there is a ready criterion, with roots deep in the common law, of the minimal expectation of privacy that *exists,* and that is acknowledged to be *reasonable.* To withdraw protection of this minimum expectation would be to permit police technology to erode the privacy guaranteed by the Fourth Amendment. We think that obtaining by sense-enhancing technology any information regarding the interior of the home that could not otherwise have been obtained without physical "intrusion into a constitutionally protected area," * * * constitutes a search—at least where (as here) the technology in question is not in general public use. **[d]** This assures preservation of that degree of privacy against government that existed when the Fourth Amendment was adopted. **[e]** On the basis of this criterion, the information obtained by the thermal imager in this case was the product of a search.

The Government maintains, however, that the thermal imaging must be upheld because it detected "only heat radiating from the external surface of the house." * * * The dissent makes this its leading point, contending that there is a fundamental difference between what it calls "off-the-wall" observations and "through-the-wall surveillance." But just as a thermal imager captures only heat emanating from a house, so also a powerful directional microphone picks up only sound emanating from a house—and a satellite capable of scanning from many miles away would pick up only visible light emanating from a house. We rejected such a mechanical interpretation of the Fourth Amendment in *Katz,* where the eavesdropping device picked up only sound waves that reached the exterior of the phone booth. **[f]** Reversing that approach would leave the homeowner at the mercy of advancing technology—including imaging technology that could discern all human activity in the home. While the technology used in the present case was relatively crude, the rule we adopt must take account of more sophisticated systems that are already in use or in development. **[g]** The dissent's reliance on the distinction between "off-the-wall" and "through-the-wall" observation is entirely incompatible with the dissent's belief * * * that thermal-imaging observations of the intimate details of a home are impermissible. The most sophisticated thermal-imaging devices continue to measure heat "off-the-wall" rather than "through-the-wall"; the dissent's disapproval of those more sophisticated thermal-imaging devices * * * is an acknowledgment that there is no substance to this distinction. As for the dissent's extraordinary assertion that anything learned through "an inference" cannot be a search, * * * that would validate even the "through-the-wall" technologies that the dissent purports to disapprove. Surely the dissent does not believe that the through-the-wall radar or ultrasound technology produces an 8-by-10 Kodak glossy that needs no analysis (*i.e.,* the making of inferences). And, of course, the novel proposition that inference insulates a search is blatantly contrary to *United States v. Karo,* (1984), where the police "inferred" from the activation of a beeper that a certain can of ether was in the home. The police activity was held to be a search, and the search was held unlawful.

The Government also contends that the thermal imaging was constitutional because it did not "detect private activities occurring in private areas." * * * It points out that in *Dow Chemical* we observed that the enhanced aerial photography did not reveal any "intimate details." * * * *Dow Chemical,* however, involved enhanced aerial photography of an industrial complex, which does not share the Fourth Amendment sanctity of the home. The Fourth Amendment's protection of the home has never been tied to measurement of the quality or quantity of information obtained. In *Silverman,* for example, we made clear that any physical invasion of the structure of the home, "by even a fraction of an inch," was too much, * * * and there is certainly no exception to the warrant requirement for the officer who barely cracks open the front door and sees nothing but the nonintimate rug on the vestibule floor. **[h]** In the home, our cases show, *all* details are intimate details, because the entire area is held safe from prying government eyes. Thus, in *Karo,* the only thing detected was a can of ether in the home; and in *Arizona v. Hicks,* (1987), the only thing detected by a physical search that went beyond what officers lawfully present could observe in "plain view" was the registration number of a phonograph turntable. These were intimate details because they were details of the home, just as was the detail of how warm—or even how relatively warm—Kyllo was heating his residence.

[It would be extremely difficult, if not impossible, to determine what is an "intimate detail" and what is a "nonintimate detail" in a house. Even if a rule could make out this distinction, police would not know in advance if the search with a thermal imager or other high-tech device would disclose an intimate or nonintimate detail.]

Where, as here, the Government uses a device that is not in general public use, to explore details of the home that would previously have been unknowable without physical intrusion, the surveillance is a "search" and is presumptively unreasonable without a warrant.

Since we hold the Thermovision imaging to have been an unlawful search, it will remain for the District Court to determine whether, without the evidence it provided, the search warrant issued in this case was supported by probable cause—and if not, whether there is any other basis for supporting admission of the evidence that the search pursuant to the warrant produced.

* * *

[d] Notice that the definition of a search has two parts. What are they? Also notice that the sentence preceding Justice Scalia's definition of a search is a statement of policy—a concern that a different definition could erode in-home protections.

[e] Notice this reference to the expectations of Congress and the states in 1791. As in Justice Thomas's *Wilson v. Arkansas* (1995) opinion, Justice Scalia, the other originalist on the Court, feels that the legitimacy of a ruling depends on whether it squares with the purported intent of the Framers and their common law environment.

[f] This statement seems to answer the question raised in Comment [a]: The Court always deals in questions of constitutional policy and has to consider the consequences of its decisions.

[g] One consequence, as Justice Scalia states, is to attempt to foresee a future when highly intrusive technology would allow easy observation into the privacy of houses and apartments. In a footnote, the opinion said, "The ability to 'see' through walls and other opaque barriers is a clear, and scientifically feasible, goal of law enforcement research and development."

[h] Is this distinction between business premises and a home sound? What if a person operates a business out of a home office? For purposes of a search, is this a home or a business? Similarly, is a fully mobile home, such as a recreational vehicle, a home, or a vehicle?

The judgment of the Court of Appeals is reversed; the case is remanded for further proceedings consistent with this opinion.

It is so ordered.

JUSTICE STEVENS, with whom THE CHIEF JUSTICE, JUSTICE O'CONNOR, and JUSTICE KENNEDY join, dissenting.

* * *

I

* * * [S]earches and seizures of property in plain view are presumptively reasonable. * * * Whether that property is residential or commercial, the basic principle is the same: "'What a person knowingly exposes to the public, even in his own home or office, is not a subject of Fourth Amendment protection.'" That is the principle implicated here.

[i] Was the heat emanating from Kyllo's house in *plain* view if it took a heat sensor to detect it?

While the Court "takes the long view" and decides this case based largely on the potential of yet-to-be-developed technology that might allow "through-the-wall surveillance," * * * this case involves nothing more than off-the-wall surveillance by law enforcement officers to gather information exposed to the general public from the outside of petitioner's home. **[i]** All that the infrared camera did in this case was passively measure heat emitted from the exterior surfaces of petitioner's home; all that those measurements showed were relative differences in emission levels, vaguely indicating that some areas of the roof and outside walls were warmer than others. As still images from the infrared scans show, * * * no details regarding the interior of petitioner's home were revealed. Unlike an x-ray scan, or other possible "through-the-wall" techniques, the detection of infrared radiation emanating from the home did not accomplish "an unauthorized physical penetration into the premises," * * * nor did it "obtain information that it could not have obtained by observation from outside the curtilage of the house." ***

Indeed, the ordinary use of the senses might enable a neighbor or passerby to notice the heat emanating from a building, particularly if it is vented, as was the case here. Additionally, any member of the public might notice that one part of a house is warmer than another part or a nearby building if, for example, rainwater evaporates or snow melts at different rates across its surfaces. * * * **[j]**

[j] Is this the same as thermal imaging by a government agent?

Thus, the notion that heat emissions from the outside of a dwelling is a private matter implicating the protections of the Fourth Amendment (the text of which guarantees the right of people "to be secure *in* their . . . houses" against unreasonable searches and seizures [emphasis added]) is not only unprecedented but also quite difficult to take seriously. Heat waves, like aromas that are generated in a kitchen, or in a laboratory or opium den, enter the public domain if and when they leave a building. A subjective expectation that they would remain private is not only implausible but also surely not "one that society is prepared to recognize as 'reasonable.'" * * *

* * * In my judgment, monitoring such emissions with "sense-enhancing technology," * * * and drawing useful conclusions from such monitoring, is an entirely reasonable public service.

On the other hand, the countervailing privacy interest is at best trivial. After all, homes generally are insulated to keep heat in, rather than to prevent the detection of heat going out, and it does not seem to me that society will suffer from a rule requiring the rare homeowner who both intends to engage in uncommon activities that produce extraordinary amounts of heat, and wishes to conceal that production from outsiders, to make sure that the surrounding area is well insulated. * * * The interest in concealing the heat escaping from one's house pales in significance to "the chief evil against which the wording of the Fourth Amendment is directed," the "physical entry of the home," * * * and it is hard to believe that it is an interest the Framers sought to protect in our Constitution.

Since what was involved in this case was nothing more than drawing inferences from off-the-wall surveillance, rather than any "through-the-wall" surveillance, the officers' conduct did not amount to a search and was perfectly reasonable.

II

[The application of the Court's holding to technology that is "not in general public use" means that as intrusive technology becomes commonplace, it will allow searches of private areas to be held constitutional. The dissent noted that over ten thousand thermal-sensing units had been manufactured and could be purchased by anyone. Another criticism is that the holding was limited to privacy only in the home; if new technology has the effect of getting information that otherwise could be obtained only by having an officer enter a place, under the expectation of privacy doctrine, it should apply to commercial places as well as to homes.]

* * *

I respectfully dissent.

In *Amos v. United States* (1921), two federal "revenuers" looking for untaxed whiskey came to Amos's house without a warrant. He was not there; his wife opened the door. They told her "that they were revenue officers and had come to search the premises 'for violations of the revenue law'; that thereupon the woman opened the store and the witnesses entered, and in a barrel of peas found a bottle containing not quite a half-pint of illicitly distilled whisky, which they called 'blockade whisky.'" A unanimous Court summarily dismissed the contention that the officers were let in voluntarily because they *demanded* entry under *government authority*. A similar case is ***Bumper v. North Carolina*** (1968). Bumper, an at-large murder suspect, "lived with his grandmother, Mrs. Hattie Leath, a 66-year-old Negro widow, in a house located in a rural area at the end of an isolated mile-long dirt road." Four officers came to the house and told Mrs. Leath that they had a *search warrant*. In response, she allowed them to search the house, and they discovered a weapon. It was later determined that there never was a search warrant. The Supreme Court held that Mrs. Leath, who did not appear at all intimidated, nevertheless did not give valid consent to the warrantless search:

> A search conducted in reliance upon a warrant cannot later be justified on the basis of consent if it turns out that the warrant was invalid. The result can be no different when it turns out that the State does not even attempt to rely upon the validity of the warrant, or fails to show that there was, in fact, any warrant at all.
>
> When a law enforcement officer claims authority to search a home under a warrant, he announces in effect that the occupant has no right to resist the search. The situation is instinct with coercion—albeit colorably lawful coercion. Where there is coercion there cannot be consent.
>
> We hold that Mrs. Leath did not consent to the search, and that it was constitutional error to admit the rifle in evidence against the petitioner. (*Bumper v. North Carolina,* 1968)

Officers who falsely claim to have a warrant or who demand entry as if the law required it are acting under color of law, and *Amos* and *Bumper* deem such action to be *legal coercion*. But it is not coercion for a police officer to ask a person, in a nonthreatening manner, if he or she may enter a home, search a car, or view a backpack and the like. If a person agrees, she has voluntarily relinquished her Fourth Amendment right to privacy. It does not matter whether the officer believes that the person is a suspect.

Despite these earlier cases, "it was not until 1973, in ***Schneckloth v. Bustamonte*** that the Supreme Court clearly articulated the requirements for a voluntary consent search consistent with the Fourth Amendment."[60] In *Schneckloth,* the Supreme Court found that the following scenario resulted in a voluntary consent to search the trunk of an automobile:

> While on routine patrol in Sunnyvale, California, at approximately 2:40 in the morning, Police Officer James Rand stopped an automobile when he observed that one headlight and its license plate light were burned out. Six men were in the vehicle. Joe Alcala and the respondent, Robert Bustamonte, were in the front seat with Joe Gonzales, the driver. Three older men were seated in the rear. When, in response to the policeman's question, Gonzales could not produce a driver's license, Officer Rand asked if any of the other five had any evidence of identification. Only Alcala produced a license, and he explained that the car was his brother's. After the six occupants had stepped out of the car at the officer's request and after two additional policemen had arrived, Officer Rand asked Alcala if he could search the car. Alcala replied, "Sure, go ahead." Prior to the search no one was threatened with arrest and, according to Officer Rand's uncontradicted testimony, it "was all very congenial at this time." Gonzales testified that Alcala actually helped in the search of the car, by opening the trunk and glove compartment. In Gonzales' words: "The police officer asked Joe [Alcala], he goes, 'Does the trunk open?' And Joe said, 'Yes.' He went to the car and got the keys and opened up the trunk." Wadded up under the left rear seat, the police officers found three checks that had previously been stolen from a car wash. (*Schneckloth v. Bustamonte,* 1973)

The majority decided (6–3) that Alcala's consent was voluntary and the checks were admissible. Justice Stewart, in his majority opinion, said the "precise question in this case, then, is what must the prosecution prove to demonstrate that a consent was 'voluntarily' given." The issue included the subsidiary question of whether the police have to *inform* those from whom they request consent to search that they have a constitutional right to refuse, where police do not have probable cause or reasonable suspicion to force a search (discussed in the next section). In concluding that Alcala voluntarily consented, the Court noted that the atmosphere surrounding the search was said to be "congenial," there had been no discussion of any crime, and Alcala even tried to aid in the search.

Regarding voluntariness in general, Justice Stewart turned to the more than thirty Supreme Court confessions cases that explored their voluntariness under the due process "facts and circumstances" test. (See Chapter 7.) He concluded that there is no formula to determine whether a consent is voluntary. On the one hand, even a person subjected to torture retains some level of choice in deciding whether to talk, while on the other it can be said that consent is never voluntary because a person would never give up his or her rights "in the absence of official action of some kind." As a result, the Court was guided, in sorting out voluntary from involuntary confessions, by "the complex of values implicated in police questioning of a suspect." This involved balancing the need of law enforcement to question suspects against a "set of values reflecting society's deeply felt belief that the criminal law cannot be used as an instrument of unfairness." The Court accommodated these competing interests in confessions cases by looking at several circumstances: the suspect's age, education, and intelligence; the length of detention; the repeated and prolonged nature of the questioning; and the use of physical punishment. The decision in each case depended on a qualitative evaluation of factors. In sum, "whether a consent to a search was in fact 'voluntary' or was the product of duress or coercion, express or implied, is a question of fact to be determined from the totality of all the circumstances."

Professor Marcy Strauss suggests that the voluntariness test "is so vague that it provides little guidance to courts, litigants or police officers."[61] Moreover, although *Schenckloth* emphasized subjective factors about the suspect's understanding of events, "lower courts may ignore or short-change subjective factors of the suspect because judges may believe that *Schneckloth* has been overturned sub silentio, or, at a minimum, may be confused about the appropriate standard to apply. Recent Supreme Court decisions . . . seem to be moving the law away from subjective considerations and towards an *objective* standard."[62] Thus if the voluntariness of consent is determined exclusively by objective factors of police behavior (e.g., whether the officer brandished a gun), determining whether the suspect's will was *in fact* overborne will disappear as a test.

Chapter 4 presents many cases in which the validity of a person's search turns on whether the person was arrested, temporarily stopped on the basis of reasonable suspicion, or gave consent. *United States v. Mendenhall* (1980) demonstrates the difficulty of determining consent and the use of an objective standard for a seizure. Sylvia Mendenhall deplaned at the Detroit Metropolitan Airport. She was observed by two DEA agents, who thought her conduct appeared "characteristic of persons unlawfully carrying narcotics." They approached Mendenhall, identified themselves as federal agents, and *asked* to see her identification and airline ticket. The name on her driver's license, Sylvia Mendenhall, and that on the ticket, Annette Ford, did not match. When asked why, she replied that she "just felt like using that name." One agent then specifically identified himself as a narcotics agent, and Mendenhall "became quite shaken, extremely nervous. She had a hard time speaking." She was then asked if she would accompany the agents to offices just fifty feet away. Once there, she was asked if she would allow a search of her person and handbag. She was told she had the right to decline if she desired. She responded, "Go ahead." A female police officer asked Mendenhall if she consented to the search and she replied that she did. Heroin was found in her undergarments, and she was arrested and convicted. The District Court concluded that Mendenhall had consented to the search.

Two justices, Stewart and Rehnquist, believed that Mendenhall had *consented* to the initial stop. Justice Stewart's **plurality opinion** reasoned that not every police–citizen encounter is a seizure of the person requiring reasonable suspicion or probable cause to be lawful. The test that distinguishes between a consent stop and a seizure is whether, in view of all the facts and circumstances, a reasonable person would believe that he or she is not *free to leave*; "a person is 'seized' only when, by means of physical force or show of authority, his freedom of movement is restrained." The plurality opinion therefore concluded that Mendenhall could have walked away from the agents at any point. No grabbing or touching occurred. The agents were not in uniform, and no weapons were displayed. The initial encounter occurred in public. They asked, but did not demand, to see her identification. The consequences of this objective test will be discussed in the next section.

Three justices (Burger, Powell, and Blackmun) felt that the initial stop was a *seizure* but that it was constitutional because the officers had *reasonable suspicion* to believe that Mendenhall was a drug courier. These five justices agreed that she had consented to going to the office and to the search of her person—that is, that there was no arrest until the heroin was found. Four dissenting justices (White, Brennan, Marshall, and Stevens) concluded, to the contrary, that Mendenhall was *seized without reasonable suspicion* and subject to an unconstitutional arrest and that the search was unconstitutional. Although the legality of airport drug stops has been clarified by the Court's acceptance of drug courier profiles as constituting reasonable suspicion, the inability of nine Supreme Court justices in *Mendenhall* to agree demonstrates the difficulty of sorting out the facts that constitute consent.

Knowledge of One's Rights

A major issue in *Schenckloth v. Bustamonte* (1973) was whether consent is possible when a defendant has no knowledge that he or she has a right to refuse a police request to search. The court of appeals had held that "a consent was a *waiver* of a person's Fourth and Fourteenth Amendment rights, and that the State was under an obligation to demonstrate, not only that the consent had been uncoerced, but that it had been given with an understanding that it could be freely and effectively withheld. Consent could not be found, the court held, solely from the absence of coercion and a verbal expression of assent. Since the District Court had not determined that Alcala had *known* that his consent could have been withheld and that he could have refused to have his vehicle searched, the Court of Appeals vacated the order denying the writ and remanded the case for further proceedings" (emphasis added). In reversing the decision, the Supreme Court held that the police are under no obligation to inform those from whom they seek consent to search that they have a constitutional right to refuse.

One reason was the fear that police, without probable cause or reasonable suspicion, would have no other way of getting evidence. "In situations where the police have some evidence of illicit activity, but lack probable cause to arrest or search, a search authorized by a valid consent may be the only means of obtaining important and reliable evidence" (*Schneckloth*, 1973). The Court did not define "some evidence," so the police could be requesting to search based only on a hunch or perhaps on categorical information (e.g., the person is a white male). Another reason is that a consent search could clear an innocent person of suspicion and stop the police from applying for a warrant where they have probable cause (but are in error) that contraband is in a place. A further reason is that it may be difficult to prove the person's subjective understanding of his or her rights, and after a consent search any defendant "could effectively frustrate the introduction into evidence of the fruits of that search by simply failing to testify that he in fact knew he could refuse to consent" (*Schneckloth*, 1973).

Borrowing from the Fifth and Sixth Amendments' *Miranda* and right-to-counsel cases, where a defendant must be informed of his or her rights, Bustamonte had argued that there is a Fourth Amendment obligation on the police to inform a person that he or she has a right to refuse consent. The Court rejected this contention. A Fourth Amendment consent is not the same as a *waiver* of the rights to silence or an attorney under the Fifth or Sixth Amendments. Waivers are valid only if made knowingly, and to ensure knowledge, suspects or defendants must be informed of these rights before giving them up. Waivers are "applied only to those rights which the Constitution guarantees to a criminal defendant in order to *preserve a fair trial.. .*.The requirement of a 'knowing' and 'intelligent' waiver was articulated in a case involving the validity of a defendant's decision to forgo a right constitutionally guaranteed to protect a fair trial and the *reliability* of the truth-determining process" (*Schneckloth*, 1973, emphases added). Violations of the privilege against self-incrimination or right to counsel might result in the conviction of innocent persons. "The protections of the Fourth Amendment are of a wholly different order, and have nothing whatever to do with promoting the fair ascertainment of truth at a criminal trial" (*Schneckloth*, 1973). Consents to search that result in the seizure of evidence of crime provide good evidence that might not otherwise be obtained. This analysis demonstrated that the Court's majority believed that Fourth Amendment rights are of lesser importance than other provisions of the Bill of Rights.

In addition, the Court believed it "would be unrealistic to expect that in the informal, unstructured context of a consent search, a policeman, upon pain of tainting the evidence obtained, could make the detailed type of examination" that occurs in courthouses when informing a defendant of his or her right to counsel. Similar considerations precluded extending the reasoning of *Miranda v. Arizona* (1966) to consent situations. The impracticality of obtaining written consents to search is a reasonable argument, although the extension of modern technology makes it less so, and many police departments utilize written consent-to-search forms. The Court did say that the suspect's knowledge, and whether he or she was informed of the right to refuse consent, are factors in assessing voluntariness.

In a brief dissent, Justice Brennan wrote: "It wholly escapes me how our citizens can meaningfully be said to have waived something as precious as a constitutional guarantee without ever being aware of its existence. In my view, the Court's conclusion is supported neither by 'linguistics,' nor by 'epistemology,' nor, indeed, by 'common sense'" (*Schneckloth v. Bustamonte,* 1973, Brennan, J., dissenting). A more elaborate dissent by Justice Marshall offered a different basis for accepting the validity of consent searches. He felt that the Court was mistaken to rely on the confessions cases because consent cases do not deal with the "coercion" present during custodial interrogation. Rather than extolling consent, as did the majority, Justice Marshall noted that police have weaker interests when they lack probable cause, suggesting that the Court ought not encourage police to seek consents. He put the basis of consent on a different footing: "[C]onsent searches are permitted, not because such an exception to the requirements of probable cause and warrant is essential to proper law enforcement, but because we permit our citizens to *choose* whether or not they wish to exercise their constitutional rights" (*Schneckloth v. Bustamonte,* 1973, Marshall, J., dissenting, emphasis added). In this view, consent is a freedom to give up a constitutional right and as such should be narrowly construed. This disagreed sharply with Justice Stewart's view that consent is a law enforcement tool that courts should broadly construe and support.

Indeed, Justice Marshall was sharply critical of the majority: "[W]hen the Court speaks of practicality, what it really is talking of is the continued ability of the police to capitalize on the ignorance of citizens so as to accomplish by subterfuge what they could not achieve by relying only on the knowing relinquishment of constitutional rights" (*Schneckloth v. Bustamonte,* 1973). But more than ignorance may be at work in consent searches. Quoting from the Ninth Circuit opinion, Justice Marshall concluded that "under many circumstances a reasonable person might read an officer's 'May I' as the courteous expression of a demand backed by force of law." This alludes to what Prof. Strauss called the "fiction of consent"—the observation supported by substantial scholarship and common sense "that most people would not feel free to deny a request by a police officer," a position that some judges agree with.[63] Sylvia Mendenhall, for example, was told that she had a right to not be searched, but she agreed anyway (*United States v. Mendenhall,* 1980).

To the extent that this is true, *Schneckloth*'s consent rules significantly weaken Fourth Amendment protections. Potential solutions, if desired, include (1) partially overruling *Schneckloth* and requiring police to inform people that they have a constitutional right to refuse to a search when asking for consent, a position that only three states have followed;[64] (2) requiring that police have reasonable suspicion before requesting consent, a rule that has been imposed on New Jersey state troopers in a consent decree following a major racial profiling case;[65] (3) allowing racial minorities to raise cultural arguments that, in view of the history of racially biased police action, the subjective attitude of blacks and Hispanics is to see most police requests for consent as coercive—a rule that Strauss believes would be difficult for courts to apply and would raise claims that the system is unfair in allowing this "strange form of affirmative action";[66] or (4) overruling *Schneckloth* and abolishing the consent exception to searches based on evidence, a position supported by Strauss.[67]

Schneckloth's approach was confirmed in **Ohio v. Robinette** (1996). A police officer stopped a motorist for speeding and issued a *warning* but did not tell him that he was "free to go," as was then required under a controversial Ohio Supreme Court decision.[68] In answer to the officer's question, Robinette said he was not carrying any contraband. The officer then asked if he could search the car. Robinette consented and the officer uncovered contraband. The Supreme Court found that the search was constitutional because Robinette consented voluntarily and that the officer did not have to inform him that he was "free to go." After the U.S. Supreme Court's decision, the Ohio Supreme Court rescinded its 1995 decision that required police to warn motorists that they did not have to allow a police search without individualized suspicion, finding that the added warning was not required under the state constitution.[69] An empirical study of written and verbal warnings issued by the Ohio Highway Patrol (OHP) during the year and a half that the Ohio Supreme Court required "*Robinette* warnings" shows that the number and rate of requests for consent by OHP officers *increased* during the period that they had to issue *Robinette* warnings. This finding allays the fears underlying *Schneckloth* that consent warnings would undermine law enforcement effectiveness.[70]

CONSENT-ONCE-REMOVED   A somewhat related "knowledge" issue is whether consent, validly given to an undercover agent who deceives an occupant about his true identity, can be extended to other police who forcibly enter a premises to search for contraband. This so-called "consent-once-removed" doctrine was upheld in several federal circuits when the undercover agent was a police official. The reasoning was that one police agent could extend his or her consent to a fellow officer. There was less support for the rule when the consent to enter was initially given not to a police agent, but to a "confidential informant," who typically is a drug user seeking to avoid prosecution. The Supreme Court indirectly approved of consent-once removed by holding that an officer who is signaled to enter by a confidential informant is entitled to qualified immunity from a civil suit (***Pearson v. Callahan,*** 2009). In *Callahan* a confidential informant was invited to Callahan's house to buy drugs. He was fitted with a wire and gave a signal as soon as he made the purchase. Police entered without a warrant and seized the contraband. The "'consent-once-removed' doctrine applies when an undercover officer [or confidential informant] enters a house at the express invitation of someone with authority to consent, establishes probable cause to arrest or search, and then immediately summons other officers for assistance."

Third-Party Consent

When two or more people share a room or common area, one person may voluntarily consent to a police search of the *common area*. Evidence found that incriminates the other party may be admitted in evidence. The prosecution need only show by a *preponderance of the evidence* that the person who gave consent had authority to do so, based on her or his relationship to the property.

In the leading third-party consent search case, ***United States v. Matlock*** (1974), police searched the bedroom of a house, with the consent of Gayle Graff, who was living with Matlock. Evidence of a bank robbery was found and admitted to prove guilt. The fact that the couple was not married was irrelevant for Fourth Amendment purposes to negate consent. The authority of a third party to consent to the search depends not on property law concepts or on rules of evidence that apply in a trial, "but rests rather on *mutual use* of the property by persons generally having joint access or control for most purposes, so that it is reasonable to recognize that any of the coinhabitants has the right to permit the inspection in his own right and that the others have assumed the risk that one of their number might permit the common area to be searched" (*United States v. Matlock*, 1974, emphasis added). Similarly, a roommate who shares a duffel bag may consent to its search (*Frazier v. Cupp,* 1969).

In contrast to *Matlock,* the Court held in ***Stoner v. California*** (1964) that a *hotel clerk* did not have authority to consent to a police search of a guest's room. The Court said, "It is important to bear in mind that it was the petitioner's constitutional right which was at stake here, and not the night clerk's or the hotel's." Although *Stoner* was decided before the "expectation of privacy" principle of *Katz* (1967) was enunciated, as a rule of thumb it seems that only those with an expectation of privacy over an area may consent to a search. *Stoner* was preceded by *Chapman v. California* (1967), which held that a *landlord* may not give consent to a police search into a tenant's apartment or house, even though the landlord has a general right of entry for normal inspection purposes.

Illinois v. Rodriguez (1990) upheld a warrantless entry into a man's apartment when consent was given by a person with reasonably *apparent authority*. Gail Fisher complained to Chicago police that Edward Rodriguez had beaten her. Officers accompanied Fisher from her mother's to Rodriguez's apartment to get her stuff. She let them in with a key. On the drive to Rodriguez's apartment, she referred to "our" place. The officers did not know that she had moved out a month earlier, removed her clothing, did not invite friends there, was never in the house when Rodriguez was not there, did not contribute to the rent, and did not have her name on the lease. In reality, Fusher did *not* possess common authority over the premises; but the police *reasonably believed* that she had. The Court held the entry to be *reasonable* under the Fourth Amendment. By analogy to probable cause cases, a police officer's reasonable mistake in a consent case does not violate the individual's Fourth Amendment rights.

The *Rodriguez* Court, extending the scope of third-party consent, differentiated *Stoner,* which is still good law. A motel clerk's apparent authority to enter a room can never be the basis for a third-party police search, because police know that ordinarily, motel personnel do not have general authority to enter a guest's room outside of normal cleaning and maintenance functions. On the other hand, when a woman with a key to an apartment claims that her boyfriend beat her, there is no reason why the police should not believe that she lives in the apartment.

Justice Marshall dissented in *Rodriguez* (joined by Justices Brennan and Stevens). A home entry without a warrant is *presumptively unreasonable*; police cannot dispense with a person's rights where that person has not limited his expectation of privacy by sharing his home with another. Under this analysis, the reasonableness of the police officers' action is irrelevant. The police should have obtained a warrant in this situation even if inconvenient.

In **Georgia v. Randolph** (2006), Scott and Janet Randolph had separated; she moved out and took their son. She returned to the marital residence a few months later, but after a domestic dispute with Scott called police saying that he took their son. When the police arrived, Janet told them that Scott used cocaine. Scott returned shortly, having taken his son to a neighbor's. He denied cocaine use and accused Janet of abusing drugs and alcohol. After the police went with Janet to retrieve the son, she said that Scott had drugs in the house. At the door to the house, the officer asked for consent to enter. Scott flatly refused, but Janet gave consent. Janet led the officer to Scott's bedroom, where he saw a straw with a powdery residue, which was seized. Under a warrant, police later found more evidence of drug use. Scott was convicted of cocaine possession. The Georgia appellate courts reversed the conviction on the grounds that "the consent to conduct a warrantless search of a residence given by one occupant is not valid in the face of the refusal of another occupant who is physically present at the scene to permit a warrantless search" (*Georgia v. Randolph,* 2006, quoting the Georgia Supreme Court).

The U.S. Supreme Court affirmed (5–3). The reasoning of Justice Souter's majority opinion was based on the idea that *widely shared social expectations*, a source outside the Fourth Amendment, should be used to interpret the amendment's Reasonableness Clause and the expectation of privacy. Widely shared social expectations made it reasonable for police to enter the Matlock residence when a person who obviously belonged there came to the door and voluntarily let the police in to look around. Likewise, a tenant or motel occupant does not expect that a landlord or motel clerk would have implied permission to allow others to enter the occupant's apartment or room. Therefore, "a caller standing at the door of shared premises would have no confidence that one occupant's invitation was a sufficiently good reason to enter when a fellow tenant stood there saying, 'stay out.' Without some *very good reason,* no sensible person would go inside under those conditions" (*Georgia v. Randolph,* 2006, emphasis added). In coming to this conclusion, the majority placed the "centuries-old principle of respect for the privacy of the home" above law enforcement convenience needs. "Disputed permission is . . . no match for this central value of the Fourth Amendment" (*Georgia v. Randolph,* 2006). The police could have obtained a warrant and could have prevented the residents from destroying any property while waiting for the warrant (*Illinois v. McArthur,* 2001). The majority noted that its decision was in accord with the preference for search warrants (*United States v. Ventresca,* 1965). It took special pains to make it clear that its decision did not prevent police from entering a premises for the very good reason that an occupant made a complaint about domestic violence, which was not a factor in this case. The majority also made it clear that the police have no responsibility to search for another occupant who might object to the consent to enter (as long as they do not deliberately remove a potentially objecting occupant from the entrance). The Court acknowledged the contingent nature of the holding, depending as it does on the fortuitous circumstance of a consenting and an objecting occupant standing at the entrance to the premises.

Chief Justice John Roberts dissented. He pointed out that a number of differing social situations could give rise to different social expectations about entering where two occupants differ, as where the entering person is a close friend or relative, or where the premises of the "feuding roommates" is a single room or a spacious house; or where there are more than two occupants and a majority invite a guest in. The dissent's basic reasoning is that the Fourth Amendment protects privacy, and when the privacy of an area is shared, the occupant assumes the risk that the privacy will be breached by the other occupant. Finally, the dissent raised an alarm that the decision would be an impediment to entry in domestic violence cases.

Scope of Consent

> Dade County police officer, Frank Trujillo, overheard . . . Enio Jimeno, arranging what appeared to be a drug transaction over a public telephone. Believing that Jimeno might be involved in illegal drug trafficking, Officer Trujillo followed his car. The officer . . . pulled Jimeno over to the side of the road in order to issue him a traffic citation [for making an illegal turn]. Officer Trujillo told Jimeno that he had been stopped for committing a traffic infraction. The officer went on to say that he had reason to believe that Jimeno was carrying narcotics in his car, and asked permission to search the car. He explained that Jimeno did not have to consent to a search of the car. Jimeno stated that he had nothing to hide and gave Trujillo permission to search the automobile. After Jimeno's spouse, respondent Luz Jimeno, stepped out of the car, Officer Trujillo went to the passenger side, opened the door, and saw a folded, brown paper bag on the floorboard. The officer picked up the bag, opened it, and found a kilogram of cocaine inside.
>
> The Jimenos were charged with possession with intent to distribute cocaine in violation of Florida law. (***Florida v. Jimeno,*** 1991, pp. 249–50)

The Florida Supreme Court ruled that the officer had to receive specific consent to open the container. The U.S. Supreme Court reversed, holding that under the Fourth Amendment the scope of a consent search depends on whether the search was reasonable. In this case, the search was reasonable because, according to Chief Justice Rehnquist, the "scope of a search is generally defined by its expressed object." Jimeno "did not place any explicit limitation on the scope of the search," and a "reasonable person may be expected to know that narcotics are generally carried in some form of a container." He stressed that Jimeno could have limited the scope of the search, and he concluded with the policy expressed in *Schneckloth* that "[t]he community has a real interest in encouraging consent, for the resulting search may yield necessary evidence for the solution and prosecution of crime."

Justice Marshall dissented, joined by Justice Stevens. He noted that under the Court's precedent, there is a lesser expectation of privacy in cars, but a heightened expectation of privacy in the content of closed containers. These "distinct privacy expectations. . . do not merge when the individual uses his car to transport the container." Also, the way in which "reasonableness" is used by the majority could lead to absurd or unacceptable results. After all, if "a reasonable person may be expected to know that drug couriers frequently store their contraband on their persons or in their body cavities," then consent to search a car could lead to a body-cavity search. He argued that Jimeno, in fact, did not consent to a search of the paper bag and the Court should interpret rights expansively and should interpret limitation of rights (such as consent) narrowly.

"Knock and Talk"

In recent years a number of cases have defined the parameters of a police practice labeled "knock and talk" (not to be confused with the search warrant knock-and-announce requirement). The Supreme Court has not yet ruled on the practice but different decisions by federal Courts of Appeal may generate a future case. Knock and talk is "a procedure used by law enforcement officers, under which they approach the door of a residence seeking to speak to the inhabitants, typically to obtain more information regarding a criminal investigation or to obtain consent to search where probable cause is lacking."[71] Police estimate that as many as 80 percent of people asked, consent to home searches at the doorstep even though the police have not probable cause or even reasonable suspicion to enter.[72] This is proper if the consent is truly voluntary, for then the search "does not trigger the Fourth Amendment's constitutional protections."[73]

Because knock and talk involves police going to residences, it involves *curtilage* issues. When police enter the curtilage in a manner that is socially prescribed for anyone approaching a residence, they do not violate the curtilage protection. This typically requires that police stay on walkways and approach at reasonable times of day. In some cases late-night knock and talks were upheld, depending on the facts and circumstances of a case. Likewise, in some cases it was deemed reasonable for police to go to the back yard of a house to knock, but in other cases it was not.[74]

A number of court decisions and commentaries have been very critical of knock and talk as a way for police to circumvent the search warrant requirement to enter homes. The Arkansas Supreme Court modified its usual rule of interpreting the Arkansas constitution in accord with the United States Supreme Court's interpretation of the Fourth Amendment, to rule in a knock and talk case that the Arkansas constitution imposed "greater restrictions on police activity" and evidence obtained in violation of Arkansas law is inadmissible in court (*Griffin v. State*, 2002).[75] In this case, four or five police officers, armed with flashlights but not with a search warrant or probable cause, hid their parked cars from Griffin's home and approached from the rear. They had one uncorroborated informant's statement that Griffin, an optician, dealt amphetamines. Griffin lived in a ground-level apartment of his parent's house; a sitting room had glass doors. It was after 10:00 p.m. and pitch-black outside. Police came upon and searched unlocked cars outside the home, finding no contraband. While Griffin was in a back room talking to his daughter on the telephone, a guest, Karen Horton, "saw a bunch of flashlights out in the vicinity of the shed coming through the woods." She told Griffin "that four or five men were approaching the house." As Griffin came into the room, the officers told Horton "not to move, and then ordered her to open the door." An officer testified that he knocked and no search began until consent was given. No written consent form was signed. Nor was Griffin advised that he could refuse to consent to search. A "sealed container containing methamphetamine in a locked cabinet in Griffin's bedroom" was found.

The Arkansas Supreme Court held that an illegal search occurred before the police knocked on the glass door to Griffin's apartment. Police, stealthily coming through the woods, with flashlights in the pitch-black night, is the antithesis of "anyone open and peaceably, at high noon, . . . walk[ing] up the steps and knock[ing] on the front door of any man's 'castle' with the honest intent of asking questions of the occupant thereof." The evidence was excluded. Three justices concurred in opinions sharply critical of knock and talk. Justice Corbin noted that before "this type of consent search became so fashionable, the police were forced to investigate anonymous or unreliable tips before they could attempt to seize evidence" suggesting one rule that would reduce errors produced by knock and talk. He also would have held that under the Arkansas constitution, knock and talk should be prohibited at night. Justice Brown alluded to the "the intimidation factor (usually two to four police officers are involved) and the message conveyed, either verbally or by insinuation, that if a consent is not given, the police officers will simply get a search warrant and come back." Such practices led the Washington Supreme Court to require police to inform householders that they have a right to refuse consent to enter.[76] Justice Brown argued that having a written consent from in knock and talk cases was better practice. Justice Hannah, in a powerful concurrence, said the "'knock and talk' practice of police poses a serious threat to the right of privacy and right against unlawful search and seizure." He argued "for greater restraints on police use of the 'knock and talk'" and would require written consent as a constitutional mandate.

A commentary reviewed a Michigan case where four police officers (two approached Frohriep while two remained hidden) got vague oral consent one May evening to "look around" Larry Frohriep's property. He opened the door to a pole barn; it was disputed whether he consented that police enter. While he was talking to one officer the others searched diligently and one shouted "Bingo" when marijuana was found in a freezer. Relying on Fourth Amendment consent search cases, the Court of Appeals upheld police practices in this case.[77] The Casenote pointed out that federal statutes impose greater limits on the behavior of door-to-door salespersons than the Fourth Amendment, as interpreted by the Michigan court, imposed on the police. It viewed any request for consent to enter a *home* as far more intrusive than other kinds of requests for consent to search. "The special sanctity afforded the home under the Fourth Amendment should protect citizens from having to shoo away police that do not even have reasonable articulable suspicions."[78] While this could lead to a warrant requirement, the Casenote advocated that police audiotape all knock and talks, that police be required to inform householders that they have a right to refuse to consent, that they may revoke consent at any time, and that they may limit consent to particular areas of their home.[79]

Aside from the issue of voluntariness, which can evaporate when police act in egregious ways, a couple of other problems arise with knock and talk. One is *constructive entry*, whereby "police use tactics that force the individual to exit his home" or "conduct a 'knock and talk' with weapons drawn, while yelling at the occupant, using a bullhorn, or while preventing the occupant from leaving the premises."[80] The other is when the police knock and talk creates an exigency that is then used by the police as a reason to enter and search. In *U.S. v. Gomez-Moreno*,[81] the exigency of a man running out of a house was created by ten to twelve police and Immigration and

Customs Enforcement Officers in labeled jackets, accompanied by an overhead helicopter, swarming around a house, trying the front door handle, and shouting "Police! Police! Open the door." This was not a knock to inquire about a crime but a way to generate an unwarranted raid for illegal aliens. In the case of suspicion of drug possession, an exigency may be created by police without warrants announcing themselves, and then breaking in if they "hear people running around" on the fear that drugs are being destroyed.[82] Several federal circuit Courts of Appeal, including the Third, Fifth and Sixth, explore the deliberate intentions or bad faith of police officers in using these tactics as pretexts to gain entry without warrants. This contrasts with the Second Circuit, which relies on objective factors regarding the tactics used by the police.[83] These Circuit differences could provide a basis for the Supreme Court to rule on knock and talk.

LAW IN SOCIETY:

Police Perjury and the Fourth Amendment

A decade ago, police perjury was "the dirty little secret of our criminal justice system."[84] Now it is common knowledge, thanks in large part to the exposed perjury of Detective Mark Fuhrman in the O. J. Simpson murder trial.[85] A law professor reports that his students frequently interrupt classroom hypotheticals involving illegal police conduct with questions like "What if the police just lie about what happened?"[86] And this, indeed, is the critical point. People in all walks of life, from presidents on down, have been known to lie; and it is necessary for society to prosecute business fraud, for professional organizations to investigate and sanction falsehoods by their members, and so forth. "What distinguishes police officers is their unique power—to use force, to summarily deprive a citizen of freedom, to even use deadly force, if necessary—and their commensurately unique responsibilities—to be the living embodiment of the 'law' in our communities, as applied fairly to every member."[87] If police officers routinely commit perjury about the legality of arrests or searches and routinely get away with it, then the true result is not a personal benefit (a good arrest record) or even a misguided belief that this enhances public safety—it effectively destroys the basic constitutional rights of every person who is subject to such illegal action and threatens the rights of the rest of us (including cops) who have not yet been framed by police lies. This kind of perjury occurs most frequently in drug enforcement.

It is important to begin with Professor Morgan Cloud's observation that it's not true that "all police officers lie under oath, or that most officers lie, or that even some officers lie all the time."[88] An insightful article by Professor Andrew McClurg notes a profound paradox: "Most police officers are honorable, moral persons," yet "many of these same police officers lie in the course of their official duties." Any resolution of the problem of police perjury requires understanding the pressures that proliferate police perjury.

The kind of police perjury most likely to undermine Fourth Amendment rights occurs when (1) a police officer thinks that a defendant was in possession of contraband or incriminating evidence, (2) the officer obtained the evidence by an unconstitutional act, and (3) in a suppression hearing the officer "embellishes" the truth by testifying so as to make it appear as if the stop, arrest, or search was performed in a constitutional manner. "Routine" perjury is a greater threat to rights than more outrageous action, such as planting evidence on innocent individuals or "booming" (illegally breaking into homes without a warrant or pretense of legality),[89] because most cops, being honorable, draw the line at such over-the-top behavior. But they will "shade" the truth if they view constitutional rights as "mere technicalities"—as impediments to effective law enforcement. Professor Richard Uviller, who spent a year observing a New York Police Department street crimes unit, notes that like most people, "cops were raised with a strong sense of justice, and they naturally apply it when the occasion arises."[90]

Scholars who have studied this issue believe that routine perjury in regard to the seizure of incriminating evidence began as a result of the federalization of the exclusionary rule in *Mapp v. Ohio* (1961). A frequently cited 1971 article by Irving Younger, a former prosecutor and judge, noted that before *Mapp,* police easily testified to making illegal stops and finding contraband—"This had the ring of truth." After *Mapp,* judges suppressed evidence obtained in this way. Police officers then discovered "that if the defendant drops the narcotics on the ground, after which the policeman arrests him, then the search is reasonable and the evidence is admissible." Hence "dropsy" testimony increased enormously.[91] Younger's observations were substantiated by a before–after empirical study of police testimony in misdemeanor narcotics arrests showing that the percent of arrests where narcotics were "hidden on the body" dropped from about 25 percent of all arrests to about 5 percent, while "dropsy" cases, which accounted for about 10 to 15 percent of arrests before *Mapp,* increased to 41 percent for narcotics officers.[92]

"Routine" perjury is close to impossible for defense lawyers, prosecutors, or judges to detect because it is so simple:

> Lying about search and seizure matters "was part of everyday police work" according to a former New York City police officer interviewed for an article announcing that cops in New York must now go to school to learn to tell the truth. The Mollen Commission cataloged a "litany" of manufactured search and seizure tales uncovered by its investigation:
>
> For example, when officers unlawfully stop and search a vehicle because they believe it contains drugs or guns, officers will falsely claim in police reports and under oath that the car ran a red light (or committed some other traffic violation) and that they subsequently saw contraband in the car in plain view. To conceal an unlawful search of an individual who officers believe is carrying drugs or a gun, they will falsely assert that they saw a bulge in the person's pocket or saw drugs and money changing hands. To justify unlawfully entering an apartment where officers believe narcotics or cash can be found, they pretend to have information from an unidentified civilian informant or claim they saw the drugs in plain view after responding to the premises on a radio run. To arrest people they suspect are guilty of dealing drugs, they falsely assert that the defendants had drugs in their possession when, in fact, the drugs were found elsewhere where the officers had no lawful right to be.[93]

A Harvard Law School conference held shortly after the verdict in the O. J. Simpson case concluded: "There are no national studies or statistics on police perjury, and there is considerable disagreement on how widespread the problem is."[94] Nevertheless, a great deal of anecdotal evidence from police commissions and others indicates that police perjury is widespread.[95] A study of twenty-six Chicago narcotics detectives asked them: "In your experience, do police officers ever shade the facts a little (or a lot) to establish probable cause when there may not have been probable cause in fact?" Sixteen officers responded "yes," and five responded "no."[96] Of course, the actual number is unknown because "[b]y their very nature, successful lies will remain undetected, and we would expect a perjurer to attempt to conceal his crime."[97] Former Kansas City and San Jose police chief and Hoover Institution research fellow Joseph D. McNamara estimated "that hundreds of thousands of law-enforcement officers commit felony perjury every year testifying about drug arrests." He based this estimate on the fact that about one million drug arrests a year are for possession, not selling, and that hundreds of thousands of police swear under oath that the drugs were in plain view or that the defendant gave consent to a search. "This may happen occasionally but it defies belief that so many drug users are careless enough to leave illegal drugs where the police can see them or so dumb as to give cops consent to search them when they possess drugs."[98]

"Routine" perjury has serious consequences. First, there is the danger that police fabrication will lead to the charging or conviction of innocent people. In some cases, the police have convinced themselves, against the evidence, that the victim of their lies was guilty. Well-known cases include Richard Jewell, suspected of bombing Olympic Park at the 1996 Atlanta Olympics, and Rolando Cruz, who was on death row in Illinois, but there are many others.[99]

Second, the frequent commission of "pious perjury" creates an enabling atmosphere that allows a minority of "rogue cops" to go over the top by planting evidence on innocent people or booming. There is no way of knowing whether such abuses are widespread. Commission reports and the anecdotes of police and lawyers do not indicate that such practices are routine. Nevertheless, when such cases do occur, they are reported, and quite a few have appeared in the last decade:

- In Philadelphia's 39th District scandal, six "rogue cops" planted evidence on many innocent people, including a grandmother who pestered them with questions when they came looking for her grandson and spent two years in prison for her verbal challenges. The city paid out at least seven million dollars, and fourteen hundred cases were reviewed.[100]

- In the mid–1990s NYPD 30th Precinct scandal, wrongful arrests and booming were connected to police participation in illegal drug sales.[101]
- Five New York State Troopers were convicted of faking fingerprint evidence in thirty cases. In one case, they lifted fingerprints from a corpse and planned to plant the evidence on anyone charged with the crime.[102]
- In Hartford, Connecticut, police officers committed perjury to cover up a police ring that systematically shook down drug dealers.[103]
- Eufrasio G. Cortez, a California narcotics Officer of the Year, was convicted after he admitted that he stole a half million dollars from drug busts, committed perjury thirty times, beat suspects on twenty occasions, and used false statements in search warrants one hundred times over his fifteen-year police career.[104]

Third, the practice cannot be kept hidden and eventually leads to a loss of public confidence in the police. As a result, jurors become skeptical of police testimony, which undermines fair prosecutions; minorities become less willing to call the police for protection; and the public is less interested in law enforcement as a career.[105]

Fourth, the practice undermines the morale and diminishes the sense of pride felt by honest officers.[106] When police lie to cover their corruption, the professional self-esteem of honest cops is injured. Uviller noted in honest cops "a sense of betrayal by the corrupt members who have demeaned the job and made it harder for the rest to convince the public of their probity."[107]

Fifth, the practice leads to corrupt police work, including the use of drugs by undercover officers who then lie to the jury about such practices. East Texas police officer and FBI undercover agent Kim Wozencraft admitted routinely planting evidence, using drugs with suspects, and lying about it in court. She was convicted of perjury, served time, and later resumed her life as a novelist and editor of *Prison Life* magazine.[108]

Sixth, police perjury forces honest cops into the risky role of becoming whistle-blowers and suffering the consequences, or joining the "blue wall of silence" and tolerating the corruption around them. Officer Michael McEvoy of the Arlington Heights, Illinois, Police Department "blew the whistle" on a case of police perjury and would have been fired by his chief, but the Arlington Heights Board of Fire and Police Commissioners reinstated McEvoy when his account was substantiated by a third officer.[109] It is not implausible to believe that a number of whistle-blowers were not as lucky as McEvoy.

Seventh, the practice drives a wedge between judges who occasionally suppress evidence and police who become angry at judges who do not accept their lies. Judge Joseph Q. Koletsky of Hartford, Connecticut, threw out evidence of a crime after the testimony of arresting police officers was clearly contradicted by physical evidence. Detectives told a plausible story of stopping a suspect next to his truck. He was arrested because he reached behind himself, establishing the basis for an arrest and a search incident to arrest during which cocaine was supposedly found. However, spilled powder cocaine in the cab of the truck supported the defendant's testimony that the officers simply drew guns and arrested him, illegally, in his truck. After the evidence was suppressed, the detectives insisted that they did the right thing. "It's a bad decision, but what can you do?" Officer Murzin said. "Some people live in the real world and some people don't."[110] In the "real world," people with power can lie and get away with it.

In a more famous case, federal judge Harold Baer suppressed evidence in a New York City drug bust. A former member of the Mollen Commission on Police Corruption, he had expressed skepticism of the police in his decision. After media coverage, it quickly became a national issue during the 1996 presidential campaign. In an unusual move, the judge ordered a second hearing, heard more testimony, and decided that the search and seizure had been lawful.[111]

Finally, and most important, police perjury diminishes liberty and undermines the constitutional order. In addition to the growing subcultural belief that the Constitution is an impediment to be overcome, judicial acceptance of police perjury undermines the very rationale given for the exclusionary rule: deterrence of police illegality.

An important reason why police perjury is pervasive is that it is in large measure condoned by the courts. According to Alan Dershowitz, "[a] judge in Detroit after listening on one day to more than a dozen 'dropsy' cases . . . chastised the police for not being more 'creative,' but nonetheless accepted their testimony."[112] Cloud gives five reasons why judges accept police perjury:

1. It can be difficult to determine if a witness is lying.
2. Judges dislike the exclusionary rule.
3. Judges cynically believe that "most defendants in the criminal justice system are guilty," and "even if they are innocent of these specific crimes, [they] are guilty of something." Therefore "it is not too disturbing that evidence will not be suppressed."
4. Judges assume that criminal defendants will commit perjury and so distrust the testimony of suspects.
5. "Judges simply do not like to call other government officials liars—especially those who appear regularly in court. It is distasteful; it is indelicate; it is bad manners."[113]

To this list McClurg adds that "judges do not want to generate adverse publicity that portrays them as being 'soft on crime.'" Elected judges, in particular, "are afraid of jeopardizing their chances of reelection."[114]

Numerous proposals have been made to deal with this issue, and many involve modifying legal rules and procedures:

- Eliminating the exclusionary rule.
- Eliminating the exclusionary rule for violent crimes but not for crimes like drug possession.
- Expanding the use of judicial warrants to all nonexigent searches and seizures while narrowing the exigency exception.
- Admitting polygraphs of witnesses in suppression hearings.
- Making probable cause more flexible to allow commonsense judgments.
- Permitting impeachment of police testimony through proof of bias and motive to lie and by allowing evidence of the prevalence of the blue wall of silence.
- Allowing judges to order discovery and allow cross-examination where there is an initial showing of police perjury in a suppression hearing.[115]

Some of these proposals are implausible, but some may have a limited impact on police perjury. Institutional changes have been proposed. Jerome Skolnick and James Fyfe propose major changes in police departments and a move toward community policing as a way to ameliorate the problem.[116] McClurg believes that "[w]e cannot rely with confidence on external actors or institutions to control police lying" and that "[p]olice lying will be substantially reduced only when more police officers come to view it as an unacceptable practice."[117] He believes that police perjury is so pervasive because of the contradiction between the fact that most police officers are moral persons and that many will commit "routine" perjury, which causes cognitive dissonance. To reduce the tension, the officers rationalize their behavior by coming to believe that lying is moral behavior.[118] To deal effectively with police perjury, he proposed a system of police academy training and on-the-street mentoring to show that the "end justifies the means" reasoning that supports perjury is shortsighted and injurious. He suggests fortifying the initial decency that rookies bring to the academy before it becomes hardened into cynicism.[119] The details of this interesting proposal are beyond the scope of this section. Clearly, though, it can work only if the head of the law enforcement agency and the political leadership of the municipality support it.

To sum up, "routine" police perjury is pervasive, and it seriously threatens the existence of Fourth Amendment rights. As noted in Chapter 1, the most important aspect of the Rule of Law is "congruence." The practices of the government must be congruent with the law as written. The glorious promises of procedural justice enshrined in the Bill of Rights can quickly become hollow and breed a terrible cynicism against government and law if they are routinely ignored. Such cynicism is widespread, and it is vital that judges and especially the police take rights seriously.

Summary

The Supreme Court has expressed a preference for search warrants over warrantless searches. Most important, a warrant places the judgment of a detached and neutral judicial officer between the police and the citizen in deciding whether probable cause exists to effect a search. A judicial officer who receives fees from warrants issued or who becomes too closely attached to the police search effort is not a neutral and detached magistrate. To obtain a search warrant, an officer must present a written affidavit to a magistrate and swear to the truth of the facts in an *ex parte* hearing that purports to show probable cause. An officer who serves a patently deficient warrant is personally liable. A statute can authorize a telephonic warrant. The place to be searched must be precisely described, but a reasonable mistake in describing the place will not make the search illegal.

Search warrants for materials protected by the First Amendment must describe the materials exactly. Anticipatory warrants authorize police to seize evidence from places that do not contain contraband at the time the warrant is issued, but reasonably expect the contraband to be delivered to the location. Anticipatory search warrants are constitutional.

A defendant can obtain a hearing to challenge an executed search warrant where a preliminary showing indicates that the officer who made out the affidavit intentionally lied about material facts or made statements with reckless disregard for the truth. Search warrants must be executed within ten days of issuance. Business papers and items in news offices can be seized under warrants rather than requested by subpoena. The Fourth Amendment requires that police officers knock and announce their presence when executing a warrant; the "knock and announce" element can be set aside by a magistrate in a no-knock warrant where potential danger to officers or loss of evidence is likely if the police knock and announce. However, a blanket no-knock policy violates the Fourth Amendment. The exclusionary rule does not apply if the knock-and-announce rule is violated. After warrant execution, the officer must inventory each item seized, and return copies to the court and the premises owner. "Sneak and peek" warrants allow officers to enter without seizing evidence and delay notification of the search.

In the 1960s, search and seizure law was modernized by creating the "expectation of privacy" doctrine (*Katz v. United States*), eliminating the mere evidence rule, by utilizing the Fourth Amendment Reasonableness Clause to weaken the particularity requirement for administrative search warrants, and to authorize investigative stops on less than probable cause (*Terry v. Ohio*). These changes made Fourth Amendment interpretation more flexible. The "expectation of privacy" doctrine includes a subjective and an objective, or societal, measure of privacy. Under the "expectation of privacy" doctrine, electronic eavesdropping was authorized and controlled by statute. Property interests are still protected by the Fourth Amendment, but the Court looks to the subjective and objective expectation of privacy balanced against the needs of effective law enforcement. The expectations given the greatest weight are those of the privacy of the home and bodily integrity. Under *Camara v. Municipal Court*, nonpolice government employees can enter homes without the owner's consent to enforce administrative ordinances with a judicial area warrant that need not be as specific as a criminal search warrant. The Fourth Amendment does not prohibit the use of undercover agents who are invited into homes and private areas under false pretense. Such an agent cannot conduct a general search of the premises but can testify as to any criminal activity that occurs in his or her presence.

Probable cause is defined as known facts that could lead a reasonably prudent person to draw conclusions about unknown facts. It is a standard of evidence sufficiency that allows a law enforcement official to arrest a person, obtain a warrant, or perform a warrantless search. Probable cause may be based on hearsay. When the hearsay is provided by a secret informant, the Supreme Court has required magistrates to examine the affidavits carefully. Under the older *Aguilar–Spinelli*

two-pronged test, the magistrate had to be convinced that the officer's affidavit supplied credible information about the informant's veracity and his or her basis of knowledge. The Court in *Illinois v. Gates* replaced the two-pronged test with a "totality of the circumstances" test, which it applied to an anonymous tip so that a deficiency in one prong can be compensated for by a strong showing as to the other or by some other indicia of reliability in determining the overall reliability of a tip.

The plain view doctrine allows the seizure of contraband when a police officer who makes the seizure is lawfully in the place (by a warrant or by virtue of being in a public place) and the illegal nature of the thing seized is immediately apparent. "Plain view" pertains to the five senses, and allows "plain feel" search and seizures. The "immediately apparent" rule is, in effect, a rule of probable cause. A police officer cannot create plain view by illegally entering a premises or by manipulating evidence beyond that authorized by the purpose of the officer's mandate. Open fields are not protected by the Fourth Amendment; evidence seized by officers who trespass on open land is admissible. The curtilage, the area and buildings immediately surrounding a house, is protected by the Fourth Amendment to the extent that the expectation of privacy in the area is secured. Airplane and helicopter flyovers may lawfully obtain evidence of what is visible in a curtilage, even if fenced, because commercial overflights have eliminated the expectation of privacy from the air. Ordinary devices, such as flashlights and field glasses, that enhance the senses do not undermine the "immediately apparent" rule. The use, without a warrant, of an enhancement device such as a beeper or a thermal imager that detects movement within a home and suggests criminal activity violates the Fourth Amendment. A warrant must be obtained for enhancement devices that are not in general public use (*Kyllo v. United States*).

A person may consent to relinquish to a law enforcement officer his or her Fourth Amendment right to privacy. An officer seeking consent to search need not have reasonable suspicion or probable cause to do so. An officer need not inform a person, when requesting consent to search, that the person has a constitutional right to refuse. Facts and circumstances of a consent encounter must show that the consent was voluntary. The burden of proof is on the government to show voluntariness. Entry under the pretense of having a search warrant negates consent. An undercover officer or agent invited into a house may transfer consent to enter to other officers when the informer has probable cause that contraband is present.

A person who shares a common area with another may give consent to the police to search, as may a person who reasonably appears to share a place. Landlords or hotel keepers cannot give consent for a criminal search. Police may rely on consent given by a person who reasonably appears to have shared control over an area even if, in fact, the person has no authority or control over the area. Consent to search an area, such as a car, gives police the right to open containers located in the area. When two people have apparent authority over a place and one gives police permission to enter but the other does not, the police have not received valid consent and must obtain a warrant to lawfully enter the premises.

Legal Puzzles

HOW HAVE COURTS DECIDED THESE CASES?

Search Warrant

3-1. Thomas was shot and injured. A friend called 911. Two officers responded to Thomas's residence, located at 3958 Balley Castle Court. While attending to Thomas the officers smelled a strong odor of marijuana inside the residence. Based upon this information, a detective with the Drug Task Force submitted an affidavit and application for a warrant to search for marijuana and drug-related documents and paraphernalia at "3958 Balley Castle Court." A magistrate granted the search warrant at 11:28 p.m., but the warrant listed the address for the search as "5365 Williams Road, Georgia, Gwinnett." The warrant did not name Thomas or any other owner or occupant. The warrant also provided that the affidavit submitted by the detective "shall not be served upon the premises—only the [search warrant] shall be served." After obtaining the search warrant the detective and the two responding officers searched Thomas's residence (3958 Balley Castle Court) early the next morning and found more than 42 pounds of marijuana.

Was the search warrant valid?

Held: NO

3-1. The detective who submitted the affidavit and application for the search warrant had created the documents using a template on her computer, which inadvertently contained an address from a prior warrant application. It was this proposed search warrant that the magistrate signed, resulting in the warrant having the wrong address. Where, as here, "the name of the owner or occupant is not given in the warrant, the description of the premises must be exact." Hence, "where the premises are described by street and number, that description will not authorize a search of the premises at another street or number." The search warrant in this case, contained an entirely different address from that which was searched, was unconstitutional.

The error was not a mere technical irregularity. (1) The warrant did not contain other elements of description sufficiently particular to identify the premises to be searched. (2) Nor did the accurate affidavit accompany the warrant. (3) The fact that the officers executing the warrant knew facts about the place to be searched (omitted from the warrant) that were essential to a proper description, will not correct the omission. A purpose of having a particularized warrant is to "assure[ ] the individual whose property is searched or seized of the lawful authority of the executing officer, his need to search, and the limits of his power to search," a purpose that goes unfulfilled if the particularized information justifying the warrant is not made available to the individual presented with the warrant.

Groh v. Ramirez (2004); *Thomas v. State*, 287 Ga.App. 262, 651 S.E.2d 183 (Ga. Court of Appeals 2007).

Scope of Search Warrant; Expectation of Privacy

3-2. Dayle Lynn Johnson operated the Village Pub, operating on the ground floor of a colonial-style house. The upper stories were Johnson's living space and storage. Johnson's closely regulated business required a liquor license and was subject to inspection by agents of the liquor licensing authority. Maine's drug agency (MDEA) received information that marijuana was being cultivated on the Village Pub premises. Also alleged was that Johnson began unauthorized renovations of the pub's bathrooms that required approval from the liquor inspectors and/or the state fire marshal. Agents of the MDEA, the liquor board, and the fire marshal agreed to have regulators inspect the pub, and if they detected marijuana, bring in MDEA agents, who had a draft search warrant affidavit. This was done and marijuana leaves were found by the fire marshal on the third floor landing of the stairwell that connected the three floors of the building, not in the pub. No administrative warrants were obtained. Knowledge of the marijuana was the basis of criminal search warrants that were executed, finding evidence that led to a conviction for possession.

(1) Was the administrative search of the pub appropriate without an administrative warrant? (2) Was the search of the premises for drugs invalid as a pretext administrative search? (3) Was the fire marshals' inspection, during which marijuana was found, appropriate as a third party who "aided in the execution of the warrant?" (4) Did the scope of the search exceed the lawful scope of the administrative searches?

Holding available from instructor.

Plain Feel Rule

3-3. Police officer Davis, assigned as a housing authority agent, was patrolling a residential complex around 12:40 a.m. in December. He approached Darrio Cost, sitting in the passenger seat of a vehicle in a parking lot designated for housing complex residents. Cost immediately reached across his body toward his left front pants pocket. Davis asked Cost what he was reaching for, but Cost did not answer. Davis told Cost to get away from his pocket, but Cost reached toward the pocket again. Davis then directed Cost to exit the vehicle. Upon exiting the vehicle, Cost immediately told Officer Davis, "You can't search me, but you can pat me down." Davis conducted a "pat down" search of Cost for concealed weapons. In doing so, Davis immediately frisked the left front pants pocket toward which Cost had been reaching. When Davis touched the pocket, he felt numerous capsules inside. Davis reached into Cost's pocket and removed a plastic bag containing twenty capsules. Subsequent analysis of the contents of those capsules showed that they contained heroin.

Davis contended that upon feeling the capsules in Cost's pocket he "knew" that they were heroin because "through my training and experience, I know that that's what heroin is packaged in." On cross-examination, Davis admitted that over-the-counter medications such as "Motrin, Tylenol, or something along those lines" are sometimes "packaged in capsules."

Was the search (entry) into Cost's pocket constitutional?
Holding available from instructor.

Dog Sniff; *Kyllo*

3-4. Officer Pedraja obtained a warrant to search the Jardines's house for marijuana, based on a crime stoppers tip, a dog sniff (by a dog who was previously reliable) conducted at the door of Jardines's house alerting for marijuana, and the fact that the air-conditioning unit of the residence ran continuously without recycling. Jardines argued that the dog sniff was a through-the-door intrusion into the privacy of his home and a violation of the Fourth Amendment.

Was the dog sniff evidence admissible to obtain the search warrant?

Holding available from instructor.

Consent

3-5. Police agents, acting on a tip that prison escapee Purcell was at a motel, went there and arrested him outside without incident. Fearing an explosion resulting from methamphetamine manufacture, police knocked on the door of Purcell's room. They heard a shower running and a fan blowing. After three minutes Purcell's girlfriend, Yolande Crist, opened the door. She gave agents consent to take a quick look around. The agents observed "two duffel type bag suitcases near the door" and a green-brown backpack located between the bed and window. Some items in the room looked suspicious. Agents received permission from Crist to conduct a more complete search. Asked if there was anything dangerous in the room, Crist replied that a firearm was in one of the bags but did not indicate which one.

An agent pointed toward one duffel bag and asked, "Is it this bag?" Crist responded that "it might be." The agent opened that first duffel bag near the door, and as he searched it Crist "said that was her bag because she set her purse on top of it." Upon opening the bag, the agent discovered marijuana but no firearm. The bag did not contain Crist's personal effects, but instead contained only men's clothing, indicating it was actually Purcell's bag, which he did not share with her. The agent did not ask her to verify whether she owned any of the other bags in the room. Shortly thereafter, another agent found the firearm in the brown-green backpack. After discovering the firearm, Crist said that she gave the backpack to Purcell for his use. The firearm was introduced to convict Purcell.

Did Crist give authority to conduct a warrantless search of the green-brown backpack for the firearm?

Holding available from instructor.

Further Reading

Craig M. Bradley, *The Failure of the Criminal Procedure Revolution* (Philadelphia: University of Pennsylvania Press, 1993).

Fred P. Graham, *The Due Process Revolution: The Warren Court's Impact on the Criminal Law* (New York: Hayden, 1970).

Barbara J. Shapiro, *"Beyond Reasonable Doubt" and "Probable Cause": Historical Perspectives on the Anglo-American Law of Evidence* (Berkeley: University of California Press, 1991).

Useful Web Sites

Police Foundation

http://www.policefoundation.org/

Includes a research-based publication and links to Internet sites on diverse topics, including domestic violence policing and racial profiling.

Police Executive Research Forum (PERF)

http://www.policeforum.org/

Publications on many issues related to criminal procedure, such as police use of force. Free document library includes a variety of topics, such as policing and terrorism. PERF members lead large police agencies.

End Notes

1. Jeremy D. Mayer, "9–11 and the Secret FISA Court: From Watchdog to Lapdog?" *Case Western Reserve Journal of International Law* 34 (2002): 249–52; and J. Christopher Champion, "Special Project Note: The Revamped FISA; Striking a Better Balance between the Government's Need to Protect Itself and the 4th Amendment," *Vanderbilt Law Review* 58 (2005): 1671–703.

2. Eric Lichtblau, *Bush's Law: The Remaking of American Justice* (New York; Pantheon Books, 2008); James Risen, *State of War: The Secret History of the CIA and the Bush Administration* (New York; Free Press, 2006).

3. B. Drummond Ayres Jr., "The Simpson Case: The Law; for Judge, a Case Where Circumstances Outweigh Safeguards," *New York Times*, July 8, 1994.

4. Scott Turow, "Policing the Police: The D.A.'s Job," in Jeffrey Abramson, ed., *Postmortem: The O.J. Simpson Case* (New York: Basic Books, 1996), 190.

5. H. R. Uviller, *Tempered Zeal* (Chicago: Contemporary Books, 1988), 125–26.

6. Commentary to *Federal Rules of Criminal Procedure*, 1987–88, Educational Edition (St. Paul: West, 1987), 129, quoting *United States ex rel., Pugh v. Pate*, 401 F.2d 6 (7th Cir. 1968).

7. Justin H. Smith, "Press One for Warrant: Reinventing the Fourth Amendment's Search Warrant Requirement through Electronic Procedures," *Vanderbilt Law Review* 55 (2002): 1591–696, 1595; and Walter Gerash, "Next Two Days Critical for Simpson Hearing," *Rocky Mountain News*, July 6, 1994. (In Colorado, telephonic warrants were obtained in an hour and a half.)

8. John Henry Hingson III, "Telephonic and Electronic Search Warrants: A Fine Tonic for an Ailing Fourth Amendment—Part One," *Champion* 29 (September/October 2005): 38.

9. Hingson, "Telephonic and Electronic Search Warrants."

10. P. Pringle, "Officer Explains Search of Simpson's Property: Police Say They Saw Blood, Feared a Life at Stake," *Dallas Morning News*, July 6, 1994; and S. Estrich, "Who's on Trial, O.J. or Cops?" *USA Today*, September 22, 1994.

11. Smith, "Press One," 1604.

12. *Lyons v. Robinson*, 783 F.2d 737 (8th Cir. 1985), citing *U.S. v. Gitcho*, 601 F.2d 369, 371 (8th Cir. 1979).

13. James A. Adams, "Anticipatory Search Warrants: Constitutionality, Requirements, and Scope," *Kentucky Law Journal* 79 (1991): 681–733, 695.

14. Adams, "Anticipatory Search Warrants," 705–6, n. 67.

15. Adams, "Anticipatory Search Warrants," 698–99.

16. Adams, "Anticipatory Search Warrants," 720–21.

17. Adams, "Anticipatory Search Warrants," 715, 727–29.

18. Adams, "Anticipatory Search Warrants," 709–10.

19. *United States v. Ruminer*, 786 F.2d 381 (10th Cir. 1986).

20. *Ker v. California* (1963).

21. Robert M. Duncan Jr., "Surreptitious Search Warrants and the USA PATRIOT Act: 'Thinking Outside the Box but within the Constitution,' or a Violation of Fourth Amendment Protections?" *New York City Law Review* 7 (2004): 1–38, 6–24.

22. Duncan, "Surreptitious Search Warrants," 24–28.

23. Duncan, "Surreptitious Search Warrants," 32–35.

24. George Orwell, *1984: A Novel* (New York: Harcourt and Brace, 1983).

25. Josh Meyer, "Five Years after; Hidden Depths to U.S. Monitoring," *Los Angeles Times*, September 11, 2006.

26. Stanley I. Kutler, *The Wars of Watergate* (New York: Alfred A. Knopf, 1990), 222–26.

27. M. Zalman, "The Federal Anti-Riot Act and Political Crime: The Need for Criminal Law Theory," *Villanova Law Review* 20 (1975): 897–937.

28. Michelle Mittelstadt, "Patriot Act Available against Many Types of Criminals," *Dallas Morning News*, September 8, 2003.

29. Bob Barr, "Patriot Act Games: It Can Happen Here," *The American Spectator* (August–September 2003).

30. Information from the *Denver Post*, February 4, 2000, July 18, 2000; and the *Denver Rocky Mountain News*, February 5, 2000, February 6, 2000, March 14, 2000, June 28, 2000; and Police Crimes.com, http://flyservers.com/members5/policecrime.com/killed/co_police.html (accessed July 14, 2006).

31. Radley Balko, *Overkill: The Rise of Paramilitary Police Raids in America* (Cato Institute, 2006), available at http://www.cato.org/pub_display.php?pub_id=6476 (accessed August 30, 2006).

32. *Federal Communications Act of 1934*, § 605.

33. Walter F. Murphy, *Wiretapping on Trial: A Case Study in the Judicial Process* (New York: Random House, 1965).

34. Bruce Allen Murphy, *Wild Bill: The Legend and Life of William O. Douglas* (New York: Random House, 2003).

35. This rule is expertly criticized by Donald L. Doernberg, "'Can You Hear Me Now?': Expectations of Privacy, False Friends, and the Perils of Speaking under the Supreme Court's Fourth Amendment Jurisprudence," *Indiana Law Review* 39 (2006): 253–308.

36. *On Lee v. United States* (1952); *Lopez v. United States* (1963); *United States v. White* (1971) (plurality opinion); and 18 U.S.C. § 2511 (2) (c) and (d).

37. Robert R. Reinertsen and Robert J. Bronson, "Informant Is a Dirty Word," in James N. Gilbert, ed., *Criminal Investigation: Essays and Cases* (Columbus, OH: Merrill, 1990), 99–103.

38. Reinertsen and Bronson, "Informant," 99.

39. "Snitches" have been implicated in many cases of wrongful conviction. See Clifford Zimmerman, "From the Jailhouse to the Courthouse: The Role of Informants in Wrongful Convictions," in Saundra D. Westervelt and John A. Humphrey, eds., *Wrongly Convicted: Perspectives of Failed Justice* (New Brunswick, N.J.: Rutgers University Press, 2001), 55–76.

40. C. Whitebread, "The Burger Court's Counter-revolution in Criminal Procedure: The Recent Criminal Decisions of the United States Supreme Court," *Washburn Law Journal* 24 (1985): 471–98.

41. See Wayne R. LaFave, "Fourth Amendment Vagaries (of Improbable Cause, Imperceptible Plain View, Notorious Privacy, and Balancing Askew)," *Journal of Criminal Law and Criminology* 74 (1983): 1171–224.

42. Corey Fleming Hirokawa, "Making the 'Law of the Land' the Law on the Street: How Police Academies Teach Evolving Fourth Amendment Law," *Emory Law Journal* 49, no. 1 (2000): 295–334, 319–20.

43. Charles H. Whitebread and Christopher Slobogin, *Criminal Procedure: An Analysis of Cases and Concepts*, 4th ed. (New York: Foundation Press, 2000), 225.

44. *Whren v. United States* (1996). See Chapter 4.

45. Vanessa Rownaghi, "Comment: Driving into Unreasonableness: The Driveway, the Curtilage, and Reasonable Expectations of Privacy," *American University Journal of Gender, Social Policy & the Law*, 11(2003): 1165–1198, 1166.

46. Carrie Leonetti, "Open Fields in the Inner City: Application of the Curtilage Doctrine to Urban and Suburban Areas," *George Mason University Civil Rights Law Journal* 15 (2005): 297–320, 302.

47. Leonetti, "Open Fields," 310.

48. Leonetti, "Open Fields," 304.

49. William J. Broad, "Ideas and Trends: We're Ready for Our Close-ups Now," *New York Times*, January 16, 2000, Sec. 4, p. 4.

50. The Joint Operations Command Center, operational in Washington, D.C., since September 11, 2001, and shared by the Metropolitan Police Department, the FBI, the Secret Service, the State Department, and the Defense Intelligence Agency, quickly allowed writer Matthew Brzezinski to view on a screen the lawn furniture and plantings in his backyard in a Washington, D.C., neighborhood. "Theoretically, with a few clicks of the mouse the system could also link up with thousands of closed-circuit cameras in shopping malls, department stores and office buildings, and is programmed to handle live feeds from up to six helicopters simultaneously." Matthew Brzezinski, "Fortress America," *New York Times Magazine*, February 23, 2003, Sec. 6, p. 38.

51. F. J. Remington et al., *Criminal Justice Administration, Materials and Cases*, 1st ed. (Indianapolis: Bobbs-Merrill, 1969), 32.

52. Marcy Strauss, "Reconstructing Consent," *Journal of Criminal Law and Criminology* 92 (2001): 211–72, 214.

53. Paul Sutton, "The Fourth Amendment in Action: An Empirical View of the Search Warrant Process," *Criminal Law Bulletin* 22 (1986): 405, 415.

54. Illya Lichtenberg, "Police Discretion and Traffic Enforcement: A Government of Men?" *Cleveland State Law Review* 50 (2002): 425–53.

55. Strauss, "Reconstructing Consent," 211–72, 259, quoting David S. Kaplan and Lisa Dixon, "Coerced Waiver and

Coerced Consent," *Denver University Law Review* 74 (1997): 941–56, 948.

56. Kaplan and Dixon, "Coerced Waiver," 948.

57. *Schneckloth v. Bustamonte* (1973), 222 (emphasis added).

58. *United States v. Santiago*, 428 F.3d 699 (7th Cir. 2005); and *Reasor v. State*, 988 S.W.2d 877 (Tex. App., 4th Dist. 1999).

59. L. A. Bradshaw, "Validity of Consent to Search Given by One in Custody of Officers," *American Law Reports*, 3rd series 9 (1966, updated 2009): 858.

60. Strauss, "Reconstructing Consent," 216.

61. Strauss, "Reconstructing Consent," 221.

62. Strauss, "Reconstructing Consent," 229 (emphasis added).

63. Strauss, "Reconstructing Consent," 236–44; *State v. Johnson*, 346 A.2d 66, 68 (N.J. 1975); and *Commonwealth v. Cleckley*, 738 A.2d 427, 434 (Pa. 1999) (Nigro, J., dissenting).

64. *Cleckley*, 738 A2d 427, 432 listed decisions of the supreme courts of Mississippi, New Jersey, and Hawaii as requiring individuals to be informed of their right to refuse a search.

65. Strauss, "Reconstructing Consent," 265, n. 194, referencing Consent Decree, *United States v. State of New Jersey*, C.A. No. 99-5970 (D.N.J. 1999), and other cases.

66. Strauss, "Reconstructing Consent," 256–58.

67. Strauss, "Reconstructing Consent," 258–71.

68. Ilya Lichtenberg, "The Impact of a Verbal Warning on Police Consent Search Practices," *Journal of Criminal Justice*, 32 (2004): 85–87.

69. Lichtenberg, "The Impact of a Verbal Warning"; and *State v. Robinette*, 80 Ohio St.3d 234, 685 N.E. 2d 762 (1997).

70. Lichtenberg, "The Impact of a Verbal Warning."

71. Fern L. Kletter, "Construction and Application of Rule Permitting Knock and Talk Visits under Fourth Amendment and State Constitutions" *American Law Reports 6th Series*, 15 (2008): 515.

72. *Griffin v. State*, 347 Ark. 788, 798, 67 S.W.3d 582, 589 (2002).

73. Bryan M. Abramoske, "Note: It Doesn't Matter What They Intended: The Need for Objective Permissibility Review of Police-Created Exigencies in 'Knock and Talk' Investigations," *Suffolk University Law Review*, 41 (2008): 561–85, 564.

74. Kletter, "Knock and Talk Visits."

75. *Griffin v. State*, 347 Ark. 788, 67 S.W.3d 582 (2002).

76. *State v. Ferrier*, 136 Wn.2d 103, 960 P.2d 927 (Wash. 1998).

77. See Herbert Gaylord, "Casenote: What Good Is the Fourth Amendment? 'Knock and Talk' & *People v. Frohriep*" *Thomas M. Cooley Law Review*, 19 (2002): 229–245; *People v. Frohriep*, 247 Mich. App. 692, 637 N.W.2d (2001).

78. Gaylord, "What Good," 238.

79. Gaylord, "What Good," 241–43.

80. Abramoske, "It Doesn't Matter," 567–68.

81. 479 F.3d 350 (5th Cir. 2007).

82. *U.S. v. Coles*, 437 F.3d 361 (3d Cir. 2006).

83. Abramoske, "It Doesn't Matter", 575–77.

84. Morgan Cloud, "The Dirty Little Secret," *Emory Law Journal* 43 (1994): 1311–49, 1311.

85. Scott Turow, "Simpson Prosecutors Pay for Their Blunders," *New York Times*, October 4, 1995; *Larry King Live*, 9:00 p.m. ET, CNN, August 28, 1995, transcript no. 1524-2, "Will O.J. Testify?" (guests: Alan Dershowitz, Simpson defense attorney; and Bill Hodes, professor of law, Indiana University); David Margolick, "Forget O. J.—The Question Becomes: Is Fuhrman the Question?" *New York Times*, September 10, 1995; Carl Rowan, "Fuhrman Tips the Scale at Simpson Trial," *Chicago Sun-Times*, September 10, 1995; and Charles L. Lindner, "The

Simpson Trial: When You Can't See the Forest for the Leaf," *Los Angeles Times*, September 3, 1995.

86. Andrew J. McClurg, "Good Cop, Bad Cop: Using Cognitive Dissonance Theory to Reduce Police Lying," *University of California at Davis Law Review* 32 (1999): 389–453, 398.

87. David N. Dorfman, "Proving the Lie: Litigating Police Credibility," *American Journal of Criminal Law* 26 (1999): 462–503.

88. Cloud, "The Dirty Little Secret," 1313, footnote omitted.

89. George James, "Officer Admits Illegal Apartment Entries," *New York Times*, January 10, 1996, B6. The officer claimed that the precinct's most senior officers raided and searched a building without first obtaining a warrant, and "[i]t was kind of implied that this was what they wanted." This account was hotly denied by Commissioner Bratton, who claimed that it was not corroborated: Barbara Ross and Wendell Jamieson, "Bratton Slams Dirty 30 Sgt.," *New York Daily News*, January 12, 1996.

90. Uviller, *Tempered Zeal*, 158.

91. Irving Younger, "The Perjury Routine," *The Nation*, 1967, 596–97, cited in Cloud, "The Dirty Little Secret," 1317; as a judge, he noted the problem in *People v. McMurtry*, 314 N.Y.S.2d 194 (Crim. Ct. 1970).

92. Sarah Barlow, "Patterns of Arrests for Misdemeanor Narcotics Possession: Manhattan Police Practices, 1960–62," *Criminal Law Bulletin* 4 (1968): 549–81. See Paul Chevigny, "Comment," *Criminal Law Bulletin* 4 (1968): 581.

93. McClurg, "Good Cop, Bad Cop," 398–99, footnotes omitted.

94. Sarah Terry, "Experts Try to Pin Down Extent of Police Misconduct," *New York Times*, November 19, 1995.

95. See Joseph D. Grano, "A Dilemma for Defense Counsel: *Spinelli-Harris* Search Warrants and the Possibility of Police Perjury," *University of Illinois Law Forum* (1971): 405, 409, cited in Cloud, "The Dirty Little Secret," 1312, n. 4. Other legal commentators cited in Cloud include Alan Dershowitz, *The Best Defense*, xxi–xxii (1982); and "Police Perjury in Narcotics 'Dropsy' Cases: A New Credibility Gap," *Georgetown Law Journal* 60 (1971): 507. Professors Cloud, McClurg, "Good Cop, Bad Cop," 396–404, and Dorfman, "Proving the Lie," 460–62, review all these materials, and they all believe that these kinds of practices are routine.

96. Myron W. Orfield Jr., "The Exclusionary Rule and Deterrence: An Empirical Study of Chicago Narcotics Officers," *University of Chicago Law Review* 54 (1987): 1016–69, 1050–51.

97. Cloud, "The Dirty Little Secret," 1313, footnote omitted.

98. Joseph D. McNamara, "Law Enforcement: Has the Drug War Created an Officer Liars' Club?" *Los Angeles Times*, February 11, 1996.

99. McClurg, "Good Cop, Bad Cop," 417–19; and Daniel Jeffreys, "Last Hope on Death Row: Call McCloskey; He Gave up a Lucrative Career in Business to Help People Wrongly Imprisoned. He Has Saved Four Lives: So Far," *Independent*, January 3, 1996.

100. Don Terry, "Philadelphia Shaken by Criminal Police Officers," *New York Times*, August 28, 1995; and Barbara Whitaker, "Philadelphia Still Reeling from Police Scandal: Officials Review More Than 1,400 Arrests Made by Six Officers Charged with Theft, Framing Suspects," *Dallas Morning News*, September 3, 1995.

101. "Officer Is Acquitted in Theft and Perjury," *New York Times*, January 26, 1996. (Earlier, Officer John Arena had been cleared by a federal jury in Manhattan; *New York Times*,

January 5, 1996.) Seth Faison, "In Plea Deal, Officer Agrees to Give Details of Corruption," *New York Times*, May 24, 1994; and James, "Officer Admits Illegal Apartment Entries."

102. "Ex-Trooper Admits a Plot to Falsify Fingerprints," *New York Times*, December 29, 1995; and "Prosecutor Tries to Make Trooper Talk on Tampering," *New York Times*, January 4, 1996.

103. Lynne Tuohy, "Grand Juror Details Police Abuse of Power; 6 Arrests Made, More Expected; Police Corruption Probe Leads to Six Arrests in Hartford," *Hartford Courant*, December 2, 1993; and "Police Arrested in Corruption Probe; State Trooper, Hartford Officer in Custody after 9-Month Inquiry," *Hartford Courant*, December 1, 1993.

104. Victor Merina, "Officers Marked Sobel for Death, Jury Told; Trial: Ex-deputy Says He and Colleagues Wanted to Eliminate the Sheriff's Sergeant When They Learned He Secretly Cooperated with Prosecutors," *Los Angeles Times*, March 21, 1992.

105. Joe Sexton, "Jurors Question Honesty of Police," *New York Times*, September 25, 1995, B3; and McClurg, "Good Cop, Bad Cop," 419–23.

106. Uviller, *Tempered Zeal*, 115.

107. Uviller, *Tempered Zeal*, 12–13.

108. Keith Kachtick, "Rush to Justice," *Texas Monthly*, January 1996, 56.

109. Marco Buscaglia, "Board Clears Officer of Misconduct Charges," *Chicago Tribune*, January 5, 1996.

110. Matthew Kauffman, "Judge Doubts City Officers' Account of Arrest," *Hartford Courant*, February 6, 1996.

111. Dorfman, "Proving the Lie," 471, n. 73; and McClurg, "Good Cop, Bad Cop," 406–11.

112. Alan Dershowitz, "Police Tampering: How Often, Where," *Buffalo News*, February 21, 1995.

113. Cloud, "The Dirty Little Secret," 1321–24, footnotes omitted.

114. McClurg, "Good Cop, Bad Cop," 405.

115. The many sources of these proposals are found in Dorfman, "Proving the Lie." The last proposal is Dorfman's.

116. Jerome K. Skolnick and James J. Fyfe, *Above the Law: Police and the Excessive Use of Force* (New York: Free Press, 1993).

117. McClurg, "Good Cop, Bad Cop," 410.

118. McClurg, "Good Cop, Bad Cop," 412–15, 424–29.

119. McClurg, "Good Cop, Bad Cop," 412–13, 428–53.

JUSTICES OF THE SUPREME COURT

Roosevelt's Liberals: Douglas, Murphy, Jackson, and Rutledge

Franklin Roosevelt appointed no justices during his first term in office and yet ended up appointing more justices (nine) than any president except George Washington, thanks in large part to his unprecedented four terms in office. Roosevelt's primary goal was to name individuals who would support New Deal legislation on economic and labor issues. For a half century, a conservative Supreme Court had, on behalf of the wealthy, more or less restricted the ability of the Democratic branches of government to pass legislation to improve working conditions and to benefit workers, farmers, and the lower middle class.

The ascendancy of the Roosevelt administration during the great economic crisis of the 1930s finally led to a liberalization of the bench. As the Supreme Court reduced its role in passing on the wisdom of economic legislation, a new wave of civil rights cases began to press forward for hearing. The civil liberties cases of the 1940s and 1950s included freedom of speech, freedom of the press, religious freedom, freedom of conscience regarding loyalty issues, and criminal procedure. It was not a foregone conclusion that justices who were liberal on economic matters would also be liberal on civil rights and criminal procedure questions. Four of Roosevelt's appointees—Justices Hugo Black, William O. Douglas, Frank Murphy, and Wiley B. Rutledge—were "liberal" in favoring the incorporation of the Bill of Rights into the Fourteenth Amendment. They tended to vote for criminal defendants and, when joined by Justices Felix Frankfurter and Robert H. Jackson, placed limits on local police officers whose actions were found to have violated the Due Process Clause of the Fourteenth Amendment.

Justices Douglas, Rutledge, and Jackson have been ranked as "near great" and Justice Murphy as average by a poll of scholars, but Murphy's originality in criminal procedure stands as a real contribution to criminal jurisprudence, as it defined the actual position taken during the due process revolution of the 1960s.

William O. Douglas

Connecticut, 1898–1980

Democrat

Appointed by Franklin Delano Roosevelt

Years of Service: 1939–1975

Collection of the Supreme Court of the United States. Photographer: Harris and Ewing.

Life and Career.   Douglas grew up in relative poverty in Yakima, Washington; he was six years old when his father, a Presbyterian missionary, died. He entered Whitman College in 1916 and taught school for a few years before entering law school. He graduated second in his class at Columbia Law School, practiced briefly at a Wall Street law firm, and then taught at Columbia and Yale law schools, gaining recognition as an expert in financial law and as a proponent of the pragmatic jurisprudence of legal realism.

Douglas joined President Roosevelt's New Deal administration in 1934 to work on the Securities and Exchange Commission (SEC), a new watchdog agency designed to regulate the stock market. He became a member of the SEC in 1936 and its chairman in 1937. First known as antibusiness, Douglas built bridges to the business world and tried to stimulate internal reform in the stock exchange to minimize governmental intrusion. He became an advisor to the president and was Roosevelt's fourth nominee to the Court at the young age of forty. Intensely ambitious, Douglas was seen as a potential presidential candidate before President Roosevelt ran for a third term, and he was a leading candidate for the vice presidential post in 1940 and 1944 after he had been appointed to the Supreme Court.

A restless man and a hard worker, he traveled to all parts of the world, authored thirty-two books (many were travelogues), was a frequent speaker on issues of foreign policy, and was a staunch environmentalist long before the environment was a popular issue. When not traveling, he spent his summers hiking and camping in Washington State. He was married four times and divorced three times, indicating a somewhat chaotic personal life.

Contribution to Criminal Procedure.   Despite his enormous output of cases, Justice Douglas wrote relatively few criminal procedure opinions. In his early years on the Court, he was tentative in taking a consistent liberal position; in fact, he wrote a 1944 opinion holding that an arrest in a public place involving public property was not entitled to the same protection as a search of the home, a decision severely criticized by Justice Frankfurter. Nevertheless, he became a very liberal justice and consistently voted for the "incorporation plus" doctrine. His solid liberal vote on criminal issues under five chief justices was a critical element in the due process revolution.

Signature Opinion.   *Griffin v. California* (1965). In this case, the Court held that a state judge could not tell a jury that although a defendant had a right to remain silent, the jury could take the defendant's failure to deny or explain facts in the case into consideration in determining whether the facts were true. The Court held that the federal rule against such comment was based on the Fifth Amendment privilege against self-incrimination and that it therefore applied to the states via the Due Process Clause of the Fourteenth Amendment. "For comment on the refusal to testify is a remnant of the 'inquisitorial system of criminal justice,' which the Fifth Amendment outlaws. It is a penalty imposed by courts for exercising a constitutional privilege."

Assessment.   Justice Douglas served longer than any other justice: thirty-six years. He was steeped in the philosophy of legal realism, which holds that a judge's policy preferences are the prime determiner of the judge's decisions. His outspoken activism made him one of the most controversial justices. He was a hard worker; he wrote a large number of opinions (many on antitrust and economic issues), but he wrote them very quickly. Despite his acknowledged brilliance, his opinions did not always spell out the doctrinal foundation of his decisions. His *Douglas v. California* (1963) opinion, holding that a defendant has a right to counsel on first appeal, did not clarify whether the decision rested on due process or equal protection.

In addition to his contributions to the law of business regulation, Justice Douglas helped to advance an absolutist concept of free speech with his dissent in *Dennis v. United States* (1951), arguing against the conviction of Communist Party leaders for advocating the violent overthrow of the government. His dissent became the law in the 1970s. He wrote, "Free speech has occupied an exalted position because of the high service it has given our society. Its protection is essential to the very existence of a democracy." His *Griswold v. Connecticut* (1965) contraception law opinion established the right of privacy, based on values inherent in the First, Fourth, and Fifth amendments. *Griswold* laid the foundation for the *Roe v. Wade* (1973) abortion rights ruling.

Further Reading

Bruce Allen Murphy, *Wild Bill: The Legend and Life of William O. Douglas* (New York: Random House, 2003).

Frank Murphy

Michigan, 1890–1949
Democrat
Appointed by Franklin Delano Roosevelt
Years of Service: 1940–1949

Collection of the
Supreme Court of the
United States.
Photographer: Pach
Brothers Studio.

Life and Career.   Murphy, a native of Michigan, obtained his undergraduate and law degrees from the University of Michigan. He had an extensive public career prior to his appointment to the Court. He served as an army officer in World War I; a federal assistant prosecutor; a judge of the Detroit Recorder's Court; mayor of Detroit from 1930 to 1933, when he gained national fame for innovative attempts to ease the burden of the Great Depression; governor-general of the Philippines from 1933 to 1937, on a presidential appointment; governor of Michigan from 1937 to 1939, during which time he refused to order the violent suppression of automobile workers' sit-down strikes; and attorney general of the United States from 1939 to 1940, when he established the civil rights division. His vigor and compassion made him a leading political figure and even a potential presidential candidate despite the fact that he was Catholic, a handicap at that time.

Contribution to Criminal Procedure.   In criminal procedure cases, Justice Murphy voted in favor of the defendant's right to counsel in every case; wrote a majority opinion that struck down the systematic exclusion of day laborers from juries; and dissented in cases that allowed the government to wiretap and electronically eavesdrop without a warrant. With one exception, he sided with the defendant in coerced confessions cases.

Signature Opinion.   Dissent in *Adamson v. California* (1947). The majority held that the Fifth Amendment is not incorporated into the Fourteenth Amendment. Justice Black dissented, arguing for total incorporation. Justice Murphy's dissent best anticipated the due process revolution of the 1960s by establishing the "incorporation plus" concept, which supported both the incorporation of the Bill of Rights into the Fourteenth Amendment *and* the independent use of the Due Process Clause to strike down unfair government action. "Occasions may arise where a proceeding falls so far short of conforming to fundamental standards of procedure as to warrant constitutional condemnation in terms of a lack of due process despite the absence of a specific provision in the Bill of Rights."

Assessment.   Justice Murphy was, with Justices Douglas and Rutledge, one of the most liberal justices on the Court in the 1940s. He dissented in the case upholding the removal of Japanese Americans from their homes to relocation centers during World War II. He wrote many pro-worker opinions in the field of labor law. He consistently favored the expansion of First Amendment rights, opposed racial segregation, favored gender equality, and generally supported the underdog.

Murphy was not a great legal stylist or a profound legal thinker and has been rated an average justice by scholars. He probably delegated more drafting to his law clerks than other justices did. However, he brought to the Court his extensive experience in public life and "a great heart attuned to the cries of the weak and suffering." His unwavering commitment to civil liberties strengthened the "solid minority" of criminal procedure liberals in the Stone and Vinson Courts and helped pave the way to the due process revolution.

Further Reading

J. Woodford Howard Jr., *Mr. Justice Murphy: A Political Biography* (Princeton, N.J.: Princeton University Press, 1968).

Collection of the
Supreme Court of the
United States.
Photographer: Harris
and Ewing.

Robert H. Jackson

New York, 1892–1954
Democrat
Appointed by Franklin Delano Roosevelt
Years of Service: 1941–1954

Life and Career.   Robert Jackson developed a reputation as the most skillful government litigator in Washington, D.C., in the heady days of the New Deal. Yet his formal educational background consisted only of high school and a year at Albany Law School. He trained for the law as an apprentice in a law office and opened his own practice in Jamestown, New York, in 1913. Over the next twenty years, he developed a prosperous practice and became a respected attorney in his region.

Treasury Secretary Henry Morgenthau persuaded Jackson to join the New Deal administration in 1934 as general counsel for the Bureau of Internal Revenue. His reputation soared by winning complex cases for the government. He was appointed assistant attorney general in charge of the Antitrust Division in 1936 and argued ten cases for the government before the Supreme Court. He won the important case upholding the Social Security Act on broad grounds that made the laws easier to administer. He supported President Roosevelt's "court-packing" plan. He became solicitor general in 1938, where he "showed a remarkable insight into both basic governmental policy and the tactics of advocacy." His service as attorney general from January 1940 to mid-1941 was marked more by careful legal advice than by administrative innovations. His most brilliant achievement was his Attorney General's Opinion justifying President Roosevelt's controversial "lend-lease" program in the dark days before America's entry into World War II, whereby fifty over-age destroyers were transferred to the British navy in return for military bases in Bermuda.

Contribution to Criminal Procedure.   Justice Jackson generally joined Justice Frankfurter in opposing incorporation. His votes were mixed; in some Fourth Amendment cases, he was quite critical of abusive police work, but he was not as consistently liberal as Justices Black, Douglas, Murphy, and Rutledge. He believed in judicial restraint and was a strong proponent of federalism. Thus, in state confessions cases he often voted to uphold the confession under the Due Process Clause, especially where a very serious crime was charged, unless the police action made it perfectly clear that the confession was obtained involuntarily.

Signature Opinion.   *Johnson v. United States* (1948). Police standing outside a hotel room smelled opium and entered without a warrant. In holding that this was a violation of the Fourth Amendment, Justice Jackson issued the classic statement about the value of a search warrant: "The point of the Fourth Amendment, which often is not grasped by zealous officers, is not that it denies law enforcement the support of the usual inferences which reasonable men draw from evidence. Its protection consists in requiring that those inferences be drawn by a neutral and detached magistrate instead of being judged by the officer engaged in the often competitive enterprise of ferreting out crime."

Assessment.   Justice Jackson generally was liberal on civil rights issues, writing the decisive compulsory flag-salute opinion (holding that requiring schoolchildren to salute the flag violated First Amendment rights). In substantive criminal law, he wrote a ringing affirmation of the common law principle that the government cannot create a legislative definition of a serious crime, such as theft, without the element of criminal intent (*mens rea*).

He was a great stylist, and many of his opinions are filled with engaging and quotable passages. He was interested in the improvement of criminal justice and chaired the American Bar Association's special committee on the administration of criminal justice. He interrupted his service as a justice for over a year after World War II to serve as the chief American prosecutor at the Nuremberg War Crimes trials of the top Nazi leaders. In this role, he made an abiding contribution to international law and the development of human rights.

Further Reading

Glendon Schubert, ed., *Dispassionate Justice: A Synthesis of the Judicial Opinions of Robert H. Jackson* (Indianapolis: Bobbs-Merrill, 1969).

Collection of the
Supreme Court of the
United States.
Photographer: Harris
and Ewing.

Wiley B. Rutledge

Iowa, 1894–1949
Democrat
Appointed by Franklin Delano Roosevelt
Years of Service: 1943–1949

Life and Career.   Rutledge was the son of a fundamentalist Baptist minister who preached in Kentucky, Tennessee, and North Carolina. A biographer notes that "although in later life he became a Unitarian, his father's fervor was reflected in his zeal for justice and right." He graduated from the University of Wisconsin in 1914, taught school for a few years, and nearly died from tuberculosis. Following his recovery, he received his LL.B. degree from the University of Colorado in 1922. After two years of law practice in Boulder, he became a law professor and then dean of the University of Iowa College of Law in the 1930s. He developed a reputation as an inspiring teacher and civic activist.

Moved by the plight of the poor and unemployed during the Great Depression, he spoke out publicly against the Supreme Court's rulings that struck down New Deal legislation. As one of the few academics to support President Roosevelt's "court-packing" scheme in 1937—a stance that led several Iowa state legislators to threaten to withhold law school salaries in reprisal—Rutledge came to the attention of the Roosevelt administration. He was appointed to the U.S. Court of Appeals for Washington, D.C., in 1939 and served for four years before his nomination to the Supreme Court.

Contribution to Criminal Procedure.   Rutledge joined Justice Black in supporting incorporation of the Bill of Rights in *Adamson* (1947), helping to make incorporation a respectable, if controversial, position. Indeed, he joined the more liberal "incorporation plus" position with Justices Murphy and Douglas.

Signature Opinion.   *Brinegar v. United States* (1949). Writing for the majority in upholding an automobile search of a bootlegger, Justice Rutledge stated the classical definition of probable cause that has been oft-repeated by the Court: "In dealing with probable cause, however, as the very name implies, we deal with probabilities. These are not technical; they are the factual and practical considerations of everyday life on which reasonable and prudent men, not legal technicians, act. . . . Requiring more would unduly hamper law enforcement. To allow less would be to leave law-abiding citizens at the mercy of the officers' whim or caprice."

Assessment.   Justice Rutledge's tenure on the Court was marked by a fierce dedication to the principles of liberty. His most famous opinion, a dissent in the *Yamashita* (1946) case, acknowledged the authority of the United States to try the former Japanese commander of the Philippines, who was accused of authorizing or allowing atrocities by his troops, but he dissented bitterly that the proceeding was characterized by none of the hallmarks of due process. He agreed with the Court in another case that a naturalized citizen could not have his citizenship revoked merely because he had belonged to the Communist Party at the time of his naturalization.

Further Reading

Landon G. Rockwell, "Justice Rutledge on Civil Liberties," *Yale Law Journal* 59 (1949): pp. 27–59.

CHAPTER 4

Arrest and Stop under the Fourth Amendment

Because the strongest advocates of Fourth Amendment rights are frequently criminals, it is easy to forget that our interpretations of such rights apply to the innocent and the guilty alike.

—JUSTICE THURGOOD MARSHALL, *United States v. Sokolow*, 490 U.S. 1, 11 (1989)

CHAPTER OUTLINE

KEY TERMS

internal passport	police officer expertise	scope of a search incident to	stop
inventory search	pretext search	arrest	stop and frisk
investigative stop	protective sweep	search incident to arrest	strip search
least intrusive means	public duty doctrine	seizure of the person	sui generis
merchant's privilege	reasonable force	sobriety checklane	*Terry* stop
mistaken arrest	roadblock	source city	vagrancy statute

OVERVIEW OF THE LAW OF PERSONAL DETENTION

Even a routine **arrest**—physically detaining a person—is a drastic event. For some people being arrested, even when justifiably, is psychologically traumatic. For the police officer, a routine detention may quickly escalate into a life-threatening episode, although firearms are not used in 99.8 percent of all arrests. Only 5.1 percent of arrests involve the use or display of weapons of any type. Indeed, in 84 percent of all arrests, police use no tactics at all—the arrestees simply submit.[1] Nevertheless, all seizures of people are, by law, forcible detentions in that they are not consensual.

Arrests and Investigative Stops

A police detention of a person can be *lawful* or *illegal*. Because liberty has priority in American political theory and constitutional law, all detentions by government officers must be justified by legal standards. In the past, the only dividing line between lawful or unlawful detention was whether probable cause existed to make an arrest. In ***Henry v. United States*** (1959), FBI agents suspected two men of interstate thefts of whiskey based on a vague tip by their employer. The agents watched the men loading a few boxes into a car during the daytime, followed them for a short period, and stopped the car. "The agents searched the car, placed the cartons (which bore the name 'Admiral' and were addressed to an out-of-state company) in their car, took the merchandise and [the men] to their office and held them for about two hours when the agents learned that the cartons contained stolen radios. They then placed the men under formal arrest." The Supreme Court reversed the conviction and ruled that an arrest took place when the car was stopped. At that point, the two men were forcibly detained (although they offered no resistance). The Court ruled that the agents did not have probable cause, making the arrest illegal.

Terry v. Ohio (1968) modified the old rule. There is now a lesser type of detention known as a **stop** or **investigative stop** that is predicated on a lesser standard of evidence, which is typically called "reasonable suspicion." Under the Fourth Amendment, both arrests and stops are seizures. Seizures are lawful if justified by probable cause or reasonable suspicion, but a detention or seizure is illegal if police act on hunches or arbitrarily.

There is no seizure, however, in consensual encounters, where a person voluntarily agrees to talk to officers or to allow his or her belongings to be searched. As discussed in Chapter 3, no evidentiary standard is necessary for consent searches. The same is true when officers simply observe or follow people in public places. Both scenarios, important to police work, "intrude[] upon no constitutionally protected interest" (*United States v. Mendenhall*, 1980).

This chapter explores the legal standards of arrests, stops, and consensual encounters. They have been developed both in criminal cases testing the admissibility of evidence and in civil lawsuits against the police for wrongful arrests. (See Chapter 2). A few distinctions and definitions provide useful guideposts:

- When *arrested*, a person is in the **custody** of the police and loses his or her freedom; the person may be taken to a police station for booking and jailed during the pretrial process; the arrest is executed for the purpose of initiating a criminal prosecution. In contrast, a *stop* confers limited powers allowing an officer to temporarily detain a person; its purpose is to give the officer a short time to question the detainee to determine whether suspicious circumstances are criminal or innocent, and not to initiate a criminal prosecution.
- An arrested person may be thoroughly searched for weapons and for incriminating evidence. A person held briefly under a ***Terry*** stop may be subjected only to a brief pat-down of outer clothing to determine whether he or she is armed.

- If a person is properly stopped based on reasonable suspicion, but the search becomes too intrusive or the person is held for too long a time, the officer has overstepped the bounds and has, unlawfully, turned the stop into an arrest. Likewise, a consensual encounter may escalate into an investigative stop or an arrest if the encounter becomes coercive. It then becomes a Fourth Amendment seizure, justified only by the requisite level of evidence.

The Supreme Court can create new legal categories to meet the needs of an ordered society. It did so in *Terry v. Ohio* (1968) by legitimating the investigative stop, which brought police practices within the scope of judicial control. The Court believed that the investigative stop function (**field interrogation** in police lingo) is necessary to police work and, when conducted properly, balances law enforcement needs with individual liberty. The Court has also considered other kinds of detention that only partially fit the arrest and stop categories and has, up to a point, made special rules to deal with them. Two examples are detentions for investigative purposes and detention while executing a search warrant.

Detention to Investigate

Physical personal characteristics—such as fingerprints, a voiceprint (*United States v. Dionisio*, 1973), or a handwriting sample (*United States v. Mara*, 1973)—are not protected by the expectation of privacy. They may be rightfully "obtained" or identified during an investigation when a defendant is lawfully in custody. A person in custody can therefore be required to appear at a lineup and cannot hide his or her face during a trial. In Fourth Amendment terms, observing a defendant's face is not a seizure.

However, may police detain a person for investigation purposes without probable cause or reasonable suspicion? The Supreme Court twice held that detaining suspects to fingerprint them violated the Fourth Amendment but held open the possibility that a one-time detention for fingerprinting might be lawful in some circumstances. In **Davis v. Mississippi** (1969), police rounded up twenty-five African-American teenagers to collect fingerprint samples, attempting to match those found at the scene of a crime. These mass arrests, justified only by a witness's statement that the offender was black, were not authorized by a judicial warrant. The detentions did not focus on a specific group of people on whom some suspicion fell and involved a second fingerprinting session and interrogations. This violated the Fourth Amendment. Yet the Court, in dictum, stated that a brief detention for fingerprinting may be reasonable because (1) fingerprinting does not intrude into a person's thoughts or belongings, (2) fingerprints can be obtained briefly during normal business hours and need be taken only once, and (3) fingerprints are an inherently reliable means of identification. In **Hayes v. Florida** (1985), a majority of the Court, again in dictum, suggested that fingerprinting at the crime scene might be permissible. In this case, however, the Court found that fingerprinting at the station house was impermissible because the defendant was forcibly taken to the station house without probable cause.

The Court categorically stated that the police have no authority to detain people at will and take them to the police station—without probable cause, reasonable suspicion, or consent—to investigate a crime. In **Dunaway v. New York** (1979), an informant told Rochester police that Dunaway was involved in a murder and robbery. Without gaining any more evidence, the detective in charge ordered officers to "pick up" Dunaway and "bring him in" for questioning. At that point, the police did not have sufficient evidence to obtain an arrest warrant. Dunaway was not told that he was under arrest, but he would have been restrained if he had attempted to leave. He made incriminating statements during the interrogation and was later convicted of murder. The Court reversed and refused to extend the *Terry* principle; if police have reasonable suspicion against a person, they can briefly detain and question him where he is found, but they cannot take him into custody. Dunaway was unlawfully arrested without probable cause.

In **Kaupp v. Texas** (2003), the Supreme Court said that the evidence in this case "points to arrest even more starkly than the facts in *Dunaway v. New York* (1979)." Although Robert Kaupp, age seventeen, was suspected of involvement in a murder, he passed a polygraph examination, and a magistrate refused to issue an arrest warrant. Detectives nevertheless went to his house at 3 a.m. on a January morning, were let in by his father, and woke him with a flashlight. Told "we need to go and talk," Robert said, "Okay." The Court ruled that this was not consent but "a mere submission to a claim of lawful authority."

Kaupp was then handcuffed. Shoeless and dressed only in boxer shorts and a T-shirt, he was taken to the station house, where he made incriminating statements during an interview after being read *Miranda* warnings. The Supreme Court held that Kaupp was seized and arrested without probable cause. Because the arrest was illegal, the confession was excluded as the "fruits of the poisonous tree" under *Brown v. Illinois*. (See Chapter 2.)

Detention and Search during the Execution of a Search Warrant

In *Michigan v. Summers* (1981), Detroit police officers executed a valid search warrant of a house for narcotics. They encountered Summers, the owner, walking down the front steps, and asked his assistance in entering the house. The police detained him during the search, and arrested him after discovering narcotics in the basement. A search incident to the arrest revealed an envelope with heroin in Summers's pocket. Although the police did not have probable cause to believe that Summers was carrying drugs before the arrest, the seizure was nevertheless upheld. The Supreme Court concluded that there was reasonable suspicion for the initial stop; the arrest and search were justified by finding drugs in his house.

Summers is general authority for a categorical rule that police may detain homeowners or others present in a place while executing a search warrant. The individual's significant right to liberty is outweighed by law enforcement needs. Giving police routine "command of the situation" reduces the likelihood of harm to the officers and residents that may be caused by sudden violence or frantic efforts to conceal or destroy evidence. Detaining a resident facilitates the orderly completion of the search with minimal damage to property because the resident can open locked doors and cabinets. Detention in the person's own home also avoids the public stigma and inconvenience of being taken to the police station. Further, there is a legitimate law enforcement interest in preventing the flight of a person if incriminating evidence is found. The length of the detention, however, is limited to the time it takes to search the house.

In contrast to the *Summers* rule, which categorically allows police to detain people while executing a warrant, *Muehler v. Mena* (2005) held that police may handcuff a resident detained during a search if it is reasonable to do so. A federal jury found that police violated Iris Mena's Fourth Amendment rights by handcuffing her arms behind her back for two to three hours while conducting a search of her house. The jury awarded her $60,000 in compensatory and punitive damages. Police in Simi Valley, California, investigating a gang-related drive-by shooting, obtained a warrant to search Mena's house because a particular gang member, Romero, rented a room there. The warrant authorized a "broad search" of the house and premises for the gang member, deadly weapons, and evidence of gang membership. Supposedly because of the danger, a SWAT team of eighteen officers executed the search, although a simultaneous search of the home of Romero's mother, who had cooperated with the police in the past, did not use a SWAT team. Romero was found and arrested at his mother's house.

The search of Mena's property was executed at 7 a.m. She was alone in the house. Three others who lived in trailers on her property, along with Mena, were detained in a garage, handcuffed, for three hours. "To get to the garage, Iris, who was still in her bedclothes, was forced to walk barefoot through the pouring rain. . . . Although she requested [the police] to remove the handcuffs, they refused to do so. For the duration of the search, two officers guarded Iris and the other three detainees. A .22 caliber handgun, ammunition, and gang-related paraphernalia were found in Romero's bedroom, and other gang-related paraphernalia was found in the living room. Officers found nothing of significance in Iris' bedroom" (*Muehler v. Mena*, 2005, Stevens, J., concurring).

In light of the dangers involved, the use of force to effectuate this search—in the form of handcuffs—was reasonable. Chief Justice William Rehnquist, for the majority, noted that the use of handcuffs was more intrusive than the detention in the garage, and he wrote that here "the governmental interests outweigh the marginal intrusion" (*Muehler v. Mena*, 2005). Further, the Court held that the length of detention was reasonable. "The duration of a detention can, of course, affect the balance of interests. . . . However, the 2 to 3-hour detention in handcuffs in this case does not outweigh the government's continuing safety interests. . . . [T]his case involved the detention of four detainees by two officers during a search of a gang house for dangerous weapons" (*Muehler v. Mena*, 2005).

Justice Anthony Kennedy concurred "to help ensure that police handcuffing during searches becomes neither routine nor unduly prolonged" (*Muehler v. Mena*, 2005, Kennedy, J., concurring). Justice John Paul Stevens, writing for three other concurring justices, felt that the Court of Appeals made mistakes and that it was proper to remand the case "to consider whether the evidence supports Iris Mena's contention that she was held longer than the search actually lasted" (*Muehler v. Mena*, 2005, Stevens, J., concurring). The case stands for the proposition that handcuffing people present during the execution of a search warrant may be reasonable if the circumstances are fraught with danger. Five justices believed that the handcuffing in this case was objectively reasonable, and four concurring justices seemed to believe that the jury was justified in finding that the extent of the handcuffing was excessive.

Summers did not create a rule that allows police to automatically search anyone present in a premises during the execution of a warrant. In *Ybarra v. Illinois* (1979), police had a valid warrant to search a bar and a bartender for drugs, but not to search the patrons. Police entered the bar and announced to a dozen patrons that they would all be frisked for weapons. Ybarra, a bar patron, was searched. A cigarette pack was retrieved from his pants pocket, and heroin was found inside. The Supreme Court overturned Ybarra's conviction. There was no probable cause to search Ybarra or any of the patrons. Simply because Ybarra was a patron in a bar where drugs were sold was no indication that he participated in purchases. "[A] person's mere propinquity to others independently suspected of criminal activity does not, without more, give rise to probable cause to search that person." The patrons' passive behavior when the raid was announced gave rise to no facts amounting to a reasonable suspicion that they were armed and presently dangerous.

The Supreme Court in *Illinois v. McArthur* (2001) ruled that, where reasonable, police can prevent a householder from entering his or her home while awaiting the arrival of a search warrant. Officers accompanied Tera McArthur to the trailer where she lived with her husband, Charles, to keep the peace while she removed her belongings. The police stayed outside. After Tera removed her belongings, she told the officers that "Chuck had dope in there" and that she had seen Chuck "slide some dope underneath the couch." Charles refused to consent to a search of the trailer. He was then prevented from reentering his home without an officer present for about two hours in the afternoon until one of the officers had obtained a search warrant. A search turned up marijuana, and Charles was charged with misdemeanors. The Illinois courts suppressed the evidence.

The Supreme Court held that the police acted reasonably under the Fourth Amendment. The search and seizure, and the temporary removal of Charles McArthur from his home, were constitutional. There was *probable cause* (the police positively assessed Tera's reliability) and an *exigency* (a good chance that if left alone, Charles would destroy the marijuana). The Court reasoned that the police "made reasonable efforts to reconcile their law enforcement needs with the demands of personal privacy" and "imposed a significantly less restrictive restraint, preventing McArthur only from entering the trailer unaccompanied" rather than searching without a warrant. The restriction on McArthur's freedom to enter his home was for a limited and reasonable period of time. Justice Stevens, dissenting, argued that the balance should be struck in favor of liberty where the offense was a minor one, relying on the rule of *Welsh v. Wisconsin*. (See Chapter 5.) "[S]ome offenses may be so minor as to make it unreasonable for police to undertake searches that would be constitutionally permissible if graver offenses were suspected."

Police in *Los Angeles County v. Rettele* (2007) obtained valid warrants to search two houses during the day, seeking African-American drug suspects. No ownership checks were performed. One house had been sold to Max Rettele, a white person. The warrant was executed at 7:15 a.m. by knocking on the front door. Six police were let in by Chase Hall. Rettele and his girlfriend were awoken in their bedroom. They were held, naked, for about two minutes until the police discovered that the suspects were not present. The police apologized and left within 15 minutes of the entry. Rettele argued that once the police saw that he and his companion were not African Americans they should have immediately allowed them privacy and withdrawn. The Supreme Court disagreed. The brief, if humiliating, encounter was reasonable because it is reasonable to surmise that African Americans and whites collaborate in criminal enterprises and suspects have been known to keep loaded weapons in their beds.

ARREST

Arrest and Police Discretion

Fourth Amendment cases examine arrest from the defendant's perspective to ensure that police act within the law; there is no Fourth Amendment issue if police do not arrest. Police discretion to *not* arrest is widely acknowledged and may be wise in cases involving minor offenses or juveniles. From the victim's perspective, however, is there an enforceable legal right to police protection? These issues arise in civil tort suits against police officers and their agencies by injured parties. The general rule—the **public duty doctrine**—is that a law enforcement officer's "specific duty to preserve the peace is one which the officer owes to the public generally, and not to particular individuals, and that the breach of such duty accordingly creates no liability on the part of the officer to an individual who was damaged by the lawbreaker's conduct."[2] A different rule could open police departments to lawsuits by all crime victims, or at least those who could plausibly argue that the police were in a position to protect them.

The public duty doctrine has been modified in states that have mandated arrest in domestic violence cases. (See the "Law in Society" section in this chapter.) Several state cases held that domestic violence mandatory arrest statutes imposed obligations on police officers to arrest those who violated domestic protection orders. The Supreme Court faced the issue of whether such mandatory state laws created a *property right* to personal protection in a victim when police fail to enforce a protection order in *Town of Castle Rock v. Gonzales* (2005). Jessica Gonzales's restraining order against her estranged husband was violated when he picked up their three daughters (ages ten, nine, and seven) about 5:30 one afternoon while they were playing in their yard. Jessica went to the Castle Rock, Colorado, police station or called the police station at 7:30 p.m., 8:30 p.m., 10:10 p.m., 12:10 a.m., and 12:50 a.m., asking the police to look for her husband and children. She informed them of the restraining order and its violation. At 8:30 p.m., she notified the police that her husband had taken the children to an amusement park in Denver. At each contact, the police refused to act and told Jessica to call later. At 3:20 a.m., the husband was killed in a shoot-out at the police station. The three children were found in the car, shot to death by Jessica's husband.

A 1994 Colorado statute was designed to correct the type of official inaction that Jessica Gonzales faced. The law stated that a peace officer "*shall* use every reasonable means" to enforce a protection order; when an officer has probable cause that the "restrained person" violated the protection order, the officer "*shall* arrest, or, if an arrest would be impractical under the circumstances, seek an arrest warrant against the restrained person." Despite the statute's mandatory language and the clear intent of the legislature that police officers should not ignore restraining order violations, the Supreme Court held that the police inaction did not violate Gonzales's due process rights under the Fourteenth Amendment.

In past cases, the Supreme Court held that where state law created a "property interest" in tangible and intangible rights, those substantive rights are protected by procedural due process. These state-created property interests included welfare benefits, disability benefits, public education, utility services, and government employment. Arbitrary termination or failure to supply such benefits was held to violate the Due Process Clause. In *Castle Rock*, seven justices held that Colorado did not create a personal entitlement to the enforcement of restraining orders. Justice Antonin Scalia, whose judicial philosophy includes "textualism" as well as an "originalism," authored the opinion:

> The procedural component of the Due Process Clause does not protect everything that might be described as a "benefit": To have a property interest in a benefit, a person clearly must have more than an abstract need or desire and more than a unilateral expectation of it. He must, instead, have a legitimate claim of entitlement to it. (*Castle Rock v. Gonzales*, 2005, internal quotations omitted)

In effect, the majority said that the mandatory language in Colorado's law and on Ms. Gonzales's protection order did not change the common law public duty doctrine. Several reasons were given. First, despite the law's mandatory language, "a well established tradition of police discretion has long coexisted with apparently mandatory arrest statutes." Next, the statute "does not specify the precise means of enforcement" when the restrained person is not present: The statute's command that police seek an arrest warrant if an arrest is impractical was deemed vague, undermining the special duty that purports to override the public duty doctrine. An entitlement guaranteed by procedural due process cannot be vague. Enforcement of the protection order was deemed to be an indirect rather than a direct benefit to Jessica Gonzales. Calling a property interest in the enforcement of restraining orders "vague and novel," the Court concluded that its creation cannot simply go without saying.

Justice Stevens, joined by Justice Ginsburg, dissented. He refuted every argument that the majority put forward regarding the nature of the Colorado protection order. The majority superficially examined general arrest laws with mandatory provisions and did not properly account for the difference between such laws and domestic violence mandatory arrest laws. Colorado has joined other states in responding to a crisis in the underenforcement of domestic violence laws and protection orders. The fact that police had an option to get an arrest warrant when immediate arrest was impractical did not make the law vague. The "crucial point is that, under the statute, the police were *required* to provide enforcement; *they lacked the discretion* to do nothing" (*Castle Rock v. Gonzales*, 2005, Stevens, J., dissenting; emphasis in original). Justice Stevens also argued that the majority undermined proper federalism by not giving due weight to the clear language of the state law and the intent of the state legislature. More important, the majority refused to send the case to the Colorado courts, in a procedure known as "certification," to allow state courts to determine whether the statute created a property interest. This means that no language used by a state legislature can ever create a §1983 property interest in enforcing protection orders that is federally enforceable without the Supreme Court's approval.

Consequences of Arrest

A person seized by police officers is in their custody. The lawful "purpose of an arrest at common law . . . was 'only to compel an appearance in court'" (*Albright v. Oliver*, 1994, Ginsburg, J., concurring). The judicial process will put the arrested person through various "screens" (initial appearance, preliminary hearing, grand jury) to determine whether to charge the person with a crime and to adjudicate guilt. Because of this goal, there is a belief that a "real" arrest does not occur until *administrative formalities* occur at the police station, including fingerprinting, identification, and a criminal history check. The colorful phrase—"**booking** the suspect" indicates the bureaucratic process of filling out forms, doing a criminal background and fingerprint check, entering the arrest in computer files, and the like to begin court processing.

Legally, these formalities are not the essence of arrest. Arrest occurs at the moment a police officer significantly interferes with a person's liberty and takes him or her into custody. The lawfulness of an arrest is determined by what happens at the moment of the seizure. Custody means that a suspect loses his or her freedom of movement and most rights of personal privacy. A major consequence of arrest is that the person is subject to a "search incident to arrest" (discussed later in this chapter). The search incident to arrest is a major exception to the Fourth Amendment warrant requirement.

Arrested people have no right to prevent police officers from observing their movements and activities. In *Washington v. Chrisman* (1982), the Court announced a clear rule: "[I]t is not 'unreasonable' for a police officer, as a matter of routine, to monitor the movements of an arrested person, as his judgment dictates, following an arrest. The officer's need to ensure his own safety—as well as the integrity of the arrest—is compelling." In this case, a campus police officer arrested an apparently underage student for possessing a bottle of gin. The officer followed the student into his dormitory room as he retrieved his identification. While standing outside the door, the officer saw what appeared to be marijuana seeds and a pipe lying on a desk. The officer entered the room, confirmed that the seeds were marijuana and determined that the pipe smelled of marijuana. The Court ruled that the officer had a right to follow the arrested student into the room—without a warrant—to maintain secure custody; any motivation the officer had for observing the room in addition to keeping the arrested person under custody was irrelevant. Because the contraband was in plain view and the officer was lawfully in the room, the marijuana was lawfully seized.

The Supreme Court held in *Atwater v. City of Lago Vista* (2001) that an officer can take a person into custody for an offense punishable with only a minor fine. Gail Atwater, an established resident of Lago Vista, Texas, was driving at about 15 miles per hour with her two young children (ages three and five) in the front seat. None were wearing seatbelts, a misdemeanor in Texas punishable with a $25 fine for the first offense and $50 for the second offense. She was pulled over by Officer Bart Turek. The children began to scream; Ms. Atwater asked Officer Turek to lower his voice because he was scaring the children. The officer jabbed his finger in her face and said, "You're going to jail." She asked if her children could be brought to a neighbor's house, but Turek told her that the children would also be brought to the police station. Neighborhood children called an adult neighbor, who took Ms. Atwater's children. "With the children gone, Officer Turek handcuffed Ms. Atwater with her hands behind her back, placed her in the police car, and drove her to the police station. Ironically, Turek did not secure Atwater in a seat belt for the drive." At "the local police station, . . . booking officers had her remove her shoes, jewelry, and eyeglasses, and empty her pockets. Officers took Atwater's 'mug shot' and placed her, alone, in a jail cell for about one hour, after which she was taken before a magistrate and released on $310 bond." She later pleaded no contest to the misdemeanor and paid the $50 fine.

The Supreme Court decided (5–4), in a Section 1983 suit against the police, that Atwater's arrest and custody were constitutional. The majority maintained a **bright-line rule**—officers do not have to guess whether an offense is or is not jailable or whether the arrested person is a flight risk. Guessing wrong could subject officers to lawsuits. Justice Sandra Day O'Connor, dissenting, noted that a full-custody arrest imposes severe limitations on liberty. Atwater could have been detained for up to forty-eight hours before seeing a magistrate, could have been jailed with potentially violent offenders, and could have received a permanent arrest record. Justice O'Connor argued that a flat ban on arrests for nonjailable misdemeanors created no problem because an officer who decides that an exception applies and detains the person has immunity from civil liability for making erroneous judgment calls. She concluded that the decision, allowing the detention of nonjailable misdemeanants, were unreasonable and therefore violated basic Fourth Amendment principles. The balance between liberty and security should have been struck in favor of liberty.

The state of Virginia does not have an exclusionary rule for violations of state arrest laws. In ***Virginia v. Moore*** (2008) police officers wrongly *arrested* Moore for driving under a suspended license, when under state law they should have issued a *summons*. The arrest, although prohibited by state law, was made with probable cause that he was driving without a license. A search incident to the arrest disclosed crack cocaine and Moore was convicted for illegal drug possession. The Virginia Supreme Court held that the arrest violated the Fourth Amendment and suppressed the drug evidence. The United States Supreme Court reversed and held that when an arrest is made with probable cause it is by definition *reasonable* and therefore constitutional, even if the arrest violated state law. The Court reasoned that there was no historical evidence that the Framers intended Fourth Amendment decisions to be guided by statutory law. Stating that a reasonable arrest upheld some state interests even where the arrest was illegal under a statute, the Court chose to be guided by traditional standards of reasonableness.

There is an important distinction between a **mistaken arrest** and an **illegal arrest**, and each has different consequences. An illegal arrest occurs if a person is taken into custody by a government officer without probable cause. Cases of illegal arrests usually occur without any malicious intent on the part of the law enforcement officers. Nevertheless, having violated the Constitution, the arrest is illegal because the probable cause standard for arrest is objective, not subjective. The most important consequence of an illegal arrest is that any evidence seized as a result of the arrest is inadmissible under the exclusionary rule. This gives arrested defendants found with contraband an incentive to challenge the legality of the arrest. An officer can also be held civilly liable for an illegal arrest.

Another way in which an arrest can be illegal is if the arresting officer had *no jurisdiction* to make the arrest. This occurred in ***Frisbie v. Collins*** (1952), when police officers from southwest Michigan traveled to Chicago to arrest Collins for a murder rather than seeking extradition or requesting that the arrest be made by an Illinois law enforcement agency. Collins argued that this illegal arrest, possibly a violation of the Federal Kidnapping Act, deprived the trial court of jurisdiction to try him and that his conviction was a nullity. The Supreme Court upheld the common law rule that a court does not lose jurisdiction to try a defendant who is brought to the court by illegal means. Once a court has ***in personam* jurisdiction**, or physical custody over a criminal defendant, it does not inquire into the means by which the person was brought into court. The Supreme Court stood by this rule in a much criticized case, *United States v. Alvarez-Machain* (1992), in which American agents had the defendant abducted in Mexico and transferred to the United States for trial.[3] Likewise, ***I.N.S. v. Lopez-Mendoza*** (1984), which upheld the deportation of undocumented aliens who had been illegally arrested, stated: "The 'body' or identity of a defendant or respondent in a criminal or civil proceeding is never itself suppressible as a fruit of an unlawful arrest, even if it is conceded that an unlawful arrest, search, or interrogation occurred."

A *mistaken* arrest occurs when an officer makes an arrest with probable cause but it turns out that in fact the wrong person was arrested. The only consequence is that the person arrested must be released if no evidence of criminality is discovered. An innocent person has no civil cause of action against the police because the officer acted in a reasonable manner. However, a *search* conducted pursuant to the mistaken arrest is *valid* insofar as it discovered any contraband.

The rule reflects the idea that probable cause does not require certainty but only an assessment of facts that would lead a prudent person to believe that the suspect was involved in a crime. In **Hill v. California** (1971), the Supreme Court ruled that police had probable cause to arrest Hill. Two men, using Hill's car, were arrested for narcotics possession. A search of the car produced evidence of a robbery. The two men admitted to the robbery and implicated Hill. The police verified Hill's ownership of the car, his description, and his association with one of the men. Armed with this probable cause, the police went to Hill's motel room to arrest him. They knocked, and the door was opened by Miller, who fit Hill's description. Miller was arrested despite the fact that he produced identification indicating he was Miller. Articles seized in plain view and incident to the search were used to convict Hill of robbery.

Miller's arrest was supported by probable cause; he could not satisfactorily explain why he was in Hill's room, and his personal identification could have been fabricated. This probable cause was based on reasonable facts and circumstances and not on the subjective good faith of the police. As a result, contraband seized during the arrest was admissible. Because it can be difficult to ascertain the true motives of police officers, the distinction between an illegal and a mistaken arrest turns on the objective reasonableness of the officers' behavior, not on subjective motives.

Defining a Fourth Amendment Seizure and Arrest

The Supreme Court has offered two definitions for an arrest: the *Mendenhall* definition and the *Hodari D.* definition. In *United States v. Mendenhall* (1980), the Court said: "[A] person has been 'seized' within the meaning of the Fourth Amendment only if, in view of all of the circumstances surrounding the incident, a reasonable person would have believed that he was not free to leave." A person, therefore, can be arrested even though not physically held or even touched by an officer. Also, there are no specific words that have to be spoken to effect an arrest: Neither an announcement that a person is under arrest, nor a description of a crime for which a person is arrested, nor a reading of *Miranda* warnings (a popular misconception) is required. Examples of personal seizure offered by the Court in *Mendenhall* include: "the threatening presence of several officers, the display of a weapon by an officer, some physical touching of the person of the citizen, or the use of language or tone of voice indicating that compliance with the officer's request might be compelled."

The *Mendenhall* definition, however, does not encompass every situation. The Court amended the *Mendenhall* definition in *California v. Hodari D.* (1991) to rule that a seizure (and hence an arrest) occurs *only* when an assertion and intent to arrest, on the part of an officer, are followed by submission of the arrested party. The rationale for the *Hodari D.* definition and the issues raised by the case are explored later in this chapter.

A Fourth Amendment seizure can occur in a variety of ways. In *Tennessee v. Garner* (1985), the Court ruled that a person who is shot by the police is arrested: "there can be no question that apprehension by the use of deadly force is a seizure subject to the reasonableness requirement of the Fourth Amendment." A **roadblock** set up intentionally to intercept a driver fleeing from the police becomes the instrument of an arrest if the driver plows into it (*Brower v. Inyo County*, 1989). This is an arrest because there has been an "intentional acquisition of physical control" over the person by the use of the roadblock. "[A] roadblock is not just a significant show of authority to induce a voluntary stop, but is designed to produce a stop by physical impact if voluntary compliance does not occur." Finally, a person, after hearing that a warrant has been issued for his or her arrest and voluntarily surrendering to the police, is seized for purposes of the Fourth Amendment (*Albright v. Oliver*, 1994, Ginsburg, J., concurring).

In each of these cases, the police *intended* to gain actual custody of the suspect. If there is no intent or actual custody, there is no seizure. The intent element was clarified in *County of Sacramento v. Lewis* (1998), a civil lawsuit against an officer, engaged in a high-speed pursuit of a speeding motorcycle, whose patrol car hit and killed a passenger thrown from the motorcycle. Applying *Brower v. Inyo County*, the Court in *Lewis* found that the officer had no *intent* to seize the passenger, and, therefore, the death caused by the high speed chase was not a Fourth Amendment seizure. As a result the lawsuit could be brought under the Due Process Clause, rather than the more specific and objective test in civil lawsuits against police for allegedly illegal arrests or excessive violence. (Discussed later in this chapter in the Use of Force section.) In a trial a jury could find that the officer deprived the passenger of the substantive due process right to life if the officer acted arbitrarily.

Probable Cause to Arrest

Probable cause to arrest can be determined by a magistrate issuing an arrest warrant. Most arrests, however, are made without warrants, and in such cases the officer must make a probable cause determination.

> Whether that arrest was constitutionally valid depends in turn upon whether, at the moment the arrest was made, the officers had probable cause to make it—whether at that moment the facts and circumstances within their knowledge and of which they had reasonably trustworthy information were sufficient to warrant a prudent man in believing that the petitioner had committed or was committing an offense. (*Beck v. Ohio*, 1964, p. 91)

In *Beck v. Ohio* (1964), police officers in a squad car saw William Beck driving his car and stopped and arrested him without a warrant. One officer testified that he knew what Beck looked like and had heard only general reports that Beck had a criminal record and was involved in gambling. A search of Beck's person at the police station disclosed betting slips in his shoe. The Supreme Court ruled this arrest *illegal*. At the time the police stopped the car, the officers did not have a level of evidence that would have satisfied a magistrate that Beck was then transporting betting slips. Beck's appearance and prior record were not "inadmissible or entirely irrelevant upon the issue of probable cause. But to hold that knowledge of either or both of these facts constituted probable cause would be to hold that anyone with a previous criminal record could be arrested at will." Thus hearsay can be lawfully used to support probable cause, but it must be more reliable than simple rumors or reputation.

Ultimately, a *court* will review whether probable cause existed to make a warrantless arrest, and courts must be given *facts* to make the decision; they cannot rely on the officer's good faith:

> We may assume that the officers acted in good faith in arresting the petitioner. But "good faith on the part of the arresting officers is not enough." If subjective good faith alone were the test, the protections of the Fourth Amendment would evaporate, and the people would be "secure in their persons, houses, papers, and effects," only in the discretion of the police. (*Beck v. Ohio*, 1964)

Thus the probable cause standard for arrest is objective, not subjective.

In a typical case, probable cause is established by the officer's observation of a crime in progress or by the report of an eyewitness. In *Peters v. New York* (1968), a companion case to *Terry v. Ohio* (1968), a police officer observed two men in his apartment building tiptoeing in the hallway. In the twelve years he had been living there, Officer Lasky had never seen these men. The men were still there when the officer had completed a phone call. When he approached them, they fled. He apprehended Peters, who gave no satisfactory reason for his actions. Lasky searched him and found burglar's tools. The Supreme Court ruled that "[i]t is difficult to conceive of stronger grounds for an arrest, short of actual eyewitness observation of criminal activity." While Lasky did not actually see Peters trying to jimmy a lock, the other evidence supplied probable cause: facts that would lead a prudent person to believe that Peters was engaged in an attempt to break and enter.

In *Chambers v. Maroney* (1970), a light blue compact station wagon carrying four men was stopped by police on a spring evening in North Braddock, Pennsylvania, about one hour after the robbery of a Gulf service station and about two miles from the station. Chambers, one of the men in the car, was wearing a green sweater, and there was a trench coat in the car:

> Two teen-agers, who had earlier noticed a blue compact station wagon circling the block in the vicinity of the Gulf station, then saw the station wagon speed away from a parking lot close to the Gulf station. About the same time, they learned that the Gulf station had been robbed. They reported to police, who arrived immediately, that four men were in the station wagon and one was wearing a green sweater. [The station attendant] told the police that one of the men who robbed him was wearing a green sweater and the other was wearing a trench coat. A description of the car and the two robbers was broadcast over the police radio.

This is a typical example of police obtaining probable cause from reliable (and non-secret) informants. Although hearsay, it is fully reliable. Of course, such information should never be taken for absolute proof of a crime. In rare cases, the initial information may be given as a mis-guided prank or out of malice. In many cases, facts are garbled and eyewitness identification of key facts may be wrong, especially about the identity of an offender. (See Chapter 8.)

Probable cause must focus on a specific individual. In **Johnson v. United States** (1948), an officer standing outside an apartment smelled burning opium in the hallway but was not sure who occupied the apartment. The officer knocked and announced his presence. Anne Johnson opened the door, and the officer told her, "Consider yourself under arrest." The Supreme Court held that the entry into the home without a warrant was a Fourth Amendment violation. Further, the arrest itself was illegal because "the arresting officer did not have probable cause to arrest [Johnson] until he had entered her room and found her to be the sole occupant."

Another common problem confronting police is whether probable cause exists to arrest a person who is in close proximity to another person who is lawfully arrested. Mere proximity to a person committing a crime does not create probable cause. For example, in **United States v. Di Re** (1948), an informer, Reed, told investigators that he was going to buy counterfeit ration coupons from one "Buttitta at a named place in the City of Buffalo, New York." Agents fol-lowed a car driven by Buttitta. Michael Di Re was the front seat passenger, and Reed sat in the back. Di Re was not known to the agents. The car was stopped, and Buttitta and Di Re were arrested. Di Re was searched at the station house after the arrest, and counterfeit ration coupons were found in an envelope concealed between his shirt and underwear. The Supreme Court ruled that this evidence was seized illegally because the agents did not have probable cause to believe that Di Re was involved in the crime, invalidating the arrest. Reed had not named Di Re as a suspect. The police suspicion against Buttitta was based on the word of their informant, Reed. "But the officer had no such information as to Di Re. All they had was his presence, and if his presence was not enough to make a case for arrest for a misdemeanor, it is hard to see how it was enough for the felony" of possessing illegal coupons with knowledge that they were counterfeit. The Court also dismissed the argument that there was a conspiracy simply because Di Re was in the car.

In contrast to *Di Re* is **Ker v. California** (1963). (See Chapter 3.) By their own observations and the word of an informer, police had probable cause to believe that George Ker was dealing marijuana from his house. The Court held that the police entered lawfully without a warrant. After entering, an agent saw George Ker sitting in the living room and Diane Ker emerging from the kitchen. The officer observed "through the open doorway a small scale atop the kitchen sink, upon which lay a "brick-like—brick-shaped package containing the green leafy substance which he recognized as marijuana." The Court conceded that the police did not have probable cause to arrest Diane Ker when they entered the apartment. But it ruled that viewing the marijuana in plain view established probable cause to believe that she was involved in the illicit business with her husband. This was not simply guilt by association, but a rational inference. In *Di Re*, the po-lice could not infer, to the level of probable cause, that Di Re possessed counterfeit ration coupons. But Diane Ker had to know that there was marijuana in the kitchen, which she had just left, and given the probable cause that police had that George Ker was illegally dealing, it was a rational inference that she was "in joint possession with her husband." This amounted to proba-ble cause to believe that she was "committing the offense of possession of marijuana in the pres-ence of the officers."

In **Maryland v. Pringle** (2003), police officers stopped a car at 3:16 a.m. for speeding. Partlow was driving, Pringle sat in the front seat, and Smith was in the backseat. When Partlow opened the glove compartment to retrieve the vehicle registration, the officer observed a large roll of cash. A consent search of the vehicle uncovered five plastic glassine baggies containing cocaine behind the upright rear seat armrest. None of the three men admitted to owning the drugs, and all three were arrested. Pringle later confessed to owning the drugs. The issue in the case was whether finding drugs in the rear seat gave police probable cause to arrest Pringle. This is not a case of guilt by association. Unlike the tavern patrons in *Ybarra v. Illinois* (1979), Pringle was in a small car with two men he knew, and car passengers are often involved in a "common enterprise with the driver." Unlike *United States v. Di Re* (1948), this was not a case where the police had previous probable cause to suspect only the driver. The Supreme Court held that under the facts of the case, there was probable cause to arrest Pringle. It was objectively reasonable for the officer on the scene to believe "that any or all three of the occupants had knowledge of, and exercised dominion and control over, the cocaine. Thus a reasonable officer could conclude that there was probable cause to believe Pringle committed the crime of possession of cocaine, either solely or jointly" (*Maryland v. Pringle*, 2003).

JUDICIAL DETERMINATION OF PROBABLE CAUSE If police arrest without a warrant, their probable cause determination must be reviewed by a judge or magistrate as soon as possible. A Florida law allowed a person to be arrested on a prosecutor's bill of information and held for a month before being brought before a magistrate. This law was struck down as a Fourth Amendment violation in *Gerstein v. Pugh* (1975):

> [A] policeman's on-the-scene assessment of probable cause provides legal justification for arresting a person suspected of crime, and for a brief period of detention to take the administrative steps incident to arrest. Once the suspect is in custody, however, the reasons that justify dispensing with the magistrate's neutral judgment evaporate. There no longer is any danger that the suspect will escape or commit further crimes while the police submit their evidence to a magistrate. And, while the State's reasons for taking summary action subside, the suspect's need for a neutral determination of probable cause increases significantly. The consequences of prolonged detention may be more serious than the interference occasioned by arrest. Pretrial confinement may imperil the suspect's job, interrupt his source of income, and impair his family relationships. Even pretrial release may be accompanied by burdensome conditions that effect a significant restraint on liberty. When the stakes are this high, the detached judgment of a neutral magistrate is essential if the Fourth Amendment is to furnish meaningful protection from unfounded interference with liberty. Accordingly, we hold that the Fourth Amendment requires a judicial determination of probable cause as a prerequisite to extended restraint on liberty following arrest. (*Gerstein v. Pugh*, 1975)

The law in every state and for the federal government, based on common law practice, has long required police to bring arrested persons promptly before a magistrate for initial processing. The Florida rule was quite unusual. The Court in *Gerstein* did not define what constituted a prompt arraignment.

The Supreme Court clarified the time period for which a person can be held after arrest before being brought before a magistrate in *County of Riverside v. McLaughlin* (1991). The majority, in an opinion by Justice O'Connor, ruled that a jurisdiction must bring an arrested person before a magistrate for a probable cause hearing as soon as is reasonably feasible, but in no event later than forty-eight hours after arrest. Where an arrested person does not receive a probable cause determination within forty-eight hours, the burden of proof shifts to the government to demonstrate the existence of a bona fide emergency or other extraordinary circumstance, which cannot include intervening weekends. Under the county's rule, which excluded weekends, a "person arrested on Thursday may have to wait until the following Monday before they receive a probable cause determination" or up to seven days over a Thanksgiving holiday. The Court also suggested that holding off bringing a person before a magistrate in order to gather additional evidence was not a bona fide emergency.

There were two dissents—by liberal and by conservative/originalist justices. The liberal position (per Justice Thurgood Marshall) was that the proper constitutional rule is that a person must be brought before a magistrate immediately upon completion of the administrative steps incident to arrest. Justice Scalia opted for a twenty-four-hour time period based on his "originalist" research, which found that such a time period was common in the late eighteenth and early nineteenth centuries. In the past, lengthy postarrest detention without recourse to a magistrate was used to force confessions out of suspects. Such a practice tempts police to abuse their control over a suspect. The rules of *Gerstein* and *Riverside County* rightfully make constitutional what is now standard practice.

USE OF SECONDARY INFORMATION A police officer may depend on a reliable informant to establish probable cause to arrest. An informant could be an impartial witness, a victim, or an "undercover" informant who works for the police or receives lenient treatment in return for information about crimes such as drug sales (*Draper v. United States*, 1959; *McCray v. Illinois*, 1967).

In this era of high mobility and instantaneous communications, police often rely on the radio bulletins or computer notifications from other police departments as a basis for probable cause to arrest. In **Whiteley v. Warden** (1971), the Court ruled that police may rely on a radio bulletin from another police department informing them that an arrest warrant was issued. In *Whiteley*, the original arrest warrant was defective; the magistrate erred in finding probable cause. As a result, the arrest was illegal, and the evidence seized in a search incident to the arrest was not admissible. The clear implication of *Whiteley*, however, was that the officers who made the arrest reasonably relied on the radio bulletin and should not be held civilly liable for the arrest. They acted reasonably even if there was no probable cause for the original arrest warrant.

Arizona v. Evans (1995) and *Herring v. United States* (2009) (Chapter 2) upheld the constitutionality of arrests based on wrong information in police computers, whether derived from bad court or police records. Aside from the constitutional issues, serious concerns about error-filled law enforcement data bases were raised by an amicus brief filed in *Herring* by the Electronic Privacy Information Center (EPIC). Recent years have seen dramatic increases in the number of law enforcement data bases and electronic information sharing. More than seventy **fusion centers** combine homeland security data bases such as terrorist watch lists, criminal data bases such as the NCIC (National Crime Information Center) data base, and commercial data bases that, together, include huge amounts of data on citizens. "These government and commercial databases are filled with errors, according to the federal government's own reports."[4] As a result, many people are subjected to unconstitutional arrests.

THE FELONY/MISDEMEANOR RULE   The traditional common law rules for felony and misdemeanor arrests by law enforcement officers differ. A police officer may arrest a person for a felony when he or she has probable cause to believe that a crime has been committed and that the arrestee is the perpetrator.[5] For a misdemeanor arrest to be lawful, however, the misdemeanor must have been committed in the officer's presence. The reason for this distinction is that the public safety requires swift arrests for more serious crimes. Because petty crimes are often the result of squabbles between individuals, an arrest based on a complainant's say-so may result in instances of false arrest and legally sanctioned harassment. The victim of a misdemeanor had to obtain an arrest warrant from a judge via a formal complaint in order to initiate the criminal process. In recent years, the **in-presence rule** has come under severe criticism because it has prevented police from making arrests in cases of domestic violence. State legislatures have rethought the rule, and virtually all have modified it to allow or require an officer to arrest in cases of domestic violence. (See the "Law in Society" section in this chapter.) Statutes have also modified the misdemeanor arrest rule for traffic-related misdemeanors not observed directly by a police officer.[6]

CITIZEN'S ARRESTS   Private individuals have the right to arrest a felon. However, the personal consequences for a sworn law enforcement officer and a private person making a mistaken arrest differ. A police officer who makes a mistaken arrest (e.g., arrests the wrong person) that is based on probable cause cannot be held civilly liable for the tort of false arrest because the officer acted reasonably. A private person who effects a **citizen's arrest** is held strictly accountable to the arrested person for any errors made during the arrest. No matter how reasonable the citizen's arrest, if a mistake was made, the person making the arrest may be successfully sued for the tort of **false arrest**. The rule places a high premium on individual liberty to be free from unwarranted interference. The relaxation of the common law rule of strict liability for law enforcement officers is evidence of a policy that encourages officers to be less fearful of the consequences of their acts so that they will not shirk their duty. This recognizes the difficulties that confront law enforcement officers when hard decisions must be made with little time for reflection and under circumstances of heightened stress.

This common law rule has great effect on security guards; they cannot arrest a person for theft, for example, without the threat of liability unless they are actually correct. "Unless the owner has given consent, a security guard's search of private property will generally constitute a trespass. And arrests or detentions not authorized by state law generally will expose a security guard to civil and criminal liability for false imprisonment and, if force is involved, for assault."[7] On the other hand, "most states have codified a **'merchant's privilege'** that allows store investigators, and in some instances other categories of private security personnel, to conduct brief investigatory detentions that would be tortious or criminal if carried out by ordinary citizens."[8]

The Use of Force

"The criminal justice process rests basically on force, the authority of the state to use raw power, properly and appropriately applied, to apprehend, detain, try, and imprison. The basis of force pervades and colors the whole criminal justice system."[9] The system's force may be mute, as in prison walls or symbolized by the judge's robe and the patrol officer's uniform, or it may be mostly held in reserve; but when consent and compliance fail, the system, and especially the police, are required to use physical power to carry out its functions. The use of force is problematic because liberty is primary in the American constitutional scheme, but it is justified by the goal of enforcing public law.

The application of force, however, must be appropriate and lawful. The common law of arrest provides a simple, but ambiguous, rule: The force used to effect an arrest must be reasonable; it must not be excessive. What is **reasonable force**? Few guidelines exist. One guideline is that the force must be commensurate with the resistance offered by a person whom the police try to arrest. If a person resists with non-lethal force, then the police may use nonlethal force to subdue him. If a person resists with deadly force, then the police can reply in kind.

THE "FLEEING FELON" RULE   Under the common law, a police officer could use deadly force to subdue and arrest a "fleeing felon" even though the felon had not used deadly force. Presumably because most common law felonies were punishable by death, their seriousness tended to increase the likelihood that felons were dangerous to the life of others. The "fleeing felon" rule served as a substitute for the executioner! In America, the **"fleeing felon" rule** had been controversial and seriously criticized in the decades since 1960, as the use of the death penalty decreased and many felonies were no longer dangerous to life. By 1980, most states had modified the "fleeing felon" rule by statute, and many police departments altered their policies so that deadly force could be used only when a suspect presented clear evidence of violent intentions. These states felt that a blanket rule allowing police to shoot at any fleeing felon was excessive.

The issue came before the Supreme Court, giving it a rare opportunity to discuss the police use of force from a constitutional perspective, in *Tennessee v. Garner* (1985). The Court modified the "fleeing felon" rule as a matter of Fourth Amendment law and held, in an opinion by Justice Byron White, that

> [t]he use of deadly force to prevent the escape of all felony suspects, whatever the circumstances, is constitutionally unreasonable. It is not better that all felony suspects die than that they escape. Where the suspect poses no immediate threat to the officer and no threat to others, the harm resulting from failing to apprehend him does not justify the use of deadly force to do so. (*Tennessee v. Garner*, 1985)

The "fleeing felon" rule violated the Fourth Amendment rather than the Due Process Clause of the Fourteenth Amendment. *Garner* created a flat rule: A statute that allows police to shoot to kill *any* fleeing felon is void. A due process rule would have subjected the issue to painstaking case-by-case analysis. Deadly force against a fleeing felon is still allowed where reasonable: "Where the officer has probable cause to believe that the suspect poses a threat of serious physical harm, either to the officer or to others, it is not constitutionally unreasonable to prevent escape by using deadly force." Thus the Court in *Garner* upheld the common law framework: The legality of the use of force by police is based on what was reasonable under all the facts and circumstances of a case; all the Court did was to announce that under the Constitution, a flat use-of-deadly-force rule in all fleeing felon circumstances was unreasonable.

Justice O'Connor dissented, joined by Chief Justice Warren Burger and Justice Rehnquist. A teenager of average height was shot and killed by a police officer while trying to get over a fence after running from a nonviolent house burglary. "[T]he officer fired at the upper part of the body, using a 38-calibre pistol loaded with hollow point bullets, as he was trained to do by his superiors at the Memphis Police Department. He shot because he believed the boy would elude capture in the dark once he was over the fence. The officer was taught that it was proper under Tennessee law to kill a fleeing felon rather than run the risk of allowing him to escape."[10] The youth died of the gunshot wound. On his person was ten dollars and jewelry he had taken from the house. Justice O'Connor pointed out that no matter how regrettable were the consequences of this case, it was not unreasonable for an officer to shoot at a fleeing burglar at night since it was not known whether the burglar was armed or what had happened in the burglarized house. "With respect to a particular burglary, subsequent investigation simply cannot represent a substitute for immediate apprehension of the criminal suspect at the scene." The dissent was more willing to grant unreviewed discretion to the police than the majority.

The "real-world" effects of legal rules are often unknown. *Tennessee v. Garner*, however, has had a positive effect, stimulating police departments to modify policies and practices that have had lifesaving effects, not only for suspects but also for police. Jerome Skolnick and the late James Fyfe, leading police scholars, write:

> When police have started their attempts to develop policy with the principle that good policing in any situation consists of the actions that best meet the primary police responsibility to protect life, the results have been remarkably successful. Deadly force policies that, in both philosophy and substance, emphasize the sanctity of life over the need to apprehend suspects have reduced killings by police—and the backlash that often follows—without negative effects on the safety of citizens or the safety and effectiveness of officers.[11]

STANDARDS OF REASONABLE FORCE   Section 1983 lawsuits against police officers for using excessive force offer guidance on the legal meaning of excessive force. In **Graham v. Connor** (1989), Officer Connor stopped Dethorne Graham a half mile from a crowded convenience store in Charlotte, North Carolina, after seeing him hastily enter and then leave. Connor did not know that Graham, a diabetic, was driven to the store by a friend so he could buy orange juice to counteract an insulin reaction. Graham left the store because of a long line to go to a friend's house to get sugar. When stopped, Graham told Connor about the insulin reaction. Connor told him to wait until he returned to the store to discover what happened and to call for backup forces. Graham was handcuffed, his pleas for sugar were ignored by one officer who said, "I've seen a lot of people with sugar diabetes that never acted like this. Ain't nothing wrong with the M. F. but drunk. Lock the S. B. up." Graham passed out twice. He asked an officer to look into his wallet for a diabetic decal and was told to "shut up." A friend brought some orange juice to the patrol car for Graham, but the officers refused to let him have it. After discovering that nothing criminal occurred at the convenience store, the police drove Graham home and released him. Graham sustained a broken foot, cuts on the wrist, a bruised forehead, and an injured shoulder. Lower federal courts held that Officer Connor did not violate Graham's rights.

Did the police violate Graham's Fourth Amendment rights? Did they act reasonably? The Supreme Court provided the standards to be used to answer such questions. It ruled that where an officer seizes a person, as occurred here, reasonableness must be decided under the *Fourth Amendment* rather than the more general rules of substantive *due process* under the Fourteenth Amendment. Therefore whether excessive force was used is to be decided by *objective* factors. The officer's *motive* is irrelevant. "An officer's evil intentions will not make a Fourth Amendment violation out of an objectively reasonable use of force; nor will an officer's good intentions make an objectively unreasonable use of force constitutional" (*Graham v. Connor*, 1989). Next, the

> reasonableness of a particular use of force must be judged from the perspective of a *reasonable officer on the scene*, rather than with the 20/20 vision of hindsight. . . . The calculus of reasonableness must embody allowance for the fact that police officers are often forced to make split-second judgments—in circumstances that are tense, uncertain, and rapidly evolving—about the amount of force that is necessary in a particular situation. (*Graham v. Connor*, 1989, emphasis added)

Under the more open-ended substantive due process analysis that most courts had used prior to *Graham*, looking at the amount of force used under the circumstances, the extent of injuries, and the motive of the officer, plaintiffs may have had greater leeway to prevail in Section 1983 action. Nevertheless, the Court's decision was unanimous. The case was remanded for reconsideration by lower courts.

Brower v. Inyo County (1989) established that a roadblock can be an instrument of force that effects an arrest. Brower stole a car and eluded the police in a high-speed twenty-mile chase. A police roadblock was set up consisting of an unilluminated eighteen-wheel tractor-trailer blocking both lanes of a road behind a curve, with a police car's headlights pointing at the on-coming traffic. Brower was killed when his car hit the roadblock. This constituted an arrest. The remaining question was whether *excessive* force was used. The Supreme Court, indicating that this was a factual issue depending on the circumstances of the roadblock, remanded the case for further proceedings to determine if setting up an immoveable roadblock behind a blind curve with a police car headlights positioned so that Brower would be "blinded" on his approach was reasonable.

FLEEING MOTORISTS   High-speed police pursuits are a controversial topic, with critics com-plaining that many are unnecessary and put innocent drivers and pedestrians at risk. In *Scott v. Harris* (2007), a case with unknown but possibly enormous constitutional ramifications, the Supreme Court relied on its *own viewing* of a police car video of an automobile chase to rule that a civil suit by an injured fleeing motorist had to be dismissed. Victor Harris, left a quadriplegic after his high-speed pursuit was ended by Deputy Timothy Scott's supervisor-authorized manuever of bumping into Harris's vehicle and sending it into a crash, sued Harris for using *excessive force* resulting in an unreasonable seizure. Before the case went to the jury, Deputy Scott filed a motion for summary judgment based on qualified immunity (see Chapter 2). The Court of Appeals, upholding the District Court, "concluded that Scott's actions could constitute 'deadly force' under *Tennessee v. Garner*" and so could be sent to the jury to determine if the Deputy's action was reasonable. Under established legal rules the facts on a summary judgment motion have to be viewed "in the light most favorable to the party asserting the injury" (Harris) because a trial judge or jury had not yet adjudicated the facts.

Harris's version of the six-minute, ten-mile chase, with speeds up to 85 miles per hour on a two-lane road noted that "he did not did run any motorists off the road. Nor was he a threat to pedestrians. . . ." Justice Scalia, writing for the eight-justice majority, noted sarcastically that Harris's account gave the impression that he "was attempting to pass his driving test" rather than fleeing from the police. "The videotape tells quite a different story." In Scalia's account, The video showed Harris's "vehicle racing down narrow, two-lane roads in the dead of night at speeds that are shockingly fast." It swerved past a dozen cars, crossed the double-yellow line, forced cars off the road, ran red lights, and traveled for considerable periods in the center left-turn-only lanes. "Far from being the cautious and controlled driver the lower court depicts, what we see on the video more closely resembles a Hollywood-style car chase of the most frightening sort, placing police officers and innocent bystanders alike at great risk of serious injury." Justice Breyer, concurring, admitted that the video changed his mind about his vote.

As a matter of procedural law, *Scott v. Harris* ruled that the Supreme Court could accept its interpretation of the video because it had to accept the facts most favorable to the party opposing the motion to dismiss only if there is a "genuine" dispute of the facts. After viewing the video, which, according to the majority, blatantly contradicted Harris's version, the Court felt there was no factual dispute. The Court then held that Deputy Scott did not violate the Fourth Amendment. His forceful seizure of Harris was objectively reasonable based on all the fact of the case. Two factors seem to portend courts finding in favor of police in lawsuits following car-chase injuries. First, the majority distinguished the facts of *Garner*: "*Garner* had nothing to do with one car striking another or even with car chases in general. . . . A police car's bumping a fleeing car is, in fact, not much like a policeman's shooting a gun so as to hit a person" (*Scott v. Harris*, 2007, citation to a Court of Appeals case omitted). Second, in assessing whether high-speed pursuits are reasonable, "We think it appropriate in this process to take into account not only the number of lives at risk, but also their relative *culpability*. It was respondent, after all, who intentionally placed himself and the public in danger by unlawfully engaging in the reckless, high-speed flight. . . ." (*Scott v. Harris*, 2007, emphasis added). This rule will make it more difficult for plaintiffs to question the judgment of police in deciding to undertake high-speed pursuits rather than other means of responding to fleeing motorists. The majority layed down what it called a "more sensible rule: A police officer's attempt to terminate a dangerous high-speed car chase that threatens the lives of innocent bystanders does not violate the Fourth Amendment, even when it places the fleeing motorist at risk of serious injury or death."

Justice Stevens's dissent put the majority's factual conclusions, which omitted some facts, in quite a different light. Harris was pursued for a traffic offense; the police had his license plate number and could have found him without a chase; part of the chase at higher speeds occurred on a four-lane (not a two-lane) road, cars pulled off the road in response to police sirens, the pursuit took place at night "on a lightly traveled road in Georgia where no pedestrians or other 'bystanders' were present; and the majority's view that if the police discontinued the chase other drivers would be endangered was "uninformed speculation." Not only does Justce Stevens's dissent point out the basic idea that different people can view "facts" differently, it raised the more fundamental question that the court's decision "has usurped the jury's factfinding function and, in doing so, implicitly labeled the four other judges to review the case unreasonable. [It] implies that no reasonable person could view the videotape and come to the conclusion that deadly force was unjustified" (*Scott v. Harris*, 2007, Stevens, J. dissenting). His point was butressed by an empirical study of a diverse sample of 1,350 Americans who viewed a version of the video in this case. The results tended to show that the video did not "speak for itself" but was viewed differently by different segments of the community, with those holding egalitarian and communitarian views "more likely to see the police, not Harris, as the source of the risk to the public and to conclude that use of deadly force was not a justifiable response" and those with hierarchical and individualistic outlooks forming "views emphatically in line with those of the Court majority."[12] The authors were not so much arguing a specific resolution of the pursuit issue, but raising a concern that the Court's resort to "brute sense impressions to justify its decision" would undermine the voice of jurors with diverse cultural perspectives.

THE ARREST WARRANT REQUIREMENT

The need to obtain an **arrest warrant**, and the form the warrant takes, is determined by the circumstances and settings under which the suspect is to be taken into custody. This section reviews the law that pertains to arresting suspects (1) in public, (2) in their own homes, and (3) in the homes of third parties. It also reviews the question of detaining and searching people while executing a search warrant.

Arrest in Public

United States v. Watson (1976) upheld the authority of the police to arrest felons in public places without a warrant.

Read Case and Comments: *United States v. Watson.*

Watson left several questions unresolved, the most important of which was whether an arrest warrant is necessary to enter a home in order to make an arrest. This question was answered four years later in *Payton v. New York* (1980).

Arrest in the Home

Payton v. New York (1980) held that, absent an exigency, police are required to have an arrest warrant to enter a person's home to make an arrest. In this case, police had probable cause to believe that Payton had committed a murder and robbery. Around 7:30 a.m., six officers went to Payton's apartment without an arrest warrant, intending to arrest him. Lights were on and music was heard in the apartment, but there was no response to their knock on the metal door. About thirty minutes later, the police used crowbars to break open the door and enter the apartment. No one was there, but a .30-caliber shell casing in plain view was seized and admitted into evidence at Payton's murder trial. Payton moved to suppress the shell casing as the product of an illegal arrest.

The majority (per Justice Stevens) held that entering the home to make a routine felony arrest without a warrant violated the Fourth Amendment. The government argued that the Fourth Amendment was designed only to prevent "general warrants" and not to require warrants when the police had probable cause to arrest. The Court replied, "[T]he evil the Amendment was designed to prevent was broader than the abuse of a general warrant. Unreasonable searches or seizures conducted without any warrant at all are condemned by the plain language of the first clause of the Amendment."

Was this ruling consistent with *Watson*, which overlooked the literal words of the Fourth Amendment? The Court did not disturb the *Watson* rule but instead distinguished arrests made in the home from arrests made in public places: "[H]owever, . . . [a] greater burden is placed . . . on officials who enter a home or dwelling without consent. Freedom from intrusion into the home or dwelling is the archetype of the privacy protection secured by the Fourth Amendment." The "right of a man to retreat into his own home and there be free from unreasonable governmental intrusion" stands at the very core of the Fourth Amendment. *Payton* is one of several post-*Katz* cases that place a special emphasis on the privacy of the home rather than treating all "expectations of privacy" the same. The majority supported its position with common law history and trends among the states: A "long-standing, widespread practice is not immune from constitutional scrutiny. But neither is it to be lightly brushed aside." As for the concern by law enforcement that the rule would undermine public safety, the Court made it clear that the police may enter a home without a warrant when there is an exigency.

Justice White dissented, joined by Chief Justice Burger and Justice Rehnquist, giving four reasons to uphold the rule that had allowed police to enter a house without a warrant to make an arrest: (1) The rule was limited to felonies and did not apply to misdemeanors, (2) the privacy of the resident was protected by the "knock and announce" rule, (3) the arrest had to be made in the daytime, and (4) such arrest was lawful only if supported by "stringent probable cause." These are rather weak arguments since the dissent restates conditions that would exist in any event. If pushed to the extreme, such arguments could totally eliminate the requirement for arrest warrants for home arrests, just as *Watson* had, in effect, destroyed any constitutional underpinning for arrest warrants in public places.

The difference between the *Watson* and *Payton* decisions is, at one level, explained by the factual difference between an arrest in public and an arrest in one's home. Yet there is enough similarity in these cases to illustrate how "middle-of-the-road" or "swing" justices influence Supreme Court decision making. In these cases, two consistently liberal justices, William Brennan and Thurgood Marshall, voted for a warrant in both *Watson* and *Payton*. Similarly, three more conservative justices—Byron White, William Rehnquist, and Warren Burger—voted against the warrant in both cases. The different outcomes in the two cases may be explained by the thinking of the three swing justices—Potter Stewart, Harry Blackmun, and Lewis Powell—who voted against a warrant in *Watson* (1976) but in favor of a warrant in *Payton* (1980). The swing justices were joined by Justice John Paul Stevens, who was appointed to the Court between the two cases. Thus the facts alone did not explain the different holding in *Watson* and *Payton*. Rather, the attitudes of the justices who evaluated those facts were decisive. The pre-existing leanings in favor of or against law enforcement of the "conservative" and "liberal" justices made their votes unresponsive to the differing facts of *Watson* and *Payton*. The justices with less ideological leanings concerning this issue were able to evaluate the cases differently. This "political" evaluation of the Supreme Court does not explain every case, but it does show that justices' personalities, temperaments, life experiences, and belief systems come into play in fashioning the rules and doctrines of constitutional law.

EXIGENT CIRCUMSTANCES   *Payton* held that police may enter the suspect's home to make an arrest without a warrant when exigent circumstances exist. The Supreme Court has been highly protective of the expectation of privacy in one's home and has narrowly viewed police claims that they have entered under an "exigency." For example, in *Welsh v. Wisconsin* (1984) (see Chapter 5), police entered a suspect's home without a warrant or consent in "hot pursuit" of a person suspected in a non-jailable, first-time civil traffic offense of driving under the influence. The police tried to justify the entry on an exigency basis: that the blood alcohol level of a suspected drunk driver was decreasing over time. The Court found that this "exigency" simply did not outweigh the sanctity of the home.

In *Minnesota v. Olson* (1990), police made a warrantless entry into an apartment in which Olson was a guest and discovered incriminating evidence. The Court first held that Olson had a legitimate expectation of privacy. Did the police breach that privacy by entering without a warrant? In this case, the crime—a robbery and murder—was far more serious than in *Welsh*. The Minnesota Supreme Court applied a "totality of the circumstances approach" to find there was no exigency compelling the police to enter the home without a warrant. That court looked at the gravity of the crime, whether the suspect was reasonably believed to be armed, the strength of the probable cause against the defendant, and the likelihood of escape.[13] In this case, Olson was not clearly identified as the driver of a car involved in a robbery and murder. The only link was a few papers found in the car and identified by an unverifiable, anonymous tip. The police did not rush to arrest him when they learned of his identity and knew that he was in the apartment with women who called the police. They had sufficient time to obtain a warrant. There was no hot pursuit of a dangerous felon. The destruction of incriminating evidence was not imminent. The apparent danger of violence or escape was low in light of the police actions. The Minnesota courts found that no exigency existed and suppressed the incriminating evidence. The U.S. Supreme

CASE AND COMMENTS

United States v. Watson

423 U.S. 411, 96 S.Ct. 820, 46 L.Ed.2d 598 (1976)

MR. JUSTICE WHITE delivered the opinion of the Court.

This case presents questions under the Fourth Amendment as to the legality of a warrantless arrest. * * *

I

[A reliable informant, Khoury, informed postal inspectors that Watson would furnish stolen credit cards. Acting under their instructions, Khoury arranged a meeting with Watson five days later in a restaurant.] Khoury had been instructed that if Watson had additional stolen credit cards, Khoury was to give a designated signal. The signal was given, the officers closed in, and Watson was forthwith arrested. [No stolen credit cards were found on Watson, but some were found in his automobile. The court of appeals ruled that the arrest was a violation of the Fourth Amendment because there was no arrest warrant and no exigency; consequently, evidence obtained from the search of Watson's automobile and seizure of the credit cards had to be excluded as the fruits of an illegal arrest.]

II

* * *

Contrary to the Court of Appeals' view, Watson's arrest was not invalid because executed without a warrant. **[a]** Title 18 U.S.C. sec. 3061(a)(3) expressly empowers the * * * Postal Service to authorize Postal Service officers and employees "performing duties related to the inspection of postal matters" to

"make arrests without warrant for felonies * * * if they have reasonable grounds to believe that the person to be arrested has committed or is committing such a felony."

* * * Because there was probable cause in this case to believe that Watson had violated [the law], the inspector and his subordinates, in arresting Watson, were acting strictly in accordance with the governing statute and regulations. **[b]** The effect of the judgment of the Court of Appeals was to invalidate the statute as applied in this case and as applied to all the situations where a court fails to find exigent circumstances justifying a warrantless arrest. We reverse that judgment.

Under the Fourth Amendment, the people are to be "secure in their persons, houses, papers, and effects, against unreasonable searches and seizures, * * * and no Warrants shall issue, but upon probable cause. * * *" **[c]** Section 3061 represents a judgment by Congress that it is not unreasonable under the Fourth Amendment for postal inspectors to arrest without a warrant provided they have probable cause to do so. This was not an isolated or quixotic judgment of the legislative branch. Other federal law enforcement officers have been expressly authorized by statute for many years to make felony arrests on probable cause but without a warrant. * * * **[d]**

* * * [T]here is nothing in the Court's prior cases indicating that under the Fourth Amendment a warrant is required to make a valid arrest for a felony. Indeed, the relevant prior decisions are uniformly to the contrary.

"The usual rule is that a police officer may arrest without warrant one believed by the officer upon reasonable cause to have been guilty of a felony. . . ." * * * **[e]** Just last Term, while recognizing that maximum protection of individual rights could be assured by requiring a magistrate's review of the factual justification prior to any arrest, we stated that "such a requirement would constitute an intolerable handicap for legitimate law enforcement" and noted that the Court "has never invalidated an arrest supported by probable cause solely because the officers failed to secure a warrant." *Gerstein v. Pugh.* * * *

The cases construing the Fourth Amendment thus reflect the ancient common-law rule that a peace officer was permitted to arrest without a warrant for a misdemeanor or felony committed in his presence as well as for a felony not committed in his presence if there was reasonable ground for making the arrest. * * * This has also been the prevailing rule under state constitutions and statutes. * * * **[f]**

The balance struck by the common law in generally authorizing felony arrests on probable cause, but without a warrant, has survived substantially intact. It appears in almost all of the States in the form of express statutory authorization. * * * [The American Law Institute's *Model Code of Pre-arraignment Procedure* in 1975 adopted] "the traditional and almost universal standard for arrest without a warrant."

* * * Congress has plainly decided against conditioning warrantless arrest power on proof of exigent circumstances. Law enforcement officers may find it wise to seek arrest warrants where practicable to do so, and their judgments about probable cause may be more readily accepted where backed by

[a] The Court states its decision at the outset. What follows are the reasons for this decision. The court of appeals invalidated the statute under its reading of the Fourth Amendment. Does the statute's authorization of warrantless arrests end the constitutional reasoning process?

[b] Would *you* nevertheless require the police to get a judicial arrest warrant in investigations where they have plenty of time to get one?

[c] Does the judgment of Congress violate the Fourth Amendment's plain words?

[d] *Entick v. Carrington* (1765) said that an illegal practice does not become legal simply because it has been practiced for a long time. Does this point weaken Justice White's argument?

[e] Is the need for law enforcement efficiency a constitutional reason? Could this reasoning lead to the total elimination of arrest warrants?

[f] This assumes that the Fourth Amendment absorbed common law practice. Another perspective is that the amendment changed common law practices to expand the protection of individual liberty.

[g] If this makes arrest warrants totally discretionary, of what use is the Fourth Amendment?

[h] It is interesting that a practice could exist for centuries before being challenged legally. There was greater acceptance of the legal status quo in the past.

[i] Justice Powell politely says that the majority opinion has skirted the main question.

[j] Does this argument undermine the Court's decision? How can the Court avoid the "logic" of the Fourth Amendment?

[k] Is this too easy an out? Does this mean that the Court need not follow the Constitution just because it has not been followed for a long time?

[l] Does Justice Marshall's analysis (requiring arrest warrants for non-life-threatening crimes) make more sense than the majority's? Would such a rule undermine effective law enforcement?

a warrant issued by a magistrate. * * * **[g]** But we decline to transform this judicial preference into a constitutional rule when the judgment of the Nation and Congress has for so long been to authorize warrantless public arrests on probable cause rather than to encumber criminal prosecutions with endless litigation with respect to the existence of exigent circumstances, whether it was practicable to get a warrant, whether the suspect was about to flee, and the like.

Watson's arrest did not violate the Fourth Amendment, and the Court of Appeals erred in holding to the contrary.

* * *

MR. JUSTICE POWELL, concurring.

* * * Today's decision is the first square holding that the Fourth Amendment permits a duly authorized law enforcement officer to make a warrantless arrest in a public place even though he had adequate opportunity to procure a warrant after developing probable cause for arrest. **[h]**

On its face, our decision today creates a certain anomaly. There is no more basic constitutional rule in the Fourth Amendment area than that which makes a warrantless search unreasonable except in a few "jealously and carefully drawn" exceptional circumstances. * * * On more than one occasion this Court has rejected an argument that a law enforcement officer's own probable cause to search a private place for contraband or evidence of crime should excuse his otherwise unexplained failure to procure a warrant beforehand. * * * **[i]**

Since the Fourth Amendment speaks equally to both searches and seizures, and since an arrest, the taking hold of one's person, is quintessentially a seizure, it would seem that the constitutional provision should impose the same limitations upon arrests that it does upon searches. Indeed, as an abstract matter an argument can be made that the restrictions upon arrest perhaps should be greater. **[j]** A search may cause only annoyance and temporary inconvenience to the law-abiding citizen, assuming more serious dimension only when it turns up evidence of criminality. An arrest, however, is a serious personal intrusion regardless of whether the person seized is guilty or innocent. Although an arrestee cannot be held for a significant period without some neutral determination that there are grounds to do so, * * * no decision that he should go free can come quickly enough to erase the invasion of his privacy that already will have occurred. * * * Logic therefore would seem to dictate that arrests be subject to the warrant requirement at least to the same extent as searches.

But logic sometimes must defer to history and experience. **[k]** [Justice Powell then goes on to argue that historical practice shows that the Fourth Amendment was not intended to require arrest warrants and that to adopt such a rule would severely hamper law enforcement.]

* * *

MR. JUSTICE MARSHALL, with whom MR. JUSTICE BRENNAN joins, dissenting.

* * *

There is no doubt that by the reference to the seizure of persons, the Fourth Amendment was intended to apply to arrests. * * *

The Court next turns to history. It relies on the English common-law rule of arrest and the many state and federal statutes following it. There are two serious flaws in this approach. First, as a matter of factual analysis, the substance of the ancient common-law rule provides no support for the far-reaching modern rule that the Court fashions on its model. Second, as a matter of doctrine, the longstanding existence of a Government practice does not immunize the practice from scrutiny under the mandate of our Constitution.

The common-law rule was indeed as the Court states it. * * * To apply the rule blindly today, however, makes [little] sense * * * without understanding the meaning of * * * words in the context of their age. For the fact is that a felony at common law and a felony today bear only slight resemblance, with the result that the relevance of the common-law rule of arrest to the modern interpretation of our Constitution is minimal.

* * * Only the most serious crimes were felonies at common law, and many crimes now classified as felonies under federal or state law were treated as misdemeanors. * * * **[l]**

* * * To make an arrest for any of these crimes [misdemeanors] at common law, the police officer was required to obtain a warrant, unless the crime was committed in his presence. Since many of these same crimes are commonly classified as felonies today, however, under the Court's holding a warrant is no longer needed to make such arrests, a result in contravention of the common law.

Thus the lesson of the common law, and those courts in this country that have accepted its rule, is an ambiguous one. Applied in its original context, the common-law rule would allow the warrantless arrest of some, but not all, of those we call felons today. Accordingly, the Court is simply historically wrong when it tells us that "[t]he balance struck by the common law in generally authorizing felony arrests on probable cause, but without a warrant, has survived substantially intact." As a matter of substance, the balance struck by the common law in accommodating the public need for the most certain and immediate arrest of criminal suspects with the requirement of magisterial oversight to protect against mistaken insults to privacy decreed that only in the most serious of cases could the warrant be dispensed with. This balance is not recognized when the common-law rule is unthinkingly transposed to our present classifications of criminal offenses. Indeed, the only clear lesson of history is contrary to the one the Court draws: the common law considered the arrest warrant far more important than today's decision leaves it.

* * * [T]he Court's unblinking literalism cannot replace analysis of the constitutional interests involved. [m] While we can learn from the common law, the ancient rule does not provide a simple answer directly transferable to our system. Thus, in considering the applicability of the common-law rule to our present constitutional scheme, we must consider *both* of the rule's two opposing constructs: the presumption favoring warrants, as well as the exception allowing immediate arrests of the most dangerous criminals. The Court's failure to do so, indeed its failure to recognize any tension in the common-law rule at all, drains all validity from its historical analysis.

* * *

[m] Does Justice Marshall's analysis better comport with the "originalist" idea of adhering to the "intent of the Framers"?

Court upheld this fact-based application of the lower court's suppression of the evidence and agreed that there was no exigency to override the *Payton* rule.

Arrests and Searches in Third-Party Homes

Is a search warrant needed to arrest a person who is in the home of a third party, or is an arrest warrant for the suspect sufficient? In ***Steagald v. United States*** (1981), police obtained an arrest warrant for Ricky Lyons. Two days later, they proceeded to Steagald's home, where they believed Lyons was hiding. Outside the premises, they stopped and frisked Gary Steagald and an acquaintance and then entered the home to look for Lyons. Lyons was not present, but the police observed cocaine in plain sight. Based on that observation, a search warrant was obtained, and large quantities of cocaine were seized. The Supreme Court held that the initial intrusion into the home was unconstitutional. There was neither an exigency nor a search warrant nor consent to authorize or allow entry into the home of a third party to look for Lyons: An arrest warrant does not give officers the right to enter the home of a third party who knows the person named in the arrest warrant. Even if the officers had a reasonable belief that the suspect was in the house, that belief was not "subjected to the detached scrutiny of a judicial officer." The privacy interests of the homeowner superseded the authority of the police to enter under these circumstances.

SEARCH INCIDENT TO ARREST

The police have the authority to conduct a warrantless search of a person for weapons and evidence whenever a person is lawfully arrested upon probable cause for any crime. An arrest always creates an exigency—the risk of injury to the officer and the likelihood of destruction of evidence. Under the warrant-preference construction of the Fourth Amendment, the **search incident to arrest** is one of three well-accepted warrant exceptions; the other two are entry into a home in hot pursuit and automobile searches. Waiting for a magistrate's warrant to search a person just arrested would indeed undermine legitimate law enforcement interests.

The Scope of a Search Incident to Arrest

The question of the **scope of a search incident to arrest** proceeds in two directions—toward and away from the arrested person. First, how intrusive may a lawful search of an arrestee's body and clothing be? Second, how far away from the suspect may a search incident to arrest lawfully extend?

The first part of the "scope" rule was clarified in ***United States v. Robinson*** (1973). Officer Jenks of the Washington, D.C., Police Department saw Robinson driving an automobile and knew that Robinson's driver's license had been revoked four days earlier. Having reason to believe that Robinson was driving without a license, Jenks stopped Robinson and cited him for driving without a license. Under Washington, D.C., law, driving without a license was a crime for which a person could be brought into custody at a police station. According to police department procedures, Officer Jenks patted down Robinson's clothing. "He felt an object in the left breast pocket of the heavy coat" Robinson was wearing, could not tell what it was, and reached into the pocket and pulled out a "crumpled up cigarette package." The officer opened it and found fourteen gelatin capsules of heroin.

Writing for the Court, Justice Rehnquist distinguished between the search that may be made of the person and a search of the area under his control following a lawful arrest, the issue decided four years earlier in *Chimel v. California* (1969). Unlike the area of control rule, which had varied over time, courts have consistently upheld the right of the police to thoroughly search a person incident to arrest in order to secure and preserve evidence of crime and "to disarm the suspect in order to take him into custody." These reasons are in force when a police officer has probable cause and makes a **custodial arrest**. When a person is taken into custody, a *Terry* pat-down does not afford the officer sufficient protection against weapons that may be concealed and could be used during the transport to a police station. The arrest was considered proper, and the search was allowed under the Fourth Amendment, making the evidence admissible.

Four dissenting judges argued that an arrest for a traffic violation does not raise suspicion of drug possession and that the extent of the search must be limited by the nature of the crime. The majority, however, refused to limit the authority of the police in such a manner. "A police officer's determination as to how and where to search the person of a suspect whom he has arrested is necessarily a quick *ad hoc* judgment which the Fourth Amendment does not require to be broken down in each instance into an analysis of each step in the search. The authority to search the person incident to a lawful custodial arrest, while based upon the need to disarm and to discover evidence, does not depend on what a court may later decide was the probability in a particular arrest situation that weapons or evidence would in fact be found upon the person of the suspect." The Court thus created a bright-line rule: Police do not have to weigh each arrest situation on the street to guess whether this particular crime justifies a particular level of search. The constitutional rule is that the police may conduct a thorough search of the person upon arrest, without having to account for whether the search was related to the crime or the circumstances of the arrest.

The rule of *Atwater v. City of Lago Vista* (2001), discussed earlier in this chapter, authorizing an officer to take a person into custody for a fine-only offense, means that there is no longer such a thing as a noncustodial arrest. There are two situations in which a personal search is not authorized after a person is seized by police. The first is a temporary investigative stop made under the authority of *Terry v. Ohio* (1967), which authorized only a brief pat-down of the outer clothing for weapons. The second situation came into play in ***Knowles v. Iowa*** (1998). A police officer stopped an automobile driver for speeding, issued the driver a citation rather than arresting him, and, with neither the driver's consent nor probable cause, conducted a full automobile search, yielding a bag of marijuana and a "pot pipe." Iowa statutes allow either an officer to arrest a person for a traffic offense and bring the person before a magistrate or "the far more usual practice of issuing a citation in lieu of arrest or in lieu of continued custody after an initial arrest." The statutes also authorize officers to make a full-custody search of a stopped car, even though a citation has been issued. The Supreme Court held that the search in this case violated the Fourth Amendment, even though authorized by state law. The two rationales for the *Robinson* search incident to arrest rule are not strongly supported here. "The threat to officer safety from issuing a traffic citation . . . is a good deal less than in the case of a custodial arrest." As for the second rationale: "Nor has Iowa shown the second justification for the authority to search incident to arrest—the need to discover and preserve evidence. Once Knowles was stopped for speeding and issued a citation, all the evidence necessary to prosecute that offense had been obtained. No further evidence of excessive speed was going to be found either on the person of the offender or in the passenger compartment of the car." The Court also rejected Iowa's contention that a full-blown search of the car might turn up evidence of another, undetected crime.

Chimel v. California (1969) deals with the other "direction" of the scope of a search incident to arrest: How far *away* from the arrested individual may the search be conducted? Although the right to conduct a warrantless search incident to arrest has never been questioned, the Supreme Court had, over a half-century period from 1914 to 1969, issued an inconsistent string of rulings on the scope question. In *Chimel*, the Supreme Court sought to finally resolve the issue by handing down a clear statement concerning the proper extent of boundaries of warrantless searches around the person following an arrest.

Read Case and Comments: *Chimel v. California*.

Following *Chimel*, the Supreme Court encountered difficulty in establishing a workable rule concerning searches incident to arrest that occurred in and around automobiles that also maintained some limits on law enforcement. These cases (*New York v. Belton*, 1981; *Robbins v.*

CASE AND COMMENTS

Chimel v. California

395 U.S. 752, 89 S.Ct. 2034, 23 L.Ed.2d 685 (1969)

MR. JUSTICE STEWART delivered the opinion of the Court.

This case raises basic questions concerning the permissible scope under the Fourth Amendment of a search incident to a lawful arrest.

* * * Late [one] afternoon * * * three police officers arrived at the * * * home of the petitioner with a warrant authorizing his arrest for [a] burglary. * * * The officers knocked on the door, identified themselves to the petitioner's wife, and asked if they might come inside. She ushered them into the house, where they waited 10 or 15 minutes until the petitioner returned home from work. **[a]** When the petitioner entered the house, one of the officers handed him the arrest warrant and asked for permission to "look around." The petitioner objected, but was advised that "on the basis of the lawful arrest," the officers would nonetheless conduct a search. No search warrant had been issued.

Accompanied by the petitioner's wife, the officers then looked through the entire three-bedroom house, including the attic, the garage, and a small workshop. In some rooms the search was relatively cursory. In the master bedroom and sewing room, however, the officers directed the petitioner's wife to open drawers and "to physically move contents of the drawers from side to side so that [they] might view any items that would have come from [the] burglary." **[b]** After completing the search, they seized numerous items—primarily coins, but also several medals, tokens, and a few other objects. The entire search took between 45 minutes and an hour.

[Items seized during the search were admitted in evidence against Chimel at a criminal trial.] * * *

[The Court assumed that the arrest was valid.] This brings us directly to the question whether the warrantless search of the petitioner's entire house can be constitutionally justified as incident to that arrest. The decisions of this Court bearing upon that question have been far from consistent, as even the most cursory review makes evident.

[Dictum in *Weeks v. United States* (1914) referred in passing to a well-known exception to the warrant requirement: "to search the person of the accused when legally arrested."] That statement made no reference to any right to search the *place* where an arrest occurs. * * * Eleven years later the case of *Carroll v. United States* (1925) brought the following embellishment of the *Weeks* statement:

> "When a man is legally arrested for an offense, whatever is found upon his person *or in his control* which it is unlawful for him to have and which may be used to prove the offense may be seized and held as evidence in the prosecution." * * * (Emphasis added.)

[Another 1925 case, *Agnello v. United States*, "still by way of dictum" said:] **[c]**

> "The right without a search warrant contemporaneously to search persons lawfully arrested while committing crime and to search the place where the arrest is made in order to find and seize things connected with the crime as its fruits or as the means by which it was committed, as well as weapons and other things to effect an escape from custody, is not to be doubted." * * *

And in *Marron v. United States* (1927), two years later, the dictum of *Agnello* appeared to be the foundation of the Court's decision, [where agents with a search warrant to seize liquor and a still also seized a ledger. **[d]** The ledger was seized as incident to the arrest of the illicit producers at the still.] The Court upheld the seizure of the ledger by holding that since the agents had made a lawful arrest, "[t]hey had a right without a warrant contemporaneously to search the place in order to find and seize the things used to carry on the criminal enterprise." * * *

That the *Marron* opinion did not mean all that it seemed to say became evident, however, a few years later in *Go-Bart Importing Co. v. United States* (1931), and *United States v. Lefkowitz* (1932). * * * [In these cases, the Supreme Court limited the *Marron* ruling to situations where the things seized incident to arrest "were visible and accessible and in the offender's immediate custody."] * * * [I]n *Lefkowitz*, * * * the Court held unlawful a search of desk drawers and a cabinet despite the fact that the search had accompanied a lawful arrest. * * * **[e]**

The limiting views expressed in *Go-Bart* and *Lefkowitz* were thrown to the winds, however, in *Harris v. United States*, decided in 1947. * * * [Harris] was arrested [on an arrest warrant] in the living room of his four-room apartment, and in an attempt to recover two canceled checks thought to have been used in effecting the forgery, the officers undertook a thorough search of the entire apartment. Inside a

[a] Why did the officers wait for Chimel to return home before searching the home? If Chimel's wife had refused them entry and they arrested Chimel outside his house, would a search of his house be just as reasonable? Justified? Could they have demanded entry under the arrest warrant?

[b] A magistrate specifies the things to be searched for in a search warrant. By searching without a warrant or under an arrest warrant, does an officer potentially have a greater scope for the search than if a search warrant had been obtained?

[c] The words "in his control" and "search the place" could logically apply to the actions of the police in Chimel's house.

[d] Does the *Marron* decision appear to authorize the search of an entire house where an arrest is made?

[e] If *Lefkowitz* or *Go-Bart* did not explicitly overrule *Marron*, does this inject uncertainty into the law? Or does the most recent case control?

desk drawer they found a sealed envelope marked "George Harris, personal papers." The envelope, which was then torn open, was found to contain altered Selective Service documents, and those documents were used to secure Harris' conviction for violating the Selective Training and Service Act of 1940. The Court rejected Harris' Fourth Amendment claim, sustaining the search as "incident to arrest." * * *

Only a year after *Harris*, however, the pendulum swung again. In *Trupiano v. United States*, [1948], [the Court invalidated the seizure of evidence at an illegal distillery made without a search warrant but pursuant to arrests.] The opinion stated:

* * *

"A search or seizure without a warrant as an incident to a lawful arrest has always been considered to be a strictly limited right. It grows out of the inherent necessities of the situation at the time of the arrest. But there must be something more in the way of necessity than merely a lawful arrest." * * *

[f] Two of the most liberal justices, Frank Murphy and Wiley Rutledge, died in 1949 and were replaced by more conservative justices, Tom Clark and Sherman Minton.

In 1950, two years after *Trupiano*, came *United States v. Rabinowitz*, the decision upon which California primarily relies in the case now before us. **[f]** In *Rabinowitz*, federal authorities * * * [armed with an arrest warrant, arrested the defendant] at his one-room business office. At the time of the arrest, the officers "searched the desk, safe, and file cabinets in the office for about an hour and a half," * * * and seized 573 stamps with forged overprints. * * * The Court held that the search in its entirety fell within the principle giving law enforcement authorities "[t]he right to search the place where the arrest is made in order to find and seize things connected with the crime." * * * The test, said the Court, "is not whether it is reasonable to procure a search warrant, but whether the search was reasonable." * * * **[g]**

[g] On a sheet of paper, trace the zigzag of the Court's rulings on the scope of the search incident to arrest.

* * * [The *Rabinowitz*] doctrine, however, at least in the broad sense in which it was applied by the California courts in this case, can withstand neither historical nor rational analysis.

* * *

[The Court then noted that the line of cases supporting the *Rabinowitz* rule was quite wavering. Furthermore, the historic background of the Fourth Amendment was the strongly felt abuses of general warrants, hated by the American colonists, implying that] * * * the general requirement that a search warrant be obtained is not lightly to be dispensed with, and "the burden is on those seeking [an] exemption [from the requirement] to show the need for it." * * *

Only last Term in *Terry v. Ohio* (1968), we emphasized that "the police must, whenever practicable, obtain advance judicial approval of searches and seizures through the warrant procedure," * * * and that "[t]he scope of [a] search must be 'strictly tied to and justified by' the circumstances which rendered its initiation permissible." * * *

A similar analysis underlies the "search incident to arrest" principle, and marks its proper extent. When an arrest is made, it is reasonable for the arresting officer to search the person arrested in order to remove any weapons that the latter might seek to use in order to resist arrest or effect his escape. **[h]** Otherwise, the officer's safety might well be endangered, and the arrest itself frustrated. In addition, it is entirely reasonable for the arresting officer to search for and seize any evidence on the arrestee's person in order to prevent its concealment or destruction. And the area into which an arrestee might reach in order to grab a weapon or evidentiary items must, of course, be governed by a like rule. A gun on a table or in a drawer in front of one who is arrested can be as dangerous to the arresting officer as one concealed in the clothing of the person arrested. **[i]** There is ample justification, therefore, for a search of the arrestee's person and the area "within his immediate control"—construing that phrase to mean the area from within which he might gain possession of a weapon or destructible evidence.

[h] The dual purposes of the search incident to arrest of the person are extended to the search of the immediate area around the arrest. The Court here states the operative rule of *Chimel*.

[i] The search of a closed drawer is consistent with *Lefkowitz* (1932).

There is no comparable justification, however, for routinely searching any room other than that in which an arrest occurs—or, for that matter, for searching through all the desk drawers or other closed or concealed areas in that room itself. Such searches, in the absence of well-recognized exceptions, may be made only under the authority of a search warrant. The "adherence to judicial processes" mandated by the Fourth Amendment requires no less.

* * *

It is argued in the present case that it is "reasonable" to search a man's house when he is arrested in it. But that argument is founded on little more than a subjective view regarding the acceptability of certain sorts of police conduct, and not on considerations relevant to Fourth Amendment interests. **[j]** Under such an unconfined analysis, Fourth Amendment protection in this area would approach the evaporation point. It is not easy to explain why, for instance, it is less subjectively "reasonable" to search a man's house when he is arrested on his front lawn—or just down the street—than it is when he happens to be in the house at the time of arrest. * * * Thus, although "[t]he recurring questions of the reasonableness of searches" depend upon "the facts and circumstances—the total atmosphere of the case," * * * those facts and circumstances must be viewed in the light of established Fourth Amendment principles.

[j] The *Chimel* case is evaluated through the lens of the warrant-preference construction of the Fourth Amendment rather than the general-reasonableness construction.

* * *

[The Court noted that the *Rabinowitz* rule creates the possibility for "pretext" arrests, where the police deliberately attempt to arrest a suspect at home so as to avoid the necessity to obtain a search warrant, especially where probable cause does not exist. Thus, in effect, police could operate as if they had general warrants.]

Rabinowitz and *Harris* have been the subject of critical commentary for many years and have been relied upon less and less in our own decisions. **[k]** It is time, for the reasons we have stated, to hold that on their own facts, and insofar as the principles they stand for are inconsistent with those that we have endorsed today, they are no longer to be followed.

Application of sound Fourth Amendment principles to the facts of this case produces a clear result. The search here went far beyond the petitioner's person and the area from within which he might have obtained either a weapon or something that could have been used as evidence against him. There was no constitutional justification, in the absence of a search warrant, for extending the search beyond that area. The scope of the search was, therefore, "unreasonable" under the Fourth and Fourteenth Amendments, and the petitioner's conviction cannot stand.

Reversed.

[Justice White dissented, joined by Justice Black. He argued that the broad "search incident to arrest" rule of *Rabinowitz* was correct because the searches must adhere to a general rule of reasonableness. In this case, the search was reasonable because the arrest alerted Mrs. Chimel, and she would have been in a position to get rid of incriminating evidence after the police had left the house.]

[k] The Court here explicitly overrules cases that allowed a broad interpretation of the scope of a search incident to arrest. This clarifies the wavering line of prior cases and seeks to put a definite end to the Court's "pendulum swings."

California, 1981; *Thornton v. United States*, 2004; and *Arizona v. Gant*, 2009) are examined in the part of Chapter 5 dealing with automobile searches.

The Protective Sweep Exception

Maryland v. Buie (1990) established the **protective sweep** warrant exception under the Fourth Amendment. Justice White's majority opinion defined a protective sweep as "a quick and limited search of a premises, incident to an arrest and conducted to protect the safety of police officers or others. It is narrowly confined to a cursory visual inspection of those places in which a person might be hiding." It can be thought of as a "frisk" of a house to search for persons other than the arrested person who might endanger the officers.

In *Buie*, two robbers, one wearing a red running suit, held up a pizza parlor and fled. An arrest warrant was obtained against Jerome Buie and his alleged accomplice, Lloyd Allen. Buie's house was placed under surveillance. Two days later, the arrest warrant was executed by seven officers who entered the house after verifying that Buie was home. They knew that the robbery had been committed by a pair of men and could not be sure that Buie was alone in the house. Upon entering, the officers "fanned out through the first and second floors." A corporal shouted down to the basement, and Buie, hiding there, surrendered and "emerged from the basement." He was arrested and handcuffed. A detective then entered the basement "in case there was someone else down there." He spotted a red running suit lying on a stack of clothes in plain view and seized it as evidence. If the detective's entry into the basement was an improper intrusion on Buie's expectation of privacy, the running suit would be inadmissible as the fruit of an illegal search.

The Court held the running suit admissible under the plain view doctrine: The officer was legitimately in the basement, although Buie had already been arrested. The majority justified the officer's going into another part of the house on the basis of police officer *safety*. When police enter a house under an arrest warrant, in hot pursuit, or under a valid exigency (as in *Arizona v. Hicks*, 1987), they can go throughout the house looking for the suspect in any likely places where the suspect might reasonably hide. It is true that once the person has been seized, the arrest warrant is executed or the exigency is at an end. At that point, the underlying expectation of privacy in the home comes into play.

However, Buie's expectation of privacy in his home, once he was arrested, did not immunize other rooms from entry after his arrest. The balancing approach of Fourth Amendment analysis of *Terry v. Ohio* shows a basic concern for officers' safety by allowing them to frisk potentially armed suspects. The protective sweep, similarly, is designed to protect the arresting officers by allowing them "to take steps to assure themselves that the house in which a suspect is being or had just been arrested is not harboring other persons who are dangerous and who could unexpectedly launch an attack" (*Maryland v. Buie*, 1990). The risk of danger in a home arrest is as great as, if not greater than, an on-the-street or roadside investigatory encounter:

> A frisk occurs before a police-citizen confrontation has escalated to the point of arrest. A protective sweep, in contrast, occurs as an adjunct to the serious step of taking a person into custody for the purpose of prosecuting him for a crime. Moreover, unlike an encounter on the street or along a highway, an in-home arrest puts the officer at the disadvantage of being on his adversary's "turf." An ambush in a confined setting of unknown configuration is more to be feared than it is in open, more familiar surroundings. (*Maryland v. Buie*, 1990)

Once holding that a protective sweep was reasonable, the Court had to determine the standard of evidence needed by police to go beyond the room in which the person sought was arrested: (1) probable cause, (2) reasonable suspicion, or (3) no evidence at all? In *Buie*, the prosecution argued for position 3—that the police should be permitted to conduct a protective sweep whenever they make an in-home arrest for a violent crime. The Maryland courts and the U.S. Supreme Court disagreed. The Maryland courts had ruled that for officers to go beyond the place of arrest in a home, they were required to have probable cause (position 1) to believe that other people were present.

The Supreme Court instead created a two-part rule. First, "there must be articulable facts which, taken together with the rational inferences from those facts, would warrant a reasonably prudent officer in believing that the area to be swept harbors an individual posing a danger to those on the arrest scene." A protective sweep of the entire house must be based on reasonable suspicion. Second, however, the Court also held "that as an incident to the arrest the officers could, as a precautionary matter and without probable cause or reasonable suspicion, look in closets and other spaces *immediately adjoining* the place of arrest from which an attack could be immediately launched." Thus the "sweep" of the entire house is differentiated from a search of the "adjoining space."

Justice White emphasized that the protective sweep of an entire house is *limited* only to protecting the safety of arresting officers if justified by the circumstances, may extend only to a cursory inspection of those spaces where a person may be found, and is limited to that period necessary to dispel the reasonable suspicion of danger "and in any event no longer than it takes to complete the arrest and depart the premises."

Justice Brennan, joined by Justice Marshall, dissented. He said that the narrow *Terry* exception swallowed the general rule that searches are reasonable only if based on probable cause. He argued that the majority's characterization of a protective sweep as a "minimally intrusive" search akin to a *Terry* frisk "markedly undervalues the nature and scope of the privacy interests involved." As he saw it, a protective sweep was not far removed from the full-blown search that was disallowed in *Chimel v. California:*

> A protective sweep would bring within police purview virtually all personal possessions within the house not hidden from view in a small enclosed space. Police officers searching for potential ambushers might enter every room including basements and attics; open up closets, lockers, chests, wardrobes, and cars; and peer under beds and behind furniture. The officers will view letters, documents and personal effects that are on tables or desks or are visible inside open drawers; books, records, tapes, and pictures on shelves; and clothing, medicines, toiletries and other paraphernalia not carefully stored in dresser drawers or bathroom cupboards. While perhaps not a "full-blown" or "top-to-bottom" search, a protective sweep is much closer to it than to a "limited patdown for weapons."

Searching at the Station House

INVENTORY SEARCH   When an arrested person is brought to a police lockup or a jail for booking, it is standard practice for officers to inventory every item of property that the arrestee has on his or her person. In **Illinois v. Lafayette** (1983), Ralph Lafayette was arrested for disturbing the peace. He was taken to the Kankakee police station where, in the process of booking him, a warrantless search of his shoulder bag, made for the purpose of inventorying his possessions, turned up amphetamine pills. The Illinois Appellate Court, ruling that the privacy interest in an item of personal luggage like a shoulder bag during an **inventory search** is greater than that in an automobile inventory search, suppressed the evidence of the drugs. The U.S. Supreme Court reversed.

In the Court's opinion, Chief Justice Burger ruled that because an inventory search does not rest on probable cause, the lack of a warrant is immaterial. The inventory search constitutes a well-defined exception to the warrant requirement: It "is not an independent legal concept but rather an incidental *administrative* step following arrest and preceding incarceration" (emphasis added). An inventory search of a jailed person's backpack or similar items is justified by balancing privacy interests in the bag versus the government's interests. The Court found that the state's interests outweighed those of the individual—the routine inventorying of all items in a person's possession is therefore reasonable under the Fourth Amendment. The Illinois Supreme Court's ruling was reversed, and the plain view seizure of the amphetamines was upheld.

The governmental and individual interests that support the conclusion that a station house inventory search is reasonable include

- Protecting the arrestee's property from theft by police officers.
- Protecting police from false claims of theft by the arrestee. ("A standardized procedure for making a list or inventory as soon as reasonable after reaching the station house not only deters false claims but also inhibits theft or careless handling of articles taken from the arrested person.")
- Accurately determining the identity of the arrested person.
- Ensuring the safety of everyone in jail. ("Dangerous instrumentalities—such as razor blades, bombs, or weapons—can be concealed in innocent-looking articles taken from the arrestee's possession.")

Chief Justice Burger stated that "[t[he governmental interests underlying a stationhouse search of the arrestee's person and possessions may in some circumstances be even greater than those supporting a search immediately following arrest." He dismissed the suggestion of the Illinois court that it was feasible in such situations to secure the property of arrestees in secure lockers and thus preserve their individual rights of privacy.

In dictum, the chief justice referred to whether or not a person can be ordered to undress at the station house: "Police conduct that would be impractical or unreasonable—or embarrassingly intrusive—on the street can more readily—and privately—be performed at the station. For example, the interests supporting a search incident to arrest would hardly justify disrobing an arrestee on the street, but the practical necessities of routine jail administration may even justify taking a prisoner's clothes before confining him, although that step would be rare."

WARRANTLESS STATION HOUSE SEARCH FOR EVIDENCE   A locked footlocker that police take into custody following an arrest, with probable cause to believe it contains drugs, cannot be opened by the police without having obtained a search warrant (*United States v. Chadwick*, 1977). It constitutes an "effect" protected by the Warrant Clause of the Fourth Amendment.

To the contrary, station house investigative seizures are allowed where an exigency exists that the suspect can destroy evidence. In **United States v. Edwards** (1974), police had probable cause to believe that the clothing worn by Edwards, who was arrested and in a police lockup, contained evidence of a crime—paint chips from the scene of a burglary. The Court held that the police could, without a warrant, require him to exchange his clothing for other clothing, even ten hours after his jailing. The time delay was reasonable because the police waited until morning, when a substitute set of clothing could be purchased. *Edwards* fell within the search incident to arrest exception and made clear that when a person is in a police lockup or jail, the exigency that supports the search incident to arrest (i.e., the destruction of evidence) may continue for considerable periods of time. The exchange of clothing could also be allowed at the time of an inventory.

A warrantless search was also upheld in **Cupp v. Murphy** (1973). The search and seizure consisted of police at a police station taking dry blood scrapings from the finger of a man who voluntarily appeared at a police station after the strangulation death of his wife. When the police noticed the stain and the man held his hands behind his back, an exigency arose because he might have destroyed evidence. *Cupp* is problematic because at the time the blood was scraped from the individual's finger, there was no formal custodial arrest. In that case, the police had only reasonable suspicion that the man murdered his wife, but their action was a very limited intrusion and the evidence was the kind that could be readily destroyed. Under these circumstances, the search and seizure were held to be constitutional.

STRIP SEARCHES   The Supreme Court has not decided whether a **strip search** of a person held in jail on a *minor offense* is reasonable. In **Bell v. Wolfish** (1979), the Court upheld the **body cavity searches** of pretrial detainees, who were held on *serious charges* in federal jails that also housed convicted prisoners, after every contact visit with a person from outside the institution. The practice was deemed necessary to discover and deter the "smuggling of weapons, drugs, and other contraband into the institution." Strip searches under such conditions were deemed reasonable under the Fourth Amendment general reasonableness construction. "A detention facility is a unique place fraught with serious security dangers."

On the other hand, federal and state courts have struck down blanket strip search or body cavity search regulations and practices as unreasonable for minor crimes. An important early Seventh Circuit Court of Appeals case, *Mary Beth G. v. City of Chicago* (1983),[14] described strip searches as "demeaning, dehumanizing, undignified, humiliating, terrifying, unpleasant, embarrassing, repulsive, signifying degradation and submission." A Chicago policy in force from 1952 to 1980 required *all female* detainees to be subjected to strip searches, regardless of the charges, while all *male* detainees were patted down. In *Mary Beth G.*, women were strip searched after arrests for outstanding parking tickets, failing to produce a driver's license, and disorderly conduct. Although these were searches incident to arrest and the women were brought to lockups, the circuit court applied the balancing test to distinguish *Bell v. Wolfish*. These cases differed because the plaintiffs "are minor offenders who were not inherently dangerous and who were being detained only briefly while awaiting bond." The Chicago strip searches bore an insubstantial relationship to security needs and, when balanced against the plaintiff's privacy interests, could not be considered reasonable.[15]

Despite such rulings, municipal police departments in many places have continued to use strip and body cavity searches in inappropriate situations and have lost substantial lawsuits as a result. Some departments have instituted regulations to utilize these searches when reasonable. "Two states, New Jersey and Tennessee, have passed statutes requiring a search warrant or consent in order to perform a visual body cavity search." In neither state have police departments complained that these laws made their lockups unsafe.[16] Yet, the inability of many police departments to act on their own initiative to institute reasonable policies has led not only to the continuation of degrading practices, but to the rise of a small, specialized group of lawyers who litigate strip search cases. A study reports that there have been "nearly a hundred jail strip-search **class actions**, and there have been hundreds more individual cases, both affirmative civil actions and criminal cases in which criminal defendants seek the suppression of evidence by attacking the strip-search that led to its discovery."[17]

An illustrative case is Stacey Hartline's. She was 21 years old in 2003 when stopped driving her pick-up truck while running errands for her employer in the Village of Southampton, New York, at 9:30 a.m. She was stopped by Officer Anthony Gallo because her truck was missing a rear license plate. When she opened her door Gallo saw marijuana plant stem on the floor and arrested Stacey. She was strip searched at the police station pursuant to department policies, by a female officer, which included a visual inspection of her orifices and removing her upper garments and lifting her bra. "Hartline was 'crying hysterically' during this process." When returned to the female cell, Stacey noticed "a video camera trained on the area in the cell in which she had been strip searched. The camera appeared to her to be turned on." After booking Stacey was released. "As she passed Gallo on her way out, she saw a television monitor near him, showing a cell. She asked him whether the cell shown on the monitor was the one she had been in. He answered that it was." The misdemeanor marijuana charges were later dismissed. Stacey brought a $1 million lawsuit against Officer Gallo and the Southampton Police Department. The case was dismissed by a federal district court but reinstated in 2008 by the Second Circuit Court of Appeals. That court said that it was unreasonable for Officer Gallo to suspect that Stacey was "illicitly concealing drugs on her person" given the complete lack of facts that typically point to drug crimes.[18]

STOP AND FRISK

This section explores the second major category of personal seizure: the investigative stop.

Establishing the Constitutional Authority to Stop

Arrest law is rooted in common law cases going back hundreds of years. Virtually no law existed regarding the temporary stopping of individuals by the police in order to obtain information. Organized police forces, however, exercised this power as a matter of custom since their inception in the nineteenth century. In the 1960s, state statutes and cases began to define the so-called **stop and frisk** power. These laws generated constitutional challenges that soon landed on the Supreme Court's doorstep. The basic rules were formulated in *Terry v. Ohio* (1968).

Terry was handed down during an explosive moment in American history—an extended period of intense racial conflict that boiled over into hundreds of inner-city riots between 1964 and 1972, reaching its highest pitch in the summers of 1967 and 1968. The immediate catalysts of these riots often were episodes between largely all-white police forces and mostly young male African Americans who felt that the promises of the civil rights movement were not being fulfilled.[19] Given the overheated political climate of 1968, some commentators suggest that the liberal Warren Court justices voted to extend the powers of the police in part as a way of mollifying the bitter attacks on the Court by the police establishment and by many conservatives in Congress following the 1966 decision in *Miranda v. Arizona*.[20] Journalist Fred Graham, in this skeptical vein, noted that "[t]he Supreme Court has never conceded that it intentionally compensates for a tough decision on one point by handing down a soft ruling on another, but its actions occasionally give that impression."[21] Thus, within two years after *Miranda*, the Court upheld the use of informers and electronic eavesdropping, dropped the mere evidence restriction on searches, and authorized stop and frisk on less than probable cause. This does not prove that the Court acted from narrow political motives, but it does fuel speculation that the Supreme Court's decisions are not entirely divorced from major national events.

Read Case and Comments: Terry v. Ohio.

TERRY AND VAGRANCY LAWS: CLOSING A LEGAL LOOPHOLE   While *Terry* can be viewed as a conservative turn for the decidedly liberal Warren Court, several years later, in **Papachristou v. City of Jacksonville** (1972), the more conservative Burger Court took a "liberal" stance in restricting the use of overly broad or vague **vagrancy statutes**. These laws had for centuries given police in England and the United States a "cover" to stop and question individuals who merely appeared suspicious but against whom no probable cause to arrest existed.[22] Vagrancy laws were used not only to question those suspected of a crime but also to control and harass social deviants and the poor. A destructive aspect of these laws was their use as "cover" charges: A police officer ensured against a lawsuit for false arrest by charging a person stopped with "vagrancy." The Supreme Court, by openly recognizing the field-interrogation power of the police in *Terry*, and by shutting down the abusive extremes of overly broad vagrancy laws in *Papachristou*, eliminated a source of hypocrisy in police work and in theory brought this area of police activity under judicial scrutiny.

After *Papachristou*, the states could continue to rely on loitering laws but tended to narrowly tailor them to specifically target disruptive behavior, such as prowling around homes, streetwalking prostitution, and conducting on-the-street drug sales. These laws provided very detailed definitions of loitering. The change worked by *Papachristou* was that now citizens could turn to the courts to determine if such specifically targeted laws met due process criteria.

The Supreme Court has applied the stop and frisk doctrine in a variety of cases in the years following *Terry*. While some cases have limited the power of police officers to stop, most have expanded the investigative stop doctrine beyond a strict reading of *Terry*. Most commentators believe that a rough balance between police rights and individual rights established during the Burger Court years has given way to a legal regime that decidedly favors police in the Rehnquist Court. The mostly Republican-appointed Court has been charged with creating a "drug exception" to the Fourth Amendment linked to the nation's "war on drugs."[23]

In the cases that follow in this chapter, the Court often has had to determine whether police action constituted an arrest, a *Terry* stop, or a consensual encounter, and if a seizure occurred, whether the seizure was justified by probable cause or reasonable suspicion. Instead of organizing the cases in a purely chronological fashion, they are presented, somewhat artificially, by the source of reasonable suspicion and the place in which the stop occurs.

The Sources of Reasonable Suspicion

FRISKING FOR A WEAPON   *Terry* was ambiguous about whether a frisk of a person for weapons had to be preceded by reasonable suspicion that the person was about to commit or in the process of committing a crime. The Court held, in **Arizona v. Johnson** (2009), "that, in a traffic-stop setting, the first *Terry* condition—a lawful investigatory stop—is met whenever it is lawful for police to detain an automobile and its occupants pending inquiry into a vehicular

CASE AND COMMENTS

Terry v. Ohio

392 U.S. 1, 88 S.Ct. 1868, 20 L.Ed.2d 889 (1968)

MR. CHIEF JUSTICE WARREN delivered the opinion of the Court.

This case presents serious questions concerning the role of the Fourth Amendment in the confrontation on the street between the citizen and the policeman investigating suspicious circumstances.

Petitioner Terry was convicted of carrying a concealed weapon. * * * Officer McFadden testified that while he was patrolling in plain clothes in downtown Cleveland [one] afternoon * * * his attention was attracted by two men, Chilton and Terry, standing on the corner of Huron Road and Euclid Avenue. * * * [H]e was unable to say precisely what first drew his eye to them. However, he testified that he had been a policeman for thirty-nine years. * * * [H]e had developed routine habits of observation over the years[;] * * * he would "stand and watch people or walk and watch people at many intervals of the day." **[a]** He added: "Now, in this case when I looked over they didn't look right to me at the time."

* * * [Officer McFadden saw them pace up and down the block five or six times each, pausing frequently to look into the window of a jewelry store and to confer.] After this had gone on for 10 to 12 minutes, the two men walked off together [following a third]. * * *

* * * He testified that * * * he suspected the two men of "casing a job, a stick-up," and that he considered it his duty as a police officer to investigate further. He added that he feared "they may have a gun." **[b]** * * * Deciding that the situation was ripe for direct action, Officer McFadden approached the three men, identified himself as a police officer and asked for their names. At this point his knowledge was confined to what he had observed. * * * When the men "mumbled something" in response to his inquiries, Officer McFadden grabbed petitioner Terry, spun him around * * * and patted down the outside of his clothing. In the left breast pocket of Terry's overcoat Officer McFadden felt a pistol. * * * At this point, * * * the officer ordered all three men to enter Zucker's store. As they went in, he removed Terry's overcoat completely [and] removed a .38-caliber revolver from the pocket. * * * [Pat-downs of Chilton and Katz produced a gun on Chilton but not on Katz.] The officer testified that he only patted the men down to see whether they had weapons, and that he did not put his hands beneath the outer garments of either Terry or Chilton until he felt their guns.

* * *

I

* * * Unquestionably petitioner was entitled to the protection of the Fourth Amendment as he walked down the street in Cleveland. * * * The question is whether in all the circumstances of this on-the-street encounter, his right to personal security was violated by an unreasonable search and seizure.

* * * [T]his question thrusts to the fore difficult and troublesome issues regarding a sensitive area of police activity[:] * * * the power of the police to "stop and frisk"—as it is sometimes euphemistically termed—suspicious persons.

* * *

[The police claim that they need authority to deal with street encounters and that the brief detention of a "stop and frisk" not amounting to arrest should not be governed by the Fourth Amendment. It is a petty indignity. **[c]** The defendant argues that unless the police have probable cause to arrest, they have no power under the Fourth Amendment to forcibly detain a person temporarily or to *frisk* him or her.]

In this context we approach the issues in this case mindful of the limitations of the judicial function in controlling the myriad daily situations in which policemen and citizens confront each other on the street. * * *

* * * [I]n some contexts the [exclusionary] rule is ineffective as a deterrent [to police misconduct]. Street encounters between citizens and police officers are incredibly rich in diversity. They range from wholly friendly exchanges of pleasantries or mutually useful information to hostile confrontations of armed men involving arrests, or injuries, or loss of life. Moreover, hostile confrontations are not all of a piece. Some of them begin in a friendly enough manner, only to take a different turn upon the injection of some unexpected element into the conversation. Encounters are initiated by the police for a wide variety of purposes, some of which are wholly unrelated to a desire to prosecute for crime. **[d]** Doubtless some police "*field interrogation*" conduct violates the Fourth Amendment. But a stern refusal by this Court to condone such activity does not necessarily render it responsive to the exclusionary rule. Regardless of how effective the rule may be where obtaining convictions is an important objective of the police, it is powerless to deter invasions of constitutionally guaranteed rights where the police either have no interest in prosecuting or are willing to forgo successful prosecution in the interest of serving some other goal.

---

[a] The case does not indicate that Terry and Chilton were African Americans and the third who joined them, Katz, was a white male. Should this be suspicious?

[b] Is Officer McFadden's suspicion based on facts? Are they reasonable? Does probable cause exist to arrest these men on the basis of what he saw? For what crime?

[c] The police are asking that their forcible stops of persons *never* be subject to court review unless they make an arrest. Terry argues that the police should have *no* right to stop him without probable cause.

[d] The Court admits that bringing the stop and frisk power within the Constitution will not enable courts to supervise instances of police misconduct where the stop does not result in an arrest and the person is simply let go.

* * * The wholesale harassment by certain elements of the police community, of which minority groups, particularly Negroes, frequently complain, will not be stopped by the exclusion of any evidence from any criminal trial. * * * **[e]** Nothing we say today is to be taken as indicating approval of police conduct outside the legitimate investigative sphere. Under our decision, courts still retain their traditional responsibility to guard against police conduct which is overbearing or harassing, or which trenches upon personal security without the objective evidentiary justification which the Constitution requires. When such conduct is identified, it must be condemned by the judiciary and its fruits must be excluded from evidence in criminal trials. * * *

> **[e]** The Court signals its awareness and condemnation of widespread police misconduct and racism, which were rampant in that era.

* * * [W]e turn our attention to the quite narrow question posed by the facts before us: whether it is always unreasonable for a policeman to seize a person and subject him to a limited search for weapons unless there is probable cause for an arrest. * * *

II

Our first task is to establish at what point in this encounter the Fourth Amendment becomes relevant. That is, we must decide whether and when Officer McFadden "seized" Terry and whether and when he conducted a "search." * * * It must be recognized that whenever a police officer accosts an individual and restrains his freedom to walk away, he has "seized" that person. And it is nothing less than sheer torture of the English language to suggest that a careful exploration of the outer surfaces of a person's clothing all over his or her body in an attempt to find weapons is not a "search." * * * It is a serious intrusion upon the sanctity of the person. * * * **[f]**

> **[f]** Thus by stopping and frisking Terry, Officer McFadden seized and searched him. Note that the frisk is defined as a limited search for one purpose only.

* * * This Court has held in the past that a search which is reasonable at its inception may violate the Fourth Amendment by virtue of its intolerable intensity and scope. * * * The scope of the search must be "strictly tied to and justified by" the circumstances which render its initiation permissible. * * *

* * * We therefore reject the notions that the Fourth Amendment does not come into play at all as a limitation upon police conduct if the officers stop short of something called a "technical arrest" or a "full-blown search."

[The next question is whether this seizure and search were unreasonable—that is, whether the officer's action was justified at its inception and whether it was reasonably related in scope to the circumstances that justified the interference in the first place.]

III

* * * [W]e deal here with an entire rubric of police conduct—necessarily swift action predicated upon the on-the-spot observations of the officer on the beat—which historically has not been, and as a practical matter could not be, subjected to the warrant procedure. **[g]** Instead, the conduct involved in this case must be tested by the Fourth Amendment's general proscription against unreasonable searches and seizures.

> **[g]** *Terry* here solidifies the general-reasonableness construction of the Fourth Amendment.

Nonetheless, the notions which underlie both the warrant procedure and the requirement of probable cause remain fully relevant in this context. * * * **[h]** [I]n justifying the particular intrusion the police officer must be able to point to specific and articulable facts which, taken together with rational inferences from those facts, reasonably warrant that intrusion. The scheme of the Fourth Amendment becomes meaningful only when it is assured that at some point the conduct of those charged with enforcing the laws can be subjected to the more detached, neutral scrutiny of a judge who must evaluate the reasonableness of a particular search or seizure in light of the particular circumstances. **[i]** And in making that assessment it is imperative that the facts be judged against an objective standard: would the facts available to the officer at the moment of the seizure or the search "warrant a man of reasonable caution in the belief" that the action taken was appropriate? * * * Anything less would invite intrusions upon constitutionally guaranteed rights based on nothing more substantial than inarticulate hunches, a result this Court has consistently refused to sanction. * * * And simple "'good faith on the part of the arresting officer is not enough.' * * * If subjective good faith alone were the test, the protections of the Fourth Amendment would evaporate, and the people would be 'secure in their persons, houses, papers, and effects,' only in the discretion of the police." * * *

> **[h]** What is an "articulable fact"? It seems to be any reason other than a hunch. This suggests a lower standard than probable cause, which is defined as facts that would lead a prudent person to conclude that a crime is occurring or has occurred.

> **[i]** Here the Court provides a standard closer to traditional probable cause. Note that this paragraph does not use the words "reasonable suspicion," although later cases concluded that this lower standard is the rule.

[The Court noted that the police have an interest to prevent and detect crime that necessitates temporary stops of individuals to inquire into suspicious circumstances.]

The crux of this case, however, is not the propriety of Officer McFadden's taking steps to investigate petitioner's suspicious behavior, but rather, whether there was justification for McFadden's invasion of Terry's personal security by searching him for weapons in the course of that investigation. **[j]** * * * Certainly it would be unreasonable to require that police officers take unnecessary risks in the performance of their duties. American criminals have a long tradition of armed violence, and every year in this country many law enforcement officers are killed in the line of duty. * * *

> **[j]** The Court turns its attention to the frisk and devotes more attention to this subject than to the stop.

In view of these facts, we cannot blind ourselves to the need for law enforcement officers to protect themselves and other prospective victims of violence in situations where they may lack probable cause for an arrest. * * *

We must still consider, however, the nature and quality of the intrusion on individual rights which must be accepted if police officers are to be conceded the right to search for weapons in situations where probable cause to arrest for crime is lacking. Even a limited search of the outer clothing for weapons constitutes a severe, though brief, intrusion upon cherished personal security, and it must surely be an annoying, frightening, and perhaps humiliating experience. **[k]** Petitioner contends that such an intrusion is permissible only incident to a lawful arrest, either for a crime involving the possession of weapons or for a crime the commission of which led the officer to investigate in the first place. However, this argument must be closely examined.

* * * [Terry] says it is unreasonable for the policeman to [disarm a suspect] until such time as the situation evolves to a point where there is probable cause to make an arrest. When that point has been reached, petitioner would concede the officer's right to conduct a search of the suspect for weapons, fruits or instrumentalities of the crime, or "mere" evidence, incident to the arrest.

There are two weaknesses in this line of reasoning, however. First, it fails to take account of traditional limitations upon the scope of searches, and thus recognizes no distinction in purpose, character, and extent between a search incident to an arrest and a limited search for weapons. **[l]** The former, although justified in part by the acknowledged necessity to protect the arresting officer from assault with a concealed weapon, * * * is also justified on other grounds, and can therefore involve a relatively extensive exploration of the person. A search for weapons in the absence of probable cause to arrest, however, must, like any other search, be strictly circumscribed by the exigencies which justify its initiation. * * * Thus it must be limited to that which is necessary for the discovery of weapons which might be used to harm the officer or others nearby, and may realistically be characterized as something less than a "full" search. * * *

* * * [Second,] [a]n arrest is a wholly different kind of intrusion upon individual freedom from a limited search for weapons, and the interests each is designed to serve are likewise quite different. An arrest is the initial stage of a criminal prosecution. It is intended to vindicate society's interest in having its laws obeyed, and it is inevitably accompanied by future interference with the individual's freedom of movement, whether or not trial or conviction ultimately follows. **[m]** The protective search for weapons, on the other hand, constitutes a brief, though far from inconsiderable, intrusion upon the sanctity of the person. It does not follow that because an officer may lawfully arrest a person only when he is apprised of facts sufficient to warrant a belief that the person has committed or is committing a crime, the officer is equally unjustified, absent that kind of evidence, in making any intrusions short of an arrest. Moreover, a perfectly reasonable apprehension of danger may arise long before the officer is possessed of adequate information to justify taking a person into custody for the purpose of prosecuting him for a crime. * * *

IV

* * * We think * * * a reasonably prudent man would have been warranted in believing petitioner was armed and thus presented a threat to the officer's safety while he was investigating his suspicious behavior. * * * **[n]** We cannot say [Officer McFadden's] decision at that point to seize Terry and pat his clothing for weapons was the product of a volatile or inventive imagination, or was undertaken simply as an act of harassment; the record evidences the tempered act of a policeman who in the course of an investigation had to make a quick decision as to how to protect himself and others from possible danger, and took limited steps to do so.

* * *

* * * **[o]** The sole justification of the search in the present situation is the protection of the police officer and others nearby, and it must therefore be confined in scope to an intrusion reasonably designed to discover guns, knives, clubs, or other hidden instruments for the assault of the police officer.

* * *

V

* * * We merely hold today **[p]** that where a police officer observes unusual conduct which leads him reasonably to conclude in light of his experience that criminal activity may be afoot and that the persons with whom he is dealing may be armed and presently dangerous, where in the course of investigating this behavior he identifies himself as a policeman and makes reasonable inquiries, and where nothing in the initial stages of the encounter serves to dispel his reasonable fear for his own or others' safety, he is entitled for the protection of himself and others in the area to conduct a carefully limited search of the outer clothing of such persons in an attempt to discover weapons which might be used to assault him. Such a search is a reasonable search under the Fourth Amendment, and any weapons seized may properly be introduced in evidence against the person from whom they were taken.

Affirmed.

MR. JUSTICE HARLAN, concurring.

* * *

---

[k] In this case, Officer McFadden placed his hands on Terry's coat (the frisk) simultaneously with the stop. He did not have probable cause to believe Terry was armed. Terry was arrested *after* the frisk disclosed a gun. Thus the case facts do not fit the rules of a search incident to arrest.

[l] The Court draws a fairly clear distinction between a full search after arrest and a limited frisk (pat-down) after or accompanying a stop.

[m] The Court slips back to explaining and justifying a stop and compares it to a full custody arrest. This analysis of the stop is interleaved with that of the frisk, making it difficult to untangle the two issues.

[n] The general rules laid down in the case are applied to the specific facts. The Court concludes that Terry's seizure was based on more than a hunch.

[o] The Court reemphasizes the limited scope of the frisk.

[p] This paragraph summarizes the case.

* * * [I]f the frisk is justified in order to protect the officer during an encounter with a citizen, the officer must first have constitutional grounds to insist on an encounter, to make a *forcible* stop. * * * I would make it perfectly clear that the right to frisk in this case depends upon the reasonableness of a forcible stop to investigate a suspected crime. **[q]**

Where such a stop is reasonable, however, the right to frisk must be immediate and automatic if the reason for the stop is, as here, an articulable suspicion of a crime of violence. Just as a full search incident to a lawful arrest requires no additional justification, a limited frisk incident to a lawful stop must often be rapid and routine. There is no reason why an officer, rightfully but forcibly confronting a person suspected of a serious crime, should have to ask one question and take the risk that the answer might be a bullet. * * *

* * *

MR. JUSTICE DOUGLAS, dissenting.

I agree that petitioner was "seized" within the meaning of the Fourth Amendment. I also agree that frisking petitioner and his companions for guns was a "search." But it is a mystery how that "search" and that "seizure" can be constitutional by Fourth Amendment standards, unless there was "probable cause" to believe that (1) a crime had been committed or (2) a crime was in the process of being committed or (3) a crime was about to be committed. **[r]**

* * * If loitering were in issue and that was the offense charged, there would be "probable cause" shown. But the crime here is carrying concealed weapons; and there is no basis for concluding that the officer had "probable cause" for believing that that crime was being committed. * * * [A] magistrate would, therefore, have been unauthorized to issue [a warrant], for he can act only if there is a showing of "probable cause." We hold today that the police have greater authority to make a "seizure" and conduct a "search" than a judge has to authorize such action. We have said precisely the opposite over and over again. **[s]**

* * *

To give the police greater power than a magistrate is to take a long step down the totalitarian path. Perhaps such a step is desirable to cope with modern forms of lawlessness. But if it is taken, it should be the deliberate choice of the people through a constitutional amendment. * * *

* * *

[q] Justice Harlan's point is that officers need have no additional reasonable suspicion to believe that the person stopped is armed; a legal frisk is justified solely by the legality of the stop. As with his concurrence in *Katz*, Justice Harlan's point came to be accepted as part of the *Terry* rule.

[r] Justice Douglas, perhaps the most liberal member of the Warren Court, here combines a liberal policy result with a nonactivist position of adhering to established rules of law.

[s] By putting his point this way, Justice Douglas created a startling and appalling conclusion—that the Court gave police greater power than judges over the liberty of citizens. Was this the first step toward a police state?

violation. The police need not have, in addition, cause to believe any occupant of the vehicle is involved in criminal activity. To justify a patdown of the driver or a passenger during a traffic stop, however, just as in the case of a pedestrian reasonably suspected of criminal activity, the police must harbor reasonable suspicion that the person subjected to the frisk is armed and dangerous."

In this case, Tucson gang task force officers on patrol in a Crips gang neighborhood stopped a vehicle with three occupants whose registration had been suspended, a civil infraction warranting a citation. There was no reason to suspect anyone in the vehicle of criminal activity. While the two other officers dealt with the driver and front seat passenger, Officer Maria Trevizo noticed that passenger Lemon Johnson looked back at the officers and was wearing clothing consistent with Crips membership. He also had a scanner in his jacket pocket, which was unusual and cause for concern because most people would not carry a scanner that way unless they were going to commit a crime or were going to evade the police by listening to the scanner. Trevizo questioned Johnson and learned that he lived in a Crips gang neighborhood, had served time in prison for burglary, and had been out for about a year.

Wanting to question Johnson away from the passenger to gain gang intelligence, Treviso asked him to get out of the car. Johnson complied. Based on her observations and Johnson's answers to her questions while he was still seated in the car, Trevizo suspected that he might have a weapon on him. She therefore patted him down "for officer safety" as soon as he exited the car. A gun was retrieved. Under the rule stated earlier, the *Terry* frisk was proper and the gun was lawfully admitted into evidence. The *Johnson* ruling clarified the authority of police to conduct a frisk under *Terry*.

HEARSAY   At first, it seemed that the novel *Terry* rule, allowing a Fourth Amendment seizure on less than probable cause (on "reasonable suspicion"), had to be based on the personal observations of an experienced police officer. *Terry* stated: "[I]n determining whether the officer acted reasonably in such circumstances, due weight must be given, not to his inchoate and unparticularized suspicion or 'hunch,' but to the specific reasonable inferences which he is entitled to draw from the facts in light of his experience." Nevertheless, the Court soon established that reasonable suspicion can be based upon reliable hearsay.

In *Adams v. Williams* (1972), a person known to Police Sergeant Connolly approached him at 2:15 a.m. in a high-crime area and told him that an individual in a nearby car was carrying narcotics and had a gun at his waist. Sergeant Connolly approached the car, tapped on the driver's window, and asked the occupant to open the door. Williams, who was alone in the car, rolled down the window instead, and the officer reached in and seized a loaded gun from Williams's waistband. Based on the discovery of the gun, Connolly arrested Williams for illegal possession of a weapon, searched him, and discovered drugs that were admitted into evidence. Unlike Officer McFadden in *Terry*, who personally saw suspicious behavior, Sergeant Connolly did not personally see the gun or corroborate this fact before simultaneously stopping and frisking (i.e., searching and seizing) Williams. The Court expressly ruled that reliable hearsay may be the basis of an officer's investigative stop, which occurred when Sergeant Connolly tapped on the window and demanded that the occupant step out.

Adams v. Williams also extended the *Terry* ruling in another way. It extended the stop and frisk authority to crimes of possession. Some felt *Terry* should be limited to violent crimes or thefts. This extension has made stop and frisk a potent tool in the "war on drugs" and has also been at the center of the bitter controversy over racial profiling. (See the "Law in Society" section in Chapter 5.) *Adams* predicted the rule that was clarified and confirmed in *Arizona v. Johnson* (2009), that a frisk need not be supported by independent reasonable suspicion to stop if an officer has reasonable suspicion that a person who is otherwise stopped is armed.

ANONYMOUS TIPS   The Court in *Adams* noted that "[t]his is a stronger case than obtains in the case of an anonymous telephone tip." Such a situation was resolved by the Court in *Alabama v. White* (1990). At 3 p.m., Montgomery police received "a telephone call from an anonymous person, stating that Vanessa White would be leaving 235-C Lynwood Terrace Apartments at a particular time in a brown Plymouth station wagon with the right taillight lens broken and that she would be going to Dobey's Motel and would be in possession of about an ounce of cocaine inside a brown attaché case." The police did not know Vanessa White or what she looked like, but they corroborated most of the facts (White was not carrying an attaché case) and stopped White in her car shortly before she reached Dobey's Motel. The officers told her she was stopped because she was suspected of carrying cocaine; they obtained consent to look into a locked, brown attaché case that was in the car. They found drugs in the attaché case.

The Supreme Court held (6–3) that "the tip, as corroborated by independent police work, exhibited sufficient indicia of reliability to provide reasonable suspicion to make the investigatory stop." The decision was assisted to some extent by the ruling of *Illinois v. Gates* (see Chapter 3), in which the Court approved a "totality of circumstances" approach to determining whether an anonymous informant who supplied probable cause for a search warrant was reliable and truthful and had a basis of knowledge. In *White*, the Court applied this approach to find that the totality of circumstances apparently indicated that the informant was so familiar with Vanessa White's movements as to be reliable and truthful and have a basis of knowledge. In the course of its opinion, the Court made an important distinction between probable cause and reasonable suspicion. Reasonable suspicion not only is a lesser quantum of proof, but it is also less reliable. "[R]easonable suspicion can arise from information that is less reliable than that required to show probable cause." This language gives police greater leeway to stop individuals, without great concern that the information supplied is unreliable, than to search.

Justice Stevens, dissenting, saw these facts differently. "An anonymous neighbor's prediction about somebody's time of departure and probable destination is anything but a reliable basis for assuming that the commuter is in possession of an illegal substance." He suggested that White may have been a room clerk at the motel and offered a much more troubling suggestion—that in cases like this, the tipster could be another police officer who has a "hunch" about a person. This is not mere surmise, but it is a technique used by corrupt police, as noted in a book on the subject:

> There happened to be money missing on a job they went on, and the guy who lost the money came into the precinct bitching. It was a set-up job. It wasn't a real radio run. They [the police] had dropped a dime on the guy. They had called 911 themselves and then responded to the bogus call to get inside the building.[24]

The Supreme Court has limited the acceptability of anonymous information that presented only general information. In *Florida v. J. L.* (2000), an anonymous caller reported to the Miami-Dade police that a young black male standing at a particular bus stop and wearing a plaid shirt was carrying a gun. Officers went to the bus stop and saw three black males, one of whom, respondent J. L., was wearing a plaid shirt. Apart from the tip, the officers had no reason to suspect any of the three of illegal conduct. The officers did not see a firearm or observe any unusual movements. One of the officers frisked J. L. and seized a gun from his pocket. J. L., who was then almost sixteen years of age, was charged under state law with carrying a concealed firearm without a license and possessing a firearm while under the age of eighteen. In its unanimous opinion, the Court distinguished *Alabama v. White* by noting that although the tip itself in *White* did not amount to reasonable suspicion, once "police observation showed that the informant had accurately predicted the woman's movements, . . . it become reasonable to think the tipster had inside knowledge about the suspect and therefore to credit his assertion about the cocaine" (*Florida v. J. L.*, 2000). Justice Ginsburg, in her opinion, called *White* a "borderline" decision:

> The tip in the instant case lacked the moderate indicia of reliability present in *White* and essential to the Court's decision in that case. The anonymous call concerning J. L. provided no predictive information and therefore left the police without means to test the informant's knowledge or credibility. That the allegation about the gun turned out to be correct does not suggest that the officers, prior to the frisks, had a reasonable basis for suspecting J. L. of engaging in unlawful conduct. The reasonableness of official suspicion must be measured by what the officers knew before they conducted their search. All the police had to go on in this case was the bare report of an unknown, unaccountable informant who neither explained how he knew about the gun nor supplied any basis for believing he had inside information about J. L. If *White* was a close case on the reliability of anonymous tips, this one surely falls on the other side of the line. (*Florida v. J. L.*, 2000)

POLICE BULLETIN   The *Terry* basis of reasonable suspicion was also expanded in ***United States v. Hensley*** (1985). *Hensley* ruled that police may stop a suspect based on information contained in a flyer or bulletin they receive from another law enforcement department. If the flyer has been issued on the basis of articulable facts supporting a reasonable suspicion that the wanted person has committed an offense (rather than probable cause), then it justifies a stop to check identification, to pose questions to the person, or to detain the person briefly while attempting to obtain further information. *Hensley* therefore held that stops not only may be made to prevent a future crime or to stop ongoing offenses, as was the case in *Terry*, but also may be used to inquire about past criminal acts. Justice O'Connor maintained that although the crime prevention rationale and the exigency present in *Terry* did not exist in *Hensley*, the ability to stop a suspect for questions based on reasonable suspicion promotes the government interest of solving crime and prevents the chance that a suspect might flee.

Terry on the Streets

Several post-*Terry* cases held that police stopped individuals without reasonable suspicion, violating their liberty rights. ***Sibron v. New York*** (1968) was a **companion case** to *Terry*. An NYPD patrol officer saw Sibron "hanging around" a street corner for many hours in the late afternoon and evening in a place where drug sales were believed to occur, talking to known drug addicts. Sibron went into a diner and, as he was eating pie and drinking coffee, was ordered outside by the officer. The officer had seen no evidence of a drug sale, but he approached Sibron, said "You know what I'm after," reached into Sibron's pocket, and found a packet of heroin. The Court held that this seizure was not based on reasonable suspicion and therefore was an unreasonable and unconstitutional stop. There were no articulable objective facts to establish drug dealing or possession. The officer clearly was not "frisking" Sibron for a weapon but simply searching for drugs. The drugs were suppressed as the product of an illegal search and seizure. *Sibron* illustrates the line between legal and illegal stops.

IDENTIFICATION AND LOITERING LAWS   General loitering statutes must adhere to *Terry* boundaries. The Supreme Court has held that statutes giving police the power to obtain the identification of people walking in public are not valid in the absence of reasonable suspicion to effect a stop. In ***Brown v. Texas*** (1979), an officer in a high-crime area in El Paso saw Brown and a man in an alley around noon. The officer testified that the situation "looked suspicious, but he was unable to point to any facts supporting that conclusion. There is no indication in the record that it was unusual for people to be in the alley." Brown angrily refused to give identification when asked. He was arrested, jailed, convicted, and fined $20 for violating a Texas statute making it a crime for a person to intentionally refuse to report his name and address to a police officer who has lawfully stopped the person and requested such information. The Court ruled that the application of the statute violated the Fourth Amendment because the police had no grounds for stopping Brown in the first place. The mere fact that the area was frequented by drug users was not reasonable suspicion to stop him.

The Court went a step beyond *Brown v. Texas* in favoring individual liberty in **Kolender v. Lawson** (1983), holding that a California statute violated *due process*. The statute required those who "loiter or wander on the streets" to identify themselves and account for their presence when asked to do so by a peace officer. Edward Lawson, an African-American business consultant in his mid-thirties who wore his hair in dreadlocks was detained or arrested under this statute, while walking in residential neighborhoods in San Diego, on approximately fifteen occasions between March 1975 and January 1977. After being prosecuted twice and convicted once he brought a civil suit to have the law declared unconstitutional. California courts limited the application of the statute only to instances where a police officer "has reasonable suspicion of criminal activity sufficient to justify a *Terry* detention."

The Supreme Court ruled that even as construed, the statute still violated the Fourteenth Amendment because it was "void for vagueness." This doctrine states that a law violates due process if it is not sufficiently definite, so that ordinary people are unable to understand what conduct is prohibited. The essential fault with a vague law is that it gives police open-ended and standardless authority; this encourages arbitrary and discriminatory law enforcement. The California statute gave police virtually complete discretion to determine whether a suspect offered "credible and reliable" identification. It violated the due process of law *as applied*. Justice O'Connor's majority opinion stated the values that underpin these rules: "Our Constitution is designed to maximize individual freedoms within a framework of ordered liberty."

Justice Brennan, concurring, argued that the statute was *facially unconstitutional* under the *Fourth Amendment*—that is, it was unconstitutional *however applied*. Justices White and Rehnquist dissented on the ground that people given actual notice of the application of the statute cannot challenge it on vagueness grounds because they are apprised of the law's impact.

A distinguishing hallmark of American life is the lack of a general requirement that citizens carry official identification at all times. Many democratic nations require their citizens to carry **internal passports**. But even if reasonable, internal passports are opposed because of the powerful cultural norms of individuality and freedom that mark the American character, norms that help to explain the *Kolender v. Lawson* ruling. However, after 9/11 some have called for a national identification card or a system that links driver's licenses to a national registry.[25]

The Court reconsidered a loitering statute in **City of Chicago v. Morales** (1999). A Chicago "gang congregation" ordinance prohibited loitering together in any public place by two or more people if at least one individual was a "criminal street gang member." It defined *loitering* as remaining in any one place with no apparent purpose. A police officer observing what was reasonably believed to be loitering was required to order the group to disperse on threat of criminal penalties. The Chicago Police Department promulgated guidelines to prevent arbitrary or discriminatory enforcement of the ordinance. These allowed only designated gang squad officers to use the ordinance, established detailed criteria for determining street gangs and membership, and limited enforcement to areas with high gang activity (not disclosed to the public). The Court struck down the ordinance on the grounds of due process vagueness.

The ordinance had been vigorously enforced: Forty-two thousand people were arrested for loitering in three years. Justice Stevens, a Chicago native, wrote for the majority. There was no dispute that gang violence imperils safety and disrupts normal street life, he wrote. As *Papachristou v. City of Jacksonville* (1972) made clear, however, a person has a right to "loiter"—that is, "to remove from one place to another according to inclination." Such "loitering" is "an attribute of personal liberty" protected by the Constitution. The Court held that the ordinance specifically violated the Due Process Clause by not clearly defining terms like *disperse* and leaving the *locality*. What exactly would purported gang members have to do to "disperse"? How quickly did they have to move? How far would they have to go? Also, the ordinance did not adequately define "loitering" with the specificity seen in loitering ordinances that targeted drug dealing or prostitution. It therefore "necessarily entrusts lawmaking to the moment-to-moment judgment of the policeman on his beat." Finally, the ordinance could apply to essentially peaceful activity and not to underlying activities that are dangerous. In sum, the ordinance violated the Due Process Clause.

STOP AND IDENTIFY STATUTES   In *Hiibel v. Sixth Judicial District Court* (2004), the Supreme Court answered a question left open in *Brown v. Texas* (1979) and upheld a law requiring a person who was lawfully stopped by police to give his or her name. "Stop and identify statutes often combine elements of traditional vagrancy laws with provisions intended to regulate police behavior in the course of investigatory stops. The statutes vary from State to State, but all permit an officer to ask or require a suspect to disclose his identity. . . . In some States, a suspect's refusal to identify himself is a misdemeanor offense or civil violation; in others, it is a factor to be considered in whether the suspect has violated loitering laws. In other States, a suspect may decline to identify himself without penalty" (*Hiibel*, 2004).

In the *Hiibel* case, a Nevada sheriff's department received a call about a man assaulting a woman in a red and silver GMC truck on Grass Valley Road. The deputy sheriff who was dispatched to investigate found the truck parked on the side of the road, Hiibel standing outside the truck, and a young woman sitting inside it. Skid marks in the gravel behind the vehicle indicated that the truck had come to a sudden stop. Hiibel was arrested after being asked for his name eleven times and refusing to give it. He was convicted and fined for obstructing a public officer in discharging his duty. Under Nevada's stop and identify statute, the officer had a right to ask only for the name of a stopped person and no right to ask for a driver's license or any other document.

The issue in this case was not whether an officer could properly ask a suspect to identify himself in the course of a *Terry* stop. This practice was recognized in many cases. The issue was whether a lawfully detained suspect could be arrested and prosecuted for failing to give his or her name. The source of Hiibel's obligation to answer the officer was a state law, not the Fourth Amendment. The Supreme Court found that the statutory obligation is consistent with *Terry*'s principles of reasonably balancing police officers' needs with suspects' expectation of privacy. This conclusion was linked to the majority's positive view of identification:

> Obtaining a suspect's name in the course of a *Terry* stop serves important government interests. Knowledge of identity may inform an officer that a suspect is wanted for another offense, or has a record of violence or mental disorder. On the other hand, knowing identity may help clear a suspect and allow the police to concentrate their efforts elsewhere. Identity may prove particularly important in cases such as this, where the police are investigating what appears to be a domestic assault. Officers called to investigate domestic disputes need to know whom they are dealing with, in order to assess the situation, the threat to their own safety, and possible danger to the potential victim. (*Hiibel v. Sixth Judicial District Court*, 2004)

Four justices dissented. Justice Stevens believed that the Fifth Amendment privilege against self-incrimination was violated because a person forced to give his or her name provides a *testimonial* communication. The person's name can be used to incriminate him or her:

> A person's identity obviously bears informational and incriminating worth, even if the [name] itself is not inculpatory. A name can provide the key to a broad array of information about the person, particularly in the hands of a police officer with access to a range of law enforcement databases. And that information, in turn, can be tremendously useful in a criminal prosecution. It is therefore quite wrong to suggest that a person's identity provides a link in the chain to incriminating evidence only in unusual circumstances. (*Hiibel v. Sixth Judicial District Court*, 2004, Stevens, J., dissenting, internal quote marks and citations omitted)

Justices Breyer, Souter, and Ginsburg based their dissent on the Fourth Amendment, arguing that the rule against requiring identification during a stop was well established.

FLEEING FROM THE POLICE   Among the most hotly contested post-*Terry* cases have been those concerning scenarios in which a police officer follows or chases a person. *Michigan v. Chesternut* (1988) held that police "intrusion" did not amount to an illegal detention and search. Chesternut, standing on a Detroit street corner, began to run when he saw a police car drive near. The patrol car turned the corner and followed to see where he was going. The car quickly caught up with him and drove alongside for a short distance. The officers saw Chesternut discard packets from his right-hand pocket; when they retrieved the packets, they found pills that one officer, who was trained as a paramedic, identified as codeine. Chesternut was arrested and searched, and more drugs were found on his person. The Michigan courts held that the police were engaged in an "investigatory pursuit" that amounted to a seizure under *Terry*.

A unanimous Supreme Court reversed, holding that the police conduct of driving along-side the defendant did not constitute a stop or a Fourth Amendment seizure. The police used no flashers or siren, drew no weapons, and did not order the defendant to stop. The car was not operated in an aggressive way to block Chesternut's course or otherwise control his speed or movement. "While the very presence of a police car driving parallel to a running pedestrian could be somewhat intimidating, this kind of police presence does not, standing alone, constitute a seizure. . . . The police therefore were not required to have 'a particularized and objective basis for suspecting [Chesternut] of criminal activity,' in order to pursue him" (*Michigan v. Chesternut*, 1988). *Chesternut* is an example of the rule that police need no evidentiary basis for observing on-the-street behavior, even if the observation becomes obvious.

In *California v. Hodari D.*, the police did not simply follow, but clearly chased, a person on foot.

Read Case and Comments: California v. Hodari D.

One commentator sees *Hodari D.* as the "culmination of a struggle between two factions of the Supreme Court," and a victory by the group led by conservative Justices Kennedy and Scalia. If the *Mendenhall* Court meant what it said when it proposed that a seizure is to be measured by the reasonable understanding of the individual, then the majority in *Hodari D.* created a new rule when it added a "physical restraint" element to Fourth Amendment seizures.[26] A year before *Hodari D.*, a leading scholar accepted as an established rule that "[w]hen a cop accosts a citizen on the street, the constitutional standard for measuring whether a seizure occurs is whether—in light of the totality of the circumstances—a reasonable person would feel free to leave the scene."[27] Professor Tracey Maclin saw this as a matter of commonsense reality: "In the typical street encounter, few persons, if any, feel free to ignore or leave the presence of a police officer who has approached and questioned them. . . . [T]he average individual who is approached by a police officer does not feel free to leave."[28] The implication of a pure *Mendenhall* rule plus "what everyone knows about being approached by the police" was that a police officer who "rushes" an individual without reasonable suspicion has seized that person; and if the person flees and tosses away contraband, its seizure is the product of an illegal search and seizure. The *Hodari D.* modification allows the tossed contraband to be taken and used as "abandoned" property.

The unresolved issue in *Hodari D.*—whether mere flight from the sight of a police officer established reasonable suspicion for an officer to give chase—was settled in favor of the police in **Illinois v. Wardlow** (2000). A four-car police caravan was cruising through a high-crime neighborhood, looking for on-the-street drug deals. Sam Wardlow was standing alone and holding an opaque bag; he made eye contact with an officer in the last car and "fled." Two officers in the car watched Wardlow run through a passageway and an alley and eventually cornered him on the street. One officer exited his car, stopped Wardlow, "and immediately conducted a protective pat-down search for weapons because in his experience it was common for there to be weapons in the near vicinity of narcotics transactions. During the frisk, Officer Nolan squeezed the bag respondent was carrying and felt a heavy, hard object similar to the shape of a gun. The officer then opened the bag and discovered a .38-caliber handgun with five live rounds of ammunition. The officers arrested Wardlow."

The Court emphasized the rule of *Brown v. Texas* (1979)—the simple presence of a person in a high-crime area does not give officers reasonable suspicion to stop a person. On the other hand, the Court ruled that unprovoked flight from the police, coupled with "commonsense judgment . . . and inferences about human behavior," constitutes reasonable suspicion. The Court did not say that flight is a per se factor that always established reasonable suspicion. While simple unprovoked flight tends to be a basis of reasonable suspicion, under this view, the officer may also take into account other factors, such as the belief that a neighborhood is a high-crime area. Four justices in *Wardlow*—Stevens, Souter, Ginsburg, and Breyer—concurred in part and dissented in part. The concurring opinion kept alive the idea that under some conditions flight will not be viewed as reasonable suspicion for a stop.

The ruling creates some tension with another rule of *Terry:* that a person against whom the police do not have reasonable suspicion may refuse to talk to the officer and, citing *Bostick*, that "any 'refusal to cooperate, without more, does not furnish the minimal level of objective justification needed for a detention or seizure.'" If a police officer, with no reasonable suspicion, approaches a person on the street to ask if the person will consent to talk to the officer and the person "flees," this could invoke reasonable suspicion. Much would depend on the facts of such a scenario. *Wardlow* does not fully define what is meant by flight. Thus, under the facts of *Wardlow*, it is unclear whether flight occurs if a person, after looking at an officer, gets on a bicycle and rides away, hails a taxi and drives off, or enters the building he was standing in front of.[29] Such issues will be resolved in future cases. *Wardlow* clearly expands the actual authority of police to control the streets.

Terry on the Road

Many *Terry* cases have developed auxiliary rules for interpreting the stop and frisk authority in automobile stop situations. The scope of a warrantless automobile search based on probable cause is dealt with in Chapter 5.

SCOPE OF A TERRY STOP AND FRISK   Most *Terry* cases involve a frisk of a person. **Michigan v. Long** (1983) held that when police stop a driver without arresting him or her, they may make a quick and cursory examination of the car's interior—a frisk of the car, so to speak. In *Long*, sheriff's deputies stopped a speeding and erratically driven car. The driver pulled into a ditch and exited the car. The door was left open. The driver, David Long, did not produce identification when asked to do so. Long began to walk back to the car but was stopped and frisked. No weapons were found. The deputies saw a hunting knife on the floorboard of the driver's side of the car. One deputy peered into the car with a flashlight and saw something protruding from under the armrest on the front seat. He knelt in the vehicle and lifted the armrest, saw an open pouch on the front seat, and, upon flashing his light on the pouch, determined that it contained what appeared to be marijuana. Long was arrested, and a search of the car's trunk revealed seventy-five pounds of marijuana.

The Court held the search constitutional under the principles of *Terry*. One reason is that "investigative detentions involving suspects in vehicles are especially fraught with danger to police officers." Thus, to protect their safety, police officers who stop cars may engage in a cursory examination of the passenger areas of the vehicle to look for weapons in those areas in which a weapon may be placed or hidden when they have a reasonable belief based on articulable facts that the suspect poses a danger and may gain immediate control of the weapons.

INFERENTIAL REASONING AND REASONABLE SUSPICION   *Terry* defines reasonable suspicion, which justifies a stop, as "specific and articulable facts which, taken together with *rational inferences from those facts*, reasonably warrant that intrusion" (*Terry v. Ohio*, 1968; emphasis added). This important part of the *Terry* doctrine was clarified and extended in **United States v. Cortez** (1981). U.S. Border Patrol officers, alerted by distinctive footprints and tire tracks in a sparsely settled area of desert thirty miles north of the Mexican border, deduced that a truck capable of holding eight to twenty people would approach from the east and stop between 2 a.m. and 6 a.m. near milepost 122 on Highway 86. As the officers surveyed the road on a particularly bright moonlit night, a camper passed traveling west and then returned approaching from the east at about the time it would take to return from milepost 122. Agents stopped the camper, and illegal aliens were found inside. The Court unanimously held that this stop was based on reasonable suspicion. Chief Justice Burger established a structure for reasonable suspicion analysis:

> Courts have used a variety of terms to capture the elusive concept of what cause is sufficient to authorize police to stop a person. Terms like "articulable reasons" and "founded suspicion" are not self-defining; they fall short of providing clear guidance dispositive of the myriad factual situations that arise. But the essence of all that has been written is that the totality of the circumstances—the whole picture—must be taken into account. . . .
>
> The idea that an assessment of the whole picture must yield a particularized suspicion contains two elements, each of which must be present before a stop is permissible. First, the assessment must be based upon all the circumstances. The analysis proceeds with various objective observations, information from police reports, if such are available, and consideration of the modes or patterns of operation of certain kinds of lawbreakers. From these data, a trained officer draws inferences and makes deductions—inferences and deductions that might well elude an untrained person.
>
> The process does not deal with hard certainties, but with probabilities. . . .

CASE AND COMMENTS

California v. Hodari D.

499 U.S. 621, 111 S.Ct. 1547, 113 L.Ed.2d 690 (1991)

JUSTICE SCALIA delivered the opinion of the Court.

Late one evening in April 1988, Officers Brian McColgin and Jerry Pertoso were on patrol in a high-crime area of Oakland, California. They were dressed in street clothes but wearing jackets with "Police" embossed on both front and back. Their unmarked car proceeded west on Foothill Boulevard, and turned south onto 63rd Avenue. **[a]** As they rounded the corner, they saw four or five youths huddled around a small red car parked at the curb. When the youths, [including Hodari D.], saw the officers' car approaching they apparently panicked, and took flight. * * *

The officers were suspicious and gave chase. **[b]** McColgin remained in the car * * *; Pertoso left the car [and chased on foot]. Hodari [emerged from an alley and did not see] Pertoso until the officer was almost upon him, whereupon he tossed away what appeared to be a small rock. A moment later, Pertoso tackled Hodari, handcuffed him, and radioed for assistance. Hodari was found to be carrying $130 in cash and a pager; and the rock he had discarded was found to be crack cocaine.

In the juvenile proceeding brought against him, Hodari moved to suppress the evidence relating to the cocaine. The court denied the motion without opinion. The California Court of Appeal reversed, holding that Hodari had been "seized" when he saw Officer Pertoso running towards him, that this seizure was unreasonable under the Fourth Amendment, and that the evidence of cocaine had to be suppressed as the fruit of that illegal seizure. The California Supreme Court denied the State's application for review. We granted certiorari. * * *

As this case comes to us, the only issue presented is whether, at the time he dropped the drugs, Hodari had been "seized" within the meaning of the Fourth Amendment. **[c]** If so, respondent argues, the drugs were the fruit of that seizure and the evidence concerning them was properly excluded. If not, the drugs were abandoned by Hodari and lawfully recovered by the police, and the evidence should have been admitted. (In addition, of course, Pertoso's seeing the rock of cocaine, at least if he recognized it as such, would provide reasonable suspicion for the unquestioned seizure that occurred when he tackled Hodari. * * *).

We have long understood that the Fourth Amendment's protection against "unreasonable . . . seizures" includes seizure of the person. * * * From the time of the founding to the present, the word "seizure" has meant a "taking possession." * * * For most purposes at common law, the word connoted not merely grasping, or applying physical force to, the animate or inanimate object in question, but actually bringing it within physical control. **[d]** A ship still fleeing, even though under attack, would not be considered to have been seized as a war prize. * * * To constitute an arrest, however—the quintessential *seizure of the person* under our Fourth Amendment jurisprudence—the mere grasping or application of physical force with lawful authority, whether or not it succeeded in subduing the arrestee, was sufficient. * * *

To say that an arrest is effected by the slightest application of physical force, despite the arrestee's escape, is not to say that for Fourth Amendment purposes there is a *continuing* arrest during the period of fugitivity. If, for example, Pertoso had laid his hands upon Hodari to arrest him, but Hodari had broken away and had *then* cast away the cocaine, it would hardly be realistic to say that that disclosure had been made during the course of an arrest. * * * The present case, however, is even one step further removed. It does not involve the application of any physical force; Hodari was untouched by Officer Pertoso at the time he discarded the cocaine. His defense relies instead upon the proposition that a seizure occurs "when the officer, by means of physical force *or show of authority*, has in some way restrained the liberty of a citizen." *Terry v. Ohio* (emphasis added). Hodari contends (and we accept as true for purposes of this decision) that Pertoso's pursuit qualified as a "show of authority" calling upon Hodari to halt. The narrow question before us is whether, with respect to a show of authority as with respect to application of physical force, a seizure occurs even though the subject does not yield. We hold that it does not.

The language of the Fourth Amendment, of course, cannot sustain respondent's contention. The word "seizure" readily bears the meaning of a laying on of hands or application of physical force to restrain movement, even when it is ultimately unsuccessful. ("She seized the purse-snatcher, but he broke out of her grasp.") It does not remotely apply, however, to the prospect of a policeman yelling "Stop, in the name of the law!" at a fleeing form that continues to flee. That is no seizure. **[e]** Nor can the result respondent wishes to achieve be produced—indirectly, as it were—by suggesting that Pertoso's uncomplied-with show of authority was a common-law arrest, and then appealing to the principle that all common-law arrests are seizures. An arrest requires *either* physical force (as described above) *or*, where that is absent, *submission* to the assertion of authority. * * *

---

[a] Does a group of huddled teenagers provide grounds to arrest them? To forcibly stop them under *Terry?*

[b] Do you think that a teen who runs from the sight of a cop should be chased? If caught, should he be arrested or subjected to field interrogation?

[c] California conceded that the flight of the youths upon seeing the police was not in itself reasonable suspicion for a *Terry* stop. Although Justice Scalia thought the point was arguable, he was bound by this concession. The issue was left open for a later case.

[d] Is the chase of a sailing ship on the high seas a good analogy for a police officer chasing a youth through a city neighborhood?

[e] As *Watson* demonstrated, a strict reading of the language of the Constitution does not always bind the Court. Is it reasonable to view a chase as a seizure if the police officer is close to the person running and is likely to capture him?

We do not think it desirable, even as a policy matter, to stretch the Fourth Amendment beyond its words and beyond the meaning of arrest, as respondent urges. Street pursuits always place the public at some risk, and compliance with police orders to stop should therefore be encouraged. * * *

Respondent contends that his position is sustained by the so-called *Mendenhall* test, . . . "A person has been 'seized' within the meaning of the Fourth Amendment only if, in view of all the circumstances surrounding the incident, a reasonable person would have believed that he was not free to leave." * * * **[f]** In seeking to rely upon that test here, respondent fails to read it carefully. It says that a person has been seized "only if," not that he has been seized "whenever"; it states a *necessary*, but not a *sufficient* condition for seizure—or, more precisely, for seizure effected through a "show of authority." *Mendenhall* establishes that the test for existence of a "show of authority" is an objective one: not whether the citizen perceived that he was being ordered to restrict his movement, but whether the officer's words and actions would have conveyed that to a reasonable person. * * *

[This case is like the chase in *Brower v. Inyo County* (1989): there was no arrest until Brower crashed into the roadblock.]

In sum, assuming that Pertoso's pursuit in the present case constituted a "show of authority" enjoining Hodari to halt, since Hodari did not comply with that injunction he was not seized until he was tackled. The cocaine abandoned while he was running was in this case not the fruit of a seizure, and his motion to exclude evidence of it was properly denied. We reverse the decision of the California Court of Appeal, and remand for further proceedings not inconsistent with this opinion.

JUSTICE STEVENS, with whom JUSTICE MARSHALL joins, dissenting.

The Court's narrow construction of the word "seizure" represents a significant, and in my view, unfortunate, departure from prior case law construing the Fourth Amendment. * * * [T]he Court now adopts a definition of "seizure" that is unfaithful to a long line of Fourth Amendment cases. Even if the Court were defining seizure for the first time, which it is not, the definition that it chooses today is profoundly unwise. **[g]** In its decision, the Court assumes, without acknowledging, that a police officer may now fire his weapon at an innocent citizen and not implicate the Fourth Amendment—as long as he misses his target.

For the purposes of decision, the following propositions are not in dispute. First, when Officer Pertoso began his pursuit of respondent, the officer did not have a lawful basis for either stopping or arresting respondent. * * * Second, the officer's chase amounted to a "show of force" as soon as respondent saw the officer nearly upon him. * * * Third, the act of discarding the rock of cocaine was the direct consequence of the show of force. * * * Fourth, as the Court correctly demonstrates, no common-law arrest occurred until the officer tackled respondent. * * * Thus, the Court is quite right in concluding that the abandonment of the rock was not the fruit of a common-law arrest.

It is equally clear, however, that if the officer had succeeded in touching respondent before he dropped the rock—even if he did not subdue him—an arrest would have occurred. **[h]** * * * In that event (assuming the touching precipitated the abandonment), the evidence would have been the fruit of an unlawful common-law arrest. The distinction between the actual case and the hypothetical case is the same as the distinction between the common-law torts of assault and battery—a touching converts the former into the latter. Although the distinction between assault and battery was important for pleading purposes, * * * the distinction should not take on constitutional dimensions. The Court mistakenly allows this common-law distinction to define its interpretation of the Fourth Amendment.

At the same time, the Court fails to recognize the existence of another, more telling, common-law distinction—the distinction between an arrest and an attempted arrest. As the Court teaches us, the distinction between battery and assault was critical to a correct understanding of the common law of arrest. * * * ("An arrest requires either physical force . . . *or*, where that is absent, *submission* to the assertion of authority"). However, the facts of this case do not describe an actual arrest, but rather, an unlawful *attempt* to take a presumptively innocent person into custody. Such an attempt was unlawful at common law. **[i]** Thus, if the Court wants to define the scope of the Fourth Amendment based on the common law, it should look, not to the common law of arrest, but to the common law of attempted arrest, according to the facts of this case.

* * *

[The dissent goes on to criticize the majority for taking a narrow view of seizure that goes against the policy purposes of *Katz* that broadened the range of behaviors that came within the scope of Fourth Amendment seizures, such as the stop and frisk in *Terry v. Ohio*. *Terry* said that a Fourth Amendment seizure occurs when an officer, by means of physical force or show of authority, has in some way restrained a citizen's liberty. Such an interference with liberty occurred in this case, and so the majority's common law reasoning fails to comport with the constitutional dimensions of Fourth Amendment law after *Terry*.]

Even though momentary, a seizure occurs whenever an objective evaluation of a police officer's show of force conveys the message that the citizen is not entirely free to leave—in other words, that his or her liberty is being restrained in a significant way. * * *

* * *

[f] Would it not seem to a reasonable person, from the officer's actions, that Hodari D. believed he was not free to leave? Does this conclusion help Hodari D.'s argument?

[g] If a police officer, without probable cause or reasonable suspicion, fired a gun at you and missed, should you be able to claim a violation of your Fourth Amendment rights in a civil suit against the officer? If so, this example undermines Justice Scalia's argument.

[h] A touching would manifest the officer's intent to arrest and would make the person liable for resisting arrest. Should constitutional rights turn on whether the officer "tagged" the fleeing youth?

[i] This challenges the accuracy and completeness of Justice Scalia's common law analysis—an especially sharp attack because Justice Scalia, as an originalist, relies heavily on the common law.

The second element contained in the idea that an assessment of the whole picture must yield a particularized suspicion is the concept that the process just described must raise a suspicion that the particular individual being stopped is engaged in wrongdoing. (*United States v. Cortez*, 1981)

Cortez continues to support the concept of **police officer expertise**, which was a basis of finding reasonable suspicion in the *Terry* case.

Inferences were key to the decision in ***United States v. Arvizu*** (2002). Arvizu was driving a minivan with his wife and children on an unpaved road in a remote area in the Coronado National Forest of southeastern Arizona known for drug trafficking. Border patrol checkpoints are staffed intermittently, and roving patrols are used to apprehend smugglers trying to circumvent the checkpoints. Magnetic sensors facilitate agents' efforts in patrolling these areas. A sensor was triggered around 2:15 p.m. This timing coincided with the point when agents begin heading back to the checkpoint for a shift change, leaving the area unpatrolled. Alien smugglers do extensive scouting and seem to be most active when agents are returning to the checkpoint. An agent told Agent Stoddard that the same sensor had gone off several weeks before, leading to the apprehension of a drug-carrying minivan using the same route.

Stoddard proceeded to the area and observed the minivan passing. As it approached, it slowed dramatically, from about 50 miles per hour to 25 or 30 miles per hour. He saw five occupants inside: two adults in the front seat and three children in the back. The driver appeared stiff and his posture very rigid. He did not look at Stoddard and seemed to be trying to pretend that Stoddard was not there. Stoddard thought this suspicious because in his experience on patrol most people look over and see what is going on, and in that area most drivers give border patrol agents a friendly wave. Stoddard noticed that the knees of the two children sitting in the very back seat were unusually high, as if their feet were propped up on some cargo on the floor. As Stoddard followed the minivan, all of the children, still facing forward, put their hands up at the same time and began to wave at Stoddard in an abnormal way. It looked to Stoddard as if the children were being instructed. Their odd waving continued on and off for about four to five minutes. A registration check disclosed that the minivan was registered to an address in Douglas, Arizona, four blocks north of the border in an area notorious for alien and narcotics smuggling. Stoddard stopped the van, asked if he could search, and Arvizu agreed. A duffel bag containing 128.85 pounds of marijuana was found.

The U.S. Court of Appeals struck down the stop, by isolating the factors and noting that each was innocent. For example, that court noted that slowing down after seeing an officer is common. It dismissed entirely the children's waving, saying, "If every odd act engaged in by one's children . . . could contribute to a finding of reasonable suspicion, the vast majority of American parents might be stopped regularly within a block of their homes."

The Supreme Court reversed the decision and unanimously upheld the stop. It emphasized that the totality of the circumstances must be considered. "This process allows officers to draw on their own experience and specialized training to make inferences from and deductions about the cumulative information available to them that 'might well elude an untrained person.'" The Court noted that it has deliberately avoided reducing reasonable suspicion to "a neat set of legal rules." Giving due weight to the factual inferences drawn by Stoddard and the district court judge, the Court ruled that the agent had reasonable suspicion to believe that Arvizu was engaged in illegal activity.

BREVITY REQUIREMENT   Another automobile stop and frisk case clarified an important *Terry* rule: A legal detention must be reasonably brief. In ***United States v. Sharpe*** (1985), a Drug Enforcement Agency (DEA) agent patrolling a road under surveillance for suspected drug trafficking noticed an overloaded pickup truck with an attached trailer being followed closely by a Pontiac. After following the two vehicles for twenty miles, the officer decided to make an investigatory stop and radioed the South Carolina Highway Patrol for assistance. When the DEA agent and the state police officer indicated that the two vehicles were to pull over, the Pontiac did so, but the truck continued along the road in an attempt to evade the state police. The driver of the Pontiac was detained for twenty minutes while the DEA agent followed the truck, approached it after it was stopped, smelled marijuana in it, and returned to the detained Pontiac. While the Court found that the officer had reasonable suspicion to make the initial stop, at issue was whether a twenty-minute detention was too long under the *Terry* doctrine because it violated the **brevity requirement** for stops. The Supreme Court held that whether a stop is too long (and thus becomes an arrest) depends not only on the length of time of the stop but also on the surrounding circumstances. The question is whether the length of time employed was reasonable. In *Sharpe*, the delay occurred because of the evasive action of the driver of the truck. The Court found that because the police acted diligently to ascertain the facts without creating unnecessary delays, *Terry* was not violated. Note that a twenty-minute stop was sufficiently long so that a special reason had to be supplied to justify it. *Terry* stops are supposed to be just long enough for an officer to ask questions to determine, based on objective factors, whether there is probable cause to arrest or no basis for further detention.

AUTHORITY TO STOP AN AUTOMOBILE   In *Delaware v. Prouse* (1979), a patrol officer made a "routine" stop of a car, explaining, "I saw the car in the area and wasn't answering any complaints, so I decided to pull them off." Prior to the vehicle stop, he did not observe any traffic or equipment violations or any suspicious activity. He made the stop merely to check the driver's license and registration. The officer did not act pursuant to any standards, guidelines, or procedures pertaining to document spot checks as defined by his department or the state attorney general. During the stop, the officer smelled marijuana and made an arrest and seizure.

Lower courts had split on whether this kind of vehicle stop, without reasonable suspicion or probable cause, violated the Fourth Amendment. The Supreme Court, holding this kind of stop and seizure unconstitutional, was not writing on a blank slate. Four years earlier, it had decided in *United States v. Brignoni-Ponce* (1975) that Border Patrol agents conducting roving patrols near the international border violated the Fourth Amendment by stopping vehicles at random. Although intercepting illegal aliens was important, the Court felt that it was unconstitutional to stop cars—not at the border or at fixed checkpoints—but on roads within one hundred miles of the Mexican border, without establishing reasonable suspicion. The reasons are that such stops (1) interfere with freedom of movement, (2) are inconvenient and time consuming, and (3) may create substantial anxiety for a driver who is pulled over for no apparent reason. In contrast, a motorist does not feel the same anxiety at a roadblock or fixed checkpoint where other motorists are observed going through the same drill. The Court dismissed the arguments that an automobile stop is an administrative search or that people have a lesser expectation of privacy in a car than in a home:

> An individual operating or traveling in an automobile does not lose all reasonable expectation of privacy simply because the automobile and its use are subject to government regulation. Automobile travel is a basic, pervasive, and often necessary mode of transportation to and from one's home, workplace, and leisure activities. Many people spend more hours each day traveling in cars than walking on the streets. Undoubtedly, many find a greater sense of security and privacy in traveling in an automobile than they do in exposing themselves by pedestrian or other modes of travel. Were the individual subject to unfettered governmental intrusion every time he entered an automobile, the security guaranteed by the Fourth Amendment would be seriously circumscribed. (*Delaware v. Prouse*, 1979)

The stop in *Prouse* was unconstitutional, and the evidence had to be suppressed.

An important related issue is whether a police officer can stop a car based on reasonable suspicion of a traffic offense when the *true motive* of the officer is to search for drugs—the **pretext search** issue. This question is highly contentious because police departments, especially those astride busy highways, "earn" billions of dollars in drug asset forfeitures of cars and cash and so have an incentive to stringently enforce traffic laws. The question has become politically explosive because it has been shown that this practice has been accompanied with "racial profiling" that disproportionately targets minorities. (See the "Law in Society" section in Chapter 5.)

A unanimous Supreme Court resolved the pretext search issue in favor of the police in *Whren v. United States* (1996) by making it clear that an automobile stop and arrest are valid whenever the police have objective evidence of probable cause of a traffic violation. On a June evening,

> plainclothes vice-squad officers of the District of Columbia Metropolitan Police Department were patrolling a "high drug area" of the city in an unmarked car. Their suspicions were aroused when they passed a dark Pathfinder truck with temporary license plates and youthful occupants waiting at a stop sign, the driver looking down into the lap of the passenger at his right. The truck remained stopped at the intersec-

tion for what seemed an unusually long time—more than 20 seconds. When the police car executed a U-turn in order to head back toward the truck, the Pathfinder turned suddenly to its right, without signaling, and sped off at an "unreasonable" speed. The policemen followed, and in a short while overtook the Pathfinder when it stopped behind other traffic at a red light. They pulled up alongside, and Officer Ephraim Soto stepped out and approached the driver's door, identifying himself as a police officer and directing the driver, petitioner Brown, to put the vehicle in park. When Soto drew up to the driver's window, he immediately observed two large plastic bags of what appeared to be crack cocaine in petitioner Whren's hands. Petitioners were arrested, and quantities of several types of illegal drugs were retrieved from the vehicle. (*Whren v. United States*, 1996)

Whren argued that the stop was not "really" for the traffic infractions—that the traffic stop was a pretext for searching for drugs. The Supreme Court, however, ruled that the Fourth Amendment review standard is objective, rather than subjective, placing examination of the officer's motives off limits. Whren then argued that D.C. police regulations "permit plainclothes officers in unmarked vehicles to enforce traffic laws 'only in the case of a violation that is so grave as to pose an immediate threat to the safety of others.'" In light of these regulations, he suggested that for an auto stop for a traffic violation to be valid, in addition to having probable cause of the traffic infraction, the stop must be one that would typically be made for a traffic infraction.

The Court refused to establish such a rule. The motives of officers are irrelevant in inventory searches, administrative searches, maritime searches, and searches incident to arrest as long as there is an objective legal standard—probable cause—to support the intrusion. The only cases in which the Court has balanced the interests of a defendant against the state to find that probable cause is not a sufficient standard are cases involving

> searches or seizures conducted in an extraordinary manner, unusually harmful to an individual's privacy or even physical interests—such as, for example, seizure by means of deadly force, [*Tennessee v. Garner* (1985)], unannounced entry into a home, [*Wilson v. Arkansas* (1995)], entry into a home without a warrant, [*Welsh v. Wisconsin* (1984)], or physical penetration of the body, [*Winston v. Lee* (1985)]. The making of a traffic stop out-of-uniform does not remotely qualify as such an extreme practice, and so is governed by the usual rule that probable cause to believe the law has been broken "outbalances" private interest in avoiding police contact. (*Whren v. United States*, 1996)

Field interrogation following an automobile search was an issue in ***Ornelas v. United States*** (1996). On an early December morning in Milwaukee, an experienced detective spotted a 1981 two-door Oldsmobile with California license plates in a motel parking lot. The car was registered to Ornelas, who with no reservations had checked into the motel with another man at 4 a.m. "The car attracted [the detective's] attention for two reasons: because older model, two-door General Motors cars are a favorite with drug couriers because it is easy to hide things in them; and because California is a 'source State' for drugs." To confirm this "profile" information, a check of the DEA's "Narcotics and Dangerous Drugs Information System (NADDIS), a federal database of known and suspected drug trafficker," revealed that both names of the motel guests appeared as known or suspected drug dealers.

The two men were subjected to a *Terry* stop when entering the car later that morning. The officers, who had searched two thousand cars for drugs over a period of nine years, looked into the car. One "noticed that a panel above the right rear passenger armrest felt somewhat loose and suspected that the panel might have been removed and contraband hidden inside. . . . [He] dismantled the panel and discovered two kilograms of cocaine." Was there reasonable suspicion to stop the men and probable cause to remove the panel? The district court ultimately answered each question in the affirmative.

The trial judge found that reasonable suspicion existed because "the model, age, and source-State origin of the car, and the fact that two men traveling together checked into a motel at 4 o'clock in the morning without reservations, formed a *drug-courier profile*. This profile, together with the NADDIS reports, gave rise to reasonable suspicion of drug-trafficking activity. . . . [R]easonable suspicion became probable cause when [the officer] found the loose panel."

Although the Supreme Court remanded the case to the Court of Appeals to review the District Court's decision, Chief Justice Rehnquist, a Milwaukee native who had moved to the warmer climate of Arizona, recited specific local facts to guide that court. "For example, what may not amount to reasonable suspicion at a motel located alongside a transcontinental highway at the height of the summer tourist season may rise to that level in December in Milwaukee." Given Milwaukee's cold temperatures in December, it is "a reasonable inference that a Californian stopping in Milwaukee in December is either there to transact business or to visit family or friends." *Ornelas* also indicates that the use of drug courier profiles is now pervasive in American policing.

CONTROLLING PEOPLE IN THE STOPPED AUTOMOBILE   The Supreme Court has given police almost complete control either to order the driver and passengers to remain in the automobile when it is stopped or to order the driver and passengers out. The primary rationale in these case is the safety of the officer.

In *Pennsylvania v. Mimms* (1977), an automobile was stopped for an expired license plate. On ordering the driver out, the officer noticed a bulge under the driver's sports jacket. A frisk produced a loaded revolver in Mimms's waistband. Balancing the interests of individual privacy against the safety of law enforcement officers, the Court unanimously upheld the officer's frisk and noted that many police officers are killed during routine traffic stops. Against this, the added intrusion of requiring that a driver exit the car momentarily is so minimal that it hardly rises to the level of a "petty indignity"; at most, it is a mere inconvenience that cannot prevail against legitimate concerns for the officer's safety.

The rule of *Mimms* was extended to passengers in *Maryland v. Wilson* (1997). Police stopped a speeding automobile—a rental car with no regular license plate. The officer ordered the driver and the passengers to exit the car. There was no legal suspicion that the passengers were engaged in any illegal activity. As Wilson, a passenger, got out of the car, an amount of crack cocaine fell to the ground. Maryland's highest court suppressed the evidence on the ground that the police had no authority to order passengers out of the car without some level of individualized suspicion. The court viewed the order to exit as a Fourth Amendment personal seizure. The Supreme Court, in an opinion by Chief Justice Rehnquist, reversed. The *Mimms* rationale—the officer's safety—applied equally to passengers. Indeed, the presence of additional people in the car increases the danger to the police. Despite the lack of probable cause or reasonable suspicion against the passenger, and the fact that a passenger has a greater liberty interest than the driver, as a practical matter the passenger is already stopped by the police detaining the vehicle. This case is analogous to *Michigan v. Summers* (1981), which states that police may temporarily detain a person whose home is being searched under a search warrant.

Justice Stevens dissented, arguing that statistics show no greater danger to police from passengers in stopped cars; the decision intrudes on personal liberty without solid reason. Justice Kennedy dissented, saying, "Traffic stops, even for minor violations, can take upwards of 30 minutes. When an officer commands passengers innocent of any violation to leave the vehicle and stand by the side of the road in full view of the public, the seizure is serious, not trivial." This decision, plus *Whren* (pretextual stops), "puts tens of millions of passengers at risk of arbitrary control by the police." When the *Wilson* rule is combined with the decision of *Wyoming v. Houghton* (1999) (see Chapter 5), which allows the police to search the handbag of a passenger when there is probable cause to search the automobile, and with the *Atwater* rule, which authorizes the custodial seizure for any arrest, an officer's control over a stopped automobile is complete.[30]

Terry in Tight Places

The nature of a stop was explored in *Immigration and Naturalization Service v. Delgado* (1984). In that case, INS officers looking for illegal immigrants walked through a factory with the owner's consent. They briefly questioned workers at their workstations and, if reasonable, asked to see immigration papers. Agents were posted at the factory exits. The Supreme Court held that the illegal workers were not seized within the meaning of the Fourth Amendment, reasoning that "police questioning, by itself, is unlikely to result in a Fourth Amendment violation." The factory workers were not free to leave, but the "detention" was caused not by the police but by the workers' normal employment requirements. The Court held that the agents were simply questioning people and that these encounters were consensual. Justices Brennan and Marshall dissented, arguing that the show of authority by the immigration officials was sufficiently substantial to "overbear the will of any reasonable person." Based on this show of authority, reasoned the dissenters, the factory workers were forcibly stopped within the meaning of *Terry*.

The use of drug courier profiles at airports (discussed later in this chapter) spawned similar practices at bus and train stations. In ***Florida v. Bostick*** (1991), decided shortly after *Hodari D.*, the Supreme Court confirmed its sharp swing toward supporting the police in investigatory stops.

> Two [Broward County sheriff's] officers, complete with badges, insignia and one of them holding a recognizable zipper pouch, containing a pistol, boarded a bus bound from Miami to Atlanta during a stopover in Fort Lauderdale. Eyeing the passengers, the officers admittedly without articulable suspicion, picked out the defendant passenger and asked to inspect his ticket and identification. The ticket, from Miami to Atlanta, matched the defendant's identification and both were immediately returned to him as unremarkable. However, the two police officers persisted and explained their presence as narcotics agents on the lookout for illegal drugs. In pursuit of that aim, they then requested the defendant's consent to search his luggage. (*Florida v. Bostick*, 1991)

Cocaine was found in the bag. Before they began this encounter, the officers had no reasonable suspicion or probable cause to believe that Terrance Bostick was carrying drugs.

The issue was whether Bostick consented to the search or whether he was seized. Justice O'Connor's majority opinion held that Bostick consented: "Our cases make it clear that a seizure does not occur simply because a police officer approaches an individual and asks a few questions. So long as a reasonable person would feel free to disregard the police and go about his business, . . . the encounter is consensual and no reasonable suspicion is required" (*Florida v. Bostick*, 1991, internal quotation marks modified). It is curious that the Court cited *Hodari D.* for this proposition rather than relying exclusively on *Mendenhall*. The Court's majority in these cases appears to have selected a different theory in each case to ensure the decision would favor law enforcement: Under *Hodari D.*, one who flees is not seized; under *Mendenhall-Bostick*, one who relents, consents. This seems to create a "heads I win, tails you lose" rule, with the police holding the coin.

Justice Marshall dissented, joined by Justices Blackmun and Stevens. He harshly castigated this form of investigation: "These sweeps are conducted in 'dragnet' style," noting that this high-volume practice (sweeps of three thousand buses in a nine-month period) inconveniences a large number of innocent people (one case found that sweeps of a hundred buses resulted in seven arrests). The heart of the dissent was that the police questioning is inherently coercive, undermining consent:

> To put it mildly, these sweeps "are inconvenient, intrusive, and intimidating." They occur within cramped confines, with officers typically placing themselves in between the passenger selected for an interview and the exit of the bus. Because the bus is only temporarily stationed at a point short of its destination, the passengers are in no position to leave as a means of evading the officers' questioning. (*Florida v. Bostick*, 1991, Marshall, J. dissenting)

The majority pointed out, to the contrary, that

> [t]he present case is analytically indistinguishable from *Delgado*. Like the workers in that case, Bostick's freedom of movement was restricted by a factor independent of police conduct—i.e., by his being a passenger on a bus. Accordingly, the "free to leave" analysis on which Bostick relies is inapplicable. In such a situation, the appropriate inquiry is whether a reasonable person would feel free to decline the officers' requests or otherwise terminate the encounter. (*Florida v. Bostick*, 1991)

Indeed, Bostick was told he had a right to refuse; the pouched gun was never removed, nor did the officers ever point it at Bostick or use it in a threatening manner; and Bostick agreed to open his bag. These factors, according to the majority, negated coercion and supported the conclusion that Bostick volunteered to open his bag.

In **United States v. Drayton** (2002), a bus sweep case with facts very similar to *Bostick*, the Supreme Court held that the police need not inform a bus rider that he has a right to refuse to consent to a search of his baggage, relying on *Ohio v. Robinette* (1996) and *Schneckloth v. Bustamonte* (1973). Justice Souter dissented, joined by Justices Stevens and Ginsburg. He argued that if three officers approached a person on the street, hemmed him in very closely, and asked if they could search any luggage, this would be intimidation that undermines consent. The same is the case in the close quarters of a bus with an aisle fifteen inches wide, cramped seats, the police in apparent control of the bus, and officers saying that they were "conducting a bus interdiction" and "wanted cooperation."

Most scholarly commentators agree with the dissent in *Bostick* and refer to the decisions in this case and *Hodari D.* as the "no seizure" rule. Professor Gerald Ashdown, for example, writes, "Hardly anyone who is confronted and questioned by armed officers, asked for identification and permission to search, believes he is free to do much of anything, certainly not to refuse to answer or to walk away. Anyone with a lick of sense knows that doing these things will only aggravate the situation and cause him more trouble."[31]

AUTOMOBILE CHECKLANES   In *Delaware v. Prouse* (1979), discussed earlier in this chapter, the Court held that a car cannot be stopped while proceeding in traffic unless an officer has specific suspicion to believe that it was engaged in a traffic violation or a criminal act. *Prouse* distinguished on-the-road stops from stops at roadblocks or fixed checkpoints, contending that motorists do not feel the same anxiety in the latter situations because they observe other motorists going through the same drill. The Supreme Court specifically upheld sobriety checklanes in **Michigan Department of State Police v. Sitz** (1990). These stops are not Fourth Amendment seizures.

In deciding that **sobriety checklanes** are not a violation of a person's reasonable expectation of privacy, the Court relied on border search fixed checkpoint cases: *United States v. Ortiz* (1975) and *United States v. Martinez-Fuerte* (1976). Those cases compared the subjective and psychological level of intrusion of fixed checkpoints on the highway as compared to stops made by roving patrols. Since at the fixed checkpoint the motorist sees other vehicles being briefly detained and sees the visible indicia of the police officers' authority, "he is much less likely to be frightened or annoyed by the intrusion" (*United States v. Ortiz*, quoted in *United States v. Martinez-Fuerte*). These findings were applied to the Michigan sobriety checklane situation: "Here, checkpoints are selected pursuant to the guidelines, and uniformed police officers stop every approaching vehicle. The intrusion resulting from the brief stop at the sobriety checkpoint is for constitutional purposes indistinguishable from the checkpoint stops we upheld in *Martinez-Fuerte*" (*Michigan Department. of State Police v. Sitz*). Chief Justice Rehnquist's majority opinion also pointed out that drunk driving is a serious national problem resulting in approximately twenty-five thousand deaths annually. The idea of the checklane as a regulatory device played some role in the decision.

In *Sitz*, the Court also considered whether the *effectiveness* of checklanes in combating drunk driving was a factor of Fourth Amendment balancing. Sitz argued that other methods were more effective. The Court ruled that the choice of enforcement modalities was up to the legislature and the executive branches—politically accountable officials—rather than allowing the courts to determine which law enforcement techniques to employ to deal with a serious public danger.

Justice Stevens, dissenting, disagreed with the Court's finding that sobriety checklanes are essentially the same as border checklanes. Sobriety checklanes, for example, occur at night, are not at fixed checkpoints but are set up quickly to effect the element of surprise, and are less standardized than a review of registration papers, for the officer must visually assess the sobriety of the driver.

An important ruling, **City of Indianapolis v. Edmond** (2000), limited the *Sitz* ruling to sobriety checklanes. The Court decided (6–3) that a roadblock whose primary purpose was general law enforcement and the detection of ordinary criminal wrongdoing, and not traffic safety, violated the Fourth Amendment. Indianapolis police set up roadblocks identified as "narcotics checkpoints," detained drivers for about two to three minutes each, examined each driver's license and registration, and had a narcotics-detection dog walk around the vehicle. In finding this practice unconstitutional, the Court distinguished the reasoning of pretext stops (*Whren*), of brief checkpoint stops for purposes of detecting alcohol-impaired drivers or illegal aliens (*Sitz* and *Martinez-Fuerte*), and special needs (*National Treasury Employees Union v. Von Raab*, 1989). The city argued that all other checkpoint stops upheld by the Court employed arrests and criminal prosecutions in pursuit of other goals that were essentially not the enforcement of the criminal law. In a statement that captured the deep policy concerns of the Court, Justice O'Connor, in her majority opinion, replied:

> If we were to rest the case at this high level of generality, there would be little check on the ability of the authorities to construct roadblocks for almost any conceivable law enforcement purpose. Without drawing the line at roadblocks designed primarily to serve the general interest in crime control, the Fourth Amendment would do little to prevent such intrusions from becoming a routine part of American life. (*City of Indianapolis v. Edmond*, 2000)

After a raft of cases that expanded the ability of police to stop virtually any car, control the passengers, and examine all containers, the Court was faced with a line, which if crossed might have made the total surveillance of anyone walking abroad subject to inspection. The Court was informed by a brief by the National League of Cities that many cities were prepared to initiate narcotics checkpoints depending on the outcome of *Edmond*. What was left unsaid was that a ruling favorable to the government in *Edmond* could have opened the door to virtually unrestricted on-the-street surveillance with drug-sniffing dogs and with highly intrusive electronic and thermal-sensing devices that penetrated the clothing of individuals. It is noteworthy that the three most conservative justices—Rehnquist, Scalia, and Thomas—dissented but that swing justices—O'Connor and Kennedy—voted to declare such practices unconstitutional.

Edmond was held not to prevent informational roadblocks. In ***Illinois v. Lidster*** (2004), police in Lombard, Illinois, partially blocked a highway to force cars into a single lane. At the checkpoint, an officer asked the occupants whether they had seen anything happen there the previous weekend. Each driver was handed a flyer that said "ALERT . . . FATAL HIT & RUN ACCIDENT." It requested "assistance in identifying the vehicle and driver in this accident which killed a 70 year old bicyclist." Each stop lasted about ten to fifteen seconds. As Lidster approached the roadblock, he swerved, nearly hit an officer, and was arrested and convicted for driving under the influence of alcohol. He challenged the constitutionality of the roadblock stop. The Supreme Court held that a roadblock of this type is constitutional as long as it is reasonably tailored to the particular circumstances of the case and to a legitimate law enforcement function. The stop in this case was constitutional for a variety of reasons. The primary purpose of the stop was not to investigate the occupants for criminal activity but to obtain information about an unsolved fatal hit-and-run that had occurred in the same area a few days before. Such stops are brief and not likely to produce anxiety. Police are not likely to ask incriminating questions, any more than would police questioning pedestrians in the vicinity of a crime as to whether they have seen anything suspicious. Voluntary requests for information "play a vital role in police investigatory work." The traffic delays that result "should prove no more onerous than many that typically accompany normal traffic congestion." The crime being investigated was serious, and the informational checkpoint in this case was narrowly tailored to getting specific information about it. The law enforcement needs and the reasonableness of the intrusion outweighed the minimal interference with liberty in this case.

Terry at the Airport: Drug Stops and Drug Courier Profiles

The typical scenario of the cases in this section, previously described in ***United States v. Mendenhall*** (1980) (see Chapter 3), is for narcotics agents to ask to speak with a person at an airport. The officers regularly scan airports and other transportation hubs for people who may be transporting illegal drugs. These cases differ from those in which agents have been tipped off by informants that a specific courier is arriving at an airport. Instead, the officers approach a person on a hunch that he or she (often young people of college age) may be carrying drugs or based on a person fitting a "profile" of variables that seem to be characteristic of drug couriers. The cases in this section ask whether the facts amount to a voluntary consent encounter, a *Terry* stop and search, or an arrest. They also describe the path of the Court's cases that eventually accepted the drug courier profile as a constitutional basis for an investigative stop.

The **drug courier profile** was developed in the early 1970s by DEA agent Paul Markonni, who was working out of the Detroit Metropolitan Airport. He borrowed the idea from an airplane hijacker profile developed in the late 1960s. The use of drug profiles spread to airports throughout the nation.[32] "Because even local police officers now receive high quality training by the DEA, street level drug interdiction programs have resulted in surprisingly few complaints of individual police officer misconduct, such as unjustified, armed threats or arbitrary harassment."[33] Stephen Hall briefly describes how drug courier profiles are used:

> One or more DEA agents (or other law enforcement officers) observe individuals at an airport for characteristics that match the profile. Agents single out an individual as a match, approach the suspect, and identify themselves as law enforcement officers. They then ask the suspect's name and destination. If the Agents are still suspicious, they usually ask the suspect to accompany them to another location for further questioning. At this point, agents ask the suspect to consent to a search of his person, luggage or both.[34]

In *Mendenhall* (1980), a young woman who deplaned at Detroit Metropolitan Airport was politely approached by DEA agents and asked to accompany them to a room. (See "Consent Searches" in Chapter 3.) After some discussion, Mendenhall agreed to be searched by a female officer in private, and drugs were found on her person. *Mendenhall* can be read for three purposes. First, given the numerous opinions of the justices, it demonstrates the difficulty of sorting out the facts to determine whether they amounted to a consent encounter or a personal seizure. Second, it shows a concern with drug courier profiles. Third, it established the test for a seizure: Did the person reasonably believe that he or she was not free to leave in view of all of the circumstances surrounding the incident? Although the *Mendenhall* test was modified to fit the contours of the chase in *Hodari D.*, it was, and still is, the standard that is applied in airport scenarios.

The stop of Mendenhall at the airport was triggered by her supposedly fitting the characteristics of a drug courier profile. Justice Powell spoke favorably of this device. He referred to "highly skilled agents" carrying out a "highly specialized law enforcement operation" being assigned to the Detroit airport "as part of a nationwide program to intercept drug couriers transporting narcotics between major drug sources and distribution centers in the United States." He noted, "During the first 18 months of the program, agents watching the Detroit Airport searched 141 persons in 96 encounters. They found controlled substances in 77 of the encounters and arrested 122 persons" (*United States v. Mendenhall*, 1980, Powell, J., concurring). Despite this endorsement, neither the lead opinion nor the concurrence in *Mendenhall* was based on a blanket acceptance of the profile. The tone of Justice White's dissent was less enthusiastic: "[T]he Government sought to justify the stop by arguing that Ms. Mendenhall's behavior had given rise to reasonable suspicion because it was consistent with portions of the so-called 'drug courier profile,' an informal amalgam of characteristics thought to be associated with persons carrying illegal drugs" (*United States v. Mendenhall*, 1980, White, J., dissenting). Although the majority in *Mendenhall* held that the encounter did not violate the Fourth Amendment, it did so on the basis of consent. *Mendenhall* did not constitutionalize the drug courier profile.

The Supreme Court expressed skepticism of profiles and found no basis of reasonable suspicion in **Reid v. Georgia** (1980, *per curiam*). The mere fact that a man who got off a plane in Atlanta from Fort Lauderdale, Florida (a "principal place of origin of cocaine sold elsewhere in the country"), and, exiting in a single-file line, occasionally looked back in the direction of another man carrying a similar shoulder bag, who caught up with Reid and exchanged a few words with him, is hardly the kind of fact that creates a drug courier profile or establishes reasonable suspicion to support an investigative stop.

In **Florida v. Royer** (1983), the Supreme Court held that a seizure at the airport violated Mark Royer's Fourth Amendment rights, but the justices could not agree on a reason. Royer was approached by two county narcotics officers at the Miami International Airport because he purportedly fit a drug courier profile: He had purchased a one-way ticket to New York City, was carrying two American Tourister suitcases that appeared to be heavy, was casually dressed, appeared pale and nervous, paid for his ticket in cash with a large number of bills, and wrote only a name on the airline identification tag. The officers identified themselves and asked Royer if he had a "moment" to speak with them. He said yes. Without oral consent, he produced his ticket and a driver's license upon request. He explained a discrepancy between his name and the name "Holt" written on the baggage tag by saying that a friend named Holt had made the reservations. The officers did not return the ticket or license but asked Royer to accompany them to a room forty feet away. In the small office, Royer was told that he was suspected of transporting narcotics and was asked if he would consent to a search of the suitcases. Without orally responding, Royer produced a key, opened the baggage, and marijuana was found. These events took about fifteen minutes.

The Court's five-judge majority found that, by holding onto Royer's ticket and driver's license, the officers had in effect arrested him without probable cause. When police officers retain these important documents, a reasonable person could not believe that he is free to leave. Thus when Royer went along with the police to the room, he did not consent but had to follow or give up his ticket and license! Holding these documents was the equivalent of a show of force.

Four of the majority justices (White, Powell, Marshall, and Stevens) also believed, however, that facts in *Royer* established reasonable suspicion that would have supported a temporary stop and questioning of Royer to confirm or dispel the suspicion. Because a majority did not share this view, the *Royer* case did not establish the constitutionality of drug courier profiles. It did indicate that a number of justices were leaning in that direction. Nevertheless, the majority felt that the police actions of obtaining the key to Royer's luggage went beyond that justified by a *Terry* stop. This was not a frisk for weapons, but a search for evidence.

Justice Brennan, concurring, thought the majority was wrong to comment on its belief that reasonable suspicion existed. Four dissenting justices (Burger, Blackmun, Rehnquist, and O'Connor) believed that the acts of the police officers were reasonable and would have upheld the encounter as based on consent.

The next airport search case, ***United States v. Place*** (1983), held the stop unconstitutional because the brevity requirement of *Terry* was violated. Raymond Place aroused the suspicions of DEA agents at the Miami International Airport. They briefly detained him for questioning. He agreed to a search of his luggage, but because his airplane was departing, the search was postponed. The agents called ahead to LaGuardia Airport in New York City, where another team of DEA agents observed Place when he arrived. Their suspicions also aroused, they detained him and told Place that they believed he was carrying narcotics. Place did not consent to a search of his luggage. The agents seized the bags, giving Place information as to where they could be retrieved. The bags were then sent to Kennedy Airport, unopened, where a trained narcotics detection dog indicated the presence of drugs. This process took ninety minutes. After the positive identification, as it was Friday afternoon, the bags were held until Monday, when a search warrant was obtained and drugs were found in the bags.

Because Place was detained, not on probable cause but at best on reasonable suspicion, the extent of the detention must be "minimally intrusive of the individual's Fourth Amendment interests." By holding a person's luggage, the person is detained by the police although the person is technically free to go. "[S]uch a seizure can effectively restrain the person since he is subjected to the possible disruption of his travel plans in order to remain with his luggage or to arrange for its return." Thus the seizure of luggage at the airport effectively "seizes" a person. Indeed, the *Terry* brevity principle was violated simply by the length of the detention of Place's luggage. Justice O'Connor noted:

> Although the 90-minute detention of respondent's luggage is sufficient to render the seizure unreasonable, the violation was exacerbated by the failure of the agents to accurately inform respondent of the place to which they were transporting his luggage, of the length of time he might be dispossessed, and of what arrangements would be made for return of the luggage if the investigation dispelled the suspicion. In short, we hold that the detention of respondent's luggage in this case went beyond the narrow authority possessed by police to detain briefly luggage reasonably suspected to contain narcotics. (*United States v. Place*, 1983)

The constitutionality of drug courier profiles was finally upheld in ***United States v. Sokolow*** (1989). Andrew Sokolow was forcibly stopped by DEA agents at the Honolulu airport because he fit the following profile elements: He paid $2,100 for two airplane tickets from a roll of $20 bills; he traveled under a name that did not match the name under which his telephone number was listed; his original destination was Miami, a **source city** for illicit drugs; he stayed in Miami for only forty-eight hours even though a round-trip flight from Honolulu to Miami takes twenty hours; he appeared nervous during his trip; and he checked none of his luggage. He wore the same black jumpsuit with gold jewelry on both his outgoing and returning trips. In Honolulu, Sokolow and a traveling companion were forcibly stopped. They were taken to a DEA office at the airport, where a canine sniff indicated the presence of drugs. Sokolow was arrested, warrants were obtained to search his luggage, and over a thousand grams of cocaine were found.

The Supreme Court held that a suspect fitting a drug courier profile raises the mere suspicion of the agent to the level of reasonable suspicion that allows a *Terry* stop. The majority held that the profile elements in this case amounted to reasonable suspicion. Although each of the facts separately is not indicative of criminality, taken together they were out of the ordinary and amounted to reasonable suspicion. Justice Rehnquist wrote, "While a trip from Honolulu to Miami, standing alone, is not a cause for any sort of suspicion, here there was more: surely few residents of Honolulu travel from that city for 20 hours to spend 48 hours in Miami during the month of July." Second, the Court ruled explicitly that reasonable suspicion may be established even though each articulable element of suspicion is innocent. It is not necessary that there also be evidence of ongoing criminal activity to establish reasonable suspicion, as the lower court had held. Finally, the majority also ruled that it was not necessary for the officers to use the "**least intrusive means** available to verify or dispel their suspicions that he was smuggling narcotics," for example, by approaching the suspect and speaking with him, rather than forcibly detaining him. The least intrusive rule "would unduly hamper the police's ability to make swift on-the-spot decisions—here, respondent was about to get into a taxicab—and it would require courts to 'indulge in "unrealistic second-guessing"'" (*United States v. Sokolow*, 1989).

Justice Marshall offered a spirited attack on the drug courier profiles in *Sokolow* but failed to convince a majority that profiles are flawed. He noted that many cases applying *Terry* required evidence of ongoing criminality—such as taking evasive action, "casing" a store, using an alibi, or being pinpointed by an informant—to trigger the reasonable suspicion standard. No such indicator of criminality existed in this case. Next, he warned that the mechanistic application of a profile would "dull the officer's ability and determination to make sensitive and fact-specific inferences 'in light of his experience.'" Most telling, he observed that what constituted profile factors seemed to shift from case to case. Citing specific cases, previously decided by lower courts, he pointed out that the profile has been held to be established by

- The fact that the suspect was the first to deplane, or was the last to deplane, or got off in the middle.
- That the suspect purchased a one-way ticket or a round-trip ticket.
- That the suspect took a nonstop flight or that the suspect changed planes.
- That the suspect had one shoulder bag or that the suspect had a new suitcase.
- That the suspect was traveling alone or that the suspect was traveling with a companion.
- That the suspect acted too nervously or that he acted too calmly.

Justice Marshall thus demonstrated that the majority's belief that drug courier profiles are sufficiently stable and reliable to authorize investigatory stops is belied by the cases that show that the elements of the profile may shift from case to case.

There is little research on the effectiveness of these profiles, but a reporter's sampling of records at the New York, Miami, and Houston airports indicates "a success rate of about fifty–fifty." A DEA spokesperson conceded that innocent persons are stopped as often as guilty ones, adding, "It's not a science, . . . [i]t's a technique." The story noted that those stopped under a profile are often handcuffed and held for several hours, including being taken to a hospital for x-rays, before being released. The story also suggested that African Americans and Hispanics are stopped more frequently than whites, although the DEA does not keep records of airport stops that can confirm these observations. Finally, the reporter also noted that drug courier profiles are used on highways, in train stations, and on interstate buses, although less frequently than in airports.[35]

Most scholarly commentators are skeptical or critical of these profiles. A primary reason is given by Justice Marshall: "[N]o uniform drug courier profile exists throughout the nation. Instead, agents create their own individual profiles based on their own professional experiences and observations."[36] A trial court noted that the profile consists of "anything that arouses the agent's suspicion."[37] Professors W. R. Janikowski and D. J. Giacopassi point out that unlike the Federal Aviation Administration's "skyjacker profile," which was formulated by psychologists and tested on half a million passengers yielding 1,406 stops and sixteen arrests, "there is some concern as to whether a profile truly exists or whether the profile is, in reality, a loose and malleable compilation of characteristics based on experiential knowledge of the drug trade and the exigencies of the situation."[38] A highly detailed analysis of the use of the profiles by Morgan Cloud, predating *Sokolow*, confirms Justice Marshall's analysis that the profiles are not predictive. By relying on the profiles, the courts are abdicating their constitutional responsibilities.[39]

Terry and Canine Detection Cases

The Court in *United States v. Place* (1983) commented favorably on the canine sniff as an important investigative technique because a "'canine sniff' by a well-trained narcotics detection dog "... does not require opening the luggage. It does not expose noncontraband items that otherwise would remain hidden from public view, as does, for example, an officer's rummaging through the contents of the luggage. Thus, the manner in which information is obtained through this investigative technique is much less intrusive than a typical search." This premise depended on a second, that the sniff or alerting of trained dogs "discloses only the presence or absence of narcotics, a contraband item." If this is true, then the dog sniff reveals information that is limited to contraband, to which the possessor has no constitutionally protected right. The Court created a special niche for the dog sniff technique: "In these respects, the canine sniff is **sui generis**. We are aware of no other investigative procedure that is so limited both in the manner in which the information is obtained and in the content of the information revealed by the procedure." As a result, *Place* held that where police have reasonable suspicion that a person possesses drugs, a trained drug-sniffing canine can properly be used to confirm its presence.

The Supreme Court extended the scope of the dog-sniffing technique in ***Illinois v. Caballes*** (2005), which upheld the use of a trained dog to sniff the car of a motorist stopped for a traffic offense, where the stop did not exceed the time needed to process the traffic matter and was not accompanied by any suspicion against the driver. Caballes was stopped for speeding (6 miles per hour over the speed limit) on an interstate highway. A member of the State Police Drug Interdiction Team overheard the radio report and immediately headed for the scene with his narcotics-detection dog. The dog was walked around the stopped vehicle and alerted at the trunk. "Based on that alert, the officers searched the trunk, found marijuana, and arrested respondent. The entire incident lasted less than 10 minutes." Caballes was convicted of a narcotics offense. The Illinois Supreme Court ruled the marijuana inadmissible because the dog sniff was made without articulable facts to suspect drug activity: It "unjustifiably enlarged the scope of a routine traffic stop into a drug investigation."

The Supreme Court (6–2) reversed. Justice Stevens's brief majority opinion essentially reiterated the logic of *Place*. The traffic stop was lawful, and the dog sniff did not extend the time of that stop. The sniff of the exterior of the car does not compromise any legitimate interest in privacy and so is not a search subject to the Fourth Amendment.

Justice Souter's dissent threw cold water on the use of trained dogs: "The infallible dog, however, is a creature of legal fiction." He cited numerous cases that indicated error rates in the use of dogs from 7 to 38 percent. If a dog sniff is erroneous, then "the dog does not smell the disclosed contraband; it smells a closed container" (*Illinois v. Caballes*, 2005, Souter, J., dissenting). Since the dog sniff is a police action used to find incriminating evidence, it should be treated as a search, limited by *Terry*, and allowed only when police have reasonable suspicion that contraband is present.

In her dissent, Justice Ginsburg argued that the fact that the procedure in *Caballes* did not extend the length of time of the stop did not mean that the scope of the search was not extended. Caballes was stopped only for speeding, and his car was sniffed only after he refused to give consent to search, although it does not appear that the officer who stopped his vehicle called for the dog unit. In this view, "A drug-detection dog is an intimidating animal" (*Illinois v. Caballes*, 2005, Ginsburg, J., dissenting). Even if trained dogs are effective, "The Court has never removed police action from Fourth Amendment control on the ground that the action is well calculated to apprehend the guilty." Justice Ginsburg raised the concern that "[t]oday's decision, in contrast, clears the way for suspicionless, dog-accompanied drug sweeps of parked cars along sidewalks and in parking lots." Both dissenting justices made it clear that their opinions were contextually related to drug detection and did not apply to dogs trained to sniff out explosives, dangerous chemicals, or biological weapons. A dog sniff for such purposes "would be an entirely different matter" because in its Fourth Amendment cases, the "Court has distinguished between the general interest in crime control and more immediate threats to public safety" (*Illinois v. Caballes*, 2005, Ginsburg, J., dissenting).[40] *Caballes* is not likely to be the last case on the use of drug-detection dogs.

LAW IN SOCIETY

Domestic Violence and Arrest

Domestic violence is a serious problem. "Approximately 20% of emergency department visits for trauma and 25% of homicides of women involve intimate partner violence (IPV)."[41] In 2001, there were 588,000 nonfatal violent crimes against female intimate partners and 103,000 against male intimate partners, according to national victimization surveys. This was a decline of 50 percent in nonfatal IPV since 1994, mirroring the general decline in crime in the late 1990s, but still a very large number.[42] It is estimated that only half of IPV incidents are reported to police.[43]

Before police forces existed, arrests were executed by court-appointed constables or citizens acting on their own or organized into posses. Arrests for traditional felonies like burglary and felony assault were purely reactive. For the most part, wife beating was condoned in English and American society, and perpetrators were not subject to arrest or prosecution, with the short-lived exception of the Puritan communities in the Massachusetts Bay Colony, where family violence was viewed as sinful and "threatened the individual's and the community's standing before God."[44] When nosy neighbors and pastoral intervention failed to end family violence, the courts intervened with criminal punishment.[45] The Puritan example faded from history, and domestic violence was forgotten as a social problem and was ignored by organized police forces until the mid-1970s.[46]

However, "[d]uring the last 25 years, social definitions of domestic violence have evolved from private wrongs to acts meriting an aggressive response from the criminal justice system. The change reflects the impact of the women's movement, civil liability lawsuits, changing criminal justice system ideology and academic research."[47] Feminist demands for gender equality empowered women and "forced society at large to shake off the selective social vision that formerly took little notice of the physical abuse of spouses."[48] The arrest of suspected batterers became a central issue in this major shift in social attitudes.

Prior to the 1970s, police called to the scene of a domestic disturbance were prevented from making arrests in some cases because the common law misdemeanor arrest doctrine did not allow arrests unless the crime took place in the officer's presence. Arrests might be made for violent felonies where a spouse was severely injured, but much depended on the officer's discretion. Officers who absorbed cultural norms that condoned spousal abuse were disinclined to arrest.

Feminist arguments of the 1970s concerning violence against women coincided with conservative "tough on crime" political agendas and were broadly accepted. The common law misdemeanor arrest rule was quickly changed by every state legislature to allow police officers to arrest if they had probable cause to believe that a suspect had committed a misdemeanor involving domestic violence.[49] This change was important because two-thirds of domestic violence cases are classified as misdemeanors,[50] and half of female victims of IPV reported a physical injury.[51]

In the 1970s, the New York Police Department (NYPD) pioneered a proactive approach to domestic violence that emphasized counseling the alleged batterer but leaving him (most perpetrators were male) in the premises. This approach was almost immediately criticized by feminists who understood male violence not simply as a private problem but as a public problem. Those concerned with women's safety lobbied for the passage of mandatory arrest laws.[52] Changing norms were having an effect on police practices.

Changing Norms and Domestic Violence Laws

By the mid-1980s, in addition to eliminating the misdemeanor arrest rule in domestic violence cases, all state legislatures provided legal and material assistance to domestic violence victims, including judicial protection orders, shelters for battered women, and diversion programs for offenders subjected to prosecution.[53] Without legislation, some police departments began to adopt a law enforcement approach to domestic violence by the mid-1970s.[54] Police resistance to arresting batterers was partly overcome by experience with enforcing protection orders and by several successful civil lawsuits against police departments based on cases where police virtually abandoned abused wives to vicious spouses.[55]

A national shift in mood was signaled by the U.S. Attorney General's Task Force on Family Violence, which in 1984 declared, "Family violence should be recognized and responded to as a criminal activity."[56] Women's and victim's rights groups "were particularly vocal in their support of a more punitive approach."[57]

Impediments to Change: Police Discretion and Domestic Violence

Legal rules regarding arrest define probable cause, the use of force, the scope of a search incident, and when a warrant is required. Yet no common law or constitutional doctrine guides the vital question of discretion: When is it proper for a police officer to arrest or not arrest a suspect? Total enforcement of criminal law is impossible. Police discretion to arrest is inevitable for several reasons:[58] Some laws (e.g., disorderly conduct) are vague or open-ended;[59] police departments are understaffed; and enforcing every minor offense to the maximum extent is excessively rigid and unfair. Police discretion typically is exercised by the lowest-ranking officers with minimal guidance from supervisors—a "low-visibility" practice that often undermines the equal application of the law. Ideally, police use discretion to arrest all serious offenders and to mitigate the harshness of the crime according to "common sense," but it does not always work that way.

Discretion can also breed unfairness if it is shaped by warped "commonsense" values that support widespread racist or sexist discrimination.[60] Thus a response to a domestic call—whether by arrest, avoidance, lecturing, or clinical-type counseling—was not a matter of departmental policy but depended on the individual police officer's beliefs about the acceptability of spousal abuse.[61] The police reflected the larger society that traditionally condoned spousal abuse to such an extent that it was not considered a criminal act by many.[62] Yet the crimes committed by a batterer "include assault and/or battery, aggravated assault, intent to assault or to commit murder, and, in cases where the woman is coerced sexually, rape."[63] The combination of traditional views and police discretion thus discouraged the arrest of batterers before 1970.

Into this volatile mix of social and ideological change bearing down on police practices came one of the most influential social science studies ever published: the Minneapolis experiment.[64]

The Minneapolis Experiment and the Replication Experiments

A 1984 report described a small-sample experiment in the Minneapolis Police Department that randomly assigned the type of police intervention to misdemeanor domestic violence cases before the police entered the house. Professors Lawrence Sherman and Richard Berk showed that arresting batterers reduced the number of domestic violence reports for six months, when compared to giving the parties on-the-spot mediation or simply separating the couple.[65]

The report, suggesting that arrest alone deterred spousal abuse, caused a sensation. Criminologists were skeptical because the results contradicted substantial research evidence that specific programs generally do not measurably deter crime. Nevertheless, the report had a tremendous impact and accelerated police policies in favor of arresting domestic violence perpetrators. Sherman publicized the research in the news media and to the general public and police chiefs.[66] The study was published at a time when a trend toward arresting batterers was already under way and likely accelerated and legitimized the trend.[67]

Because the findings were controversial and the issue was important, in the 1980s the National Institute of Justice funded replications of the Minneapolis experiment in Charlotte, Colorado Springs, Miami, Milwaukee, and Omaha. The results of these experiments unleashed a new barrage of controversy: Most found no evidence of an unambiguous deterrent effect of arrest on domestic violence recidivism. In a book summarizing the Minneapolis experiment and the Spouse Assault Replication Project (SARP), Sherman, who conducted one of the replications, summarized the paradoxical and contradictory findings. First, the studies, viewed individually, showed that arrest reduces domestic violence in some cities but increases it in others. One study suggested that arrest may reduce domestic violence only among employed people. Another indicated that arrest might increase domestic violence in the long run. Sherman argued that police can predict which couples are most likely to suffer future violence, but our society values privacy too highly to encourage preventive action.[68]

It would clearly be incoherent and unconstitutional to fine-tune an arrest policy that mandates arrests of employed batterers but not those without a job! Ultimately, Sherman favored repealing mandatory arrest laws, allowing warrantless misdemeanor arrests, and encouraging police departments to develop local policies. He also favored special units and policies to focus on chronically violent couples.[69]

Mandatory Arrest: Policies, Polemics, and Findings

Despite the Minneapolis experiment and the adoption of pro-arrest policies by many police departments, as of 1992 only seven states mandated arrest. The criminal trial of O. J. Simpson for the killing of his wife, Nicole Brown, whom he had allegedly abused, galvanized the majority of states to pass mandatory or preferred arrest laws. As of 2005, thirty states had passed laws mandating arrest when probable cause exists to believe that a protection order was violated, and another twenty-six plus the District of Columbia had laws with either a mandatory or a pro-arrest policy for domestic violence, whether or not a protection order was violated.[70]

The SARP findings created controversy within feminist ranks. Joan Zorza, a senior attorney with the National Center on Women and Family Law, continued to support the mandatory arrest of batterers in an article critical of the replication studies. She correctly pointed to the need for broader coordinated efforts to deal effectively with domestic violence, but her conclusion about mandatory arrest did not entirely come to grips with the SARP findings.[71]

A number of legal writers support mandatory arrest.[72] Even mandatory arrest policies and laws, however, may not result in more arrests—a point borne out in a study by Professor Kathleen Ferraro, who observed arrest patterns by Phoenix police officers in domestic cases under a mandatory arrest law. Police discretion shaped how officers assessed the existence of probable cause, leading to questionable no-probable-cause decisions.[73] Mandatory arrest laws, therefore, are needed to counteract police bias and send a message that arrest is the appropriate response to battering. The point of heated controversy among feminists concerns the argument that mandatory arrest removes the decision to arrest from the victim's control, where her fear and powerlessness in an abusive relationship are likely to prevent her from demanding the arrest of her batterer. Proponents argue that mandatory arrest laws may thus empower victims by giving them the courage to call the police in the first place. Also, a lax criminal justice system strengthens cultural norms that tolerate domestic assaults, which in turn perpetuate the social and political subjugation of women.[74]

Other legal writers oppose mandatory arrest laws and their prosecutorial "no-drop" counterparts. They are skeptical of the lasting deterrent effect of mandatory arrest and worry that mandatory arrest and prosecution will lead to retaliation by the abusing spouse and the loss of economic support, putting the victim in a worse situation. But the most heated point of contention that raises ideological differences is the concern that mandatory arrest laws will disempower women who have been battered by their spouses or boyfriends, undermine their autonomy, and fail to consider the unique circumstances of each case.[75]

Mandatory Arrest: Empirical Studies

More recent empirical studies shed light on this issue but do not provide unambiguous policy direction. One study by Christopher D. Maxwell and colleagues combined all of the SARP data and examined the reduction of assaults using two measures: official arrest records and interviews with female victims six months after the initial police call. Official records indicated increases in assault in the follow-up period, while victim interviews indicated a reduction in assault. Unfortunately, 30 percent of the victims could not be interviewed six months after the initial assault. Not knowing whether the missing were victims of retaliatory assaults casts some doubt on the deterrent findings of those who were interviewed. Further, even where arrest was shown to have a deterrent effect, the strength of the arrest factor was weak and overshadowed by factors such as the offender's prior criminal record.[76]

A national study by Richard B. Felson and colleagues, using victimization data that were more representative of the nation than the SARP data, found that the effect of arrest on reoffending was not statistically significant; it tended toward deterrence, but it was small. On the other hand, the reporting of abuse by victims had a strong, statistically significant deterrent effect. This supports the women's empowerment argument.[77]

An analysis of the interviews of victims in the Dade County SARP study indicated that arrest did have a short-term deterrent effect; 14 percent of the victims of assault where batterers were arrested experienced an episode of violence within six months, compared to 21 percent overall. The arrest of suspects was not related to the victim's perception of personal power, was negatively related to the victim's sense of legal power, and was positively related to the victim's sense of safety. The latter finding, however, varied considerably among the victims, and the best predictor of recurrent violence was the level of stress in the relationship. On the whole, Miller concluded that Dade County victims "were unlikely to have experienced long-term benefits as a consequence of suspect arrest."[78]

Rodney F. Kingsnorth and Randall C. MacIntosh's study of more than five thousand domestic violence cases processed through the Sacramento County prosecutor's office examined victim support for arrest and prosecution. The researchers found that support varied depending on the victim's race or ethnicity, sex, and age; marital, cohabitation, and parental status; the severity of the attack and injury; whether there was medical treatment; prior incidents; and whether there was a protective order. The study suggested that "victims are engaged in a complex decision making process in which they seek to weigh the costs and benefits of involving criminal justice system officials in their lives."[79] The study strongly suggested that a victim's wishes usually ought to be taken into account.

Laura Dugan examined domestic victimization using national data and comparing states with strong versus weak protection order laws and mandatory arrest provisions. She concluded that "those households residing in states with aggressive legislation have a lower probability of domestic violence."[80]

Conclusion

Overall, the studies tend to show that mandatory arrest alone has at best a weak deterrent effect on the reoccurrence of domestic violence; some studies have found no effect. Further, the effect of mandatory arrest differs by population, and victims usually make rational decisions about the overall effects that the arrest and prosecution of their abusers will have on their lives. This in turn suggests that policies that allow and even encourage arrest and prosecution are preferable to strict mandatory arrest policies. Unfortunately, the rational weighing and discussion of policies with great effects on people's lives tend to be nonexistent in the political arena. Having "found" mandatory arrest and prosecutorial no-drop policies, politicians can be expected to vigorously endorse these policies.[81]

Even proponents of mandatory arrest laws support the need for additional services.[82] Within law enforcement, coordinated domestic violence teams and prosecutors' victim support units increase victim support for these services, and an unusual experiment with intensive bail supervision found a deterrent effect on repeat victimization.[83] Recently, police have formed partnerships with communities, and many communities have established coordinated responses to domestic violence.[84]

The police continue to play a critical role as gatekeeper in domestic violence cases. The arrest experiments have shed light on the exercise of police discretion and are a part of the larger arenas of study and action concerning domestic violence and violence against women. Much needs to be done in these areas, but this exploration demonstrates the value of scientific inquiry into legal and police processes.

Summary

Legal detentions, which are Fourth Amendment seizures, fall into two categories: arrests supported by probable cause and investigative stops supported by reasonable suspicion; seizures may be legal or illegal. In addition, a person may consent to speak with a law enforcement officer, which requires no level of evidence. Police have no right to detain people to investigate crimes unless they have probable cause. A lawful arrest authorizes an officer to take a person into custody to begin the process of prosecution. An officer with only reasonable suspicion may temporarily detain a person for brief questioning to confirm or dispel the suspicion. When executing a warrant, police may detain residents during the time the search is executed, and may handcuff them for the duration of the search, if reasonable. An arrested person may be thoroughly searched for evidence of crime or weapons. A person briefly detained for an investigatory stop may only be subjected to a "frisk": a brief pat-down of outer clothing to detect the presence of a weapon. The police have a general duty to the public to arrest criminal perpetrators. They do not have a specific duty to crime victims that is enforceable by civil lawsuits—except in rare instances where they establish a protective relationship that a person relies on for protection.

The Supreme Court has issued two definitions of *arrest*: (1) An arrest occurs when a person believes he or she is not free to leave (*Mendenhall*), and (2) an arrest occurs when a person is physically stopped (*Hodari D.*). A person fleeing from a police officer is not seized until the person is physically stopped. An arrested person loses his or her right to privacy and may be kept in view of police at all times. An officer must have probable cause *before* making an arrest. Probable cause is an objective standard supported by facts, not by the officer's good faith. Proximity to a crime alone does not establish probable cause. Every warrantless arrest is subjected to a probable cause determination by a judicial officer soon after an arrest—and typically within forty-eight hours. Probable cause can also be based on direct observation of an officer, hearsay, or reports from other police departments. Misdemeanor arrests can be made only for offenses committed in the officer's presence, except that in most states, by statute, misdemeanor arrests can be made on probable cause in domestic violence cases. An arrested person can be taken into custody even if the underlying offense does not carry a jail term. An arrest made with probable cause is constitutional under the Fourth Amendment even if it is not legal under state law. An illegal arrest does not deprive a court of jurisdiction over a case. Evidence seized during an illegal arrest is inadmissible, but evidence obtained during an arrest based on probable cause that was in fact mistaken is admissible. A citizen's arrest may be made on probable cause, but if mistaken, the person making the arrest is strictly liable for the tort of false arrest. Police may use reasonable force to make an arrest; they may use deadly force where it is reasonable. The common law rule allowing an officer to shoot to kill a fleeing felon even without evidence that the felon is armed and dangerous violates the Fourth Amendment because it is excessive and unreasonable.

The Fourth Amendment does not require an arrest warrant for a lawful arrest that is made in a public place, even if the police had time to obtain a warrant. On the other hand, police must have an arrest warrant to enter a person's home to arrest that person unless the entry is justified by an exigency. An exigency is not created merely because the crime for which the arrest is made is serious. Police cannot rely on an arrest warrant to enter the home of a third party to arrest a person—such an entry has to be justified with a search warrant.

A person arrested for a crime that authorizes the officer to take the person into custody may be thoroughly searched for weapons and for evidence. The evidence from a search incident to arrest need not pertain to the crime for which a person was arrested. A police officer who stops a speeding car and issues a citation rather than making an arrest has no justification to search the car. When a person is arrested, the police may search the area within the person's immediate control for weapons or evidence but may not go beyond to search a house or other premises. When police enter a premises and arrest a person, they may look into the adjoining room, without any evidentiary basis, to look for another person who could injure the officers. However, to conduct a protective sweep of the entire premises to look for a confederate of the arrested person, police must have reasonable suspicion to believe that another person is in the house. Police may conduct an inventory of all of an arrested person's belongings at a police lockup or jail; this is not a Fourth Amendment search for evidence but an administrative procedure designed to promote safety and to deter theft and false claims of theft of the prisoner's goods. A search incident to arrest may be made at the police station. Pretrial detainees held in a jail may be subjected to strip and body cavity searches only when reasonable.

The Court has recognized the law enforcement power to briefly detain suspects who are reasonably believed to be involved in criminal activity in order to question them about their suspicious activity and to frisk them for weapons. The standard of evidence for such a stop and frisk is reasonable suspicion, a lesser standard than probable cause to believe that a crime has been committed and that the suspect committed it. Reasonable suspicion can be based on an officer's expertise in drawing inferences from observed facts, on an informant's hearsay, from a verified and reliable anonymous call, or from a police bulletin. Reasonable suspicion is based on a totality of the circumstances, including inferences from facts. An investigatory stop must be brief and nonintrusive.

A person cannot be stopped on the street simply for identification under an indefinite vagrancy statute or because he or she is standing in a high-crime neighborhood. A gang loitering ordinance that makes it a crime for a gang member to simply "loiter" and not disperse when so ordered violates the "void for vagueness" doctrine of the Fourteenth Amendment. Statutes that require lawfully stopped persons to provide their names are constitutional. A person who is chased by a police officer is not seized until the person is physically caught, and any property that the person throws away before being caught has been abandoned and is not protected by the Fourth Amendment expectation of privacy. A person who flees from a police officer without provocation establishes reasonable suspicion for an investigatory stop.

Automobile drivers cannot be stopped at random on the highway by police for a registration and license check without probable cause or reasonable suspicion of a crime or a motor vehicle violation. When a person is stopped in a car for an investigatory stop, officers may visually scan the interior of the car for weapons. There is no Fourth Amendment violation if an officer who stops a car for an existing traffic offense did so for the purpose of searching for drugs—a pretext search is constitutional. A drug courier profile can be the basis for making a stop of a person in an automobile. Reasonable suspicions to stop of a car may be based on a combination of innocent facts. Once a car is stopped, the officer may, for safety's sake, order the driver and passengers to exit the automobile.

When police officers accost a person in a nonthreatening manner in a space where the person would not ordinarily be free to move about, such as at a factory workstation or in an intercity bus, that fact alone does not turn a consensual encounter into a seizure. A motorist stopped in an open sobriety checklane is not seized for Fourth Amendment purposes. Police who accost a person at an airport and ask to speak to him or her about drug transportation do not seize that person unless they retain the passenger's ticket or luggage for more than a few moments. A sniff of luggage or the exterior of a car (that has been lawfully stopped) by a trained narcotics dog is not a Fourth Amendment search. A person who gets off an airplane from Florida on an early morning flight and looks behind him for a companion does not fit a drug courier profile. A drug courier profile may be based on a series of innocent facts that, when taken together, allows an officer to draw a reasonable conclusion that the person is a drug courier. Police have reasonable suspicion to stop a person who fits a drug courier profile.

Legal Puzzles

HOW HAVE COURTS DECIDED THESE CASES?

Handcuff during Warrant Execution

4-1. Federal agents obtained search warrants in 2002 alleging that the Islamic Institute of Islamic Thought ("IIIT"), a tax-exempt organization located in Herndon, Virginia, illegally laundered and funneled money to terrorists. Iqbal Unus, Ph.D., was employed by IIIT. Dr. Unus, his wife, Aysha, and their two teenage daughters, including Hanaa, aged eighteen, lived in a two-story, single-family residence in Herndon. The Unus's are U.S. citizens and none had a criminal record.

On March 20, 2002, at 10:30 a.m., eleven federal agents and three uniformed police officers executed a warrant to search the Unus residence. (Warrants were executed against fourteen homes and offices that day). They pounded on the front door, ordering the occupants to open it. Aysha Unus was in the living room at rear of the home and Hanaa Unus was upstairs, asleep in her bedroom. Aysha heard the pounding and a voice commanding her to open the door, and saw a gun through a side window as she inched toward the door. Frightened and confused, Aysha began screaming for Hanaa, who came downstairs. They retreated to the rear, went into the living room, and called 911. At this time, the officers broke through the front door with a battering ram and an agent entered with a firearm drawn. Hanaa reported that an agent "pointed [a gun] at me, and he was yelling at me to drop the phone and put my hands up." Agents handcuffed Aysha and Hanaa behind their backs, and placed them on a chair and sofa in the living room.

During the search, Aysha and Hanaa Unus remained handcuffed in the family room for nearly four hours. They were permitted to use the restroom upon request; Aysha was allowed to self-administer her diabetes medication. Around 2:00 p.m., the women were allowed to perform afternoon prayers, in accordance with their Muslim faith, with handcuffs removed. Aysha and Hanaa were not allowed to pray outside the presence of the male agents, nor were they allowed to wear head scarves or cover their hands while the male agents were present, or while being photographed. After prayers the two women were no longer handcuffed, but remained confined to the living room for the duration of the search. Computers and documents were seized. Agents left a copy of the warrant and a written inventory of the items seized. (According to news accounts, no criminal action had been taken as of 2008). The Unus' filed a civil suit against the agents and the government.

Did the handcuffing and means of detention during the execution of the warrant violate the Fourth Amendment rights of Aysha and Hanaa Unus?

Held: NO

4-1. Handcuffing is constitutional under the Fourth Amendment, if reasonable, while occupants are detained during the execution of a search warrant. In *Muehler v. Mena* (2005) a two- to three-hour detention of a woman handcuffed in her garage was reasonable because officers were searching in a gang house for dangerous weapons and a wanted gang member. The government's continuing safety interests were held to outweigh the "marginal" intrusion.

In this case agents executed a facially valid search warrant. Although they were searching only for financial documents, and

not for weapons or persons, a reasonable officer would have had legitimate safety concerns. The search was one of many conducted that day, at a residence believed to contain evidence of money laundering by entities suspected of assisting international terrorism. Viewed objectively, the agents did not know whether they would be confronted by resistance. Upon entry into the Unus residence, the agents encountered hectic conditions. "Excitement" in the plaintiffs' voices, and the fact that the plaintiffs were "clearly concerned and worried and agitated" created a "possibility that the women would take some action that would make an unstable situation and that the agents would have to do something to get control again." The agent's decision to initially handcuff the women upon entry was reasonable.

It was reasonable for the agents to keep the women detained in handcuffs for nearly four hours because the agents were executing a "terrorism-related warrant" and because the women had "acted a certain way at the time of entry." After "things had calmed down a bit," the agents moved the handcuffs from the back to the front of the plaintiffs to make them more comfortable. The agents reassessed the situation as the search progressed, however, entirely removing the handcuffs after the women performed their afternoon prayers.

Unus v. Kane, 565 F.3d 103 (2d Cir. 2009).

Arrest—Use of Force

4-2. At 7:50 a.m. Bruce Weigel struck Wyoming State Trooper Broad's patrol car from the rear on I-25. Weigel careened to the other side of the highway. Weigel told the troopers he did not need medical attention and blamed the accident on his car's faulty steering linkage. While producing his vehicle documents, Trooper Henderson smelled alcohol on Weigel's breath. Weigel agreed to perform a field sobriety test. As they approached the interstate to return to Trooper Henderson's patrol car, a van approached; the Trooper told Weigel to step back. Weigel walked forward and was struck in the chest by the passing van's sideview mirror. At 7:54 a.m. Trooper Broad radioed for an ambulance. Weigel continued trying to cross the interstate and other witnesses described his behavior as bizarre and erratic.

Concerned for Weigel's safety, Trooper Henderson wrestled him to the ground in a ditch alongside the highway. Weigel fought vigorously. Trooper Henderson put Weigel in a chokehold but Weigel continued to resist and fight, even after being handcuffed. A bystander lay across the back of Weigel's legs. The troopers maintained Weigel in a face-down position. Trooper Broad applied pressure to Weigel's upper body, including his neck and shoulders, by using either one or both knees and his hands. Weigel was bound with plastic cord. Weigel ceased to struggle, as Trooper Henderson went to radio in a dispatch. Before 8:00 a.m. Weigel stopped breathing and went into cardiac arrest. Attempts to resuscitate him were unsuccessful. The autopsy revealed the most likely cause of Weigel's death was "mechanical asphyxiation caused by inhibition of respiration by weight applied to the upper back."

Was excessive force used when Trooper Broad applied pressure to Weigel's upper body with his knees while Weigel was lying face down and by keeping Weigel in a face-down position? Holding available from instructor.

Stop and Frisk—Reasonable Suspicion

4-3. At approximately 3:40 a.m. on 24 July 2006, Officer Coyle of the Carrboro PD responded to a report of a breaking and entering (B&E) in progress on South Peak Drive. Coyle arrived within three minutes. While driving toward the location he turned onto Old Pittsboro Road and observed someone riding a bicycle on the road, within a quarter of a mile of the B&E location. Old Pittsboro Road does not intersect with South Peak Drive, but is connected to it via Daffodil Lane. The rear of the bicycle had a flashing red light. Officer Coyle did not observe anyone else in the area. He radioed other officers information about the bicycle rider and proceeded to the house on South Peak Drive. He observed that a window had been opened with "a small, flathead screwdriver or a pry tool," and notified other officers of that information.

Officer Gandy was on patrol in her police vehicle. She responded to the B&E call, received Officer Coyle's call concerning the bicyclist, and observed a man (Anthony Campbell) riding a bicycle and turning from Old Pittsboro Road onto South Greensboro Street. Campbell had an illuminated light on his cap and the bicycle had a headlight and two flashing rear reflectors. Officer Gandy recognized Campbell by face but not by name. She drove past Campbell, turned around, drove back past him, and pulled off the road. She watched Campbell turn onto a highway uphill on-ramp and stop at the top of the hill. Officer Gandy turned on her spotlights and observed Campbell "play with something" in his backpack.

Officer Gandy then approached Campbell, exited her vehicle, and asked Campbell for his name and identification. After this stop, Lt. Taylor arrived; he recognized Campbell as having an extensive history of B&Es. Campbell was detained, handcuffed, and frisked. A small flashlight and a Swiss Army-type knife, which could have used to open the window, were retrieved. Campbell was arrested and a search incident to arrest of his backpack yielded jewelry and burglar's tools.

> *Did Officer Gandy have reasonable suspicion to stop Campbell?*
> *Holding available from instructor.*

Stop and Frisk—Providing Identification

4-4. A party of about twenty people, including Hispanics and African Americans, turned violent when a fight erupted and two black men were evicted. They returned shortly with Torrence Stratton, who was described as wearing a "bright" shirt. They brandished guns, were forced out, but returned immediately and fired shots, striking several party-goers.

Pasco Police Officer Chavez, patrolling in an audio/video-equipped car, was notified by dispatch about the shooting. He spotted and followed a vehicle matching the dispatch description, and pulled in behind the suspect vehicle when it parked on a side street. He saw a black male dressed in a yellow shirt walking away; he was Torrance Stratton. Officer Chavez testified that Stratton "didn't want to talk to me." Defense counsel objected; the court sustained the objection and instructed the jury to disregard that testimony. However, a video of Officer Chavez stopping Stratton was played to the jury. The man identified as Stratton did not clearly respond when asked his name three times.

> *Was Stratton's Fifth Amendment right against self-incrimination violated when the jury was shown a video with him refusing to identify himself to Officer Chavez during a* Terry *stop?*
> *Holding available from instructor.*

Further Reading

Human Rights Watch, *Shielded from Justice: Police Brutality and Accountability in the United States* (New York: Human Rights Watch, 1998).

William Ker Muir Jr., *Police: Streetcorner Politicians* (Chicago: University of Chicago Press, 1977).

Lawrence P. Tiffany, Donald M. McIntyre Jr., and Daniel L. Rotenberg, *Detection of Crime* (Boston: Little, Brown, 1967).

Useful Web Sites

National District Attorneys Association and American Prosecutors Research Institute

http://www.ndaa-apri.org/

Provides information about prosecutors. The American Prosecutors Research Institute lists many relevant publications and offers downloadable reports.

Domestic Violence and Sexual Assault Data Resource Center

http://www.jrsa.org/dvsa-drc/index.html

Provides information on data collection and use in the states. Identifies types of information currently obtained by state and local agencies and includes all aspects of domestic violence.

End Notes

1. Kenneth Adams et al., *Use of Force by Police: Overview of National and Local Data* (Washington, D.C.: National Institute of Justice and Bureau of Justice Statistics, October 1999).

2. Robert A. Shapiro, "Annotation: Personal Liability of Policeman, Sheriff, or Similar Peace Officer or His Bond, for Injury Suffered as a Result of Failure to Enforce Law or Arrest Lawbreaker," *American Law Reports*, 3rd series, 41 (1972, updated weekly): 700; and Licia A. Esposito Eaton, "Annotation: Liability of Municipality or Other Governmental Unit for Failure to Provide Police Protection from Crime," *American Law Reports*, 5th series, 90 (2001, updated weekly): 273.

3. Michael J. Glennon, "International Kidnapping: State-Sponsored Abduction: A Comment on *United States v. Alvarez-Machain*," *American Society of International Law Newsletter* 86 (October 1992): 746.

4. Brief of Amici Curiae Electronic Privacy Information Center (EPIC), Privacy and Civil Rights Organizations, and Legal Scholars and Technical Experts in Support of Petitioner, *Herring v. United States*, p. 6 (May 16, 2008).

5. These rules may have originated in the late eighteenth and nineteenth centuries. See Thomas Y. Davies, "Recovering the Original Fourth Amendment," *Michigan Law Review* 98, no. 3 (1999): 547–750, 634–42, 724–26.

6. See J. Bradley Ortins, "District of Columbia Survey: Warrantless Misdemeanor Arrest for Drunk Driving Found Invalid in *Schram v. District of Columbia*," *Catholic University Law Review* 34 (1985): 1241–54.

7. David A. Sklansky, "The Private Police," *UCLA Law Review* 46 (1999): 1165–1287, 1183.

8. Sklansky, "Private Police," 1184.

9. F. J. Remington et al., *Criminal Justice Administration: Materials and Cases*, 1st ed. (Indianapolis: Bobbs–Merrill, 1969), 20.

10. *Garner v. Memphis Police Department*, 710 F.2d 240 (6th Cir. 1983).

11. Jerome H. Skolnick and James J. Fyfe, *Above the Law: Police and the Excessive Use of Force* (New York: Free Press, 1993), 246.

12. Dan M. Kahan, David A. Hoffman, and Donald Braman, "Whose Eyes Are You Going to Believe? *Scott v. Harris* and the Perils of Cognitive Illiberalism," *Harvard Law Review* 122 (2009): 837–906, 903.

13. *Dorman v. United States*, 435 F.2d 385, 392–93 (D.C. Cir. 1970).

14. *Mary Beth G. v. City of Chicago*, 723 F.2d 1263 (7th Cir. 1983).

15. Robin Lee Fenton, "Comment: The Constitutionality of Policies Requiring Strip Searches of All Misdemeanants and Minor Traffic Offenders," *University of Cincinnati Law Review* 54 (1985): 175–89, 180–81.

16. William J. Simonitsch, "Comment: Visual Body Cavity Searches Incident to Arrest: Validity under the Fourth Amendment," *University of Miami Law Review* 54 (2000): 665–88, 681–82.

17. Margo Schlanger, "Jail Strip-Search Cases: Patterns and Participants," *Law and Contemporary Problems*, 71(2008): 65–103, 73.

18. *Hartline v. Gallo*, 546 F.3d 95 (2d Cir. 2008).

19. D. Caute, *The Year of the Barricades: A Journey through 1968* (New York: Harper and Row, 1988).

20. However, one biographer read *Terry* at face value as a balancing of law enforcement needs against privacy rights: G. Edward White, *Earl Warren: A Public Life* (New York: Oxford University Press, 1982), 276–78.

21. F. Graham, *The Due Process Revolution: The Warren Court's Impact on Criminal Law* (New York: Hayden, 1970), 22–23.

22. P. Chevigny, *Police Power: Police Abuses in New York City* (New York: Pantheon, 1969).

23. M. Lippman, "The Drug War and the Vanishing Fourth Amendment," *Criminal Justice Journal* 14 (1992): 229–308.

24. M. McAlary, *Buddy Boys: When Good Cops Turn Bad* (New York: Putnam's, 1987), 87.

25. Daniel J. Steinbock, "National Identity Cards: Fourth and Fifth Amendment Issues," *Florida Law Review* 56 (2004): 697–760.

26. T. J. Devetski, "Fourth Amendment Protection against Unreasonable Seizure of the Person: The New (?) Common Law Arrest Test for Seizure," *Journal of Criminal Law and Criminology* 82 (1992): 747–72.

27. Tracey Maclin, "Book Review: Seeing the Constitution from the Backseat of a Police Squad Car," *Boston University Law Review* 70 (1990): 543–91, 550 (emphasis added).

28. Maclin, "Book Review," 550.

29. Marvin Zalman, "Fleeing from the Fourth Amendment," *Criminal Law Bulletin* 36, no. 2 (2000): 129–47.

30. David Moran, "The New Fourth Amendment Vehicle Doctrine: Stop and Search Any Car at Any Time," *Villanova Law Review* 47 (2002): 815–38.

31. G. G. Ashdown, "Drugs, Ideology, and the Deconstitutionalization of Criminal Procedure," *West Virginia Law Review* 95 (1992): 1–54, 22 (paragraph breaks omitted).

32. M. Cloud, "Search and Seizures by the Numbers: The Drug Courier Profile and Judicial Review of Investigative Formulas," *Boston University Law Review* 65 (1985): 843–921, 844–45, 847–48; and S. E. Hall, "A Balancing Approach to the Constitutionality of Drug Courier Profiles," *University of Illinois Law Review* 1993 (1993): 1007–36, 1009–10.

33. S. Guerra, "Domestic Drug Interdiction Operations: Finding the Balance," *Journal of Criminal Law and Criminology* 82 (1992): 1109–61, 1114.

34. Hall, "A Balancing Approach," 1010.

35. Lisa Belkin, "Airport Anti-Drug Nets Snare Many People Fitting 'Profiles,'" *New York Times*, March 20, 1990, 1.

36. Hall, "A Balancing Approach," 1010–11.

37. Cases cited in Hall, "A Balancing Approach," 1011, n. 35.

38. W. R. Janikowski and D. J. Giacopassi, "Pyrrhic Images, Dancing Shadows, and Flights of Fancy: The Drug Courier Profile as Legal Fiction," *Journal of Contemporary Criminal Justice* 9 (1993): 60–69.

39. Cloud, "Search and Seizures by the Numbers," n. 32.

40. Justice Ginsberg cited *Michigan Department of State Police v. Sitz* (1990) and *City of Indianapolis v. Edmond* (2000) in support.

41. L. Bensley, et al., "Prevalence of Intimate Partner Violence and Injuries—Washington, 1998," *Journal of the American Medical Association* 284, no. 5 (August 2, 2000): 559–60 (from the Centers for Disease Control and Prevention: Morbidity and Mortality Weekly Report).

42. Callie Marie Rennison, *Crime Data in Brief: Intimate Partner Violence, 1993–2001* (Washington, D.C.: Bureau of Justice Statistics, NCJ 197838, February 2003).

43. Callie Marie Rennison and Sarah Welchans, *Special Report: Intimate Partner Violence* (Washington, D.C.: Bureau of Justice Statistics, NCJ 178247, May 2000).

44. Elizabeth Pleck, *Domestic Tyranny* (New York: Oxford University Press, 1987), 17.

45. Pleck, 18.

46. Pleck, 182.

47. Rodney F. Kingsnorth and Randall C. MacIntosh, "Domestic Violence: Predictors of Victim Support for Official Action," *Justice Quarterly* 21, no. 2 (2004): 301–28, 301–2.

48. M. Zalman, "The Courts' Response to Police Intervention in Domestic Violence," in E. S. Buzawa and C. G. Buzawa, eds., *Domestic Violence: The Changing Criminal Justice Response* (Westport, Conn.: Auburn House, 1992), 79–110, 82.

49. Lisa G. Lerman, "Statute: A Model State Act: Remedies for Domestic Abuse," *Harvard Journal on Legislation* 21 (1984): 61–143, 126–27.

50. Patrick A. Langan and Christopher A. Innes, *Special Report: Preventing Domestic Violence against Women* (Washington, D.C.: Bureau of Justice Statistics, 1986).

51. Rennison and Welchans, *Special Report: Intimate Partner Violence*.

52. Marion Wanless, "Note: Mandatory Arrest: A Step toward Eradicating Domestic Violence, But Is It Enough?" *University of Illinois Law Review* 1996 (1996): 533–75, 539–40.

53. Lerman, "Statute."

54. International Association of Chiefs of Police, *Training Key 245: Wife Beating* (Gaithersburg, Md.: International Association of Chiefs of Police, 1976): "The officer who starts legal action may give the wife the courage she needs to realistically face and correct her situation."

55. Ruth Gundle, "Civil Liability for Police Failure to Arrest: *Nearing v. Weaver*," *Women's Rights Law Reporter* 9, no. 3–4 (1986): 259–65, 259–60, 262. Injunction suits were brought: *Bruno v. Codd*, 90 Misc.2d 1047, 396 N.Y.S.2d 974 (Sup Ct. Special Term 1977), rev'd in part, appeal dismissed in part, 64 A.D.2d 582, 407 N.Y.S.2d 165 (1978), aff'd, 47 N.Y.2d 582, 393 N.E.2d 976 (1979) (class action; consent decree entered to enforce protection orders); *Scott v. Hart*, No. C–76–2395 (N.D., Cal., filed Nov. 24, 1976); and *Raguz v. Chandler*, No. C–74–1064 (N.D., Ohio, filed Nov. 20, 1974).

56. U.S. Attorney General's Task Force on Family Violence, *Report* (Washington, D.C.: U.S. Department of Justice, 1984).

57. A. Binder and J. Meeker, "The Development of Social Attitudes toward Spousal Abuse," in Buzawa and Buzawa, eds., *Domestic Violence*, 3–19, 12.

58. American Bar Association, *Standards Relating to the Urban Police Function* (1972), 116; J. Goldstein, "Police Discretion Not to Invoke the Criminal Process: Low-Visibility Decisions in the Administration of Justice," *Yale Law Journal* 69 (1960): 543–94; and William Ker Muir Jr., *Police: Streetcorner Politicians* (Chicago: University of Chicago Press, 1977).

59. Indeed, legislatures at times assume that laws they pass will not be strictly enforced by the police. See M. Zalman, "Mandatory Sentencing Legislation: Myth and Reality," in M. Morash, ed., *Implementing Criminal Justice Policies* (Beverly Hills, Calif.: Sage, 1982), 61–69.

60. K. C. Davis, *Discretionary Justice: A Preliminary Inquiry* (Baton Rouge: Louisiana State University Press, 1969), 3, 5.

61. Muir, *Police*, 57, 82–100.

62. Lloyd Ohlin and Michael Tonry, "Family Violence in Perspective," in Ohlin and Tonry, eds., *Family Violence* (Chicago: University of Chicago Press, 1989), 1–18. A 1970 survey found that 25 percent of the male respondents and 17 percent of the females approved of a husband's slapping his wife under certain circumstances. Irene H. Frieze and Angela Browne, "Violence in Marriage," in Ohlin and Tonry, eds., *Family Violence*, 165.

63. Del Martin, *Battered Wives*, rev. ed. (San Francisco: Volcano Press, 1981), 87–88.

64. R. B. Felson, J. M. Ackerman, and C. A. Gallagher, "Police Intervention and the Repeat of Domestic Assault," *Criminology* 43, no. 3 (2005): 563–88, 564.

65. The report was published in the *Police Foundation Reports* (1984) and was based on a scholarly article: L. Sherman and R. Berk, "The Specific Deterrent Effects of Arrest for Domestic Violence," *American Sociological Review* 49, no. 2 (1984): 261–72. The article was cautious in drawing policy conclusions.

66. R. Lempert, "Humility Is a Virtue: On the Publicization of Policy-Relevant Research," *Law and Society Review* 23 (1989): 146–61.

67. J. Zorza, "Must We Stop Arresting Batterers? Analysis and Policy Implications of New Police Domestic Violence Studies," *New England Law Review* 28 (1994): 929–90, 935–36.

68. The Minneapolis report, L. Sherman's replication report, and a general analysis of these issues are found in L. Sherman, *Policing Domestic Violence: Experiments and Dilemmas* (New York: Free Press, 1992).

69. Sherman, *Policing Domestic Violence*, 22–24.

70. G. Kristian Miccio, "A House Divided: Mandatory Arrest, Domestic Violence, and the Conservatization of the Battered Women's Movement," *Houston Law Review* 42 (2005): 237–323, n. 2.

71. Zorza, "Must We Stop Arresting Batterers?" 985.

72. Wanless, "Note: Mandatory Arrest," 533–75; and Catherine Popham Durant, "Note: When to Arrest: What Influences Police Determination to Arrest When There Is a Report of Domestic Violence?" *Southern California Review of Law and Women's Studies* 12 (2003): 301–35.

73. K. J. Ferraro, "Policing Women Battering," *Social Problems* 36, no. 1 (1989): 61–74.

74. E. S. Buzawa and C. G. Buzawa, "Domestic Violence," in Buzawa and Buzawa, *Domestic Violence*, 20.

75. Miccio, "A House Divided"; Jessica Dayton, "Student Essay: The Silencing of a Woman's Choice: Mandatory Arrest and No Drop Prosecution Policies in Domestic Violence Cases," *Cardozo Women's Law Journal* 9 (2003): 281–97; and Erin L. Han, "Note: Mandatory Arrest and No-Drop Policies: Victim Empowerment in Domestic Violence Cases," *Boston College Third World Law Journal* 23 (2003): 159–91.

76. C. D. Maxwell, J. H. Garner, and J. A. Fagan, "The Effects of Arrest in Intimate Partner Violence: New Evidence from the Spouse Assault Replication Program," National Institute of Justice Research in Brief (NCJ 188199, July 2001).

77. Felson, Ackerman, and Gallagher, "Police Intervention," 581–82.

78. Joann Miller, "An Arresting Experiment: Domestic Violence Victim Experiences and Perceptions," *Journal of Interpersonal Violence* 18, no. 7 (2003): 695–716, 708.

79. Kingsnorth and MacIntosh, "Domestic Violence," 301–28, 321–22.

80. Laura Dugan, "Domestic Violence Legislation: Exploring Its Impact on the Likelihood of Domestic Violence, Police Involvement, and Arrest," *Criminology and Public Policy* 2, no. 2 (2003): 283–312, 303.

81. See press release of Governor George Pataki of New York, "Governor: Keep Mandatory Arrest in Domestic Violence Law" (March 9, 2001), http://www.ny.gov/governor/press/01/march9_01.htm (accessed July 24, 2006).

82. Wanless, "Note: Mandatory Arrest," 562.

83. Thomas S. Whetstone, "Measuring the Impact of a Domestic Violence Coordinated Response Team," *Policing* 24, no. 3 (2001): 371–98; and James Lasley, "The Effect of Intensive Bail Supervision on Repeat Domestic Violence Offenders," *Policy Studies Journal*, 31, no. 2 (2003): 187–207.

84. M. Reuland et al., *Police-Community Partnerships to Address Domestic Violence* (PERF, COPS, Department of Justice, n.d.); and Alissa P. Worden, *Models of Community Coordination in Partner Violence Cases* (NCJ 187351, 2001).

JUSTICES OF THE SUPREME COURT

Stalwart Conservatives, 1938–1962: Reed, Vinson, Burton, Minton, and Whittaker

These five justices, appointees of Presidents Franklin D. Roosevelt, Harry S. Truman, and Dwight D. Eisenhower, were instrumental in delaying the implementation of the due process "incorporation" revolution of the 1960s. They were largely conservative in their criminal procedure rulings, both in denying the validity of the incorporation argument and in construing the Due Process Clause narrowly. For the most part, legal commentators rank these justices as not especially distinguished: Their vision of the Court's role tended to be cramped, and they failed to explain their positions with intellectual force. They typically followed the lead of justices with more manifest abilities, especially Justices Felix Frankfurter and John Marshall Harlan II. They displayed basic legal competence but little independence in their decisions, and their opinions were not written with the high craft that is critical to shaping the law.

This group of justices, with Justice Tom Clark, formed a majority of the Court from 1949 to 1953 (excluding Justice Whittaker, who sat from 1957 to 1962). From 1953 to 1962, a combination of centrist and less dyed-in-the-wool conservatives kept the Court from breaching the *Palko* doctrine until Justice Clark's decision in *Mapp*. With Justice Frankfurter's retirement and replacement by Justice Arthur Goldberg in 1962, the Court took a decidedly liberal turn that marked the Warren Court of the 1960s.

Collection of the Supreme
Court of the United States.
Photographer: Harris and Ewing.

Stanley F. Reed

Kentucky, 1884–1980

Democrat

Appointed by Franklin Delano Roosevelt

Years of Service: 1938–1957

Life and Career.   Reed held B.A. degrees from Kentucky Wesleyan College and Yale University and studied law at the Sorbonne, Columbia University, and the University of Virginia without graduating. He completed his legal studies by reading law in a Kentucky lawyer's office, and he practiced from 1910 to the 1920s. He entered government service under President Herbert Hoover but remained in the attorney general's office as a faithful New Dealer under President Roosevelt. As solicitor general from 1935, he argued some of the key New Deal cases before the Supreme Court and developed a good reputation for legal craftsmanship. He was President Roosevelt's second appointment to the Supreme Court.

Contribution to Criminal Procedure.   He was a stalwart supporter of Justice Frankfurter and helped to block the movement toward incorporation, applying the criminal provisions of the Bill of Rights to the states.

Signature Opinion.   *Adamson v. California* (1947). Justice Reed's majority opinion in *Adamson* kept the Court's anti-incorporation position intact. Adamson was tried for murder; he did not take the stand in his own defense, knowing that if he did so, prior convictions for burglary, larceny, and robbery would have been introduced into evidence to impeach him. California law allowed the judge to comment to the jury on the defendant's silence. Writing for the majority, Reed relied on a long train of cases, including *Twining v. New Jersey* (1908), for the proposition that the Self-Incrimination Clause was not a fundamental right incorporated into the Due Process Clause of the Fourteenth Amendment. He relied on the *Palko* case, noting that this ruling allowed the states to pursue their own criminal procedure policies unfettered by rules under the Bill of Rights that had limited the federal government. "It accords with the constitutional doctrine of federalism by leaving to the states the responsibility of dealing with the privileges and immunities of their citizens except those inherent in national citizenship."

In addition, Justice Reed made it clear that he did not entirely disapprove of the practical impact of a judge's telling a jury that they could take the defendant's refusal to testify into account in weighing the evidence, even though by 1947 a majority of the states had abolished the practice by statute or state constitutional rule. Adamson argued that this placed a penalty on his right to silence under the California constitution and shifted the burden of proof from the government to him. Justice Reed, to the contrary, noted: "[W]e see no reason why comment should not be made upon his silence. It seems quite natural that when a defendant has opportunity to deny or explain facts and determines not to do so, the prosecution should bring out the strength of the evidence by commenting upon defendant's failure to explain or deny it. The prosecution evidence may be of facts that may be beyond the knowledge of the accused. If so, his failure to testify would have little if any weight. But the facts may be such as are necessarily in the knowledge of the accused. In that case a failure to explain would point to an inability to explain."

Assessment.   Justice Reed's record was "liberal" in regard to New Deal economic issues. He was a strong believer in judicial restraint and feared what he called "krytocracy," or government by judges. He was a judicial conservative in many civil liberties areas, and he voted consistently with Justice Frankfurter's bloc. On the question of school desegregation, he had consistently voted against segregated facilities under the "separate but equal" doctrine but was at first reluctant to overturn the doctrine in *Brown v. Board of Education* (1954). After Chief Justice Vinson died during deliberations, Chief Justice Earl Warren persuaded Reed to join a unanimous Court in overruling *Plessy v. Ferguson* (1896).

Further Reading

John D. Fassett, *New Deal Justice: The Life of Stanley Reed of Kentucky* (New York: Vantage, 1994).

Collection of the Supreme
Court of the United States.
Photographer: Harris and Ewing.

Fred M. Vinson

Kentucky, 1890–1953

Democrat

Appointed Chief Justice by Harry Truman

Years of Service: 1946–1953

Life and Career.   Vinson, born in Kentucky, was educated at Kentucky Normal School and Centre College, where he excelled in athletics and received a law degree. Vinson practiced law from 1911 to 1931. Elected to the House of Representatives in 1924, he rose to a position of power on the Ways and Means Committee and, as a loyal ally to Roosevelt, was instrumental in developing New Deal tax and coal programs. He was appointed to the U.S. Circuit Court for the District of Columbia in 1938 but resigned during World War II to become director of economic stabilization and later director of war mobilization. He developed a strong friendship with President Truman, who appointed him secretary of the treasury.

Vinson's public philosophy, including his theory of the Supreme Court's role, was shaped by these momentous events. He believed the federal government needed the power to solve the enormous problems threatening the nation. He was pragmatic and, while serving in all three branches, had participated in the process through which big government won the greatest war in history and tamed the worst political-economic crisis in the life of the United States. He had faith born of experience that American political institutions and the American public had the judgment to successfully resolve competing interests for the public good.

Contribution to Criminal Procedure.   In 1946, a liberal bloc of four justices (Hugo Black, William O. Douglas, Frank Murphy, and Wiley Blount Rutledge) came close to inaugurating the incorporation of the Bill of Rights. Justice Vinson opposed this action, and during his tenure, the number of justices opposed to incorporation increased as Murphy and Rutledge were replaced by Clark and Minton. Justices Felix Frankfurter and Robert H. Jackson, while of a more liberal temperament and more willing to find for defendants under the Due Process Clause, were also opposed to the incorporation doctrine.

Signature Opinion.   *Stack v. Boyle* (1951). Although Justice Vinson voted in favor of the federal government in its heavy-handed repression of American Communists in loyalty cases during the cold war, he drew the line at the use of the courts to stifle traditional rights. The right to bail came up in *Stack v. Boyle* (1951). Pretrial bail was set at $50,000 each for leaders of the American Communist Party on trial for the theoretical advocacy of the violent overthrow of the government. Writing for the Court, Justice Vinson held that the bail was excessive because it was set at a figure higher than reasonably calculated to ensure that the defendants would return to stand trial and submit to sentence. He wrote: "This traditional right to freedom before conviction permits the unhampered preparation of a defense, and serves to prevent the infliction of punishment prior to conviction. Unless this right to bail before trial is preserved, the presumption of innocence, secured only after centuries of struggle, would lose its meaning."

Assessment.   Justice Vinson believed in judicial restraint. Having seen a conservative Supreme Court subvert the political will at the beginning of the New Deal, Vinson consistently voted to uphold the power of government in civil liberties (in loyalty oath and Communist conspiracy cases), in economic affairs, and in criminal law. He was appointed chief justice in part to calm several personal antagonisms that had developed among more brilliant justices, but his lack of constitutional vision and craft made him an ineffective chief justice.

Further Reading

Melvin I. Urofsky, *Division and Discord: The Supreme Court under Stone and Vinson, 1941–1953* (Columbia: University of South Carolina Press, 1997).

Collection of the Supreme
Court of the United States.
Photographer: Harris and Ewing.

Harold Burton

Ohio, 1888–1964

Republican

Appointed by Harry S. Truman

Years of Service: 1945–1958

Life and Career.   Burton was born in Jamaica Plain, Massachusetts, was educated at Bowdoin College and Harvard Law School, and practiced law in the west before settling in Cleveland. His political career included service in the Ohio House of Representatives from 1929, election to mayor of Cleveland in 1935—serving two terms—and election to the U.S. Senate in 1941. Although a Republican mayor, he cooperated with the national government, a position taken by few midwestern Republicans. Although sometimes critical of the Democratic administration, Burton supported the economic and social policies of the New Deal and the entry of the United States into the United Nations. These positions made Burton an acceptable Republican nominee by a Democratic president. As with all of Truman's nominees, the president and Senator Burton were friends; Burton had been a member of Truman's committee to investigate wartime fraud.

Contribution to Criminal Procedure.   Justice Burton was a stalwart conservative in opposing the incorporation doctrine. In confessions cases, he was unwilling to use the Due Process Clause to exclude confessions that the Court's majority found coercive. On the other hand, he was in the minority in a case that held that a person who was electrocuted and lived could be executed a second time without violating any constitutional provision, including the fundamental fairness aspect of due process.

Signature Opinion.   *Rovario v. United States* (1957). Writing for a six-to-one majority, Justice Burton held that the identity of a secret undercover informant must be made known to the defendant, Rovario, during a trial for heroin possession where the informer had taken a material part in bringing about Rovario's possession of the drugs, had been present with him while the crime occurred, and might have been a material witness as to whether he knowingly transported the drugs. Justice Burton ruled that the so-called informer's privilege is in reality the government's privilege to withhold from disclosure the identity of those who furnish information of violations of law to officers charged with enforcing that law. This "privilege" assists effective law enforcement by encouraging people to inform about crime, but where it conflicts with fundamental fairness, it must give way to the defendant's right to a fair trial. In effect, where a conviction depends on the disclosure of the identity of a secret informant, the government must either divulge the informant's identity or dismiss the prosecution. *Rovario* indicates that the stalwart conservatives in criminal procedure, while tending to favor the prosecution, adhered to fundamental standards of a fair trial.

Assessment.   On the Court, Justice Burton's conservative positions on civil liberties were close to those of Justice Reed. As Chief Justice Vinson and Justices Minton and Clark were appointed, they joined to form what seemed to be a voting bloc that upheld the government's loyalty oath programs.

Further Reading

Mary Frances Berry, *Stability, Security, and Continuity: Mr. Justice Burton and Decision-Making in the Supreme Court, 1945–1958* (Westport, Conn.: Greenwood Press, 1978).

Collection of the Supreme Court of the United States. Photographer: Harris and Ewing.

Sherman Minton

Indiana, 1890–1965

Democrat

Appointed by Harry S. Truman

Years of Service: 1949–1956

Life and Career.   Minton was born in Indiana, graduated at the head of his class at Indiana University, studied law at Yale University, and returned home to practice law while engaging in local politics. In 1933, he was appointed counselor to Indiana's Public Service Commission. He played a significant role in developing a state version of the New Deal and was elected in 1934 to the U.S. Senate, where he was a staunch supporter of the Roosevelt administration. His legal knowledge and militant manner in debate led to his rise to a Senate leadership role in which he supported Roosevelt's "court-packing" plan. Minton was an internationalist, a position that was not too popular in the Midwest, and he lost his Senate seat in 1940. He worked as a presidential assistant for the next year and was appointed to the U.S. Court of Appeals for the Seventh Circuit (Indiana, Illinois, and Wisconsin) in 1941. It was Minton's good fortune to be seated next to another freshman senator, Harry S. Truman, in 1934. They became and remained good friends, which was a key element in each of Truman's appointments to the Supreme Court.

Contribution to Criminal Procedure.   As a stalwart conservative on criminal matters, Justice Minton joined the Frankfurter-led bloc to halt any advance toward incorporation.

Signature Opinion.   *United States v. Rabinowitz* (1950). He wrote the majority opinion in *Rabinowitz*, which established the rule that a search incident to arrest could justify the search of the entire premises. This rule stood until overturned by the *Chimel* decision in 1969. Justice Minton wrote: "What is a reasonable search is not to be determined by any fixed formula. The Constitution does not define what are 'unreasonable' searches and, regrettably, in our discipline we have no ready litmus-paper test. The recurring questions of the reasonableness of searches must find resolution in the facts and circumstances of each case." In *Rabinowitz*, Justice Minton viewed the search as reasonable because the search and seizure were incident to a valid arrest; the place of the search was a business room to which the public was invited; the room was small and under the immediate and complete control of the respondent; the search did not extend beyond the room used for unlawful purposes; and the possession of the forged stamps was a crime. The Court was clearly influenced by the Crime Control Model of criminal justice: "A rule of thumb requiring that a search warrant always be procured whenever practicable may be appealing from the vantage point of easy administration. But we cannot agree that this requirement should be crystallized into a *sine qua non* to the reasonableness of a search. . . . The judgment of the officers as to when to close the trap on a criminal committing a crime in their presence or who they have reasonable cause to believe is committing a felony is not determined solely upon whether there was time to procure a search warrant. Some flexibility will be accorded law officers engaged in daily battle with criminals for whose restraint criminal laws are essential."

Assessment.   Justice Minton replaced liberal Justice Rutledge and was thought by most observers at the time to be in the liberal mold. However, he fit very closely into the Vinson–Reed–Burton camp; as a New Dealer, he acquiesced to Congress in economic matters, but in civil rights issues, he had the most conservative record, voting for the government even more than Chief Justice Vinson. As a judicial conservative, he strongly maintained that the Court had no special obligation to support civil rights and that the Court had no power to legislate.

Further Reading

Harry L. Wallace, "Mr. Justice Minton: Hoosier Justice on the Supreme Court," *Indiana Law Journal* 34 (1959): 145–205.

Charles E. Whittaker

Missouri, 1901–1973

Republican

Appointed by Dwight D. Eisenhower

Years of Service: 1957–1962

Collection of the Supreme Court of the United States. Photographer: Abdon Daoud Ackad.

Life and Career.   Whittaker was born and raised on a modest Kansas farm, where he trapped small animals and tracked game to supplement his family's income. He attended the University of Kansas City Law School at night while working as a clerk in a law firm, graduating in 1924. From then until 1954 (as partner from 1930), he practiced law in the same firm, which represented many large corporations doing business in Missouri. He was first a litigator and later an advisor to the firm's large business clients. He was active in bar association activities and became president of the Missouri State Bar Association. In 1954, he was appointed by President Eisenhower as a federal district judge and, in 1956, as a judge to the U.S. Court of Appeals for the Eighth Circuit. Known for his hard work and efficiency as a judge, he established conservative credentials in ruling that a tenured professor in a private university could be dismissed for refusing to answer questions asked by a congressional committee and the university's board of trustees about possible Communist Party affiliations. He was selected by President Eisenhower as a conservative Republican judge to replace Justice Reed.

Contribution to Criminal Procedure.   Justice Whittaker strove to put aside ideological considerations and decide cases on their merits alone. This led to a somewhat inconsistent position. While he voted for the defendant in a number of cases, he also opposed the incorporation of the Fourth Amendment exclusionary rule in *Mapp v. Ohio* (1961).

Signature Opinion.   *Draper v. United States* (1959). Writing for a six-to-one majority, Whittaker ruled that probable cause existed to arrest Draper based on evidence given by a known reliable informant. An officer was told that Draper, a known drug peddler in Denver, would return by train from Chicago with a supply of heroin. The informant described the clothing that Draper would be wearing (a light-colored raincoat, brown slacks, and black shoes). The Court held that probable cause existed because the officer, having corroborated every factual element about Draper, except the possession of drugs when he detrained, "had 'reasonable grounds' to believe that the remaining unverified bit of [the informant's] information—that Draper would have the heroin with him—was likewise true."

Assessment.   On the Court, Justice Whittaker aligned himself with such conservatives as Justices Frankfurter, Harlan, Clark, Burton, and Potter Stewart to maintain a slim majority in several civil liberties and criminal procedure cases. Unlike these conservative justices, he never was able to articulate a coherent philosophy of judging by which to guide his opinions. Thus, when he did rule in favor of defendants, his votes appeared to be based more on emotional factors of sympathy than on a firm understanding of the role of the federal judiciary. It would appear that he did not outgrow his position as a district court judge who could achieve success in applying the law; as a Supreme Court justice, it is necessary to expound the contours of the Constitution in novel and difficult cases. It is possible that Justice Whittaker's abilities were overtaxed, for he apparently put in an enormous number of hours and worried substantially about the cases. He fell ill in March 1962, apparently exhausted from his work. He resigned from the Court that year and accepted a position as a legal advisor to the General Motors Corporation.

Further Reading

Barbara B. Christensen, "Mister Justice Whittaker: The Man on the Right," *Santa Clara Law Review* 19 (1979): 1039–62.

CHAPTER 5

Warrantless Searches

[T]he most basic constitutional rule in this area is that "searches conducted outside the judicial process, without prior approval by judge or magistrate, are per se unreasonable under the Fourth Amendment—subject only to a few specifically established and well-delineated exceptions." . . . In times of unrest, whether caused by crime or racial conflict or fear of internal subversion, this basic law and the values that it represents may appear unrealistic or "extravagant" to some. But the values were those of the authors of our fundamental constitutional concepts.

—JUSTICE POTTER STEWART, *Coolidge v. New Hampshire,* 403 U.S. 443, 455 (1971)

KEY TERMS

administrative search
automobile search
border
border search

crime scene investigation exception
emergency aid doctrine
exigency exception
extraterritorial

fixed checkpoint
hot pursuit
impound
in loco parentis
inventory search

pervasively regulated industry
roving patrol
special needs doctrine
warrantless search

Warrantless searches are of enormous practical importance to police work. Despite the Supreme Court's preference for a search warrant, warrantless searches are far more common. Every warrantless search is conducted without prior judicial review but is subject to judicial review after the fact. Nevertheless, a search based on an officer's assessment of probable cause is more likely to be arbitrary than one subjected to the warrant process.

This text has already discussed several kinds of warrantless searches: plain view, consent, search incident to arrest, and the *Terry* stop and frisk. Each is based on a different rationale and is held to different legal standards. An item lawfully seized in plain view, for example, involves no Fourth Amendment interest or expectation of privacy because the officer is in a public or other lawful place when the "plain view" occurs. A consent search is not burdened by the Fourth Amendment because the person has voluntarily given up the right of privacy, even if the officer does not have probable cause or reasonable suspicion to believe that the person is carrying contraband. The Fourth Amendment, however, imposes one absolute standard on all warrantless searches—they must be *reasonable*. Thus, for example, consent must be truly voluntary, and an item in plain view must be immediately apparent as contraband.

In contrast to consent searches and plain view seizures, which do not directly interfere with Fourth Amendment rights, a group of warrantless searches are valid even though they *directly interfere* with personal rights under the search and seizure amendment. These warrantless searches impinge on a person's expectation of privacy but are deemed reasonable because each occurs under *emergency* conditions. These **exigency exceptions** include (1) home entries under a condition of hot pursuit, (2) the "automobile exception," and (3) search incident to arrest (see Chapter 4). The Supreme Court has also allowed forcible warrantless searches for evidence in a few miscellaneous cases that Professors Whitebread and Slobogin have labeled "evanescent evidence." That is, when evidence may be destroyed or may disappear, police can forcibly restrain a suspect and take the evidence, as long as the methods are not brutal.[1] This includes taking blood from a vehicular homicide suspect (*Schmerber v. California,* 1966; see Chapter 3) or scrapings of dried blood from the finger of a homicide suspect (*Cupp v. Murphy,* 1973; see Chapter 4). In addition, warrantless entries into premises are allowed for exigencies, as in police officers entering a home in *Arizona v. Hicks* (1987) (see Chapter 3) and firefighters entering a burning building (this chapter).

For an exigency search to be lawful, an officer must have *probable cause* to believe that contraband is in the place or vehicle being entered or probable cause to arrest the person being searched incident to arrest. These exigency exceptions are compatible with the warrant-preference construction of the Fourth Amendment (see "The Fourth Amendment's Structure" in Chapter 2):

> Thus the most basic constitutional rule in this area is that "searches conducted outside the judicial process, without prior approval by judge or magistrate, are *per se* unreasonable under the Fourth Amendment—subject only to a few specifically established and well-delineated exceptions." The exceptions are "jealously and carefully drawn," and there must be "a showing by those who seek exemption . . . that the exigencies of the situation made that course imperative." (*Coolidge v. New Hampshire,* 1971)

The exigency exceptions existed under common law and, because of their obvious necessity, do not undermine the warrant requirement. The warrant-preference construction warns against creating new categories of exceptions. Recently, however, the Court has indeed weakened the warrant-preference policy of the Fourth Amendment by extending the scope of automobile searches and by creating a class of warrantless searches justified by "special needs beyond the normal need for law enforcement." This chapter also reviews other kinds of nonexigency warrantless searches: inventory searches, administrative searches, and border searches.

To reiterate, the basic rule that justifies all warrantless searches under the Fourth Amendment is *reasonableness*. Beyond this basic requirement, the exigency exceptions require the prior existence of probable cause. Some warrantless searches dispense with probable cause and rely on reasonable suspicion (e.g., *Terry* stops and searches of public school students' bags by teachers). Other warrantless searches require no probable cause or reasonable suspicion (e.g., automobile inventory searches). And still others dispense with particularized suspicion against a specific person (e.g., automobile sobriety checklanes).

HOT PURSUIT AND OTHER EXIGENCY SEARCHES

Hot Pursuit

Hot pursuit occurs when a dangerous criminal suspect is being chased by police and enters a place that is protected by the Fourth Amendment expectation of privacy, such as the suspect's home. The suspect presents a danger to society: He or she may flee, harm someone, or destroy evidence. Police officers need to enter the premises immediately to make an arrest and to search for weapons and contraband. The immediacy of a hot pursuit makes it absurd to "stop the action" to obtain a search warrant to enter. A greater danger to the public and to the police might develop if police cordoned off a house because it gives the suspect an opportunity to destroy evidence and to fortify the residence. As a result, the hot pursuit exception allows the police to enter immediately, without an arrest or search warrant, to make an arrest. If evidence of a crime is observed in plain view during the hot pursuit entry for purposes of arrest, it may be seized and is admissible in a criminal trial.

In *Warden v. Hayden* (1967), cab drivers followed Hayden to a house after he had robbed the taxi company office. They transmitted the information to the taxi dispatcher, who in turn relayed the information to the police. Police officers arrived at Hayden's home "within minutes" of receiving the call, knocked on his door, and entered when the door was opened by his wife. They searched through the house looking for the suspect and found incriminating evidence in a washing machine: a jacket and trousers similar to that worn by the robber. This evidence would be admissible only if the initial entry was lawful. The Supreme Court, holding the entry and search constitutional, explained the basis of the hot pursuit exception to the warrant requirement:

> The Fourth Amendment does not require police officers to delay in the course of an investigation if to do so would gravely endanger their lives or the lives of others. Speed here was essential, and only a thorough search of the house for persons and weapons could have ensured that Hayden was the only man present and that the police had control of all weapons which could be used against them or to effect an escape. (*Warden v. Hayden,* 1967)

Several legal principles of the hot pursuit exception can be derived from this case. *First*, the hot pursuit warrant exception, as an exigency exception, must be based on *probable cause* to believe that the person who has just entered the premises has committed a felony or is dangerous to the safety of others. *Second*, hot pursuit may be based either on the officer's personal observations or on *reliable hearsay*. *Third*, the pursuit need not be immediate; there may be a *short time lapse* between the suspect's entry into the house and the arrival of the police. The *fourth* rule concerns the *scope* of the search pursuant to the hot pursuit entry. "The permissible scope of search must, . . . at the least, be as broad as may reasonably be necessary to prevent the dangers that the suspect at large in the house may resist or escape" (*Warden v. Hayden,* 1967). In other words, until the offender is found, the police may search the entire premises for suspects, weapons, and evidence of the crime. However, once the offender has been apprehended, the police may not search beyond the limits of a search incident to an arrest.

Most hot pursuits proceed from public property onto private property. **United States v. Santana** (1976) established a *fifth rule*: The pursuit *may begin on private property*. Officers had reliable information that "Mom" Santana was in possession of marked money from a heroin buy. As the police approached her house, Santana was standing in the doorway holding a paper bag. She retreated to a vestibule, where the police seized her. In a brief struggle, heroin packets fell from the bag and were lawfully seized by the police. Here, although the pursuit technically began on private property, the Court held that for Fourth Amendment purposes, it was a public place. The *Santana* ruling, however, does not allow the police to enter a house where there is no exigency and thereby "create" one. Santana also indicates a *sixth rule*: there must be a *pursuit*. A "'hot pursuit' means some sort of a chase, but it need not be an extended hue and cry in and about the public streets. The fact that the pursuit here ended almost as soon as it began did not render it any the less a 'hot pursuit' sufficient to justify the warrantless entry into Santana's house." (*U.S. v. Santana*, 1976, quotes and text modifications omitted).

The *seventh rule*, established by **Welsh v. Wisconsin** (1984), concerns the *gravity* of the offense: Police may enter a premises without a warrant in hot pursuit only for serious crimes. A minor offense does not create an exigency that overrides the Fourth Amendment rule that police must obtain an arrest warrant in order to arrest a suspect in his or her home (*Payton v. New York,* 1980). The offense in *Welsh* was a civil infraction of driving while intoxicated (DWI). Welsh's erratic driving resulted in his car's careening off a road and into a ditch on a rainy night. A witness saw the apparently intoxicated driver walk off into the night and called the police, who arrived at Welsh's nearby home within the hour. They entered the house without a warrant or the consent of Welsh's stepdaughter, found Welsh in bed, arrested him, and took him to the police station, where he refused to submit to a breath analysis test. His refusal could result in a license revocation only if the arrest was legal, and this, in turn, depended on the legality of the forcible, warrantless home entry. The state's only rationale for a constitutional entry was hot pursuit.

The Wisconsin Supreme Court upheld the warrantless entry because of the need to prevent harm to the offender and the public resulting from drunk driving and to prevent the "destruction" of the blood alcohol evidence by its dissipation before testing could be completed. The U.S. Supreme Court reversed. It discounted the weak public safety reasoning because the offender was in bed and thus no longer a threat to anyone. Preservation of evidence is a basis of the hot pursuit exigency, but the Court held "that an important factor to be considered when determining whether any exigency exists is the gravity of the underlying offense for which the arrest is being made." Under Wisconsin law, the underlying offense in this case—first-offense DWI—was a noncriminal violation subject to a $200 fine. Justice Brennan, writing for the majority, noted that a warrantless entry into a home is presumptively unreasonable and that the burden of proof is on the government to show that an exigency makes a warrantless entry reasonable. The Court felt that a hot pursuit entry for a minor crime is presumptively unreasonable and difficult for the government to rebut.

The entry and search in this case violated the Fourth Amendment because (1) "there was no immediate or continuous pursuit of the petitioner from the scene of a crime," (2) Welsh had arrived home and abandoned his car so there was little remaining threat to the public safety, and (3) the exigency of ascertaining Welsh's blood-alcohol level was outweighed by the fact that first-offense DWI was classified as a civil offense. The majority believed that this would be "unreasonable police behavior that the principles of the Fourth Amendment will not sanction."

Justice Byron White's dissent noted that a warrantless entry into a home is as serious a Fourth Amendment intrusion for a person wanted for a serious felony as for a minor crime. He disagreed with the majority's assessment of gravity because of the danger to highway safety by drunk drivers. The warrantless intrusion into Welsh's bedroom promoted the "valid and substantial state interests" of prosecuting drunk driving. He also suggested that police are better served by bright-line rules so that what constitutes a serious offense—justifying hot pursuit—is not open to interpretation. The dissent also urged the Court to defer to the state's judgment as to the seriousness of the offense.

Welsh does not indicate what constitutes a nonserious crime, beyond the civil offense of first-time DWI punishable by a fine. Justice William Brennan implied that a simple bright-line division between felonies and misdemeanors is not the proper line between serious and nonserious offenses. Even if the *Welsh* rule does not apply only to civil offenses punishable by a fine, the case itself does not establish the serious–nonserious criterion. Perhaps, then, it is the penalty, such as imprisonment for thirty days or six months. Or possibly, hot pursuit is not proper for some nonviolent felonies but is for some violent misdemeanors. Another uncertainty left by *Welsh* is whether the hot pursuit exception for minor crimes applies in premises other than the home.

The Supreme Court held in ***Minnesota v. Olson*** (1990) that being wanted for a serious felony does not in itself create an exigency. Police suspected that Olson, a murder suspect, was in a house, and they entered without a warrant. Their attempt to justify the warrantless entry on the basis of hot pursuit was undercut by several factors:

- The suspect was thought to be the driver of a get-away car and not the shooter.
- The police had already recovered the murder weapon.
- There was no suggestion of danger to other people from the suspect.
- The entry occurred a day after the murder-robbery.
- Three or four police squads surrounded the house, which was secured.

Minnesota v. Olson demonstrates that the finding of an exigency is a factual determination made by a court assessing all of the circumstances of the case.

Other Exigencies

The hot pursuit warrant exception is an example of a general rule that police may enter a premises or conduct a search without a warrant when exigent circumstances justify the search or intrusion. The exigent circumstance may be an imminent threat to the life or safety of people that no police officer should ignore. In *Arizona v. Hicks* (1987) (see Chapter 3), the officer properly entered an apartment to search for a man who had shot a bullet through the floor into another apartment, injuring an occupant and creating an obvious and continuing threat to life and safety. In *Hicks,* there was probable cause to believe that a person had committed a felony. There was no hot pursuit as such, but the entry met the reasonableness criterion of an exigency exception. Warrantless entry into homes by government agents who are not police officers enforcing the criminal law must also be supported by a real exigency: firefighting is a prime example (*Michigan v. Tyler,* 1978; *Michigan v. Clifford,* 1984).

The warrantless entry in *Arizona v. Hicks* (1987) was made under what has come to be recognized as the **emergency aid doctrine (*Brigham City v. Stuart,* 2006)**. The duty of police to come to the aid of those who are in danger of losing life or limb is so apparent that it gives rise to relatively little litigation. In *Stuart,* police were called to a loud house party at 3 a.m., heard loud shouting, walked down a driveway, and saw two teenagers drinking beer in the yard. Through a screen door and windows, they saw a fight in the kitchen between four adults and a juvenile, who punched the face of one of the adults, causing him to spit blood in the sink. The other adults pushed the juvenile up against a refrigerator to restrain him. "At this point, an officer opened the screen door and announced the officers' presence. Amid the tumult, nobody noticed. The officer entered the kitchen and again cried out, and as the occupants slowly became aware that the police were on the scene, the altercation ceased." Under these circumstances, the officer's warrantless entry was justified. As a matter of Fourth Amendment law, the test of the entry's reasonableness is objective. The circumstances made it objectively reasonable for an officer to believe that the injured adult needed medical aid and that the violence in the kitchen might continue. "Nothing in the Fourth Amendment required [the officers] to wait until another blow rendered someone 'unconscious' or 'semiconscious' or worse before entering. The role of a peace officer includes preventing violence and restoring order, not simply rendering first aid to casualties; an officer is not like a boxing (or hockey) referee, poised to stop a bout only if it becomes too one-sided" (*Brigham City v. Stuart,* 2006).

An immediate warrantless search and seizure is constitutional where essential to prevent the destruction of criminal evidence. In **Schmerber v. California** (1966), a driver was arrested in a hospital while being treated for injuries suffered in an automobile accident. A police officer directed a physician to draw blood for alcohol testing. The sample was admitted into evidence to convict Schmerber of driving while intoxicated. This critical evidence would have been lost if the blood were not promptly drawn. The seizure was reasonable because the routine collection of blood by medical workers is not dangerous, overly invasive, or humiliating, and is likely to produce highly accurate evidence. Probable cause existed to believe Schmerber committed the crime and the intrusion on privacy interests was minimal.

Other cases have upheld warrantless searches as reasonable because of the exigency that evidence might be destroyed. In these cases, privacy rights were minimal, and the cases did not precisely fit the search incident to arrest warrant exception. *United States v. Edwards* (1974) involved taking potentially incriminating paint chips from the clothing of a police lockup inmate who was ordered to exchange his clothing for jail issue. *Cupp v. Murphy* (1973), discussed in Chapter 4, upheld the removal of what was apparently dried blood from the finger of a potential murder suspect, who had not been arrested, at a police station.

REJECTING THE CRIME SCENE INVESTIGATION EXCEPTION   The Supreme Court *rejected* a **crime scene investigation exception** to the warrant requirement in **Mincey v. Arizona** (1978). A police officer was killed in a drug raid in the Tucson, Arizona, apartment of Rufus Mincey, who was apparently shot by the slain officer. Backup officers entered the apartment, located other people, called for emergency assistance, and refrained from further investigation. Ten minutes later, homicide investigators arrived, arranged for the removal of the fatally injured officer and the suspects, and then secured the apartment. They then proceeded to gather evidence.

Their search lasted four days, during which period the entire apartment was searched, photographed, and diagrammed. The officers opened drawers, closets, and cupboards, and inspected their contents; they emptied clothing pockets; they dug bullet fragments out of the walls and floors; they pulled up sections of the carpet and removed them for examination. Every item in the apartment was closely examined and inventoried, and 200 to 300 objects were seized. In short, Mincey's apartment was subjected to an exhaustive and intrusive search. No warrant was ever obtained. (*Mincey v. Arizona,* 1978)

The evidence obtained in the search was introduced at trial to convict Mincey of homicide and drug possession. The Arizona Supreme Court upheld the warrantless search as reasonable when conducted to investigate "the scene of a homicide—or of a serious personal injury with likelihood of death where there is reason to suspect foul play" as long as "the purpose [is] limited to determining the circumstances of death and the scope [does] not exceed that purpose. The search must also begin within a reasonable period following the time when the officials first learn of the murder (or potential murder)."

The Supreme Court unanimously reversed, holding that this warrantless search violated the Fourth Amendment. Although Mincey was a suspect, he retained some reasonable expectation of privacy in his home. To strip a suspect of all rights of privacy in the home "would impermissibly convict the suspect even before the evidence against him was gathered." The fact that Mincey was arrested and was in custody does not lessen "his right to privacy in his entire house" (*Mincey v. Arizona,* 1978). An exigency after the violent crime authorized the initial entry into Mincey's apartment, the protective sweep, the securing of the apartment, and the seizure of contraband items in plain view. But "a four-day search that included opening dresser drawers and ripping up carpets can hardly be rationalized in terms of the legitimate concerns that justify an emergency search" (*Mincey v. Arizona,* 1978). The Court also rejected the idea that special promptness was required to search the scene of a homicide, suggesting that an exception for that crime would lead to a blanket crime scene warrant exception and the argument that dispensing with a warrant would be more efficient. There was no suggestion that a search warrant could not have been easily and conveniently obtained. The Supreme Court later held that a warrantless, thorough, sixteen-hour homicide investigation of a cabin violated the *Mincey* ruling (*Flippo v. West Virginia,* 1999).

THE AUTOMOBILE EXCEPTION

An Overview of Vehicle Search Rules

The stop and search of mobile vehicles by police raises a variety of constitutional issues, some of which are discussed in Chapters 3, 4, and 7.

1. *Stopping I:*   Probable cause or reasonable suspicion is required to stop a mobile vehicle (*Delaware v. Prouse,* 1979; see Chapter 4).
2. *Stopping II:*   Innocent behavior can be the basis for stopping an automobile on reasonable suspicion grounds (*United States v. Arvizu,* 2002; see Chapter 4).
3. *Automobile exception: search of vehicle:*   What is the scope of an officer's authority to search a stopped mobile vehicle without a warrant? (See *United States v. Ross,* 1982, in this chapter.)
4. *Automobile exception: search of containers:*   What is the scope of an officer's authority to look into or to search closed areas or closed containers in a stopped mobile vehicle without a warrant? (See *California v. Acevedo,* 1991, in this chapter.)
5. *Pretext stops:*   An officer may stop a car with objective reasonable suspicion or probable cause of a traffic violation even though the real (subjective) reason for the stop is to search for drugs and there is no legal basis to stop the car for drugs (*Whren v. United States,* 1996; see Chapter 4).
6. *Stop and frisk:*   An officer may enter an automobile to frisk a suspect or to inspect the interior (*Adams v. Williams,* 1972; *Michigan v. Long,* 1983; see Chapter 4).
7. *Control of driver and passengers:*   An officer may order the driver and passengers to remain in or exit the vehicle (*Pennsylvania v. Mimms,* 1977; *Maryland v. Wilson,* 1997; *Brendlin v. California,* 2009; see Chapter 4).

8. ***Knowledge and consent:***   An officer need not inform a driver that he or she is free to go before obtaining consent to search a vehicle (*Schneckloth v. Bustamonte,* 1973; *Ohio v. Robinette,* 1996; see Chapter 3).

9. ***Scope of consent:***   Consent to search a car includes consent to search a container in the car (*Florida v. Jimeno,* 1991; see Chapter 3).

10. ***Questioning:***   An officer need not read *Miranda* warnings for a routine stop or for most aspects of a stop for drunk driving (*Berkemer v. McCarty,* 1984; *Pennsylvania v. Muniz,* 1990; see Chapter 7).

11. ***Checklanes:***   Mobile vehicles may be stopped at checklanes to examine drivers for sobriety but not for illegal drug possession (*Michigan Department of State Police v. Sitz,* 1990; *City of Indianapolis v. Edmond,* 2000; see Chapter 4).

12. ***Dog sniff of stopped vehicles:***   Can police bring a drug-sniffing dog to examine the exterior of a stopped vehicle? (*Illinois v. Caballes,* 20005, see Chapter 4).

13. ***Impounded vehicles:***   What rules guide the inventory search of impounded vehicles? (See *Florida v. Wells,* 1990, in this chapter).

Clearly, an **automobile search** is a complex legal area. The development of various auto search rules over the last three decades has been one of the most confusing and contentious areas of criminal procedure. Most legal scholars have criticized the Supreme Court automobile search rulings that cut into the Fourth Amendment, accusing the Court of twisting principles to ensure that police officers can search automobiles almost at will. One scholar states, "Although the Court has described warrantless searches as presumptively invalid, more than twenty seemingly haphazard exceptions to the warrant clause in fact have swallowed the warrant requirement."[2] The relentless pressure by police to search cars is driven by the "war on drugs" and by the fact that police departments can augment their budgets by the forfeiture of automobiles found to be transporting illegal drugs.[3] The constitutional debate has recently become an explosive law enforcement and political issue as the practice of racial profiling has been exposed. (See the "Law in Society" section in this chapter.)

The discussion of the automobile exception, narrowly defined, usually focuses on the first four categories just listed. However, in the "real world" of policing, all of the rules and exceptions listed come together to produce a powerful regime of rules that makes it possible for a police officer to search virtually any car that he or she has a mind to stop. Driving is a pervasive activity in America, and it is nearly impossible for anyone to drive without violating some motor vehicle law, including speeding, driving over a line, changing lanes without signaling, inoperative taillight, headlights not on one-half hour after sunset to one-half hour before sunrise "and at such other times as atmospheric conditions render visibility as low as or lower than is ordinarily the case during that period," having an excessively loud muffler, and so forth.[4] Therefore a police officer following a vehicle is likely to spot a violation at some point and, upon stopping that car, can utilize one of the various automobile search rules to engage in some level of lawful search. The potential—and the reality—of the pervasive stopping of black and Hispanic drivers in large numbers on pretextual grounds has led Professor David Harris to claim that "[i]ndeed, it is no exaggeration to say that in cases involving cars, the Fourth Amendment is all but dead."[5] To Professor David Moran this trend culminated in *United States v. Arvizu* (2002), which found reasonable suspicion based on a family driving in a camper and "scrupulously obeying all traffic laws. . . . The Court's new vehicle doctrine is now complete: The police may lawfully stop any car at any time and virtually always search the car."[6] The following section demonstrates how the basic automobile search doctrine was fashioned.

The Automobile Exception

The Supreme Court has upheld warrantless searches of automobiles for two reasons:

> Our first cases establishing the automobile exception to the Fourth Amendment's warrant requirement were based on the automobile's "ready mobility," an exigency sufficient to excuse failure to obtain a search warrant once probable cause to conduct the search is clear. . . . *Carroll v. United States* (1925). More recent cases provide a further justification: the individual's reduced expectation of privacy in an automobile, owing to its pervasive regulation. (*Pennsylvania v. Labron,* 1996)

Early on, the Supreme Court applied the "automobile" exception to a boat, and lower courts have applied the rule to searches of such mobile vehicles as trains, airplanes, ferries, and houseboats (*United States v. Lee,* 1927).

Carroll v. United States (1925) is the foundation case for the automobile exigency exception. Chief Justice William Howard Taft wrote:

> The guaranty of freedom from unreasonable searches and seizures by the Fourth Amendment has been construed, practically since the beginning of the government, as recognizing a difference between a search of a store, dwelling house or other structure in respect of which a proper official search warrant readily may be obtained, and a search of a ship, motor boat, wagon or automobile for contraband goods, where it is not practicable to secure a warrant, because the vehicle can be quickly moved out of the locality or jurisdiction in which the warrant must be sought. (*Carroll v. United States,* 1925)

The *Carroll* rule requires that (1) police have probable cause to believe that the vehicle contains contraband, and (2) there is a "mobility exigency"—the vehicle will be driven off if it is not immediately seized. It is absurd for the police to leave a suspected vehicle to obtain a warrant. In *Carroll,* the officers had probable cause to believe that bootleggers were transporting illegally imported liquor in violation of the Prohibition laws when they spotted the "Carroll boys" driving toward Grand Rapids, Michigan. The officers stopped the car, felt the back seat, noticed that it was hard, and proceeded to rip and destroy the seat in order to get to the bottles of whiskey. The Court did not comment on this, indicating that the authority to search for contraband may reasonably include the destruction of some property necessary to get to the evidence.

The second rationale for a warrantless automobile search, a lesser expectation of privacy than exists in homes or in luggage, was explained in *California v. Carney* (1985):

> Even in cases where an automobile was not immediately mobile, the lesser expectation of privacy resulting from its use as a readily mobile vehicle justified application of the vehicular exception. In some cases, the configuration of the vehicle contributed to the lower expectation of privacy; for example . . . because the passenger compartment of a standard automobile is relatively open to plain view, there are lesser expectations of privacy. But even when enclosed "repository" areas have been involved, we have concluded that the lesser expectations of privacy warrant application of the exception. We have applied the exception in the context of a locked car trunk, a sealed package in a car trunk, a closed compartment under the dashboard, the interior of a vehicle's upholstery, or sealed packages inside a covered pickup truck.
>
> These reduced expectations of privacy derive not from the fact that the area to be searched is in plain view, but from the pervasive regulation of vehicles capable of traveling on the public highways. (*California v. Carney,* 1985)

The pervasive regulation includes periodic inspection and licensing requirements, and ticketing for driving with expired license plates or inspection stickers or for such violations as exhaust fumes or excessive noise. Furthermore, all members of the public are fully aware of these regulations and know that they can be stopped while driving for such errors.

The mobility rationale—a traditional, common law exigency exception to the warrant requirement—easily fits into the warrant-preference construction of the Fourth Amendment. It is a commonsense explanation for dispensing with a warrant. Professor Steinberg states that the lesser expectation of privacy rationale, however, "makes no sense. Under this line of reasoning, a state could eviscerate Fourth Amendment protections simply by heavy regulation of an activity or location." Also, although houses are "regulated extensively by building codes," police cannot search them without a warrant.[7] It suggests a policy preference on the part of the Supreme Court's conservative majority to simply give police a free hand when searching in and around an automobile. This conclusion is drawn by Harris, who believes the Court is motivated by "the desire that the police have wide latitude to investigate and the safety of the officers while they carry out these duties."[8]

THE MOBILITY FACTOR   In *Coolidge v. New Hampshire* (1971), a plurality of the Court ruled that the exception does not apply to immobilized vehicles. The defendant was arrested and detained for murder. Two days later, his car was impounded by police and searched pursuant to a search warrant that was later found to be defective. The state argued that the search was nevertheless constitutional under the automobile search exception. The Court rejected this argument, holding that the exception does not apply simply because an automobile was searched:

> The word "automobile" is not a talisman in whose presence the Fourth Amendment fades away and disappears. And surely there is nothing in this case to invoke the meaning and purpose of the rule of *Carroll v. United States*—no alerted criminal bent on flight, no fleeting opportunity on an open highway after a hazardous chase, no contraband or stolen goods or weapons, no confederates waiting to move the evidence, not even the inconvenience of a special police detail to guard the immobilized automobile. In short, by no possible stretch of the legal imagination can this be made into a case where "it is not practicable to secure a warrant," . . . and the "automobile exception," despite its label, is simply irrelevant. (*Coolidge v. New Hampshire*, 1971)

The Court, unfortunately, has not strictly held to this aspect of *Coolidge*. It has in numerous cases invoked the automobile exception to uphold the search of a parked automobile where mobility was not a factor. *Coolidge* appeared to say that the mobility exigency was based on actual mobility—the immediate, or almost immediate, possibility that the car would be driven away by the suspect. More recently, the Court has diluted this rationale by leaning toward the potential mobility of the vehicle. Thus, in **Pennsylvania v. Labron** (1996), the Court upheld the search of a car belonging to a suspect who had been arrested for a drug transaction. There was no confederate to take the car away, and a warrant could have been obtained. The Pennsylvania Supreme Court ruled that a warrant was required. The U.S. Supreme Court reversed, stating: "If a car is *readily* mobile and probable cause exists to believe it contains contraband, the Fourth Amendment thus permits police to search the vehicle without more" (*Pennsylvania v. Labron*, 1996, emphasis added).

TIME FRAME OF THE EXIGENCY   The rights of drivers have also been weakened in cases dealing with the time frame of the exigency, both before and after the search. In *Coolidge*, the automobile was searched two and a half weeks after the police obtained probable cause, far after the time that any real exigency might have existed. The Court, however, has expanded the time frame within which an exigency is said to exist in ways that do not seem reasonable. The foundation for this approach was laid in a Prohibition Era case of the same vintage as *Carroll*: **Husty v. United States** (1931). A reliable informant told a Prohibition officer that Husty, a previously convicted bootlegger, "had two loads of liquor in automobiles of a particular make and description, parked in particular places on named streets." The agent proceeded to one of the cars, although he had sufficient time to obtain a warrant. He saw Husty and two other men get into the car. At that point, the agent approached, and the two other men fled. The car was searched, and contraband was found. In response to the argument that the agents had sufficient time to obtain a warrant, Justice Harlan Fiske Stone reasoned that the agent "could not know when Husty would come to the car or how soon it would be removed. In such circumstances we do not think the officers should be required to speculate upon the chances of successfully carrying out the search, after the delay and withdrawal from the scene of one or more officers which would have been necessary to procure a warrant" (*Husty v. United States*, 1931). Under these circumstances, an actual exigency existed.

Four decades later, the Supreme Court moved the time frame from the actual to the potential exigency and beyond. When an automobile is stopped by police with probable cause to believe that it contains contraband, the police can search on the spot or perhaps uphold a strict reading of the Fourth Amendment by securing the vehicle until a warrant has been obtained. The Supreme Court properly rejected the argument that a warrant had to be obtained in **Chambers v. Maroney** (1970): "For constitutional purposes, we see no difference between on the one hand seizing and holding a car before presenting the probable cause issue to a magistrate and on the other hand carrying out an immediate search without a warrant. Given probable cause to search, either course is reasonable under the Fourth Amendment." Although the Court has stated a preference for a search warrant, holding a person at the roadside until a warrant can be obtained is a severe intrusion of liberty. Justice John M. Harlan II, dissenting, preferred the latter course; he thought that the warrantless search was more intrusive because it could lead to a criminal conviction. He believed that a person with nothing to hide would give police consent to search the car. Despite this reasoning, requiring police to obtain a warrant to search a stopped vehicle can create unnecessary risks and burdens on law enforcement.

In *Chambers,* the police stopped a car at night because the car and its four passengers fit the description of a car recently involved in a gas station robbery. Under these circumstances, it was neither practical nor safe for the officers to conduct the search on the roadside; consequently, the car was searched at the police station after the suspects were detained. No warrant was obtained to search the car. The Supreme Court held the search to be constitutional as an automobile search. This is a difficult decision because the time of the exigency had ended. Perhaps it was possible for a confederate or a stranger to enter the automobile and destroy evidence, but this reasoning stretches belief. The *Chambers* decision demonstrates that the Court ignored the mobility rationale of *Carroll,* even before establishing the lesser expectation of privacy rationale for automobile searches. In more recent years, as a practical matter, the ad hoc custody of the automobile practiced in *Chambers* has been replaced by the more routine police practice of impounding all seized vehicles and subjecting them to a detailed inventory search.

Chambers may be explained in part by the Court's desire to protect police officers' safety. This made it reasonable for the officer to take the car to the station house instead of searching it on the road at night; there was a real exigency when the car was first seized. But in **Texas v. White** (1975), the Court allowed the search of a vehicle at the station house, although there was, at best, a potential exigency when the car was seized. White was arrested at 1:30 p.m. while attempting to pass fraudulent checks at a drive-in window of a bank, after police had a report of a similar incident at another bank earlier that day by a person matching White's description. He was ordered to park his car, and a bank employee and an officer observed him attempting to stuff something between the seats of his car. White was driven to the station house while another officer drove his car there. After thirty to forty-five minutes of questioning, White refused to consent to a search of his car, but the officers proceeded to search it anyway. During the search, four wrinkled checks corresponding to those White had attempted to pass at the first bank were discovered. The Court, in a brief *per curiam* opinion, upheld the search on this reading of *Chambers:* "[P]olice officers with probable cause to search an automobile on the scene where it was stopped could constitutionally do so later at the station house without first obtaining a warrant." Justice Thurgood Marshall, joined by Justice Brennan, dissented. He took the majority to task for misreading the holding of *Chambers.* The facts in *Chambers* included a nighttime stop of a car with four suspected armed robbers, a clearly perilous scenario. "*Chambers* simply held [the station house search] to be the rule when it is *reasonable* to take the car to the station house in the first place" (*Texas v. White,* 1975, emphasis added). By ignoring these facts, the Court created a per se rule that allows a car seized with probable cause to be searched, even if the car's mobility was at an end.

The decisions in *Chambers* and *White* stretch the time frame of an "exigency" to mythic proportions. A commonsense understanding of an exigency indicates that no true exigency was present when the police searched the cars in these two cases. It is useful to note that these cases occurred before the Supreme Court validated the routine inventory search (discussed later in this chapter). A routine inventory search is not an exigency search and serves other constitutional interests than those of a probable cause search. Nevertheless, as a functional matter, if not as a matter of constitutional law, routine inventory searches in effect allow the seizure of all contraband found in a car that is searched well after an arrested person has been taken into custody. In any event, the creation of the lesser expectation of privacy rationale and the "stretching" of the time frame for an exigency were vital elements in the Court's expansion of the power of police to search cars. The next step was the Court's willingness to authorize warrantless automobile searches of parked cars.

WHAT IS AN AUTOMOBILE?   *California v. Carney* (1985) gave a precise definition of an automobile for Fourth Amendment purposes. Carney lived in a fully mobile motor home. Police, suspicious that he was trading drugs for sex, had his motor home under surveillance while it was parked in a downtown San Diego public parking lot not far from the courthouse. They observed a youth enter the vehicle and stay there for an hour and a quarter. When the youth emerged, he was stopped by the police and told them that he received marijuana in return for allowing Carney sexual contact. The police and the youth went to the motor home, knocked, and after Carney stepped out, entered it without a warrant and seized illegal drugs.

Carney argued that because this vehicle was also his home, it had to be given the same Fourth Amendment protection as a stationary home—that is, the police could not search it without obtaining a warrant. The Supreme Court disagreed, holding that such a motor home is a mobile vehicle, subject to similar licensing and regulation requirements as an automobile; therefore, the reasonable (i.e., objective) expectation of privacy in a motor home is equivalent to what one expects in an automobile, not a home. These factors brought the vehicle under the exigency exception to the warrant requirement: "Our application of the vehicle exception has never turned on the other uses to which a vehicle might be put."

Justice John Paul Stevens dissented in *Carney* on the grounds that there was no exigency. He urged the Court to rule that the automobile exception should not apply to a parked vehicle where there is time to obtain a warrant, but only to vehicles in motion along the highway. The majority refused to adopt this restriction. However, in *Coolidge v. New Hampshire* (1971), there was time to obtain a warrant, and the search was held to violate the Fourth Amendment. The Court in *Carney* distinguished *Coolidge* on its facts. The seizure in *Coolidge* was preceded by a two-week investigation, and the vehicle was in full police control, while in *Carney* the surveillance of the van lasted for a little over an hour. The police had ample time to plan their action in *Coolidge,* while the police in *Carney* acted with less preparation or planning, although they apparently had the ability to obtain a warrant. In *Coolidge,* the car was taken to the police station, while in *Carney,* the mobile home was in a public parking lot. In *Coolidge,* neither the defendant nor anyone associated with him had access to the car, while Carney was in his vehicle and could have driven it away if he was not arrested. The Court stated in *Carney,* "[T]he respondent's motor home was readily mobile. Absent the prompt search and seizure, it could readily have been moved beyond the reach of the police."

The Supreme Court is clearly reluctant to add any qualification or addition to the automobile exigency rule that benefits defendants. In **Maryland v. Dyson** (1999), police had advance warning, amounting to probable cause, that a specific vehicle would come into the jurisdiction with illegal drugs. An intermediate Maryland appellate court ruled that because the police had time to obtain a warrant, there was no exigency, and a search warrant was required. The Court, in a *per curiam* opinion, reversed. "[U]nder our established precedent, the 'automobile exception' has no separate exigency requirement." Nevertheless, the *Dyson* decision does not seem consistent with the principle, if not the precise facts, of *Coolidge v. New Hampshire* (1971).

THE VIN RULE   The Supreme Court demonstrated its creativity in upholding the legality of a warrantless police entry into a vehicle in **New York v. Class** (1986) by fabricating a limited right of intrusion into a car without probable cause in order to view a vehicle identification number (VIN) not viewable from outside the car. Police stopped a car for speeding. The driver produced a registration certificate and proof of insurance but no driver's license. The officer could not see the VIN on the dashboard so he "reached into the interior of the car to move some papers obscuring the area of the dashboard where the VIN is located in all post–1969 models. In doing so, the officer saw the handle of a gun, and respondent was promptly arrested." With a valid entry, the gun was in plain view and thus admissible. The Court reasoned that the VIN is needed to protect safety and property and is required by federal regulations to be in a place that can be easily read by someone standing outside the automobile. Combining the special requirements of the VIN with the lesser expectation of privacy in an automobile, the Court felt justified in creating a warrant exception authorizing such an entry without probable cause to believe there was contraband in the car. *Class* created a limited police power, because police cannot enter a vehicle if the VIN is observable from the car's exterior, and newer-model cars are designed to make it impossible to cover the VIN.

SEIZURE OF A CAR SUBJECT TO FORFEITURE   In *Florida v. White* (1999), officers observed Tyvessel Tyvorus White make cocaine deliveries in his car in July and August 1993 but did not arrest him. Under the Florida Contraband Forfeiture Act, his car was subject to forfeiture. Several months later, White was arrested at his workplace on charges unrelated to the cocaine delivery. Police officers went to the employee parking lot, where White's car was parked, and seized it without a warrant. A subsequent inventory search disclosed cocaine. The Florida Supreme Court ruled the warrantless seizure to be unconstitutional. The U.S. Supreme Court reversed and offered two reasons for upholding the warrantless seizure: (1) Although the police had no probable cause to believe that the car contained contraband, "they certainly had probable cause to believe that the vehicle *itself* was contraband under Florida law," and the mobility rationale applies to the warrantless seizure of contraband in a mobile vehicle and the mobile vehicle itself; and (2) "our Fourth Amendment jurisprudence has consistently accorded law enforcement officials greater latitude in exercising their duties in public places." The Court treated the owner's private property as a public place for Fourth Amendment purposes and concluded that "the Fourth Amendment did not require a warrant to seize respondent's automobile" (*Florida v. White,* 1999).

Justice Stevens dissented in *White,* joined by Justice Ruth Bader Ginsburg. Under *Soldal v. Cook County* (1992), the Fourth Amendment protects property as well as privacy interests. There was no exigency here. White had been arrested, and there was sufficient time to obtain a search warrant. The car is not inherent contraband, such as drugs or firearms, so its seizure is not required to preserve public safety. A "warrant application interjects the judgment of a neutral decisionmaker, one with no pecuniary interest in the matter." Justice Stevens found it "particularly troubling. . . not that the State provides a weak excuse for failing to obtain a warrant either before or after White's arrest, but that it offers us no reason at all" and concluded that "the officers who seized White's car simply preferred to avoid the hassle of seeking approval from a judicial officer." The simple convenience of officers was thought too feeble a reason to override Fourth Amendment rights. Although the majority paid lip service to the warrant requirement, "its decision suggests that the exceptions have all but swallowed the general rule."

CONTROLLING PEOPLE IN THE STOPPED AUTOMOBILE   The Supreme Court has given police almost complete control either to order the driver and passengers to remain in the automobile when it is stopped or to order the driver and passengers out. The primary rationale in these case is the safety of the officer.

In *Pennsylvania v. Mimms* (1977), an automobile was stopped for an expired license plate. On ordering the driver out, the officer noticed a bulge under the driver's sports jacket. A frisk produced a loaded revolver in Mimms's waistband. Balancing the interests of individual privacy against the safety of law enforcement officers, the Court unanimously upheld the officer's frisk and noted that many police officers are killed during routine traffic stops. Against this, the added intrusion of requiring that a driver *exit the car* momentarily is so minimal that it hardly rises to the level of a "petty indignity"; at most, it is a mere inconvenience that cannot prevail against legitimate concerns for the officer's safety.

The rule of *Mimms* was extended to passengers in *Maryland v. Wilson* (1997). Police stopped a speeding automobile—a rental car with no regular license plate. The officer ordered the driver and the passengers to exit the car. There was no legal suspicion that the passengers were engaged in any illegal activity. As Wilson, a passenger, got out of the car, an amount of crack cocaine fell to the ground. Maryland's highest court suppressed the evidence on the ground that the police had no authority to order passengers out of the car without some level of individualized suspicion. The court viewed the order to exit as a Fourth Amendment personal seizure. The Supreme Court, in an opinion by Chief Justice Rehnquist, reversed. The *Mimms* rationale—the *officer's safety*—applied equally to passengers. Indeed, the presence of additional people in the car increases the danger to the police. Despite the lack of probable cause or reasonable suspicion against the passenger, and the fact that a passenger has a greater liberty interest than the driver, as a practical matter the passenger is already stopped by the police detaining the vehicle. This case is analogous to *Michigan v. Summers* (1981), which states that police may temporarily detain a person whose home is being searched under a search warrant.

Justice Stevens dissented, arguing that statistics show no greater danger to police from passengers in stopped cars; the decision intrudes on personal liberty without solid reason. Justice Kennedy dissented, saying, "Traffic stops, even for minor violations, can take upwards of 30 minutes. When an officer commands passengers innocent of any violation to leave the vehicle and stand by the side of the road in full view of the public, the seizure is serious, not trivial." This decision, plus *Whren* (pretextual stops), "puts tens of millions of passengers at risk of arbitrary control by the police." When the *Wilson* rule is combined with the decision of *Wyoming v. Houghton* (1999), which allows the police to search the handbag of a passenger when there is probable cause to search the automobile, and with the *Atwood* rule, which authorizes the custodial seizure for any arrest, an officer's control over a stopped automobile is complete.[9]

Brendlin v. California (2007) answered a question implied in *Maryland v. Wilson* and squarely held that when an officer makes a traffic stop, passengers are seized by the stop as well as the driver. Police stopped a car that they knew was operating legally, under soon-to-expire license plate tags, ostensibly to check its registration. The officer recognized passenger Bruce Brendlin as a parole violator with an outstanding no-bail warrant and arrested him. A search of the car disclosed methamphetamine paraphernalia and Brendlin was charged with possession. If a passenger is seized when a car is stopped, Brendlin could argue that his search was the product of an illegal auto stop. If a passenger is not seized unless and until an officer directs attention to and seizes the passenger, then the state could argue that Brendlin was lawfully seized under the outstanding warrant.

A unanimous Supreme Court held that Brendlin was seized the moment the car was stopped. A seizure of the person normally requires physical force or the show of authority. But when an individual's submission to police action takes the form of "passive acquiescence," the test of whether the person has been seized is the *Mendenhall* (1980) test—that in view of all the circumstances "a reasonable person would have believed that he was not free to leave." The Court has "said over and over in dicta that during a traffic stop an officer seizes everyone in the vehicle, not just the driver." Any reasonable passenger has the societal expectation and understanding that he or she cannot simply walk away from a stopped vehicle as if there was no police officer present. The Fourth Amendment test for seizures is objective. The rule the state argues for would require courts to delve into the motives of police officers when seizing passengers of stopped vehicles, adding possible confusion to relatively clear legal rules. As a result, the case was remanded, allowing Brendlin to challenge the legality of the car stop.

Search Incident to Arrest Meets the Automobile Search

Following the decision in *Chimel v. California* (1969) (see Chapter 4), limiting the scope of a search incident to arrest to the area within the suspect's "immediate control," the Supreme Court encountered cases where a person was arrested while in a car, or got out, or was ordered out of the vehicle. Under *Chimel*, was the entire car under the arrestee's control, including closed containers and locked compartments? The cases posed a problem similar to that in *Chimel*, namely, giving the police reasonable authority to enforce the law while maintaining some constitutional limits. These cases also overlap with those discussed in the next section that concern the search of containers within seized automobiles. Although separating the cases into distinct sections is somewhat artificial, the division provides some doctrinal clarity.

In *New York v. Belton* (1981), the Supreme Court conflated the automobile exigency exception to the search warrant with the search incident to arrest rationale to uphold a search. A lone New York State trooper stopped a speeding car on the New York Thruway, discovered that none of the four men in the car owned it, smelled burnt marijuana, and saw an envelope marked "Supergold" on the floor of the car characteristic of envelopes containing marijuana. The trooper ordered the men out of the car and separated them. He arrested all four occupants for possession of marijuana, secured them with handcuffs, searched them individually, and returned to the car to pick up the envelope. The trooper then found a leather jacket belonging to Roger Belton, one of the occupants. He unzipped one of the pockets and discovered cocaine. The issue is whether the opening of the zippered jacket pocket was a constitutional search.

The Court relied on the search incident to arrest rule, bolstered in part by the automobile search situation, to hold the search valid under the Fourth Amendment. "[W]e hold that when a policeman has made a lawful custodial arrest of the occupant of an automobile, he may, as a contemporaneous incident of that arrest, search the passenger compartment of that automobile." And as an extension of that rule, the Court stated that "the police may also examine the *contents of any containers* found within the passenger compartment, for if the passenger compartment is *within reach* of the arrestee, so also will containers be within his reach" (emphasis added). This language was inconsistent with the *Chadwick-Sanders* rule (explained later in this Chapter). The rationale for the holding was that police needed a bright-line rule to guide them in postarrest searches of persons arrested in automobiles. Like pre-*Chimel* law, the flat *Belton* rule seemed to say that whenever a police officer, with probable cause, arrested a person in a car or ordered out of a car, the officer had carte blanche to search the car for contraband. Was the *Chimel* search incident rule stretched too far? The suspects were not near the interior of the car when the search was actually made. The majority offered limited reasoning to support its decision beyond the need for a bright-line rule. One might reason that *Belton* was not an unjustifiable extension of *Chimel* because the officer was outnumbered by four arrestees. Even though he had secured them outside the car, he could not be certain that one of them would not bolt for the car and find a concealed weapon. *Belton*'s bright-line holding, however, precluded the argument that under some circumstances a search incident to arrest at a vehicle is unreasonable, as, for example, when two police officers arrest a sole driver.

Justice Brennan, dissenting, called the *Belton* bright-line rule an arbitrary extension of existing law under *Chimel*. The *Chimel* exception to the Fourth Amendment warrant requirement was based on (1) the officer's safety and (2) the need to preserve easily concealed or easily destroyed evidence. Neither rationale is present to search the passenger compartment of a vehicle when the occupants are out of the car and secured. According to Justice Brennan, given that New York courts found that the occupants were no longer any danger, this expansion of the permissible scope of searches incident to arrest "ignores both precedent and principle." He predicted that under this "dangerous precedent" the result would be the same even if a handcuffed Belton and companions were placed in the patrol car. This, indeed, came to pass in the next case examining this issue.

In ***Thornton v. United States*** (2004), Officer Nichols became suspicious that Marcus Thornton was driving in a way to avoid the officer, who was driving an unmarked police vehicle but was in uniform. A license tag check revealed that they were issued to a 1982 Chevy two-door and not to the Lincoln Town Car that Thornton was driving. Before Nichols could pull Thornton over, he drove into a parking lot and got out of the car. Nichols approached and told Thornton that the license tags did not match. Thornton appeared nervous. When asked, Thornton said he had no drugs or weapons on him. Concerned for his safety, Officer Nichols obtained consent to pat down Thornton and felt a bulge. Thornton then admitted to carrying drugs and pulled bags of marijuana and crack cocaine out of his pockets. Nichols *handcuffed* Thornton, informed him that he was under arrest, and placed him in the *back seat* of the *patrol car*. He then searched the Lincoln Town Car and found a BryCo .9-millimeter handgun under the driver's seat. Thornton was found guilty of possessing a firearm as a previously convicted felon and in furtherance of drug trafficking.

The issue raised was whether *Belton*'s bright-line rule allowing the search of a car's passenger compartment only applied "where the officer initiated contact with an arrestee while he was still an occupant of the car." Chief Justice Rehnquists's plurality opinion (joined by Justices Kennedy, Thomas, and Breyer) upholding the search rested on the need for a bright-line rule and the notion that whether the arrestees were in or out of the car played no role in the *Belton* decision. What was significant for the future development of rules guiding the search of automobiles incident to the arrest of a driver who had exited or was ordered out were the concerns and reasoning of three concurring justices. Justice O'Connor, joining Justice Scalia's concurring opinion, expressed concern that police had taken the *Belton* rule and run with it to the point that they were no longer constrained by the Constitution: "lower court decisions seem now to treat the ability to search a vehicle incident to the arrest of a recent occupant as a police entitlement rather than as an exception justified by the twin rationales of *Chimel*" (officer safety and the need to prevent destruction or concealment of evidence). She referred to *Belton*'s foundation as "shaky."

In his lengthy concurrence, Justice Scalia, joined by Justice Ginsburg, reasoned that the risk that Thornton could get out of the police car and grab a weapon or evidence from his own caw was "remote in the extreme." The government could not point to a single case where that scenario ever occurred. He disagreed with the rationale that "since the officer could have conducted the search at the time of arrest (when the suspect was still near the car), he should not be penalized for having taken the sensible precaution of securing the suspect in the squad car first." The problem is that "conducting a *Chimel* search is not the Government's right; it is an exception—justified by necessity—to a rule that would otherwise render the search unlawful." If the police secure the situation they can still search the car after obtaining a warrant. Finally, the value of a bright-line rule becomes questionable when the cost is, in the words of a federal appellate judge, that "we have now abandoned our constitutional moorings and floated to a place where the law approves of purely exploratory searches of vehicles during which officers with no definite objective or reason for the search are allowed to rummage around in a car to see what they might find."

Justice Scalia then engaged in a historical analysis to show that a broad vision of the search incident to arrest, exemplified in the *Rabinowitz* (1950) decision that was overturned by *Chimel*, competed with *Chimel*'s narrow vision. The broad vision was not based on *Chimel*'s dual rationale but "on a more general interest in *gathering evidence relevant to the crime* for which the suspect had been arrested." (*Thornton*, 2004, emphasis added). Urging that there is "nothing ir-rational" about this policy, Justice Scalia proposed that "I would therefore limit *Belton* searches to cases where it is reasonable to believe evidence relevant to the crime of arrest might be found in the vehicle." This reasoning bore fruit.

The Supreme Court, in ***Arizona v. Gant*** (2009), adopted the rule proposed by Justice Scalia in *Thornton*. Gant was arrested for driving on a suspended licence even though the police officers were more interested in his possible involvement in drugs. After the arrest Gant and other associates were handcuffed and placed in police vehicles. A search of his car thereafter turned up drugs. "When asked at the suppression hearing why the search was conducted, Officer Griffith responded: 'Because the law says we can do it.'" After conviction the Arizona Supreme Court held the drugs inadmissible and the State appealed. The Supreme Court, noting that the bright-line rule of *Belton* "has long been criticized and probably merits reconsideration," affirmed (5–4).

Justice Stevens's opinion began with the bedrock rule that "searches conducted outside the judicial process, without prior approval by judge or magistrate, are *per se* unreasonable under the Fourth Amendment—subject only to a few specifically established and well-delineated exceptions." An exception is a far cry from the entitlement that, according to Justice O'Connor, police felt they had, as expressed by Officer Griffith's candid reply. Although there was a basis for reading *Belton* as limited by its facts, the case had come to be "widely understood to allow a vehicle search incident to the arrest of a recent occupant even if there is no possibility the arrestee could gain access to the vehicle at the time of the search." As a result, the Court issued a two-part holding. First, "the *Chimel* rationale authorizes police to search a vehicle incident to a recent occupant's arrest only when the arrestee is unsecured and within reaching distance of the passenger compartment at the time of the search." Second, "we also conclude that circumstances unique to the vehicle context justify a search incident to a lawful arrest when it is 'reasonable to believe evidence relevant to the crime of arrest might be found in the vehicle,'" citing *Thornton*.

Justice Stevens believed that the bright-line reading of *Belton* was not as clear as it appeared and that the dual rules in *Gant* would not seriously impede law enforcement work. Most important,

> [T]he State seriously undervalues the privacy interests at stake. . . . It is particularly significant that *Belton* searches authorize police officers to search not just the passenger compartment but every purse, briefcase, or other container within that space. A rule that gives police the power to conduct such a search whenever an individual is caught committing a traffic offense, when there is no basis for believing evidence of the offense might be found in the vehicle, creates a serious and recurring threat to the privacy of countless individuals. Indeed, the character of that threat implicates the central concern underlying the Fourth Amendment—the concern about giving police officers unbridled discretion to rummage at will among a person's private effects. (*Arizona v. Gant*, 2009)

Justice Scalia, concurring, was concerned that the *Chimel* rationale used to support the *Belton*–*Thornton* rule was patently ridiculous and thought that the "charade" should be ended by overruling those cases and abandoning *Chimel* reasoning in automobile search incident cases altogether. "I would hold that a vehicle search incident to arrest is *ipso facto* 'reasonable' only when the object of the search is evidence of the crime for which the arrest was made, or of another crime that the officer has probable cause to believe occurred. Because respondent was arrested for driving without a license (a crime for which no evidence could be expected to be found in the vehicle), I would hold in the present case that the search was unlawful." As no other justice agreed with setting aside *Chimel* in automobile search incident to arrest cases, he concurred. Justice Alito, dissenting (joined by Chief Justice Roberts and Justices Kennedy and Breyer), attacked Justice Stevens's opinion as improperly setting aside precedent and suggested that his ruling was a plurality and not a majority because of the nature of Juistice Scalia's concurring opinion.

Searches of Containers in Mobile Vehicles

A hotly contested automobile search issue in the 1970s and 1980s was the scope of searches of closed areas and containers in seized vehicles. The "container" cases demonstrate that visions of constitutional interpretation are shaped by judges' ideologies. On the one side stood liberal justices Brennan, Marshall, and Stevens, who believed that warrants were required to search containers in vehicles that had been secured by police. This is the position of the warrant-preference construction of the Fourth Amendment and reflects the Due Process Model of criminal justice. On the other side stood the Court's growing conservative majority, who found the Crime Control Model of criminal justice more congenial. Despite some doctrinal difficulties, they ultimately ruled that under the general-reasonableness construction of the Fourth Amendment, warrants are not needed to open closed areas and containers in automobiles if there is probable cause to believe that the containers contain contraband.

SEARCHES OF CONTAINERS NOT IN AUTOMOBILES   In *Carroll v. United States* (1925), the Supreme Court held that when the automobile exception comes into play, officers could search any part of the car in which the contraband could reasonably be found. The officer's determination of what to search was coextensive with that of a magistrate. In *Carroll,* an agent determined that the *hard* back seat of a roadster established probable cause that bootleg liquor was stowed there. The Court agreed and upheld the agent's act of *tearing up* the seat cushion. The destruction of parts of the car within which contraband was stored was therefore allowed if reasonably necessary to seize the contraband.

In contrast to the *Carroll* case, **United States v. Chadwick** (1977) held that a person's "effects" cannot be searched without a warrant, even if an officer has probable cause to believe that the person's "container" holds contraband. In *Chadwick,* Amtrak officials in San Diego became suspicious when two people, one of whom fit the profile of a drug trafficker, loaded a footlocker that was unusually heavy for its size and leaking talcum powder (used to mask the odor of marijuana) on a Boston-bound train. Federal narcotics agents in Boston were on hand two days later when the footlocker arrived. They had no arrest or search warrant, but a trained dog signaled the presence of a controlled substance inside the trunk. Three people took possession of the footlocker and loaded it into the trunk of a car. At that moment, the agents arrested the three men and seized the footlocker, which was taken to the federal building. An hour and a half later, the agents obtained the key to the footlocker, opened it, and found large amounts of marijuana.

The Supreme Court (7–2), in an opinion authored by Chief Justice Warren Burger, held that this warrantless search violated the Fourth Amendment. Although the agents had probable cause to believe that the footlocker contained illicit drugs, it was protected by the Warrant Clause, which "makes a significant contribution to . . . protection" against unreasonable searches and seizures. As early as 1878, the Supreme Court had said that "[l]etters and sealed packages . . . are as fully guarded from examination and inspection, except as to their outward form and weight, as if they were retained by the parties forwarding them in their own domiciles" (*Ex Parte Jackson,* 1878). Important privacy interests are at stake when a person sends a locked trunk to another place, both subjective and reasonable (socially objective). There is a constitutional expectation of privacy in such a container. The Court ruled that brief contact of the footlocker with a car did not turn this into an automobile search case. The Court also found that under the facts of the case, a warrantless search of the footlocker could not be justified as a search incident to arrest. The *Chadwick* Court distinguished a footlocker (an "effect") from an automobile. Although a footlocker is mobile, it is afforded greater Fourth Amendment protection because it is not the subject of pervasive government regulation as is an automobile. Furthermore, once the footlocker's general mobility was ended and it was secured in the Boston federal building under the exclusive control of the police, there was no exigency that required an on-the-spot search without a warrant. "With the footlocker safely immobilized, it was unreasonable to undertake the additional and greater intrusion of a search without a warrant" (*United States v. Chadwick,* 1977).

SEARCHES OF MOBILE CONTAINERS IN AUTOMOBILES   If *Chadwick* were strictly followed, when police search an automobile under the automobile exigency exception, and they discover a container that does not immediately indicate that it holds contraband (e.g., the hardness of the back seat of the roadster in *Carroll* indicated bottles of whiskey), they should seize but not open the container and obtain a search warrant. The court followed this line of reasoning in **Arkansas v. Sanders** (1979). Police had probable cause, supplied by a reliable informant's tip, that Sanders would arrive at an airport with drugs. Sanders deplaned with a suitcase and entered a taxicab. The police followed the cab for several blocks and pulled it over. Without asking permission, they took the suitcase from the cab, opened it, and found over nine pounds of marijuana. The Supreme

Court held that although the police had probable cause to believe that the suitcase contained drugs, and although they were justified in stopping the taxi and seizing the suitcase, the suitcase could not be opened and searched without a search warrant because the mobility exigency regarding the suitcase had ended. The *Sanders* decision was a straightforward application of *Chadwick:* "[W]e hold that the warrant requirement of the Fourth Amendment applies to personal luggage taken from an automobile to the same degree it applies to such luggage in other locations."

The *Sanders* rule proved to be unstable and short-lived. The five majority justices included moderates and liberals (Justices Powell, Brennan, Stewart, White, and Marshall). Justices Blackmun and Rehnquist dissented on the grounds that *Chadwick* was not correctly decided and that even if it were, where police have probable cause to believe a container in a mobile vehicle holds contraband, it should be subject to the rules of *Carroll* (1925) and *Chambers v. Maroney* (1970); that is, the police should be able to open it on the spot without a warrant. The dissent stressed the "untoward costs on the criminal justice system of this country in terms of added delay and uncertainty" caused by the *Chadwick–Sanders* rule. Quite significant, two concurring justices (Chief Justice Burger and Justice Stevens) argued that the situation in *Sanders* was not an automobile exigency search, thus clouding an understanding of the scope of a search of containers found in a mobile vehicle, and opening the door to later cases.

Sanders was followed by *New York v. Belton* (1981), which, as noted, blurred the lines between a search incident to arrest and an automobile search exception to the warrant requirement. The issue was further confused by the Court's fractured decision in **Robbins v. California** (1981), a companion case to *Belton*. Police stopped a station wagon traveling erratically. An officer smelled marijuana smoke when Robbins emerged, searched him, and found a vial of liquid. The officer searched the interior of the car and found marijuana. Police officers then opened the tailgate of the station wagon and raised the cover of a recessed luggage compartment, in which they found two packages wrapped in green opaque plastic. The police unwrapped the packages and discovered a large amount of marijuana in each. The issue was whether the opening of the two packages violated the Fourth Amendment. The Supreme Court, in a plurality opinion by Justice Stewart, held this an unreasonable search and seizure on the authority of *Chadwick* and *Sanders:* (1) the outward appearance of the package did not undermine Robbins's expectation of privacy; and (2) there was no constitutional difference between a footlocker (a "worthy" container) and a plastic bag or package (an "unworthy" container). Concurring Justice Powell and Chief Justice Burger, however, expressed reservations about the decision and suggested a line of reasoning that would soon undermine the *Chadwick–Sanders* rule, namely that "when the police have probable cause to search an automobile, rather than only to search a particular container that fortuitously is located in it, the exigencies that allow the police to search the entire automobile without a warrant support the warrantless search of every container found therein." Support for the *Chadwick–Sanders* approach to the search of containers found in automobiles was waning.

BRIGHT-LINE RULES FOR THE SCOPE OF AUTOMOBILE EXCEPTION SEARCHES   The reasoning of *Robbins* undermined its strength as a precedent. In the following year, Justice Stewart retired and was replaced by the more conservative Justice Sandra Day O'Connor. This allowed reconsideration of the doubts raised in *Robbins*. Indeed, the Court overturned *Robbins* the next year in **United States v. Ross** (1982). In *Ross* and *California v. Acevedo* (1991), a conservative tide on the Court swept away the *Chadwick–Sanders* rule in two waves, finally establishing the bright-line rule that allowed police to search automobiles and *any* closed compartments or containers in them without a search warrant whenever probable cause existed to believe that contraband was in the car generally or in a specific container. Their rules are simple. *Ross* holds that when police have probable cause to believe that contraband is located in an automobile, they may, under the automobile exception, open any closed container in the car that may logically hold the contraband; this overrules *Robbins*. *Acevedo* holds that when an officer has probable cause to believe that a specific container located in a car contains contraband, the officer may, upon lawfully stopping the car and gaining access to its interior, open the container. This overrules *Sanders* but not *Chadwick*, because *Chadwick* was not treated as an automobile exception case.

In *Ross,* a known reliable informant telephoned a police detective and told him that an individual known as "Bandit" was selling narcotics that he kept in the trunk of a "purplish maroon" Chevrolet Malibu parked at a specific street location. The informant had just observed "Bandit" complete a sale and said that "Bandit" told him that additional narcotics were in the trunk. Police officers drove to the street address and saw a maroon Malibu parked there. The officers completed a computer check and discovered that the car was registered to Albert Ross, who fit the informant's description and who used the alias "Bandit." The officers drove through the neighborhood twice but did not observe anyone matching Ross's description. They returned five minutes later and saw the maroon Malibu being driven off by a man matching the informant's description. The officers stopped the car and ordered Ross out of the car. Officers observed a bullet on the front seat so they searched the interior of the car and found a pistol in the glove compartment, whereupon they arrested and handcuffed Ross. A detective took Ross's keys, opened the trunk, and found a closed brown paper bag that was found to contain a number of glassine bags filled with a white powder that was later determined to be heroin. At the station house, the car trunk was searched without a warrant, and a zippered red leather pouch was found and opened. It contained $3,200 in cash. Did the officers have constitutional authority to open the paper bag in the trunk of Ross's automobile?

Ross squarely presented the issue of the scope of an automobile search wherein police had probable cause to believe that contraband was located somewhere in the car or the trunk, but not in a specific bag or container. On the one hand, *Carroll* allowed police, without a warrant, to rip open the upholstery of a car stopped at the side of the road to get at the contraband. On the other hand, *Chadwick* ruled that the container can be seized and held (but not opened) until a search warrant was obtained. The Court opted for the *Carroll* approach. The details of *Ross* were not the same as the facts of *Sanders,* where police had probable cause to believe that there was contraband in a *specific container* located in a moving car, but no probable cause to believe that there was contraband elsewhere in the car. For the time being, *Chadwick* controlled *Sanders*-type situations.

The Court advanced several reasons for its decision in *Ross.* It noted that from the *Carroll* case in 1925 up to *Chadwick* in 1977, decisions of lower courts and the Supreme Court never questioned the right of police to open bags of suspected contraband found in lawfully stopped cars. The practical benefits of the *Carroll* rule would be largely nullified by not allowing police to open closed containers reasonably suspected of housing contraband because illegal materials are usually secured to be kept out of sight. Also, *Carroll* did not increase the scope of a lawful search, but instead "merely relaxed the requirements for a warrant on grounds of practicability" (*Henry v. United States,* 1959). Thus a search warrant allowing a search for contraband implies that officers may open containers in the premises that could logically hold the kind of contraband sought.

> When a legitimate search is under way, and when its purpose and its limits have been precisely defined, nice distinctions between closets, drawers, and containers, in the case of a home, or between glove compartments, upholstered seats, trunks, and wrapped packages, in the case of a vehicle, must give way to the interest in the prompt and efficient completion of the task at hand. (*United States v. Ross,* 1982)

This rule applies to all containers; the Court upheld the concept of *Robbins* that a constitutional distinction between "worthy" and "unworthy" containers (e.g., suitcases versus paper bags) was improper, as long as the container shielded its contents from plain view. Finally, because a search under the automobile exception was as valid as a search incident to arrest or a search under a warrant, the suspect loses the expectation of privacy to the same extent as in these cases, which allow the opening of "some containers." In conclusion, the "scope of a warrantless search of an automobile . . . is not defined by the nature of the container in which the contraband is secreted [but] by the object of the search and the places in which there is probable cause to believe that it may be found" (*United States v. Ross,* 1982). Significantly, the majority rejected the holding of *Robbins* but upheld the specific holding in *Sanders,* thus allowing police to seize but not search containers where they have probable cause to believe that the *specific container* holds contraband.

Justice Marshall dissented, joined by Justices Brennan and White, harshly accusing the Court of "repeal[ing] the Fourth Amendment warrant requirement itself" and "utterly disregard[ing] the value of a neutral and detached magistrate." He reiterated the value of a search warrant and the positive effect of the warrant process on officers who had to write affidavits to justify searches. He noted that in many automobile warrant exception cases there was an *actual exigency* that justified the police in searching without a warrant. To the contrary, however, Fourth Amendment principles are undermined when the automobile exigency exception is applied to *every* search of an automobile, even when the suspect is arrested and there is no likelihood that another person will get to the car. Ignoring this difference was deemed a sleight of hand by the majority. Fourth Amendment principles required the Court to apply *Chadwick* to a search of a vehicle when the exigency is over. Finally, the majority's ruling in *Ross* was inconsistent with the rule of *Sanders*. Prophetically, Justice Marshall stated, "This case will have profound implications for the privacy of citizens traveling in automobiles."

A decade later, the Court dropped the other shoe and, in **California v. Acevedo** (1991), overruled *Arkansas v. Sanders* (1979). Between 1982 and 1991, the composition of the Court had become considerably more conservative, with Justice Rehnquist becoming Chief Justice upon the retirement of Chief Justice Burger, the addition of Justices Antonin Scalia, Anthony Kennedy, and David Souter to the Court, and the retirement of Justices Powell and Brennan. Justice Blackmun, who had dissented in *Sanders,* now had the opportunity to bury that decision in his majority opinion, and he was joined by Chief Justice Rehnquist and Justices O'Connor, Kennedy, and Souter. Justice Scalia concurred with the majority. Justices White, Stevens, and Marshall dissented.

In *Acevedo,* marijuana lawfully seized by the Drug Enforcement Administration (DEA) in Hawaii was shipped to Officer Coleman of the Santa Ana, California, Police Department. He set up a controlled delivery to one Jamie Daza, who picked up the package from a Federal Express office at 10:30 a.m. Daza, package in hand, was followed to his apartment. At 11:45 a.m., Daza left the apartment and dropped the marijuana container's wrapping into a trash bin. Officer Coleman left the scene to get a search warrant. At 12:30 p.m., respondent Charles Steven Acevedo arrived. He entered Daza's apartment, stayed for about ten minutes, and emerged carrying a brown paper bag that appeared to be full. Other officers observing the scene noticed that the bag was the size of one of the wrapped marijuana packages sent from Hawaii. Acevedo walked to a silver Honda in the parking lot, placed the bag *in the trunk of the car*, and started to drive away. Fearing the loss of evidence, officers in a marked police car stopped him. They opened the trunk and the bag and found marijuana. The California Court of Appeals suppressed the marijuana on the basis of *Chadwick* (instead of *Ross*) because the officers had probable cause to believe that the *paper bag* contained drugs but lacked probable cause to suspect that Acevedo's car itself otherwise contained contraband.

The reasons given by the majority for allowing a warrantless search of a closed container in an operative vehicle, which had become immobilized and the driver taken into custody, began with an observation on *Ross:* Where police have probable cause to believe that contraband is located in a car but have not pinpointed a specific container, "the time and expense of the warrant process would be misdirected if the police could search every cubic inch of an automobile until they discovered a paper sack, at which point the Fourth Amendment required them to take the sack to a magistrate for permission to look inside." The majority forthrightly noted

> that a container found after a general search of the automobile and a container found in a car after a limited search for the container are equally easy for the police to store and for the suspect to hide or destroy. In fact, we see no principled distinction in terms of either the privacy expectation or the exigent circumstances between the paper bag found by the police in *Ross* and the paper bag found by the police here. Furthermore, by attempting to distinguish between a container for which the police are specifically searching and a container which they come across in a car, we have provided only minimal protection for privacy and have impeded effective law enforcement. (*California v. Acevedo,* 1991)

Put this way, it seems clear that the fine line between *Chadwick–Sanders* (specific probable cause) cases and *Carroll–Ross* (general probable cause) cases is a thin one and that it would be better for the cases to be decided consistently: Either *all containers can be opened* by the police, or *all containers should be held for a warrant* based on a magistrate's ruling on the police officer's assessment of probable cause.

Which way is best? The path chosen by the majority was based, first, on its stated assumption that the *Ross* rule provided "minimal protection for privacy" because in the *Chadwick–Sanders* situation, the suspicious package is seized and held for a warrant in any event. Next, the Court noted that the clear theoretical distinction is not always clear to a police officer in the field searching a car. Doubts about the locus of probable cause in an automobile search case would have defendants arguing that the probable cause existed as to the *container* and *not* the *entire vehicle* to get *Chadwick–Sanders* protection, causing unneeded litigation. Alternatively, police might try to circumvent the *Chadwick–Sanders* rule by needlessly searching an *entire* car to make it seem as if the *Ross* rule operates when they really had probable cause to believe that the contraband is located in a specific container. Further, the opening of a container is less physically intrusive than a full search of an automobile: "If destroying the interior of an automobile is not unreasonable, we cannot conclude that looking inside a closed container is." Justice Blackmun's majority opinion argued that the dichotomy between the two automobile search rules has created confusion in the lower courts and impeded effective law enforcement. "The *Chadwick–Sanders* rule is the antithesis of a 'clear and unequivocal' guideline." The Supreme Court thus overruled *Arkansas v. Sanders* (1979) and stated that it had returned all automobile search cases to the basic rule of *Carroll*.

Justice Stevens's dissent was unusually blunt and specifically referred to the Court's relying "on arguments that *conservative judges* have repeatedly rejected in past cases" (emphasis added). Justices are aware of their and their colleagues' ideological leanings, but they rarely state this so forthrightly in an opinion. Because a *dissent* is the justice's *personal statement*, it is often more freewheeling or idiosyncratic than a majority opinion, which reflects the judgment of each justice who joins the opinion. By stating that "conservative justices" supported *Sanders* in the past, Justice Stevens suggested that *Acevedo*'s majority justices are extremists. His opinion began with an exposition on constitutional policy favoring the use of warrants and reminding that "[t]he Fourth Amendment is a restraint on Executive power." The burdens of obtaining warrants "are outweighed by the individual interest in privacy that is protected by advance judicial approval." He then argued that *Ross* and *Chadwick–Sanders* were not inconsistent; *Ross* applied to the scope of an automobile search, whereas *Sanders* applied to the search of all closed containers, whether found in automobiles or not. He also noted, as did Justice Marshall dissenting in *Ross,* that the *Chadwick–Sanders* rule allows for exigency exceptions.

Justice Stevens challenged three specific points made in Justice Blackmun's majority opinion. First, the majority claimed that the existence of the *Chadwick–Sanders* rule and the *Ross* rule was confusing and anomalous. Justice Stevens recited cases that seemed to have no difficulty in distinguishing between the two and so disagreed as to the confusion. If there was an anomaly in the law, it was created by the majority, "[f]or, surely it is anomalous to prohibit a search of a briefcase while the owner is carrying it exposed on a public street yet to permit a search once the owner has placed the briefcase in the locked trunk of his car" (*California v. Acevedo,* 1991). Justice Stevens thought that making the automobile search rules the same by eliminating the warrant requirement in both was the worse solution because the person had the same expectation of privacy in the container, whether found in or out of a car.

Second, he disagreed that the *Chadwick–Sanders* rule does not protect any significant interest in privacy. "Every citizen clearly has an interest in the privacy of the contents of his or her luggage, briefcase, handbag or any other container that conceals private papers and effects from public scrutiny. . . . Under the Court's holding today, the privacy interest that protects the contents of a suitcase or a briefcase from a warrantless search when it is in public view simply vanishes when its owner climbs into a taxicab. Unquestionably the rejection of the *Sanders* line of cases by today's decision will result in a significant loss of individual privacy."

The majority's third argument was that the older rules impede effective law enforcement. Justice Stevens noted that the Court cited no authority for this contention. Even if true, it was, "in any event, an insufficient reason for creating a new exception to the warrant requirement." From a Due Process Model approach to the Constitution, the convenience of the police is hardly a powerful argument when compared to the expectation of privacy by citizens.

Ross and *Acevedo* are significant cases because, by creating bright-line rules, they resolved the tangled legal threads on the scope of automobile and sealed container searches. To the dissenting justices, these cases seriously undermine Fourth Amendment rights and give the police carte blanche to search cars. Each majority opinion, however, mandates that there must be a clear connection between *probable cause* and the scope of a search. Doctrinally, *Ross* and *Acevedo* do not grant police unbridled searching power; for example, police cannot search the locked trunk of a car if its driver is arrested for driving under the influence of alcohol or a controlled substance. However, the real fear is that lenient rules will be applied by the police as license to use their discretion to search, guided only by their common sense and innate sense of decency, and that when police step over the legal line, lower court judges will excuse such behavior. Indeed, as suggested at the beginning of this section, it appears that the totality of automobile search rules provides very little restraint on auto searches.

The *Ross* rule was extended to automobile passengers in *Wyoming v. Houghton.*

Read Case and Comments: *Wyoming v. Houghton.*

CASE AND COMMENTS

Wyoming v. Houghton

526 U.S. 295, 119 S.Ct. 1297, 143 L.Ed.2d 408 (1999)

JUSTICE SCALIA delivered the opinion of the Court.

This case presents the question whether police officers violate the Fourth Amendment when they search a passenger's personal belongings inside an automobile that they have probable cause to believe contains contraband.

I

[a] Suppose you are driven to classes by a friend and the car is stopped for speeding. The officer orders your friend out of the car and notices a single marijuana cigarette on the floor. Should the officer be able to search your backpack, which is sitting on the back seat? Should it matter if you claim the backpack as your property?

In the early morning hours * * * a Wyoming Highway Patrol officer stopped an automobile for speeding and driving with a faulty brake light. There were three passengers in the front seat of the car: David Young (the driver), his girlfriend, and respondent. While questioning Young, the officer noticed a hypodermic syringe in Young's shirt pocket. He left the occupants under the supervision of two backup officers as he went to get gloves from his patrol car. Upon his return, he instructed Young to step out of the car and place the syringe on the hood. The officer then asked Young why he had a syringe; with refreshing candor, Young replied that he used it to take drugs. **[a]**

[The two female passengers were ordered out of the car. Asked for identification, Houghton falsely identified herself as "Sandra James." In light of Young's admission, the officer searched the passenger compartment of the car for contraband, and found a purse on the backseat that Houghton claimed as hers. He removed her wallet containing her driver's license.] When the officer asked her why she had lied about her name, she replied: "In case things went bad." [The officer then removed a brown pouch and a black wallet-type container. Houghton denied that the pouch was hers] and claimed ignorance of how it came to be there. [It contained] drug paraphernalia and a syringe with 60 cc of methamphetamine. . . . The officer also found fresh needle-track marks on Houghton's arms. He placed her under arrest.

[The trial court denied Houghton's motion to suppress evidence obtained from the purse as the fruit of a Fourth Amendment violation. She was convicted of felony possession of methamphetamine. The trial court] held that the officer had probable cause to search the car for contraband and, by extension, any containers therein that could hold such contraband.

[The Wyoming Supreme Court, reversing the conviction, ruled that where an officer has probable cause to believe that contraband is somewhere in a lawfully stopped car, the officer may search all containers in the car *except* containers that the officer knows or should know are personal effects of a passenger who is not suspected of criminal activity, "*unless* someone had the opportunity to conceal the contraband within the personal effect to avoid detection."]

II

* * *

* * * [I]n the present case [] the police officers had probable cause to believe there were illegal drugs in the car. **[b]** *Carroll v. United States* (1925) * * * held that "contraband goods concealed and illegally transported in an automobile or other vehicle may be searched for without a warrant" where probable cause exists.

[b] Notice that the exigency reasoning of *Carroll* is not mentioned.

We have furthermore read the historical evidence to show that the Framers would have regarded as reasonable (if there was probable cause) the warrantless search of containers *within* an automobile. **[c]** In *Ross* we upheld as reasonable the warrantless search of a paper bag and leather pouch found in the trunk of the defendant's car by officers who had probable cause to believe that the trunk contained drugs. * * *

[c] As an "originalist," Justice Scalia justifies Fourth Amendment rulings by "finding" what he thinks the Framers would have ruled in 1791.

Ross summarized its holding as follows: "If probable cause justifies the search of a lawfully stopped vehicle, it justifies the search of *every part of the vehicle and its contents* that may conceal the object of the search." (emphasis added). **[d]** And our later cases describing *Ross* have characterized it as applying broadly to *all* containers within a car, without qualification as to ownership. * * *

[d] This logically includes Houghton's purse.

* * *

In sum, neither *Ross* itself nor the historical evidence it relied upon admits of a distinction among packages or containers based on ownership. When there is probable cause to search for contraband in a car, it is reasonable for police officers—like customs officials in the Founding era—to examine packages and containers without a showing of individualized probable cause for each one. **[e]** A passenger's personal belongings, just like the driver's belongings or containers attached to the car like a glove compartment, are "in" the car, and the officer has probable cause to search for contraband *in* the car.

[e] *Ross* did not involve passengers and so does not establish direct precedent for a rule that allows an officer to open a passenger's purse.

Even if the historical evidence, as described by *Ross*, were thought to be equivocal, we would find that the balancing of the relative interests weighs decidedly in favor of allowing searches of a passenger's belongings. Passengers, no less than drivers, possess a reduced expectation of privacy with regard to the property that they transport in cars, which "travel public thoroughfares." * * *

In this regard—the degree of intrusiveness upon personal privacy and indeed even personal dignity—the two cases the Wyoming Supreme Court found dispositive differ substantially from the package search at issue here. **[f]** *United States v. Di Re* (1948), held that probable cause to search a car did not justify a body search of a passenger. And *Ybarra v. Illinois,* (1979), held that a search warrant for a tavern and its bartender did not permit body searches of all the bar's patrons. These cases turned on the unique, significantly heightened protection afforded against searches of one's person. * * *

Whereas the passenger's privacy expectations are, as we have described, considerably diminished, the governmental interests at stake are substantial. **[g]** Effective law enforcement would be appreciably impaired without the ability to search a passenger's personal belongings when there is reason to believe contraband or evidence of criminal wrongdoing is hidden in the car. As in all car-search cases, the "ready mobility" of an automobile creates a risk that the evidence or contraband will be permanently lost while a warrant is obtained. In addition, a car passenger—unlike the unwitting tavern patron in *Ybarra*—will often be engaged in a common enterprise with the driver, and have the same interest in concealing the fruits or the evidence of their wrongdoing. **[h]** A criminal might be able to hide contraband in a passenger's belongings as readily as in other containers in the car,—perhaps even surreptitiously, without the passenger's knowledge or permission. * * *

To be sure, these factors favoring a search will not always be present, but the balancing of interests must be conducted with an eye to the generality of cases. To require that the investigating officer have positive reason to believe that the passenger and driver were engaged in a common enterprise, or positive reason to believe that the driver had time and occasion to conceal the item in the passenger's belongings, surreptitiously or with friendly permission, is to impose requirements so seldom met that a "passenger's property" rule would dramatically reduce the ability to find and seize contraband and evidence of crime. [Litigation would increase over the issue of whether the police officer should have believed a passenger's claim of ownership.] We think they militate in favor of the needs of law enforcement, and against a personal-privacy interest that is ordinarily weak.

* * *

We hold that police officers with probable cause to search a car may inspect passengers' belongings found in the car that are capable of concealing the object of the search. The judgment of the Wyoming Supreme Court is reversed.

[Justice Breyer concurred.]

JUSTICE STEVENS, with whom JUSTICE SOUTER and JUSTICE GINSBURG join, dissenting.
* * *

* * * In the only automobile case confronting the search of a passenger defendant—***United States v. Di Re,*** (1948)—**[i]** the Court held that the exception to the warrant requirement did not apply (addressing searches of the passenger's pockets and the space between his shirt and underwear, both of which uncovered counterfeit fuel rations). In *Di Re,* as here, the information prompting the search directly implicated the driver, not the passenger. Today, instead of adhering to the settled distinction between drivers and passengers, the Court fashions a new rule that is based on a distinction between property contained in clothing worn by a passenger and property contained in a passenger's briefcase or purse. **[j]** In cases on both sides of the Court's newly minted test, the property is in a "container" (whether a pocket or a pouch) located in the vehicle. Moreover, unlike the Court, I think it quite plain that the search of a passenger's purse or briefcase involves an intrusion on privacy that may be just as serious as was the intrusion in *Di Re.*

Even apart from *Di Re,* the Court's rights-restrictive approach is not dictated by precedent. **[k]** For example, in *United States v. Ross* (1982), we were concerned with the interest of the driver in the integrity of "his automobile," and we categorically rejected the notion that the scope of a warrantless search of a vehicle might be "defined by the nature of the container in which the contraband is secreted," . . . "Rather, it is defined by the object of the search and the places in which there is probable cause to believe that it may be found." We thus disapproved of a possible container-based distinction between a man's pocket and a woman's pocketbook. * * *

Nor am I persuaded that the mere spatial association between a passenger and a driver provides an acceptable basis for presuming that they are partners in crime or for ignoring privacy interests in a purse. Whether or not the Fourth Amendment required a warrant to search Houghton's purse, at the very least the trooper in this case had to have probable cause to believe that her purse contained contraband. The Wyoming Supreme Court concluded that he did not.

[f] *Di Re* is central to Justice Steven's dissent. The majority does not overrule *Di Re* but instead distinguishes it, so that the rule of *Di Re* still exists, but so too does the rule of *Houghton.*

[g] Given the control that the police had over the car in this case (the driver arrested, the car subject to impoundment), do references to "ready mobility" become a smoke screen that allows police to search a car and all its contents simply because it is a car?

[h] The real difference between the majority and the dissenters is that the majority imposes a per se, bright-line rule allowing no *Ross* exception for the belongings of a passenger. The dissent allows a search of a passenger's bag if an officer has probable cause to believe that it holds contraband. Justice Scalia suggests that such a rule would lessen the number of seizures from automobiles and enmesh police in fine-tuned adjudications of probable cause.

[i] See *Di Re* in Chapter 4. In that case, an informer was riding in the car and would have seen the driver pass contraband to Di Re.

[j] If *Di Re* is still good law and the search of Houghton's purse is constitutional, could an officer lawfully open a "fanny pack" worn by a passenger on a belt?

[k] Although *Ross* is not direct precedent for the search of a passenger's bag, the "object" of the search in *Ross* was drugs located somewhere in the car, not in a specific container, making the extension of *Ross* to a passenger's belongings logical. Justice Stevens, the author of the *Ross* opinion, did not mention a pocket or pocketbook in that opinion. The *Ross* case made no reference to *Di Re.* Does Justice Stevens regret the *Ross* decision or simply believe that the majority is going too far?

Finally, in my view, the State's legitimate interest in effective law enforcement does not outweigh the privacy concerns at issue. I am as confident in a police officer's ability to apply a rule requiring a warrant or individualized probable cause to search belongings that are—as in this case—obviously owned by and in the custody of a passenger as is the Court in a "passenger-confederate[']s" ability to circumvent the rule. Certainly the ostensible clarity of the Court's rule is attractive. But that virtue is insufficient justification for its adoption. Moreover, a rule requiring a warrant or individualized probable cause to search passenger belongings is every bit as simple as the Court's rule; it simply protects more privacy.

* * *

AUTOMOBILE INVENTORY SEARCHES

Statutes and local ordinances provide several reasons to **impound** vehicles:

- To remove vehicles involved in accidents to permit the flow of traffic and preserve evidence.
- To remove damaged vehicles from the highways.
- To tow away automobiles that violate parking ordinances.
- To remove cars after the driver has been arrested.
- To impound automobiles subject to forfeiture.

Of course, a vehicle seized after the driver's felony arrest may also be impounded and subjected to an **inventory search**. Unlike these numerous administrative reasons for vehicle impoundment, an inventory of an arrested person's property at a police lock-up or a jail is legal only if the underlying arrest is legal. (See Chapter 4.) Impounded vehicles have been placed in the unsecured private lot of a local garage (*Cady v. Dombrowski,* 1973) (rural area; lot seven miles from the police station) or in an impoundment lot operated by a municipality (*South Dakota v. Opperman,* 1976).

An inventory search of an impounded motor vehicle by law enforcement officers is an **administrative search**, deemed reasonable under the Fourth Amendment and designed to perform a caretaking function. An inventory is a list of all items found in an impounded car. A vehicle inventory search is not a search for evidence that requires a warrant and probable cause. Any contraband disclosed in an inventory is in plain view and hence is admissible in a criminal prosecution.

Consequently, inventory searches do not come under the automobile exigency warrant exception of *Carroll v. United States* (1925). Neither a judicial warrant, probable cause, nor reasonable suspicion is needed to justify an inventory search. Indeed, an inventory search is the opposite of an exigency search—it must be conducted under standardized rules and regulations so that each inventory search is as much like another as possible. The Supreme Court has ruled that the inventory's administrative "interests outweighed the individual's Fourth Amendment interests" (*Colorado v. Bertine,* 1987). In *Cady v. Dombrowski* (1973), Justice Rehnquist explained that "[l]ocal police officers . . . frequently investigate vehicle accidents in which there is no claim of criminal liability and engage in what, for want of a better term, may be described as community caretaking functions, totally divorced from the detection, investigation, or acquisition of evidence relating to the violation of a criminal statute."

REASONS FOR THE INVENTORY SEARCH   The purposes of the inventory of an automobile and the inventory of a person taken into custody are similar. First, the routine listing of the contents of the vehicle protects the owner's property against theft or careless handling by the police while it remains in police custody. Second, the inventory protects the police against false claims or disputes over lost or stolen property by the owner. Third, it protects the police from potential danger. Additionally, the inventory helps determine whether a vehicle has been stolen (*South Dakota v. Opperman,* 1976). A prime reason to inventory people taken into custody in police lockups—to prevent them from injuring themselves or others with weapons or dangerous instruments—is rarely the case in vehicle inventories. In unusual cases, however, explosives or weapons may be present, which, if stolen from an impounded vehicle, can pose a threat to the public. Also, opening a vehicle containing explosives endangers the lives of officers.[10]

SCOPE OF AN INVENTORY SEARCH   The cases show that an inventory search can be extremely thorough. In *South Dakota v. Opperman* (1976), the Supreme Court upheld the inventory of items in the unlocked glove compartment of an automobile. In *Michigan v. Thomas* (1982), the Court upheld the inventory search of a car's locked trunk, the space under the front seat and under the dashboard, and the opening of air vents under the dashboard, where a loaded revolver was found. The Court rejected the argument that the search of the air vents was improper because that is not a place where personal items are normally stored. In a *per curiam* opinion in *Florida v. Meyers* (1984), the Court upheld, without explanation, a second inventory search of an automobile made eight hours after the car was first searched and impounded. In *Illinois v. Lafayette* (1983), a police lockup inventory case (see Chapter 4), the police searched a purse-type shoulder bag belonging to a person taken into custody; the Supreme Court held that the police were under no obligation to place it in a secure box or locker, even if this was less intrusive than the inventory search. "The reasonableness of any particular governmental activity does not necessarily or invariably turn on the existence of alternative 'less intrusive' means" (*Illinois v. Lafayette,* 1983).

The issue of the scope of an inventory was revisited in **Colorado v. Bertine** (1987) to determine whether *United States v. Chadwick* (1977)—holding warrantless searches of closed trunks and suitcases to violate the Fourth Amendment—modified the rule for vehicle inventory searches. *Bertine* reaffirmed the *Opperman* decision. A van was impounded after the driver was arrested for driving under the influence of alcohol. The van's contents were subjected to a detailed inspection and inventory in accordance with local police procedures. An officer then opened a closed backpack and found drugs. The Supreme Court found that the search was legal and the drugs admissible in evidence. Chief Justice Rehnquist, for the majority, said that an inventory search is made for regulatory reasons and is not a search for criminal evidence. There was no proof that the police had acted in bad faith for the sole purpose of investigation, and the police department's regulations mandated the opening of closed containers and the listing of their contents. Justice Marshall, dissenting, argued that, in fact, the procedures were not standardized, thereby making the action a criminal search rather than an inventory. He wrote that the search was conducted in a "slipshod" manner that undermined the purposes of an inventory procedure and that the rule of *Chadwick* should apply to a backpack.

THE NECESSITY OF STANDARDIZED RULES   The Supreme Court's motor vehicle inventory doctrine has evolved from allowing an *ad hoc* inventory when made for inventory purposes (*Cady v. Dombrowski,* 1973) to a rule that requires that a police department have in place standardized inventory rules and procedures in order for an inventory search to be constitutional (*Florida v. Wells,* 1990).

In *Colorado v. Bertine* (1987), the Court emphasized the importance of written, standardized procedures to guide the inventory search. No such procedures apparently existed in **Cady v. Dombrowski** (1973), which involved the warrantless search of a car for the express purpose of finding the weapon in the private vehicle of a drunk driver who was a police officer. The inventory search was upheld because it was clearly performed for administrative purposes and not as a search for criminal evidence. A driver involved in a serious single-car accident was taken into custody one evening for drunk driving in a rural Wisconsin town. He stated that he was a Chicago police officer. The Wisconsin officers believed that Chicago police officers were required by regulation to carry their service revolvers at all times. They were concerned that someone would steal the weapon from the car, which was placed in an unsecured lot. As a result, they looked into the passenger compartment and glove box but found no service revolver. A tow truck arrived and removed the disabled car to a garage seven miles from the police station, where it was left unguarded. Dombrowski, the driver, was hospitalized after lapsing into a coma. Hours later, after midnight, an officer went to the car to search for Dombrowski's police weapon. The officer testified that the effort to find the revolver was "standard procedure in our department." He opened the trunk of Dombrowski's car and did not find a gun but did find his police uniforms, a Chicago police baton with his name imprinted on it, and fresh blood that was introduced into evidence to convict Dombrowski of first-degree murder. Under these circumstances, the Court treated this search as a valid administrative search and not as a search for criminal evidence. "Where, as here, the trunk of an automobile, which the officer reasonably believed to contain a gun, was vulnerable to intrusion by vandals, we hold that the search was not 'unreasonable' within the meaning of the Fourth and Fourteenth Amendments" (*Cady v. Dombrowski,* 1973).

From the somewhat loose procedure upheld in *Dombrowski,* the Court has moved to a position that, for an inventory search to be constitutionally reasonable, it must be authorized by (1) departmental policy and regulations that establish standard procedures, or (2) established routine. The rationale is that one inventory search should be conducted like another and that the procedure should actually produce an inventory—a list. The goal is to limit the discretion of the officer as to the manner in which the inventory is to be conducted. "The individual police officer must not be allowed so much latitude that inventory searches are turned into 'a purposeful and general means of discovering evidence of crime'" (*Florida v. Wells,* 1990, citing *Colorado v. Bertine,* 1987).

Florida v. Wells (1990) is an example of an officer turning a routine inventory into a search for evidence because he overstepped administrative regulations. Wells was stopped for speeding and was arrested for DWI after an officer smelled alcohol on his breath. An inventory search of the car revealed two marijuana cigarette butts in an ashtray and a locked suitcase in the trunk. There was no departmental inventory policy. The officer used his discretion to order the suitcase forced open. Large quantities of marijuana were found. The U.S. Supreme Court agreed with the Florida Supreme Court that the evidence should be suppressed as a Fourth Amendment violation because the police department had no inventory policy at all. In the course of his majority opinion, Chief Justice Rehnquist said:

> A police officer may be allowed sufficient latitude to determine whether a particular container should or should not be opened in light of the nature of the search and characteristics of the container itself. Thus, while policies of opening all containers or of opening no containers are unquestionably permissible, it would be equally permissible, for example, to allow the opening of closed containers whose contents officers determine they are unable to ascertain from examining the containers' exteriors. The allowance of the exercise of judgment based on concerns related to the purposes of an inventory search does not violate the Fourth Amendment. (*Florida v. Wells,* 1990)

This quote was treated as dictum by four justices who disagreed with it. Thus the question of whether an officer has discretion to open some containers has not been finally resolved. The concurring justices felt that the officer should not have such discretion—that is, that an inventory policy should order an officer to open all containers or none. Justice Brennan expressed concern that "police may use the excuse of an 'inventory search' as a pretext for broad searches of vehicles and their contents."

BORDER AND EXTRATERRITORIAL SEARCHES

Border Searches

Every sovereign nation has a right to control its **borders** to determine who or what shall come into or exit the country, to collect customs, and to control smuggling. To enforce this plenary power, a country may search entering persons and luggage. As a general rule, the Fourth Amendment does not apply to routine searches and seizures at the border of the United States. As Justice Rehnquist noted:

> Since the founding of our Republic, Congress has granted the Executive plenary authority to conduct routine searches and seizures at the border, without probable cause or a warrant, in order to regulate the collection of duties and to prevent the introduction of contraband into this country. . . . This Court has long recognized Congress' power to police entrants at the border. (*United States v. Montoya de Hernandez,* 1985)[11]

United States v. Ramsey (1977) described **border searches** as "reasonable" simply because a person or item enters into the country from outside, without any regard to the existence of probable cause or recourse to a judicial warrant. In practice, any automobile or passenger entering the United States at the Canadian or Mexican border, or any international traveler entering at an international seaport or airport, may be searched at random by customs officers. Such a practice, of course, would be intolerable and blatantly unconstitutional if it were conducted by law enforcement officers within the United States.

In recent decades, as the United States has dealt with mounting problems of drug importation, illegal aliens, and foreign terrorists, issues concerning border searches have proliferated.

Along with thorny political and law enforcement issues, the constitutional law of border searches has become complex because the Supreme Court has had to resolve issues arising from variations on the location of the "border" search and specific kinds of intrusions. The cases deal with five types of border searches:

1. At the actual border.
2. At a **fixed checkpoint** miles from the border.
3. **Roving patrols** by the Border Patrol up to a hundred miles from the border.
4. Search of international mail.
5. Boarding ships in open waters.

SEARCHES AT THE ACTUAL BORDER   For routine searches by customs officers, the general rule is alive and well—any person seeking entry may be stopped and searched without probable cause or reasonable suspicion. In 1999, acting on a hunch, a customs officer stopped an Algerian national at the small Port Angeles, Washington, checkpoint on the U.S.–Canadian border. She discovered explosives in the wheel well of the Algerian's car. As it turned out, the suspect, Ahmed Ressam, was then thought to have ties to Osama bin Laden.[12] After the 9/11 attacks, Ressam, who was awaiting sentencing for plotting to bomb the Los Angeles International Airport during the 2000 millennium celebrations, provided federal authorities with new information about people involved in al Qaeda–related terrorist cells.[13] A search not based on reasonable suspicion that lasts for one or two hours, during which a technician removes the gas tank of an automobile for inspection to find if it contains contraband, is a routine border search for purposes of allowing contraband discovered by such a search into evidence (*U.S. v. Flores-Montano*, 2004).

For nonroutine border searches, the Fourth Amendment requires that officials have reasonable suspicion of a crime to justify search and detention. In **United States v. Montoya de Hernandez** (1985), Rosa Elvira Montoya de Hernandez arrived in Los Angeles on a flight from Bogotá, Colombia. An experienced customs agent thought she was smuggling drugs by having swallowed drug-filled balloons. An airline refused to return her to Colombia because she did not have a proper visa. As a result, she was held without a warrant in a locked room for sixteen hours, during which she "refused all offers of food and drink, and refused to use the toilet facilities." She "exhibited symptoms of discomfort consistent with 'heroic efforts to resist the usual calls of nature.'" Ultimately, a court order was obtained and a medical examination determined the existence of a foreign substance in her rectal canal. Subsequently, she "passed 88 balloons containing a total of 528 grams of 80 percent pure cocaine hydrochloride."

The Supreme Court found that the customs officer had *reasonable suspicion* to believe she was smuggling drugs, and this was sufficient grounds for the court order and the body cavity search. She said she came to Los Angeles to purchase merchandise for her husband's store. However, because she arrived from a "source city" for drugs, could not speak English, and did not have family or friends in the United States, her explanation was questionable. She had not scheduled appointments with merchandise vendors nor made hotel reservations. Even though she carried $5,000 in cash (mostly $50 bills), she did not have a billfold, nor did she possess checks, waybills, credit cards, or letters of credit, and she did not recall how her ticket was purchased. She told an implausible story that she "planned to ride around Los Angeles in taxicabs visiting retail stores such as J.C. Penney and K-Mart in order to buy goods for her husband's store with the $5,000." These articulable facts "clearly supported a reasonable suspicion that respondent was an alimentary canal smuggler."

Was the sixteen-hour detention without a warrant and the delay in summoning medical personnel "reasonably related in scope to the circumstances which justified it initially"? The Court rejected a hard-and-fast time limit as to what is reasonable. In this case, Montoya refused to be X-rayed, falsely claiming to be pregnant. The alternatives were to hold her for observation or allow her into the interior of the country.

Justice Brennan dissented, joined by Justice Marshall. He felt that more intrusive border detentions and searches are constitutionally reasonable only if authorized by a judicial officer upon probable cause of criminality. There was no exigency in this case, and a warrant could have been obtained at the outset. The majority replied that "not only is the expectation of privacy less at the border than in the interior, . . . [but] the Fourth Amendment balance between the interests of the Government and the privacy right of the individual is also struck much more favorably to the Government at the border."

STOPS AND SEARCHES AT FIXED CHECKPOINTS   Permanent or fixed checkpoints may be located up to one hundred miles from the U.S. boundary. The Supreme Court has applied standard Fourth Amendment reasoning to fixed checkpoint searches, employing the concepts of administrative searches, stop and frisk, and arrest. The rule is that no level of evidence sufficiency is needed to stop a vehicle at a fixed checkpoint, but that probable cause is required to search a car that has been stopped.

A well-marked checkpoint at San Clemente, California, warned motorists a mile in advance that they would have to slow down or stop. At the checkpoint, a "point" agent visually screened all northbound traffic. Standing between two lanes of traffic, the agent directed some cars to a secondary inspection area where the driver and passengers were questioned for three to five minutes. If the stop produced proof that the passengers were illegal aliens, they were arrested and returned to Mexico. In *United States v. Martinez-Fuerte* (1976), a detected illegal alien challenged his conviction on the basis that the stop at the San Clemente checkpoint was without reasonable suspicion, probable cause, or a warrant and therefore violated the Fourth Amendment.

The Court agreed "that checkpoint stops are 'seizures' within the meaning of the Fourth Amendment," but held that they are a reasonable and valid governmental response to a serious problem. A requirement that the stops be based on reasonable suspicion "would be too impractical because the flow of traffic tends to be too heavy to allow the particularized study of a given car that would enable it to be identified as a possible carrier of illegal aliens." The intrusion of these stops "is quite limited" and involves only a brief detention during which a few questions must be answered. "Neither the vehicle nor its occupants are searched, and visual inspection of the vehicle is limited to what can be seen without a search." Unlike a roving patrol, checkpoint stops involve less discretion, and notice of the checkpoint is clearly given to those approaching it; checkpoints do not create the same concern or fear that may be generated during a stop along a road by a patrol car. As a result, no evidentiary requirement is necessary for a fixed checkpoint stop.

The Supreme Court held unanimously in *United States v. Ortiz* (1975) that the trunk of a car cannot be opened (i.e., searched) during a checkpoint stop unless the officers have probable cause to believe that contraband or illegal aliens are present in the closed area. The Court reasoned that Fourth Amendment considerations come to the fore when a brief stop at a checkpoint, miles from the border, moves beyond a brief visual inspection and the asking of a few questions, which is a seizure, to a more intrusive search by customs officials. The Court noted that many factors could be taken into account by the Border Patrol officers to determine probable cause, including "the number of persons in a vehicle, the appearance and behavior of the driver and passengers, their inability to speak English, the responses they give to officers' questions, the nature of the vehicle, and indications that it may be heavily loaded." No such factors were apparent in *Ortiz,* and the Court found the search to be unconstitutional.

STOPS AND SEARCHES BY ROVING CUSTOMS PATROLS   Because of the difficulties involved in enforcing customs and immigration rules along our extensive borders, Congress authorized the Border Patrol to conduct roving patrols along the roads and in off-road areas within one hundred air miles of the border. Roving patrol stops by the Border Patrol are more intrusive than checkpoint stops, and therefore *United States v. Brignoni-Ponce* (1975) held that they must be justified with reasonable suspicion. An officer must be "aware of specific articulable facts, together with rational inferences from those facts, that reasonably warrant suspicion" that a vehicle contains illegal aliens. Four years later, the reasoning in *Brignoni-Ponce* led the Court to extend the same right to drivers throughout the United States in *Delaware v. Prouse* (1979). Earlier, *Almeida-Sanchez v. United States* (1973), held that the search of an automobile stopped by Border Patrol officers is a great intrusion on personal privacy mandating the need for probable cause for the search to be constitutional. The majority was concerned that allowing roving patrol searches up to one hundred miles from the border would destroy the Fourth Amendment rights of local residents.

INSPECTIONS AND INVESTIGATION OF INTERNATIONAL MAIL   *United States v. Ramsey* (1977) held that customs officials may inspect incoming mail from outside the United States if they have reasonable suspicion to believe that the mail contains contraband. While examining a sack of international mail from Thailand, a customs inspector noticed eight bulky envelopes bound for four different locations in the Washington, D.C., area. The addresses had apparently been typed on the same typewriter. He felt and weighed the envelopes and determined that they contained items other than paper. He opened the envelopes and in each found plastic bags containing heroin placed between cardboard. A warrant was then obtained, and the presence of heroin reconfirmed. The packages were resealed and delivered, which ultimately led to the arrest of the defendant.

The Supreme Court held that the more exacting probable cause standard was not required to justify opening the mail under the Fourth Amendment because (1) the federal statute that guided this action imposes a less stringent requirement than that of probable cause required for the issuance of warrants, and (2) mail inspection is justified by the greater authority that the government has to make stops at the border. Justice Stevens dissented in *Ramsey*, joined by Justices Brennan and Marshall. He argued that the 1866 statute that authorized mail stops was intended to apply to large packages and that until 1971, the post office opened mail only in the presence of the addressee or under the authority of a court order supported by probable cause.

CONTROLLED DELIVERIES   In *Illinois v. Andreas* (1983), the Supreme Court ruled that an initial inspection of international shipments that discloses contraband may lead to a "controlled delivery" to suspects in the interior of the country. Those to whom contraband-laden packages are delivered may be arrested and the packages searched without a warrant when they take possession of the delivered contraband. In *Andreas*, customs agents found marijuana in a table shipped from India, repackaged it, and had police officers posing as deliverymen convey it. The defendant accepted the package and was arrested less than an hour later as he exited his house. The warrantless arrest and search were justified by the initial customs inspection that found contraband, thus creating a lesser expectation of privacy for Andreas. Resealing the package does not function to revive or restore the lawfully invaded privacy rights. After the first inspection, the contraband was, in effect, in plain view. The lapse of time during which the police could not see the defendant did not reinstate his privacy rights. The Court noted that perfectly controlled deliveries are not always possible, and the arrest and search were not unreasonable because there was a "substantial likelihood" that the illegal contents of the container were not changed.

BOARDING AND SEARCHING SEAGOING VESSELS   Under federal law in force continuously since 1790, Coast Guard and customs officers may, without a warrant or reasonable articulable suspicion of criminal activity, hail, stop, and board any vessel located in waters that provide ready access to the open sea. The purpose is to inspect the ship's manifest and other documents. In contrast, automobiles may not be stopped without probable cause or reasonable suspicion of a traffic violation or crime (*United States v. Brignoni-Ponce*, 1975; *Delaware v. Prouse*, 1979). This rule for ships was held to be reasonable in **United States v. Villamonte-Marquez** (1983) because at sea it is impossible to establish the equivalent of border checkpoints or roadblocks. Although checkpoints could be established in ports, smugglers could easily avoid ports by anchoring at obscure points along the shore or by transferring cargo to other vessels. Also, the documentation requirements for vessels are different and more complex than automobile licensure, and information about the ship's registry and travel manifests cannot be known without boarding to inspect the documents, as the identity of ships involved in smuggling may be falsified.[14] The intrusion on a ship's Fourth Amendment interests by the Coast Guard boarding is limited, constituting "a brief detention while officials come on board, visit public areas of the vessel, and inspect documents." In *Villamonte-Marquez*, a forty-foot sailboat named the *Henry Morgan II* was packed with tons of marijuana, and the odor gave customs officials plain view authority to search. Justice Brennan, joined by Justice Marshall, dissented in *Villamonte-Marquez*, arguing that as a practical matter, ships in a channel can be funneled into a checkpoint area that allows the uniform checking of documents of all ships.

Extraterritorial Arrests and Searches

This section examines the **extraterritorial** reach of the Constitution: whether an illegal arrest in a foreign country deprives a federal court of jurisdiction to try a defendant, whether the Fourth Amendment exclusionary rule applies to searches conducted in other countries, and whether officers are liable for their actions in other countries. After the 9/11 terror attacks, an FBI senior legal advisor noted that, "as a result of the globalization of crime and the emergence of international terrorism, the apprehension of those who violate American criminal laws will often have to take place abroad."[15] Even before 9/11, the FBI established permanent offices in dozens of cities overseas to fight organized crime and terrorism.[16] The Supreme Court had to decide whether the Constitution "follows the flag"—that is, whether the constitutional limitations on government power apply to the activities of U.S. civilian law enforcement personnel in other countries.

KIDNAPPING AND ILLEGAL ARRESTS   The Supreme Court has ruled that the illegal arrest or even kidnapping of a defendant within the United States does not divest a court of the jurisdiction to try the defendant (*Frisbie v. Collins*, 1952; see Chapter 4). The Supreme Court extended this rule to cases where a defendant was seized in another country (***United States v. Alvarez-Machain***, 1992). The *Alvarez-Machain* case began in 1985 when a Drug Enforcement Administration (DEA) agent, Enrique Camarena Salazar, was kidnapped, tortured, and killed by Mexican drug dealers, an event that strained relations between the United States and Mexico. The United States indicted nineteen Mexicans, including high-level government officials, for Camarena's torture-killing. Among those indicted was Dr. Humberto Alvarez-Machain, a gynecologist practicing in Guadalajara, Mexico.[17] In 1990, the DEA hired Mexican bounty hunters to kidnap Dr. Alvarez-Machain and bring him to the United States, where he was arrested and put on trial for Camarena's murder. "The arrest of Alvarez took place without an extradition request by the United States, without the involvement of the Mexican judiciary or law enforcement, and under protest by Mexico."[18]

Did the United States have jurisdiction to try Alvarez-Machain? In a six-to-three decision before the trial, the Supreme Court held that it did. Although an extradition treaty existed between Mexico and the United States, the treaty did not specifically address the question of forcible abductions. Therefore, according to Chief Justice Rehnquist's majority opinion, the treaty and its procedural history did not prohibit forcible abductions. The treaty, in this view, did not specify the *only* way that one country could gain custody over a citizen of the other country. The Supreme Court refused to interpret the treaty beyond its terms, even if the actions of the DEA agents were "shocking" and "in violation of general international law principles." Justice Stevens, dissenting for himself and Justices Blackmun and O'Connor, argued that the majority's interpretation in effect nullified the extradition treaty, breaking faith with Mexico. Justice Stevens showed that the trial of Dr. Alvarez-Machain violated the rules of customary international law concerning jurisdiction. The world would view the majority's decision as "monstrous" and the ruling would weaken America's quest to strengthen the Rule of Law in the international arena by demonstrating that the United States did not live up to international law.

The case ended badly for the United States. Dr. Alvarez-Machain was acquitted of murder and torture in the Los Angeles Federal District Court in December 1992. The trial judge threw out the case, calling the prosecution's case the "wildest speculation" after discovering that the wrong doctor was kidnapped. Others were convicted for the murder. The incident caused much resentment of the United States in Mexico, and as a result, the Clinton administration promised Mexico that the United States will not engage in any cross-border kidnapping of Mexican citizens pending a revised extradition treaty. International opinion and international law scholars roundly criticized the United States.

Dr. Alvarez-Machain sued federal law enforcement officials for $20 million in damages for kidnapping, torture, and false imprisonment. After lengthy litigation, the Ninth Circuit ruled en banc that the doctor had a right to sue the United States under the Alien Tort Claims (ATC) Act and the Federal Tort Claims Act (FTCA).[19] The Supreme Court, however, reversed, finding that the FTCA's exception for acts committed in foreign countries precluded the liability of the government and its agents and employees. The Court also held that the ATC Act, which was enacted as a jurisdictional statute in 1789, did not support Alvarez-Machain's claim, although it would support some claims under international law. The Court cautiously ruled that "federal courts should not recognize private claims under federal common law for violations of any international law norm with less definite content and acceptance among civilized nations than the historical paradigms familiar when [the ATC] was enacted." It further found that no act of Congress or treaty of international law clearly established a substantive right claimed by Alvarez-Machain (***Sosa v. Alvarez-Machain***, 2004).

In contemporary terms, the *Alvarez-Machain* cases have legitimated "rendition to justice," or "the covert transfer of a suspected criminal from one state to another for the purpose of an investigation or trial"[20]—in other words, the kidnapping of suspects from foreign countries.

EXTRATERRITORIAL APPLICATION OF THE FOURTH AMENDMENT   The Supreme Court held in *United States v. Verdugo-Urquidez* (1990) that the Fourth Amendment does not apply when U.S. officers search the premises of an alien in a foreign country. This is true even if the alien is lawfully in federal custody on American soil at the time of the search and the purpose of the search is to obtain evidence for his or her conviction of a federal crime in a U.S. court. Verdugo-Urquidez, a reputed drug dealer, was arrested in Mexico by Mexican officers at the request of American authorities and was charged in federal court for the kidnapping and murder of DEA special agent Enrique Camarena Salazar. A joint Mexican Police–DEA task force carried out a raid of Verdugo-Urquidez's home in Mexico, and the evidence obtained was used by the DEA to prosecute him. No approval or warrant was sought from U.S. attorneys or magistrates for the raid. The Ninth Circuit Court of Appeals held that a warrant was required for such a search. Although the warrant would have no legal validity in Mexico, it would "define the scope of the search" for American authorities. In rejecting this argument, Chief Justice Rehnquist, writing for the majority, noted that the Fourth Amendment had never been extended to protect aliens on foreign soil. The fact that Verdugo-Urquidez was in custody on American soil at the time of the raid is a "fortuitous circumstance" that should not dictate the outcome of the case.

Foreign relations activities may have influenced the *Verdugo-Urquidez* decision. While the case was being considered, the United States invaded Panama to rid that country of its military dictator, Manuel Noriega, who was under federal indictment for drug dealing. Noriega surrendered to U.S. forces and was transported to the United States for trial.[21] Chief Justice Rehnquist noted that the United States had employed its armed forces over two hundred times on foreign soil. "Application of the Fourth Amendment to those circumstances could significantly disrupt the ability of the political branches to respond to foreign situations involving our national interest." The Court clearly thought it would be bad policy to impose the burden or concern on the president and members of Congress "as to what might be reasonable in the way of searches and seizures conducted abroad" before authorizing such military actions.

Justice Brennan, dissenting, noted that in recent years the extraterritorial reach of American criminal law against foreign nationals has been increasing under U.S. drug, antitrust, securities, antiterrorist, and piracy statutes. If the United States can extend its criminal law overseas, then the Fourth Amendment should "travel with" American agents who go abroad to exercise criminal jurisdiction. It is unlikely that the Supreme Court will adopt such a rule in the context of what will probably be a very long war on terrorism worldwide.[22]

REGULATORY SEARCHES AND THE SPECIAL NEEDS DOCTRINE

Origins of the Doctrine and Administrative Searches

In *New Jersey v. T.L.O.* (1985), the Supreme Court ruled that a public high school student has a Fourth Amendment expectation of privacy in her purse. Nevertheless, the Court ruled that when the circumstances make it reasonable, a public school official can inspect the content of the student's purse, looking for materials that violate school rules and that could subject the student to criminal prosecution, without first obtaining a warrant and even without probable cause to believe that the purse contains illegal contraband. *T.L.O.* set off a chain of rulings that have collectively come under a rule known as the **special needs doctrine**. It is not clear that the Court intended to create a doctrine, for the cases that have relied on the reasoning of "special needs *beyond the need for normal law enforcement*" involve different factual settings and allow searches based on different evidentiary foundations. In some cases, a government official must have *reasonable suspicion* of wrongdoing before searching without a warrant, whereas under other factual circumstances there need be *no individualized suspicion* for a search to take place. What the cases have in common is that in each case the search is conducted by a government officer who is *not* a police officer engaged in the enforcement of criminal law.

The special needs cases are closely related to *administrative searches*—a type of search that the Supreme Court brought under the aegis of the Fourth Amendment in 1967. Chapter 3 discussed four 1960s cases that "revolutionized" the Fourth Amendment. The *Katz* (1967) "expectation of privacy" doctrine replaced the idea that privacy protection depended on property rights and expanded Fourth Amendment protection. *Warden v. Hayden* (1967) abolished the "mere property" rule, allowing police to seize a defendant's property for the duration of a prosecution to be used at trial. *Terry v. Ohio* (1968) modified search and seizure jurisprudence by making it more *flexible*, thus allowing police to stop a person on less evidence than probable cause. Together these cases made Fourth Amendment law more functional and flexible.

The fourth "revolutionary" case, *Camara v. Municipal Court* (1967), applied the Fourth Amendment not only to police officers investigating felonies, but to entry by administrative officers enforcing municipal safety, health, or occupancy ordinances. *Camara* overruled an earlier case that held that the Fourth Amendment did not apply at all to these kinds of essentially noncriminal searches (*Frank v. Maryland*, 1959). The *Camara* Court recognized that the Fourth Amendment protected against all official intrusions into the privacy of a home, whether by police officers or by other government officers. By extending the Fourth Amendment to administrative searches, *Camara* allowed householders or business owners to refuse entry to inspectors without *search warrants*. This created a dilemma. To be effective, inspectors need to enter every home or business to enforce ordinances. But it is often close to impossible for inspectors to obtain *probable cause* to believe that *this* particular householder or business is in violation of codes. *Camara*'s warrant requirement threatened to undermine the effectiveness of inspection programs. The Supreme Court got around this sticking point by holding that administrative search warrants could be obtained by proving to a court that the conditions *in an area* made inspections necessary. Without quite saying so, the Supreme Court watered down the Fourth Amendment's *particularity requirement* by ruling that an "area warrant" was *reasonable*. In effect, the Supreme Court authorized *general warrants*, so hated by the Framers of the Constitution.

The Supreme Court applied the administrative search doctrine, with its "area warrants," to inspections of commercial establishments (*See v. City of Seattle*, 1967). Indeed, the Court soon held that even area warrants could be dispensed with when inspectors entered a **pervasively regulated industry**, such as liquor stores or gun dealerships, as long as they did so during normal business hours and did not use force. Dealers who refused inspections could lose their licenses (*Colonnade Catering v. United States,* 1970; *United States v. Biswell,* 1972). Under the administrative search rules, unannounced safety inspections of mines without a warrant was permissible under the Mine Safety and Health Act because the law was known to all mine owners and provides a constitutionally adequate substitute for a warrant (*Donovan v. Dewey,* 1981). The Supreme Court did require area warrants for worker safety inspections under the Occupational Safety and Health Administration (OSHA). It ruled that simply requiring safety and health regulations does not transform monitored industries into "pervasively regulated industries" (*Marshall v. Barlow's, Inc.,* 1978).

The *flexible interpretation* of the Fourth Amendment established by the administrative search cases, then, made the Court receptive to relying on the Reasonableness Clause of the Fourth Amendment to uphold a variety of warrantless searches under the "special needs" rubric.

Fire Inspections

Determining the cause of a blaze involves an inspection, which is conducted for both administrative and criminal investigation purposes, after the fire. Rules for these kinds of searches were established in *Michigan v. Tyler* (1978) and *Michigan v. Clifford* (1984) and provide a mix of administrative search and criminal search rules:

Rule 1. "A burning building creates an exigency that justifies a warrantless entry by fire officials to fight the blaze."

Rule 2. "Moreover,. . . once in the building, officials need no warrant to remain for 'a reasonable time to investigate the cause of a blaze after it has been extinguished.'"

Rule 3. "Where, however, reasonable expectations of privacy remain in the fire-damaged property, additional investigations begun after the fire has been extinguished and fire and police officials have left the scene, generally must be made pursuant to a warrant or the identification of some new exigency."

Rule 4. "If the primary object [of a renewed search] is to determine the cause and origin of a recent fire, an administrative warrant will suffice. To obtain such a warrant, fire officials need show only that a fire of undetermined origin has occurred on the premises, that the scope of the proposed search is reasonable and will not intrude unnecessarily on the fire victim's privacy, and that the search will be executed at a reasonable and convenient time."

Rule 5. "If the primary object of the [renewed] search is to gather evidence of criminal activity, a criminal search warrant may be obtained only on a showing of probable cause to believe that relevant evidence will be found in the place to be searched."

Rule 6. "If evidence of criminal activity is discovered during the course of a valid administrative search [or during the initial firefighting], it may be seized under the 'plain view' doctrine. . . . This evidence then may be used to establish probable cause to obtain a criminal search warrant."

In *Michigan v. Tyler* (1978), a fire broke out in a furniture store at midnight. At 2 a.m., just as the firefighters were "watering down smoldering embers," fire inspectors arrived to determine the cause, and they seized two plastic containers of flammable liquid. A police detective arrived at 3:30 a.m. and took photographs of the suspected arson. Shortly thereafter, the police investigator abandoned the investigation because the smoke and darkness made careful observation of the crime scene impossible. The fire inspectors returned briefly at 8 a.m. after the fire had been fully extinguished and the building was empty. They left and returned with the police investigator at 9:30 a.m. During this search, they discovered more evidence of arson: pieces of tape on a stairway with burn marks and pieces of carpet suggesting a fuse trail. The investigators left to obtain tools, returned, and seized the incriminating evidence. Three weeks later, an investigator with the state police arson section returned to take pictures. All the entries were made without consent or warrants.

The Court held that the Fourth Amendment applied to searches following a fire, noting that a magistrate must not be a "rubber stamp" when issuing an administrative search warrant. Instead, the magistrate must ensure that the investigation does not stray beyond reasonable limits. The magistrate's role is to prevent undue harassment of property owners and to keep the inspection to a minimum.

Applying the search rules to the facts of *Tyler,* the Court held that the warrantless entry and search immediately after the fire was proper (Rules 1 and 2). The search at 9:30 the next morning was construed by the Court as a continuation of the search begun a few hours before: that search was cut off owing to the smoke and darkness, and "[l]ittle purpose would have been served by their remaining in the building, except to remove any doubt about the legality of the warrantless search and seizure later that same morning." The photographs taken by the state police investigator, however, were not admissible without a warrant: Too much time had elapsed, and suspicion had accrued.

Michigan v. Clifford involved an early-morning house fire. Firefighters arrived on the scene at 5:40 a.m., extinguished the blaze, and left the scene shortly after 7 a.m. One hour later, a police fire investigator received an order to investigate. Because he was working on other cases, he did not arrive on the scene until 1 p.m. When he arrived, a work crew hired by the owner was boarding up the house and pumping water out of the basement. Clifford was out of town on a vacation and was communicating about the situation through his insurance agent and a neighbor. After the work crew departed, the investigators entered the basement of the house without obtaining consent or an administrative warrant and quickly found evidence of arson (a strong odor of fuel and a crock pot attached to a timer set for 3:45 a.m. that stopped at 4 a.m.). This evidence was seized and marked. The officer proceeded through the remainder of the house, much of which was still intact, and seized other suspicious evidence.

The Supreme Court held this seizure to be a Fourth Amendment violation. The owner, by hiring a crew to board up and pump out his house, clearly maintained an expectation of privacy in his home. Therefore, before entry, the officer should have obtained an administrative search warrant. The time lapse meant that there was no longer an exigent circumstance. Once the officer found incriminating items in the basement, it was necessary to halt the search and take the evidence to a magistrate to seek a criminal search warrant. Thus all the evidence was inadmissible.

In sum, fire officials have the right to enter burned premises immediately after a fire in an attempt to determine the cause of the fire. Owners or residents, however, do not lose their right to privacy; more extensive, long-term investigations and searches must be accompanied by a warrant.

Early Special Needs Cases: Creating a Doctrine

The special needs doctrine originated in *New Jersey v. T.L.O.* (1985), although that case did not announce the creation of any doctrine. Rather, in the course of deciding a case that did not fit easily into preexisting categories, the Court laid a conceptual foundation that later cases recognized as a basis for what came to be called the special needs doctrine, and was later applied to dissimilar kind of cases.

In *T.L.O.*, a teacher discovered a fourteen-year-old public high school freshman smoking in a lavatory in violation of a school rule. She was brought to the principal's office and questioned by an assistant vice principal. The girl, T.L.O., denied that she had been smoking and claimed that she did not smoke at all. The assistant vice principal then demanded to see her purse, opened the purse, and found a pack of cigarettes. Upon removing the cigarettes, he noticed a pack of cigarette rolling papers. Rolling papers are closely associated with the use of marijuana. The assistant vice principal proceeded to search the purse thoroughly and found a small amount of marijuana, a pipe, a number of empty plastic bags, a substantial quantity of one-dollar bills, an index card listing students who owed T.L.O. money, and two letters implicating T.L.O. in marijuana dealing. This discovery led to T.L.O.'s adjudication as a delinquent and a one-year probation sentence.

Did the vice principal's search of the purse violate T.L.O.'s constitutional rights? *State action* existed in this case because a public school is established by a local government. Its administrators and teachers exercise legitimate control over students by virtue of their positions. Justice White's majority opinion first asked whether T.L.O. had a Fourth Amendment privacy interest in her purse. The Court's unanimous decision on this point rested on a close analysis of the actualities of school life in the 1980s:

> Students at a minimum must bring to school not only the supplies needed for their studies, but also keys, money, and the necessaries of personal hygiene and grooming. In addition, students may carry on their persons or in purses or wallets such nondisruptive yet highly personal items as photographs, letters, and diaries. Finally, students may have perfectly legitimate reasons to carry with them articles of property needed in connection with extracurricular or recreational activities. In short, school children may find it necessary to carry with them a variety of legitimate, noncontraband items, and there is no reason to conclude that they have necessarily waived all rights to privacy in such items merely by bringing them onto school grounds. (*New Jersey v. T.L.O.*, 1985)

The state argued that public school students had *no* reasonable expectation of privacy in school. The Court rejected this argument along with the idea that teachers stood ***in loco parentis***—in the place of parents. Under such a rule school authorities could search the belongings of high school students *at will*. The old-fashioned idea that parents transfer their personal authority to teachers does not fit the modern reality that schools are in many ways large bureaucracies.

Deciding that public high school students enjoy an expectation of privacy did not answer whether the vice principal's search violated T.L.O.'s rights, which had to be balanced against schools' interests in maintaining order by enforcing such school rules as bans on smoking. Two further issues needed answers: Was a *warrant* necessary? And if not, what was the proper *standard of evidence* for a lawful warrantless search in a school setting? As to the first, all the justices agreed that the "warrant requirement, in particular, is unsuited to the school environment: requiring a teacher to obtain a warrant before searching a child suspected of an infraction of school rules (or of the criminal law) would unduly interfere with the maintenance of the swift and informal disciplinary procedures needed in the schools."

The Court decided that the search of the purse was constitutionally reasonable as long as the vice principal had *reasonable suspicion*. Since T.L.O. denied smoking, it was reasonable. . . to resolve the dispute between the teacher and student, for the assistant vice principal to open the purse where cigarettes would be carried. When he saw the rolling papers, he had some suspicion that T.L.O. might be in possession of marijuana, although a less likely but innocent use would have been to roll tobacco. She may have been carrying the rolling papers for another student or person. In short, the observation of the rolling papers did *not* establish probable cause, but did provide the assistant vice principal with reasonable suspicion that T.L.O. had marijuana in her purse. The Court rejected the probable cause standard. After *Terry v. Ohio* (1968), probable cause it is not an irreducible requirement of a valid search. The decision was an application of the general-reasonableness construction of the Fourth Amendment to the specific facts of this school search.

Justice Brennan, joined by Justices Marshall and Stevens, dissented. Fourth Amendment warrant exceptions were allowed in past cases only where there was a pressing emergency. The facts in this case did not rise to such a level of seriousness as to cause the constitutional balance to tip in favor of the school's interests when measured against the student's right to privacy. The suspected infraction, smoking, was not a crime. "Considerations of the deepest significance for the freedom of our citizens counsel strict adherence to the principle that no search may be conducted where the official is not in possession of probable cause" (*New Jersey v. T.L.O.*, 1985, Brennan, J., dissenting). Justice Stevens, also dissenting, stated that the kind of search involved in this case would have been justified if there had been an allegation involving in-school violence.

T.L.O. provides an example of how legal doctrines evolve. In a footnote, Justice White wrote that "the *special needs* of the school environment require assessment of the legality of such searches against a standard less exacting than that of probable cause." Justice Blackmun, in a concurring opinion, wrote that "[o]nly in those *exceptional circumstances in which special needs, beyond the normal need for law enforcement*, make the warrant and probable-cause requirement impracticable, is a court entitled to substitute its balancing of interests for that of the Framers" (*New Jersey v. T.L.O.* 1985, concurring opinions, emphasis added). The use of the term *special needs* was probably not meant to define a new doctrine but simply to explain the basis of the Court's ruling.

Two years after *T.L.O.*, however, the Supreme Court decided three cases that relied on *T.L.O.* as precedent and used the "special needs" language as justification for the decisions. These cases established the idea that the ruling of *New Jersey v. T.L.O.* established a new doctrine. None of the cases involved public school searches.

O'Connor v. Ortega (1987) was a civil suit in which a supervisor thoroughly searched the office, desk, and filing cabinet of Dr. Ortega, a psychiatrist employed by a state hospital. Ortega was suspected of fraud and was also charged with sexual harassment of female employees and inappropriate disciplining of a resident. There was state action because the search was ordered by the executive director of a state hospital. The Supreme Court found that Dr. Ortega had a reasonable expectation of privacy in his office, but also stated that an expectation of privacy can be overcome if a governmental interest outweighs an individual's privacy interests. In her majority opinion justifying the search, Justice O'Connor relied heavily on the incipient rule in Justice Blackmun's *T.L.O.* concurrence and quoted his special needs formulation (i.e., "special needs, beyond the normal need for law enforcement") as a reason for upholding the search of a public employee's office on less than probable cause. Both Justice O'Connor and Justice Scalia referred to these words, but both omitted the opening words in Justice Blackmun's sentence in *T.L.O.*, recognizing a "special needs" exception only in "exceptional circumstances." If *T.L.O.* had been known as the "exceptional circumstances" doctrine, perhaps it would have been less frequently employed.

In the next special needs case, the Court combined that doctrine with the pervasively regulated industry exception to administrative search warrants. ***New York v. Burger*** (1987) held that evidence found in plain view during a police inspection of automobile junk shops could be admitted in a criminal case. A state statute required vehicle dismantlers to maintain records of cars in their junkyards and to allow police or motor vehicle inspectors to examine the records during working hours. Failure to produce records was a misdemeanor. NYPD officers, who were part of a team that conducted five to ten administrative junk shop inspections daily, identified stolen vehicles by their VINs during such an inspection.

The Court upheld this search and seizure even though the police had no warrant nor *any* suspicion of wrongdoing. The Court relied on three reasons: (1) junkyards are a pervasively regulated industry providing a reduced expectation of privacy; (2) warrantless inspections are necessary to make the inspection system work and are of limited scope; and (3) the statute is not a pretext for criminal searches without a warrant. As to the last point, the Court said that a state can address a major social problem through both the administrative system and penal sanctions. In this regard, the police officers were treated simply as regulatory agents. This last point is rather weak, as the major "social problem" targeted by the New York law was the dismantling of *stolen cars*. If this logic were pushed to its extreme, every crime could be declared a social problem, and constitutional protections would be eliminated by treating investigations as inspections.

The last special needs case of 1987, ***Griffin v. Wisconsin***, ruled that a probationer's home could be entered and searched without a warrant by probation officers as long as there were reasonable grounds to believe contraband was present, as was required by state law. Justice Scalia offered this justification: "The search of Griffin's home satisfied the demands of the Fourth

Amendment because it was carried out pursuant to a regulation that itself satisfies the Fourth Amendment's reasonableness requirement under well-established principles."

> A probationer's home, like anyone else's, is protected by the Fourth Amendment's requirement that searches be "reasonable." Although we usually require that a search be undertaken only pursuant to a warrant (and thus supported by probable cause, as the Constitution says warrants must be), . . . we have permitted exceptions when "special needs, beyond the normal need for law enforcement, make the warrant and probable-cause requirement impracticable."

In support, Justice Scalia cited *New Jersey v. T.L.O., O'Connor v. Ortega,* and the administrative search cases. The creation of a new doctrine requires a certain amount of maneuvering. Strictly speaking, neither *T.L.O.* nor *O'Connor v. Ortega* applied to a home. Justice Scalia also cited *Payton v. New York* (1980), which held that an arrest warrant is necessary for entry into a home to make a felony arrest. But instead of treating the search of a probationer's home as a home search, the Court instead treated it as part of a probation system "like [the] operation of a school, government office or prison, or . . . supervision of a regulated industry." A probationer's punishment includes correctional supervision and only conditional liberty in the community, which diminishes his or her expectation of privacy, even in the home.

These initial special needs cases demonstrate how new legal doctrines are formed. First, a case is decided that does not precisely fit earlier precedent. In its opinion, the Court *provides a phrase* that helps to explain the decision. Subsequent cases *apply the phrase* as a basis for decisions to cases that are not precisely the same as the first. The phrase is now becoming a doctrine—*a legal category* that can be used as a *framework* to decide future cases. This produces the appearance that the system of common law reasoning is more inductive than deductive.[23] By organizing the cases under a doctrine, the Court attempts to offer a *consistent and satisfactory explanation* to police officers and lower court judges who must decide novel cases.

The creation of a doctrine is not simply a neutral process of logic. In the example of the special needs doctrine, the new category allowed a conservative Court to advance a theory that relied on the Reasonableness Clause and the general-reasonableness construction of the Fourth Amendment. (See "The Fourth Amendment's Structure" Section in Chapter 2.) This made it feasible to get around the obstacles of the Warrant Clause and the probable cause requirement to uphold action by government officers that intruded on Fourth Amendment privacy in different situations. Liberal justices saw the special needs cases as assaults on fundamental rights. As Justice Thurgood Marshall wrote, "In the four years since this Court, in *T.L.O.,* first began recognizing "special needs" exceptions to the Fourth Amendment, the clarity of Fourth Amendment doctrine has been badly distorted, as the Court has eclipsed the probable-cause requirement in a patchwork quilt of settings" (*Skinner v. Railway Labor Executives' Association,* 1989).

Drug Testing

The personal and societal costs of alcoholism and drug abuse have made them prime domestic issues. Government agencies and private employers, including major league sports franchises, have turned to random or mandatory drug testing as a way to deter drug use and to identify users. The pervasiveness and visibility of drug testing has assured court challenges. Drug testing by private businesses is not a Fourth Amendment concern, just as searches in private schools do not infringe on a constitutional right of privacy; drug testing by government agencies, on the other hand, involves state action and comes under the Fourth Amendment. The Supreme Court has decided a number of special needs cases concerning drug testing.

EARLY CASES   The first two such cases were decided in favor of government-mandated testing programs. One upheld the mandatory testing of every train crew member after a major rail accident (*Skinner v. Railway Labor Executives' Association,* 1989). The other allowed the U.S. Customs Service to test virtually all of its agents for drugs at some point in their careers (*National Treasury Employees Union v. Von Raab,* 1989).

An initial issue in both cases was whether taking and testing blood and urine samples intruded on reasonable expectations of privacy. As noted in Chapter 3, under *Katz* the Court held that urine collection and its testing to ascertain the presence of drugs in a person's body intrudes upon expectations of privacy that society has long recognized as reasonable. "There are few activities in our society more personal or private than the passing of urine. Most people describe it by euphemisms if they talk about it at all. It is a function traditionally performed without public observation; indeed, its performance in public is generally prohibited by law as well as social custom" (*Skinner v. Railway Labor Executives' Association,* 1989). The Court noted that this expectation of privacy is not only rooted in the traditional dictates of modesty, but also in the fact that the chemical analysis of urine, like that of blood, can reveal a host of medical facts about a person. Although urine testing in order to detect drugs or alcohol infringes on Fourth Amendment privacy, it is allowed under certain conditions (*Skinner v. Railway Labor Executives' Association,* 1989).

The second issue in both cases concerned the *standards* needed to ascertain the constitutionality of drug testing. In each case, the Court applied the *special needs* doctrine to find these drug-testing programs reasonable under the Fourth Amendment, even though no warrant was required and *no level of individualized suspicion* was needed to trigger drug testing. Each case was decided on the particular facts of the respective testing program. The linchpin of the holdings in *Skinner* and *Von Raab* was that the *purposes* of these laws were essentially *administrative,* although the discovery of the presence of drugs could lead to criminal prosecution.

In **Skinner v. Railway Labor Executives' Association** (1989), the Court upheld a federal law that mandated drug testing of all on-site employees after a major train accident, whether the employees worked for a *private* railroad company or a line run by the government. *State action* was based on the fact that the program was *mandated by law for the public safety.* The Court's decision that mandatory testing was reasonable and constitutional was based on several points: (1) preserving the life and safety of train passengers is of great importance; (2) employees subjected to testing are involved in safety-sensitive tasks; (3) absolute prohibition of alcohol and drug use while on the job is a reasonable requirement; and (4) the usual sanction for on-the-job intoxication is dismissal and not criminal prosecution. The warrant requirement would add little to further the aims of the drug-testing program because the tests were standardized. The fact that blood alcohol levels drop at a constant rate requires swift testing and creates an exigency. Waiting to get a warrant before testing would effectively undermine the usefulness of the testing.

The railway union argued in *Skinner* that there must be a *particularized suspicion* against specific railroad employees after an accident before they could be tested. The Court disagreed and concluded that mandatory and comprehensive testing was constitutional for the following reasons:

- Blood and urine testing are relatively limited encroachments on railway employees' expectations of privacy because they are job- and safety-related requirements in a pervasively regulated industry.
- The testing is limited in time, intrusiveness, and ancillary risk.
- The state's interest in testing without individualized suspicion is compelling because it is not easy for supervisors to spot workers who have used a drug and are still under its influence.
- A mandatory testing and dismissal rule has a greater deterrent effect than a weaker nonmandatory testing policy.
- Accident scenes are chaotic, and it may be extremely difficult for supervisors to sort out who is to be tested and who is not to be tested on the basis of individualized suspicion.
- The fact that drug tests are not, in themselves, conclusive proof of impairment does not render the program unconstitutional, because statistical evidence obtained from mandatory, across-the-board testing is useful to the railway industry in assessing the causes of accidents.

The balance of interests in **National Treasury Employees Union v. Von Raab** (1989) differed in several respects. The challenged rule of the U.S. Customs Service required the automatic drug testing of all officers who (1) are directly involved in *drug interdiction* or drug law enforcement, (2) are required to carry *firearms,* or (3) *handle classified material* that would be useful to drug smugglers and could be relinquished through the bribery or blackmail of drug-dependent employees. This testing program was not triggered by a particular negative incident but was required for *all* who were hired or promoted into sensitive posts. The government interest was not preventing on-the-job impairment but was to ensure that the three categories of customs officers would lead drug-free lives. The theory was that drug-addicted customs agents are targets for bribery and cannot carry out their functions in a positive manner. Like government employees in sensitive jobs (i.e., U.S. Mint employees or intelligence officers), customs officers "have a diminished expectation of privacy in respect to the intrusions occasioned by" their positions.

Justice Anthony Kennedy, writing for the majority, held, as he did in *Skinner,* that neither a warrant nor individualized suspicion would serve a useful purpose in such a program. The majority agreed with the first two rationales presented by the Customs Service, upholding the program of drug testing for those agents directly involved in drug law enforcement and for those who carried firearms. It could not agree on the reasonableness of the third rationale, preventing the compromise of agents handling classified information, and remanded the case for further fact-finding.

Justice Marshall, joined by Justice Brennan, dissented in both *Skinner* and *Von Raab* on the grounds that their special needs analyses were flawed. For them, the goals and methods of the two programs provided no reasonable basis to dispense with the individualized suspicion usually required by the Fourth Amendment before interfering with a person's constitutional rights. He felt that the need for individualized suspicion would not undermine these programs, and accused the majority of submitting to popular pressure generated by public hysteria over the drug problem and giving away precious rights.

Justices Scalia and Stevens concurred in *Skinner* but dissented in *Von Raab.* Justice Scalia's dissent noted that the factual predicate for the two cases differed. In *Skinner,* the government gave evidence to show that a substantial number of train accidents were caused by intoxicated railroad employees. In *Von Raab,* on the other hand, "neither the frequency of use nor connection to harm is demonstrated or even likely. In my view the Customs Service rules are a kind of immolation of privacy and human dignity in symbolic opposition to drug use." Justice Scalia noted that the government did not supply even one example in which the purported state interest of preventing bribe taking, poor intentions, unsympathetic law enforcement, or the compromise of classified information was endangered by drug use. Some of the government's arguments were weak. For example, the fact that an agent uses drugs does not necessarily mean the officer would be hostile or indifferent to drug enforcement. Calling the Customs Service's reasons "feeble," Justice Scalia noted that its commissioner said that the drug-testing program would "set an important example in our country's struggle with this most serious threat to our national health and security." In effect, Justice Scalia agreed with Justice Marshall's point, that the testing of customs officers was an unnecessary sacrifice of constitutional freedoms as a result of pandering to public and political pressure.

DRUG TESTING OF POLITICAL CANDIDATES   The Supreme Court drew the line at mandatory drug testing in ***Chandler v. Miller*** (1997). A Georgia law required every candidate for statewide office to be drug tested. Two libertarian candidates for statewide offices challenged the law as an infringement of their Fourth Amendment rights. The Supreme Court (8–1), per Justice Ginsburg, agreed. Drug testing under the law was not based on individualized suspicion against the candidate. Indeed, the program was "relatively noninvasive" because it permitted a candidate to provide a urine specimen in the office of his or her private physician. The results are then given to the candidate, who controls further dissemination of the report. The Court held that requiring certification of drug testing before a person's name could be placed on the ballot is not a special need beyond the normal needs of law enforcement and was unconstitutional. "Nothing in the record hints that the hazards respondents broadly describe [i.e., drug-addicted candidates] are real and not simply hypothetical for Georgia's polity. The statute was not enacted . . . in response to any fear or suspicion of drug use by state officials" (*Chandler v. Miller,* 1997). The testing program was simply too weak to identify or to deter candidates who violate antidrug laws. In contrast to other drug-testing programs designed to deal with real dangers of illicit drug use, Justice Ginsburg wrote that the actual purpose of the Georgia law was simply to project an "image" of being tough on drugs. "By requiring candidates for public office to submit to drug testing, Georgia displays its commitment to the struggle against drug abuse. The suspicionless tests, according to respondents, signify that candidates, if elected, will be fit to serve their constituents free from the influence of illegal drugs" (*Chandler v. Miller,* 1997). A law that is merely *symbolic* does not create the special need that allows an individual's right to privacy to be overridden without a warrant and individualized suspicion. Chief Justice Rehnquist, the lone dissenter, found no infringement on a personal right and, displaying his pro-state philosophy, wrote, "Nothing in the Fourth Amendment or in any other part of the Constitution prevents a State from enacting a statute whose principal vice is that it may seem misguided or even silly to the members of this Court" (*Chandler v. Miller,* 1997).

DRUG TESTING OF PREGNANT WOMEN   The Supreme Court again drew a line against the special needs justification for drug testing pregnant women enrolled in a public prenatal care program in ***Ferguson v. City of Charleston*** (2001). Staff members at a Charleston, South Carolina, public hospital in 1988 were concerned that patients receiving prenatal treatment were using cocaine. A policy to identify and test pregnant patients suspected of drug use, and refer those who tested positive to the county substance abuse commission for counseling and treatment, did not reduce the incidence of cocaine use among patients.

A new policy developed by a task force *in conjunction with the local prosecutor and police* drug-screened all women in the program who met one of nine criteria, including "late prenatal care after 24 weeks gestation," "incomplete prenatal care," "abruptio placentae," "IUGR [intrauterine growth retardation] 'of no obvious cause,'" "previously known drug or alcohol abuse," or "unexplained congenital anomalies." The new policy had a treatment component but also *required* that information about drug use be *forwarded to police authorities for prosecution.* The policy also prescribed in detail the precise offenses with which a woman could be charged, depending on the stage of her pregnancy, from simple possession to possession and distribution to a person under the age of eighteen, and unlawful neglect of a child. Although women in the prenatal care program signed consent forms, it was not clear that they were informed of the possibility of prosecution for receiving health care. The Court assumed that the women did not know they were being tested for drugs and that the results were forwarded to law enforcement officials for prosecution.

The Supreme Court decided the case on the issue of whether there were special needs beyond the normal need for law enforcement that justified the drug testing of these women without a search warrant or any individualized suspicion. In reaching its conclusion that the testing program was unconstitutional, the Court concluded that the nine criteria used to initiate testing did not amount to probable cause or even reasonable suspicion that a woman had ingested cocaine. Justice Stevens's majority opinion noted that there was no "evidence in the record indicating that any of the nine search criteria was more apt to be caused by cocaine use than by some other factor, such as malnutrition, illness, or indigency." The Circuit Court's decision upholding the testing program rested "on the premise that the policy would be valid even if the tests were conducted randomly" (*Ferguson v. City of Charleston,* 2001).

The key factor that distinguished *Ferguson* from the earlier drug-testing special needs cases is that in the earlier cases there was some *administrative* rationale or consequence, such as dismissal from a position or discipline for substance use. In *Ferguson,* on the other hand, the goal of preventing cocaine use by pregnant women was secondary. "[T]he central and indispensable feature of the policy from its inception was the use of law enforcement to coerce the patients into substance abuse treatment." However beneficent the policy's ultimate goal, "the purpose actually served by the [hospital's] searches 'is ultimately indistinguishable from the general interest in crime control'" (*Ferguson v. City of Charleston,* 2001, citing *City of Indianapolis v. Edmond,* 2000). In fact, Charleston police and prosecutors "were extensively involved in the day-to-day administration of the policy." This close involvement had the effect of so closely involving hospital staff in law enforcement that they had "a special obligation to make sure that the patients are fully informed about their constitutional rights, as standards of knowing waiver require" (*Ferguson v. City of Charleston,* 2001).

Justice Scalia dissented, joined by Chief Justice Rehnquist and Justice Clarence Thomas. He argued, weakly, that drug testing is not a search, but at most "a 'derivative use of the product of a past unlawful search,' which, of course, 'works no new Fourth Amendment wrong' and 'presents a question, not of rights, but of remedies'" (*Ferguson v. City of Charleston,* 2001, Scalia, J., dissenting). Thus the dissenters were attempting to have the case decided as a matter of the applicability of the exclusionary rule.

Writing in 1999, Lynn Paltrow, program director of the National Advocates for Pregnant Women (NAPW), noted that "[i]n the name of fetal rights, over 200 pregnant women or new mothers in approximately twenty states have been arrested. Most of the women arrested have been low-income women of color with untreated drug addictions. Thus, the arrests focus on those people and issues that are hardest to defend in the court of public opinion. Wrongly prejudged as irresponsible and uncaring, the public has expressed little support for them."[24] She viewed these prosecution programs as an assault on the reproductive rights of women. Some justification for this is that "[m]any more children are harmed every year from prenatal alcohol use than by cocaine or marijuana. Yet fetal alcohol syndrome, which is characterized by retardation, is not prosecuted under such laws, because alcohol, like other possible detriments to a healthy baby, is legal."[25] Recent studies have shown that the impairment of fetuses from alcohol use is far worse than that resulting from cocaine, and that impairment previously attributed to cocaine use was the result of alcohol ingestion.[26]

DRUG TESTING AND STRIP SEARCHES OF HIGH SCHOOL STUDENTS   In two cases, the Supreme Court has upheld the mandatory testing of all high school students who are involved in athletics and extracurricular activities. In *Vernonia School District 47J v. Acton* (1995), the Court upheld a policy of mandatory drug testing of all students involved in interscholastic athletic programs. As in *Skinner* (1989) and *Von Raab* (1989), the Court upheld intrusions on Fourth Amendment privacy by searches conducted without a warrant or any level of individualized suspicion. *Vernonia* went beyond *T.L.O.*, in which the search of a student's belongings was based on individualized suspicion of wrongdoing and a violation of a school rule. Justice Scalia's majority opinion gave several reasons for finding that the blanket searches, not based on individual suspicion, were reasonable:

- Drug use had become evident in the school system and was believed to be widespread. The school district was concerned that student athletes using drugs were prone to injury.
- Urine testing constitutes a Fourth Amendment search.
- The actual privacy interests of student athletes, however, are "negligible." Public schools have "custodial and tutelary responsibility for children"; students are subject to physical examinations and vaccinations for health purposes; and "school sports are not for the bashful," as the athletes bathe in communal showers.
- The intrusion is limited. The school personnel who collect the urine samples do not directly observe the function; all student athletes are subject to testing; laboratories reveal only the presence of illicit drugs and not other health information; the results are known only by a limited group of school personnel; and results are not turned over to police.
- The state's interest is very important because drug use is especially harmful to youngsters.

As a result, the district need not base its testing on individualized suspicion. The state is not required to select the "least intrusive" method of search; it can balance the practicalities and select this method. The Court noted that focusing on "troublesome" students for testing could lead to arbitrary testing decisions.

Justice Ginsburg, concurring, noted that the decision does not determine whether routine testing of all public school students in a school or a district, not just those enrolled in interscholastic athletics, is allowable. A spirited dissent in *Vernonia* was written by Justice O'Connor, joined by Justices Stevens and Souter. She focused on the lack of individualized suspicion. The Court's decision means that *millions* of student athletes, the "overwhelming majority" of whom have given school officials "no reason whatsoever to suspect they use drugs at school, are open to an intrusive bodily search." The Framers of the Constitution were concerned with general searches as well as with general warrants. "[M]ass, suspicionless searches" are unreasonable in the criminal law enforcement context, and each "special needs" case that dispenses with individualized suspicion has to advance a "sound reason[] why such a regime would likely be ineffectual under the usual circumstances." Furthermore, her careful review of the facts discounted the costs of not drug testing. The failure to test school athletes simply did not put the lives and safety of many people at risk. Therefore, the district cannot simply decide to discard individualized suspicion. Without specific and compelling reasons to show that eliminating individualized suspicion is reasonable, the requirement is constitutionally necessary.

We cannot know the deeper reasons why two conservative justices split in this case. I speculate that the *Vernonia* opinions offer glimpses into the justices' constitutional norms, their views of political theory, and even their personal backgrounds. Justice O'Connor gave the following reason for her dissent:

Searches based on individualized suspicion also afford potential targets considerable control over whether they will, in fact, be searched because a person can avoid such a search by not acting in an objectively suspicious way. And given that the surest way to avoid acting suspiciously is to avoid the underlying wrongdoing, the costs of such a regime, one would think, are minimal. (*Vernonia School District 47J v. Acton,* 1995)

This logical, deterrence-based argument connects the Fourth Amendment's individualized suspicion requirement to a political philosophy of individualism and a willingness to give young citizens a choice whether to act lawfully or unlawfully *before* subjecting them to drug searches. The Constitution balances public safety against individual liberty. The Framers have commanded later generations of Americans to take risks in regard to public safety by trusting its citizens to make their own personal decisions to obey the law. Perhaps this strong leaning toward individualism can be explained, in part, by Justice O'Connor's upbringing. She "spent her early years on the Lazy B ranch doing the chores expected of a child growing up on a ranch—driving tractors, fixing fences, branding cattle. Sandra learned to be independent at an early age."[27]

In contrast, Justice Scalia's majority opinion can be seen as reflecting a philosophy of statist regimentation. The Vernonia District formulated a school policy that emphasizes public control over all student athletes, under the pain of penalty, rather than individual self-control. Justice Scalia's opinion refers positively to the fact that teachers in private schools "stand *in loco parentis* over the children entrusted to them." This had no direct bearing on a case involving public schools, but it offers insight into his authority-based reasoning in this and later cases. We can speculate that Justice Scalia's comfort with an authoritarian regime of drug testing is not entirely unrelated to the fact that he attended high school at a Roman Catholic military academy.[28] Finally, to return to Justice O'Connor's dissent, she writes: "Blanket searches, because they can involve 'thousands or millions' of searches, 'pose a greater threat to liberty' than do suspicion-based ones, which 'affect one person at a time,'" citing her dissent in *Illinois v. Krull* (1987). As suggested in Chapter 2, this concern by a conservative justice may have been generated by her experience as a state legislator.

In *Board of Education of Independent School District No. 92 of Pottawatomie County v. Earls* (2002), the Court (5–4) extended the rule of *Vernonia v. Acton* to high school students engaged in *extracurricular activities*. The basis for the majority ruling in *Earls* was much weaker than in *Vernonia*. For example, although there was no evidence of a widespread drug problem in the Tecumseh, Oklahoma, schools, Justice Thomas's majority opinion suggested that the national problem of teen drug use had grown worse since 1995. As for Tecumseh, the entire basis for the rural school district's concern was the testimony of two teachers that a student once appeared to be under the influence of drugs and another was overheard talking about drugs, a drug dog detected marijuana cigarettes near the school's parking lot, and that "[p]olice officers once found drugs or drug paraphernalia in a car driven by a Future Farmers of America member" (*Earles,* 2002).

Justice Ginsburg's dissent (joined by Justices Stevens, O'Connor, and Souter) pointed out that the facts in *Vernonia* included two good reasons for its decision: that drug use could be physically harmful for athletes and that athletes were leaders of an aggressive drug cult. Neither reason applies to all extracurricular activities. It borders on the comical to be concerned about potential injury to band members lifting heavy instruments, Future Farmers guiding livestock, and Future Homemakers of America using sharp knives. It appears, then, that the majority based its special needs determination of allowing drug testing of all students engaged in extracurricular activity on a *generalized* concern about drug use among teens. Justice Thomas, supporting the majority decision, noted that "the test results are not turned over to any law enforcement authority" (*Earls,* 2002). The majority characterized the urine collection and testing as "minimally intrusive" and concluded that "the invasion of students' privacy is not significant" (*Earls,* 2002).

The dissent noted that although extracurricular activities are nominally voluntary, large numbers of students engage in them. "Participation in such activities is a key component of school life, essential in reality for students applying to college, and, for all participants, a significant contributor to the breadth and quality of the educational experience" (*Earls,* 2002, Ginsburg, J., dissenting). Ironically, a cited study indicated that students enrolled in extracurricular activities are *less* likely to develop substance abuse problems than their peers. It seems, then, that the majority decision is close to allowing schools to require mandatory drug testing for all students. The dissent viewed the school policy as closer to the *symbolic* program adopted in *Chandler v. Miller* (1997).

Although *Earls* allows school districts to adopt drug-testing programs, a study of school administrators in one suburban district found that the level of support for drug testing was mixed and that the *Earls* case itself did not lead to the adoption of random testing in schools without such policies.[29] Thus the case may have limited practical effect. In this vein, a large study of 76,000 high school students nationwide found that drug use was no different in schools with or without random drug-testing programs. A newspaper article reporting the study noted that "[m]ost schools have shied away from drug testing." and that "only 18 percent of the nation's schools did any kind of screening from 1998 to 2001."[30]

The special needs doctrine has garnered scholarly criticism. Robert Dodson, citing eight critical law review articles, notes that "[c]onsiderable doubt exists over whether the Court should have ever adopted the special needs doctrine."[31] As Justice Marshall noted, there is no textual support for this doctrine, which weakens civil liberties, in the Fourth Amendment. Dodson notes that the "Court has never adequately defined what it means by special need."[32] He proposes that the special needs doctrine be modified to ensure that warrantless searches be allowed only if the program affects the safety of large numbers of people and only if the courts can identify factors that make the policy truly special. He notes that evidence obtained under the special needs doctrine has indeed led to a large number of prosecutions, and he recommends that an exclusionary rule apply to these instances to prevent the perversion of the doctrine into another tool of law enforcement.

SCHOOL STRIP SEARCH   It is not clear whether criticism of the special needs doctrine as such has caused the Supreme Court to back away from expanding it as a basis of its reasoning. It is interesting that in ***Safford Unified School District v. Redding*** (2009), the Court held (8–1) that the *strip search* of 13-year-old middle school student Savana Redding was unconstitutional, based on the precedent of *New Jersey v. T. L. O.* (1985), without once mentioning the special needs doctrine. A boy in the school told the principal and assistant principal Kerry Wilson that students were bringing drugs and weapons on campus and a week later gave Wilson a white pill given to him by student Marissa Glines. The pill was ibuprofen 400 mg, available only by prescription. The school had a policy strictly prohibiting the nonmedical possession of any prescription or over-the-counter drug on school grounds, unless permission was granted.

Called out of class, Marissa turned out her pockets and opened her wallet and produced a blue pill (a 200-mg dose of anti-inflammatory drug naproxen), several white ones, and a razor blade. Marissa, who was in possession of Savana's day planner, said she got the pills from Savana Redding. Wilson did not ask Marissa any follow-up questions to determine whether there was any likelihood that Savana presently had pills, neither asking when Marissa received the pills from Savana nor where Savana might be hiding them. Marissa was subjected to a strip search similar to the one subsequently endured by Savana, which revealed no drugs or pills.

Savana Redding, an honors student, was brought to Wilson's office where he showed her the day planner, unzipped and open flat on his desk, in which there were several knives, lighters, a permanent marker, and a cigarette. Savana said she lent her planner to Marissa a few days before and that none of the other items belonged to her. She denied knowing anything about the pills and denied that she was giving pills to fellow students. She agreed to let Wilson and Helen Romero, an administrative assistant, search her belongings. They searched Savana's backpack and found nothing. "At that point, Wilson instructed Romero to take Savana to the school nurse's office to search her clothes for pills. Romero and the nurse, Peggy Schwallier, asked Savana to remove her jacket, socks, and shoes, leaving her in stretch pants and a T-shirt (both without pockets), which she was then asked to remove. Finally, Savana was told to pull her bra out and to the side and shake it, and to pull out the elastic on her underpants, thus exposing her breasts and pelvic area to some degree. No pills were found."

In his last opinion in his Supreme Court career, Justice Souter held that Assistant Principal Wilson had sufficient suspicion to justify a search of Savana's backpack and outer clothing. "If a student is reasonably suspected of giving out contraband pills, she is reasonably suspected of carrying them on her person and in [her backpack]. If Wilson's reasonable suspicion of pill distribution were not understood to support searches of outer clothes and backpack, it would not justify any search worth making. And the look into Savana's bag, in her presence and in the relative privacy of Wilson's office, was not excessively intrusive, any more than Romero's subsequent search of her outer clothing." The reasonable suspicion standard that determines the legality of a school administrator's search of a student was established in *New Jersey v. T.L.O.*

(1985). It is not possible to precisely define the boundaries of this standard: "At the end of the day, however, we have realized that [specified] factors cannot rigidly control, and we have come back to saying that the standards are fluid concepts that take their substantive content from the particular contexts in which they are being assessed" (*Safford Unified v. Redding*, 2009, internal quotes omitted).

The strip search, however, was not justified in this case. The facts of the search and "both subjective and reasonable societal expectations of personal privacy support the treatment of such a search as categorically distinct, requiring distinct elements of justification on the part of school authorities for going beyond a search of outer clothing and belongings." Savana had a societally reasonable expectation of privacy, the violation of which she subjectively described as "embarrassing, frightening, and humiliating." Studies of student strip searches support her reaction. Unlike changing for gym, which is getting ready for play, "exposing for a search is responding to an accusation reserved for suspected wrongdoers and fairly understood as so degrading that a number of communities have decided that strip searches in schools are never reasonable and have banned them no matter what the facts may be" (*Safford Unified v. Redding*, 2009).

In some settings a humiliating strip search may be reasonable, but in the school setting, *T.L.O.* ruled that scope of a permissible search must not be "excessively intrusive in light of the age and sex of the student and the nature of the infraction." In this case, "the content of the suspicion failed to match the degree of intrusion." Wilson knew beforehand that the pills in question were pain relievers and had no reason to suspect that large amounts of the drugs were being passed around in quantities to do immediate harm. "Nor could Wilson have suspected that Savana was hiding common painkillers in her underwear." It was common knowledge that students bringing banned medications to school would likely hide them in clothing or backpacks. "But when the categorically extreme intrusiveness of a search down to the body of an adolescent requires some justification in suspected facts, general background possibilities fall short; a reasonable search that extensive calls for suspicion that it will pay off." There was no evidence that middle school students were hiding pills in their underwear.

The Court in *Redding* was continuing the policy of *T. L. O.* that school searches have to be reasonable in scope. A strip search had to be supported by the reasonable suspicion of danger of students hiding contraband in their underwear before a school official "can reasonably make the quantum leap from outer clothes and backpacks to exposure of intimate parts. The meaning of such a search, and the degradation its subject may reasonably feel, place a search that intrusive in a category of its own demanding its own specific suspicions" (*Safford Unified v. Redding*, 2009).

LAW IN SOCIETY

Racial Profiling and Constitutional Rights

Confronting the continuing roles played by race and racism is essential to understanding law enforcement and constitutional rights. The brutal subjugation of blacks during slavery and the legal segregation and lynching of the Jim Crow era no longer exist. The blatant racism common in America until the 1970s has faded. Nevertheless, more subtle forms of racism continue to influence criminal justice.[33] The use of racial profiling in highway stops in an effort to interdict drugs shows these lingering effects. "The essence of racial profiling is a judgment that the targeted group . . . —usually African Americans or Hispanics— . . . is more prone to crime in general, or to a particular type of crime, than other racial or ethnic groups"[34] At worst, this stereotyping attributes criminality to all minority group members.

Racial profiling is not primarily a problem of racist white cops harassing minorities for the purposes of social and political repression, although this does happen.[35] Indeed, a 1999 national study of police vehicle stops and searches found "that officers' race does not have a statistically significant influence on the use of coercive actions toward drivers."[36] This suggests that "historic discrimination" has been replaced not by color-free attitudes, but by the complex reality of "contemporary discrimination."[37] Policing now occurs in a social matrix with a substantial black middle class and a substantial black underclass.[38] Increased political participation of African Americans has "not led to equality with whites commensurate to that achieved in civil status."[39] Residential segregation remains high.[40] And closer to our inquiry, "there has been a steady increase in support among white Americans for *principles* of racial equality, but substantially less support for *policies* intended to implement principles of racial equality."[41] These themes mark race relations in all aspects of American life and are reflected in racial profiling.

Racial Profiling and the "War on Drugs"

Racial and ethnic profiling exists in different contexts and at different places. Profiling for terrorists at airports may involve different considerations than profiling drivers on interstate highways. Profiles of drug couriers may differ from profiles of tax cheaters. And profiling differs from the use of race to identify a suspect in a particular crime.

The profiling of minorities by police can take place in a number of venues—on the streets, in airports and bus stations, while shopping, and even at home.[42] There is good reason, however, to focus on highway stops of minorities by police searching for drugs. For one thing, "traffic stops were the most common reason cited for contact between citizens and police."[43] A national study estimated that 16.8 million drivers were stopped by the police in 2002, and of those, 838,000 resulted in vehicle or driver searches. Studies show that while the proportion of minorities who are stopped only slightly exceeds that of white drivers, the search rates are clearly disproportionate: 3.5 percent of white drivers are searched, compared to 10.2 percent of black drivers and 11.4 percent of Hispanic drivers.[44] This disproportion alone does not indicate that racial profiling has occurred, however.

The aggressive stopping and searching of drivers are, however, a result of the so-called "war on drugs." In the 1980s, the Drug Enforcement Administration "initiated a program named Operation Pipeline, a nationwide highway interdiction program that focuses on private motor vehicles." The DEA trained local officers around the country to look for telltale factors that might identify a car carrying drugs. Operation Pipeline was "an 'intensified enforcement' program to find illegal drugs by generating a very high volume of legal traffic enforcement stops to screen for criminal activity, which may include drug trafficking."[45] It created the impetus for more aggressive highway stops and searches in an apparently failed attempt to end the problem of drug use and addiction.

A 1999 national statistical study of drivers confirmed the disparities that occur as a consequence of these traffic stops. "[C]ontrolling for other relevant extralegal and legal factors, the odds of *citation*, *search*, *arrest*, and *use of force* for black drivers are 1.5, 1.5, 1.8, and 2.1 times higher, respectively, than for white drivers."[46]

An argument can be made that African Americans and Hispanics are stopped and searched at higher rates not because of race but because of other factors not listed in the data. This is countered, first, by the virtually complete police discretion to stop cars:

> [T]he police may, if they want, stop just about any car that is driving down the highway. The laws regulating driving are so elaborate, so detailed, and so unrealistic that virtually every driver violates one or another almost all the time—or at least there is probable cause to believe she might be, which is all that's required to justify a stop. [Studies] confirm what everybody knows: almost all cars on interstate highways speed. But even the rare driver who doesn't speed may be stopped if an officer has probable cause to believe that he has a burned-out license-plate light, an obscured tag or rear-view mirror, a cracked windshield, misaligned headlights, or is not wearing a seat belt. As one California Highway Patrol Officer put it: "The vehicle code gives me fifteen hundred reasons to pull you over."[47]

Next, the Supreme Court has "enabled" the use of racial profiling through its automobile rulings. A narcotics officer is authorized to stop a car for any traffic violation, no matter how trivial, when the real reason is to search for drugs, even if the police used race as the only reason or one of several reasons for the stop.[48] Once a motor vehicle is stopped, the police have complete control over whether the driver and passengers should exit, allowing further inspection for drugs.[49] Although police are authorized to stop a car only on probable cause or reasonable suspicion of a crime or traffic violation, reasonable suspicion can be based on entirely innocent factors.[50] Even if an officer has no right to search a stopped automobile, the officer can ask for consent without informing the driver of his or her right to refuse.[51] Professor Tracey Maclin concludes that a "huge gap exists between the law as theory and the law that gets applied to black males on the street,"[52] but it may be the case that the Supreme Court justices who created the permissive automobile search rules when the "war on drugs" was a major domestic policy understood how the rules would be applied.

The data support the link among lenient Supreme Court rulings, the proactive highway stops for drugs, and open-ended police discretion to create a foundation for suspecting racial profiling. Thus the national study of police stops found that

> [o]f the drivers who were stopped by police, officers asked 2.9% if they could search their person and/or their vehicle. Of these 2.9% of drivers, nearly all (97.7%) gave consent to be searched. Officers' requests to search, however, differed significantly by drivers' race-ethnicity. Officers asked for consent to search 2.5% of white drivers, compared to 3.9% of black drivers, 4.1% of Hispanic drivers, and 3.9% of drivers of other races. . . . Contraband was discovered on 12.5% of those who gave consent to be searched.[53]

Further, whites were more likely than minorities to be stopped for speeding (52 percent compared to 41 percent), while minorities (40 percent) were more likely than whites (31 percent) to be stopped for other traffic offenses or for vehicle defects. Yet drivers who were stopped for reasons other than speeding "were significantly more likely to be searched, arrested, and have force used against them. . . . Note, however, that it is unknown if police are inappropriately stopping minorities for minor offenses. It is possible that racial and ethnic minorities, who are overrepresented in low-income groups, may be more likely to drive vehicles with equipment violations."[54] The data, to this point, only suggest that minority drivers stopped on the highway are targeted because of their race or ethnicity. This point will be pursued in the following paragraphs.

The Discovery of Racial Profiling

In the 1990s, racial profiling was well known to minorities and was half-jokingly referred to as DWB—driving while black—in the African-American community.[55] Racial profiling became a major political issue only after 1998, and the DWB "joke," along with general knowledge of racial profiling, has since become mainstream.[56] Up to that time, the evidence for racial profiling was largely anecdotal. It is indicative of the socioeconomic divide among African Americans that many, if not most, of the anecdotes related to upper- and middle-class blacks being stopped and even harassed.

"It has happened to actors Wesley Snipes, Will Smith, Blair Underwood, and LeVar Burton. It has also happened to football player Marcus Allen, and Olympic athletes Al Joyner and Edwin Moses."[57] The late Johnnie Cochran, lead attorney in the O. J. Simpson murder trial, was stopped by police while driving with his children when he was a Los Angeles assistant district attorney; police released him quickly when they realized that "they had made what could be a career-ending mistake."[58] Similar stories are documented about African-American and Hispanic judges and lawyers in New Jersey, Michigan, and Texas.[59] Prominent black writers experienced racial profiling.[60] A black, Los Angeles psychologist took to leaving his work identification badge on during his drive home from work to show police that he was a professional and not a criminal.[61] A former police officer, an African American, was stopped by Long Beach, California, police officers while driving, and during questioning he was pushed through a plate glass window. He was documenting police discrimination, and the incident was filmed by NBC News.[62] The stories can be multiplied.[63]

Professor R. Richard Banks has noted the middle-class slant of the anecdotal evidence of racial profiling:

> The media and civil rights groups have featured those victims of racial profiling and police mistreatment who are not only innocent, but also respectable and middle class: the Harvard-educated lawyer driving home from a relative's funeral who was detained on the highway in the freezing rain, the military officer made to sit handcuffed in the police car while his young son watched, the four young men on their way to a college basketball tryout who were stopped by police officers and nearly fatally wounded, without any evidence of wrongdoing. Commentators have highlighted these sorts of sympathetic plaintiffs.[64]

These class-based anecdotes may reflect an underlying reality of the "increasing polarization of the black population into middle-class and disadvantaged segments."[65] A national survey by Ronald Weitzer and Steven Tuch based on a Gallup poll found that "better educated African Americans are more likely than the less educated to disapprove of profiling, to view it as a pervasive practice, and to say that they have personally experienced it."[66] This may reflect a greater media awareness of these respondents, the greater likelihood that middle-class minorities would be driving in mixed or "white" neighborhoods, and the stereotyping of police who appraise the symbols of success differently for whites and for minorities.[67]

The anecdotes provided moving evidence of the harm and resentments inflicted by racial profiling but did not prove that the traffic stops were statistically disproportionate, because other innocent minority drivers had never been stopped in pretextual drug searches.[68] In the late 1990s, at least three empirical studies found such evidence (which has since been confirmed by the national surveys referred to earlier). Studies of stops on the New Jersey Turnpike and I–95 in Maryland by state troopers were conducted by Dr. John Lamberth of Temple University, who was given access to official data as a result of lawsuits brought by stopped drivers against the state police agencies. Also, a study of four Ohio cities by law professor David Harris provided statistical evidence to show that blacks and Hispanics were stopped in far greater numbers than whites in comparable situations.[69]

Lamberth and colleagues developed a baseline of the proportion of drivers by race by direct observation of forty-two thousand cars on the New Jersey Turnpike and compared these figures to police records of stops, tickets, and arrests on the same stretch of road. They found that the speeding rates of black and white drivers were similar and that while blacks were 13.5 percent of all drivers, they were 35 percent of all drivers stopped and 73.2 percent of all drivers arrested. Lamberth concluded that the odds of these results occurring by chance was "substantially less than one in one billion" and that "it would appear that the race of the occupants and/or drivers of the cars is a decisive factor" for stops and arrests.[70]

Similar findings surfaced in the Maryland I–95 study, where blacks constituted 17.5 percent of the population violating the traffic code but more than 72 percent of those stopped and searched. "The disparity between 17.5 percent black and 72 percent stopped includes 34.6 standard deviations. Such statistical significance, Lamberth said, 'is literally off the charts.'" He concluded that "[w]hile no one can know the motivation of each individual trooper in conducting a traffic stop, the statistics presented herein, . . . show without question a racially discriminatory impact on blacks . . . from state police behavior along I–95. The disparities are sufficiently great that taken as a whole, they are consistent and strongly support the assertion that the state police targeted the community of black motorists for stop, detention, and investigation."[71]

The Political Reaction to Racial Profiling

In a formal sense, the political campaign against racial profiling has been a success. In 2000, a rally in Washington, D.C., drew tens of thousands of demonstrators, and national news coverage focused on the issue of racial profiling.[72] A federal anti-racial-profiling bill passed the House of Representatives but died in the Senate due to law enforcement opposition.[73] Despite this setback, by 2004, twenty-nine states had passed laws against racial profiling, although some statutes are limited.[74] "As a result of the campaign against racial profiling, law enforcement agencies and government officials now publicly disavow the practice. Numerous jurisdictions have prohibited it, as has the Bush administration for federal law enforcement agencies."[75] By 2004, "[n]ew reporting requirements and data collection efforts by over four hundred law enforcement agencies across the country—including entire states such as Maryland, Missouri, and Washington—are producing a continuous flow of new evidence on highway police searches"[76]

Public opinion supports these laws and monitoring efforts. Weitzer and Tuch's national survey found widespread disapproval of racial profiling, although the results indicated the different experiences of white and black respondents: 94 percent of African-American respondents disapproved, compared to 84 percent of white respondents. While 82 percent of black respondents thought that racial profiling was widespread, 60 percent of white respondents thought so. And as for personal experience, 40 percent of black respondents felt they had been stopped by police because of their race, while only 5 percent of white respondents felt that way.[77]

Despite the laws, the monitoring requirements, and the broad disapproval of racial profiling, the evidence is that minorities continue to be stopped and searched at disproportionate rates as drug enforcement continues.[78] What is going on? A major intellectual debate is now under way. Empirical studies and legal analyses by "[e]conomists, civil liberties advocates, legal and constitutional scholars, political scientists, lawyers, and judges . . . [are] reaching, in many cases, quite opposite conclusions about racial profiling."[79]

Is Racial Profiling a Rational Policy?

An influential 2001 study of racial profiling data by economists concluded that the racial dispro-portions in stops and searches in the Maryland I–95 study did not reflect discrimination against blacks but rather "a bias against white motorists."[80] They came to this conclusion by subjecting "hit rates"—the percentage of searches resulting in drug confiscations—to econometric analysis. The raw data indicated that the rates of finding any drugs on stopped drivers, by their race or eth-nicity, was 34 percent for African Americans, 32 percent for whites, and 11 percent for Hispanic drivers. Furthermore, when looking not at any amount, but at large ("felony") quantities of drugs, the hit rates are 13 percent for African Americans, 3 percent for whites, and 6 percent for Hispanic drivers.[81] The study concluded that "the probabilities of being found with drugs in any amount are equal across African Americans and whites which is consistent with maximizing be-havior by police who are not racially prejudiced." This shows that police "are trying to maximize the number of successful searches." On the other hand, the smaller percentage of drug finds among Hispanics "suggests that police may be biased against Hispanics."[82] Other hit rates pro-duce different conclusions. Thus a study of Missouri drivers in which hit rates for drugs were higher for whites than for African Americans or Hispanics concluded that "the data are consis-tent with racial prejudice rather than statistical discrimination."[83]

The economists have challenged the idea that the strong racial disproportion of searches of stopped drivers is automatically unconstitutional or improper racial profiling. This challenge has generated an interesting debate that widens our thinking about the purposes and context of racial profiling on the highways. The most complete response has been published by University of Chicago law professor Bernard Harcourt.[84]

Harcourt moves the debate beyond racial profiling to challenge the value of criminal pro-filing as an effective crime-fighting tool. He argues that several factors must be considered be-fore concluding that racial (or criminal) profiling is worthwhile. First, we must go beyond hit rates as a measure of success and ask whether the profiling reduces the amount of profiled crime. Next, we must consider whether profiling has a ratchet effect, by which the more police focus on minorities the greater the conviction rates of minorities above that of a comparable group of whites. Others call this effect a "racial tax."[85] An additional factor to consider is whether police resources are allocated efficiently. Finally, the costs of racial profiling on innocent motorists and on the minority community must be taken into account.

Underlying much of Harcourt's analysis is his use of the economics term *elasticities* to in-dicate that neither offending rates nor law enforcement practices remain static. Over time, the proportion of drivers who carry drugs may change. If it becomes known, for example, that state troopers disproportionately stop and search minorities, over time fewer minorities and more whites will carry drugs on that stretch of road. These elasticities result from the deterrent and in-capacitation effects of law enforcement on the highway. If troopers continue to target minorities because they continue to get "hits," this will ratchet up the proportion of guilty blacks subjected to stops compared to guilty whites who carry drugs but are not stopped and searched. Not only is this an inefficient enforcement strategy, but it inflicts real harm on the vast majority of innocent minority drivers who are stopped.

If this scenario is the case, the "narrow efficiency" of police officers in targeting minority drivers, who may have higher rates of carrying felony quantities of drugs, may have the ironic ef-fect of increasing the overall amount of drugs being transported on the highway because there are more white drivers. Harcourt establishes this effect by employing econometric analysis. The narrow efficiency of officers (who do not necessarily harbor any malice toward minorities but still believe that racial profiling is good police work) does not answer "the key question of racial profiling, namely whether it is racist. If targeting minority motorists increases long-term offend-ing on the highways or the overall costs to society, then it is in effect racially prejudiced. It may be inadvertent and mistaken, but it is effectively racist because it uses a racial category without any benefit to society."[86]

Harcourt notes that the data are inadequate to make firm statements about the comparative offending elasticities of white and minority populations. National self-report survey data suggest that drug use is about the same among Hispanics, whites, and African Americans, although med-ical data imply higher use among minorities.[87] Nevertheless, summarizing all of his analysis, he concludes that making conservative assumptions about a lower relative elasticity of offending among minorities and "slightly higher natural total offending rates among minority motorists—it is fair to infer that racial profiling on the highways may *increase* the total number of persons transporting drug contraband on the roads."[88] Also, given the fact that 85 percent of the hits were for trace or personal amounts of drugs, it is fanciful to think that highway interdiction seriously impedes the flow of drugs.

Next, given that police are disproportionately searching minority motorists, it is likely that police are more likely to base stops and searches of whites on neutral and crime-related factors (e.g., luxury vehicle, third-party vehicle, late-model cars with tinted windows, bumper stickers). This in turn produces equal or lower hit rates for minority drivers that may mask higher offending by "comparably situated minority motorists," undermining "any reliable conclusion as to the narrow efficiency of highway searches."[89] This means that police resources are inefficiently allocated.

Finally, Harcourt concludes that "[r]acial profiling on the highways likely has a significant ratchet effect on the profiled population . . . that has a significant cost to minority families and communities."[90] In addition, racial profiling imposes real costs on innocent minority drivers who are stopped and has a negative effect on the general public (white and minority) vis-à-vis law enforcement.

What are the implications of Harcourt's analysis for the law? Under current Fourth Amendment doctrines, as shown earlier, the tactics used by police are constitutional. Of course, simply because a policy is constitutional does not mean that it is wise. Harcourt suggests that the kind of economic analysis he undertakes could be used to challenge (and to defend) racial profiling under the Equal Protection Clause, where the use of race is a suspect category that can be overcome if the government can show a compelling state interest, such as reducing crime. No court has yet received such a challenge, but "in the jurisdictions where the new [racial profiling] data reveal disparities, a reviewing court should find the statistical evidence of racial profiling on the highways to be sufficient evidence of unconstitutional police practices."[91]

The Costs of Racial Profiling

As noted earlier, the African-American community has become increasing polarized into middle-class and disadvantaged segments. Disadvantaged minorities commit a disproportionate number of serious "street felonies," resulting in much higher rates of conviction and imprisonment by race. There is a good case to be made that these rates are in part a result of social inequities that are maintained and exacerbated by the continuation of subtle racism. Nevertheless, careful studies of the modern criminal justice system, from the point of investigation and arrest, do not find that racism plays a significant role in enforcing laws against murder, robbery, and the like.[92]

To the contrary, there is strong evidence that since the mid-1980s, the expanded and intensive use of discretionary police power in enforcing ever-more-harsh drug laws has selectively targeted minorities, increasing their proportion in the U.S. penal population. One major consequence has been to severely depress the voting power of minorities in their home communities while increasing the electoral base in rural and predominantly white electoral districts where prisons are located but where prisoners do not vote.[93]

One lesson is that the issue of racial profiling cannot be rationally discussed or dealt with without addressing the larger issue of the "war on drugs" and the overpenalization that characterizes American culture. The other lesson is that the way in which police overgeneralize and see most African Americans as criminals has a real negative effect on the "roughly 97.9 percent of the national population of blacks [who] in any given year will not be arrested for committing a crime"[94] Studies by social psychologists Tom Tyler and Cheryl Wakslak show that people believe that racial profiling exists, whether or not they believe they have personally been profiled, and the stronger the belief that racial profiling exists, the lower the support for and belief in the legitimacy of the police, especially for minorities.[95] This coincides with the conclusions of Weitzer and Tuch that "[s]tops by police officers can have lasting, adverse effects on citizens, especially when the stop appears to be motivated by race."[96]

In conclusion, racial profiling was a by-product of a misguided national law enforcement strategy that had no impact on illicit drug use or sales. It is supported by lingering racial stereotypes rather than the racial prejudice of individual officers. On its face it seems to be rational to the police, but on closer examination it promotes inefficient and counterproductive law enforcement policies. Even so, police may continue to support profiling because occasional large drug busts are seen as good police work and may result in the forfeiture of the cars carrying the drugs. The ratcheting effect imposes extra costs on black and Hispanic underclass communities, while racial profiling alienates middle-class minorities from the police. Racial profiling makes a substantial proportion of the citizenry suspicious of police and acts counter to the community policing ethic. The Supreme Court has helped to encourage racial profiling in its rulings. Current statutes are not likely to stop the disproportionate stops of minorities on the highways, but data-collection efforts, along with better analysis, may convince police and policymakers that the costs of the policy outweigh any benefits.

Summary

Warrantless searches are routine and highly practical for police work. Different types of warrantless search are based on separate rationales. Every warrantless search must meet the minimum constitutional requirement of reasonableness. Three classic exigency exceptions to the warrant requirement, which allow searches, require probable cause to believe that contraband is present: hot pursuit home entries, the automobile exception, and search incident to arrest. Other exigencies, such as the emergency aid doctrine, allow police entry to deal with the emergency. There is no crime scene investigation exigency to remain in crime scenes; once the place is secure, police must obtain a warrant to remain.

Hot pursuit occurs when a dangerous criminal suspect is chased by police and enters a premises protected by Fourth Amendment privacy. A constitutional hot pursuit exigency entry must be based on probable cause, may be based on hearsay, may occur a few minutes after the suspect has entered the premises, may begin on private property outside the premises, authorizes the police to search the entire premises to find the suspect, and is limited to chases involving suspects of serious crimes.

Warrantless automobile searches are based on the exigency of mobility and on the lesser expectation of privacy accorded to people in vehicles. In addition to the automobile exigency exception, an automobile search involves other warrantless search rules, including consent, plain view, stop and frisk, and pretext searches. Police who arrest a car driver or passenger with probable cause of illegal possession may search the car without a warrant even if the suspect is out of the car, in secure custody, and the car is immobilized; this rule does not apply and such a search is unconstitutional if the arrest is for a driving offense (*Arizona v. Gant*, 2009). Any operative motor vehicle is an automobile for purposes of the exception, even if it is also a person's home. The automobile exception applies even if police have time to obtain a warrant. A car subject to forfeiture may be seized from a public area without warrant. The stop of a car by a police officer seizes the driver and passengers.

A "container"—whether a footlocker or a closed paper bag—is an "effect" and is protected by Fourth Amendment privacy rights. A warrant is required to search a seized closed container, even if police have probable cause to believe it contains contraband (unless it is searched incident to arrest). However, when police have probable cause to believe that contraband is located in a automobile, they may, under the automobile exception, open any closed container located in the car that could logically hold the contraband (*United States v. Ross*, 1982). When an officer has probable cause to believe that a specific container located in a car contains contraband, the officer may, upon lawfully stopping the car and gaining access to its interior, open the container (*California v. Acevedo*, 1991). *Ross* was extended to passengers: Police officers with probable cause to search a car may inspect passengers' bags found in the car if they are capable of concealing the object of the search (*Wyoming v. Houghton*, 1999).

Automobile inventory searches are regulatory searches based on a routine policy to make an inventory of items contained in all cars that are impounded by police for traffic or other violations. No probable cause is required. The purposes for making inventories are to protect owners' property against theft or careless handling by the police, to protect the police against false claims or disputes over lost or stolen property, and to protect the police from potential danger. Inventory searches must be made routinely and under standards and procedures that limit the discretion of the officer. Officers conducting inventory searches may look into an unlocked glove compartment, a locked trunk, the space under the front seat and under the dashboard, and the opening of air vents under the dashboard as well as the passenger compartment. Any contraband found in the course of an inventory search is seized in plain view and is admissible in evidence.

Border searches are based on national sovereign power to control entry and egress of people and goods; this require no warrant or probable cause. In addition to searches at the actual border, case law covers roving patrols and fixed checkpoints. Although there is a lesser expectation of privacy at the border, aliens and citizens retain some Fourth Amendment protections. At the border, or its functional equivalent, a person may be detained and searched at random, but the search must be reasonable. Reasonable suspicion must exist before border agents may subject a person to a body cavity search. Border agents operating fixed checkpoints or roving patrols must have probable cause to search parties who have been stopped under reasonable suspicion by roving patrols or under no suspicion at fixed checkpoints. Reasonable suspicion of contraband is required before international mail can be searched. Because of well-established rules for ships, the complex nature of ships' documents, and the special difficulties of stopping seagoing vessels, government agents may stop and board vessels for document inspections without warrants or reasonable suspicion. The Fourth Amendment does not apply to extraterritorial (foreign) arrests or searches.

Searches by government employees infringe Fourth Amendment interests but may be allowed without a warrant or probable cause if they are conducted for "special needs beyond the normal need for law enforcement." This has been applied to a public school administrator searching the bag of a student who is reasonably suspected of violating a school no-smoking rule; the search of the office of a psychiatrist hired by a state hospital and suspected of violating rules; the warrantless search of the home of a probationer for violating a condition of probation (no reasonable suspicion required); and a police inspection of automobile junk shops without a warrant under a regulatory law.

An administrative search warrant may be forgone for searches of pervasively regulated industries (such as gun and liquor dealers) or safety inspections of mines. OSHA safety inspections require warrants.

Firefighters who enter a premises to extinguish a fire intrude on an expectation of privacy but may do so because the fire creates an exigency. They may stay after the fire is extinguished to investigate the cause of the blaze. If the firefighters leave the site of a fire and the owner retains an expectation of privacy, they must obtain an administrative warrant before returning to determine the cause and origin of a recent fire and must obtain a criminal search warrant if they are suspicious of arson.

Drug testing by government agencies intrudes on a reasonable expectation of privacy but may be upheld if special needs beyond the normal need for law enforcement make it reasonable. The Supreme Court has upheld the drug testing of railway workers after a crash without individualized suspicion, the drug testing of Customs Service officers who are in drug enforcement positions or who carry firearms, and the testing of high school varsity athletes. The Court found that the required testing of candidates for state office without particularized suspicion did not meet the criteria of special needs. Special needs has supported warrantless and suspicionless drug testing of public high school students but not the strip search of middle school children.

Legal Puzzles

HOW HAVE COURTS DECIDED THESE CASES?

Hot Pursuit

5-1. At approximately 2:50 p.m., officer Russo received a dispatched call regarding a theft at a gas station, directly across the street from a shopping plaza where the officer was patrolling. Upon his arrival moments later, Russo observed a crowd of people yelling and pointing down the street. After conducting witness interviews, Russo was told that Hathcock had entered the gas station and left with unpaid merchandise. Gas station attendants followed Hathcock outside and confronted him. Hathcock then turned on his car's ignition and one of the attendants jumped on the hood. Hathcock drove erratically from side to side, dislodging the attendant.

A witness who knew Hathcock directed Russo to Hathcock's home, only four blocks away. Russo arrived at Hathcock's house no more than twelve or fifteen minutes after he had first arrived at the gas station. Other officers arrived and they ascertained that Hathcock was in the house. Hathcock refused to exit after a request and the officers decided to enter the house and arrest him.

Was the entry made in hot pursuit of Hathcock?

Held: NO

5-1. *Warden v. Hayden* (1967) permits the warrantless entry into a home when there is a risk of danger to the police or the public. In *Warden*, the risk was apparent based on the suspect's use of a weapon to commit the crime and the possibility that the weapon would be used to escape and elude the police. Exigencies include (1) danger of flight or escape, (2) danger of harm to police officers or the general public, (3) risk of destruction of evidence, and (4) hot pursuit of a fleeing suspect. A hot pursuit requires some sort of chase.

In this case, exigent circumstances did not exist to permit the officers to enter Hathcock's house without a warrant and effectuate an arrest. There was no evidence that Hathcock was armed when he shoplifted the items or that he had access to weapons thereafter. There was no evidence of endangerment to the public. Hathcock possessed no evidence that was at risk of destruction pending the obtaining of an arrest warrant. There was no risk of flight because his house was surrounded.

The District Court found, in this Section 1983 action, that the law of hot pursuit was clearly established so that the officers did not have qualified immunity. Because Hathcock did not suffer any actual damage, he was entitled to a nominal damage award of $1.00.
Hathcock v. Cohen, 547 F. Supp.2d 1271 (S.D. Fla. 2008)

Automobile Exception

5-2. Around 1:00 a.m., Rene Gomez was stopped by Officer Burpo for swerving across the center yellow line twice while traveling on a highway. As Officer Burpo asked Gomez for his license and registration, he smelled alcohol and saw two six-pack alcoholic beverage containers inside Gomez's car. The visible containers were unopened, but one container was missing. Officer Burpo directed Gomez to get out of the vehicle because he wanted to search the car for an open container. Officer Burpo began to search the immediate driver's area of Gomez's car. Before Officer Burpo began searching, Gomez clearly stated that he did not consent to the search. As Officer Burpo searched the driver's immediate area, he noticed the center console lid was ajar and opened it. Inside the console was an open bottle of alcohol. Burpo lifted the bottle and underneath the bottle he found a glass pipe, a small amount of methamphetamine, and a digital scale.

Was Officer Burpo's search of the car's interior justified by the automobile/vehicle exception to the warrant requirement

to allow the introduction of the methamphetamine as evidence?
Holding available from instructor.

Auto Inventory

5-3. Lancaster, Pennsylvania, police officers recognized Devon Smith. . . in the passenger seat of an automobile operated by Danny Santiago, as subject to an outstanding arrest warrant. The officers stopped the vehicle, arrested Smith, and arrested Santiago after he got into fight with an officer. Neither Smith nor Santiago claimed to own the car or know the owner and registration papers were not available. There was no one else available at the scene to take possession of the car. The officers believed that they should not leave the vehicle in a bad neighborhood where it might be damaged, vandalized, or stolen. Therefore, one officer impounded the vehicle and drove it to the police station. At the station during a routine warrantless inventory search of the vehicle, the other officer found a loaded semi-automatic handgun in its glove department. He then interrupted the search, obtained a search warrant, and resumed the search.

The gun was introduced in a trial against Smith, who was convicted on a charge of a felon in possession of a weapon. Testimony established that the officer conducting the inventory was exercising his discretion when he opted to impound the vehicle. The Lancaster PD had no standardized policy regarding the impoundment of vehicles and had established routines but no written policies guiding the conduct of the inventory search.

Was the gun seized in the automobile admissible against Smith as lawfully seized in plain view as the product of a proper inventory search?
Holding available from instructor.

Border Search

5-4. In 2004, Sawsaan Tabbaa and four other plaintiffs, U.S. citizens and practicing Muslims, were among an estimated thirteen thousand individuals from across North America who attended the Reviving the Islamic Spirit Conference ("RIS Conference") at the Skydome in Toronto, Canada. Tabbaa returned to the United States via the Buffalo, New York, border crossing. The conference, which lasted three days, included religious and cultural activities, musical performances, a series of prominent Islamic speakers, and communal prayer three times a day. The plaintiffs had no criminal records and the government had no individualized suspicion of their being associated with terrorism.

The U.S. Bureau of Customs and Border Protection ("CBP") received intelligence (which was examined by the court) that persons with known terrorist ties would attend the conference. Federal regulations give the CBP authority to enforce immigration and customs laws, secure the border, and prevent the entry of terrorists into the United States. Based on the intelligence, CBP ordered border officials to identify conference attendees, contact CBP's data center to determine if the individuals seeking entry posed a threat, and to question attendees about their activities. Fingerprinting and photographing of conference attendees was permitted.

When plaintiffs told CBP agents that they attended the Skydome conference, they were ordered to pull their cars into a separate area. They entered a building that included other RIS Conference attendees. Plaintiffs had to fill out several forms. They were questioned about past travels, relationships to other vehicle occupants, and why they attended and what occurred at the RIS Conference. Plaintiffs were frisked, fingerprinted, and photographed, and their cars were searched. They were not told why they were being fingerprinted and photographed, or why they were detained and inspected so thoroughly. Plaintiffs who questioned the process were told they would not be released until all of the screening measures had been completed. Regarding two of the plaintiffs, CBP officers forcibly kicked the feet open and almost knocked down some plaintiffs in order to effectuate pat-downs. Plaintiffs' hands were grabbed to take the fingerprints. Each plaintiff was detained and searched for between four and six hours, after which he or she was released into the United States. Within seven days, the government removed plaintiffs' fingerprints and photographs from its databases, but continued to hold some information about them, including the details of their 2004 detentions.

The plaintiffs seek a declaratory judgment that the searches violated their Fourth Amendment rights and expungement of their records.

Were these border searches nonroutine and thus Fourth Amendment violations?
Holding available from instructor.

Fire Inspection

5-5. On a July evening a power line running between a power pole and a metal warehouse, which O'Keefe rented, was arcing and sparking. Melting wire from the power line caused molten metal to drip onto the ground, which ignited a grass fire approximately ten feet from the warehouse. Fire officials responded and, after the grass fire was contained, the captain of the fire department arrived. The captain determined that an electrical problem inside the warehouse could have caused the power line to arc and spark and that such an electrical problem could have caused a fire inside. There were no visible signs that the warehouse was on fire, but the captain was unable to see inside the building because the windows were blackened. The fire captain also concluded that an electrical problem inside could again cause the power line to arc and spark, allowing another fire to ignite once electricity was restored to the warehouse. The captain therefore concluded that it was necessary to enter the warehouse to inspect the circuits.

A firefighter entered the warehouse through a second floor window and noticed drying marijuana plants and the odor of marijuana. Once the captain could see marijuana plants he notified the police. Responding police secured the warehouse and obtained and executed a search warrant.

Was the initial entry into the warehouse justified as a fire inspection exigency, allowing the introduction of the marijuana as evidence to convict O'Keefe?
Holding available from instructor.

Further Reading

Randall Kennedy, *Race, Crime, and the Law* (New York: Pantheon, 1997).

Leonard W. Levy, *A License to Steal: The Forfeiture of Property* (Chapel Hill: University of North Carolina Press, 1996).

Jeffrey Toobin, *The Nine: Inside the Secret World of the Supreme Court* (New York: Doubleday, 2007).

Useful Web Site

Northeastern University Racial Profiling Data Collection Resource Center

http://www.racialprofilinganalysis.neu.edu

Funded by the U.S. Department of Justice, Bureau of Justice Assistance. Designed as a central clearinghouse for information

about current data-collection efforts, legislation and model policies, police–community initiatives, and methodological tools to collect and analyze data.

End Notes

1. Charles Whitebread and Christopher Slobogin, *Criminal Procedure: An Analysis of Cases and Concepts*, 4th ed. (New York: Foundation Press, 2000), 216–23.
2. David E. Steinberg, "The Drive toward Warrantless Auto Searches: Suggestions from a Back Seat Driver," *Boston University Law Review* 80, no. 2 (2000): 545–75.
3. Marvin Zalman, "Judges in Their Own Case: A Lockean Analysis of Drug Asset Forfeiture," *Criminal Justice Review* 21, no. 2 (1996): 197–230; and Eric Blumenson and Eva Nilsen, "Policing for Profit: The Drug War's Hidden Economic Agenda," *University of Chicago Law Review* 65 (1998): 35–114.
4. David Harris, "Car Wars: The Fourth Amendment's Death on the Highway," *George Washington Law Review* 66 (1998): 556–91, 560–61.
5. Harris, "Car Wars," 556.
6. David Moran, "The New Fourth Amendment Vehicle Doctrine: Stop and Search Any Car at Any Time," *Villanova Law Review* 47 (2002): 815–38, 835, 837.
7. Steinberg, "The Drive toward Warrantless Auto Searches," 549.
8. Harris, "Car Wars," 566–67.
9. David Moran, "The New Fourth Amendment Vehicle Doctrine: Stop and Search Any Car at Any Time," *Villanova Law Review* 47 (2002): 815–38.
10. Whitebread and Slobogin, *Criminal Procedure,* 309.
11. See *Carroll v. United States* (1925); and *United States v. 12 200—Foot Reels of Film* (1973).
12. Robin Wright, "Bin Laden Tie Seen in Border Arrest," *Los Angeles Times,* December 19, 1999.
13. Timothy Egan, "A Nation Challenged: The Convicted Terrorist; Man Caught in 2000 Plot Is Helping Investigators," *New York Times,* September 27, 2001.
14. See William Langewiesche, "Anarchy at Sea," *The Atlantic,* September 2003.
15. Roberto Iraola, "A Primer on Legal Issues Surrounding the Extraterritorial Apprehension of Criminals," *American Journal of Criminal Law* 29 (2001): 1–27, 4.
16. "F.B.I. Plans to Open an Office in Poland," *New York Times,* July 2, 1994; and David Johnston, "Fighting the Mob; The F.B.I. Makes Friends in (of All Places) Moscow," *New York Times,* July 10, 1994, sec. 4; and David Johnston, "Strength Is Seen in a U.S. Export: Law Enforcement," *New York Times,* April 17, 1995.
17. Richard L. Berke, "2 Ex-Mexican Aides Charged in Slaying of U.S. Drug Agent," *New York Times,* February 1, 1990.
18. *Alvarez-Machain v. United States,* 331 F.3d 604 (9th Cir. 2003).
19. *Alvarez-Machain v. United States,* 331 F.3d 604 (9th Cir. 2003). See Michael J. Glennon, "International Kidnapping: State-Sponsored Abduction: A Comment on *United States v. Alvarez-Machain,*" *American Society of International Law Newsletter* 86 (October 1992): 746.
20. Beth Henderson, "Note and Comment: From Justice to Torture: The Dramatic Evolution of U.S.-Sponsored Renditions," *Temple International and Comparative Law Journal* 20 (2006): 189–218, 189.
21. Andrew Rosenthal, "Noriega Gives Himself up to U.S. Military; Is Flown to Florida to Face Drug Charges," *New York Times,* January 4, 1990.
22. See Robert A. Pape, "Dying to Kill Us," *New York Times,* September 22, 2003 (arguing on the basis of research that the number of suicide bombings is increasing and is due not to religion but to a secular and specific goal to compel liberal democracies to withdraw from territory that terrorists consider their homelands).
23. See Edward Levi, *An Introduction to Legal Reasoning* (Chicago: University of Chicago Press, 1949, 1961).
24. Lynn M. Paltrow, "Pregnant Drug Users, Fetal Persons, and the Threat to *Roe v. Wade,*" *Albany Law Review* 62 (1999): 999–1055, 1002–3.
25. Editorial, "Policing of Pregnancies Won't Protect Children," *New York Times,* August 4, 1996, sec. 4.
26. Linda Carroll, "Alcohol's Toll on Fetuses: Even Worse Than Thought," *New York Times,* November 4, 2002, sec. F.
27. Nancy Maveety, *Justice Sandra Day O'Connor: Strategist on the Supreme Court* (Lanham, Md.: Rowman and Littlefield, 1996), 12–13. See Sandra Day O'Connor and H. Alan Day, *Lazy B: Growing up on a Cattle Ranch in the American Southwest* (New York: Random House, 2002).

28. David A. Schultz and Christopher E. Smith, *The Jurisprudential Vision of Justice Antonin Scalia* (London: Rowman and Littlefield, 1996), xiii; for a sophisticated analysis, see George Kannar, "The Constitutional Catechism of Antonin Scalia," *Yale Law Journal* 99 (1990): 1297–1357.

29. Cynthia Kelly Conlon, "Urineschool: A Study of the Impact of the *Earls* Decisions on High School Random Drug Testing Policies," *Journal of Law and Education* 32 (2003): 297–319.

30. Greg Winter, "Study Finds No Sign That Testing Deters Students' Drug Use," *New York Times,* May 17, 2003.

31. Robert D. Dodson, "Ten Years of Randomized Jurisprudence: Amending the Special Needs Doctrine," *South Carolina Law Review* 51 (2000): 258–89, 278.

32. Dodson, "Ten Years of Randomized Jurisprudence," 284.

33. Randall Kennedy, *Race, Crime, and the Law* (New York: Pantheon, 1997); Michael Tonry, *Malign Neglect-Race, Crime, and Punishment in America* (New York: Oxford University Press, 1995); and David C. Anderson, *Crime and the Politics of Hysteria: How the Willie Horton Story Changed American Justice* (New York: Times Books/Random House, 1995).

34. Samuel R. Gross and Katherine Y. Barnes, "Road Work: Racial Profiling and Drug Interdiction on the Highway," *Michigan Law Review* 101 (2002): 651–754, 654–55.

35. An Ohio lawsuit uncovered a group of Reynoldsburg, Ohio, police officers who identified themselves as a "SNAT" ("special nigger arrest team"). The courts found that this was, at best, "a crude and offensive joke" but, at worst, that these officers "intentionally discriminated against blacks" (*Murphy v. Reynoldsburg,* 1991 WL 150938 [Ohio Court App. 10th App. Dist. Franklin Co. (1991)]) "in an attempt to keep blacks out of the city" (*Murphy v. Reynoldsburg,* 65 Ohio St. 3d 356, 604 N.E.2d 138 [1992]).

36. Robin Shepard Engel and Jennifer M. Calnon, "Examining the Influence of Drivers' Characteristics during Traffic Stops with Police: Results from a National Survey," *Justice Quarterly* 21, no. 1 (2004): 49–90, 78–79.

37. W. J. Wilson, *The Truly Disadvantaged* (Chicago: University of Chicago Press, 1987).

38. G. J. Jaynes and R. M. Williams Jr., *A Common Destiny: Blacks and American Society* (Washington, D.C.: National Academy Press, 1989), 6, 274.

39. Jaynes and Williams, *A Common Destiny,* 258.

40. Jaynes and Williams, *A Common Destiny,* 88–91.

41. Jaynes and Williams, *A Common Destiny,* 117 (emphasis added).

42. Amnesty International, *Threat and Humiliation: Racial Profiling, Domestic Security, and Human Rights in the United States* (New York: Amnesty International, 2004), 3–12.

43. Michael R. Smith and Geoffrey P. Alpert, "Searching for Direction: Courts, Social Science, and the Adjudication of Racial Profiling Claims," *Justice Quarterly* 19, no. 4 (2002): 673–703, 674, n. 1 (quotations omitted).

44. Erica L. Smith and Matthew R. Durose, *Special Report: Characteristics of Drivers Stopped by Police, 2002* (Washington, D.C.: Bureau of Justice Statistics, NCJ 211471, June 2006).

45. Gross and Barnes, "Road Work," 671 (internal quotations omitted); and Engel and Calnon, "Drivers' Characteristics," 50–53.

46. Engel and Calnon, "Drivers' Characteristics," 77 (emphasis added).

47. Gross and Barnes, "Road Work," 670–71 (footnotes omitted).

48. *Whren v. United States* (1996).

49. *Pennsylvania v. Mimms* (1977); and *Maryland v. Wilson* (1997).

50. *Delaware v. Prouse* (1979); *United States v. Arvizu* (2002).

51. *Schneckloth v. Bustamonte* (1973); and *Ohio v. Robinette* (1996).

52. T. Maclin, "'Black and Blue Encounters'—Some Preliminary Thoughts about Fourth Amendment Seizures: Should Race Matter?" *Valparaiso University Law Review* 26 (1991): 243–79, 252.

53. Engel and Calnon, "Drivers' Characteristics," 76.

54. Engel and Calnon, "Drivers' Characteristics," 70, 80.

55. Henry Louis Gates Jr., "Thirteen Ways of Looking at a Black Man," *New Yorker,* October 23, 1995, cited in Kennedy, *Race, Crime, and the Law,* 151–52.

56. John L. Burris (with Catherine Whitney), *Blue vs. Black: Let's End the Conflict between Cops and Minorities* (New York: St. Martin's Press, 1999); and Kenneth Meeks, *Driving while Black: Highways, Shopping Malls, Taxicabs, Sidewalks* (New York: Broadway, 2000).

57. David A. Harris, "The Stories, the Statistics, and the Law: Why 'Driving while Black' Matters," *Minnesota Law Review* 84 (1999): 265–326.

58. K. B. Noble, "A Showman in the Courtroom, for Whom Race Is a Defining Issue," *New York Times,* January 20, 1995.

59. Judge Claude Coleman, cited in Tonry, *Malign Neglect,* 50–51; Judge Dennis Archer, who later became a Michigan Supreme Court justice, mayor of Detroit, and president of both the Michigan and the American Bar Associations, and his son, attorney Dennis Archer Jr.: Robyn Meredith, "Near Detroit, a Familiar Sting in Being a Black Driver," *New York Times,* July 16, 1999; and federal judge Filemon B. Vela: Jim Yardley, "Some Texans Say Border Patrol Singles Out Too Many Blameless Hispanics," *New York Times,* January 26, 2000.

60. Tonry, *Malign Neglect,* 51, describing the experiences of Brent Staples, a *New York Times* editorial board writer, and philosopher Cornel West.

61. A. Wallace and S. Chavez, "Understanding the Riots Six Months Later: Separate Lives/Dealing with Race in L.A.; Can We All Get Along?" *Los Angeles Times,* November 16, 1992.

62. Maclin, "'Black and Blue Encounters,'" 243–79, 254.

63. Amnesty International, Threat and Humiliation; and David Rudovsky, "Law Enforcement by Stereotypes and Serendipity: Racial Profiling and Stops and Searches without Cause," *University of Pennsylvania Journal of Constitutional Law* 3 (2001): 296–366, 296–98.

64. R. Richard Banks, "Beyond Profiling: Race, Policing, and the Drug War," *Stanford Law Review* 56 (2003): 571–603, 576–7 (footnotes omitted).

65. Ronald Weitzer and Steven A. Tuch, "Perceptions of Racial Profiling: Race, Class, and Personal Experience," *Criminology* 40, no. 2 (2002): 435–56, 437.

66. Weitzer and Tuch, "Perceptions of Racial Profiling," 450.

67. Weitzer and Tuch, "Perceptions of Racial Profiling," 450–51.

68. Bill Johnson, "The Answer to Driving while Black Is Not More Racial Profiling," *Detroit News,* July 30, 1999.

69. Information about the three studies is taken from Harris, "The Stories."

70. Harris, "The Stories," 279.

71. Harris, "The Stories," 281.

72. Cindy Loose and Chris L. Jenkins, "Rallying to 'Redeem the Dream': Rights' Leaders Target Racial Profiling," *Washington Post,* August 27, 2000.

73. Harris, "The Stories," 319–21.

74. Amnesty International, *Threat and Humiliation*, vii, 28–29.

75. R. Richard Banks, "Beyond Profiling: Race, Policing, and the Drug War," *Stanford Law Review* 56 (2003): 571–603, 574–5 (footnotes omitted).

76. Bernard E. Harcourt, "Rethinking Racial Profiling: A Critique of the Economics, Civil Liberties, and Constitutional Literature, and of Criminal Profiling More Generally," *University of Chicago Law Review* 71 (2004): 1275–1381, 1275 (footnote omitted).

77. Weitzer and Tuch, "Perceptions of Racial Profiling," 441–42.

78. Gross and Barnes, "Road Work," 661.

79. Harcourt, "Rethinking Racial Profiling," 1276.

80. John Knowles, Nicola Persico, and Petra Todd, "Racial Bias in Motor Vehicle Searches: Theory and Evidence," *Journal of Political Economy* 109 (2001): 203–29, 2007.

81. Knowles, Persico, and Todd, "Racial Bias in Motor Vehicle Searches," 222.

82. Knowles, Persico, and Todd, "Racial Bias in Motor Vehicle Searches," 228.

83. Harcourt, "Rethinking Racial Profiling," 1293, citing Rubén Hernández-Murillo and John Knowles, "Racial Profiling or Racist Policing? Testing in Aggregated Data" (working paper, April 18, 2003).

84. Other responses include Gross and Barnes, "Road Work"; Banks, "Beyond Racial Profiling"; and William J. Stuntz, "Local Policing after the Terror," *Yale Law Journal* 111 (2002): 2137–94. Stuntz would allow the limited use of group profiling and seek to control it. Gross and Barnes and Banks conclude that racial profiling, even if the product of police who are not racially prejudiced and who seek to interdict drugs, has virtually no effect on stopping the flow of drugs and inflicts harm on innocent drivers. Gross and Barnes, while not claiming that the data in the Maryland I–95 study are entirely flawed, show that police have manipulated highway stop data to "improve" their success rates.

85. Kennedy, *Race, Crime, and the Law,* 159; and Banks, "Beyond Racial Profiling," 589.

86. Harcourt, "Rethinking Racial Profiling," 1306–7.

87. Harcourt, "Rethinking Racial Profiling," 1361–71.

88. Harcourt, "Rethinking Racial Profiling," 1371 (emphasis added).

89. Harcourt, "Rethinking Racial Profiling," 1372.

90. Harcourt, "Rethinking Racial Profiling," 1372–73.

91. Harcourt, "Rethinking Racial Profiling," 1354.

92. Tonry, *Malign Neglect*, 65–68; and Alfred Blumstein, "On the Racial Disproportionality of United States' Prison Populations," *Journal of Criminal Law and Criminology* 73 (1982): 1259–81.

93. Tonry, *Malign Neglect*, 10–12; Anderson, *Crime and the Politics of Hysteria;* and Jason Belmont Conn, "Note: Felon Disenfranchisement Laws: Partisan Politics in the Legislatures," *Michigan Journal of Race and Law* 10 (2005): 495–539.

94. "Developments in the Law: Race and the Criminal Process," *Harvard Law Review* 101 (1988): 1472–1641, 1508.

95. Tom R. Tyler and Cheryl J. Wakslak, "Profiling and Police Legitimacy: Procedural Justice, Attributions of Motive, and Acceptance of Police Authority," *Criminology* 42, no. 2 (2004): 253–81.

96. Weitzer and Tuch, "Perceptions of Racial Profiling," 452.

JUSTICES OF THE SUPREME COURT

Thoughtful Conservatives: Clark, Harlan II, Stewart, and White

Justices Tom Clark, John Marshall Harlan II, Potter Stewart, and Byron White were appointed by presidents with differing political philosophies (Harry S. Truman, Dwight D. Eisenhower, and John F. Kennedy). Nevertheless, these four justices exhibited several similarities. On criminal procedure issues, all were conservative in that they generally opposed incorporation and tended to find for the prosecution. On the other hand, all were receptive to the civil rights claims of African Americans. Clark, as a key architect of President Truman's anticommunist loyalty oath program, was fiercely opposed to easing the application of these rules. All of these justices were thorough and thoughtful in their review of cases, and each had at times ruled in support of criminal defendants in significant cases.

Among these justices, John Harlan ranks as the most acute legal thinker. Known as a lawyer's justice, he carefully crafted opinions without ambiguity to be applied by practicing lawyers and trial judges. Potter Stewart was the most centrist in criminal procedure matters. He dissented in *Miranda v. Arizona* (1966), but his opinions in such cases as *Chimel v. California* (1969) (reach-and-lunge rule) and *Coolidge v. New Hampshire* (1971) (warrant-preference interpretation) were quite liberal. His opinion in *Katz v. United States* (1967) was the keystone in modernizing Fourth Amendment law.

Justice White may have been a surprise; nominated by a liberal president, he quickly joined the conservative wing of the Court on many issues, especially criminal procedure. In this regard, he stands in sharp contrast to Kennedy's other appointee, Arthur Goldberg. Justice White's influence on the Court was enhanced by his lengthy tenure and his practice of at times shifting to the center of the Court so as to occupy the pivotal middle ground.

Collection of the Supreme Court of the United States.
Photographer: Harris and Ewing.

Tom C. Clark

Texas, 1899–1977

Democrat

Appointed by Harry S. Truman

Years of Service: 1949–1967

Life and Career.   The son of a Dallas lawyer, Clark served in the U.S. Army during World War I, graduated from the University of Texas Law School, and practiced in his father's law firm from 1922 to 1927. Thereafter, he held appointed posts as civil district attorney and assistant (criminal) district attorney for Dallas. His involvement in politics led to his appointment to the U.S. Justice Department in 1937, where he worked on a variety of issues, including war claims, antitrust, the evacuation of Japanese Americans from the West Coast to camps during World War II, and war frauds. In 1943, he was appointed assistant attorney general and headed the antitrust and the criminal divisions.

He supported Truman for the vice presidential nomination in 1944 and was appointed by Truman as attorney general in 1945. Clark was a vigorous attorney general, instituting 160 antitrust cases, supporting civil rights actions designed to end racial segregation, and playing a key role in developing President Truman's anticommunist loyalty oath program, generated by cold war fears of internal subversion.

In 1967, Justice Clark resigned from the Court as a gesture of paternal love when his son, Ramsey Clark, was appointed by President Lyndon Johnson as attorney general. If he had continued to serve, a conflict of interest would have arisen in every Supreme Court case involving the U.S. government. For the next decade of his life, he actively participated as a judge in the various federal circuits and contributed to numerous programs designed to enhance the quality of the American judiciary.

Contribution to Criminal Procedure.   Justice Clark more often than not voted in favor of the state in cases involving criminal procedure issues. For example, he dissented in *Miranda v. Arizona* (1966). He dissented in a case that held that probable cause could not be based on a person's general reputation (*Beck v. Ohio,* 1964); he dissented in a case that excluded evidence seized from one person pursuant to an illegal arrest of another person (*Wong Sun v. United States,* 1963); and he joined Justice Sherman Minton's decision in *United States v. Rabinowitz* (1950). Nevertheless, he wrote the majority opinion in the breakthrough incorporation decision of *Mapp v. Ohio* (1961), and he was a staunch supporter of fair trials, as seen in his opinions finding constitutional error because of excessive pretrial publicity.

Signature Opinion.   *Mapp v. Ohio* (1961). Why did a justice who was generally conservative on criminal matters support the incorporation of the exclusionary rule? In a revealing interview after retirement, Justice Clark told seminar students that as a young lawyer, he defended his cook's son against a Prohibition charge (possessing liquor) after Dallas police simply entered the accused's room, ripped open a mattress, and gave the bottle of liquor they found to federal agents. Clark was shocked that police could do this. Thus, although as a justice he was loath to curb the legitimate power of police officers, the facts of *Mapp* were excessive. To Justice Clark, the exclusionary rule, applied to the states as well as the federal government, simply made sense, and as he wrote in *Mapp,* "there is no war between the Constitution and common sense."

Assessment.   Clark replaced the staunch liberal Justice Frank Murphy in 1949, tilting the Vinson Court in a more conservative direction. Clark generally joined Justices Stanley Reed, Felix Frankfurter, Robert Jackson, and Harold Burton, although he was somewhat more liberal than Chief

Justice Fred Vinson. During the 1950s, he supported the government in antitrust and loyalty cases, where his experiences as attorney general shaped his approaches, thus taking a liberal stance in the first area and a conservative stance in the latter. His positions on First Amendment issues, voting district reapportionment, and racial segregation were in sync with the liberal Warren Court.

Further Reading

Richard Kirkendall, "Tom C. Clark," in Leon Friedman and Fred L. Israel, eds., *The Justices of the United States Supreme Court, 1789–1969*, vol. 4 (New York: Chelsea House, 1969), 2665–95.

Collection of the Supreme Court of the United States.
Photographer: Harris and Ewing.

John M. Harlan II

New York, 1899–1971
Republican
Appointed by Dwight D. Eisenhower
Years of Service: 1955–1971

Life and Career.   The grandson of a Supreme Court justice by the same name, Harlan was viewed as a "progressive Republican" when appointed. He was born in Chicago, was educated at private schools, and served briefly in World War I. He received his bachelor's degree from Princeton in 1920, was a Rhodes Scholar at Oxford, and completed his legal studies at New York Law School in 1924. He practiced law in New York with a prestigious Wall Street law firm up until his appointment to the Second Circuit Court of Appeals in early 1954. However, his background also included years of public service. He prosecuted a former U.S. attorney general for corruption when he was an assistant U.S. attorney in the 1920s, acted as a special prosecutor for New York State in a major investigation of municipal graft in the 1930s, directed a critical unit of experts advising the commanding general of the Eighth Air Force on bombing operations in Europe during World War II, and was chief counsel of an organized crime investigation for the state of New York in the early 1950s. After less than a year on the Second Circuit Court of Appeals, he was nominated by President Eisenhower to the Supreme Court.

Contribution to Criminal Procedure.   Justice Harlan opposed incorporation and dissented in *Mapp v. Ohio* (1961) and *Miranda v. Arizona* (1966); he believed the federal government should be held to higher standards of procedural regularity under the Bill of Rights than states under the Fourteenth Amendment. He was generally conservative and voted for the state, but not slavishly so. Thus he concurred on extending the right to counsel to all felony defendants (*Gideon v. Wainwright,* 1963); he concurred in extending the right to counsel to juveniles (*In re Gault,* 1967; *Katz v. United States,* 1967). He dissented in *United States v. White* (1971), arguing that police agents should not be able to wear body mikes without a prior judicial warrant.

Signature Opinion.   *Spinelli v. United States* (1969). Justice Harlan's opinion upheld the two-prong test for determining when the hearsay evidence of a confidential informant can amount to probable cause for a search warrant. He closely examined the facts put forth by the FBI and penetrated the affidavit's veneer of certainty to show that the agency was, in effect, asking for a blank check on its decision. The opinion highlights the vital importance of judicial scrutiny of police affidavit requests to the preservation of Fourth Amendment privacy and liberty.

Assessment.   Justice Harlan developed a close intellectual friendship with Justice Frankfurter; with the latter's resignation in 1962, Harlan took on the mantle of the chief spokesperson for judicial restraint and traditional judicial conservatism. During the entire period of the due process revolution, Justice Harlan wrote the most exhaustive and penetrating dissents against the incorporation doctrine.

Justice Harlan was "a lawyer's judge"—he closely examined cases and often based decisions on fine factual distinctions rather than upon broad generalizations, and his opinions reflected his desire to give lawyers and judges clear guidance in applying the rules of the case. He had a profound respect for judicial precedent and felt that the Court should interfere as little as possible into the political workings of both state and federal governments. His incorporation dissents noted that "the American federal system is itself constitutionally ordained, that it embodies values profoundly making for lasting liberties in this country" (*Pomtar v. Texas,* 1965). He was skeptical about the ability of courts to ensure true liberty by their rulings, believing that liberty "can rise no higher or be made more secure than the spirit of a people to achieve and maintain it." (*Pomtar v. Texas,* 1965) He also believed that federalism encouraged differences between the states and that it was not the role of the Supreme Court to eradicate these differences by applying the Bill of Rights as a steamroller over variations of state procedure.

Further Reading

Tinsley E. Yarbrough, *John Marshall Harlan: Great Dissenter of the Warren Court* (New York: Oxford University Press, 1992).

Potter Stewart

Collection of the Supreme Court of the United States.
Photographer: Harris and Ewing.

Ohio, 1915–1985
Republican
Appointed by Dwight D. Eisenhower
Years of Service: 1958–1981

Life and Career.   Born into a politically active Republican family with "a strong tradition of public service," Stewart was educated at the Hotchkiss School, Yale University (where he was a Phi Beta Kappa), and Yale Law School, where he generally supported the New Deal. He served as a deck officer on an oil tanker during World War II, which put him in contact with men of a different background than he would meet at Yale or in corporate law practice. He practiced law in his hometown of Cincinnati from 1946 to 1954. His political activity (he was twice elected to the Cincinnati City Council) and his support of Eisenhower's bid for the Republican presidential nomination in 1952 against Ohio senator Robert Taft led President Eisenhower to name him to the Sixth Circuit Court of Appeals in 1954 at the young age of thirty-nine. His reputation as an excellent judge led to his nomination to the Supreme Court in 1958.

Contribution to Criminal Procedure.   Although known as a middle-of-the-road justice who did not automatically side with either the liberals or the conservatives, Justice Stewart wrote a large number of Fourth Amendment opinions for the Supreme Court that tended to expand defendants' rights. On the liberal, or pro-defendant, side were *Vale v. Louisiana* (1970) (a doorstep arrest does not authorize a general search of a premises) and *Coolidge v. New Hampshire* (1971) (supporting the warrant-preference construction of the Fourth Amendment). On the conservative, or pro-prosecution, side, Justice Stewart opposed incorporation, dissented in *Miranda v. Arizona* (1966), and wrote the majority opinion in *Schneckloth v. Bustamonte* (1973), holding that the police need not warn suspects of their Fourth Amendment rights before requesting consent to search.

Justice Stewart had a talent for turning a pithy phrase that encapsulates a rule, and he wrote logical, well-organized opinions. This was seen in his most important Fourth Amendment opinion, *Katz v. United States* (1967), where his emblematic statement—"For the Fourth Amendment protects people, not places"—nicely summed up the major shift in Fourth Amendment jurisprudence from its foundations in property law to its new basis on an expectation of privacy.

Signature Opinion.   *Chimel v. California* (1969). His majority opinion in *Chimel* ended the long zigzag course of opinions on the scope of a search incident to arrest. It confirmed that while officers may reasonably search the area within the immediate control of an arrested suspect to seize weapons and contraband, they may not use the arrest as an excuse to search a premises without a warrant.

Assessment.   Justice Stewart's approach to constitutional law was cautious and restrained. His middle-of-the-road votes made him a "swing justice" in many areas. His judicial philosophy appeared to be that a judge should first defer to legislative and executive branch authority but not hesitate to exercise judicial review in order to maintain essential procedural safeguards and to prevent abuses of power. Justice Stewart favored narrow rulings and preferred that cases be resolved on the specific facts when necessary. He was a lone dissenter in the case that held school prayer to violate the First Amendment, but he voted for free speech in censorship cases. On the death penalty, he held it to be unconstitutional as applied in 1972, but he voted to uphold revised death penalty laws in 1976 that incorporated the element of guided discretion. He decided a very large number of criminal procedure cases. Ultimately, it is not possible to classify Justice Stewart simply as a liberal or conservative or as an activist or passivist judge.

Further Reading

Tinsley E. Yarbrough, "Justice Potter Stewart: Decisional Patterns in Search of Doctrinal Moorings," in Charles M. Lamb and Stephen C. Halpern, eds., *The Burger Court: Political and Judicial Profiles* (Urbana: University of Illinois Press, 1991), 375–406.

Byron R. White

Colorado, 1917–2002

Democrat

Appointed by John F. Kennedy

Years of Service: 1962–1993

Collection of the Supreme Court
of the United States.
Photographer: Joseph Bailey.

Life and Career.   White's youth was filled with hard work in the beet fields of rural Colorado and on railroad section crews. He was an excellent student and an outstanding athlete in high school and at the University of Colorado, where he was elected to Phi Beta Kappa, graduated first in his class in 1938, and attracted national attention as a star tailback (nicknamed "Whizzer") on Colorado's unbeaten football team. He also won varsity letters in basketball and baseball. Between 1938 and 1942, White spent a year at Oxford University as a Rhodes Scholar (where he met Ambassador Joseph Kennedy's son, John), was the highest paid professional football player in America, and began law school. While serving as a naval intelligence officer in the South Pacific during World War II, White again met John F. Kennedy. He completed his law degree at Yale after the war, clerked for Chief Justice Fred Vinson (1946–1947), and while in Washington, had numerous opportunities to meet with John Kennedy, then a freshman congressman from Massachusetts. In 1947, he returned to Colorado and the private practice of law.

In 1959, White led the Colorado organization on behalf of Kennedy's efforts to gain the Democratic presidential nomination. He was appointed deputy U.S. attorney general in 1961 and won recognition as an able administrator, effectively acting as "chief of staff" of the Justice Department. During the tense days in May 1961, when Attorney General Robert Kennedy dispatched four hundred federal marshals to Alabama to protect the Freedom Riders, White calmly and competently supervised the marshals and deputies. As deputy attorney general, he ably screened candidates for federal judgeships.

Contribution to Criminal Procedure.   Justice White was generally conservative on criminal procedure issues; he dissented strongly in *Escobedo v. Illinois* (1964) and *Miranda v. Arizona* (1966) and was clearly opposed to the incorporation of the Fourth Amendment exclusionary rule. On occasion, he decided in favor of the defendant. In *Duncan v. Louisiana* (1968), however, he effectively ended the *Palko* (1937) approach to fundamental rights, arguing that if a Bill of Rights procedure is fundamental to the American system of justice, it ought to be incorporated.

His pro-government rulings include the late-1980s ruling that a helicopter overflight of a backyard at four hundred feet is not a search; there is no expectation of privacy in abandoned trash; an indicted defendant may waive his right to counsel and be interrogated without his attorney present; and government forfeiture of funds to prevent paying an attorney does not violate the right to counsel. On the other hand, in *Arizona v. Fulminante* (1991), he led a liberal coalition in holding that a confession was coerced and dissenting against a new rule that a coerced confession can be harmless error.

Signature Opinion.   *United States v. Leon* (1984). Justice White's most significant Fourth Amendment opinion held that evidence obtained without probable cause by a police officer relying in good faith on a faulty judicial warrant was admissible. *Leon* was the first clear exception to the *Mapp v. Ohio* (1961) exclusionary rule and a significant victory for conservative justices opposed to the expansion of the rights of criminal suspects. *Leon*'s reasoning relied heavily on a balancing analysis and to some extent on shaky empirical research.

Assessment.   Justice White was generally a middle-of-the-road or swing justice. In the 1960s, he supported governmental authority over individual liberty in cases involving the investigation of communists and other groups. On the other hand, his votes on the civil rights of minorities usually favored integration, school busing, and affirmative action. Justice White has puzzled commentators because of his apparent lack of a clear judicial philosophy. Thus, despite his generally strong support for civil rights and "one man, one vote," he ruled inconsistently on occasion. Some inconsistent decisions can be explained by his concern with the specific factual and procedural contours of each case.

Further Reading

Dennis J. Hutchinson, *The Man Who Once Was Whizzer White: A Portrait of Byron R. White* (New York: Free Press, 1998).

CHAPTER **6**

The Right to Counsel

It is a fundamental principle of our constitutional scheme that government, like the individual, is bound by the law. We do not subscribe to the totalitarian principle that the Government is the law, or that it may disregard the law even in pursuit of the lawbreaker.

—JUSTICE ABE FORTAS, DISSENTING, *Alderman v. United States*, 394 U.S. 165, 202 (1969)

It is during our most challenging and uncertain moments that our Nation's commitment to due process is most severely tested; and it is in those times that we must preserve our commitment at home to the principles for which we fight abroad.

—JUSTICE SANDRA DAY O'CONNOR, *Hamdi v. Rumsfeld*, 542 U.S. 507, 532 (2004)

CHAPTER OUTLINE

KEY TERMS

actual imprisonment rule
appointed counsel
asset forfeiture
assigned counsel
authorized imprisonment rule
conflict of interest

continuance
counsel
critical stage
deficient performance
formal charge rule
indigent
multiple representation

parallel right
prejudice the case
pro bono publico
pro se defense
public defender
recoupment
retained counsel

self-representation
special circumstances rule
standby counsel
waiver of counsel

A defense lawyer stands next to her criminal client in court. Both face judge and jury while awaiting verdict. The defendant will suffer the penalty for a guilty verdict, but their standing together is a powerful reminder that the attorney is the defendant's surrogate—the lawyer "stands in the defendant's shoes." The attorney owes the client an undivided duty of representation, within the law, marked by "warm zeal." The attorney is cloaked with the attorney–client privilege, which preserves a criminal client's right against self-incrimination. Without adequate representation, a fair trial is impossible.

The link between a fair trial and a competent lawyer was not always so. Attorneys were not permitted in the English common law jury trial from its origins in the Middle Ages until the nineteenth century—criminal defendants defended themselves. Also, except in major treason trials, public prosecutors did not exist. An English criminal trial was a "long argument" between the defendant and a private accuser.[1] English law first allowed a defendant the right to legal representation in treason trials only in 1695. Lawyers began to advise ordinary felony defendants shortly after that date, but by law they were barred from speaking in the trial. This rule was seen as unjust and was at times breached in practice.[2] Nevertheless, it was not until 1836 that English defendants gained the ability to be represented by a paid lawyer in a felony trial.

In contrast to England, colonial America embraced the use of attorneys in criminal trials. John Adams, later the second president of the United States, was hired as a defense lawyer in many criminal cases. In the celebrated Boston Massacre case, Adams, although a member of the pro-liberty party, vigorously defended and won acquittals for the British soldiers who fired in self-defense on a large stone-throwing mob of zealous patriots.[3] Many early state constitutions guaranteed **counsel** in criminal cases.[4] Despite the guarantee of counsel in the federal Bill of Rights and states' bill of rights, most **indigent** defendants represented themselves in those days. Judges ideally took special care to advise such indigent defendants, to ensure that they did not completely ruin their defenses. The right to counsel existed only for those who could afford a lawyer. In death penalty cases, however, judges often ordered lawyers to donate their services free of charge as a professional obligation.

The Constitution's Framers viewed the right to counsel favorably, even if not intending to provide free lawyers for indigent defendants. The Sixth Amendment is the primary source of the right to counsel: "In all criminal prosecutions, the accused shall enjoy the right . . . to have the Assistance of Counsel for his defence."[5] The Sixth Amendment right is limited to criminal prosecutions. In other proceedings, counsel may be guaranteed on the basis of other rights. The due process (Fifth and Fourteenth Amendments) fairness concept is the basis for providing counsel in probation revocation hearings, depending on facts and circumstances. The Fourteenth Amendment Equal Protection Clause has been applied by the Supreme Court to guarantee equitable treatment in the trial process by relieving indigent defendants of paying filing fees or the costs of transcripts if they are important for the defense. The Due Process and Equal Protection Clauses, combined, guarantee a lawyer for a convicted defendant's first appeal as of right. The right to counsel at a custodial interrogation, a right made famous by the *Miranda* warnings, is based on the Fifth Amendment privilege against self-incrimination. Also, prior to the incorporation of the Sixth Amendment right to counsel into the Due Process Clause in 1963 by *Gideon v. Wainwright*, the Due Process Clause of the Fourteenth Amendment was an important vehicle for guaranteeing the provision of counsel in certain state proceedings.

Before the mid-twentieth century, the Sixth Amendment right to counsel meant that a court or statute could not abolish a defendant's right to be represented in court by a paid, licensed lawyer of his or her choosing. At first, the right did not mean that the state had to pay for a defense lawyer. Until the early twentieth century, it was constitutionally acceptable for a poor person to defend him- or herself without a lawyer in a felony trial, with whatever help the judge was disposed to grant. In complex or death penalty cases, judges might order local lawyers to represent indigent defendants for no charge, ***pro bono publico***, but the practice was not uniform. The development of the right to counsel in the twentieth century has centered on the practical issue of whether the state has to pay for lawyers for persons who are themselves too poor to pay.

Professional lawyers are essential to ensure fair trials in the adversarial trial by jury, where the truth is thought to emerge from the "clash of evidence" provided by prosecution and defense. The trial is a technical and intimidating process requiring expertise. Good criminal attorneys are trained in substantive criminal law, which can be intricate and can change, know the latest rules of criminal procedure, have the rules of evidence at their fingertips, and have developed the practical skills to bring these rules to life in the conduct of trials. In addition to trial advocacy, attorneys direct pretrial investigations (for evidence of innocence and for defenses such as insanity) and protect the defendant's rights in legally complex pretrial hearings. Motions for bail, discovery, suppression of illegally obtained evidence, change of venue in notorious cases, and the conduct of plea negotiations require experienced attorneys. Plea bargaining, contrary to common belief, is quite adversarial. Attorneys who prepare negotiated cases as if they were going to trial learn strengths and weaknesses of the case and are in a position to back up their negotiating position with a resort to trial if needed. The adversarial nature of American trials pervades the entire adjudication process and makes even routine cases dependent on the abilities of trained, professional advocates. A defendant without a lawyer is at a severe disadvantage.

The benefits of a defense attorney were once available only to those who could afford one. The critical issue running through the Supreme Court's counsel cases in the first half of the twentieth century was whether the state had to provide counsel for indigents—those who were too poor to pay for a lawyer.

THE DEVELOPMENT OF THE RIGHT TO COUNSEL TO 1961

The growth of urban populations and bureaucratic, multi-judge courts in the twentieth century required that *ad hoc* methods of providing lawyers for indigents be replaced with more formal legal aid and defender systems. Some cities and states, but not all, began to do this. The U.S. Constitution was not thought to oblige federal or state governments to provide lawyers for the defendants they prosecuted, in order to ensure fair trials. In 1932, the Supreme Court began to change that view and to define the right to counsel. Thirty years later, it applied the Sixth Amendment right to the states by *incorporating* that right into the Fourteenth Amendment Due Process Clause (see Chapter 1). The constitutional journey began with one of the most celebrated trials in American history, the infamous Scottsboro case. In ***Powell v. Alabama*** (1932), the Court found that under certain circumstances the Due Process Clause required state courts to provide criminal defendants with free counsel.

Powell v. Alabama: The Scottsboro Case

Nine African-American teens, arrested after a fistfight with several white boys on a freight train rolling through Alabama in 1931, were falsely accused of rape by two white female passengers. The teens were tried for a capital crime in Scottsboro, Alabama. Thus began one of the great trial sagas in American history. It did not end until the last of the defendants was released from prison decades later.[6] The "Scottsboro boys" were tried three times in a climate dripping with racism; they were sentenced to death, gained national notoriety, grew to maturity in prison, and were saved by appeals, stays of execution, and commutations. Twice they saw their cases go before the U.S. Supreme Court.[7]

The first trials were one-day affairs held on successive days. Eight of the teens were sentenced to death. The Alabama Supreme Court affirmed seven of the capital sentences. The U.S. Supreme Court accepted the case and reversed the convictions in November 1932. Justice George Sutherland's majority opinion in *Powell v. Alabama* (1932) held that the defendants' due process rights had been violated.

The issue in *Powell* was whether the defendants' due process rights were violated by the denial of the right to counsel, "with the accustomed incidents of consultation and opportunity of preparation for trial." Prior to 1932, the Supreme Court had not incorporated any of the criminal procedure rights in the Bill of Rights, which included the guarantee of the assistance of counsel. The Supreme Court, however, had ruled less than a decade before that a state prosecution obtained through the pressure of a lynch mob infringed a state defendant's constitutional rights under the Fourteenth Amendment Due Process Clause (*Moore v. Dempsey*, 1923; see Chapter 1). "Mob justice" was not the precise basis of the *Powell* decision, although Justice Sutherland did note that the atmosphere surrounding the trials was one of "tense, hostile and excited public sentiment."

How were the defendants represented in the Scottsboro case? The transcript indicated that lawyers for the defendants examined and cross-examined witnesses and made arguments. On this basis, the Alabama Supreme Court ruled that Ozie Powell and the other youths had been represented by counsel and not denied due process. Why did the U.S. Supreme Court conclude otherwise? Justice Sutherland noted that the defendants, who were young and poor strangers in

Scottsboro, were not asked if they had access to lawyers. They were not given much time to contact their families in other states to arrange for counsel:

> It is hardly necessary to say that, the right to counsel being conceded, a defendant should be afforded a fair opportunity to secure counsel of his own choice. Not only was that not done here, but such designation of counsel as was attempted was either so indefinite or so close upon the trial as to amount to a denial of effective and substantial aid in that regard. (*Powell v. Alabama*, 1932)

Indeed, the trial transcript disclosed that in fact none of the lawyers was willing to definitely be a lawyer for a specific defendant. Steven Roddy, a Tennessee lawyer, was asked by the court whether he intended to appear for the defendants. Roddy replied that he was not really hired although he "would like to appear along with counsel that the court might appoint."[8] Ultimately, no single lawyer was appointed for all the defendants, nor was each defendant appointed individual counsel. Instead, the trial judge "appointed all the members of the bar for the purpose of arraigning the defendants" and continued that arrangement for the trial when neither Roddy nor any of the local lawyers would stand up to be *the* attorney of record.[9] The white lawyers were obviously unwilling to vigorously defend poor African-American teens and drifters accused of the rape of two white women in the segregated South. In the critical time period before trial, when a lawyer could have organized an investigation into the facts and marshaled legal arguments, no one focused on this task. This lack of resolution and focus clearly offended Justice Sutherland:[10]

> It is not enough to assume that counsel thus precipitated into the case thought there was no defense, and exercised their best judgment in proceeding to trial without preparation. Neither they nor the court could say what a prompt and thoroughgoing investigation might disclose as to the facts. No attempt was made to investigate. No opportunity to do so was given. Defendants were immediately hurried to trial. . . . Under the circumstances disclosed, we hold that defendants were not accorded the right of counsel in any substantial sense. To decide otherwise, would simply be to ignore actualities. (*Powell v. Alabama*, 1932)

Did Justice Sutherland's holding—that the defendants were not accorded the right to counsel in any substantial sense—incorporate the Sixth Amendment? That is, did it directly apply the Sixth Amendment's assistance of counsel right to the state courts in all felony trials? Although his bare words can give that impression, Justice Sutherland based his decision on the Due Process Clause alone. His review of history showed that twelve of the original states established the right to counsel when no such right existed in England, demonstrating its importance. Indeed, some colonies required the appointment of defense counsel in death penalty cases, as did Alabama by statute in 1931.

Addressing the incorporation issue, Justice Sutherland noted that *Hurtado v. California* (1884), standing alone, held that the federal courts could not incorporate a Bill of Rights provision into the Fourteenth Amendment Due Process Clause, making it a state requirement. But *Hurtado* did not stand alone. *Chicago, Burlington and Quincy Railroad Co. v. Chicago* (1897) held that the states, as a matter of Fourteenth Amendment due process, had to grant just compensation when the state took private property for public use, even though a Just Compensation Clause existed in the Fifth Amendment. Furthermore, "freedom of speech and of the press are rights protected by the Due Process Clause of the Fourteenth Amendment, although in the First Amendment, Congress is prohibited in specific terms from abridging the right."[11] Therefore, a right found in the Bill of Rights, which limited the *federal* government, could also exist as a **parallel right** within the Due Process Clause to limit the *states*. This "parallel right" approach is clearly not the "total incorporation" under the Privileges or Immunities Clause (desired by Justices John Harlan I and Hugo Black), nor is it the modern approach of "selective incorporation." Yet it seems clear that Justice Sutherland was influenced by the "fundamental rights" reasoning of *Twining v. New Jersey* (1908). (See Chapter 1.)

Although Justice Sutherland and the Court did not cleanly incorporate the Sixth Amendment right to counsel, his opinion came rather close to calling it a fundamental right. Philosopher Hadley Arkes suggests that Justice Sutherland was concerned with basic principles: "To begin at the root, the purpose of a trial was to do justice, to punish the guilty and vindicate the innocent. The central task was to make reasoned discriminations between the innocent and the guilty and arrive at verdicts that were substantially just."[12] At minimum, due process requires notice, a fair hearing, and a competent tribunal. Justice Sutherland's classic passage explains the vital importance of a fully committed defense attorney to fulfilling the ideal of a fair trial:

> What, then, does a hearing include? Historically and in practice, in our own country at least, it has always included the right to the aid of counsel when desired and provided by the party asserting the right. The right to be heard would be, in many cases, of little avail if it did not comprehend the right to be heard by counsel. Even the intelligent and educated layman has small and sometimes no skill in the science of law. If charged with crime, he is incapable, generally, of determining for himself whether the indictment is good or bad. He is unfamiliar with the rules of evidence. Left without the aid of counsel he may be put on trial without a proper charge, and convicted upon incompetent evidence, or evidence irrelevant to the issue or otherwise inadmissible. He lacks both the skill and knowledge adequately to prepare his defense, even though he had a perfect one. He requires the guiding hand of counsel at every step in the proceedings against him. Without it, though he be not guilty, he faces the danger of conviction because he does not know how to establish his innocence. If that be true of men of intelligence, how much more true is it of the ignorant and illiterate, or those of feeble intellect. If in any case, civil or criminal, a state or federal court were arbitrarily to refuse to hear a party by counsel, employed by and appearing for him, it reasonably may not be doubted that such a refusal would be a denial of a hearing, and, therefore, of due process in the constitutional sense. (*Powell v. Alabama*, 1932)

With this, the Court easily ruled that the Fourteenth Amendment due process rights of the Scottsboro defendants were violated, and a new trial was required.

Note, however, that *Powell v. Alabama* did not rule that the states *had* to provide a lawyer for *every* indigent defendant in every felony trial. The scope of its application was narrower. The decision was based on the facts and circumstances of the case.

> All that it is necessary now to decide, as we do decide, is that in a capital case, where the defendant is unable to employ counsel, and is incapable adequately of making his own defense because of ignorance, feeble mindedness, illiteracy, or the like, it is the duty of the court, whether requested or not, to assign counsel for him as a necessary requisite of due process of law. (*Powell v. Alabama*, 1932)

As a Due Process Clause precedent, *Powell* became known as the **special circumstances rule:** That is, due process requires counsel in cases where "special circumstances" exist.

After *Powell:* Toward Incorporation

Six years after *Powell*, Justice Hugo Black's majority opinion in **Johnson v. Zerbst** (1938) forcefully made the assistance of counsel in a federal case—directly applying the Sixth Amendment, uncluttered by states' rights or special circumstances considerations—an absolute right. Two soldiers on leave in South Carolina, convicted in a federal prosecution of passing counterfeit currency, were tried without the assistance of counsel. The case shows why a lawyer is necessary. The defendants presented a defense that was not artful at best and one that a jury could read as an evasion of guilt. Johnson misused his time by attempting to answer minor, possibly prejudicial, statements by the prosecutor (e.g., that he was a "hoodlum from New York"). Johnson also failed to challenge the evidence and neglected to raise legal challenges that could have mitigated the crime or won an acquittal.

Justice Black's majority opinion secured two important constitutional rules. First, it held for the first time that a federal felony trial conducted without a defense lawyer, unless properly waived, is a *jurisdictional violation*. It is not a mere technical mistake but an infringement of the Sixth Amendment that deprives the court of "the power and authority to deprive an accused of his life or liberty" (*Johnson v. Zerbst*, 1938).

> This is [a] safeguard[] . . . deemed necessary to ensure fundamental human rights of life and liberty. [It is an] essential barrier[] against arbitrary or unjust deprivation of human rights. The Sixth Amendment stands as a constant admonition that if the constitutional safeguards it provides be lost, justice will not "still be done." (*Johnson v. Zerbst*, 1938, p. 462)

Second, the case specified the rules for **waiver of counsel**. There is a presumption against the waiver of such a fundamental right. Even if the defendant goes silently along with the conduct of a trial without complaining about the lack of counsel, his or her silence does not amount to a waiver. A waiver is defined as "an intelligent relinquishment or abandonment of a known right or privilege." For a waiver to be constitutional, the defendant must know that he or she has a right to counsel and must voluntarily give it up knowing that the right to claim it exists. The Supreme Court later required trial judges to carefully investigate waivers of counsel and make a written record of any waivers (*Von Moltke v. Gillies*, 1948). "Presuming waiver from a silent record is impermissible. The record must show . . . that an accused was offered counsel but intelligently and understandably rejected the offer" (*Carnley v. Cochran*, 1962). These rules became the standard for all Fifth and Sixth Amendment waivers, including waivers of the right to remain silent after having been read the *Miranda* warnings.

Betts v. Brady (1942), decided a decade after *Powell*, was a setback to the incorporation of the Sixth Amendment. *Betts* confirmed the special circumstances rule of *Powell*. Betts, a farmhand, was indicted for noncapital robbery. Not having the money to hire a lawyer, he asked the judge for **appointed counsel** at his arraignment. The judge refused, saying that the Carroll County Court appointed counsel for indigent defendants only in prosecutions for murder and rape. Betts pleaded not guilty and defended himself in a nonjury trial before the judge.

> At his request witnesses were summoned in his behalf. He cross-examined the State's witnesses and examined his own. The latter gave testimony tending to establish an alibi. Although afforded the opportunity, he did not take the witness stand. The judge found him guilty and imposed a sentence of eight years. (*Betts v. Brady*, 1942)

The issue before the Supreme Court, sharpened by Betts's explicit request for a lawyer, was (as in *Powell*) whether a state felony trial conducted without defense counsel was a deprivation of Fourteenth Amendment due process liberty. The majority, in an opinion by Justice Owen Roberts, clearly rejected incorporation: "[T]he Sixth Amendment of the national Constitution applies only to trials in federal courts." Relying on *Palko v. Connecticut* (1937), it refused to apply the *Johnson v. Zerbst* rule to state cases and decided the case exclusively under the Due Process Clause special circumstances test as set out in *Powell v. Alabama* to decide, on an "appraisal of the totality of facts in a given case," whether a trial without defense counsel is "a denial of fundamental fairness, shocking to the universal sense of justice" (*Betts v. Brady*, 1942).

Applying *Powell*, Justice Roberts concluded that special circumstances did not exist in Betts's case. Due process, therefore, did not require the state to appoint counsel. The case was not complicated: Did Betts commit a robbery? He put alibi witnesses on the stand, and the issue for the judge was a simple matter of witness credibility. Unlike the Scottsboro defendants, Betts was "not helpless, but was a man forty-three years old, of ordinary intelligence, and [able] to take care of his own interests on the trial of that narrow issue. He had once before been in a criminal court, pleaded guilty to larceny and served a sentence and was not wholly unfamiliar with criminal procedure" (*Betts v. Brady*, 1942). None of the lynch-mob racism of *Powell* infected this run-of-the-mill case. In affirming Betts's uncounseled noncapital felony conviction, the majority was satisfied that its holding did not violate "natural, inherent, and fundamental principles of fairness."

Federalism played a large part in the reasoning of the majority. Uncounseled defense was a common practice to "those who have lived under the Anglo-American system of law." Most states then provided an attorney at no charge to the defendant in noncapital cases only at the discretion of the court and not as a mandatory right. The provision of counsel was seen as a legislative or political issue, not as a fundamental right, and Maryland law required the appointment of counsel if special circumstances existed. The Supreme Court worried that a flat rule would burden states with the cost of providing counsel even in "small crimes tried before justices of the peace" and in "trials in the Traffic Court."

Justice Black's spirited dissent, joined by Justices Douglas and Murphy, urged incorporation of the Sixth Amendment right to counsel into the Fourteenth Amendment. Failing that, he argued that Justice Sutherland's logic in *Powell*—that it is difficult for any layperson to adequately defend him- or herself in a criminal trial—means that a felony trial conducted without defense counsel is always unfair and a due process violation. Justice Black sought to extend *Johnson v. Zerbst* to state cases. The former populist senator emphasized the greater risks of unjust conviction to poor people. "A practice cannot be reconciled with 'common and fundamental ideas of fairness and right,' which subjects innocent men to increased dangers of conviction merely because of their poverty. . . . Denial to the poor of the request for counsel in proceedings based on charges of serious crime has long been regarded as shocking to the 'universal sense of justice' throughout this country" (*Betts v. Brady*, 1942).

Justice Black was later vindicated in *Gideon v. Wainwright* (1963). In the two decades following *Betts*, the Court undermined the special circumstances test by finding that special circumstances existed in many instances. The Court held that counsel was required by due process in all death penalty trials (*Bute v. Illinois*, 1948), in all capital case arraignments (*Hamilton v. Alabama*, 1961), and in cases involving an unsworn defendant who wishes to make a statement (*Ferguson v. Georgia*, 1961). Justice Stanley Reed revealed that the Court was divided as to noncapital cases but that several justices felt that "the Due Process Clause . . . requires counsel for all persons charged with serious crimes" (*Uveges v. Pennsylvania*, 1948). These cases paved the way to *Gideon*.

The Equal Protection Approach

Griffin v. Illinois (1956) held (5–4) in an opinion written by Justice Black that under the Fourteenth Amendment Equal Protection Clause, indigent defendants, with some restrictions, are entitled to free trial transcripts in order to facilitate appeals. A transcript, which is expensive to produce, clearly makes it easier for judges to decide whether to grant an appeal and makes it easier for appellate judges to review potential trial errors. Without a transcript, an indigent defendant has to rely on a judge's discretion to authorize an appeal and might not get one where a wealthier defendant who could afford a transcript would. This relatively technical topic, with its focus on providing equal justice on appeal rather than at a criminal trial, does not seem directly relevant to the issue raised in *Johnson v. Zerbst* (1938) and *Betts v. Brady* (1942). It seems that the Court's liberal justices were seeking to establish an alternate constitutional basis for the right to counsel on appeal. This is inferred in part from Justice Black's dictum in *Griffin*: "There can be no equal justice where the kind of *trial* a man gets depends on the amount of money he has" (emphasis added). This seems to be a logical derivation from *Griffin*'s principle: that the state should eliminate the differences between the rich and the poor so as to ensure equal justice. If people with the means had an absolute right to counsel, and if counsel is essential to a fair trial, should not a lawyer be provided for indigents? As it turned out, however, the Equal Protection Clause was not the platform for the rule requiring trial counsel.

The dissent expressed a concern for federalism by noting that a free transcript should be provided by the states as they saw fit and not required by federal constitutional law. They also expressed concern that an equal protection ruling saying that rich and poor had to be treated equally would lead to "leveling," by abolishing all laws that had any disparate economic impact on the rich and the poor (e.g., disallowing fixed taxes such as a sales tax).

GIDEON V. WAINWRIGHT AND ITS AFTERMATH

In *Gideon v. Wainwright*, the Supreme Court finally guaranteed the right to counsel to all state felony defendants by incorporating the Sixth Amendment into Fourteenth Amendment due process.

Read Case and Comments: *Gideon v. Wainwright*.

Does *Gideon* Apply to Misdemeanor Trials?

In *Argersinger v. Hamlin* (1972), the Supreme Court found no constitutional basis for distinguishing between a misdemeanor and a felony for purposes of **assigned counsel** for indigents. It held that counsel was required by the Sixth Amendment in misdemeanor cases where a defendant is actually sentenced to imprisonment. The Court reserved the issue of whether counsel is constitutionally required in cases involving imprisonment as an authorized punishment, but the defendant does not actually lose liberty.

CASE AND COMMENTS

Gideon v. Wainwright

372 U.S. 335, 83 S.Ct. 792, 9 L.Ed.2d 799 (1963)

[a] Justice Black had the pleasure of writing the opinion in a landmark decision overruling a case in which he had strenuously dissented two decades before.

[b] This was the Supreme Court's third criminal procedure incorporation case of the 1960s. As in other incorporation cases, the federal rule interpreting a Bill of Rights provision was more favorable to the defendant's rights than the state rule.

[c] Justice Black seems to be stretching a fair reading of the "older precedent" of *Powell v. Alabama* by viewing it as having guaranteed the right of counsel to indigents in *all* felony cases. Compare this reading of precedent to that made in the concurrence by Justice Harlan.

[d] The case was remanded, and Earl Clarence Gideon was tried again in Panama City, Florida, this time represented by counsel. Anthony Lewis's celebrated book *Gideon's Trumpet* recounts the second trial. Gideon's lawyer, Fred Turner, prepared the case carefully by thoroughly reviewing the facts and observing the pool hall. His skillful cross-examination of the lead prosecution witness raised the real possibility that the teen who had identified Gideon as the criminal was himself the burglar. Gideon was acquitted.

MR. JUSTICE BLACK delivered the opinion of the Court. **[a]**

[Gideon, charged with breaking into a pool hall, a felony, demanded (because of his indigence) and was refused appointed counsel. He conducted his own defense.] He made an opening statement to the jury, cross-examined the State's witnesses, presented witnesses in his own defense, declined to testify himself, and made a short argument "emphasizing his innocence to the charge contained in the Information filed in this case." The jury returned a verdict of guilty, and petitioner was sentenced to serve five years in the state prison. [The Court characterized the facts as similar to *Betts v. Brady* (this text) and set the case for review to reconsider the *Betts* rule because of the "continuing source of controversy and litigation in both state and federal courts" that the *Betts* rule presented.]

* * * Upon full reconsideration we conclude that *Betts v. Brady* should be overruled.

We have construed [the Sixth Amendment] to mean that in federal courts counsel must be provided for defendants unable to employ counsel unless the right is competently and intelligently waived. [Justice Black reviewed *Betts v. Brady*, noting that it held the Sixth Amendment right of counsel not to be fundamental and thus not incorporated into the Due Process Clause of the Fourteenth Amendment.] **[b]**

We accept *Betts v. Brady*'s assumption, based as it was on our prior cases, that a provision of the Bill of Rights which is "fundamental and essential to a fair trial" is made obligatory upon the States by the Fourteenth Amendment. We think the Court in *Betts* was wrong, however, in concluding that the Sixth Amendment's guarantee of counsel is not one of these fundamental rights. Ten years before *Betts v. Brady*, this Court, after full consideration of all the historical data examined in *Betts*, had unequivocally declared that "the right to the aid of counsel is of this fundamental character." *Powell v. Alabama.* * * * While the Court at the close of its *Powell* opinion did by its language, as this Court frequently does, limit its holding to the particular facts and circumstances of that case, its conclusions about the fundamental nature of the right to counsel are unmistakable. * * *

* * * The fact is that in deciding as it did—that "appointment of counsel is not a fundamental right, essential to a fair trial"—the Court in *Betts v. Brady* made an abrupt break with its own well-considered precedents. In returning to these old precedents, sounder we believe than the new, we but restore constitutional principles established to achieve a fair system of justice. **[c]** Not only these precedents but also reason and reflection require us to recognize that in our adversary system of criminal justice, any person haled into court, who is too poor to hire a lawyer, cannot be assured a fair trial unless counsel is provided for him. This seems to us to be an obvious truth. Governments, both state and federal, quite properly spend vast sums of money to establish machinery to try defendants accused of crime. Lawyers to prosecute are everywhere deemed essential to protect the public's interest in an orderly society. Similarly, there are few defendants charged with crime, few indeed, who fail to hire the best lawyers they can get to prepare and present their defenses. That government hires lawyers to prosecute and defendants who have the money hire lawyers to defend are the strongest indications of the widespread belief that lawyers in criminal courts are necessities, not luxuries. The right of one charged with crime to counsel may not be deemed fundamental and essential to fair trials in some countries, but it is in ours. From the very beginning, our state and national constitutions and laws have laid great emphasis on procedural and substantive safeguards designed to assure fair trials before impartial tribunals in which every defendant stands equal before the law. This noble ideal cannot be realized if the poor man charged with crime has to face his accusers without a lawyer to assist him. * * *

The judgment is reversed. * * * **[d]**

[Justices Douglas and Clark concurred in separate opinions.]

MR. JUSTICE HARLAN, concurring.

I agree that *Betts v. Brady* should be overruled, but consider it entitled to a more respectful burial than has been accorded, at least on the part of those of us who were not on the Court when that case was decided.

I cannot subscribe to the view that *Betts v. Brady* represented "an abrupt break with its own well-considered precedents." * * * In 1932, in *Powell v. Alabama*, * * * a capital case, this Court declared that under the particular facts there presented—"the ignorance and illiteracy of the defendants, their youth, the circumstances of public hostility * * * and above all that they stood in deadly peril of their lives" * * *—the state court had a duty to assign counsel for the trial as a necessary requisite of due process of law. It is evident that these limiting facts were not added to the opinion as an afterthought; they were repeatedly emphasized, * * * and were clearly regarded as important to the result.

Thus when this Court, a decade later, decided *Betts v. Brady*, it did no more than to admit of the possible existence of special circumstances in noncapital as well as capital trials, while at the same time insisting that such circumstances be shown in order to establish a denial of due process. The right to appointed counsel had been recognized as being considerably broader in federal prosecutions [*Johnson v. Zerbst*], but to have imposed these requirements on the States would indeed have been "an abrupt break" with the almost immediate past. The declaration that the right to appointed counsel in state prosecutions, as established in *Powell v. Alabama*, was not limited to capital cases was in truth not a departure from, but an extension of, existing precedent.

The principles declared in *Powell* and in *Betts*, however, have had a troubled journey throughout the years. * * * [e]

[More and more capital and noncapital cases found "special circumstances," even in doubtful instances.] The Court has come to recognize, in other words, that the mere existence of a serious criminal charge constituted in itself special circumstances requiring the services of counsel at trial. In truth the *Betts v. Brady* rule is no longer a reality.

This evolution, however, appears not to have been fully recognized by many state courts, in this instance charged with the front-line responsibility for the enforcement of constitutional rights. To continue a rule which is honored by this Court only with lip service is not a healthy thing and in the long run will do disservice to the federal system.

The special circumstances rule has been formally abandoned in capital cases, and the time has now come when it should be similarly abandoned in noncapital cases, at least as to offenses which, as the one involved here, carry the possibility of a substantial prison sentence. (Whether the rule should extend to *all* criminal cases need not now be decided.) This indeed does no more than to make explicit something that has long since been foreshadowed in our decisions.

[Justice Harlan then stated his disagreement with the majority over the incorporation question, stating that in his opinion, the *Gideon* decision falls under the Fourteenth Amendment only and not the Sixth.]

On these premises I join in the judgment of the Court.

[e] Justice Harlan correctly points out that in the twenty years between *Betts* and *Gideon*, many narrow decisions began to shift toward granting the right to counsel in more and more cases. He posits a less absolutist view of constitutional rights and constitutional change than does Justice Black. In Justice Harlan's view, the meaning of constitutional provisions can change gradually over time to take into account new social realities. This was anathema to Justice Black, who strenuously rejected what he saw as judicial lawmaking.

Justice Lewis Powell, concurring in *Argersinger*, urged the Court to choose a due process special circumstances rule rather than the majority's incorporation approach of requiring counsel if a defendant was to spend even one day in jail. For example, complex legal issues in a case would be a special circumstance. It would be up to a trial court in its discretion to find special circumstances and appoint an attorney. Justice Powell was concerned with requiring states to shoulder the costs of providing counsel in each and every case, no matter how straightforward and simple the issues.

The issue reserved in *Argersinger* was decided in a case concerning a shoplifter who was convicted without the assistance of a lawyer and fined $50, although the law *authorized* a jail term. In *Scott v. Illinois* (1979), the Court ruled that *Argersinger* meant that *actual imprisonment* differs from a penalty of a fine or a threat of jailing. Therefore, "the Sixth and Fourteenth Amendments to the United States Constitution require only that no indigent criminal defendant be sentenced to a term of imprisonment unless the State has afforded him the right to assistance of appointed counsel in his defense." The mere fact of being tried under a statute authorizing incarceration does not automatically guarantee counsel. Justice William Brennan, dissenting, argued that *Argersinger* required appointment of counsel if there is actual incarceration *or* if the crime charged is punishable by more than six months in prison. He thus urged the Court to adopt an **authorized imprisonment rule** rather than an **actual imprisonment rule**.

Scott injects an illogical element into the Sixth Amendment: A person charged with a felony must have a lawyer, even if not sentenced to prison, but this is not so for a misdemeanor defendant in the same circumstance. Justice Powell, concurring, expressed some concern that the actual imprisonment rule would lead judges to guess in advance of the trial what the likely outcome would be and thus distort the judicial process. He concurred because he thought the Court should substitute the flexible due process rule rather than the rigid Sixth Amendment requirement to misdemeanor trials.

RECOUPMENT OF COSTS   The governmental unit that pays for indigents' assigned counsel may constitutionally seek to recoup the costs of the defense if, later, the defendant acquires the means to pay. According to *Fuller v. Oregon* (1974), a **recoupment** law does not violate the Equal Protection Clause, provided that it allows the indigent person to claim all the exemptions granted to other judgment debtors in the state's civil code and does not require payment if the defendant remains or again becomes indigent. Indigents who were *acquitted* cannot be asked to pay for their free defense, and the Supreme Court held that this exception in the law also does not violate equal protection because it is a rational distinction. Dissenting justices felt that recoupment would have a "chilling effect" on the right to counsel; an indigent defendant would decline to accept free counsel knowing that he or she may have to repay the costs of the defense. However, Justice Potter Stewart thought this unlikely because of the protections in the statute ensuring that an indigent cannot be compelled to pay. The Court also noted that defendants whose financial status places them just above the poverty line may have to go into debt in order to pay the costs of a criminal defense. "We cannot say that the Constitution requires that those only slightly poorer must remain forever immune from any obligation to shoulder the expenses of their legal defense, even when they are able to pay without hardship."

THE RIGHT TO COUNSEL AFTER *GIDEON*

Choosing a Paid Lawyer and Limitations on the Right to Choose

RIGHT TO CHOOSE RETAINED COUNSEL   The right to retain one's own counsel for a criminal defense is basic and in all cases there is a presumption in favor of a defendant's counsel of choice. That right, however, is not absolute, and under some circumstances a trial judge can refuse to allow an attorney to represent a defendant. "Regardless of his persuasive powers, an advocate who is not a member of the bar may not represent clients (other than himself) in court. Similarly, a defendant may not insist on representation by an attorney he cannot afford or who for other reasons declines to represent the defendant. Nor may a defendant insist on the counsel of an attorney who has a previous or ongoing relationship with an opposing party, even when the opposing party is the government" (*Wheat v. United States*, 1988).

The issue in **United States v. Gonzalez-Lopez** (2006) was whether a convicted defendant has an automatic right to a retrial when a trial judge erroneously refused to allow the defendant's paid lawyer to represent him. The Supreme Court held (5–4), in an opinion authored by Justice Scalia, that he does. A federal magistrate judge presiding over a drug case in which three defense lawyers were involved refused, for reasons found to be erroneous by the appellate court, to admit an out-of-state lawyer *pro hac vice* (for this case only). The Supreme Court found that this "violated respondent's Sixth Amendment right to paid counsel of his choosing," which is "an element" of the Sixth Amendment right to the assistance of counsel. The government argued that despite this violation of respondent's basic right he was not entitled to a new trial because his actual trial, in which he was convicted for a drug conspiracy, was fair. The prosecution argued that to get a new trial, Gonzalez-Lopez had to show how the case would have resulted differently if he had his counsel of choice. The dissent supported this argument by asserting that a defendant does not have a right to "counsel" as such but "the right 'to have the Assistance of Counsel' [which] carries with it a limited right to be represented by counsel of choice" (*Gonzalez-Lopez*, 2006, Alito, J., dissenting).

Justice Scalia would have none of this reasoning designed to whittle away a basic right. The government's argument is that respondent's basic right is to a fair trial, and as long as he received a fair trial, the specific rights of the Sixth Amendment can be discarded. The Court rejected this kind of reasoning in regard to the Confrontation Clause in *Crawford v. Washington* (2004) (See Chapter 11). "So also with the Sixth Amendment right to counsel of choice. It commands, not that a trial be fair, but that a particular guarantee of fairness be provided—to wit, that the accused be defended by the counsel he believes to be best. . . . In sum, the right at stake here is the right to counsel of choice, not the right to a fair trial; and that right was violated because the deprivation of counsel was erroneous. No additional showing of prejudice is required to make the violation 'complete.'"

Justice Scalia added that it would be nearly impossible for Gonzalez-Lopez to prove how the counsel of choice would have produced a different result. The majority held that wrongly depriving a defendant of counsel of choice is, for purposes of harmless error analysis, a "structural defect" that infects the entire trial and not a specific "trial error" because different "attorneys will pursue different strategies with regard to investigation and discovery, development of the theory of defense, selection of the jury, presentation of the witnesses, and style of witness examination and jury argument. And the choice of attorney will affect whether and on what terms the defendant cooperates with the prosecution, plea bargains, or decides instead to go to trial."

In **Wheat v. United States** (1988) the Court upheld a trial court's denial of a defendant's counsel of his choice when the district court found that the representation carried a substantial possibility of a **conflict of interest**. This ruling, unlike *Gonzalez-Lopez*, subordinates the right to counsel to that of a fair adversary trial. In *Wheat*, the Court was concerned that **multiple representation** of three drug-sale defendants in separate trials by the same lawyer would undermine the lawyer's ability to cross-examine his clients. Thus, even though the defendants were willing to waive their right to a trial free of conflict of interest, the Court refused to accept their waivers. Four dissenting justices agreed that the right to select a lawyer is not absolute, but argued that the trial court's basis for inferring a conflict of interest was thin. In a stinging dissent, Justice Stevens characterized the Court's decision as paternalistic and said, "This is not the first case in which the Court has demonstrated 'its apparent unawareness of the function of the independent lawyer as a guardian of our freedom.'" Even the majority recognized a hidden danger in its decision— that the prosecution would manufacture "implausible conflicts" in order to remove very effective and successful defense lawyers as opposing counsel.

In some contentious cases that followed, the Supreme Court denied defendants their right to the lawyers they chose by less direct means.

PAYMENT AND ASSET FORFEITURE   Two 1989 decisions upheld congressional acts that allow prosecutors to *freeze assets* of suspected organized crime members and drug dealers "before trial [and] without regard to whether the person will have enough money left to hire a lawyer."[13] The **asset forfeiture** law, used aggressively by federal prosecutors, was thought by many to undermine the Sixth Amendment right to adequate representation. **Caplin & Drysdale v. United States** (1989) was a suit by a law firm for its legal fees, which had been placed in escrow before trial and which the government tried to seize after the client's conviction. In **United States v. Monsanto** (1989), pretrial freezing of assets forced the defendant to rely on a **public defender**. The Supreme Court (5–4) found both practices to be constitutional.

The forfeiture law made assets that were proceeds of crime *government property* from the time of the commission of the crime (*ab initio*). The theory was that the defendant was paying his or her lawyer with, in effect, someone else's (i.e., the government's) money. Relying on *Wheat v. United States*, the Court said that "a defendant may not insist on representation by an attorney he cannot afford." The law created some exceptions allowing payments to owners of stolen property and to some innocent retailers, but none for attorneys' fees.

Four dissenting justices felt that the constitutional requirement of adequate representation required the Court to create an *exemption* for legal fees so that the alleged proceeds of a crime could be used for lawyers. They argued that pretrial asset freezing would "undermine the adversary system as we know it" because it gives the government "an intolerable degree of power over any private attorney who takes on the task of representing a defendant in a forfeiture case." It allows prosecutors to

> use the forfeiture weapon against a defense attorney who is particularly talented or aggressive on the client's behalf—the attorney who is better than what, in the Government's view, the defendant deserves. The spectre of the Government's selectively excluding only the most talented defense counsel is a serious threat to the equality of forces necessary for the adversarial system to perform at its best. (*Caplin & Drysdale v. United States*, 1989)

MEANINGFUL ATTORNEY–CLIENT RELATIONSHIP   *Morris v. Slappy* (1983) held that the Sixth Amendment does not guarantee a "meaningful" relationship between defendant and appointed counsel. A deputy public defender represented Slappy at a preliminary hearing and supervised an extensive investigation in his rape prosecution. Shortly before trial, this lawyer was hospitalized for emergency surgery and a senior trial attorney from the public defender's office was assigned to the case. Slappy claimed the attorney did not have enough time to prepare and moved for a **continuance**. The newly assigned attorney stated that he was prepared and that a further delay would not benefit him in presenting the case. The trial court denied Slappy's motion. The trial continued and Slappy was found guilty by a jury on three counts. During a second trial of counts left unresolved in the first trial, Slappy refused to cooperate with or even speak to his attorney. The jury returned a guilty verdict on the other counts. The federal appeals court, in a federal habeas corpus action, held that the Sixth Amendment includes the right to a meaningful attorney–client relationship.

The Supreme Court reversed and held that, under the circumstances of this case, there was no Sixth Amendment violation by the trial court's refusal to delay the case when the attorney himself did not want one. The Court rejected the novel idea that an indigent defendant is guaranteed a "meaningful" relationship with assigned counsel; furthermore, an indigent defendant does not have an unqualified right to the appointment of counsel of his or her own choosing. Justice Brennan, while concurring in the decision, noted that lower federal courts have recognized the importance of a defendant's relationship with his or her attorney so that a defendant with retained counsel was seen to have "a qualified right to continue that relationship." The qualified right to a meaningful attorney–client relationship is *not* the guarantee of "rapport" between them. Rather, according to Justice Brennan, where an attorney has put sufficient work into a case so that he or she has become knowledgeable of its intricacies, a court should take into account the length of delay before allowing another attorney to try the case.

When Does the Right to Counsel "Attach" for an Indigent Defendant?

With the Sixth Amendment applicable in state as well as federal court under *Gideon v. Wainwright*, a number of interesting cases have defined the contours of the right to counsel. The Sixth Amendment guarantees its rights "in all criminal *prosecutions*." This clearly applied to a *trial* at common law. In modern criminal justice, however, a host of pretrial processes (such as preliminary hearings) and ancillary factors (such as the availability of psychiatrists to evaluate a defendant's sanity) that are important to the outcome of trials, and post-trial procedures (such as appeals and probation revocation hearings) where lawyers can play an important role raise the question whether counsel is required under the sixth Amendment, or perhaps under the due process special circumstances test that was in vogue before *Gideon*.

The Supreme Court has applied different concepts and theories to resolve the issues. Before reviewing these cases the reader should note that issues discussed in this section appear in Chapters 7 and 8, which focus on limits to *police interrogation* after a criminal prosecution has begun and a defendant has or is entitled to counsel and the right to counsel at live or photographic *lineups*. Those cases have helped to define when the right to counsel begins and are discussed in this section to the extent that they help to elucidate concepts.

The Court has employed different concepts or theories in solving the question of when the right to counsel "attaches." In some instances a procedure or process is not part of the criminal prosecution and there is simply no right to counsel. In other instances a procedure is not part of the criminal prosecution but a limited or discretionary right to counsel may be available under the Due Process or Equal Protection Clauses of the Fourteenth Amendment. Other cases deal with the boundary line at which the criminal prosecution begins; these cases draw on two concepts, one being that "a person's Sixth and Fourteenth Amendment right to counsel attaches only at or after the time that adversary judicial proceedings have been initiated against him" (*Kirby v. Illinois*, 1972), and the other is that counsel is required in any procedure that is a "critical stage" because what "happens there may affect the whole trial, [and] available defenses may be as irretrievably lost, if not then and there asserted" (*Hamilton v. Albama*, 1961).

PROCEDURES WHERE NO RIGHT TO COUNSEL ATTACHES   What criminal case procedures are deemed to *not* be a part of the criminal prosecution so that a defendant has no right to an attorney? An obvious case is *police investigation*. No court has ever held that a lawyer must accompany police in conducting interviews or in gathering physical evidence of a crime. A lawyer has no traditional role to play during investigation, and any problems with the evidence may be exposed during discovery or by cross-examination. Counsel is not required in investigative hearings, such as grand jury and legislative hearings,[14] or when taking fingerprints, handwriting samples, or voice exemplars.[15] This question has arisen in these instances because the Supreme Court famously held in *Miranda v. Arizona* (1966) that a suspect can demand to remain silent during custodial police interrogation without the advice of a lawyer (see Chapter 7). The Court also in *United States v. Wade* (1967) held that counsel is required in post-indictment lineups, but somewhat inconsistently ruled that a lawyer is not required in a pre-indictment lineup or in photographic lineups (see Chapter 8)[16]. Counsel was extended in these two procedures because they are especially prone to being unfair and might possibly finger innocent suspects. Any errors in routine police investigation can be exposed by cross-examination at a trial.

PROCEEDINGS THAT MAY BE SIMILAR TO CRIMINAL TRIALS   One month after deciding *Gideon v. Wainwright* (1963), the Supreme Court held that the assistance of counsel is as important *in plea bargaining* as it is in the felony trial (**White v. Maryland,** 1963). An arraignment or other pretrial procedure conducted without counsel is unconstitutional. When a lawyer is not present at a critical stage, the Court does "not stop to determine whether prejudice resulted: 'Only the presence of counsel could have enabled this accused to know all the defenses available to him and to plead intelligently'. . . . [A]n intelligent assessment of the relative advantages of pleading guilty is frequently impossible without the assistance of an attorney" (*White v. Maryland*).

Recognizing that a criminal trial is fundamentally unfair when an indigent defendant cannot have access to an essential witness, the court held in **Ake v. Oklahoma** (1985) that a psychiatrist must be provided for an indigent defendant whenever insanity is reasonably raised as an issue. The holding was based on a combination of equal protection and due process reasoning. According to Justice Thurgood Marshall, reviewing the right to counsel decisions, "Meaningful access to justice has been the consistent theme of these cases. . . . [A] criminal trial is fundamentally unfair if the State proceeds against an individual defendant without making certain that he has access to the raw materials integral to the building of an effective defense."

Another question is "when does the criminal prosecution terminate," after a verdict or entry of a guilty plea or after sentencing? The Supreme Court included both typical *sentencing* conducted at a set time after a verdict and *deferred sentencing* as being part of the criminal prosecution in **Mempa v. Rhay** (1967). Jerry Mempa was convicted of "joyriding" and sentenced to two years of probation and one month in jail, with the jail sentence deferred. The suspension was revoked and Mempa sent to jail when the prosecutor charged seventeen-year-old Jerry with involvement in a burglary, supported only by a probation officer's statement. He had no lawyer at his deferred sentencing hearing and was never asked if he wished to have a lawyer. Jerry admitted to the burglary and did not cross-examine the probation officer. Without taking any evidence, the judge sentenced Jerry ten years in prison, with a recommendation of release in one year to the parole board. Justice Thurgood Marshall, writing for a unanimous Court, announced a broad Sixth Amendment principle: "appointment of counsel for an indigent is required at every stage of a criminal proceeding where substantial rights of a criminal accused may be affected." A lawyer was important in this procedure because the judge's recommended sentence was relied on heavily by the parole board and it is obvious that a lawyer is helpful "in marshaling the facts, introducing evidence of mitigating circumstances and in general aiding and assisting the defendant to present his case as to sentence." Also, appeals could be taken only after sentencing was completed and Mempa lost any right to appeal because a lawyer was not present.

The Court held in **In re Gault** (1967) that a *juvenile delinquency adjudication* is not a criminal prosecution within the contemplation of the Sixth Amendment. Yet, under the Due Process Clause, the Court held that an adjudication of juvenile delinquency, which may result in commitment to an institution, is so much like an adult criminal trial that the provision of counsel is essential. If the child or parents cannot afford counsel, the state is required to appoint a lawyer to represent the child.

To the contrary of *Gault*, the Court held in **Middendorf v. Henry** (1976) that a *summary court-martial* was not a criminal prosecution within the meaning of the Sixth Amendment and that a lawyer was not constitutionally required. This was because the maximum penalty could not exceed thirty days' confinement, and a summary court-martial's "purpose 'is to exercise justice promptly for relatively minor offenses under a simple form of procedure'" for purposes of military discipline. In contrast, counsel is provided in special and general court-martials, which are more formal and try serious crimes.

PRETRIAL PROCEEDINGS AND THE ATTACHMENT OF THE RIGHT TO COUNSEL   The most important cases defining the moment at which the right to counsel attaches have concerned various pretrial proceedings. They are part of the complex system of modern justice that expanded in the twentieth century to expedite large numbers of criminal cases and to provide substantial justice (see Chapter 10). These cases have developed the general rule that a lawyer must be provided to an indigent defendant in every **critical stage** of the criminal process. The critical stage doctrine was developed prior to *Gideon*. A unanimous Court in **Hamilton v. Alabama** (1961) ruled that, under Alabama law, an *arraignment* in a *capital case* was a critical stage because it was the only point in the criminal process at which a defendant could raise an insanity defense without the approval of the trial judge. Other important motions, such as a challenge to the systematic exclusion of one race from the grand jury, had to be made at arraignment. "Available defenses may be as irretrievably lost, if not then and there asserted, as they are when an accused represented by counsel waives a right for strategic purposes" (*Hamilton v. Alabama*, 1961). If an arraignment is a simple formality where no important decision is made (such as arranging for bail), then the lack of counsel is not a due process or Sixth Amendment violation. Otherwise, a defendant must be represented by an attorney.

The reasoning of *Hamilton* was applied to the *preliminary examination*. In **Coleman v. Alabama** (1970), the Supreme Court ruled that a preliminary examination is a critical stage requiring assistance of counsel. Under Alabama law, the defendant was not required to raise a defense there, but if he was without counsel to cross-examine prosecution witnesses, any testimony taken was inadmissible at trial (see Chapters 10 and 11). The Alabama courts saw this as a fair rule that prevented the lack of counsel from causing prejudice to the defendant's case. Yet Justice Brennan's majority opinion noted that (1) a lawyer's skilled cross-examination of witnesses can expose fatal weaknesses in the prosecution's case that will lead a magistrate to dismiss; (2) cross-examination of witnesses may establish a basis for impeaching witnesses at the trial; (3) trained counsel can use the hearing as a way of discovering prosecution information that can prove helpful in devising a defense strategy; and (4) counsel can be influential in making arguments for bail or for a psychiatric examination. "The inability of the indigent accused on his own to realize these advantages of a lawyer's assistance compels the conclusion that the Alabama preliminary hearing is a 'critical stage' of the State's criminal process at which the accused is 'as much entitled to such aid [of counsel]. . . as at the trial itself'" (*Coleman v. Alabama*, 1970).

The Supreme Court did not go so far as to hold that counsel was required at every pretrial proceeding. In *Gerstein v. Pugh* (1975) the Court held that although a person could not be detained for a substantial time after arrest without a probable cause hearing (see Chapter 4), because "of its limited function and its nonadversary character, the *probable cause determination* is not a 'critical stage' in the prosecution that would require appointed counsel." The Court found that a magistrate's decision as to whether probable cause existed was not critical because it would not impair a defense on the merits. Although the *Gerstein v. Pugh* no-counsel rule still applies to any magistrate's hearing that *only* decides on whether probable cause to arrest existed, its practical holding seems to have been undercut by the more recent decision of **Rothgery v. Gillespie County** (2008), which affirmed the rule that the right to counsel attaches at an *initial appearance* before a magistrate shortly after arrest.

On July 15, 2002, a few weeks after Walter Rothgery and his wife arrived from Arizona to take a job managing an RV park in Gillespie County, Texas, he was arrested for carrying a gun as a convicted felon.[17] This was based on a mistake in a computer database. In fact Rothgery had never been convicted of a felony. He was taken before a magistrate and in a brief, informal, and routine hearing (known as a 15.17 hearing after the provision in the Texas code) the magistrate verified the charge and the officer's affidavit, informed Rothgery of the accusation, set his bail at $5,000, and committed him to jail. He was released after his wife used their last $500 to release Walter and he posted a surety bond. No lawyer was provided at this hearing.

"Rothgery had no money for a lawyer. [He] made several oral and written requests for appointed counsel, which went unheeded." In January 2003 he was indicted by a grand jury and rearrested the next day. Bail was increased to $15,000. During the half year between his initial arrest and indictment, Walter was out of steady work and broke because of the charges hanging over his head when "all of the potential employers he contacted knew or learned of the criminal charge pending against him." He was sent back to a county jail one hundred miles from his home, where he sat for three weeks. He was released only after a sympathetic warden helped Walter find an attorney to obtain documentation showing he had no felony record. He was released and the weapons charge finally was dropped.

After his release he filed a Section 1983 suit for damages resulting from a violation of his constitutional rights. The precise issue in *Rothgery v. Gillespie County* was *not whether* "the right to counsel guaranteed by the Sixth Amendment applies at the first appearance before a judicial officer at which a defendant is told of the formal accusation against him and restrictions are imposed on his liberty." The Court had already held that to be the law in cases concerning the consequences of police interrogation of defendants whose right to counsel attached (*Brewer v. Williams*, 1977; *Michigan v. Jackson*, 1986, see Chapter 7). The general rule is that the right to counsel, is "pegged [to] commencement [of] 'the initiation of adversary judicial criminal proceedings—whether by way of formal charge, preliminary hearing, indictment, information, or arraignment.'"

The issue in *Rothgery* was "whether Texas's article 15.17 hearing" marks the point when the state is obliged "to appoint counsel *within a reasonable time* once a request for assistance is made" (*Rothgery v. Gillespie County*, 2008, emphasis added). Justice Souter's review of precedent held (8–1) that it was. The facts in *Rothgery* fit the underlying rule that a prosecution begins at "the point at which the government has committed itself to prosecute, the adverse positions of government and defendant have solidified, and the accused finds himself faced with the prosecutorial forces of organized society, and immersed in the intricacies of substantive and procedural criminal law (*Rothgery v. Gillespie County*, 2008, internal quotation marks and citations omitted). Therefore,

> by the time a defendant is brought before a judicial officer, is informed of a formally lodged accusation, and has restrictions imposed on his liberty in aid of the prosecution, the State's relationship with the defendant has become solidly adversarial. And that is just as true when the proceeding comes before the indictment (in the case of the initial arraignment on a formal complaint) as when it comes after it (at an arraignment on an indictment). (*Rothgery v. Gillespie County*, 2008)

To support its ruling, the Court pointed out that forty-three states by statute require that counsel be appointed before, at, or just after the initial appearance. The majority brushed aside various arguments, such as Texas's assertion that defense counsel should be provided when the prosecutor becomes aware of charges. Such a rule would be unworkable and subject to manipulation.

Following Walter Rothgery's Supreme Court victory, his lawsuit culminated in a $40,000 settlement approved by the Gillespie County Commissioners. While less than he wished, his lawyer said that he would get some compensation for the three weeks he spent in jail unnecessarily and for other losses he suffered while waiting for the county to appoint him an attorney. On a broader scale, news accounts indicated that a number of Texas counties were taking steps to improve their indigent legal defense programs to provide counsel earlier, as is the general practice. One news account quoted Rothgery as saying "Texas really is part of America now."

Justice Alito, concurring in *Rothgery*, raised the point that the decision did not hold that an attorney must be present during the initial appearance, a point quietly acknowledged in Justice Souter's majority opinion. Therefore, as the law now stands, it is possible for counsel to "attach" in a proceeding that is not a critical stage. In several cases the Supreme Court has ruled that counsel is not required in proceedings held to not be "criminal prosecutions" because the state has not yet formally committed itself to prosecute, even though they could have been interpreted as critical stages. This included a pre-indictment lineup (*Kirby v. Illinois*, 1972) and a period during which prisoners are held in administrative detention under suspicion of having committed in-prison crimes but are not yet formally charged (*United States v. Gouveia*, 1984).

GRANTS OF RIGHT TO COUNSEL BY STATUTE—CLEMENCY HEARINGS Many states extend the right to counsel to defendants in various proceedings by *legislation* in proceedings where the Supreme Court has held that there is no *constitutional* right to counsel. Exploring such statutes in detail is beyond the scope of this text. ***Harbison v. Bell*** (2009) provides an example of statutorily created right to counsel for proceedings other than trial. The Supreme Court interpreted a federal statute that allows the federal appointment of an attorney to pursue federal habeas corpus on behalf of an indigent defendant sentenced to death in a state court. The statute also provided for indigent counsel in federal death penalty cases. The issue was whether a portion of the statute that extended the appointment to "represent the defendant in . . . [subsequent] proceedings for executive or other clemency as may be available to the defendant" applied only to federal defendants or to state defendants as well. The Court held that the statute extended the appointment to state defendants. It decided that this was correct from the *plain meaning* of the text and from its *legislative history*. For example, federal clemency is vested exclusively in the executive (the president) while in some states clemency is vested in pardon boards or the legislature. It thus makes sense that "other clemency" referred to state proceedings. The Court also dismissed the government's fears that this interpretation would require appointing federal counsel to the retrial of successful habeas defendants in state courts because retrials are not subsequent but new procedures. Finally, the Court ruled that clemency is not simply a matter of grace but is a "fail safe" in the criminal justice system, and that an attorney who has prepared a habeas corpus petition has generated substantial information about a case that "may provide the basis for a persuasive clemency application."

Counsel in Correctional Procedures

PROBATION AND PAROLE REVOCATION   The Supreme Court ruled in *Gagnon v. Scarpelli* (1973) (probation) and *Morrissey v. Brewer* (1972) (parole) that "[p]robation revocation, like parole revocation, is not a stage of a criminal prosecution, but does result in a loss of liberty" (*Gagnon v. Scarpelli*, 1973). As a result, neither probation nor parole can be revoked without a formal due process hearing that requires notice, disclosure of evidence, an opportunity to be heard, a neutral hearing body, and written statements of the fact-finders. In neither case, however, was counsel required by the Sixth Amendment. Instead of holding that counsel be required as a matter of due process fundamental fairness, the Court established more flexible due process rules. The Court offered guidelines in *Gagnon:*

> Presumptively, . . . counsel should be provided in cases where, after being informed of his right to request counsel, the probationer or parolee makes such a request, based on a timely and colorable claim (i) that he has not committed the alleged violation of the conditions upon which he is at liberty; or (ii) that, even if the violation is a matter of public record or is uncontested, there are substantial reasons which justified or mitigated the violation and make revocation inappropriate, and that the reasons are complex or otherwise difficult to develop or present. In passing on a request for the appointment of counsel, the responsible agency also should consider, especially in doubtful cases, whether the probationer appears to be capable of speaking effectively for himself. (*Gagnon v. Scarpelli*, 1973)

Gagnon in effect resurrected the *Betts v. Brady* special circumstances test for the requirement of counsel for indigent defendants at probation revocation hearings.

PRISON DISCIPLINARY HEARINGS   Prisoners have even fewer procedural rights in disciplinary hearings than do probationers or parolees facing revocation, since they have much less freedom to lose than probationers or parolees. In *Wolff v. McDonnell* (1974), the Court required a due process hearing before an inmate could be subjected to major institutional forms of discipline involving losses of liberty, such as placement in solitary confinement or a loss of good time. But the dangerous reality of prisons, when combined with the lesser liberty interest of prisoners, led the Court to conclude that inmates had no absolute right to confront and cross-examine witnesses and were, therefore, at the mercy of the prison hearing officer's discretion. As for counsel, the Court, after reviewing its ruling in *Gagnon*, said, "At this stage of the development of these procedures we are not prepared to hold that inmates have a right to either retained or appointed counsel in disciplinary proceedings." Thus, whereas a probationer facing revocation has a right to the assistance of **retained counsel**, a prisoner has no Fourteenth Amendment right to a paid lawyer's presence in an administrative prison disciplinary hearing. In the interests of inmate safety and prison security, a prison may legitimately bar all attorneys from disciplinary hearings.

The Right to Counsel on Appeal

"[E]very state and the federal system provide some means of review to defendants in criminal cases. However, according to a long line of Supreme Court opinions, there is no constitutional mandate that states provide any type of review process for defendants convicted in their criminal courts."[18] If so, does this mean that there is no right to counsel on appeal? The appellate process is not included within the wording of the Sixth Amendment's "criminal prosecution." The Supreme Court analyzed the question of the right to counsel on appeal in state courts under the Fourteenth Amendment and has applied a functional analysis. It has concluded that counsel is required on first appeals as of right but is not required for subsequent, discretionary appeals.

RIGHT TO COUNSEL ON FIRST, MANDATORY APPEAL   *Douglas v. California* (1963) held that the Fourteenth Amendment guarantees a defendant the right to representation of counsel on a *first, mandatory appeal*. By 1963, every state granted a convicted criminal defendant the right to one mandatory appeal, but not every state guaranteed counsel for these appeals. In California, the rule allowed a court after reviewing part of the trial record to appoint counsel for an indigent convicted person *only* if in the court's discretion an attorney would serve any useful purpose. In contrast, counsel was always appointed for indigents on mandatory first appeals from convictions in federal court, whether or not the federal court thought that a lawyer was needed.

The U.S. Supreme Court held that the California procedure was invidious discrimination against those who were too poor to hire a lawyer to assist them on appeal. It relied on the *Griffin v. Illinois* "equality principle." The majority thought it unfair that a person with means will present his or her case to the appellate court with "the full benefit of written briefs and oral argument by counsel," while a person who cannot afford a lawyer has to rely on a judge to review the record without the benefit of partisan legal analysis and argument. A case often has hidden merit, and a neutral reviewer, rather than a partisan attorney, can miss it. Justice William O. Douglas's majority opinion was not a model of doctrinal clarity, and his writing mixed up Due Process Clause fairness concerns with Equal Protection Clause equality concerns, a point that was challenged by the dissent. This decision did not apply to second, discretionary appeals, such as writs of habeas corpus or petitions for certiorari. The decision also acknowledged that some differences based on wealth can stand as long as the state does not draw pernicious lines between the rich and the poor. For example, an indigent granted counsel cannot insist on the most highly paid lawyer available.

Justice Harlan's dissenting opinion concluded that the Equal Protection Clause is not the proper basis for a holding. Rather, the issue should be whether California's procedure violated the fair trial rule of the Due Process Clause. He felt that it did not. In his view, there was no equal protection violation because the state does not deny appeals to indigents and because the state cannot lift all disabilities flowing from economic differences. As for the due process issue, he noted that appellate review is not required by the Fourteenth Amendment, and therefore issues of fairness had to be decided in the context of the state's providing a discretionary benefit. He felt that issues that arise on appeal are not as complex as factual issues at a trial, and so it was fair to allow state judges to review a case to see whether a lawyer was needed in a particular appeal.

Halbert v. Michigan (2005) held, under the precedent of *Douglas*, that counsel must be appointed for an indigent defendant who *pleaded guilty* and was first appealing to an intermediate court of appeals, whose role was to correct errors in defendants' convictions. Michigan amended its constitution to make first appeals discretionary where defendants waived trials and pleaded guilty. The Supreme Court noted that complicated issues could confront defendants who pleaded guilty, including constitutional defects irrelevant to factual guilt, jurisdictional defects, preserved entrapment claims, mental competency claims, and the like. Furthermore, at least two-thirds of inmates, most of whom pleaded guilty, suffer from illiteracy or very low reading skills, failure to complete high school, learning disabilities (like Antonio Halbert), or mental illness, making it unlikely that they could properly prepare the papers required to file leaves to appeal.

RIGHT TO COUNSEL ON SECOND, DISCRETIONARY APPEALS   A decade after *Douglas v. California*, a more conservative Supreme Court refused to extend the guarantee of counsel to *second, discretionary appeals*. *Ross v. Moffitt* (1974) involved two convictions against Claude Moffitt for uttering forged instruments in two different North Carolina counties. In both cases, Moffitt appealed as of right, represented by assigned counsel, and lost both appeals. He then sought the appointment of counsel to pursue a discretionary habeas corpus writ to the state supreme court. After a failure in the state appeal, he sought appointment of counsel to prepare petitions for a writ of certiorari to the U.S. Supreme Court. North Carolina opposed the granting of counsel as a matter of constitutional right. The U.S. Court of Appeals for the Fourth Circuit ruled that the principle of *Douglas v. California* applied even when a convicted person was taking a second appeal to a court that had discretion to deny the appeal. Many state supreme courts, like the U.S. Supreme Court, may decline to take cases, or decide to hear them primarily because the issue raised is of significant public importance. They may deny appeals even if a particular case might have been wrongly decided against a petitioner's interest. Nevertheless, according to the Court of Appeals,

[a] defendant with adequate resources to engage counsel has a meaningful right to seek access to the state's highest court. An indigent should be afforded counsel to give him a comparably meaningful right. . . . Denied the assistance of a competent lawyer, the quality of justice for the indigent has been substantially impaired in comparison with the quality of justice afforded his more affluent brothers. (*Moffitt v. Ross*, 483 F.2d 650, 653, 4th Cir. 1973)

The Supreme Court reversed in an opinion by Justice Rehnquist, borrowing somewhat from Justice Harlan's dissent in *Douglas*. Justice Rehnquist first ruled that the Due Process Clause does not require a state to provide a convicted person—who has been represented by counsel at trial and by counsel at the one appeal as of right—with counsel on his discretionary appeal to the state supreme court. Relying on the fact that the Constitution does not mandate appeals and that a defendant in Moffitt's position is seeking to overturn a conviction, he reasoned that there would be unfairness "only if indigents are singled out by the State and denied meaningful access to the appellate system because of their poverty." Viewing the issue as one better analyzed under equal protection, he turned to that clause.

The "Fourteenth Amendment 'does not require absolute equality or precisely equal advantages.' . . . It only requires that the state appellate system be 'free of unreasoned distinctions.'" The majority noted that because the indigent person had already "received the benefit of counsel in examining the record of his trial" in the appeal as of right, there was no "unreasoned distinction" in allowing a wealthier person with a lawyer to pursue a writ while not providing counsel for an indigent petitioner. The high court will have the transcript and appellate papers prepared by counsel for the earlier appeal. This is especially so because the purpose of discretionary appeals "is not whether there has been 'a correct adjudication of guilt' in every individual case, . . . but rather whether 'the subject matter of the appeal has significant public interest,' [or] whether 'the cause involves legal principles of major significance to the jurisprudence of the State.'"

Justice William Douglas, at the twilight of his career, dissented in *Ross* on the equality and fairness grounds specified in *Douglas*. He quoted from *Douglas v. California* that the "same concepts of fairness and equality, which require counsel in a first appeal of right, require counsel in other and subsequent discretionary appeals." But that belief, so resonant to an older generation, failed to convince a newer generation of justices that the Constitution required state and local governments to pay for counsel in the context of discretionary appeals.

RIGHT TO COUNSEL FOR DISCRETIONARY APPEAL BY INDIGENT DEATH-ROW INMATES
Murray v. Giarratano (1989) held that, under *Ross*, indigent death-row inmates seeking postconviction review of their death sentences, after their first appeals, had no Fourteenth Amendment right to counsel at the expense of the state. The majority was unmoved by the petitioner's three arguments, which four dissenting justices saw as valid: (1) Death-row inmates are under greater emotional stress than other inmates and thus less able to write adequate legal briefs; (2) Virginia's law postponed some issues normally heard at first appeal to the postconviction proceedings, thus making these second appeals more like first appeals for death-row inmates; and (3) "a grim deadline imposes a finite [time] limit on the condemned person's capacity for useful research." In rejecting these arguments, the Court emphatically limited the right to counsel on Fourteenth Amendment equal protection and due process grounds in procedures other than the trial. While indigents retain the same basic rights as wealthier persons, there are limits to what the state must do to remedy the infirmities in the justice system caused by economic inequality.

THE RIGHT TO SELF-REPRESENTATION

The Sixth Amendment right to the assistance of counsel co-exists with a defendant's seemingly contradictory but perhaps more fundamental right of self-representation. Before the Supreme Court constitutionalized a defendant's right to proceed *pro se*—in one's own behalf—federal statutes and the laws of thirty-six states upheld such a right.[19] **Self-representation** reflects the American value of self-reliance and a distrust of lawyers. Some have defended themselves in notorious political trials in order to publicize their perspectives. Angela Davis, an African-American communist and philosophy instructor, was tried in California for abetting the murder of a judge in the Soledad Brothers case. She represented herself, with some legal assistance, and won an acquittal in 1972.

An excellent empirical study estimates that the prevalence of ***pro se* defense** in federal and state felony cases is approximately 0.3 to 0.5 percent annually, or about 3,000 to 5,000 cases.[20] The study supports the view that *pro se* defense is most likely when a defendant becomes frustrated with the actual or perceived incompetence of assigned counsel or a public defender, or when a defendant sharply disagrees with counsel's legal strategy.[21] An indigent defendant, who has no right to select a particular lawyer, may also demand self-representation as leverage to get rid of an obviously incompetent lawyer after a request for a new lawyer is denied.[22] Finally, a small proportion of *pro se* defendants, perhaps 10 percent, will represent themselves to promote an ideological cause, such as the unconstitutionality of the tax system.[23]

Faretta v. California

In ***Faretta v. California*** (1975), the Supreme Court decided (6–3) that the Sixth Amendment established a right to self-representation and set down guidelines for *pro se* defense. Justice Stewart, writing for the majority, said that the issue "is whether a State may constitutionally hale a person into its criminal courts and there force a lawyer upon him, even when he insists that he wants to conduct his own defense" (*Faretta v. California*, 1975). Faretta, charged with grand theft, had previously defended himself in court. He believed his assigned counsel in the Los Angeles Superior Court was too burdened with a large caseload to adequately assist him. The trial judge questioned Faretta about the hearsay rule and the law regarding challenges to potential jurors and ruled that he had no constitutional right to self-representation. The trial was conducted with appointed counsel.

The core of the Supreme Court's decision was the significance of the Sixth Amendment's text:

> The Sixth Amendment does not provide merely that a defense shall be made for the accused; it grants to the accused personally the right to make his defense. It is the accused, not counsel, who must be "informed of the nature and cause of the accusation," who must be "confronted with the witnesses against him," and who must be accorded "compulsory process for obtaining witnesses in his favor." Although not stated in the Amendment in so many words, the right to self-representation—to make one's own defense personally—is thus necessarily implied by the structure of the Amendment. The right to defend is given directly to the accused; for it is he who suffers the consequences if the defense fails.
>
> . . .
>
> The counsel provision supplements this design. It speaks of the "assistance" of counsel, and an assistant, however expert, is still an assistant. The language and spirit of the Sixth Amendment contemplate that counsel, like the other defense tools guaranteed by the Amendment, shall be an aid to a willing defendant—not an organ of the State interposed between an unwilling defendant and his right to defend himself personally. To thrust counsel upon the accused, against his considered wish, thus violates the logic of the Amendment. In such a case, counsel is not an assistant, but a master; and the right to make a defense is stripped of the personal character upon which the Amendment insists. It is true that when a defendant chooses to have a lawyer manage and present his case, law and tradition may allocate to the counsel the power to make binding decisions of trial strategy in many areas. . . . This allocation can only be justified, however, by the defendant's consent, at the outset, to accept counsel as his representative. An unwanted counsel "represents" the defendant only through a tenuous and unacceptable legal fiction. Unless the accused has acquiesced in such representation, the defense presented is not the defense guaranteed him by the Constitution, for, in a very real sense, it is not his defense. (*Faretta v. California*, 1975)

Therefore, the right to counsel announced in *Gideon v. Wainwright* was not inconsistent with the right to self-representation: "Personal liberties are not rooted in the law of averages. The right to defend is personal" (*Faretta v. California*, 1975).

On the other hand, self-representation is not a license. To accept a waiver of counsel, a judge has to be convinced that a defendant has the minimal ability to conduct the trial. "A defendant need not himself have the skill and experience of a lawyer in order competently and intelligently to choose self-representation" (*Faretta v. California*, 1975). A judge cannot deny self-representation to a defendant simply because the defendant does not have expert knowledge of criminal law and procedure. The record in the case showed "that Faretta was literate, competent, and understanding, and that he was voluntarily exercising his informed free will." The trial judge was in error in denying him the right to represent himself, even if he did not have expert knowledge of hearsay rules (*Faretta v. California*, 1975).

Chief Justice Burger dissented in *Faretta*. He saw the basic right as the Sixth Amendment right to a fair trial. The entire justice system and the people at large have a stake in a fair and competent trial system. "That goal is ill-served, and the integrity of and public confidence in the system are undermined, when an easy conviction is obtained due to the defendant's ill-advised decision to waive counsel." Furthermore, the dissent saw the majority opinion as undermining the authority of the trial judge, who should retain final discretion on this question, because the judge "is in the best position to determine whether the accused is capable of conducting his defense."

In sum, the waiver of counsel is an unusual and extreme step. When requested, a judge should personally inform the defendant who wishes to defend *pro se* "of the many procedural complications of representing oneself, that he will be given no special treatment, and that waiving counsel is generally unwise."[24] In the colloquy with the defendant, the judge takes pains to ensure that the waiver is voluntary, that it is unequivocal and expressed, that it is knowing and intelligent, and that the defendant is mentally able to make the waiver. The verbal exchange between the judge and the defendant is placed on the record. If, after all this, the defendant meets the minimum standard of competency and continues to insist on self-representation, the judge has no right to deny self-representation.

The Supreme Court ruled, in **Martinez v. Court of Appeal** (2000), that *Faretta* does not create a right to *pro se* representation *on appeal*. Martinez, a self-described self-taught paralegal with extensive law firm experience, represented himself at trial and was convicted of fraud. California refused to allow his self-representation on appeal. The Supreme Court found historical record of a self-representation right on appeal. Criminal appeals, in fact, did not exist at common law and were not common in American states until the early twentieth century.

Because the Sixth Amendment, which applies to "criminal prosecutions," simply "does not include any right to appeal," any self-representation right on appeal has to be based on due process or equal protection grounds. The right to self-representation at trial balances a defendant's autonomy with the state's need for fair and orderly trials, and the defendant's rights under *Faretta* are not absolute. Having dashed cold water on *pro se* representation, Justice Stevens found that in "the appellate context, the balance between the two competing interests surely tips in favor of the State," which supported the holding that the constitution does not require a state to allow *pro se* representation on appeal.

Justice Stevens's opinion for a unanimous Court was so hostile to self-representation that Justice Scalia wrote a concurrence supporting that basic right, which was given constitutional protection in *Faretta*. These opposing views erupted again in *Indiana v. Edwards* (2008), discussed in a following section.

Standby Counsel

The practice of the judge appointing **standby counsel** to assist a *pro se* defendant was upheld by the Supreme Court in **McKaskle v. Wiggins** (1984). Justice Sandra Day O'Connor ruled that a defendant's Sixth Amendment rights are not violated when standby counsel is appointed, even over the defendant's objection. To ensure that standby counsel does not overwhelm the defendant's personal right to make a defense, two rules guide the conduct of such counsel and determine when the attorney might have undermined the defendant's rights:

> First, the *pro se* defendant is entitled to preserve actual control over the case he chooses to present to the jury. . . . If standby counsel's participation over the defendant's objection effectively allows counsel to make or substantially interfere with any significant tactical decisions, or to control the questioning of witnesses, or to speak instead of the defendant on any matter of importance, the *Faretta* right is eroded.

Second, participation by standby counsel without the defendant's consent should not be allowed to destroy the jury's perception that the defendant is representing himself. The defendant's appearance in the status of one conducting his own defense . . . exists to affirm the accused's individual dignity and autonomy. (*McKaskle v. Wiggins*, 1984)

Dissenting justices suggested that this two-pronged rule actually gives trial judges little guidance on how to restrain standby counsel from taking over the case from the self-represented defendant. Also, the dissenters sharply differed with the majority about whether the activity of standby counsel in this case (including over fifty interventions in a three-day trial precipitating some disagreements that were observed by the jury) amounted to a violation of the *Faretta* self-representation right.

Four reasons support the regular appointment of standby counsel. First, if a *pro se* defendant, purposely or out of confusion, decides during trial to ask for a lawyer, there will be no delay—standby counsel will be able to immediately continue the case. Second, by providing expert advice, standby counsel helps the *pro se* defendant "exercise his right of self-representation more effectively and begins to level the playing field in the courtroom."[25] Third, standby counsel can assist "a defendant of questionable mental or emotional fortitude" who still meets the low appointment standard of *Godinez v. Moran* (1993) in making a meaningful defense and thus maintain the fairness of the judicial process.[26] Finally, standby counsel eliminates the appearance of bias created when the judge gives the defendant practice pointers during the trial.

Some problems may occur from the use of standby counsel, however. As *McKaskle v. Wiggins* noted, when standby counsel interferes too much, the defendant may feel that his or her right to self-representation is infringed. Also, it is unwise for a court to appoint as standby counsel the lawyer whom the defendant dismissed. Finally, "hybrid representation," where both the defendant and standby counsel appear before the jury, should be disallowed. It causes confusion in the jury's mind and may **prejudice the case**. To correct this, Marie Williams suggests that (1) standby counsel be appointed in every *pro se* defense, (2) the jury be instructed as to the constitutionality and nature of standby counsel, and (3) that hybrid representation not be allowed except when the defendant is cross-examining the victim and when the defendant takes the stand to testify.[27] Empirical evidence suggests that standby counsel is appointed in the overwhelming majority of self-representation cases, as high as 88 percent in one federal sample.[28]

Standards for Self-Representation—Limiting the Right?

In *Indiana v. Edwards* (2008) the Supreme Court held that a trial court could deny a defendant suffering from schizophrenia the right to defend himself *pro se* even though Edwards had the capacity to knowingly and voluntarily waive counsel and was competent to stand trial. The majority decision reflected a growing, and possibly misguided, skepticism about the value of *pro se* representation and the mental competence of those who desire to represent themselves.

The *Indiana v. Edwards* Court refused to overrule *Faretta* and refused to set a bright-line standard to guide trial judges as to when a defendant is competent to represent him- or herself. *Faretta* suggested that the bar against self-representation be set low. The Court in *Godinez v. Moran* (1993) held that the standard of competency to waive counsel is the same as the standard to stand trial. That standard includes "both (1) whether the defendant has a rational as well as factual understanding of the proceedings against him and (2) whether the defendant has sufficient present ability to consult with his lawyer with a reasonable degree of rational understanding" (*Indiana v. Edwards*, internal quotations and emphases omitted). The essential facts in *Godinez v. Moran* were that a murder case defendant dismissed his attorneys and pled guilty. Psychologists declared him competent to stand trial. The judge further decided that Moran knew the consequences of entering a guilty plea and was able to waive the right of counsel knowingly and intelligently. He was sentenced to death. On appeal the Supreme Court held that although the decision to plead guilty is a profound one, such a decision is no more complicated than the decisions a criminal defendant during trial must make to consult with and assist his counsel. The Court ruled that a more exacting "capacity for reasoned choice" among alternatives available to a defendant was not required.

Justice Breyer, writing for the majority in *Indiana v. Edwards*, distinguished *Godinez*. The competence in *Edwards* was the competence to *conduct a trial*, not simply the competence to assist counsel, to waive a trial, and to plead guilty. Relying on the need for and *appearance* of a *fair trial*, "the most basic of the Constitution's criminal law objectives," the court held that "the Constitution permits States to insist upon representation by counsel for those competent enough to stand trial . . . but who still suffer from severe mental illness to the point where they are not competent to conduct trial proceedings by themselves."

In a spirited dissent, Justice Scalia, joined by Justice Thomas, pointed out that an attorney was forced on Edwards who pursued a defense with which his client disagreed. In sync with his views on the importance of specific trial rights (see Chapter 11, "Confrontation" section), Justice Scalia raised the value of free choice in this situation above that of what may be seen as a fair trial:

> When a defendant appreciates the risks of forgoing counsel and chooses to do so voluntarily, the Constitution protects his ability to present his own defense even when that harms his case. . . . [T]he defendant's choice must be honored out of that respect for the individual which is the lifeblood of the law. What the Constitution requires is not that a State's case be subject to the most rigorous adversarial testing possible— after all, it permits a defendant to eliminate *all* adversarial testing by pleading guilty. What the Constitution requires is that a defendant be given the right to challenge the State's case against him using the arguments *he* sees fit. (*Indiana v. Edwards*, 2008, Scalia, J., dissenting, internal quotations and citations omitted, emphasis in original).

He also characterized the "appearance of a fair trial" basis of the decision, which allowed a judge to impose a lawyer on a competent defendant who was quite able to represent himself when lucid, as "the epitome of both actual and apparent unfairness."

The majority opinion in *Edwards* seems motivated in part by the view of some judges that *pro se* defense has led to "trials that are unfair." A number of highly publicized cases have portrayed self-representation making a mockery of justice, including a trial conducted by the psychotic defendant Colin Ferguson, who killed six and wounded nineteen commuters on the Long Island Rail Road in 1993,[29] or the bizarre antics of Zacarias Moussaoui, a conspirator in the September 11, 2001, terror attack in his pretrial hearings.[30] In the absence of data, these all-too-real anecdotes have created the appearance that all *pro se* defendants are mentally ill and that they do not fare well at trial. An excellent study by Professor Erica Hashimoto, which was quoted by Justice Breyer in *Edwards* and may have played a role in the decision to *not* overrule *Faretta*, refutes both of these contentions. She used two large state and federal trial data sets and a smaller set from federal criminal dockets that provided sufficient information to draw qualified conclusions about *pro se* defendants. First, as to the mental disabilities of pro se defendants, she noted that federal judges order competency hearings if a defendant shows any signs of instability, for fear of having convictions overturned. Only 22 percent of the defendants in the large federal court data base were referred to observation. The fact that 9 percent were sent to observation *after* they asked to represent themselves may reflect the biases of federal judges. On average, 10 to 30 percent of state defendants referred to observation are declared incompetent. Hashimoto inferred that the overwhelming majority of *pro se* defendants are competent.[31]

The other issue is whether *pro se* defendants are inevitably convicted. Her state court sample did *better* than average. A smaller percent pled guilty, but twice the proportion of *pro se* felony defendants pled guilty to *misdemeanors* as represented defendants. Twice the proportion also had cases dismissed. Of those who went to trial, the acquittal rate, based on the entire sample and not just of those who went to trial, was the *same* for *pro se* and represented defendants. Results for federal defendants showed that *pro se* defendants did slightly worse than represented defendants and, as in the state sample, the overall acquittal rate was the same.[32] These findings, despite limitations of the data, show that "defendants choose to represent themselves not because they suffer from mental illness, but instead because they are dissatisfied with counsel."[33]

Prof. Hashimoto made it clear that her findings did not undermine the importance of the *Gideon* rule requiring legal representation, but only that given the serious deficiencies with legal representation in America (see "Law in Society" section, this chapter), *pro se* representation is a rational choice for a very small and select group. She also suggested that court systems look into the possibility that unqualified defendants are being pressured to represent themselves in misdemeanor cases for improper reasons and that advice to defendants who desire to represent themselves be thorough. She also suggested that courts take mental illness into account for defendants who show signs of instability, although that does not seem to be much of a problem after *Indiana v. Edwards* (2008). She concluded by strongly supporting the importance of appointing standby counsel.

THE EFFECTIVE ASSISTANCE OF COUNSEL

In 1970, the Supreme Court ruled that the Sixth Amendment assistance of counsel guarantee in criminal cases means the *effective* assistance of retained and appointed counsel (*McMann v. Richardson*, 1970). The Court clarified the meaning of "effective assistance" in *Strickland v. Washington* (1984) and established rules for interpreting this standard in practice.

Read Case and Comments: *Strickland v. Washington.*

Applying the *Strickland* Test

Strickland's rules apply not only to felony trials and death penalty sentencing, but also at plea bargaining (*Hill v. Lockhart*, 1985). **Glover v. United States** (2001) held that an attorney's failure to argue a point under the federal sentencing guidelines, possibly resulting in an increase in the defendant's sentence of *six months' imprisonment*, was a sufficiently large loss to raise an effective assistance of counsel argument. Under *Strickland v. Washington*, a defendant establishes prejudice when a trial court makes a sentencing guidelines error, the attorney fails to argue against the error, and as a result the defendant's sentence is increased. It is not clear whether *Glover* applies to state sentencing processes that are entirely indeterminate, discretionary, and unstructured. These proceedings involve standardless discretion where what constitutes attorney error is not clear and it may be impossible to establish criteria of effective assistance. Capital sentencing and guideline sentencing, however, have elements of an adversary trial so that the standards of *Strickland*'s two-pronged test can be applied.

The Supreme Court has applied commonsense reasoning combined with deference to the judgment of defense lawyers in not requiring them to go to extreme and unnecessary lengths in defending clients. Thus, an attorney's representation was competent, in a capital case, where evidence of guilt was overwhelming, the client refused to cooperate despite the lawyer's attempts to communicate, and the lawyer decided to "concentrate the defense on establishing, at the penalty phase, cause for sparing the defendant's life" (**Florida v. Nixon,** 2004). Likewise, the Court held that an attorney is not required to go through a hopeless proceeding simply on the ground that the defendant had "nothing to lose." In this case Nixon was tried for killing his nineteen-year-old cousin, after stabbing her nine times with a hunting knife and shooting her four times, in a bifurcated trial that included a guilt phase and a not guilty by reason of insanity (NGI) phase. The strategy was to enter evidence of insanity at the guilt phase to negate premeditation, followed by the NGI phase. The jury found defendant guilty of first-degree murder, and defendant's parents, disheartened, refused to testify for him at the NGI trial. The only evidence at the NGI trial was the evidence of insanity presented at the guilt phase. On counsel's recommendation, defendant withdrew the NGI plea. The Supreme Court rejected a "nothing to lose" standard for evaluating claims under *Strickland* (*Knowles v. Mirzayance*, 2009).

PROOF OF INEFFECTIVE ASSISTANCE   *United States v. Cronic* (1984) ruled that ineffective assistance of counsel must be *affirmatively proven*; it must not be inferred. Cronic, convicted of mail fraud, claimed ineffective assistance of counsel because (1) his lawyer was inexperienced; (2) the charge was serious; (3) the case facts were complex; (4) the time to investigate was limited to thirty days; and (5) some witnesses were inaccessible. The *Strickland* standard puts the *burden of proof on the convicted complainant* to prove that his or her lawyer's assistance was ineffective. Cronic raised a set of relevant factors but *could not point to any specific action* by his lawyer that showed deficient performance. If Cronic's position were accepted, the Court could find ineffective assistance even though the lawyer's performance was flawless. None of the factors in the case, alone or in combination, deprived Cronic of a fair trial: Relevant evidence was supplied, and the government's evidence was cross-examined. The Court also noted in *Cronic* that the test of adequate performance did not require that the lawyer perform flawlessly in a trial. "When a true adversarial criminal trial has been conducted—even if defense counsel may have made demonstrable errors—the kind of testing envisioned by the Sixth Amendment has occurred."

CASE AND COMMENTS

Strickland v. Washington

466 U.S. 668, 104 S.Ct. 2052, 80 L.Ed.2d 674 (1984)

JUSTICE O'CONNOR delivered the opinion of the Court.

* * *

I

A

[Respondent, David Leroy Washington, was found guilty and sentenced to death in Florida for a crime spree that included three murders, torture, kidnapping, and theft. He confessed to the police. Against the advice of his experienced, assigned defense lawyer, Washington waived a jury trial and pleaded guilty, telling the judge that he accepted responsibility for his acts. Against counsel's advice, once again, Washington also waived an advisory jury on the death penalty issue.] **[a]**

[After his trial, conviction, and death sentence, Washington appealed as of right to the Florida Supreme Court, which upheld his conviction and sentence. A collateral state appeal on the grounds of ineffective assistance of counsel resulted in a ruling, upheld by the Florida Supreme Court, that Washington's lawyer was competent. Washington then filed a petition for a writ of habeas corpus in federal district court; an evidentiary hearing resulted in finding the lawyer competent. An en banc decision of the federal circuit court ultimately reversed and remanded. Florida petitioned the federal decision to the U.S. Supreme Court, which reversed the court of appeals, finding that the federal district court was correct in denying the writ of habeas corpus.]

* * *

In preparing for the sentencing hearing, counsel spoke with respondent about his background. He also spoke on the telephone with respondent's wife and mother, though he did not follow up on the one unsuccessful effort to meet with them. He did not otherwise seek out character witnesses for respondent. **[b]** * * * Nor did he request a psychiatric examination, since his conversations with his client gave no indication that respondent had psychological problems. * * *

Counsel decided not to present and hence not to look further for evidence concerning respondent's character and emotional state. That decision reflected trial counsel's sense of hopelessness about overcoming the evidentiary effect of respondent's confessions to the gruesome crimes. * * * It also reflected the judgment that it was advisable to rely on the plea colloquy for evidence about respondent's background and about his claim of emotional stress: the plea colloquy communicated sufficient information about these subjects, and by foregoing the opportunity to present new evidence on these subjects, counsel prevented the State from cross-examining respondent on his claim and from putting on psychiatric evidence of its own.

Counsel also excluded from the sentencing hearing other evidence he thought was potentially damaging. He successfully moved to exclude respondent's "rap sheet." **[c]** * * * Because he judged that a presentence report might prove more detrimental than helpful, as it would have included respondent's criminal history and thereby undermined the claim of no significant history of criminal activity, he did not request that one be prepared. * * *

At the sentencing hearing, counsel's strategy [stressed Washington's remorse, his acceptance of responsibility, the stress that he claimed he was under at the time of the crime spree, and his apparently clean prior criminal record]. The State put on evidence and witnesses largely for the purpose of describing the details of the crimes. Counsel did not cross-examine the medical experts who testified about the manner of death of respondent's victims.

[The trial judge found that the aggravating circumstances outweighed the mitigating circumstances and sentenced Washington to death.]

* * *

B

* * * Respondent challenged counsel's assistance in six respects. He asserted that counsel was ineffective because he failed to move for a continuance to prepare for sentencing, to request a psychiatric report, to investigate and present character witnesses, to seek a presentence investigation report, to present meaningful arguments to the sentencing judge, and to investigate the medical examiner's reports or cross-examine the medical experts. **[d]** In support of the claim, respondent submitted 14 affidavits from friends, neighbors, and relatives stating that they would have testified if asked to do so. He also submitted one psychiatric report and one psychological report stating that respondent, though not under the

[a] For purposes of effective assistance of counsel, the guilt phase and the death penalty phase of a capital trial are treated the same; the jury's binary decision of one of two sentences, death or life, parallels the guilty/not guilty verdict.

[b] Character witnesses testify only about a defendant's general reputation and rarely make negative statements. Judges are less likely to be impressed by character witnesses than are jurors.

[c] Washington's lawyer seems to be doing little to present mitigating factors and some of the positive and human sides of his client, but he also keeps damaging information out of consideration by this strategy.

[d] This information was gathered by Washington's appellate lawyers, who sought to reverse the death penalty by showing that it resulted from the ineffectiveness of his trial attorney.

influence of extreme mental or emotional disturbance, was "chronically frustrated and depressed because of his economic dilemma" at the time of his crimes.

[Florida courts found Washington's six claims to be groundless: (1) there was no legal basis for seeking a continuance; (2) state psychiatric examinations of Washington disclosed no mental abnormalities; (3) character witnesses would not have rebutted aggravating circumstances and would have added no mitigating circumstances; (4) a presentence report would have brought out the respondent's prior criminal record, which was otherwise kept out of the proceedings; (5) counsel presented an "admirable" argument for the respondent in light of the overwhelming nature of the aggravating circumstances; and (6) cross-examination of the state's medical witnesses could have led the prosecution, on rebuttal, to undermine Washington's claim that he was under stress when he went on his crime spree.]

* * * [T]he trial court concluded * * * "there is not even the remotest chance that the outcome would have been any different. The plain fact is that the aggravating circumstances proved in this case were completely *overwhelming*. * * *"

II

* * * The right to counsel plays a crucial role in the adversarial system embodied in the Sixth Amendment, since access to counsel's skill and knowledge is necessary to accord defendants the "ample opportunity to meet the case of the prosecution" to which they are entitled. * * * [e]

* * * That a person who happens to be a lawyer is present at trial alongside the accused, however, is not enough to satisfy the constitutional command. The Sixth Amendment recognizes the right to the assistance of counsel because it envisions counsel's playing a role that is critical to the ability of the adversarial system to produce just results. An accused is entitled to be assisted by an attorney, whether retained or appointed, who plays the role necessary to ensure that the trial is fair.

For that reason, the Court has recognized that "the right to counsel is the right to the effective assistance of counsel." * * *

* * * The benchmark for judging any claim of ineffectiveness must be whether counsel's conduct so undermined the proper functioning of the adversarial process that the trial cannot be relied on as having produced a just result. [f]

III

A convicted defendant's claim that counsel's assistance was so defective as to require reversal of a conviction or death sentence has two components. [g] First, the defendant must show that counsel's performance was deficient. This requires showing that counsel made errors so serious that counsel was not functioning as the "counsel" guaranteed the defendant by the Sixth Amendment. Second, the defendant must show that the **deficient performance** prejudiced the defense.

This requires showing that counsel's errors were so serious as to deprive the defendant of a fair trial, a trial whose result is reliable. Unless a defendant makes both showings, it cannot be said that the conviction or death sentence resulted from a breakdown in the adversary process that renders the result unreliable.

A

[T]he proper standard for attorney performance is that of reasonably effective assistance. * * * When a convicted defendant complains of the ineffectiveness of counsel's assistance, the defendant must show that counsel's representation fell below an objective standard of reasonableness. [h]

More specific guidelines are not appropriate. The Sixth Amendment * * * relies instead on the legal profession's maintenance of standards sufficient to justify the law's presumption that counsel will fulfill the role in the adversary process that the Amendment envisions. * * * The proper measure of attorney performance remains simply reasonableness under prevailing professional norms. [i]

* * * Counsel's function is to assist the defendant, and hence counsel owes the client a duty of loyalty, a duty to avoid conflicts of interest. * * * From counsel's function as assistant to the defendant derive the overarching duty to advocate the defendant's cause and the more particular duties to consult with the defendant on important decisions and to keep the defendant informed of important developments in the course of the prosecution. Counsel also has a duty to bring to bear such skill and knowledge as will render the trial a reliable adversarial testing process. * * *

These basic duties neither exhaustively define the obligations of counsel nor form a checklist for judicial evaluation of attorney performance. In any case presenting an ineffectiveness claim, the performance inquiry must be whether counsel's assistance was reasonable considering all the circumstances. Prevailing norms of practice as reflected in American Bar Association standards and the like * * * are guides to determining what is reasonable, but they are only guides. No particular set of detailed rules for counsel's conduct can satisfactorily take account of the variety of circumstances faced by defense counsel or the range of legitimate decisions regarding how best to represent a criminal defendant.

[e] The right to counsel is placed in the context of the right to a fair trial; thus it serves the interests of society while benefiting the individual defendant.

[f] Justice O'Connor's "benchmark" means that some errors by counsel can be overlooked *if* the overall result of the trial was just.

[g] The Court establishes a two-prong test for the effective assistance of counsel. The "performance" prong is discussed in III.A. and the "prejudice" prong in III.B.

[h] "Reasonableness" is not a precise standard; what standard of reasonableness does the Court rely on? Note that the burden of proof is on the convicted defendant to prove that his or her lawyer was ineffective.

[i] The "objective" measure is the performance of other lawyers. Only general guidelines of effective (or deficient) performance by a criminal defense lawyer are provided here. Thus deficient performance must be determined from case-by-case decisions of the courts.

Any such set of rules would interfere with the constitutionally protected independence of counsel and restrict the wide latitude counsel must have in making tactical decisions. * * *

Judicial scrutiny of counsel's performance must be highly deferential. **[j]** It is all too tempting for a defendant to second-guess counsel's assistance after conviction or adverse sentence, and it is all too easy for a court, examining counsel's defense after it has proved unsuccessful, to conclude that a particular act or omission of counsel was unreasonable. * * * [A] court must indulge a strong presumption that counsel's conduct falls within the wide range of reasonable professional assistance. * * * There are countless ways to provide effective assistance in any given case. Even the best criminal defense attorneys would not defend a particular client in the same way. * * *

[Intense scrutiny of attorneys' performances by appellate courts would produce a flood of ineffectiveness challenges that would make lawyers less willing to represent criminal defendants and would undermine trust between attorney and client.]

* * * A convicted defendant making a claim of ineffective assistance must identify the acts or omissions of counsel that are alleged not to have been the result of reasonable professional judgment. The court must then determine whether, in light of all the circumstances, the identified acts or omissions were outside the wide range of professionally competent assistance.

* * *

B

An error by counsel, even if professionally unreasonable, does not warrant setting aside the judgment of a criminal proceeding if the error had no effect on the judgment. * * * The purpose of the Sixth Amendment guarantee of counsel is to ensure that a defendant has the assistance necessary to justify reliance on the outcome of the proceeding. **[k]** Accordingly, any deficiencies in counsel's performance must be prejudicial to the defense in order to constitute ineffective assistance under the Constitution.

In certain Sixth Amendment contexts, prejudice is presumed. Actual or constructive denial of the assistance of counsel altogether is legally presumed to result in prejudice. * * * Prejudice in these circumstances is so likely that case-by-case inquiry into prejudice is not worth the cost. * * *

One type of actual ineffectiveness claim warrants a similar, though more limited, presumption of prejudice. In *Cuyler v. Sullivan* (1980), the Court held that prejudice is presumed when counsel is burdened by an actual conflict of interest. In those circumstances, counsel breaches the duty of loyalty, perhaps the most basic of counsel's duties. * * * Prejudice is presumed only if the defendant demonstrates that counsel "actively represented conflicting interests" and that "an actual conflict of interest adversely affected his lawyer's performance." * * * **[l]**

Conflict of interest claims aside, actual ineffectiveness claims alleging a deficiency in attorney performance are subject to a general requirement that the defendant affirmatively prove prejudice. * * * Attorney errors come in an infinite variety and are as likely to be utterly harmless in a particular case as they are to be prejudicial. They cannot be classified according to likelihood of causing prejudice. Nor can they be defined with sufficient precision to inform defense attorneys correctly just what conduct to avoid. Representation is an art, and an act or omission that is unprofessional in one case may be sound or even brilliant in another. Even if a defendant shows that particular errors of counsel were unreasonable, therefore, the defendant must show that they actually had an adverse effect on the defense.

* * *

[The defendant cannot argue that his or her conviction would likely not have occurred because the jury would have nullified the law. The prejudice prong must be assessed on the basis of assuming that a conscientious jury would have applied legal standards impartially.]

* * * When a defendant challenges a conviction, the question is whether there is a reasonable probability that, absent the errors, the fact-finder would have had a reasonable doubt respecting guilt. **[m]** When a defendant challenges a death sentence such as the one at issue in this case, the question is whether there is a reasonable probability that, absent the errors, the sentencer * * * would have concluded that the balance of aggravating and mitigating circumstances did not warrant death.

In making this determination, a court hearing an ineffectiveness claim must consider the totality of the evidence before the judge or jury. Some of the factual findings will have been unaffected by the errors, and factual findings that were affected will have been affected in different ways. Some errors will have had a pervasive effect on the inferences to be drawn from the evidence, altering the entire evidentiary picture, and some will have had an isolated, trivial effect. Moreover, a verdict or conclusion only weakly supported by the record is more likely to have been affected by errors than one with overwhelming record support. **[n]** Taking the unaffected findings as a given, and taking due account of the effect of the errors on the remaining findings, a court making the prejudice inquiry must ask if the defendant has met the burden of showing that the decision reached would reasonably likely have been different absent the errors.

---

[j] "Deferential" review means that the benefit of doubt is resolved in favor of finding a lawyer's performance competent.

[k] The "prejudice" prong asks whether counsel's performance substantially contributed to the guilty verdict or sentence of death. It does not mean "discrimination" in this context.

[l] Two kinds of "automatic prejudice" eliminate the defendant's need to prove prejudice: (1) no assistance of counsel and (2) conflict of interest. In other cases, prejudice must be proven beyond a reasonable doubt on the facts.

[m] The appellate court must decide whether the outcome would likely have differed if the attorney had not made the errors that established deficient performance under the first prong.

[n] A "facts and circumstances" or "totality of the evidence" standard is open-ended; it is the antithesis of a bright-line rule. As with the "deficient-performance" prong, standards will develop incrementally as the courts decide specific cases.

[In Part V, the Court applied the standards announced in Parts II and III to the facts of the case. The majority concluded that the conduct of Washington's lawyer was adequate and was not the cause of the death penalty sentence.]

JUSTICE MARSHALL, dissenting.

* * *

I

A

My objection to the performance standard adopted by the Court is that it is so malleable that, in practice, it will either have no grip at all or will yield excessive variation in the manner in which the Sixth Amendment is interpreted and applied by different courts. To tell lawyers and the lower courts that counsel for a criminal defendant must behave "reasonably" and must act like "a reasonably competent attorney," is to tell them almost nothing. In essence, the majority has instructed judges called upon to assess claims of ineffective assistance of counsel to advert to their own intuitions regarding what constitutes "professional" representation, and has discouraged them from trying to develop more detailed standards governing the performance of defense counsel. [o] In my view, the Court has thereby not only abdicated its own responsibility to interpret the Constitution, but also impaired the ability of the lower courts to exercise theirs.

* * *

B

I object to the prejudice standard adopted by the Court for two independent reasons. First, it is often very difficult to tell whether a defendant convicted after a trial in which he was ineffectively represented would have fared better if his lawyer had been competent. Seemingly impregnable cases can sometimes be dismantled by good defense counsel. On the basis of a cold record, it may be impossible for a reviewing court confidently to ascertain how the government's evidence and arguments would have stood up against rebuttal and cross-examination by a shrewd, well-prepared lawyer. The difficulties of estimating prejudice after the fact are exacerbated by the possibility that evidence of injury to the defendant may be missing from the record precisely because of the incompetence of defense counsel. [p] In view of all these impediments to a fair evaluation of the probability that the outcome of a trial was affected by ineffectiveness of counsel, it seems to me senseless to impose on a defendant whose lawyer has been shown to have been incompetent the burden of demonstrating prejudice.

Second and more fundamentally, the assumption on which the Court's holding rests is that the only purpose of the constitutional guarantee of effective assistance of counsel is to reduce the chance that innocent persons will be convicted. In my view, the guarantee also functions to ensure that convictions are obtained only through fundamentally fair procedures. The majority contends that the Sixth Amendment is not violated when a manifestly guilty defendant is convicted after a trial in which he was represented by a manifestly ineffective attorney. [q] I cannot agree. Every defendant is entitled to a trial in which his interests are vigorously and conscientiously advocated by an able lawyer. A proceeding in which the defendant does not receive meaningful assistance in meeting the forces of the State does not, in my opinion, constitute due process.

* * *

[o] If Justice Marshall is correct, is it possible to specify good lawyering? Should Washington's lawyer have performed each of the six acts not done?

[p] Justice Marshall would eliminate the "prejudice" prong entirely. Would this make it very difficult to uphold convictions on appeal?

[q] Justice Marshall was the most experienced trial attorney sitting on the Court. As an African-American lawyer challenging racial segregation in southern courts in the 1930s, 1940s, and 1950s, he often worked under extremely hostile circumstances. Should his experience give his views special weight?

A death penalty was appealed on the grounds of ineffective assistance of counsel in **Bell v. Cone** (2002). Gary Cone was convicted for a brutal murder; his insanity defense was rejected. At the death penalty phase, the prosecutor established aggravating factors warranting the death penalty. After the junior prosecutor gave a low-key closing, defense counsel *waived final argument* in order to prevent the lead prosecutor, by all accounts an extremely effective advocate, from arguing in rebuttal. The defense counsel cross-examined the prosecution witnesses but called no other witnesses. He directed the jury's attention to the mitigating evidence presented at trial, relating to Gary Cone's substance abuse and posttraumatic stress disorders resulting from his Vietnam military service; the jury was reminded that his mother testified that Cone had returned from Vietnam a changed person. The jury found four aggravating factors and no mitigating circumstances, which required the imposition of the death penalty.

The Supreme Court upheld the state appellate court's finding that the performance of Cone's counsel was within the permissible range of competency under the attorney-performance standard of *Strickland v. Washington*. The Supreme Court agreed that the state court's application of *Strickland* was reasonable, especially in light of the guideline that "judicial scrutiny of a counsel's performance must be highly deferential" and that "every effort [must] be made to eliminate the distorting effects of hindsight, to reconstruct the circumstances of counsel's challenged conduct, and to evaluate the conduct from counsel's perspective at the time" (*Bell v. Cone*, 2002, citing *Strickland*). In this light, the defense attorney's decision to not make a closing statement so as to preclude an effective close by an experienced prosecutor, plus his cross-examination and bringing out mitigating factors, can reasonably be considered sound trial strategy.

EXAMPLES OF INEFFECTIVE ASSISTANCE   An example of deficient performance is found in *Kimmelman v. Morrison* (1986). The defense lawyer in a rape prosecution failed to object to the introduction of illegally seized evidence, filed a late motion for the suppression of evidence, and did not ask for discovery of police reports that would have indicated that the seizure of evidence was arguably unconstitutional. The attorney's excuse was that he believed it was the state's responsibility to turn over all relevant evidence. Since there is no such general obligation, the Supreme Court ruled that the lawyer's failure to take normal and routine steps before trial to obtain relevant evidence was inexcusable negligence, amounting to deficient performance. The Court remanded to determine if the deficient performance prejudiced the outcome of the case.

In *Williams v. Taylor* (2000), the Supreme Court reinstated a trial court's finding that counsel was ineffective at the death penalty phase of a trial, after the Virginia Supreme Court ruled that the performance was reasonable. In this robbery and capital murder case, the trial judge found that defense counsel had *not presented and explained the significance of all the available mitigating factors*. If they had, the cumulative mitigation evidence would have raised a reasonable probability that the result of the sentencing proceeding would have been different. Defense counsel began to prepare for the capital sentencing only a week before the trial and failed to conduct an investigation that would have uncovered extensive records of mitigation— not because of any strategic calculation, but because the attorneys incorrectly thought that state law barred access to such records. The mitigating factors would have included Terry William's borderline mental retardation; his parents' conviction for neglect; his severe and repeated beatings by his father; his stay in an abusive foster home; his return to his abusive parents after their release from prison; prison records indicating that Williams received commendations for helping to crack a prison drug ring and for returning a guard's missing wallet; and testimony of prison officials who described Williams as among the inmates least likely to act in a violent, dangerous, or provocative way.

In *Rompilla v. Beard* (2005), two public defenders were held to be deficient in *failing to examine the court file* on Ronald Rompilla's prior conviction for the death penalty phase of a Pennsylvania murder trial. The attorneys interviewed Rompilla, who was recalcitrant and unhelpful, and family members and medical experts who were equally unhelpful in uncovering mitigating factors. Prior to the trial, the prosecutor notified defense counsel and the court that it would use Rompilla's court file containing his prior criminal conviction as a basis for finding aggravating factors. The prosecutor introduced Rompilla's prior felony conviction as an aggravating factor; the mitigating factors consisted of family members pleading for mercy. Rompilla was sentenced to death. When appellate lawyers looked at the prior conviction file, they "found a range of mitigation leads that no other source had opened up." The information showed that Rompilla had a horrendous upbringing by a violent father and an alcoholic mother who drank during her pregnancy with Ronald. His father severely beat his mother and beat young Ronald with his hands, fists, leather straps, belts, and sticks. His mother once stabbed his father. Rompilla had run-ins with juvenile authorities, a drinking problem, and a third-grade level of cognition after nine years of schooling. He was diagnosed as bordering on schizophrenia. The Rompilla children lived in terror and in isolation from other children; there were no expressions of parental love, affection, or approval; Rompilla and his brother Richard were locked in a small wire mesh dog pen that was filthy and filled with excrement. The Rompilla house had no indoor plumbing; Ronald slept in the attic with no heat, and the children attended school in rags.

These were clearly mitigating factors. The Court's majority held that the public defenders' defense was deficient in failing to adhere to the "norms of adequate investigation in preparing for the sentencing phase of a capital case." Further, the evidence found in the sentencing file "has shown beyond any doubt that counsel's lapse was prejudicial." Justice O'Connor concurred, noting that the defense counsel did not fail to look at the prior conviction file as a matter of trial strategy but claimed that they were overworked. Four dissenting justices, in an opinion by Justice Anthony Kennedy, were concerned that a *"per se* rule requiring counsel in every case to review the records of prior convictions used by the State as aggravation evidence is a radical departure from *Strickland"* and would impose impossible burdens in future cases.

EFFECTIVE ASSISTANCE AND TRUTH   The attorney's obligation to maintain the integrity of the trial process and to elicit the truth can appear to conflict with the specific obligation to provide the best defense. It is fundamental to the adjudication process that evidence cannot be fabricated. A lawyer has no obligation to support a defendant with false testimony. In *Nix v. Whiteside* (1986), a defendant charged with murder claimed self-defense. He told his lawyer that he did not actually see a gun in his assailant's hand but believed it was there. He wanted to testify that he saw "something metallic" because a jury would be more likely to believe the assailant had a gun. Counsel told Whiteside that as a matter of law, it was not necessary for the defendant to see a gun to prove self-defense. Counsel told Whiteside that they would not allow him to commit perjury, would not themselves suborn perjury, would advise the judge if he did commit perjury, and would seek to withdraw their representation if he did so. Whiteside was convicted and argued that the lawyer's advice amounted to ineffective assistance. The Supreme Court ruled that because there is no right, constitutional or otherwise, to testify falsely, the lawyer's assistance was not deficient.

Conflict of Interest

Multiple representation occurs when a retained or assigned attorney represents two or more co-defendants. In *Cuyler v. Sullivan* (1980), attorneys DiBona and Peruto represented three defendants. DiBona was primarily responsible for Sullivan's trial, while Peruto, responsible for the trial of Sullivan's co-defendants, advised DiBona in the Sullivan trial. The Supreme Court held that this constituted multiple representation, but the multiple representation did not, in itself, violate an attorney's obligations to adequately defend and to give full and complete attention to the client's defense. Multiple representation, therefore, is not automatically a conflict of interest. This rule takes economic realities of providing counsel into consideration. As Justice Stevens said in *Burger v. Kemp* (1987), "Particularly in smaller communities where the supply of qualified lawyers willing to accept the demanding and unrewarding work of representing capital prisoners is extremely limited, the defendants may actually benefit from the joint efforts of two partners who supplement one another in their preparation. Moreover, we generally presume that the lawyer is fully conscious of the overarching duty of complete loyalty to his or her client."

A conflict of interest arises when, in the circumstance of multiple representation, an attorney renders less effective assistance to one client out of consideration for the interests of the other client. The long-standing rule is that where a conflict of interest exists, the defendant establishes ineffective assistance of counsel *per se* and need not show that the conflict of interest prejudiced the case (*Glasser v. United States*, 1942). A trial judge is not obligated to hold a hearing into the possibility of a conflict of interest in every case of multiple representation (*Cuyler v. Sullivan*, 1980). However, should an assigned attorney raise a timely objection to multiple representation on the grounds that it constitutes a conflict of interest, the trial judge is required to hold a hearing to make certain that there is no genuine conflict before the trial can proceed (*Holloway v. Arkansas*, 1978).

A conflict of interest can be difficult to prove, as the defendant "must demonstrate that an actual conflict of interest adversely affected his lawyer's performance" (*Cuyler v. Sullivan*, 1980). *Burger v. Kemp* (1987) is an example where the mere possibility of a conflict of interest does not amount to ineffective assistance of counsel under *Strickland*. Burger first argued that his lawyer failed in an appellate brief to raise, as a death penalty mitigation, the argument that Burger was less culpable for the killing than a co-defendant. The Supreme Court rejected this contention because (1) the lesser culpability defense was raised and rejected at trial; (2) Burger actually killed the victim; (3) the Georgia Supreme Court found his acts to be "inhuman"; and (4) lower courts found that it was not deficient performance by the attorney to forgo this avenue on appeal.

Burger next claimed that the lawyer failed to obtain a plea bargain resulting in a life sentence. However, the facts indicated that the defense lawyer attempted to obtain a plea, but the prosecutor simply refused to agree to a plea bargain. Finally, Burger claimed that the lawyer failed to bring out mitigating circumstances at the death penalty sentencing hearing. The omission of some mitigating information was deemed a tactical decision by the lawyer, designed to keep the defendant off the stand and thereby keep aggravating information from the court. Over the vigorous dissent of four justices, the Supreme Court held in this case that there was no deficient performance or conflict of interest.

LAW IN SOCIETY

The Unmet Promise of Equal Justice

Gideon v. Wainwright (1963), *Argersinger v. Hamlin* (1972), and *Strickland v. Washington* (1984) guarantee a competent attorney for every defendant facing a serious criminal charge—even if the defendant is too poor to pay for legal services. A legal guarantee "on the books" is only as good as its enforcement, however. The promise of equal justice is meaningless if the lawyers, courts, county commissions, state legislators, and governors—and ultimately the American people—fail to implement it substantially. Have the legal community and responsible government units responded to the guarantee of equal justice?

It is true that the nation established several methods for providing lawyers for indigent defendants in criminal cases.[34] Different cities, counties, and states either assign lawyers, fund legal aid and public defenders' agencies, or establish contract systems by which bar associations of private firms agree to provide indigent defense for a set fee. As a result, a lawyer always represents an indigent client at public expense. Nevertheless, fees are usually capped and quite low for assigned counsel, and public defenders often have unrealistically large caseloads. It is a struggle to obtain adequate investigators or expert witnesses. The lack of funding for indigent defense undermines the ability even of competent attorneys to provide adequate defense. Proper criminal defense work is an expensive, labor-intensive, expert undertaking. Sadly, America's people and its governmental servants have grown increasingly insensitive in the last few decades to the promise of equal justice.

The Expense of Private Criminal Defense

The cost of retaining a private defense lawyer can be enormous. A 1996 survey by journalists of indigent cases in Houston found that retained lawyers "often can earn $25,000 to $75,000 to defend a felony case, depending on the complexity of the case and the probability that it will go to trial. Several top criminal defense attorneys acknowledged that fees for complex, high-profile cases can run into the hundreds of thousands of dollars."[35] As the following examples show, effective assistance of counsel is a major professional undertaking that is very expensive.

- A car service dispatcher in Queens, New York, who was charged with felonious assault in 1995, claimed self-defense. A seasoned attorney charged $15,000 and hired an investigator at $50 an hour to find witnesses. The dispatcher was found guilty of a lesser charge "and probably avoided prison time." His father mistakenly believed that the money would be returned if his son was found not guilty.[36]
- In the notorious Wenatchee, Washington, "witch hunt," police officer Robert Perez accused Pentecostal Minister Robert Roberson, his wife, Connie, and more than forty parishioners of conducting orgies with children. The case ultimately collapsed after several poor and mentally retarded parishioners were imprisoned. Attorney Robert Van Siclen, who volunteered to defend Mr. Roberson, estimated that the case cost his firm $100,000. He planned to sue the county in an effort to recoup the cost of defending his client during the six-week trial.[37]
- Karen and Jeffrey Wilson, a paralegal and a high school teacher, respectively, were charged with child abuse when their seven-month-old son, Brock, was treated for a head injury. They spent $60,000 in legal fees to regain custody of Brock, who was taken from them by the social services department. Charges were dismissed by the family court.[38]
- Between January and March 2000, Representative Earl Hilliard spent $37,500 in legal fees, out of the $40,000 that he raised for his reelection campaign, to defend himself against an ethics investigation involving his previous race.[39]
- An injured trucker, accused of perpetrating criminal workers' compensation fraud, spent more than $100,000 in attorneys' fees fighting criminal allegations. The trucker was vindicated.[40]
- In late 1999, seven big vitamin companies pleaded guilty to price fixing and agreed to pay more than $1 billion in damages. Their attorneys' fees were estimated at $122 million.[41]
- Linda Tripp, whose Maryland charges for wiretapping in the Whitewater and Lewinsky scandals were ultimately dismissed, ran up legal bills of about $750,000. A defense fund was set up to help her pay her debt.[42]

- Monica Lewinsky, a central figure in the scandal that led to the impeachment of President Bill Clinton, was represented by top lawyers Plato Cacheris and Jacob Stein, who charge about $400 per hour. At the time she hired this team, it was predicted that "she'll likely owe more than $300,000 to her first legal team," which was led by William Ginsburg, whom she dismissed.[43]

- President Clinton's bill for legal services in his impeachment trial exceeded $10 million. To pay these bills, President Clinton created a legal defense fund to receive private donations.[44]

- Murder cases are in a special league. "'In a murder case, practically every defendant is indigent,' says Larry Hammond, a criminal lawyer in Phoenix, Arizona. 'They may not have started that way, but for anyone other than the super-rich, they will be indigent before the case is over.'" Dr. Dale Bertsch, an anesthesiologist accused of murdering his ex-wife in a case with no physical evidence against him, was quoted fees in the $250,000 range. Hammond took the case for the sum total of Bertsch's liquidated assets, which came to about $160,000. He could not pay for an evidentiary hearing, which would have required $50,000, or a mock jury for $30,000. Dr. Bertsch was convicted.[45]

- As for the "super-rich," O. J. Simpson, whose net worth before his trial was said to be $10 million, took out a $3 million credit line on his Brentwood home. He spent $100,000 for a jury consultant, paid a fee of $100,000 a month for twelve months to Robert Shapiro, and paid Johnnie Cochran Jr. "a large flat fee," to mention only the lead attorneys.[46]

- Multimillionaire Robert Durst, acquitted of murdering a neighbor and dismembering the corpse while living in obscurity in a run-down Galveston, Texas, neighborhood, was taped in a jail conversation with his wife mentioning $1.2 million as the cost of his defense, but defense attorneys declined to say what Durst paid for their successful representation.[47]

Funding for Indigent Defense

The underfunding of indigent criminal defense makes a mockery of the constitutional ideal of equal justice. The "largely hospitable funding environment" for indigent defense of the 1960s has given way to "public outcry over the neglect of . . . crime victims" and a steering of "resources toward law enforcement and away from indigent defense."[48] The late David Bazelon, chief judge of the Washington, D.C., U.S. Court of Appeals, wrote in 1984 that the "battle for equal justice is being lost in the trenches of the criminal courts," as the poor, uneducated, and unemployed are being represented all too often by "walking violations of the sixth amendment."[49]

In all jurisdictions, the amounts paid to assigned counsel are significantly below what retained counsel charge. As of May 2000, New York State had not raised fees for assigned attorneys in fourteen years.[50] In 1999, the federal Criminal Justice Act, which since 1964 has provided funding for assigned counsel in federal cases, set a maximum fee of $60 per hour for in-court time and $40 per hour for out-of-court time, far below going rates for retained lawyers.[51] Virginia placed a cap of $845 on the amount an attorney can receive for representing a defendant on a murder charge, but its general assembly approved a 24 percent increase in fees, effective July 1, 2001. "That level of funding will keep Virginia at or near the bottom of the rankings for payment of court-appointed attorneys' fees."[52]

As for public defenders' offices, in most places, the caseloads of public defenders are so high, because of underfunding, that the ability of defenders to perform at the best of their abilities is diminished. There is no survey that assesses the total picture in the United States, but there is substantial evidence of real underfunding of indigent defense.

. . . Across the nation, the bulk of criminal justice funds go to the police, prosecutors, and jails. Only 2.3% of the seventy-four billion dollars spent on the justice system in 1990 went to pay for attorneys for indigent defendants while 7.4% went to the prosecution. However, the number of defendants unable to afford an attorney had risen dramatically, from forty-eight percent in 1982 to eighty percent today. Public defenders handle over 11 million of the 13 million cases which are tried annually. Yet, as of 1990, the United States Department of Justice found that nationally, public defenders are receiving less than one-third of the resources provided to the prosecution. Prosecutors' offices received $5.5 billion from federal, state, local, county, and municipal governments, as opposed to the $1.7 billion provided for public defense by the same government sources. Moreover, defense lawyers are further overwhelmed by additional resources provided to prosecutors, including a great deal of investigatory work by law enforcement which are officially classified as "police expenditures."[53]

The following examples provide a glimpse of the conditions and pressures that cause ineffective assistance of counsel.

- An assistant public defender in the western United States admitted in open court to doing an inadequate job. She testified that she had collapsed in court and that her health was seriously threatened by a caseload of two thousand cases per year. She resigned from the public defenders' office, saying that she was "actually doing the defendants more harm by just presenting a live body than if they had no representation at all."[54]
- A New Orleans public defender, representing 418 clients in the first seven months of 1991 and with seventy cases pending trial, obtained a court ruling that his excessive caseload precluded effective representation to the clients. "Not even a lawyer with an 'S' on his chest," the judge ruled, "could handle this docket."[55]
- In 1992, New Jersey eliminated $2.9 million budgeted to the Department of the Public Advocate to pay for counsel in cases where a conflict of interest barred the public defender. This left some indigent defendants jailed without an attorney to represent them. The public advocate resigned "in disgust" to protest the budget reductions.[56]
- A survey in the late 1980s showed an annual starting salary of $24,259 for public defenders and an average salary of $34,787 for a defender with five years' experience. This may not have improved by the late 1990s, as the legal profession became "saturated."[57]

The Crisis in Death Penalty Cases

The most serious cases, involving capital punishment, are among the most severely affected by underfunding and incompetent attorneys. Here are some examples:

- George Alec Robinson, charged with capital murder in Virginia, was vigorously defended by two appointed attorneys who worked a combined total of six hundred hours. Robinson was found guilty but was spared death by the electric chair. The attorneys submitted a bill of approximately $55,000 at prevailing rates for private clients. During this trial, the attorneys neglected their private practices and even their personal lives under the pressure of having responsibility for a man's life. The state of Virginia paid them $573 each. "The two lawyers subsequently removed their names from the list of attorneys willing to accept appointments. They joined an increasing number of experienced attorneys nationwide who are no longer willing to provide their services at such great personal and financial sacrifice."[58]
- Calvin Jerold Burdine was released by a federal court from a Texas prison after spending sixteen years on death row. His lawyer had no co-counsel and had slept through substantial portions of his trial. The Texas Court of Criminal Appeals did not think that this constituted ineffective assistance of counsel. Burdine's case was one of several of Texas prisoners on death row whose lawyers slept during their trials. In 1999, George W. Bush, then the governor of Texas, vetoed a bill to improve the quality of legal representation of poor defendants, expressing satisfaction with the Texas justice system.[59]
- Frederico Martinez-Macias, a common laborer convicted of a double murder, was defended by a court-appointed attorney who was paid $11.84 an hour. His attorney did no legal research to correct his erroneous view about key evidence and failed to call an alibi witness who would have placed the defendant miles away from the crime. After Martinez-Macias was sentenced to death, a Washington firm took his case *pro bono*. Full investigation established his innocence.[60] The *pro bono* lawyers invested about $1 million of billable hours, spent $11,599 for psychological testimony, and found eyewitnesses who did not identify Martinez-Macias at the murder scene.[61] Other cases like this exist.[62]
- Attorney Mike Williams, a small-town Alabama lawyer, was assigned the capital murder case of James Wyman Smith. Williams was given no money for an investigator and estimated that he received $4.98 per hour to prepare for the defense. Another Alabama solo practitioner in Birmingham, Wilson Meyers, submitted an itemized bill for $13,399 to the trial court for representing an indigent in a capital murder trial. The judge reduced the amount of payment to $4,128. The court agreed that Meyers had put in the time but called the fees too excessive. After paying his investigator and paralegal, Meyers netted $5.05 an

hour on this case. As a result, earnest lawyers like Mike Williams and Wilson Myers drop out of defending indigents in capital cases because of the financial burden, leaving inexperienced or incompetent lawyers to take such cases.[63]

- Some lawyers are forced to take assigned capital cases or face contempt of court. They may put in about fifty hours on death penalty cases when, according to experts, adequate preparation requires five hundred to one thousand hours.[64]

Causes of Ineffective Counsel

What causes the diminished funding for indigent defense?

- *Tough-on-crime attitudes.* "Providing free attorneys to accused criminals is probably one of the government's least popular functions. In recent years, 'victim's rights' movements have become increasingly popular. Many politicians, being sensitive to public opinion, are concerned with appearing to be 'tough on crime.' Citizens and politicians alike often have little understanding of or sympathy for the needs of the adversary system, at least insofar as it requires a strong defense advocate. Defense attorneys are often seen as obstacles to justice."[65]
- *Rising caseloads.* From 1982 to 1984, there was a 40 percent increase in caseloads for the nation's indigent defense systems. A 1990 study, commissioned by Chief Justice Rehnquist, concluded that the most pressing problem for federal courts was the unprecedented number of federal drug prosecutions. In 1964, federal courts made sixteen thousand compensated appointments of counsel under the Criminal Justice Act of that year. By 1993, that number rose to eighty-nine thousand indigent appointments in federal courts.[66]
- *Diminishing government resources.* "Recently, many local governments, the primary locus of funding of defense services, have seen their resources dwindle, as tax-cutting measures are passed by the electorate and federal funds for local programs are cut."[67]
- *Greater demands on defense attorneys.* Prosecutors have either limited or eliminated plea bargaining for certain crimes, have increased the number of charges filed against defendants, and have charged more serious crimes. All of this requires greater defense efforts. New crimes and harsher penalties passed by legislatures require defense attorneys to spend time learning the law, developing appellate challenges to the new provisions, and offering a more dogged defense against higher penalties.[68]

Solving the Problem of Ineffective Counsel

Several steps can be taken to solve the problem of the ineffective assistance of counsel, including these suggestions:

- Modify the rule of *Strickland v. Washington* (1984) to make it easier for courts to find ineffective assistance of counsel.
- Improve the efficiency of public defenders' offices through the widespread use of advanced technology for managing information in complex cases, in case tracking, and for information exchange.[69]
- Reengineer the role of chief public defenders from that of narrow and defensive managers to spokespeople for the need for adequate funding for indigent defense. This may include developing better relations with legislators, prosecutors, police, corrections, the media, and community groups in an effort to advocate the need for indigent defense and to sponsor community crime-prevention programs.[70]
- Tie the expenditure of indigent defense (all systems) to a percentage of funding of public prosecution, at a suggested rate of 75 percent.[71]
- Allow public defenders' offices to negotiate reasonable caseload limits with courts and funding agencies.
- Require a minimum level of experience before assigning major cases to counsel.[72]
- Eliminate the practice of judges' compelling attorneys to take major cases on a *pro bono* basis.[73]
- Finance indigent defense in part with a portion of court fees.
- Reduce the enforcement component of the "war on drugs," with its draconian punishments for low-level crimes, and replace this with more treatment options.

Until such practical solutions are implemented, the promise of the Constitution—equal justice under the law—will go unfulfilled.

Summary

The right to the assistance of counsel in a criminal prosecution is guaranteed by the Sixth Amendment. It is fundamental to the proper conduct of criminal trials and the adversary system of justice. In other proceedings, a right to counsel has been guaranteed by the Due Process and Equal Protection Clauses of the Fourteenth Amendment as well as the Fifth Amendment right against self-incrimination. Defense counsel is more important in common law trials than in trials under the European civil law system. The actual use of lawyers in trials was a late common law development.

Prior to its incorporation into the Fourteenth Amendment in *Gideon v. Wainwright* (1963), the Sixth Amendment right applied only to federal prosecutions. Under federal law, a defendant had to be represented and could waive counsel only if it specifically appeared on the record that the defendant did so knowingly and voluntarily (*Johnson v. Zerbst*, 1938). In state cases, lack of counsel violated a defendant's Fourteenth Amendment due process right to a fair trial only when special circumstances existed—for example, the death penalty, the defendant's immaturity or ignorance, complex issues, or an atmosphere of prejudice (*Powell v. Alabama*, 1932). *Griffin v. Illinois* (1956) held that under the Fourteenth Amendment Equal Protection Clause, in which the state allows certain legal benefits to those who can afford them, the state must provide indigent defendants with free benefits, such as transcripts for appeals.

Gideon v. Wainwright (1963) incorporated the Sixth Amendment right to counsel into the Fourteenth Amendment Due Process Clause. The right to counsel was later applied to all misdemeanor cases in which the defendant was actually imprisoned. The Sixth Amendment right to counsel attaches when a suspect is brought before a magistrate for the initial appearance, and counsel must be present at all critical stages (preliminary examination, capital arraignment, and sentencing), but not to postconviction correctional processes (probation revocation, parole revocation, or prison disciplinary hearings). The Sixth Amendment requires appointment of a psychiatric expert when necessary to decide an insanity issue. A critical stage is one in which a factual determination can be made that determines the outcome of a case.

In proceedings that are not Sixth Amendment prosecutions, counsel is authorized by the Due Process Clause in some proceedings (probation and parole revocations, juvenile delinquency adjudication) but not in others (prison discipline, summary court martial). In probation revocation hearings, courts have discretion to appoint counsel to indigents when special circumstances exist, but in juvenile adjudication, counsel must be provided. A federal statutory right to counsel in state capital cases extends to representation in clemency hearings.

Courts can prevent those who are not licensed in the practice of law from serving as counsel and can bar an attorney from representing a person if the court believes there will be a conflict of interest. However, a retrial is required if a court wrongly prevents a defendant from being represented by retained (paid) counsel of choice. A federal forfeiture statute that allows the confiscation of attorneys' fees before trial does not violate the Sixth Amendment right to counsel. The Sixth Amendment does not guarantee a meaningful relationship between a defendant and assigned counsel. When counsel is provided without cost to an indigent defendant, the state has a right to seek compensation at a later time when the defendant has obtained the money to repay the costs.

Counsel is guaranteed on a first appeal under the Due Process and Equal Protection Clauses (*Douglas v. California*, 1963). The Court limited the extension of this rule in *Ross v. Moffitt* (1974) so that counsel is not constitutionally required for indigent litigants pursuing discretionary, second appeals or habeas corpus proceedings, as long as the state allows indigent prisoners to pursue such appeals.

The right to representation at a criminal trial is personal, and a defendant has a right to waive the assistance of counsel and to conduct a defense *pro se* (*Faretta v. California*, 1975). A waiver requires the trial judge to closely examine the defendant to be sure he or she understands the benefits of counsel and waives appointed counsel voluntarily and to be sure that the defendant has the minimum skills needed to conduct a reasonable defense. The court cannot disqualify a *pro se* defense because the defendant does not have expert knowledge of the law or of the trial process. A trial court must find that a *pro se* defendant has the competence to conduct a trial. In instances of *pro se* defense, the court may appoint standby counsel over the defendant's objection.

The Sixth Amendment requires that the assistance afforded to a defendant be effective. The basic rules of effective assistance are, first, that the attorney's conduct must be reasonable, or not deficient, according to the prevailing standards of practicing attorneys in the locality and, second, that if the attorney's performance was deficient, this must have prejudiced the defendant's case so that the conviction was a result of the deficient performance. The complaining defendant has the burden of proving ineffective assistance. Ineffective assistance will not be presumed. It is not deficient performance to refuse to assist a client in committing perjury. In cases involving a real conflict of interest, ineffective assistance is presumed, but the mere fact that an attorney represented two clients is not in itself a conflict of interest. If an attorney raises a reasonable possibility of a conflict of interest, a trial judge must hold a hearing to inquire into the matter.

Legal Puzzles

HOW HAVE COURTS DECIDED THESE CASES?

Choosing Retained Counsel

6-1. Goldsberry and Myers were tried together for murder and robbery while selling drugs. Goldsberry was found guilty. During a pretrial motion to sever the trials of Myers and Goldsberry, Myers's lawyer informed the trial judge that Attorney Mckenzie spoke to her client about the case while Myers was represented, potentially violating rules of professional ethics. She argued that the conversation prejudiced Myers because possible cross-examination by Mckenzie might undercut Myers's decision to testify. Mckenzie said that Myers made no incriminating admissions to him. Goldsberry's other lawyer, Andrew Jezic, told the court, and the court accepted, that he and Mckenzie did not discuss the conversation with Myers—the two maintained a "Chinese wall" about that conversation. The trial court ruled that Mckenzie could not continue to represent Goldsberry but could remain at the trial table.

The prosecutor then informed the court that a state witnesses, Ms. Davis, testified to the grand jury that she was "coached" by McKenzie and Goldsberry, and that the prosecutor might have to call McKenzie as a witness. The court prohibited McKenzie from sitting at the trial table.

Did the trial judge's refusal to allow Mr. McKenzie to represent Goldsberry deny Goldsberry his right to be represented by the counsel of his choice?

HELD: NO.

6-1. Though the potential conflicts in this case were different from those in *Wheat*, the trial court here similarly acted within its discretion in determining that Goldsberry's right to counsel of choice was outweighed by the countervailing interests of fairness, maintaining ethical standards, and avoiding conflicts of interest. Continued representation by McKenzie could have violated Maryland's legal ethics rules and Myers's right to a fair trial. McKenzie's "coaching" of Ms. Davis made him a possible witness in the case, possibly violating the rule prohibiting a lawyer from acting as an advocate in trial where the lawyer is likely to be called as a witness. Also, Goldsberry was not deprived of his right to counsel of choice as he was still represented by Mr. Jezic, whom he selected, and the trial court's ruling permitted Mr. McKenzie to assist in appellant's defense by consulting with Jezic as long as they did not discuss the conversation with Mr. Myers. Thus, the trial court's ruling properly balanced Goldsberry's qualified right to counsel against competing factors that weighed against continued unrestricted representation by McKenzie.

Goldsberry v. State, 182 Md. App. 394, 957 A.2d 1110 (Maryland Court of Appeals 2008).

Self-Representation

6-2. Gabby Tennis, nineteen, was convicted for first-degree murder in the 2003 killing of ninety-one-year-old Albert Vassella. His co-defendant and girlfriend, Sophia Adams, sixteen, pled guilty to second-degree murder and testified against Tennis at trial. Tennis was sentenced to death. The motive was money to pay Liza Boltos, Sophia Adams's mother, for the "right" to marry Sophia. Tennis claims that he was in Vasella's house but did not murder him. Liza Boltos had been a house cleaner for Vassella.

Tennis made two requests to represent himself. In April 2005, Tennis filed a motion to dismiss counsel, alleging that counsel failed to "perfect a defense," ignored Tennis's attempts to contact him, and refused to investigate Liza Boltos's participation in the murder. At a hearing the judge denied the motion to dismiss counsel. In June 2005 Tennis filed another motion to dismiss counsel, alleging a conflict of interest with his counsel and that counsel failed to prepare for trial. In a hearing the trial court asked Tennis for substantiation. Tennis referred to an out-of-court verbal confrontations between his family and counsel. Tennis stated, "I refuse to go to trial with him. I would like to go *pro se*, instead of having two prosecutors against me, I'll do it myself. Even though I don't know what I'm doing, I will have a better fighting chance." The trial court found that counsel was competent and did not address Tennis's alternative request to represent himself. Tennis then made two additional written motions to represent himself.

Was the trial judge's refusal to allow Tennis to proceed pro se without specifically ruling on his request appropriate under Indiana v. Edwards (2008)?
Holding available from instructor.

Standby Counsel

6-3. Marco Allen Chapman pled guilty to murder and volunteered for the death penalty after firing his attorneys. He was allowed to represent himself after the trial court held a hearing and ruled that Chapman was competent to fire his attorneys, to plead guilty, and to seek death. Over the objections of both Chapman and his former attorneys, the trial court appointed the same attorneys Chapman fired to act as his standby counsel. Chapman alleged a communication breakdown and irreconcilable differences between him and his attorneys, but in fact they continued to confer. Chapman was sentenced to death.

Did the trial judge abuse his discretion by appointing lawyers who were fired by the defendant as his standby counsel when he represented himself pro se?
Holding available from instructor.

Effective Assistance

6-4. Bryant was found guilty of manslaughter in the first degree. The prosecution case was that Fournier and Jones purchased illicit drugs from a dealer and Bryant, and began to drive off without paying. Bryant held onto their car and eventually beat Jones to death with repeated kicks. The prosecution's evidence was based on the eyewitness testimony of Fournier, described as uncooperative and intoxicated at the time, and Ewan Sharpe, a teen who did not come forward until four years after the fact, and only while undergoing police interrogation for an unrelated felony. The medical examiner made a thorough autopsy of Jones' body and testified that the cause of Jones' death was blunt head trauma.

An alternate scenario was available, based on statements to police of four witnesses. Thomas Davis (1), a Marine Corps veteran and security guard, was driving in a company vehicle at the time and place of the killing and heard gunshots when Fournier and Jones's Ford Escort crashed into his car, while emerging the wrong way from a one-way street with the driver slumped over the steering wheel. A white Cadillac pursued the Ford, stopped, and a light-skinned Hispanic man exited. He approached Davis's vehicle with an object in his hand. Believing the neighborhood to be dangerous, Davis displayed his own firearm, and the man departed. Davis did not see anyone beat or kick the occupant. Melissa Young-Duncan (2) and John Gartley (3) were experienced emergency medical technicians at the incident. They promptly arrived

at the scene and provided the initial medical treatment to Jones. They both noticed what appeared to be a gunshot wound to Jones's left temple as well as what appeared to be a powder burn. Rene Fleury (4), Fournier's girlfriend and owner of the ford Escort, spoke with Fournier after he arrived home from the hospital and Fournier told her that "there had been an incident with three Hispanic males and a gun."

Bryant's defense counsel, David Smith, decided to not call the four alternate witnesses because (1) there was no evidence to support the theory of the involvement of a gunman because there was no forensic evidence of a gunshot wound and (2) introducing the possibility that a gun had been involved might have increased Bryant's sentence.

Was attorney Smith's decision to not call the four witnesses ineffective assistance of counsel?
Holding available from instructor.

Further Reading

David J. Bodenhamer, *Fair Trial: Rights of the Accused in American History* (New York: Oxford University Press, 1992).
James Goodman, *Stories of Scottsboro* (New York: Pantheon, 1994).

David Feige, *Indefensible: One Lawyer's Journey into the Inferno of American Justice* (New York: Little, Brown, 2006)
Anthony Lewis, *Gideon's Trumpet* (New York: Vintage, 1964).

Useful Web Sites

National Association of Criminal Defense Lawyers

http://www.nacdl.org/public.nsf/freeform/WhoWeAre?OpenDocument

Site of membership organization. Offers informative press releases, *amicus curiae* briefs, and articles in *Champion Magazine*, as well as data on indigent defense, the death penalty, and more.

National Legal Aid and Defenders Association

http://www.nlada.org/

Site of organization representing public defenders; materials on the right to counsel; timely news items.

End Notes

1. *Faretta v. California* (1975), quoting Holdsworth, *History of English Law;* C. Rembar, *The Law of the Land* (New York: Simon and Schuster, 1980), 181; and L. Levy, *Origins of the Fifth Amendment* (New York: Oxford University Press, 1968), 19.

2. William Blackstone, *Commentaries on the Laws of England, Volume 4—of Public Wrongs* (Chicago: University of Chicago Press, 1979, facsimile of 1st ed., 1769), 349–50; John H. Langbein, *The Origins of Adversary Criminal Trial* (Oxford, UK: Oxford University Press, 2003), 106–77.

3. Hiller B. Zobel, *The Boston Massacre* (New York: W. W. Norton, 1970).

4. *Powell v. Alabama* (1932), citing the right to counsel in the first constitutions of Maryland, Massachusetts, New Hampshire, New York, Pennsylvania, Delaware, New Jersey, and Connecticut (not adopted until 1818), the statutes of North Carolina and South Carolina, and the later constitutions of Georgia and Rhode Island.

5. In England and Canada and in the colonies and early republican United States, the word was spelled *defence*. The modern American spelling is *defense*.

6. Two excellent histories of the Scottsboro case are D. T. Carter, *Scottsboro: A Tragedy of the American South*, rev. ed. (Baton Rouge: Louisiana State University Press, 1979), and J. Goodman,

Stories of Scottsboro (New York: Pantheon, 1994). The case narrative is taken from these sources.

7. The second appeal to the U.S. Supreme Court, *Norris v. Alabama* (1934), held that the exclusion of African Americans from juries violated the defendants' right to equal protection under the Fourteenth Amendment.

8. H. Arkes, *The Return of George Sutherland: Restoring a Jurisprudence of Natural Rights* (Princeton, N.J.: Princeton University Press, 1994).

9. Arkes, *The Return of George Sutherland*.

10. Arkes, *The Return of George Sutherland*, 265.

11. Justice Sutherland cited *Gitlow v. New York* (1925), *Stromberg v. California* (1931), and *Near v. Minnesota* (1931).

12. Arkes, *The Return of George Sutherland*, 268.

13. Linda Greenhouse, "High Court Backs Seizure of Assets in Criminal Cases," *New York Times*, June 22, 1989.

14. *In re Groban* (1957) (dictum).

15. *Davis v. Mississippi* (1969); *Gilbert v. California* (1967); and *United States v. Dionisio* (1973).

16. *Kirby v. Illinois* (1972); *United States v. Ash* (1973).

17. The facts in this section are taken from the case and the following news sources: News, *The Bismarck Tribune*, June 24, 2008;

Zeke MacCormack, "Gillespie County paying for legal mistake," *San Antonio Express-News*, April 30, 2009; Laura B. Martinez, "Expensive Defenders: Cameron County Steps up Indigent Legal Defense," *The Brownsville* (Texas) *Herald*, February 15, 2009. Unattributed direct quotations are from *Rothgery v. Gillespie County* (2008).

18. David Rossman, "'Were There No Appeal': The History of Review in American Criminal Courts," *Journal of Criminal Law and Criminology* 81, no. 3 (1990): 518–66, 519.

19. Marie Higgins Williams, "Comment: The Pro Se Criminal Defendant, Standby Counsel, and the Judge: A Proposal for Better Defined Roles," *University of Colorado Law Review* 71 (2000): 789–818, 795–97.

20. Erica J. Hashimoto, "Defending the Right of Self-Representation: An Empirical Look at the Pro Se Felony Defendant," *North Carolina Law Review* 85 (2007): 423–488, 447.

21. Hashimoto, "An Empirical Look," 429, 460-63.

22. Hashimoto, "An Empirical Look," 464–65, 465 n. 153.

23. Hashimoto, "An Empirical Look," 429–30, 473–75.

24. Williams, "The Pro Se Criminal Defendant," 801.

25. Williams, "The Pro Se Criminal Defendant," 805.

26. Williams, "The Pro Se Criminal Defendant," 805.

27. Williams, "The Pro Se Criminal Defendant," 809–15.

28. Hashimoto, "An Empirical Look," 485.

29. J. T. McQuiston, "In the Bizarre L.I.R.R. Trial, Equally Bizarre Confrontations," *New York Times*, February 5, 1995; D. Van Biema, "A Fool for a Client; Accused L.I.R.R. Killer Colin Ferguson Is Defending Himself, and That May Be Something of a Crime," *Time*, February 6, 1995.

30. Philip Shenon, "Judge Lets Man Accused in September 11 Plot Defend Himself," *New York Times*, June 14, 2002; Philip Shenon, "Judge Bars 9/11 Suspect from Being Own Lawyer," *New York Times*, November 15, 2003.

31. Hashimoto, "An Empirical Look," 456–59.

32. Hashimoto, "An Empirical Look," 447–54.

33. Hashimoto, "An Empirical Look," 486.

34. See the Spangenberg Group, *Indigent Defense and Technology: A Progress Report* (Bureau of Justice Assistance, NCJ 179003 November 1999).

35. Bob Sablatura, "Study Confirms Money Counts in County's Courts: Those Using Appointed Lawyers Are Twice as Likely to Serve Time," *Houston Chronicle*, October 17, 1999.

36. "I Think You Get All the Justice You Can Afford," *Time*, June 19, 1995, 46–47.

37. Gregg Herrington, "Sex Ring Attorney Looks to Civil Trial," *Columbian*, December 15, 1995; T. Egan, "Pastor and Wife Are Acquitted on All Charges in Sex-Abuse Case," *New York Times*, December 12, 1995; and D. Nathan, "Justice in Wenatchee," *New York Times*, December 19, 1995. See Dorothy Rabinowitz, *No Crueler Tyrannies* (New York: Wall Street Journal Book Publishing, 2003).

38. D. West, "Cleared of Child Abuse, but the Anguish Lingers," *New York Times*, October 19, 1995.

39. Bulletin Broadfaxing Network, The Bulletin's Frontrunner, April 26, 2000: "Legal Fees Reduce Hilliard's Warchest to $149; Blames Racism for His Problem."

40. "CHSWC Okays New Study on Drug Costs," *Workers' Comp Executive* 9, no. 22 (December 1, 1999).

41. David Lawsky, "$1 Billion Settlement Reported in Vitamin Suit," *Toronto Star*, November 4, 1999, business sec.

42. Del Quentin Wilber, "Tripp Seeks Help Paying Lawyers," *Des Moines Register*, November 18, 1999.

43. Jill Abramson, "The Nation: The Price of Being Lewinsky; Dream Team, Nightmare Tab," *New York Times*, June 7, 1998, sec. 4.

44. Don Van Natta Jr., "Fewer Donations Coming in for Clinton Defense Fund," *New York Times*, August 13, 1999.

45. "I Think You Get All the Justice You Can Afford," *Time*, June 19, 1995.

46. E. Gleick, "Rich Justice, Poor Justice," *Time*, June 19, 1995.

47. Kevin Moran, "Durst Told Wife He Would Be Acquitted," *Houston Chronicle*, November 13, 2003.

48. Kim Taylor-Thompson, "Effective Assistance: Reconceiving the Role of the Chief Public Defender," *Journal of the Institute for the Study of Legal Ethics* 2 (1999): 199–200.

49. David Bazelon, quoted in R. Klein, "The Emperor *Gideon* Has No Clothes: The Empty Promise of the Constitutional Right to Effective Assistance of Counsel," *Hastings Constitutional Law Quarterly* 13 (1986): 625–93, 656.

50. Editorial, "Judicial Reforms in Albany," *New York Times*, May 26, 2000.

51. Martha K. Harrison, "Note: Claims for Compensation: The Implications of Getting Paid When Appointed under the Criminal Justice Act," *Boston University Law Review* 79 (1999): 553–76, 555, n. 15.

52. Alan Cooper, "Appointed Lawyer's Low Fee Ruled No Bar to Fair Trial," *Richmond Times Dispatch*, May 5, 2000.

53. R. Marcus, "Racism in Our Courts: The Underfunding of Public Defenders and Its Disproportionate Impact upon Racial Minorities," *Hastings Constitutional Law Quarterly* 22 (1994): 219–67, 228–29 (footnotes omitted, emphasis added).

54. S. Mounts, "The Right to Counsel and the Indigent Defense System," *New York University Review of Law and Social Change* 14 (1986): 221–41, 221, citing *Cooper v. Fitzharris*, 551 F.2d 1162, 163 n. 1 (9th Cir. 1977).

55. R. L. Spangenberg and T. J. Schwartz, "The Indigent Defense Crisis Is Chronic," *Criminal Justice* (Summer 1994): 13, citing *State v. Peart*, 621 So.2d 780 (La. 1993).

56. Spangenberg and Schwartz, "The Indigent Defense Crisis," citing *National Law Journal*, August 20, 1992.

57. R. L. Spangenberg, "We Are Still Not Defending the Poor Properly," *Criminal Justice* (Fall 1989): 11–131, 12.

58. S. E. Mounts and R. J. Wilson, "Systems for Providing Indigent Defense: An Introduction," *New York University Review of Law and Social Change* 14 (1986): 193–201, 194, citing *Washington Post*, June 25, 1984.

59. Ross E. Milloy, "Judge Frees Texas Inmate Whose Lawyer Slept at Trial," *New York Times*, March 2, 2000; and Paul Duggan, "George W. Bush: The Record in Texas; Attorneys' Ineptitude Doesn't Halt Executions," *Washington Post*, May 12, 2000.

60. S. Bright, "Counsel for the Poor: The Death Sentence Not for the Worst Crime but for the Worst Lawyer," *Yale Law Journal* 103 (1994): 1835–83, 1838–39.

61. A. Cohen, "The Difference a Million Makes," *Time*, June 19, 1993.

62. "Another Wrongly Convicted Man," *Indianpolis Star*, February 10, 2000; and Bright, "Counsel for the Poor."

63. Sara Rimer, "Questions of Death Row Justice for Poor People in Alabama," *New York Times*, March 1, 2000.

64. Rimer, "Questions of Death Row Justice."

65. Mounts and Wilson, "Systems for Providing Indigent Defense," 200–201.

66. Spangenberg and Schwartz, "The Indigent Defense Crisis," 14; and J. J. Cleary, "Federal Defender Services: Serving the

System or the Client?" *Law and Contemporary Problems* 58 (1995): 65–80, 65.

67. Mounts and Wilson, "Systems for Providing Indigent Defense," 200–201.

68. Spangenberg and Schwartz, "The Indigent Defense Crisis."

69. Spangenberg Group, *Indigent Defense and Technology*, 1999.

70. Taylor-Thompson, "Effective Assistance."

71. Taylor-Thompson, "Effective Assistance," 207–8.

72. Jo Becker, "Rules Set for Death Row Lawyers," *St. Petersburg (Fla.) Times*, October 30, 1999.

73. Stafford Henderson Byers, "Delivering Indigents' Right to Counsel While Respecting Lawyers' Right to Their Profession: A System 'between a Rock and a Hard Place,'" *St. John's Journal of Legal Commentary* 13 (1999): 491–526.

JUSTICES OF THE SUPREME COURT

Warren Court Liberals: Warren, Goldberg, and Fortas

The liberal reputation of the Warren Court (1953–1969) rests primarily on its work in four major areas: destroying legalized racial segregation, mandating equal voting power through the apportionment of voting districts so that each voter's vote was of approximately equal weight, expanding First Amendment rights, and incorporating most of the criminal procedure provisions of the Bill of Rights. The last achievement, in fact, began in 1961 with *Mapp v. Ohio* and gathered momentum only with the appointment of Justice Arthur Goldberg upon the retirement of Justice Felix Frankfurter. The incorporation cases often, but not invariably, hinged on the votes of a slim majority—Chief Justice Earl Warren and Justices Hugo Black, William Douglas, William Brennan, and Arthur Goldberg (and Justice Abe Fortas after him). This is not surprising to constitutional scholars because important constitutional innovations often embody one side of a large conflict of ideals of the society. The competing ideals of liberty and security are both essential, so the law of criminal procedure is bound to exhibit some tension and shift. The adoption of a competing ideal in a particular case is less a matter of "right and wrong" in a factual sense than a value choice between the approaches and a response to differing perceived needs of the nation at a given time. This may explain why American electoral politics, policy choices, and constitutional doctrines are subject to broad swings over the decades; there may be no other way to maintain peaceful continuity in a nation so vast and so varied.

Collection of the Supreme Court of the United States. Photographer: Abdon Daoud Ackad.

Earl Warren

California, 1891–1974

Republican

Appointed Chief Justice by Dwight D. Eisenhower

Years of Service: 1953–1969

Life and Career.   The son of a Norwegian immigrant railroad car inspector, Warren received his undergraduate and law degrees from the University of California, Berkeley. After army service in World War I, he entered public service and became the district attorney of Alameda County, California, in 1925. His vigorous prosecution of corrupt politicians and organized crime helped to elevate him to California's attorney general in 1938. In that role, he backed the relocation of Japanese Americans from their homes to internment camps for the duration of World War II. He was elected governor of California in 1943, and he ran for vice president of the United States in 1948 on the losing Republican ticket with Thomas Dewey of New York. His support of a rule that allowed Dwight Eisenhower to win the nomination of the Republican Party led to his appointment as chief justice in 1953.

Contribution to Criminal Procedure.   After his first two terms on the Court, Chief Justice Warren became a critical liberal vote, and with the appointment of Justice Goldberg to replace Justice Frankfurter in 1962, the way was clear to accomplish the due process revolution by which most of the criminal provisions of the Bill of Rights were incorporated. His important majority opinions include *Terry v. Ohio* (1968) (stop and frisk), *Sherman v. United States* (1958) (entrapment), and *Klopfer v. North Carolina* (1967) (incorporating the Sixth Amendment right to a speedy trial). Chief Justice Warren, who had been a tough prosecutor, knew well how such public servants could abuse their great powers of office to overwhelm the will of the individual.

Signature Opinion.   *Miranda v. Arizona* (1966). *Miranda* is the case that revolutionized the law of confessions. In his majority opinion, Chief Justice Warren characteristically devoted relatively little space to a discussion of precedents, which would ordinarily be critical to justify a decision, and instead devoted the lion's share of the opinion to documenting the numerous ways that law enforcement officers "subjugated the individual to the will of his examiner." The decision in *Miranda* spelled out practical rules and their application for police and prosecutors, an approach that has been derided by critics as judicial legislation. *Miranda* was characteristic of Chief Justice Warren's activism and liberalism and of his willingness to ignite controversy if he believed his position was the fair course to take.

Assessment.   Earl Warren is ranked as a great chief justice, not because he had a brilliant legal mind or because of his judicial craft in writing opinions, but for his leadership. He was a progressive with strong streaks of moralism and populism, as well as a superb administrator who knew how to motivate people and get things done. He is remembered for his masterful ability to take a Court divided on the monumental issue of school segregation and steer it to a unanimous opinion in *Brown v. Board of Education* (1954), a feat considered to be the hallmark of judicial statesmanship. During an oral argument, he often cut through technical presentations to ask lawyers if the position they were supporting was fair, a question some saw as unsophisticated. However, this approach provided the framework for rulings that transformed American politics, law enforcement, and society. Under Chief Justice Warren, the Supreme Court was marked by activism, liberalism, and populism. It outlawed racial segregation, ended unrepresentative voting districts in the states, extended First Amendment rights, and vigorously upheld antitrust laws.

Further Reading

Bernard Schwartz, *Super Chief: Earl Warren and His Supreme Court—A Judicial Biography* (New York: New York University Press, 1983).

Arthur J. Goldberg

Illinois 1908–1990

Democrat

Appointed by John F. Kennedy

Years of Service: 1962–1965

Life and Career.   The youngest of eleven children of Russian immigrants, Goldberg was educated in Chicago public schools and received his bachelor's and law degrees from Northwestern University, graduating first in his law school class. He practiced law in Chicago until World War II and, in 1938, began to practice labor law. During the war, he served in the Office of Strategic Services in charge of labor espionage behind enemy lines.

After the war, he became a leading labor lawyer and, in 1948, became general counsel for the United Steelworkers Union. He played a central role in the merger of the American Federation of Labor and the Congress of Industrial Organizations (AFL-CIO) and became the group's general counsel. In 1957, he led the fight to expel the crime-ridden Teamsters Union from the labor body. Through this work and his excellent reputation as a negotiator, Goldberg gained national prominence. He became an advisor to Senator John F. Kennedy in his 1960 bid for the presidency and was selected by President Kennedy to be secretary of labor, where he played an active role in settling several major strikes. In 1962, he was nominated by Kennedy to replace Justice Frankfurter.

In 1965, President Lyndon Johnson persuaded Justice Goldberg to resign his seat on the Court to become ambassador to the United Nations in the hope that his negotiating skills would help in bringing a speedy end to the Vietnam War.

Contribution to Criminal Procedure.   Despite his short period of service, Justice Goldberg's appointment created a liberal majority on the Court and inaugurated the due process revolution of applying the Bill of Rights to the states in criminal procedure.

Signature Opinion.   *Escobedo v. Illinois* (1964). In *Escobedo*, the Court held that police refusal of a lawyer's request to see a client violated the right to counsel and that a confession obtained under those conditions was inadmissible in court. This breakthrough case paved the way for *Miranda v. Arizona* (1966).

Assessment.   Justice Goldberg was a liberal who believed that the Court has a legitimate problem-solving role and an important role in democracy by imposing constitutional majoritarian restraints to protect minority rights. He was a creative justice and established himself as the leading liberal spokesperson on a wide variety of explosive civil rights issues. In *Griswold v. Connecticut* (1965), the contraceptive case that established a framework for abortion rights, Goldberg concurred on the intellectually daring position that the rarely used Ninth Amendment should be the basis for removing criminal penalties against physicians who dispense, and married people who seek, contraception advice. He argued that the Court should look to the "traditions and [collective] conscience of our people" to discover which rights are fundamental and beyond the reach of the legislature. He also opposed the death penalty, arguing in 1963 that the Court should decide its constitutionality, an issue that the Court did not confront until the 1970s. He took a bold approach to civil rights, urging the Court to go beyond declaring discriminatory laws unconstitutional and instead require the states to act affirmatively to guarantee civil rights, a position shared by only two other justices.

Further Reading

Stephen J. Friedman, "Arthur Goldberg," in Leon Friedman and Fred L. Israel, eds., *The Justices of the United States Supreme Court, 1789–1969*, vol. 4 (New York: Chelsea House, 1969), 2977–90.

Abe Fortas

Tennessee, 1910–1982

Democrat

Appointed by Lyndon Johnson

Years of Service: 1965–1969

Life and Career.   A native of Memphis and the son of a poor tailor, Fortas graduated from Southwest College and Yale Law School. At Yale, he came to the attention of Professor William O. Douglas, who brought Fortas to Washington, D.C., during the New Deal. Fortas was a tough and brilliant government lawyer. At age thirty-two, as undersecretary of the interior, he argued unsuccessfully against the removal of Japanese Americans from the West Coast.

After World War II, he went into private law practice in Washington, D.C. The firm of Arnold, Porter, and Fortas developed a reputation for effectively representing large corporations and for courageously defending the civil liberties of people hounded by the government during the anticommunist hysteria of the late 1940s and early 1950s. Fortas skillfully represented Texas Congressman Lyndon Johnson, under charges of election fraud, in a notorious 1948 Senate primary election vote recount that secured Johnson a Senate seat. Fortas then became a close advisor to Johnson.

As a private lawyer, Fortas took several *pro bono* cases that significantly changed criminal law and procedure. *Durham v. United States* (District of Columbia Court of Appeals, 1954, later reversed) made a major change in the insanity defense in Washington, D.C. He argued for the defendant in *Gideon v. Wainwright* (1963), playing an important role in advancing the incorporation doctrine and expanding the right to counsel.

Fortas was appointed to the Supreme Court by President Johnson in 1965, and after Earl Warren announced his *prospective* retirement in 1968, Johnson nominated him to be chief justice. Johnson did not seek a new term because of the intense politics surrounding the Vietnam War. As a result, Republicans in the Senate blocked Justice Fortas's appointment, and he eventually withdrew it. During the nomination process, the press discovered that he was a major presidential advisor while sitting on the bench and that he was receiving an annual payment of $20,000 from the family foundation of a businessman who had gone to prison for stock manipulation. In 1969, under intense public scrutiny and abetted by inside pressure from President Nixon's attorney general, John Mitchell, Justice Fortas resigned, although he had done nothing illegal.

Contribution to Criminal Procedure.   As a Warren Court liberal, Justice Fortas voted for the incorporation doctrine and for the expansion of suspects' and defendants' procedural rights in several important cases, providing the crucial fifth majority vote in *Miranda v. Arizona* (1966). He had a special interest in the rights of juvenile delinquents, a novel area for the Court, and his majority opinion in *Kent v. United States* (1966) held that a juvenile is entitled to a hearing under the Due Process Clause before a delinquency case can be transferred from juvenile court into the adult criminal system.

Signature Opinion.   *In re Gault* (1967). This case resulted in major changes in the way that juvenile court proceedings would be conducted. Before being adjudged delinquent, juveniles were entitled to many of the same procedural guarantees afforded to adults, including counsel, notice, the confrontation of witnesses, cross-examination, a written transcript, and appellate review. Justice Fortas's opinion was powerful because it recognized that a benevolent governmental purpose can mask oppression in practice. It emphasized that the procedural rights of the Constitution are critical to the legitimacy of American courts, even special courts designed to help juveniles and not merely to punish. No matter how noble the goal of the state, the Due Process Clause applies whenever any person, including a minor, is stripped of life, liberty, or property.

Assessment.   Justice Fortas was a solid liberal in all civil rights areas, but unlike most liberal justices, in antitrust matters he was not opposed to big business and usually did not vote against corporate mergers. His resignation allowed an additional appointment by President Nixon, thus shifting the Court from a liberal to a moderate-conservative stance in the area of criminal procedure.

Further Reading

Laura Kalman, *Abe Fortas: A Biography* (New Haven: Yale University Press, 1990).

CHAPTER 7

Interrogation and the Law of Confessions

The Constitution of the United States stands as a bar against the conviction of any individual in an American court by means of a coerced confession. There have been, and are now, certain foreign nations with governments dedicated to an opposite policy: governments which convict individuals with testimony obtained by police organizations possessed of an unrestrained power to seize persons suspected of crimes against the state, hold them in secret custody, and wring from them confessions by physical or mental torture. So long as the Constitution remains the basic law of our Republic, America will not have that kind of government.

—JUSTICE HUGO BLACK, *Ashcraft v. Tennessee,* 322 U.S. 143, 155 (1944)

KEY TERMS

admission	exculpatory	material witness	third degree
compulsion	immunity	privilege	voluntariness test
confession	inculpatory	real evidence	
cruel trilemma	interrogation	supervisory authority	
dying declaration	involuntary confession	testimonial evidence	

INTRODUCTION

"The cases before us raise questions which go to the roots of our concepts of American criminal jurisprudence: the restraints society must observe consistent with the Federal Constitution in prosecuting individuals for crime." The opening line of Chief Justice Warren's majority opinion in *Miranda v. Arizona* (1966) dispassionately itemizes the poles of the continuum of justice in a decent society: effectiveness in law enforcement balanced against fair and legal treatment. Few criminal justice practices have produced and continue to produce such white-hot controversy as police interrogation and the production of confessions. Today, police almost never torture suspects and it appears that the use of physical force during interrogation is minimal. Yet, evidence shows that alongside restrained interrogation, police routinely manipulate, harangue, harass, and lie to suspects to get them to confess. Police do not openly defend the outer limits of such behaviors, but there is little doubt that the methods are seen as necessary to convict a number of serious criminals. Critics point to a large number of known false confessions. In this chapter, the legal rules generated by the Supreme Court to control excesses in police interrogation are explored, and the "Law in Society" section takes a more direct look at interrogation practices.

Interviewing witnesses and interrogating suspects are essential police investigation techniques.[1] Interviewing witnesses helps police understand what occurred at a crime scene. Police will interrogate an arrested suspect to obtain **admissions** or **confessions** of guilt that can be used in court to convict the suspect. Abusive interrogation, including torture, was common in American policing until the 1940s. Instances of excessive force still occur, and the potential for brutality must constantly be guarded against.[2] Furthermore, recent research shows that contemporary practices of "psychological interrogation" produce many false confessions by the innocent.[3] (See the "Law in Society" section in this chapter.)

The Supreme Court has developed three areas of constitutional law designed to check abusive **interrogation**: (1) *due process* to prevent torture and abuse of suspects, (2) the *privilege against self-incrimination* to preserve a suspect's right to silence, and (3) the *right to counsel for post-indictment questioning* of defendants. Since 1966, *Miranda v. Arizona* (1966) and other Self-Incrimination Clause cases have been the major focus of interrogation law. Although *Miranda* includes a Fifth Amendment right to counsel that applies during pre-indictment custodial interrogation, the Sixth Amendment Right to Counsel Clause requires a lawyer for all questioning of a person who has been formally charged with a crime under *Massiah v. United States* (1964).

In a nutshell, (1) the Due Process Clauses (Fifth and Fourteenth Amendments) prohibit the introduction of **involuntary confessions**; (2) the *Miranda* doctrine holds that police interrogation of a *suspect* in custody is *inherently coercive* and any confession or admission is presumed to be the product of **compulsion** unless a suspect is informed of his or her rights and voluntarily waives the right of silence under the privilege against self-incrimination; (3) the right to counsel prohibits questioning a criminal *defendant* to elicit incriminating statements without the defendant's lawyer being present; and (4) suspects and defendants can *waive* their Fifth and Sixth Amendment rights, giving police an opening to persuade them to give up their constitutional protections.

The Privilege against Self-Incrimination

The Self-Incrimination Clause appears to focus *only* on criminal trial testimony: "No person . . . shall be compelled in any criminal *case* to be a witness against himself" (emphasis added). Nevertheless, the Supreme Court ruled that the **privilege** against self-incrimination applies to police interrogation in *Miranda v. Arizona* (1966). Despite a large number of cases interpreting the privilege, the meaning of this famous rule is even now not fully settled. The state of confessions law has been in flux since *Miranda* was decided. A decision in 2000 declaring the *Miranda* rule to be constitutional (*Dickerson v. United States*) was followed by a civil case that added confusion concerning the effect of the privilege *Miranda* (*Chavez v. Martinez,* 2003). More recent cases have only partially determined that *Miranda* is enforceable, and conservative justices seem ready to neuter the *Miranda* rule. These cases, discussed in this chapter, require a basic understanding of contemporary self-incrimination law.

Despite its text, the Self-Incrimination Clause, which clearly allows a defendant to remain silent in a criminal trial and have counsel conduct the defense entirely by cross-examination, applies in other proceedings. Also, a prosecutor or judge who mentions a defendant's silence, except at the defendant's behest, violates his or her right against self-incrimination (*Griffin v. California*, 1965; *Lakeside v. Oregon*, 1978). Jurors may believe that a defendant who does not take the stand has something to hide, but a hint by a judge or prosecutor so unbalances the scales of justice in the state's favor as to undermine a fair adversary trial. Prosecutorial or judicial comment also puts pressure ("compulsion") on the defendant to give up the right to silence.

CLAIMING THE PRIVILEGE   To ensure that the right is not destroyed before a criminal prosecution begins, a person may refuse to testify under the Fifth Amendment in a variety of proceedings where he or she is called as a witness. These include criminal and civil cases (*McCarthy v. Arndstein*, 1924; *United States v. Monia*, 1943), administrative proceedings (*Malloy v. Hogan*, 1964), congressional investigations (*Watkins v. United States*, 1957), and grand juries (*Counselman v. Hitchcock*, 1892). If witnesses testify in these proceedings, their preserved testimony, if incriminating, can later be introduced against them in a criminal trial.

The privilege has to be actively *invoked* in these proceedings because it is an exception to the general rule that individuals have an obligation to testify (either voluntarily or under subpoena) to assist the state in prosecuting crimes and gathering information for legitimate purposes. State officers may request information in informal and formal proceedings. A police officer who asks residents for information about a criminal incident, which is not a formal proceeding, cannot compel a person to provide information. Given Americans' well-honed sense of privacy, many may refuse to "get involved." Nevertheless, as Chief Justice Earl Warren stated, "It is an act of responsible citizenship for individuals to give whatever information they may have to aid in law enforcement" (*Miranda v. Arizona*, 1966). A person not in custody who *does respond* to questions of a federal police officer, however, has an obligation to answer questions *truthfully* and may face criminal charges for lying (*Brogan v. United States*, 1998).

In contrast, persons lawfully subpoenaed to formal hearings have a general obligation to testify under oath. Prosecutors have the power to arrest and confine **material witnesses** if a judge believes the person has information material to the prosecution of a pending criminal charge or grand jury investigation and the person may flee.[4] Persons formally subpoenaed by judicial, executive, or legislative bodies or by grand juries or held as material witnesses must give testimony *unless* they have a legal privilege or right to refuse to testify. Failure to testify can lead to a finding of contempt, punishable with fines or even jail. The law recognizes several privileges that exempt a person from providing information to lawful authority. Religious, medical, or legal practitioners need not divulge information given in professional confidence; the marital privilege protects the natural privacy of spouses;[5] and the privilege against self-incrimination exempts a person from confessing to crimes.

VALUES PROTECTED BY THE PRIVILEGE   The privilege against self-incrimination "is widely regarded as both fundamental to human liberty and venerable in the history of the development of civil rights."[6] It is related to modern notions of privacy and is a mainstay of the adversary system. It supports the rule that the burden of proof of guilt rests on the prosecution and that guilt must be proven beyond a reasonable doubt.

The privilege against self-incrimination stands in contrast to brutal legal measures in ancient Rome and medieval continental Europe that allowed the use of torture to obtain evidence of serious crime.[7] It also contrasts with the far more civilized European criminal justice systems of today that many view as more effective in getting at the truth, in which defendants routinely talk to police and prosecutors.[8] The Supreme Court, listing seven values, stated that the privilege

reflects many of our fundamental values and most noble aspirations: our unwillingness to subject those suspected of crime to the **cruel trilemma** of self-accusation, perjury or contempt; our preference for an accusatorial rather than an inquisitorial system of criminal justice; our fear that self-incriminating statements will be elicited by inhumane treatment and abuses; our sense of fair play which dictates a fair state-individual balance by requiring the government to leave the individual alone until good cause is shown for disturbing him and by requiring the government in its contest with the individual to shoulder the entire load; our respect for the inviolability of the human personality and of the right of each individual to a private enclave where he may lead a private life; our distrust of self-deprecatory statements; and our realization that the privilege, while sometimes a shelter to the guilty, is often a protection to the innocent. (*Murphy v. Waterfront Commission of New York Harbor,* 1964, internal references and quotation marks omitted)

Truth values underlie the Fifth Amendment privilege. It is a trial right said by the Court to be closely related to the "correct ascertainment of guilt." As such, the privilege itself and the *Miranda* rule that followed serve to "guard against the use of unreliable statements at trial" (*Withrow v. Williams,* 1993, citing similar cases).

Prior to 1964, the privilege applied only to the federal government. In *Malloy v. Hogan* (1964), it was *incorporated* into the Fourteenth Amendment Due Process Clause and held to "secure . . . against state invasion the same privilege that the Fifth Amendment guarantees against federal infringement—the right of a person to remain silent unless he chooses to speak in the unfettered exercise of his own will, and to suffer no penalty . . . for such silence."

APPLICATION OF THE PRIVILEGE   The privilege applies only to "natural persons." It cannot be claimed on behalf of corporations or other business entities by their officers, even sole proprietorships; they are deemed to be "artificial persons" for self-incrimination purposes (*Wilson v. United States,* 1911; *Bellis v. United States,* 1974; *United States v. Doe,* 1984). Tax records created by an individual and delivered to his or her attorney are not immune from subpoena power (*Fisher v. United States,* 1976). The privilege applies only to **testimonial evidence**—evidence given by a live witness (or in personal writings such as a diary) that is of a "communicative nature." Testimony conveys information based on what the witness knows or believes he or she knows. A testimonial communication "must itself, explicitly or implicitly, relate a factual assertion, or disclose information" that expresses "the contents of an individual's mind" (*Doe v. United States,* 1988). This is important because even if testimony is not directly self-incriminating, a witness who speaks reveals something about his or her mental process to the listener. This opens up the witness's mind and psychological process to the listener's scrutiny. A witness who testifies raises the possibility that his or her statements will lead the listener to infer that the witness has admitted to an incriminating fact, even if no explicit confession is made.

The privilege against self-incrimination does not apply to physical evidence, also called **real evidence**, no matter how incriminating, because it is not testimonial. Justice Oliver Wendell Holmes Jr. ruled that a suspect has no right to prevent the court, jury, or witnesses from viewing the suspect's face and person (***Holt v. United States***, 1910). The government can "compel a person to: (1) reenact a crime; (2) shave a beard or mustache; (3) try on clothing; (4) dye his or her hair; (5) demonstrate speech or other physical characteristics; (6) furnish handwriting samples, hair samples, or fingerprints; (7) have his or her teeth and gums examined; (8) submit to blood-alcohol, breathalyzer, or urine tests; or (9) provide DNA samples."[9] A suspect can be photographed or measured, have tattoos and scars examined, and be required to stand in a lineup. Police can require a person to provide blood samples taken by medical personnel where blood-alcohol levels are relevant evidence (***Schmerber v. California***, 1966). A driver stopped for driving under the influence (DUI) who refuses to take a breathalyzer test may have his or her driving license revoked, and the fact of *refusal* can be used against the driver at a subsequent criminal trial, even if the police did not inform the driver of that fact, because the refusal was not compelled (*South Dakota v. Neville,* 1983). Blood taking is distinguished from a "lie detector" session, which not only gathers physiological attributes but also may elicit testimonial responses. Police departments uniformly give *Miranda* warnings before administering polygraph examinations.

COMPULSION   Compulsion is an element of the right against self-incrimination. A purely voluntary admission of guilt to a friend or to an undercover agent is not made under compulsion; therefore the listener can later testify to what was said. An ordinary witness in a trial or grand jury hearing need not be warned of his or her privilege because the witness is not deemed to be under such compulsion, even though subpoenaed and sworn to testify (***United States v. Monia***, 1943). In other words, the privilege against self-incrimination is *not self-executing* and must be *claimed* by the witness or it will be lost.

Although the Fifth Amendment's text appears to absolutely prohibit prosecutorial compulsion against a suspect or against a witness who claims the privilege, this is not so. The state can *lawfully compel* a witness to testify by granting **immunity** from prosecution, and in this way the state can achieve its legitimate goal of gathering information in an inquiry or furthering a prosecution. (This type of immunity differs from immunity to civil suits discussed in Chapter 2.)

Immunity is granted when the prosecutor believes that a witness who claims the privilege has relevant information. If immunity from prosecution is granted and the witness continues to refuse to testify, the courts have power "to compel testimony . . . by use of civil contempt and coerced imprisonment" (*Lefkowitz v. Turley*, 1973, citing *Shillitani v. United States,* 1966).

An important consequence of granting immunity—for understanding the most recent controversy regarding confessions law—is that once immunity is granted, the statement made *cannot be used against the witness* in *any* way. "Testimony given in response to a grant of legislative immunity is the *essence of coerced testimony*. In such cases there is no question whether physical or psychological pressures overrode the defendant's will; the witness is told to talk or face the government's coercive sanctions, notably, a conviction for contempt" (**New Jersey v. Portash**, 1979, emphasis added). Therefore, grand jury testimony compelled by a grant of immunity cannot be used later in a trial to *impeach the witness's credibility*. As will be seen later in this chapter, the rule is different under *Miranda* law.

The government can also compel testimony, for purposes other than criminal prosecution, in the so-called *penalty cases*. Police officers were required to testify before an administrative body about corruption or forfeit their jobs; no immunity was offered. Such testimony was held to be compelled under the Fifth Amendment and excluded from use in prosecutions (*Garrity v. New Jersey,* 1967). The upshot, however, is that compulsion to testify on the pain of losing one's public job is lawful, as long as such compelled testimony is not later admitted in a criminal case. Also, although an officer who refused to testify about his own conduct could be fired for refusing to testify, and officer who refused to waive immunity could not be fired for this "refusal to waive a constitutional right" (*Gardner v. Broderick,* 1968). These early cases implied that the state could not compel the officers to testify, but as the Court later made clear, the state can require officers to testify on pain of losing their jobs and can require contractors to testify on pain of losing contracts, as long as they were granted immunity from criminal prosecution (*Lefkowitz v. Turley,* 1973). The result of these cases is to treat penalties (e.g., loss of jobs or contracts) as compulsion, but to allow the compulsion as long as the witnesses are immunized from the use of their testimony in later criminal prosecutions.

The act of a police officer simply asking questions of a person is not Fifth Amendment compulsion. *Miranda v. Arizona* (1966), however, held that when questions are asked of a suspect during *custodial interrogation,* Fifth Amendment compulsion exists. In this case, the privilege is not self-executing, and the police must inform the suspect of his or her rights by reading several warnings. (Cases that distinguish between police interviewing and interrogation are reviewed later in this chapter.)

INCRIMINATION   Under the privilege, a person cannot lawfully refuse to testify to protect another, to avoid trouble with private parties, or for any reason *except* to avoid being prosecuted *personally* for a crime or for juvenile delinquency, as the penalties for a delinquency adjudication are essentially penal in nature (*In re Gault,* 1967). Similarly, any incriminating statements obtained from a defendant who spoke with a state psychiatrist in a pretrial hearing to determine competence to stand trial cannot be introduced in the defendant's sentencing hearing unless the defendant waived his or her right against self-incrimination at the hearing following *Miranda* warnings (**Estelle v. Smith**, 1981).

On the other hand, the Court has not extended self-incrimination protection to proceedings under sexual offender statutes that lead to incarceration or additional penalties. These programs are declared *civil*, and *not penal*, in nature. In **Allen v. Illinois** (1986), sexual assault charges were dropped against the defendant, and the state proceeded against him under the Sexually Dangerous Persons Act. Examining psychiatrists for the state testified at the bench trial on the state's commitment petition. The trial court found that the state proved Allen had a mental disorder and a propensity to commit sexual assaults. Based on the psychiatrists' testimony, and that of the sexual assault victim, the court found Allen to be a sexually dangerous person. The act authorized potentially indefinite (life) commitment to the "sex deviate facility" located *in* the Wisconsin State Prison. Allen claimed that information elicited from him violated his right against self-incrimination. The Supreme Court held (5–4) that the program was one of *civil commitment*, despite the fact that the act provides safeguards applicable in criminal trials (counsel, jury trial, confrontation and cross-examination of witnesses), that the state had to prove dangerousness beyond a reasonable doubt, and that a person adjudged sexually dangerous is committed to a maximum-security institution that also houses convicts needing psychiatric care.

In *McKune v. Lile* (2002), a prison inmate convicted of rape was ordered into a treatment program a few years before his scheduled release. To participate, Robert Lile had to answer questions that would disclose criminal activity. No immunity was granted for any incriminating disclosures. Lile refused to participate. As a result, his prison privileges were reduced. He lost visitation rights, earnings, work opportunities, the ability to send money to family, canteen expenditures, access to a personal television, and other privileges. He also was transferred to a potentially more dangerous maximum-security unit. The Supreme Court held (5–4) that the requirement to disclose criminal information did not violate the Self-Incrimination Clause. In a plurality opinion, Justice Anthony Kennedy reasoned that although prisoners have Fifth Amendment rights, the program does not compel prisoners to testify because the lost privileges and transfer to a maximum-security unit "are not [consequences] that compel a prisoner to speak about his past crimes despite a desire to remain silent." The loss of privileges that Lile suffered was, furthermore, related to the objectives of a program that had legitimate penological goals. There was no self-incrimination violation as long as the program objectives did not constitute atypical and significant hardships. Justice John Paul Stevens, dissenting, felt that the penalties imposed for not participating were severe. More fundamentally, Lile was punished for exercising his rights under the Self-Incrimination Clause.

Allen was criticized because it "is insensitive to the reality of the commitment system" that makes it very much like an indefinite prison sentence.[10] The kinds of programs upheld in *Allen* and *McKune* are politically popular attempts to deal with highly predatory criminals. Nevertheless, there is evidence that some offenders placed in these programs do not fit the profiles of mentally aberrant patients and that the programs may be covert ways of imposing virtual life sentences. The evidence used to place prisoners in programs may consist more of their prior record than any medical information.[11]

The privilege protects only against incrimination in American courts. A former Nazi camp guard, unprosecutable in the United States because the statute of limitations had run out, was subpoenaed to testify in deportation hearings. He claimed self-incrimination protection because his testimony could be used to prosecute him in other countries, including Lithuania or Germany. The Supreme Court held that the Self-Incrimination Clause refers only to *American* procedures, as do the other clauses of the Fifth Amendment (Grand Jury, Double Jeopardy, Due Process, and Just Compensation) (*United States v. Balsys,* 1998).

THE ACT OF PRODUCING EVIDENCE   Federal appellate courts have held that although "the *contents* of voluntarily produced papers are not protected by the Fifth Amendment, the *act of producing* such documents is protected . . . if the act itself is both testimonial and incriminating."[12] A person who complies with a subpoena and produces the evidence shows that he had possession, knew the evidence existed and was authentic, and believed the documents matched the terms of a subpoena. These facts could be incriminating (*Fisher v. United States,* 1976). The Supreme Court has not established a bright-line rule that immunizes compelled production of records from prosecution. Each case must be resolved on its own facts. Where a court determines that production itself is incriminating, the individual may still have to produce the records but may be granted immunity, although this is not automatic (*United States v. Doe,* 1984).

Certainly, the oddest and most dramatic act-of-production case is **Baltimore Department of Social Services v. Bouknight** (1990). The Baltimore City Department of Social Services (BCDSS), fearing child abuse, removed an infant, Maurice, from his mother, Jacqueline Bouknight. He was returned to her a few months later, under various conditions. Eight months later, fearing for Maurice's safety, the juvenile court ordered his return to BCDSS custody. Bouknight refused to turn over the boy. A diligent search by police and relatives failed to produce him. Bouknight was held in contempt of court for failing to produce Maurice and was jailed. She challenged this in the U.S. Supreme Court on the ground that the compelled production of Maurice might tend to incriminate her.

The Supreme Court held that Bouknight had no Fifth Amendment claim because Maurice's physical condition was not testimonial evidence. She argued that "her implicit communication of control over Maurice at the moment of production might aid the State in prosecuting [her]." The Court also ruled that even if the boy's production were testimonial, it still did not give her the right to refuse the order "because she has assumed *custodial duties* related to production [of Maurice] and production is required as a part of a *noncriminal regulatory scheme*" (emphasis added). The Court did not answer the question of whether the Fifth

Amendment would protect Bouknight against prosecution if she complied with the order, produced Maurice, and was prosecuted for child abuse because of evidence obtained from her act of production.

Having lost her case, Bouknight remained in jail for contempt of court for seven and a half years, one of the longest terms for contempt in U.S. history. She was released in October 1995. The judge who ordered the release said that continued imprisonment was no longer an effective tool to force the information from her. Her lawyers called Bouknight a hero of civil disobedience, but the judge who had held her in contempt expressed fears that the child might be dead.[13]

The Due Process Voluntariness Test

English and American courts around 1800 developed a common law *exclusionary rule* not allowing the introduction of *coerced confessions* into evidence in criminal trials. Courts did not develop this rule under the common law privilege against self-incrimination, although the privilege may have influenced its creation. Under the voluntariness test, police could question suspects, and incriminating statements could be used in evidence against them, as long as the statements were not "induced by force, threat of force, or promise of leniency from a person in authority, for if it has been so obtained, it is considered 'involuntary' and excluded."[14] These common law courts, utilizing their powers of fashioning binding rules in the course of deciding cases, were motivated by reasons akin to those outlawing torture: guarding against false confessions and upholding civilized standards of conduct.

In 1912, the English courts advanced the protection offered to a suspect from coercive interrogation by establishing the so-called Judges' Rules for the guidance of police officers. The Judges' Rules stated that before asking a person about to be charged with a crime if he or she wished to say anything in answer to the charges, that person should be told, "You are not obliged to say anything unless you wish to do so, but whatever you say will be taken down in writing and may be given in evidence."[15] A failure to give the warning rendered a statement improper, and it could be excluded from consideration at trial. The English Judges' Rules were well known to American jurists and established the idea that it is proper to inform suspects of their basic right against self-incrimination. These Rules did not include a specific exclusionary rule; it was simply assumed that English police officers would act properly. Some American police agencies, such as the FBI, decided as a matter of good law enforcement administration to require agents to warn suspects of their rights.

The **voluntariness test** was established in each American state by the late nineteenth century. The U.S. Supreme Court, in **Bram v. United States** (1897), held that coerced confessions in *federal* cases were guided by the Fifth Amendment right against self-incrimination. The test of admissibility under *Bram,* however, was essentially the voluntariness test established as a common law rule by states. In both state and federal law, therefore, coerced or involuntary confessions were excluded from evidence, although no warning requirement was yet established. Because the Bill of Rights criminal justice amendments had not been incorporated before 1961, *Bram*'s self-incrimination rule did not apply to the states.

In practice, state courts were often reluctant to exclude confessions even when there was compelling evidence of coercion. As a result, defendants whose confessions were the product of coercion turned to the federal courts, claiming that coerced confessions violated the Fourteenth Amendment Due Process Clause and were inadmissible. From 1936 until 1966, the Supreme Court decided more than thirty confessions cases from the states under the Due Process Clause. In 1964, the Fifth Amendment self-incrimination rule was incorporated, paving the way to *Miranda v. Arizona* (1966). A brief review of the due process voluntariness test helps us appreciate the significance of the "*Miranda* revolution." It is important to keep in mind that the due process voluntariness test *co-exists* with the *Miranda* rule and can be used today by defendants to challenged coerced confessions.

Brown v. Mississippi (1936) was the first Supreme Court case to review a confession obtained by state or local officers. Three African-American men confessed to committing a murder after being subjected to *torture* during their interrogation by the local sheriff and others. Their treatment included being hung by a rope from a tree, being let down, and being hung again, and whipping "with a leather strap with buckles on it" that cut their backs to pieces. After resisting these tortures over three days, they were told that it would continue until they signed a confession dictated by a deputy. The Supreme Court held that confessions obtained by such physical torture were "not consistent" with Fourteenth Amendment due process of law. Such trials and convictions were void because they were "a mere pretense where the state authorities have contrived a conviction resting solely upon confessions obtained by violence" (*Brown v. Mississippi*, 1936). The legal foundation of *Brown* was not a specific Bill of Rights provision but the "fair trial" idea of the Fourteenth Amendment Due Process Clause, first adopted by the Court in *Moore v. Dempsey* (1923). (See Chapter 1.)

The due process approach toward involuntary confessions initiated by *Brown* was not limited to physical torture. The Court soon applied the voluntariness test to lesser forms of coercion. The basic question was whether, under the facts and circumstances of the case, a particular confession was voluntary. Was it made of the defendant's free will? Was it obtained by police interrogation tactics that overcame the defendant's will? In case after case, the Supreme Court moved inexorably toward more refined standards. In ***Ashcraft v. Tennessee*** (1944), for example, the police did not beat the defendant but questioned him "in relays" for thirty-six hours with no interruption and no sleep until he confessed to murdering his wife. The Supreme Court held that the long period of straight questioning was itself sufficient coercion so that his statements were not voluntary but compelled. Justice Hugo Black cited the Wickersham Commission's report of 1930 that condemned this kind of police behavior, known as the **third degree**, "as a secret and illegal practice."[16] The third degree, common in that era, ranged from severe questioning to police beatings of suspects to force confessions out of them. The Court's stream of state confessions cases, enforcing the involuntary confessions rule, was aimed at pressuring police departments to adopt more civilized interrogation methods. *Chambers v. Florida* (1940), a coerced confessions case, "clearly acknowledged that the federal government had a duty to guarantee fair trials in state as well as federal courts."[17]

Other practices held to undermine the defendant's will and induce involuntary confessions in violation of the Fourteenth Amendment included

- Defendant moved to *secret places* so that family, lawyers, or friends could not contact him (*Chambers v. Florida*, 1940; *Ward v. Texas*, 1942).
- Defendant kept *naked* for several hours (*Malinski v. New York*, 1945).
- Defendant told by a state-employed psychiatrist that the doctor was there to help him and would provide medical assistance, thus gaining the defendant's *false confidence* and incriminating information (*Leyra v. Denno*, 1954).
- Suspect, a young African American, *threatened* that he would be handed over to a lynch mob (*Payne v. Arkansas*, 1958).
- Defendant, in his cell, told by a police officer, who had been his childhood friend, over a period of days that the *officer would lose his job* if he did not get a statement (*Spano v. New York*, 1959).
- Vigorous interrogation of a *mentally defective* or insane suspect (*Blackburn v. Alabama*, 1960; *Culombe v. Connecticut*, 1961).
- Use of "*truth serum*" (*Townsend v. Sain*, 1963).
- Defendant told that her children's welfare assistance would be cut off and *her children taken from her* if she failed to cooperate with police (*Lynumn v. Illinois*, 1963).

The justices were clearly appalled by these excessive and coercive methods. Indeed, the Supreme Court held that where police action in forcing a confession was so egregious as to clearly violate due process, the police could be subject to prosecution under the federal criminal laws (*Williams v. United States*, 1951). As a court of law, however, the Supreme Court could not directly require police to follow more civilized procedures. Through its due process jurisdiction, the Court could only indirectly influence police practices by reversing convictions when police went too far. By progressively refining the standard of what constituted an involuntary confession, the Court signaled the police community to eliminate coercive methods of interrogation. On the positive side, the due process approach balanced the operating realities of policing with an expression of society's highest values. The negative side was that the Court's piecemeal approach seemed to hardly make a dent in the problem of police coercion.

PROBLEMS WITH THE VOLUNTARINESS RULE. The due process approach is subjective; it provided no clear guidance for lower courts and police and was deemed unsatisfactory to many judges and lawyers. This piecemeal method gave the police examples of what to avoid, but no clear-cut or bright-line rule explaining how constitutional interrogation should be conducted.

This growing dissatisfaction was a reason why the Court adopted the seemingly clear, rulelike guidelines in *Miranda*. Professor Richard Cortner comments:

> Adhering to the fair trial approach to the Due Process Clause, the Court followed a meandering and ofttimes puzzling course in state criminal cases during the 1950s . . . [T]he Court's performance under the Due Process Clause was such as to involve it in unpredictable intrusions into the state criminal process on the basis of standards nowhere satisfactorily articulated—with the result that serious federal-state strains developed.[18]

This "totality of the circumstances" approach to coerced confessions was *ad hoc*, case-by-case decision making that seemed the opposite of firm constitutional policy.

More fundamentally, the Court based the due process voluntariness test on different constitutional reasons: "(1) ensuring that convictions are based on *reliable* evidence; (2) *deterring* improper police conduct; or (3) assuring that a defendant's confession is the product of his *free and rational choice*."[19] The Court shuttled between these rationales, leaving lawyers and trial judges in confusion. In early cases like *Brown* and *Ashcraft*, all three elements coincided: Excessive police conduct overpowered the suspect's will and raised real doubts about the accuracy of the confession. In some later cases, the Court seemed to focus primarily on the reliability or accuracy of confessions. *Lyons v. Oklahoma* (1944) ruled that a confession would be upheld if the state "employed a fair standard in adjudicating common law in voluntariness claims" as long as it appeared that the confession was *true*—a rationale that would have *narrowed* the scope of the voluntariness rule. In *Lyons*, for example, a first confession was deemed involuntary because there was some evidence of violence and because the Oklahoma sheriff resorted to the goulish expedient of placing a pan containing the murder victim's bones on Lyons's lap to unnerve him. Nevertheless, the Supreme Court held that a voluntary confession given eleven days later was admissible.

But in other cases, the Court set aside convictions even where the confession's truthfulness was substantially corroborated, because the *police misconduct* was too great to ignore (**Watts v. Indiana**, 1949). In *Watts* the murder suspect was held for *six days*, at first in solitary confinement (in "the hole") and then under mean conditions, and questioned for hours on end by relays of six to eight officers before he confessed. Only after a prosecutor had the confession put in perfect legal form was Watts brought to a magistrate. A police misconduct rationale would *broaden* the Court's control over police behavior. Indeed, without signaling a clear intention to do so, the Court in the 1950s seemed to be shifting toward a police conduct test, concerned less with the accuracy of the confession or its actual voluntariness and more with controlling egregious police conduct. In **Rogers v. Richmond** (1961), for example, the Court struck down a seemingly accurate and voluntary confession because the police tricked the suspect into thinking that they were going to arrest his ailing wife for questioning. The Court, nevertheless, did not rely on *Rogers* as a vehicle to sharply limit police interrogation practices. It thus produced inconsistent results by emphasizing different purposes in different cases. The lack of clarity of the rules and the underlying purposes of its due process cases led the Court to search for *bright-line* confessions rules to give police firmer guidance.

THE FEDERAL "TIME TEST"   In *McNabb v. United States* (1943) and **Mallory v. United States** (1957) the Supreme Court, exercising its **supervisory authority** over federal law enforcement, held that *all* confessions, even voluntary ones, were excluded from evidence if there was "unnecessary delay" in bringing an arrested suspect before a magistrate (*United States v. Upshaw*, 1948). This strict rule, which does not apply to state and local law enforcement officers, enforces the Federal Rules of Criminal Procedure, which require that a person arrested in the United States for a federal crime must be taken "without unnecessary delay" to a federal magistrate or a state or local judicial officer for an initial appearance. *McNabb* stated that the goal of the rule was to eliminate "secret interrogation" by police so as to reduce opportunities of coercion and third-degree practices. *Mallory* repeated this rationale, noting that an important function of the judge at the initial appearance is to inform a suspect of his or her right to remain silent.

The dangers inherent in the police holding suspects in custody without bringing them to a judge were seen in *Watts v. Indiana* (1949) and were highlighted shortly before *Miranda* in **Davis** *v. North Carolina* (1966). Elmer Davis Jr., an African American with low mental functioning who had escaped from a prison camp, was held as a suspect in a rape-murder for sixteen days in a police lockup cell measuring six by ten feet and was questioned every day in order to obtain a confession. A written station house order instructed police not to allow anyone to have contact with Davis. Only after confessing was he taken before a magistrate, despite the state rule requiring that an arrested person be brought before a magistrate within a reasonable period of time. The Supreme Court ruled Davis's confession to be involuntary.

Other places in this text (Chapter 1; later in this chapter) describe the national furor created by the 1966 *Miranda* decision, as it became a lightening rod of criticism of the Supreme Court by the law enforcement community.[20] Politicians quickly picked up on and inflamed this anger. Presidential candidate Richard Nixon made it a major campaign attack point against liberal justices in 1968, blaming them for increases in crime. Congress was so incensed by *Miranda* that it passed a law purporting to abolish it, 18 U.S.C. §3501, part of the Omnibus Crime Control and Safe Streets Act of 1968. Subsection (a) tried to overrule *Miranda* by making all voluntary confessions admissible, and reducing warnings of rights to the level of factors to be taken into consideration by courts deciding voluntariness. As will be described later in this chapter, the Supreme Court in *Dickerson v. United States* (2000) held that Congress cannot override a constitutional ruling of the Supreme Court and found that because *Miranda* was a constitutional ruling, §3501(a) had no effect.

Another section, 3501(c), modified the *Mc-Nabb–Mallory* rule. It read that in any federal prosecution, "a confession made . . . by . . . a defendant therein, while such person was under arrest . . . , shall not be inadmissible solely because of delay in bringing such person before a magistrate judge . . . if such confession is found by the trial judge to have been made voluntarily . . . and if such confession was made . . . within six hours [of arrest]"; the six-hour time limit is extended when further delay is "reasonable considering the means of transportation and the distance to be traveled to the nearest available [magistrate]." In *Corley v. United States* (2009) the Supreme Court held (5–4) that this statute, alone or in conjunction with 3501(a), which stated that any confession shall be admissible if it is voluntarily given, did not overrule *McNabb–Mallory*. Instead, *McNabb–Mallory* was modified so that any confession taken within a six-hour safe-harbor period is presumed to be admissible if voluntary, but confessions made after six hours of custody, even if voluntary, are presumed to be inadmissible. The majority's disagreement with the dissent was focused mainly on issues of statutory interpretation, but policy statements by Justice Souter made it clear that the majority believed that *McNabb–Mallory* continues to be a critical rule:

> In a world without *McNabb–Mallory*, federal agents would be free to question suspects for extended periods before bringing them out in the open, and we have always known what custodial secrecy leads to. No one with any smattering of the history of 20th-century dictatorships needs a lecture on the subject, and we understand the need even within our own system to take care against going too far. "[C]ustodial police interrogation, by its very nature, isolates and pressures the individual, . . . and there is, mounting empirical evidence that these pressures can induce a frighteningly high percentage of people to confess to crimes they never committed."[21] (*Corley v. United States*, 2009)

The wisdom of the six-hour safe harbor may be inferred from the fact that lengthy interrogation is a factor in false confessions. Research on false confessions has shown that in "[In] fifteen of the sixteen proven or probable false confession cases in which Leo and Ofshe specify the length of the interrogation, the police interrogated the suspect for more than six hours."[22]

RIGHT TO COUNSEL   The *secrecy* of police interrogation was a major concern. Without representation by counsel, the defendant is alone and vulnerable to improper police tactics. In two late 1950s cases, *Crooker v. California* (1958) and *Cicenia v. LaGay* (1958), dissenting justices argued that voluntary confessions should be excluded on the grounds that defendants' *requests* for attorneys were denied. The majority, however, held that a mere denial to see one's attorney was not in itself a due process violation. This position began to erode in *Spano v. New York* (1959), which held that overbearing police tactics led to an involuntary confession. Four concurring justices in *Spano* argued that the defendant had a right of access to counsel, noting that he had been formally indicted before confessing. *Gideon v. Wainwright* (1963), decided four years later, incorporated the right to counsel at trial and increased the pressure to view police interrogation as a critical stage in the prosecution. Furthermore, in 1964 the Court in *Massiah v. United States* (this chapter) held that an indicted defendant who had already obtained counsel could not be secretly taped or questioned by the police without the consent of the defendant's lawyer.

The turning point in the move to replace the voluntariness test with a clearer rule came in ***Escobedo v. Illinois*** (1964). It held that a preindictment suspect had a Sixth Amendment right to counsel during police interrogation, but only if the lawyer had been hired before the interrogation began. The *Escobedo* case was, according to Fred Graham, "enigmatic" because its holding was based on a complicated set of facts, and it was not clear which of these facts would be crucial in extending the right to counsel during interrogation in later cases.[23] In *Escobedo,* a lawyer was hired by the family of a murder suspect. The lawyer made repeated attempts over a period of three or four hours to see his client at the police station. At one point, Escobedo and his lawyer made eye contact, but the police refused to allow them to meet. The Court held that although Escobedo's confession was made voluntarily, it was unconstitutional because his Sixth Amendment right to counsel had been violated. Was *Escobedo* another "special circumstances" case (like *Powell v. Alabama* and *Betts v. Brady* regarding the right to counsel), or was it a first step toward requiring attorneys during every police interrogation?

The Court's opinion muddied the Sixth Amendment basis for its holding by injecting Fifth Amendment concerns: "Without informing him of his absolute right to remain silent in the face of this accusation, the police urged him to make a statement." *Escobedo* was an important case, but it was clearly not the final word or a firm rule for the guidance of police interrogation. First, the holding was fact-specific, limiting its future application to other scenarios. Also, it was problematic to base a right to counsel at police interrogation on the Sixth Amendment because the amendment applies to the "criminal prosecution," which does not commence until formal charges have been issued against a defendant. *Escobedo* left many questions unanswered. The Supreme Court expected a trickle of appeals designed to clarify the case's ambiguities but instead received a flood. Within two years it startled the legal community with its monumental *Miranda* decision. *Miranda* took a new turn and, "decid[ing] to answer all of the questions at once," placed state confessions law firmly on a Fifth Amendment foundation.[24]

THE *MIRANDA* DECISION

Miranda was not an incorporation case. The recently incorporated rights to counsel and against self-incrimination gave the Supreme Court the impetus to forge a new approach to establish a definitive confessions rule after three decades of due process cases. The *Miranda* majority chose the Fifth Amendment, not the Sixth Amendment, as the constitutional foundation of confessions law. *Miranda* was, for a time, one of the most severely criticized cases in the Court's history, referred to by some as a "self-inflicted wound." Many lawyers were offended by the unprecedented and legislative-like style of the ruling, while police officials and conservative politicians denounced the Court for its pro-defendant ruling.[25]

After the Supreme Court decision excluding Ernesto Miranda's confession, he was retried for rape and convicted in 1967 on the testimony of his common law wife. He was later paroled but continued to get into trouble. Miranda was stabbed to death on January 31, 1976, in the restroom of a cheap bar in Phoenix, Arizona, after a fistfight. Police caught the man who had assailed Ernesto and read him his *Miranda* warnings.[26]

Read Case and Comments: *Miranda v. Arizona.*

An Interpretation of *Miranda*

Was *Miranda* a revolutionary break with the voluntariness rule, as claimed by its critics? *Miranda* can be seen as an *extension* of that test because the underlying rationale of the Self-Incrimination and the Due Process Clauses is the same: *forbidding compelled testimony.* The voluntariness test *evolved* over time from outlawing torture to finding that certain psychological pressure tactics were unconstitutional. In this light, *Miranda* has *continued* the progressive *civilizing* approach of the voluntariness exclusionary rule by attacking the source of undue compulsion. If the Court was correct that modern police interrogation is so highly manipulative as to amount to compulsion, then *Miranda* can be seen as a *conservative* ruling that *preserved* police interrogation. If the Court had followed *Spano*'s (1959) lead, it could have *abolished* all secret interrogation, forbidding all interrogation of suspects unless a lawyer was actually present, and "any lawyer worth his salt will tell the suspect in no uncertain terms to make no statement to police under any circumstances" (*Watts v. Indiana*, Jackson, J., concurring).

Miranda can also be seen as a logical and not very extreme extension of the privilege against self-incrimination. As noted earlier, a witness can invoke the privilege in any official venue when subpoenaed to testify, whether at a criminal trial, civil trial, administrative hearing, grand jury proceeding, or legislative inquiry. It makes sense to extend the privilege to a suspect in the station house. A court cannot order a witness claiming the privilege to talk on the witness stand under a threat of a contempt citation and then use what is said against the witness in a criminal trial. Likewise, not protecting a suspect's ability to remain silent in the station house would entirely nullify the defendant's absolute right to silence at the trial.

There is an irony about *Miranda*. The Court's desire—to replace numerous case-specific decisions under the "facts and circumstances" approach of the voluntariness test with one bright-line rule for determining the constitutionality of confessions—was not to be. After *Miranda,* the Court had to deal with a cascade of cases litigating its meaning. These cases are reviewed in subsequent sections.

Voluntariness after *Miranda*

Miranda v. Arizona did not eliminate the due process voluntariness test. A suspect can obviously be coerced into confessing after being read *Miranda* warnings. Such a confession is inadmissible under the Fifth or Fourteenth Amendment Due Process Clauses. Additionally, a coerced confession cannot be used to impeach a defendant who chooses to testify at trial.

Mincey v. Arizona (1978) is a blatant example of involuntariness. Rufus Mincey was shot and left semiconscious after a shoot-out with a police officer. He was brought to a hospital intensive care unit (ICU) in *critical condition.* That evening, Detective Hust went to the ICU, told Mincey he was under arrest for murdering a police officer, administered *Miranda* warnings, and proceeded to question him about the shoot-out. Mincey asked repeatedly that the interrogation stop until he could get a lawyer, but Hust continued to question him until almost midnight. Throughout, Mincey was heavily medicated by an intravenous device; tubes were inserted into his throat to help him breathe and through his nose into his stomach to keep him from vomiting; and a catheter was inserted into his bladder. Mincey could not talk, so answers were written on pieces of paper.

When asked by Detective Hust, "Did you shoot anyone?" it seemed clear to the Court that Mincey's reply, "I can't say. I have to see a lawyer," was evidence of a clear desire not to speak. Yet he was pressured by the detective and made an incriminating statement. Justice Potter Stewart wrote:

> It is hard to imagine a situation less conducive to the exercise of "a rational intellect and a free will" than Mincey's. He had been seriously wounded just a few hours earlier, and had arrived at the hospital "depressed almost to the point of coma," according to his attending physician. Although he had received some treatment, his condition at the time of [the] interrogation was still sufficiently serious that he was in the [ICU]. He complained to Hust that the pain in his leg was "unbearable." He was evidently confused and unable to think clearly about either the events of that afternoon or the circumstances of his interrogation, since some of his written answers were on their face not entirely coherent. Finally, while Mincey was being questioned he was lying on his back on a hospital bed, encumbered by tubes, needles, and breathing apparatus. He was, in short, "at the complete mercy" of Detective Hust, unable to escape or resist the thrust of Hust's interrogation. (*Mincey v. Arizona,* 1978)

Despite the fact that Mincey had made some coherent statements, the Court found that his statements "were not the product of his free and rational choice," violated due process, and held that the state could not use Mincey's statements for *impeachment* purposes.

In a five-to-four decision, the Supreme Court held a confession to be involuntary in ***Arizona v. Fulminante*** (1991). Fulminante, in federal prison for a weapons offense, was suspected of having murdered his stepdaughter. He was befriended by another inmate, Anthony Sarivola, a former police officer who became a paid FBI informant. Masquerading as an organized crime figure,

Sarivola promised to protect Fulminante against violence from other inmates if they discovered he had killed his daughter, but only if he told Sarivola whether he committed the crime. Fulminante admitted the crime to Sarivola, who later testified to Fulminante's confession at his murder trial. The Supreme Court affirmed the Arizona Supreme Court's decision that "the confession was obtained as a direct result of extreme coercion and was tendered in the *belief that the defendant's life was in jeopardy if he did not confess*. This is a true coerced confession in every sense of the word" (emphasis added). Both courts drew on the common knowledge that prisoners are known to assault and even murder child abusers and, thus, could conclude that Fulminante had spoken out of fear for his life.

Crane v. Kentucky (1986) held that when a defendant raises the issue of a coerced confession under the Due Process Clause at trial, he or she must be allowed to introduce evidence of "the physical and psychological environment in which the confession was obtained." Even if a judge finds a confession to be voluntary in a pretrial hearing, a jury may disagree and find that the confession was involuntary or decide not to give it great weight. Innocent suspects have made voluntary confessions that they later regret. It would be difficult or impossible for a defendant alleging a coerced confession to prove it, if he or she could not introduce evidence about the environment in which the confession was taken.

It is worth keeping in mind that *Miranda* violations and voluntariness rule violations are not entirely distinct. In **Withrow v. Williams** (1993), a defendant claimed that his *Miranda* rights were violated when at a police station during an "interview" (i.e., supposedly not an interrogation), police told Williams to "give us the truth" or else "we're simply gonna charge you and lock you up and you can tell it to a defense attorney and let him try and prove differently." In deciding that federal courts could hear *Miranda* claims under habeas corpus jurisdiction, the Court noted that if it decided otherwise, state prisoners could simply convert *Miranda* claims into due process claims that their convictions were based on involuntary confessions.

MIRANDA AS A CONSTITUTIONAL RULE

Attacking the Constitutional Basis of *Miranda*

Theories of **Miranda** A theoretical debate with real-world consequences about the nature of *Miranda* warnings had divided the Court for decades. At first, conservative justices appointed by President Nixon, and generally hostile to Warren Court rulings, seemed poised to overrule *Miranda*.[28] Instead they reinterpreted it, saying that *Miranda* warnings were *not themselves constitutional* rules. They were said to be only prophylactic rules designed to protect the underlying privilege against self-incrimination. As a result, statements taken during custodial interrogation that violated *Miranda*, because of defective warnings or because no warnings were given, although inadmissible at trial, could be *used for collateral purposes*. These peripheral purposes included impeaching a defendant who testified at trial or using the statements as a lead to other incriminating evidence. In contrast, as noted earlier, statements obtained by "pure" compulsion to testify under a grant of immunity (Fifth Amendment violations) (*New Jersey v. Portash*, 1979), or involuntary confessions produced by egregious police behavior (due process violations) (*Mincey v. Arizona*, 1978), cannot be used for collateral purposes.

If *Miranda* was not a constitutional ruling, as implied by the collateral use cases, then it would appear that the Court had *no jurisdiction* to impose a supervisory rule on the states, an issue that the Court simply ignored.[29] Instead of overruling *Miranda,* the Court continued to narrow its application in decisions favoring the state and allowing the use of confessions. Having "defanged" the rule, the Court became somewhat supportive of the case. As Chief Justice Burger said in dictum: "The meaning of *Miranda* has become reasonably clear and law enforcement practices have adjusted to its strictures; I would neither overrule *Miranda,* disparage it, nor extend it at this late date" (*Rhode Island v. Innis,* 1980, concurring). Reasons for this position included (1) a concern that overruling *Miranda* might be misread by the police as tacitly condoning abusive police tactics, (2) a desire to maintain the Court's symbolic role as a guarantor of individual liberties, and, most important, (3) a realization by 1980 that *Miranda* did not stop police from obtaining confessions.

The Court seemed to shift direction in *Dickerson v. United States* (2000), holding that a statute purporting to overrule *Miranda* was void because *Miranda* was in fact a constitutional rule. This, however, did not change the Court's collateral use position. *Chavez v. Martinez* (2003)

CASE AND COMMENTS

Miranda v. Arizona

384 U.S. 436, 86 S.Ct. 1602, 16 L.Ed.2d 694 (1966)

[In four consolidated cases none of the defendants were fully informed of their constitutional rights, although some were informed of their right to remain silent. **[a]** In *Miranda v. Arizona,* Miranda confessed to a rape after being interrogated for only two hours at a police station. In *Vignera v. New York,* a robbery suspect questioned by police made an oral admission in the afternoon and a written confession to a prosecutor that evening. In *Westover v. United States,* local police arrested Westover for a robbery and interrogated him that evening. The next day, FBI agents began to interrogate the defendant at 9 a.m. He was read warnings at noon and confessed at 2:00 p.m. In *Stewart v. California,* the defendant was interrogated nine times over five days by the police and was held incommunicado until he confessed. He was then taken before an examining magistrate. There was no evidence of threats or violence in any of these cases. The majority opinion discussed the facts of the cases after fifty pages of constitutional analysis.]

 MR. CHIEF JUSTICE WARREN delivered the opinion of the Court.

 The cases before us raise questions which go to the roots of our concepts of American criminal jurisprudence: the restraints society must observe consistent with the Federal Constitution in prosecuting individuals for crime. **[b]** More specifically, we deal with the admissibility of statements obtained from an individual who is subjected to custodial police interrogation and the necessity for procedures which assure that the individual is accorded his privilege under the Fifth Amendment to the Constitution not to be compelled to incriminate himself.

* * *

We start here, as we did in *Escobedo,* with the premise that our holding is not an innovation in our jurisprudence, but is an application of principles long recognized and applied in other settings. **[c]** * * *

* * *

Our holding * * * briefly stated is this: the prosecution may not use statements, whether **exculpatory** or **inculpatory**, stemming from custodial interrogation of the defendant unless it demonstrates the use of procedural safeguards effective to secure the privilege against self-incrimination. By custodial interrogation, we mean questioning initiated by law enforcement officers after a person has been taken into custody or otherwise deprived of his freedom of action in any significant way.

I

* * * [All the cases here] share salient features—incommunicado interrogation of individuals in a police-dominated atmosphere, resulting in self-incriminating statements without full warning of constitutional rights. **[d]**

An understanding of the nature and setting of this in-custody interrogation is essential to our decisions today. The difficulty in depicting what transpires at such interrogations stems from the fact that in this country they have largely taken place incommunicado. From extensive factual studies undertaken in the early 1930s, including the famous Wickersham Report to Congress by a Presidential Commission, it is clear that police violence and the "third degree" flourished at that time. In a series of cases decided by this Court long after these studies, the police resorted to physical brutality—beatings, hanging, whipping—and to sustained and protracted questioning incommunicado in order to extort confessions. * * *

* * *

Again we stress that the modern practice of in-custody interrogation is psychologically rather than physically oriented. * * * ["T]his Court has recognized that coercion can be mental as well as physical, and that the blood of the accused is not the only hallmark of an unconstitutional inquisition." * * * **[e]** Interrogation still takes place in privacy. Privacy results in secrecy and this in turn results in a gap in our knowledge as to what in fact goes on in the interrogation rooms. A valuable source of information about present police practices, however, may be found in various police manuals and texts which document procedures employed with success in the past, and which recommend various other effective tactics. * * *

 The officers are told by the manuals that the "principal psychological factor contributing to a successful interrogation is privacy—being alone with the person under interrogation." * * *

 To highlight the isolation and unfamiliar surroundings, the manuals instruct the police to display an air of confidence in the suspect's guilt and from outward appearance to maintain only an interest in confirming certain details. **[f]** The guilt of the subject is to be posited as a fact. The interrogator should direct his comments toward the reasons why the subject committed the act, rather than court failure by asking the subject whether he did it. Like other men, perhaps the subject has had a bad family life, had

[a] The Supreme Court stated that these facts did not make the confessions unconstitutional under the due process voluntariness test. In Part V of the majority opinion, it applied the general rules of the decision and found that in each case the self-incrimination rights of the defendants had been violated.

[b] The Court clearly specifies the factual predicate of these cases (custodial police interrogation) and the decision's constitutional basis (the privilege against self-incrimination).

[c] This is disingenuous. As the dissenters state, this case was clearly a constitutional innovation.

[d] The case is decided not on the specific facts in each of the four consolidated cases, but merely on the fact that in each there was police custodial interrogation and rights were not explained to the defendants. There was no physical or psychological coercion in these cases. A review of interrogation techniques found in police manuals substituted for finding specific case facts.

[f] Are these practices outrageous or simply like high-pressure sales tactics used to get the suspect to admit to the crime?

an unhappy childhood, had too much to drink, had an unrequited desire for women. The officers are instructed to minimize the moral seriousness of the offense, to cast blame on the victim or on society. These tactics are designed to put the subject in a psychological state where his story is but an elaboration of what the police purport to know already—that he is guilty. Explanations to the contrary are dismissed and discouraged. * * *

* * *

When the techniques described above prove unavailing, the texts recommend they be alternated with a show of some hostility. One ploy often used has been termed the "friendly-unfriendly" or the "Mutt and Jeff" act. * * *

[g] Is using tricks and lies ethical if it is the only way to get a "guilty" person to confess? What if the suspect is in fact not guilty? Should there be a limit to trickery?

The interrogators sometimes are instructed to induce a confession out of trickery. **[g]** The technique here is quite effective in crimes which require identification or which run in series. In the identification situation, the interrogator may take a break in his questioning to place the subject among a group of men in a line-up [and to coach a witness to identify the suspect]. * * * A variation on this technique is called the "reverse line-up":

> "The accused is placed in a line-up, but this time he is identified by several fictitious witnesses or victims who associated him with different offenses. It is expected that the subject will become desperate and confess to the offense under investigation in order to escape from the false accusations."

* * *

[h] These examples from police manuals are not scientifically drawn random samples of police activity; nevertheless, there is no reason to believe that they are uncommon. In your opinion, are they inherently coercive?

From these representative samples of interrogation techniques, the setting prescribed by the manuals and observed in practice becomes clear. **[h]** In essence, it is this: To be alone with the subject is essential to prevent distraction and to deprive him of any outside support. The aura of confidence in his guilt undermines his will to resist. He merely confirms the preconceived story the police seek to have him describe. Patience and persistence, at times relentless questioning, are employed. To obtain a confession, the interrogator must "patiently maneuver himself or his quarry into a position from which the desired objective may be attained." When normal procedures fail to produce the needed result, the police may resort to deceptive stratagems such as giving false legal advice. It is important to keep the subject off balance, for example, by trading on his insecurity about himself or his surroundings. The police then persuade, trick, or cajole him out of exercising his constitutional rights.

* * *

In the cases before us today, given this background, we concern ourselves primarily with this interrogation atmosphere and the evils it can bring. * * *

[i] The Court puts the finishing touch on its argument: (1) The self-incrimination clause forbids compelled testimony; (2) secret police interrogation is inherently compelling; therefore (3) safeguards are required in order to "dispel" compulsion.

In these cases, we might not find the defendants' statements to have been involuntary in traditional terms. **[i]** Our concern for adequate safeguards to protect precious Fifth Amendment rights is, of course, not lessened in the slightest. * * * The fact remains that in none of these cases did the officers undertake to afford appropriate safeguards at the outset of the interrogation to insure that the statements were truly the product of free choice.

It is obvious that such an interrogation environment is created for no purpose other than to subjugate the individual to the will of his examiner. This atmosphere carries its own badge of intimidation. To be sure, this is not physical intimidation, but it is equally destructive of human dignity. * * * Unless adequate protective devices are employed to dispel the compulsion inherent in custodial surroundings, no statement obtained from the defendant can truly be the product of his free choice.

* * *

[Part II of the opinion reviewed the history of the right against self-incrimination in English and American law and its incorporation into the Fourteenth Amendment in *Malloy v. Hogan* (1964), which established the constitutional jurisdiction for the Court to apply the Fifth Amendment's privilege against self-incrimination to the states.]

III

Today, then, there can be no doubt that the Fifth Amendment privilege is available outside of criminal court proceedings and serves to protect persons in all settings in which their freedom of action is curtailed in any significant way from being compelled to incriminate themselves. We have concluded that without proper safeguards the process of in-custody interrogation of persons suspected or accused of crime contains inherently compelling pressures which work to undermine the individual's will to resist and to compel him to speak where he would not otherwise do so freely. In order to combat these pressures and to permit a full opportunity to exercise the privilege against self-incrimination, the accused must be adequately and effectively apprised of his rights and the exercise of those rights must be fully honored.

[j] The suggestion that other protective techniques could replace the warnings became an extremely controversial point. A more conservative Court used this statement to argue that *Miranda* warnings are not rules required by the Constitution.

It is impossible for us to foresee the potential alternatives for protecting the privilege which might be devised by Congress or the States in the exercise of their creative rule-making capacities. **[j]**

Therefore we cannot say that the Constitution necessarily requires adherence to any particular solution for the inherent compulsions of the interrogation process as it is presently conducted. Our decision in no way creates a constitutional straitjacket which will handicap sound efforts at reform, nor is it intended to have this effect. We encourage Congress and the States to continue their laudable search for increasingly effective ways of protecting the rights of the individual while promoting efficient enforcement of our criminal laws. However, unless we are shown other procedures which are at least as effective in apprising accused persons of their right of silence and in assuring a continuous opportunity to exercise it, the following safeguards must be observed.

At the outset, if a person in custody is to be subjected to interrogation, he must first be informed in clear and unequivocal terms that he has the right to remain silent. **[k]** For those unaware of the privilege, the warning is needed simply to make them aware of it—the threshold requirement for an intelligent decision as to its exercise. More important, such a warning is an absolute prerequisite in overcoming the inherent pressures of the interrogation atmosphere. * * *

[k] The first warning. Are the reasons for it convincing?

The Fifth Amendment privilege is so fundamental to our system of constitutional rule and the expedient of giving an adequate warning as to the availability of the privilege so simple, we will not pause to inquire in individual cases whether the defendant was aware of his rights without a warning being given. * * *

The warning of the right to remain silent must be accompanied by the explanation that anything said can and will be used against the individual in court. **[l]** This warning is needed in order to make him aware not only of the privilege, but also of the consequences of foregoing it. It is only through an awareness of these consequences that there can be any assurance of real understanding and intelligent exercise of the privilege. Moreover, this warning may serve to make the individual more acutely aware that he is faced with a phase of the adversary system—that he is not in the presence of persons acting solely in his interest.

[l] The second warning.

The circumstances surrounding in-custody interrogation can operate very quickly to overbear the will of one merely made aware of his privilege by his interrogators. **[m]** Therefore, the right to have counsel present at the interrogation is indispensable to the protection of the Fifth Amendment privilege. * * *

[m] The third warning. It is *not* based on the Sixth Amendment; it is required to protect Fifth Amendment rights.

* * *

In order fully to apprise a person interrogated of the extent of his rights under this system then, it is necessary to warn him not only that he has the right to consult with an attorney, but also that if he is indigent a lawyer will be appointed to represent him. **[n]** Without this additional warning, the admonition of the right to consult with counsel would often be understood as meaning only that he can consult with a lawyer if he has one or has the funds to obtain one. * * *

[n] The fourth warning.

Once warnings have been given, the subsequent procedure is clear. If the individual indicates in any manner, at any time prior to or during questioning, that he wishes to remain silent, the interrogation must cease. **[o]** At this point he has shown that he intends to exercise his Fifth Amendment privilege; any statement taken after the person invokes his privilege cannot be other than the product of compulsion, subtle or otherwise. Without the right to cut off questioning, the setting of in-custody interrogation operates on the individual to overcome free choice in producing a statement after the privilege has been once invoked. If the individual states that he wants an attorney, the interrogation must cease until an attorney is present. At that time, the individual must have an opportunity to confer with the attorney and to have him present during any subsequent questioning. If the individual cannot obtain an attorney and he indicates that he wants one before speaking to police, they must respect his decision to remain silent.

[o] Consequences of the warnings. The suspect can "invoke" the privilege and lawfully refuse to answer by "just saying no" when asked to talk by the police, even after answering some questions.

This does not mean, as some have suggested, that each police station must have a "station house lawyer" present at all times to advise prisoners. * * *

If the interrogation continues without the presence of an attorney and a statement is taken, a heavy burden rests on the government to demonstrate that the defendant knowingly and intelligently waived his privilege against self-incrimination and his right to retained or appointed counsel. **[p]** * * * Since the State is responsible for establishing the isolated circumstances under which the interrogation takes place and has the only means of making available corroborated evidence of warnings given during incommunicado interrogation, the burden is rightly on its shoulders.

[p] The burden of proof of a voluntary waiver is on the state; the state must produce some proof of a waiver.

An express statement that the individual is willing to make a statement and does not want an attorney followed closely by a statement could constitute a waiver. But a valid waiver will not be presumed simply from the silence of the accused after warnings are given or simply from the fact that a confession was in fact eventually obtained. * * *

* * *

The warnings required and the waiver necessary in accordance with our opinion today are, in the absence of a fully effective equivalent, prerequisites to the admissibility of any statement made by a defendant. No distinction can be drawn between statements which are direct confessions and statements which amount to "admissions" of part or all of an offense. **[q]** The privilege against self-incrimination protects the individual from being compelled to incriminate himself in any manner; it does not distinguish degrees of

[q] This paragraph closes potential loopholes in the *Miranda* rules. A suspect might be led to say things he *thinks* will clear him (*exculpatory* statements) but that instead lead to independent evidence of guilt. These too are covered by the *Miranda* warnings.

[r] This is a critical point. The Fifth Amendment privilege applies prior to formal charges during custodial police interrogation, and not only at judicial-like hearings as the dissenters argued.

[s] Some critics feared that the Supreme Court would make all extra-judicial confessions illegal. The Court tries to allay these fears.

[t] Recent scholarship casts some doubt on Justice White's historical argument.[27]

[u] Justice White accuses the majority of fabricating the constitutional element of coercion by assuming that the police manuals describe the reality of every interrogation, without proof of coercion in each specific case.

incrimination. Similarly, for precisely the same reason, no distinction may be drawn between inculpatory statements and statements alleged to be merely "exculpatory." If a statement made were in fact truly exculpatory it would, of course, never be used by the prosecution. In fact, statements merely intended to be exculpatory by the defendant are often used to impeach his testimony at trial or to demonstrate untruths in the statement given under interrogation and thus to prove guilt by implication. These statements are incriminating in any meaningful sense of the word and may not be used without the full warnings and effective waiver required for any other statement. In *Escobedo* itself, the defendant fully intended his accusation of another as the slayer to be exculpatory as to himself.

The principles announced today deal with the protection which must be given to the privilege against self-incrimination when the individual is first subjected to police interrogation while in custody at the station or otherwise deprived of his freedom of action in any significant way. **[r]** It is at this point that our adversary system of criminal proceedings commences, distinguishing itself at the outset from the inquisitorial system recognized in some countries. * * *

Our decision is not intended to hamper the traditional function of police officers in investigating crime. * * *

* * *

In dealing with statements obtained through interrogation, we do not purport to find all confessions inadmissible. Confessions remain a proper element in law enforcement. Any statement given freely and voluntarily without any compelling influences is, of course, admissible in evidence. * * * There is no requirement that police stop a person who enters a police station and states that he wishes to confess to a crime, or a person who calls the police to offer a confession or any other statement he desires to make. **[s]** Volunteered statements of any kind are not barred by the Fifth Amendment and their admissibility is not affected by our holding today.

* * *

[Part IV presented policy arguments in favor of the warnings requirement; noting that warnings were required in England and many Commonwealth nations and were routinely given by FBI agents and military police without any loss of effective law enforcement.]

[Justices Clark (concurring in *Stewart v. California*), Harlan, and White each wrote dissenting opinions.]

MR. JUSTICE WHITE, with whom MR. JUSTICE HARLAN and MR. JUSTICE STEWART join, dissenting. * * *

I

The proposition that the privilege against self-incrimination forbids in-custody interrogation without the warnings specified in the majority opinion * * * has no significant support in the history of the privilege or in the language of the Fifth Amendment. * * * The rule excluding coerced confessions matured about 100 years [after the privilege against self-incrimination did,] "but there is nothing in the reports to suggest that the theory has its roots in the privilege against self-incrimination. . . ." * * * **[t]**

* * *

* * * [T]he Fifth Amendment privilege was . . . extended to encompass the then well-established rule against coerced confessions * * * [in] *Bram v. United States.* * * *

* * *

Bram, however, itself rejected the proposition which the Court now espouses. The question in *Bram* was whether a confession, obtained during custodial interrogation, had been compelled. * * * [T]he Court declared that:

> "* * * the mere fact that the confession is made to a police officer, while the accused was under arrest in or out of prison, or was drawn out by his questions, does not necessarily render the confession involuntary; but, as one of the circumstances, such imprisonment or interrogation may be taken into account in determining whether or not the statements of the prisoner were voluntary" * * *

* * *

III

* * * Rather than asserting new knowledge, the Court concedes that it cannot truly know what occurs during custodial questioning, because of the innate secrecy of such proceedings. **[u]** It extrapolates a picture of what it conceives to be the norm from police investigatorial manuals, published in 1959 and 1962 or earlier, without any attempt to allow for adjustments in police practices that may have occurred in the wake of more recent decisions of state appellate tribunals or this Court. But even if the relentless application of the described procedures could lead to involuntary confessions, it most assuredly does not follow that each and every case will disclose this kind of interrogation or this kind of consequence.

Insofar as appears from the Court's opinion, it has not examined a single transcript of any police interrogation, let alone the interrogation that took place in any one of these cases which it decides today. * * * [T]he factual basis for the Court's premise is patently inadequate.

* * *

* * * [E]ven if one assumed that there was an adequate factual basis for the conclusion that all confessions obtained during in-custody interrogation are the product of compulsion, the rule propounded by the Court would still be irrational, for, apparently, it is only if the accused is also warned of his right to counsel and waives both that right and the right against self-incrimination that the inherent compulsiveness of interrogation disappears. **[v]** But if the defendant may not answer without a warning a question such as "Where were you last night?" without having his answer be a compelled one, how can the Court ever accept his negative answer to the question of whether he wants to consult his retained counsel or counsel whom the court will appoint? * * * The Court apparently realizes its dilemma of foreclosing questioning without the necessary warnings but at the same time permitting the accused, sitting in the same chair in front of the same policemen, to waive his right to consult an attorney. * * *

* * * By considering any answers to any interrogation to be compelled regardless of the content and course of examination and by escalating the requirements to prove waiver, the Court not only prevents the use of compelled confessions but for all practical purposes forbids interrogation except in the presence of counsel. That is, instead of confining itself to protection of the right against compelled self-incrimination the Court has created a limited Fifth Amendment right to counsel—or, as the Court expresses it, a "need for counsel to protect the Fifth Amendment privilege." * * * The focus then is not on the will of the accused but on the will of counsel and how much influence he can have on the accused. Obviously there is no warrant in the Fifth Amendment for thus installing counsel as the arbiter of the privilege.

In sum, for all the Court's expounding on the menacing atmosphere of police interrogation procedures, it has failed to supply any foundation for the conclusions it draws or the measures it adopts.

IV

* * *

In some unknown number of cases the Court's rule will return a killer, a rapist or other criminal to the streets and to the environment which produced him, to repeat his crime whenever it pleases him. **[w]** As a consequence, there will not be a gain, but a loss, in human dignity. The real concern is not the unfortunate consequences of this new decision on the criminal law as an abstract, disembodied series of authoritative proscriptions, but the impact on those who rely on the public authority for protection and who without it can only engage in violent self-help with guns, knives and the help of their neighbors similarly inclined. * * *

Nor can this decision do other than have a corrosive effect on the criminal law as an effective device to prevent crime. A major component in its effectiveness in this regard is its swift and sure enforcement. The easier it is to get away with rape and murder, the less the deterrent effect on those who are inclined to attempt it. This is still good common sense. * * *

* * *

[w] There is always a trade-off between security and liberty in criminal procedure; Justice White sees little gain in civil liberties by limiting the power of the police in this area.

held that the mere failure to read *Miranda* warnings to a suspect is not a violation of the right against self-incrimination. The use of leads was continued in *United States v. Patane* (2004), and a "cured statement" use was only qualified in *Missouri v. Seibert* (2004). These cases are discussed in greater detail later in this chapter.

COLLATERAL USE OF MIRANDA-VIOLATED STATEMENTS *Harris v. New York* (1971) held that a confession that violated *Miranda*, because obtained without police giving complete *Miranda* warnings, could still be introduced at trial, not to prove guilt but to *impeach* the credibility of a defendant whose testimony contradicted his earlier confession. This implied that *Miranda* was not based on the privilege against self-incrimination. Justice Brennan, dissenting, quoted a passage from *Miranda* explicitly stating that incriminating statements taken without the full warnings being given *cannot* be used to impeach the defendant's testimony at trial. Chief Justice Burger's majority opinion, however, got around this by declaring the passage in *Miranda* to be mere *dictum* that "was not at all necessary to the Court's holding and cannot be regarded as controlling." Recall that *New Jersey v. Portash* (1979) held that grand jury testimony compelled by a grant of immunity could not be used to impeach the witness at a later trial because such use violated the Self-Incrimination Clause. The Court in *Harris* began to chip away at the theory that *Miranda* warnings are constitutional rules.

The *Harris* rule was confirmed by **Oregon v. Hass** (1975). Hass, arrested for theft and burglary, was read *Miranda* warnings. On the way to the police station, Hass said he wanted to call his attorney. Instead of ceasing to question him, the officer said that Hass could do so when they reached the station. Hass then made incriminating statements in the police car. At the trial Hass claimed he was innocent, testifying that a friend impulsively stole a bicycle and threw it into Hass's truck and that Hass was arrested after the police traced the truck to him. In rebuttal, the officer testified that Hass made incriminating statements in the patrol car after asking for his attorney. The trial court allowed the officer's testimony in order to evaluate Hass's credibility as a witness (i.e., to impeach him) but not as proof of guilt.

The Supreme Court applied the *Harris* rule and upheld the trial court even though the officer's continuing interrogation after Hass asked for a lawyer violated *Miranda*. Justice Harry Blackmun, for the majority, wrote that "the shield provided by *Miranda* is not to be perverted to a license to testify inconsistently, or even perjuriously, free from the risk of confrontation with prior inconsistent utterances" (*Oregon v. Hass,* 1975). Justice Brennan, dissenting, repeated his point in *Harris* that "[a]n incriminating statement is as incriminating when used to impeach credibility as it is when used as direct proof of guilt and no constitutional distinction can legitimately be drawn." He noted that once *Miranda* warnings were given, the state has no incentive to obey the rule, for by continuing to question, the "police may obtain a statement which can be used for impeachment if the accused has the temerity to testify in his own defense."

Michigan v. Tucker (1974) allowed *evidentiary leads* derived from *Miranda* violations to be introduced into evidence, continuing to undermine *Miranda*. Deficient *Miranda* warnings were given to Tucker before interrogation (he was not informed of the right to appointed counsel). Tucker gave police the name of a supposedly favorable witness whose statements nevertheless incriminated him. Nothing that Tucker said was used against him, but evidence *derived* from his statement (i.e., the witness's statement) was used against him to prove his guilt of a rape.[30]

In *Tucker* the Supreme Court adopted Justice Rehnquist's reasoning that *Miranda* warnings are *prophylactic rules* designed to protect the underlying Fifth Amendment right of silence, but *not constitutional rules* in their own right. The police failure to give warnings therefore did not violate Tucker's privilege against self-incrimination but only *Miranda*'s protective rules. Justice Rehnquist based this conclusion on a *selective reading* of *Miranda* by quoting the following sentence: "We cannot say that the Constitution necessarily requires adherence to any particular solution for the inherent compulsions of the interrogation process as it is presently conducted" (*Miranda v. Arizona,* 1966). However, he failed to quote a passage appearing three sentences later: "However, unless we are shown other procedures which are at least as effective in apprising accused persons of their right of silence and in assuring a continuous opportunity to exercise it, *the following safeguards must be observed*" (*Miranda v. Arizona,* 1966, emphasis added).

It is clear that *Miranda*'s majority based its mandatory warnings on the Fifth Amendment privilege and that the *Tucker* Court *changed the meaning of Miranda*. The *Tucker* majority did so by interpreting the second sentence as *dictum*, and not as a rule. The police, therefore, did not violate Tucker's right against compulsory self-incrimination "but rather failed to make available to him the full measure of procedural safeguards associated with that right since *Miranda*." Since a violation of *Miranda* warnings did not violate the right against self-incrimination, it did not require the exclusion of derivative evidence. The majority added that no additional deterrence to police misconduct could be expected by the use of evidence derived from a good faith failure to follow the *Miranda* rules.

Oregon v. Elstad (1985) provides a third way in which a *Miranda* violation did not prevent the use of a defendant's admission taken in violation of *Miranda:* by allowing a second or "cured" statement. Police, armed with an arrest warrant, arrested eighteen-year-old Michael Elstad in his home. He was suspected of stealing $150,000 worth of art objects and furnishings from the home of his friend and neighbor. Just after his arrest, Elstad, in the presence of his mother, made incriminating statements to the police upon being questioned about the burglary. He was not warned of his rights. At the sheriff's offices later in the day, Elstad was again questioned, but this time *Miranda* warnings were read and he initialled a waiver form. He again made incriminating statements, and these "cured" statements were admitted into evidence. The Court ruled that the "fruits of the poisonous tree" doctrine did not bar the second confession: It was not "tainted" as a result of the prior, unwarned, admission. Justice O'Connor ruled that the police action did not in itself violate the self-incrimination privilege. She noted that "[t]he *Miranda* exclusionary rule, however, serves the Fifth Amendment and sweeps more broadly than the Fifth Amendment itself. It may be triggered even in the absence of a Fifth Amendment violation" (*Oregon v. Elstad,* 1985).

Justice Brennan dissented strongly. He argued that the *Elstad* example was a *classic ploy* designed to break a suspect's will. The first question might have been asked of eighteen-year-old Michael Elstad to "soften him up" into a confessing mood. This made him more willing to waive his rights and talk at the police station, since the "cat was out of the bag." The majority and the dissenters clearly differed as to whether *Miranda* is a constitutional rule. Justice Brennan believed that "*Miranda* clearly emphasized that warnings and an informed waiver are essential to the Fifth Amendment privilege itself." Although Justice Brennan may be correct that once a person confesses he may think that it is futile to assert one's right to silence thereafter, the facts in *Elstad* do not appear to show that the police deliberately set up Michael to talk when he was arrested.

The Public Safety Exception

The doctrinal foundation laid in *Harris, Hass,* and *Tucker* bore full fruit in **New York v. Quarles** (1984), a case that created a *public safety exception* to *Miranda.* By creating an explicit exception to *Miranda* based on a balancing test, the Court seemed to confirm its view that the *Miranda* warnings were not themselves constitutional requirements.

At 12:30 a.m., two police officers were approached by a woman who told them that she had just been raped by a black male. She described his jacket with the name "Big Ben" printed in yellow letters on the back and told the officers that the man had just entered a nearby supermarket carrying a gun. The officers spotted the man in the supermarket and arrested him after a brief chase through the aisles. When frisked, the man, Benjamin Quarles, was found to be wearing an empty shoulder holster. After handcuffing him, Officer Kraft asked him where the gun was. Quarles nodded in the direction of some empty cartons and responded, "The gun is over there." Officer Kraft then retrieved a loaded .38-caliber revolver from a carton, formally placed Quarles under arrest, and read him his *Miranda* rights from a printed card. Quarles said that he would be willing to answer questions. When Officer Kraft asked him if he owned the gun and where he had purchased it, Quarles answered that he did own it and that he had purchased it in Miami.

The New York courts, at every level, excluded Quarles's initial statement and the gun from evidence in the trial because he had not been read *Miranda* warnings before the question was asked; they also excluded the statement about the ownership and purchase of the gun as being derived from an illegal interrogation. The Supreme Court agreed that the brief scenario in *Quarles* constituted custodial police interrogation, a situation that requires warning a suspect of his rights under *Miranda* before a statement can be admitted into evidence. Nevertheless, the Court (6–3) reversed the New York Court of Appeals, that state's highest court.

The basis of the Court's holding was that "this case presents a situation where concern for public safety must be paramount to adherence to the literal language of the prophylactic rules enunciated in *Miranda.*" The Court thus injected something like the Fourth Amendment balancing test and an exigent circumstances exception into a Fifth Amendment area. Were *Miranda* a constitutional rule, this would not be permissible because "the Fifth Amendment's strictures, unlike the Fourth's, are not removed by showing reasonableness" (*New York v. Quarles,* 1984), In other words, the Fifth Amendment privilege is *absolute*. Since *Quarles* creates an exception to the *Miranda* warnings requirement, the warnings cannot be the same as the privilege because, in theory, an exception cannot be made for the privilege. The Court characterized the warnings as "'practical reinforcement' for the Fifth Amendment right" by making it less likely that the police would commit "constitutionally impermissible practices" during interrogation (*New York v. Quarles,* 1984, citing *Michigan v. Tucker,* 1974).

Justice Rehnquist, writing for the majority, held that

> on these facts there is a "public safety" exception to the requirement that *Miranda* warnings be given before a suspect's answers may be admitted into evidence, and that the availability of that exception does not depend upon the motivation of the individual officers involved. In a kaleidoscopic situation such as the one confronting these officers, where spontaneity rather than adherence to a police manual is necessarily the order of the day, the application of the exception which we recognize today should not be made to depend on . . . the subjective motivation of the arresting officer. Undoubtedly most police officers, if placed in Officer Kraft's position, would act out

of a host of different, instinctive, and largely unverifiable motives—their own safety, the safety of others, and perhaps as well the desire to obtain incriminating evidence from the suspect. (*New York v. Quarles,* 1984)

The holding was criticized by three dissenting justices. Justice Marshall wrote that because the "Court in *Miranda* determined that custodial interrogations are inherently coercive . . . [it] therefore created a *constitutional presumption* that statements made during custodial interrogations are compelled in violation of the Fifth Amendment and are thus inadmissible in criminal prosecutions" (*New York v. Quarles,* 1984, Marshall, J., dissenting, emphasis added). He chided the majority for substituting its view that a threat to public safety existed, when the New York courts unanimously found no threat to public safety: The store was deserted in the middle of the night; there was no indication that Quarles had a confederate who might use the gun; the police were certain that the gun was in the immediate area of the arrest; Quarles was handcuffed; and "the arresting officers were sufficiently confident of their safety to put away their guns." Justice Marshall noted that if there was a genuine threat of violence, the officers could violate *Miranda* to get the weapon, but the statement should not be admissible.

The dissent noted that conservative justices often defer to state court evaluations of the facts in a case, suggesting that the majority's analysis of the facts was wrong and hypocritical. It is as if the majority wanted to create an exception and manipulated the facts of the case to ensure the "proper" outcome. Justice O'Connor concurred, raising a concern that the exception blurred *Miranda*'s bright-line rule.

Rehabilitating *Miranda*?

In **Dickerson v. United States** (2000), the Supreme Court finally confronted the issue of whether *Miranda* was a constitutional ruling. To the surprise of many, the Court held that it is. Charles Dickerson was indicted by a federal grand jury for bank robbery and related crimes. He moved to suppress a statement made to FBI agents during an interrogation because he had not received *Miranda* warnings. The district court granted the motion to suppress because of technical errors in warning Dickerson and specifically ruled that the confession was *otherwise voluntary*. Federal prosecutors appealed to the Court of Appeals for the Fourth Circuit, reputed to be the most conservative federal court of appeals in the nation.[31] That court held (2–1) that although the *Miranda* warnings were defective, the confession was *admissible* under 18 U.S.C. §3501, which says that in any federal prosecution a confession "shall be admissible in evidence if it is voluntarily given."

This federal statute was passed in 1968, shortly after the *Miranda* decision, expressing political outrage against the decision. Under the law, being advised of one's right to remain silent is not required for a confession to be admissible but is only one factor to be taken into account to determine if the confession is voluntary. The law sought, in effect, to overrule *Miranda*. One commentator called it "the most sweeping attack on the Supreme Court since Franklin Roosevelt tried to expand its membership in 1937."[32] The law had not been used by federal prosecutors or the Justice Department prior to the *Dickerson* case because they did not want to create a constitutional clash between the Court and Congress. At this point, the Clinton administration, through a letter from Attorney General Janet Reno to Congress, asserted that insofar as Section 3501 sought to overrule *Miranda*, it was unconstitutional.

In upholding the admissibility of Dickerson's confession, the court of appeals noted that "Congress, pursuant to its power to establish the rules of evidence and procedure in the federal courts, acted well within its authority in enacting §3501, [and] §3501, rather than *Miranda*, governs the admissibility of confessions in federal court." The stage was set for a showdown between the Supreme Court and Congress over *Miranda*.

It is fundamental to American constitutionalism that Congress can by legislation only modify or void a Court-made rule based on a common law basis or statutory interpretation. But Congress cannot overrule a Court-made constitutional law doctrine. When the Supreme Court establishes a constitutional doctrine through its interpretation of a constitutional provision, the only way in which that can properly be modified is by the Court itself overruling its own rulings (e.g., *Gideon v. Wainwright* overruled *Betts v. Brady*) or by constitutional amendment (e.g., the first sentence of the Fourteenth Amendment "overruled" the *Dred Scott* case).

In a 7–2 opinion for the Court, Chief Justice Rehnquist, acknowledging that Congress had intended to overrule *Miranda,* wrote:

We hold that *Miranda,* being a constitutional decision of this Court, may not be in effect overruled by an Act of Congress, and we decline to overrule *Miranda* ourselves. We therefore hold that *Miranda* and its progeny in this Court govern the admissibility of statements made during custodial interrogation in both state and federal courts. (*Dickerson v. United States,* 2000)

The majority opinion in *Dickerson* declared the portion of federal statute relating to *Miranda* unconstitutional for a number of reasons:

- Chief Justice Rehnquist simply brushed away decades of calling *Miranda* a prophylactic rule: "[W]e concede that there is language in some of our opinions that supports the view" that *Miranda* is not a constitutional rule.
- He reasoned, tautologically, that *Miranda* was not based on the Court's supervisory power (which applies only to federal courts and agents) because it had applied the *Miranda* rule to the states from the very beginning.
- Further, the justices in the *Miranda* case, both the majority and the dissenters, understood the Court's ruling as a constitutional rule; the *Miranda* case itself stated that it was giving "concrete *constitutional* guidelines" to law enforcement officers, a point that was trounced by a later Court in *Tucker.*
- Another reason adopted the argument of the dissenters in *Tucker:* The warnings required by *Miranda* have not been superseded by other methods of securing a suspect's right to remain silent in the coercive atmosphere of a police station.
- As for cases like *Quarles* and *Harris* that created exceptions to *Miranda* or that allowed collateral use of *Miranda,* the answer was (1) that the Court had also broadened the scope of *Miranda* in a few cases and (2) that a constitutional rule can have exceptions.
- Chief Justice Rehnquist relied heavily on the concept of *stare decisis,* or precedent:

  Whether or not we would agree with *Miranda*'s reasoning and its resulting rule, were we addressing the issue in the first instance, the principles of *stare decisis* weigh heavily against overruling it now. . . . While *stare decisis* is not an inexorable command, particularly when we are interpreting the Constitution, even in constitutional cases, the doctrine carries such persuasive force that we have always required a departure from precedent to be supported by some special justification.

  We do not think there is such justification for overruling *Miranda. Miranda* has become embedded in routine police practice to the point where *the warnings have become part of our national culture.* (*Dickerson v. United States,* 2000, internal citations and quotations omitted, emphasis added)

- A final reason was that the due process voluntariness test "is more difficult than *Miranda* for law enforcement officers to conform to, and for courts to apply in a consistent manner."

Ultraconservative justices Antonin Scalia and Clarence Thomas, dissenting, accurately accused some majority justices of having reversed their prior decisions. Justice Scalia's dissent also suggests that the majority did not fully establish the constitutionality of *Miranda* warnings by using phrases like "*Miranda* is a constitutional decision," "*Miranda* is constitutionally based," and *Miranda* has "constitutional underpinnings," without saying "that custodial interrogation that is not preceded by *Miranda* warnings or their equivalent violates the Constitution of the United States" (*Dickerson v. United States,* 2000, Scalia, J., dissenting). The dissent viewed the *Dickerson* decision as constitutionally *unprincipled.* Chief Justice Rehnquist's adroit opinion, on the other hand, can be seen as a mature reflection of the fact that constitutional government can be based on understandings—constitutional norms—that develop over time. The decision also signals to Congress that it cannot tread on an area within the preserve of the Supreme Court's authority.

Dickerson was silent on whether the collateral uses of statements taken in violation of *Miranda* (e.g., impeachment, derivative use) had to be eliminated now that *Miranda* was declared to be a constitutional rule, to be consistent with *New Jersey v. Portash* (1979) and *Mincey v. Arizona* (1978). **Chavez v. Martinez** (2003) provided mixed signals. Two police officers were questioning a person about drug dealing in an open area when Oliverio Martinez, a field worker, rode by on his bicycle. Martinez, who had no drugs on him, was detained and severely injured when a frisk and scuffle led to an officer shooting Martinez five times, leaving him blind and paralyzed. Sergeant Chavez arrived with paramedics and interrogated Martinez for about ten minutes during a forty-five-minute drive in the ambulance. The interrogation was audio-recorded. Sergeant Chavez suspected, erroneously, that Martinez attempted to murder the officers. Concerned that Martinez might die before providing information or an admission, *Miranda* warnings were never administered. Martinez intermittently cried out in pain, begged for treatment, and expressed fear of dying. He answered Chavez's questions inconsistently, at one point admitting to pointing Officer Salinas's gun at him, after having denied it.

Martinez was never charged with a crime. He sued Chavez and the municipality under Section 1983 for violating his rights under the Due Process and Self-Incrimination Clauses by interrogating him without reading *Miranda* warnings and for abusive interrogation. In regard to the due process issue, Justice Kennedy recognized that police interrogation can occur under difficult situations that might involve taking a **dying declaration**, and he noted that there "is no rule against interrogating suspects who are in anguish and pain" in exigency situations (*Chavez v. Martinez*, 2003). A due process violation would occur if Chavez gave the impression that Martinez would be treated *only if* he answered the questions. This was the equivalent of the police creating the injuries to Martinez in order to get him to talk and was akin to *torture*. A five-justice majority in effect signaled that they believed there was a due process violation, but remanded the case to the lower courts to decide the due process issue.

As for the self-incrimination issue, all nine justices agreed that the *simple failure* of a police officer *to read Miranda* warnings to a suspect prior to custodial interrogation does not violate the suspect's privilege against self-incrimination. Beyond this agreement, the justices offered sharply different views of the Self-Incrimination Clause. A plurality of four justices (Thomas, Rehnquist, O'Connor, and Scalia), viewing the clause *as an exclusionary rule*, posited that what happens during interrogation, even torture, could *never* be a violation of the Fifth Amendment privilege because it can only be violated by the *introduction* of tainted evidence into a criminal trial.[33]

Justice Souter wrote for the five-justice majority on the due process issue and concurred on the self-incrimination issue (joined only by Justice Breyer). He agreed with the majority that the core of the Fifth Amendment is its application at trial as an exclusionary rule, not allowing compelled evidence to be introduced. He also felt that in cases of *outrageous conduct* by the police there may be a constitutional violation, but it "must sound in substantive due process." He remanded the case to the lower courts to make appropriate findings.

Justice Kennedy (joined by Justices Stevens and Ginsburg), dissenting, would hold that "the Self-Incrimination Clause is applicable at the time and place police use compulsion to extract a statement from a suspect." This position views the Self-Incrimination Clause as more than an exclusionary rule. Although a simple failure to read *Miranda* warnings is not a violation of the suspect's privilege against self-incrimination, "an actionable violation arose at once under the Self-Incrimination Clause (applicable to the States through the Fourteenth Amendment) when the police, after failing to warn, used *severe compulsion or extraordinary pressure* in an attempt to elicit a statement or confession" (*Chavez v. Martinez,* 2003, Kennedy, J., dissenting, emphasis added). Justice Stevens, writing more forcefully in dissent, said "the interrogation of [Martinez] was the functional equivalent of an attempt to obtain an involuntary confession from a prisoner by torturous methods. As a matter of law, that type of brutal police conduct constitutes an immediate deprivation of the prisoner's constitutionally protected interest in liberty" (*Chavez v. Martinez,* 2003, Stevens, J., dissenting).

Extraterritoriality and *Miranda*

The holding of *Chavez v. Martinez* (2003), that the Fifth Amendment is an exclusionary rule, or is at its core an exclusionary rule that excludes compelled statements from trials, is why *Miranda* has extraterritorial effect. That is, extraterritorial interrogations must adhere to at least a modified version of the *Miranda* warnings. Mohamed Rashed Daoud Al-'Owhali, a member of al Qaeda, was prosecuted in 2001 in a New York federal court for the 1998 bombing of the U.S. embassy in Nairobi, Kenya. He claimed that his statements, made during his interrogation in Kenya by an FBI special agent and an Assistant U.S. Attorney, violated his right against self-incrimination. Federal Judge Leonard Sand ruled, in a case of first impression, that U.S. law enforcement personnel interrogating suspects abroad with the consent of the host country for purposes of prosecuting the suspects in U.S. courts must abide by *Miranda:*

> [A] principled, but realistic application of *Miranda*'s familiar warning/waiver framework, in the absence of a constitutionally-adequate alternative, is both necessary and appropriate under the Fifth Amendment. Only by doing so can courts meaningfully safeguard from governmental incursion the privilege against self-incrimination afforded to all criminal defendants in this country—wherever in the world they might initially be apprehended—while at the same time imposing manageable costs on the transnational investigatory capabilities of America's law enforcement personnel . . .
>
> . . . We therefore hold that a defendant's statements, if extracted by U.S. agents acting abroad, should be admitted as evidence at trial only if the Government demonstrates that the defendant was first advised of his rights and that he validly waived those rights.[34]

Judge Sand noted that prior case law required warnings when U.S. agents were involved in questioning by foreign police personnel. He specifically held that a suspect questioned on foreign soil must be warned of the right to silence. "He must also be told that anything he does say may be used against him in a court in the United States or elsewhere. This much is uncontroversial."[35] However, the need to warn a suspect that he or she has a right to the presence of counsel depends on whether that is a right that exists under the law of the host country:

> *Miranda* does not require law enforcement to promise that which they cannot guarantee or that which is in fact impossible to fulfill. No constitutional purpose is served by compelling law enforcement personnel to lie or mislead subjects of interrogation. Nor does *Miranda* mandate that U.S. agents compel a foreign sovereign to accept blind allegiance to American criminal procedure, at least when U.S. involvement in the foreign investigation is limited to mutual cooperation.[36]

Judge Sand rejected the prosecution argument that giving the warnings, with modifications as necessary, would impose intolerable costs on international investigations with cooperating nations or on America's ability to deter transnational crime. Indeed, the federal agents did read extensive warnings to Al-'Owhali, relying on an "Overseas FBI Advice of Rights Form." Judge Sand held that the form was facially deficient because it only informed the suspect that he would have a right to counsel if he was in the United States, creating the impression that no such right was available in the country in which the interrogation occurred. Indeed, Kenyan law raised the possibility that counsel might be available at interrogation. As a result, five days of Al-'Owhali's interrogation were suppressed.

Al-'Owhali later indicated that he wished to inculpate himself in exchange for a guarantee that he be tried in the United States; statements taken on that day were admissible because they were preceded by an oral statement by a U.S. attorney that he could have an attorney present. Al-'Owhali got his wish. He and three others were found guilty of the embassy bombing in the U.S. federal court in Manhattan, just weeks after the 9/11 attacks. They were sentenced to life in a U.S. prison without any chance of release.[37]

The decision in the Al-'Owhali case anticipated the theory accepted in *Chavez v. Martinez* (2003) that *Miranda* rights and the right against self-incrimination are essentially exclusionary rules, violations of which occur at the time and place that compelled statements are introduced in court. This is some indication that Supreme Court decisions build on bodies of legal doctrine. However much a judge's ideological inclinations may persuade him or her to see a solution to a legal question as the right one, it does not mean that Supreme Court decisions are simple political expedients.

Collateral Use of *Miranda*-Violated Statements Post-*Dickerson*

If *Dickerson* held that *Miranda* is a constitutional decision, *Chavez v. Martinez* left open the specific nature and the effectiveness of the *Miranda* warnings. Were the warnings in and of themselves constitutional rights? Justice Thomas's plurality opinion in *Chavez* continued to describe the warnings as "judicially crafted prophylactic rules" and did *not once* cite *Dickerson*.

If the failure to warn a suspect cannot lead to civil liability, it means either that the warnings themselves are *not* constitutional requirements or that only very serious violations of *Miranda* rise to the level of constitutional violations, which seems to be Justice Kennedy's minority view.

The most important post-*Chavez* question was whether the collateral use approach to *Miranda* law still existed. This has tremendous practical effect because in the 1990s some police departments began to deliberately violate *Miranda* in order to obtain a statement for impeachment use or to get leads against a suspect.[38] When done deliberately, this was known as "interrogation outside *Miranda*." For example, if a suspect invokes the right to silence or asks for an attorney, according to *Miranda,* interrogation must cease. The interrogator may believe that it is worth it to violate the suspect's *Miranda* rights to obtain statements that can be used for collateral purposes. This is especially so after the ruling in *Chavez v. Martinez* that the simple failure to give warnings does not impose any civil liability on police officers. The practical effect of wide-open police flouting of *Miranda*'s rules would be to severely limit the practical effectiveness of the case.

In 2004, the Court decided two collateral consequences cases, one involving the *derivative evidence exception* to *Miranda* and the other involving the *cured statement* exception. In *United States v. Patane* (2004), the Court continued to uphold the derivative evidence exception of *Michigan v. Tucker* (1974), where *Miranda* violations appeared to be inadvertent. To the contrary, in *Missouri v. Seibert* (2004), the Supreme Court held that the *cured statement exception* of *Oregon v. Elstad* (1985) did not extend to *Miranda* violations that are deliberate.

Samuel Patane was arrested by Officer Fox just outside his house for violating a domestic violence restraining order. Fox was accompanied by Detective Benner, who was investigating Patane's alleged illegal gun possession (he was a convicted felon). Immediately after the arrest, Benner began advising Patane of his *Miranda* rights but only got as far as the right to silence when Patane said that he knew his rights. No further *Miranda* warnings were given. Benner continued to question Patane about guns, and Patane said that a Glock pistol was in his bedroom. Benner obtained permission to enter the house and seized the gun where Patane said it was. The government conceded that Patane's *Miranda* rights had been violated and that the statements made to Benner were inadmissible.

The Supreme Court held in **United States v. Patane** (2004) that the gun was admissible. Justice Thomas's plurality opinion (joined by Justices Rehnquist and Scalia) held that the "fruits of the poisonous tree" doctrine does not exclude physical evidence taken on the basis of information obtained as a result of incomplete *Miranda* warnings because "police do not violate a suspect's constitutional rights (or the *Miranda* rule) by negligent or even deliberate failures to provide the suspect with the full panoply of warnings prescribed by *Miranda*" (*United States v. Patane,* 2004). Justice Kennedy (joined by Justice O'Connor) agreed but felt it was unnecessary for the plurality to suggest that a failure to give warnings might not be a *Miranda* violation or that as long as an incriminating statement was not admitted into evidence, there were no deterrence concerns. Justice David Souter's dissent, joined by Justices Stevens and Ginsburg, was based squarely on the need to deter deliberate police violations of *Miranda*. "There is no way to read this case except as an unjustifiable invitation to law enforcement officers to flout *Miranda* when there may be physical evidence to be gained" (*United States v. Patane,* 2004). Justice Stephen Breyer, dissenting, would apply the "fruits of the poisonous tree" doctrine to evidence derived from a *Miranda* violation unless the violation occurred in good faith. *Patane* leaves open the question of whether a deliberate *Miranda* violation can be the basis for the introduction of a lead derived from the statement.

In **Missouri v. Seibert** (2004), a woman suspected of involvement in a homicide resulting from an arson was awakened at 3 a.m. in a hospital where her son was being treated for burns incurred during the arson. She was taken to a police station, deliberately not read *Miranda* warnings, and questioned for forty minutes in a suggestive manner designed to elicit an admission of guilt. After she confessed, Seibert was given a twenty-minute coffee break, advised of her *Miranda* rights, and interrogated after waiving her rights. She made another confession. The issue was whether this deliberate two-step process came under the cured statement rule of *Oregon v. Elstad* (1985), allowing the use of the second confession. Justice Souter's plurality opinion (joined by Justices Stevens, Ginsburg, and Breyer) argued that *Miranda* warnings are designed to provide a suspect with a real choice between talking and not talking. The question-first technique employed in the two-step procedure is designed to render *Miranda* warnings ineffective by waiting to give them until after the suspect has already confessed. The method effectively disabled Seibert from freely choosing whether to speak and thus undermined a basic purpose of *Miranda*. This practice is not protected by the *Elstad* ruling, which does not authorize admission of a confession repeated under the question-first strategy. Unlike the brief and tentative unwarned question in *Elstad,* here the questioning was systematic, exhaustive, and managed with psychological skill.

Justice Breyer concurred on the ground that "[c]ourts should exclude the 'fruit' of the initial unwarned questioning unless the failure to warn was in good faith." This made clear the distinction between inadvertent and deliberate failures to administer warnings to suspects. Justice Kennedy also concurred in the judgment of the Court. He wrote that not every *Miranda* violation leads to the exclusion of evidence, and so he supported the existing exceptions, including *Elstad.* He agreed with Justice Souter's conclusion and wrote that the two-step procedure "relies on an intentional misrepresentation of the protection that *Miranda* offers and does not serve any legitimate objectives that might otherwise justify its use." However, he appeared inclined to give police more leeway in the future in how interrogations and warnings can be structured: "The admissibility of postwarning statements should continue to be governed by the principles of *Elstad* unless the deliberate two-step strategy was employed." Thus he suggested that a two-step procedure may be allowable where there is "a substantial break in time and circumstances" between the two interrogation sessions.

Justice O'Connor (joined by Justices Rehnquist, Scalia, and Thomas) dissented in a formalistic opinion that, while recognizing the psychological impact of a two-step interrogation, noted that the Court in *Elstad* refused "to 'endow' those 'psychological effects' with 'constitutional implications.'" Further, the dissent would shift confessions law back to the voluntariness standard: "I would analyze the two-step interrogation procedure under the voluntariness standards central to the Fifth Amendment." This would harken back to *Bram v. United States* (1897), which ruled that involuntary confessions violated the privilege and would be a way for the Court to sidestep *Miranda* in many circumstances.

The decisions in *Patane* and *Seibert* are not the last word on the collateral use exceptions under *Miranda.* An open question following *Seibert* involves the length of the break between the first, non-*Mirandized,* and the second, *Mirandized,* interrogation sessions. Given the Court's focus on the specific policies underlying different exceptions, it seems likely that the impeachment collateral use will continue, as it is designed to prevent a defendant from taking advantage of a misrepresentation of what was said before taking the stand.

INTERPRETING *MIRANDA*

Miranda v. Arizona (1966) spawned scores of cases interpreting each part of the decision. Most of the rulings have provided sufficient flexibility to ensure that they do not unduly hamper police interrogations. In some areas, however, the Court has strengthened protections of interrogated suspects.

Adequacy of Warnings

Police officers need not use *Miranda*'s precise words, or any rigid formula, as long as they *adequately convey the substance* of each warning to suspects prior to interrogation (*California v. Prysock*, 1981). Randall Prysock, a minor, was arrested for murder and declined to talk to his interrogator, Sergeant Byrd. His parents spoke with Randall at the sheriff's office, and he agreed to talk. In a taped interrogation, Byrd informed Randall and his parents of Randall's *Miranda* rights, plus his right as a juvenile to have his parents present. Byrd stated the right to have counsel provided for an indigent person with these words: "You all, uh—if—you have the right to have a lawyer appointed to represent you at no cost to yourself." The Supreme Court majority found that "[i]t is clear that the police in this case fully conveyed to respondent his rights as required by *Miranda.*" Justice Stevens dissented because, as the California courts found, the warning failed to inform Prysock "that the services of a free attorney were available *prior* to the impending questioning." It was more likely that Prysock would have decided not to talk until he had a lawyer had the warning been clearer.

In *Duckworth v. Eagan* (1989), the Court again refused (5–4) to find somewhat "nonstandard" language in the warnings given to a defendant to be inadequate. Eagan was told, as part of otherwise complete *Miranda* warnings:

> You have a right to talk to a lawyer for advice before we ask you any questions, and to
> have him with you during questioning. You have this right to the advice and presence

of a lawyer even if you cannot afford to hire one. *We have no way of giving you a lawyer, but one will be appointed for you, if you wish, if and when you go to court.* If you wish to answer questions now without a lawyer present, you have the right to stop answering questions at any time. You also have the right to stop answering at any time until you've talked to a lawyer. (*Duckworth v. Eagan,* 1989, emphasis added)

Chief Justice Rehnquist, for the majority, noted that the warnings as a whole "touched all of the bases required by *Miranda.*" The additional phrase that a lawyer will be appointed "if and when you go to court" merely informs the suspect of the normal routine of how lawyers are appointed. He also noted that under *Miranda,* lawyers need not be producible on call, nor do police stations need to have attorneys on the premises at all times to advise suspects.

Justice Marshall, for the dissenters, thought the warnings given here would mislead the average suspect into believing that only suspects who could afford lawyers could have one immediately; others "not so fortunate" must wait. Also, "a warning qualified by an 'if and when' caveat still fails to give a suspect any indication of when he will be taken to court. Upon hearing the warnings given in this case, a suspect would likely conclude that no lawyer would be provided until trial" (*Duckworth v. Eagan,* 1989, Marshall, J., dissenting). The dissents in *Prysock* and *Eagan* aimed at making *Miranda* protections clear and unambiguous to defendants, even to the point of expanding the content of the required warnings. *Prysock* adheres more closely to the contours of *Miranda* on this issue, while *Duckworth* appears to undercut the value of warnings.

The Supreme Court has not added new warnings or additional information to the four basic warnings. In **Colorado v. Spring** (1987), Spring was questioned twice while in jail, about three months apart, first by federal agents and a second time by Colorado officers. Complete *Miranda* warnings were administered both times, and Spring signed waiver forms. The federal agents questioned Spring about a firearms violation. They knew he was a homicide suspect and asked him, during the questioning, if he had ever shot anyone. "Spring admitted that he had 'shot [a] guy once. '" This statement was later used in evidence against him in his Colorado murder trial. The Supreme Court held that it was not necessary, under *Miranda,* for the federal officers to tell Spring that they knew he was a murder suspect or that he would later be approached by Colorado officers about that crime. "The Constitution does not require that a criminal suspect know and understand every possible consequence of a waiver of the Fifth Amendment privilege . . . Here, the additional information could affect only the wisdom of a *Miranda* waiver, not its essential voluntary and knowing nature." Justice Marshall, dissenting, saw this as a psychological ploy designed to undermine Spring's will to remain silent. Under these circumstances, he argued, a failure to give the suspect additional information nullified the voluntary, knowing, and intelligent nature of the waiver of rights, making the confession unconstitutional.

Waiver of Rights

Miranda v. Arizona (1966) held that if a confession is obtained, "a *heavy burden* rests on the Government to demonstrate that the defendant *knowingly* and *intelligently* waived his privilege against self incrimination and his right to retained or appointed counsel." The Court allowed an oral waiver but stated that "a valid waiver will not be presumed simply from the silence of the accused after warnings are given or simply from the fact that a confession was in fact eventually obtained."

The "heavy burden" of proving a voluntary waiver was met in **North Carolina v. Butler** (1979). Butler was read his rights and refused to sign a waiver form. The officer told him that he did not have to speak or sign the form but that he wanted to talk to Butler. Butler replied, "I will talk to you, but I am not signing any form." Justice Stewart ruled this a valid waiver:

An express written or oral statement of waiver of the right to remain silent or of the right to counsel is usually strong proof of the validity of that waiver, but is not inevitably either necessary or sufficient to establish waiver. The question is not one of form, but rather whether the defendant in fact knowingly and voluntarily waived the rights delineated in the *Miranda* case. As was unequivocally said in *Miranda* mere silence is not enough. That does not mean that the defendant's silence, coupled with an understanding of his rights and a course of conduct indicating waiver, may never support a conclusion that a defendant has waived his rights. (*North Carolina v. Butler,* 1979)

The majority found, after examining the facts and circumstances, that the defendant had knowingly and voluntarily waived his rights. The minority view, expressed by Justice Brennan for three dissenting justices, interpreted *Miranda* to require an affirmative waiver. They therefore considered Butler's confession invalid. While an affirmative waiver, such as signing a *Miranda* form, is the normal practice today, *Butler* indicates that where the state meets its heavy burden of proving a voluntary waiver, a verbal agreement to speak can constitute a waiver of rights. *Butler* is an example of the Court's reluctance to strictly enforce the rules of *Miranda*.

The "heavy burden" was not met in ***Tague v. Louisiana*** (1980), where the state produced no evidence to show that the defendant knowingly or voluntarily waived his rights. In *Butler,* the record indicated that the full complement of warnings was read and that the defendant understood them. In *Tague,* the arresting officer who testified at the hearing to suppress the confession could not recall whether the defendant understood his rights. Without a record, it was an error to presume that the suspect understood the warnings.

Connecticut v. Barrett (1987) held that a suspect can partially waive *Miranda* rights. After warnings were read to him, Barrett said he was willing to talk to the police but would not sign a statement without a lawyer present. As a general rule, questioning should have ceased. In this case, however, Barrett was very clear that he was willing to talk about the crime but wanted a lawyer's advice as to whether he should sign a statement. He repeated this at his trial. The Supreme Court held his incriminating statements to be admissible. Here, his "affirmative announcements of his willingness to speak with the authorities" overrode his limited request for a lawyer. This is an exceptional case, and the general rule is that a request for a lawyer ends a confession session.

Termination and Resumption of Questioning

Once warnings have been given, the subsequent procedure is clear. If the individual indicates in any manner, at any time prior to or during questioning, that he wishes to remain silent, the interrogation must cease. At this point he has shown that he intends to exercise his Fifth Amendment privilege; any statement taken after the person invokes his privilege cannot be other than the product of compulsion, subtle or otherwise. Without the right to cut off questioning, the setting of in-custody interrogation operates on the individual to overcome free choice in producing a statement after the privilege has been once invoked. (*Miranda v. Arizona,* 1966)

Chief Justice Warren, an experienced former prosecutor, knew it was quite common for interrogating officers to badger suspects—that is, to continue questioning them even after they invoke their right to remain silent. Although the passage may seem clear on its face, the Supreme Court later thought that it was ambiguous:

This passage . . . does not state under what circumstances, if any, a resumption of questioning is permissible. The passage could be literally read to mean that a person who has invoked his "right to silence" can never again be subjected to custodial interrogation by any police officer at any time or place on any subject. Another possible construction of the passage would characterize "any statement taken after the person has invoked his privilege" as "the product of compulsion" and would therefore mandate its exclusion from evidence, even if it were volunteered by the person in custody without any further interrogation whatever. Or the passage could be interpreted to require only the immediate cessation of questioning, and to permit a resumption of interrogation after a momentary respite. (***Michigan v. Mosley***, 1975)

Richard Mosley was arrested for a robbery. During questioning at Detroit police headquarters, after having been read his rights, Mosley said he did not want to talk about the case, whereupon questioning ceased. A few hours later, Mosley was taken from his fourth-floor cell to the homicide division on the fifth floor of the same building. He was read his rights, agreed to talk, and made an incriminating statement that led to evidence that was used to convict him of a homicide. The Supreme Court ruled that Mosley's second statement was admissible at trial. Justice Stewart fashioned a "facts and circumstances" rule that allows the police to question a defendant who has invoked his rights about an entirely different crime after a lapse of time.

Mosley's statement was admissible in evidence because he was properly warned and never requested a lawyer. Also, when he had asked earlier that questioning cease, his request was immediately honored. The mere fact that he once terminated the interrogation, however, did not bar questioning for a different criminal act.

The *Mosley* test is treated as a "totality of the circumstances" test. Lower courts have identified five *Mosley* factors that support the use of a statement after a suspect has invoked his or her right of silence: (1) Initial *Miranda* warnings were given; (2) police immediately ceased interrogation when the suspect invoked the right to silence; (3) a significant time period elapsed between the two interrogations; (4) a fresh *Miranda* warning was given before the second interrogation; and (5) the second interrogation was for a different crime than that investigated in the first interrogation or was triggered by new circumstances (e.g., a confession by a confederate).[39]

Invoking the Right to Counsel

> [A]n individual held for interrogation must be clearly informed that he has the right to consult with a lawyer and to have the lawyer with him during interrogation . . . This warning is an absolute prerequisite to interrogation. No amount of circumstantial evidence that the person may have been aware of this right will suffice to stand in its stead. (*Miranda v. Arizona*, 1966)

Once a defendant claims a desire to see an attorney, questioning must stop. The Supreme Court has, with a few exceptions, interpreted this requirement favorably for suspects.

For example, in **Smith v. Illinois** (1984), an eighteen-year-old robbery suspect, while in custody, was read the required *Miranda* warnings. Told that he had a right to consult with a lawyer and have a lawyer present while being questioned, he replied, "Uh, yeah. I'd like to do that." Despite this, the officer continued to advise Smith of his rights and asked, "Do you wish to talk to me at this time without a lawyer being present?" Smith replied, "Yeah and no, uh, I don't know what's what really." To this, the officer said, "Well. You either have [to agree] to talk to me this time without a lawyer being present and if you do agree . . . you can stop at any time you want to." Smith replied, "All right. I'll talk to you then." He subsequently confessed.

The Court found that Smith invoked his right to counsel by his *first* statement in a clear and unambiguous way. While statements made after the first request for counsel may have been ambiguous, the Court held that "[w]here nothing about the request for counsel or the circumstances leading up to the request would render it ambiguous, all questioning must cease" (*Smith v. Illinois*, 1984). The Court also ruled that "an accused's postrequest responses to further interrogation may not be used to cast retrospective doubt on the clarity of the initial request itself. Such subsequent statements are relevant only to the distinct question of waiver." Justice Rehnquist, writing for three dissenters, believed that the interrogation had not yet begun but that police were still in the process of giving Smith his warnings. Noting that Smith had not been badgered, he felt that the *Miranda* warning process should be examined in its totality. The holding of *Smith v. Illinois*, however, demonstrates that invocation of the right to *counsel* is defined strictly by the Supreme Court.

NONLEGAL ADVISERS   The Court's strict posture regarding requests for counsel is not extended to requests for help from other individuals or officials. In **Fare v. Michael C.** (1979), a juvenile in custody asked to see his probation officer during a murder interrogation. Justice Blackmun held that a request for a probation officer was not equivalent to a *Miranda* request for an attorney. "The *per se* aspect of *Miranda* [was] based on the unique role the lawyer plays in the adversarial system of criminal justice." A probation officer is a state employee who is a peace officer and does not act unequivocally on behalf of the suspect. Justice Marshall dissented (joined by Justices Brennan and Stevens), reinterpreting *Miranda* to say that questioning should stop whenever a juvenile requests an adult who is obligated to represent his or her interests. He suggested that it is unrealistic to expect a juvenile to call for a lawyer; it is more likely for a youth to turn to parents or another adult, such as a welfare worker, as the only means of securing legal counsel. However reasonable this point is, the Court was not willing to expand *Miranda* rights.

THIRD-PARTY INVOLVEMENT   What happens if third parties—such as parents, friends, or relatives—request an attorney for suspects being held by the police, even though the accused themselves have not invoked their *Miranda* rights? The Court has ruled that this is *not* an invocation of Fifth Amendment rights by the suspect personally, and any confession made while an attorney is trying to contact the suspect does not violate the *Miranda* rule.

In ***Moran v. Burbine*** (1986), Brian Burbine was arrested for breaking and entering and was suspected of an earlier murder. After the arrest, his sister called the public defender's office to obtain an attorney's assistance. Allegra Munson, a staff attorney, called the police department. Advised that Burbine was in custody, she told the police, over the telephone, that she was representing him in the event he was questioned or placed in a lineup. The unidentified officer told Munson that Burbine would not be questioned that night. An hour later, however, police did *Mirandize* and question Burbine, who waived his rights and ultimately made incriminating statements.

Burbine raised issues of waiver and the right to counsel. Regarding waiver, Justice O'Connor, for the majority, held that "[e]vents occurring outside of the presence of the suspect and entirely unknown to him surely can have no bearing on the capacity to comprehend and knowingly relinquish a constitutional right." Even the officer's deception of attorney Munson, whether inadvertent or not, unethical or not, does not change the fact that Burbine knowingly and intelligently waived his rights. The Court refused to add a requirement to *Miranda* that the police must inform a defendant of an attorney's attempts to reach him or her, citing practical problems that such a requirement would raise.

That someone had procured counsel for Burbine before he was questioned did not change the complexion of his rights. Justice O'Connor stated:

> [T]he suggestion that the existence of an attorney-client relationship itself triggers the protections of the Sixth Amendment misconceives the underlying purposes of the right to counsel. The Sixth Amendment's intended function is not to wrap a protective cloak around the attorney-client relationship for its own sake any more than it is to protect a suspect from the consequences of his own candor. Its purpose, rather, is to assure that in any "criminal prosecutio[n]" the accused shall not be left to his own devices in facing the "prosecutorial forces of organized society." (*Moran v. Burbine,* 1986)

Because Burbine had not yet been charged by a grand jury or by information, the Sixth Amendment right to an attorney did not yet apply. The majority refused to apply *Escobedo v. Illinois,* which had come to be reinterpreted as a case concerned more with the right against self-incrimination than the right to counsel. In effect, the *Escobedo* ruling became a dead letter.

Justice Stevens wrote a scathing dissent. "Until today, incommunicado questioning has been viewed with the strictest scrutiny by this Court; today, incommunicado questioning is embraced as a societal goal of the highest order that justifies police deception of the shabbiest kind" (*Moran v. Burbine,* 1986). He noted that the rulings of many state courts and the standards of the American Bar Association find that statements taken after the deception of a client's attorney should be excluded from evidence. Furthermore, police "interference with communications between an attorney and his client is a recurrent problem." The ruling in *Moran* would do nothing to curb this kind of improper police behavior.

TERMINATION AND RESUMPTION OF QUESTIONING   The Supreme Court protects the rights of suspects who invoke the right to counsel more strictly than those who terminate questioning without asking for the assistance of counsel. In ***Edwards v. Arizona*** (1981), Robert Edwards was arrested for robbery, burglary, and murder. Questioned at the police station after being given proper *Miranda* warnings, he told the officers that he wanted to "make a deal," but the police terminated the discussion when he said, "I want an attorney before making a deal." The next day, detectives came to the lockup and reinterrogated him. After playing him the taped statement of an alleged accomplice, Edwards agreed to talk as long as it was not tape-recorded, and he implicated himself in the crime. The Supreme Court reversed his conviction. Although a person may validly waive rights, Justice Byron White, for the majority, held that

> when an accused has invoked his right to have counsel present during custodial interrogation, a valid waiver of that right cannot be established by showing only that he responded to further police-initiated custodial interrogation even if he has been advised of his rights. We further hold that an accused, such as Edwards, having

expressed his desire to deal with the police only through counsel, is not subject to further interrogation by the authorities until counsel has been made available to him, *unless the accused himself initiates* further communication, exchanges, or conversations with the police. (*Edwards v. Arizona,* 1981, emphasis added)

The *Edwards* rule, strongly protective of defendants' rights, was weakened in the next two cases. ***Oregon v. Bradshaw*** (1983) decided that a suspect *had* initiated further questioning. In this case, interrogation ceased after Bradshaw requested counsel. During the trip from the police station to the jail Bradshaw asked: "Well, what is going to happen to me now?" He was again read his rights, and in a "general conversation," agreed to take a lie detector test. The next day, Bradshaw took a lie detector test, preceded by *Miranda* warnings, which resulted in an incriminating admission. A four-justice plurality said that Bradshaw's question, although ambiguous, "evinced a willingness and a desire for a generalized discussion about the investigation." A four-justice dissent, written by Justice Marshall, found this interpretation of Bradshaw's words by the plurality to be preposterous:

If respondent's question had been posed by Jean-Paul Sartre before a class of philosophy students, it might well have evinced a desire for a "generalized" discussion. But under the circumstances of this case, it is plain that respondent's only "desire" was to find out where the police were going to take him. (*Oregon v. Bradshaw,* 1983)

The Supreme Court, in ***Davis v. United States*** (1994), held that in order to invoke the protection of *Edwards,* the request for counsel must be made *clearly.* Naval investigators suspected that Robert L. Davis beat another sailor to death with a pool cue. Davis was arrested, was advised of his rights under military law, and waived his rights to remain silent. An hour and a half into the interview, Davis said, "Maybe I should talk to a lawyer." A Navy investigator testified:

We made it very clear that we're not here to violate his rights, that if he wants a lawyer, then we will stop any kind of questioning with him, that we weren't going to pursue the matter unless we have it clarified is he asking for a lawyer or is he just making a comment about a lawyer, and he said, "No, I'm not asking for a lawyer," and then he continued on, and said, "No, I don't want a lawyer." (*Davis v. United States,* 1995)

The investigators took a short break and then reminded Davis of his rights to remain silent and to counsel. They continued the interview for another hour, during which he made an incriminating statement. Soon thereafter Davis said, "I think I want a lawyer before I say anything else" and questioning ceased. The Court held that the incriminating statement was admissible and that Davis's rights under *Edwards* were not violated.

Analytically, there are three possible options to determine if a suspect's mention of a lawyer invoked the right to counsel: (1) Any mention of counsel, however ambiguous, *invokes* counsel; (2) the *Edwards* protection is invoked if the suspect's request meets a "threshold" standard of *clarity*; or (3) whenever a suspect mentions a lawyer, questioning must cease, but *interrogators may ask "narrow questions* designed to clarify the earlier statement and the [suspect's] desires respecting counsel." The Court selected the second option.

Noting that *Edwards*'s prohibition on questioning is not itself a constitutional right but, like the *Miranda* rule, a protection for the Fifth Amendment, Justice O'Connor, writing for the Court, held that "after a knowing and voluntary waiver of the *Miranda* rights, law enforcement officers may continue questioning until and unless the suspect clearly requests an attorney." Justice O'Connor said that asking "clarifying questions" (option number three), while good police practice, is not required. *Davis* upholds the bright-line rule of *Edwards* by not forcing interrogating officers "to make difficult judgment calls about whether the suspect in fact wants a lawyer even though he hasn't said so, with the threat of suppression if they guess wrong."

Although the *Bradshaw* plurality strained in order to rule in favor of the state, and *Davis* burdens a suspect's rights under *Edwards,* the following cases show that, for the most part, the Supreme Court has interpreted the *Edwards* "bright-line rule" in favor of suspects.

Arizona v. Roberson (1988) strengthened the *Edwards* rule in two ways. First, once a suspect asks to see a lawyer before speaking, this knowledge applies not only to the officer who first

Mirandized the suspect but to every officer in the same agency. This is a necessary corollary to the *Edwards* rule since it would be too easy for police officers to sidestep *Edwards* by claiming ignorance that invocation of rights was made to another officer. Justice Stewart, favoring bright-line rules, noted that "custodial interrogation must be conducted pursuant to established procedures, and those procedures in turn must enable an officer who proposes to initiate an interrogation to determine whether the suspect has previously requested counsel." Second, after a suspect invoked counsel during a first interrogation, police cannot initiate a second interrogation about a different crime than the one inquired into at the first interrogation. The accused had expressed the view during the first interrogation "that he is not competent to deal with the authorities without legal advice." This explains why, under *Mosley*, police may reinitiate questioning under some circumstances after a suspect has invoked the right to silence, but not after invoking counsel. Although the Court did not refer specifically to police strategies to badger suspects to get them to talk despite having invoked silence or counsel after receiving *Miranda* warnings, in a more general way it reiterated the concern with "the pressures of custodial interrogation" as support for its holding.

The *Edwards* rule was solidified in **Minnick v. Mississippi** (1990). An in-jail interrogation ceased after Minnick invoked the right to counsel. He was thereafter allowed to consult with a lawyer. After that, he was again interrogated without counsel present and made an incriminating admission. The Supreme Court held (6–2) that simply allowing the suspect to confer with counsel does not satisfy *Edwards*. A suspect who asks to speak to a lawyer is demanding a right to have a lawyer *present during* interrogation. Unless a subsequent uncounseled conversation is initiated by the suspect, as required by *Edwards,* the police cannot reinterrogate. A different standard would dilute the clarity of *Edwards*'s bright-line rule and could create confusion whereby a suspect would gain *Edwards* protection at several points during custody by invoking the right to counsel and then lose it after conferring with an attorney. Justice Kennedy's majority opinion emphasized that the *Edwards* rule prevents the police from badgering suspects as well as making it easier for judges to decide whether a suspect's *Miranda* and *Edwards* rights were complied with. "A single consultation with an attorney does not remove the suspect from persistent attempts by officials to persuade him to waive his rights, or from the coercive pressures that accompany custody and that may increase as custody is prolonged."

Defining Custody

> By custodial interrogation, we mean questioning initiated by law enforcement officers after a person has been taken into custody or deprived of his freedom of action in any significant way. (*Miranda v. Arizona,* 1966)

The Supreme Court expanded *Miranda*'s definition of *police custody* beyond the station house. The basic question is: Does the setting in which a confession is given create the compulsion contemplated by the Fifth Amendment privilege that brings the *Miranda* requirement and its exclusionary rule into play? Is the interrogation setting coercive? The Fifth Amendment does not forbid interrogation, but looks instead to see whether the questioning is accompanied by compulsion.

HOME   Being questioned in one's own home may be custodial depending upon the facts. There was custody in *Orozco v. Texas* (1969) when police entered the defendant's house at 4 a.m. and questioned him while he was under arrest, not free to leave, and surrounded by police officers. There was no custody in **Beckwith v. United States** (1975). Beckwith was the target of a criminal tax investigation. Internal Revenue Service (IRS) agents came to his home during the day, politely requested admittance, and gave him time to finish dressing. The interview was conducted in a friendly and relaxed manner at Beckwith's dining room table. He was not pressed to answer questions and was told at the beginning of the interview that he had a right to refuse to answer questions. On these facts, the interview was not conducted in custody; therefore, *Miranda* warnings did not have to be given even though Beckwith, as an investigation target, could have legally refused to answer questions had he been subpoenaed.

PRISON   *Mathis v. United States* (1968) holds that all interrogations of inmates that occur in prison must be preceded by *Miranda* warnings. IRS agents interviewed Mathis in prison, without issuing *Miranda* warnings, about tax issues unrelated to the reason for his imprisonment. Based on his custody status, the Supreme Court found a *Miranda* violation and overturned the conviction. Justice White, dissenting, believed that the underlying rationale of *Miranda* "rested not on the mere fact of physical restriction but on a conclusion that coercion—pressure to answer questions—usually flows from a certain type of custody, police station interrogation," of a suspect. Since Mathis was in familiar surroundings when questioned, even though confined, Justice White felt he was under no pressure to talk.

POLICE STATION   Interrogation in a police station does not become custodial merely because of the location; it depends instead on the circumstances of the interrogation atmosphere. The majority in *Oregon v. Mathiason* (1977) found no custody or significant curtailment of freedom of action when a suspect voluntarily complied with a police request that he come to the station house for an interview. Carl Mathiason, a parolee, was identified as a probable burglar. A police officer left a card at Mathiason's residence asking him to call. A meeting was held at the police station at Mathiason's convenience. The officer shook Mathiason's hand when he came to the station, and they met in a closed office with the officer sitting across a desk. The officer falsely told Mathiason that his fingerprints were found, whereupon he confessed. Only then were *Miranda* warnings read and another confession obtained.

The Court concluded that Mathiason was *not* in custody before he confessed, and so no *Miranda* warnings had to be read. The Court admitted that "[a]ny interview of one suspected of a crime by a police officer will have coercive aspects to it, simply by virtue of the fact that the police officer is part of a law enforcement system which may ultimately cause the suspect to be charged with a crime." This kind of pressure, a sort of "background radiation" that attaches to police officers, is different from the *heightened compulsion* that occurs when a person is taken into custody. Justice Marshall dissented. He felt that Mathiason's freedom of movement was curtailed in a true sense and that he was in custody even though not formally placed under arrest. The Court reached the same result in *California v. Behler* (1983) on similar facts, except that the defendant went voluntarily to the police station to tell the police that he was at the scene of a homicide, although he had been drinking earlier in the day and was emotionally distraught.

The test of custody is an *objective* determination of whether the suspect was deprived of freedom in any significant way. In *Stansbury v. California* (1994), a police detective investigating the abduction and rape-murder of a ten-year-old girl questioned Robert Stansbury, one of two ice cream truck drivers whom the girl had spoken to on the day she was killed. Stansbury was not read *Miranda* warnings because the detective thought the other driver was the likely suspect. During the interview, Stansbury described a borrowed car he drove on the night of the murder that was similar to a description of the car given by a witness. This aroused the officer's suspicion, and *in his mind* he focused on Stansbury as a suspect. Stansbury had no way of reading the officer's mind. The officer did not, by word or deed, convey to Stansbury that he was not free to leave. Under the objective standard, therefore, Stansbury was not yet in custody, and his incriminating statement about the car was admissible. As the questioning continued, Stansbury said that he had prior convictions for rape, kidnapping, and child molestation. At this point, the officer terminated the interview and another officer read Stansbury his *Miranda* warnings. The Court ruled that "an officer's subjective and undisclosed view concerning whether the person being interrogated is a suspect is irrelevant to the assessment whether the person is in custody."

In *Yarborough v. Alvarado* (2004), the Supreme Court (5–4) held that a stationhouse interrogation of a seventeen-year-old questioned as an accessory to a murder for two hours in a closed room without his parents present was *not* custodial. During the questioning Michael Alvarado admitted to helping a friend commit a carjacking, during which the friend shot and killed the victim. The majority and dissenting justices differed sharply over the facts, although both applied an objective test based on cases like *Mathiason*, *Behler*, and *Stansbury*. The majority did not take into account Alvadado's youth and inexperience with the police while the dissenters did.

According to Justice Kennedy's majority opinion, custody could be inferred from the fact that Alvarado was interviewed at the police station and was not told that he was free to leave, the interview lasted two hours compared to the thirty-minute interview in *Mathiason*, and Michael could not easily get away from the station personally because his parents drove him there. Despite this, the majority concluded that Alvarado was not in custody because police did not pick him up and drive him to the station, did not threaten him or place him under arrest, told him and his parents that the interview would not be long (although it was), focused on his accomplice being the shooter (although the questioning was intended to get Michael to admit he was an accessory), appealed to his interest in telling the truth and being helpful to a police officer, and at the end of the interview, Michael went home.

The view expressed in Justice Breyer's dissenting opinion was that as a matter of common sense, the "obvious answer" to the question, "Would a reasonable person in Alvarado's position have felt he was at liberty to terminate the interrogation and leave?"—in light of all of the circumstances surrounding the interrogation including his youth—is "no."

PROBATION INTERVIEW   The Supreme Court held in **Minnesota v. Murphy** (1984) that a probation interview is not custody for *Miranda* purposes, even though a probationer is legally required to attend probation interviews and a condition of probation is that he or she answer all questions truthfully. The probationer, Marshall Murphy, was not under arrest, nor was his freedom of movement seriously restrained. In this case, Murphy's probation officer planned in advance to ask him about previous crimes in an effort to elicit incriminating information. She gave Murphy no prior warning of such questions. He admitted to previously committing a rape and murder, and the statement to the probation officer was admissible in his first-degree murder trial.

The reason Murphy's statement was not compelled is that, except for the *Miranda* situation, the Fifth Amendment privilege against self-incrimination is not self-executing. Incriminating statements are not automatically excluded simply because a person makes them to a listener. With the exception of a police custodial interrogation, in which a person must be informed of his rights, a person must claim the privilege in order to rely on it. Once a person utters an incriminating statement, it is presumed voluntary, and the listener can tell what he or she heard to prosecutorial authorities (or anyone else) and may testify in court as to what was heard.

Murphy claimed that the probation condition that required truthful answers to the probation officer's questions amounted to compulsion. The Court disagreed. The probationer is in a similar situation as a witness subpoenaed before a grand jury. Both are legally compelled to attend and to answer truthfully, and they are not granted immunity. The probation conditions did not deprive Murphy of his Fifth Amendment rights. He could have refused to answer the questions that could have incriminated him. Murphy claimed that he feared revocation of probation if he did not answer. There was no proof, however, that Minnesota law or practice punished a probationer who claimed the protection of the Fifth Amendment.

TRAFFIC STOPS   A motorist stopped for a moving violation, whether a misdemeanor or a felony, such as speeding or operating under the influence of drugs or alcohol, is detained for the time it takes to write a ticket or to proceed to an arrest. Writing for a nearly unanimous Court in ***Berkemer v. McCarty*** (1984), Justice Marshall held that "persons temporarily detained pursuant to" police roadside stops of vehicles for traffic violations "are not 'in custody' for the purposes of *Miranda*." Such stops do not significantly restrain the freedom of movement to such an extent as to deprive them of their will, as contemplated by *Miranda,* for two simple reasons. First, "detention of a motorist pursuant to a traffic stop is presumptively temporary and brief." Second, the stop occurs in public so that the motorist does not feel completely at the mercy of the police. Thus, although the motorist is detained, these factors "mitigate the danger that a person questioned will be induced 'to speak where he would not otherwise do so freely'" (*Berkemer v. McCarty,* 1984, quoting *Miranda*). The stopped motorist is far less likely, under this reasoning, to be coerced into giving up Fifth Amendment rights.

McCarty was stopped by a trooper who saw his car weaving in traffic. After he failed a field sobriety test, he was told he would be taken into custody. Asked if he had taken any intoxicants, McCarty said that "he had consumed two beers and had smoked several joints of marijuana a short time before." At the jail, McCarty was again asked questions and gave incriminating answers. At no time were *Miranda* warnings read. McCarty's roadside statements were admitted into evidence.

Berkemer v. McCarty, however, did hold that once a motorist has been arrested or taken into custody on traffic felony or misdemeanor charges, *Miranda* warnings must be read prior to interrogation. The Court equated traffic misdemeanors with felonies in order to uphold the "simplicity and clarity of the holding of *Miranda*." An exception from warnings for traffic misdemeanors would create confusion and the potential for endless litigation. For example, some crimes escalate from misdemeanors to felonies depending on the number of prior convictions, and it is not clear at the time of the vehicle stop whether a driving offense is a misdemeanor or felony. Thus admissions made by McCarty on the roadside were admissible, but those made at the police station were inadmissible.

Pennsylvania v. Muniz (1990) further clarified the application of *Miranda* when a driver is stopped for driving under the influence (DUI) and is ordered to undergo a field sobriety test. The Supreme Court held that *Miranda* warnings were not required simply for stopping a driver for DUI. The fact that the driver's speech is slurred, however incriminating, does not come under *Miranda* because physical inability to articulate words is not testimonial evidence. Similarly, ordering a driver to perform and videotaping standard physical sobriety tests—the horizontal gaze nystagmus test, the walk-and-turn test, and the one-leg stand test—are not testimonial. The officer ordered the DUI suspect to perform the tests in "carefully scripted instructions as to how the tests were to be performed. These instructions were not likely to be perceived as calling for any verbal response and therefore were not 'words or actions' constituting custodial interrogation." As a result, *Miranda* warnings are not required. Furthermore, an officer can ask a driver's name, address, height, weight, eye color, date of birth, and current age. The Court held that answers to these questions are admissible under a "routine booking question" exception to *Miranda*. Biographical data needed to complete booking or pretrial services and requested for record-keeping purposes only are reasonably related to police administrative concerns. In this case, Muniz made unsolicited, incriminating statements that he had been drinking while the officer read him another carefully prepared script concerning the nature of Pennsylvania's implied consent law and a request to submit to a breathalyzer test. The only questions asked of Muniz were whether he understood the instructions and whether he wished to submit to the test. "These limited and focused" questions were a part of legitimate police procedure and were not designed or likely to be perceived as calling for an incriminating response. Therefore Muniz's statements that he had been drinking were admissible.

The Court held that *Miranda* warnings were required only as to one question posed by the officer: "Do you know what the date was of your sixth birthday?" This was held to be testimonial interrogation; Muniz's incoherent response implied that he was intoxicated. This was not admissible because the question was asked before *Miranda* warnings were administered. Justice Brennan, for the majority, reasoned that the *content* of the answer allowed the police officer to infer that the driver's mental state was confused. Because the incriminating inference was drawn from a testimonial act rather than a physical fact, the question confronted the suspect with the classic "trilemma" of self-incrimination, perjury, or contempt. Chief Justice Rehnquist disagreed on this point, claiming that Justice Brennan's assumption about human behavior was wrong. Given the nature of the question to Muniz, which was basically to check how well he could add the number six to his date of birth, there was no real incentive for Muniz to lie and commit perjury. In this view, the question was closer to the physical tests and the "booking questions" that did not violate the Fifth Amendment in this case.

The Nature of Interrogation

Miranda v. Arizona (1966) applies to custodial interrogation. ***Rhode Island v. Innis*** (1980) ruled that

> *Miranda* safeguards come into play whenever a person in custody is subjected to either *express questioning* or its *functional equivalent.* That is to say, the term "interrogation" under *Miranda* refers not only to express questioning, but also to any words or actions on the part of the police (other than normally attendant to arrest and custody) that the police should know are reasonably likely to elicit an incriminating response from the suspect. (*Rhode Island v. Innis,* 1980, emphasis added)

The functional equivalent of express interrogation can be discovered from the facts and circumstances of cases.

Police arrested Innis at 4:30 a.m. on suspicion of murdering a taxicab driver with a shotgun. They advised him of his rights. He said he wanted to speak with a lawyer, terminating any interrogation. Innis was placed in the back of a patrol car and driven to the station. On the way to the station, Officer Gleckman spoke to Officer McKenna about the shotgun, saying there was a school for handicapped children in the area "and God forbid one of them might find a weapon with shells and they might hurt themselves." McKenna agreed and suggested that they should continue to search for the shotgun. At that point, Innis interrupted the conversation, stating that he could lead the officers to the gun, which he did. This incriminating statement and the shotgun were admitted into evidence to convict him.

Was this exchange the functional equivalent of interrogation? Justice Stewart, writing for the majority, said "no." He characterized the comments as only a few offhand remarks that the police could not have known would suddenly move Innis to make a self-incriminating response. A lengthy and more pointed "harangue" might become interrogation, but not the conversation here. The Court suggested that an example of a functional equivalent of interrogation is a "reverse lineup" where the police plant a "witness" in the lineup room to vocally accuse the suspect of a fictitious crime to induce him to confess to the actual crime. The Court added an important embellishment to its "functional equivalent" rule:

> But, since the police surely cannot be held accountable for the unforeseeable results of their words or actions, the definition of interrogation can extend only to words or actions on the part of police officers that they *should have known* were reasonably likely to elicit an incriminating response. (*Rhode Island v. Innis*, 1980)

To go further, police knowledge includes not only the likely effect of words on a hypothetical person, but also on a suspect with known weaknesses or susceptibilities.

Justice Marshall concurred with the definition of *interrogation* but dissented from its application to the facts in this case. He noted that appeals to the decency and the honor of the suspect are classic interrogation ploys and that "[o]ne can scarcely imagine a stronger appeal to the conscience of a suspect." Justice Stevens, also dissenting, suggested a different definition of *interrogation:* "[A]ny statement that would normally be understood by the average listener as calling for a response is the functional equivalent of a direct question, whether or not it is punctuated by a question mark." This definition focuses on the intention of the officers to some degree. The majority's rule, however, "focuses primarily upon the perceptions of the suspect, rather than the intent of the police."

The *Innis* definition was applied in **Arizona v. Mauro** (1987). William Mauro was arrested for the murder of his son after turning himself in at a local K-Mart store. He refused to make statements without a lawyer present, and he was not questioned. Police interviewed Mrs. Mauro at the station house. She insisted on speaking with her husband and was allowed to after some resistance on the part of the police. She was told that an officer would be present, and a tape recorder was placed prominently on the table. William Mauro told his wife not to answer questions until a lawyer was present. At trial, the taped conversation was admitted into evidence to refute Mauro's insanity defense.

The Court held (5–4), in an opinion by Justice Powell, that the recording of the conversation was not the functional equivalent of interrogation under *Miranda* or *Innis*. The police did not send Mrs. Mauro in to speak with her husband, and the presence of the officer during their conversation was not improper. The mere possibility that a suspect in custody will incriminate himself under these circumstances does not amount to interrogation. "[T]he actions in this case were far less questionable than the 'subtle compulsion' that we held *not* to be interrogation in *Innis* . . . Officers do not interrogate a suspect simply by hoping that he will incriminate himself."

Justice Stevens, for the dissenters, reasoned that the police used a "powerful psychological ploy" when they allowed Mrs. Mauro to speak to her husband; it was bound to generate some discussion after he had manifested a clear desire to remain silent. The legitimacy of the police presence is irrelevant to this finding, for on the witness stand, the police captain admitted that one reason for allowing the meeting was to obtain statements that could "shed light on our case." Also, a police detective testified that a standard police technique used to get juveniles to talk is to bring their parents into the police station. It is noteworthy that in both the *Innis* and *Mauro* cases, the state supreme courts believed that interrogation, or its functional equivalent under *Miranda,* had occurred.

Colorado v. Connelly (1986) is an example of noninterrogation. Francis Connelly, a chronic schizophrenic, traveled from Boston to Denver because the "voice of God" commanded him to do so. He approached a police officer on a downtown Denver street "and, without any prompting, stated that he had murdered someone and wanted to talk about it." Connelly was immediately informed of his rights, but he insisted he wanted to speak. He gave a confession on the street, after two additional *Miranda* warnings, and appeared at that point to be mentally normal.

Connelly's confession was held to be valid because it was a purely voluntary statement not barred by the Fifth Amendment. Justice Brennan dissented, joined by Justice Marshall, finding the admission of a statement by a person diagnosed with chronic paranoid schizophrenia to be a due process violation. "Today the Court denies Mr. Connelly his fundamental right to make a vital choice with a sane mind, involving a determination that could allow the State to deprive him of liberty or even life. This holding is unprecedented" (*Colorado v. Connelly*, 1986, Brennan, J., dissenting).

The Use of Deception

Police who lie to suspects during interrogation to get them to confess do not violate the Constitution unless the deception tactics coerce the confessions. Deception may be necessary, in some cases, to convince suspects to incriminate themselves. Common ploys range from secretly wiretapping jail inmates to issuing false threats, and include police falsely telling suspects that a confederate ratted on them or that a fingerprint or blood test put them at the crime scene.[40] Police believe that a truly guilty party may at that point confess, while a truly innocent person will deny such charges. A risk is that police deception, combined with forceful and prolonged interrogation, has also led innocent people to confess.[41] (See the "Law in Society" section in this chapter.)

Support for police deception is found in *Frazier v. Cupp* (1969), which involved a confession given before *Miranda* was decided. Frazier was arrested for a murder and interrogated by the police. After a time, an officer told the defendant that his cousin, who was also a suspect, had confessed. This was a lie. "Petitioner [Frazier] still was reluctant to talk, but after the officer sympathetically suggested that the victim had started a fight by making homosexual advances, petitioner began to spill out his story." Frazier argued that the misrepresentation about his cousin's confession rendered the confession inadmissible as a due process violation. The Court disagreed. The false statement, while relevant, was deemed insufficient to make an otherwise voluntary confession inadmissible.

Illinois v. Perkins (1990) stands for the general proposition that an undercover police agent who falsely holds himself out as a friend of a suspect and gets the suspect to confess to a crime is not required to give the suspect *Miranda* warnings. This is the case even if the false friend scenario occurs in a jail. Perkins made a detailed confession about a murder he committed to a jail "plant"—a police undercover agent—who was inserted into the jail as an inmate in order to obtain an incriminating statement. The police believed Perkins had committed the murder because a man who had earlier shared a cell with Perkins in prison said Perkins admitted the crime and he provided details of the murder that were not well known. It was true that Perkins was in custody at the time he made his confession to the undercover agent, but the Supreme Court held (8–1) that the conversation between the undercover agent and Perkins was not interrogation because the essential *Miranda* ingredients of a "police-dominated atmosphere" and compulsion were missing. Perkins had no idea he was speaking to a police officer; there was simply no element of coercion or compulsion to talk in his mind. Likewise, for the purposes of *Miranda*, Perkins was not in custody because he didn't know that he was talking with a government agent, and the psychological pressures that weaken a suspect's will in police custodial interrogation were not present. Justice Kennedy noted that a certain amount of deception by law enforcement officers is allowed under *Miranda* as long as the deception does not become coercive.

Perkins was distinguished from *United States v. Henry* (1980) and *Maine v. Moulton* (1985), discussed later in this chapter, which were decided under the *Massiah* Sixth Amendment right to counsel rule. Those cases involved interactions between undercover agents and suspects *after* the suspects had been *formally charged* and had attorneys. In *Perkins*, no charges had been filed regarding the murder that was subject of the interrogation, so the Sixth Amendment did not come into play. *Perkins* allows the use of a valuable investigation tool, although law enforcement should be vigilant about abuses that can occur in using inmates as snitches.

Lower courts cases hold that deception does not extend to express lies about the waiver of rights, suggesting, for example that a suspect cannot see a lawyer.[42] A notable state case has held that police deception violated due process and compelled a confession where police, with the knowledge of the prosecutor, fabricated two scientific *written* reports, with one false report prepared on stationery of the Florida Department of Criminal Law Enforcement and the other the on stationery of a scientific testing organization. The false reports indicated that semen stains on the rape victim's underwear came from the defendant. The police showed the reports to the defendant and after some time he confessed. The Florida Court of Appeals reasoned that a suspect, entering the uncertain arena of police interrogation, and not expecting to be confronted with a fabricated official-(looking) report, "is more impressed and thereby more easily induced to confess when presented with tangible, official-looking reports as opposed to merely being told that some tests have implicated him." Such a report "impresses one as being inherently more permanent and facially reliable than a simple verbal statement." The court laid down a bright-line rule against this kind of deception. It also raised a number of practical objections, noting that such a report could be filed and at some later time be accepted as truly *official* and *accurate*.[43]

QUESTIONING AFTER FORMAL CHARGING: THE SIXTH AMENDMENT

Interrogation of suspects in police custody is limited by the due process voluntariness test and by *Miranda*, under the Self-Incrimination Clause. Once the suspect is *formally charged*, however, the legal picture changes. Formal charging can occur by grand jury indictment, a prosecutor's information, or a magistrate's bind-over after a preliminary examination. At this point, the *criminal prosecution* defined by the Sixth Amendment has begun and the right to counsel "attaches." Once a defendant is charged, different and *more stringent* constraints on police questioning and eavesdropping apply. In theory, post-indictment statements obtained by the police surreptitiously, or in disregard of the defendant's right to counsel, are excluded from the trial. In practice the Supreme Court has relaxed the rules regarding *waiver* of counsel so that police have almost as much freedom after indictment to approach and question suspects as they do before.

The general rule was established in *Massiah v. United States* (1964). Winston Massiah, a crew member on a ship from South America, was charged in New York with transporting cocaine into the United States, indicted, and released on bail. While on bail, Massiah's co-defendant, Colson, agreed to cooperate with the government. A listening device placed in Colson's car transmitted Massiah's incriminating statements. A government agent testified to the incriminating statements at Massiah's trial. The Supreme Court held that introducing the testimony violated Massiah's Sixth Amendment right to counsel. The Court said that counsel has long been considered essential during the pretrial stages and held that secretly obtaining incriminating statements from an indicted defendant interfered with his right to legal representation.

Justice Stewart's majority opinion repeated his views in *Spano v. New York* (1959), a pre-*Miranda* confession case decided under the voluntariness test. He noted that obtaining a confession from an indicted defendant without notifying an attorney "might deny a defendant 'effective assistance of counsel at the only stage when legal aid and advice would help him'" (*Massiah v. United States*, 1964, quoting *Spano*). That is, secretly taping incriminating statements virtually convicts the defendant, in effect creating a critical stage where counsel has to be present. The same goes for open interviews between police or prosecutors and the defendant. If a plea arrangement is desired, the defendant's lawyer must be present.

Justice White, dissenting, believed that there was no interference with Massiah's right to counsel. Unlike the Canon of Professional Ethics that prevents an attorney from interviewing an opposing party, he argued that there is no ethical restriction on investigators' contacting a criminal defendant. "Law enforcement may have the elements of a contest about it, but it is not a game" (*Massiah v. United States*, White, J., dissenting). Justice White's view failed to acknowledge that once the investigator speaks to or overhears a suspect and gets incriminating statements, the value of a lawyer's advice is nullified.

Cases decided under *Massiah* deal with similar functional issues to those that arise under *Miranda,* including the definition of interrogation and the validity of a waiver. Such questions arose in the notorious Christian burial speech case of *Brewer v. Williams* (1977). Williams, incidentally, was retried and found guilty. The Supreme Court upheld the second conviction under the doctrine of inevitable discovery in *Nix v. Williams* (1984), also referred to as *Williams II*; see Chapter 2.

Read Case and Comments: *Brewer v. Williams*.

The *Massiah* Right after *Brewer v. Williams*

A dozen decisions in post-*Massiah* cases display a struggle between justices whose attitudes fit the Crime Control Model versus the Due Process Model in determining how suspects are to be treated. There is a level of idealism about the adversary trial that animates the Due Process Model, captured in Prof. Yale Kamisar's wonderful metaphor of the "mansions and the

CASE AND COMMENTS

Brewer v. Williams

430 U.S. 387, 97 S.Ct. 1232, 51 L.Ed.2d 424 (1977)

MR. JUSTICE STEWART delivered the opinion of the Court.

I

[a] Numerous facts are stated. Which are essential to the holding of the case?

* * * [Robert Williams, a mental hospital escapee, turned himself in to Davenport, Iowa, police for the murder of a ten-year-old girl at a Des Moines YMCA on December 26, 1968. [a] He was arrested, formally arraigned (charged) for the crime, and advised of his rights by the judge, who noted that Williams was represented by attorney McKnight in Des Moines and attorney Kelly in Davenport. McKnight spoke to Williams on the phone in the presence of Des Moines police detective Leaming. He informed Williams that Des Moines officers would drive to Davenport, pick him up, and would not interrogate him or mistreat him. He warned Williams not to talk to the officers about the crime. When Detective Leaming picked up Williams, Kelly, the Davenport lawyer, was denied a request to ride back to Des Moines with them. Kelly repeated to Detective Leaming that Williams was not to be questioned on the ride back.]

[b] Do you think Detective Leaming made the speech to deliberately elicit incriminating evidence or just to pass the time?

[On the 160-mile ride to Des Moines, Williams expressed no desire to be interrogated without his lawyer present; he said he would tell the whole story at the end of the trip. Leaming knew Williams was a deeply religious man and engaged him in a general discussion. Soon after the trip began, Leaming delivered the so-called] "Christian burial speech." Addressing Williams as "Reverend," the detective said: [b]

> "I want to give you something to think about while we're traveling down the road. . . . Number one, I want you to observe the weather conditions, it's raining, it's sleeting, it's freezing, driving is very treacherous, visibility is poor, it's going to be dark early this evening. They are predicting several inches of snow for tonight, and I feel that you yourself are the only person that knows where this little girl's body is, that you yourself have only been there once, and if you get a snow on top of it you yourself may be unable to find it. And, since we will be going right past the area on the way into Des Moines, I feel that we could stop and locate the body, that the parents of this little girl should be entitled to a Christian burial for the little girl who was snatched away from them on Christmas [E]ve and murdered. And I feel we should stop and locate it on the way in rather than waiting until morning and trying to come back out after a snow storm and possibly not being able to find it at all."

[c] The call for silence at this point allowed Leaming's speech to work on Williams's mind.

Williams asked Detective Leaming why he thought their route to Des Moines would be taking them past the girl's body, and Leaming responded that he knew the body was in the area of Mitchellville—a town they would be passing on the way to Des Moines. [c] Leaming then stated: "I do not want you to answer me. I don't want to discuss it any further. Just think about it as we're riding down the road."

As the car approached Grinnell, a town approximately 100 miles west of Davenport, Williams asked whether the police had found the victim's shoes. When Detective Leaming replied that he was unsure, Williams directed the officers to a service station where he said he had left the shoes; a search for them proved unsuccessful. As they continued towards Des Moines, Williams asked whether the police had found the blanket, and directed the officers to a rest area where he said he had disposed of the blanket. Nothing was found. The car continued towards Des Moines, and as it approached Mitchellville, Williams said that he would show the officers where the body was. He then directed the police to the body of Pamela Powers.

* * *

[This evidence was introduced and used to convict Williams of murder. The Iowa courts ruled that Williams waived his right to counsel, but the lower federal courts, on a writ of habeas corpus, ruled the evidence inadmissible on the alternative grounds of denial of assistance of counsel, a *Miranda* violation, and that his statements were involuntary.]

II

B

[d] As noted in Chapter 6, the right to counsel attaches pretrial at critical stages. *Hamilton v. Alabama* (1961) required counsel at arraignment.

* * * [*Miranda v. Arizona* does not apply to this case.] For it is clear that the judgment before us must in any event be affirmed upon the ground that Williams was deprived of a different constitutional right—the right to the assistance of counsel. [d]

This right, guaranteed by the Sixth and Fourteenth Amendments, is indispensable to the fair administration of our adversary system of criminal justice. [It is a] vital need at the pretrial stage. * * *

* * * Whatever else it may mean, the right to counsel granted by the Sixth and Fourteenth Amendments means at least that a person is entitled to the help of a lawyer at or after the time that judicial proceedings have been initiated against him—"whether by way of formal charge, preliminary hearing, indictment, information, or arraignment." * * *

There can be no doubt in the present case that judicial proceedings [by arraignment] had been initiated against Williams before the start of the automobile ride from Davenport to Des Moines. * * * **[e]**

There can be no serious doubt, either, that Detective Leaming deliberately and designedly set out to elicit information from Williams just as surely as—and perhaps more effectively than—if he had formally interrogated him. Detective Leaming was fully aware before departing for Des Moines that Williams was being represented in Davenport by Kelly and in Des Moines by McKnight. Yet he purposely sought during Williams' isolation from his lawyers to obtain as much incriminating information as possible. Indeed, Detective Leaming conceded as much when he testified at Williams' trial. * * *

The circumstances of this case are thus constitutionally indistinguishable from those presented in *Massiah v. United States. * * * **[f]**

That the incriminating statements were elicited surreptitiously in the *Massiah* case, and otherwise here, is constitutionally irrelevant. * * * Rather, the clear rule of *Massiah* is that once adversary proceedings have commenced against an individual, he has a right to legal representation when the government interrogates him. * * *

III

The Iowa courts recognized that Williams had been denied the constitutional right to the assistance of counsel. **[g]** They held, however, that he had waived that right during the course of the automobile trip from Davenport to Des Moines. * * *

[The Iowa courts applied a totality of circumstances test to ascertain whether Williams waived his right to counsel. The federal courts held that this was the wrong standard under the constitutional guarantee to counsel: There must be an affirmative waiver.]

* * *

The [lower federal courts] were also correct in their understanding of the proper standard to be applied in determining the question of waiver as a matter of federal constitutional law—that it was incumbent upon the State to prove "an intentional relinquishment or abandonment of a known right or privilege." * * * **[h]** We have said that the right to counsel does not depend upon a request by the defendant, * * * and that courts indulge in every reasonable presumption against waiver. * * * This strict standard applies equally to an alleged waiver of the right to counsel whether at trial or at a critical stage of pretrial proceedings. * * *

We conclude, finally, that the Court of Appeals was correct in holding that, judged by these standards, the record in this case falls far short of sustaining petitioner's burden. It is true that Williams had been informed of and appeared to understand his right to counsel. **[i]** But waiver requires not merely comprehension but relinquishment, and Williams' consistent reliance upon the advice of counsel in dealing with the authorities refutes any suggestion that he waived that right. [He spoke to both the Des Moines and Davenport attorneys numerous times before the trip.] Throughout, Williams was advised not to make any statements before seeing McKnight in Des Moines, and was assured that the police had agreed not to question him. His statements while in the car that he would tell the whole story *after* seeing McKnight in Des Moines were the clearest expressions by Williams himself that he desired the presence of an attorney before any interrogation took place. But even before making these statements, Williams had effectively asserted his right to counsel by having secured attorneys at both ends of the automobile trip, both of whom, acting as his agents, had made clear to the police that no interrogation was to occur during the journey. Williams knew of that agreement and, particularly in view of his consistent reliance on counsel, there is no basis for concluding that he disavowed it.

Detective Leaming proceeded to elicit incriminating statements from Williams. Leaming did not preface this effort by telling Williams that he had a right to the presence of a lawyer, and made no effort at all to ascertain whether Williams wished to relinquish that right. The circumstances of record in this case thus provide no reasonable basis for finding that Williams waived his right to the assistance of counsel.

The Court of Appeals did not hold, nor do we, that under the circumstances of this case Williams *could not,* without notice to counsel, have waived his rights under the Sixth and Fourteenth Amendments. It only held, as do we, that he did not.

IV

The crime of which Williams was convicted was senseless and brutal, calling for swift and energetic action by the police to apprehend the perpetrator and gather evidence with which he could be convicted.

[e] Is this obvious? If so, is there any logic in Justice Blackmun's dissent? Should the Supreme Court allow blatant violations of rights if the crime is horrible?

[f] This clarifies the *Massiah* ruling. It is, essentially, a right-to-counsel case and is not limited to cases where government agents eavesdrop.

[g] Part III deals with whether Williams properly waived his right to counsel.

[h] This is the test of *Johnson v. Zerbst* (1938), which is the test for waiver of counsel at trial.

[i] The state had the burden of proof that Williams voluntarily waived his right to counsel. The majority thinks the burden was not met. Compare this to Justice White's dissent. Should Detective Leaming have informed Williams of his right to counsel and given him the chance to waive that right?

[j] The majority refuses to "bend the rules" of constitutional rights to gain a conviction in a terrible crime. Compare the remarks of Chief Justice Burger.

[k] This is political "tough on crime" rhetoric. Does it belong in a Supreme Court opinion? Do suspects have too many rights? Can this rhetoric lead to the permanent loss of rights?

[l] What is Justice White's logic? Can this logic make legal any incriminating statement except those obtained by torture? Was Williams's admission spontaneous?

[m] A question not settled by this case is whether it is ever possible for police to interview a suspect without his or her lawyer present after formal charges.

[n] Do the first two points made by Justice Blackmun pass the "giggle test"?

[o] Like *Rhode Island v. Innis* and *Arizona v. Mauro*, the case is also about the functional equivalent of interrogation. If Detective Leaming's speech is not the functional equivalent, what is?

[j] No mission of law enforcement officials is more important. Yet, "[d]isinterested zeal for the public good does not assure either wisdom or right in the methods it pursues." * * * Although we do not lightly affirm the issuance of a writ of habeas corpus in this case, so clear a violation of the Sixth and Fourteenth Amendments as here occurred cannot be condoned. The pressures on state executive and judicial officers charged with the administration of the criminal law are great, especially when the crime is murder and the victim a small child. But it is precisely the predictability of those pressures that makes imperative a resolute loyalty to the guarantees that the Constitution extends to us all.

The judgment of the Court of Appeals is affirmed.

It is so ordered.

[Justices Marshall, Powell, and Stevens concurred in separate opinions.]

MR. CHIEF JUSTICE BURGER, dissenting. **[k]**

The result in this case ought to be intolerable in any society which purports to call itself an organized society. It continues the Court—by the narrowest margin—on the much-criticized course of punishing the public for the mistakes and misdeeds of law enforcement officers, instead of punishing the officer directly, if in fact he is guilty of wrongdoing. It mechanically and blindly keeps reliable evidence from juries whether the claimed constitutional violation involves gross police misconduct or honest human error.

* * *

[Further in his opinion, the CHIEF JUSTICE argued that the exclusionary rule should not apply to nonegregious police conduct.]

MR. JUSTICE WHITE, with whom MR. JUSTICE BLACKMUN and MR. JUSTICE REHNQUIST join, dissenting.

* * *

Respondent relinquished his right not to talk to the police about his crime when the car approached the place where he had hidden the victim's clothes. **[l]** Men usually intend to do what they do, and there is nothing in the record to support the proposition that respondent's decision to talk was anything but an exercise of his own free will. Apparently, without any prodding from the officers, respondent—who had earlier said that he would tell the whole story when he arrived in Des Moines—spontaneously changed his mind about the timing of his disclosures when the car approached the places where he had hidden the evidence. However, even if his statements were influenced by Detective Leaming's above-quoted statement, respondent's decision to talk in the absence of counsel can hardly be viewed as the product of an overborne will. The statement by Leaming was not coercive; it was accompanied by a request that respondent not respond to it; and it was delivered hours before respondent decided to make any statement.

Respondent's waiver was thus knowing and intentional.

* * *

MR. JUSTICE BLACKMUN, with whom MR. JUSTICE WHITE and MR. JUSTICE REHNQUIST join, dissenting.

* * *

What the Court chooses to do here, and with which I disagree, is to hold that respondent Williams' situation was in the mold of *Massiah v. United States,* **[m]** that is, that it was dominated by a denial to Williams of his Sixth Amendment right to counsel after criminal proceedings had been instituted against him. The Court rules that the Sixth Amendment was violated because Detective Leaming "purposely sought during Williams' isolation from his lawyers to obtain as much incriminating information as possible." I cannot regard that as unconstitutional *per se.*

First, the police did not deliberately seek to isolate **[n]** Williams from his lawyers so as to deprive him of the assistance of counsel. * * * The isolation in this case was a necessary incident of transporting Williams to the county where the crime was committed.

Second, Leaming's purpose was not solely to obtain incriminating evidence. The victim had been missing for only two days, and the police could not be certain that she was dead. Leaming, of course, and in accord with his duty, was "hoping to find out where that little girl was," * * * but such motivation does not equate with an intention to evade the Sixth Amendment. * * *

Third, not every attempt to elicit information should be regarded as "tantamount to interrogation." * * * **[o]** I am not persuaded that Leaming's observations and comments, made as the police car traversed the snowy and slippery miles between Davenport and Des Moines that winter afternoon, were an interrogation, direct or subtle, of Williams. * * * In summary, it seems to me that the Court is holding that *Massiah* is violated whenever police engage in any conduct, in the absence of counsel, with the subjective desire to obtain information from a suspect after arraignment. Such a rule is far too broad. Persons in custody frequently volunteer statements in response to stimuli other than interrogation. * * * When there is no interrogation, such statements should be admissible as long as they are truly voluntary. * * *

* * *

gatehouses" of American criminal procedure.[44] The "mansion" of the criminal trial is replete with formal rights and the proper treatment of defendants who, cloaked with the presumption of innocence, may sit silent while the state's prosecutor labors to prove to a disinterested jury of peers that the defendant is guilty beyond a reasonable doubt. This is of little concern to the state if in the "gatehouse" of the police system the defendant is badgered and manipulated into becoming "the deluded instrument of his own conviction" (*Culombe v. Connecticut*, 1961). The justices who wrote and voted for the majority opinion in *Miranda v. Arizona* (1966) clearly intended to temper police interrogation to accord with the ideals of adversary treatment. This effort has had limited success. Under *Miranda* torture and physical beatings by police are rare, but psychological interrogation techniques continue to make suspects objects to be used by police to get preordained results in cases that stand in sharp contrast to the way in which defendants have to be treated in courts.[45]

The limited success of *Miranda* raises the question of whether a defendant who has been *formally charged*, and is no longer a suspect but is now a defendant, will be treated more like a *suspect* in the police "gatehouse" or more like a *defendant* in the courthouse "mansion" before trial. The pretrial defendant has paid for or has been assigned a criminal defense lawyer working to protect the client's interests and to ensure that the state meets its legal and constitutional obligations to gain a conviction only by legal means. The ruling in *Massiah v. United States* (1964) seems to suggest "mansion" treatment, as a nearly apoplectic Chief Justice Burger realized in his dissent in *Brewer v. Williams* (1977). The idea that a defendant can be cordoned off from the police by his defense lawyer derives in part from the norms of civil law, where the parties are genuinely equal adversaries in law and a party to a lawsuit cannot be approached by opposing counsel without the knowledge of that party's lawyer. Indeed, *Massiah* and *Brewer* seemed almost to put a defendant on the same basis as a civil lawsuit party. The Supreme Court, however, in a series of cases, largely annulled the wall of protection created by the right to counsel afforded to a defendant charged with a crime.

There have been twelve Supreme Court decisions interpreting *Massiah* between 1977 and 2009. Every one of four early decisions (three between 1977 and 1985 and one in 1986) favored the defendant's claim. In 1986 and 1988 Justices Scalia and Kennedy were seated as associate justices. They swung the balance to the government side in every subsequent case. One decision in 1986 and six decisions in the years following resolved *Massiah* cases in favor of the prosecution. The only case decided by a unanimous vote, *Fellers v. United States* (2005), was neutral in its impact. *Fellers* upheld the basic rule of *Massiah* and agreed with the lower courts in excluding a deliberately elicited statement. The Court made it clear that the issue was *not* whether there was *interrogation* of an indicted person who was not read *Miranda* warnings, but whether his incriminating statement was deliberately elicited. Because of the erroneous basis of the lower court decision, the Supreme Court reserved for future decision whether a later statement by Fellers, taken after *Miranda* warnings were issued, are excludable as "fruits" of the deliberately elicited statement.

Massiah (1964) and *Brewer v. Williams* (1977) firmly established the rule that in pretrial proceedings, after the formal initiation of charges and the attachment of the right to counsel under the Sixth Amendment, the state may not *deliberately elicit* an incriminating statement from a defendant. The *Massiah* rule is not connected to the *Miranda* Fifth Amendment predicate of the custodial interrogation of suspects. Incriminating statements obtained from defendants are inadmissible whether or not there was interrogation. Although the rule continues to exist, it was significantly narrowed after 1986.

The most significant practical way in which *Massiah* was diminished, and which tends mostly to reduce the status of a defendant (in the "mansion") to that of a suspect (in the "gatehouse"), was the ruling that a defendant can be approached by police, and by waiving the right to counsel after receiving *Miranda* warnings, waive counsel both under the Fifth and the Sixth Amendments (*Patterson v. Illinois*, 1988). While *Patterson* viewed the Fifth and Sixth Amendments as similar (for purposes of expanding the government's power), they were viewed as different when that interpretation was necessary to diminish the defendant's rights. Therefore, when a *defendant* invokes *Massiah*, the Court held that the invocation is *crime specific*, allowing police the question a *Mirandized* defendant for a different crime, even one arising out of a factually related crime that occurred in the same criminal transaction as the crime that was protected from deliberate elicitation by *Massiah* (*McNeil v. Wisconsin*, 1991; *Texas v. Cobb*, 2001). Also, the Court has ruled that the *Massiah* rule is prophylactic and not itself a Sixth Amendment right.

As a result, statements taken in violation of *Massiah* can be used at trial to impeach the defendant (*Michigan v. Harvey*, 1990; *Kansas v. Ventris*, 2009).

One early case, *Maine v. Moulton* (1985) was factually the same as *Massiah*. A co-defendant, working for the prosecution for dropped charges, testified to incriminating statements made by Moulton while they planned trial strategy while free on bail. The Court held the statements inadmissible under *Massiah* and wrote in strong support of defendants' rights. A charged defendant has a "right to rely on counsel as a 'medium' between him and the State." The government has an "affirmative obligation not to act in a manner that circumvents the protections" of *Massiah*. The state cannot knowingly exploit "an opportunity to confront the accused without counsel being present." The majority in *Moulton* did note that *Massiah* does not prevent the police from continuing to investigate a case before trial or from investigating an indicted defendant for other, nonindicted crimes.

The "deliberate elicitation" rule played out in two early cases involving the use of jail inmates who became government informants for pay or other benefits. In *United States v. Henry* (1980), an incriminating statement made by Henry, indicted for a bank robbery, to a jail cellmate/informant was thrown out as a *Massiah* violation. The informant "deliberately elicited" the statement by engaging in conversations that produced it. On the other hand, *Kuhlman v. Wilson* (1986) distinguished *Henry* on the facts and allowed testimony regarding the incriminating statement. The informant did not initiate any conversations about the crime but "only listened" to Wilson and took notes later. The rule, then, is that the police can place a *passive listener* in a cell who acts like a *listening device*. A cellmate or snitch can report an incriminating statement as long as the agent does not start conversations that are likely to lead the suspect to incriminate himself. This ruling, favorable to the prosecution, does not take into account the human tendency of an inmate to talk to a cellmate, increasing the likelihood of making incriminating statements.

The high point of Supreme Court support for defendants' rights under *Massiah* was *Michigan v. Jackson* (1986) (later overruled), which extended the rule of *Edwards v. Arizona* (1981) to *Massiah* cases. *Edwards* held that when a suspect asks for a lawyer while being interrogated, and the interrogation properly ceases, police cannot approach the suspect to get him or her to talk about the crime that was the subject of the first interrogation or any other crime. Reinterrogation is allowed only if the desire to talk to police without counsel present is initiated by the suspect. Justice Stevens's majority opinion blurred the distinction between the Fifth and Sixth Amendment rights to counsel and stressed that "the reasons for prohibiting the interrogation of an uncounseled prisoner who has asked for the help of a lawyer are even stronger after he has been formally charged with an offense than before." The reason for this belief is that after a formal accusation the "person who had previously been just a 'suspect' has become an 'accused' within the meaning of the Sixth Amendment," and the "constitutional right to the assistance of counsel is of such importance" that the state can no longer deliberately elicit incriminating statements without counsel under *Massiah* and *Brewer v. Williams*. Support was found in the stringent standard for waiving the Sixth Amendment right to counsel in *Johnson v. Zerbst* (1938), which stated that the Court should "indulge every reasonable presumption against waiver of fundamental constitutional rights." *Michigan v. Jackson* held that a defendant who is arraigned and who *requests* a lawyer may not thereafter be approached by police to get the suspect to talk.

Justice Rehnquist dissented. In his view *Edwards* was a prophylactic rule that applied *only* to prevent police from badgering suspects, who asserted their Fifth Amendment right to silence under *Miranda*, into talking. No such prophylactic rule is needed to support the right to counsel: "The Court does not even suggest that the police commonly deny defendants their Sixth Amendment right to counsel. Nor, I suspect, would such a claim likely be borne out by empirical evidence." *Jackson* was relied on in subsequent cases but was questioned as unsound by a number of justices, and overruled in *Montejo v. Louisiana* (2009).

After *Jackson*, the court whittled down the scope of *Massiah-Brewer* protection. As noted earlier, *Patterson v. Illinois* (1988) held (5–4) that an *indicted* defendant who was read *Miranda* warnings, waived his Sixth Amendment, *Massiah*, right to counsel as well as the Fifth Amendment right. As a result, his post-indictment confession to the police was admissible. Justice White's majority opinion emphasized that, as a pragmatic matter, *Miranda* warnings fully apprised the defendant of the *nature* and the *consequences* of a waiver of his rights—namely that a confession could be used to convict him. Justice White admitted that "a more searching or formal inquiry" than a simple warning is required before a defendant can waive the right to counsel for a trial. This is so because the "dangers and disadvantages during questioning are less substantial and more obvious to an accused than they are at trial" (*Patterson v. Illinois*, internal quotation omitted). Justice Stevens, dissenting, disagreed and noted that *Miranda* warnings do not begin to inform a defendant of the various functions that a lawyer can perform aside from advising at interrogation. A lawyer can detect legal flaws in charges against the defendant and "is likely to be considerably more skillful at negotiating a plea bargain." Justice White and the majority strongly resisted the idea of adding any additional warnings to the *Miranda* quartet. Justice Stevens also emphasized that it is *unethical* for investigators or prosecutors during trial preparation to go behind the backs of their adversaries and communicate with a defendant in order to get a confession.

The Court further limited *Massiah* rights in *McNeil v. Wisconsin* (1991). A defendant who invokes the right to counsel for one crime (and cannot be questioned about it) is not automatically protected against police questioning for *another crime*. The Court held that the Sixth Amendment right to counsel is *offense-specific*, unlike the right to counsel created by the Supreme Court in *Miranda* to protect Fifth Amendment rights. The reason for this distinction is that the purpose of the Sixth Amendment right to counsel is to protect the unaided layperson at a critical confrontation. The purpose of the *Miranda–Edwards* rule, however, is to protect a suspect's desire to deal with police only through counsel. The offense-specific concept was taken one step further in *Texas v. Cobb* (2001), where the Court held (5–4) that police could question an indicted defendant about a different legal charge (a murder) that was part of the same criminal transaction as the crime that Cobb had been indicted for (a burglary). The Court, per Chief Justice Rehnquist, held that the definition of an offense under the Double Jeopardy Clause of the Fifth Amendment applies to determining whether questioning a defendant for the same or a different crime. Under the double jeopardy test, violations of two distinct statutory crimes that arise out of the same criminal act or transaction are different crimes if "each provision requires proof of a fact which the other does not." Both the dissenters, having joined in Justice Breyer's dissenting opinion, and the respondent, felt that the majority ruling "threatens to diminish severely the additional protection that . . . the Sixth Amendment provides when it grants the right to counsel to defendants who have been charged with a crime and insists that law enforcement officers thereafter communicate with them through that counsel" (*Texas v. Cobb*, Breyer, J., dissenting). The Court dismissed the respondent's stronger concern that "the offense-specific rule will prove 'disastrous' to suspects' constitutional rights and will 'permit law enforcement officers almost complete and total license to conduct unwanted and uncounseled interrogations," as a "parade of horribles" that has not occurred in jurisdictions that have applied the *McNeil* rule. As will be discussed regarding *Montejo*, later in this chapter, whether the results of these rules are viewed as negative or salutary depends in large measure on the criminal justice ideology of the beholder. A concurring opinion in *Cobb*, written by Justice Kennedy and joined by Justices Scalia and Thomas, took aim at the underlying theory of *Michigan v. Jackson* (1986).

Another example of conservative activism in *Massiah* cases is found in the reasoning that has allowed the use of statements taken in violation of *Massiah* to be used at a trial to *impeach* the defendant who chooses to testify. *Michigan v. Harvey* (1990) held that a statement taken in violation of one's *Massiah* rights under *Michigan v. Jackson* (1986) can be used at a trial to *impeach* the defendant who chooses to testify. The majority viewed *Jackson*, as an analogy of *Edwards v. Arizona* (1981) to be a prophylactic rule and thus, like *Miranda*, to allow collateral use of statements that violated the rule. Justice Stevens, dissenting (joined by Justices Brennan, Marshall, and Blackmun), argued that the true basis of a *Massiah* right is the Sixth Amendment right to counsel itself, and that neither *Massiah* nor *Jackson* is a prophylactic rule. In this case, according to the dissent, Harvey's right to see his lawyer was violated by a police officer who told a confused Harvey that he didn't have to see his lawyer.

Kansas v. Ventris (2005) (7–2) extended the impeachment use of deliberately elicited statements by a jailhouse informant taken in violation of *Massiah*. An issue in *Ventris* was whether the *Massiah* right to counsel is a trial right that comes into play when illegally seized evidence is introduced. Justice Scalia, writing for the majority, concluded "that the *Massiah* right is a right to be free of uncounseled interrogation, and is infringed at the time of the interrogation." That is the point at which counsel is denied and it "is *that* deprivation which demands a remedy" (*Kansas v. Ventris*, 2009, emphasis in original). Justice Stevens, joined by Justice Ginsburg, and viewing *Massiah* rights as complete constitutional rights and not as prophylactic protections, disagreed. "While the constitutional breach began at the time of interrogation, the State's use of that evidence at trial compounded the violation. The logic that compels the exclusion of the evidence during the State's case in chief extends to any attempt by the State to rely on the evidence, even for impeachment." In a footnote he alluded to an amicus curiae brief warning that the "likelihood that evidence gathered by self-interested jailhouse informants may be false cannot be ignored." Taking aim at the Crime Control Model empathy of the majority, Justice Stevens noted that the Court once again "has privileged the prosecution at the expense of the Constitution." He felt that instead of strengthening the trial, the *Ventris* rule weakens the adversary process by limiting the opportunity of defense counsel to block the use of dissembling jailhouse snitches.

Montejo v. Louisiana (2009), a major decision under *Massiah*, overruled *Michigan v. Jackson* (1986) and moved formally charged defendants firmly into the police gatehouse of the criminal justice system. Jesse Montejo was arrested on September 6 in connection with a robbery and murder.[46] He waived *Miranda* rights, and after a partially videotaped interrogation stretching from the late afternoon and evening of September 6 to the early morning of September 7, confessed to the crime. Montejo claims that the detectives repeatedly lied to him, that he was deprived of sleep, and that he clearly asked for a lawyer but revoked this request after being badgered. On the morning of September 10 he was brought before a judge for a preliminary hearing, called a "72-hour hearing" in Louisiana, was charged with first-degree murder, and was ordered held without bail. The judge assigned counsel by ordering the public defender's office to name an attorney to represent him. Under state procedures Montejo did not have to *request* the assigned counsel. Before the named attorney met with Montejo, two police detectives came to the prison and asked him to accompany them to a lake where he said he threw the gun. After hesitating, Montejo agreed to go. He claims that he told the detectives he was assigned an attorney but that one detective said he checked and erroneously said that no attorney was appointed. "[D]uring the excursion [to the lake], he wrote an inculpatory letter of apology to the victim's widow, using legal terms that were probably suggested by the detectives. Only upon their return did Montejo finally meet his court-appointed attorney, who was quite upset that the detectives had interrogated his client in his absence." According to Monetjo's appellate brief, this inculpatory letter of apology was critical to the prosecution's case because there was "relatively little physical evidence" that Montejo killed the robbery victim. (The murder weapon and money bag were never found; there was no blood spatter in Montejo's van or on any of this clothing; there were no eyewitnesses. Police did not follow up on exculpatory evidence claimed by Montejo. There *was* DNA evidence matching Montejo under the victim's fingernails, which Montejo explained as the result of "an altercation with the victim before the fatal shooting.")

Montejo moved to exclude the inculpatory letter on the grounds that counsel had been *assigned*, and that under *Michigan v. Jackson* (1986) police could not initiate a conversation to get Montejo to waive his rights and talk. The sticking point was that unlike the procedures in *Jackson*, where a defendant had to *request* counsel, Montejo did not have to request counsel under Louisiana procedures. Both the majority and dissenters agreed that a rule that depended on whether state procedures required a request before the right counsel attached is impractical and unsound. The way they would solve the dilemma, however, differed sharply. The four dissenters would apply *Jackson* across the board and not allow police to approach a defendant who was assigned counsel at a preliminary hearing, whether or not a request was made for questioning. The majority solved the problem by overruling *Jackson*. The views expressed by Justice Scalia in support of overruling *Jackson* and those of Justice Stevens, opposing this decision, display the deeper values that animate each of the models of criminal justice.

The majority opinion noted that if *Jackson*'s rule (that police cannot initiate interrogation after counsel is assigned) were made uniform by eliminating the need for a defendant to *request* counsel (as was the case in *Jackson*), a likely result would be that police could *never* interrogate defendants who are formally charged. As for Montejo's case, the majority saw his voluntary waiver being negated by the presumption of *Jackson* that the waiver was invalid. The majority, viewing *Edwards* and *Jackson* as prophylactic rules, viewed the benefits too few and the costs too high.

> Which brings us to the strength of *Jackson*'s reasoning. When this Court creates a prophylactic rule in order to protect a constitutional right, the relevant "reasoning" is the weighing of the rule's benefits against its costs. The value of any prophylactic rule . . . must be assessed not only on the basis of what is gained, but also on the basis of what is lost. We think that the marginal benefits of *Jackson* (viz., the number of

confessions obtained coercively that are suppressed by its bright-line rule and would otherwise have been admitted) are dwarfed by its substantial costs (viz., hindering society's compelling interest in finding, convicting, and punishing those who violate the law. (*Montejo v. Louisiana*, internal citations and quotations omitted)

This is a straightforward expression of the basic value position of the Crime Control Model, which holds that because crime suppression advances social order and the enjoyment of liberties more than extending civil rights to suspects and defendants, crime suppression is a preferred outcome where the two are in conflict. Another attribute of that model is to view the operations of the criminal justice process as largely competent and error free.

A bright-line rule like that adopted in *Jackson* ensures that no fruits of interrogations made possible by badgering-induced involuntary waivers are ever erroneously admitted at trial. But without *Jackson*, how many would be? The answer is few if any. (*Montejo v. Louisiana*)

A reason for this conclusion is that compelled self-incrimination is blocked by the effects of the prophylactic rules of *Miranda*, *Edwards*, and *Minnick*. "These three layers of prophylaxis are sufficient. . . . *Jackson* was policy driven, and if that policy is being adequately served through other means, there is no reason to retain its rule. *Miranda* and the cases that elaborate upon it already guarantee not simply noncoercion in the traditional sense, but what Justice Harlan [in *Miranda*] referred to as 'voluntariness with a vengeance'" (*Montejo v. Louisiana*). Having revealed his distaste for even the *Miranda* regime, Justice Scalia presses on, drawing on cases that give full-throated support to full-court-press police interrogation tactics:

On the other side of the equation are the costs of adding the bright-line *Jackson* rule on top of *Edwards* and other extant protections. The principal cost of applying any exclusionary rule is, of course, letting guilty and possibly dangerous criminals go free. *Jackson* not only operates to invalidate a confession given by the free choice of suspects who have received proper advice of their *Miranda* rights but waived them nonetheless, but also deters law enforcement officers from even trying to obtain voluntary confessions. The ready ability to obtain uncoerced confessions is not an evil but an unmitigated good. Without these confessions, crimes go unsolved and criminals unpunished. These are not negligible costs, and in our view the *Jackson* Court gave them too short shrift. (*Montejo v. Louisiana*, internal citations and quotations omitted)

Whether Justice Scalia's assertions are empirically verifiable is a matter of debate, but their forceful assertion completes the analysis and undergirds the decision: "In sum, when the marginal benefits of the *Jackson* rule are weighed against its substantial costs to the truth-seeking process and the criminal justice system, we readily conclude that the rule does not pay its way. *Michigan v. Jackson* should be and now is overruled" (*Montejo v. Louisiana*, internal citations and quotations omitted).

The dissent was just as powerfully motivated by views reflective of the Due Process Model. Justice Stevens denied that *Massiah* and *Jackson* are prophylactic rules and accused Justice Scalia of "flagrantly misrepresent[ing] *Jackson*'s underlying rationale and the constitutional interests the decision sought to protect." Their ratioanle is not simply the protective one of preventing police from badgering a defendant from asserting or maintaining his or her right to counsel (as apparently happened in Montejo's case), in part because *Jackson* did not even mention that reason. Rather

Jackson emphasized that the purpose of the Sixth Amendment is to protect the unaided layman at critical confrontations with his adversary, by giving him the right to rely on counsel as a 'medium' between himself and the State. Underscoring that the commencement of criminal proceedings is a decisive event that transforms a suspect into an accused within the meaning of the Sixth Amendment, we concluded that arraigned defendants are entitled to "at least as much protection" during interrogation as the Fifth Amendment affords unindicted suspects. . . . Thus, . . . the rules adopted in . . . *Jackson* did not rely on the reasoning of *Edwards* but remained firmly rooted in the unique protections afforded to the attorney-client relationship by the Sixth Amendment. (*Montejo v. Louisiana*, Stevens, J. dissenting; internal citations, quotations, and modifications omitted)

Jackson aside, the dissent also saw the police action in this case as having deliberately elicited Montejo's letter under pre-*Jackson Massiah* cases. Additionally, the dissent was critical of "the dubious decision in *Patterson,*" which held that a *Miranda* warning provides sufficient information to allow a defendant to waive his or her Sixth Amendment right to counsel.

Because *Miranda* warnings do not hint at the ways in which a lawyer might assist her client during conversations with the police, I remain convinced that the warnings prescribed in *Miranda*, while sufficient to apprise a defendant of his Fifth Amendment right to remain silent, are inadequate to inform an unrepresented, indicted defendant of his Sixth Amendment right to have a lawyer present at all critical stages of a criminal prosecution. The inadequacy of those warnings is even more obvious in the case of a *represented* defendant. While it can be argued that informing an indicted but unrepresented defendant of his right to counsel at least alerts him to the fact that he is entitled to obtain something he does not already possess, providing that same warning to a defendant who has *already* secured counsel is more likely to confound than enlighten. By glibly assuming that that the *Miranda* warnings given in this case were sufficient to ensure Montejo's waiver was both knowing and voluntary, the Court conveniently avoids any comment on the actual advice Montejo received, which did not adequately inform him of his relevant Sixth Amendment rights or alert him to the possible consequences of waiving those rights. (*Montejo v. Louisiana*, Stevens, J. dissenting, footnotes omitted)

Viewing the majority's opinion in the light of these considerations, the dissent saw the Court's decision to scrap *Jackson* as "acting on its own" rather than under the law (and "[p]aying lip service to the rule of *stare decisis*"), as condoning a "police interrogation [that] clearly violated petitioner's Sixth Amendment right to counsel," and as undermining the public's interest in knowing that defendants can rely on lawyers to represent them when dealing with the police. Expressing the Due Process Model that valorizing crime suppression above civil rights endangers both in the long run, Justice Stevens concluded by warning that "The Court's decision to overrule *Jackson* is unwarranted [and] the dubious benefits it hopes to achieve are far outweighed by the damage it does to the rule of law and the integrity of the Sixth Amendment right to counsel."

LAW IN SOCIETY

The Social Reality of Confessions

The Acceptance of *Miranda*

Despite its bitter reception by police and others in 1966, the *Miranda* ruling has since been accepted by the legal and law enforcement communities. Chief Justice Warren Burger stated in 1980, "The meaning of *Miranda* has become reasonably clear and law enforcement practices have adjusted to its strictures; I would neither overrule *Miranda,* disparage it, nor extend it at this late date" (*Rhode Island v. Innis*). This signaled that *Miranda*'s opponents could now live with it, in part because the case did not undermine effective policing. Chief Justice Burger also wanted to avoid another round of appeals designed to clarify a major legal revolution in established and well-known confessions rules.

Many police see *Miranda,* and the study of constitutional law in general, as enhancing the professional status of policing. Some officers accept that without legal strictures, their crime-fighting behavior could turn to lawlessness. Others have internalized the *Miranda* rules and are happy to apply them to the extent that they accord with what they believe is "fair and decent" behavior.[47] In this light, it is important to be clear that "*Miranda* has not failed to achieve its limited goals"[48]—which were *not* to eliminate interrogation and confessions or to completely equalize the power relationship between a suspect and the police or to lower confession rates.

Miranda was designed to reduce the compulsion of the interrogation process. Understanding this, police officers are happy to follow the letter of the *Miranda* decision if the goals of law enforcement can be generally realized.[49] This has resulted in police adaptation to the *Miranda* requirements.

Police Interrogation Today: Adapting to *Miranda*

What do we know about how custodial interrogation is conducted? "During the first few years after *Miranda,* empirical studies suggested that *Miranda*'s impact was minimal."[50] Few studies of *Miranda*'s effect appeared for some time, but since 1996 several have enlarged our understanding of *Miranda,* and some have generated a lively debate over the "costs" to law enforcement of the need to warn interrogated suspects of their rights.

How Are Interrogations Conducted?

As a routine practice, third-degree tactics—the use and threats of beatings—have disappeared as police interrogation techniques. Police today use sophisticated psychological techniques to "persuade" recalcitrant defendants to admit their guilt. A study by Professor Richard Leo of 182 interrogations observed in three California police departments in 1992 and 1993 provided a picture of contemporary interrogation. Most of the suspects were young working-class African-American males. Seventy percent of the primary detectives conducting the questioning were white, and 90 percent were males. In 69 percent of the cases, interrogation was conducted by one officer, and in 31 percent, two officers interrogated. Forty-three percent of the cases were for robberies, 24 percent were for assault, 12 percent were for homicide, and the other 21 percent were for burglaries, thefts, and other crimes.

Only 22 percent of the suspects invoked their *Miranda* rights after they were read. Suspects with prior felony records invoked their rights more often (30 percent) than those with no record (8 percent) or with prior misdemeanor involvement (11 percent) in the criminal justice system. Thirty-six percent of the suspects made no incriminating statement, 22 percent made an incriminating statement, 18 percent made a partial admission, and 24 percent made a full confession. Thirty-five percent of the interrogations lasted less than thirty minutes, 36 percent lasted thirty to sixty minutes, 21 percent lasted for one to two hours, and 8 percent lasted more than two hours.[51] Leo concluded that under legal criteria, only four out of 182 cases, or 2 percent, "rose to the level of 'coercion.'"[52]

Leo provides six in-depth vignettes from the cases he observed. In each, the officers used a variety of psychological ploys to get confessions. A suspect accused of smashing in a car's window and stealing its contents was told that several witnesses saw him do this. "The detective was, of course, fabricating evidence against the suspect, but the suspect did not know this."[53] The interrogation lasted more than an hour; the suspect admitted breaking into the car and, on a plea bargain, received a one-year sentence. Another suspect, a twenty-one-year-old Hispanic male, was accused of kidnapping a fourteen-year-old girl from a party and brutally raping and anally and orally sodomizing her before returning the girl to the party with a warning that he would shoot her if she spoke. The victim immediately told a friend, who called the police. A swift medical examination confirmed severe physical injury. During the interrogation, the detective, a Hispanic female, "went from somewhat formal language (which it appeared he didn't understand) to slang, crude, and even profane language to ask him questions about the sexual acts." He appeared nervous, but "she quickly put her hand on his in a friendly gesture, smiled, and told him to trust her, that she wouldn't be embarrassed by anything he told her." The suspect invoked counsel, ending the interrogation after thirty-four minutes. He pleaded guilty to statutory rape and received a one-month sentence plus four years of "formal probation."[54] This indicates that failure to obtain confessions in some cases may allow guilty parties to go free or receive less than adequate punishment.

Why Do Suspects Waive Their Miranda Rights?

Observations of police interrogation practices show that a variety of psychological methods are used to get suspects to talk. If the police follow the spirit of *Miranda,* they at least deliver the warnings in a neutral way at the beginning of an interrogation session. Some do. But many others de-emphasize the importance of *Miranda* waivers in several ways. They may indicate that the waiver is an unimportant bureaucratic detail (a mere formality) or may build rapport and engage in small talk before mentioning *Miranda*. Another "selling" technique is to stress the importance of the suspect's "telling his side of the story."[55] A more insidious technique is to weave the warnings into questions and answers over a long period of time so that the suspect waives rights and after this is read the warnings in a block—a method dubbed "participating *Miranda*" by Professors Peter Lewis and Harry Allen.[56]

Leo describes the process by characterizing police interrogation as a "confidence game." Like a "con man," or perhaps any good salesperson, the police interrogator must psychologically "size up" and figure out how to manipulate the suspect. This requires knowledge of the crime, the victim, and the suspect. Unlike a true confidence man, a police interrogator cannot select or "qualify" the "mark." The officer "cultivates" the suspect by projecting a friendly and sincere image, offering coffee, and engaging in light banter. Simultaneously, the barren interrogation room, the thick case folder with the suspect's name prominently attached, and various interrogation techniques, such as pitting the suspect against a shadowy but fearsome prosecutor or judge and jury, are designed to raise the suspect's anxiety. The police frame their questions with admonitions about telling the truth; telling the truth will "make it go better" for the suspect and make him or her feel better. To elicit a confession, the police draw on various techniques of persuasion, deception, and neutralization: contradicting false statements, minimizing the immoral nature of what was done, posing false statements, and many more. Finally, the officers, knowing that the confessions will be attacked once defense lawyers come into the case, "cool the mark" by complimenting the suspect for his or her honesty and cooperation and maintaining a neutral tone and a positive reaction to the defendant to the end.[57]

Interrogation "Outside" Miranda.

As noted in the body of this chapter, a troubling interrogation practice known as "interrogation outside *Miranda*" has become prevalent in some places. In this practice, police deliberately violate a suspect's *Miranda* rights in order to gain the collateral use of evidence. The Supreme Court is examining the practice, the existence of which reveals the need for vigilance in protecting individual rights.[58]

The Benefits of Miranda.

Leo asserts that *Miranda* has had four positive long-range social effects. In his view, conservative critics of the 1980s were wrong to contend that *Miranda* has undermined effective law enforcement, and liberals have been shortsighted in saying that *Miranda*'s effects have been more symbolic than real.[59] First, Leo says, "*Miranda* has exercised a civilizing influence on police behavior inside the interrogation room" by accelerating a process that was in place in 1966. This has helped to make the police more professional by establishing objective and written standards of police behavior. As a result, "American police in the last thirty years have, by necessity, become more solicitous of suspects' rights, more respectful of their dignity, and more concerned with their welfare inside the interrogation room."[60] Second, *Miranda* "has transformed the culture—the shared norms, values and attitudes—of police . . . by fundamentally re-framing how police talk and think about the process of custodial interrogation."[61] Third, *Miranda* has increased public awareness of constitutional rights. Finally, "*Miranda* has inspired police to develop more specialized, more sophisticated and seemingly more effective interrogation techniques with which to elicit inculpatory statements from custodial suspects."[62] Thus *Miranda* is part of a larger and longer-term trend in Western society in which government power is "more controlling of its subjects" but at the same time "more subject to control itself [in the areas of] legal institutions, professional standards, and social norms."[63]

Improving Miranda: Videotaping.

This does not mean that police interrogation is without its problems. As will be explored later, numerous false confessions raise concerns about how interrogation is conducted. To ensure that interrogation becomes more professional and effective, Leo, borrowing from a 1993 Department of Justice study, has urged that courts mandate the videotaping of interrogations as a matter of due process.[64] There are many good reasons for videotaping interrogations: (1) It creates an "objective, reviewable record of custodial questioning that protects [police] against false accusations—accusations such as 'softening up' a suspect prior to *Miranda*, failing to correctly read the *Miranda* warnings, or eliciting a confession through improper inducements." (2) It is "likely to improve the quality of police work and thus contribute to more professional and more effective interrogation practices. Officers and detectives who know they will be videotaped are more likely to prepare their strategies beforehand and to be more self-conscious about their conduct during questioning." (3) Tapes can be used for training. (4) Videotaping can increase law enforcement effectiveness because it "facilitates the identification, prosecution, and conviction of guilty offenders." For example, it "preserves the details of a suspect's statement that may not have been initially recorded in a detective's notes but may subsequently become important." (5) Videotapes are believed to have helped prosecutors negotiate a higher percentage of guilty pleas and obtain longer sentences because they provide "a more complete record with which to better assess the state's case against the accused," including "the demeanor and sophistication of the suspect." As a result, some defense attorneys oppose videotaping confessions because it makes it more difficult to challenge the stories of detectives, although public defenders with high caseloads appreciate videotapes because it helps them to more quickly cut through clients' lies and produce accurate guilty pleas.

Why Do Innocent People Confess?

The English common law harbors a traditional distrust of confessions (found in the rule that uncorroborated confessions are inadmissible in court) out of fear that psychological manipulation would induce innocent people to confess. This problem still exists, despite *Miranda*, and requires precautions in how interrogation is conducted. As improbable as it may seem, when police use modern "psychological interrogation" rather than torture (e.g., *Brown v. Mississippi,* 1936), they still get innocent people to confess.

How Innocent People Confess.

Professors Richard Leo and Richard Ofshe, drawing on prior scholarship regarding false confessions and on their own inquiry, have explored many cases of false confessions. They review sixty cases of allegedly false confessions and, after examining available court and news media records, classify them into three groups: thirty-four confessions that were proven false, eighteen highly probable false confessions, and eight probable false confessions.[65] In other writings, Ofshe and Leo acknowledge that the actual number of false confessions cannot be known because (1) police do not keep complete records of interrogations, making it difficult to evaluate the reliability of the interrogation or whether there was any undue pressure; (2) no criminal justice agency keeps records or collects statistics on the number or frequency of interrogations; and (3) many cases of false confession are not reported.[66] Nevertheless, there are so many documented cases just in the past decade that false confessions must be seen as an important policy area to be addressed.[67]

Leo and Ofshe have intensively explored false confessions in a lengthy article that relies heavily on field data—transcripts of both true and false confessions—to display how certain processes lead to false confessions by the innocent.[68] They identify four types of false confessions: [69]

- *Stress-compliant false confessions.* The modern psychological interrogation is stressful by design, and for some individuals—especially those with an abnormal reactivity to stress, those who may be phobic, or those with intellectual limitations who cope by becoming submissive—the pressure requires alleviation by saying, "I did it."
- *Coerced-compliant false confessions.* These false confessions often result from the familiar "accident scenario technique" or "maximization/minimization." This is a subtle promise and threat (traditionally outlawed in England) by which the police convince the suspect that what he or she did was not all that serious because there is a legal excuse or mitigation and that by confessing, he or she will receive lenient treatment.
- *Voluntary and involuntary persuaded false confessions.* These are instances where, after a good deal of interviewing and subtle or not-so-subtle badgering, the innocent person becomes so confused that confidence in his own memory is shattered. He reports that despite no overt memory of committing the crime, he agrees that the interrogators' recitation of events and (fabricated) "facts" must mean he is guilty.

Ofshe and Leo do not suggest that confessions be abolished. They recommend safeguards because the process by which the innocent confess is very close to the process by which investigators obtain confessions from the guilty. The steps by which confessions are obtained in the era of psychological interrogation show why this is so. Detectives have two categories of suspects: "likely suspects, for whom there exists solid evidence suggesting their guilt; and possible suspects, which includes everyone whose name comes up during an investigation." Interrogation is superficially the same for both types. The detective may begin with an interview rather than interrogation format, especially for a possible suspect, to gain rapport and lull the interviewee into forgetting the adversarial nature of the encounter. Once *Miranda* warnings are read, neither "an innocent nor a guilty party is likely to appreciate the full significance of the . . . warnings." The innocent person thinks that he or she has nothing to hide. At that point, the tone and content of the interaction become confrontational and demanding. To get the suspect to say, "I did it," an investigator must strongly reject denials and insist that objective evidence points to guilt. At this point, a truly innocent person "is likely to experience considerable shock and disorientation . . . because he is wholly unprepared for the confrontation and accusations that are the core of the process, and will not understand how an investigator could possibly suspect him." The tragedy of wrongful confessions occurs because the responses to questioning by the guilty and the innocent "are often indistinguishable to an investigator." The investigator must now convince the suspect that arrest is imminent and get the suspect to make an admission. Once this watershed is crossed, the investigator then moves the process toward obtaining a full confession.[70]

An Example of a False Confession.

In 1986, Thomas F. Sawyer, a thirty-six-year-old groundskeeper, was charged with the murder of his next-door neighbor, a single twenty-five-year-old woman, in Clearwater, Florida, on the basis of a confession. Janet Staschak was found strangled, nude, face down on her bed with wire and tape marks on her ankles. Sawyer, a recovering alcoholic, was extremely shy, suffered from bouts of anxiety, and often turned red and sweated profusely in ordinary social situations. When Sawyer was initially questioned by police officers, they noted his odd mannerisms and targeted him as a suspect. However, hair and blood samples obtained from Sawyer before his interrogation did not match samples found on the dead woman.

Although there was no corroborating evidence, two Clearwater detectives, John Dean and Peter Fire, obtained a confession from Sawyer. Before, during, and after the interrogation, Sawyer maintained his innocence. Then how or why would an innocent person confess?[71]

Understanding Sawyer's confession in this case is aided by the transcript of what occurred during the entire taped sixteen-hour interrogation session, which stretched from 4:00 p.m. to 8:00 a.m., with time out for a ninety-minute nap. After several hours of questioning, the detectives asked Sawyer to pretend he was a police officer and to suggest methods and motives for the crime. Later during the questioning, they would take his statements and say that he knew too much about the crime to have guessed about the state of the room and the way in which the crime was carried out. Yet police officers had for some time before the questioning been back and forth between Sawyer's and Staschak's apartment, and he may have heard a good deal about the crime; furthermore, the transcript, at this point, included a good deal of prompting by the detectives.

At about 8:00 p.m., four hours after the questioning began in a small room at the police station, the officers warned Sawyer of his rights, an example of "participating *Miranda*":

DEAN: All right. We got this squared away. Now Tom, because this is a criminal investigation, obviously, what we've been doing—There's a new phase we have to enter into now. And before I do that, I have to read you your rights. You watch television. You know. So just let me read you these. You have the right to remain silent. Do you understand that?

SAWYER: Uh-huh.

DEAN: Anything you say can and will be used against you in a court of law. Do you understand that? *[Sawyer nods.]*

FIRE: You got to go "yes."

SAWYER: Yes.

FIRE: Okay.

DEAN: You have the right to talk to a lawyer—

FIRE: No, wait a minute. You don't *have* to say yes. You answer the way you want to answer, but we have to hear you. I know you're saying yes with your nod, okay? You nodded yes, but—Okay?

SAWYER: Yeah. Okay.

DEAN:	You have the right to talk to a lawyer. Have him present with you while you are being questioned. Do you understand that?
SAWYER:	Yes.
DEAN:	If you can't afford to hire a lawyer, one will be appointed to represent you before any questioning if you wish. Do you understand that?
SAWYER:	Say it again. I wasn't—
DEAN:	Okay. If you cannot afford to hire a lawyer, one will be appointed to represent you before any questioning if you wish. Do you understand that?
SAWYER:	Yes.
DEAN:	Okay. You can decide at any time to exercise your rights and not answer any questions or make any statements. Do you understand that?
SAWYER:	Yes.
DEAN:	Okay.
FIRE:	Okay. So you understand everything. Okay. Listen, Tom. John and I— we've been talking to you all evening about this. Right? Okay? So why don't you tell us what happened. Tell us what happened.

This was followed by continuous denials by Sawyer and insistent statements by Dean and Fire that Sawyer was guilty.

SAWYER:	I didn't do it.
FIRE:	Tommy, it's not the truth.
SAWYER:	Yes, it is.
FIRE:	No it's not. Tom. Tell me the truth. Tell me what happened. It was an accident, Tom. I know it was. I know it was an accident. I need for you to tell me what happened.
SAWYER:	I was never there. I never did it.
FIRE:	Tom.
SAWYER:	I'll look you in the eye and say that all night.
FIRE:	I know, we got all night.

Throughout the session, Sawyer believed that his hair samples matched those found on Janet Staschak and that a polygraph test indicated he was lying.[72] Playing on this, the detectives suggested to Sawyer that he had "blacked out" during the crime and committed it, although he did not remember anything. Throughout the session, Dean and Fire told Sawyer that he was an intelligent and good person, that the crime was not premeditated, that he would feel a great sense of relief if he confessed. Worn down, Sawyer finally confessed not only to a murder, but also to having raped Janet Staschak when in fact there was no physical evidence of sexual penetration. Many of the facts he admitted to were stated only after several false starts with persistent prompting by Fire and Dean. He made his confession conditional on the physical evidence: "The only reason I believe I did it is if my hairs were in her car and on her body and in her apartment."

At the preliminary examination, the trial court, lacking corroborating physical evidence, threw out the confession in a detailed decision. By fastening onto the closest possible suspect, the police apparently did not diligently follow up possible leads. Staschak had taken in roommates to help pay her rent; at first a heterosexual couple who were dealing drugs and later a homosexual couple. She had evicted both couples, and both had left her in some fear. It seems likely that by fastening on Sawyer, the Clearwater officers let the real culprits escape. The trial judge described the interrogation session as an intellectual wrestling match. The Florida Court of Appeals agreed and upheld the suppression of the confession.

Preventing False Confessions.

As noted, Ofshe and Leo do not recommend abolishing police interrogation, but they do have recommendations to lessen the possibility of false confessions. One recommendation, discussed earlier, is that custodial interrogations be videotaped. A lengthy interrogation contains so many subtle, forward-moving points of persuasion-threat-coercion, such as maximization-minimization techniques, that "it is beyond human ability to remember just what happened." Since interrogators are zealous in achieving their goal of obtaining confession, they are naturally biased and simply will not see that they did anything that might induce a false confession.

Ofshe and Leo's central point is that false confessions come about when commonplace interrogation methods (including the verbal fabrication of "evidence") are used improperly, inappropriately, or ineptly.[73] Therefore, police training is critical to avoiding false confessions. Police need to be educated in the facts of false confessions and to understand that they do occur. Since there is a subtle difference between the proper and improper use of the psychological interrogation, the most important factor is for police to be aware that when they have a possible suspect, as opposed to a likely suspect, they should seek corroborating evidence. "If police and prosecutors recognized that the mere admission 'I did it' is not necessarily a true statement, they would be far less likely to arrest and prosecute suspects who give false confessions."[74]

The last recommendation is that trial judges "should evaluate the reliability of confession statements," as they do hearsay statements, to determine whether they should be allowed into evidence. "Oddly, the constitutional law of criminal procedure has no substantive safeguards in place to specifically prevent the admission of even demonstrably false confessions." The constitutional rules for confessions under the Fifth and Sixth Amendments are designed to ensure procedural regularity but not reliability, and the same has become true under the due process voluntariness test. Given this constitutional vacuum, it is critically important for judges to perform this task. The stakes for fairness are high: "It has been shown that placing a confession before a jury is tantamount to an instruction to convict, even when the confession fails to accurately describe the crime, fails to produce corroboration, and is contradicted by considerable evidence pointing to a suspect's innocence." Therefore, judges should demand that confessions display a minimal level of reliability. This can be done without any change in statutes or court rules. Judges routinely rule on admissibility and would, for example, not allow a jury to see a photograph that had been doctored. "A false confession is analogous to a doctored photograph. The mechanism for creating it is the ancient technology of human influence carried forward into the interrogation room."

A short decade ago, there was at best a vague awareness that false confessions were a rare and tragic human failing. Recent scholarship has brought the problem to the forefront. Judges, prosecutors, leaders of the bar, and police officials have no reason to claim ignorance. It remains to be seen if the legal world will respond to this challenge.

Summary

The Constitution protects against abusive interrogation by the due process involuntary confessions exclusionary rule, the Fifth Amendment privilege against self-incrimination (pre-indictment), and the Sixth Amendment right to counsel for formally charged defendants. The privilege against self-incrimination allows "natural persons" who are sworn to testify to claim the privilege if their testimony would tend to incriminate them. The privilege does not bar the taking and use of physical evidence, including a person's appearance and evidence from his or her body (e.g., hair, blood, DNA), to convict that person. The privilege prevents a person from having to face the "cruel trilemma" of self-accusation, perjury, or contempt. When applicable, the privilege against self-incrimination is an absolute bar against the use of compelled testimony taken from natural persons. The privilege may not be claimed to protect against civil commitment, as under Sexually Dangerous Person Acts.

Under the Due Process Clause, confessions or admissions are inadmissible if they are not made voluntarily. Statements obtained by threats, promises, the use of force, or undue psychological pressure are involuntary and inadmissible as due process violations. Different reasons have been proposed for the voluntariness rule: to ensure accurate confessions, to prevent egregious police behavior, and to ensure that a confession is the product of a free and rational choice. Federal law presumes confessions made within a six-hour "safe harbor" are voluntary. Judicial displeasure with the subjectivity of the voluntariness test led the Supreme Court to seek a more concrete rule. In 1963 and 1964, the Supreme Court incorporated the Sixth Amendment right to the assistance of counsel and the privilege against self-incrimination. *Miranda v. Arizona* (1966) held police custodial interrogation to be inherently coercive, requiring that police inform suspects of their rights under the privilege against self-incrimination in order to dispel the coercive atmosphere of police custody. Four warnings are required: the suspect has a right to remain silent; any statement may be used as evidence against him; he has a right to the presence of an attorney; and if he cannot afford an attorney, one will be appointed. A defendant may voluntarily, knowingly, and intelligently waive these rights.

Following *Miranda*, a more conservative Supreme Court declared that *Miranda* warnings were not themselves constitutional rights but prophylactic rules designed to protect the underlying Fifth Amendment right against self-incrimination. As a result, statements taken in violation of *Miranda* could be used to impeach the defendant and to lead to other evidence. The Court also allowed admission of a warned confession taken after *Miranda* violations in a prior interrogation. A public safety exception was created under this theory, allowing the admission into evidence of unwarned statements made in answers to questions designed to protect the safety of arresting officers and others in the immediate area (*New York v. Quarles*, 1984).

Despite this, *Dickerson v. United States* (2000) held that the *Miranda* warnings were constitutional rules that could not be overridden by Congress, purporting to reinstate the voluntariness test as the sole measure of the constitutionality of confessions in federal cases. *Miranda* had become so widely accepted that *stare decisis* compelled a recognition of the rule as being constitutional. But the effect of *Dickerson* was put into question by *Chavez v. Martinez* (2003), which held that a simple failure to read *Miranda* warnings is not a violation of any right. A plurality of the Court held that the privilege and the *Miranda* warnings operate only as exclusionary rules, so that violations occur only when compelled evidence is sought to be introduced.

More recently, the Supreme Court has continued to interpret *Miranda* as a rule with exceptions, even though deemed constitutional. Physical evidence obtained in violation of *Miranda* is admissible (*U.S. v. Patane*, 2004). Police, however, cannot rely on the rule of *Oregon v. Elstad* (1985) to "cure" a statement taken in violation of *Miranda* by administering warnings and reinterrogating a suspect where the "second" interrogation is part of a single interrogation session (*Missouri v. Seibert*, 2004). The Fourteenth Amendment due process voluntariness test exists as a backstop to, and not a replacement for, the *Miranda* rule.

Numerous cases clarify *Miranda*'s meaning. Warnings need not be given in the precise language found in *Miranda* as long as the correct understanding of the warnings is conveyed. Police do not have to add anything to the warnings, such as the consequences of confessing or their knowledge that the suspect may have committed crimes that are not the immediate subject of the questioning. The prosecution has the burden of proving that a waiver is made voluntarily. A waiver is not presumed from silence, and an oral waiver is allowable as long as it was made expressly and is shown on the record. Written waivers are the common form of proving that the rights to silence and counsel were waived voluntarily.

Police must cease questioning a suspect who has waived his or her rights but indicates during interrogation the wish to terminate the interrogation. However, police may resume questioning at a later time if the resumption is reasonable. Police must cease questioning a suspect who personally and clearly invokes a desire to see an attorney but not another kind of counselor. The police may not thereafter resume questioning unless it is initiated by the suspect. This rule is violated if an officer in a department reinterrogates a suspect who invoked counsel in ignorance of his or her prior request for an attorney. Simple consultation with a lawyer does not dispel *Edwards* protection; a defendant has a right, after invoking counsel, to be questioned by police or prosecutors only with counsel present.

A person is in *Miranda* custody if the circumstances or surroundings are objectively coercive. Depending on the circumstances, interviews in one's home, at a police station, or by a probation officer may not be coercive. Interrogation in prison, even for a crime unrelated to the original crime, requires *Miranda* warnings. Questioning by a patrol officer after a routine traffic stop is generally not custodial because this kind of common detention is in public and lacks the coercive atmosphere of the police station. Questions designed to produce an incriminating answer or questions asked after a person has been arrested at the roadside constitute custodial interrogation.

Interrogation consists of express questioning or its functional equivalent: words or actions on the part of the police (other than normally attendant to arrest and custody) that the police should know are reasonably likely to elicit an incriminating response from the suspect. Deception by police interrogators is allowed. Undercover agents, in or out of jail, are not required to give *Miranda* warnings when they ask incriminating questions because the interrogation is not conducted in a coercive atmosphere.

Once a person is formally arraigned, the police may not question or eavesdrop on him or her without a lawyer present, a rule established by *Massiah v. United States* (1964). This rule was violated in *Brewer v. Williams* (1977) when an officer made the functional equivalent of an interrogation designed to elicit a response by delivering a "Christian burial" speech to an isolated mental patient. Undercover agents who investigate a person who has been formally charged must not ask any questions or deliberately elicit conversations likely to generate incriminating statements. They may, however, listen for such statements, which are then admissible. Deliberately elicited statements, however, are admissible to impeach a defendant. A defendant may waive the Sixth Amendment right to counsel and consent to interrogation after being read *Miranda* warnings. A charged defendant who invokes counsel under *Massiah* for one crime may still be asked to waive his rights for another crime, even one arising out of the same criminal transaction, because the Sixth Amendment was held to be crime-specific. Once a charged defendant invokes *Massiah* rights, the police may initiate a conversation with the defendant to request that he waive the right to counsel and submit to an interrogation.

Legal Puzzles

HOW HAVE COURTS DECIDED THESE CASES?

Self-Incrimination / Voluntariness

7-1. Christopher Brown was prosecuted for aggravated battery and abuse of a child. The Kansas Department of Social and Rehabilitation Services (SRS) identified the Browns as perpetrators of child abuse. This was based on a single incident of a skull fracture and other injuries to the Browns' one-month-old baby. No drug use or other family problems were found. The SRS moved to terminate the Browns' parental rights over all their children. Brown was told that he could regain custody of his children if he would, among other tasks, admit how the injuries occurred. On the date that the Browns' parental rights were to be terminated, Brown went to the sheriff's office, sought out a detective who had been involved in the investigation, and told him that he was ready to make a statement. After being *Mirandized*, Brown gave a statement admitting that on the night in question, the baby would not stop crying, was driving him "freaking crazy," and Brown "squeezed him too hard."

> *(1) Was the threat of the loss of parental rights a penalty that made Brown's confession the product of Fifth Amendment compulsion? (2) Was the confession coerced?*

HELD: (1) Yes. (2) Yes. The confession was properly suppressed by lower courts.

7-1. Pressure that compels a person to admit to a crime may be created by any state agent or officer, not just police officers. The privilege may be raised in any proceeding, civil or criminal, formal or informal, where testimonial evidence may incriminate the individual in future criminal proceedings. (1) When a parent is essentially compelled to choose between confessing guilt in abusing his or her own child or losing his or her parental rights, the choice is between two fundamental rights under the Constitution. This is Fifth Amendment compulsion—a "classic penalty" situation. In such case the privilege against self-incrimination was not self-executing and Brown can challenge his confession if it is used against him in a criminal prosecution.

(2) Under the totality of the circumstances test, the government has the burden to prove by the preponderance of the evidence that the confession was voluntary. The same facts that proved a substantial Fifth Amendment penalty proved that Brown's will was overcome by state actors. *State v. Brown*, 286 Kan. 170, 182 P.3d 1205 (Kan. Supreme Court 2008)

Voluntariness

7-2. Cindi Rush, a twenty-year old woman with a ninth-grade education and no involvement in the criminal justice system, was arrested for first-degree murder as part of a household robbery. She was read *Miranda* warnings, interrogated, and confessed. During interrogation she gave several versions of what happened but always maintained that she did not pull the trigger. Parts of the interrogation transcript read:

RUSH: How, why am I bein' charged with first degree murder?

DETECTIVE: Darlin', darlin', well, until we get all the details as to exactly what happened, how things laid out, there's no way we can get around this.

* * *

DET.:   Well darlin', you're a part of the whole thing until we can get all the details as exactly what happened. We can't narrow the scope down until we know every little detail about what happened. * * * Until that happens, and we know exactly what happened that day and why it happened, I've got a warrant for ya for first degree murder. Now —

RUSH: I didn't kill anybody —

* * *

DET.:   Cindi, I'm not saying you did. I know you didn't. I know you didn't. And that seems like a whole lot, a huge burden on your shoulders about this. But I know you're part of it. I know that you played a part in this because there's no other way. There's no other connection to that family other than through you. There's no other connection. Now, you can sit here and take the ride, take the charge —

* * *

DET.:   Now, ya know, there, there could be some salvation here. . . . Neither one of you pulled the trigger in this. Neither one of you went inside. Neither one of you are the person that Jeffrey Gilbert was. So let's get it all out of exactly what happened and why it happened so we can resolve this and get it over with. But you sittin' here lyin' to me is not gonna do it.

A confession induced by police threats, promises, or inducements render the confession involuntary and inadmissible. Mere exhortations to tell the truth and appeals to a suspect's inner conscience, in and of themselves, are not improper promises.

> *Did the detective make improper inducements?*
> *Holding available from instructor.*

Adequacy of *Miranda* Warnings

7-3. Defendant, a twenty-year old woman with a ninth-grade education and no involvement in the criminal justice system, was arrested for murder and was interrogated. Prior to administering *Miranda* warnings the detective asked the defendant "Do you know why you are here?" He established her education, lack of a GED, and her ability to read. The *Miranda* warnings read to the defendant stated: "You have the right to talk to a lawyer before you're asked any questions. You have the right, you have, you have the right to have a lawyer with you while being questioned. If you want a lawyer and can't afford one, one will be provided to you **at some time at no cost.**" Defendant waived her rights and confessed.

> *Did the phrase "at some time at no cost" in the Miranda warnings make the warnings inadequate, requiring that the confession be ruled inadmissible?*
> *Holding available from instructor.*

Two-Step Interrogation

7-4. Megan Morris was charged with manslaughter in conjunction with the death of a child, Romeo, whom she babysat. She maintained that Romeo accidentally hit his head on a bed guardrail. At about 2:00 p.m. one afternoon, Morris, her fiancé, and her mother went to the police station at the request of the police for interviews.

In an interview room, Morris was told she was not under arrest, was free to leave, and was given no *Miranda* warnings. She maintained her story to a lieutenant and left after twenty minutes. She began to walk home but a police captain went to her in the parking lot and told her that he wanted to resolve the case. They spoke in the parking lot and police station lobby for about thirty minutes. She was not read *Miranda* warnings. The captain then led Morris to an interview room and conducted a recorded interview from 4:55 p.m. to 5:45 p.m. No *Miranda* warnings were issued. In response to questions, Morris replied that no promises were made to her. She again went to the lobby to wait for her fiancé.

During the second interview the captain asked, "Okay, have I promised you anything?" Morris responded, "Only that I could go home." At the conclusion of this statement, the captain said, "Have I ever told you, you couldn't leave?" Morris responded, "No, but you said it was in my best interest to" [a Court footnote noted that she surely meant "in her best interest not to"].

A sergeant present during the second interview approached Morris and requested a third interview. They went to an interview room where Morris was told she was not under arrest and was free to leave, but he did not advise of her of her *Miranda* rights. The sergeant and Morris talked from 5:50 p.m. to 6:30 p.m. He told her that based on the autopsy reports, there was no way that the child's head wound had been accidentally inflicted. Morris then said she struck Romeo in the back of the head with her fist.

At 6:34 p.m., Morris was given *Miranda* warnings for the first time, signed a waiver form and gave a recorded statement, at 7:00 p.m., in which she reiterated that she had become frustrated with Romeo's crying and had struck him on the back of the head with her fist. After giving this statement, Morris was allowed to leave the police station. She was arrested the next day.

(1) Was Morris under custodial interrogation during the third interview? (2) Was Morris's confession admissible under Seibert v. Missouri (2004)?
Holding available from instructor.

Deliberately Elicited Statements

7-5. James Oliveira was arrested on charges of sexually molesting his six-year-old grandson. The state filed a complaint against him on August 13, the day on which he was presented in district court, referred to the public defender's office, and held without bail. On October 29 he was indicted on two counts of first-degree child molestation. Laurie Moriarty, a Department of Children, Youth and Families (DCYF) child protective investigator, was assigned to the child's case. The DCYF, by law, investigates all child abuse allegations. The goals of a DCYF investigation are to determine the validity of reported allegations and to assure the safety and well-being of children. It is DCYF policy that investigators interview each involved adult, including alleged perpetrators. It is also DCYF protocol to work in conjunction with law enforcement personnel.

On August 24, Moriarty went to the Child Advocacy Center where she interviewed the boy and his mother, and met with the detectives and prosecutor in this case. She was informed that there was enough evidence to press charges against Oliveira. The next day, August 25, Moriarty went to the jail and interviewed Oliveira. She did not ascertain whether he was represented by counsel. During the jail interview Oliveira admitted that he sexually molested his grandson. At trial, after refreshing her memory by reviewing her report, Moriarty told the jury what the defendant told her, which included details of the sexual acts. Oliveira was convicted.

(1) When did Oliveira's Sixth Amendment right to counsel attach? (2) Was Moriarty a state officer for purposes of enforcing Oliveira's rights under Massiah v. United States (1964) and Maine v. Moulton (1985)?
Holding available from instructor.

Further Reading

Liva Baker, *Miranda: Crime, Law and Politics* (New York: Atheneum, 1985).

R. H. Helmholz et al., *The Privilege against Self-Incrimination: Its Origins and Development* (Chicago: University of Chicago Press, 1997).

Richard A. Leo, *Police Interrogation and American Justice* (Cambridge, Mass.: Harvard University Press, 2008).

Useful Web Sites

American Civil Liberties Union

http://www.aclu.org/

Information on criminal justice, the death penalty, and other topics from a liberal/individual rights–oriented perspective.

Cato Institute

http://www.cato.org/index.html

Publications and reports on criminal justice topics from a conservative/libertarian perspective.

End Notes

1. See, e.g., George Seibel, *Enlightened Police Questioning: Interviewing, Interrogation and Investigation* (Mesilla, N.M.: Prairie Avenue Press, 2003); and Charles R. Swanson, Neil C. Chamelin, and Leonard Territo, *Criminal Investigation,* 8th ed. (Boston: McGraw Hill, 2003).

2. Human Rights Watch, *Shielded from Justice: Police Brutality and Accountability in the United States* (New York: Human Rights Watch, 1998); and Malcolm Holmes, "Minority Threat and Police Brutality: Determinants of Civil Rights Criminal Complaints in U.S. Municipalities," *Criminology* 38, no. 2 (2000): 343–67.

3. See Steven A. Drizin and Richard A. Leo, "The Problem of False Confessions in the Post-DNA World," *North Carolina Law Review* 82 (2004): 891.

4. Stacey M. Studnicki and John P. Apol, "Witness Detention and Intimidation: The History and Future of Material Witness Law," *St. John's Law Review* 76 (2002): 483–533.

5. Amanda H. Frost, "Updating the Marital Privileges: A Witness-Centered Rationale," *Wisconsin Women's Law Journal* 14 (1999): 1–44.

6. R. H. Helmholz, "Introduction," in R. H. Helmholz et al., *The Privilege against Self-Incrimination: Its Origins and Development* (Chicago: University of Chicago Press, 1997), 1.

7. John H. Langbein, *Torture and the Law of Proof: Europe and England in the Ancien Régime* (Chicago: University of Chicago Press, 1977); and Edward Peters, *Torture* (Oxford: Basil Blackwell, 1985).

8. Richard S. Frase, "Review Essay: The Search for the Whole Truth about American and European Criminal Justice" (review of William T. Pizzi, *Trials without Truth* [New York: New York University Press, 1999]), *Buffalo Criminal Law Review* 3 (2000): 785–849.

9. "Annual Review of Criminal Procedure," *Georgetown Law Journal Annual Review of Criminal Procedure* 37(2008): 608–09 (footnotes omitted).

10. Charles H. Whitebread and Christopher Slobogin, *Criminal Procedure: An Analysis of Cases and Concepts,* 4th ed. (New York: Foundation Press, 2000), 379.

11. Laura Mansnerus, "Questions Rise over Imprisoning Sex Offenders Past Their Terms," *New York Times,* November 17, 2003.

12. "Project: Twenty-ninth Annual Review of Criminal Procedure," *Georgetown Law Journal* 88 (2000), 879, 1431–32 (footnotes omitted, emphasis added).

13. P. W. Valentine, "Woman, Jailed for Contempt, Freed after 7 Years; Md. Mother Failed to Reveal Son's Location," *Washington Post,* November 1, 1995; and "Mother Ends 7-Year Jail Stay, Still Silent about Missing Child," *New York Times,* November 2, 1995.

14. Delmar Karlen, *Anglo-American Criminal Justice* (New York: Oxford University Press, 1967), 121; and David J. Bodenhamer, *Fair Trial: Rights of the Accused in American History* (New York: Oxford University Press, 1992), 53–4. Some scholars suggest that the rule excluding the admission of coerced confessions at trial may have had an organic connection with the privilege against self-incrimination; see Lawrence Herman, "The Unexplored Relationship between the Privilege against Compulsory Self-Incrimination and the Involuntary Confession Rule," *Ohio State Law Journal* 53 (1992): 101–209, 497–553.

15. Karlen, *Anglo-American Criminal Justice,* 122.

16. See Samuel Walker, *Popular Justice: A History of American Criminal Justice* (New York: Oxford University Press, 1980), 173–75, 189, 231. Richard Leo, *Police Interrogation and American Justice* (Cambridge, Mass.: Harvard University Press, 2008), 41–77, examined the third degree and suggested that the practice declined because of increasing police professionalism, changing attitudes, and changes in legal doctrine.

17. Bodenhamer, *Fair Trial,* 101.

18. Richard C. Cortner, *The Supreme Court and the Second Bill of Rights* (Madison: University of Wisconsin Press, 1981), 150.

19. "Note: Developments in the Law of Confessions," *Harvard Law Review* 79 (1966): 935, 963–83 (emphasis added).

20. Fred P. Graham, *The Due Process Revolution: The Warren Court's Impact on Criminal Law* (New York: Hayden, 1970), 184–86.

21. The Court cited Steven A. Drizin and Richard A. Leo, "The Problem of False Confessions in the Post-DNA World," *North Carolina Law Review* 82 (2004): 891–1007, 906–907.

22. Christopher Slobogin, "Lying and Confessing", *Texas Tech Law Review,* 39 (2007): 1275–1292, 1290, n. 87, citing Welsh S. White, "Confessions in Capital Cases," *University of Illinois Law Review,* 2003: 1021, drawing on Richard A. Leo and Richard J. Ofshe, "The Consequences of False Confessions: Deprivations of Liberty and Miscarriages of Justice in the Age of Psychological Interrogation," *Journal of Criminal Law and Criminology,* 88 (1998): 429, 430.

23. Graham, *The Due Process Revolution,*154.

24. Graham, *The Due Process Revolution,* 155.

25. Graham, *The Due Process Revolution,* 153–93; Liva Baker, *Miranda: Crime, Law and Politics* (New York: Atheneum, 1985).

26. Baker, *Miranda,* 191–94, 408–9.

27. Herman, "The Unexplored Relationship," 101–209, 497–553.

28. Politicians and police officials sharply criticized the liberal majority that decided *Miranda.* Richard Nixon denounced *Miranda* and the liberal Warren Court in his 1968 presidential campaign, and as president he appointed four conservatives to the Court (Chief Justice Burger and Justices Blackmun, Powell, and Rehnquist) after three liberals and one conservative retired (Chief Justice Warren and Justices Black, Harlan, and Fortas), creating a pro-prosecution, centrist-to-conservative Court. See Baker, *Miranda,* 221–324, 346; and C. M. Lamb and S. C. Halpern, eds., *The Burger Court: Political and Judicial Profiles* (Urbana: University of Illinois Press, 1991).

29. The issue was raised by a leading conservative scholar, Joseph D. Grano, *Confessions, Truth and the Law* (Ann Arbor: University of Michigan Press, 1993), 173–222, who felt that *Miranda* should be overruled. See Yale Kamisar, *Police Interrogation and Confessions: Essays in Law and Policy* (Ann Arbor: University of Michigan Press, 1980). Both sides are presented in Richard A. Leo and George C. Thomas III, eds., *The Miranda Debate: Law, Justice and Policing* (Boston: Northeastern University Press, 1998).

30. The interrogation occurred before *Miranda* was decided, but the trial took place after the *Miranda* decision. Therefore, the *Miranda* ruling applied to this case.

31. The moving force behind the appeal invoking Section 3501, which federal prosecutors had studiously avoided for three decades, was the passionate advocacy of Paul Cassell, then a

law professor, who mounted a crusade to overturn *Miranda*. See George C. Thomas and Richard Leo, "The Effects of *Miranda v. Arizona:* 'Embedded' in Our National Culture?" *Crime and Justice: A Review of Research* 29 (2002): 203–71, 264; and Roger Parloff, "*Miranda* on the Hot Seat," *New York Times Magazine,* September 26, 1999, who describes Professor Cassell as "an indefatigable, ideologically driven young law professor at the University of Utah" who has made a career of trying to get the courts to use Section 3501 to overrule *Miranda.* "For seven years, Cassell filed such briefs in one or two cases a year, primarily in the District of Utah or in the Fourth Circuit. These were his current and former stomping grounds and two of the most inviting venues legally, based on controlling Federal precedents in those regions."

32. Richard Harris, *The Fear of Crime* (New York: Praeger, 1969), 58.

33. Arnold H. Loewy, "Police-Obtained Evidence and the Constitution: Distinguishing Unconstitutionally Obtained Evidence from Unconstitutionally Used Evidence," *Michigan Law Review* 87 (1989): 907–39, 926: "[T]he fifth amendment does not contain an exclusionary rule; it is itself an exclusionary rule."

34. *United States v. Usama Bin Laden,* 132 F.Supp.2d 168, 185–86, 187 (S.D.N.Y. 2001).

35. *United States v. Usama Bin Laden,* 132 F.Supp.2d 168, 188 (S.D.N.Y. 2001).

36. *United States v. Usama Bin Laden,* 132 F.Supp.2d 168, 188 (S.D.N.Y. 2001).

37. Benjamin Weiser, "Four Are Sentenced to Life in Prison in 1998 U.S. Embassy Bombing," *New York Times,* October 19, 2001. The jury had voted nine to three for the death sentence; execution required a unanimous verdict of death.

38. Charles D. Weisselberg, "Saving Miranda," *Cornell Law Review* 84 (1998): 109–92, citing Devallis Rutledge, *Questioning "Outside Miranda," Did You Know . . .* (Sacramento: California District Attorneys Association, June 1995), 133; M. Zalman, "The Coming Paradigm Shift on *Miranda:* The Impact of *Chavez v. Martinez,*" *Criminal Law Bulletin* 39 (2003): 334–52; and M. Zalman, "Reading the Tea Leaves of *Chavez v. Martinez:* The Future of *Miranda,*" *Criminal Law Bulletin* 40, no. 4 (2004): 299–368.

39. *Weeks v. Angelone,* 176 F.3d 249 (4th Cir. 1999).

40. A list of ploys is found in Slobogin, *Lying and Confessing,* 1285–86.

41. See *Gauger v. Hendle,* 2002 U.S. Dist. LEXIS 18002 (U.S. Dist. Ct. N.D. Ill. 2002).

42. Jackson v. Litscher, 194 F.Supp.2d 849 (E.D.Wis. 2002), rev'd, *Jackson v. Frank,* 348 F.3d 658 (7th cir. 2003).

43. *State v. Cayward,* 552 So. 2d 971 (Fla. Ct. App. 2d Dist.1989).

44. Yale Kamisar, "Equal Justice in the Gatehouses and Mansions of American Criminal Procedure: from *Powell* to *Gideon,* from *Escobedo* to . . . ," in *Criminal Justice in Our TIME* (A. E. Dick Howard ed., Charlottesville: University Press of Virginia, 1965), 11–38.

45. Charles D. Weisselberg, "Saving Miranda," *Cornell Law Review* 84 (1998): 109–92.

46. The facts recited herein are taken from the Supreme Court's opinions and from the Brief for Petitioner.

47. T. Jacoby, "Fighting Crime by the Rules," *Newsweek,* July 18, 1988, reviewing R. Uviller, *Tempered Zeal.*

48. Leo, *Police Interrogation in America,* 335.

49. Leo, *Police Interrogation in America,* 336–42.

50. Richard A. Leo and Welsh S. White, "Adapting to *Miranda:* Modern Interrogators' Strategies for Dealing with the Obstacles Posed by *Miranda,*" *Minnesota Law Review* 84 (1999): 397–472, 402, n. 18 lists some of the early studies.

51. Leo, *Police Interrogation in America,* 258–68, 276–77. Leo's dissertation has been published in several articles: "Inside the Interrogation Room," *Journal of Criminal Law and Criminology* 86 (1996): 266–303; and "*Miranda's* Revenge: Police Interrogation as a Confidence Game," *Law and Society Review* 30 (1996): 259–88.

52. Leo, *Police Interrogation in America,* 271.

53. Leo, *Police Interrogation in America,* 191.

54. Leo, *Police Interrogation in America,* 212–20.

55. Leo and White, "Adapting to *Miranda,*" 431–47.

56. P. W. Lewis and H. E. Allen, "'Participating *Miranda':* An Attempt to Subvert Certain Constitutional Safeguards," *Crime and Delinquency* 23, no. 2 (1977): 75–80.

57. See Leo, *Police Interrogation in America,* 230–51; and D. Simon, *Homicide: A Year on the Killing Streets* (Boston: Houghton Mifflin, 1991).

58. Weisselberg, "Saving *Miranda*"; and Leo and White, "Adapting to *Miranda,*" 447–50.

59. Leo, *Police Interrogation in America,* 354.

60. Leo, *Police Interrogation in America,* 357–59.

61. Leo, *Police Interrogation in America,* 359–60.

62. Leo, *Police Interrogation in America,* 361–63.

63. Leo, *Police Interrogation in America,* 416.

64. Richard Leo, "The Impact of *Miranda* Revisited," *Journal of Criminal Law and Criminology* 86 (1996): 621–92, 683–84, relying on William A. Geller, *Videotaping Interrogations and Confessions* (U.S. Department of Justice, March 1993).

65. Richard A. Leo and Richard J. Ofshe, "The Consequences of False Confessions: Deprivations of Liberty and Miscarriages of Justice in the Age of Psychological Interrogation," *Journal of Criminal Law and Criminology* 88 (1998): 429–96.

66. Richard A. Leo and Richard J. Ofshe, "Missing the Forest for the Trees: A Response to Paul Cassell's 'Balanced Approach' to the False Confession Problem," *Denver University Law Review* 74 (1997): 1135.

67. In Jim Dwyer, Peter Neufeld, and Barry Scheck, *Actual Innocence* (New York: Doubleday, 2000), 78–106. The law professors who operate the "innocence project" list false confessions as one of several problems that contribute to what DNA testing has disclosed is a major problem of convicting the innocent.

68. Richard J. Ofshe and Richard A. Leo, "The Decision to Confess Falsely: Rational Choice and Irrational Action," *Denver University Law Review* 74 (1997): 979–1122.

69. Ofshe and Leo, "The Decision to Confess Falsely," 997–1000.

70. Ofshe and Leo, "The Decision to Confess Falsely," 986–94.

71. The information on the Sawyer case is derived from a 292-page transcript of the police interrogation. The secondary sources used that reprinted parts of the transcript are found in "Readings: [Transcript] True Confession?" *Harper's,* October 1989, 17–201; and Philip Weiss, "Untrue Confessions," *Mother Jones,* September 1989, 18–24+.

72. The lie detector examination was given during the evening when he was under great stress. A later polygraph examination indicated that Sawyer's denial of the murder was truthful.

73. Leo and Ofshe, "Missing the Forest," n. 49.

74. Ofshe and Leo, "The Decision to Confess Falsely," 1119–20, n. 51.

JUSTICES OF THE SUPREME COURT

Enduring Liberals: Brennan and Marshall

When William Brennan was appointed by President Dwight Eisenhower and Thurgood Marshall by President Lyndon Johnson, the Supreme Court was representative of the ascendant liberal ideology of the day. Their backgrounds, experiences, and beliefs about the Court's role well suited them to play a part in expanding the rights of society's outcasts. As justices with long tenures, their careers coincided with the long swing of the political pendulum, from liberal to conservative, that has marked American politics since the 1960s. The careers of Justices Brennan and Marshall exemplify an important institutional aspect of the Supreme Court: Presidents nominate individuals who represent the political aspirations of the day, but with life tenure, justices who sit for several decades can extend their philosophies over time. This places the Court somewhat above the political passions of the period and offers a form of stability. The disadvantage is that at times it makes the Court unresponsive to the needs and demands of the polity.

The resignation of Justices Arthur Goldberg and Abe Fortas and Chief Justice Earl Warren between 1965 and 1969 led to a change in the Court's composition that reflected and possibly accelerated a shift toward conservatism on some issues. This has persisted since 1970, as the ten nominees of Republican Presidents Richard Nixon, Gerald Ford, Ronald Reagan, and George H. W. Bush moved the Court progressively to the right. Democratic President Jimmy Carter had no opportunity to nominate a justice, and President Clinton carefully selected moderate rather than liberal justices.

Thus for two decades, Justices Brennan and Marshall, the enduring liberals, penned more than a normal share of dissents in many criminal procedure cases. At times, their dissents expressed outrage and dire warnings that the conservative justices were subverting constitutional rights. Less frequently, they joined with at least three moderate justices to rule in favor of the defendant. For the most part, their dissents after 1970 were written not so much for the present but for the future, in the hope that a new generation of justices would be more open to defendants' claims.

Collection of the Supreme Court of the United States.
Photographer: Robert Oakes.

William J. Brennan Jr.

New Jersey, 1906–1997

Democrat

Appointed by Dwight Eisenhower

Years of Service: 1956–1990

Life and Career.   The son of an Irish immigrant who became a political leader in Newark, New Jersey, noted for integrity and efficiency, William Brennan grew up in comfortable circumstances. He graduated from the Wharton School of the University of Pennsylvania with honors and was in the top 10 percent of his class at Harvard Law School in 1931. He practiced law with a prestigious Newark firm that specialized in labor issues for corporate clients. During World War II, he was a labor productivity troubleshooter for the undersecretary of war, rising to the rank of colonel. After the war, he became associated with the judicial reform efforts of New Jersey's renowned Chief Justice Arthur Vanderbilt and, as a result, was appointed a trial judge. As an associate justice of the New Jersey Supreme Court, Brennan came to the attention of U.S. Attorney General Brownell at a conference on judicial administration, where he sat in for Vanderbilt. The next year, when a vacancy appeared on the Court, Brennan fit the political requirements for the job: He was a Catholic, an easterner, and a nominal Democrat acceptable to Republicans. The only senator to vote against his confirmation to the Supreme Court was Joseph McCarthy, the demagogic communist hunter who may have been angered by Brennan's earlier public criticism of "McCarthyism."

Contribution to Criminal Procedure.   Justice Brennan wrote few criminal procedure majority opinions in the 1960s, although he consistently voted for incorporation and defendants' rights. Under a more conservative Court, he authored many criminal procedure dissents, including *United States v. Leon* (1984) (good faith exception to exclusionary rule), *Illinois v. Gates* (1983) (abolishing the *Spinelli* two-pronged test for reliability of informant), *United States v. Calandra* (1974) (use of illegally obtained evidence in grand jury is constitutional), *Florida v. Riley* (1989) (helicopter overflights not a search subject to Fourth Amendment warrant requirement), *Hampton v. United States* (1976) (no entrapment if government agent supplies illegal drug), *Michigan v. Mosley* (1975) (reinterrogation allowed after a suspect claims right to silence), *United States v. Ash* (1973) (*Wade* lineup rule does not apply to photographic identification), and *Kuhlman v. Wilson* (1986) (passive jail informant does not violate a suspect's right to counsel under the *Massiah* doctrine).

In many dissents, he was outspokenly critical of the majority, often accusing it of ignoring facts or twisting precedent simply to arrive at a desired outcome—the same charge of result-oriented jurisprudence that was hurled at the activist Warren Court during the 1960s. In reaction to the curtailment of defendants' rights, Justice Brennan called on state court judges to apply their own state constitutions to afford more rights to suspects than were granted under the current reading of the Bill of Rights. This indeed has been a growing trend and is an ironic twist for a justice who championed federal rights in the 1960s.

Signature Opinion.   Dissenting opinion in *Illinois v. Gates* (1983). In this tour de force, Justice Brennan directly attacked the ideological basis of the conservative Court's criminal procedure rulings as "code words for an overly permissive attitude toward police practices in derogation of the rights secured by the Fourth Amendment."

Assessment.   Justice Brennan was called "a towering figure in modern law who embodied the liberal vision of the Constitution as an engine of social and political change," and many commentators referred to the Warren Court as the "Brennan Court," so great was the influence of his prolific opinions and his ability to gain majorities for his opinions. He strongly influenced all the major areas of the Warren Court's liberal agenda, including free speech, free press, separation of church and state, voting apportionment, school busing, and criminal procedure.

Further Reading

Kim Isaac Eisler, *Justice for All: William J. Brennan, Jr., and the Decisions That Transformed America* (New York: Simon and Schuster, 1993).

Thurgood Marshall

New York, 1908–1993
Democrat
Appointed by Lyndon Johnson
Years of Service: 1967–1991

Collection of the Supreme Court of the United States.
Photographer: Joseph Lavenburg.

Life and Career.   Marshall had one of the most distinguished and significant legal careers in American constitutional history. Born in Baltimore into a middle-class family, this great-grandson of a slave graduated from Lincoln University (Chester, Pennsylvania) and was first in his class at Howard University Law School. From 1933 to 1938, he was the counsel for the National Association for the Advancement of Colored People (NAACP) in Baltimore, and from 1938 to 1960, he was the chief counsel of the Legal Defense Fund, the legal organization spun off from the NAACP to defend the civil rights of African Americans in a then legally segregated society. He led the legal battle to overturn segregation laws and thus played a central role in the civil rights movement. He appeared before the Supreme Court thirty-two times and won thirteen of the sixteen cases in which he was the principal attorney. His most significant victories were *Shelly v. Kramer* (1948), which declared restrictive covenants on real estate deeds unenforceable in the courts, and *Brown v. Board of Education* (1954), the most important case of the twentieth century, which overturned the "separate but equal doctrine" and outlawed school segregation. In 1961, President John F. Kennedy named Marshall to the Court of Appeals for the Second Circuit, and in 1965, President Johnson named him as the solicitor general, the chief federal attorney to argue cases before the Supreme Court. Two years later, Marshall was appointed to the Court.

Contribution to Criminal Procedure.   As the Court moved steadily to the right after 1970, Justice Marshall, along with Justice Brennan and on occasion Justices Harry Blackmun and John Paul Stevens, dissented in most criminal procedure cases. His opinions were often trenchant and eloquent denunciations of what he saw as the conservative majority's oppressive misreading of the Bill of Rights and its attempt to dismantle constitutional protections. In *Schneckloth v. Bustamonte* (1973) (knowledge of rights not required to give valid consent to search), for example, he stated, "I have difficulty in comprehending how a decision made without knowledge of available alternatives can be treated as a choice at all."

Along with Justice Brennan, he held that the death penalty is a flat violation of the Cruel and Unusual Punishment Clause of the Eighth Amendment and voted to overturn each capital punishment case, a position adopted by Justice Blackmun a few months before his retirement. On occasion, he wrote a majority opinion for a unanimous Court, as in the ruling that a brief roadside stop of a motorist for a traffic violation does not constitute the kind of custodial interrogation that triggers the need for *Miranda* warnings (*Berkemer v. McCarty,* 1984).

Signature Opinion.   Concurring opinion in *Batson v. Kentucky* (1986). Although the Court's majority issued a "liberal" decision, that the exclusion of a juror on account of race in a single trial could be challenged, Marshall moved beyond the frontiers of the decision and argued that the use of peremptory challenges during voir dire perpetuates the potential for discrimination and should be eliminated altogether.

Assessment.   Marshall was a staunch supporter of civil rights. He consistently voted throughout the Burger Court era and into the Rehnquist Court era to uphold liberal positions that were staked out during the 1960s. He dissented powerfully in cases that limited the scope of school integration orders to districts that had practiced deliberate discrimination. Marshall was often an engaging, blunt, and humorous speaker, but he issued critical dissents and was sharply critical of his successor on the bench, Clarence Thomas. Nevertheless, Thurgood Marshall exuded great warmth and, when he retired, was praised by his colleagues. Even those who did not agree with him respected his convictions, accomplishments, and fierce candor.

Further Reading

Michael E. Davis and Hunter R. Clark, *Thurgood Marshall: Warrior at the Bar, Rebel on the Bench,* rev. ed. (New York: Citadel Press, 1994).

CHAPTER 8

Identification of Suspects: Lineups and Showups

Law enforcement may have the elements of a contest about it, but it is not a game.

—JUSTICE BYRON WHITE,

DISSENTING IN *MASSIAH V. UNITED STATES*, 377 U.S. 201, 213 (1964)

CHAPTER OUTLINE

KEY TERMS

cross-examination	identification parade	showup	testimonial evidence
exoneration	lineup	suggestibility	wrongful conviction
eyewitness			

THE PERSISTENCE OF MISTAKEN IDENTIFICATION

Eyewitness identification is the most important source of truth in most criminal cases and, ironically, the leading source of error that results in the conviction of innocent people. The use of eyewitnesses at every stage of the criminal process is self-evident. A street mugging victim sits in a police car and is asked whether a suspect matches her description. A store clerk at a police station **lineup** is asked whether each person in the lineup is or is not the armed robber. At a trial, a homeowner sitting in the witness box is asked to identify the burglar; he raises his arm, points to the person sitting next to the defense lawyer, and says, "That's the man; I'd know him anywhere."

Honestly mistaken identification is recognized by commonsense psychology. An attorney conducting a **cross-examination** of an eyewitness in a criminal trial asks commonsense questions to cast doubt on the accuracy of the witness's perception. How long did the witness observe the perpetrator? Was the witness wearing eyeglasses? What were the lighting conditions? The legal system places great faith in the ability of cross-examination to ferret out the truth. A century ago,

Dean John Wigmore of Northwestern University Law School called cross-examination "the greatest legal engine ever invented for the discovery of truth."[1] The Supreme Court said that "cross-examination is the principal means by which the believability of a witness and the truth of his testimony are tested" (*Davis v. Alaska,* 1974). Nevertheless, it has been known for a century that human identification is fraught with error. Classroom experiments by psychologist Hugo Münsterberg were published in 1908 and dramatically demonstrated that human recall of recent events is filled with errors.[2] In 1932, Professor Edwin Borchard of Yale Law School published *Convicting the Innocent: Sixty-five Actual Errors of Criminal Justice,* telling stories of people found guilty of felonies and later proven to be completely innocent.[3] Most of these miscarriages of justice were caused by mistaken eyewitness identification and some by the misconduct of prosecutors. A few of the innocent were given monetary compensation by special acts of state legislatures. A similar 1957 book by jurist Jerome Frank and Barbara Frank documented thirty-four case of innocents convicted in American courts.[4] When asked to estimate the percentage of innocent people convicted of felonies, criminal justice officials—judges, police chiefs, prosecutors, and defense lawyers—from the 1980s to the present estimate from .5 percent to 2 percent.[5] Although estimates are subject to criticism, this translates into 5,000 to 20,000 innocents convicted of felonies *every year* out of approximately one million convictions, with 60 percent incarcerated in jails or prisons. More precise estimates of **exonerations** in capital cases concur with the estimates of justice system personnel and have identified error rates of 3.5 to 5 percent in recent *death penalty* cases.[6]

News accounts of the exoneration of the innocent appear with astonishing regularity.[7] In a 1974 New York case, a person was jailed for armed robbery for a year based on a photo identification but no voice identification. When the victim discovered a year later that the suspect had a thick West Indian accent, the innocent man was released.[8] A New York assistant prosecutor charged with attempted rape in 1985 was released when a look-alike confessed.[9] A Roman Catholic priest, Father Bernard Pagano, was mistaken for the "gentleman robber" in Delaware.[10] Reports showed that by 1990 five innocent people convicted in Dallas had been freed.[11] Eyewitness evidence convicted Lenel Geter, a young African-American engineer, of a fast-food franchise robbery, over testimony of coworkers that he was at work fifty miles from the robbery site. In truth he bore little resemblance to the robber's description. "Intense national publicity, including a story on CBS's *60 Minutes,*" forced Geter's release.[12] The case of Randall Dale Adams, sentenced to death for murdering Dallas police officer Robert Wood in 1977, was brought to light by a riveting documentary film, *The Thin Blue Line,* produced by Errol Morris. It exposed a combination of prosecutorial overzealousness and fabricated eyewitness testimony that elicited a virtual confession from the real killer, David Harris, and led to Adams's release.[13]

These stories supplied evidence of **wrongful convictions** based on eyewitness error but generated no significant impetus for reform. That began to change after 1990 as DNA testing became common and led to the exonerations of a more and more innocents. Under Attorney General Janet Reno the Justice Department published a report in 1996 whose title conveyed its message: *Convicted by Juries, Exonerated by Science: Case Studies in the Use of DNA Evidence to Establish Innocence after Trial.*[14] By the 1990s studies of cognitive psychologists created a huge store of knowledge about eyewitness identification and suggested ways to conduct lineups to reduce honest witness error (this will be discussed in detail in the "Law in Society" section, this chapter). The creation of innocence projects assisted the exoneration of innocent prisoners and provided a source of information about the problems of eyewitnesses and wrongful convictions.[15]

A poignant and now famous case of mistaken identification leading to the conviction of an innocent man is the story of rape victim Jennifer Thompson, who wrongly identified Ronald Cotton in 1984.[16] His DNA exoneration in 1996 led to momentous changes in both their lives that led to friendship and joint work to advance the cause of exonerations. In June 2000, Jennifer wrote a moving article detailing her experience of identifying the wrong man after making efforts to recall her assailant. Thompson wrote, "If anything good can come out of what Ronald Cotton suffered because of my limitations as a human being, let it be an awareness of the fact that eyewitnesses can and do make mistakes."[17] Thompson urged Texas to halt the execution of Gary Graham, who was convicted of murder largely on the testimony of a single witness who said she saw him from thirty to forty feet away through her car windshield. No physical evidence linked Graham to the crime. Tests showed that the gun he was carrying was not the murder weapon. Two witnesses who were never called to testify said they had seen the killer—and it was not Graham. He was represented by a court-appointed lawyer who failed to mount a meaningful defense. Despite these substantial indications of doubt, the then-Texas governor refused to intervene in the pardon process, asserting that "there has not been one innocent person executed since I've been governor"; he had presided over 135 executions. Gary Graham was executed on June 22, 2000.[18]

The number of wrongful convictions can be reduced, generally speaking, by police procedures (administrative) and by legal means. How police investigate cases, interview witnesses, and conduct lineups can increase or lower investigation errors. Traditionally, cross-examination was the only legal mechanism to correct eyewitness identification errors. Changes in administrative measures that could effectively improve accuracy and reduce identification errors became possible by the 1990s based on the work of cognitive psychologists. In 1999 the National Institute of Justice issued a report, *Eyewitness Evidence: A Guide for Law Enforcement,* recommending specific guidelines for conducting initial reports, composing "mug books," interviewing witnesses, field identification procedures (showups), and lineups. The report was based on psychological research and spurred by the stunning revelations of wrongful convictions generated by forensic DNA testing.

The legal world decided to act earlier. By the 1960s, problems with eyewitness identification were sufficiently known to be a concern among criminal justice professionals and lawyers. Motivated by this problem, the Warren Court established novel constitutional rules to remedy identification process deficiencies in two constitutional areas: the Sixth Amendment right to counsel during a lineup and the due process right to a fair lineup or **showup** (under the Fifth and Fourteenth Amendments). The Court also considered whether lineup participants had rights under the Self-Incrimination Clause, but narrowly rejected this expansion of rights.

In truth, refined legal procedures, such as providing an attorney at lineups, are marginally helpful in reducing mistaken eyewitness identification. These procedures do not get at the heart of the problem—the psychology of perception—that mostly leads to the misidentification of defendants. On the other hand, given the lack of action on the part of the criminal justice system, the Supreme Court's involvement raised the visibility of this issue.

IDENTIFICATION AND THE RIGHT TO COUNSEL

The Supreme Court turned its attention to lineup identification in 1967, just four years after *Gideon v. Wainwright* and one year after *Miranda v. Arizona.* The tide of the Court's due process revolution was still riding high, and the lineup cases were a logical sequel. Yet these cases startled the legal community because the issue lacked precedents. Unlike search and seizure, confessions, and the right to appointed counsel, which had been the subject of litigation for decades and which rested on ancient legal principles, the lineup rules were created by imaginative lawyers who, imbued with the innovative spirit of the due process revolution, suggested ways of expanding the frontiers of the Bill of Rights. This annoyed conservative jurists. In 1965, four years prior to his elevation to chief justice of the Supreme Court, Warren Burger, then a judge on the U.S. Court of Appeals, said, "Such 'Disneyland' contentions as that absence of counsel at the police line-up voids a conviction are becoming commonplace."[19]

The Right to Counsel at Post-indictment Lineups

United States v. Wade (1967) and its companion case, *Gilbert v. California,* held that a post-indictment lineup is a *critical stage* requiring the presence of defense counsel. In addition, *Stovall v. Denno* (1967) applied due process fairness principles to lineups. *Stovall* also ruled that the lineup right to counsel was not to be applied retroactively to earlier cases in which lineups were conducted without counsel.

Read Case and Comments: *United States v. Wade.*

Did *Wade* require that a lawyer be present when police apprehend a suspect immediately after a crime, based on a victim's or witness's description, and show the stopped suspect to the victim or witness? This standard practice has the dual benefit of immediately exonerating innocent look-alikes and presenting an identification opportunity to a witness when recall is the strongest. To delay such a showup until a lawyer can be secured can multiply injustices for both the victim and the defendant.[20] Faced with the unpalatable possibility of extending the right to counsel rule to on-the-street situations, in 1969 the liberal U.S. Court of Appeals for the District of Columbia Circuit carved out an exception to the right to counsel for immediate postarrest showups.[21] The need for such an exception became unnecessary after the Supreme Court dealt with the timing of the right to counsel at lineups in *Kirby v. Illinois* (1972).

CASE AND COMMENTS

United States v. Wade

388 U.S. 218, 87 S.Ct. 1926, 18 L.Ed.2d 1149 (1967)

MR. JUSTICE BRENNAN delivered the opinion of the Court.

The question here is whether courtroom identifications of an accused at trial are to be excluded from evidence because the accused was exhibited to the witnesses before trial at a postindictment line-up conducted for identification purposes without notice to and in the absence of the accused's appointed counsel. **[a]**

[In September 1964, a bank was robbed by a man with a small strip of tape on each side of his face. He forced a teller and bank officer, at gunpoint, to fill a pillowcase with money. He escaped with an accomplice who was waiting in a stolen car. In March 1965, Wade and two others were indicted for conspiracy and bank robbery.] **[b]** Wade was arrested on April 2, and counsel was appointed to represent him on April 26. Fifteen days later an FBI agent, without notice to Wade's lawyer, arranged to have the two bank employees observe a lineup made up of Wade and five or six other prisoners and conducted in a courtroom of the local county courthouse. **[c]** Each person in the line wore strips of tape such as allegedly worn by the robber and upon direction each said something like "put the money in the bag," the words allegedly uttered by the robber. Both bank employees identified Wade in the lineup as the bank robber.

At trial, the two employees, when asked on direct examination if the robber was in the courtroom, pointed to Wade. The prior lineup identification was then elicited from both employees on cross-examination. **[d]** At the close of testimony, Wade's counsel moved for a judgment of acquittal or, alternatively, to strike the bank officials' courtroom identifications on the ground that conduct of the lineup, without notice to and in the absence of his appointed counsel, violated his Fifth Amendment privilege against self-incrimination and his Sixth Amendment right to the assistance of counsel. The motion was denied, and Wade was convicted. The Court of Appeals for the Fifth Circuit reversed the conviction and ordered a new trial at which the in-court identification evidence was to be excluded, holding that, though the lineup did not violate Wade's Fifth Amendment rights, "the lineup, held as it was, in the absence of counsel, already chosen to represent appellant, was a violation of his Sixth Amendment rights. . . ." **[e]** * * * We reverse the judgment of the Court of Appeals and remand to that court with direction to enter a new judgment vacating the conviction and remanding the case to the District Court for further proceedings consistent with this opinion.

I

[The Court ruled that no Fifth Amendment violation occurred by requiring Wade to participate in the lineup, by placing strips of tape on his face, or by having him repeat what was said at the robbery. Providing physical evidence of one's identity is not the kind of "testimonial evidence" protected by the privilege against self-incrimination.] **[f]**

II

[This part reviewed the Sixth Amendment right to counsel, deemed indispensable to protect the right to a fair trial. Dissenters said that lawyers had never participated in lineups and had no proper role to play at lineups. In Part II, Justice Brennan replied: "The Framers of the Bill of Rights envisaged a broader role for counsel than under the practice then prevailing in England of merely advising his client in 'matters of law,' and eschewing any responsibility for 'matters of fact.'" The Sixth Amendment requires counsel at any critical stage of the criminal proceedings, which can include a lineup if it brings potential substantial prejudice to defendants' rights.]

III

The Government characterizes the lineup as a mere preparatory step in the gathering of the prosecution's evidence, not different—for Sixth Amendment purposes—from various other preparatory steps, such as systematized or scientific analyzing of the accused's fingerprints, blood sample, clothing, hair, and the like. **[g]** We think there are differences which preclude such stages being characterized as critical stages at which the accused has the right to the presence of his counsel. Knowledge of the techniques of science and technology is sufficiently available, and the variables in techniques few enough, that the accused has the opportunity for a meaningful confrontation of the Government's case at trial through the ordinary processes of cross-examination of the Government's expert witnesses and the presentation of the evidence of his own experts. The denial of a right to have his counsel present at such analyses does

[a] This narrow statement of the issue is linked to the "remedy" in Part V of the opinion. There are other legal issues in the case.

[b] Wade's indictment prior to the lineup seems like a minor detail. It became an important factor in determining the scope of the right to counsel in later cases.

[c] Additional facts are found in Part IV. Case facts are sometimes scattered through an opinion, making them difficult to read.

[d] Note the *two* identifications—in the courtroom and at the lineup.

[e] The Court of Appeals, believing that the witnesses might not have identified Wade if they had not participated in the lineup, simply eliminated their in-court identification. Compare the Supreme Court's remedy in Part V.

[f] The issue in Part I is discussed later in this chapter.

[g] Taking and analyzing physical evidence is clear-cut, and errors can be ascertained by cross-examination; it is *not* a critical stage. To the contrary, suggestive identification at the lineup is not clear-cut and cannot be reconstructed by cross-examination.

not therefore violate the Sixth Amendment; they are not critical stages since there is minimal risk that his counsel's absence at such stages might derogate from his right to a fair trial.

IV

But the confrontation compelled by the State between the accused and the victim or witnesses to a crime to elicit identification evidence is peculiarly riddled with innumerable dangers and variable factors which might seriously, even crucially, derogate from a fair trial. **[h]** The vagaries of eyewitness identification are well-known; the annals of criminal law are rife with instances of mistaken identification. * * * A major factor contributing to the high incidence of miscarriage of justice from mistaken identification has been the degree of suggestion inherent in the manner in which the prosecution presents the suspect to witnesses for pretrial identification. A commentator has observed that "[t]he influence of improper suggestion upon identifying witnesses probably accounts for more miscarriages of justice than any other single factor—perhaps it is responsible for more such errors than all other factors combined." **[i]** * * * Suggestion can be created intentionally or unintentionally in many subtle ways. And the dangers for the suspect are particularly grave when the witness' opportunity for observation was insubstantial, and thus his susceptibility to suggestion the greatest.

Moreover, "[i]t is a matter of common experience that, once a witness has picked out the accused at the lineup, he is not likely to go back on his word later on, so that in practice the issue of identity may (in the absence of other relevant evidence) for all practical purposes be determined there and then, before the trial." **[j]**

The pretrial confrontation for purpose of identification may take the form of a lineup, also known as an "**identification parade**" or "showup," as in the present case, or presentation of the suspect alone to the witness. * * * It is obvious that risks of suggestion attend either form of confrontation and increase the dangers inhering in eyewitness identification. But as is the case with secret interrogations, there is serious difficulty in depicting what transpires at lineups and other forms of identification confrontations. * * * For the same reasons, the defense can seldom reconstruct the manner and mode of lineup identification for judge or jury at trial. **[k]** Those participating in a lineup with the accused may often be police officers; in any event, the participants' names are rarely recorded or divulged at trial. The impediments to an objective observation are increased when the victim is the witness. Lineups are prevalent in rape and robbery prosecutions and present a particular hazard that a victim's understandable outrage may excite vengeful or spiteful motives. * * * [T]he accused's inability effectively to reconstruct at trial any unfairness that occurred at the lineup may deprive him of his only opportunity meaningfully to attack the credibility of the witness' courtroom identification.

* * *

The potential for improper influence is illustrated by the circumstances, insofar as they appear, surrounding the prior identifications in the three cases we decide today. In the present case, the testimony of the identifying witnesses elicited on cross-examination revealed that those witnesses were taken to the courthouse and seated in the courtroom to await assembly of the lineup. **[l]** The courtroom faced on a hallway observable to the witnesses through an open door. The cashier testified that she saw Wade "standing in the hall" within sight of an FBI agent. Five or six other prisoners later appeared in the hall. The vice president testified that he saw a person in the hall in the custody of the agent who "resembled the person that we identified as the one that had entered the bank."

The lineup in *Gilbert* [a companion case], was conducted in an auditorium in which some 100 witnesses to several alleged state and federal robberies charged to Gilbert made wholesale identifications of Gilbert as the robber in each other's presence, a procedure said to be fraught with dangers of suggestion. **[m]** And the vice of suggestion created by the identification in *Stovall* was the presentation to the witness of the suspect alone handcuffed to police officers. It is hard to imagine a situation more clearly conveying the suggestion to the witness that the one presented is believed guilty by the police. * * *

The few cases that have surfaced therefore reveal the existence of a process attended with hazards of serious unfairness to the criminal accused. * * * We do not assume that these risks are the result of police procedures intentionally designed to prejudice an accused. Rather we assume they derive from the dangers inherent in eyewitness identification and the **suggestibility** inherent in the context of the pretrial identification. * * * **[n]** "[T]he fact that the police themselves have, in a given case, little or no doubt that the man put up for identification has committed the offense, and that their chief pre-occupation is with the problem of getting sufficient proof, because he has not 'come clean,' involves a danger that this persuasion may communicate itself even in a doubtful case to the witness in some way. . . ." * * *

* * * [E]ven though cross-examination is a precious safeguard to a fair trial, it cannot be viewed as an absolute assurance of accuracy and reliability. Thus in the present context, where so many variables and pitfalls exist, the first line of defense must be the prevention of unfairness and the lessening of the hazards of eyewitness identification at the lineup itself. The trial which might determine the accused's fate may well not be that in the courtroom but that at the pretrial confrontation, with the State

---

[h] Should the Court intervene if the problem of misidentification results only from human failings?

[i] "Suggestion" is not simply a human failing. It is something done by the police, thus providing the "state action" necessary for the Court to intervene.

[j] This is a virtual definition of a *critical stage;* the lineup determines the outcome of the trial.

[k] The inability to reconstruct lineup events suggests the role of a lawyer—to observe and report.

[l] This is a "showup" and is highly suggestive of guilt.

[m] The "contagion effect" in *Gilbert* is clear. *Stovall* is also a showup.

[n] Suggestibility is so well known in medical trials that "double-blind" procedures require the person dispensing the drug or placebo to not know which is which.

aligned against the accused, the witness the sole jury, and the accused unprotected against the overreaching, intentional or unintentional, and with little or no effective appeal from the judgment there rendered by the witness—"that's the man."

* * * [T]here can be little doubt that for Wade the postindictment lineup was a critical stage of the prosecution at which he was "as much entitled to such aid [of counsel] . . . as at the trial itself." * * * Thus both Wade and his counsel should have been notified of the impending lineup, and counsel's presence should have been a requisite to conduct of the lineup, absent an "intelligent waiver." **[o]** * * * No substantial countervailing policy considerations have been advanced against the requirement of the presence of counsel. Concern is expressed that the requirement will forestall prompt identifications and result in obstruction of the confrontations. As for the first, we note that in the two cases in which the right to counsel is today held to apply, counsel had already been appointed and no argument is made in either case that notice to counsel would have prejudicially delayed the confrontations. [Substitute counsel might also reduce delay.] And to refuse to recognize the right to counsel for fear that counsel will obstruct the course of justice is contrary to the basic assumptions upon which this Court has operated in Sixth Amendment cases. * * * In our view counsel can hardly impede legitimate law enforcement; on the contrary, for the reasons expressed, law enforcement may be assisted by preventing the infiltration of taint in the prosecution's identification evidence. That result cannot help the guilty avoid conviction but can only help assure that the right man has been brought to justice. **[p]**

Legislative or other regulations, such as those of local police departments, which eliminate the risks of abuse and unintentional suggestion at lineup proceedings and the impediments to meaningful confrontation at trial may also remove the basis for regarding the stage as "critical." But neither Congress nor the federal authorities have seen fit to provide a solution. What we hold today "in no way creates a constitutional straitjacket which will handicap sound efforts at reform, nor is it intended to have this effect." * * *

V

We come now to the question whether the denial of Wade's motion to strike the courtroom identification by the bank witnesses at trial because of the absence of his counsel at the lineup required, as the Court of Appeals held, the grant of a new trial at which such evidence is to be excluded. **[q]** We do not think this disposition can be justified without first giving the Government the opportunity to establish by clear and convincing evidence that the in-court identifications were based upon observations of the suspect other than the lineup identification. * * * Where, as here, the admissibility of evidence of the lineup identification itself is not involved, a *per se* rule of exclusion of courtroom identification would be unjustified. * * * A rule limited solely to the exclusion of testimony concerning identification at the lineup itself, without regard to admissibility of the courtroom identification, would render the right to counsel an empty one. **[r]** The lineup is most often used, as in the present case, to crystallize the witnesses' identification of the defendant for future reference. We have already noted that the lineup identification will have that effect. The State may then rest upon the witnesses' unequivocal courtroom identification, and not mention the pretrial identification as part of the State's case at trial. Counsel is then in the predicament in which Wade's counsel found himself—realizing that possible unfairness at the lineup may be the sole means of attack upon the unequivocal courtroom identification, and having to probe in the dark in an attempt to discover and reveal unfairness, while bolstering the government witness' courtroom identification by bringing out and dwelling upon his prior identification. Since counsel's presence at the lineup would equip him to attack not only the lineup identification but the courtroom identification as well, limiting the impact of violation of the right to counsel to exclusion of evidence only of identification at the lineup itself disregards a critical element of that right.

We think it follows that the proper test to be applied in these situations is that quoted in *Wong Sun v. United States* [1963], "'[W]hether, granting establishment of the primary illegality, the evidence to which instant objection is made has been come at by exploitation of that illegality or instead by means sufficiently distinguishable to be purged of the primary taint.' * * * " **[s]** Application of this test in the present context requires consideration of various factors; for example, the prior opportunity to observe the alleged criminal act, the existence of any discrepancy between any pre-lineup description and the defendant's actual description, any identification prior to lineup of another person, the identification by picture of the defendant prior to the lineup, failure to identify the defendant on a prior occasion, and the lapse of time between the alleged act and the lineup identification. **[t]** It is also relevant to consider those facts which, despite the absence of counsel, are disclosed concerning the conduct of the lineup.

We doubt that the Court of Appeals applied the proper test for exclusion of the in-court identification of the two witnesses. * * * [The judgment of the Court of Appeals was vacated and the case remanded for further proceedings.]

[o] The substantive rule of the case is stated here, as well as a reply to the dissenters.

[p] Justice Brennan was three decades ahead of his time. The prosecution is helped by defense counsel who prevent the conviction of innocent persons. Legislation is finally beginning to address lineups.

[q] This part concerns the remedy. How does the Supreme Court's remedy differ from that of the Court of Appeals?

[r] The courtroom identification is linked to whether the witness is recalling the defendant from the crime or from the lineup.

[s] What is the "primary illegality" in the lineup situation? What is the "exploitation of that illegality"?

[t] What are these factors designed to do?

[Chief Justice Warren and Justices Black, Douglas, and Fortas concurred but believed that compelling Wade to wear tape and speak at the lineup violated his Fifth Amendment privilege against self-incrimination. Justice Clark concurred in the majority opinion.]

MR. JUSTICE BLACK, dissenting in part and concurring in part.

[Justice Black agreed that a lineup is a critical stage at which counsel is required. However, he found fault with the Court's remedy (in Part V) on both practical and constitutional grounds. He would have allowed the witness to identify the defendant at the trial and voted to uphold the conviction.] **[u]**

In the first place, even if this Court has power to establish such a rule of evidence, I think the rule fashioned by the Court is unsound. The "tainted fruit" determination required by the Court involves more than considerable difficulty. I think it is practically impossible. How is a witness capable of probing the recesses of his mind to draw a sharp line between a courtroom identification due exclusively to an earlier lineup and a courtroom identification due to memory not based on the lineup? What kind of "clear and convincing evidence" can the prosecution offer to prove upon what particular events memories resulting in an in-court identification rest? How long will trials be delayed while judges turn psychologists to probe the subconscious minds of witnesses? All these questions are posed but not answered by the Court's opinion. * * *

MR. JUSTICE WHITE, whom MR. JUSTICE HARLAN and MR. JUSTICE STEWART join, dissenting in part and concurring in part.

* * *

I share the Court's view that the criminal trial, at the very least, should aim at truthful factfinding, including accurate eyewitness identifications. I doubt, however, on the basis of our present information, that the tragic mistakes which have occurred in criminal trials are as much the product of improper police conduct as they are the consequence of the difficulties inherent in eyewitness testimony and in resolving evidentiary conflicts by court or jury. **[v** I doubt that the Court's new rule will obviate these difficulties, or that the situation will be measurably improved by inserting defense counsel into the investigative processes of police departments everywhere.

But, it may be asked, what possible state interest militates against requiring the presence of defense counsel at lineups? After all, the argument goes, he *may* do some good, he *may* upgrade the quality of identification evidence in state courts and he can scarcely do any harm. Even if true, this is a feeble foundation for fastening an ironclad constitutional rule upon state criminal procedures. Absent some reliably established constitutional violation, the processes by which the States enforce their criminal laws are their own prerogative. * * *

* * *

When Does the Right to Counsel at Lineups Attach?

The lineup in *Wade* occurred *after* Wade had been indicted. The issue in ***Kirby v. Illinois*** (1972) was whether the right to counsel applied to a lineup that was conducted *before* a suspect was indicted. The facts of *Kirby* were simple. Willie Shard, a robbery victim, was asked to identify two suspects who were detained in a police station the day after the incident. Shard immediately identified suspects Thomas Kirby and Ralph Bean, who had been found with Shard's traveler's checks and Social Security card. No lawyer was present during the identification. The suspects did not ask for a lawyer, nor were they advised of any right to the presence of counsel. They were indicted for the robbery six weeks later. At trial, Shard identified Kirby and Bean and testified to his police station identifications. The Illinois Supreme Court upheld the legality of this identification process. Kirby argued that the benefits of counsel to dispel or record suggestive action by police officers are equally important in a *pre-indictment* lineup as in a *post-indictment* lineup. The Supreme Court upheld Kirby's conviction.

Justice Potter Stewart, who dissented in *Wade,* wrote the *plurality* opinion in *Kirby*. The *Wade–Gilbert* right to counsel was based on the Sixth Amendment, not the Fifth Amendment privilege against self-incrimination, and all previous Sixth Amendment cases held that the right to counsel "attaches at the time of arraignment" or the "initiation of judicial criminal proceedings." The right to counsel in *Miranda,* by contrast, was based on vindicating the privilege against self-incrimination. Therefore, reasoned the plurality justices, the Sixth Amendment right to counsel does not apply to pre-indictment lineups but only to lineups and showups "at or after the time that adversary judicial proceedings have been initiated against him."

To justify the decision, Justice Stewart noted that

[t]he initiation of judicial criminal proceedings is far from a mere formalism. It is the starting point of our whole system of adversary criminal justice. For it is only then

---

[u] Justice Black also attacked the majority for exercising what he believed was unconstitutional power under the Due Process Clause to make new law.

[v] Justice White argues, in contrast to Justice Brennan, that the problem is not suggestibility but the fallibility of human memory. Thus there is no "state action" and no basis for the jurisdiction of federal courts. This argument displays a belief in federalism.

that the government has committed itself to prosecute, and only then that the adverse positions of government and defendant have solidified. It is then that a defendant finds himself faced with the prosecutorial forces of organized society, and immersed in the intricacies of substantive and procedural criminal law. (*Kirby v. Illinois,* 1972)

If any abuses were alleged to occur during a pre-indictment lineup or showup, the defendant could seek a remedy under the due process rule announced in *Stovall v. Denno* (1967), which is discussed later in this chapter.

Justice Brennan's dissent in *Kirby* (joined by Justices Douglas and Marshall), like his majority opinion in *Wade,* argued that the right to counsel is designed to ensure a fair trial. Having a lawyer present at a police station showup is necessary to prevent the suggestibility that influences a witness and thus is crucial to a fair trial. The essence of the *Wade–Gilbert* rule is that an attorney be present at a *pretrial* identification confrontation, for the unfairness of suggestibility can equally infect a pre-indictment or a post-indictment showup or lineup. In this regard, "an abstract consideration of the words 'criminal prosecutions' in the Sixth Amendment" should not limit the extension of the right to counsel at all station house identification procedures. Justice Brennan virtually accused the majority of willfully misconstruing the real meaning of the *Wade* and *Gilbert* cases by inflating the importance of the fortuitous circumstance that the lineups in those cases occurred after indictments. Indeed, "every United States Court of Appeals that has confronted the question has applied *Wade* and *Gilbert* to preindictment confrontations," as did the appellate courts of thirteen states. Against this, only five states at that time ruled, as did Illinois, that the *Wade* rule applied only to postindictment lineups.

Kirby is an example of the judicial politics of the Supreme Court. There is little doubt that had the Warren Court that decided *Wade* also decided *Kirby,* the right to counsel would have been extended to pre-indictment as well as post-indictment lineups. But by 1972 the Court included four justices appointed by President Nixon who had run on reversing "liberal" criminal procedure cases like *Miranda* and *Mapp.* Although Supreme Court justices have "ideological" leanings, they do not simply vote according to the ideological valence of a particular rule. They are also guided by their judicial philosophies and by institutional concerns about the Court's stature. Thus, for example, Justice Byron White, who had dissented in *Wade,* now wrote a dissent without joining Justice Brennan's *Kirby* dissent. He expressed the philosophy of "judicial conservatism," namely precedent or *stare decisis,* by noting that *Wade* and *Gilbert* "govern this case and compel reversal of the judgment below." That is, having "lost" in *Wade,* he felt duty bound to support the law that had been established only five years before. Justice Powell, more pointedly, was concerned that it was one thing to inject an inconsistent wrinkle in the law (by requiring lawyers at lineups depending on whether formal charges had been filed), but another to overrule a recently established precedent. Such a true "counter-revolution" would have exposed the Court as a nakedly political institution. His one-sentence concurrence, "As I would not extend the *Wade-Gilbert per se* exclusionary rule, I concur in the result reached by the Court"—made it clear that he prevented Justice Stewart's plurality opinion from becoming a majority that would have lead to *Wade*'s overruling.

Kirby revealed Burger Court discontent with the *Wade* rule by limiting it. But having established a complex rule by *distinguishing Wade,* based on its different facts, the Court stood by the *Wade* rule. In **Moore v. Illinois** (1977), a rape victim gave police a description of her attacker. She examined two sets of photographs in the week following the crime and whittled possible suspects down to two or three from two hundred photographs. One was Moore. He was arrested and presented at a *preliminary examination* the next day to determine whether he should be formally charged by the grand jury. Police officers accompanied the victim to the preliminary examination, during which she was to view Moore and to "identify him if she could." She positively identified him, and the detectives had her sign a complaint naming Moore as her assailant. Moore, unrepresented by a lawyer at this point, was bound over.

Moore challenged the introduction of the identification, arguing that the preliminary hearing "marked the initiation of adversary judicial criminal proceedings against him. Hence, under *Wade, Gilbert,* and *Kirby,* he was entitled to the presence of counsel at that confrontation." The Supreme Court agreed with Moore. *Kirby* applied the *Wade* counsel rule not only after indictment but "at or after the initiation of adversary judicial criminal proceedings," including proceedings instituted "by way of formal charge [or] preliminary hearing." Thus not only did the showup in the *Moore* case fall within the *Kirby* rule, it was obviously a *critical stage*: Moore faced a state prosecutor at the hearing; it was a hearing at which the charges could have been dismissed; the state had to produce evidence against the defendant at that point or drop the case; and, of course, the defendant was identified at that proceeding.

The Supreme Court, incidentally, made it absolutely clear that the *Wade–Gilbert–Kirby* rules apply to a *showup* of one suspect as well as to a *lineup* of several look-alikes:

> Although *Wade* and *Gilbert* both involved lineups, *Wade* clearly contemplated that counsel would be required in both situations. * * * Indeed, a one-on-one confrontation generally is thought to present greater risks of mistaken identification than a lineup.... There is no reason, then, to hold that a one-on-one identification procedure is not subject to the same requirements as a lineup. (*Moore v. Illinois*, 1977)

Finally, the prosecution argued that the victim's identification testimony should be automatically introduced at trial because there was an "independent source" for it. That is, the victim said that she thought she had seen Moore at a neighborhood bar. The Supreme Court rejected this argument. It ruled that the prosecution cannot violate the *Wade–Gilbert* rules and then simply allow the defendant to be identified in the "case in chief" based on the theory that the identification was based on the crime or other encounter. The case was remanded to determine whether the victim's memory was based on the incident or the showup. Justice Rehnquist grudgingly concurred, noting that he would prefer that *Wade–Gilbert*'s *per se* exclusionary rule of the lineup/showup identification be replaced with a "totality of the circumstances" approach. In conclusion, although the Supreme Court erected a somewhat artificial distinction in *Kirby*, it maintained the doctrinal integrity of the *Kirby* rule in *Moore v. Illinois*.

Does the Right to Counsel Apply to Photographic Identification?

A year after *Kirby,* the Supreme Court decided that an attorney was *not* required to be present at a post-indictment "photographic lineup." Victims and witnesses are sometimes shown single photos of a suspect, in a photographic counterpart of a showup. Photo lineups can be in the form of an array of six photos of similar-looking individuals (a "sixpack") or a stack of head shots, or photos gathered in "mug books."

In *United States v. Ash* (1973), the Supreme Court rejected the *Wade–Kirby* Sixth Amendment approach to photographic identification and held that under the Sixth Amendment, a lawyer is never required when photographs that include the suspect's likeness are shown to a witness. Instead, the admissibility of photographs depends on whether their display violated due process fairness.

An informant told FBI agents that Charles J. Ash, Jr. had been involved in a bank robbery. Prior to pressing formal charges, the agents "showed five black-and-white mug shots of Negro males of generally the same age, height, and weight, one of which was of Ash, to four witnesses. All four made uncertain identifications of Ash's picture." Prior to trial, after Ash had been formally charged, the prosecutor "decided to use a photographic display to determine whether the witnesses he planned to call would be able to make in-court identifications. Shortly before the trial, an FBI agent and the prosecutor showed five color photographs to the four witnesses who previously had tentatively identified the black-and-white photograph of Ash. Three of the witnesses selected the picture of Ash, but one was unable to make any selection." Ash claimed that this process violated his right to counsel at a critical stage of the prosecution. The trial judge denied this claim. At trial, the three witnesses who had been inside the bank identified Ash as the gunman, but they were unwilling to state that they were certain of their identifications. The trial judge ruled that all five color photographs would be admitted into evidence. The jury convicted Ash. The Court of Appeals applied the *Wade–Gilbert* rule and held that Ash's right to counsel was violated when his attorney was not given the opportunity to be present at the *post-indictment* pretrial photographic displays.

The Supreme Court (6–3) reversed. Several reasons for the decision can be discerned in Justice Blackmun's lengthy and murky majority opinion. One reason is that the suspect is not physically present at a photo lineup, and therefore "no possibility arises that the accused might be misled by his lack of familiarity with the law or overpowered by his professional adversary" (*United States v. Ash,* 1973). Because a suspect is not subjected to testimonial questioning at a lineup, this point refers to a scenario in which police have the suspect say more or do more at a live lineup that makes him stand out to the witnesses. This, however, falls logically under the category of suggestibility that can also affect a photo identification, if, for example, an officer pauses at greater length at the suspect's photo.

Related to this reason is the point that "the counsel guarantee would not be used to produce equality in a trial-like adversary confrontation" where "the function of the lawyer has remained essentially the same as his function at trial" (*United States v. Ash,* 1973). This means that the Supreme Court is reluctant to extend the right to counsel to settings that do not have some of the attributes of a trial where the lawyer's forensic skill is used: questioning witnesses, cross-examining, and projecting and analyzing legal arguments. The Court, however, had indeed extended the right to counsel in non-trial-like settings for post-indictment lineups (*Wade*) but illogically drew the line at pre-indictment lineups (*Kirby*). The Court clearly desired not to further expand the right to counsel beyond arraignments, pretrial examinations, and the like, where counsel acts "as a spokesman for, or advisor to, the accused" (*United States v. Ash,* 1973).

Another point was that although the use of photography in criminal investigation was relatively new, witnesses had been questioned by magistrates and police for hundreds of years without the presence of defense counsel. The Court may have been concerned that a ruling in Ash's favor could lead to bringing police interrogation under the Sixth Amendment, however remote the possibility.

The Court's weakest argument was that photo identification is *less suggestive* than live lineups and can be more easily cured by cross-examination at trial. This point was made by Justice Stewart, concurring, as well as by Justice Blackmun:

> A photographic identification is quite different from a lineup, for there are substantially fewer possibilities of impermissible suggestion when photographs are used, and those unfair influences can be readily reconstructed at trial. It is true that the defendant's photograph may be markedly different from the others displayed, but this unfairness can be demonstrated at trial from an actual comparison of the photographs used or from the witness' description of the display. Similarly, it is possible that the photographs could be arranged in a suggestive manner, or that by comment or gesture the prosecuting authorities might single out the defendant's picture. But these are the kinds of overt influence that a witness can easily recount and that would serve to impeach the identification testimony. In short, there are few possibilities for unfair suggestiveness—and those rather blatant and easily reconstructed. Accordingly, an accused would not be foreclosed from an effective cross-examination of an identification witness simply because his counsel was not present at the photographic display. For this reason, a photographic display cannot fairly be considered a "critical stage" of the prosecution. (*United States v. Ash,* 1973, Stewart, J., concurring)

It seems, however, that Justice Brennan, dissenting with Justices Douglas and Marshall, had the better argument on this point. In a photo identification, "as in the lineup situation, the possibilities for impermissible suggestion in the context of a photographic display are manifold" (*United States v. Ash,* 1973). Indeed, Justice Stewart suggested some of the ways in which a police officer, even inadvertently, could suggest that a certain photo is that of the suspect. Without an attorney present to observe the showing, how would it be possible for the defense lawyer to form cross-examination questions that are on the mark? As a matter of logic and experience, Justice Stewart's views on the ability of cross-examination to detect suggestibility are not very convincing except in the most outrageous examples. He limits his examples only to overt suggestibility and says nothing about other factors discussed by Justice Brennan, including "the manner in which the photographs are displayed to the witness" by, for example, emphasizing the suspect's photograph by leaving it out longer, arraying it in a way to point it out, and so forth, and by "gestures or comments of the prosecutor at the time of the display [that] may lead an otherwise uncertain witness to select the 'correct' photograph." In this regard, Justice Brennan touched on the powerful psychological effect that is conveyed even by unintentional cues: "More subtly, the prosecutor's inflection, facial expressions, physical motions, and myriad other almost imperceptible means of communication might tend, intentionally or unintentionally, to compromise the witness' objectivity" (*United States v. Ash,* 1973, Brennan, J., dissenting). In these situations, reconstruction of the suggestion is next to impossible.

Justice Brennan's conclusion was that the Court's logic was "a triumph of form over substance" (*Ash*) because in past instances where the Court found that a critical stage existed, requiring the presence of counsel, the essential point was that the stage of the criminal process was one in which unfairness would undermine the fairness of the trial itself. Since, in the view of the dissenters, the uncorrectable suggestibility of the photographic identification would taint the trial, it was a critical stage.

United States v. Ash (1973), like *Kirby v. Illinois* (1972), is a clear example of the conservative Burger Court's limiting expansive Warren Court rulings, not by overruling them but by trimming them back or preventing further expansion. The Court now emphasized the Crime Control Model over the Due Process Model of constitutional analysis as explained by Professor Herbert Packer.[22] (See Chapter 1.) The majority was concerned with creating rules that might interfere with the work of police and prosecutors as the "war on crime" became a seemingly permanent feature of American political and social life. The dissenters displayed greater concern with the overall fairness of the process and were willing to make the investigation process less efficient for the purpose of reducing the possibility of wrongful convictions. Indeed, as later research and analysis indicated, numerous miscarriages of justice resulted from improper photo identification.[23]

IDENTIFICATION AND THE FIFTH AMENDMENT

United States v. Wade (1967) held that "[n]either the lineup itself nor anything . . . that Wade was required to do in the lineup violated his privilege against self-incrimination." This holding can be divided into two rules. The first, unanimously supported by the Court, is that the simple display of a person at trial or at a lineup so that he or she can be identified as a suspect does not violate the Fifth Amendment privilege against self-incrimination. The Fifth Amendment prohibits only the compulsion of **testimonial evidence**:

> We have no doubt that compelling the accused merely to exhibit his person for observation by a prosecution witness prior to trial involves no compulsion of the accused to give evidence having testimonial significance. It is compulsion of the accused to exhibit his physical characteristics, not compulsion to disclose any knowledge he might have. (*United States v. Wade*, 1967)

Wade raised another argument that was accepted by four dissenting justices: Justice Hugo Black in a separate dissent, and Justice Abe Fortas in a dissent joined by Chief Justice Warren and Justice Douglas. Wade, along with other lineup participants, was required to wear strips of tape on each side of his face, as the robber had, and to speak words that the robber had spoken. *Wade*'s second self-incrimination is that this kind of compelled behavior, which goes beyond the simple display of a suspect's face, also does not violate the privilege.

Justice Brennan's dissent relied on the precedent of **Schmerber v. California** (1966). Blood was drawn from Schmerber by medical personnel after he was arrested at the scene of a car crash for a drunk driving. The Supreme Court held that the self-incrimination principle was to protect individuals from divulging information "of a communicative nature." This means that the Fifth Amendment privilege prohibits the state from forcing a person to admit guilt by spoken words, actions that convey meaning, or writings that convey a sense of guilt. The state, in enforcing the law, however, may have access to any physical evidence, including the *sound* of a voice, that is probative and that may be obtained without violating due process or Fourth Amendment protections.

The *Schmerber* principle has allowed the use of different kinds of physical evidence, including blood samples; handwriting exemplars;[24] voice exemplars;[25] body evidence such as fingerprints, photographs, hair samples, and cell scrapings from which DNA tracers can be identified; and one's name.[26]

The dissenters thought that what Wade was required to do "is more than passive, mute assistance to the eyes of the victim or of witnesses. It is the kind of volitional act—the kind of forced cooperation by the accused—which is within the historical perimeter of the privilege against compelled self-incrimination." Nevertheless, as Justice Brennan pointed out for the majority, the precedent of *Holt v. United States* (1910), authored by Justice Oliver Wendell Holmes Jr., upheld the right of the state to require a suspect at a lineup to wear an article of clothing that was worn at the crime.

DUE PROCESS AND EYEWITNESS IDENTIFICATION

Stovall v. Denno (1967) ruled that *suggestive* lineups or showups are controlled by the Fifth or Fourteenth Amendment's Due Process Clause. Unnecessarily suggestive pretrial identification procedures are fundamentally unfair. Fairness is a flexible test that requires a court to examine the totality of the circumstances. A due process rule, therefore, is more a general standard than a clear-cut or bright-line rule. As a result, in due process litigation, the Court frequently is faced with finely differentiated fact situations that require careful examination.

Stovall v. Denno (1967) demonstrates that under some circumstances, even suggestive showups are admissible; the necessities of law enforcement may override the purity of the identification process. A physician, Dr. Behrendt, was stabbed to death in the kitchen of his home at midnight on August 23. His wife, also a physician, entered the kitchen and jumped at the assailant. He knocked her to the floor and stabbed her eleven times. Physical clues led the police to Stovall, and he was arrested on the afternoon of August 24. The wife was hospitalized for major surgery to save her life that same day.

> The police, without affording [Stovall] time to retain counsel, arranged with her surgeon to permit them to bring petitioner to her hospital room about noon of August 25, the day after the surgery. Petitioner was handcuffed to one of five police officers who, with two members of the staff of the District Attorney, brought him to the hospital room. [Stovall] was the only Negro in the room. Mrs. Behrendt identified him from her hospital bed after being asked by an officer whether he "was the man" and after petitioner repeated at the direction of an officer a "few words for voice identification." None of the witnesses could recall the words that were used. Mrs. Behrendt and the officers testified at the trial to her identification of the petitioner in the hospital room, and she also made an in-court identification of petitioner in the courtroom. (*Stovall v. Denno,* 1967)

A federal appellate court, on a habeas corpus petition, reversed the state conviction on the ground that the eyewitness identification violated Stovall's right to counsel. The Supreme Court, in a majority opinion by Justice Brennan, reversed this part of the holding and decided in *Stovall* that the *Wade–Gilbert* rule did not apply retroactively, concerned "that retroactive application of *Wade* and *Gilbert* 'would seriously disrupt the administration of our criminal laws.'" As the lack of counsel at the showup was not an issue, the remaining question was whether a new trial should be ordered with evidence of the showup excluded because the identification procedure "was so unnecessarily suggestive and conducive to irreparable mistaken identification that he was denied due process of law" (*Stovall v. Denno,* 1967).

Justice Brennan, noting that the "practice of showing suspects singly to persons for the purpose of identification, and not as part of a lineup, has been widely condemned," nevertheless ruled against Stovall and allowed the introduction of the identification made in the hospital room.

> Here was the only person in the world who could possibly exonerate Stovall. Her words, and only her words, "He is not the man" could have resulted in freedom for Stovall. The hospital was not far distant from the courthouse and jail. No one knew how long Mrs. Behrendt might live. Faced with the responsibility of identifying the attacker, with the need for immediate action and with the knowledge that Mrs. Behrendt could not visit the jail, the police followed the only feasible procedure and took Stovall to the hospital room. Under these circumstances, the usual police station lineup, which Stovall now argues he should have had, was out of the question. (*Stovall v. Denno,* quoting the Court of Appeals decision)

Although the showup in *Stovall* was surely suggestive, under the circumstances—which included the reasonable possibility that the only eyewitness to the serious crime might soon die, the impossibility to construct a lineup, and the fact that the suspect was not chosen at random but was tied to the crime scene by physical evidence—the choice was between a suggestive identification procedure or none at all. These circumstances resulted in the conclusion that the showup in this case was not fundamentally unfair.

Foster v. California (1969) was a clear example of a lineup that violated due process fairness standards. Foster, a thin, six-foot-tall robbery suspect, wearing a leather jacket similar to the robber's, was placed in a lineup with two other men who were approximately five-foot-five and were not wearing leather jackets. Despite these discrepancies, the witness could not identify Foster, so he was brought into a room with the witness and made to speak. "Even after this one-to-one confrontation [the witness] still was uncertain whether petitioner was one of the robbers: 'Truthfully—I was not sure,' he testified at trial." In a second lineup a week later, Foster was the only individual from the first lineup. At this point, the witness was convinced. Justice Fortas's opinion, finding that due process was violated, relied on the element of reliability: "The suggestive elements in this identification procedure made it all but inevitable that [the witness] would identify [Foster] whether or not he was in fact 'the man.' In effect, the police repeatedly said to the witness, 'This is the man.'… This procedure so undermined the reliability of the eyewitness identification as to violate due process" (*Foster v. California,* 1969).

The Supreme Court refused to hold that the showing of a suspect's photograph to crime victims during the investigation of a crime, while the suspect was still at large, violated due process (***Simmons v. United States***, 1968). Although such a procedure is necessarily suggestive, "this procedure has been used widely and effectively in criminal law enforcement, from the standpoint both of apprehending offenders and of sparing innocent suspects the ignominy of arrest by allowing eyewitnesses to exonerate them through scrutiny of photographs" (*Simmons v. United States*, 1968). Any risk of misidentification can be corrected at trial through cross-examination.

The Supreme Court has substantially reduced the protection offered by the due process test in the last two due process cases decided by the Supreme Court. These cases no longer allow the use of showups only when there is a real exigency, as in *Stovall v. Denno,* and have established the rule that identification resulting from a suggestive showup may be allowed into evidence if the suggestibility is offset by strong indicia of reliability.

In ***Neil v. Biggers*** (1972) a rape victim who had directly viewed her assailant from fifteen minutes to a half hour indoors and under a full moon outdoors, and gave a detailed description, identified Biggers at a show up. The show up was conducted because police could not locate individuals at the city jail or juvenile home fitting Biggers's unusual physical description. The victim, a practical nurse by profession, had viewed many suspects prior to the show up and at each said the suspect was not the rapist. She testified that she had "no doubt" that Biggers was her assailant.

The Supreme Court, disagreeing with lower courts, held that the confrontation was *not* so suggestive as to violate due process. The primary concern in identification cases is to avoid "a very substantial likelihood of irreparable misidentification." Simply stated, it is critical that the identification in issue show a strong liklihood that the actual perpetrator was selected by the witness. The *Stovall* precedent showed that "the admission of evidence of a showup without more does not violate due process." In this case it was true that the show up was suggestive. The identification, nevertheless, was deemed reliable because several factors of reliability were present: the victim had a good *opportunity to view* the criminal at the time of the crime, her *degree of attention* was high, her *prior description* of the criminal was good, her *level of certainty* at the showup was high. One factor that cut against reliability was that the *length of time between the crime and the confrontation*, seven months, was long. The Court concluded that "On balance, the identification did not violate Biggers's right to due process in an identification."

The *Biggers* factors were confirmed in the lead case on due process in identification procedures, ***Manson v. Brathwaite*** (1977). The facts in *Manson* were that Glover, a narcotics undercover police officer, and Brown, an informant, went to a suspected apartment building in Hartford, Connecticut, during daylight, to make a controlled narcotics buy. Glover and Brown were observed by backup officers D'Onofrio and Gaffey. Glover and Brown knocked on a third-floor door in an area illuminated by natural light from a window in the hallway. A man opened the door; Brown asked for "two things" of narcotics; Glover handed over a $10 bill and observed the man in the apartment; the door closed; a moment later, the man opened the door and handed Glover two glassine bags of heroin; Glover was within two feet of the seller and observed his face.

At headquarters, Glover, who is African American, described the seller to D'Onofrio as "a colored man, approximately five feet eleven inches tall, dark complexion, black hair, short Afro style, and having high cheekbones, and of heavy build. He was wearing at the time blue pants and a plaid shirt." D'Onofrio thought that Brathwaite might be the seller and left a photograph of him at Glover's office. Two days later, Glover viewed the photograph for the first time and identified Brathwaite as the seller. At the trial, eight months after the sale, the identification photograph was received in evidence without defense objection. Glover said he had no doubt that the person in the photograph was the seller, and he made an in-court identification. No explanation was offered by the prosecution for the failure to utilize a photographic array or to conduct a line-up. State courts upheld the conviction finding that no "substantial injustice resulted from the admission of this evidence." On a habeas corpus petition, the federal Court of Appeals ruled that the photograph should have been excluded, regardless of reliability, because the examination of the single photograph was unnecessary, suggestive, and possibly unreliable. The Supreme Court reversed.

In this case, Glover's viewing of a single photograph left for him *was* suggestive and *unnecessary*, since D'Onofrio could have prepared a photographic array. The precedent of *Biggers,* however, was that a suggestive and unnecessary showup was not *per se* excluded. (The showup in *Stovall* was *necessary* because of Mrs. Behrendt's condition). The Court recognized that a *per se* exclusionary rule would tend to make identification more reliable, lessen the opportunity of mistaken identification, and more likely deter improper police procedures. A more flexible "totality of the circumstances" approach, while possibly allowing more instances of injustice, was instead upheld. The totality rule adopted also guarded against impropriety, since a suggestive showup or lineup might be excluded, but did not go as far as the *per se* rule to protect innocent suspects. The trade-off was that under a *per se* approach, a guilty party was more likely to go free. On balance, the Court continued to uphold the due process "totality of circumstances" approach in evaluating the admissibility of suggestive identification procedures, again indicating a preference for the Crime Control Model over the Due Process Model of criminal justice.

The Court then analyzed each of the *Biggers* factors and found that the "indicators of Glover's ability to make an accurate identification are hardly outweighed by the corrupting effect of the challenged identification itself."

1. *The opportunity to view.* The facts indicated that Glover had natural lighting and two to three minutes to observe Brathwaite from two feet away.
2. *The degree of attention.* Glover was a trained on-duty police officer specializing in narcotics enforcement, was an African American, and could be expected "to pay scrupulous attention to detail, for he knew that subsequently he would have to find and arrest his vendor" and testify about this in court.
3. *The accuracy of the description.* Glover's description was given to D'Onofrio within minutes after the transaction and included the seller's race, height, and build, the color and style of his hair, and the high-cheekbone facial feature. It also included a description of the clothing the seller wore. D'Onofrio reacted positively, and two days later, when Glover was alone, he viewed the photograph and identified its subject as the narcotics seller.
4. *The witness's level of certainty.* Glover, when questioned about whether the photograph was that of the seller, testified: "There is no question whatsoever." As will be discussed in the Law in Society section, psychological studies show little or no correlation between certainty and accuracy. This is one factor where "common sense" is probably wrong.
5. *The time between the crime and the confrontation-identification was very short.* The Court concluded that "we cannot say that under all the circumstances of this case there is 'a very substantial likelihood of irreparable misidentification.'"

LAW IN SOCIETY

Reducing the Error of Eyewitness Identification

The obligation that police, prosecutors, judges, and juries have to detect, prosecute, and convict the guilty carries an obligation not to convict the innocent. Studies persistently show that eyewitnesses are frequently mistaken in their identifications of suspects and that half of the wrongfully convicted are victims of mistaken eyewitness identification.[27] The criminal justice system has perennially accepted wrongful convictions based on misidentification as the inevitable failing of a human system. Lawyers believed, with some justification, that properly conducted criminal trials keep mistaken identification to a minimum. An experienced defense attorney with sufficient time and resources to investigate a case prior to trial and skillful in cross-examining witnesses was sufficient to ferret out the truth. This faith might have been justified up to the beginning of the twentieth century. The growing findings of modern scientific psychological research, however, demonstrate the variability of human memory, and legal scholars have become more aware that an alarming number of completely innocent people are wrongfully convicted.[28]

By the 1960s, this knowledge led the Warren Court to augment the legal protections of the common law jury trial with constitutional rules meant to prevent wrongful conviction. This effort had limited success as the more conservative Burger Court restricted the right to counsel at identification procedures (*Kirby v. Illinois,* 1972; *United States v. Ash,* 1973; *Manson v. Brathwaite,* 1977). Of greater significance, the right to counsel during identification procedures and due process rules concerning suggestiveness are crude tools to prevent and correct misidentification.

Since the 1960s, several factors have laid a foundation for a major breakthrough in the problem of wrongful conviction. First, extensive research by psychologists has led to better explanations of human identification and misidentification, establishing a scientific foundation for improvements. They have also designed studies to find out which kinds of questioning and identification procedures are more likely to provide accurate identification. This research has been disseminated to the legal community, making it more aware of its shortcomings, although prosecutors believe in the accuracy of eyewitnesses far more than do defense lawyers.[29] At the same time, celebrated cases of wrongful conviction, such as those of Rubin "Hurricane" Carter, Dr. Sam Sheppard, and Randall Adams, and the dramatic moratorium on executions by Illinois governor George Ryan after half of those on death row were exonerated, have sensitized the wider public to the fact that misidentification is a persistent problem.

The factor that has had the greatest impact since 1990 has been DNA testing. It has revealed that the worst fears of critics have been justified: An unacceptably high proportion of people who are charged with crimes and convicted are innocent. The DNA breakthrough is not a prescription for complacency. The authors of *Actual Innocence,* who run the Innocence Project at Cardozo Law School, write:

> Most of the lessons of the DNA era have nothing to do with high-tech gizmos or biotechnical wizardry. "Jurors should get innocence training," says Kevin Green [a wrongly convicted man]. They need to be told: "'You're doing this because we have to find the truth. The police haven't necessarily found the truth. The district attorney hasn't found the truth. Only you can.'"[30]

The authors note that England established "an official Criminal Cases Review Commission that investigates claims of innocence,"[31] and North Carolina has established an Innocence Inquiry Commission to review and re-adjudicate claims of actual innocence.[32] Barry Scheck and Peter Neufeld, attorneys who have done as much as anyone to force authorities to allow inmates with credible claims to have DNA tests, warn that these tests are not a panacea for correcting wrongful convictions:

> In a few years, the era of DNA exonerations will come to an end. The population of prisoners who can be helped by DNA testing is shrinking, because the technology has been used widely since the early 1990s, clearing thousands of innocent suspects before trial. Yet blameless people will remain in prison, stranded because their cases don't involve biological evidence. . . .
>
> From Borchard's review of cases stretching back to the dawn of the American republic, all the way to the dawn of the twenty-first century, the causes of wrongful conviction remain the same. Clarity is manufactured about moments of inherent confusion. Witnesses swear they can identify the man who held the gun or knife. Police officers then coax or force confessions from suspects they believe guilty. Prosecutors bury exculpatory evidence and defense lawyers sleep on the job.[33]

Steps can and should be taken to improve the accuracy of identification throughout the investigation and trial process. Before a sound program of accurate identification can be put in place, a foundation of scientific knowledge about the nature of memory and recall is required.

Understanding Memory and Recall

Research has generated a better understanding of human perception, memory, and recall than "common sense," even if an integrated theory of perception has not been fully developed.[34] This information helps us better understand eyewitness testimony.

An important starting point is the wide agreement in perception research that eyewitness testimony is often unreliable. This contradicts the beliefs of many people and the experience of jurors:[35] Under experimental conditions, such as a staged crime before a class, "witnesses have been proven to be remarkably inaccurate."[36] An experiment by Robert Buckhout had a New York television news program run a staged robbery for twelve seconds. A six-man lineup was then shown, and viewers were invited to call in to pick out the perpetrator. Over two thousand viewers called in, and only 14.1 percent picked the correct man, a result that was no better than a random guess.[37] Because psychological experiments can modify the elements of perception and recall, the percentage of accurate recall in various experiments has varied from no better than chance to 90 percent.[38]

A field experiment by John Brigham and colleagues assessed the accuracy of facial recall in a real-life setting.[39] Two men, one white and one African American, entered seventy-three convenience food stores within five minutes of one another, posing as customers. One paid for a pack of cigarettes entirely with pennies and asked for directions. The other asked for directions after fumbling around for change. Two hours later, two men pretending to be law interns asked the clerk to identify each "customer" from two photo arrays, one of six whites and one of six African Americans. The overall rate of accurate identifications was 34.2 percent, which increased to 46.8 percent when instances of "no identification" were omitted. This is significantly higher than the 16.7 percent rate (one out of six) that would be expected by random guessing, but it also confirms a large number of incorrect identifications. The correct recall of convenience store clerks fell to chance when the "law interns" presented the photo arrays more than twenty-four hours after the "customers" left the store.

This study also found, in accord with other research, that identification accuracy of a person of one's own race is higher and that the ability of white clerks to identify the African-American "customer" was significantly related to each clerk's amount of cross-racial experience. The African-American clerks in this study had higher accuracy rates than the white clerks: They were 13 percent more accurate in identifying the white "customer" and 23 percent more accurate in identifying the African-American "customer." As expected, recognition was higher for the "customers" who were more attractive or distinctive and from lineups using larger pictures.

Elizabeth Loftus's summary of research findings notes that the memory process is selective. Humans do not simply record events like a videotape recorder but process information at the acquisition stage when the event is perceived, during the retention stage, and again at the retrieval stage during which a person recalls stored information.[40] A complex event consists of a vast amount of information; an individual's sensory mechanism selects only certain aspects of the visual stimulus. People are therefore much better at remembering salient facts of an event than peripheral details.[41]

Acquisition is affected by event factors: retention time and frequency (the longer or more frequently something is viewed, the more information is stored) and the type of fact observed (people have great difficulty in assessing speed and time; violent and emotional events produce lower accuracy of memory).[42] "Studies also show that the amount of time perceived as going by is overestimated under conditions of danger and that the overestimation tends to increase as the stress increases."[43] Witness factors also affect observation. The "role that stress plays at the time a witness is perceiving a complex event is captured in the Yerkes-Dodson Law[:]...that strong motivational states such as stress or other emotional arousal facilitate learning and performance up to a point, after which there is a decrement."[44] Much social-psychological research demonstrates that individual bias affects perception, whether the bias is a result of situational expectations, personal or cultural prejudice, or expectations from past experience.[45]

The retention stage is affected by the time lapse between the event and recall. More unnerving, the memory of an event can change. "Postevent information can not only enhance existing memories but also change a witness's memory and even cause nonexistent details to become incorporated into a previously acquired memory."[46] This underlines the danger of *suggestibility*, so prominent in the *Wade–Gilbert–Stovall* trilogy of cases. Studies have shown that (1) the likelihood of recall of an event is enhanced simply by mentioning it; (2) postevent suggestion can cause the memory to compromise between what was originally seen and what is reported; and (3) mentioning a nonexistent object to a witness can cause the witness to later report having seen it. Not only simple facts but also subjective recollections about the violence of an event can be modified by postevent suggestion.

Verbal cues subtly influence retention. Subjects shown a filmed traffic accident were asked if they saw broken glass, although there was none. Seven percent of those asked about cars that "hit" reported broken glass, compared to 16 percent of those asked about cars that "smashed" into each other. Both original information and external information acquired after the event become merged into one memory. Labeling a situation influences memory, as does the practice of witnesses guessing at information if they are not sure of their original memory. The dangers of inaccuracy during memory retention are worsened by a freezing effect: A person who makes a statement about an event tends to more strongly remember the statement at a later time, and this applies to objectively true elements of the original event as well as false information.[47]

Similar memory modification occurs during the retrieval stage. Accuracy of recall is increased when a person relays it in a familiar and comfortable setting and in a narrative form rather than answering controlled questions. Increased status of the questioner enhances the quantity and accuracy of responses. The wording of questions influences responses. An experiment demonstrated that more witnesses who were asked to describe "the" event said they saw something not present in a film compared to those who were asked about "an" event.[48]

Toward More Accurate Identification

It is utopian to believe that wrongful convictions can be entirely eliminated. Nevertheless, police agencies can apply practical knowledge to substantially reduce this injustice. As noted earlier, in 1999 the NIJ issued a forty-four-page report, *Eyewitness Evidence: A Guide for Law Enforcement,* compiled by a group of law enforcement professionals, defense lawyers, and psychologists. It does not provide the background research but, rather, lists precise procedural suggestions for law enforcement agencies. The guide goes a long way toward establishing national criteria, although it has some weaknesses. Professor Donald Judges's thorough review of the guide states that it is "faithful to research findings in its recommendations to avoid instruction bias."[49] On the other hand, he faults it for not recommending double-blind and sequential lineup procedures.[50]

The guide offers recommendations to police in five areas: (1) the initial report of a crime, (2) the preparation of "mug books" and composites and the instruction of witnesses who view them, (3) follow-up interviews of witnesses, (4) field identification (showup) procedure, and (5) lineup procedures for eyewitness identification of suspects. Under lineups, procedures are recommended for composing photo and live lineups, instructing witnesses prior to lineups, and conducting identification procedures. The NIJ supplemented the guides with training criteria for these procedures.[51] It notes that no validation studies have been authorized and that changes may be recommended in the future.

In general terms, the guide's recommendations are designed to improve the accuracy of police interviewing and identification. In regard to the initial interviews and follow-up interviews with witnesses, the guide adopts many research findings of what is known as the cognitive interview.[52] Police are instructed to ask open-ended questions and to augment answers with closed-ended questions, to avoid asking suggestive or leading questions, to separate witnesses, to instruct witnesses to avoid discussing details of the incident with other witnesses, to encourage witnesses to volunteer information without prompting, to encourage witnesses to report all details—even if they seem trivial, to caution witnesses not to guess, to avoid interrupting witnesses, and so forth. According to Professor Judges, the guide misses some points:

> For example, in its statements of principle or policy, the Guide does not explicitly state the concepts underlying the components of the cognitive interview, including the witness-centered control of information. Other specific recommendations from CI [Cognitive Interview] are either lacking or only obliquely referred to, such as inviting narrative presentation, witness-compatible questioning (i.e., tailoring questions to witnesses' mental representation of the event, such as a witness who viewed the perpetrator from the side or rear only), and the varied-retrieval method (e.g., having the witness recall the event in reverse chronological order).[53]

The remainder of this section reviews some methods that experts have proposed to improve lineups.

Improving Lineups

Based on extensive psychological research, the adoption of the following procedures are likely to reduce the number of erroneous identifications made during lineups:

- *Establish double-blind procedures.*   The dangers of suggestibility or contamination of witnesses by even subtle or unintended emphasis is very well established and uniformly supported by psychological research.[54] Professor Judges urges that "eyewitness identification procedures should be conducted only by persons who are ignorant of which lineup member is the suspect. . . . Use of 'double-blind' procedures—which has long been standard practice in human-subject research—would preclude the possibility of contamination even from inadvertent or subtle feedback cues from the investigator."[55]

- *Conduct lineups in a sequential manner, not simultaneously.*   The problem with the more typical simultaneous lineup, where all the individuals are viewed while standing together, is that it forces the witness to engage in relative (comparative) judgment ("Does this person look more like the suspect than that person?") instead of absolute judgment ("That's the man."). A review of research found that "critical tests of this hypothesis have consistently shown that a sequential procedure produces fewer false identifications than does a simultaneous procedure with little or no decrease in rates of accurate identification." This manipulation, because it directly addresses the cognitive source of the problem, is an especially important component of the set of recommendations advanced by researchers in this area for reducing the risk of false identifications.[56]

- Utilize lineup context cues.   Lineup context cues improve the accuracy of lineup identifications. Brian Cutler and Steven Penrod recommend

> that lineup procedures should ensure the use of voice samples and should show the lineup members from three-quarter poses and, whenever possible and appropriate, allow the witness to watch the lineup members walking in and out of the observation room. Such cues should also be taken into consideration when photographs are taken for the purpose of mug books.[57]

- *Construct lineups fairly.*   This seems to be axiomatic, but police in the past have been tempted to construct the lineup so that the suspect stands out. The NIJ guide urges fairness. Lindsay and Wells note that as nonsuspects ("foils") in a lineup come to resemble the suspect more, more witnesses can be expected to erroneously identify the foils, suggesting a trade-off between a high probability of selecting the suspect in unfair (low-similarity) lineups and a high probability of selecting an innocent person in high-similarity lineups. Using experimental lineups with a "criminal" present and a "criminal" absent, Lindsay and Wells found that the choice of a "guilty" suspect fell from 71 percent in unfair lineups to 58 percent in fair ones in the criminal-present mode. However, choosing the "innocent suspect" (a look-alike to the "criminal") fell from 70 percent to 31 percent in the criminal-absent mode. Lindsay and Wells developed diagnosticity ratios that indicated mathematically that the fair lineups improve the relative quality of both identifications and no identifications over the unfair lineups. The practical value of this experiment is to dissuade police from setting up unfair lineups in the hope of highlighting suspects who they are "certain" are guilty.[58] After all, since the selection and conviction of an innocent person leave the real criminal at large, law enforcement, prosecution, and defendants share a real desire to make lineups more fair.

- *Have an officer of the same race as the suspect construct the lineup.*   Research shows that same-race identification tends to be more accurate than recognition of other-race faces. If other-race faces tend to look similar, there is a risk that, for example, a white officer who constructs a lineup of a black suspect and black foils for black witnesses may construct a lineup of faces that look alike to him but appear dissimilar to the witnesses.[59] This point is conjectural and has not yet been subject to rigorous research.

- *Use expert witnesses or closing arguments to rebut errors about eyewitness identification.* This has been strenuously resisted by prosecutors for fear that experts would undermine juror confidence in eyewitnesses. Courts and scholars are split on whether to allow experts to testify. Huff, Rattner, and Sagarin would always allow expert witnesses on the issue of reliability, while Judges is skeptical of its value.[60] Attorneys could utilize closing statements to inform jurors about known information about eyewitness identification. For example, an area in which research contradicts common sense is witness certainty and accuracy of a prior description. Many studies show little or no correlation between the confidence that witnesses express in their certainty and the accuracy of their observations, while others do.[61] The common finding of no confidence-accuracy correlation is counterintuitive; in fact, the Supreme Court in *Neil v. Biggers* (1972) and *Manson v. Brathwaite*

(1977) relied on confidence as one of five indicia of certainty, thus possibly injecting an element of factual injustice into some cases. An expert could be useful in bringing this to the attention of a jury, as well as alerting them to other possibly relevant issues.

This list does not exhaust all of the ways in which identification procedures can be made more accurate. The NIJ guide is only a first step, and it has flaws. It is probably the case that very few law enforcement departments conduct lineups in a double-blind fashion, and given the disruption of routine, it is not expected that many will change rapidly. It is worth keeping in mind that research will continue to refine knowledge in the area of witness perception. The hopeful sign is that for the first time serious national attention has been given to the issue. Time will tell whether real advances will be made in making the identification process more accurate or whether these efforts will soon be forgotten.

Summary

Eyewitness identification is an important source of truth in the justice process but is often mistaken and leads to the unwarranted conviction of innocent people. Legal rules are less important in preventing mistaken eyewitness identification than proper police procedures. Identification can be made by identifying one suspect in a procedure known as a showup. A lineup—live or photographic—is a police identification procedure in which a witness views a suspect to the crime along with others with similar physical characteristics.

The Supreme Court has established rules for the admissibility of eyewitness identification. *United States v. Wade* (1967) held, under the Sixth Amendment, that a suspect is entitled to counsel during a post-indictment police lineup. Counsel's role at lineup is to prevent suggestiveness or to detect and record it. A witness may not identify a defendant in a trial after viewing the suspect in an uncounseled post-indictment lineup unless the government can show by clear and convincing evidence that witness's memory is based on observations made at the time of the crime. The *Wade* rule is based on the potential for police suggestiveness at a lineup.

In *Kirby v. Illinois* (1972), the Court limited this right to counsel only to post-indictment lineups. A lawyer is not required at a pre-indictment lineup. The Court held that suspects are entitled to counsel only after an adversary judicial proceeding has been directed against them. Counsel is required at a lineup held after a defendant has been processed at a preliminary examination.

There is no right to counsel at photographic identification procedures, whether held before or after indictment.

A photo array is determined not to present the same dangers of suggestibility as a lineup, any suggestive behavior can be cured by cross-examination at trial, and the defendant is not present at a photo identification, eliminating the need for counsel to protect the defendant's rights.

The Fifth Amendment protection is against compelled testimonial evidence and therefore does not prevent the state from exhibiting the defendant at a lineup or trial for identification purposes. Further, the suspect may be required to wear distinctive clothing or to speak words to improve his or her identification.

Due process requires that identification procedures be conducted fairly. The due process rule is a totality of the circumstances test; the Court has rejected a narrower per se rule. In deciding whether a defendant's due process rights have been violated, the necessity to conduct a showup may be taken into account. A showup is justified if a witness might die or if any suggestibility is offset by procedures that ensure reliability. Pictures of a lone suspect may be shown to witnesses prior to arrest to aid in apprehension. Identification after a grossly unfair lineup in which the suspect is made to stand out violates due process and results in the suppression of the identification.

Five factors may be taken into account in determining whether a suggestive showup has been offset by indicia of reliability: (1) the witness's opportunity to view the suspect at the scene of the crime; (2) the witness's degree of attention; (3) the accuracy of the witness's original description; (4) the witness's level of certainty; and (5) the time elapsed between the crime and the identification procedure.

Legal Puzzles

HOW HAVE COURTS DECIDED THESE CASES?

Right to Counsel

8-1. Joseph Lloyd Cook was sentenced to death for a murder committed in the course of a robbery of two elderly people for whom he did yard work. The killing occurred on July 9. At about 6:00 that day, Cook arrived at his brother's house driving the victims' white pickup truck, with the victims' large stereo speakers, which Cook sold to his brother for $150. On July 13 police administered *Miranda* warnings to Cook; he asked for counsel after hearing his rights but none was appointed and the interrogation ceased.

Witnesses Gina and Cruz Wilcox identified Cook as the man they saw standing next to a white pickup truck in front of their house on July 10, 1992, about a half-mile from Cook's residence. Gina Wilcox had selected Cook's photo from a photo book. Cook was kept in custody on a parole hold.

A live lineup was held on July 22. No defense counsel was present. By that day no criminal complaint had yet been filed. The prosecutor was in the process of deciding whether to charge Cook with a capital crime. Police decided to hold the live lineup without the prosecutor's knowledge. At the lineup Cruz Wilcox selected Cook as the man standing beside the victims' truck. At the time of the lineup, law enforcement officers were still investigating the case and gathering evidence. A criminal complaint was filed later the same day.

Did the lack of a defense lawyer at the lineup violate Cook's right to counsel because suspicion had focused on him as the killer and he had asked for counsel?

Held: NO

8-1. The rule of *Wade*(1967) is that defendants are entitled to counsel at a *post-indictment* lineup to preserve their basic right to a fair trial. In *Kirby* (1972) a plurality of the U.S. Supreme Court reaffirmed that the right to counsel does not attach until a judicial criminal proceeding such as an indictment is initiated or a complaint is filed.

Defendant argues that *Kirby* is factually distinguishable from the present case, in that here Cook had been in custody on a parole hold for more than a week before the lineup was held, and the investigation had already begun, whereas in *Kirby* the showup at the police station was held the same day the defendant was arrested, and he was not charged until many weeks later.

Nothing in *Kirby* indicates that these distinguishing facts would have made a difference in the ultimate conclusion that, until formal charges were filed, counsel was not required to be present at the lineup under the federal Constitution. Accordingly, there was no violation of the defendant's right to counsel under the federal Constitution.

People v. Cook, 40 Cal.4th 1334, 157 P.3d 950, 58 Cal. Rptr.3d 340 (California Supreme Court 2007)

Suggestiveness

8-2. A man on a bicycle approached Benjamin Valentin after midnight while Valentin sat in his car waiting for traffic to pass. The man punched Valentin to unconsciousness. When Valentin came to his car was gone. Valentin described his assailant to police as a Hispanic male, about 5'7", with a husky build and a scar on his face, who was wearing something white and red. Carmello Herrera was taken into custody to administer a breathalyzer test at about 1:00 a.m. after being found intoxicated next to a damaged vehicle in the roadway with the front passenger side tire missing. The damaged car was discovered to be Valentin's. A showup was arranged at about 2:50 a.m. at a hospital where Herrera had been taken; Valentin was told by police that his car was recovered and they wanted him to identify somebody found in it. As soon as Valentin entered the hospital emergency room he identified Herrera, who was about six feet away, as the man who had attacked him. The other persons in the emergency room were two police officers and nurses.

Was the showup identification evidence admissible at Herrera's carjacking trial?

Holding available from instructor.

Suggestiveness

8-3. Timothy Hiltsley, drinking and "buzzed," left a bar at approximately 1:00 a.m. with Boyd. He met a group of men he knew, including Tyronne Dubose, an African American. Hiltsley invited two of the men and Boyd to his residence to smoke marijuana. At Hiltsley's apartment, Dubose allegedly held a gun to Hiltsley, took his and Boyd's money, and left with his companion. Within minutes, a neighbor called police to report a possible burglary. She described two fleeing African-American men, one wearing a large hooded flannel shirt. Hiltsley and Boyd chased Dubose and the other man. They met police officers responding to the burglary call, and described the suspects as African American, one standing about 5 feet 6 inches, and the other a little taller.

Dubose, not wearing a flannel shirt, was captured by police. He said he had an argument with his girlfriend and had just left her house; that he ran because he thought she might have called them. He was arrested, searched, and no weapons, money, or contraband was found. Dubose was placed in the back of a squad car. Hiltsley was placed in the back seat of a second squad car, which was parked so that its rear window was three feet apart from the rear window of the squad car containing Dubose. The dome light was turned on in the car containing Dubose. The officers told Hiltsley that Dubose was possibly one of the men who had robbed him at gunpoint, and asked Hiltsley if he could identify the man in the other squad car. Hiltsley told the police that he was 98 percent certain that Dubose was the robber, due to his small, slender build and hairstyle. Dubose sat alone in the back seat of the other squad car.

Was the showup suggestive? Was it admissible?

Holding available from instructor.

Civil Liability

8-4. At noon two senior citizens were robbed by a man who followed them into their apartment. Mrs. Feldman called 911 and described the robber as a black man around 5'8" tall with a medium complexion and dark hair, who was wearing a black leather jacket and a "beige-y" shirt; the perpetrator did not use a weapon. A building employee, Dade, saw the robber, followed him, and was told to back away. The robber ran off.

Alerted police officers saw Christopher Pitt, who matched the perpetrator's description. They followed his car; he was not speeding. Pitt was stopped, arrested, and handcuffed. His clothes and physical characteristics matched the description of the robber. A consent search of Pitt's vehicle revealed a hunting knife and a BB gun. Pitt worked as a courier and kept the weapons for protection. He provided the police list of his deliveries and receipts for recent deliveries to the Kuwait embassy.

Police officers brought the Feldmans and Dade to the arrest site. In a showup Mrs. Feldman told police that she got a good look at the robber and that she was certain he was not Pitt. Mr. Feldman said he did not think the robber was Pitt. Dade could not be sure whether Pitt was the robber. A police lieutenant who viewed building security tapes of the robbery said he thought Pitt was the robber. The court noted that the video shows that the perpetrator clearly had a receding hairline, while Pitt has a full head of hair, and to be stockier than Pitt.

At that time Detective Bovino investigated Pitt's alibi about making embassy deliveries. A guard at the Kuwaiti Embassy later testified at the civil trial that a "Chris" had been at the embassy on the day of the robbery, but a detective testified that the guard told him that "he hasn't seen Chris today."

The arrest affidavit made by Officers Adams and Baxter contained absolutely no mention of the Feldmans' negative identifications.

Pitt spent ten days in custody. The case was later dismissed. Pitt sued Officers Adams and Baxter and Detective Bovino and the District of Columbia for false arrest and malicious prosecution. Such a suit depends in part on whether there was sufficient evidence for the police to arrest a suspect.

Did probable cause exist to continue to hold Pitt in custody after the showup? Were police malicious in continuing to hold Pitt in custody after the showup?

Holding available from instructor.

Further Reading

Edward Connors et al., *Convicted by Juries, Exonerated by Science: Case Studies in the Use of DNA Evidence to Establish Innocence after Trial* (National Institute of Justice, NCJ 161258, June 1996).

James M. Doyle, *True Witness: Cops, Courts, Science, and the Battle against Misidentification,* (New York: Palgrave Macmillan, 2005).
Elizabeth Loftus, *Eyewitness Testimony* (Cambridge, Mass.: Harvard University Press, 1979).

Useful Web Site

The Innocence Project

http://www.innocenceproject.org/

Site of the first innocence project, located at Cardozo Law School. Lists and describes cases of individuals exonerated by DNA; offers information on causes and remedies.

Endnotes

1. John H. Wigmore, *Evidence in Trials at Common Law* (John H. Chadbourn, rev. ed., 1974), Vol. 5, sec. 1367.
2. Noted in James Marshall, *Law and Psychology in Conflict* (Indianapolis: Bobbs-Merrill, 1966).
3. Edwin M. Borchard, *Convicting the Innocent: Sixty-five Actual Errors of Criminal Justice* (Garden City, N.Y.: Doubleday, 1932).
4. Jerome Frank and Barbara Frank, *Not Guilty* (Garden City, N.Y.: Doubleday, 1957).
5. C. R. Huff, A. Rattner, and E. Sagarin, *Convicted but Innocent: Wrongful Conviction and Public Policy* (Thousand Oaks, Calif.: Sage, 1996); R. J. Ramsey and J. Frank, "Wrongful Conviction: Perception of Criminal Justice Professionals Regarding the Frequency of Wrongful Conviction and the Extent of System Errors," *Crime & Delinquency* 53 (2007): 436–70; M. Zalman, B. Smith, and A. Kiger, "Officials' Estimates of the Incidence of 'Actual Innocence' Convictions." *Justice Quarterly* 25 (2008) 72–100.
6. S. R. Gross, K. Jacoby, D. J. Matheson, N. Montgomery, & S. Patil, "Exonerations in the United States, 1989 through 2003." *Journal of Criminal Law & Criminology* 95 (2005): 523–60; D. M. Risinger, "Innocents Convicted: An Empirically Justified Factual Wrongful Conviction Rate," *Journal of Criminal Law and Criminology* 97 (2007): 761–806.
7. See Scott Christianson, *Innocent: Inside Wrongful Conviction Cases* (New York: New York University Press, 2004).
8. R. Hermann, "The Case of the Jamaican Accent," *New York Times Magazine*, December 1, 1974, p. 30.
9. S. Raab, "Man Wrongfully Imprisoned by New York to Get $600,000," *New York Times*, January 18, 1985, p. 1.
10. Mentioned in E. Loftus, "Trials of an Expert Witness," *Newsweek*, June 29, 1987, p. 10.
11. "Freedom for Another Dallas Prisoner," *New York Times* (national ed.), February 16, 1990, p. A10.
12. C. R. Huff, A. Rattner, and E. Sagarin, "Guilty until Proven Innocent: Wrongful Conviction and Public Policy," *Crime and Delinquency* 32, no. 4 (1986): 518–44.
13. P. Applebome, "Overturned Murder Conviction Spotlights Dallas-Style Justice," *New York Times* (national ed.), March 7, 1989, p. 11; and R. D. Adams, with W. Hoffer and M. M. Hoffer, *Adams v. Texas* (New York: St. Martin's, 1991).
14. E. Connors, T. Lundregan, N. Miller, and T. McEwan, *Convicted by Juries, Exonerated by Science: Case Studies in the Use of DNA Evidence to Establish Innocence after Trial* (National Institute of Justice, NCJ 161258, June 1996).
15. See the Website of The Innocence Project, http://www.innocenceproject.org/ (accessed June 14, 2009).
16. J. Thompson-Cannino and R. Cotton with E. Torneo, *Picking Cotton: Our Memoir of Injustice and Redemption* (New York: St. Martin's Press, 2009); PBS Frontline, *What Jennifer Saw* (1997).
17. Jennifer Thompson, "I Was Certain, but I Was Wrong," *New York Times*, June 18, 2000, sec. 4, p. 15.
18. "Editorial: Irreversible Error in Texas," *New York Times*, June 23, 2000, p. A22; and Jim Yardley, "In Death Row Dispute, a Witness Stands Firm," *New York Times*, June 16, 2000, p. A22.
19. The quote is from *Williams v. United States*, 345 F.2d 733, 736 (D.C. Cir. 1965), reprinted in Fred P. Graham, *The Due Process Revolution* (New York: Hayden, 1970), 223.
20. Graham, *The Due Process Revolution*, 236–37, referring to the unreported case of *United States v. Beasley*.

21. *Russell v. United States*, 408 F.2d 1280 (D.C. Cir. 1969); see comments on this case in Graham, *The Due Process Revolution*, 238.

22. Herbert L. Packer, "Two Models of the Criminal Process," *University of Pennsylvania Law Review* 113 (1964): 1–68.

23. Connie Mayer, "Due Process Challenges to Eyewitness Identification Based on Pretrial Photographic Arrays," *Pace Law Review* 13 (1994): 815–61.

24. *Gilbert v. California* (1967); and *United States v. Mara* (1973).

25. *United States v. Dionisio* (1973).

26. *California v. Byers* (1971), upholding a law that required drivers involved in an accident to stop and leave their names; such activity does not provide testimonial or communicative evidence.

27. Jennifer L. Devenport, Steven D. Penrod, and Brian Cutler, "Eyewitness Identification Evidence: Evaluating Commonsense Evaluations," *Psychology, Public Policy and Law* 3 (1997): 338–58.

28. Donald P. Judges, "Two Cheers for the Department of Justice's Eyewitness Evidence: A Guide for Law Enforcement," *Arkansas Law Review* 53 (2000): 231–97, 283–91.

29. J. C. Brigham and M. P. Wolfskiel, "Opinions of Attorneys and Law Enforcement Personnel on the Accuracy of Eyewitness Identifications," *Law and Human Behavior*, 7 (1983): 337–39.

30. Scheck, Neufeld, and Dwyer, *Actual Innocence*, 245.

31. Scheck, Neufeld, and Dwyer, *Actual Innocence*, 246, n. 19. See Lissa Griffin, "The Correction of Wrongful Convictions: A Comparative Perspective," *American University International Law Review* 16 (2001): 1241–1308. The Web site of England's Criminal Cases Review Commission is http://www.ccrc.gov.uk/ (accessed December 14, 2003).

32. Jerome M. Maiatico, "Note: All Eyes on Us: A Comparative Critique of the North Carolina Innocence Inquiry Commission," *Duke Law Journal* 56 (2007): 1345–1376.

33. Scheck, Neufeld, and Dwyer, *Actual Innocence*, 250.

34. See, for example, E. F. Loftus, *Eyewitness Testimony* (Cambridge, Mass.: Harvard University Press, 1979); A. D. Yarmey, *The Psychology of Eyewitness Testimony* (New York: Free Press, 1979); and John C. Yuille, "A Critical Examination of the Psychological and Practical Implications of Eyewitness Research," *Law and Human Behavior* 4, no. 4 (1980): 335–45.

35. Loftus, *Eyewitness Testimony*, 19.

36. Yuille, "Critical Examination," 336.

37. R. Buckhout, "Nearly 2,000 Witnesses Can Be Wrong," quoted in Loftus, *Eyewitness Testimony*, 135–36.

38. Woodhead et al., recounted in Loftus, *Eyewitness Testimony*, 166–70.

39. J. Brigham et al., "Accuracy of Eyewitness Identifications in a Field Setting," *Journal of Personality and Social Psychology* 42, no. 4 (1982): 673–81.

40. Loftus, *Eyewitness Testimony*, 21 (citations omitted).

41. Loftus, *Eyewitness Testimony*, 21, 25–27.

42. Loftus, *Eyewitness Testimony*, 23–32.

43. Yarmey, *The Psychology of Eyewitness Testimony*, 52.

44. Loftus, *Eyewitness Testimony*, 33.

45. Loftus, *Eyewitness Testimony*, 32–51.

46. Loftus, *Eyewitness Testimony*, 55.

47. Loftus, Eyewitness Testimony, 52–87.

48. Loftus, *Eyewitness Testimony*, 88–104.

49. Judges, "Two Cheers," 277.

50. Judges, "Two Cheers," 238–39, 253, 262–63, 270.

51. Technical Working Group for Eyewitness Evidence. *Eyewitness Evidence: A Trainer's Manual for Law Enforcement.* (Washington: NIJ #188678, September, 2003).

52. Warren E. Leary, "Novel Methods Unlock Witnesses' Memories," *New York Times* (national ed.), November 15, 1988, p. 25; and Ronald P. Fisher, "Interviewing Victims and Witnesses of Crime," *Psychology, Public Policy and Law* 1, no. 4 (1995): 732–64.

53. Judges, "Two Cheers," 274.

54. Gary L. Wells and Eric P. Seelau, "Eyewitness Identification: Psychological Research and Legal Policy on Lineups," *Psychology, Public Policy and Law* 1 (1995): 765; and other sources noted in Judges, "Two Cheers."

55. Judges, "Two Cheers," 270.

56. Judges, "Two Cheers," 263, citing Wells and Seelau, "Eyewitness Identification."

57. Brian Cutler and Steven Penrod, "Improving the Reliability of Eyewitness Identification: Lineup Construction and Presentation," *Journal of Applied Psychology* 72, no. 2 (1988): 281–90, 289.

58. R. C. L. Lindsay and Gary L. Wells, "What Price Justice? Exploring the Relationship of Lineup Fairness to Identification Accuracy," *Law and Human Behavior* 4, no. 4 (1980): 303–13.

59. John C. Brigham, "Perspectives on the Impact of Lineup Composition, Race, and Witness Confidence on Identification Accuracy," *Law and Human Behavior* 4, no. 4 (1980): 315–21, 318; and Christian A. Meissner and John C. Brigham, "Thirty Years of Investigating the Own-Race Bias in Memory for Faces: A Meta-Analytic Review," *Psychology, Public Policy and Law* 7 (2001): 3–35.

60. Huff, Rattner, and Sagarin, *Convicted but Innocent*; and Judges, "Two Cheers," 289–90.

61. Yarmey, *The Psychology of Eyewitness Testimony*, 150–51, 156; Loftus, *Eyewitness Testimony*, 100–101; and Brigham et al., "Accuracy of Eyewitness Identifications."

JUSTICES OF THE SUPREME COURT

Nixon's Conservatives: Burger and Rehnquist

President Richard Nixon had the good political fortune to name four justices during his first term in office and thus was able to significantly mold the Court's direction. He attacked the Warren Court as a campaign issue in 1968 and was only too happy to fill retiring Chief Justice Earl Warren's seat with Warren Burger, an outspoken critic of the Warren Court's criminal procedure rulings. Justice William Rehnquist, appointed in 1972 from a position in the Justice Department, was the most consistently conservative justice over the next three decades.

The Burger Court's output, while more conservative than that of the Warren Court, did not achieve the radical conservative counterrevolution contemplated by the extreme right. The Burger Court supported gender equality, was moderately supportive of prisoners' rights, and did not significantly inhibit freedom of expression. Indeed, the Court's 1973 abortion rights decision has been a constant lightning rod for criticism from conservatives. Its criminal procedure cases were generally conservative; they halted the expansion of suspects' rights without overruling Warren Court decisions. On the whole, the Burger Court probably reflected a nation that could be better described as moderate (or perhaps vacillating), rather than strictly conservative, in social issues.

Justice Rehnquist was elevated to chief justice in 1986, upon Warren Burger's retirement; he was only the third sitting associate justice to have been so promoted. (The other two were Edward D. White and Harlan Fiske Stone. Charles Evans Hughes, a retired associate justice, was later named chief justice.) Although a chief justice has only one vote among nine, when in the majority he appoints the writer of the opinion and thus has an additional opportunity to shape the emphasis of American constitutional law.

Collection of the Supreme Court of the United States. Photographer: Robert S. Oakes.

Warren Earl Burger

Virginia, 1907–1995

Republican

Appointed Chief Justice by Richard Nixon

Years of Service: 1969–1986

Life and Career.   Burger, a Minnesota native, graduated magna cum laude from the St. Paul College of Law and practiced with a substantial St. Paul law firm from 1931 to 1956. Active in political affairs, he supported Governor Harold Stassen's bid for the presidential nomination on the Republican ticket in 1948. At the 1952 nominating convention, Burger played a key role in swinging Stassen's delegates to Dwight Eisenhower, ensuring his nomination over Ohio's Senator Robert Taft. Later, President Eisenhower's attorney general, Herbert Brownell, brought Burger to the Justice Department as an assistant attorney general. He was appointed to the U.S. Court of Appeals for the District of Columbia in 1956, where he gained recognition as a highly competent jurist who was outspoken in criticizing the Warren Court's expansion of the rights of criminal suspects. This reputation was an important factor in Burger's nomination by President Nixon, whose 1968 presidential campaign included sharp criticism of the liberal Supreme Court's criminal justice decisions.

Contribution to Criminal Procedure.   Chief Justice Burger was quite conservative, calling for the abolition of the exclusionary rule and limiting its scope wherever possible (e.g., noncoerced statements obtained in violation of *Miranda* can be used to impeach a witness; the exclusionary rule is not a constitutional right but merely a Court-created police deterrent). On the other hand, in *U.S. v. Chadwick* (1977), he upheld the plain text of the Fourth Amendment by ruling that a warrant was required to search a footlocker.

Signature Opinion.   Dissent in *Bivens v. Six Unknown Named Agents* (1971). In an opinion by Justice William Brennan, the Court held, for the first time, that a person whose Fourth Amendment rights are violated by federal law enforcement officers may bring a civil, tort lawsuit in federal court against the officers. Chief Justice Burger dissented, arguing that the Fourth Amendment itself created no such lawsuit and that, under the separation of powers, the Court should not authorize such a suit but should wait for Congress to establish a federal civil remedy. In his opinion, he wrote broadly on the exclusionary rule, trying to narrow its scope by characterizing it as resting only "on the deterrent rationale—the hope that law enforcement officials would be deterred from unlawful searches and seizures" if the products of such searches were suppressed.

Assessment.   In other areas, Chief Justice Burger was often moderate to conservative and pragmatic. In First Amendment law, he broadened the scope of what is considered obscenity but struck down a gag order on the press in criminal trials. In civil rights, he upheld busing to integrate deliberately segregated school systems but not where segregation was not intended; he upheld the denial of federal tax credits to schools that discriminate but voted against holding that inequitable school taxes violated the Equal Protection Clause. He concurred in *Roe v. Wade* (1973) (abortion rights), and in *United States v. Nixon* (1974) he wrote for a unanimous Court that President Nixon's claim of executive privilege did not override a court order to turn over tapes of his Watergate conversations. He was not known as an especially effective leader as chief justice, and during his tenure Justices Brennan, Rehnquist, and Powell were more influential with their fellow justices. In 1987, Burger stepped down to head the national celebration of the bicentennial of the Constitution, a fitting role after eighteen years of service as chief justice of the United States.

Further Reading

Charles M. Lamb, "Chief Justice Warren E. Burger: A Conservative Chief for Conservative Times," in Charles M. Lamb and Stephen C. Halpern, eds., *The Burger Court: Political and Judicial Profiles* (Urbana: University of Illinois Press, 1991), 129–62.

William H. Rehnquist

Arizona, 1924–2005

Republican

Appointed by Richard Nixon and as Chief Justice by Ronald Reagan

Years of Service: Associate Justice, 1972–1986; Chief Justice, 1986–2005

Life and Career.   Rehnquist was born in Milwaukee, Wisconsin, and attended Stanford University after service during World War II. He received a master's degree in political science and graduated first in his class from Stanford Law School. He clerked for Justice Robert Jackson and practiced law in Phoenix, Arizona, from 1953 to 1969. He was active in conservative Republican politics and in 1969 became an assistant attorney general in the Nixon administration. He was appointed to the Court at the relatively young age of forty-seven and at that time was the most conservative member of the Court. He faced strong opposition in his initial appointment and again in 1986, when President Ronald Reagan nominated him to the position of chief justice.

Collection of the Supreme Court of the United States. Photographer: Dane Penland.

Contribution to Criminal Procedure.   Chief Justice Rehnquist was a prolific opinion writer in criminal procedure cases and helped shape a very conservative view of Fourth Amendment rights. His majority opinions restricted Fourth Amendment standing to those with property-like interests; replaced the two-pronged rule for using the hearsay of a secret informant to obtain a search warrant with the more lenient "totality of the circumstances" test; held that *Miranda* warnings were only protective devices and not themselves constitutionally protected rights; created a public safety exception to the *Miranda* rule; expanded *Terry* stops to crimes of possession based on hearsay; limited the right to counsel on second appeals; and held that drug courier profiles constituted reasonable suspicion for a stop. More recently, he held that prosecuting a higher proportion of African Americans for possession of crack cocaine, which carries a heavier penalty than powdered cocaine, is not selective prosecution; that a law that allows the forfeiture of a wife's interest in her car, which her husband used for a tryst with a prostitute, does not violate due process; and that a lawyer's failure to object to an aggravating factor at a death penalty trial does not prejudice the defendant's case.

Signature Opinion.   *Dickerson v. United States* (2000). Chief Justice Rehnquist, for a seven-to-two majority, upheld the *Miranda* ruling, calling it "a constitutional rule that Congress may not supersede legislatively." His adroit opinion seemed to go against his many earlier opinions, which established the rule that "[t]he prophylactic *Miranda* warnings therefore are not themselves rights protected by the Constitution but are instead measures to insure that the right against compulsory self-incrimination is protected"—Rehnquist's own words in the majority opinions of *Michigan v. Tucker* (1974) and *New York v. Quarles* (1984). Indeed, *Dickerson*'s reasoning, while plausible in some respects, did not easily square with the earlier pronouncements of the chief justice and the Court. The explanation seems to be that Rehnquist saw the institutional role of the Supreme Court as outweighing doctrinal purity in this case. The nation had come to rely on *Miranda* warnings to such an extent that they "have become part of our national culture." As such, the dictates of *stare decisis*, a doctrine that Rehnquist never thought was paramount in constitutional adjudication, nevertheless carried the day here.

Assessment.   Chief Justice Rehnquist's judicial philosophy dictated the outcome of many of his cases. He believed that American federalism requires the Court to play a small role in the affairs of the states and of other branches of government. He disfavored the incorporation doctrine and preferred that the states make their own decisions in regard to defendants' rights. He wrote that the Supreme Court does not have a special position as the ultimate guardian of individual rights because that was not a role intended by the Framers of the Constitution. Chief Justice Rehnquist's constitutional philosophy of strict federalism and deference to the elected branches of government can be seen as democratic in giving the majority a greater voice while reducing the Court's role as a "guardian" of minorities.

Further Reading

Sue Davis, *Justice Rehnquist and the Constitution* (Princeton, N.J.: Princeton University Press, 1989).

CHAPTER 9

Entrapment

"Fidelity" to the commands of the Constitution suggests balanced judgment rather than exhortation. The highest "fidelity" is not achieved by the judge who instinctively goes furthest in upholding even the most bizarre claim of individual constitutional rights, any more than it is achieved by a judge who instinctively goes furthest in accepting the most restrictive claims of governmental authorities. The task of this Court, as of other courts, is to "hold the balance true."

—JUSTICE WILLIAM H. REHNQUIST, *Illinois v. Gates*, 462 U.S. 213, 241 (1983)

CHAPTER OUTLINE

KEY TERMS

agent provocateur
covert facilitation
criminal law
   approach

criminal procedure
   approach
decoy
due process defense

encouragement
entrapment
hypothetical person test
inducement

objective test
outrageous conduct test
predisposition
subjective test

INTRODUCTION

Entrapment is a complete defense to a crime; if a court or jury concludes that a defendant was entrapped, the indictment is dismissed or the defendant is acquitted. It seems a strange rule because the absolved defendant did indeed "commit" the crime charged. Nevertheless, the defendant is released under the law when it appears to judge or jury that police used tactics that planted the idea of the crime in the defendant's mind. The rule is not based on the Constitution. Therefore, each state is free to adopt its own entrapment rule or to have no entrapment rule. It is fair to say that although the defense of entrapment is not based directly on the Due Process Clauses of the Fifth or Fourteenth Amendments, it originated in the sense of fairness and limits on government power that underlie due process. The entrapment defense announces that there is a limit to what the police will be allowed to do to ferret out crime.

Classification and Origins of the Entrapment Defense

Entrapment differs from other criminal procedure doctrines in that it is classified as a rule of substantive criminal law (as a defense to crime) *and* as a rule of criminal procedure.[1] How can this be? Entrapment was created as a criminal law defense by state supreme courts in the late nineteenth and early twentieth centuries. Their decisions interpreted criminal statutes to declare that legislatures intended to criminalize only those whose criminal intent was not conceived by the police. As this criminal law defense concerns the restraint of excessive police action, it is also properly a subject of criminal procedure. Entrapment is a uniquely American rule that is not the product of the English common law and has had no counterpart in the civil law jurisdictions of Europe.[2] In most Western European legal systems, actions by police undercover agents that entrap defendants are viewed as criminal complicity—that is, crimes by the police.[3]

As a criminal law defense, lawyers argued that where police overreached and drew the defendant into crime, courts should "condemn excessive police encouragement [and] completely absolve any individuals who commit the encouraged acts."[4] Some sympathetic courts at first simply condemned police manipulation that led weak people into crime but upheld the convictions. Earlier courts felt that a defendant who gave in to temptation—even if manufactured by the police—should not have a criminal defense.[5] By 1878, as seen in the Michigan case of *Saunders v. State,*[6] courts began to recognize, in dictum, that an entrapment defense should exist. A lawyer improperly asked a police officer to leave a courtroom unlocked so that he could have access to records. The officer, instead of refusing, laid a trap and arrested the attorney. The court held that this was not entrapment, but rather only furnished an opportunity to commit the crime. Nonetheless, it ruled that evidence of the "entrapment context of the crime ought to be available to the jury."[7] In a proper case, therefore, a jury could acquit a person because government officers caused the defendant to commit the crime. A concurring justice in *Saunders* noted that "human nature is frail enough at best, and requires no encouragement in wrong-doing."[8] Over time, state supreme courts went from condemning extreme police encouragement to adopting entrapment as a defense. In the century after *Saunders,* every state adopted a form of entrapment defense either by court ruling or by statute.

A brilliant analysis by Rebecca Roiphe links the emergence of the entrapment defense in the late nineteenth century to the creation, expansion, and bureaucratization of local, state, and federal police forces. "Entrapment caught the attention of judges and academics in the context of this rapidly transforming system of law enforcement. It gradually took hold amidst the increasingly interrelated and invasive tactics of both federal and local police."[9] In the mid-nineteenth century, courts praised law enforcement tactics involving trickery and deceit to catch criminals at a time when police forces were new and small and most relations between the individual and the government were still personalized. But by the late 1870s and 1880s, the courts began to denounce "the involvement of the state in their overzealous pursuit of undercover investigations and prosecutions."[10] What happened? Courts came to view entrapment "as a way of ascertaining voluntariness in the context of a prevalent and powerful state using increasingly sophisticated law enforcement techniques."[11] Thus, from the outset, the entrapment defense was concerned with the basic function of constitutional criminal procedure: to maintain a balance between effective law enforcement and basic individual liberties. As the state grew more powerful, the need for added citizen protections also grew.

The distinction between entrapment as a criminal law rule and entrapment as a criminal procedure rule suggests different theories of entrapment. Under the **criminal law approach**, the main purpose of entrapment is to protect the essentially, or "otherwise," innocent person. This "subjective" theory (or **subjective test**) emphasizes whether the defendant had a **predisposition** to commit the crime in the first place. In the **criminal procedure approach**, on the other hand, the emphasis is on the **inducement** offered by the police to commit the crime. In this view, the goal of the entrapment rule is to deter excessive police activity. The "objective" theory (or **objective test**) requires courts to determine when police participation goes too far, whatever the defendant's predisposition. The debate is not entirely theoretical, as different approaches can result in more or fewer entrapment acquittals or dismissals for different sorts of defendants, as explained in this chapter.

An important limit is that the entrapment defense "is unavailable when causing or threatening bodily injury is an element of the offense."[12] Entrapment is most often claimed as a defense in vice crimes (e.g., drug dealing and manufacture, prostitution, loan-sharking, liquor bootlegging), bribery and corrupt practices (e.g., prison guards smuggling contraband, kickbacks in awarding government contracts), buying or selling stolen property, extortion, counterfeiting, white-collar crimes, money laundering, and the like. No cases appear to involve crimes of violence.

Before continuing to explore the entrapment defense, we briefly review the constitutionality of police "encouragement" tactics and undercover techniques.

Covert Facilitation and Undercover Policing

Covert facilitation (also called **encouragement**) and undercover police investigation are lawful and necessary police functions. Because they involve deception, however, they are prone to abuse, and entrapment is the prime example. Entrapment occurs when police undercover agents or informants go too far in using techniques of encouragement. Covert techniques are most useful in enforcing such crimes as drug dealing or bribery, where the perpetrator and victim are willing participants in an illicit business transaction that they conceal from public scrutiny. It may be impossible to penetrate organized or white-collar crime without covert policing techniques.

Lawful encouragement has been defined as

> the activity of the police officer or police agent (a) who acts as a victim; (b) who intends, by his actions, to encourage a suspect to commit a crime; (c) who actually communicates this encouragement to the suspect; and (d) who has thereby some influence upon the commission of the crime. Encouragement does not usually consist of a single act but a series of acts, part of the normal interplay between victim and suspect.[13]

A police **decoy** poses as a "street person" or a taxicab driver and makes an arrest when attacked by a mugger or a cab robber. By playing the role of a potential victim, he provides only the opportunity for crime, but little or no encouragement. An undercover officer who poses as a prostitute, who buys drugs from a dealer, or who offers a bribe to a public official goes further to encourage a targeted suspect to commit a specific crime. The undercover officer communicates to the target that she is a willing participant in an illicit transaction and thus influences the target to engage in the illegal act.

A double lie envelops undercover agents: their identity and the true motives of the transaction. This alone, however, is not entrapment. However lawful and necessary to prosecute secretive crimes, encouragement is inherently unethical conduct that is justified by concepts of the "greater good." Thus encouragement must not "manufacture" crime. Some officers who regularly engage in deceit, however, may also lie about the specifics of suspects' behavior in borderline cases in order to make questionable arrests "stick." (See the "Law in Society" section in Chapter 3.) Courts therefore became suspicious of overzealous police officers who try to convince suspects to commit crimes. When the crime is one the suspect would not "otherwise" have committed, encouragement slips into entrapment—the criminal intent is implanted in the mind of a law-abiding citizen by police inducement.

Consider, for example, the common scenario of a female police officer dressed as a "lady of the evening." She pretends to be a consenting participant in the "victimless" crime of prostitution. If a potential "customer" approaches her and she accepts an illicit offer, her behavior is lawful encouragement because it only provides the opportunity for the crime. On the other hand, if the officer actively solicits males walking by and arrests one who accepts her advances, the officer's actions might be considered entrapment by a judge or jury, because it cannot be shown that the passerby would otherwise have agreed to engage in sex for hire had he not been approached. It is true that the "John" made the illegal offer, but it may be that he had no prior intention to do the illegal act until he was tempted by the officer's active solicitation. The real danger is that police entrapment *manufactures* crime.

UNDERCOVER AGENTS AND INFORMERS   In addition to undercover officers, entrapment involves civilian undercover informers role-playing as criminal participants in return for money, nonprosecution, or other benefits. ***Hoffa v. United States*** (1966) held that the simple use of undercover informers or agents violates no constitutional provision. Jimmy Hoffa, the president of the national Teamsters Union, was on trial in Nashville, Tennessee, on federal charges related to union matters. During the trial, Edward Partin, a local Teamsters official in criminal trouble with the federal government, spent time at Hoffa's Nashville apartment with the knowledge and support of federal agents. During this espionage, Partin learned that Hoffa was engaged in jury tampering and divulged this information to the federal agents in exchange for leniency in his own case and money for his wife. Hoffa was later prosecuted for jury tampering, and he claimed that the use of Partin's testimony, based on his undercover role, violated Hoffa's Fourth, Fifth, Sixth, and Fourteenth Amendment rights.

The Supreme Court, in an opinion by Justice Potter Stewart, held that an undercover agent's entry into a home does not violate the pre-*Katz* (1967) "constitutionally protected area" doctrine of the Fourth Amendment. Also, no interest protected by the amendment was violated. "Neither this Court nor any member of it has ever expressed the view that the Fourth Amendment protects a wrongdoer's misplaced belief that a person to whom he voluntarily confides his wrongdoing will not reveal it." Even under the *Katz* "expectation of privacy" doctrine, the misplaced confidence in a false friend does not violate the right to be free from illegal search and seizure.

Neither does an undercover agent violate the right to be free from compelled self-incrimination. The Fifth Amendment prohibits the government from compelling a person to testify. The statements in *Hoffa* were wholly voluntary. The undercover agent's deception is not a substitute for Fifth Amendment compulsion. Nor was Hoffa's Sixth Amendment right to counsel violated, because Hoffa could not prove that Partin heard privileged statements between Hoffa and his lawyer. The right to counsel does include "the right of a defendant and his counsel to prepare for trial without intrusion upon their confidential relationship by an agent of the Government, the defendant's trial adversary." However, Partin's mere presence in the apartment while Hoffa conferred with his lawyers did not violate the Constitution. The Court also ruled that the government has no obligation to arrest a person as soon as it has enough evidence to support probable cause, so as to protect the right to counsel. "There is no constitutional right to be arrested." An investigation may continue after the police have probable cause to arrest so as to gather more convincing evidence for use at a trial.

The Court rejected Hoffa's claim that using an undercover agent violated his due process right to fundamental fairness because the use of informers is an odious practice, and given Partin's motives, there was a high probability that Hoffa would commit perjury. Quoting Learned Hand, a renowned federal judge, the Court rejected these arguments: "Courts have countenanced the use of informers from time immemorial; in cases of conspiracy, or in other cases when the crime consists of preparing for another crime, it is usually necessary to rely upon them or upon accomplices because the criminals will almost certainly proceed covertly."[14] As for the risk of perjury by Partin, it could be uncovered through cross-examination. Informers are bound by the legal and constitutional restrictions that apply to all witnesses and governmental agents. In sum, "the use of secret informers is not *per se* unconstitutional."

Chief Justice Earl Warren, perhaps disturbed by Attorney General Robert Kennedy's personal vendetta to indict Hoffa, dissented,[15] but he did not seek an absolute ban on undercover police work. He voted to reverse the conviction under a flexible rule allowing a court to throw out evidence obtained by an undercover agent in specific cases "in order to insure that the protections of the Constitution are respected and to maintain the integrity of federal law enforcement." The chief justice believed that the Court should use its supervisory power over federal criminal justice to exclude evidence or to order new trials in flagrant circumstances. No other justice joined this view.

THE SUBJECTIVE AND OBJECTIVE TESTS OF ENTRAPMENT

Development of Federal Entrapment Law

At the time that state courts began to develop the entrapment defense, a federal case stated in dictum that a court should not "lend its countenance to a violation of positive law, or to contrivances for inducing a person to commit a crime."[16] A federal appeals court first reversed a conviction on the grounds that it was obtained by entrapment in 1915. In **Woo Wai v. United States**, federal undercover agents, who had no reason to believe that Woo Wai was smuggling aliens into the United States, nevertheless spent several months pressuring him to assist them in bringing Chinese aliens into the country from Mexico. He continually resisted their pleas, saying that to do so was illegal. He finally relented and was convicted. The Ninth Circuit Court of Appeals overturned the conviction. "We are of the opinion that it is against public policy to sustain a conviction obtained" in this way, "and a sound public policy can be upheld only by denying the criminality of those who are thus induced to commit acts which infringe the letter of the law."[17]

The Supreme Court first unanimously adopted the entrapment defense in **Sorrells v. United States** (1932), dividing only on the proper theory. Chief Justice Charles Evans Hughes, writing for the majority, explained the subjective theory: A defendant not predisposed to commit a crime may claim an entrapment defense if the idea for the crime was implanted by the police. An undercover Prohibition agent, pretending to be an out-of-town businessman, was introduced to Sorrells by a third person. They visited at Sorrells's home for an hour and a half, sharing their mutual war experiences. The agent said, four or five times, that he would like to bring home some whiskey. Sorrells said he "did not fool with whiskey." After repeated requests, however, Sorrells left his home and returned a half hour later with a half-gallon of liquor, which he sold to the undercover agent. There was no evidence that Sorrells was a professional "rum runner."

Chief Justice Hughes ruled that although the National Prohibition Law contained no statutory defense of entrapment, it was within the authority of the Court to interpret the statute to find such a defense. To read the statute literally would produce a clear injustice. "We are unable to conclude that it was the intention of Congress in enacting this statute that its processes of detection and enforcement should be abused by the instigation by government officials of an act on the part of persons otherwise innocent in order to lure them to its commission and to punish them." Merely using an "artifice or stratagem" to catch criminals by enabling law enforcement to "reveal the criminal design" is legal and often necessary. However, "[a] different question is presented when the criminal design originates with the officials of the Government, and they implant in the mind of an innocent person the disposition to commit the alleged offense and induce its commission in order that they may prosecute." In such cases, the defendant may raise to the jury the defense that he or she was entrapped and may be acquitted on that ground.

Justice Owen Roberts, joined by Justices Louis Brandeis and Harlan Fiske Stone, concurred in finding entrapment but would have based entrapment on a different theory. He criticized the majority's reasoning that Congress intended to create an entrapment defense in a Prohibition statute that was silent on the subject. "This seems a strained and unwarranted construction of the statute; and amounts, in fact, to judicial amendment. It is not merely broad construction, but addition of an element not contained in the legislation." He then proposed, as the true basis of entrapment, a judicial policy of fair law enforcement:

> The doctrine rests, rather, on a fundamental rule of public policy. The protection of its own functions and the preservation of the purity of its own temple belongs only to the courts. It is the province of the court and of the court alone to protect itself and the government from such prostitution of the criminal law. The violation of the principles of justice by the entrapment of the unwary into crime should be dealt with by the court no matter by whom or at what stage of the proceedings. . . . Proof of entrapment, at any stage of the case, requires the court to stop the prosecution, direct that the indictment be quashed, and the defendant set at liberty. If in doubt as to the facts it may submit the issue of entrapment to a jury for advice. But whatever may be the finding upon such submission the power and the duty to act remain with the court and not with the jury." (*Sorrells v. United States*, 1932, Roberts, J., concurring)

Twenty-five years later, the Court clarified and continued the *Sorrells* doctrine in *Sherman v. United States* (1958), in which the Court again unanimously upheld the entrapment defense based on the subjective theory, while a concurring minority urged the objective theory as the rationale for entrapment. The facts of the *Sorrells* and *Sherman* cases exhibit some similarities. Sherman, a heroin addict under a physician's treatment, was befriended in the doctor's office by a government informer, one Kalchinian, in August 1951, who was also a heroin addict. After spending some time and several meetings getting to know Sherman, Kalchinian asked if he knew of a good source of narcotics, claiming that he was not responding to treatment. Sherman avoided the issue, but over time Kalchinian repeatedly asked Sherman for a source when they met. Sherman finally gave in and obtained a personal amount of drugs, which he shared with Kalchinian at cost. After several such sales, Kalchinian informed Bureau of Narcotics agents that he had another seller for them. On three occasions during November 1951, the agents observed Sherman selling narcotics to Kalchinian in return for money supplied by the government. Sherman was convicted by a jury, which rejected his entrapment defense, and was sentenced to ten years in prison.

Chief Justice Warren's majority opinion held that entrapment was made out as a matter of law under the *Sorrells* rule. Several factors showed that Sherman was not predisposed to sell drugs when he first met Kalchinian and that he was induced to sell by Kalchinian. The idea of selling drugs originated with Kalchinian, who was an active informer. He had recently led narcotics agents to two other prosecutions before entrapping Sherman. Although Kalchinian was not paid money, in 1951 he was under criminal charges for illegally selling narcotics and had not yet been sentenced. The federal agent in charge of the case never bothered to question Kalchinian about the way in which he made contact with Sherman. It appeared that Kalchinian was seeking a sentence reduction and the government was interested in getting convictions.

There was no evidence that Sherman was a dealer. Two prior convictions for narcotics possession in 1942 and 1946 were not evidence of being in the business of selling drugs. A search of his house produced no narcotics. He made no profit from the multiple sales, which were not evidence of predisposition, because each was induced by Kalchinian's pleas for help—they were "the product of the inducement." This was not a case where Sherman was offered an opportunity to deal and he quickly accepted it. Kalchinian had to repeatedly ask Sherman for a source of drugs before he agreed to find one. As in *Sorrells,* the facts here showed that the government was manufacturing crime, that the criminal conduct was "the product of the creative activity" of law enforcement officials. Entrapment was established because the government crossed the line "drawn between the trap for the unwary innocent and the trap for the unwary criminal." The government played on an innocent party's weaknesses and led him to commit crimes that he otherwise would not have attempted. "Law enforcement does not require methods such as this."

Four justices—both liberal (William Douglas and William Brennan) and conservative (Felix Frankfurter and John Marshall Harlan II)—concurred. Justice Frankfurter's concurring opinion argued that entrapment should not be based on the legal fiction that the drug statute included a "silent" defense based on the defendant's lack of predisposition. Sherman knew that it was illegal to sell drugs to Kalchinian, even if for no profit. "If [the defendant] is to be relieved from the usual punitive consequences, it is on no account because he is innocent of the offense described. In these circumstances, conduct is not less criminal because the result of temptation, whether the tempter is a private person or a government agent or informer."

In place of the subjective theory, Justice Frankfurter argued that while undercover policing, with its deceptions, is proper, "in holding out inducements [the police] should act in such a manner as is likely to induce to the commission of crime only these persons and not others who would avoid crime and through self-struggle resist ordinary temptations." This test shifts the Court's focus away from the defendant's weaknesses and "to the conduct of the police and the likelihood, objectively considered, that it would entrap only those ready and willing to commit crimes" (*Sherman v. United States,* 1958, Frankfurter, J., concurring). This would later come to be known as the **hypothetical person test**.

The objective test highlighted the real policy for the entrapment defense: that "the methods employed on behalf of the Government to bring about conviction cannot be countenanced" or "tolerated by an advanced society." The legal authority for the Supreme Court to impose this restriction on federal law enforcement officers is the Court's supervisory authority, not any constitutional provision. As for the argument that a strict reading of the statute *required* a conviction if the facts were proven, Justice Frankfurter noted that laws are enacted with the presupposition that the entire legal order will operate properly. Thus a criminal conviction is proper only following a trial that adheres to all the rules of due process, is based on properly seized evidence, and is free from entrapment.

Despite Justice Frankfurter's belief that the police conduct rule "is as objective a test as the subject matter permits," in order to determine which "lawless" police actions constituted entrapments, trial judges would have to intuit which police methods violated "rationally vindicated standards of justice," hardly a clear standard. His opinion more effectively pointed out problems with the subjective test. That test, for example, depended on evidence of the defendant's past criminal behavior. This could prejudice a jury, deflect attention away from police methods, and result in successful entrapment defenses only for "good people." This would violate the principle of equality under the law "and would espouse the notion that when dealing with the criminal classes anything goes."

Applying the Subjective Test

The subjective and objective tests overlap. Both are concerned with police conduct, and both seek "to determine whether the government's involvement is the principal cause of the crime."[18] This meshing of concerns is observed in ***Jacobson v. United States*** (1992), the most recent Supreme Court entrapment case.

Read Case and Comments: *Jacobson v. United States.*

Keith Jacobson was entrapped by one of several U.S. Postal Service investigations of child pornography, named Project Looking Glass. Many of the investigations were aimed at commercial child pornography dealers. The Postal Service claims that one-third of the suspects arrested for child pornography offenses have also sexually abused children. Project Looking Glass resulted in 165 convictions.[19] "There were also four suicides, including another Nebraska farmer and a Wisconsin man who left a note saying he had been 'cursed with a demon for a sexual preference.'"[20] This suggests that this particular sting, unlike the interception of active and ongoing "kiddy porn" groups, may have cast its net too widely. An operation that trawls for and badgers individuals against whom little evidence exists seems like a prescription for entrapment.[21]

While reaffirming the subjective test, *Jacobson* is preoccupied with heavy-handed law enforcement practices. "[W]hat is new in *Jacobson* is the extent to which the Court was willing to take its disapproval of police methods as authorization to immunize the defendant."[22] Justice Byron White dwelled on the facts of government excess: twenty-six months of repeated mailings, phony front organizations, and appeals to genuine First Amendment rights to snag a person who, despite his sexual inclinations, was not an avid purchaser of child pornography.

PROOF OF PREDISPOSITION   Proving predisposition involves the difficult task of proving the defendant's state of mind. Some courts have held that only the defendant's general intent or purpose to commit *a* crime when the opportunity is provided is sufficient. Other courts have ruled that the predisposition must be to commit *the specific* crime charged, which may be more difficult to prove. In either case, courts rely on a "totality of the circumstances" approach toward proving predisposition.[23]

The kind of evidence needed to prove predisposition generally falls into six categories: (1) the defendant's character or reputation, including any prior criminal record; (2) whether the government agent was the first to suggest criminal activity; (3) whether the defendant was engaged in the criminal activity for profit; (4) whether the defendant showed reluctance to commit the offense, overcome only by repeated government inducement or persuasion; (5) the nature of the inducement or persuasion supplied by the police; and (6) whether the defendant had the ability to carry out the crime.[24]

These factors are not mechanically applied. For example, in *Sherman v. United States* (1958), Sherman's two drug convictions were several years old, suggesting that he was an addict and not a drug dealer. Also, in *Jacobson* (1992), the Supreme Court made it clear that the relevant inquiry is to prior crimes, not to prior acts. The kind of crime makes a difference. Prosecutors could not introduce an expressed willingness to deal in stolen property in a firearms case because the two kinds of dealing are quite different.[25] Sophistication about how to commit a crime is a good sign of predisposition, but the inability to carry out a crime does not necessarily mean a lack of predisposition.[26]

EXPERT TESTIMONY   Because predisposition involves an individual's psychological state, courts have held that "expert testimony about a defendant's susceptibility to inducement generally is admissible if it will substantially assist the trier of fact to understand the evidence or to

CASE AND COMMENTS

Jacobson v. United States

503 U.S. 540, 112 S.Ct. 1535, 118 L.Ed.2d 174 (1992)

JUSTICE WHITE delivered the opinion of the Court.

On September 24, 1987, petitioner Keith Jacobson was indicted for violating a provision of the Child Protection Act of 1984 which criminalizes the knowing receipt through the mails of a "visual depiction [that] involves the use of a minor engaging in sexually explicit conduct. . ." Petitioner defended on the ground that the Government entrapped him into committing the crime through a series of communications from undercover agents that spanned the 26 months preceding his arrest. Petitioner was found guilty after a jury trial. The Court of Appeals affirmed his conviction, holding that the Government had carried its burden of proving beyond reasonable doubt that petitioner was predisposed to break the law and hence was not entrapped. **[a]**

Because the Government overstepped the line between setting a trap for the "unwary innocent" and the "unwary criminal," *Sherman v. United States* (1958), and as a matter of law failed to establish that petitioner was independently predisposed to commit the crime for which he was arrested, we reverse the Court of Appeals' judgment affirming his conviction.

I

In February 1984, petitioner, a 56-year-old veteran-turned-farmer who supported his elderly father in Nebraska, ordered two magazines and a brochure from a California adult bookstore. The magazines, entitled Bare Boys I and Bare Boys II, contained photographs of nude preteen and teenage boys. [Jacobson] testified that he had expected to receive photographs of "young men 18 years or older." * * * The young men depicted in the magazines were not engaged in sexual activity, and petitioner's receipt of the magazines was legal under both federal and Nebraska law. Within three months, the law with respect to child pornography changed; Congress passed the Act illegalizing the receipt through the mails of sexually explicit depictions of children. In the very month that the new provision became law, postal inspectors found petitioner's name on the mailing list of the California bookstore that had mailed him Bare Boys I and II. There followed over the next 2½ years repeated efforts by two Government agencies, through five fictitious organizations and a bogus pen pal, to explore petitioner's willingness to break the new law by ordering sexually explicit photographs of children through the mail.

[In January 1985, Postal Service agents targeted Jacobson, and others, with mailings not directly offering child pornography for sale. Instead, "prohibited mailing specialists" sent mailings from sham organizations that blended civil liberties and free speech messages with hints at sexual interests. The first came from the "American Hedonist Society," advocating the "right to read what we desire,... discuss similar interests with those who share our philosophy, and finally. . . to seek pleasure without restrictions being placed on us by outdated puritan morality." This anodyne message included a membership application and a "sex survey." Jacobson checked a box labeled "enjoy" to indicate that preteen sex gave him pleasure but indicated that he was opposed to pedophilia.]

[A May 1986 mailing from "Midlands Data Research" extolled the "joys of sex and the complete awareness of those lusty and youthful lads and lasses" without specifying whether it referred to minors or young adults. Jacobson responded, expressing an interest in teenage sexuality and requesting "Please keep my name confidential." A similar solicitation, from another fictitious organization, "Heartland Institute for a New Tomorrow" (HINT), promoted "sexual freedom and freedom of choice." Jacobson indicated that his interest in "preteen sex-homosexual" material was above average, but not high. An agent then sent personal letters, under a pseudonym. He "mirrored" Jacobson's interests and asked for letters indicating Jacobson's sexual interests. In reply Jacobson wrote, "As far as my likes are concerned, I like good looking young guys (in their late teens and early 20's) doing their thing together," but made no reference to child pornography. Jacobson stopped writing after two letters.] **[b]**

By March 1987, 34 months had passed since the Government obtained petitioner's name from the mailing list of the California bookstore, and 26 months had passed since the Postal Service had commenced its mailings to petitioner. Although petitioner had responded to surveys and letters, the Government had no evidence that petitioner had ever intentionally possessed or been exposed to child pornography. The Postal Service had not checked petitioner's mail to determine whether he was receiving questionable mailings from persons—other than the Government—involved in the child pornography industry.

[This was followed by a Customs Service solicitation from its own child pornography sting, to which Jacobson responded, but an order for materials was never filled. Finally, another Postal Service solicitation from another fictitious government-front organization, the "Far Eastern Trading Company

[a] The government concedes that it induced Jacobson or at least offered him child pornography. The case turns on the question of whether Jacobson was predisposed to make the purchase. Notice that the Supreme Court majority drew a different conclusion from the same facts available to the Court of Appeals. The dissenters in this case agree with the way in which the Court of Appeals interpreted Jacobson's state of mind.

[b] Do these efforts seem to be an efficient way of discovering child pornography rings? Should the government play on individuals' "weaknesses" or predilections in this way?

Ltd.," was made. Jacobson sent for a catalog, from which he] ordered Boys Who Love Boys, a porno-graphic magazine depicting young boys engaged in various sexual activities. Petitioner was arrested after a controlled delivery of a photocopy of the magazine.

When petitioner was asked at trial why he placed such an order, he explained that the Government had succeeded in piquing his curiosity:

> "Well, the statement was made of all the trouble and the hysteria over pornography and I wanted to see what the material was. It didn't describe the—I didn't know for sure what kind of sexual action they were referring to in the Canadian letter."

[c] How significant is the lack of child pornography, other than the mailing sent by the government, in Jacobson's home?

In petitioner's home, the Government found the Bare Boys magazines and materials that the Government had sent to him in the course of its protracted investigation, but no other materials that would indicate that petitioner collected, or was actively interested in, child pornography. **[c]** * * *

II

There can be no dispute about the evils of child pornography or the difficulties that laws and law en-forcement have encountered in eliminating it. * * * Likewise, there can be no dispute that the Government may use undercover agents to enforce the law. * * *

[d] This statement announces a rule that is significant to the outcome in this case. The government must prove that Jacobson's predisposition, if any, existed in February 1984, when his name first came to the attention of the Postal Service, and not after years of "working on him."

In their zeal to enforce the law, however, Government agents may not originate a criminal design, implant in an innocent person's mind the disposition to commit a criminal act, and then induce commis-sion of the crime so that the Government may prosecute. Where the Government has induced an individ-ual to break the law and the defense of entrapment is at issue, as it was in this case, the prosecution must prove beyond reasonable doubt that the defendant was disposed to commit the criminal act prior to first being approached by Government agents. **[d]**

[e] The Court makes it clear that its ruling is not designed to disrupt typical undercover law enforcement.

Thus, an agent deployed to stop the traffic in illegal drugs may offer the opportunity to buy or sell drugs and, if the offer is accepted, make an arrest on the spot or later. In such a typical case, or in a more elaborate "sting" operation involving government-sponsored fencing where the defendant is simply pro-vided with the opportunity to commit a crime, the entrapment defense is of little use because the ready commission of the criminal act amply demonstrates the defendant's predisposition. Had the agents in this case simply offered petitioner the opportunity to order child pornography through the mails, and petitioner—who must be presumed to know the law—had promptly availed himself of this criminal opportunity, it is unlikely that his entrapment defense would have warranted a jury instruction. **[e]**

But that is not what happened here. By the time petitioner finally placed his order, he had already been the target of 26 months of repeated mailings and communications from Government agents and fictitious organizations. Therefore, although he had become predisposed to break the law by May 1987, it is our view that the Government did not prove that this predisposition was independent and not the product of the attention that the Government had directed at petitioner since January 1985. **[f]**

[f] While it is not sensible to think that Jacobson's underlying sexual proclivities were caused by the government's inducement, it seems to make sense that a defendant's predisposition to commit a specific offense could be stimulated by the government's inducement in some cases.

* * * The sole piece of preinvestigation evidence is petitioner's 1984 order and receipt of the Bare Boys magazines. But this is scant if any proof of petitioner's predisposition to commit an illegal act, the criminal character of which a defendant is presumed to know. It may indicate a predisposition to view sexually oriented photographs that are responsive to his sexual tastes; but evidence that merely indicates a generic inclination to act within a broad range, not all of which is criminal, is of little probative value in establishing predisposition.

Furthermore, petitioner was acting within the law at the time he received these magazines. * * * Evidence of predisposition to do what once was lawful is not, by itself, sufficient to show predisposition to do what is now illegal, for there is a common understanding that most people obey the law even when they disapprove of it. **[g]** This obedience may reflect a generalized respect for legality or the fear of prosecution, but for whatever reason, the law's prohibitions are matters of consequence. Hence, the fact that petitioner legally ordered and received the Bare Boys magazines does little to further the Government's burden of proving that petitioner was predisposed to commit a criminal act. This is par-ticularly true given petitioner's unchallenged testimony that he did not know until they arrived that the magazines would depict minors.

[g] The Court here adds another element of the federal entrapment defense—prior *legal* acts cannot be used to prove current illegal activity.

[Justice White reviewed Jacobson's responses to the questions asked in the numerous solicita-tions by undercover agents posing behind front organizations. He concluded that they did not prove that Jacobson was predisposed to purchasing child pornography. The responses] were at most indicative of certain personal inclinations, including a predisposition to view photographs of preteen sex and a will-ingness to promote a given agenda by supporting lobbying organizations. Even so, petitioner's respons-es hardly support an inference that he would commit the crime of receiving child pornography through the mails. Furthermore, a person's inclinations and "fantasies. . . are his own and beyond the reach of government. . . ."

On the other hand, the strong arguable inference is that, by waving the banner of individual rights and disparaging the legitimacy and constitutionality of efforts to restrict the availability of sexually ex-plicit materials, the Government not only excited petitioner's interest in sexually explicit materials banned by law but also exerted substantial pressure on petitioner to obtain and read such material as part of a fight against censorship and the infringement of individual rights. * * * [h]

Petitioner's ready response to these solicitations cannot be enough to establish beyond reasonable doubt that he was predisposed, prior to the Government acts intended to create predisposition, to commit the crime of receiving child pornography through the mails. The evidence that petitioner was ready and willing to commit the offense came only after the Government had devoted $2\frac{1}{2}$ years to convincing him that he had or should have the right to engage in the very behavior proscribed by law. Rational jurors could not say beyond a reasonable doubt that petitioner possessed the requisite predisposition prior to the Government's investigation and that it existed independent of the Government's many and varied approaches to petitioner. As was explained in *Sherman,* where entrapment was found as a matter of law, "the Government [may not] play on the weaknesses of an innocent party and beguile him into committing crimes which he otherwise would not have attempted."

Law enforcement officials go too far when they "implant in the mind of an innocent person the *disposition* to commit the alleged offense and induce its commission in order that they may prosecute." *Sorrells,* (emphasis added). * * * When the Government's quest for convictions leads to the apprehension of an otherwise law-abiding citizen who, if left to his own devices, likely would have never run afoul of the law, the courts should intervene.

Because we conclude that this is such a case and that the prosecution failed, as a matter of law, to adduce evidence to support the jury verdict that petitioner was predisposed, independent of the Government's acts and beyond a reasonable doubt, to violate the law by receiving child pornography through the mails, we reverse the Court of Appeals' judgment affirming the conviction of Keith Jacobson.

JUSTICE O'CONNOR, with whom THE CHIEF JUSTICE and JUSTICE KENNEDY join, and with whom JUSTICE SCALIA joins except as to Part II, dissenting.

Keith Jacobson was offered only two opportunities to buy child pornography through the mail. Both times, he ordered. Both times, he asked for opportunities to buy more. He needed no Government agent to coax, threaten, or persuade him; no one played on his sympathies, friendship, or suggested that his committing the crime would further a greater good. [i] In fact, no Government agent even contacted him face to face. The Government contends that from the enthusiasm with which Mr. Jacobson responded to the chance to commit a crime, a reasonable jury could permissibly infer beyond a reasonable doubt that he was predisposed to commit the crime. I agree.

* * *

I

* * *

Today, the Court holds that Government conduct may be considered to create a predisposition to commit a crime, even before any Government action to induce the commission of the crime. In my view, this holding changes entrapment doctrine. [j] Generally, the inquiry is whether a suspect is predisposed before the Government induces the commission of the crime, not before the Government makes initial contact with him. There is no dispute here that the Government's questionnaires and letters were not sufficient to establish inducement; they did not even suggest that Mr. Jacobson should engage in any illegal activity. If all the Government had done was to send these materials, Mr. Jacobson's entrapment defense would fail. Yet the Court holds that the Government must prove not only that a suspect was predisposed to commit the crime before the opportunity to commit it arose, but also before the Government came on the scene.

[h] Suppose a person targeted by the Postal Service with these materials was taking a college class and was doing research on the First Amendment freedom of speech for a term paper. Sexually explicit Web sites are now common. Should law enforcement officers be allowed to target all who access such sites?

[i] Do you find Justice White's or Justice O'Connor's depiction of what went on in Jacobson's mind more persuasive?

[j] Under this view, the question is whether a defendant is predisposed to commit a crime after government agents worked on his or her predilections for several years. Is this fair?

determine a fact in issue."[27] In *State v. Shuck* (1997), a bizarrely controlling male employer came to the attention of the police after breaking into a female employee's apartment to castigate her and a male friend about their relationship. Another female employee, who told a police investigator that Shuck made statements that seemed like threats against the other woman, agreed to wear a wire. She said that in an unrecorded statement Shuck said he would forgive a debt in return for help in "getting rid" of the woman he tried to control and her husband. An undercover law enforcement officer then came into the case as a prospective "hit man." Over a period of time, the employee wearing the wire kept discussing the "hit man." A meeting was finally arranged, Shuck and the officer reached an agreement, and he paid $500 and was arrested and convicted.

To support its entrapment theory, the defense sought to introduce expert testimony from a neuropsychologist that Shuck suffered from a cognitive decline, that the significant deterioration of his cognitive abilities rendered him more susceptible to the persuasion of others to commit a crime, and that he was particularly susceptible to the persuasion of a trusted employee and confidante. The trial judge ruled that the testimony was not admissible because it would invade the province of the jury. The Tennessee Supreme Court reversed, ruling that the trial judge abused his discretion by not allowing the expert witness, and remanded for a new trial. The general criterion for the admissibility of an expert witness is whether the expert testimony will substantially assist the trier of fact to understand the evidence or to determine a fact in issue. Unlike the relaxed federal rule that allows expert testimony that "merely assists the trier of fact," the Tennessee rule was one of necessity—where "the subject under examination must be one that requires that the court and jury have the aid of knowledge or experience such as men not specially skilled do not have, and such therefore as cannot be obtained from ordinary witnesses."[28] Because the neuropsychologist did not seek to testify as to whether Shuck was entrapped (the ultimate issue of fact), but only on his susceptibility "based upon observation, intelligence tests, and other assorted data," this would have assisted the jury and it was an abuse of discretion to not allow it. The testimony of a psychologist, based on observation and tests, can be invaluable, as, for example, in a drug case where the defendant claims to be of subnormal intelligence, but the trial judge usually has a good deal of latitude in deciding whether the expert will assist or confuse the jury.[29]

OTHER TESTS: DUE PROCESS AND OUTRAGEOUS CONDUCT

Federal and state courts have considered alternatives to the subjective and objective tests. In 1971, a federal court for the first time threw out the conviction of predisposed whiskey bootleggers because a government agent was their business collaborator for two and a half years and the government was their only buyer! Although entrapment as such did not exist, the court was offended by outrageous governmental conduct that violated its sense of justice.[30]

The Supreme Court twice considered whether an **outrageous conduct test** existed under the Due Process Clause. In both cases, the Court (1) applied the subjective test and found the defendants were predisposed and (2) announced that a **due process defense** was theoretically possible in cases of outrageous governmental conduct.

In *United States v. Russell* (1973), Joe Shapiro, a federal undercover narcotics agent, got to know three men operating a methamphetamine laboratory. Shapiro supplied them with the chemical phenyl-2-propanone—a legal but hard-to-get essential ingredient in manufacturing methamphetamine—in return for one-half of the drug produced. Shapiro visited the laboratory and watched the drug being produced. The defendants were convicted. The Ninth Circuit Court of Appeals overturned the conviction on grounds of "an intolerable degree of governmental participation in the criminal enterprise." First, the court held that entrapment existed whenever the government furnished contraband to a suspect. The second rationale was an outrageous government conduct test, finding that a prosecution is "repugnant to the American criminal justice system" when a government investigator becomes "enmeshed" in the criminal activity.[31] Both rationales "are premised on fundamental concepts of due process and evince the reluctance of the judiciary to countenance overzealous law enforcement."[32]

The U.S. Supreme Court reversed. Justice William Rehnquist, writing for five justices, instead applied the *Sherman* predisposition test and upheld the conviction of the predisposed meth lab operators. The majority pointed out that the chemical could have been obtained from other sources and therefore the government was not an exclusive supplier, a fact that was disputed in Justice Stewart's dissent. The majority disapproved of the discretion that the due process rule would place in the hands of judges:

> [T]he defense of entrapment. . . was not intended to give the federal judiciary a "chancellor's foot" veto over law enforcement practices of which it did not approve. The execution of the federal laws under our Constitution is confided primarily to the Executive Branch of the Government, subject to applicable constitutional and statutory limitations and to judicially fashioned rules to enforce those limitations. We think that the decision of the Court of Appeals in this case quite unnecessarily introduces an unmanageably subjective standard which is contrary to the holdings of this Court in *Sorrells* and *Sherman*. (*United States v. Russell*, 1973)

The majority opinion, however, added: "While we may some day be presented with a situation in which the conduct of law enforcement agents is so outrageous that due process principles would absolutely bar the government from invoking judicial processes to obtain a conviction, . . . the instant case is distinctly not of that breed" (*United States v. Russell,* 1973). "This 'some day' dicta, as the passage has come to be known, has been so widely cited in connection with the outrageous government conduct defense that it has effectively become a battle cry for the defense's proponents."[33] Subsequently, Justice Rehnquist tried, but failed, to kill the possibility of the Court's ever adopting a due process entrapment defense.

In *Hampton v. United States* (1976), the Court once again refused to apply a due process theory of entrapment. Hampton, an addict, twice sold heroin to two Drug Enforcement Administration (DEA) agents posing as dealers, after a conversation he had with an informant with whom he was shooting pool. Hampton said he needed money, and the informant said he could find buyers. The sales were for $145 and $500. The government claimed that Hampton found the supplier on his own, but Hampton claimed that the informant put him in touch with a pharmacist/seller who sold him what he thought were counterfeit drugs. Hampton's claim was that the government sold illegal drugs to him and purchased them from him, but the trial judge refused to instruct the jury that they must acquit whenever the government supplies drugs to a suspect before arresting him. Hampton was convicted.

The Supreme Court upheld the conviction, with five justices finding that Hampton was predisposed to sell heroin. What is interesting is that the five majority justices split: A plurality opinion by Justice Rehnquist (joined by the chief justice and Justice White) tried to "kill off" even the possibility of a federal due process test by writing that an outrageous conduct test could *never* apply to a predisposed defendant. This reversed the meaning of the "same day" dictum in *Russell*. He also wrote that there was no essential difference between the government's supplying a legal substance, as was the case in *Russell*, and its supplying an illegal drug. Finally, Justice Rehnquist argued that a due process defense could operate only when the outrageous conduct of undercover agents also violated another constitutional right. This would eliminate a freestanding outrageous conduct test based on the Due Process Clause. Two concurring justices, however (Justices Lewis Powell and Harry Blackmun), while agreeing that the government conduct in this case was not outrageous, felt that in future cases the Court could use its supervisory power "to bar conviction of a predisposed defendant because of outrageous police conduct," keeping the outrageous conduct test alive in theory. Three dissenting justices (Brennan, Stewart, and Thurgood Marshall) would have (1) adopted the objective theory of entrapment, (2) found that Hampton was entrapped under the subjective approach, (3) supported the existence of the outrageous conduct test, and (4) found that the police activity was outrageous in this case because the police supplied contraband and were too heavily involved in this government setup.

After *Hampton,* the due process approach has rarely succeeded in lower federal courts and has been rejected in principle by some circuits.[34] *United States v. Twigg* (1978)[35] is an example of a successful application of the due process test. Robert Kubica, a convicted methamphetamine manufacturer, agreed to apprehend illegal drug dealers for the DEA in order to reduce a four-year prison sentence. Kubica contacted an old friend, Henry Neville, to discuss setting up a "speed" laboratory, and over a period of months Kubica drew Neville into the scheme. They worked together to set up a lab. Kubica's contributions were funded by the government, including two and a half gallons of phenyl-2-propanone costing $475. Seven months later, Neville introduced Kubica to William Twigg, who got involved in the operation to repay a debt to Neville. Twigg played a minor role in the process, often running errands for groceries or coffee. He was present in the lab while Kubica actually produced six pounds of methamphetamine hydrochloride during the one week that the lab was in operation. Twigg was convicted for the manufacture of illegal drugs.

A federal court of appeals reversed the convictions. "The nature and extent of police involvement in this crime [were] so overreaching as to bar prosecution of the defendants as a matter of due process of law. Although no Supreme Court decision has reversed a conviction on this basis, the police conduct in this case went far beyond the behavior found permissible in previous cases" (*United States v. Twigg,* 1978). Essentially, the government set up a criminal enterprise, actively worked at it, and then prosecuted its collaborators. Significantly, the criminal scheme was *initiated* by the government through a convicted felon seeking to reduce the severity of his sentence. A major factor in the reversal was that the government supplied a substantial amount of the funds and materials for the laboratory when it was not clear that the parties had the means to obtain the chemicals on their own. Indeed, the DEA made arrangements with chemical suppliers to circumvent regulations needed to get controlled chemicals. "Neither defendant had the know-how with which to actually manufacture methamphetamine.

The assistance they provided was minimal and then at the specific direction of Kubica" (*United States v. Twigg,* 1978).

Although Neville and Twigg were predisposed, they would not have gotten into the drug-manufacturing business if Kubica had not proposed the scheme. "This egregious conduct on the part of government agents generated new crimes by the defendant merely for the sake of pressing criminal charges against him when, as far as the record reveals, he was lawfully and peacefully minding his own affairs. Fundamental fairness does not permit us to countenance such actions by law enforcement officials and prosecution for a crime so fomented by them will be barred" (*United States v. Twigg,* 1978). It should be noted that the outrageous conduct test is a special kind of objective test.

CONTEMPORARY ENTRAPMENT LAW

The Declining Number of Entrapment Cases

In recent years, a number of states have, by legislation and case law, experimented with the subjective approach, the objective approach, various hybrid tests of entrapment, and state outrageous conduct tests under the due process clauses of state constitutions. Before examining these developments, we note Professor Dru Stevenson's study of reported entrapment cases, which raises the fascinating likelihood that "[e]ntrapment cases are disproportionately concentrated in a few states. They are declining almost everywhere, even including these concentration points."[36] This is very odd because law enforcement continues to pursue drug crimes even as serious felonies declined in the 1990s. "There is no reason to think. . . that undercover or sting operations themselves are decreasing."[37] Further, there has been no wholesale change in the rules of entrapment since the 1980s, and Stevenson discounts the possibility that many more defendants are successful in claiming entrapment. "An easy acquittal technique would be adopted by everyone, even those with marginal claims to the defense," leading to a reduction in plea bargains, more trials, and more losses leading to entrapment claims showing up as issues in appellate cases.[38]

State entrapment appeals declined from 164 in 1993 to 84 in 2003, while federal entrapment appeals declined from 184 to 50 in the same period.[39] The declines are not reflected in whether a state had adopted the subjective or the objective approach to entrapment.[40] Stevenson's research indicates that in the early 2000s, entrapment cases tended to be concentrated in California, Florida, Michigan, Ohio, Tennessee, Texas, and Washington, but *not* in other heavily populated states such as New York, Pennsylvania, New Jersey, and Illinois.[41]

She suggests three factors that would explain the concentration of the entrapment defense in some states: "undercover or sting operations being favored by local law enforcement chiefs, peer influence among the local defense bar, and a state of uncertainty about the legal rules in a given jurisdiction."[42] She suggests that uncertainty in legal rules affects the number and methods of undercover police work and the reliance on the entrapment defense by defendants' attorneys. This conjecture is supported by spikes in the number of "entrapment cases [occurring] in almost every state in the three years between 1988 and 1991, followed by a second large spike in the three years between 1992 and 1995. There was a significant drop-off after 1995, and a continuing decline to the present."[43] These spikes followed the 1988 Supreme Court ruling of *Mathews v. United States* (1988), which "held that defendants are entitled, as a matter of law, to jury instructions regarding entrapment whenever there is sufficient evidence to indicate the possibility of entrapment,"[44] and the Court ruling of *Jacobson v. United States* (1992). "The U.S. Supreme Court's jurisprudence on entrapment is naturally very influential even in states using other tests. [Although *Mathews*] was not an obvious expansion of the entrapment defense, its subtle tinkering created uncertainty about how to apply the rules to various fact patterns, allowing more fodder for litigation."[45] Likewise, *Jacobson* "led to a flurry of speculation in academic journals about the rules being relaxed since the defendant won."[46]

"*Jacobson* also generated a spate of new attempts to use the entrapment defense by hopeful parties. The rules were uncertain." After a few rounds of cases and appeals, however, it became clear that the entrapment defense "would be applicable to only a narrow set of circumstances or facts and the furor subsided."[47] Thereafter, because entrapment is "often a second-best defense" that is not popular with judges or juries except in egregious cases, the numbers have dropped off.[48] The use of entrapment by attorneys has shifted to novel uses, as part of ineffective assistance of counsel arguments or claims that entrapment was used to increase sentences. Stevenson's analysis provides a glimpse into the relationship between the legal doctrine that is established by lawmaking bodies and the way in which that doctrine affects practices in line-level cases.

The Current Scene: A Mixed Approach toward Entrapment

The majority and concurring opinions in *Sorrells* (1932) and *Sherman* (1958) posited the subjective and objective approaches to an entrapment rule almost as polar opposites. In theoretical terms, the goals of the two approaches were said to be protection of the innocent (subjective approach) versus deterring excessive police techniques (objective approach). The objective test and its later variation, the outrageous conduct–due process test, was thought by most early commentators to be the real reason for having an entrapment rule. The objective test approach won the adherence of the prestigious American Law Institute in 1962 in its *Model Penal Code,*[49] as a rule that "fit better with the more progressive agenda of having juridical, and more mechanical, regulation of law enforcement."[50] It defined *entrapment* as the action of a "public law enforcement official or a person acting in cooperation with such an official" who, for "the purpose of obtaining evidence of the commission of an offense," induces a person to commit a crime by "employing methods of persuasion or inducement that create substantial risk that such an offense will be committed by persons other than those who are ready to commit it."[51] This hypothetical person test was suggested by Justice Frankfurter's concurrence in *Sherman*—that police encouragement should be of such a nature "as is likely to induce to the commission of crime only these persons [who are ready and willing to commit the crime] and not others who would normally avoid crime and through self-struggle resist ordinary temptations." Under the *Model Penal Code,* a defendant "shall be acquitted if he proves by a preponderance of evidence that his conduct occurred in response to an entrapment."[52] To be entirely sure that this was not to be seen as a partially subjective approach, the explanatory note to this section stated that the Code's entrapment provision did not "turn on the character of the particular defendant." By focusing on a "hypothetical" or "average" person, the objective test avoids the problem of having to introduce potentially prejudicial evidence about the defendant's past crimes to the jury in order to prove predisposition.

Despite the clarity of the objective approach, a majority of states have adhered to the subjective approach. Recall that because entrapment is not a constitutional defense, states are free to develop their own rules. While a few states have adopted the objective approach, the situation is actually more complex. The reason is that many states have both approaches, or various subjective-objective hybrids. In addition, a number of states have imposed outrageous conduct–due process tests on top of their subjective or objective approaches. Further, state legislation and cases deal with the issue of whether entrapment should be decided by a judge or a jury and whether facts known before trial establish entrapment as a matter of law (requiring dismissal) or only as an issue that can go to the jury (which may or may not acquit on the grounds of entrapment).

SELECTING THE SUBJECTIVE TEST   States that stay with the subjective test, like the Ohio Supreme Court in ***State v. Doran*** (1983),[53] do so because of problems with the objective test. For one thing, police may engage in undercover work that might not entrap a hypothetical person but inveigles a really innocent person into committing the crime, especially a person of subnormal intelligence who may be unusually prone to suggestiveness.[54] The other side of the coin is that the police may use tactics that go over the line, resulting in the freeing of a "real" (predisposed) criminal who regularly engages in crime.

Although the subjective approach has been criticized for imprecision in deciding whether a defendant is predisposed and was "really" induced to commit the crime, in practice the objective test also involves difficulties of proof. A fundamental problem is that determining whether the behavior would entrap a hypothetical person is also speculative. On a practical level, because the acts that lead to claims of entrapment usually occur in private, "swearing contests" as to what the police actually did also occur in cases under the objective test. In *Doran,* while the Ohio Supreme Court selected the subjective test because it posed fewer problems, it also expressed a concern that the use of reputation evidence, standing alone as proof of predisposition, could produce its own injustices.

Still, several weaknesses accompany the subjective test. As noted, it is based on a legal fiction about legislative intent. It is difficult to maintain that it fits into criminal law theory because, as noted, it is not available for violent crimes and is not a defense when a nonpredisposed person is induced to commit a crime by a private person. The fact that the identical inducement by an undercover police agent does constitute a defense shows that even the subjective test is mainly concerned with improper government action.[55]

SELECTING THE OBJECTIVE TEST   Alaska was the first state to explicitly adopt the objective test in a case where an undercover agent convinced a tavern owner that he befriended, apparently not a regular drug dealer, to obtain and sell personal quantities of illegal drugs. *Grossman v. State* (1969),[56] paraphrasing the *Model Penal Code,* defined entrapment as inducement by a law enforcement official "which would be effective to persuade an average person, other than the one who is ready and willing, to commit such an offense." Examples of objective entrapment included "extreme pleas of desperate illness; appeals based primarily on sympathy, pity, or close personal friendship; and offers of inordinate amounts of money." The Alaska Supreme Court, however, was concerned that "real criminals" could escape and said, "[W]e do not intend that entrapment should become a ready escape hatch for those who are engaged in a course of criminal enterprise. But, under standards of civilized justice, there must be some control on the kind of police conduct which can be permitted in the manufacturing of crime."

Michigan followed suit in a similar case in which a sheriff's deputy befriended a small business owner who was not involved in drug dealing and convinced him to find and sell personal amounts of drugs by playing on his sympathy. The business owner even lectured the undercover agent on the harmful effects of marijuana and heroin. A majority of the Michigan Supreme Court held that this was entrapment as a matter of law and adopted the objective formulation. Recalling its heritage as the first state to adopt the entrapment defense, the court noted: "This is the type of overreaching by the police condemned by our Court in *Saunders v. People* (1878)."[57]

Other states have created a specific objective rule where, in effect, state agents sold drugs to themselves, through a set-up defendant. This occurred when police used informants who were themselves drug addicts or dealers and were desperate to entrap anyone to stay out of jail. They would supply the defendant with drugs that would then be sold to an undercover agent. In such cases, the informants' acts were not known to the police.[58] A state could have this special objective rule for circular drug sales, as per se entrapment, while otherwise maintaining the subjective test.[59] This rule echoes Justice Brennan's dissent in *Hampton v. United States* (1976)—that the "Government is doing nothing less than buying contraband from itself through an intermediary and jailing the intermediary." This is an example of states creating situation-specific entrapment rules to deal with persistent problems of police overreaching.

Cases in "subjective" states show concerns about police operations, and cases in "objective" states tend to discuss defendants' attributes. This tends to show that "separation of the objective and subjective approaches is unworkable. Inducement cannot be considered in isolation from predisposition."[60] While about thirty-five states rely on the subjective test and twelve the objective test, a number have adopted hybrid tests.[61]

HYBRID TESTS   The hybrid approach includes states with both subjective and objective tests. They come in two flavors: the *composite hybrid approach,* where a defendant has to prove entrapment under both the subjective and the objective approaches, and a *discrete hybrid approach,* where a defendant has to prove entrapment under either the subjective or the objective approach in order to be released.[62] The composite hybrid approach is unfair to defendants because it forces a genuinely nonpredisposed defendant to show that the nature of the police inducement would also lead a hypothetical person into crime. The benefit of the objective test in disallowing prejudicial evidence of the defendant's past is negated by the composite approach because past crimes are still allowed into evidence. Also, this approach may require both the objective and the subjective tests to be decided by a jury, as was required by the New Jersey entrapment statute.[63]

The discrete hybrid approach "gives a defendant greater latitude to assert an entrapment defense while reducing the burden of persuasion. It provides the nonpredisposed defendant with a defense against the government's overwhelming power to coerce, and it also gives the nonpredisposed defendant a defense against egregious police conduct."[64]

LAW IN SOCIETY

Undercover Policing and Its Control

Undercover police work, fascinating and varied, includes dangerous tactics by courageous officers to uncover major crimes, sleazy and routine vice enforcement, and questionable tactics by which police manufacture crime. Undercover work often includes encouragement or covert facilitation[65] but may involve spying to gather background information about crime. Undercover policing is an essential tool of law enforcement for detecting consensual crimes (e.g., vice, white-collar crime) and organized crime. Yet it poses so many undesirable side effects that it must be carefully monitored by police agencies.

The Nature and Growth of Undercover Policing

According to Professor Gary Marx's classic study, undercover policing has three major functions: intelligence, prevention, and facilitation. "Intelligence operations use covert and deceptive tactics to gather information about crimes that" have occurred, might be planned, or are in progress. An example is a police agent befriending a suspect in order to gather more information and get a confession.[66] This happened in *Arizona v. Fulminante* (1991) when Anthony Sarivola—an imprisoned former police officer—played a "mobster" in prison and befriended Fulminante to gain a confession to the murder of his stepdaughter. (See Chapter 7.) This was not entrapment, but the confession was coerced because of the implied threats to Fulminante's life. Intelligence gathering includes placing snitches in jail cells. Prevention occurs when police infiltrate an organization, such as an extremist political group, and convince its members to refrain from violence. In contrast, a government infiltrator, known by the French term **agent provocateur**, infiltrates a clandestine political group to deliberately stir up violent protest among its members in order to discredit and ultimately destroy the group. Facilitation, or encouragement, is the form of undercover policing most likely to result in entrapment. In using facilitative techniques, agents can pose either as victims (e.g., decoys) or as co-conspirators.[67]

Prior to 1975, most undercover activity focused on vice—public soliciting for prostitution, operating after-hours bars, selling drugs, and the like— although FBI monitoring and infiltration of radical political organizations occurred too.[68] Since the 1970s, undercover police activity has expanded to many new areas. *Decoy officers* pose as potential victims, such as "skid-row bums" or elderly people who are easy prey for muggers. In New York City, decoy officers drove taxicabs after a rash of cab driver robbery-murders.[69] *Sting operations* also became popular, where police set up fictitious criminal enterprises to do business with burglars or car thieves. Police have posed as major drug dealers, selling to or buying from wholesale drug traffickers. Undercover operations develop in response to a changing society. The rapid growth of Internet use has spawned computer crime. A particularly odious form—sexual predation of minors by pedophiles—has been met by the now-common practice of police officers' going online and posing as young teens on sexually oriented chat lines. The explosive growth of popular Web sites like MySpace has increased the risks of predatory sexual crimes against children.[70]

After the 1970s, undercover work grew enormously, shifting in focus to target white-collar crime, organized crime, and political corruption.[71] Justice Department appropriations for undercover activities increased from $1 million in 1977 to $12 million in 1984.[72] Marx estimated that in 1982, "the proportion of all police arrests involving undercover work has roughly doubled in the last 15 years."[73] The number of federal undercover operations investigating political corruption in the United States jumped from 50 in the late 1970s to 463 in 1981.[74] This trend has continued. Between 1985 and 1995, federal spending on informers alone increased from $25 million to about $100 million a year—a figure that does not include local law enforcement expenditures.[75]

Organized crime organizations, long thought to be immune from infiltration, have been penetrated by government agents, including the famous seven-year undercover operation of FBI Agent Joseph Pistone, who as "Donnie Brasco" infiltrated the leadership of the Bonanno crime family.[76] Undercover work can be part of a larger strategy to disrupt organized crime by intelligence gathering, electronic surveillance, and coordinated police and prosecution strategies.[77] A 1990 FBI operation known as Cat-com (for catch communications), for example, put a dent in cocaine importation. For three years, federal agents infiltrated a Miami communications shop used as a meeting point for drug dealers. Hidden video cameras gathered evidence that led to the breakup of the drug importation ring, the arrest of sixty-eight suspects, the seizure of several million dollars in cash and property, and the seizure of drugs worth several hundred million dollars. The operation, which generated eight hundred reports, gave federal authorities a better picture of Colombian cocaine-trafficking patterns.[78]

Since the Watergate scandal in the early 1970s, federal investigation of local government corruption has become routine. Rumors of judicial corruption in Chicago, for example, led to an astonishing investigation called "Operation Greylord." A downstate Illinois judge was transferred to Chicago and "wired" to record incriminating statements of corrupt fellow judges. This resulted in the conviction of nine local Chicago judges, thirty-seven attorneys, and nineteen court officers and clerks by mid-1988.[79] Integrity testing is also important in police and correctional agencies to ensure that police and correctional officers do not succumb to the temptations that regularly come their way. Recent sting operations in New York City revealed that about 1 percent of police officers were not honest.[80]

The most extensive corruption probe was Abscam (short for "Abdul scam"). The two-year probe began in 1978 when an informant involved in a stolen art sting told investigators that the mayor of Camden, New Jersey, was taking bribes. The FBI set up a fictitious company, "Abdul Enterprises, Ltd.," supplied the company with furnished offices and a yacht, and played on the then-popular theme of oil-rich Arabian sheiks with vast wealth seeking to buy favors. The "sheik" (FBI agent Anthony Amoroso) worked with Melvin Weinberg, a convicted "con man," who made connections with politicians. The FBI allowed Weinberg to design what, in effect, became a major integrity-testing program. In the course of discussing supposedly legitimate investment and immigration matters, the Abscam players offered huge sums of money to political figures and operatives. Camden's mayor, for example, was videotaped receiving $125,000 in return for promising to help get permission for "Abdul Ltd." to open a casino in Atlantic City. The sting operation snowballed. Congressmen were to be paid $50,000 to introduce private bills to allow fictitious "sheiks" refugee status.[81] Abscam middlemen spread tales about huge sums of money available for returning favors. "The operation was finally forced to shut down due to the large number of minor politicians seeking bribe money from the sheik."[82] By 1980, Abscam had exposed "six United States congressmen, one United States senator, a United States Immigration Service official, three members of the Philadelphia City Council, the mayor of Camden, New Jersey, and assorted bagmen, middlemen, and corrupt lawyers."[83] Was Abscam entrapment? The courts said no and upheld the convictions of the politicians and middlemen. Some appellate judges expressed concern that the huge sums offered, "in excess of real-world opportunities," might have created crimes.[84] Most judges, however, saw this as creating a grapevine to which corrupt and greedy politicians responded.[85]

White-collar crime milks billions of dollars from consumers and honest business firms, creates dangers that cause injuries and deaths, and undermines public confidence in business. Past violations were treated as administrative errors, and even after prosecution, penalties were light.[86] After the Watergate scandal, which included revelations of illegal business payoffs to politicians, local and federal prosecutors began to prosecute white-collar crimes with greater vigor—judicial sentences included prison terms for corporate executives. In this climate of opinion, the government has utilized undercover agents in some unusual areas.

For example, an elaborate FBI operation to investigate corruption in the Chicago Board of Trade (the "Merc") ran from 1987 to 1989.[87] Suspicion arose that traders were overcharging customers, not paying full proceeds of sales, and using knowledge of customers' orders to first trade for themselves. Archer-Daniels-Midland Company, a large agricultural concern, complained about abuses and aided the FBI sting by "hiring" two agents to work for the company's trading subsidiary. Getting information was difficult because Merc traders formed tight-knit cliques where much depended on mutual trust. Over a two-year period, four undercover agents lived the fast-paced lives of Chicago futures traders with false identities, fabricated college degrees (verified by cooperating universities), expensive apartments and cars, memberships in trendy health clubs, and seats on the Merc so they could work regularly as traders. They infiltrated the trader culture so as to win other traders' confidence. "Once into the sting operation, the agents tape recorded traders in restaurants, at parties, in health clubs and on the noisy floors of the exchanges themselves." At the conclusion of the operation, the agents had sufficient incriminating evidence to subpoena fifty traders and others for various securities violations and frauds.

White-collar sting operations can be expensive to run and can involve immense stakes. At times, they expose links between big business and political corruption. Some investigations have international repercussions, and prosecution plans may become entangled with conflicting policies of the State Department, the Commerce Department, and even the White House.[88] In other white-collar stings, big business mixes with ordinary crime. The flamboyant automobile entrepreneur John Z. DeLorean desperately needed $10 million to finance a sinking enterprise to build sports cars in Ireland. He was approached by a former neighbor—a narcotics dealer and FBI informant—with the prospect of raising money through a cocaine deal. When DeLorean could not raise the cash for the drug deal, the agent proposed that he sign over his company as collateral. DeLorean might have been convicted if the subjective test of entrapment had been adhered to strictly, but he was acquitted. The jury apparently disapproved of the government's unrelenting tactics and the singling out of the defendant because of his high visibility.[89]

Problems with Covert Policing

Undercover work is subject to abuses and unintended consequences, aside from entrapment. First, despite the heroic TV and movie image of undercover work, some officers are psychologically or physically damaged by the high-stress effort required to play a negative role, thus raising moral dilemmas that often go unresolved. In extreme cases, agents cannot return to normal work; some turn criminal. Covert work puts greater-than-ordinary strains on officers' family lives. Undercover police are sometimes mistaken for real criminals and mistreated by uniformed officers. In an extreme example, a Detroit robbery decoy unit set up in the late 1960s resulted in three officers and sixteen civilians being killed before the unit was disbanded.[90] In 2000, New York City was rocked by the killing of a completely innocent man in a reverse sting. Patrick Dorismond, twenty-six, father of two, and an off-duty security guard, was hailing a cab outside a Midtown Manhattan bar when he was rushed by an undercover police officer who wanted to buy marijuana. Dorismond, offended, brushed him off. They argued and scuffled, and the undercover detective called for backup. In a moment, Dorismond, who was African American, was shot and killed.[91]

Higher rates of entrapment can be expected, for example, when police use notoriously unreliable drug informants to make unobserved buys.[92] Informants may be motivated by revenge and are sometimes paid for their work. Police recruits may be selected because they are not known to local criminals. To ensure their credibility and the lack of a "police attitude," they are put on the street before entering the academy with virtually no training or briefing. Since these agents may remain on the street for many months, making hundreds of buys before terminating their covers, the dangers of lost evidence and misidentification are multiplied.[93] Unfortunately, undercover officers have been known to falsify drug purchase reports by not including information that could clear a defendant; since they work in secret, this form of perjury is hard to detect. Some studies show that officers' reports adhere to the letter of the law even if their actions do not.[94]

Overuse of sting operations, such as a fictitious business buying stolen goods from burglars, raises serious cost/benefit questions beyond issues of entrapment. These operations are costly, and there should be an administrative determination of whether the total costs of running the operation are worth it in terms of the amount of property recovered. Another issue, which is difficult to measure, is whether a sting operation increases the quantity of crime. A new sting operation might stimulate people with no record as burglars to commit crimes when they hear that there is money to be made at this "new outlet."[95]

Undercover work poses risks to citizens as a result of administrative bungling. A chilling example was documented by R. E. Payne, a Covington, Louisiana, newspaper reporter.[96] Payne went to the FBI with a tip about an organized crime murder of a tow-truck operator and agreed to go undercover to detect a political corruption connection. He met with a businessman, K. T. Fogg, who was a local official, and requested a bribe for silence about incriminating information. Payne was not wired for sound; what he did not know was that Fogg had become an undercover operative for a *separate* FBI political corruption unit and was wearing a recording device. As a result of their conversation, Payne was indicted for conspiracy, and his FBI handler refused to acknowledge that Payne was working undercover! Payne was saved from conviction when his attorney obtained a memorandum proving his undercover status. As undercover work expands, so will the danger of more administrative mismanagement, leading to botched cases and gross injustice. Close administrative supervision is essential in any espionage work, whether it involves national security or civilian criminal justice.

Appalling cases of confidential informant abuse occurred when the FBI failed to adequately supervise agent John Connolly, Jr. He had for years allowed James J. "Whitey" Bulger and Stephen J. "The Rifleman" Flemmi, *leaders* of South Boston's Winter Hill Gang, continue their ongoing organized crime enterprise because they were confidential informants (C.I.s) supplying information about La Cosa Nostra. Connolly breached FBI regulations requiring him to fully inform his supervisors and federal prosecutors. This came to light when Bulger and Flemmi were indicted for their racketeering activities. Connolly was convicted and sentenced in 2002 to ten years imprisonment of racketeering and obstruction of justice.

Two horrible consequences resulted from the gross misuse of *organized crime leaders* as C.I.s. First, Connolly had "leak[ed] to Bulger and Flemmi the names of several cooperating individuals who were later killed."[97] In a related case, the FBI withheld information that would have revealed that Flemmi, their informant, had killed a low-level mobster, Edward Deegan in 1965. Instead, they allowed four innocent men to be convicted for the murder on the testimony of "government's primary witness, a mob hit man named Joseph Barboza who was known as the Animal." This extreme miscarriage of justice was finally revealed three decades later, but only after two of the innocent men, Henry Tameleo and Louis Greco, died in prison. They were exonerated in 2001, along with Joseph Salvati, who was paroled in 1997 and Peter Limone, "who was released after 33 years in prison." The government paid more than $100 million in damages to the estates of the deceased exonerees and to Salvati and Limone, believed to be the highest amount ever paid for this kind of abuse.[98]

Covert policing also carries political risks to democratic government. For most of the twentieth century, the FBI used informers not only to infiltrate foreign espionage cells but also to spy on citizens' groups with extremist political views. In the turbulent days of the late 1960s, FBI agents provocateurs, often criminals, infiltrated groups of antiwar protesters to provoke violent incidents that would lead to arrests. The worst case involved an informer in the Chicago Black Panther Party who provided a diagram of the Panthers' apartment, indicating where everyone slept. The FBI passed it to a Chicago police unit and persuaded the police to make the 1969 predawn raid in which Fred Hampton, the local leader, was killed in his bed by a hail of police bullets. The FBI role was not discovered for several years.[99]

Despite the risks of abuse, poorly defined benefits, and dangers of generating crime and entrapment, undercover policing is necessary. It would be impossible or outrageously expensive to police criminal behavior that is secret and where victims do not come forward to complain. The question, then, is how to appropriately control abuses.

Judicial and Administrative Control of Undercover Policing

There are limits to the judicial control of undercover work. The entrapment defense, useful in marking the outer limits of covert facilitation, does not provide appropriate guidance of undercover policing. Some scholars advocate further legal and judicial control of undercover operations: that police not engage in covert facilitation unless reasonable suspicion or probable cause exists to believe that known or unknown suspects are engaged in the crime targeted by the covert facilitation and that a judge has approved the covert facilitation "for only one integrity test."[100] These suggestions are misplaced. Undercover policing is not a search, so warrants are not constitutionally required.[101] Even if created by statute, undercover probable cause warrants would go beyond traditional judicial case-by-case reasoning. Judges would have to enter into administrative oversight and pass on the wisdom of police work, a task for which they are not trained. Courts have assumed administrative control of prisons and other executive agencies only in extreme cases to preserve the constitutional rights of inmates and others. The quasi-administrative role of supervising undercover work could tarnish the judicial role. Conversely, judicial involvement can hamper proper undercover work: Some judges might unnecessarily restrict creative policing, while others would rubber-stamp unwise stings. Judge shopping can cause even greater inconsistencies.

The U.S. Attorney General has established guidelines for C.I.s used by federal law enforcement agencies and federal prosecutors in domestic but not in foreign intelligence cases. The guidelines apply to the FBI, the DEA, the U.S. Marshals Service, immigration enforcement officers, and the Department of Justice Office of the Inspector General. The Justice Department requires each agency to establish a Confidential Informant Review Committee (CIRC) to review decisions regarding the registration and use of C.I.s. Under the guidelines, only prosecutors with "primary jurisdiction to prosecute" a C.I. for criminal activity can authorize immunity from prosecution, not federal law enforcement officers. Officers have a "duty of candor" which means that they have to share their information about C.I.s with supervisors and relevant prosecutors. They also have a duty to "take the utmost care to avoid conveying any confidential investigative information to a CI. . . other than what is necessary and appropriate for operational reasons." Federal prosecutors are required to keep the identity of C.I.s secret "unless obligated to disclose it by law or Court order."[102]

The use of informants has become bureaucratized. Their suitability to serve must be reviewed. The review must show how and why they could provide useful information. The review must consider the negative aspects of a potential C.I.: any "risk that the person might adversely affect a present or potential investigation or prosecution," "the person's reliability and truthfulness," past criminal history, potential for being the subject of a pending investigation, possible danger to the public, whether a substance abuser, the person's record as an informant, and the risk of danger to the informant's immediate family or close associates. Each C.I. must be reviewed annually for suitability.[103]

In fact, the Guidelines provide for "long-term" C.I.s and for the registration of each C.I. A revealing news article exploring corruption between a Baltimore police officer and a C.I. asserts that unlike the movies where "cops slip their snitches $20 or $50 in a back alley," in "real life, informants get their money, sometimes in five- and six-figure amounts, in the form of checks from the U.S. Treasury Department. And in real life, informants get bonuses for exceptional work." This information is not provided by the Justice Department but is apparently known to lawyers and former federal prosecutors, who describe "a whole industry in 'cultivating, protecting and paying informants.'"[104]

The most troublesome but necessary aspects of the guidelines is that paid "informants can break some laws to help law enforcement, but the guidelines warn that they must be carefully supervised and that they are not, under any circumstances, allowed to 'participate in an act of violence.' They also cannot break laws that cops themselves can't break, such as enter a home without a search warrant or tape a conversation without approval from a judge."[105]

The use of C.I.s is a necessary evil. They are used in the investigations hard to get at crimes and criminal organizations, such as of organized crime, domestic terrorism, white collar crime, drug crimes, international terrorism, civil rights crimes, crimes against the national infrastructure, computer intrusion and cyber crime, major thefts, and violent gangs. In addition to detailing notorious errors and abuses of the use of C.I.s, as noted, a 2005 Justice Department report showed real deficiencies in the way that the FBI monitored its C.I.s. This careful and detailed study found that "the FBI's compliance with. . . Investigative Guidelines differed considerably by Guideline and field office. The most significant problems were failures to comply with the Confidential Informant Guidelines. For example, we identified one or more Guidelines violations in *87 percent* of the confidential informant files we examined."[106]

The Guidelines have attempted to stave off lawsuits based on failures to follow them by providing that "[n]othing in these Guidelines is intended to create or does create an enforceable legal right or private right of action by a CI or any other person." Nevertheless, lawsuits have occurred and are necessary to curb government abuses and the conviction of innocent people.[107] It is imperative that the Justice Department and federal law enforcement agencies take vigorous steps to comply with best practices regarding informants, and that state and municipal law enforcement agencies follow suit.

The effective use of guidelines ensures that law enforcement controls an essential function, assures the public that abuses will be kept to a minimum, and avoids overreliance on the entrapment defense, which is not well suited to the routine guidance of police undercover work.

Summary

Entrapment is a complete defense to crime based on the concept that the idea for the crime was implanted in the defendant's mind by police. It is both a criminal law defense and a doctrine of criminal procedure. It is not a constitutional defense; rather, it's a judge-made doctrine of statutory interpretation designed to protect "unwary innocents" from overbearing and entrepreneurial police tactics. The defense is not applied to crimes of violence.

Covert police work—encouragement and undercover policing—involves the lawful use of deception. Undercover police pretend to be victims (decoys) or participants in crime.

They may or may not use the technique of encouragement. Encouragement is police activity in which an undercover agent pretends to be a participant in crimes and furnishes an opportunity for a person to engage in crime. Undercover work does not, in itself, violate any provision of the Constitution.

There are two theories of entrapment. The subjective test—favored by a majority of states and the federal courts—views entrapment as occurring when a law enforcement officer implants a criminal idea in the mind of a person who otherwise would not have engaged in an illegal act. A person predisposed to commit a crime cannot claim entrapment under the subjective test. Proof of entrapment allows the introduction into evidence of such prejudicial facts as prior criminal acts. The objective test—favored by some Supreme Court justices in the past and by a few states—holds that entrapment occurs when government agents perform acts that would tend to draw average persons into crime. Both the subjective and objective tests are concerned with predisposition and excessive police behavior.

Under the subjective test, the defendant must establish that the government has induced an individual to break the law and that the defense of entrapment is at issue. The prosecution must then prove beyond reasonable doubt that the defendant was disposed to commit the criminal act prior to first being approached and induced by government agents.

Another test, suggested by the U.S. Supreme Court and applied by a few courts, is that particularly outrageous law enforcement action used to draw a person into crime violates the defendant's due process rights. Some state rules declare that outrageous conduct occurs when government agents sell drugs to a suspect and then buy them back from him. The Supreme Court has held this not to be entrapment if the defendant was predisposed to commit the crime. In recent years the number of cases employing the entrapment defense has declined.

Most states follow the subjective test. Several have adopted hybrid tests that combine the subjective and objective tests. A composite hybrid approach requires a defendant to prove that entrapment occurred under both the subjective and the objective approaches; the discrete hybrid approach allows the defendant to prove entrapment under either the subjective or the objective approach. The subjective and objective tests overlap in their goal of limiting excessive police actions that draw essentially innocent people into crime.

Legal Puzzles

HOW HAVE COURTS DECIDED THESE CASES?

Predisposition

9-1. Undercover State Trooper "Vinny," assigned to an FBI task force investigating local motorcycle clubs suspected of selling narcotics, was introduced to members of the Longriders Motorcycle Club in Ludlow by "cooperating informant" (snitch) William Donais. (Donais agreed to cooperate with authorities after being arrested for a traffic incident. He was paid more than $100,000 for his work over a period of several years and received other benefits including housing and a motorcycle, which was necessary to maintain his role as a member of the Longriders Club.) Willie the snitch introduced "Vinny" to James Doyle (the defendant), a former president of the Longriders Club.

On June 4, 1999, "Vinny" attempted to arrange a $500 purchase of cocaine from Doyle Longriders Club's clubhouse, using Donais as an intermediary. Doyle took "Vinny" into the clubhouse's bathroom, locked the door, gave "Vinny" his money back, said he needed more time to procure the cocaine, and said that he did not do business over the telephone.

On July 8, 1999, "Vinny" again met Donais and Doyle at the clubhouse and purchased cocaine for $650. "Vinny" protested the increased price; Doyle explained that the price was higher "because he was getting it from a different guy now; and that the other guy was in jail and the police were attempting to deport him."

Doyle based his entrapment defense at his 2003 trial on the testimony of numerous witnesses (all Doyle's friends and associates) that he had undergone treatment for a cocaine addiction in 1997 and was no longer addicted or predisposed to use or sell cocaine at the time that the government, through Donais, infiltrated the Longriders Club in January 1998. They testified about Donais's persistent attempts to persuade Doyle to use and procure cocaine and about Donais's intimidating physical appearance. The defense also presented evidence that Donais was a cocaine addict but the judge refused to admit evidence showing that Donais died of a cocaine overdose in 2003.

Was Doyle predisposed to sell drugs as a drug dealer?

HELD: Yes.

9-1. Doyle offered sufficient evidence to meet the low threshold entitling him to an instruction on entrapment simply by testifying that Donais, a government agent, induced him to sell the drugs to "Vinny." Once an entrapment defense is adequately raised, the prosecution is required to prove beyond a reasonable doubt that the defendant was already predisposed to commit the crime. The central inquiry then becomes, "Was the defendant, initially not ready or willing to break the law, enticed or ensnared by the Commonwealth into overcoming his reluctance or resistance and doing so? Or did the Commonwealth merely provide the defendant, already ready and willing—already 'predisposed'—to commit the crime, an opportunity to do so?"

The Commonwealth's evidence—particularly Doyle's manifested willingness to engage in a drug transaction on June 4, 1999, and admitted ability to obtain drugs on short notice at that time—if believed, negated any rational inference that when Doyle sold the cocaine to "Vinny" on July 8, 1999, he lacked predisposition because he was an innocent beguiled into committing crimes that he otherwise would not have attempted. The jury was not required to believe the "very feeble" defense version of events regarding Doyle's purported lack of predisposition to sell drugs and were entitled to discredit any or all of Doyle's and his witnesses' testimony. *Commonwealth v. Doyle*, 67 Mass.App.Ct. 846, 858 N.E.2d 1098 (Appeals Court of Massachusetts 2006).

Inducement: Derivative Entrapment

9-2. Robert Luisi, an admitted member of the "La Cosa Nostra" (LCN) crime family, was convicted of cocaine dealing stemming from an FBI investigation. The FBI employed Ronald Previte a paid "cooperating witness" (undercover informant) and a captain or "capo regime" in LCN. Luisi admitted his involvement in the cocaine transactions. His defense was entrapment. He claimed that Previte, acting for the government along with another undercover FBI agent (McGowan), had improperly tried to induce him to commit drug crimes. When Luisi resisted, Previte persuaded Philadelphia LCN boss Joseph Merlino to order Luisi to engage in the drug deals.

Merlino was Luisi's superior in the LCN, and the government was aware that Luisi faced death if he refused to follow Merlino's order.

Luisi and McGowan had a number of conversations about obtaining stolen goods and some about a diamonds-for-cocaine swap. Luisi made comments that expressed reluctance to go ahead with the deal and indicated that Luisi had "nothing to do with" the cocaine business. Luisi explained to McGowan that "in the last ... three years I lost over a dozen and a half guys to that. . . . And I have to make a stern, a firm stand here. . . . I don't wanna have nothing to do with it." After this Previte, still cooperating with the FBI, had a conversation with Merlino and convinced Merlino to order Luisi to close the diamonds-for-cocaine swap. Luisi's theory is that Merlino's order was concocted by the FBI and was government inducement.

The district court instructed the jury on the entrapment defense, but the court's instructions foreclosed the jury from considering Merlino's role in the asserted government entrapment of Luisi.

Was the trial court in error in issuing instructions that prevented the jury from considering the order of the crime boss as part of the inducement in regard to the claimed entrapment?

Holding available from instructor.

Entrapment

9-3. Munoz, the owner of "Video Den," was charged with the sale of harmful materials to a minor. A sheriff's office received an anonymous complaint that minors were able to rent X-rated videotapes from the "Top Banana" video store. The sheriff's office decided to spread the investigation to other video stores in the county that rented X-rated movies. The names of the other video stores renting X-rated videotapes were obtained by searching the Yellow Pages of the local phone book. Video Den was totally unconnected to Top Banana. The sheriff's office had received no complaints regarding Video Den and had no independent knowledge as to whether Video Den was renting X-rated movies to minors. The sheriff's office decided to target Video Den in its investigation.

The sheriff's office obtained a false membership card from Video Den under the fictitious name of Brian Jackson, indicating that Jackson was thirty-four years old. The sheriff's office also obtained the assistance of a sixteen-year-old girl who had recently been arrested for negotiating the purchase of a pound of marijuana. The juvenile informant appeared to be at least eighteen

years of age. The membership card was given to the juvenile informant. She was instructed to rent an X-rated videotape from Video Den, to lie about her age, and to say that she was either the sister or girlfriend of Jackson.

On two occasions the underage informant purchased X-rated videotapes from Video Den, after lying about her age and relationship to "Brian Jackson." The videotapes were kept in a separate room and a posted sign explicitly stated that no person under the age of 18 was allowed to enter the room.

Was Munoz entrapped as a matter of law?

Holding available from instructor.

Entrapment Sufficiency

9-4. Jose Reyes Ortega-Gonzalez (Ortega), a Mexican banker, was videotaped at a meeting set up by undercover agents agreeing to launder money and helping to perfect a money-laundering scheme. This was part of Operations Checkmark and Casablanca, the largest undercover money-laundering and drug investigations in U.S. history, aimed at destroying the Colombian Cali and Juarez cocaine cartels.

Ortega claims that prior to his money-laundering activities, four armed men entered his father's house and threatened him, Ortega's immediate family, and the family of Ortega's wife, and asked about Ortega's willingness and ability to launder money. Ortega reported this incident to his bank's security head, but not to the Mexican police, believing them to be corrupt. Ortega then began to notice a strange car parking outside his residence. He was then contacted by Navarro, a low-level money launderer for the Cali cartel, who invited him to Los Angeles to meet "potential investors," who turned out to be several undercover agents who had gained Navarro's confidence. The men at the meeting requested that Ortega facilitate the money laundering, which he did. Ortega claims that Mendoza made a number of veiled threats and repeatedly alluded to the Cali cartel's well-known reputation for violence. Ortega asserts that he feared for the lives and safety of his family, that he had never been involved in money laundering, and that he became involved only out of fear for himself and his family.

Did Ortega present sufficient evidence to require the trial judge to instruct the jury on entrapment?

Holding available from instructor.

Further Reading

Gary Marx, *Undercover: Police Surveillance in America* (Berkeley: University of California Press, 1988).

Scott Turow, *Personal Injuries* (Toronto: HarperCollins, 1999).

David Wise, *The American Police State: The Government against the People* (New York: Random House, 1976).

Useful Web Site

The National Security Archive

http://www.gwu.edu/~nsarchiv/index.html

An independent nongovernmental research institute and library located at George Washington University, the Archive collects and publishes declassified documents obtained through the Freedom of Information Act. Useful source of information relating to justice in a time of terror.

End Notes

1. The subject is found in criminal law and criminal procedure textbooks: W. LaFave and A. W. Scott Jr., *Handbook on Criminal Law* (St. Paul, Minn.: West, 1972), 369–74; and C. Whitebread and C. Slobogin, *Criminal Procedure,* 4th ed. (New York: Foundation, 2000), 503–20.

2. Paul Marcus, "The Development of Entrapment Law," *Wayne Law Review* 33 (1986): 5–37, 5–9; C. Robton Perelli-Minetti, "Comment: Causation and Intention in the Entrapment Defense," *UCLA Law Review* 28 (1981): 859–905; and George Fletcher, *Rethinking Criminal Law* (Boston: Little, Brown, 1978), 541. Mark M. Stavsky, "The 'Sting' Reconsidered: Organized Crime, Corruption and Entrapment," *Rutgers Law Journal* 16 (1985): 937–89, notes that in New Zealand, entrapment may result in the exclusion of evidence, and Canadian dictum indicates that entrapment is a legitimate defense.

3. Jacqueline E. Ross, "Tradeoffs in Undercover Investigations: A Comparative Perspective," *University of Chicago Law Review* 69 (2002): 1501–41, 1521–22.

4. Stavsky, "The 'Sting' Reconsidered," 949.

5. *Board of Commissioners v. Backus,* 29 How. Pr. 33, 42 (New York, 1864), quoted in Marcus, "The Development of Entrapment Law," 9. A sophisticated analysis of the nineteenth-century cases demonstrates that the entrapment defense arose out of contract notions of consent as a defense to crime: Rebecca Roiphe, "The Serpent Beguiled Me: A History of the Entrapment Defense," *Seton Hall Law Review* 33 (2003): 257–302.

6. *Saunders v. State,* 38 Mich. 218 (1878), commented on by Marcus, "The Development of Entrapment Law." The Michigan Supreme Court was one of the most highly respected state supreme courts in the mid- to late-nineteenth century under Chief Justice Thomas M. Cooley, a leading legal scholar.

7. Marcus, "The Development of Entrapment Law," 10.

8. Justice Marston in *Saunders v. State,* 38 Mich. 218 (1878), commented on by Marcus, "The Development of Entrapment Law."

9. Roiphe, "The Serpent Beguiled Me," 270.

10. Roiphe, "The Serpent Beguiled Me," 274.

11. Roiphe, "The Serpent Beguiled Me," 275.

12. American Law Institute, *Model Penal Code* (Philadelphia: American Law Institute, 1985), § 2.13(3) (emphasis added) [the complete text of the *Model Penal Code* as adopted at the 1962 meeting of the American Law Institute].

13. Lawrence P. Tiffany, Donald M. McIntyre Jr., and Daniel L. Rotenberg, *Detection of Crime* (Boston: Little, Brown, 1967), 207–82, 210. In this text, illegal entrapment is distinguished from lawful encouragement, but the *Model Penal Code* and some state statutes use these terms synonymously.

14. *Hoffa v. United States* (1966), quoting from *United States v. Dennis,* 183 F.2d 201, 224 (2nd Cir. 1949) (prosecution of leaders of the American Communist Party).

15. See Victor Navasky, *Kennedy Justice* (New York: Atheneum, 1971).

16. *United States v. Whittier,* 28 F. Cas. 591 (C.C.E.D. Mo. 1878) (No. 16,688), discussed in Marcus, "The Development of Entrapment Law," 12.

17. *Woo Wai v. United States,* 223 F. 412 (9th Cir. 1915), reported in Marcus, "The Development of Entrapment Law," 12–13.

18. Kenneth Lord, "Entrapment and Due Process: Moving toward a Dual System of Defenses," *Florida State University Law Review* 25 (1998): 463–517, 465. "Although theoretically distinct, inquiries into the existence of inducement and predisposition in practice often overlap": Anthony M. Dillof, "Unraveling Unlawful Entrapment," *Journal of Criminal Law and Criminology* 94 (2004): 827–96, 834.

19. Lawrence Maxwell, *Testimony before the Senate Judiciary Committee* (Federal Document Clearing House Congressional Testimony, October 15, 2003).

20. Ruth Marcus, "Fair Sting or Foul Trap? Child Pornography Investigation Challenged," *Washington Post,* November 6, 1991, p. A1.

21. John Holliman, "Postal Service Delivers Child Pornography Ring," CNN News, May 9, 1996, transcript no. 1221–1.

22. Nancy Y. T. Hanewicz, "Comment: *Jacobson v. United States:* The Entrapment Defense and Judicial Supervision of the Criminal Justice System," *Wisconsin Law Review* (1993): 1163–93, 1191.

23. Lord, "Entrapment and Due Process," 475–76.

24. Lord, "Entrapment and Due Process," 478, 489–90, citing *United States v. Kaminski,* 703 F.2d 1004 (7th Cir. 1983).

25. Lord, "Entrapment and Due Process," 479–80, citing *United States v. Swiatek,* 819 F.2d 721 (7th Cir. 1987).

26. Lord, "Entrapment and Due Process," 89–90, citing *Gossmeyer v. State,* 482 N.E.2d 239 (Ind. 1985); *United States v. Aikens,* 64 F.3d 372 (8th Cir. 1995) (defendant predisposed, demonstrated selling crack cocaine to undercover officer); *United States v. Hernandez,* 31 F.3d 354 (6th Cir. 1994) (sophisticated advice to undercover officer about cocaine trafficking shows defendant not innocent dupe); *Collins v. State,* 520 N.E.2d 1258 (Ind. 1988); and *United States v. Hollingsworth,* 27 F.3d 1196 (7th Cir. 1994) (en banc).

27. *State v. Shuck,* 953 S.W.2d 662, 663; 70 A.L.R.5th 743 (Tenn. 1997).

28. *State v. Shuck,* 953 S.W.2d 662, 668; 70 A.L.R.5th 743 (Tenn. 1997).

29. See *United States v. Hill,* 655 F.2d 512 (3rd Cir.1981); *United States v. Newman,* 849 F.2d 156 (5th Cir. 1988).

30. *Greene v. United States,* 454 F.2d 783 (9th Cir. 1971); and Lord, "Entrapment and Due Process," 504–5.

31. Quoted in *United States v. Russell* (1973) 428.

32. Quoted in *United States v. Russell* (1973), 428 (internal quotation marks omitted).

33. Lord, "Entrapment and Due Process," 509.

34. *United States v. Tucker,* 28 F.3d 1420 (6th Cir. 1994).

35. *United States v. Twigg,* 588 F.2d 373 (3rd Cir. 1978).

36. Dru Stevenson, "Entrapment by Numbers," *Florida Journal of Law and Public Policy* 16 (2005): 1–75, 16.

37. Stevenson, "Entrapment by Numbers," 18–19.

38. Stevenson, "Entrapment by Numbers," 21.

39. Stevenson, "Entrapment by Numbers," 38.

40. Stevenson, "Entrapment by Numbers," 24.

41. Stevenson, "Entrapment by Numbers," 21–24 (footnotes omitted).

42. Stevenson, "Entrapment by Numbers," 25.

43. Stevenson, "Entrapment by Numbers," 27.

44. Stevenson, "Entrapment by Numbers," 28.

45. Stevenson, "Entrapment by Numbers," 28–29.

46. Stevenson, "Entrapment by Numbers," 29.

47. Stevenson, "Entrapment by Numbers," 30.

48. Stevenson, "Entrapment by Numbers," 35.

49. *Model Penal Code* § 2.13.

50. Stevenson, "Entrapment by Numbers," 11.

51. *Model Penal Code* § 2.13 (1) (b).

52. *Model Penal Code* § 2.13 (2).

53. *State v. Doran,* 5 Ohio St. 3d 187, 449 N.E.2d 1295 (1983), commented on in Margaret Baker, "Comment: Criminal Law: Entrapment in Ohio," *Akron Law Review* 17 (1984): 709–15.

54. See *United States v. Hill,* 655 F.2d 512 (3d Cir. 1981).

55. Lord, "Entrapment and Due Process," 465, 489–90.

56. *Grossman v. State,* 457 P.2d 226 (Alaska 1969) (remanded to determine whether entrapment made out under facts).

57. *People v. Turner,* 390 Mich. 7, 210 N.W.2d 336 (1973).

58. *State v. Talbot,* 71 N.J. 160, 364 A.2d 9 (1976); and *People v. Strong,* 21 Ill. 2d 320, 172 N.E.2d 765 (1961).

59. See John S. Knowles III, "Casenote: Criminal Procedure— Entrapment as a Matter of Law: Contraband Supplied to Defendants by Government Agents—*Epps v. State,* 417 So. 2d 543 (Miss. 1982)," *Mississippi College Law Review* 4 (1983): 99–111, 105–7.

60. Hanewicz, "The Entrapment Defense," 1182.

61. See Erich Weyand, "Comment: Entrapment: From *Sorrells* to *Jacobson*—The Development Continues," *Ohio Northern University Law Review* 20 (1993): 293–317, 299, 303–4; and Lord, "Entrapment and Due Process," 496, 498, 502.

62. Lord, "Entrapment and Due Process," 498–504.

63. See *State v. Rockholt,* 96 N.J. 570, 476 A.2d 1236 (1984); Lord, "Entrapment and Due Process," 498–501; Brian Victor, "Comment: The Citizen and the Serpent: *State v. Rockholt* and Entrapment in New Jersey," *Rutgers Law Review* 38 (1984): 589–617, 589, 611–16.

64. Lord, "Entrapment and Due Process," 502.

65. John Braithwaite, Brent Fisse, and Gilbert Geis, "Covert Facilitation and Crime: Restoring Balance to the Entrapment Debate," *Journal of Social Issues* 43 (1987): 5–41.

66. Gary Marx, *Undercover: Police Surveillance in America* (Berkeley: University of California Press, 1988), 61.

67. Marx, *Undercover,* 60–65.

68. Tiffany, McIntyre, and Rotenberg, *Detection of Crime.* For FBI infiltration of the Communist Party and the Ku Klux Klan under J. Edgar Hoover, see Richard Gid Powers, *Secrecy and Power: The Life of J. Edgar Hoover* (New York: Free Press, 1987).

69. See Bruce Hay, "Sting Operations, Undercover Agents, and Entrapment," *Missouri Law Review* 70 (2005): 387–431, 390–91.

70. Mary Swerczek, "Cops Snare Suspected Internet Predators; State, Local Police Set up Sting," *New Orleans Times-Picayune,* August 20, 2006; and Bill Hewitt et al., "MySpace Nation: The Controversy," *People,* June 5, 2006.

71. Stavsky, "The 'Sting' Reconsidered," 955: White-collar crimes include tax evasion, bribery, embezzlement of pension funds, and some forms of political corruption; much organized crime includes intimidation-type crimes such as protection rackets, loan-sharking, blackmail, and simple extortion, which are often "invisible crimes" because victims are reluctant to come forward. This new focus was due in large measure to the FBI's changed priorities after the death of J. Edgar Hoover in 1972: Powers, *Secrecy and Power.*

72. Maura F. J. Whelan, "Lead Us Not into (Unwarranted) Temptation: A Proposal to Replace the Entrapment Defense with a Reasonable-Suspicion Requirement," *University of Pennsylvania Law Review* 133 (1985): 1193–1230, 1194, n. 6, citing a 1984 congressional subcommittee report.

73. See Gary T. Marx, "Who Really Gets Stung? Some Issues Raised by the New Police Undercover Work," in Gerald M. Caplan, ed., *ABSCAM Ethics: Moral Issues and Deception in Law Enforcement* (Washington, D.C.: Police Foundation, 1983), 65–99.

74. Stavsky, "The 'Sting' Reconsidered," 956. David Katz, "The Paradoxical Role of Informers within the Criminal Justice System: A Unique Perspective," *University of Dayton Law Review* 7 (1981): 51–71, 55–56, reports that in the late 1970s the FBI engaged twenty-eight hundred "operators" and paid nearly $1.5 million to informants, resulting in twenty-six hundred arrests. James B. Stewart, *The Prosecutors: Inside the Offices of the Government's Most Powerful Lawyers* (New York: Simon and Schuster/Touchstone, 1987), 91.

75. Stephen Labaton, "The Nation: The Price Can Be High for Talk That's Cheap," *New York Times,* April 2, 1995.

76. Howard Abadinsky, *Organized Crime,* 2nd ed. (Chicago: Nelson-Hall, 1988), 295; Robert P. Rhodes, *Organized Crime: Crime Control vs. Civil Liberties* (New York: Random House, 1984); and Arnold H. Lubasch, "F.B.I. Infiltrator Says Mob Chief Told of Slayings," *New York Times,* August 4, 1982.

77. Ralph Blumenthal, "New Technology Helps in Effort to Fight Mafia," *New York Times,* November 24, 1986.

78. Jeff Gerth, "A Covert and Major Victory Is Reported in the Drug War," *New York Times,* April 23, 1990.

79. James Tuohy and Rob Warden, *Greylord: Justice, Chicago Style* (New York: G. P. Putnam's Sons, 1989).

80. Erika Martinez, "8 Lawbreaking Cops Get an F on Integrity Test," *New York Post,* April 19, 2005.

81. Whelan, "Lead Us Not into (Unwarranted) Temptation," 1200–1203; and Stavsky, "The 'Sting' Reconsidered," 956–61.

82. Stavsky, "The 'Sting' Reconsidered," 957.

83. Whelan, "Lead Us Not into (Unwarranted) Temptation," 1200.

84. *United States v. Kelly,* 707 F.2d 1460 (D.C. Cir. 1983), by then Judge Ruth Bader Ginsburg.

85. *United States v. Kelly,* 707 F.2d 1460 (D.C. Cir. 1983), by Judge MacKinnon. A spirited defense of the Abscam operation is presented by its Justice Department coordinator: Irvin B. Nathan, "ABSCAM: A Fair and Effective Method for Fighting Public Corruption," in Gerald M. Caplan, ed., *ABSCAM Ethics: Moral Issues and Deception in Law Enforcement* (Washington, D.C.: Police Foundation, 1983), 1–16.

86. Gilbert Geis, *White-Collar Criminal: The Offender in Business and the Professions* (New York: Atherton, 1968).

87. Eric N. Berg, "F.B.I. Commodities 'Sting': Fast Money, Secret Lives," *New York Times,* January 30, 1989.

88. Stewart, *The Prosecutors,* 92, discussing a sting of corporate executives of Hitachi, Ltd., a major Japanese manufacturer, who were attempting to illegally purchase IBM secrets regarding the design of new computers.

89. Whelan, "Lead Us Not into (Unwarranted) Temptation," 1197–1200.

90. Marx, *Undercover,* 159–79.

91. "Editorial: The Patrick Dorismond Case," *New York Times,* March 21, 2000.

92. Stavsky, "The 'Sting' Reconsidered," 953.

93. George I. Miller, "Observations on Police Undercover Work," *Criminology* 25 (1987): 27–46.

94. Miller, "Observations on Police Undercover Work," 39–40. The other studies referred to are Jerome Skolnick, *Justice without Trial* (New York: Wiley, 1975); and Peter K. Manning, "Police Lying," *Urban Life and Culture* 3 (1974): 283–306.

95. See Marx, "Who Really Gets Stung?"

96. Andrew Radolf, "Lesson Learned: Working Undercover for the FBI Nearly Lands a Louisiana Reporter in Jail; Articles by a Columnist for Another Paper Help Him Beat Extortion Rap," *Editor and Publisher,* September 24, 1988, 9–11.

97. FBI Office of the Inspector General, *Special Report: Compliance with the Attorney General's Investigative Guidelines (Redacted)* (September 2005). Retrieved October 17, 2009 from http://www.usdoj.gov/oig/special/0509/exec.htm

98. Pam Belluck, "U.S. Must Pay $101.8 Million for Role in False Convictions," *New York Times*, July 27, 2007.

99. Nelson Blackstock, *Cointelpro: The FBI's Secret War on Political Freedom* (New York: Vintage, 1975), 12–13; and John Kifner, "The Nation—Informers: A Tale in Itself," *New York Times,* January 22, 1995.

100. Braithwaite, Fisse, and Geis, "Covert Facilitation and Crime," 9–10; and Whelan, "Lead Us Not into (Unwarranted) Temptation," 1216–18.

101. Lawrence W. Sherman, "Reinventing Probable Cause: Target Selection in Proactive Investigations," *Journal of Social Issues* 43 (1987): 87–94.

102. The Attorney General's Guidelines Regarding the Use of Confidential Informants (2002), accessed October 18, 2009 from http://www.usdoj.gov/oig/special/0509/appendices.pdf

103. A.G. Guidelines for C.I.s.

104. Peter Hermann, "Crime Scenes: The Murky World of Informants," *Baltimore Sun*, October 4, 2009, accessed from www.baltimoresun.com/news/maryland/crime/bal-md.hermann04oct04,0,6499881.story

105. Ibid.

106. FBI Office of the Inspector General, *Special Report: Compliance with the Attorney General's Investigative Guidelines (Redacted)* (September 2005, emphasis added). Retrieved October 17, 2009 from http://www.usdoj.gov/oig/special/0509/exec.htm

107. Alexandra Natapoff, "Beyond Unreliable: How Snitches Contribute to Wrongful Convictions," *Golden Gate University Law Review* 37 (2006):107-129.

JUSTICES OF THE SUPREME COURT

The Nixon–Ford Moderates: Blackmun, Powell, and Stevens

To a significant degree, these moderate justices—Harry Blackmun, Lewis Powell, and John Paul Stevens—really defined the agenda of the Burger Court. With staunch liberals (Justices William Douglas, William Brennan, and Thurgood Marshall) and conservatives (Justices Warren Burger and William Rehnquist), and with Justice Byron White joining various sides depending on the issue, Justices Blackmun, Powell, and Stevens were often the "swing" votes that determined the outcome of cases in the 1970s and 1980s. At the beginning of his career on the Supreme Court, it appeared that Justice Blackmun would be a clone of Chief Justice Burger (they were irreverently dubbed "the Minnesota twins"). But in the late 1970s, his voting patterns began to shift away from the Court's conservative wing, and he often voted with Justices Brennan and Marshall, but not so consistently to have been labeled a liberal. *Roe v. Wade,* his abortion rights opinion in 1973 blocking states from prohibiting first-trimester abortions, was by far the most controversial liberal decision in past decades.

In civil liberties areas, including obscenity, school prayer, public religious displays, and free press, the Burger Court did not decide cases in ways favored by the extreme right. In these and in civil rights cases, Justices Blackmun, Powell, and Stevens took moderate or liberal positions. On the other hand, Justice Powell tended generally to rule for the prosecution in criminal cases, with Justices Blackmun and Stevens voting for defendants more often than Justice Powell but not as often as Justices Brennan and Marshall. In the affirmative action decisions, the Court was so evenly balanced that Justice Powell's compromise opinions became the law of the land.

This kaleidoscope of opinions should make it abundantly clear that it is a gross oversimplification to label the Supreme Court at a particular time as liberal or conservative in general. Even in specific areas of law, it is more meaningful to pay close attention to the reasoning of the justices in order to obtain a better understanding of the Court's work.

Collection of the Supreme Court of the United States. Photographer: Joseph D. Lavenburg.

Harry A. Blackmun

Minnesota, 1908–1999
Republican
Appointed by Richard Nixon
Years of Service: 1970–1994

Life and Career.   A lifelong friend of Warren Burger, Harry Blackmun graduated summa cum laude from Harvard University, where he majored in mathematics, and from Harvard Law School in 1931. He clerked for a federal judge and practiced estate and tax law from 1934 to 1950 with a Minneapolis firm; he also engaged in public service and taught law. He was resident counsel for the Mayo Clinic in Rochester, Minnesota, during the 1950s, an association that may have influenced his famous *Roe v. Wade* (1973) abortion rights decision. Appointed to the U.S. Court of Appeals for the Eighth Circuit (Missouri, Minnesota, Arkansas, Iowa, Nebraska, South Dakota, and North Dakota) in 1959, he developed a reputation as a conservative but not inflexible judge, usually denying a criminal defendant's claims but holding that whipping inmates was cruel and unusual punishment. In the turbulent Vietnam War era, he expressed dismay at the militant antiestablishment views of many young people.

Contribution to Criminal Procedure.   It is difficult to characterize Justice Blackmun's position because although he was at first a moderate-conservative on criminal procedure issues, after 1988 he began to shift to the left, and by 1992 his votes put him on the liberal wing of a Court that was growing progressively more conservative. On the conservative side, he joined Chief Justice Burger's campaign to overturn the exclusionary rule, holding that illegally seized evidence need not be excluded from civil proceedings (*United States v. Janis,* 1976). He also ruled that the right to counsel does not extend to photographic identification procedures after a defendant has been formally charged (*United States v. Ash,* 1973); he ruled against a juvenile defendant's right to a jury trial (*McKeiver v. Pennsylvania,* 1971); and he dissented in the Christian burial speech case, claiming that police could interrogate a formally charged suspect in the absence of his or her lawyer.

Justice Blackmun began to diverge from a solidly conservative position by joining the dissenters in three cases that upheld aerial surveillance by fixed-wing aircraft and helicopters. His decisions regarding confessions were mixed, agreeing that a confession made while an attorney was trying to contact his or her client is admissible (*Moran v. Burbine,* 1986) but joining the dissent in *Arizona v. Mauro* (1987) (taped conversation between husband-suspect and wife after the murder of their child constituted an interrogation). He wrote the dissent protesting the decision that upheld the law allowing the confiscation of funds used for the payment of attorney fees. Shortly before his retirement, his growing concern over the application of the death penalty led him to hold that it was not possible to apply the death penalty in a constitutional manner, and he would henceforth vote against every application of capital punishment (*Collins v. Collins,* 1994).

Signature Opinion.   *California v. Acevedo* (1991). For a six-to-three majority, Blackmun ruled that police having probable cause could search a container in an automobile without a warrant. Although Blackmun generally upheld an individual's Fourth Amendment right of privacy in the home, he ruled in such a way as to defer to the needs of police in automobile searches, giving them a bright-line rule that allowed the opening of containers, regardless of whether probable cause extended to the entire car or to the specific container.

Assessment.   Despite his pro-prosecution rulings in the 1970s, a generally conservative stance in free speech and obscenity cases, and inconsistent positions in equal protection cases, Justice Blackmun produced several major surprises. He authored three opinions that upset the older "commercial speech" doctrine, which said that First Amendment protections do not apply to commercial speech. He was the author of *Roe v. Wade* (1973), the abortion rights decision, the most controversial opinion of the Burger Court and an issue that has continued to spark public, political, and legal contention.

Further Reading

Linda Greenhouse, *Becoming Justice Blackmun: Harry Blackmun's Supreme Court Journey* (New York: Times Books, 2005).

Lewis F. Powell Jr.

Virginia, 1907–1998
Democrat
Appointed by Richard Nixon
Years of Service: 1972–1987

Collection of the Supreme Court of the United States. Photographer: Joseph Bailey.

Life and Career.   Powell, from a well-to-do background in Norfolk, Virginia, graduated first in his class at Washington and Lee College, where he was class president. He completed a three-year law program at Washington and Lee in two years, again graduating first in his class, and after studying law at Harvard University for a year, he entered the private practice of law in Richmond, Virginia. His practice was primarily in corporate law, representing some of the nation's largest businesses. During World War II, he served as a U.S. Air Force intelligence officer in North Africa. Powell was always involved in substantial public and professional service activities. While serving as president of the Richmond School Board from 1952 to 1961, his moderation and leadership fostered the peaceful racial integration of the public schools. He served as president of the American Bar Association, the American College of Trial Lawyers, and the Virginia State Board of Education and was a member of President Johnson's Crime Commission in the late 1960s.

Contribution to Criminal Procedure.   Justice Powell generally voted in favor of the state. In *Stone v. Powell* (1976), he ruled that federal habeas corpus should not be open to state defendants who argued the issues before state courts, thus cutting off access of a large group of cases to the Supreme Court. He ruled against an absolute right to counsel at probation revocation hearings but allowed for a due process "totality of the circumstances" rule that would require counsel if special circumstances existed (*Gagnon v. Scarpelli,* 1973). If core values of the Bill of Rights were attacked, he would rule against the government; for example, he ruled that the president cannot issue electronic eavesdropping orders without a warrant (*United States v. U.S. District Court,* 1972).

Signature Opinion.   *United States v. Calandra* (1974). In this case, Justice Powell raised the theory that the purpose of the exclusionary rule is primarily to deter police misconduct. While this arguably misread the intent of *Mapp v. Ohio* (1961), it was a potent approach that gave the Burger and Rehnquist Courts the intellectual ammunition to curtail the scope of the exclusionary rule, which paved the way to the *Leon* exception, which allowed illegally seized evidence to be introduced into evidence if it was seized by police relying in good faith on a bad search warrant.

Assessment.   At the time he retired, Justice Powell was called the most powerful man in America because he often provided the deciding vote in important Supreme Court cases. Outside of his generally conservative stance in criminal procedure, he tended to be a nondoctrinaire judge. Under the Equal Protection Clause, he voted against gender inequality or laws that imposed extra fiscal burdens on indigents. He precisely analyzed competing interests in cases. In a First Amendment case, for example, he ruled that a shopping mall did not have to allow the distribution of leaflets because, unlike in a company town, the leaflet distributors could find other places to make their views known.

His greatest "balancing act" was in the *Regents of University of California v. Bakke* (1978) medical school admissions affirmative action case. Affirmative action programs posed an explosive issue for the Court. If racial quotas were upheld, a white backlash could wipe out the programs, while a finding of unconstitutionality could produce resentment and even violence in parts of the minority community. In *Bakke,* eight justices split in these liberal and conservative directions. Justice Powell's opinion split the difference by ruling that numeric quotas were unconstitutional but that race could legitimately be taken into account in admissions decisions to achieve the laudable goals of affirmative action. This statesmanlike decision legitimated affirmative action programs in a way designed to be most acceptable to the entire society.

Further Reading

John C. Jeffries Jr., *Justice Lewis F. Powell, Jr.* (New York: Charles Scribner's Sons, 1994).

John Paul Stevens

Illinois, 1920–

Republican

Appointed by Gerald Ford

Years of Service: 1975–

Collection of the Supreme Court of the United States. Photographer: Steve Petteway.

Life and Career.   Born into a wealthy Chicago family, Stevens graduated Phi Beta Kappa from the University of Chicago, served as a naval officer during World War II, graduated first in his class from Northwestern University Law School, clerked for Supreme Court Justice Wiley Rutledge, and practiced law in Chicago from 1948 to 1970. His expertise in antitrust law led to adjunct teaching at prominent Chicago-area law schools, the publication of articles on the subject, and his advising of Congress on antitrust reform. Appointed to the U.S. Court of Appeals for the Seventh Circuit in 1970, he gained a reputation as one of the best appellate judges in the country. His first written opinion—a dissent urging that a legislature could not use its contempt power to summarily imprison one who disrupted a legislative session—was adopted by the Supreme Court, which held that due process required a hearing before imprisonment. President Gerald Ford nominated Stevens to the Supreme Court partly because he was a centrist. After the resignation of President Richard Nixon, Ford was not in a political position to appoint a sharply conservative person to the Court.

Contribution to Criminal Procedure.   As the Supreme Court shifted to the right in his more than thirty years of service, Justice Stevens came to have the most liberal voting record in criminal procedure cases on the Rehnquist and Roberts Courts. Although he does not adhere to an overriding judicial philosophy, like the originalism of Justices Antonin Scalia and Clarence Thomas, his work has been characterized as preferring standards to rules, striving to avoid wrong decisions, paying close attention to the facts of cases, and being "keenly aware of the specific consequences of decisions."

Justice Stevens has staunchly supported the equal protection rights of minorities: In *Illinois v. Wardlow* (2000), he noted that poor minority members believe "contact with the police can itself be dangerous." His lone dissent in *United States v. Armstrong* (1996) highlighted the disproportionate burden of federal drug penalties on African Americans. His dissent in *Purkett v. Elem* (joined by Justice Stephen Breyer) criticized racial discrimination in peremptory challenges.

Opinions favoring the police include *United States v. Ross* (1982) (extending the automobile search exception to closed containers where the police have probable cause to search the entire vehicle) and *Michigan v. Summers* (1981) (allowing police to detain the owner of a premises while executing a search warrant). Dissents in *Moran v. Burbine* (1986) (police can lie to a detained suspect's lawyer about his presence) and in *McNeil v. Wisconsin* (1991) (police can try to get a waiver of silence from a detained suspect without informing his lawyer) show his strong support for the right to counsel and the adversary system.

Signature Opinion.   *Payton v. New York* (1979). In this case, Justice Stevens held that an arrest warrant is a prerequisite to a lawful entry of a person's home in order to arrest him. "In this case . . . neither history nor this Nation's experience requires us to disregard the overriding respect for the sanctity of the home that has been embedded in our traditions since the origins of the Republic."

Assessment.   In First Amendment religion cases, Justice Stevens is a reliable liberal, but less so in freedom of expression cases. In cases concerning protection for underprivileged or vulnerable groups, such as aliens, illegitimate children, or prisoners, he tends to find in favor of the rights of the underdog. His monumental "war on terror" majority opinions in *Hamdan v. Rumsfeld* (2006) (the president cannot have Guantanamo prisoners tried before unilaterally established military commissions that do not uphold basic procedural rights) and in *Rasul v. Bush* (2004) (U.S. courts have jurisdiction to hear habeas corpus petitions from foreign detainees held at the Guantanamo Bay military prison) are great victories for the rule of law.

Further Reading

Christopher E. Smith, "The Roles of Justice John Paul Stevens in Criminal Justice Cases," *Suffolk University Law Review* 39 (2006): 719–44.

CHAPTER 10

The Pretrial Process

The [prosecutor] is the representative not of an ordinary party to a controversy, but of a sovereignty whose obligation to govern impartially is as compelling as its obligation to govern at all; and whose interest, therefore, in a criminal prosecution is not that it shall win a case, but that justice shall be done. As such, he is in a peculiar and very definite sense the servant of the law, the twofold aim of which is that guilt shall not escape or innocence suffer. He may prosecute with earnestness and vigor—indeed, he should do so. But, while he may strike hard blows, he is not at liberty to strike foul ones. It is as much his duty to refrain from improper methods calculated to produce a wrongful conviction as it is to use every legitimate means to bring about a just one.

—Justice George Sutherland, *Berger v. United States,* 295 U.S. 78, 88 (1935)

KEY TERMS

absolute immunity
arraignment
bail
bail bond
bail bondsman
bind-over decision
charging
deposit bond
discovery

facial attack
formal charges
grand jury
immunity
indictment
information
initial appearance
motion
preliminary examination

preventive detention
prima facie case
qualified immunity
release on recognizance
screening
selective prosecution
separation of powers
subpoena
subpoena power

transactional immunity
trial *de novo*
true bill
use immunity
venue
vindictive prosecution
work product rule

PRETRIAL JUSTICE

The pretrial process, occurring between arrest and adjudication, is the most important part of the judicial process for most arrested people. Most criminal cases are either adjudicated by guilty plea or dismissed or diverted at the pretrial stage. In federal courts almost "all (96%) of those convicted pleaded guilty or no contest."[1] In state courts, slightly less than 95 percent of defendants found guilty of felonies pleaded guilty.[2]

Prosecutors are the prime actors in dismissing or diverting felony suspects. In 2002, federal prosecutors declined to prosecute 27 percent of the 124,335 suspects investigated for possible federal crimes.[3] As for state felony defendants, statistics of felony case processing in the nation's seventy-five largest counties found that an estimated 24 percent of all cases were dismissed and another 7 percent of cases were diverted or placed on deferred adjudication. Only about 1 percent overall were acquitted.[4] Prosecutors may exercise their discretion to dismiss even when probable cause to convict exists. Discretionary dismissals may depend on a host of factors: that the harm caused was trivial, satisfactory restitution was made, a key witness refuses to testify, an informant is being rewarded, the defendant has been granted immunity, a jury is highly unlikely to convict although probable cause exists, and so forth.

Factual investigation is as, if not more, important to securing justice in the pretrial process as legal research and procedural filings by prosecutors and defense lawyers. Prosecutorial **charging**—the decision to press charges and the determination of which specific crimes to charge—or dismissal, for example, depends in large measure on the facts that have been discovered and reported by the police. A prosecutor who reads the police report ideally asks the police whether weaknesses in the evidence or other factors would caution against proceeding with the case. According to American Bar Association standards, a prosecutor should not institute criminal charges that are not supported by probable cause or without "sufficient admissible evidence to support a conviction."[5] In major cases, and especially in complex federal investigations, a prosecutor may be part of the investigative team and will suggest what kinds of legally obtained evidence must be found in order to gain a conviction under a crime's legal definition.[6]

Likewise, a defense attorney's first step in a case is to interview the defendant. Depending on the defendant's mental capacities and willingness or ability to be entirely truthful, this task is often far from easy.[7] Again depending on the defendant's resources and the seriousness of the charges, the attorney may hire a trained investigator. The attorney's investigation typically includes questioning witnesses. A defendant free on pretrial release is often the best person to find alibi or other witnesses. But attorneys have expert knowledge of the substantive criminal law, and this knowledge helps them direct the search for facts relevant to exonerate the defendant or to establish reasonable doubt. Leading legal scholars indicate that "interviewing and fact investigation are probably the most important skills that a good defense lawyer can offer her client."[8]

Despite the overriding importance of fact investigation, the pretrial process involves a large number of legal procedures. These are likely to be utterly bewildering to the defendant and yet critically important to his or her ability to receive substantial justice and a fair trial. Pretrial release, by **bail** or personal recognizance, will determine whether the defendant sits in jail or goes free before trial. An attorney can facilitate pretrial release and, if it is refused, can continue to press for it. Defense counsel can make pretrial motions that challenge the admissibility of unconstitutionally obtained evidence. A lawyer can work for a dismissal throughout the pretrial period. These require the skills that a good attorney brings to bear in preparing for a satisfactory negotiated plea or in preparing for trial: thorough knowledge of the substantive criminal law, a careful analysis of the evidence, a sober weighing of the strengths and weaknesses of the case, and a willingness to use this information to fight for the client's interests.

At the same time, the prosecutor uses the same skills to determine which are the proper charges, whether to dismiss, and, if not, to adequately negotiate a plea. The prosecutor's preparation is necessary to present an adequate case before a grand jury in jurisdictions that require an indictment. Similarly, the prosecutor must establish a **prima facie case** at a preliminary hearing in order for a magistrate to decide to make a **bind-over decision** to hold the defendant to stand felony charges rather than dismissing. A defense lawyer plays an important role at the **preliminary examination**. He or she must cross-examine prosecution witnesses or potentially lose that opportunity if the witness fails to appear at trial. Also, defense probing prepares for a favorable plea agreement by better understanding the strength and weaknesses of the prosecutor's case.

Some critics say that the decline in trials and the heavy reliance on guilty pleas has made our justice system less fair than in the past and has undermined the adversary system.[9] But as this brief introduction indicates, the pretrial process has become lengthy and complex. Many cases are quickly dismissed, but a typical felony case is completed, on average, from six months to a year from arrest to adjudication, although only half of all murder cases are resolved within one year.[10] In contrast to the view that plea bargaining undermines justice and adversariness, Professor Malcolm Feeley suggests that despite the decline in the number of trials, the expanded use of pretrial procedures actually *strengthens* the adversary system:

> Probable cause hearings, bills of particulars, motions to suppress evidence, and the like, all shape the criminal process prior to trial and formal adjudication of guilt or innocence. In many cases, pretrial hearings—or for that matter negotiations in the shadow of the law—can become mini-trials. Whether the early review of the evidence reveals a strong or weak case or whether the testimony of a particular witness or the introduction of a specific piece of evidence will or will not be admitted into the record can make or break a case, and depending on the conclusion reached, charges may be dropped, reduced, or the accused may plead guilty or take his case to trial. So, while we have witnessed the demise of the trial, we have at the same time experienced an increase in pretrial opportunities to review in adversarial context some of the same types of issues that once were *less* carefully considered by the jury at trial.[11]

The modern pretrial process thus provides a defendant with opportunities for fair treatment. An attorney is provided early in the process. Pretrial steps allow for thorough examination of evidence. Weaker cases are removed, by dismissal or plea, leaving trials for closely contested cases or for more serious crimes.

As a result, the complex pretrial felony process is filled with many important legal steps. This chapter examines a few (but not all) of these steps: pretrial release or bail, the prosecutor's charging decision, **discovery**, and the screening institutions of the grand jury and preliminary examination. Misdemeanors are typically handled in a more perfunctory way. Some of the pretrial processes for a felony case include:

- *Initial appearance.* A suspect is brought before a magistrate within twenty-four to forty-eight hours of arrest and is informed of the charges and of his or her constitutional rights, including the right to remain silent. At the **initial appearance**, the defendant may be represented by a retained lawyer; indigents are provided with assigned counsel or a public defender. Bail or another mode of pretrial release is arranged or denied.
- *Suppression hearings.* Defendants may challenge the introduction of confessions, physical or eyewitness evidence, lineups, electronic eavesdropping evidence, and the like under constitutional or statutory exclusionary rules in special suppression hearings conducted before a judge to determine whether such evidence was obtained illegally.
- *Pretrial motions.* **Motions** are formal written requests to a judge to obtain a ruling or an order. There are standard pretrial motions, but a motion may be uniquely tailored to the case.

Judges may grant or deny motions summarily or may order that hearings be held during which attorneys make extended argument to support or oppose the motions. Suppression hearings, for example, are initiated by motion. Motion hearings are open to the public (*Waller v. Georgia,* 1984). Motion practice is critical to the fairness of the trial process. Motions for a change of **venue**, for example, play a vital role in avoiding local prejudice. Common motions include those to obtain continuances (adjournments), to request psychiatric services and competency hearings, to lower the bail amount, to waive filing fees on the ground of indigence, to be tried by jury, to strike redundant counts of an indictment, to join or sever co-defendants or charges in the same or separate trials, and so forth.

- *Discovery.*   Very few processes are as critical as discovery in major criminal cases. Unlike pretrial rules in civil cases, which expedite the exchange of factual information between the parties before a trial, criminal procedural rules have been less open. The imbalance between the state's police resources to investigate crimes and the limited resources of most indigent defendants has led the Supreme Court to mandate a level of sharing (*Brady v. Maryland,* 1963), although in recent years it has limited full disclosure. It is incumbent on competent defense lawyers to use all legal means to gain access to factual information gathered by the state.
- *Prosecutor–defense conferences.*   In many jurisdictions plea agreements or arrangements for the conduct of a trial are worked out between the prosecutor and the defense lawyer in regular meetings rather than on-the-fly. Conferences allow for rationalized discovery and exchanges of information, and a calm atmosphere in which to discuss case strengths and weaknesses. Conferences improve court efficiency and the rational handling of cases.
- *Arraignment.*   The **arraignment** is a brief procedure where the charges are read to the defendant, who is then given the opportunity to plead guilty, not guilty, or *nolo contendere* or to remain mute. The practice is a mere formality in most courts and is often the arena for the taking of pleas after plea bargaining.

THE BAIL DECISION: PRETRIAL RELEASE

The Eighth Amendment states: "Excessive bail shall not be required...." This does not guarantee pretrial release in every case, but it does reflect a policy favoring the suspect's pretrial freedom, and supports the presumption of innocence. The Bail Clause reflects the traditional method of balancing *individual freedom* with the state's need to ensure that defendants *will return to court* to stand trial. Bail is the release of a defendant before trial based on that defendant's promise to return, secured by some kind of collateral, such as money. The defendant agrees to transfer the collateral to the court if he or she does not show up for trial. Bail may be refused where it appears that no amount of bail will be sufficient to compel a defendant to return to court for trial.[12]

Bail, a legal device, has become a business. A **bail bondsman** receives a portion of the bail amount from the defendant, usually 10 percent, and in return posts a **bail bond** with the court, promising to pay the full bail amount if the defendant does not show. This results in pretrial freedom for the defendant, an income for the bail bondsman, and some assurance to the court that the defendant will show up. Some bail bondsmen employ bounty hunters to search for absconding defendants, itself a controversial practice.[13] If the defendant defaults by "skipping town," the bail bondsman must pay the full amount of the bail to the court and then find and sue the defendant for that money. Courts have the power to forgive part or all of the forfeited amount. Although this discretion may be fair in some instances, it is also an obvious source of corruption.

A defendant has a real *interest in pretrial freedom.* While on release, the defendant can continue to work, earn money, and maintain family relations. A person jailed for longer than a few days may lose his or her job and find it hard to get a new one. The defendant who is free on bail can play a more active role in finding witnesses and gathering evidence. He or she can also confer more freely with the defense attorney. The defendant, presumed to be innocent, also avoids the unpleasant reality of living under often squalid and possibly dangerous jail conditions.

The *public* may have *different interests,* for freedom also makes it possible for a defendant to hide and avoid the trial process. Witness intimidation and killing may also result. A *New York Times* investigation reports that "[a]t least 19 witnesses have been killed in New York City since 1980. Around the state in the last seven years, local district attorneys have charged at least

14 people with killing witnesses."[14] The report admitted that "[n]o one knows how many criminal cases evaporate because witnesses are threatened or assaulted.... Some prosecutors acknowledge that fear among witnesses is a staple of their work lives."[15] The problem of witness intimidation may be especially pervasive in areas infested with criminal gangs. A 1996 National Institute of Justice Report found that witness intimidation was a major problem for half of the prosecutors in large jurisdictions and for 43 percent of prosecutors in small jurisdictions.[16] This is a matter of national concern. By 2006, seventeen states had passed some form of witness intimidation law. "Massachusetts legislation provides $750,000 a year to protect witnesses from intimidation when they testify to a grand jury or at criminal trials. Witnesses in the program can receive armed police escorts, surveillance, relocation and housing and living expenses."[17] A Maryland prosecutor estimated that a quarter of nonfatal shooting cases in Baltimore are dismissed because of witness intimidation. In Albany, New York, a prosecutor used a "rare tactic against witness intimidation" by requesting news media to not publish the names of witnesses who were to testify in the trial of a teenager charged with killing a ten-year-old girl.[18] After years of effort, the House of Representatives in June 2009 passed a bill proposed by Representative Elijah E. Cummings of Maryland to authorize funds to support state efforts to combat witness intimidation.[19]

The Eighth Amendment and the Right to Bail

The Eighth Amendment does not absolutely guarantee pretrial release, although bail is *presumed* in *noncapital* cases. Under common law, *capital crimes* punishable by death were not bailable. The modern approach, in capital cases, is presumption against bail only where "the proof is evident or the presumption of guilt is great." Thus even a capital suspect may obtain bail if a magistrate finds weaknesses in the prosecutor's case. In all cases, bail can be denied or withdrawn if the prosecutor can show that a defendant attempted to destroy evidence or to intimidate witnesses.

The leading case of **Stack v. Boyle** (1951) overturned high bail set for twelve Communist Party leaders who were charged under the Smith Act with advocating the violent overthrow of the U.S. government. The bail amount for each was set at $50,000. The Supreme Court found little evidence that the defendants had a history or intention of fleeing prosecution and no support for the idea that they would "jump bail" because they were involved in a worldwide communist conspiracy. The typical bail amount for suspects charged with crimes carrying a maximum penalty of five years' imprisonment and a $10,000 fine was usually much lower than $50,000. The Supreme Court held that the high bail amount was arbitrary, excessive, and a violation of the Eighth Amendment. Chief Justice Fred Vinson said, "Unless this right to bail before trial is preserved, the presumption of innocence, secured only after centuries of struggle, would lose its meaning."

Modern Forms of Pretrial Release and Detention

Bail practice was for many years criticized as discriminatory, confining suspects who were likely to return for trial, simply because they lacked sufficient funds. Since the 1960s, most states and the federal government have established release mechanisms designed to release suspects who are likely to return for trial proceedings.

RELEASE ON RECOGNIZANCE (ROR)   A court officer interviews the defendant to determine whether personal characteristics make him or her a good prospect to return to court for additional hearings or trial. Objective characteristics include home stability, living with a family member, having a job or attending school, and prior history of escapes. If the suspect receives a high score indicating a likelihood of returning, eligibility is established for **release on recognizance (ROR)**—that is, release without posting any kind of security but by making a formal promise to return to court when summoned.

CONDITIONS OF RELEASE   Modern laws allow a judge to place *restrictions* on a suspect released before trial, in addition to bail or as part of ROR, to ensure the suspect's return to court for further proceedings. The Federal Bail Reform Act of 1984, which applies only to federal courts, mandates that the defendant follow these conditions:

1. Report to a police or probation officer on a regular basis.
2. Stay away from certain people (e.g., victim or witnesses) or places (e.g., airports, bars).
3. Be under the custody or care of an individual or treatment program to ensure the defendant's appearance and nondanger to the community.

4. Maintain employment or schooling.
5. Comply with a curfew.
6. Not possess a deadly weapon.
7. Refrain from alcohol or drug use.
8. Undergo medical, psychiatric, or drug treatment.
9. Agree to forfeit property or money on failure to appear.
10. Execute a bail bond.
11. Be jailed in the evening and on weekends.

These conditions must be reasonably related to facilitating the defendant's return and be tailored to the defendant's circumstances.

DEPOSIT BOND   A few states, to end the unsavory business of bail bondsmen and to ensure equal treatment for indigents, have created the **deposit bond**, also known as an "appearance bond," as a bail bond substitute. If a judge believes that ROR is not appropriate, a bail amount is set and the defendant must raise 10 percent of the bail amount to be released. The 10 percent is not paid to a bail bondsman but to the court. If the defendant fails to appear, he or she becomes liable for the entire amount. Defendants who return to court, on the other hand, receive the deposit amount less a 1 percent retention fee.

The Illinois deposit bond law was challenged as a due process and equal protection violation but was upheld in **Schilb v. Kuebel** (1971), which referred to bail bondsmen in harsh terms. The Supreme Court rejected the argument that the 1 percent fee ultimately retained by the courts was discriminatory against indigents. The Court said that the fee was reasonable; also, the statute had an ROR provision that the judge could use as a release mechanism for indigent defendants who were good risks, thus avoiding any discrimination. The *Schilb* decision, in addition to upholding the deposit bond system, displays faith in the nation's trial court judges to fairly administer pretrial release.

PREVENTIVE DETENTION   The traditional theory of bail—which favors defendants and accords with the Due Process Model of criminal justice—holds that the *only* reason to detain a suspect before trial is to ensure the integrity of the judicial process. Under this theory, a bail amount should be set or bail denied for only two purposes: to ensure the defendant's return for trial or to revoke bail for those who have attempted to destroy evidence or to intimidate witnesses while on bail. An alternate theory—a pro-prosecution, Crime Control Model view—is that bail also serves other functions. It was widely known that *in fact* judges often set high bail to detain a suspect feared *likely* to commit crimes while awaiting trial. Denying bail for this reason is called **preventive detention**. Congress, believing that preventive detention can be constitutional when accompanied by procedural safeguards, authorized its use in the Bail Reform Act of 1984 (18 U.S.C. §§ 3141–50). The constitutionality of the act was upheld in *United States v. Salerno* (1987).

Read Case and Comments: *United States v. Salerno.*

PROSECUTORIAL CHARGING

Prosecutors have *nearly unlimited discretion* in deciding whether to formally charge (accuse) a person with a crime, as long as probable cause supports the accusation, or to dismiss charges filed by the police. This discretion includes deciding *which crimes* to charge, whether of greater or lesser seriousness (*Ball v. United States,* 1985), whether to *plea-bargain,*[20] *when* to bring charges (*United States v. Lovasco,* 1977), whether to *grant immunity* to one or more defendants in the case,[21] and whether to seek the *death penalty.* Courts do not normally oversee or review prosecutorial charging.

Formal charges drafted by the prosecutor are either by **indictment** or by **information**. In federal prosecutions and approximately one-third of the states, formal charges are drawn up by the prosecutor and approved by a citizens' grand jury.[22] A grand jury hears witnesses and reviews relevant evidence in secret. It votes on the charges and hands up (approves) an indictment by majority vote. In states that do not require a grand jury indictment, a prosecutor initiates the prosecution by filing an information against the defendant after a preliminary examination has been held and a prima facie case established. Both indictments and information are *formal* charging instruments (documents) that list the specific crimes that the prosecutor must prove and that the

CASE AND COMMENTS

United States v. Salerno

481 U.S. 739, 107 S.Ct. 2095, 95 L.Ed.2d 697 (1987)

[a] "Clear and convincing" is a very high standard of proof. (See Table 3–1.)

[b] A **facial attack** means that the statute is unconstitutional under all circumstances, not just as applied in this case.

CHIEF JUSTICE REHNQUIST delivered the opinion of the Court.

The Bail Reform Act of 1984 (Act) allows a federal court to detain an arrestee pending trial if the Government demonstrates by clear and convincing evidence **[a]** after an adversary hearing that no release conditions "will reasonably assure … the safety of any other person and the community." * * * We granted certiorari because of a conflict among the Courts of Appeals regarding the validity of the Act. **[b]** We hold that, as against the facial attack mounted by these respondents, the Act fully comports with constitutional requirements. * * *

I

[c] Congress decided that crimes committed by defendants on bail is such a serious problem that the judge should predict whether the defendant will commit a crime while on bail.

[The Bail Reform Act is a response to "the alarming problem of crimes committed by persons on release." It gives a "judicial officer" discretion to order the pretrial detention of an arrestee if the judge "finds that no condition[s] will reasonably assure the appearance of the person as required and the safety of any other person and the community." **[c]** The law includes procedural safeguards: the presence of counsel, the right to testify, to present witnesses and evidence, and to cross-examine other witnesses. If the judge finds that no release conditions "can reasonably assure the safety of other persons and the community," the findings of fact must be stated in writing, supported by "clear and convincing evidence."]

[d] Which of these factors seem predictive of future behavior?

The judicial officer is not given unbridled discretion in making the detention determination, [but must consider several statutory factors: **[d]** (1) the nature and seriousness of the charges, (2) the substantiality of the government's evidence against the arrestee, (3) the arrestee's background and characteristics, and (4) the nature and seriousness of the danger posed by the arrestee's release. If pretrial detention is ordered,] the detainee is entitled to expedited appellate review of the detention order.

[Anthony Salerno was charged with racketeering in a twenty-nine-count indictment. Facts were presented to show that Salerno was a high-ranking "boss" in an organized crime "family." In the preventive detention hearing, the government submitted evidence from court-ordered wiretaps and offered to produce testimony of two trial witnesses who would assert that Salerno personally participated in two of the murder conspiracies charged against him. Salerno presented character witnesses. The district court, believing the government's allegations and that Salerno would intimidate witnesses if released, denied release before his trial.] **[e]**

[e] Do you agree with the decision of the district court or the Court of Appeals?

[The court of appeals reversed, concluding that detaining persons because they were thought to present a future danger to the community violates due process.] It reasoned that our criminal law system holds persons accountable for past actions, not anticipated future actions. Although a court could detain an arrestee who threatened to flee before trial, such detention would be permissible because it would serve the basic objective of a criminal system—bringing the accused to trial. * * *

II

* * * Respondents present two grounds for invalidating the Bail Reform Act's provisions permitting pretrial detention on the basis of future dangerousness. First, they rely upon the Court of Appeals' conclusion that the Act exceeds the limitations placed upon the Federal Government by the Due Process Clause of the Fifth Amendment. Second, they contend that the Act contravenes the Eighth Amendment's proscription against excessive bail. We treat these contentions in turn.

A
* * *

[f] Part II.A. addresses the due process challenge to the statute. What is the distinction that determines whether the detention ordered by the statute violates Salerno's due process liberty interests?

Respondents first argue that the Act violates substantive due process because the pretrial detention it authorizes constitutes impermissible punishment before trial. * * * The Court of Appeals assumed that pretrial detention under the Bail Reform Act is regulatory, not penal, and we agree that it is. **[f]**

As an initial matter, the mere fact that a person is detained does not inexorably lead to the conclusion that the government has imposed punishment. * * * To determine whether a restriction on liberty constitutes impermissible punishment or permissible regulation, we first look to legislative intent. * * * Unless Congress expressly intended to impose punitive restrictions, the punitive/regulatory distinction turns on "'whether an alternative purpose to which [the restriction] may rationally be connected is assignable for it, and whether it appears excessive in relation to the alternative purpose assigned [to it].'" * * *

We conclude that the detention imposed by the Act falls on the regulatory side of the dichotomy. The legislative history of the Bail Reform Act clearly indicates that Congress did not formulate the pretrial detention provisions as punishment for dangerous individuals. * * * Congress instead perceived pretrial detention as a potential solution to a pressing societal problem. * * * There is no doubt that preventing danger to the community is a legitimate regulatory goal.

Nor are the incidents of pretrial detention excessive in relation to the regulatory goal Congress sought to achieve. **[g]** The Bail Reform Act [is] carefully limit[ed] * * * to the most serious of crimes[:] * * * crimes of violence, offenses for which the sentence is life imprisonment or death, serious drug offenses, or certain repeat offenders. The arrestee is entitled to a prompt detention hearing, * * * and the maximum length of pretrial detention is limited by the stringent time limitations of the Speedy Trial Act. * * * Moreover, * * * the conditions of confinement envisioned by the Act "appear to reflect the regulatory purposes relied upon by the" Government [requiring] that detainees be housed in a "facility separate, to the extent practicable, from persons awaiting or serving sentences or being held in custody pending appeal." * * * We conclude, therefore, that the pretrial detention contemplated by the Bail Reform Act is regulatory in nature, and does not constitute punishment before trial in violation of the Due Process Clause.

[Other kinds of regulatory detention, upheld by the Supreme Court as not violating due process, include **[h]** wartime detention of persons believed to be dangerous, potentially dangerous resident aliens pending deportation proceedings, mentally unstable individuals who present a danger to the public, dangerous defendants who become incompetent to stand trial, dangerous arrested juveniles before trial, and defendants who present risks of flight or dangers to witnesses.]

* * * The Bail Reform Act * * * narrowly focuses on a particularly acute problem in which the Government interests are overwhelming. **[i]** The Act operates only on individuals who have been arrested for a specific category of extremely serious offenses. * * * Congress specifically found that these individuals are far more likely to be responsible for dangerous acts in the community after arrest. * * *

[Chief Justice Rehnquist recognized the individual's strong interest in liberty, but held that given the carefully delineated law, individual liberty must be "subordinated to the greater needs of society." He concluded this section by holding that the procedures of the Bail Reform Act were] "adequate to authorize the pretrial detention of at least some [people] charged with crimes." * * * As we stated in *Schall* [*v. Martin* (1984)], "there is nothing inherently unattainable about a prediction of future criminal conduct." * * * **[j]**

B

* * * We think that the Act survives a challenge founded upon the Eighth Amendment.

The Eighth Amendment addresses pretrial release by providing merely that "[e]xcessive bail shall not be required." This clause, of course, says nothing about whether bail shall be available at all. Respondents nevertheless contend that this Clause grants them a right to bail calculated solely upon considerations of flight. They rely on *Stack v. Boyle.* * * * In respondents' view, since the Bail Reform Act allows a court essentially to set bail at an infinite amount for reasons not related to the risk of flight, it violates the Excessive Bail Clause. **[k]** Respondents concede that the right to bail they have discovered in the Eighth Amendment is not absolute. A court may, for example, refuse bail in capital cases. And, as the Court of Appeals noted and respondents admit, a court may refuse bail when the defendant presents a threat to the judicial process by intimidating witnesses. Respondents characterize these exceptions as consistent with what they claim to be the sole purpose of bail—to ensure the integrity of the judicial process. **[l]**

* * * [W]e reject the proposition that the Eighth Amendment categorically prohibits the government from pursuing other admittedly compelling interests through regulation of pretrial release. * * *

* * * Nothing in the text of the Bail Clause limits permissible government considerations solely to questions of flight. The only arguable substantive limitation of the Bail Clause is that the government's proposed conditions of release or detention not be "excessive" in light of the perceived evil. Of course, to determine whether the government's response is excessive, we must compare that response against the interest the government seeks to protect by means of that response. Thus, when the government has admitted that its only interest is in preventing flight, bail must be set by a court at a sum designed to ensure that goal, and no more. * * * We believe that when Congress has mandated detention on the basis of a compelling interest other than prevention of flight, as it has here, the Eighth Amendment does not require release on bail.

* * *

JUSTICE MARSHALL, with whom JUSTICE BRENNAN joins, dissenting.

This case brings before the Court for the first time a statute in which Congress declares that a person innocent of any crime may be jailed indefinitely, pending the trial of allegations which are legally presumed to be untrue, if the Government shows to the satisfaction of a judge that the accused is likely to commit crimes, unrelated to the pending charges, at anytime in the future. **[m]** Such statutes, consistent with the usages of tyranny and the excesses of what bitter experience teaches us to call the police state, have long been thought incompatible with the fundamental human rights protected by our

[g] Notice the two "punishment" arguments: first, whether preventive detention *is* punishment, and second, whether preventive detention is so excessive a means to achieve the regulatory purpose of preventing crime by defendants on bail as to violate due process.

[h] Are these examples similar to preventive detention, or can they be "distinguished" as a matter of law?

[i] Does this mean that *all* defendants charged with extremely serious crimes can always be denied pretrial freedom?

[j] *Schall* upheld preventive detention for juvenile defendants.

[k] Part II.B. discusses the Eighth Amendment challenge. Is the denial of bail the same as imposing excessive bail?

[l] The integrity of the judicial process is undermined when a defendant flees from the trial, but not when he commits a crime while on bail.

Constitution. Today a majority of this Court holds otherwise. Its decision disregards basic principles of justice established centuries ago and enshrined beyond the reach of governmental interference in the Bill of Rights. * * *

II

[m] Do you agree that the law is inconsistent with the presumption of innocence?

[n] Does Justice Marshall's shocking hypothesis apply to the majority's reasoning? On the one hand, the act applies only to arrestees; on the other hand, it applies to people presumed to be innocent. Which factor best fits Marshall's hypothesis?

* * * Let us apply the majority's reasoning to a similar, hypothetical case. After investigation, Congress determines (not unrealistically) that a large proportion of violent crime is perpetrated by persons who are unemployed. It also determines, equally reasonably, that much violent crime is committed at night. From amongst the panoply of "potential solutions," Congress chooses a statute which permits, after judicial proceedings, the imposition of a dusk-to-dawn curfew on anyone who is unemployed. Since this is not a measure enacted for the purpose of punishing the unemployed, and since the majority finds that preventing danger to the community is a legitimate regulatory goal, the curfew statute would, according to the majority's analysis, be a mere "regulatory" detention statute, entirely compatible with the substantive components of the Due Process Clause. **[n]**

[Justice Marshall claims that the majority simply redefined punishment as regulation, and so allows a clear violation of the due process rights of detainees.] * * *

III

The essence of this case may be found, ironically enough, in [another] provision of the Act to which the majority does not refer, [p]rovid[ing] that "[n]othing in this section shall be construed as modifying or limiting the presumption of innocence." But the very pith and purpose of this statute is an abhorrent limitation of the presumption of innocence. The majority's untenable conclusion that the present Act is constitutional arises from a specious denial of the role of the Bail Clause and the Due Process Clause in protecting the invaluable guarantee afforded by the presumption of innocence.

* * *

[Justice Stevens dissented.]

---

defendant must oppose. They state a few facts sufficient to establish a basis—either probable cause or a prima facie case—for the prosecutor to go forward with the case.

In practice, the prosecutor has almost as much control over charges by indictment as by information, for grand juries almost always follow the prosecutor's lead. Formal charges are important because they tell the defendant that he or she will stand trial only on the crimes charged. If new facts come to light, the prosecutor can charge a defendant with additional "counts" (specific crimes) in an *amended* indictment approved by the grand jury or in an amended information approved by the judge.

Discretion and the Separation of Powers Doctrine

A prime reason for prosecutorial discretion is the **separation of powers** doctrine. The prosecutor is an *executive branch* officer and is typically an elected county official. Federal prosecutors are appointed by the president. Judges, whether elected or appointed, are responsible for "the judiciary," a separate branch of government, and do not exercise direct control over prosecutors. This is so even though prosecutors are "officers of the court," as are all lawyers. An example of the separation of powers doctrine arose in the civil rights era case of *United States v. Cox* (1965). A federal judge in Mississippi believed that African-American defendants lied in testifying that a local registrar refused to give them voting registration applications. He referred their case to a grand jury, which proceeded to hand up indictments for perjury. The U.S. attorney (i.e., the federal prosecutor) in that district, on orders of the attorney general of the United States, refused to sign the indictment, thus blocking the prosecution. The federal district court judge then held the U.S. attorney in contempt and threatened to hold the attorney general in contempt. The case was quickly appealed to the Court of Appeals, which reversed the trial court:

The discretionary power of the attorney for the United States in determining whether a prosecution shall be commenced or maintained may well depend upon matters of policy wholly apart from any question of probable cause. Although as a member of the bar, the attorney for the United States is an officer of the court, he is nevertheless

an executive officer of the Government, and it is as an officer of the executive department that he exercises a discretion as to whether or not there shall be a prosecution in
a particular case. It follows, as an incident of the constitutional separation of powers,
that the courts are not to interfere with the free exercise of the discretionary powers
of the attorneys of the United States in their control over criminal prosecutions.
(*Cox,* 5th Circuit, 1965)[23]

The basic rule, therefore, is one of *prosecutorial autonomy* from judicial control in the
charging function (*Town of Newton v. Rumery*, 1987; *United States v. Armstrong*, 1996).

There are many reasons for prosecutorial discretion in charging. One is that the same behavior can often be charged under different sections of the penal code, carrying higher or lower
maximum penalties. Confining the decision to charge with legal restrictions will make charging
more cumbersome and possibly *unjust*—the prosecutor should use his or her discretion to fit the
charge to the overall seriousness of the alleged crime. For example, the forcible taking of property can be charged as a robbery with a potential life sentence or as a theft from the person with a
lower maximum penalty, and saddling a young purse-snatcher with a possible life sentence may
be overkill. Justice may be a reason to dismiss charges against a minor participant in a crime.
Efficiency may convince a prosecutor to charge a burglar with one offense if he or she admits to
others, thus helping the police to clear a number of crimes. *Effective law enforcement* will convince a prosecutor to offer a grant of immunity to a lesser actor to ensure testimony against other
co-defendants. The charging power does gives the prosecutor substantial leverage in positioning
a case to the state's advantage at trial or in plea bargaining, and defendants often accuse prosecutors of "overcharging." In sum, the "right" level of charging requires great judgment.

Norm Maleng, the King County (Seattle) prosecutor, faced a morally difficult choice in deciding to not seek the death penalty against Gary L. Ridgway, the "Green River killer"—perhaps
the worst serial killer in American history—so that Ridgway would identify his victims and bring
closure to the victims' families. DNA evidence linked Ridgway to seven victims, but under his
plea arrangement he admitted to killing at least forty-eight women. Maleng said that the decision
had been "excruciating."[24]

Whether elected or appointed, a charging prosecutor's decisions cannot be entirely divorced from politics.[25] Most charging follows legal standards (e.g., is evidence adequate to
convict?) and legitimate policy factors (e.g., negligible harm caused by crime; restitution), but
suspicion often lingers that political factors, such as reelection, may weigh in charging decisions.
The positive side is that the policies and practices of elected prosecutors are open to public input.
On occasion, a prosecutor who pursues an unpopular course may be removed by the ballot box.
This happened to a Michigan prosecutor who was seen as overly zealous in his failed attempts to
convict Dr. Jack Kevorkian of assisted suicide.[26] The negative side is that political considerations
may warp charging decisions, which ideally are made evenhandedly according to legal criteria.
Even if political considerations are not visible, critics accuse prosecutors of using their discretion
to routinely *overcharge* defendants so that the defendants will be forced into disadvantageous
plea bargains. Prosecutors reply that they frame charges by fitting the facts to the definitions of
the penal law. In rebuttal, defense-oriented critics maintain that statutory criminal penalties are
unrealistically harsh.

Constitutional Limits: Selective and Vindictive Prosecution

Courts have extremely limited powers to set aside decisions of prosecutors. Two constitutional
rules that are rarely applied—selective and vindictive prosecution—allow courts to find that
prosecutions were improper under the Constitution.

Selective prosecution occurs when a defendant is singled out for charging on impermissible grounds, such as race, religion, or political beliefs, or for exercising constitutional rights.
Oyler v. Boles (1962) held that *some* prosecutor selectivity in deciding to prosecute offenders
under a habitual offender statute does *not* violate the Fourteenth Amendment Equal Protection
Clause *unless* the "selection was deliberately based upon an unjustifiable standard such as race,
religion, or other arbitrary classification." In federal cases selective prosecution violates the equal
protection principle inherent in the Fifth Amendment Due Process Clause (*Bolling v. Sharpe*,
1954). Selective prosecution is very difficult for defendants to prove. The discrimination has to
be blatant, as where, for example, after a fatal robbery, a prosecutor charges an African-American

defendant with capital murder while charging white co-conspirators with second-degree murder, unless a *rational factor* distinguished the co-defendants. The classic case of selective application of the law was ***Yick Wo v. Hopkins*** (1886). A San Francisco ordinance required laundries to operate in brick or stone buildings unless the board of supervisors had granted a waiver. The board granted permits to operate laundries in wooden buildings to all white applicants except one, but it denied such permits to two hundred Chinese applicants. This blatant racial discrimination in the enforcement of a reasonable law was held to violate the Equal Protection Clause.

In ***Wayte v. United States*** (1985), the Supreme Court found no selective prosecution even though only sixteen men were indicted for failing to register for the military draft out of about 674,000 who had failed to register. Wayte claimed he was singled out for prosecution because he wrote letters to the government stating that he would not register on grounds of conscience—that is, he claimed he was prosecuted for exercising his First Amendment free speech rights. The selective prosecution doctrine under the Equal Protection Clause requires a showing of both *discriminatory effect* and *discriminatory purpose*. A detailed review of government policy concluded that Wayte was not prosecuted for expressing his views but because at some point the law had to be enforced. The government had applied a "passive enforcement" of not actively investigating failure to register and not going after non-registrants unless they became known to the government. Even then, non-registrants were given several opportunities to register, after letters and even visits by FBI agents explained that failure to do so could result in prosecution. This was known as the "beg" policy. Several grace periods were extended to non-registrants. Some of the sixteen who were prosecuted had *not* protested the draft.

Even if "the Government was aware that the passive enforcement policy would result in prosecution of vocal objectors," discriminatory purpose implies more than awareness of consequences. "It implies that the decisionmaker ... selected ... a particular course of action at least in part 'because of,' not merely 'in spite of,' its adverse effects upon an identifiable group." This could not be shown in the present case. Wayte was prosecuted essentially for failing to register and not because he protested his reasons for nonregistration vocally.

One of the most blatant examples of unequal justice in recent years has been a federal drug law that imposed a mandatory five-year sentence for distribution of 500 grams of powdered cocaine or 5 grams of crack cocaine. This 100-to-1 disparity was originally thought to be reasonable because crack cocaine was thought to be a more dangerous substance that led to violence. It later became clear that there were no inherent differences between the different forms of this drug, but the sentence disparity had a major impact on blacks because crack is a preferred form of the drug among African Americans while white drug sellers and users, in much larger numbers, prefer the powdered form. The federal Sentencing Commission has recommended equal sentences since 1995 but Congress has not yet acted. This disparity, which was made worse by sentencing guidelines, was indirectly reduced by the Supreme Court in rulings that made federal sentencing guidelines advisory and then ruled that a judge can take the disparity into effect in imposing a sentence lower than the guidelines (*U.S. v. Booker*, 2005; *Kimbrough v. U.S.*, 2007).

A failed attempt to challenge the disparity was made in ***United States v. Armstrong*** (1996) by African Americans charged with selling more than 50 grams of crack cocaine who claimed they were subject to *selective prosecution* because they were black. A federal–state drug task force investigation established that they were regular dealers. The Supreme Court found that Armstrong and his co-defendants failed to meet the threshold for establishing selective prosecution because they did not show that the government declined to prosecute similarly situated suspects of other races. In other words, Armstrong had to show not only that black defendants were prosecuted but that white defendants were *not* prosecuted for crack cocaine offenses. To support its position the government produced a comprehensive report showing that the manufacture and distribution of crack was controlled by large-scale, interstate trafficking networks of Jamaicans, Haitians, and black street gangs, while whites were predominant dealers of LSD and pornography and purveyors of prostitution. The government also produced detailed affidavits showing that race played no role in the DEA investigation, but that the decision to prosecute was based on such general criteria for prosecution as the large quantity of cocaine involved, multiple sales, firearms violations connected to the sales, and the defendants' criminal histories.

Armstrong countered with extremely weak evidence. A paralegal working in a federal defender's office swore that the defendant was black in every one of the twenty-four crack cocaine cases closed by the office in one year and that there are "an equal number of caucasian users and dealers to minority users and dealers" of crack. Armstrong also submitted an affidavit from a criminal defense attorney alleging that in his experience many nonblacks are prosecuted in state court for crack offenses, and a newspaper article reporting that "federal crack criminals ... are being punished far more severely than if they had been caught with powder cocaine, and almost every single one of them is black."

The Supreme Court held that a criminal defendant alleging selective prosecution must present "clear evidence to the contrary" and added that, "Presumptions at war with presumably reliable statistics have no proper place in the analysis of this issue." One reason for the high threshhold of proving selective prosecution is that a selective-prosecution claim asks a court to exercise judicial power over a "special province" of the executive. The Attorney General and United States Attorneys, as the delegates of the president, retain *broad discretion* to enforce the nation's criminal laws to help the president discharge his constitutional responsibility to "take Care that the Laws be faithfully executed" (U.S. Const., Art. II, §3).

Vindictive prosecution occurs when new and more serious charges are brought simply because a defendant has exercised his or her statutory or constitutional rights. For example, if a defendant wins a new trial after appealing a conviction for breaking and entering, it is illegally vindictive behavior for the prosecutor to simply recharge the defendant with the more serious crime of burglary. Increasing the charge might be interpreted as the prosecutor's "getting even" with the defendant for exercising the legal right to appeal. *North Carolina v. Pearce* (1969) initiated the concept in a case involving sentencing. The scenario is one where a defendant successfully overturns a conviction on appeal (whether for constitutional or nonconstitutional errors) and is retried, reconvicted, and resentenced for the same crime. The Supreme Court ruled that vindictiveness must play no part in the resentencing. The concern was that a harsher sentence after a successful appeal was seen to punish defendants for exercising their constitutional rights to appeal. This would "chill" the right to appeal; that is, it would *cause prisoners to not pursue their rights*. In practice, this meant that the second sentencing could not be harsher than the first unless new facts came to the attention of the sentencing judge.

The *Pearce* non-vindictiveness principle, based on concepts of due process fairness, has been applied to cases in which a prosecutor has an opportunity to charge a defendant a second time. In **Blackledge v. Perry** (1974), Perry was found guilty of a *misdemeanor* and was sentenced to six months' incarceration. Under North Carolina's two-tiered trial system, instead of appealing, he was granted a **trial *de novo*** in the superior court, where "the slate is wiped clean, the prior conviction annulled, and the prosecution and defense begin anew." The prosecutor then charged Perry with the *felony* of assault with a deadly weapon. He was convicted and sentenced to a term of five to seven years in prison. On appeal to the Supreme Court, Justice Potter Stewart held that the prosecutor's enhancement of the charges constituted a *due process* violation for "vindictiveness." It was not necessary to show that the prosecutor was motivated by ill will or bad faith, only that the harsher charge was *in response to* the defendant's exercise of a *legal right*. The basis of the vindictiveness rule is "the fear that such vindictiveness may unconstitutionally deter a defendant's exercise of the right to appeal his first conviction." Due process requires that "a defendant be freed of the apprehension of such a retaliatory motivation" on the part of the prosecutor. In this instance, "[a] person convicted of an offense is entitled to pursue his statutory right to a trial *de novo* without apprehension that the State will retaliate by substituting a more serious charge for the original one thus subjecting him to a significantly increased potential period of incarceration."

United States v. Goodwin (1982) demonstrates that vindictiveness is not to be automatically inferred from new and harsher charges. Goodwin was stopped for speeding by a federal park police officer in Maryland. When he was ordered back into his car by the officer and asked to raise the front seat armrest so the officer could see what was in a clear plastic bag, Goodwin drove off and knocked the officer down. The officer filed a complaint against Goodwin in the federal district court, charging him with misdemeanor assault. The case was set for trial, but Goodwin fled the jurisdiction. He was found in custody in Virginia three years later and was returned to federal custody in Maryland. His *misdemeanor* charges were to be tried before a federal magistrate. Goodwin then requested a jury trial. The case was transferred from the magistrate's court, which had no authority to try felonies, to a felony-level court. The U.S. attorney obtained a *felony* indictment against Goodwin for forcibly assaulting a federal officer. After conviction, Goodwin claimed that the enhanced charge amounted to vindictiveness under the rule of *Blackledge*. The Court disagreed and found no vindictiveness:

> There is good reason to be cautious before adopting an inflexible presumption of prosecutorial vindictiveness in a pretrial setting. In the course of preparing a case

for trial, the prosecutor may uncover additional information that suggests a basis for further prosecution or he simply may come to realize that information possessed by the State has a broader significance. At this stage of the proceedings, the prosecutor's assessment of the proper extent of prosecution may not have crystallized. In contrast, once a trial begins—and certainly by the time a conviction has been obtained—it is much more likely that the State has discovered and assessed all of the information against an accused and has made a determination, on the basis of that information, of the extent to which he should be prosecuted. Thus, a change in the charging decision made after an initial trial is completed is much more likely to be improperly motivated than is a pretrial decision. (*United States v. Goodwin,* 1982)

Therefore, a defendant's request for a jury over a bench trial, before trial, may not trigger a presumption of vindictiveness when charges are thereafter increased. As a due process rule, vindictiveness must be determined after examining all of the facts and circumstances.

SCREENING: THE GRAND JURY AND THE PRELIMINARY EXAMINATION

Screening—eliminating cases that should not go to trial—is an essential pretrial function. Quickly screening out innocent suspects eliminates "easy" cases from trial dockets and relieves innocent suspects from further expense, inconvenience, and fear. As noted at the beginning of this chapter, most cases are screened out of the judicial process by *prosecutors* who decline to prosecute suspects arrested by the police. Two major screening institutions, the grand jury and the preliminary examination, have roots in the common law era and have the formal function to decide whether the state has presented probable cause to support a prosecution. In the unlikely event that a prosecutor does not establish probable cause, the prosecution must be dismissed.

In fact, neither of these institutions screens out very many cases today, although they play other useful pretrial functions. The **grand jury** is a panel of citizens that dates back to the origin of trial by jury in the thirteenth century. The preliminary examination, created by statute in the sixteenth century, was designed to secure information of the crime immediately after an arrest.[27] The modern preliminary examination culminates with the magistrate either binding over a case for trial or dismissing, depending on whether the prosecutor established probable cause.

The Grand Jury

During the seventeenth century, grand juries in England gained the public's respect by refusing to indict popular political opponents of the Crown. This resistance to British authority made the grand jury popular in the American colonies. Each new American state and the federal government required that criminal prosecutions be initiated by grand jury, and federal grand juries were guaranteed in the Fifth Amendment of the Bill of Rights (1791).[28]

By the mid-nineteenth century, however, over half the states had eliminated grand jury indictment as costly and cumbersome. With the expansion of the right to vote, it was believed that elected prosecutors would charge defendants fairly by information. In the noted case of **Hurtado v. California** (1884) the Supreme Court held that *states* did not have to indict defendants by citizen's grand juries, as did the federal government. (See Chapter 1.) The Fifth Amendment Grand Jury Clause in the Bill of Rights did not apply to the states—that is, it was not incorporated into the Due Process Clause. Further, the Court held that the grand jury is not so *fundamental* to liberty and justice as to be an element of Fourteenth Amendment due process. States without the indictment requirement still retain grand juries that can be called by prosecutors in special cases. These tend to be complex white-collar, organized crime, or government corruption cases where grand jury secrecy and its **subpoena** powers are useful powers.

Depending on a state's law, citizen grand juries number between twelve and twenty-three jurors. They determine by *majority vote* whether there is probable cause to hold a suspect for trial, issuing either a "**true bill**" of indictment or "no bill." The prosecutor must sign the bill of indictment to formally charge a defendant. The grand jury may rely on *hearsay evidence* in coming to its decision, such as summarizations of testimony by government agents rather than the direct testimony of witnesses (**Costello v. United States,** 1956). As noted in Chapter 2,

United States v. Calandra (1974) held that grand jury *questions* may be based on *illegally seized evidence*. The *Calandra* rule makes it considerably easier for prosecutors to gain indictments.

Grand jurors "investigate" crimes mainly by listening to witnesses. In theory, they could issue subpoenas on their own, but they rarely do. The prosecutor presents cases to the grand jury and generally guides its activities. Judges do not preside over grand juries but can decide evidentiary questions that arise during grand jury proceedings. As a citizens' body, the grand jury is not administratively or legally within any of the three branches of government.

The term of a federal grand jury is *eighteen months*, with six-month extensions. In practice, federal grand jury service lasts for a month. Then, although the grand jurors no longer meet, the grand jury retains its "legal" existence. This is important because a person who is granted **immunity** in order to testify before a grand jury, but refuses to do so, can be held in contempt and jailed during the entire life of the grand jury, even if the jury is not actively sitting.

Racial bias in the *selection* of members of a grand jury results in the *automatic reversal* of the indictment (*Ex Parte Virginia,* 1880; *Cassell v. Texas,* 1950). Legal objections to a grand jury's racial composition ordinarily must be brought before the case goes to trial. If an objection was not possible before the trial began, however, an indictment may still be reversed even though the defendant was found guilty by an unbiased petit jury. In **Vasquez v. Hillary** (1986), the appellant's conviction occurred twenty-four years before the appeal was filed. Justice Thurgood Marshall, writing for the majority, pointed out that a conviction does not erase all the damage inflicted by a biased grand jury. Even if there was probable cause, the grand jury might have charged the defendant with a lesser crime, or with fewer counts, or on a noncapital rather than a capital charge. "Once having found discrimination in the selection of a grand jury, we simply cannot know that the need to indict would have been assessed in the same way by a grand jury properly constituted." As Justice Harry Blackmun forcefully noted in *Rose v. Mitchell* (1979), the exclusion of grand jurors on account of race "destroys the appearance of justice and thereby casts doubt on the integrity of the judicial process. [It] impairs the confidence of the public in the administration of justice. [It] 'not only violates our Constitution and the laws enacted under it but is at war with our basic concepts of a democratic society and a representative government.'"

Grand Jury Functions and Powers

The grand jury functions as a "shield" to screen out cases improperly brought by the prosecutor, but also has powers that make it an effective "sword" to investigate crime. In reality, these powers are used by the *prosecutor* with the grand jury's agreement. These powers include the power to subpoena witnesses and documents, to provide grants of immunity, and to meet in secrecy.

SUBPOENA   A **subpoena** requires individuals to testify (subpoena *ad testificandum*) or to bring papers and evidence (subpoena *duces tecum*) before the grand jury in order to further a criminal investigation. There is a *general obligation* to obey grand jury subpoenas. In **Branzburg v. Hayes** (1972), the Supreme Court held that a *news reporter* does not have a First Amendment privilege to withhold information or to avoid testifying before a grand jury when the reporter promised not to reveal sources who may have been involved in criminal activity. Failure to obey a subpoena can be punished with a contempt-of-court citation. Testimony before the grand jury is under oath, so false or contradictory statements can be used later to *impeach* the witness or can be used as a basis for a *perjury* prosecution. Courts may overrule a subpoena if the requested evidence is not relevant to the investigation or if the request for documents is too vague or unreasonable.[29]

IMMUNITY   A related power is the grant of immunity to witnesses who refuse to testify on Fifth Amendment self-incrimination grounds. (See Chapter 7.) Immunity granted by a state court at a prosecutor's request also prohibits federal prosecution, and federal immunity prevents state prosecution (*Murphy v. Waterfront Commission of New York Harbor,* 1964). The scope of immunity may be either *narrow* or *broad*. Prosecutors in *Counselman v. Hitchcock* (1892) granted a limited form of **use immunity** to grand jury witnesses. This prevents the use and derivative use of testimony in future prosecutions, but does not bar future prosecutions of the defendant if evidence is obtained from an *independent source*. The Supreme Court held in 1892 that such narrow immunity was not sufficient to protect the witness's privilege against self-incrimination.

In response to *Counselman,* Congress adopted a **transactional immunity** statute that provided that a witness required to testify was granted broad immunity "for or on account of any transaction, matter, or thing concerning which he may testify or produce evidence." The Court began to shift its ground in *Murphy v. Waterfront Commission of New York Harbor* (1964), leading Congress to again narrow its immunity statute. The Supreme Court upheld the constitutionality of the narrower use immunity in *Kastigar v. United States* (1972). This narrowing of the privilege against self-incrimination is another indication of the Burger Court's Crime Control Model approach to criminal justice.

SECRECY   The grand jury meets in secrecy. Lawyers of witnesses and suspects are barred, as is the general public. The Supreme Court gives five reasons for grand jury secrecy:

1. To prevent the escape of indicted suspects.
2. To ensure great freedom of deliberation for grand jurors.
3. To prevent witness tampering.
4. To encourage the free testimony of witnesses with information about the crime.
5. To protect the identity of an innocent suspect who is exonerated (***United States v. Procter & Gamble Co.,*** 1958).

Under the Federal Rules of Criminal Procedure, grand jury information (except for the jury deliberations and vote of specific grand jurors) may be released automatically to other prosecutors or to law enforcement personnel to assist them in their official duties.[30] Otherwise, grand jury information may be released only upon a court order, with or without a request by the defendant.

Misuse of the Grand Jury and the Calls for Reform

Abuses have led to calls for the abolition or reform of the grand jury system, which in fact was abolished in England in 1933 on the grounds that it was a cumbersome institution that did little to protect defendants from improper prosecution. One perennial criticism is that the grand jury is not an independent citizens' body anymore; it has become a rubber stamp for the prosecutor, who values it only for its secrecy and enormous powers of compelling testimony. Another criticism is that it has been used to intimidate witnesses.[31]

The worst abuses in recent history occurred during the Nixon administration (1969–1974), when the Justice Department's Internal Security Division used federal grand juries to harass and intimidate antiwar activists and peaceful dissidents. Using its national jurisdiction, these prosecutors subpoenaed witnesses on short notice, flew them across the nation to a place they had never been, and grilled them for days to gain information.[32] These politically motivated abuses went a long way toward limiting federal prosecutorial authority that in the early twenty-first century is deemed necessary to prosecute terrorism cases. The excesses of the past are a reminder that the grand jury's powers can be used for oppressive purposes.

Abuses led some critics to propose *eliminating* the grand jury.[33] Other critics suggest reforming it. One reform proposal is to allow *witnesses' attorneys to be in the grand jury room* during testimony to advise their clients on the legality of questions, but not to allow them to offer substantive challenges. This would be fair and efficient, eliminating the need for delays as witnesses leave the grand jury room to confer with counsel. Today, about fifteen states allow counsel in their grand jury hearings.[34] Another reform proposal *allows the "target" of the grand jury investigation to testify voluntarily* and to present evidence before the grand jury. Although this makes a grand jury hearing resemble a trial or a preliminary hearing, about ten states now require evidence standards approaching the requirements imposed at trial.[35]

Some experienced lawyers concede that the federal grand jury is a tool of the prosecutor but still oppose these reforms. They argue that the grand jury's power is not usually abused and that it is an important cog in the government's investigatory machinery. Without the grand jury, prosecutorial charging followed by preliminary examinations in complex white-collar crime cases could lead to hearings that require weeks of judicial time. Also, questions asked by grand jurors often help the prosecutor to sharpen the focus of the indictment or to decide to terminate further investigation.[36] As the movement for grand jury abolition has waned, strengthening the grand jury and instituting some procedural reform seems to be the appropriate course for the federal and state governments.

The Preliminary Examination and Its Procedures

The preliminary examination is a trial-like adversary hearing. It is not guaranteed by the Constitution but is a statutory right in every jurisdiction.[37] Its screening function overlaps with that of the grand jury and in some jurisdictions, including the federal government, and a preliminary examination cannot be held once a grand jury has indicted.[38] This rule, over the objections of defense attorneys, has virtually eliminated preliminary examinations in some federal district courts, depriving defendants of other valuable functions of the preliminary examination.[39] Some courts have allowed preliminary hearings after grand jury indictment in states where formal charges are typically brought by information.[40] This provides an independent determination of probable cause and acknowledges the existence of informal functions of the preliminary examination.

A defendant may *waive* his or her right to a preliminary examination. This is often inadvisable, especially if the waiver is done before consulting with a lawyer. Counsel may recommend a waiver on tactical grounds, where, for example, defense counsel wants to avoid giving prosecution witnesses an opportunity to become practiced and at ease in the courtroom. Prosecutors in many jurisdictions can insist upon a preliminary examination even if the defendant waives it.

A preliminary examination is conducted much like a trial. It is open to the public and held in a courtroom before a magistrate or judge, witnesses may be called and cross-examined, and a transcript of the proceedings is made. The defendant must be present and be represented by an attorney. This is noticeably different than the grand jury, which operates in strict secrecy. Defendants rarely present witnesses at preliminary examinations but tend to probe prosecution witnesses to develop a sense of the strength of the prosecutor's case.

The goal of the preliminary examination—to determine whether *probable cause* exists—means that the testimony elicited by the prosecutor is more *limited* than that presented at trial, where the prosecutor must prove a defendant guilty beyond a reasonable doubt. The magistrate may restrict the scope of the questioning or the cross-examination if, for example, he or she believes that the questioning goes beyond an attempt to undermine probable cause and becomes a quest for discovery.[41] Also, in most states, evidence may be admitted in a preliminary examination that is not admissible at the trial.

As with a trial, a preliminary examination must be open to the public. ***Press Enterprise Co. v. Superior Court*** (1986) involved a forty-one-day preliminary examination in which the defendant was charged with murdering twelve people by administering a heart drug. The magistrate refused to release the transcript of the hearing to a news organization on the grounds that it would generate such hysteria as to prejudice the defendant's right to a fair trial. The Supreme Court reversed—the news organization's First Amendment right guaranteed access to the preliminary examination. Further, "public access plays a significant positive role in the functioning" of the preliminary examination, which is often the only public airing of a criminal prosecution. In the absence of a jury, the presence of the public helps prevent corrupt or overzealous prosecution and compliant, biased, or eccentric judges. A magistrate can legally bar the public from a preliminary examination if he or she makes a specific, on-the-record finding that demonstrates that closure is essential to preserve "higher values," such as the fairness of the trial, and is narrowly tailored to serve that interest.

The preliminary examination is a *critical stage* of the criminal prosecution under the Sixth Amendment, requiring that a defendant be *represented by counsel* unless the defendant waives this right. Counsel must be provided by the state for indigent defendants. In ***Coleman v. Alabama*** (1970), the Supreme Court reasoned that lack of counsel at the preliminary examination would undermine the defendant's right to a fair trial:

> First, the lawyer's skilled examination and cross-examination of witnesses may expose fatal weaknesses in the State's case that may lead the magistrate to refuse to bind the accused over. Second, in any event, the skilled interrogation of witnesses by an experienced lawyer can fashion a vital impeachment tool for use in cross-examination of the State's witnesses at the trial, or preserve testimony favorable to the accused of a witness who does not appear at the trial. Third, retained counsel can more effectively discover the case the State has against his client and make possible the preparation of a proper defense to meet that case at the trial. Fourth, counsel can also be influential at the preliminary hearing in making effective arguments for the accused on such

matters as the necessity for early psychiatric examination or bail. The inability of the indigent accused on his own to realize these advantages of a lawyer's assistance compels the conclusion that the Alabama preliminary hearing is a "critical stage" of the State's criminal process at which the accused is 'as much entitled to such aid [of counsel] ...as at the trial itself'; [citing *Powell v. Alabama*]. (*Coleman v. Alabama*, 1970)

Coleman demonstrated that having counsel at the preliminary examination was as crucial to a defendant's interests in a fair defense as it was at the actual trial.

The Informal Functions of the Preliminary Examination

Aside from its screening purpose, the preliminary examination serves other useful functions that are not explicitly recognized by statutes. These have lower legitimacy in the eyes of many judges. The least controversial "covert" function is to *preserve testimony* in the transcript of the examination. Because witnesses are under oath and subject to cross-examination, the preliminary examination transcripts may be used to impeach (discredit) the testimony of a witness during trial if the testimony is inconsistent.

A preliminary examination *transcript* may be introduced into evidence if a witness is unavailable for trial due to death, disability, or disappearance. This is a recognized hearsay rule exception. In **California v. Green** (1970), the defendant was charged with furnishing marijuana to Porter, a minor. On the witness stand, Porter became evasive and uncooperative and claimed a lapse of memory when asked about receiving marijuana from Green. The prosecutor then introduced the preliminary hearing transcript to prove that Porter had received illegal substances from Green. The Supreme Court upheld this practice. It ruled that the Sixth Amendment Confrontation Clause was not violated by the introduction of testimony made during a prior hearing because the witness had been *subject to* cross-examination, even if he had not actually been cross-examined. The fact that preliminary examination questioning is not usually as intense as cross-examination at trial does not alter the rule. Although the witness was physically present, he was unavailable for constitutional purposes. The state did its best to question Porter, and when he "clammed up," nothing in the Confrontation Clause prohibited the state from also relying on his prior testimony to prove its case against Green (*California v. Green*, 1970).

More controversial is the defense use of the preliminary examination as a *discovery* device to gather information and to assess the strength of the prosecution's case. This purpose is less important in jurisdictions in which prosecutors fully and promptly share factual information with the defense. On the other hand, prosecutors who keep information from the defense for tactical reasons (e.g., obtaining a favorable guilty plea despite weak evidence) encourage this covert use of the preliminary examination by defense counsel. Most judges believe that discovery is subordinate to the primary bind-over function and may limit cross-examination by the defense if it appears to be aimed only at discovering information in the prosecutor's hands rather than probing the existence of probable cause.

The preliminary examination plays a role in plea bargaining by clarifying the prosecutor's case and by observing whether it is strong or weak. This may expedite a willingness to enter a plea agreement by the party with the weaker hand. If a case does go to trial, the prosecution may benefit by having given witnesses an "audition," so they become more familiar with the courtroom setting and with their "lines." They are apt to show less nervousness when they testify at trial and will be more believable.

DISCOVERY

If justice consists of convicting the guilty and exonerating the innocent, nothing can be more important in a criminal prosecution than getting the facts before the jury. The adversary system, however, raises a number of procedural and substantive barriers to the presentation of evidence. The trial judge acts as a screener who may exclude evidence. Reasons for exclusion include the judge's assessment that the evidence is irrelevant, or even if relevant, introduced to confuse or prejudice the jury (as where it is too gory), or is barred by the hearsay rule. A number of privileges will bar the testimony of the defendant or witnesses such as a physician or spouse. Constitutional and statutory exclusionary rules may also limit the evidence that a jury hears or a judge considers in a bench trial. Despite these limits on the introduction of evidence, one of the greatest sources of injustice is the inability of the defendant to gain access to factual information in the hands of the prosecution. Why this is so requires some understanding of the process known in law as *discovery*—a process by which adversaries obtain trial-related evidence from one another.

In the early common law trials were thought of almost in terms of warfare, where each adversary kept its information secret, to be brought out to defeat the opponent at trial. This is unfair and inefficient because it does not give an adversary an opportunity to fairly learn facts and build arguments based on those facts that could properly affect the outcome of the case. Parties "surprised" by new information would request continuances or delays to gather more facts. Major nineteenth-century reforms resulted in a standardization of the right and requirement of pretrial discovery in civil cases. Before a civil case can get to trial, the parties file "interrogatories" or lists of questions that the opposing party must answer in writing and will conduct "depositions" or the interrogation of opposing witnesses, under oath and on the record, but without a judge present. Parties who oppose specific questions can object and later have the issue decided by a court. The general result is a far more efficient civil law system in which both sides develop a good understanding of the relative strengths and weaknesses of their case. This process encourages case settlement instead of trial.

Unlike civil law, there is no general or constitutional right to discovery in criminal cases. Instead, "pretrial discovery is largely governed by statutes and court rules which vary from one jurisdiction to another."[42] Some states and localities have broad discovery for defendants while the federal government and many states have more restrictive rules.[43] One kind of evidence that is not discoverable in civil or criminal cases are materials that come under the **work product rule**, which exempts both prosecution and defense materials prepared specifically for litigation, especially those that reflect the mental impressions, conclusions, opinions, or legal theories of an attorney or investigators.

DISCOVERY OF DEFENDANT'S EVIDENCE   Restrictions on discovery by prosecutors and defendants reflect different theories and policies. Defense-oriented theories restricting prosecutors from discovering any defense evidence are based on the defendant's constitutional rights, including the privilege against self-incrimination and the right to counsel. The Supreme Court in *Williams v. Florida* (1970) upheld a state law requiring defendants claiming an alibi defense to provide prosecutors with the names and addresses of the alibi witnesses and the place the defendant claimed to have been. A defendant will have to produce such witnesses at trial when they will be subject to cross-examination, so allowing the prosecution to have the names in advance will avoid surprise and delays while the prosecution gathers evidence to impeach alibi witnesses. Justice White wrote that "The adversary system of trial is hardly an end in itself; it is not yet a poker game in which players enjoy an absolute right always to conceal their cards until played." Notice-of-alibi laws do not violate due process. After the *Williams* case, prosecution discovery against the defendant expanded greatly in every state, and now includes notice of mental illness or insanity defenses, prospective defense witnesses and their statements, reports by experts hired by the defense, and tangible evidence defendants intend to introduce.[44]

The Supreme Court has made it clear that discovery must be a "two-way street" (*Weatherford v. Bursey*, 1977). *Wardius v. Oregon* (1973) established a right to *reciprocal discovery* by holding that rules requiring the defendant to disclose an intention to rely on an alibi, without requiring the prosecutor to provide discovery to the defense, were fundamentally unfair. "The State may not insist that trials be run as a 'search for truth' so far as defense witnesses are concerned, while maintaining 'poker game' secrecy for its own witnesses. It is fundamentally unfair to require a defendant to divulge the details of his own case while at the same time subjecting him to the hazard of surprise concerning refutation of the very pieces of evidence which he disclosed to the State."

DISCOVERY OF PROSECUTION EVIDENCE   State laws and court rules vary as to their generosity in allowing defendants to discover prosecution evidence. The most favorable rules are those that require prosecutors to maintain *open files policies* that allow defendants to have access to everything in prosecutors' files except work product. Open files policies are required in some states by law, but may be implemented as an administrative decision of a chief prosecutor. Such a policy, of course, cannot apply to information that is not written and could encourage some police investigators to not reduce evidence to writing. The Supreme Court has explicitly ruled that the Due Process Clause does not require prosecutors to maintain open files policies (*U.S. v. Agurs*, 1976).

All prosecution discovery rules allow prosecutors to petition courts to withhold evidence where there is a reason to believe that the defense will misuse the information or use it to intimidate witnesses. This is especially the case in disclosing lists of prosecution witnesses. This reasonable rule of caution sheds light on the general reasons why discovery is limited in criminal prosecutions. According to Mary Prosser, "A dominant perspective that informs this resistance and the overall limitations on discovery in criminal cases is an unspoken presumption of guilt of the defendant. ... While those who object to broad discovery rarely openly acknowledge that they presume that the accused are guilty, the reasons that have been advanced for denying, delaying, or limiting discovery clearly reflect that presumption."[45] This distrust creates a global fear that defendants will intimidate witnesses or tamper with evidence. Closely related to this presumption of guilt, a component of the Crime Control Model (see Chapter 1), is the "implicit assumption ... that the defendant does not need to be given all relevant information to prepare a defense because he or she was there, and therefore already knows the facts."[46]

This perspective overlooks two important matters. First, a view that assumes bad faith only on the part of the defendant, "does not acknowledge that the police and prosecutors exercise considerable power to influence witnesses by threats or rewards for particular testimony and that sometimes they have knowingly presented perjured testimony to secure a conviction."[47] In fact, studies of police and prosecutorial misconduct reveals a troubling level of just such conduct (See "Law in Society" section, this chapter). Second, the defendant may be innocent. Indeed, data and sound estimates suggest that 1 to 2 percent of felony defendants are innocent. An innocent defendant is at a huge disadvantage in the adversary system exactly because he does not have a clue about, and often has no way of countering, false evidence.

The other general "objection to broad discovery is that it would undermine the adversary system in criminal cases. ... The Supreme Court [has] endorsed the model of the adversary system as the 'primary means by which truth is uncovered' and characterized the *Brady* rule [discussed below] as a 'limited departure' from that model." It is argued that because the defendant has advantages such as the right to remain silent, and thus can withhold evidence that is discoverable through depositions in civil cases, he "should not be further advantaged ... by having access to prosecution evidence. This view ignores the greater investigatory resources of the prosecutor [and] the proliferation of reciprocal discovery provisions in many jurisdictions, which require a defendant to disclose certain defenses and defense evidence well in advance of trial."[48] Once again "the view that the defendant is advantaged by procedural protections ignores the fact that if the defendant is innocent, what he or she fails to disclose as a result of these procedural rights does not impair the government's access to relevant evidence of guilt."[49]

The Jencks Act (18 U.S.C. §3500), which allows a defendant to obtain the files of government witnesses, is a particularly restrictive rule of discovery. Among its other provisions, it does not allow this discovery to occur until *after* the government witness has testified on direct examination. This restriction is clearly grounded in the fear that prior disclosure will facilitate defense perjury, will give the defendant an advantage in preparing his or her case, may provide insight into the prosecutor's work product, and is necessary to protect witnesses. It has been argued that the only valid use of a government witness's prior statements is to impeach the witness, and disclosing the statement at trial is sufficient to achieve that goal.[50] This procedure is so cumbersome that some judges hold pretrial hearings to expedite Jencks Act reviews after each government witness testifies and some federal prosecutors allow advance notice. As an experienced litigator notes, however, "In many districts, government prosecutors rigidly adhere to the practice of refusing to produce *Jencks* statements meaningfully in advance of a witness' testimony. There is no sound policy reason supporting this approach other than the rationale that 'trial by ambush' generally favors the prosecution."[51]

LIMITED CONSTITUTIONAL RIGHT TO MATERIAL EXCULPATORY EVIDENCE   In the watershed case of **Brady v. Maryland** (1963) the Supreme Court held that under the Due Process Clause prosecutors have a duty to ensure that "criminal trials are fair" by providing defendants with favorable evidence that is "material either to guilt or to punishment" regardless of the good faith or bad faith of the prosecutor. A long train of *Brady* cases has generally restricted the beneficial scope of this rule. *Brady*'s discovery rule was based on earlier cases holding that prosecutors violated the due process rights of defendants by allowing perjured or misleading testimony about the case or about the credibility of a witness (See "Law in Society" section, this chapter).

Giglio v. United States (1972) was an important case holding that the prosecutor has an obligation to disclose exculpatory evidence that includes evidence that *impeaches* the credibility of prosecution witnesses. This is especially critical in cases where the prosecution relies on the testimony of cooperating witnesses or snitches, often criminals themselves with incentives to lie because they may receive money or leniency in their own prosecutions in return for supplying incriminating evidence. This is a well-known cause of the convictions of factually innocent prisoners.[52] Both *Giglio* and *Kyles v. Whitley* (1995) make it clear that a prosecutor cannot avoid *Brady* and *Giglio* responsibilities by hiding behind the fact that the information was known to another prosecutor or a police officer. The trial prosecutor is charged with knowledge of exculpatory evidence known to police as well as to other attorneys in his or her office, and thus the individual prosecutor has a "duty to learn of any favorable evidence known to the others acting on the government's behalf in the case, including the police."

The *Brady* rule has several features that are inherently problematic for defendants. First, whether the evidence is exculpatory or favorable to the defendant is up to the prosecutor, the very adversary who has decided that the defendant is guilty and seeks to persuade a jury or judge to render a guilty verdict. Assuming that most prosecutors are fair minded and seek justice above winning-at-all-costs, it is nevertheless psychologically questionable whether the prosecutor will see evidence as favorable to the defense in a close case.

Another limitation is that the Supreme Court ruled there is no constitutional obligation for prosecutors to present substantial exculpatory evidence in their possession to *grand juries* (*United States v. Williams*, 1992), nor are they required to disclose material impeachment evidence to the defendant prior to entering into a *plea agreement* (*United States v. Ruiz*, 2002).

Another way in which *Brady* limited its due process discovery rule was that it applied only to *material* evidence. Materiality is like the prejudice prong of the effective assistance of counsel rule of *Strickland v. Washington* (1984). That is, even if favorable to the defendant, it need not be turned over (or cause a reversal on appeal) unless the suppressed evidence might have *affected the outcome* of the case. The Supreme Court created a set of different materiality standards in *United States v. Agurs* (1976). First, if evidence has been perjured or is known to be false, then the prosecutor must turn it over if there is *any likelihood* that it could have resulted in a different verdict. This is a low standard of materiality and comes into play even if no *Brady* request has been made. Second, if the defendant made a *specific request* for evidence that was not honored (in *Brady* the defendant requested a co-defendant's confession), there is a due process violation if the material *might have affected the outcome*. This is a more stringent materiality standard. Third, if the defendant made no *Brady* request or made a general request (such as a request of the prosecutor for "all *Brady* material") there is no due process violation if the evidence *might have helped* the defense, or might have affected the outcome of trial; such evidence is not material in the constitutional sense. Thus, whether evidence is material depends in part on the procedure followed. This somewhat illogical and convoluted rule only makes sense because the Supreme Court did not want to impose a general discovery obligation on prosecutors.

In the *Agurs* case no *Brady* request was made and the prosecutor failed to disclose the prior criminal record of assault and carrying a deadly weapon (a knife) of James Sewell. Sewell checked into a motel wearing a Bowie knife in a sheath, and carried another knife in his pocket. He was found dead by motel employees who heard screams from his room and Linda Agurs on top of him. Sewell had been stabbed by Agurs, who by inference, appeared to be a drug-addicted prostitute. Agurs fled and turned herself in the next day. She claimed self-defense but was convicted of second-degree murder. The Supreme Court held that the prior-record evidence was not material because Sewell's prior record did not contradict any evidence offered by the prosecutor, and was largely cumulative of the evidence that Sewell was carrying knives. It was not requested and only might have helped her. Agurs was therefore not deprived of a fair trial.

The Supreme Court's attempts to apply and clarify the materiality standard have produced subtle shifts and have led the Supreme Court to issue fact-sensitive rulings.[53] In *United States v. Bagley* (1985) the Court seemed to simplify the rule by a single definition of materiality as occurring "only if there is a *reasonable probability* that, had the evidence been disclosed to the defense, the result of the proceedings would have been different, and defining "reasonable probability" as a probability sufficient to *undermine confidence* in the outcome.

The Court, however, did not firmly conclude whether the evidence not provided in *Bagley* was material and remanded the case to the lower courts. In this case, the defendant was charged with violating narcotics and firearms laws. He filed a discovery motion requesting the names of government trial witnesses and "any deals, promises or inducements" made to them in exchange for their testimony. The principal prosecution witnesses at trial were two state law enforcement officers assisting the federal Bureau of Alcohol, Tobacco and Firearms as undercover agents. They had signed contracts that paid them $300 for information regarding violations committed by Bagley. Not only did the government fail to turn over such information, it forwarded affidavits by the witnesses stating that they testified voluntarily without any threats or rewards, or promises of reward having been made in return for it. The District Court found that this information would not have made a difference in its verdict. The Court of Appeals reversed, but the Supreme Court ruled in favor of the prosecution, holding, as noted above, that undisclosed evidence is material under *Brady* only if it is "reasonably probable" that the trial's outcome would have been different had the evidence been disclosed to the defense. The ruling in *Bagley* weakened the effect of the specific request. One firm rule of *Bagley*, however, was to confirm the *Giglio* rule that the *Brady* obligation applied to exculpatory as well as impeachment evidence.

In *Kyles v. Whitely* (1995) the Court, in an intensely fact-specific ruling, found that the prosecutor's failure to turn over exculpatory and impeachment evidence violated the *Brady* principle and remanded for a new trial. Curtis Kyles was convicted of murder and sentenced to death for the murder of a woman outside a store, following a mistrial. "Before trial, his counsel filed a lengthy motion for disclosure by the State of any exculpatory or impeachment evidence. The prosecution responded that there was 'no exculpatory evidence of any nature,' despite the government's knowledge of" a large number of items that would fit those categories. Kyles took the stand at his trial and claimed innocence, introduced an alibi, and called witnesses who testified to circumstances that placed guilt on one "Beanie." Eyewitnesses differed as to the killer's description. The police were first put on to Kyles by Beanie, a close acquaintance, who gave the police different aliases and continuously changed his story. The police also paid Beanie $400. Nevertheless, despite much evidence that Beanie was the possible killer who was trying to shift guilt to Kyles, the police did not critically examine the evidence against him or even take Beanie's fingerprints. By failing to provide *all* eyewitnesses' statements, which would have cast a shadow on the strong eyewitnesses who did testify, the prosecution shielded the jury from evidence of doubt about the leading cause of wrongful convictions.[54] And by not disclosing the myriad of information that pointed a finger at Beanie, the prosecution not only failed to consider that perjury by the real perpetrators is a frequent cause of wrongful convictions, it also fell into the trap of tunnel vision.[55]

The next major case, *Strickler v. Greene* (1999), exposed a worrisome failure in discovery practice. Strickler, convicted of murder, argued that evidence that might have impeached a prosecution eyewitness was withheld. The witness gave a very detailed and positive description at the trial but police reports of interviews with her displayed a far less certain and unsure witness. No *Brady* request was made because the prosecutor had an open files policy. The problem is that the police reports casting doubt on the certainty of the eyewitness were not in the prosecutor's files. The Supreme Court ruled that defense counsel did not have to make motions for evidence where there was no basis to be suspicious of the prosecutor and that the prosecutor failed in his *Brady* obligation by not ensuring that all relevant police reports were placed in the prosecutor's less-than-complete open files.

Despite this, the Court found that the excluded witness report was not material under *Brady*. There was a wealth of other forensic and witness evidence on which a jury could find that Strickler was guilty of the murder and sufficiently dangerous to warrant the death penalty, even if the excluded reports entirely discredited the testimony of the eyewitness. Although there may have been a "reasonable *possibility* that either a total, or just a substantial, discount of [the eyewitness'] testimony might have produced a different result, either at the guilt or sentencing phases ... [Strickler's] burden [was] to establish a reasonable *probability* of a different result." The Supreme Court, however, sought to clarify the precise standard of materiality on appeal under *Kyles*. It "is not just a matter of determining whether, after discounting the inculpatory evidence in light of the undisclosed evidence, the remaining evidence is sufficient to support the jury's conclusions. Rather, the question is whether 'the favorable evidence could reasonably be taken to put the whole case in such a different light as to undermine confidence in the verdict.'"

In the most recent major case, ***Banks v. Dretke*** (2004), a death row murder defendant was seeking to discredit two essential prosecution witnesses in a new trial, mostly to show at the sentencing phase that he was not so dangerous as to deserve the death penalty. The prosecution hid the fact that one witness was a paid police informant (who was paid money and not prosecuted for other crimes), and hid a pretrial transcript showing that the other witness had been intensively coached by prosecutors and law enforcement officers regarding what to say at the trial. When these witnesses testified and lied on the stand, one about his informant status and the other about having been coached (he said he had not talked to any police officer about the case until a few days before the trial), the prosecutor "raised no red flag." Instead of correcting the informant's false statements, "the prosecutor told the jury that the witness 'had been open and honest with you in every way,' and that his testimony was of the 'utmost significance'" (*Banks v. Dretke*, internal citations omitted). To add to the defendant's deception and to stave off a *Brady* request, "prior to trial, the State advised Banks's attorney there would be no need to litigate discovery issues, representing: 'We will, without the necessity of motions, provide you with all discovery to which you are entitled'" (*Banks v. Dretke*, internal modifications omitted). This pattern of evasion and stonewalling was maintained by the government forces through direct state appeals and three state post-conviction proceedings an attendant appeals. The truth came out sixteen years later on a federal habeas corpus collateral appeal. The Supreme Court remanded, holding that the lower courts had to allow Delma Banks to argue his case. Entirely aside from the particular merits of Banks's own case, the ability of police and prosecutor to routinely hide impeachment information from judges and juries must be stopped not only by appellate courts but by honest and professional police investigators and prosecutors, even in the worst of cases.

LAW IN SOCIETY

Prosecutorial Misconduct and Convicting the Innocent

The Prosecutor's Power, Misconduct, and Ethics

The prosecutor is the most powerful actor in the criminal justice system,[56] with virtually unreviewable power to charge crimes or to dismiss arrests and to investigate crimes, especially using the grand jury's subpoena power. Prosecutors use "hardball" tactics such as surprise subpoenas to get parties to testify before a grand jury and subpoenaing family members to shake information loose about a suspect.[57] The Supreme Court has deliberately limited judicial control on these executive branch functions to enable the government to vigorously investigate cases and prosecute crimes. Judicial controls would give defendants with large resources (e.g., white-collar criminals) the ability to tie up prosecutors in preliminary challenges.[58] Judicial control over vindictive and selective prosecution, as noted in this chapter, is quite limited.

Civil remedies against prosecutorial misconduct are also extremely limited because prosecutors enjoy **absolute immunity** against civil lawsuits that challenge such core functions as charging, appearing in pretrial hearings, and trying a case, even if the prosecutor unknowingly presented false information (*Imbler v. Pachtman,* 1976; *Burns v. Reed,* 1991). **Qualified immunity,** opening the prosecutor to civil suit, applies only when misconduct occurs in noncore professional activity—that is, appearing at a press conference or swearing to the truth of facts in an affidavit to support a charge (*Kalina v. Fletcher,* 1997) (See Chapter 2.)

Prosecutorial misconduct takes many forms because errors and violations can be made at every stage of the pretrial and trial process.[59] Common forms include appealing to the passions and fears of jurors by inflammatory language, making innuendos of guilt unsupported by evidence, announcing that the defendant or witness took a polygraph test, and the like.[60] Even when courts find that a prosecutor violated a rule of legal ethics or due process, a case will not be reversed on appeal if the error was harmless—that is, unless the error caused the verdict.[61] This section focuses on examples of misconduct that can lead to the conviction of the innocent.

Given the lack of external controls on prosecutorial misconduct, the adherence to standards of ethics by prosecutors is profoundly important. In his 1940 address, Robert Jackson stated that "the spirit of fair play and decency … should animate the federal prosecutor." He admonished federal prosecutors "that while you are being diligent, strict, and vigorous in law enforcement you can also afford to be just. Although the government technically loses its case, it has really won if justice be done."[62] The problem is that such moral exhortations, while followed by many prosecutors, are not binding. If only a few rogue prosecutors decide to not play by the rules, they can significantly increase the convictions of innocent people.

Due Process and Truth

In three cases the Supreme Court established foundational rules to guide prosecutors in their professional ethical conduct. These cases are the foundation of the discovery cases discussed earlier in this chapter. As is true of any lawyer operating under rules of professional ethics, a prosecutor cannot fabricate evidence or knowingly allow perjured evidence to be used against a defendant, allow the introduction of misleading evidence, or shield the judge or jury from evidence that casts a shadow on witness credibility. To do so not only runs afoul of state bar ethical rules but violates a defendant's due process right to a fair trial.

Perjured or Fabricated Evidence

In **Mooney v. Holohan** (1935), the Supreme Court noted in dictum that "a deliberate deception of court and jury by the presentation of testimony known to be perjured" would violate the defendant's due process rights. The Court denied relief on procedural grounds. This case arose out of the conviction of a well-known labor radical, Tom Mooney, for setting off a bomb during a pro-military parade in San Francisco in 1916 that killed ten people and seriously injured forty. There was strong exonerating evidence, but it was a period of antiradical hysteria, and the prosecutor relied on "eyewitnesses" who were known liars. Mooney was pardoned soon after the Supreme Court's ruling.[63]

Misleading Testimony

The *Mooney* principle was applied in **Alcorta v. Texas** (1957), which held that due process is violated by introducing evidence that creates a false impression regarding a material fact if it was elicited by the prosecutor with knowledge of its inaccuracy. In *Alcorta,* a jealous husband was prosecuted for murdering his adulterous wife. Before trial, the wife's lover told the prosecutor that he and Alcorta's wife had been sexually intimate. The prosecutor told him not to volunteer such evidence but to answer questions put to him at trial truthfully. At trial, the lover testified that he had not kissed the deceased woman on the night she died and that he only had a casual affair with her. The truth was disclosed after the defendant was convicted of first-degree murder. This violated Alcorta's due process right to a fair and meaningful trial, even though the prosecutor's actions were not as deliberate as those in *Mooney* and affected the level of guilt and punishment rather than a determination of guilt or innocence.

Witness Credibility

In **Napue v. Illinois** (1959), a prosecution witness testified on direct examination that he received no promise of consideration for his testimony. The prosecutor knew that this was false but made no effort to correct the falsehood. The lie was not directly material to the issue of guilt, but it undermined the ability of the defense to properly cross-examine by impeaching the witness's credibility. This widespread kind of due process violation is a major problem in wrongful conviction cases.

Mischaracterizing Evidence

In **Miller v. Pate** (1967), an innocent taxi driver was convicted of the rape and murder of a young girl on the basis of red-stained underpants found near the murder scene and a confession that was obtained under duress. At trial, the prosecutor held up the garment and referred to it as "bloody shorts." Only after a lengthy appeal process, during which Miller spent years on Illinois's death row, did forensic tests by the defense disclose that the red stains were paint and not blood. Miller was freed from his decade-long ordeal by a Supreme Court finding that the prosecutor's trial oratory violated due process. The lesson is that prosecutors must scrupulously check the facts of their cases. A careful review of the entire case by Miller's appellate attorney makes it abundantly clear that Lloyd Miller was factually innocent.[64]

Prosecution Error and Wrongful Conviction

Various studies of wrongful conviction list prosecution misconduct as one of the major causes of sending innocent men and women to prison, including death row.

- The Innocence Project reviewed seventy-four cases of actual innocence established by DNA. Twelve factors causing the wrongful convictions were present in one or more cases. Prosecutorial misconduct was the fourth most common error, appearing in thirty-three (45 percent) of the cases.[65]
- James Liebman and colleagues found that the overall error rate in capital convictions from 1973 to 1995 was 68 percent (7 percent were completely exonerated) and that of the total cases, "prosecutorial suppression of evidence that the defendant is innocent or does not deserve the death penalty" accounted for 16 percent of state postconviction reversals.[66]
- C. Ronald Huff and colleagues estimated that of 205 wrongful convictions they identified, nineteen resulted from negligence by criminal justice officials and five from perjury by criminal justice officials.[67]
- Edwin Borchard, in the first systematic study of sixty-five wrongful convictions in the United States, found that in sixteen cases prosecutorial "fault, carelessness, or overzealousness" was present.[68]
- The Web site for the Innocence Project finds that the kinds of prosecutorial misconduct connected with cases of falsely convicted people include suppression of exculpatory evidence (37 percent); knowing use of false testimony (25 percent); coerced witnesses (11 percent); improper closing arguments (9 percent); false statements to the jury (9 percent); evidence fabrication (5 percent); and other misconduct (4 percent).[69]

It should be kept in mind that rarely is one kind of error alone the cause of a wrongful conviction. George Castelle and Elizabeth Loftus identify the "cross-contamination of evidence: when one piece of misinformation contaminates other information in a case and ultimately results in the conviction of the innocent."[70] An initial misidentification by a witness may cause the police to form a rigid idea that the correct suspect has been apprehended, and the initial error may be compounded by a failure of the prosecutor to expose the error. As Professor Brian Forst suggests, however, this is a weak excuse for prosecutors.

Prosecution Policy and the Conviction of Innocents

Forst notes that prosecutors typically measure success by such criteria as conviction rates and success in being reelected. These criteria do not probe the more vital and more difficult-to-measure goals of reducing crime, pursuing justice, ensuring evenhandedness, and enhancing the legitimacy of government, although such goals are probably part of prosecutors' unarticulated motives in deciding whether to charge a defendant and at which level of severity. Prosecutors rarely consider whether their policies are aimed at reducing the incidence of wrongful convictions. In fact, as Forst indicates, prosecutors are in a very good position to control "errors of justice."[71] Prosecutors can

> ferret out errors made by the police by screening arrests more carefully, directing postarrest investigations to resolve conflicting sources of evidence, working more diligently with victims and witnesses to establish, precisely and accurately, pertinent events that preceded and followed the episode in question, and directing the forensic processing of key items of physical evidence to resolve ambiguities involving both incriminating and exculpatory evidence.[72]

The failure of prosecutors to pursue such ends more often exposes systemic flaws in the criminal justice system.

Examples of Egregious Prosecutorial Misconduct

- Erick Jackson was convicted in 1980 for felony murder stemming from the setting of a fire in a Brooklyn, New York, supermarket in which six firefighters were killed. He supposedly confessed to having been paid to set a fire on the roof of the market. But a court, years later, found that the confession was uncorroborated and confused his statements about a different fire with the fatal blaze. After a decade in prison, Jackson won release when an appellate court ruled that the prosecutor deliberately withheld evidence that could have exonerated Jackson at trial. An investigator conducted experiments and concluded that the cause of the fire was not arson but faulty wiring. A civil attorney hired to represent the firefighters' widows later disclosed a report of the investigator that showed that in addition to the initial accidental fire, firefighters deliberately set additional fires in the building in order to aid the families of the deceased firefighters by increasing the amount of insurance money paid to them. Citing another judge in a recent case, the trial judge who dismissed the case and released Jackson said, "It is truly a scandal which reflects unfavorably on all participants in the criminal justice system."[73]

- Under the leadership of Henry Wade from the 1950s to 1986, the Dallas district attorney's office had a reputation for getting convictions at any cost. In two nationally known cases, it appeared that truth was of no consequence. Lenell Geter, an African-American electronics engineer, was convicted of a 1982 armed robbery committed in a Dallas suburb. The prosecution relied on "a photo identification by a victim, and ignored testimony from Geter's co-workers at E-Systems that he had been at work the entire time the robbery was taking place" sixty miles away. Outraged coworkers convinced CBS-TV *60 Minutes* to air a segment on this miscarriage of justice. That segment "established the guilt of another man and the likelihood that prosecutors knew Geter was innocent."[74]

- Another notorious Dallas case was that of Randall Dale Adams, who was sentenced to death in 1977 for the murder of a police officer. His case came to national attention with the release of the 1988 film *The Thin Blue Line.* The film not only exposed the real killer (in prison for another crime), demonstrated Adams's complete innocence, and revealed what should have been fatal weaknesses in the evidence against him, but also "suggests that the prosecutors *knew*" Adams did not kill the officer. Even as the case against Adams unraveled in postappeal procedures, the prosecutor's office resisted releasing him.[75]

- Dr. Sam Sheppard was convicted of killing his wife in 1956 in a Cleveland trial that took place in a "circus atmosphere" created by the news media, which convicted Sheppard in the headlines well before the trial. The police conducted a sloppy investigation and broadcast their evidence to the public. The trial judge utterly failed to control the situation. At the heart of the wrongs in the case, however, was the prosecutorial suppression of evidence contradictory to its case. A defense demand for files and records was ignored. A forensic examination of the crime scene brought out evidence favorable to Sheppard but which the prosecutor ignored. In 1966, the Supreme Court reversed the case (*Sheppard v. Maxwell,* 1966), and in a retrial with a more vigorous and focused defense counsel, F. Lee Bailey, Sheppard was acquitted on a powerful presentation of forensic evidence.[76]

- Pulitzer Prize–winning author Edward Humes recounts in detail the rise of Edward Jagels, the law-and-order prosecutor in Bakersfield, California, in the 1980s, based on political "dirty tricks" involving the filching of a confidential file from a court. An exemplar of overly aggressive prosecution, the combative Jagels actually reveled in his frequent chastisement by appellate courts for misconduct, knowing that it made him popular with the public. With his active assistance, the criminal justice system in Kern County began one of the first of the extravagant and nightmarish witch hunts of the 1980s that rounded up hundreds of innocent people accused of child molestation. In total, Kern County authorities investigated over ten child-molestation "rings," investigating over two hundred people, charging eighty-three and convicting forty. Some of the charges involved "over-the-top" allegations of satanic ritual abuse, a widely believed and never proved phenomenon in the 1980s. Of these forty convictions, most were overturned and only six remained in prison, three from the only "ring" "in which a majority of the accused appear to be genuinely guilty. ... Uniquely, all but one were members of the same household, preying upon their own child relatives." This witch hunt inflicted an enormous amount of human suffering and the disruption of lives.[77]

- The convictions of Rolando Cruz and Alejandro Hernandez in 1983 for the abduction, rape, and murder of ten-year-old Jeanine Nicarico were so riddled with prosecutorial error that the prosecutors themselves were later charged criminally with misfeasance, a virtually unheard of turn of events. At three trials of Cruz, the DuPage, Illinois, county prosecutors presented evidence that Cruz told police about the crime from a dream that he had, although the detectives had no written report of this account. The police tried to link a boot print found outside Jeanine's home to Cruz and Hernandez. An evidence technician told the prosecutors that analysis by the Nike shoe company verified that the prints came from a woman's shoe or from one that was too small for either Cruz or Hernandez. "The prosecutor put the technician on the witness stand and carefully avoided any mention of shoe size or likely gender. In fact, the defense was not told about the Nike analysis." Even worse, after the first trial, which was overturned on appeal, the real killer, Brian Dugan, a pedophile, came forward and voluntarily confessed to this and other murders to avoid the death penalty. Later DNA tests confirmed that Dugan was the killer and showed no evidence that Cruz or Hernandez participated in the crime. The prosecutors nevertheless pressed on and obtained a second conviction that was again overturned. At a third trial before a judge, the various lies of police and prosecutors were exposed, and the case was thrown out after twelve years.

- This was followed by an astonishing circumstance. The state assigned a special prosecutor to investigate the prosecution. As a result, three prosecutors and four sheriff's investigators were indicted for perjury and obstruction of justice. Charges against two of the prosecutors were dismissed, and the remaining defendants were acquitted. Barry Scheck and colleagues suggest that the reason for the acquittal was the "thin" recollection of grand jurors in the original prosecution of Cruz and Hernandez that there was some testimony about Cruz's "dream" and the suggestion to the jury that if the investigators and prosecutors were convicted, the county would be sued for astronomical sums.[78]

Correcting Prosecutorial Misconduct

The prospects for radical change in the way in which prosecutors pursue justice are limited. The elective nature of most prosecutors' offices and the very nature of the adversary system, which relies on the competitiveness of attorneys, will continue to breed attitudes that stress winning. Even prosecutors who understand the emptiness of conviction rates as a measure of success will do little to downplay this, for to do otherwise would leave the prosecutor vulnerable to electoral defeat. The wider public is not likely to be impressed with internal reforms that allow closer case monitoring. Also, prosecutors who decide to look more closely into the arrests brought to them for charging might antagonize police forces, creating interagency friction and potential political antagonism.

In many of the exonerations that have become common in recent years, prosecutors often refuse to admit that an error was made. After one such exoneration, a newspaper reported: "'I am not saying loud and clear Rudolph Holton is innocent,' Hillsborough County State Atty. Mark Ober said at a news conference. 'I am saying we cannot prove his guilt beyond a reasonable doubt.'"[79] It is psychologically difficult and professionally costly for prosecutors to admit to incompetence or worse. One prosecutor who helped to exonerate defendants in their fifth trial as a witness in a neighboring county was well positioned to comment on the prosecutorial mind-set. "'As a prosecutor, I knew they'd invested too much in [their] theory to start over,' he said. 'There's a mind-set. The theory fits as well as anything; we're going to stick with it no matter what happens.'"[80] It is easier to hide behind the "not proven" tack than to open up the case and seek the actual culprit. As a result, a double injustice often occurs.

It is highly unlikely, and perhaps unwise, for courts to exercise oversight of the prosecutor's discretionary powers. Appellate courts have exercised a useful if limited role in reversing convictions. Courts, however, have no authority to explore the factual basis of convictions and can only review for legal error. There is no place in the common law system of the United States for a factual review of possibly erroneous verdicts, although commissions to review doubtful convictions have been established in Canada and the United Kingdom.[81]

Prosecutorial misconduct is a real problem that the justice system does not appear to be adequately dealing with at present. It is time for prosecutors to take to heart a judge's charge to a jury: "The government always wins when justice is done, regardless of whether the verdict be guilty or not guilty."[82]

Summary

The pretrial process contains numerous steps, involves important constitutional rights, and adds substantial complexity and due process to the prosecution of crimes. The trade-off for this complexity is that cases are thoroughly screened so that, ideally, only those based on solid evidence and deserving of prosecution go forward to trial. Consequently, the government is able to give more formal attention to serious and important cases.

Important pretrial processes include initial appearance, bail hearings, prosecutorial charging, discovery, plea negotiations, grand jury and/or preliminary hearings, discovery, and pretrial motion hearings. Decisions at each stage can influence prosecutorial discretion to bring a case forward or to forgo further criminal prosecution.

Pretrial release, or bail, is a critical pretrial process. Defendants are entitled to "reasonable" bail that is not out of line with current practices. Disparity in who gets released has led to such reforms as release on recognizance for indigents who are good risks, and court-run deposit bond systems to lower the cost of bonds and eliminate the need for bail bondsmen. The federal preventive detention statute allows pretrial detention of suspects without bail if they are predicted to be likely to commit crimes while released on bail. *United States v. Salerno* (1987) upheld the legality of preventive detention, under due process and the Eighth Amendment, because hearings and procedural guidelines preserve the due process rights of detainees.

Prosecutors have great discretion in charging suspects. Courts, under the separation of powers doctrine, cannot dismiss charges that they think are unwise, but can dismiss where there is selective or vindictive prosecution. Selective prosecution occurs when a defendant is intentionally prosecuted on impermissible grounds, such as race, religion, or political beliefs or for exercising constitutional rights. Vindictive prosecution occurs when more serious charges are preferred against a defendant who exercised his or her constitutional rights; discriminatory intent is not an element.

The grand jury is a citizens' institution originated in the common law. It meets in secret to investigate charges and to decide whether to indict suspects. It may issue subpoenas to compel witnesses to testify or to supply evidence, and it may request immunity for witnesses who plead the privilege against self-incrimination. Grand juries are criticized for meeting in secret and for being the prosecutor's rubber stamp. The federal constitutional guarantee a prosecution only on in-dictment by grand jury is not applicable to the states. Grand jury reform proposals include allowing counsel to attend and advise witnesses and allowing the target of the investigation to attend and voluntarily address the grand jury.

The preliminary examination consists of the presentation of prosecution witnesses before a lower court judge to determine if probable cause exists to bind the defendant over for trial. Preliminary hearings are open to the public, prosecution witnesses can be cross-examined, and defendants have a right to counsel. The preliminary hearing preserves testimony for trial if a witness should become unavailable and may be a way for the defense to discover the strengths and weaknesses of the prosecutor's case as well as obtain factual information.

Unlike in civil law, there is no right to discovery of facts from opposing parties in criminal law. The prosecutor has a limited right to discover defense evidence of alibi witnesses and an insanity defense. Defendants have a due process right to obtain exculpatory evidence, when a prosecutor believes that such evidence is material to guilt or punishment. There is no constitutional requirement that prosecutors have "open files" policies, but many do.

Legal Puzzles

HOW HAVE COURTS DECIDED THESE CASES?

Excessive Bail

10-1. Bail in the amount of $2,500,000 was set for Marco Periandri. He was arrested for allegedly being part of a group of five who brutally attacked a woman who had charged Marco's brother of rape while his brother was in jail. The victim suffered multiple bruises after a sack was put over her head, and an attempt was made to strangle her with a telephone cord. She identified Marco by his voice and threats made during the attack. She was left in a parking lot and treated in a hospital.

Marco has a daughter and son, ages nine and ten. He is an iron worker with a structural building company and can work if released from jail. He and his wife bought a house two years ago and with a monthly mortgage payment of $800. In 1996, was convicted of a fifth-degree felony drug offense and successfully completed his sentence of one year probation. He does not have a passport, and he and his wife have not traveled extensively outside of Ohio.

Was the bail of $2,500,000 excessive?

HELD: Yes. The bail amount was reduced to $150,000 and conditions were imposed.

10-1. The purpose of bail is to secure attendance at trial. In determining a reasonable bail, the court must weigh factors: the nature and circumstances of the offense charged; the weight of the evidence; the accused's history of flight; his ties to the community, including his family, financial resources, and employment, and his character and mental condition.

In other cases this court found bail in the amounts of $1 and $3 million in major drug cases excessive and reduced them to $250,000 and $750,000, even though a defendant had a history of flight. In the present case, the charges are very serious allegations of very violent crimes demanding a high bond. However, the $2,500,000 bond is inconsistent with the benchmarks provided by previous cases. Also, the bond is inconsistent with current County Court Bail Guidelines, which recommend bail as low as $100,000 for aggravated murder.

Periandri presents a low risk of flight. He successfully completed probation several years ago. He does not have a passport, nor has he extensively traveled outside of Ohio. Most telling is that when he learned that there was a warrant for his arrest, he voluntarily turned himself in, within hours of being released from jail. The legitimate concern for community safety is better addressed by imposing the conditions of no contact and electronically monitored home detention than by imposing unreasonable bail, which is prohibited by the constitution.

In the Matter of Periandri v. McFaul, 142 OhioApp.3d 588; 756 N.E.2d 682 (Ohio Court of Appeals, 2001).

Selective Prosecution

10-2. Samuel Lewis, a.k.a. Shaheed Lewis, an African-American Muslim, was convicted of making false statements on federal firearms applications. He had no prior criminal record, but from 2000 to 2003 he purchased thirty-two firearms and supplied false addresses on some federal forms; he was convicted on fifteen counts. Witnesses said that Lewis said he wished to move to a country in which there was a war or a crisis, and that he had mused about wanting to die in a jihad.

Lewis claims he was selectively prosecuted because he is an African-American Muslim. He agues he should be compared to white non-Muslims who have been convicted of misstating addresses on federal firearms applications. None were prosecuted in the federal district in three years. Lewis argues that statistical probability indicates that some white non-Muslims quite probably have committed such minor infractions, but the fact that none were prosecuted established selective prosecution.

Was Lewis selectively prosecuted?

Holding available from instructor.

Discovery

10-3. Defendants were convicted, after a jury trial, of kidnapping and endangering the welfare of a child. Leslie, thirteen-years old, testified to being held hostage for a year in the apartment building where her mother, her mother's boyfriend, and her three siblings lived. She testified the kidnappers hid her just two floors away from her family's apartment. Leslie also said she had a perfectly amicable relationship with the Garcias, had had no prior disputes with them, and considered the Garcias' daughter to be her very best friend. During the entire twelve months that Leslie was held captive, no ransom demands were received.

There was evidence that Leslie was physically restrained by defendants and forced onto a plane by Melendez and taken on a flight to Puerto Rico. The prosecutor disclosed only the names of flight attendants, with no contact information or indication as to what information they possessed. These names were buried in a voluminous amount of discovery provided shortly before trial, and were not identified as *Brady* material. One of the flight attendants, whom the trial prosecutor had personally interviewed, was listed as a potential witness, giving the defense reason to believe that the flight attendant would testify favorably for the prosecution.

The prosecutor interviewed the flight attendants and each of them informed the prosecutor prior to trial that no such incident had taken place. Each said that if a thirteen-year-old child aboard the flight "cried out for help, and physically grabbed one of the flight attendants, each flight attendant responded that if the incident had happened that way, she would have remembered it."

Did the prosecution wilfully suppress evidence, that is, the information about the flight attendants, from the defense?

Holding available from instructor.

Grand Jury Secrecy

10-4. The Better Government Association (BGA) sued Governor Rod R. Blagojevich in August 2006, as governor of Illinois, under the Illinois Freedom of Information Act (FOIA), to disclose his federal grand jury subpoena. Blagojevich refused, claiming that if such subpoenas existed, disclosure is preempted by federal law. In answer to a request by the BGA, the United States Attorney for the Northern District of Illinois replied "we will only take such action as we believe is authorized by law and necessary to protect the secrecy and integrity of the federal grand jury process."

The Federal Rule imposes grand jury secrecy on (i) a grand juror, (ii) an interpreter, (iii) a court reporter, (iv) an operator of a recording device, (v) a person who transcribes recorded testimony, (vi) an attorney for the government, or (vii) a person to whom disclosure is made, whom the attorney for the government considers necessary to assist in performing that attorney's duty to enforce federal criminal law.

Does the recipient of a federal grand jury subpoena, acting as a public official for the State of Illinois, have the discretion to refuse a request to disclose that subpoena, pursuant to the Illinois Freedom of Information Act (FOIA)?

Holding available from instructor.

Further Reading

Angela J. Davis, *Arbitrary Justice: The Power of the American Prosecutor* (New York: Oxford University Press, 2007).

Gary Delsohn, *The Prosecutors: A Year in the Life of a District Attorney's Office* (New York: Plume, 2003).

Jim McGee and Brian Duffy, *Main Justice: The Men and Women Who Enforce the Nation's Criminal Laws and Guard Its Civil Liberties* (New York: Simon and Schuster, 1996).

H. Richard Uviller, *Virtual Justice: The Flawed Prosecution of Crime in America* (New Haven, Conn.: Yale University Press, 1996).

Useful Web Site

American Bar Association

http://abanet.org/

Site of the premier lawyers' association in the United States. Includes information about getting a law degree and careers in the legal profession, and offers ABA materials on criminal justice as well as other legal topics.

End Notes

1. *Federal Criminal Case Processing, 2002: With Trends, 1982–2002* (U.S. Department of Justice, Bureau of Justice Statistics, NCJ 207447, January 2005), p. 1.
2. Thomas H. Cohen and Brian A. Reaves, *Felony Defendants in Large Urban Counties, 2002* (U.S. Department of Justice, Bureau of Justice Statistics, NCJ 210818, February 2006), 24, Table 23.
3. Federal Criminal Case Processing, 2002. See Frank W. Miller, *Prosecution: The Decisions to Charge a Suspect with a Crime* (Boston: Little, Brown, 1969) regarding he prosecutor's decision to dismiss.
4. Cohen and Reaves, *Felony Defendants in Large Urban Counties, 2002,* 24.
5. American Bar Association, *Standards for Criminal Justice: The Prosecution Function,* 3rd ed., Standard 3(a) (1993).
6. Peter J. Henning, "Prosecutorial Misconduct in Grand Jury Investigations," *South Carolina Law Review* 51 (1999): 1–61, 25.
7. Joshua Dressler and George C. Thomas III, *Criminal Procedure: Principles, Policies and Perspectives,* 2nd ed. (St. Paul, Minn.: West, 2003), 820.
8. Dressler and Thomas, *Criminal Procedure.*
9. Albert W. Alschuler, "Implementing the Criminal Defendant's Right to Trial: Alternatives to the Plea Bargaining System," *University of Chicago Law Review* 50 (1983): 931–1050.
10. Cohen and Reaves, *Felony Defendants in Large Urban Counties, 2002,* 23: "For 48% of felony defendants in the 75 largest counties, adjudication of their cases occurred within 3 months of arrest, and 69% of cases were adjudicated within 6 months. ... By the end of the 1-year study period, 87% of all cases had been adjudicated."
11. Malcolm M. Feeley, "Plea Bargaining and the Structure of the Criminal Process," *Justice System Journal* 7 (1982): 338–55.
12. *United States v. Abrahams,* 575 F.2d 3 (1st Cir. 1978).
13. Jonathan Drimmer, "When Man Hunts Man: The Rights and Duties of Bounty Hunters in the American Criminal Justice System," *Houston Law Review* 33 (1996): 731–93.
14. William Glaberson, "'Lie or Die'—Aftermath of a Murder; Justice, Safety and the System: A Witness Is Slain in Brooklyn," *New York Times,* July 6, 2003.
15. Glaberson, "'Lie or Die.'"
16. Peter Finn and Kerry Murphy Healy, *Preventing Gang-and Drug-Related Witness Intimidation* (U.S. Department of Justice, National Institute of Justice, NCJ 163067, November 1996), 5.
17. Nora Lockwood Tooher, "States Move to Curb Witness Intimidation," *Lawyers Weekly USA,* February 27, 2006.
18. "DA Asks Hush on Names," *Albany (N.Y.) Times-Union,* Jan. 6, 2009.
19. Congressional Documents and Publications (News Release), "House Approves Cummings' Witness Protection Bill," June 9, 2009.
20. *United States v. Williams,* 47 F.3d 658 (4th Cir. 1995).
21. *United States v. Schweihs,* 971 F.2d 1302 (7th Cir. 1992).
22. Deborah Emerson, *Grand Jury Reform: A Review of Key Issues* (Washington, D.C.: Department of Justice, National Institute of Justice, 1983).
23. *United States v. Cox,* 342 F.2d 167 (5th Cir. 1965).
24. Sarah Kershaw, "In Plea Deal That Spares His Life, Man Admits Killing 48 Women," *New York Times,* November 6, 2003.
25. Sandra Caron George, "Current Development 2004–2005: Prosecutorial Discretion: What's Politics Got To Do with It?" *Georgetown Journal of Legal Ethics* 18 (2005): 739–758
26. L. L. Brasier and Alison Young, "Verdict Is in: Thompson Is out: Attorney Gorcyca, and Kevorkian, Beat Prosecutor," *Detroit Free Press,* August 7, 1996.
27. John H. Langbein, "The Criminal Trial before the Lawyers," *University of Chicago Law Review* 45 (1978): 263–316.
28. F.P. Hafetz and J. M. Pelletieri, "Time to Reform the Grand Jury," *Champion Magazine,* January/February 1999, p. 12.
29. *United States v. Gurule,* 437 F.2d 239 (10th Cir. 1970).
30. F.R.C.P. Rule 6(e)(3).
31. Marvin E. Frankel and Gary P. Naftalis, *The Grand Jury: An Institution on Trial* (New York: Hill and Wang, 1977).
32. Barry Winograd and Martin Fassler, "The Political Question," *Trial Magazine,* January/February 1973, pp. 16–20.
33. William J. Campbell, "Eliminate the Grand Jury," *Journal of Criminal Law and Criminology* 64 (1973): 174.
34. Bureau of Justice Statistics, *Report to the Nation on Crime and Justice,* 2nd ed. (Washington, D.C.: U.S. Department of Justice, 1988), 72.
35. Bureau of Justice Statistics, *Report to the Nation,* 72.
36. Thomas P. Sullivan and Robert D. Nachman, "If It Ain't Broke, Don't Fix It: Why the Grand Jury's Accusatory Function Should Not Be Changed," *Journal of Criminal Law and Criminology* 75 (1984): 1047–69.
37. See Federal Magistrate's Act, 18 U.S.C. § 3060; and *Federal Rules of Criminal Procedure,* Rules 5 and 5.1.
38. *Federal Rules of Criminal Procedure,* Rule 5(d). See *Sciortino v. Zampano,* 385 F.2d 132 (2d Cir. 1967); and *United States v. Quinn,* 357 F. Supp. 1348 (N.D. Ga. 1973) (an indictment obtained *during* a preliminary examination requires termination of examination).
39. Yale Kamisar, Wayne R. LaFave, and Jerold H. Israel, *Modern Criminal Procedure,* 6th ed. (St. Paul, Minn.: West, 1986), 944.
40. *People v. Duncan,* 201 N.W.2d 629 (Mich. 1972).
41. *Coleman v. Burnett,* 477 F.2d 1187 (D.C. Cir. 1973).
42. Y. Kamisar, W. R. LaFave, J. H. Israel, N. J. King, and O. S. Kerr, *Modern Criminal Procedure,* 12th ed. (Thompson/West, 2008), 1195.
43. Mary Prosser, "Reforming Criminal Discovery: Why Old Objections Must Yield to New Realities," Wisconsin Law Review 2006 (2006): 541–614, 578.
44. Kamisar et al., Modern Criminal Procedure, 1221.
45. Prosser, "Reforming Criminal Discovery," 582–83.
46. Prosser, "Reforming Criminal Discovery," 585.
47. Prosser, "Reforming Criminal Discovery," 583–84.
48. Prosser, "Reforming Criminal Discovery," 584.
49. Prosser, "Reforming Criminal Discovery," 585.
50. Kamisar et al., *Modern Criminal Procedure,* 1209–10.
51. Barry Tarlow, "Jencks Act Disclosure: Strict Construction or Trial by Ambush," *The Champion,* 20 (1996): 46, 50.
52. Alexandra Natapoff, "Beyond Unreliable: How Snitches Contribute to Wrongful Convictions," *Golden Gate University Law Review* 37 (2006): 107–129.
53. Kamisar et al., *Modern Criminal Procedure,* 1255.
54. The Justice Project, "Eyewitness Identification: A Policy Review." Available at http://www.thejusticeproject.org/press/reports/pdfs/PolPack_EyewitnessID-72dpi.pdf (Acessed June 19, 2009).

55. K. A. Findley and M. S. Scott, "The Multiple Dimensions of Tunnel Vision in Criminal Cases," *Wisconsin Law Review* (2006): 291–397.

56. Robert Jackson, "The Federal Prosecutor," *Journal of the American Institute of Criminal Law and Criminology* 31 (1940): 3–6; and Lyn Morton, "Seeking the Elusive Remedy for Prosecutorial Misconduct: Suppression, Dismissal, or Discipline?" *Georgetown Journal of Legal Ethics* 7 (1994): 1083–1116, 1085.

57. Rory K. Little, "Proportionality as an Ethical Precept for Prosecutors in Their Investigative Role," *Fordham Law Review* 68 (1999): 723–70, 729–30.

58. Henning, "Prosecutorial Misconduct in Grand Jury Investigations."

59. "Given the assortment of interactions between prosecutors, defendants, and defense counsel, it should not be surprising that the term 'prosecutorial misconduct' does not describe any particular type of act or category of violation." Peter J. Henning, "Prosecutorial Misconduct and Constitutional Remedies," *Washington University Law Quarterly* 77 (1999): 713–833, 721.

60. See Bennett L. Gershman, *Prosecutorial Misconduct* (Deerfield, Ill.: Clark Boardman Callaghan, 1995).

61. Henning, "Prosecutorial Misconduct and Constitutional Remedies," 721–22.

62. Jackson, "The Federal Prosecutor," 4.

63. Richard H. Frost, *The Mooney Case* (Stanford, Calif.: Stanford University Press, 1968).

64. Willard J. Lassers, *Scapegoat Justice: Lloyd Miller and the Failure of the American Legal System* (Bloomington: Indiana University Press, 1973).

65. Barry Scheck, Peter Neufeld, and Jim Dwyer, *Actual Innocence: When Justice Goes Wrong and How to Make It Right* (New York: Signet, 2001), 361.

66. James S. Liebman et al., "Capital Attrition: Error Rates in Capital Cases, 1973–1995," *Texas Law Review* 78 (2000): 1839–65.

67. C. Ronald Huff, Arye Rattner and Edward Sagarin. *Convicted but Innocent: Wrongful Conviction and Public Policy* (Thousand Oaks, Calif.: Sage, 1996), 64.

68. Edwin Borchard, *Convicting the Innocent: Sixty-five Actual Errors of Criminal Justice* (Garden City, N.Y.: Garden City Publishing, 1932), xv.

69. Innocence Project Web site, http://www.innocence project.org/ (accessed January 6, 2004).

70. George Castelle and Elizabeth Loftus, "Misinformation and Wrongful Convictions," in Saundra D. Westervelt and John A. Humphrey, eds., *Wrongly Convicted: Perspectives on Failed Justice* (New Brunswick, N.J.: Rutgers University Press, 2001), 18.

71. Brian Forst defines *errors of justice* as both the conviction of innocent parties and sanctions against the guilty that are less than optimal, including failures to prosecute guilty parties whose cases are not properly dismissed on the grounds of justice, e.g., trivial offenses. Brian Forst, *Errors of Justice: Nature, Sources and Remedies* (New York: Cambridge University Press, 2004), 3–6.

72. Forst, *Errors of Justice,* 112.

73. Scott Christianson, *Innocent: Inside Wrongful Conviction Cases* (New York: New York University Press, 2004), 144–47; and *People v. Jackson,* 154 Misc.2d 718, 593 N.Y.S.2d 410 (Sup. Ct. Kings. Co. 1992).

74. Richard L. Fricker, "Crime and Punishment in Dallas," *American Bar Association Journal* 75 (July 1989): 52.

75. Fricker, "Crime and Punishment in Dallas"; and Randall Dale Adams, William Hoffer, and Marilyn Mona Hoffer, *Adams v. Texas* (New York: St. Martin's Press, 1991).

76. James Neff, *The Wrong Man: The Final Verdict on the Dr. Sam Sheppard Murder Case* (New York: Random House, 2001).

77. Edward Humes, *Mean Justice* (New York: Simon and Schuster, 1999), 451 (see 128–40, 205, 228, 361–80).

78. Scheck, Neufeld, and Dwyer, *Actual Innocence,* 226–32.

79. Steve Mills and Maurice Possley, "Officials Often Insist Ex-inmates Are Guilty: Authorities Often Slow to Admit Mistakes," *Chicago Tribune,* October 27, 2003.

80. Mills and Possley, "Officials Often Insist Ex-inmates Are Guilty."

81. David Horan, "The Innocence Commission: An Independent Review Board for Wrongful Convictions," *Northern Illinois University Law Review* 20 (2000): 9–189.

82. Kenneth Bresler, "'I Never Lost a Trial': When Prosecutors Keep Score of Criminal Convictions," *Georgetown Journal of Legal Ethics* 9 (1996): 537–46, 539.

JUSTICES OF THE SUPREME COURT

Reagan's Conservative Legacy: O'Connor, Scalia, and Kennedy

Ronald Reagan's presidency capped off a dramatic political shift whereby the conservative wing of the Republican Party became dominant and sought to transform American politics as deeply as President Franklin Roosevelt had in the 1930s. Although the Senate was controlled by Republicans at the onset of the Reagan years, the Congress reverted to Democratic hands, and the sweep of the Reagan revolution was not complete. The greatest Reagan victories were in economic deregulation and a military buildup. The ideologically far-right social agenda of some conservatives has never been fully achieved. Still, the shift to the right has been felt in the Supreme Court to which Reagan appointed three justices—including the first female justice, Sandra Day O'Connor.

President Reagan's three successful Supreme Court nominees joined the Burger Court, which was better described as moderate than conservative. Justice Antonin Scalia was a brilliant academic and judicial supporter of conservative economic theories before being named to the Court. Justice Anthony Kennedy was a low-key and popular nominee after President Reagan's tumultuous failed attempts to have Judge Robert Bork and then Judge Douglas Ginsberg named to the Court.

Justices O'Connor, Scalia, and Kennedy are highly rated for their judicial craft and acuity. While each has voted for the prosecution far more often than for the defense, they do not vote in lockstep, and each has displayed independence in evaluating the facts and doctrines of criminal procedure cases, leading each to decide specific cases for the individual on the basis of carefully reasoned criteria.

Collection of the Supreme Court of the United States.
Photographer: Dane Penland.

Sandra Day O'Connor

Arizona, 1930–

Republican

Appointed by Ronald Reagan

Years of Service: 1981–2006

Life and Career.   Justice O'Connor holds the distinction of being the first woman appointed to the Supreme Court. Raised on an Arizona ranch, she graduated magna cum laude from Stanford University and was third in the 1952 Stanford Law School class in which William Rehnquist graduated first. Despite her academic attainments, she received no offers from private firms because of the gender bias of that era. She worked as a county attorney in San Mateo, California, as a civilian attorney for the U.S. Army while her husband served, and in private practice while raising a family in Phoenix, Arizona. Active in civic and political activities—and described as a "mainstream pragmatic Republican"—O'Connor served as assistant attorney general of Arizona from 1965 to 1969. She was appointed and then elected twice to the Arizona Senate, rising to Senate majority leader before becoming judge of the Maricopa County Superior Court in 1974 and judge of the Arizona Intermediate Court of Appeals in 1979.

Contribution to Criminal Procedure.   Justice O'Connor's position was generally conservative. In right-to-counsel cases, she found no constitutional violation by the forfeiture of funds to pay for counsel (*Caplin & Drysdale v. United States,* 1989). Her opinion in *Moran v. Burbine* (1986) held that the fact that an attorney has been retained and is attempting to reach a suspect does not affect the voluntariness of a confession given after *Miranda* warnings have been read and the suspect has waived the right to remain silent.

In *Illinois v. Krull* (1987), O'Connor dissented from a ruling that evidence of an illegal search based on the good faith reliance on a statute is admissible. Although she joined the conservative majority in *Leon* (1984), holding illegal evidence seized in a good faith reliance on a bad warrant is admissible, her experience as a legislator led her to distinguish a warrant from a statute. A legislature's "unreasonable authorization may affect thousands or millions," while a magistrate's error only affects the individual involved, and legislators are more subject to "political pressures that may threaten Fourth Amendment values" than are judges.

Signature Opinion.   *Strickland v. Washington* (1984). While holding that a defendant's Sixth Amendment right to counsel can be violated by the ineffective assistance of counsel, she formulated a weak standard that requires a defendant to show a serious deficiency in an attorney's performance and also requires that this performance was responsible for the verdict or sentence.

Assessment.   Justice O'Connor came to the Supreme Court as a moderate conservative, supporting the death penalty and equal rights for women and having a mixed position on abortion. These policies have generally characterized her votes as a justice. Her judicial philosophy downplayed broad ideological positions. As a judicial conservative, she changed the law incrementally, anchoring the law in precedent and the facts of cases.

By the time of her retirement, Justice O'Connor had become the pivotal "swing" justice whose middle-of-the-Court votes between more conservative and liberal justices made her fifth vote the decisive voice on the Court. This prevented the radical conservative legal revolution desired by Justices Scalia and Clarence Thomas. Justice O'Connor often influenced the law through concurring opinions, by joining a conservative majority in high-visibility abortion, death penalty, and church–state cases but preventing it from establishing sweeping doctrines. Her joint opinion in *Planned Parenthood v. Casey* (1992) (with Kennedy and Souter) prevented the Court's overruling *Roe v. Wade* (1973) on the grounds of precedent. In church–state cases, she allowed Christmas season displays, under the First Amendment, with some religious content if they were predominantly secular—a ruling that has become the Court's position.

Further Reading

Nancy Maveety, *Justice Sandra Day O'Connor: Strategist on the Supreme Court* (Lanham, Md.: Rowman and Littlefield, 1996).

Antonin Scalia

New Jersey, 1936–
Republican
Appointed by Ronald Reagan
Years of Service: 1986–

Collection of the Supreme Court
of the United States.
Photographer: Mollie Isaacs.

Life and Career.   Antonin Scalia, the son of a Sicilian immigrant and professor of romance languages at Brooklyn College, was a superb student, graduating first in his class from Xavier High School and Georgetown University. He was an editor on the *Harvard Law Review* and received his law degree from Harvard Law School in 1960. His strong conservative beliefs were pronounced even as a schoolboy. He practiced corporate law, taught at the University of Virginia Law School, and from 1971 to 1977 held several key appointments on legal advisory staffs to Presidents Richard Nixon and Gerald Ford, including assistant attorney general in charge of the Justice Department's Office of Legal Counsel. He spent a year as scholar-in-residence at the American Enterprise Institute, a conservative think tank, served four years as law professor at the University of Chicago, and was appointed to the U.S. Court of Appeals for the District of Columbia in 1982.

Scalia was a leading conservative spokesman on issues of law and economics, asserting the power of the executive branch, favoring judicial restraint, and backing deregulation of the marketplace; he blasted judicially supported affirmative action programs. These positions were evident in many of his opinions on the Court of Appeals. His opinions were forceful, and when he was appointed to replace Justice Rehnquist (who was elevated to the office of chief justice), it was thought that his charm and powers of persuasion would solidify a conservative court that would overturn *Roe v. Wade.* His nomination sailed through the Senate, and he was confirmed by a 98-to-0 vote.

Contribution to Criminal Procedure.   Justice Scalia's position on criminal procedure issues has proven to be something of a surprise. While hardly a liberal—most of his criminal law votes favor the prosecution—he has, on several occasions, taken positions in which the logic of the law led him to support the defendant. These include his opinion in *Arizona v. Hicks* (1987) (a slight movement of property to view a serial number constitutes a search) and dissenting opinions in *National Treasury Employees Union v. Von Raab* (1989) (automatic drug testing of every customs officer is not based on a real need but on political motivations and violates the Fourth Amendment) and *Maryland v. Craig* (1990) (placing a screen between a defendant and an accuser who is a minor violates the Sixth Amendment Confrontation Clause).

His many pro-prosecution opinions include *Wyoming v. Houghton* (1999) (police can search handbag of passenger of stopped car when there is probable cause to search car, despite lack of suspicion against the passenger), *Whren v. United States* (1996) (pretext search of automobile upheld), and *Vernonia School District 47J v. Acton* (1995) (special needs allows drug testing of every public high school student athlete).

Signature Opinion.   *California v. Hodari D.* (1991). A youth fleeing from the police threw away drugs before being tackled. For the Court, Scalia wrote that there was no stop or arrest before the youth was physically seized; the drugs were therefore abandoned and admissible into evidence. To reach this result, he set aside the existing rule that persons are seized when they reasonably believe they are not free to leave and replaced it with the physical restraint standard.

Assessment.   Scalia is a leading intellectual on the Court and has been instrumental in reviving the rights of property owners against government regulation. He generally votes conservatively in First Amendment and other civil rights areas, although less so than Rehnquist and Thomas. He is known for his opinions and writings, which argue that the plain text of statutes should be the leading principle as to their interpretation, and is wary of using legislative history as a guide to statutory interpretation. He has been a lone dissenter on the question of the separation of powers, where he believes that sharp lines must be drawn between the branches of government; he voted against the constitutionality of the U.S. Sentencing Commission on which judges and executive appointees join to set policy.

Further Reading

David A. Schultz and Christopher E. Smith, *The Jurisprudential Vision of Justice Antonin Scalia* (Lanham, Md.: Rowman and Littlefield, 1996).

Collection of the Supreme Court
of the United States.
Photographer: Robin Reid.

Anthony Kennedy

California, 1936–
Republican
Appointed by Ronald Reagan
Years of Service: 1988–

Life and Career.   A Sacramento, California, native, Kennedy graduated from Stanford University (member of Phi Beta Kappa) and graduated cum laude from Harvard Law School in 1961. He practiced law in San Francisco and took over his father's Sacramento law and lobbying practice in 1963. His approach to law practice was scholarly, and for twenty-three years he taught law part-time at the McGeorge School of Law. He came to Governor Reagan's attention in 1971 by drafting a tax-limitation amendment that was the forerunner of California's famous Proposition 13. On Reagan's recommendation, he was appointed to the Ninth Circuit Court of Appeals in 1975 by President Ford.

Kennedy was a respected federal judge who upheld precedent, carefully considered all sides of a case before rendering a decision, and who generally did not find in favor of women, minorities, or homosexuals in civil rights cases. His decision declaring the "legislative veto" unconstitutional (i.e., Congress delegates power to administrative agencies to overrule agency rules) was upheld by the Supreme Court.

He was quickly confirmed as associate justice after the monumental battle that blocked President Reagan's nomination of Judge Robert Bork to the Supreme Court and the failed attempt to have a second nominee, Judge Douglas Ginsburg, approved.

Contribution to Criminal Procedure.   In most cases, Justice Kennedy votes for the government and against the individual. He has voted to uphold the drug courier profile as a basis for a *Terry* stop, to find that ambiguity in a *Miranda* warning does not void a confession, that a judge can deny a defendant's free choice of attorney on grounds of conflict of interest over the defendant's objections, and that a helicopter overflight of residential backyard is not a search. In *Skinner v. Railway Labor Executives' Association* (1989) and *National Treasury Employees Union v. Von Raab* (1989), he upheld drug testing on the basis of the special needs doctrine.

Signature Opinion.   *Powers v. Ohio* (1991). A prosecutor used peremptory challenges to keep seven African Americans off the jury in a murder trial. For the majority, Justice Kennedy held that a white defendant could object. He wrote, "Jury service is an exercise of responsible citizenship by all members of the community, including those who otherwise might not have the opportunity to contribute to our civic life."

Assessment.   Aside from criminal procedure cases, Justice Kennedy is a moderate conservative who is often aligned with Justices O'Connor and Souter and not with the most conservative wing of the Court (Justices Rehnquist, Scalia, and Thomas). In a pivotal abortion case, he wrote a joint opinion with Justices O'Connor and Souter upholding a woman's right to choose based on the concept of precedent. He held that the burning of the American flag during a protest was protected speech and could not be criminal because the result was compelled by the Constitution. In a case involving the solicitation of funds and the distribution of leaflets by members of Hare Krishna at an airport, he joined the moderates on the Court in holding that while the solicitation could be banned, the leafleting was protected by the First Amendment. And in *Romer v. Evans* (1996), he wrote for the majority, which struck down a state referendum that specifically stated that homosexual orientation could not be a basis for heightened antidiscrimination protection. Kennedy viewed this law as violating the Equal Protection Clause because it singled out a certain class of citizens for disfavored legal status or general hardships.

Further Reading

Akhil Reed Amar, "Justice Kennedy and the Ideal of Equality," *Pacific Law Journal* 28 (1997): 515–32.

CHAPTER 11

The Trial Process

EQUAL JUSTICE UNDER LAW

[T]here are principles of liberty and justice, lying at the foundation of our civil and political institutions, which no State can violate consistently with that due process of law required by the Fourteenth Amendment in proceedings involving life, liberty, or property.

—JUSTICE JOHN MARSHALL HARLAN I, dissenting, *Hurtado v. California*, 110 U.S. 516, 546 (1884)

CHAPTER OUTLINE

KEY TERMS

abuse of discretion
accusatorial trial
adversarial trial
adverse comment
bench trial
challenge for cause
character witness
compulsory process
Confrontation Clause

cross-examination
direct examination
dossier
dying declaration
expert witness
hearsay
hung jury
in camera
inquisitorial trial

invidious discrimination
jury deliberation
jury pool
jury trial
"key man" method
master jury list
peremptory challenge
petty crime
presumption of innocence

prima facie case
reasonable doubt
representative cross section
secret informants
venire
verdict
voir dire
waiver trial

THE IDEAL OF THE FAIR TRIAL

All cultures develop methods to ascertain the guilt of those accused of serious norm violations or crimes. Even if offenders are caught "red-handed," there is a human tendency to conduct formal processes for declaring guilt. The trial therefore has two functions: first, to determine a suspect's guilt in a practical and efficient manner, and second, to provide a formal setting that solemnizes the conclusion that this person is guilty and must be punished. The **jury trial** performs these functions in the Anglo-American legal tradition.[1] Trial by jury was not legislated into being all at once as the best method to resolve criminal cases. Rather, it evolved over centuries in England. As a result many have argued that it is not the most efficient or effective method of separating the guilty from the innocent. Nevertheless, it is embedded in American culture and is guaranteed by Article III and by the Sixth and Seventh Amendments of the U.S. Constitution, as well as by every state constitution.

Trials in continental European countries differ substantially from English or American jury trials. In 1215 the Roman Catholic Church forbade priests from participating in trials by ordeal at the Fourth Lateran Council. Ordeals were superstitious appeals to God to decide cases where evidence pointed to a suspect but proof of guilt was uncertain. England turned to its nascent jury used to settle land claims, and gave the job of deciding guilt or innocence to twelve men. On the Continent, such cases were given to single judges, borrowing a more direct procedure promulgated by the Church for the inquisition of heretics. English juries did not explain verdicts and so could hang defendants on the basis of circumstantial evidence. European judges, who had personal responsibility for decisions, had to explain verdicts in writing and could lawfully condemn defendants only on "full proof"—eyewitnesses or confessions—but not on circumstantial evidence. The need for full proof led to the use of torture as a legal judicial method in European criminal trials until the mid-eighteenth century.[2]

Both trial by jury and the **inquisitorial trial** were advances over the superstitious and brutal methods of trial by ordeal. Of great importance in playing their expressive as well as functional roles is that in both systems of justice trials are generally open to the public:

> Legal systems to determine guilt are fundamentally different from administrative methods of determining facts, which can be carried out secretly, but with accuracy and impartiality, by police or other investigators. Legal proceedings, however, must give the appearance of being fair and accurate, and the best way—perhaps the only way—to give that appearance is by allowing the community either to witness the process through which the decision is made or to participate in some way. This lends the proceeding legitimacy, avoids suspicion and rumor of official prejudice and arbitrariness, and gives the public a feeling of security. In the second place, public adjudication proceedings perform an important function in the administration of criminal justice which cannot be achieved by administrative fact-finding: they dramatize moral issues and inform the public of the sad consequences which attend violation of the law. Through their public ceremonies adjudication proceedings condemn, educate, and deter.[3]

After the seventeenth century, the common law criminal jury trial was extolled as a guarantor of British liberty because in political trials citizens resisted authoritarian government pressure and acquitted political opponents of the state.[4] On the other hand, the jury trial has been criticized as inefficient and prone to error.[5] Professor John Langbein notes that the conduct of English criminal trials before lawyers regularly defended suspects (about 1750) left much to be desired. The defendant had to defend him- or herself, and the jury sat through as many as twenty trials a day, each typically lasting about half an hour. Decisions were made on groups of cases in open court. The judge dominated the jury and could openly influence its **verdict**.[6]

Although these earlier trials were inferior to contemporary procedures under modern standards of due process, a sense of fair play prevailed in them. The English maxim—"It is better that ten guilty go free than one innocent be convicted"—sums up the common law attitude to criminal justice. As a result, English common law trials did not utilize torture, unlike continental inquisitorial trials prior to the eighteenth century, and a defendant could have his or her say in open court before a local jury. At the core of the **adversarial trial** (or **accusatorial trial**) is the idea of a fair fight, one in which the defendant is given a full opportunity to challenge the prosecution, to present witnesses, to confront and **cross-examine** the accusers, and to present the case to an impartial group of legal equals. The prosecutor, further, has a very high burden of proof: proof beyond a reasonable doubt. In the forum of the trial court, the prosecutor is simply another party before an impartial judge and has no special status. Despite its glorious history and high repute, unpopular verdicts and the knowledge that many innocent people have been convicted have raised serious doubts about the ability of the jury trial to achieve fair verdicts.

A brief comparison of the two trial systems will sharpen an understanding of the jury trial.

Comparing Adversarial and Inquisitorial Trials

It may help to better understand the common law jury trial, which originated in England and is the form of trial in the United States, by comparing it to European criminal trials that derive from the "civil" or "Roman" justice system. Common law trials are *accusatorial* or *adversarial*, pitting the defendant, who is expected to gather evidence in his or her defense, against the prosecutor. *Inquisitorial* criminal trials in civil law countries, by contrast, are viewed more as systematic inquiries into the truth of a criminal charge conducted by trained police, prosecutorial, and judicial officers.[7]

The most obvious difference is that the common law jury—a group of ordinary citizens chosen to hear a case—being instructed on the law, decides the facts and renders the verdict, and then disperses back into the population. In the inquisitorial mode of trial, both the law and the facts are decided by trained professional judges, sometimes with the assistance of citizen-jurors. Another difference is that the judge is the central actor in the inquisitorial trial. The judge "runs" the trial, conducts most of the questioning, and shapes the introduction of evidence. In contrast, the attorneys (adversaries) decide which evidence to present and how to present it in common law trials. The common law judge is more of a referee who decides whether evidence is admissible and whether the lawyers make errors. The common law judge occasionally supplements attorneys' questions with his or her own. Another difference is that English and American judges are drawn from the ranks of practicing lawyers, while inquisitorial judges are highly trained, lifelong career professionals.

Common law trials are based primarily on oral testimony that, ideally, should be heard in a continuous process. Each side collects its own evidence and decides how to present its case. Although the sharing of physical evidence by the police and prosecutor with the defense has become more common, there is only a limited obligation on prosecutors to turn over exculpatory evidence to defendants. Written or physical evidence has to be introduced with testimony as to its authenticity. In the United States, police investigate without formal control or direction by prosecutors, who are in separate agencies.

Modern inquisitorial trials are preceded by police investigations under the formal directions of a centralized prosecution office. The heart of the inquisitorial trial is the investigation, which gathers its findings into a detailed investigation file or **dossier**. It is the dossier that is the focus of the inquisitorial trial, although the trial itself is open to the public and witnesses are sworn to testify.

The search for the truth in the adversary trial is accomplished by the "clash of evidence" presented by the prosecution and the defense. Each side's evidence is subjected to cross-examination by the other attorney, which is supposed to bring out the truth to the jury. Formal rules of evidence, such as the hearsay rule, exclude evidence that cannot be subjected to cross-examination or that can confuse or prejudice the lay jury. In contrast, the European trial allows in all relevant evidence, with a small number of privileges, for evaluation by professional judges.

The privilege against self-incrimination exists in both systems. In practice, defendants usually participate and testify in inquisitorial trials. In American jury trials, defendants often do not testify. Negative inferences may not be drawn from this silence in American trials but are now allowed to be made in England. The burden of proof is on the prosecution in both systems, and in both the defendant is presumed innocent.

The centrality of the search for the truth distinguishes these systems. The search for the truth is paramount in the modern inquisitorial system; in the multipurposed adversarial trial, truth may be subordinated to other values. Ingraham notes that the adversary system is unique in "the degree to which the question of guilt or innocence is left to the game-playing skills of two adversary lawyers."[8] Because the adversarial jury system supports goals other than the truth of the case (e.g., suppressing illegally seized evidence to deter police and prosecutorial misconduct), it is a better counterweight to political oppression. Whether one system or the other produces more accurate verdicts and is less likely to convict the innocent is subject to debate.

Steps in the Jury Trial

The modern jury has continuously evolved into a complex process involving a number of distinct steps briefly explained here.

JURY SELECTION—VOIR DIRE   A panel of about forty prospective jurors in a typical felony case is led into the courtroom. The panel should have been selected from a larger group representing a fair cross-section of the community (described later in this chapter). **Voir dire** involves *questioning* the entire panel and individual jurors, by the judge and the attorneys, to weed out biased or prejudiced jurors. Each side can *strike* jurors via an unlimited number of **challenges for cause** where the judge agrees that the prospective juror is partial. A limited number of **peremptory challenges** are granted to each side, allowing the attorneys to eliminate jurors for any or no reason, except for the deliberate elimination of jurors on the grounds of race, ethnicity, or gender. Challenges are "fast paced, made on the spot and under pressure. Counsel as well as court, in that setting, must be prepared to decide, often between shades of gray, 'by the minute'"(*U.S. v. Martinez-Salazar*, 2000).

OPENING STATEMENTS   Each lawyer outlines the main points of the case to the jury, putting the best interpretation on the case. Both in voir dire and in opening statements, lawyers also try to make good personal impressions on jurors.

THE "CASE IN CHIEF" AND CROSS-EXAMINATION   The heart of the case is the presentation of witnesses called by each side. By presenting evidence the prosecutor seeks to convince the jury that the defendant is guilty of the crime(s) charges beyond a **reasonable doubt**. The defense seeks to raise a reasonable doubt about guilt. The prosecution goes first with the **direct examination** of prosecution witnesses. Each prosecution witness may be cross-examined by the defense lawyer. The prosecutor must establish probable cause or a **prima facie case** of guilt at the end of his or her case. The defense may make a motion to dismiss at this point on the ground that probable cause of guilt was not established. The motion is typically denied, but it may succeed if the prosecutor has not offered proof as to an essential element of the crime. The prosecution case may be followed by the defense presenting witnesses, whom the prosecution may cross-examine. The defense may put on a case by the direct examination of its witnesses or may rest its case without presenting witnesses on the belief that it has raised sufficient reasonable doubt to convince the jury to acquit.

There are three types of witnesses. Ordinary witnesses can testify only as to their personal observations. A witness may also introduce documents or physical evidence. **Expert witnesses**, on the other hand, are allowed to offer *opinions* in their area of expertise. **Character witnesses** may testify only to the general good reputation of the defendant. Cross-examination, deemed a great "engine" to determine the truth, is designed to discredit witnesses' testimony or credibility with the jury. After a witness has been cross-examined, the lead attorney asks questions on redirect; these questions are limited to clarifying or rehabilitating the witness on the points specifically raised by cross-examination.

CLOSING STATEMENTS   The defense attorney first addresses the jury, followed by the prosecutor. The prosecutor has the last word because of the heavy burden of proof beyond a reasonable doubt. The attorneys bring together the various pieces of testimony and evidence, weaving together a coherent and convincing narrative. The prosecutor explains why the evidence indicates that the defendant is guilty beyond a reasonable doubt, while the defense counsel explains why the evidence establishes reasonable doubt. A pithy and famous example of reasonable doubt was Johnny Cochran's exhortation to the jury in the O. J. Simpson murder trial: "If the glove doesn't fit, you must acquit."

JURY INSTRUCTIONS   Following the presentation of evidence and closing statements, the judge instructs the jurors on the law by defining and explaining the crimes charged, the rules of evidence (especially proof beyond a reasonable doubt), and the possible verdicts that are allowed.

JURY DELIBERATIONS AND VERDICT   Jurors are sworn to follow the law as instructed by the judge and deliberate in private to review the evidence and vote on the verdict. For each count of the indictment, the jury must enter a verdict of guilty or not guilty. The verdict must be unanimous, except in states that allow a verdict based on a supermajority vote. If a jury is deadlocked and the vote is lopsided, the judge will admonish holdout jurors not to be rigid and to reasonably review the evidence as viewed by the majority. If further deliberations do not change the vote, the court declares a **hung jury**; the case is dismissed but may be retried at the prosecutor's discretion.

POSTVERDICT MOTIONS   The defense can submit a motion for judgment notwithstanding the verdict (or judgment NOV, for *non obstante verdicto*) or a motion in arrest of judgment, arguing that the jury could not have reasonably convicted the defendant based on the evidence presented. The defense can also file a motion for a new trial based on the judge's errors in admitting evidence. Such motions are rarely successful.

An actual trial involves more complex preparation, strategy, psychological penetration, and dramatic human action than this list can show.[9]

IMPORTANT CONSTITUTIONAL TRIAL RIGHTS

The trial is guided by many complex rules of criminal procedure and evidence law. This section presents an overview of some important constitutional trial rights.

The Right to Be Present

A defendant's right to be present throughout the trial is based on the **Confrontation Clause** of the Sixth Amendment (*Diaz v. United States*, 1912) and on due process. A defendant has the right to accompany the jury if it leaves the courtroom to view the scene of the crime. However, in ***United States v. Gagnon*** (1985), the Court held that there was no Sixth Amendment violation when a judge met with a juror and the defense attorney (without the defendant presence) regarding the juror's nervousness because the defendant drew sketches of the jurors during the trial. The defendant's presence at the meeting was not required to ensure fundamental fairness or a reasonable opportunity to conduct the defense. The *Gagnon* rule applies to cases where the defendant is excluded from pretrial evidence suppression hearings.

Secret trials ("kangaroo courts," "star chamber proceedings") are anathema to the adversary system and have been eliminated from civilian trials. A serious issue arises where in a trial against terrorists, corrupt government contractors, or government officials involved in foreign relations for illegal acts, the defendant seeks to introduce classified information that may harm the national security if it is leaked to the public. To balance a defendant's right to an open trial against the protection of national security, Congress passed the Classified Information Procedures Act of 1980. Under the law, the defense may use classified material, but it must notify the prosecutor in advance as to which secrets will be used. The government is then given the opportunity to submit edited statements in place of the disputed documents. If the judge is not satisfied that these statements are fair to the defense, the prosecution is then given the option of allowing the documents to be made public or to drop the charges that bring the secrets to light in the courtroom.[10]

Ray Agard, charged with sodomy and sexual assault, testified on his own behalf that the sexual encounter was consensual. In her closing statement the prosecutor said that Agard, "unlike all the other witnesses in this case . . . [had] has a benefit . . . [U]nlike all the other witnesses . . . he gets to sit here and listen to the testimony of all the other witnesses before he testifies. . . . That gives you a big advantage, doesn't it. You get to sit here and think what am I going to say and how am I going to say it? How am I going to fit it into the evidence? . . . He's a smart man. . . . He used everything to his advantage." Agard complained that the prosecutor's statements deprived him of his right to be present at the trial, by placing a burden on his presence. The Supreme Court in ***Portuondo v. Agard*** (2000) disagreed. Agard asked for a ruling like that in *Griffin v. California* (1965), which held that judicial comment on a defendant's *silence* unconstitutionally burdened his Fifth Amendment right to silence under the privilege against self-incrimination. The Court distinguished the cases. Jurors are not supposed to infer guilt from a defendant's silence, making a prosecutor's comment an invitation to engage in *prohibited* reasoning. In this case, however, Agard took the stand and testified. Having done so, it is natural and *proper* for the jury to weigh his *credibility as a witness*. Thus, the prosecutor's statement did not violate any trial right or create any fundamental unfairness under the Due Process Clause. Two justices dissented and two expressed the view that the prosecutor's statement is not one to be encouraged.

DISRUPTIVE DEFENDANTS   A defendant who behaves in a loud, obnoxious, and disruptive manner cannot force the state to delay or dismiss a case. In *Illinois v. Allen* (1970), Justice Hugo Black stated:

> It is essential to the proper administration of criminal justice that dignity, order, and decorum be the hallmarks of all court proceedings in our country. The flagrant disregard in the courtroom of elementary standards of proper conduct should not and cannot be tolerated. We believe trial judges confronted with disruptive, contumacious, stubbornly defiant defendants must be given sufficient discretion to meet the circumstances of each case. No one formula for maintaining the appropriate courtroom atmosphere will be best in all situations. We think there are at least three constitutionally permissible ways for a trial judge to handle an obstreperous defendant like Allen: (1) bind and gag him, thereby keeping him present; (2) cite him for contempt; (3) take him out of the courtroom until he promises to conduct himself properly. (*Illinois v. Allen*, 1970)

A trial judge must first be patient with and admonish a disruptive defendant, explaining that obstructionist tactics will not work, before taking the drastic steps of binding or removal. Today, defendants who have been forcibly removed from the courtroom are able to view the trial and communicate with their lawyers from a jail cell through interactive video links.

ABSCONDING DEFENDANTS   A defendant who skips out in the middle of a trial forfeits the right to be present, and the trial may continue in his or her absence. The Supreme Court rejected the argument that for the trial to continue *in absentia,* the judge had to have explicitly warned the defendant about the right to be present. This would add a meaningless formality. Defendants don't have to be told that they are required to be present and that if they abscond, the trial, "where judge, jury, witnesses and lawyers are present and ready to continue," will go on in their absence (*Taylor v. United States,* 1973).

The Appearance of Fairness

The appearance of fairness is important because jurors, as ordinary citizens, can be swayed by prejudicial factors. Consider a huge difference between French and American trials. In France, the defendant's entire life background including his past criminal record is considered by the court before rendering a verdict. French judges, as highly trained and expert legal professionals, should be able to separate out the defendant's background from the specific question of whether he or she committed the criminal act. Jurors, however, cannot be trusted to put aside prejudicial facts, and so the trial is structured in a sense like an antiseptic surgical operating room where only facts relevant to guilt or innocence are admitted. As the Court has said, "one accused of a crime is entitled to have his guilt or innocence determined solely on the basis of the evidence introduced at trial, and not on grounds of official suspicion, indictment, continued custody, or other circumstances not adduced as proof at trial" (*Taylor v. Kentucky*, 1978).

Estelle v. Williams (1976) held that due process is violated where a state compels a defendant to go to trial in a jail or prison uniform. The Court's majority held, however, that the defendant had to object to make the rule effective, while Justice Brennan, dissenting (joined by Justice Marshall), would have found that the fact that Williams went to trial in "a white T-shirt with 'Harris County Jail' stenciled across the back, oversized white dungarees that had 'Harris County Jail' stenciled down the legs, and shower thongs" constituted a violation whether or not objection was made. Chief Justice Burger's majority opinion indicated that the rule against forcing a defendant to wear jail clothes was designed in part to preserve the presumption of innocence. But he indicated that the rule was not absolute, noting, for example, that *Illinois v. Allen* (1970) permitted the shackling of a disruptive defendant. In stronger terms, Justice Brennan got to the real danger of allowing a trial to proceed under such a condition: "Identifiable prison garb robs an accused of the respect and dignity accorded other participants in a trial and constitutionally due the accused as an element of the presumption of innocence, and surely tends to brand him in the eyes of the jurors with an unmistakable mark of guilt."

The question of shackling, which the Court said may be necessary to control an obstreperous defendant, was reconsidered in **Deck v. Missouri** (2005). The Court held that whether at a trial or the penalty-phase trial in a capital case, due process does not allow "the use of physical restraints visible to the jury." Exceptions are allowed only if the trial court finds "that they are justified by a state interest specific to a particular trial." Judicial "hostility to shackling" is based on three principles. First, "[v]isible shackling undermines the presumption of innocence and the related fairness of the factfinding process." Second, shackling undermines the defendant's right to a lawyer by interfering with the "ability to communicate" with counsel both directly and by burdening, confusing, or embarrassing the defendant. Dignity of the courtroom is the third principle.

> The courtroom's formal dignity, which includes the respectful treatment of defendants, reflects the importance of the matter at issue, guilt or innocence, and the gravity with which Americans consider any deprivation of an individual's liberty through criminal punishment. And it reflects a seriousness of purpose that helps to explain the judicial system's power to inspire the confidence and to affect the behavior of a general public whose demands for justice our courts seek to serve. The routine use of shackles in the presence of juries would undermine these symbolic yet concrete objectives. As this Court has said, the use of shackles at trial "affronts" the "dignity and decorum of judicial proceedings that the judge is seeking to uphold." (*Deck v. Missouri*, 2005)

The non-shackling rule is not absolute, but in order to constitutionally shackle a defendant, the trial judge must make specific findings as to why special security needs or a heightened risk of escape requires irons.

Another question is whether action by non-state actors can create such a gross appearance of unfairness as to undermine a trial's fairness. A number of older cases decided under the Due Process Clause make it emphatically clear that the source of unfairness does not matter; what matters is whether the defendant received a fair trial. The first such case was, in fact, the first case in which the Supreme Court ever reversed a state criminal conviction under the Due Process Clause: **Moore v. Dempsey** (1923) (see Chapter 1 regarding the role of the case in the incorporation of the Bill of Rights). *Moore* held that a lynch mob present outside a court during a trial "that threatened the most dangerous consequences to anyone interfering with the desired result" undermined any semblance of a fair trial and constituted a due process violation allowing a federal court to reverse a state conviction under a federal writ of habeas corpus. Other cases held that excesses by print or television news reporters that created a "carnival atmosphere" and prejudiced the minds of the jurors violated due process (*Estes v. Texas*, 1965; *Sheppard v. Maxwell*, 1966).

Not every possible factor in a courtroom that might make a juror dwell on the defendant's guilt is a due process violation. A unanimous Court held that the presence of four armed state troopers seated behind the rail in a trial of six armed robbers was not so inherently prejudicial as to deny a defendant's right to a fair trial (**Holbrook v. Flynn**, 1986). Likewise, in **Carey v. Musladin** (2006) a unanimous Court found no due process violation where family members of a homicide victim sat in the front seat of the spectators' section during a trial and wore buttons two to four inches in diameter that only displayed his photograph. Justice Thomas's majority opinion, under convoluted new rules of habeas corpus, was only willing to rule that "the state court's decision" finding that the trial was not unfair because of the buttons, "was not contrary to or an unreasonable application of clearly established federal law." Three concurring justices (Stevens, Kennedy, and Souter), however, made it clear that the rules of cases like *Moore v. Dempsey* (1923) and *Sheppard v. Maxwell* (1966) were applicable, and that *if* trial spectators had acted in ways to create an unfair trial atmosphere the Supreme Court would have had the authority to reverse, but agreed that there was no due process violation under the facts.

Subpoena: The Right to Compulsory Process

The Sixth Amendment guarantee that the defendant shall have "**compulsory process** for obtaining witnesses in his favor"—that is, the subpoena right—is meant to eliminate barriers to relevant testimony that the defendant wishes to offer. A trial would be grossly unfair if only the state, and not the defense, had such power. The right was incorporated into the Fourteenth Amendment Due Process Clause in *Washington v. Texas* (1967). Washington was charged with murder for a killing that occurred during an argument. His defense was that he was trying to persuade Fuller, the actual killer, to leave and was not in the room when the gun went off. Fuller had been convicted and was willing to testify in Washington's defense. The state blocked his testimony by relying on a Texas law that forbade an accomplice to testify for another. The Supreme Court held that this law violated the Compulsory Process Clause. A state may prevent some defense testimony under ordinary rules of evidence (e.g., because the testimony is irrelevant or incompetent), but it may not disallow relevant evidence.

In *Webb v. Texas* (1972), the defendant's only witness was subpoenaed from prison, where he was serving a sentence. The trial judge threatened the witness with heavy-handed warnings against committing perjury and said that lying would extend the witness's prison term and be counted against him by the parole board. This so terrified the witness that he refused to testify. The Supreme Court, ruling that the trial judge's unnecessarily emphatic warning "drove the witness off the stand," reversed the judgment. This due process violation tended to undermine the defendant's subpoena right. In more recent years, the Supreme Court has weakened the right to compulsory process.

In *United States v. Valenzuela-Bernal* (1982), the Supreme Court held that the government could deport illegal immigrants before a trial in which they might be called as defense witnesses concerning their being smuggled into the United States. The defense attorney did not even have an opportunity to interview them. The Court felt that the government's legal obligation to swiftly deport aliens, the financial costs of prolonged detention, and the human costs to the detainees were more important than the defendant's Sixth Amendment right to subpoena witnesses.

In *Pennsylvania v. Ritchie* (1987), a father charged with incest sought to subpoena records from Children and Youth Services (CYS), a protective service agency, claiming that the records were necessary for the defense to cross-examine witnesses. Pennsylvania courts granted the defense request to fully examine the contents of CYS confidential files on the basis of the defendant's confrontation and compulsory process rights. The U.S. Supreme Court reversed, in part, noting that the Confrontation Clause "does not include the power to require the pretrial disclosure of any and all information that might be useful in contradicting unfavorable testimony." Since the defense counsel was able to cross-examine all prosecution witnesses fully, there was no violation of the Confrontation Clause. Justice Powell, writing for the majority, also noted that Pennsylvania law allowed a court to disclose parts of a youth's record. The Court agreed that Ritchie was entitled to have a trial judge, but not the defense lawyer, review the CYS records to determine which were material. In this way, the defendant's compulsory process right was balanced with "the Commonwealth's compelling interest in protecting its child abuse information." The *Ritchie* rule places much discretion and trust in the judge's hands, but it weakens the adversary system, which is premised on the idea that lawyers are better able to detect favorable facts in a record than judges because they are motivated to do so.

Due Process and Access to Evidence

Closely related to the *Brady* rule (discussed in Chapter 10) are attempts, thus far unsuccessful, to establish constitutionally guaranteed access to evidence. In three cases, the Supreme Court ruled against defendants seeking to make the preservation of or access to evidence held by police a due process requirement. There was no evidence of police bad faith in the preservation cases, that is, trying to evade *Brady*'s requirement that prosecutors turn over factual evidence to the defendant. At worst, the police were negligent in failing to preserve the evidence.

California v. Trombetta (1984) held that police departments do not have to preserve breath samples with alcohol readings, for testing by defendants in DUI cases. Trombetta argued that the sample would allow him to impeach the test's accuracy. The routine failure to save breath samples and the introduction of breath-analysis test *results* do not violate defendants' due process rights to a fair trial. First, "the chances are extremely low that preserved samples would have been exculpatory." The breath-analysis test is routine, and if administered properly, there is a low probability that the results will be inaccurate. Also, defendants can inspect the breath-analysis machine. A prior case held that a defendant's due process rights were not violated when evidence was admitted based on preliminary field notes taken by FBI agents (used to prepare a formal report) that were inadvertently destroyed (*Killian v. United States*, 1961). The Court hinted that imposing administrative requirements on all police departments bordered on the Court's improperly exercising its supervisory power.

A more serious case arose in ***Arizona v. Youngblood*** (1988). Youngblood was identified by the ten-year-old victim of a sexual assault in a photo lineup nine days after an abduction and anal sodomy. A hospital physical examination using a "sexual assault kit" collected samples of the boy's saliva, blood, and hair, and swabs from the boy's rectum and mouth, which were refrigerated, and the boy's underwear and T-shirt, which were not refrigerated. A blood group test was not performed at this time. Later examination found that samples in the kit were insufficient to detect any blood group substances, and that two semen stains found on the boy's clothing could not yield information of the semen depositor's blood type because the clothing had not been refrigerated. At trial Youngblood argued that the victim's identification was inaccurate and that he could have proven his innocence if the clothing had been properly refrigerated.

With *Trombetta* as precedent, Supreme Court held the police destruction of evidence by not refrigerating it was not a denial of due process even though the preserved evidence could have eliminated Youngblood as the perpetrator. The lack of a bad faith attempt by the police to hide evidence from the defendant in order to get around his *Brady* right to disclosure was an important factor in the ruling. Although properly preserved semen evidence might have exonerated Youngblood, the majority noted that the Court had in the past been reluctant to say that fundamental fairness, a central meaning of due process, imposed "on the police an undifferentiated and absolute duty to retain and to preserve all material that might be of conceivable evidentiary significance in a particular prosecution." This reflects the powerful tug of *federalism* as a continuing reason why the Supreme Court has been reluctant to impose constitutional requirements on the police. Justice Stevens, concurring, said that "Although it is not possible to know whether the lost evidence would have revealed any relevant information, it is *unlikely that the defendant was prejudiced* by the State's omission" (*Arizona v. Youngblood,* Stevens, J., concurring, emphasis added).

Justice Harry Blackmun, dissenting (joined by Justices Brennan and Marshall), argued that (1) the *Brady* line of cases did not rest on a prosecutor's bad faith, so any failure to provide evidence, even if negligent, was a constitutional wrong; (2) the real test of whether a trial is fundamentally unfair is whether the unavailable evidence was "constitutionally material"; (3) the *Trombetta* decision relied on the high accuracy level of breath-analysis tests, making the breath samples not constitutionally material; (4) a preserved semen stain could have identified a blood type marker that could clearly have exonerated Youngblood if his semen blood type marker did not match that of the semen on the victim's clothing; and (5) therefore, semen evidence is constitutionally material. Justice Blackmun noted that due process must take the burdens on law enforcement into account. In a case such as this, the state could have had the proper tests conducted in a timely fashion or could have notified the defense that it intended to discard the original evidence. This would have given the defense notice and time to have the evidence tested.

Youngblood underscores the vital importance of proper police procedures in preserving evidence. DNA testing became available soon after, allowing tests on small samples of dry body evidence. A later DNA test on the preserved semen stain on the unrefrigerated clothing showed that Larry Youngblood was not the attacker of the ten-year-old boy. He was released from custody in August 2000 after serving nine years for a crime he did not commit. When the DNA profile was entered into the national convicted offender databases, it matched the profile of Walter Cruise, who, like Youngblood, is blind in one eye. In August 2002, Cruise was convicted of the crime and sentenced to twenty-four years in prison.[11] The aftermath of *Youngblood* demonstrates the hollowness of its result, and the absolute need for police departments to comply with the best practices of evidence collection and preservation.

In ***District Attorney's Office v. Osborne*** (2009) the Supreme Court (5–4) refused to hold that a defendant has a *substantive* due process, freestanding right to DNA evidence. In his majority opinion, Chief Justice Roberts noted that the Supreme Court has been reluctant to expand the concept of substantive due process because such rulings tend to entangle the Court in legislative-like decisions regarding the details of a substantive due process right and "would force us to act as policymakers." This was an odd and complex case for a number of reasons. Osborn was convicted of kidnapping and sexual assault in 1993 and was released on parole in 2007. In a section

1983 civil rights suit (see Chapter 2), he asked for advanced DNA testing of a sperm sample from the crime, despite the fact that his lawyer refused an earlier and less precise DNA test at trial because she thought he was guilty. He had also confessed to the crime in prison in order to obtain parole. Under these conditions, Alaska, one of only four states without a statute providing post-conviction access to DNA testing, resisted Osborn's request for testing. The Court hinted that a prisoner might be able to obtain access to DNA testing in a habeas corpus appeal instead of a civil rights suit. Further, under the specific facts and post-conviction procedures in Alaska that held open the possibility of DNA testing under conditions not met by Osborn, the Supreme Court ruled that the denial of testing in this case did not violate the fundamental fairness test of *procedural* due process.

Aside from Osborn himself, did the Court's ruling cut off DNA testing access to prisoners claiming to be innocent? The majority opinion noted that "DNA testing has an unparalleled ability both to exonerate the wrongly convicted and to identify the guilty. It has the potential to significantly improve both the criminal justice system and police investigative practices." Because of this, as of 2009 the federal government and forty-six states had passed laws allowing prisoners "to move for court-ordered DNA testing under certain specified conditions." The federal act also grants money to states that enact testing statutes to subsidize testing. Courts in three of the four states without post-conviction testing laws have addressed the issue, and there has been such rapid expansion of such laws that the remaining states may pass enabling legislation.

In his dissenting opinion, Justice Stevens noted that the DNA evidence sought would conclusively establish whether Osborne committed the crime, is inexpensive, and "and its results uniquely precise. Yet for reasons the State has been unable or unwilling to articulate, it refuses to allow Osborne to test the evidence at his own expense and to thereby ascertain the truth once and for all." He argued that Osborn had a due process liberty interest that arose from various sources—from a state law that provides general post-conviction relief, and from substantive liberty interests "to have evidence made available for testing," or to be "free of arbitrary government action." As noted in Chapter 1, substantive liberty was not created by the Due Process Clause but is a more fundamental "unalienable" right listed in the Declaration of Independence, but a right that has been recognized in many areas by the Court. As of this writing it is not clear whether the decision in *Osborn* will make a great difference. The majority strongly implied that access to DNA testing has been made available and is not a concern of the federal courts. The alternate concern is that state statutory conditions for access vary, and in some states DNA evidence may become very difficult to get without the backup possibility of recourse to federal courts under the Constitution. If so, this is an issue that can re-arise as a claim under the Due Process Clause.

Right to Silence

The Fifth Amendment right guarantees that no person "shall be compelled in any criminal case to be a witness against himself." This was held to mean in ***Griffin v. California*** (1965) (overruling *Adamson v. California,* 1947) that if a defendant in a state trial chooses not to testify, the Constitution strictly forbids the judge or prosecutor from making a comment that allows a jury to draw an adverse inference. This was the federal rule (*Wilson v. United States*, 1893). **Adverse comment** on silence "is a penalty imposed by our courts for exercising a constitutional privilege. It cuts down on the privilege by making its assertion costly. . . .What the jury may infer given no help from the court is one thing. What they may infer when the court solemnizes the silence of the accused into evidence against him is quite another." Further, a prosecutor cannot introduce evidence that a defendant remained silent, after being read *Miranda* warnings, to impeach him (*Doyle v. Ohio*, 1976). This due process violation is inconsistent with the implied guarantee that silence in response to the *Miranda* warnings will carry no penalty.

Carter v. Kentucky (1978) ruled, however, that a trial judge, when requested by the defense, must instruct the jury that the defendant's silence does not lead to a negative inference. Justice Potter Stewart noted in *Carter* that a trial judge has "an affirmative constitutional obligation" to instruct the jury: "No judge can prevent jurors from speculating about why a defendant stands mute in the face of a criminal accusation, but a judge can, and must, if requested to do so, use the unique power of the jury instruction to reduce that speculation to a minimum." On the other hand, ***Lakeside v. Oregon*** (1978) held that the trial judge can constitutionally give such a protective instruction, over the objection of the defense, if the judge believes that not to do so would lead to an unfair trial. This ruling places great faith in the ability of trial judges to control their courtrooms to ensure fair trials.

Confrontation, Hearsay, and Cross-examination

A FUNDAMENTAL RIGHT   In *Pointer v. Texas* (1965) a robbery victim testified in a preliminary examination at which Pointer was present that Pointer robbed him. Pointer had no lawyer and did not try to cross-examine the witness. The witness then moved to California and did not return for trial. The state trial court allowed a transcript of the witness's statement to be introduced in evidence. The Supreme Court reversed the conviction and held "that the Sixth Amendment's right of an accused to confront the witnesses against him is [like the right to counsel] a fundamental right and is made obligatory on the States by the Fourteenth Amendment." *Pointer*, one of the historic cases that "incorporated" provisions of the Bill of Rights (see Chapter 1), intimately linked the right of confrontation to cross-examination: "It cannot seriously be doubted at this late date that the right of cross-examination is included in the right of an accused in a criminal case to confront the witnesses against him." The right of confrontation and the ability to cross-examine were deemed essential to a fair trial, the overriding goal of the Sixth Amendment.

Constitutional scholar Akhil Reed Amar, who notes that all the provisions of the Sixth Amendment have to be read together to provide an interlocking set of guarantees for a fair adversary trial, offers three reasons why the right to confrontation is necessary for a fair trial. First, confrontation in open court may discourage deliberate perjury by witnesses "who might be ashamed to tell their lies with the defendant in the room" and fear that lies will not "stand up to open scrutiny." Second, an innocent defendant who hears honestly mistaken or perjured testimony will be able to figure out the source of the lies and tell his or her lawyer how to counter them. Third, the clause "enables the defendant . . . to directly question [the witness's story] and cross-examine it—to show the jury and the public where the holes are—and to invite the witness herself to supplement or clarify or revise the story, so that the jury and the public may hear the *whole* truth."[12]

HEARSAY AND CONFRONTATION: THE EVOLUTION OF DOCTRINES   In the last three decades the Supreme Court's Confrontation Clause jurisprudence has gone through tremendous changes that affect police, prosecutors, and defense attorneys in many areas, including highly sensitive prosecutions of those accused of child sexual abuse and domestic violence. The Court's rulings have been influenced in part by changes demanded by society to make it easier to prosecute alleged abusers. In the midst of this change, Justice Antonin Scalia's voice has sounded the clearest call, both in dissent and in leading the Court, to revolutionize confrontation doctrine, for what he has seen as absolute fidelity to the text and history of the Confrontation Clause.

A bit of background is needed to put recent changes in context. We start with the common law hearsay rule. Although it can be traced back to earlier English precedents, it was really developed by American and English courts in the first half of the nineteenth century. The rule excludes the introduction of out-of-court statements (oral or written) by someone (a "declarant") other than the person testifying, offered in evidence to prove the truth of the matter asserted. Legal historian Lawrence M. Friedman suggests that the hearsay rule, which he describes as "cancerously intricate," underwent "explosive growth" in the early nineteenth century as a result of a judicial attitude of distrust toward the jury and a desire to "exclude all shaky, secondhand, or improper evidence from the eyes and ears of the jury." The problem is that excluding all second-hand evidence would make it very difficult, perhaps close to impossible, to prove anything in court. Thus, unlike the "fairly simple and rational" law of evidence in modern Europe that "lets most everything in and trust the judge to separate good evidence from bad," the Anglo-American approach "was a bizarre kind of rule—one simple, if Utopian, idea, along with a puzzle box of exceptions."[13]

In order to make trials workable the hearsay rule has many court-made and statutory exceptions. Federal rules of evidence list twenty-eight specific hearsay exceptions as well as one "residual" exception where the hearsay is found to be "more probative" than any other evidence.[14] Many of the exceptions are things like routine official or business records that are relied on as accurate. Other exceptions, which come into play in criminal prosecutions, require that a declarant be unavailable to testify at the trial, and include **dying declarations**, statements against interest, and evidence previously given at a hearing if the defendant "had an opportunity and similar motive to develop the testimony by direct, cross, or redirect examination."[15] The exceptions are based on the central idea that the kinds of evidence admitted are inherently trustworthy and can, in any event, still be subject to cross-examination at trial.

With this background, an historical overview suggested by Prof. Thomas Reed will help put the Confrontation Clause cases in context. In the first era, from 1892 to 1965, the Confrontation Clause did not apply to the states. The Supreme Court ruled in 1892, in *Mattox v. United States*, that under the clause, prosecution witnesses must appear in court and be subject to cross-examination. The one exception noted was when a witnesses testified about the crime in an earlier trial but was unavailable in the present trial. In *Mattox*, a first trial was reversed on appeal and a second ended in a hung jury. The witness, who identified Mattox at the first trials and was cross-examined, died before the third trial. The Supreme Court allowed the introduction of his earlier testimony. "For more than sixty years after *Mattox*, criminal defendants were prosecuted and convicted using unsworn hearsay statements by absent witnesses."[16]

A flavor of this practice is seen in a case that while not based on the Confrontation Clause raised closely aligned issues. Prior to **Rovario v. United States** (1957) it was the practice for police detectives to testify as to what **secret informants** said and did as testimony against defendants. The secret informant did not come into court. This was designed to protect the informant from any reprisals, but it also prevented the defendant from cross-examining the one person who did the most to convict him or her. *Rovario* held that the government may not conceal the identity of an informer who testifies at a trial. The informant must either be brought into court to personally testify or his or her testimony cannot be used. Cross-examining the police detective "was hardly a substitute for an opportunity to examine the man who had been nearest to him and took part in the transaction." In this case the informant was involved in the drug trade and helped set up a deal. The Supreme Court noted that "His testimony might have disclosed an entrapment." *Rovario* was decided on the basis of the Court's supervisory power over federal cases. Nevertheless, the "*Rovario* rule" stands for the proposition that confrontation includes the right to know the identity of one's accusers. The Supreme Court later ruled on related issues under the Confrontation Clause, holding that an undercover narcotics officer who testifies against a defendant must give his or her real name and address. Not to do so does not give the defense a full opportunity to gather information that might cast a shadow on the witness's credibility (*Smith v. Illinois*, 1968). In another case, the Court said that withholding the fact that a witness was on probation for juvenile delinquency, when that fact was relevant to the witness's possible bias, unconstitutionally weakened the defendant's ability to cross-examine the witness (*Davis v. Alaska*, 1974).

The second era of evolving Confrontation Clause jurisprudence, lasting from 1965 to 1972, revived the clauses's exclusionary rule. It began with *Pointer v. Texas* (1965), discussed earlier, which incorporated the clause and held that testimony at a preliminary hearing that had no chance of being cross-examined was inadmissible at trial. *Pointer* was followed by **Barber v. Page** (1968) and *California v. Green* (1970), which clarified the requirements of the Confrontation Clause where testimony was given by a witness at a preliminary hearing. In both cases the defendant was represented by counsel at the hearing, and in both cases the lawyer decided that it was better strategy not to cross-examine the witness.

In *Barber*, the witness, one Woods, an accomplice, was in a federal prison at the time of Barber's trial. Instead of producing Woods to testify the prosecution read a transcript of his testimony at the preliminary hearing to the jury, which convicted Barber. This violated the Confrontation Clause. The state argued that Woods was unavailable because he was outside the jurisdiction. Finding that it is feasible for state prosecutors to subpoena federal prisoners and for federal prosecutors to subpoena state prisoners, the Court noted that "the State made absolutely no effort to obtain the presence of Woods at trial other than to ascertain that he was in a federal prison outside Oklahoma." The rule is that the Confrontation Clause requires a good faith effort on the part of the prosecution to locate and produce the witness. Significantly, the Court said that it would have ruled this way even if Woods had been cross-examined at the preliminary hearing. "The right to confrontation is basically a trial right. It includes both the opportunity to cross-examine and the occasion for the jury to weigh the demeanor of the witness."

A later case dealing with the unavailability of a witness found no Sixth Amendment violation where the testimony of a witness at an earlier trial was introduced in a later trial, when the witness had become a permanent resident of a foreign country; the state trial court sent a subpoena to the witness's last address in the United states, and the state "was powerless to compel his attendance at the second trial, either through its own process or through established procedures depending on the voluntary assistance of another government" (*Mancusi v. Stubbs*, 1972).

California v. Green (1970), however, made it clear that prior testimony of a witness given at a preliminary hearing is *admissible* at trial if the defendant was represented by counsel and had an opportunity to cross-examine the witness. In this case the witness, sixteen-year-old Melvin Porter, who admitted receiving marijuana from Green at the preliminary hearing, balked when he was called to testify at the trial and said that he did not have a memory of the crime and was "unsure of the actual episode." The Supreme Court held that the Confrontation Clause was not violated when the prosecutor read portions of Porter's statement at the trial to refresh his memory. Although he was "unavailable" for cross-examination as a trial witness, it was important that Porter was put on the witness stand and admitted that he made the statement at the preliminary hearing. This was sufficient to "afford the trier of fact a satisfactory basis for evaluating the truth of the prior statement."

The third era of Confrontation Clause jurisprudence lasted from 1980 to 2004, a period when under *Ohio v. Roberts* (1980) the Supreme Court, in Professor Reed's colorful metaphor, effected "a shotgun wedding between the hearsay rule and the Confrontation Clause."[17] The era ended with a "divorce" of the clause and the rule in *Crawford v. Washington* (2004), ushering in the fourth and present era of Confrontation Clause rulings. These will be discussed after an examination of whether the clause requires face-to-face encounters in the courtroom.

DOES THE CONFRONTATION CLAUSE REQUIRE FACE-TO-FACE COURTROOM ENCOUNTERS?   In three cases the Supreme Court ruled that while the defendant normally must be able to see the face of a witness at every trial and hearing where the defendant's presence is required, exceptions are allowed under narrowly defined circumstances. These cases all involved allegations of sexual abuse of children and were decided against a background of greater societal awareness of such crimes. As a result, legislatures in many states passed laws that allowed children to testify without having to see the face of the defendant.

In **Kentucky v. Stincer** (1987) a man charged with child sexual abuse against children eight, seven, and five years of age was excluded from **in camera** (in chambers) proceedings where the judge questioned the children to determine if the two younger children were competent to testify. Stincer's lawyer was present. The Supreme Court held that Stincer's right to confrontation was not violated because his exclusion did not preclude effective cross-examination by defense counsel. Any background questions relevant to the trial could be repeated on direct examination of the child witnesses in court. "[T]he critical tool of cross-examination was available to counsel as a means of establishing that the witnesses were not competent to testify, as well as a means of undermining the credibility of their testimony." Justice Marshall, dissenting (joined by Justices Blackmun and Stevens), wrote, "Although cross-examination may be a primary means for ensuring the reliability of testimony from adverse witnesses, we have never held that standing alone it will suffice in every case. . . . Physical presence of the defendant enhances the reliability of the factfinding process."

In **Coy v. Iowa** (1988), the Supreme Court held that a trial in which two thirteen-year-old sexual abuse victims testified from behind a screen so as to avoid eye-to-eye contact with the defendant violated the Confrontation Clause. There were two possible grounds for the decision: (1) that face-to-face confrontation, "the irreducible literal meaning of the Clause," is absolutely required in a trial, or (2) that an exception from a face-to-face encounter could not be imposed by a "legislatively imposed presumption of trauma" but required *individualized* findings that the children would be traumatized by testifying while being able to view Coy. Justice Scalia's majority opinion seemed to be based on the first basis, but did indicate, under a then-prevalent interpretation of the Confrontation Clause as tightly bound to the hearsay rule, that the second basis was possible. Four justices, two dissenting and two concurring, stated that exceptions to the face-to-face requirement were possible. Support for the idea that face-to-face confrontation is essential to a fair trial resides in the common psychological understanding, as put by Justice Scalia, that "It is always more difficult to tell a lie about a person 'to his face' than 'behind his back.'"

The issue left open in *Coy* was resolved in **Maryland v. Craig** (1990), which upheld (5–4) the use of one-way closed-circuit television to transmit the testimony of a child witness where procedural safeguards were in place. Under Maryland law, closed-circuit testimony is used only where absolutely necessary and only on a case-by-case basis. The trial court had to establish that the specific witness, in this case a six-year-old allegedly victimized by the owner of a child care center, would suffer serious emotional distress such that she could not reasonably communicate in a face-to-face confrontation. The closed-circuit television hookup allowed the defendant to observe the demeanor of the witness during examination and cross-examination, and the defendant was in electronic communication with her defense counsel at all times. Counsel retained the right to object to any questions.

Justice O'Connor, for the majority, held that the Sixth Amendment does not guarantee absolute right to a face-to-face meeting at the trial. Instead, "[t]he central concern of the Confrontation Clause is to ensure the reliability of the evidence against a criminal defendant by subjecting it to rigorous testing in the context of an adversary proceeding before the trier of fact" (*Maryland v. Craig*, 1990). She noted that although face-to-face confrontation is an important aspect of the right, there are other protections found in the Maryland practice: (1) the witness must testify under oath, to impress on him or her the seriousness of the procedure and to establish the perjury penalty for lying; (2) cross-examination, the "greatest legal engine ever invented for the discovery of truth," is allowed; and (3) the jury must observe the witness's demeanor so as to assess her credibility. It is these factors together that satisfy the right of confrontation. The defendant's rights had to be balanced against the important state interest of protecting minor victim witnesses from further trauma and psychological harm.

Justice Antonin Scalia, arguing for a strict interpretation of the Constitution's words, wrote for four dissenters:

> Seldom has the Court failed so conspicuously to sustain a *categorical* guarantee of the Constitution against the tide of prevailing current opinion. . . . The purpose of enshrining [the Confrontation Clause] protection in the Constitution was to assure that none of the many policy interests from time to time pursued by statutory law could overcome a defendant's right to face his or her accusers in court. . . .
>
> . . . [The Court's] reasoning abstracts from the right to its purposes, and then eliminates the right. It is wrong because the Confrontation Clause does not guarantee reliable evidence; it guarantees specific trial procedures that were thought to *assure* reliable evidence, undeniably among which was "face-to-face" confrontation. Whatever else it may mean in addition, the defendant's constitutional right "to be confronted with the witnesses against him" means, always and everywhere, at least what it explicitly says: the "right to meet face to face all those who appear and give evidence at trial." (*Maryland v. Craig*, 1990, Scalia, J., dissenting, emphasis added)

The Supreme Court remanded the case to the Maryland Court of Appeals to determine whether the trial court made a necessary finding that the use of the closed-circuit television to cut off the physical confrontation had occurred. That court ruled in favor of Sandra Ann Craig in 1991 and reversed her conviction. Shortly thereafter the county prosecutor decided to not retry her. She had maintained her innocence throughout the case, and although she had been free on an appeal bond since 1987, she and her husband owed about $200,000 in legal fees even though her attorney defended her pro bono.[18] The charges against Ms. Craig arose at a time of national hysteria about the ritual abuse and sexual abuse of children in day care centers that generated hundreds of improbable prosecutions against totally innocent people who worked in day care centers. These prosecutions and wrongful convictions went on for more than a decade. This "moral panic," and the prosecutions that resulted from it, drenched in public hysteria, was reminiscent of the 1692 Salem witch trials.[19] Viewing *Maryland v. Craig* (1990) in light of 1980's child abuse hysteria warns against procedural innovations designed to promote convictions. This erodes trial procedures evolved over the centuries to create a sober courtroom atmosphere where the search for the truth is removed from prejudice and popular hysteria. When procedures to protect the defendant—presumed to be innocent—are weakened, the worst injustices can occur.

MARRYING THE CONFRONTATION CLAUSE AND THE HEARSAY RULE, 1990–2004: THE *OHIO V. ROBERTS* ERA　Herschel Roberts stayed in Anita Isaacs's apartment in Ohio. He was prosecuted for forging her father's checks and fraudulently using his credit card. Roberts claimed that Anita gave him the checks and cards with permission to use them. At Roberts's preliminary hearing Anita was called as a defense witness and she denied giving Herschel permission. She was not declared a hostile witness and so was not subjected to cross-examination. Roberts's trial was delayed because Anita left Ohio, could not be located, was out of touch with her family, and was last in contact with a social worker in San Francisco. The prosecutor entered a transcript of Anita's preliminary hearing testimony and Roberts was convicted. His conviction was reversed by the Ohio Supreme Court on the ground that there was no real cross-examination.

The U.S. Supreme Court could easily have reversed the Ohio court by ruling that the use of the transcript complied with *California v. Green* (1970) because the witness (Anita) was available for cross-examination. Instead, in **Ohio v. Roberts** (1980) the Supreme Court revolutionized Confrontation law by asserting "that the Confrontation Clause is intimately related to the hearsay rule because both rules curb the admissibility of hearsay. . . . This shotgun wedding made all hearsay declarations subject to the Confrontation Clause."[20] As a result, "when a hearsay declarant is not present for cross-examination at trial . . . his statement is admissible only if it bears adequate 'indicia of reliability.' Reliability can be inferred without more in a case where the evidence falls within a *firmly rooted hearsay exception*. In other cases, the evidence must be excluded, at least absent a showing of *particularized guarantees of trustworthiness*" (*Ohio v. Roberts*, 1980, emphasis added). Finding that Roberts's defense lawyer "tested Anita's testimony with the equivalent of significant cross-examination," the Supreme Court ruled that Anita's statement was sufficiently trustworthy under hearsay-rule-type reasoning to be admissible.[21] The *Ohio v. Roberts* rule thus had the potential to allow a larger number of out-of-court statements, which might have been excluded under older confrontation analysis, into court as evidence.

Confrontation Clause cases decided after *Roberts* raised concerns. Thus, wiretap recordings of co-conspirators were admitted as having some "independent evidentiary significance" under hearsay rules even though the conspirators were available to be cross-examined, but were not called, breaking one of the most fundamental confrontation rules. The Court said that the unavailability requirement was only limited to cases where the hearsay declarant gave prior testimony (*United States v. Inadi*, 1986). The weirdness of the reliance on hearsay to resolve Confrontation Clause cases can be seen in two cases involving alleged sexual abuse of very young children. In **Idaho v. Wright** (1990) the hearsay testimony of a pediatrician about what child sex abuse victims said was excluded because the state's residual hearsay exception was not a firmly rooted hearsay exception, which provides a traditional standard of trustworthiness, for Confrontation Clause purposes. Justice O'Connor, writing for the majority that included Justice Scalia in a 5–4 case, expressed the concern that were the Court to automatically admit statements under the residual hearsay exception, it would grant every statutory hearsay exception "constitutional stature, a step this Court has repeatedly declined to take." Contrary to *Wright*, the Court admitted hearsay statements in **White v. Illinois** (1992) made by a four-year-old victim to her babysitter, mother, and a police officer under the spontaneous declaration hearsay exception, and to a nurse and physician under a hearsay exception for statements made in the course of securing medical treatment. The trial court made no finding that the victim was unavailable to testify. Considering that the function of the Confrontation Clause is to guarantee the accuracy of verdicts, Professor Reed's point takes on added force: "The outcome of the Confrontation Clause objection should not turn on the prosecution's selection of a hearsay exception for this evidence."[22] According to Professor Reed, the case of *Lilly v. Virginia* (1999) constituted the "irretrievable breakdown" of the confrontation–hearsay marriage forged in *Roberts*. Although all of the justices agreed that a co-defendant's confession could not be admitted into evidence in the separate trial of another co-defendant (the confessor was unavailable to testify because he claimed the privilege against self-incrimination), they offered many different reasons. There was no majority, only a plurality opinion. Four concurring opinions offered different interpretations of whether the confession, admitting to a burglary but putting the entire blame for the homicide on the co-defendant, really fit under the statement-against-penal-interest hearsay exception. The Court seemed to be concerned that its linking of the hearsay rule with confrontation was leading states to undermine defendants' Confrontation Clause rights. Justice Breyer's concurring opinion, noting the opinion of scholars and jurists, "asserted it was time for the Court to revisit its jurisprudential support for the modern interpretation of the Confrontation Clause." Because "the Court was unable to agree on the proper doctrinal rule to support the exclusion of Mark Lilly's confession, [its decision] virtually guaranteed a reexamination of *Roberts* the next time a Confrontation Clause case came before the Court."[23]

THE CONFRONTATION CLAUSE–HEARSAY RULE DIVORCE   In *Crawford v. Washington* (2004) the Supreme Court realigned Confrontation Cause jurisprudence by overruling *Ohio v. Roberts* (1980) and returning confrontation to its historic roots. *Crawford* made it clear that the exclusion of evidence under the Sixth Amendment did not depend on whether it might be reliable under a firmly rooted hearsay exception. Police recorded a statement from Sylvia Crawford, who observed a fight in which her husband Michael stabbed Kenneth Lee. Michael confessed and claimed self-defense, saying he thought he saw a weapon in Lee's hand. Sylvia's statement to the police, which might have been against her penal interest as an accessory, tended to undercut Michael's self-defense claim. Sylvia could not testify at trial because Michael claimed the spousal privilege. Instead, the prosecution played the tape of Sylvia's statement to the jury. The Washington Supreme Court upheld the introduction of the tape because her statement "bore guarantees of trustworthiness" because it could have led to her being charged in the assault. The U.S. Supreme Court reversed, and excluded Sylvia's statement because its introduction violated Michael Crawford's right to confront his witnesses.

Justice Scalia's majority opinion, based on "originalist" constitutional theory, provided an exhaustive Confrontation Clause history beginning in English common law. The prime concern with confrontation at common law was the introduction of magistrates' *ex parte* examinations of witnesses, which were introduced as evidence instead of having witnesses testify. On this basis, the Confrontation Clause covers only *testimonial* evidence, defined as a solemn declaration or affirmation made for the purpose of establishing or proving some fact. This includes statements made to the police about a criminal investigation but not an offhand, overheard remark. The latter might be unreliable and thus excludable under the hearsay rule, but is not the concern of confrontation. Testimonial statements include "material such as affidavits, custodial examinations, prior testimony that the defendant was unable to cross-examine, or similar pretrial statements that declarants would reasonably expect to be used prosecutorially" (*Crawford v. Washington*, 2004). The second component of the confrontation rule was well established in cases like *Barber v. Page* (1968) and *California v. Green* (1970): "that the Framers would not have allowed admission of testimonial statements of a witness who did not appear at trial unless he was unavailable to testify, and the defendant had had a prior opportunity for cross-examination" (*Crawford v. Washington*, 2004).

The *Crawford* majority opinion sharply criticized the *Roberts* test, which was based on whether the evidence appeared to be reliable to a judge. "Reliability is an amorphous, if not entirely subjective, concept. . . . To be sure, the Clause's ultimate goal is to ensure reliability of evidence, but it is a procedural rather than a substantive guarantee. It commands, not that evidence be reliable, but that reliability be assessed in a particular manner: by testing in the crucible of cross-examination." This pro-defendant ruling by a conservative Court immediately raised concerns that the prosecution of domestic violence would be undermined because in many cases women would not testify against abusers after making complaints to the police. This, indeed, was the issue in the next major Confrontation Clause case before the Court.

Two domestic violence cases were consolidated in **Davis v. Washington** (2006). In both cases women verbally accused their male partner or husband of domestic violence; in both cases the women who were assaulted did not testify in trials and transcripts of their statements were allowed into evidence. The first case involved a transcript of a 911 call, which was analytically divided into two parts. The first concerned the emergency for which Michelle McCrotty called for help after being assaulted; the second part occurred after Adrian Davis, her assailant, left the house and, with the emergency ended, the operator gathered more detailed information about the assault. In the second case, police separated a husband and wife in their house, and took a statement from Amy Hammon detailing the assault on her. The defendants in both cases objected that introducing the statements violated their Confrontation Clause rights.

The Court provided a definition of testimonial statements that determined its outcome: "Statements are nontestimonial when made in the course of police interrogation under circumstances objectively indicating that the primary purpose of the interrogation is to enable police assistance to meet an ongoing emergency. They are testimonial when the circumstances objectively indicate that there is no such ongoing emergency, and that the primary purpose of the interrogation is to establish or prove past events potentially relevant to later criminal prosecution." Applying this definition to Michelle McCrotty's 911 statement, the Court ruled that the first (emergency) part was not testimonial because it was not "directed at establishing the facts of a past crime, in order to identify (or provide evidence to convict) the perpetrator." It did not come under the Confrontation Clause and was admissible. The second part of the 911 call was not before the Court because the Washington Supreme Court ruled that even if it was testimonial its admission was harmless error, and Davis did not contest that.

The Supreme Court next held that Amy Hammond's statements were testimonial and not admissible. "It was formal enough that Amy's interrogation was conducted in a separate room, away from her husband (who tried to intervene), with the officer receiving her replies for use in his 'investigat[ion].'" Like the *Mirandized* questioning in *Crawford*, Amy Hammon's "statements deliberately recounted, in response to police questioning, how potentially criminal past events began and progressed." They "took place some time after the events described were over. Such statements under official interrogation are an obvious substitute for live testimony, because they do precisely *what a witness does* on direct examination; they are inherently testimonial."

Arguments to the Court in *Davis* raised the concern that domestic violence prosecutions require "greater flexibility in the use of testimonial evidence" because this type of crime "is notoriously susceptible to intimidation or coercion of the victim to ensure that she does not testify at trial. When this occurs the Confrontation Clause gives the criminal a windfall." Justice Scalia offered two responses. The first could be seen as a remarkable statement from a conservative jurist embued with the "crime control" approach (see Chapter 1), but is in keeping with the Rule of Law approach embodied in the ancient Roman adage, "let justice be done even though the heavens might fall": "We may not, however, vitiate constitutional guarantees when they have the effect of allowing the guilty to go free." Second, this was followed by a reminder that an exception to a defendant's claim under the Confrontation Clause was that he procured or coerced silence from the non-testifying witness, a rule established by precedent and known as "forfeiture by wrongdoing."

The Court soon examined an issue under the "forfeiture by wrongdoing" exception in ***Giles v. California*** (2008). Dwayne Giles was convicted of murdering his ex-girlfriend Brenda Avie, having shot her six times shortly after his niece, from inside a house, heard them speaking in conversational tones. Avie did not carry a weapon. Giles testified at his trial and claimed self-defense. He said that Avie was jealous, had once shot a man, threatened people with a knife, threatened to kill him and his new girlfriend, and that he shot when she charged him, fearing she had something in her hand. The prosecution introduced into evidence a police report, taken about three weeks before the shooting, by a crying Avie. She told police that Giles had accused her of having an affair, that they argued, that Giles grabbed her by the shirt, lifted her off the floor, and began to choke her, that he punched her in the face and head, opened a folding knife, and threatened to kill her if he found her cheating on him. Giles objected to the introduction of this hearsay statement but the California Supreme Court ruled it admissible under *Crawford* because Giled forfeited his claim by his wrongdoing.

"The idea underlying the doctrine [of forfeiture by wrongdoing] is simple: no one should profit from wrongful conduct. . . . The Confrontation Clause should be a shield, not a sword."[24] According to Professor Tom Lininger, prior to *Giles*, a "minority of courts had conditioned forfeiture upon the *specific intent* to silence the victim as a witness, but the majority had rejected this approach. Not only was the requirement of specific intent difficult to apply—few murderers make a record that their motive is to thwart testimony—but such a rule also could create an incentive for an assailant to kill, rather than merely injure, his victim in order to cover his tracks" (footnotes omitted, emphasis added).[25]

The Court, in a majority opinion by Justice Scalia, held (6–3) that under the Confrontation Clause, before admitting a testimonial statement on the grounds of forfeiture by wrongdoing the prosecution must show that the defendant *intended* to prevent a witness from testifying. The Court so held because under its originalist interpretation, this was the meaning of eighteenth-century English common law cases. "In cases where the evidence suggested that the defendant had caused a person to be absent, but had not done so to prevent the person from testifying—as in the typical murder case involving accusatorial statements by the victim—the testimony was excluded unless it was confronted or fell within the dying-declaration exception" (*Giles v. California*, 2008).

Justice Breyer's dissent (joined by Justices Stevens and Kennedy) strenuously disputed the majority's interpretation of common law cases and struck a blow against this kind of originalism by noting that differences among judges in interpreting "a handful" of old cases is a reason to not base constitutional law on "trying to guess the state of mind of 18th century lawyers." In any event, all the justices agreed that even if the defendant did not explicitly say that he killed the victim to prevent her testimony, it might be possible to infer the intent to prevent the victim from testifying by presenting facts of an abusive relationship. Justice Scalia wrote that "Acts of domestic violence often are intended to dissuade a victim from resorting to outside help, and include conduct designed to prevent testimony to police officers or cooperation in criminal prosecutions. Where such an abusive relationship culminates in murder, the evidence may support a finding that the crime expressed the intent to isolate the victim and to stop her from reporting abuse to the authorities or cooperating with a criminal prosecution—rendering her prior statements admissible under the forfeiture doctrine" (*Giles v. California*, 2008). On that basis the case was remaded to the California courts for further consideration.

These cases, especially *Davis* and *Giles*, have raised real concerns about the future success of domestic violence that prosecutions. Professor Lininger has proposed "practical solutions that will enable effective prosecutions of domestic violence within the new parameters set by *Giles*." One would be a rule adopted by lower courts that infers that a batterer intended to prevent a victim from testifying (and thus invoking forfeiture by wrongdoing) when the batterer violated a restraining order issued for the protection of the accuser. Other *per se* rules would find the batterer's intent to prevent testimony of the domestic violence that occurred after the victim made a police report or initiated any judicial proceedings or upon evidence of a history of abuse and isolation in the relationship.[26] Such rules would operate within the framework of *Giles* to protect domestic violence victims too traumatized to appear in court.

FORENSIC SCIENCE REPORTS AND CONFRONTATION   The Supreme Court ruled that reports of government forensic scientists, such as reports giving the conclusions of the testing of substances for the presence and quantity of illicit drugs, are among the "core class of testimonial statements," that include "affidavits . . . that declarants would reasonably expect to be used prosecutorially." There was no doubt that the drug testing certificate in ***Melendez-Diaz v. Massachusetts*** (2009) was prepared to be introduced into evidence to convict the defendant of cocaine possession. Therefore, under the Confrontation Clause, scientific examiners are required to appear in court to be subjected to cross-examination by the defense as to the accuracy of their tests and reports. The case did not advance Confrontation Clause doctrine; it was characterized by Justice Scalia, writing for the majority (5–4), as "little more than the application of our holding in *Crawford v. Washington*" (2009). The majority countered several doctrinal objections raised by Justice Kennedy, dissenting (joined by Chief Justice Roberts and Breyer and Alito, JJ.), such as that examiners' reports are admissible without cross-examination as official or business records or that notice-and-demand statutes that require defendants to indicate before trial when they intend to call government lab experts shifts the burden of proof to the defense.

The majority and dissenters disagreed about the *practical impact* of the *Melendez-Diaz* rule. Prosecutors complained that requiring laboratory experts to leave their laboratories to testify would seriously disrupt their work and undermine the prosecution of drug cases. Justice Scalia noted that no such disruption occurred in the more than ten states where lab scientists may be called to testify. As a practical matter, most drug felonies are settled by plea, and defense attorneys have no incentive to call the examiners and scientists in cases where they have no reason to believe that errors or improprieties occurred. "Defense attorneys and their clients will often stipulate to the nature of the substance in the ordinary drug case. It is unlikely that defense counsel will insist on live testimony whose effect will be merely to highlight rather than cast doubt upon the forensic analysis. Nor will defense attorneys want to antagonize the judge or jury by wasting their time with the appearance of a witness whose testimony defense counsel does not intend to rebut in any fashion" (*Melendez-Diaz v. Massachusetts*, 2009).

From the perspective of accuracy in criminal prosecutions, the most important part of the majority opinion is that which sustains the *basic purpose* of the confrontation right: "Contrary to respondent's and the dissent's suggestion, there is little reason to believe that confrontation will be useless in *testing* analysts' *honesty*, *proficiency*, and *methodology*—the features that are commonly the focus in the cross-examination of experts" (*Melendez-Diaz v. Massachusetts*, 2009, emphasis added). Tragically, much expert testimony by government forensic experts has been accepted without question in the past on the mistaken idea that they are inherently trustworthy, leading to convictions of innocent persons. Indeed, forensic error and fraud is a major cause of wrongful convictions.[27] This was recognized in Justice Scalia's opinion, drawing on a prepublication version of a major report by the National Academy of Sciences (NAS) that is critical of much forensic evidence. The state of Massachusetts argued that forensic reports should be treated differently than ordinary witness testimony because the reports are the result of "neutral, scientific testing." Justice Scalia said that even if there are better ways of testing forensic evidence, when it is introduced in court, the dictates of the Constitution, requiring "testing in the crucible of cross-examination," cannot be set aside. This, of course, does not prevent the adversaries from agreeing to allow a defense expert retest the evidence.

Drawing on the NAS report and other sources, Justice Scalia stated that it is not "evident that what respondent calls 'neutral scientific testing' is as neutral or as reliable as respondent suggests. Forensic evidence is not uniquely immune from the risk of manipulation." The NAS report, critically examining the work of forensic analysts, found that "because forensic scientists [working in police-administered laboratories] often are driven in their work by a need to answer a particular question related to the issues of a particular case, they sometimes face pressure to sacrifice appropriate methodology for the sake of expediency." Some may even "feel pressure— or have an incentive—to alter the evidence in a manner favorable to the prosecution." The worst documented abuse that has been uncovered is "drylabbing, where forensic analysts report results of tests that were never performed."

> Confrontation is one means of assuring accurate forensic analysis. While it is true, as the dissent notes, that an honest analyst will not alter his testimony when forced to confront the defendant, the same cannot be said of the fraudulent analyst. . . . Like the eyewitness who has fabricated his account to the police, the analyst who provides false results may, under oath in open court, reconsider his false testimony. And, of course, the prospect of confrontation will deter fraudulent analysis in the first place. (*Melendez-Diaz v. Massachusetts*, 2009, internal citations omitted)

Although cross-examination might not eliminate every instance of forensic error that gets to the trial stage, the seriousness of the problem and the fundamental requirement of confrontation in the adversary system offer strong support for the correctness of *Melendez-Diaz*.

Presumption of Innocence and Proof beyond a Reasonable Doubt

Two fundamental and closely linked rules are central to a fair trial: (1) a defendant is clothed with the **presumption of innocence**, and (2) the state must prove the defendant guilty of every element of the crime charged by proof *beyond a reasonable doubt*. The text of the Constitution includes neither rule. They are so fundamental that they were assumed to be part of the trial-by-jury guarantee. The Supreme Court first linked them in 1970, holding in **In re Winship,** a juvenile delinquency adjudication, that the reasonable doubt standard is essential to due process.

Reasonable doubt is an elusive concept. A judge need not define it when instructing jury members that they must not convict a defendant if they have a reasonable doubt about guilt. Unfortunately, definitions of reasonable doubt often confuse more than they clarify. If a judge does define it, no special definition is required, but "taken as a whole, the instructions [must] correctly convey the *concept* of reasonable doubt to the jury" (*Holland v. United States*, 1954). In one case, **Cage v. Louisiana** (1990), the Court held that the trial judge's instruction violated due process because it made the defendant's task of establishing a reasonable doubt *more difficult* than what the Constitution requires. The instruction included two phrases—"*It must be such doubt as would give rise to a grave uncertainty*" and "*It is an actual substantial doubt*—that suggested a higher degree of doubt than is required for acquittal under the reasonable doubt standard. Also, a judge's instruction that tends to make jurors think that the defendant must raise an almost certain doubt lowers the prosecutor's burden of proof. The test of whether a judge's definition of reasonable doubt violates due process is not whether the jury "could have" applied it in an unconstitutional manner, but whether there is a reasonable likelihood that the jury did so apply the instruction (*Estelle v. McGuire*, 1991).

The archaic term *moral certainty* has tended to confuse jurors. Nevertheless, the Supreme Court in **Victor v. Nebraska** (1994) upheld a jury instruction using that term in defining reasonable doubt. The use of "moral certainty" did not violate the defendant's due process right to a fair trial because, although the term is rarely used, it means "highly probable"—which is permissible. Courts would be well advised to drop such no-longer-used words in charging juries in the serious task of evaluating trial evidence. A second issue in *Victor* was the use of "substantial doubt" to define reasonable doubt. These words might convey a sense of near certainty, thus overstating the degree of doubt necessary for acquittal. Alternatively, the term could simply mean "that [doubt] specified to a large degree." The Court ruled that taken in the context of the entire charge to the jury, the term did not mislead the jury into thinking that they had to expel virtually all doubt. The court told the jurors that a substantial doubt does not mean an imaginary doubt or a fanciful conjecture.

It is likely that the justices in *Victor* were not happy with the instructions in these cases but decided not to interfere with them, in part because they did not want to impose a rigid rule on the states. In a useful concurrence, Justice Ruth Bader Ginsburg suggested a better instruction drafted by the Federal Judicial Center:

> Proof beyond a reasonable doubt is proof that leaves you firmly convinced of the defendant's guilt. There are very few things in this world that we know with absolute certainty, and in criminal cases the law does not require proof that overcomes every possible doubt. If, based on your consideration of the evidence, you are firmly convinced that the defendant is guilty of the crime charged, you must find him guilty. If on the other hand, you think there is a real possibility that he is not guilty, you must give him the benefit of the doubt and find him not guilty. (*Victor v. Nebraska*, 1994, Ginsburg, J., concurring)

THE JURY

Constitutional Requirements

In all criminal prosecutions, the accused shall enjoy the right to a speedy and public trial, by an impartial jury of the State and district wherein the crime shall have been committed, which district shall have been previously ascertained by law, and to be informed of the nature and cause of the accusation; to be confronted with the witnesses against him; to have compulsory process for obtaining witnesses in his favor, and to have the Assistance of Counsel for his defence.
—Sixth Amendment, U.S. Constitution

INCORPORATING TRIAL RIGHTS In a unitary country the judicial system's features and rules are defined by its statutes, and in a common law country such as New Zealand, also by its high court decisions regarding the constitutionality of court-related statutes and practices. This is more complicated the United States—a federation where states have their own complete governments and court systems, and where a superordinate federal Constitution with a Supremacy Clause (U.S. Const. art. VI ¶ 2) gives the national Supreme Court authority to determine whether *state* rules comply with the U.S. Constitution. In the 1960s the Supreme Court fundamentally reshaped constitutional relationships, extending greater autonomy and civil liberty protections to American citizens against their own state and local governments when rights under the U.S. Constitution were violated. This was the Due Process Revolution process of incorporation described in Chapter 1.

When the Supreme Court imposed federal constitutional rules on the states in cases regarding trial rights, it came up against a diversity of state procedures. Would the Court impose strict uniformity on all fifty states, requiring them to follow federal rules, or would it allow some variation? The Supreme Court did both. In cases involving jury size and voting requirements the Court found that states need not adhere to the federal rules. This fractured the notion that basic constitutional rights must be uniform and made it clear that the direct application of the Bill of Rights to the federal government could differ somewhat from the application of the Bill of Rights to the states *through* the Fourteenth Amendment Due Process Clause.

Trial by jury in federal courts is guaranteed by Article III of the 1789 Constitution and by the Bill of Rights' (1791) Sixth (criminal cases) and Seventh (civil cases) Amendments. From the very beginning of the United States as an independent nation in 1776, the states had trials by jury. The Supreme Court's incorporation of the Sixth Amendment right to a jury trial in ***Duncan v. Louisiana*** (1968) did not fundamentally restructure criminal trials. Instead, it decided whether a state's trial rules were consistent with the Sixth Amendment. The standard of constitutionality in *Duncan* was the rule required of federal courts.

In *Duncan*, an interracial fight between teenage boys, sparked by disagreements over school desegregation, led to the imprisonment of Gary Duncan, an African-American teen, for sixty days for slapping a white boy. The crime carried a penalty of up to two years of imprisonment. The Supreme Court held that under the Sixth Amendment his right to a jury trial was violated because his request for a jury was denied as not allowed under state law. Justice White held: "Because we believe that trial by jury in criminal cases is fundamental to the American scheme of justice, we hold that the Fourteenth Amendment guarantees a right of jury trial in all criminal cases which—were they to be tried in federal court—would come within the Sixth Amendment guarantee" (***Duncan v. Louisiana,*** 1968). *Duncan* held that a person tried for a crime carrying a two-year maximum sentence is entitled to a jury even if sentenced to less than six months' imprisonment.

THE PETTY CRIME–SERIOUS CRIME DISTINCTION   The Court in *Duncan* reaffirmed the long-established view that so-called **petty crimes** may be tried without a jury. This old rule is designed to avoid expense and delay in prosecuting minor offenses. The rule was clarified in ***Baldwin v. New York*** (1970), which held that "no offense can be deemed 'petty' for purposes of the right to trial by jury where imprisonment for more than six months is authorized." A New York City ordinance that disallowed juries in crimes with penalties of up to one year in prison was held unconstitutional. Justices Hugo Black and William Douglas dissented on the ground that the literal terms of the Sixth Amendment, guaranteeing a jury trial in "*all* criminal prosecutions" should be given literal effect.

The *Baldwin* six-month rule is an objective rule that depends on the judgment of the legislature: *statutory* jail sentences up to six months are petty and no jury trial is required. Several cases clarified the line between petty crimes and crimes where jury trials are available. A crime punishable by up to six months' incarceration is still "petty" even though it carries additional penalties, such as a minimum jail stay and community service (***Blanton v. City of North Las Vegas***, 1989). A defendant prosecuted in a single trial for several petty crimes, whose total punishment could amount to more than six months of imprisonment, is not entitled to a jury trial because the legislature deemed the authorized maximum penalty for each offense to be six months or less (***Lewis v. United States***, 1996). The one exception is for a trial of criminal contempt of court, where the maximum term is not fixed by the legislature, and the actual aggregate term of imprisonment imposed is more than six months (***Codispoti v. Pennsylvania***, 1974).

THE SIZE OF THE JURY   *Williams v. Florida* (1970) held that a six-person felony jury did not violate the Sixth Amendment. This differed from the federal rule that requires a twelve-person jury in felony cases and reversed an eight-hundred-year common law tradition requiring twelve jurors (*Thompson v. Utah*, 1898; *Patton v. U.S.*, 1930). Justice Byron White's majority opinion relied on functional analysis. He stated that the prime "purpose of the jury trial is to prevent oppression by the Government." What was critical was that a group of laypersons deliberate and decide the case, rather than allow government professionals to make the ultimate decision. Calling the number twelve an historical accident, the majority opinion said that it made no difference whether the number of jurors was six or twelve. Six was "large enough to promote group deliberation" to be "free from outside attempts at intimidation, and to provide a fair possibility for obtaining a representative cross section of the community." An interesting combination of three justices dissented from this position, believing that the Constitution requires a twelve-person jury in felony cases: Justice Marshall who supported the incorporation doctrine, and Justices Harlan and Stewart, who opposed it (*Williams v. Florida*, 1970).

The Court drew the line on the constitutionally permissible size of a felony jury by striking down a five-person jury in ***Ballew v. Georgia*** (1978) as a violation of the Sixth Amendment; henceforth felony juries must contain at least six members. *Ballew* contained a subtle admission that *Williams*'s functional analysis was premature. Justice Blackmun's opinion noted that (1) recent studies cast doubt on the accuracy of small-jury verdicts, (2) the defense seems to be hurt by small juries, (3) minority group representation decreases in smaller juries, and (4) there are no significant gains in cost or efficiency in a five-person jury. Despite the *Williams* rule, the overwhelming majority of states require twelve-person juries in felony trials.[28]

THE VOTING REQUIREMENT: MAJORITY VERSUS UNANIMITY   The common law requires a unanimous jury verdict. A single holdout juror can cause a "hung jury," blocking a verdict either of guilt or acquittal. The government may order a retrial after a hung jury. Several states authorize felony verdicts based on less-than-unanimous votes. The Supreme Court has upheld such laws under the Sixth Amendment if they require a supermajority vote for a guilty verdict, allowing guilty verdicts by votes of eleven-to-one and ten-to-two in ***Apodaca v. Oregon*** (1972). In ***Johnson v. Louisiana*** (1972), the Court approved a law authorizing a nine-to-three verdict under the Fourteenth Amendment Equal Protection Clause. In *Apodaca*, Justice White again relied on functional analysis: A "requirement of unanimity does not materially contribute to the exercise of [the] commonsense judgment" of a group of laymen. "Requiring unanimity would obviously produce hung juries in some situations where nonunanimous juries will convict or acquit. But in either case, the interest of the defendant in having the judgment of his peers interposed between himself and the officers of the State who prosecute and judge him is equally well served." Such majority verdicts were held to not undermine the proof beyond a reasonable doubt standard.

Justice Douglas, dissenting in *Johnson* and *Apodaca,* expressed strong misgivings. "The diminution of verdict reliability flows from the fact that nonunanimous juries need not debate and deliberate as fully as must unanimous juries. As soon as the requisite majority is attained, further consideration is not required even though the dissident jurors might, if given the chance, be able to convince the majority." Justice Douglas cited an empirical study to show that such reversals by persuasion occurred in 10 percent of all **jury deliberations**.[29] Additionally, deadlocks usually occur because one, two, or three jurors hold out. Since the majority favors the prosecutions in most deadlocked cases, the majority vote rule upsets a traditional common law protection of defendants.

Concern for this point led the Court to prohibit nonunanimous verdicts in six-person misdemeanor juries. A law allowing guilty verdicts by five out of six jurors in crimes carrying less than six months of imprisonment was declared unconstitutional by a unanimous Supreme Court in **Burch v. Louisiana** (1979). Justice Rehnquist reasoned that "lines must be drawn somewhere if the substance of the jury trial right is to be preserved." Only two states at that time allowed majority verdicts in six-person juries, thus indicating that the national view favored unanimity.

WAIVER OF THE RIGHT TO A JURY   Defendants may have strategic reasons to waive a jury trial and opt for a **bench trial**, or **waiver trial**, with a judge as the sole trier of fact. They may believe that a jury would be prejudiced and unlikely to render a fair decision or that a trained judge is better able to find reasonable doubt than a lay jury. A defendant's waiver to surrender the right to a jury trial must be express and intelligent (*Patton v. United States*, 1930). This allows federal criminal trials to continue with eleven jurors if one juror becomes incapacitated, as long as both the defendant and prosecutor so stipulate.

Under federal law, the jury trial is the standard mode of adjudication and a defendant can waive a jury only if the prosecutor consents and the judge approves.[30] The Supreme Court ruled, in an opinion by Chief Justice Earl Warren, that "[a] defendant's only constitutional right concerning the method of trial is to an impartial trial by jury. The Constitution recognizes an adversary system as the proper method of determining guilt, and the Government, as a litigant, has a legitimate interest in seeing that cases in which it believes a conviction is warranted are tried before the tribunal which the Constitution regards as most likely to produce a fair result" (*Singer v. United States*, 1965). Thus a jury trial in federal court can be had at the behest of the prosecutor, over the defendant's objection. Some states, on the other hand, view the jury primarily as a protection to the defendant, and the defendant has the last word as to whether the trial will be held before a judge or a jury.

THE JURY RIGHT IN JUVENILE DELINQUENCY HEARINGS   The Supreme Court ruled, in **McKeiver v. Pennsylvania** (1971), that a jury trial is not constitutionally required in juvenile delinquency proceedings. The decision surprised juvenile justice experts because it halted a trend of decisions between 1966 and 1971 granting juvenile offenders legal rights equal to those of adults under due process in delinquency adjudications. **Kent v. United States** (1966) imposed the due process requirements of notice and counsel if a juvenile was to be transferred to the adult court system for a criminal trial. The Supreme Court in **In re Gault** (1967), noting that a delinquency determination could result in state confinement much like a criminal conviction, held that the essentials of due process and fair treatment in juvenile delinquency adjudications included notice of charges, the right to trial, confrontation and cross-examination of witnesses, and the right against self-incrimination. And **In re Winship** (1970) held that "the constitutional safeguard of proof beyond a *reasonable doubt* is as much required during the adjudicatory stage of a delinquency proceeding as are those constitutional safeguards applied in *Gault.*"

Nevertheless, the Court refused (5–3) to extend the jury right to juvenile delinquency adjudication proceedings. The Court noted in *McKeiver* that although juvenile delinquency trials are due process hearings requiring procedural safeguards, they are not Sixth Amendment criminal prosecutions where the jury right would automatically apply. Relying on a more flexible, policy-oriented approach under the Due Process Clause, Justice Blackmun noted that despite criticisms of the juvenile court system, its existence represented the view that juveniles should be processed less formally than adults, in special proceedings that allow consideration of social factors not related to factual guilt. A jury requirement would be the final blow to this concept, bringing formality, legalism, and delay, which are incompatible with the ideals of the juvenile court.

McKeiver also supported federalism, deferring to the needs of the states. Justice Blackmun expressed a desire not to impose a single national standard but to allow the states to experiment with advisory juries, if they wished, in juvenile adjudication.

Selecting an Unbiased Jury

Selecting an unbiased, impartial jury takes two steps. First, a **representative cross section** of the community is selected as a pool of potential jurors, rather than economic, social, or political elites, as had earlier been the norm. Second, actual jurors in a case are selected by "voir dire" to weed out jurors with actual or potential biases (discussed in the next section). The mechanics of selecting a representative cross section require a county or judicial district to compile a **master jury list** (also called a *jury wheel* or *master wheel*) of eligible jurors from among the citizenry. From this list, a jury pool, or venire, is selected and summoned to appear for jury service. (The term **venire** is often interchanged with **jury pool**.) At the courthouse, jury panels are drawn from the entire venire. The panel then undergoes voir dire, and the six or twelve jurors, plus alternates, are selected.

Congress, in the Federal Jury Act of 1968, introduced the selection of jury pools that reflect a representative cross section of the community, thus advancing the political theory and value of equality (see Chapter 1). To achieve this, jury master lists that begin with voter registration lists are supplemented with driver's license lists and city or telephone directories. Rigorous statistical methods are applied to ensure unbiased selection.[31] Supreme Court cases after 1968 interpreted the Fourteenth Amendment Equal Protection Clause and the Sixth Amendment impartial jury requirement to reflect the representative cross-section ideal of jury selection.

THE EQUAL PROTECTION CASES   The Equal Protection Clause declares: "No State shall . . . deny to any person within its jurisdiction the equal protection of the laws." This Fourteenth Amendment (1868) right was designed in part to promote the basic rights and political equality of African Americans. Jury service and voting are primary means by which citizens exert political influence and achieve equality. Preventing blacks from jury service or voting after the Civil War was a way to cripple their political participation and influence. Relying on this clause, the Supreme Court, in **Strauder v. West Virginia** (1880), held that a *statute* that explicitly excluded African Americans from jury service was unconstitutional. The following year, the Court held that a *practice* excluding African Americans from juries under a neutral statute was unconstitutional (**Neal v. Delaware,** 1881).

Jim Crow segregation in the South *in fact* denied civil rights to African Americans until after the civil rights struggles from the 1950s to the 1970s. Facially race-neutral laws, such as requiring jury members to be property holders, eliminated minorities from juries. **Norris v. Alabama** (1935), one of the "Scottsboro" cases, held that the *virtual exclusion* of African Americans from grand juries violated equal protection. Under this weak rule blacks continued to be underrepresented on juries. The Supreme Court did little to force the issue, holding that there was not *per se* discrimination where African Americans made up nearly 7 percent of grand jury panels in a Texas county where they comprised over 15 percent of the population (*Cassell v. Texas*, 1950). *Avery v. Georgia* (1953) held there was no discrimination where *not one* African American was selected for a jury panel of sixty people, where 5 percent of the jury list was African American. It took *color-coded jury ballots* for the Court to decide in *Avery* that there was an equal protection violation because it demonstrated intentional discrimination, which is normally very hard to prove.

The way Supreme Court justices think is influenced by broad social and political factors. The massive civil rights movement, which transformed race relations, probably changed the Court's thinking: in 1965 it held that numerical disparities in jury selection were not evidence of discrimination, but in three cases decided just a few years later, between 1967 and 1972, it did so find. **Swain v. Alabama** (1965) held that although the exclusion of a prospective juror on account of race violated the defendant's equal protection rights, there was no violation where, for over a decade, only 10 to 15 percent of jurors were black in a county where African Americans were 26 percent of the eligible voters. In truth, such a statistical pattern was virtually impossible in a fair selection system.[32] Justice White relied on the fact that Alabama did not *totally* exclude African Americans from jury venire panels to find that "[n]either the jury roll nor the venire need be a perfect mirror of the community or accurately reflect the proportionate strength of every identifiable group."

After *Swain,* the Supreme Court seemed to realize its error and finally began to recognize that a statistically significant imbalance constituted **invidious discrimination**, perhaps reflecting the political gains achieved by the civil rights movement.

- *Whitus v. Georgia (1967):*   There is a prima facie case of purposeful discrimination where three of thirty-three prospective grand jurors and seven of ninety in the petit jury venire were African Americans in a county where 43 percent of males over twenty-one years old were black.
- *Turner v. Fouche (1970):*   There is prima facie discrimination where, in a county with 60 percent black population, 37 percent of the grand jury list was African American and 171 of the 178 people disqualified for lack of "intelligence" or "uprightness" were African American.
- *Alexander v. Louisiana (1972):*   A prima facie case of discrimination existed where fewer than 7 percent of African Americans sat on grand jury panels, although nearly 14 percent of grand jury questionnaires were submitted by blacks, and the county was 21 percent African American.

Casteneda v. Partida (1977), involving grand juror selection, specified *three factors* in equal protection cases: (1) The underrepresented *group* must be a *recognizable, distinct class.* (2) The *degree of underrepresentation* must be proved by *comparing* the proportion of the group in the total population to the proportion of the group called to serve as grand jurors over a significant period of time. (3) The *selection procedure* must be susceptible to abuse or not racially neutral. If the degree of underrepresentation of a distinct group is attributed to an unfair selection method, *a prima facie case* is made out and the burden shifts to the government to rebut discrimination raised by the statistical showing.

A prima facie case was established in *Casteneda.* The county was 79 percent Mexican American but between 39 and 50 percent of the grand jurors had Spanish surnames. The **"key man" method** of jury selection, whereby the district judge selects three to five jury commissioners who in turn select fifteen to twenty people they know in the county, was not neutral. The prima facie case was not rebutted by the district judge's bare assertion that there were no prejudicial motives in the selection process. Nor was the prima facie discrimination rebutted by the theory that discrimination is impossible where the recognizable group constitutes a "governing majority" in the jurisdiction. The methods announced in *Casteneda* would be applied to voir dire analysis less than a decade later in *Batson v. Kentucky* (1986).

THE SIXTH AMENDMENT IMPARTIAL JURY CASES   A Sixth Amendment claim that a jury is not impartial is broader than an equal protection challenge under the Fourteenth Amendment because the defendant need show that *any* prospective juror was unfairly excluded, not just jurors of the defendant's ethnic or racial group or gender. Every defendant has a right to an impartial jury. The incorporation of the impartial jury provision in *Parker v. Gladden* (1966) opened the way for jury selection challenges. Thus a white defendant is entitled to a jury system that does not systematically exclude blacks (**Peters v. Kiff,** 1972), and a male defendant is entitled to a jury drawn by a selection process that does not suppress the number of women who might otherwise serve (**Taylor v. Louisiana,** 1975). These cases constitutionalized the right "to a jury drawn from a venire constituting a fair cross section of the community" (*Taylor v. Louisiana,* 1975), which began with the Jury Selection Act of 1968. Justice White explained the underlying theory of fair jury selection, which later played an important role in the voir dire cases:

> [t]he purpose of a jury is to guard against the exercise of arbitrary power—to make available the common sense judgment of the community as a hedge against the overzealous or mistaken prosecutor and in preference to the professional or perhaps overconditioned or biased response of a judge. This prophylactic vehicle is not provided if the jury pool is made up of only special segments of the populace or if large, distinctive groups are excluded from the pool. Community participation in the administration of the criminal law, moreover, is not only consistent with our democratic heritage but is also critical to public confidence in the fairness of the criminal justice system. Restricting jury service to only special groups or excluding identifiable

segments playing major roles in the community cannot be squared with the constitutional concept of jury trial. (*Taylor v. Louisiana*, 1975)

Taylor eliminated a practice whereby a woman wishing to serve on a jury had to file a written declaration of her desire. The federal rule was that women constitute a distinctive segment of the population for purposes of jury service even though they do not respond to issues as a class any more than do men (*Ballard v. United States*, 1946). The Court rejected Louisiana's argument that women play a distinctive role in society that is deterred by jury service. The Victorian notion that women must be "protected" from jury service is simply passé in an era when women are reaching numerical parity with men in the legal profession.

Duren v. Missouri (1979) expanded the *Taylor* rule by holding that the gross underrepresentation of women on jury venires (15 percent out of 54 percent of the population) as a result of rules that made it very easy for women to decline jury service (for example, by not showing up) constituted a prima facie violation of the Sixth Amendment rule that juries constitute a fair cross section of the population. The three-part test of *Casteneda* was made out in *Duren*. Federal courts restrict the distinctive groups to groups with immutable characteristics such as race, ethnicity, and gender. Defendants' arguments that other subgroups are "distinctive groups" under *Duren* (e.g., blue-collar workers, college students, less-educated people, rural inhabitants, nonregistrants to vote, or jurors with absolute scruples against imposing the death penalty) have failed.[33]

Voir Dire and Fairness

During voir dire prospective jurors are questioned for bias. Due process requires that each side has an unlimited number of *challenges for cause*. Jurors who say they cannot be fair or are shown to be biased must be excused by the judge as a matter of fundamental fairness and to meet the Sixth Amendment impartial jury requirement. Peremptory challenges are not required by the Constitution, but "are one means to achieve the constitutionally required end of an impartial jury" (*U.S. v. Martinez-Salazar*, 2000).

An important issue is whether the trial judge asks all the questions or allows the lawyers to conduct voir dire. Lawyers believe that judge-conducted voir dire fails to probe jurors sufficiently to elicit bias. Judge-conducted voir dire supposedly conserves time or prevents attorneys from "spinning" a case before the jury. Attorneys can submit questions to judges who conduct voir dire, but the judges are not obligated to ask them. An attorney can appeal a judge's refusal to ask or allow a question, but to win the attorney must meet the high legal standard of whether the denial amounts to an **abuse of discretion**.

Ham v. South Carolina (1973) ruled that a judge who disallowed questions about racial prejudice in a prosecution of a bearded African-American civil rights worker for possession of marijuana violated his right to due process. No violation occurred, however, in **Ristaino v. Ross** (1976), where the judge refused to allow questions about prejudice regarding the defendant's beard in a robbery case in which the defendant was black and the victim white. In *Ham* the context of civil rights activism might have prejudiced jurors because beards were liberal symbols in that era, while in *Ristaino* the possible prejudice regarding defendant's beard was tenuous. *Ristaino* held that the Constitution does not require such questions simply because the defendant is black and the victim white where there were no other racial animosity factors. A judge must ask questions requested by a defendant about race when racial issues are inextricably bound up with the conduct of the trial, but a trial judge must be given great latitude by appellate courts in deciding whether that is the case (*Rosales-Lopez v. U.S.*, 1981).

An exception to *Ristaino* is made in death penalty cases. "[A] capital defendant accused of an interracial crime is entitled to have prospective jurors informed of the race of the victim and questioned on the issue of racial bias" (**Turner v. Murray,** 1986). Justice White's rationale was that because the jury has greater discretion in the sentencing phase of a capital case than in the guilt-finding phase, the death sentence should not stand where the voir dire did not inquire into race prejudice. The Supreme Court also held (6–3) in *Morgan v. Illinois* (1992) that in a death penalty case, a requested voir dire question had to be asked about a juror's propensity to automatically impose the death penalty, even if mitigating factors existed.

Mu'Min v. Virginia (1991) was a murder case with substantial pretrial publicity. The judge on voir dire questioned prospective jurors about whether they had read or heard about the case and whether they had formed an opinion based on outside information. The judge, however, refused to question prospective jurors about the *content* of their information, as requested by the defense. The Supreme Court held this did not violate due process. Justice Marshall, dissenting, argued that it is constitutionally unfair to not allow attorneys to ask content questions because they (1) determine whether the type and extent of pretrial publicity would disqualify the juror as a matter of law, (2) give "legal depth" to the trial court's finding of impartiality, and (3) facilitate accurate trial court fact-finding.

PEREMPTORY CHALLENGES   In addition to unlimited challenges for cause, both sides in a criminal prosecution have a limited number of *peremptory challenges*, whereby a juror is excused without a stated cause or reason. These are often based on an attorney's "hunch" that the individual will prove unsympathetic to his or her side. Where several defendants are tried together, each is entitled to peremptory challenges, while the prosecutor may be limited to a smaller number.

In the 1980s, defendants protested that prosecutors unconstitutionally used peremptories to deliberately produce racially unbalanced juries. In 1986, the Supreme Court responded positively to this claim, making an important change in the law regarding peremptory challenges. In *Batson v. Kentucky* (1986), the Supreme Court drew on and modified the procedures for determining bias in jury selection that was first set out in *Casteneda v. Partida* (1977) and modified *Swain v. Alabama* (1965). Given the two lines of cases on fair jury selection, one under the Equal Protection Clause and the other under the Sixth Amendment impartial jury requirement, *Batson* made his claim on both. The Court decided the case on the basis of the Fourteenth Amendment.

Read Case and Comments: *Batson v. Kentucky.*

BATSON'S AFTERMATH   Cases following *Batson* relied both on the Equal Protection Clause and Sixth Amendment impartial jury reasoning to expand the rule disallowing peremptory strikes based on race, ethnicity, and gender in different situations, even when the discrimination was not against the complaining party's ethnic group or gender. The Court did this by including *jurors* as people who have a stake in unbiased jury selection. "We have recognized that whether the trial is criminal or civil, potential jurors, as well as litigants, have an equal protection right to jury selection procedures that are free from state-sponsored group stereotypes rooted in, and reflective of, historical prejudice" (*J.E.B. v. Alabama ex rel. T.B.*, 1994).

Batson reasoning regarding peremptory challenges was applied to other groups of people and types of cases:

- *White defendant.*   A white defendant has third-party standing to challenge a prosecutor's peremptory challenge to remove an African American from the jury (*Powers v. Ohio*, 1991). "A prosecutor's discriminatory use of peremptory challenges harms the excluded jurors and the community at large."
- *Civil lawsuits.*   The *Batson* rule applies to all parties in civil lawsuits; the necessary state action predicate for an equal protection violation lies in the judge's action of dismissing a challenged juror on a party's request (*Edmonson v. Leesville Concrete Co.*, 1991).
- *Hispanic jurors.*   The *Batson* rule extends to the exclusion of Hispanic jurors on account of their ethnicity. Under *Batson,* this is akin to "a cognizable racial group" (*Hernandez v. New York*, 1991).
- *Criminal defendant's peremptory.*   The prosecutor is now allowed to challenge the discriminatory exercise of a peremptory by the defendant, as was predicted by the dissent in *Batson.* "A criminal defendant's exercise of peremptory challenges in a racially discriminatory manner inflicts the harms addressed by *Batson.*" It erodes public confidence in a fair and impartial jury (*Georgia v. McCollum*, 1992).
- *Gender.*   Neither female nor male jurors can be stricken by peremptory challenges solely on the basis of their sex. The equal protection violation lies in the assumption that men and women "hold particular views simply because of their gender," and this stereotype reflects and reinforces patterns of historical discrimination (*J.E.B. v. Alabama ex rel. T.B.*, 1994).

CASE AND COMMENTS

Batson v. Kentucky

476 U.S. 79, 106 S.Ct. 1712, 90 L.Ed.2d 69 (1986)

JUSTICE POWELL delivered the opinion of the Court.

This case requires us to reexamine that portion of *Swain v. Alabama* (1965), concerning the evidentiary burden placed on a criminal defendant who claims that he has been denied equal protection through the State's use of peremptory challenges to exclude members of his race from the petit jury. **[a]**

I

Petitioner, a black man, was indicted in Kentucky on charges of second-degree burglary and receipt of stolen goods. [At the trial,] the judge conducted *voir dire* examination of the venire, excused certain jurors for cause, and permitted the parties to exercise peremptory challenges. The prosecutor used his peremptory challenges to strike all four black persons on the venire, and a jury composed only of white persons was selected. [Counsel claimed] that the prosecutor's removal of the black veniremen violated petitioner's rights under the Sixth and Fourteenth Amendments to a jury drawn from a cross section of the community, and under the Fourteenth Amendment to equal protection of the laws. [The judge denied the motion, observing] that the parties were entitled to use their peremptory challenges to "strike anybody they want to." * * * **[b]**

[Batson's conviction was upheld by the Kentucky Supreme Court, which relied on *Swain:*] a defendant alleging lack of a fair cross section must demonstrate systematic exclusion of a group of jurors from the venire. * * * We granted certiorari and now reverse.

II

In *Swain v. Alabama,* this Court recognized that a "State's purposeful or deliberate denial to Negroes on account of race of participation as jurors in the administration of justice violates the Equal Protection Clause." **[c]** * * * This principle has been "consistently and repeatedly" reaffirmed, * * * in numerous decisions of this Court both preceding and following *Swain.* We reaffirm the principle today.

A

* * * In holding that racial discrimination in jury selection offends the Equal Protection Clause, the Court in *Strauder* recognized, however, that a defendant has no right to a "petit jury composed in whole or in part of persons of his own race." * * * "The number of our races and nationalities stands in the way of evolution of such a conception" of the demand of equal protection. * * * **[d]** But the defendant does have the right to be tried by a jury whose members are selected pursuant to non-discriminatory criteria. * * * The Equal Protection Clause guarantees the defendant that the State will not exclude members of his race from the jury venire on account of race, * * * or on the false assumption that members of his race as a group are not qualified to serve as jurors.

Purposeful racial discrimination in selection of the venire violates a defendant's right to equal protection because it denies him the protection that a trial by jury is intended to secure. **[e]** "The very idea of a jury is a body . . .composed of the peers or equals of the person whose rights it is selected or summoned to determine; that is, of his neighbors, fellows, associates, persons having the same legal status in society as that which he holds." The petit jury has occupied a central position in our system of justice by safeguarding a person accused of crime against the arbitrary exercise of power by prosecutor or judge. * * * Those on the venire must be "indifferently chosen," to secure the defendant's right under the Fourteenth Amendment to "protection of life and liberty against race or color prejudice." * * *

* * *

The harm from discriminatory jury selection extends beyond that inflicted on the defendant and the excluded juror to touch the entire community. **[f]** Selection procedures that purposefully exclude black persons from juries undermine public confidence in the fairness of our system of justice. Discrimination within the judicial system is most pernicious because it is "a stimulant to that race prejudice which is an impediment to securing to [African Americans] that equal justice which the law aims to secure to all others."

B

[In this part the Court ruled that the Equal Protection Clause applies to the prosecutor's exercise of peremptory challenges.] Although a prosecutor ordinarily is entitled to exercise permitted peremptory challenges "for any reason at all, as long as that reason is related to his view concerning the outcome" of

[a] *Swain* held that race could not be a basis for excluding a juror but made it nearly impossible to prove. The issue in *Batson* is whether a defendant can prove racial bias in excluding jurors based on what happened in this case.

[b] Batson raised a Sixth Amendment (impartial jury) as well as a Fourteenth Amendment (equal protection) challenge because he was not sure he could win on equal protection grounds. In fact, this case was decided exclusively on equal protection, Fourteenth Amendment, grounds.

[c] The substantive *Swain* rule of equality means little if it is almost impossible for a defendant to prove a racially biased exercise of the prosecutor's peremptories.

[d] This remains the rule. A fair selection process cannot guarantee that a six- or twelve-person jury will include a member of one's own race or a cross section of the community.

[e] "Peers" are said to be people with the same *legal* status (i.e., any eligible jurors), *not* people who match the defendant in terms of race, age, or social class. Do you think an all-white jury will usually be as fair to a black defendant as a racially mixed jury?

[f] This gets close to saying the jurors have rights, as well as the defendant. The Supreme Court adopted this position in later peremptory challenge cases.

the case to be tried, * * * the Equal Protection Clause forbids the prosecutor to challenge potential jurors solely on account of their race or on the assumption that black jurors as a group will be unable impartially to consider the State's case against a black defendant.

III

* * * A recurring question in [the jury selection] cases, as in any case alleging a violation of the Equal Protection Clause, was whether the defendant had met his burden of proving purposeful discrimination on the part of the State. * * * That question also was at the heart of the portion of *Swain v. Alabama* we reexamine today.

A

[In this section, the Court noted that in practice the *Swain* rule made it virtually impossible for a defendant to ever challenge a prosecutor's use of peremptory challenges to excuse African-American jurors.]

B

[g] Rules regarding the nondiscriminatory selection of the jury pool are transferred below to the selection of the petit jury.

[In this section, the Court reviewed the equal protection cases regarding discrimination in selecting the jury pool, or venire. Those cases placed the burden of proof on the defendant to show that the state had a racially discriminatory purpose in its selection procedures. **[g]** Once the defendant has established a prima facie case of discrimination, the state has to explain why racial disparities in the larger jury pool were not caused by racial discrimination. Courts could examine direct and circumstantial evidence in deciding whether jury pool selection was racially biased. Further,] a defendant may make a prima facie showing of purposeful racial discrimination in selection of the venire by relying solely on the facts concerning its selection *in his case.*

C

[h] The Court here establishes the first three-step procedure by which lower courts can determine whether a prima facie case or inference of discrimination in exercising the peremptory challenge has been established.

* * * [A] defendant may establish a prima facie case of purposeful discrimination in selection of the petit jury solely on evidence concerning the prosecutor's exercise of peremptory challenges at the defendant's trial. To establish such a case, the defendant first must show that he is a member of a cognizable racial group * * * and that the prosecutor has exercised peremptory challenges to remove from the venire members of the defendant's race. Second, the defendant is entitled to rely on the fact, as to which there can be no dispute, that peremptory challenges constitute a jury selection practice that permits "those to discriminate who are of a mind to discriminate." **[h]** * * * Finally, the defendant must show that these facts and any other relevant circumstances raise an inference that the prosecutor used that practice to exclude the veniremen from the petit jury on account of their race. This combination of factors in the empaneling of the petit jury, as in the selection of the venire, raises the necessary inference of purposeful discrimination.

In deciding whether the defendant has made the requisite showing, the trial court should consider all relevant circumstances. For example, a "pattern" of strikes against black jurors included in the particular venire might give rise to an inference of discrimination. Similarly, the prosecutor's questions and statements during *voir dire* examination and in exercising his challenges may support or refute an inference of discriminatory purpose. These examples are merely illustrative. We have confidence that trial judges, experienced in supervising *voir dire,* will be able to decide if the circumstances concerning the prosecutor's use of peremptory challenges creates a prima facie case of discrimination against black jurors.

[i] The defendant's prima facie showing does not end the matter—it raises an inference of discrimination. Another set of procedures follow.

Once the defendant makes a prima facie showing, the burden shifts to the State to come forward with a neutral explanation for challenging black jurors. **[i]** Though this requirement imposes a limitation in some cases on the full peremptory character of the historic challenge, we emphasize that the prosecutor's explanation need not rise to the level justifying exercise of a challenge for cause. * * * But the prosecutor may not rebut the defendant's prima facie case of discrimination by stating merely that he challenged jurors of the defendant's race on the assumption—or his intuitive judgment—that they would be partial to the defendant because of their shared race. * * * Just as the Equal Protection Clause forbids the States to exclude black persons from the venire on the assumption that blacks as a group are unqualified to serve as jurors, * * * so it forbids the States to strike black veniremen on the assumption that they will be biased in a particular case simply because the defendant is black. **[j]** The core guarantee of equal protection, ensuring citizens that their State will not discriminate on account of race, would be meaningless were we to approve the exclusion of jurors on the basis of such assumptions, which arise solely from the jurors' race. Nor may the prosecutor rebut the defendant's case merely by denying that he had a discriminatory motive or "affirm[ing] [his] good faith in making individual selections." * * * If these general assertions were accepted as rebutting a defendant's prima facie case, the Equal Protection

[j] Blanket assumptions that people of a certain class, age, religion, ethnicity, and so on think only in one way cannot be used to justify strikes.

Clause "would be but a vain and illusory requirement." * * * The prosecutor therefore must articulate a neutral explanation related to the particular case to be tried. The trial court then will have the duty to determine if the defendant has established purposeful discrimination.

IV

The State * * * argues that the privilege of unfettered exercise of the challenge is of vital importance to the criminal justice system. **[k]**

[k] The majority wishes to keep the peremptory challenge alive but to modify it so that it will not perpetuate the known use of racial discrimination by prosecutors.

While we recognize, of course, that the peremptory challenge occupies an important position in our trial procedures, we do not agree that our decision today will undermine the contribution the challenge generally makes to the administration of justice. The reality of practice, amply reflected in many state- and federal-court opinions, shows that the challenge may be, and unfortunately at times has been, used to discriminate against black jurors. By requiring trial courts to be sensitive to the racially discriminatory use of peremptory challenges, our decision enforces the mandate of equal protection and furthers the ends of justice. In view of the heterogeneous population of our Nation, public respect for our criminal justice system and the rule of law will be strengthened if we ensure that no citizen is disqualified from jury service because of his race. * * *

[The case was remanded.]

JUSTICE MARSHALL, concurring.

I join JUSTICE POWELL's eloquent opinion for the Court, which takes a historic step toward eliminating the shameful practice of racial discrimination in the selection of juries. * * * I nonetheless write separately to express my views. The decision today will not end the racial discrimination that peremptories inject into the jury-selection process. That goal can be accomplished only by eliminating peremptory challenges entirely.

I

* * *

Misuse of the peremptory challenge to exclude black jurors has become both common and flagrant. * * *

II

* * * Cases . . . illustrate the limitations of the [Court's] approach. First, defendants cannot attack the discriminatory use of peremptory challenges at all unless the challenges are so flagrant as to establish a prima facie case. This means, in those States, that where only one or two black jurors survive the challenges for cause, the prosecutor need have no compunction about striking them from the jury because of their race. * * * Prosecutors are left free to discriminate against blacks in jury selection provided that they hold that discrimination to an "acceptable" level. **[l]**

[l] Justice Marshall's concerns were borne out in later cases that demonstrated that prosecutors' race-neutral explanations are easy to make.

Second, when a defendant can establish a prima facie case, trial courts face the difficult burden of assessing prosecutors' motives. * * * Any prosecutor can easily assert facially neutral reasons for striking a juror, and trial courts are ill equipped to second-guess those reasons. * * *

Nor is outright prevarication by prosecutors the only danger here. "[I]t is even possible that an attorney may lie to himself in an effort to convince himself that his motives are legal." * * * A prosecutor's own conscious or unconscious racism may lead him easily to the conclusion that a prospective black juror is "sullen," or "distant," a characterization that would not have come to his mind if a white juror had acted identically. . . .

* * *

CHIEF JUSTICE BURGER, joined by JUSTICE REHNQUIST, dissenting.

[Chief Justice Burger's dissent correctly predicted that the majority's rule would in the future be applied to *defendants,* limiting their ability to use peremptory challenges to strike jurors they believe believed to be biased. He also thought that the majority's ruling destroy the peremptory nature of the challenge, and would be impossible to apply.]

* * * I am at a loss to discern the governing principles here. A "clear and reasonably specific" explanation of "legitimate reasons" for exercising the challenge will be difficult to distinguish from a challenge for cause. . . . Apparently the Court envisions permissible challenges short of a challenge for cause that are just a little bit arbitrary—but not too much. While our trial judges are "experienced in supervising *voir dire,*" * * * they have no experience in administering rules like this.

* * *

Prosecutors' race-neutral explanations for exercising peremptory challenges against *Batson* categories were at first readily accepted:

- A prosecutor's exclusion of Latino jurors, on the grounds that there was some reason to believe that specific Spanish-speaking jury panel members would *not automatically accept the official translator's version of testimony* given in Spanish, was deemed race-neutral by the Supreme Court (*Hernandez v. New York*, 1991).
- The Court also held in *Hernandez* that a state court's finding of the *absence of discriminatory intent* by the party exercising a peremptory is "a pure issue of fact" that is accorded significant deference and will not be overturned on appeal unless clearly erroneous.
- A prosecutor eliminated two African-American jurors, was challenged under *Batson*, and said they were excluded not because of their race, but because each had *long unkempt hair, a mustache, and a goatee*. This "is race neutral and satisfies the prosecution's . . . burden of articulating a nondiscriminatory reason for the strike" (*Purkett v. Elem*, 1995).

This pro-prosecution tilt in accepting race-neutral explanations later become more balanced. The Court ruled it will not tolerate prosecutors' blatantly striking black jurors in **Miller-El v. Cockrell** (2003), and remanded a death penalty appeal, even under restrictive habeas corpus laws making it difficult for capital defendants to be heard in federal court, where a prosecutor peremptorily struck ten out of eleven African-American jurors. On remand, the lower court, relying on the lone *dissent* in *Miller-El* by Justice Thomas, who thought there was no racial discrimination, upheld the conviction. The case returned to the Supreme Court. In a detailed opinion, Justice Souter held that equal protection was denied where the prosecutor peremptorily struck 91 percent of the eligible black jurors, compared to 13 percent of eligible nonblack prospective jurors, and after an exhaustive and detailed review of the views of individual jurors, ordered the state court to grant relief to Miller-El, rather than remanding the case to lower court. This was insulting to the lower court. By its action the Supreme Court in effect signaled that the lower court in this case could not be trusted to enforce a ruling designed to ameliorate the effects of racism (**Miller-El v. Dretke**, 2005).

The fact-specific and more searching inquiry of *Miller-El* was continued in **Snyder v. Louisiana** (2008). The Court reversed an African-American defendant's capital murder conviction where a black juror was peremptorily struck by the prosecutor and similarly situated whites were not. Two purportedly race-neutral reasons were offered by the prosecution for striking juror David Brooks: a nervous demeanor and concern that a lengthy trial would interfere with his student-teaching obligations. The prosecutor knew the trial would be short and Mr. Brooks's concerns were allayed after talking to his supervisor. Two white jurors had business and personal concerns that seemed "substantially more pressing than Mr. Brooks' . . . [a]nd the prosecution declined the opportunity to use a peremptory strike" on them. The judge in this case did not clearly indicate which reason was accepted as race-neutral. Justice Alito's opinion thus infers that trial courts need to be more specific in placing the reasons for *Batson* decisions *on the record*. Of interest in this case is that the decision favoring a defendant and supporting a more even-handed *Batson* approach developed by the *Miller-El* cases was authored by Justice Alito and joined by Chief Justice Roberts, who have proven to be very conservative in most criminal procedure rulings. In this case Justices Thomas and Scalia dissented. The majority opinion, however, added a dictum that could come to benefit prosecutors in future cases. Borrowing from another area of discrimination law, Justice Alito suggested that once a discriminatory intent was shown on the part of the prosecutor, the *Batson* three-stage procedure might be changed to add a fourth, giving the prosecutor a chance to show that the discriminatory intent "was not determinative."

Professor Charles J. Ogletree, reviewing *Batson*'s application in the lower courts, concluded that "trial judges' acceptance of prosecutors' facially neutral explanations for peremptory strikes have undermined the protection *Batson* was meant to offer against discriminatory peremptory strikes."[34] This reinforced Justice Marshall's call for completely eliminating peremptory challenges. Others have suggested, as correctives, (1) requiring that some minority jurors be seated in the trial of a minority defendant, (2) race-conscious change-of-venue statutes, (3) increasing the number of minorities on the jury venire, (4) seating minority jurors who are struck by peremptories, and (5) reducing the number of peremptory challenges available to the prosecution.[35] Professor Ogletree adds: (6) dismissing a prosecution where a prosecutor violates *Batson* and (7) eliminating prosecution, but not defense, use of peremptory challenges.

This last seemingly unbalanced proposal is based on a concern that a total elimination of peremptories would empower trial judges to seat biased jurors. It is unlikely that the current Supreme Court or the state legislatures would adopt any of these extremely pro-defendant or racially based rules. Indeed, the Court held that an error by a state judge in mistakenly refusing to allow a defendant's *Batson* challenge is not a constitutional violation as long as the juror was not biased (i.e., challengeable for cause) (*Rivera v. Illinois*, 2009). Proposals to eliminate peremptory challenges fail to consider that were this to happen, discrimination could shift to challenges for cause, and fail to account for the benefits of peremptory challenges. The racially biased misuse of peremptories needs to be corrected by greater alertness to this problem among judges and lawyers, vigorous enforcement of *Batson* rules, and a critical review of race-neutral explanations by judges.[36]

LAW IN SOCIETY

Jury Trials and Wrongful Convictions

Convicting the Innocent

Marion Coakley was one of the first innocent prisoners freed by the Innocence Project.[37] He was a hapless fellow with a low IQ, who was identified as the perpetrator of a vicious rape and robbery because his mug shot was left in police sex crimes files. This happened when a woman he picked up at a bar, a prostitute, asked for payment *after* services were rendered. An indignant Coakley, refusing to pay, was charged with rape by the hooker as a way to extort her "fee." The complaint against him was dismissed after the woman failed to show. But his photograph was later picked out by the victim of a real rape. His case progressed to trial through a string of errors, including honestly mistaken eyewitness identification after substandard lineup procedures, an overworked and ill-prepared public defender, and sloppy police forensic investigation. Coakley, however, not only passed a polygraph examination, but had a seemingly rock-solid alibi: he was at a regularly scheduled Bible-study meeting at his sister's apartment on the night of the rape. He had hung out at that apartment building for several hours before the study meeting, chatting with friends, and he "had nine witnesses ready to say he was there, including the minister."[38] Nevertheless, an assertive victim convinced the prosecutor to go forward with a weak case. The prosecutor did not violate any of Coakley's constitutional or evidentiary rights. What she did was standard operating procedure in an adversary trial. As Scheck et al. put it, "Through pinpoint cross-examination, Assistant D.A. Reiser was able to spin the preacher like a child's top."[39] She questioned the minister about the meeting's time and place, weather conditions, the number of men present, and their precise participation in a way to befuddle him. The testimony established that Coakley was at the meeting, but the questions injected doubt about when it ended, allowing her to argue that Coakley had enough time to commit the crime.[40] Perhaps a prosecutor adhering to the "minister of justice" model would not have used cross-examination to sprinkle doubt on an honest witness. Although a standard view of the adversary system reserves that tactic only for defense lawyers,[41] what D.A. Reiser did was allowable under adversary trial rules of combat.

Was Coakley's case an aberration or a recurrent feature of American justice? Unfortunately, some limited studies and the consensus of wrongful conviction experts tends to support the view that, conservatively, 1 to 2 percent of all persons convicted for felonies, by trial and by plea, are factually innocent.[42] While this may seem like a small error rate, it amounts to five thousand to ten thousand innocent people jailed and imprisoned every year for crimes they did not commit, and a similar number placed on probation.

Every comprehensive study of wrongful convictions points to similar causes: mistaken eyewitness testimony abetted by and suggestive lineups (see Chapter 8); forensic testing errors (including "junk science," sloppy laboratory procedures, and forensic examiner perjury), false confessions (see Chapter 7); perjury (by perpetrators, witnesses, and jailhouse snitches); "tunnel vision" by police and prosecutors and failures to search for exculpatory evidence; prosecutor misconduct (including the failure to disclose exculpatory evidence, misstating facts to the jury, and minimizing reasonable doubt) (see Chapter 10); incompetent defense lawyers (including failure to object to improper evidence) (see Chapter 6); and judges who disproportionately favor the prosecution in their rulings.[43] Until recently less attention was given to the prospect that the adversary system itself may not only be inadequate at identifying and stopping such errors, but may generate errors.

Professor Daniel Givelber reviewed studies in England and the United States suggesting even higher error rates in jury trials.[44] These studies examined the agreement between jury verdicts in actual cases and the opinions of judges or courtroom observers. These disagreements do not necessarily mean that jury convictions were erroneous. Yet after careful review,

> Baldwin and McConville [England] found that 5.2% of trials ended in the conviction of an arguably innocent person. The Kalven and Zeisel [United States] data suggest a figure of about 3%. These numbers represent the percentage of all trials: because only about two-thirds of studied trials ended in convictions, the percentage of convictions involving innocent defendants is higher—7.9% in the English study and 5% in the Kalven and Zeisel study.[45]

When we consider the devastating consequences of convicting the innocent, these figures are unacceptable. Not only does an innocent person pay for another person's crime, but the guilty party remains free to inflict harm on others. Ultimately, justice is not done, and the families of victims are put through unnecessary trauma. For the public at large, the very legitimacy of the criminal justice system is weakened.

Why Trials Do Not Stop Wrongful Convictions

Can the jury trial can catch errors made earlier in the criminal justice process? Are pleas of guilty less prone to wrongful convictions? The evidence is not encouraging.

Prosecutors have enormous leverage to get defendants to plead guilty. Penalties in American jurisdictions are bizarrely harsh by European standards. The threat of years or decades in prison or a death sentence is likely to make some innocent defendants plead guilty, as happened to many in the Los Angeles Police Department Rampart scandal.[46]

Jurors begin cases with a bias toward conviction. "The state's decision to charge the defendant with the crime has considerable evidentiary weight regardless of the presumption of innocence or any other platitude. By prosecuting a case, the state does more than simply provide the jury with two conflicting stories—it suggests that the victim's story is believable."[47]

Guilt assumption is stronger in capital cases because a prospective death case juror must not have "scruples" against imposing the death penalty if the defendant is found guilty. "Many studies have shown that these exclusions [of "scrupled" jurors] make the jury more likely to convict."[48]

Prosecutors are reluctant to back down after charging a defendant with a crime, even if their case is weak. First, there is a natural human tendency to believe in one's judgments and "stick to one's guns." But prosecutors also rely on police reports that look stronger than they are, and that provide enough information to make out a prima facie case but may not be sufficiently strong for a conviction. "[T]he police are more interested in closing the case than obtaining convictions."[49] and as a result many police investigation reports are shoddy and filled with misinformation, which the prosecutor is in no position to correct.[50] Police and victims will pressure prosecutors to not dismiss weak cases, as happened to Marion Coakley.[51] Thus, "having made this decision [to prosecute], the prosecutor will not retreat easily from it without securing something in return, such as a plea, even to a lesser offense."[52]

The great imbalance of investigation resources between prosecutors and defendants, except in the case of extremely wealthy defendants, is another reason why trials do not prevent the conviction of innocents. In some miscarriages of justice exculpatory evidence was buried in police or prosecutorial files but there were no defense resources to dig it out. There is no general rule of discovery in criminal cases and "no constitutional requirement that the prosecution make a complete and detailed accounting to the defense of all police investigatory work on a case" (*Moore v. Illinois,* 1972). The rule of *Brady v. Maryland* (1963), although a great advance, only provides that due process requires the prosecutor to turn over material factual evidence that is favorable to the defendant. It is the prosecutor, a partisan, who decides what is helpful or favorable to the defendant.

[I]f the prosecutor believes in the defendant's guilt, the prosecutor probably views the helpful information as a 'red herring' with which defense counsel may make mischief, possibly leading to the guilty defendant's acquittal. If the material were truly exculpatory, arguably, the prosecutor would not have brought the case in the first instance.[53]

Some prosecutors have voluntarily adopted open files policies, but the Supreme Court has not made this better practice a requirement.[54]

Professor Brian Forst adds a lists of why lay juries make mistakes, based on substantial scholarship: juries may not be representative of the people in the community and thus lose the distinctive insight of excluded members; jurors who are not allowed to take notes may fail to recall essential elements of the case in deliberations; some jurors may be genuinely incompetent; jurors are swayed in favor of the prosecution by their sympathy for the victim in particularly gruesome crimes; judges' instructions delivered in "legalese" may be very difficult to understand and may lead to mistaken verdicts.[55]

The Adversary Trial

In the end, a statement made by an eminent comparative law scholar, after long and careful study, is instructive: he said that if he were innocent, he would prefer to be tried by a civil law court, but that if he were guilty, he would prefer to be tried by a common law court. This is, in effect, a judgment that criminal proceedings in the civil law world are more likely to distinguish accurately between the guilty and the innocent.[56]

This quote suggests an unpleasant truth: that the modern European inquisitorial trial is better at finding the truth than the American adversary trial, where so much depends on the storytelling ability of prosecutors and defense lawyers.[57] Part of the problem is that in the American trial system, the triers of fact are passive and simply receive evidence without any ability to probe what may be clear deficiencies. In the adversary system, to paraphrase Givelber, courts are unconcerned with the obligations of the police or prosecutor to conduct a thorough investigation, "to maintain comprehensive records, or even to choose wisely which potential defendants to charge. These matters—the very essence of a system concerned with actual innocence—are extra-constitutional."[58] Trials of major crimes in France are preceded by extensive investigation by one of two national police agencies, eliminating much of the unevenness of quality in police investigation that generates so much error in America. French police answer to civil service prosecutors, eliminating the differing agendas that cause police to sometimes hand half-prepared files to prosecutors here and also eliminating the political motivations that warp some prosecutorial work.[59]

Perhaps it is the very core of the adversary trial that is the problem, at least in criminal cases. Civil adversary trials produce more evidence, as each side works hard to gather evidence. But in criminal trials, the defense seems to be permanently handicapped. In France, defense counsel can request the government to carry out specific types of investigation that should be a great boon to innocent defendants. Such a request is impossible in a system where each side gathers and presents its facts. In European trials, the emphasis is on the dossier, the meticulously collected facts, and the evidence is presented in a more business-like way than in American trials. The ways in which prosecutors and defense counsel appeal to the emotions of jurors have no place, and prosecutors' attempts to outrage jurors with gory pictures are likewise out of place. Two scholars have suggested that American trials be modified in cases where specific facts are in dispute to emulate the best aspects of European trials without departing from the adversary trial, which in any event is so deeply embedded in our Constitution and legal culture that any fundamental changes are impossible.[60]

Aside from major structural changes, a number of small-scale reforms might help improve the accuracy of American trials. A rule requiring police to preserve evidence would avoid the injustice meted out to Larry Youngblood, described earlier. Without changing the adversary system, prosecutors could voluntary or under stronger laws supply defendants with exculpatory information. Eliminating incentives for jailhouse informants, and reducing the draconian prison sentences for drug and property crimes, would reduce incentives for innocent persons to plead guilty.[61] Until the judicial and criminal justice systems come to grips with such issues, we can expect to see a steady stream of news stories about wrongly convicted defendants being released from prison or death row.

Summary

The common law jury trial is a central legal institution in America. It has great symbolic and functional importance to support and ensure justice in the processing of criminal suspects. Unlike inquisitorial trial practices in civil law nations, the common law trial gives unique power to citizen jurors to be the final arbiters of case facts, and by the extent of attorney control of the trial rather than judge control, which is the norm in inquisitorial trials.

A felony jury trial includes many steps and Sixth Amendment rights. After jury selection, prosecutors and defense counsel may make opening statements. The prosecution enters evidence that is subject to cross-examination by the defense. The defense may then introduce evidence that is subject to the prosecutor's cross-examination, or it may rest without introducing evidence. A defendant has a constitutional right to be present at all phases of the trial unless the defendant voluntarily absents him- or herself or acts disruptively. This right does not include every conference between the judge and the attorneys, in camera competence hearings, or brief meetings with witnesses or jurors where the meetings are not unfair and the defense attorney is on hand. It does include visits to crime scenes. Forcing the defendant to wear prison garb or appear in restraints violates due process. Compulsory process to subpoena witnesses is another right that supports a fair trial. There is no due process right that the police preserve evidence or provide access to DNA, as long as evidence is not destroyed in bad faith. The Fifth Amendment right against self-incrimination requires that the prosecutor and the judge refrain from commenting on the defendant's absolute right not to testify unless so requested by the defendant.

Confrontation is central to the common law trial because it affords the defendant the opportunity to cross-examine prosecution witnesses. Cross-examination is a key to elicit the truth by testing witness credibility and the strength of testimony. A defense attorney seeks to establish a reasonable doubt by cross-examination. Hearsay is excluded because the out-of-court declarant cannot be cross-examined. Under due process, the identity of a secret informant must be disclosed at trial to allow full cross-examination. The elimination of eye-to-eye contact in the trial itself has been held to be a violation of the Confrontation Clause unless special circumstances are proven. Prior to 2004, hearsay not subject to cross-examination was admissible if it bore adequate indicia of reliability. This was overruled. Testimonial evidence is not admissible unless it was subject to cross-examination, making it difficult to prosecute domestic violence cases when victims refuse to testify. Forensic science reports are testimonial, and subject to cross-examination.

Due process requires proof of guilt beyond a reasonable doubt. A judge's reasonable doubt jury instruction is constitutional if, taken as a whole, it correctly conveys the idea of reasonable doubt. One that defines it as a "doubt as would give rise to a *grave uncertainty*," standing alone, violates due process because it suggests a higher degree of doubt than is required for acquittal under the reasonable doubt standard. On the contrary, a jury instruction that "[a] reasonable doubt is an *actual and substantial doubt* arising from the evidence, . . . as distinguished from a doubt arising from mere possibility, from bare imagination, or from fanciful conjecture" does not violate due process because it is tied to real facts. A jury instruction using the archaic phrase "moral certainty" does not automatically violate due process.

The Sixth Amendment guarantees a jury in the criminal trial of all but petty crimes and a jury is not required in juvenile delinquency hearings. Some constitutional variations are allowed between the federal common law jury, which requires twelve members and a unanimous verdict, and state juries, some of which consist of fewer than twelve members and allow verdicts by a "supermajority" (e.g., nine to three).

A fair jury is required under (1) the Fourteenth Amendment's Equal Protection Clause—people cannot be excluded from the jury because they share the race, ethnicity, or gender of the defendant—or (2) the Sixth Amendment requirement of an impartial jury—any jury must be selected from a panel that reflects a fair cross section of the community, whatever the relation between the defendant's race, gender, and so forth and the characteristics of jury pool members.

The petit jury, because of its small size, need not reflect a fair cross section of the community, as is required of jury pools. A prosecutor cannot use peremptory challenges to excuse prospective jurors *because of* their race, ethnicity, or gender. A challenged peremptory strike must be made for a race-neutral reason (*Batson v. Kentucky,* 1986) under the Equal Protection Clause. Post-*Batson* cases have extended its rule to civil trials and criminal defendants and to the categories of gender and ethnicity. The Court has been lenient in accepting race-neutral explanations for striking minorities from juries.

Legal Puzzles

HOW HAVE COURTS DECIDED THESE CASES?

Compulsory Process

11-1. Parents of a fourteen-year-old "Daphne" asked a neighbor and family friend, Joseph Rizzo, who previously helped them with marital problems, to counsel their daughter about her personal and disciplinary problems. Some months later "Daphne" told her parents that Rizzo touched her inappropriately during their counseling sessions; the sessions were immediately cancelled. "Daphne" was then counseled by Dr. Linda Pucci, a clinical psychologist, and "Daphne" told Dr. Pucci that an adult had been "messing with her" but did not disclose further details. Police were notified; Rizzo was convicted of several counts of sexually assaulting a child.

Before trial, Rizzo motioned the trial court to conduct an *in camera* review of Dr. Pucci's reports and records. The state provided a six-page summary prepared by Dr. Pucci, explaining her knowledge of the case and treatment of "Daphne." Her summary and testimony related to providing reasons why a molested person would be reluctant to come forward. The trial court conducted an *in camera* review of the records to determine if they contained exculpatory information. After reviewing the records, the trial judge denied Rizzo access to them. He said that Dr. Pucci's files contained the same information as her summary.

Was the court's refusal to allow Rizzo access to Dr. Pucci's clinical files a violation of his constitutional rights under the Sixth Amendment Compulsory Process Clause and the Fourteenth Amendment Due Process Clause?

Held: NO.

11-1. Under *Pennsylvania v. Ritchie* (1987) the Supreme Court held that fundamental fairness required that a father charged with sexually assaulting his thirteen-year-old daughter receive an *in camera* review of the records maintained by a child protective agency concerning his daughter, to determine whether they contained exculpatory information or information that would affect the outcome of the trial. Under the Fourteenth Amendment the government must turn over evidence in its possession that is both favorable to the accused and material to guilt or punishment. However, full disclosure to defense counsel in this type of case would unnecessarily sacrifice the state's compelling interest in protecting its child-abuse information. An *in camera* review by the trial court balances the rights of the defendant in ensuring a fair trial and the needs of the state or the individual to keep those records private. Rizzo received the same procedure as did Richie.

Rizzo v. Smith, 528 F.3d 501 (7th Cir. 2008)

Preservation of Evidence

11-2. Kofi Yevakpor was charged with importing heroin from Canada. The government's evidence included three one-minute video segments out of twenty-five minutes recorded at a border entry customs area by a series of video cameras that run continuously. The video clips were recorded during the border stop and search. The images are recorded on a DVR machine and are preserved on a compact disc. A Border Patrol supervisor directed that the three portions of the encounter with Yevakpor be preserved. The rest of the video recording was destroyed, although it would have been relatively easy and inexpensive to preserve.

The video segments do not clearly show the results of any search or a search of Yevakpor or of his companion before, during, or after the border stop. They do purport to show Yevakpor being detained at the secondary inspection area, carrying suitcases from the car into the inspection area, a search of suitcases by officers, Yevakpor's attempted use of a cellular telephone, and his allegedly giving materials or documents to a companion.

Does the introduction of three clips at Yevakpor's trial violate his due process right to a fair trial?
Holding available from instructor.

Confrontation

11-3. Scott McLaughlin was convicted of murder in the first degree and the rape of Beverly Guenther. They cohabited from 2002 to 2003, and had a stormy relationship marked by breakups and restraining orders obtained by Beverly. After the breakup, Scott was convicted of burglarizing Beverly's apartment, although he claimed he was just trying to remove his belongings.

In the guilt and penalty phases of the trial, police officers were allowed to testify about aspects of this relationship, including hearsay statements of Beverly Guenther, relating to incidents when officers escorted Beverly from her office to her car and, at her request, followed her several miles from work until she reached the highway; to McLaughlin's harassing and threatening conduct toward Beverly at her work; and to the burglary.

Did the introduction of unconfronted statements by Beverly Guenther violate McLaughlin's Confrontation Clause rights?
Holding available from instructor.

Voir Dire/Peremptory Challenge

11-4. Williamson was convicted of possession with intent to distribute a controlled substance. During voir dire questioning the trial judge asked whether "any member of the panel had any experience involving yourself, any member of your family, or any close friend that relates to the use or possession of illegal drugs or narcotics?" The judge also asked a similar question in regard to criminal matters. In response to these questions, thirteen members of the venire—including the only two black venire members—responded that they, a family member, or a close friend had some drug involvement.

During follow-up questions, the prosecution asked questions only of the black venire members, focusing on their "associations" with persons who had drug involvement, and used peremptory strikes against the two black venire members. Williamson objected, arguing that the strikes were based on race. The prosecution offered, as a race-neutral explanation, that the two struck African-American jurors were "the only persons that the government is aware of on the panel who stated that they had friends and relatives. . . . that had been convicted of drug offenses and were still using drugs and that she associated with both the friends and the relatives." The trial court overruled Williamson's *Batson* objection.

Did the prosecution's peremptory strikes violate Williamson's rights under Batson v. Kentucky (1986)?
Holding available from instructor.

Further Reading

Jeffrey Abramson, *We, the Jury: The Jury System and the Ideal of Democracy* (New York: Basic Books, 1994).

Steve Bogira, *Courtroom 302: A Year behind the Scenes in an American Criminal Courthouse* (New York: Alfred Knopf, 2005).

George P. Fletcher, *With Justice for Some: Victims' Rights in Criminal Trials* (Reading, Mass.: Addison-Wesley, 1995).

Barry Scheck, Peter Neufeld, and Jim Dwyer, *Actual Innocence: Five Days to Execution, and Other Dispatches from the Wrongly Convicted* (New York: Doubleday, 2000).

Useful Web Sites

National Center for State Courts

http://www.ncsconline.org/

Site of quasi-official agency that seeks to improve the administration of justice. Information about jobs in court administration, jury studies, family violence, and more.

American Judges Association

http://aja.ncsc.dni.us/

Site of voluntary international judges' association. Articles from *Court Review* include criminal justice topics.

End Notes

1. See Charles Rembar, *The Law of the Land: The Evolution of Our Legal System* (New York: Touchstone, 1980).

2. John H. Langbein, *Torture and the Law of Proof: Europe and England in the Ancien Regime* (Chicago: University of Chicago Press, 1977).

3. Barton L. Ingraham, *The Structure of Criminal Procedure: Law and Practice of France, the Soviet Union, China, and the United States* (New York: Greenwood Press, 1987), 86.

4. Thomas Andrew Green, *Verdict According to Conscience: Perspectives on the English Criminal Trial Jury, 1200–1800* (Chicago: University of Chicago Press, 1985), 320–21; John H. Langbein, *The Origins of Adversary Criminal Trial* (Oxford, UK: Oxford UniversityPress, 2003), 78.

5. See Jerome Frank, *Courts on Trial: Myth and Reality in American Justice* (1949; reprint, New York: Atheneum, 1963); and Stephen J. Adler, *The Jury: Disorder in the Courts* (New York: Doubleday, 1994).

6. John H. Langbein, "The Criminal Trial before the Lawyers," *University of Chicago Law Review* 45 (1978): 263–316; and Malcolm M. Feeley, "Plea Bargaining and the Structure of the Criminal Process," in George F. Cole, ed., *Criminal Justice: Law and Politics,* 5th ed. (Pacific Grove, Calif.: Brooks/Cole, 1988), 467–82.

7. See Craig M. Bradley, ed., *Criminal Procedure: A Worldwide Study*, 2nd ed. (Durham, N.C.: Carolina Academic Press, 2007); Rene David and John E. C. Brierly, *Major Legal Systems in the World Today,* 3rd ed. (London: Stephens and Sons,1985); and Richard J. Terrill, *World Criminal Justice Systems: A Survey,* 6th ed. (Cincinnati: Anderson, 2007).

8. Ingraham, *The Structure of Criminal Procedure,* 85.

9. From among a vast and fascinating literature, see Stephen Phillips, *No Heroes, No Villains* (New York: Random House, 1977); Paul and Shirley Eberle, *The Abuse of Innocence: The McMartin Preschool Trial* (Buffalo, N.Y.: Prometheus, 1993); and Stuart Taylor, Jr. and K. C. Johnson, *Until Proven Innocent: Political Correctness and the Shameful Injustices of the Duke Lacrosse Rape Case* (New York: St. Martin's Press, 2007).

10. S. Engleberg, "At Storm's Eye, a Law about Secrets," *New York Times,* February 13, 1989.

11. The Innocence Project Web site (know the cases > Larry Youngblood), http://www.innocenceproject.org/Content/303.php (accessed May 27, 2009).

12. Akhil Reed Amar, *The Constitution and Criminal Procedure: First Principles* (New Haven, CT: Yale University Press, 1997), 125.

13. Lawrence M. Friedman, *A History of American Law* [First Edition] (New York: Touchstone Book, 1973), 135.

14. Federal Rules of Evidence (F.R.E.) 803, 804, 807.

15. F.R.E. 804(b)(1).

16. Thomas J. Reed, "*Crawford v. Washington* and the Irretrievable Breakdown of a Union: Separating the Confrontation Clause from the Hearsay Rule," *South Carolina Law Review* 56 (2004) 185, 193.

17. Reed, p. 199.

18. Paul W. Valentine, "Craig Abuse Verdict Reversed 2nd Time," *Washington Post,* April 9, 1991; Stephen Buckley, "Prosecutors Reject New Trial in Sandra Craig Abuse Case," *Washington Post,* July 3, 1991.

19. See Dorothy Rabinowitz, *No Crueler Tyrannies: Accusation, False Witness and Other Terrors of Our Times* (New York: Wall Street Journal Book, 2003); Randall Grometstein, "Wrongful Conviction and Moral Panic: National and International Perspectives on Organized Child Sexual Abuse," in C. Ronald Huff and Martin Killias, eds., *Wrongful Conviction: International Perspectives on Miscarriages of Justice* (Philadelphia: Temple University Press, 2008), 11–32.

20. Reed, pp. 201–02.

21. Analysis of the disagreement between the majority and dissent over whether the state made a good faith effort to locate Anita is not included.

22. Reed, p. 207.

23. Reed, pp. 214–6.

24. Tom Lininger, "The Sound of Silence: Holding Batterers Accountable for Silencing Their Victims," *Texas Law Review* 87 (2009): 861.

25. Lininger, "Sound of Silence," pp. 861–2.

26. Lininger, "Sound of Silence," pp. 898–902.

27. "In more than 50% of the DNA exonerations nationwide, unvalidated or improper forensic science contributed to the underlying wrongful conviction." The Innocence Project, http://www.innocenceproject.org/fix/Crime-Lab-Oversight.php (accessed June 26, 2009).

28. Bureau of Justice Statistics, *State Court Organization 2004* (Washington, D.C.: U.S. Department of Justice, Bureau of Justice Statistics, 2006 NCJ 212351), Table 42, pp. 233–7, available at http://www.ojp.usdoj.gov/bjs/pub/pdf/sco04.pdf.

29. Harry Kalven and Hans Zeisel, *The American Jury* (Boston: Little, Brown, 1966), 490.

30. F.R.C.P. Rule 23(a).

31. See Hiroshi Fukurai, Edgar W. Butler, and Richard Krooth, *Race and the Jury* (New York: Plenum, 1993).

32. Michael Finkelstein, "The Application of Statistical Decision Theory to the Jury Discrimination Cases," *Harvard Law Review* 80 (1966): 338.

33. Cases collected in "Thirty-sixth Annual Review of Criminal Procedure," *Georgetown Law Journal Annual Review of Criminal Procedure* 36 (2007): 523, n. 1643.

34. Charles J. Ogletree, "Just Say No! A Proposal to Eliminate Racially Discriminatory Uses of Peremptory Challenges," *American Criminal Law Review* 31 (1994): 1099–1151, 1100.

35. Ogletree, "Just Say No!" 1113–16.

36. M. Zalman and Olga Tsoudis, "Plucking Weeds from the Garden: Lawyers Speak about Voir Dire," *Wayne Law Review* 51 (2005):163–448.

37. The Innocence Project, http://www.innocenceproject.org/ (accessed June 1, 2009)

38. Scheck et al., 25.

39. Ibid.

40. Ibid., 27–28.

41. Monroe H. Friedman, "Professional Responsibility of the Defense Lawyer: The Three Hardest Questions," *Michigan Law Review* 64 (1966): 1469–84.

42. Robert J. Ramsey and James Frank, "Wrongful Conviction: Perception of Criminal Justice Professionals Regarding the Frequency of Wrongful Conviction and the Extent of System Errors" *Crime & Delinquency* 53 (2007): 436–70; D. Michael Risinger, "Innocents Convicted: An Empirically Justified Factual Wrongful Conviction Rate," *Journal of Criminal Law and Criminology* 97 (2007): 761–806; Marvin Zalman, Brad Smith, and Angie Kiger, "Officials' Estimates of the Incidence of 'Actual Innocence' Convictions," *Justice Quarterly* 25 (2008): 72–100.

43. Brandon L. Garrett, "Judging Innocence," *Columbia Law Review* 108 (2008): 55–141.

44. Daniel Givelber, "Meaningless Acquittals, Meaningful Convictions: Do We Reliably Acquit the Innocent? *Rutgers Law Review* 49 (1997): 1317–96, 1343–44, revieweing Harry Kalven Jr. and Hans Zeisel, *The American Jury* (Boston: Little, Brown, 1966); and John Baldwin and Michael McConville, *Jury Trials* (New York: Oxford University Press, 1979).

45. Givelber, "Meaningless Acquittals," 1343.

46. Ann W. O'Neill, "Ex-prosecutor Defends Actions in Rampart Case; Courts: Now a Judge, He Says an Allegedly Tainted Conviction Seemed Like a Simple Plea Bargain," *Los Angeles Times*, October 18, 2000, B1.

47. Givelber, "Meaningless Acquittals," 1372.

48. Gross, "The Risks of Death," 494–95.

49. Givelber, "Meaningless Acquittals," 1361.

50. Stanley Z. Fisher, "Just the Facts, Ma'am: Lying and the Omission of Exculpatory Evidence in Police Reports," *New England Law Review* 28 (1993): 1–62.

51. See Gross, "The Risks of Death," 490–91.

52. Givelber, "Meaningless Acquittals," 1363 (footnotes omitted).

53. Givelber, "Meaningless Acquittals," 1375 (footnotes omitted).

54. H. Lee Sarokin and William Zuckerman, "Presumed Innocent? Restrictions on Criminal Discovery in Federal Court Belie This Presumption," *Rutgers Law Review* 43 (1991): 1089.

55. Brian Forst, *Errors of Justice* (New York: Cambridge University Press, 2004), 37–38.

56. Givelber, "Meaningless Acquittals," 1317, quoting John H. Merryman, *The Civil Law Tradition,* 2nd ed. (Stanford, Calif.: Stanford University Press, 1985), 132.

57. Sam Schrager, *The Trial Lawyer's Art* (Philadelphia: Temple University Press, 1999).

58. Givelber, "Meaningless Acquittals," 1371 (footnotes omitted). Givelber was referring specifically to Supreme Court cases, but his point applies to the role of trial judges as well.

59. Bron McKillop, "Anatomy of a French Murder Case," *American Journal of Comparative Law* 45 (1997): 527–83.

60. D. Michael Risinger, "Unsafe Verdicts: The Need for Reformed Standards for the Trial and Review of Factual Innocence Claims," *Houston Law Review* 41 (2004): 1281–1336; Tim Bakken, "Truth and Innocence Procedures to Free Innocent Persons: Beyond the Adversarial System," *University of Michigan Journal of Law Reform* 41 (2008): 547–583.

61. Givelber, "Meaningless Acquittals," 1381–94.

JUSTICES OF THE SUPREME COURT

The Twenty-First-Century Court: Souter, Thomas, Ginsburg, Breyer, Roberts, and Alito

Each of these justices previously served as a federal judge, although David Souter, a New Hampshire Supreme Court judge, had barely taken his federal appointment to the First Circuit Court of Appeals before his elevation to the Supreme Court, and Clarence Thomas had only one year of judicial experience. Justices Souter and Thomas, appointed by President George H. W. Bush, replaced the most enduring liberals on the Court: Justices William Brennan and Thurgood Marshall. Many thought that these appointments would mark the end of the politically inflammatory abortion rights decision, *Roe v. Wade,* but this was not to be. In the criminal procedure area, however, the new appointments did not change the generally pro-prosecution cast of the Court. What was lost with the retirement of Justices Brennan and Marshall was a strong liberal voice, even if in dissent. Justice Souter aligned himself with the moderate-conservative center of the Court, and Justice Thomas joined the extreme conservatives on these issues.

President Bill Clinton, appointing the first Democrats to the Court since 1967, disappointed some supporters by not naming highly liberal jurists to offset the distinctive conservatism of Justices Antonin Scalia and Clarence Thomas. Justices Ruth Bader Ginsburg and Stephen Breyer, who replaced Justices Byron White and Harry Blackmun, both had reputations as highly competent, moderate federal judges. Justice Ginsburg had been a leading litigator in women's rights cases before the Supreme Court in the 1970s and was viewed as liberal on some issues. Justice Breyer had a national reputation as an original thinker on issues of economic regulation and as a member of the federal Sentencing Commission. Neither of them was expected to modify the Court's position on criminal procedure. Indeed, they have proven to be centrists. This reflects the national mood and President Clinton's position as moderately conservative on crime issues.

Oddly, then, the only sitting justice who might fairly be called a criminal procedure liberal is Justice John Paul Stevens, who migrated to the position from a centrist posture. The Court at the beginning of the twenty-first century was best described as moderate to conservative on criminal procedure issues. The general framework of incorporation, a legacy of the Warren Court's "due process revolution," endured but has been weakened by decisions that block access to federal courts (i.e., standing and habeas corpus) and by decisions that interpret such categories as due process, reasonable suspicion, probable cause, and cruel and unusual punishment in ways that favor the state. Defendants have been able to prevail on issues associated with property rights (e.g., asset forfeiture) or race discrimination (peremptory challenges to remove jurors).

In 2005 and 2006, President George W. Bush appointed two highly competent and distinctly conservative federal judges, John Roberts and Samuel Alito, to the bench. Despite threats of a Democratic filibuster, both judges were approved by the Senate, although Alito's confirmation by a vote of fifty-eight to forty-two indicated a real fight over the Court's direction. Justice Roberts's selection as chief justice, after Chief Justice William Rehnquist died in office, basically replaced one conservative vote with another. But Judge Alito filled the seat vacated by Justice Sandra Day O'Connor, who retired. As Justice O'Connor had become the pivotal swing justice, her replacement with a sharply conservative justice seems certain to strengthen the staunchly conservative right wing of the Court.

Collection of the Supreme Court
of the United States.
Photographer: Joseph Bailey.

David H. Souter

New Hampshire, 1939–

Republican

Appointed by George H. W. Bush

Years of Service: 1990–

Life and Career.   A native of New Hampshire, Souter graduated from Harvard College magna cum laude. He spent two years at Oxford University as a Rhodes Scholar, graduated from Harvard Law School, and practiced law for two years in New Hampshire. He served for a decade (1968–1978) in the New Hampshire attorney general's department, with the last two years in the appointed top job. He developed a strong friendship with Attorney General Warren Rudman, a moderate Republican who was elected to the U.S. Senate. He served as trial judge and then was appointed to the New Hampshire Supreme Court (1983–1990) by Governor John Sununu. He quickly became the intellectual leader of the state's high court. In 1990, Souter was appointed to the First Circuit Court of Appeals, deciding only one case before he was nominated to the Supreme Court on the recommendation of John Sununu, who had become White House chief of staff. The low-key and highly professional judge had not left a paper trail concerning the "litmus test" issue of abortion and was confirmed by the Senate by a vote of ninety to nine.

Contribution to Criminal Procedure.   Although Justice Souter became a liberal justice on the Rehnquist Court, his decisions in criminal procedure cases have generally been conservative. By replacing Justice Brennan, the most liberal justice on the Court, Souter inevitably swung the Court's criminal procedure jurisprudence in favor of the state. In his first years on the Court, he tended to support the prosecution (joining the majority in *Alvarez-Machain,* 1992) but also joined the opinion in the *Jacobson* (1992) entrapment case. By 1995, he began to shift to a more overall moderate stance. One majority opinion held that a state appellate court on collateral review must grant a new trial to the defendant if a prosecutor withheld relevant evidence (*Kyles v. Whitely,* 1995). In recent years, Justice Souter has been more likely to join the liberal bloc in criminal procedure cases—joining the dissent in the *Illinois v. Wardlow* (2000) reasonable suspicion case—writing the dissenting opinion in *Pennsylvania Board of Probation and Parole v. Scott* (1998), arguing that the exclusionary rule should apply to a warrantless entry into a parolee's home by a parole officer based on a functional analysis showing that parole officers work under similar motives as police and that the deterrent rationale of the exclusionary rule should therefore apply to them.

Signature Opinion.   *Georgia v. Randolph* (2006). In this case, the Court held that police may not enter a premises when a physically present co-occupant refuses to give consent. The decision was based on the idea that the Fourth Amendment derives much of its meaning from widely shared social expectations, which are influenced by property law but not controlled by its rules. The decision would not prevent police from acting when exigencies, such as spousal abuse, were present.

Assessment.   By his third year on the Court, Souter came to be seen as an intellectual leader of the Court's moderate-conservative center and has become a distinctly liberal justice in the years since. In *Planned Parenthood v. Casey* (1992), he joined with Justices O'Connor and Kennedy in an unusual joint opinion upholding *Roe v. Wade* (by a narrow five-to-four vote) on the basis of *stare decisis. Casey* signaled that the most extreme conservative interpretations of the Constitution, espoused by Chief Justice Rehnquist and Justices Scalia and Thomas, would not become the law of the land. He dissented in *Bush v. Gore* (2000), believing that the Constitution had a procedure that allowed Congress to decide deadlocked presidential elections. In an era of extremely partisan politics, Souter became a lightning rod for conservative ire. "No more Souters!" became a slogan of conservatives frustrated that the Reagan–Bush appointees on the Supreme Court have not been able to overturn a woman's right to choose abortion, *Miranda,* and the ban on school prayer under the First Amendment.

Further Reading

Tinsley E. Yarbrough, *David Hackett Souter: Traditional Republican on the Rehnquist Court* (New York: Oxford University Press, 2005).

Collection of the Supreme Court of the United States.
Photographer: Joseph Bailey

Clarence Thomas

Virginia, 1948–

Republican

Appointed by George H. W. Bush

Years of Service: 1991–

Life and Career.   Thomas was born into a poor family in segregated Savannah, Georgia. He was raised by his grandparents, who instilled in him a sense of pride and discipline, self-reliance and hard work, commitment to black solidarity through the National Association for the Advancement of Colored People (NAACP), and a determination that education was the key to a better life. He attended Catholic school and experienced the blatant racism of fellow students in a Missouri seminary. He graduated from Holy Cross College and Yale Law School, where he developed a dislike for affirmative action. After graduation in 1974, he worked as an assistant attorney general in Missouri, as a corporate lawyer, and as legislative assistant to Senator Danforth of Missouri.

As one of the few African-American conservatives during the Reagan administration, he became chairman of the Equal Employment Opportunity Commission (EEOC), an agency to which the administration was hostile. Thomas handled this difficult assignment by ultimately abandoning the agency's affirmative action agenda and class-action suits and focusing instead on individual discrimination cases. Many criticized his EEOC leadership as failing to effectively support the claims of minorities, women, and the elderly. He was nominated to the U.S. Court of Appeals for the Washington, D.C., Circuit in 1989, an appointment that was viewed as a stepping-stone to the Supreme Court.

Thomas's confirmation process, following his nomination by President George H. W. Bush to the Supreme Court to replace retiring Justice Marshall, was extremely controversial. He was lambasted for his conservatism, his lack of high judicial qualifications, and his opposition to *Roe v. Wade.* Many thought that George Bush cynically manipulated the "black seat" on the Court to make it difficult for African Americans to oppose a black candidate. And this was *before* the sensational story broke that he had sexually harassed Anita Hill, a former employee and a law professor. The hearings on Professor Hill's testimony and Judge Thomas's impassioned defense were televised and were the scandal of the hour. Thomas denied the allegations and called the ordeal "a high-tech lynching for uppity blacks." His nomination was affirmed by a fifty-two to forty-eight vote of the Senate.

Contribution to Criminal Procedure.   From 1991 to 1995, Thomas was second only to Chief Justice Rehnquist in conservative voting in criminal procedure cases, supporting individuals in only 19 percent of cases. Although he is a solid conservative on a conservative Court, he has little influence because he is not given opportunities to write majority opinions in important cases, but typically writes majority opinions only when the justices share a strong consensus, as was the case in holding that the "knock and announce" rule of search warrant execution is a constitutional rule (*Wilson v. Arkansas,* 1995). He is the most conservative justice in death penalty, habeas corpus, and Eighth Amendment cases.

Signature Opinion.   Dissenting opinion in *Hudson v. McMillan* (1992). The Court held that excessive force by a prison guard (the beating alleged was deliberate and resulted in minor bruises, facial swelling, loosened teeth, and a cracked dental plate) may constitute cruel and unusual punishment even though the inmate does not suffer serious injury. Justice Thomas said, "In my view, a use of force that causes only insignificant harm to a prisoner may be immoral, it may be tortious, it may be criminal, and it may even be remediable under other provisions of the Federal Constitution, but it is not 'cruel and unusual punishment.'"

Assessment.   Justice Thomas has applied the theory of originalism more rigidly than Justice Scalia, and although he expresses confidently that he knows the intent of the Framers of the Constitution, it was noted that he "has shown little familiarity with the most recent scholarship" about the origin of the Fourteenth Amendment, where he seems to have mistakenly asserted that its Framers intended to create a "color-blind" Constitution, a position that supports his votes.

Further Reading

Christopher E. Smith, "Clarence Thomas: A Distinctive Justice," *Seton Hall Law Review* 28 (1997): 1–28.

Ruth Bader Ginsburg

New York, 1933–
Democrat
Appointed by William Clinton
Years of Service: 1993–

Collection of the Supreme Court of the United States.
Photographer: Steve Petteway.

Life and Career.   Ginsburg grew up in Brooklyn, New York, in a Jewish, lower-middle-class family. An excellent student, she won a scholarship to Cornell University and decided to pursue a career in the law with her husband, Martin Ginsburg. Following Martin's army service and the birth of their first child, she entered Harvard Law School a year after Martin did. She was one of only nine women in a class of five hundred students. Martin was diagnosed with cancer and underwent radiation therapy while Ruth took notes in his classes as well as her own and typed his third-year paper while caring for their child. Martin recovered and obtained a position with a New York law firm, and Ruth transferred to Columbia Law School. She was the first woman to have served on two law reviews.

After graduation, prevalent sexist attitudes prevented her from being hired by a law firm, so she clerked for a state judge. She joined the Rutgers Law School faculty in 1963; in 1972, she became the first tenured female law professor at Columbia Law School. Between 1972 and 1978, Ginsburg argued six gender-equality cases before the Supreme Court (winning five), on the basis that sex-role stereotypes violated the Equal Protection Clause. Some have called her "the Thurgood Marshall of women's rights." In 1980, she was appointed to the U.S. Court of Appeals for the District of Columbia, where she developed an excellent reputation as a leading centrist judge.

Contribution to Criminal Procedure.   Justice Ginsburg's votes in criminal cases are liberal to moderate. She has been described as pragmatic. She has sided with the government in upholding drug testing of school athletes, pretext searches, gaining consent to search cars without informing drivers of their rights, the forfeiture of a wife's interest in a car that was confiscated after her husband was found guilty of soliciting prostitution, and ordering nonsuspicious passengers out of stopped cars.

However, she has joined with liberal and moderate justices to support individual rights in dissent where fleeing from an officer has been held to constitute reasonable suspicion, where a car was seized for forfeiture without a warrant, where parole officers entered a parolee's home without a warrant, and where police searched the handbag of a nonsuspicious automobile passenger. She, along with Justice Stevens, has attacked the way in which *Michigan v. Long* (1983) has applied the adequate and independent state grounds doctrine, arguing in *Arizona v. Evans* (1995) that the Court should not overturn state court decisions that expand defendants' constitutional rights.

Signature Opinion.   *Florida v. J.L.* (2000). For a unanimous Court, Ginsburg held that an anonymous phone call "that a young black male standing at a particular bus stop and wearing a plaid shirt was carrying a gun" does not in itself establish reasonable suspicion to conduct a *Terry* stop if all that the police know is that a person at the described place fits the description given by the caller. The ruling indicates that the Court has become wary of extending the reach of police powers that clearly go beyond constitutional protections: "[A]n automatic firearm exception to our established reliability analysis would rove too far."

Assessment.   Justice Ginsburg is a moderate liberal and takes a dynamic approach to the complex issues of legal process. The major themes of her writings include the ideal of a person's day in court, court efficiency, and judicial integrity, including *stare decisis* and procedural regularity. In *United States v. Virginia* (1996), she wrote the majority opinion holding that the Virginia Military Institute could not lawfully exclude female students.

Further Reading

Laura Krugman Ray, "Justice Ginsburg and the Middle Way," *Brooklyn Law Review* 68 (2003): 629–82.

Collection of the Supreme Court of the United States.
Photographer: Steve Petteway.

Stephen G. Breyer

Massachusetts, 1938–

Democrat

Appointed by William Clinton

Years of Service: 1994–

Life and Career.   Breyer's father, a lawyer, brought him to a voting booth when he was young and helped to impart "a love for the possibilities of democracy." His mother, active in local Democratic politics and in the League of Women Voters, instilled in Stephen a sense that intellectual activity had to be balanced by an ability to work with and help people. He was a Boy Scout, worked as a delivery boy, and dug ditches for a local utility company. He graduated from Stanford University with highest honors, earned another degree at Oxford University in philosophy, politics, and economics, and graduated magna cum laude from Harvard Law School in 1964.

After law school, Breyer clerked for Justice Arthur Goldberg. He then worked as an antitrust lawyer in the Justice Department and was a Harvard Law School professor. He developed a sophisticated but pragmatic theory of the regulatory state and believes that economic regulation should maximize competition and not burden the private sector with unnecessary government restraints. He also served as an assistant on the Watergate Special Prosecution force that helped topple President Richard Nixon and as counsel to the Senate Judiciary Committee. In 1980, he was appointed to the First Circuit Court of Appeals. He was a coalition builder on that court. In 1985, Breyer was appointed to the U.S. Sentencing Commission, which was designed to rationalize federal sentencing practices, and in 1994 was elevated to the Supreme Court.

Contribution to Criminal Procedure.   As an expert in economic regulation, Breyer has written few major opinions in the criminal procedure area. His voting pattern is middle-of-the-road. He voted for the government in *United States v. Armstrong* (1996) (it is not selective prosecution to charge a disproportionate percentage of African Americans for crack cocaine offenses); *Carlisle v. United States* (1996) (motion for judgment of acquittal cannot be granted if filed one day beyond time limit); *Lewis v. Casey* (1996) (no violation of rights from inadequate law library unless actual injury shown); *Wyoming v. Houghton* (1999) (police can search handbag of a nonsuspicious automobile passenger); and *Bond v. United States* (2000) (traveler has no expectation of privacy "that strangers will not push, pull, prod, squeeze, or otherwise manipulate his luggage" on an intercity bus). He has, on occasion, joined liberal and moderate justices: in dissent where fleeing from an officer has been held to constitute reasonable suspicion; in dissent where parole officers entered a parolee's home without a warrant; and in dissent where wife's interest in car was forfeited for her husband's crime.

Signature Opinion.   Dissenting opinion in *Apprendi v. New Jersey* (2000). The majority held that a factual element of the crime used to enhance a sentence must be submitted to a jury and proved beyond a reasonable doubt. Breyer, dissenting, stated that "the real world of criminal justice cannot hope to meet" the ideal that "juries, not judges, determin[e] the existence of those facts upon which increased punishment turns. It can function only with the help of procedural compromises, particularly in respect to sentencing."

Assessment.   In *United States v. Lopez* (1995), the Court struck down a federal law based on the Commerce Clause—making it a federal crime to possess a weapon within one hundred feet of a local school—for the first time since the 1930s. Breyer wrote a sharp and detailed dissent, joined by Justices Stevens, Souter, and Ginsburg, defending federal authority to pass such a law.

Further Reading

Paul Gewirtz, "Review: The Pragmatic Passion of Stephen Breyer," *Yale Law Journal* 115 (2006): 1675–98.

Collection of the Supreme Court of the United States.
Photographer: Steve Petteway.

John G. Roberts Jr.

Maryland, 1955–
Republican
Appointed by George W. Bush
Years of Service: 2005–

Life and Career.   Roberts was raised in Indiana; his father was a steel company executive. Although always recognized as a brilliant student, he was also a "scrappy athlete" and captain of his high school football team. He graduated summa cum laude from Harvard College and was managing editor of the law review at Harvard Law School. After law school, he clerked for the noted federal judge Henry Friendly and then for Associate Justice Rehnquist. He served as a lawyer in the Justice Department and in the White House Counsel's Office from 1982 to 1986 for President Ronald Reagan. As a corporate lawyer from 1986 to 1989 and from 1993 to 2003, he represented some of the largest companies and was earning $1 million a year when he left. He served as a deputy solicitor general from 1989 to 1993, arguing cases before the Supreme Court, and was appointed to the U.S. Court of Appeals for the District of Columbia Circuit in 2005.

Roberts was originally nominated to fill Justice O'Connor's vacancy upon her retirement, but was re-nominated for the post of chief justice when Chief Justice Rehnquist died. In confirmation hearings, Roberts noted that his approach to interpreting the Constitution is more varied and flexible than the originalism subscribed to by Justices Thomas and Scalia. As a lawyer who argued thirty-nine cases before the Supreme Court, John Roberts was known as "perhaps the most impressive Supreme Court advocate of his generation, extremely intelligent, thoughtful and able—a lawyer's lawyer." Given his great legal talents and his low-key and winning personality, he was eminently qualified to be chief justice.

Contribution to Criminal Procedure.   During four terms on the Court, the Chief Justice, to no one's surprise, has proven to be a solidly conservative justice, anchoring the right wing of the Court in criminal procedure cases along with Justices Alito and Thomas. During his first term he joined the Court in diminishing the exclusionary rule in *Hudson v. Michigan* (2006), upholding a suspicionless search of a parolee (*Samson v. California*, 2006), and dissented against consent ruling that allowed a homeowner to block police from entering against the consent of a co-occupier (*Georgia v. Randolph*, 2006). He dissented against Justice Scalia's opinion in *Arizona v. Gant* (2009) and would have allowed police to search the car of a driver arrested for a vehicular offense as a search incident to arrest where the driver was handcuffed and secured in a patrol car, but joined Justice Scalia's "conservative" opinion in *Montejo v. Lousiana* (2009), which overruled *Michigan v. Jackson* (1986), that allowed police to question a defendant who was assigned a lawyer and had requested the assistance of counsel. Unlike Justices Alito, Thomas, and Scalia, who have dissented against lopsided liberal rulings, he joined the majority in *Rothgery v. Gillespie County* (2008; 8–1; the right to counsel attaches at the initial appearance); *Snyder v. Louisiana* (2008, 7–2; peremptory challenge violation found under *Batson*); and *Harbison v. Bell* (2009, 7–2; assigned counsel can pursue clemency petition).

Signature Opinion.   His majority opinion in *Herring v. U.S.* (2009) (5–4) continued the Court's trend since 1974 of viewing the Fourth Amendment exclusionary rule not as a constitutional rule or a personal right but as a device to deter only flagrant and deliberate violations. The Court held that evidence resulting from a search based in good faith reliance on erroneous information in a police database is admissible. *Herring* has made the deliberate and the flagrant misconduct of the officer the lynchpin of applying the exclusionary rule, not the fact that a person's constitutional right was violated.

Assessment.   Chief Justice Roberts has hewn to a generally conservative Crime Control Model approach to criminal procedure cases, especially in Fourth Amendment cases. His engaging writing style helps advance his substantive positions. He has proven to be less than doctrinaire by joining pro-defendant rulings in several nonunanimous Fifth and Sixth Amendment cases.

Further Reading

Barbara A. Perry, *"The Supremes": An Introduction to the U.S. Supreme Court Justices* (New York: Peter Lang, 2009).

Collection of the Supreme Court of the United States. Photographer: Steve Petteway.

Samuel A. Alito Jr.

New Jersey, 1950–

Republican

Appointed by George W. Bush

Years of Service: 2006–

Life and Career.   Alito's father was a highly regarded nonpartisan legislative drafter for the New Jersey legislature. Samuel Alito graduated from Princeton University and from Yale Law School in 1975, where he won prizes for scholarship and oral argument and published an award-winning *Yale Law Journal* note. After clerking for a federal appeals judge from 1976 to 1977, he made a career as a federal government lawyer and prosecutor, including service in the solicitor general's office and as a deputy assistant attorney general in the Reagan administration under Edwin Meese, who sought a conservative realignment of constitutional law. Alito indicated a commitment to conservative legal views. He was appointed as U.S. Attorney for New Jersey in 1987 and to the U.S. Court of Appeals for the Third Circuit in 1990.

Alito was nominated to the Supreme Court after President Bush's nomination of his legal advisor, Harriet Miers, "was withdrawn after furious attacks" by right-wing Republicans. Alito's nomination was said to galvanize the right, and he was confirmed by the Senate. Despite his strong commitment to a conservative agenda, before his nomination to the Supreme Court, Alito earned respect and friendship "across the political spectrum. Some who describe themselves as liberals say that they admire what they call his meticulousness and fair-mindedness." Several of Judge Alito's opinions were later disapproved by the Supreme Court, including *Planned Parenthood v. Casey* (1992), where he upheld a state abortion law provision requiring women to notify their husbands before they have an abortion.

Contribution to Criminal Procedure.   Justice Alito, a former prosecutor, has proven to be the most conservative justice, to the right of even Clarence Thomas. Having replaced Justice O'Connor, his vote may have been critical in several 5–4 decisions: *District Attorney v. Osborne* (2009; no due process right to DNA evidence); *Herring v. U.S.* (2009; exclusionary rule does not apply where officers rely, in good faith, on error in police database); *Montejo v. Louisiana* (2009; police may re-initiate interrogation of defendant who was assigned and requested counsel); and *Hudson v. Michigan* (2006; exclusionary rule does not apply to constitutional violation of knock-and-announce rule). He did author a pro-defendant opinion in *Snyder v. Louisiana* (2008), holding that the exclusion of an African-American juror was clear error under *Batson*, requiring a new trial in a murder case (Justices Thomas and Scalia dissented). His "conservative" dissents included *Hamdan v. Rumsfeld* (2006; extending habeas corpus to Guantanamo detainees); *Harbison v. Bell* (2009; allowing assigned counsel to represent capital defendant in a state clemency proceeding); and *Melendez-Diaz v. Massachusetts* (2009; requiring forensic examiners to be cross-examined under the Confrontation Clause). His dissent for the conservative wing of the Court in *Corley v. U.S.* (2009), which held that a federal statute did not overrule the *McNabb–Mallory* rule that excluded confessions made to federal officers who did not bring suspects to a magistrate within six hours of arrest, tenaciously supported a tenuous reading of the statute and seems little concerned that the statute would not have any enforcement mechanism.

Signature Opinion.   *Pearson v. Callahan* (2009). Writing for a unanimous Court, Justice Alito slightly expanded the "consent-once-removed" doctrine to extend the consent to enter a place without a warrant given to an undercover confidential informant to police as soon as probable cause of criminality is established. More important to the Court, *Saucier v. Katz* (2001) was overruled. It held, in civil liability qualified immunity hearings, that a court must first determine if a right was violated and then decide whether it was clearly established. *Pearson* restored discretion to trial courts to decide the order of the issues, as a matter of judicial efficiency.

Assessment.   Justice Alito has strongly supported the Crime Control Model of criminal procedure and is a very solid anchor for conservative arguments. His opinions are very thorough.

Further Reading

Barbara A. Perry, *"The Supremes": An Introduction to the U.S. Supreme Court Justices* (New York: Peter Lang, 2009).

APPENDIX A
CONSTITUTION OF THE UNITED STATES

SELECTED PROVISIONS OF THE CONSTITUTION OF THE UNITED STATES

We the People of the United States, in Order to form a more perfect Union, establish Justice, insure domestic Tranquility, provide for the common defence, promote the general Welfare, and secure the Blessings of Liberty to ourselves and our Posterity, do ordain and establish this Constitution for the United States of America.

Article. I

SECTION. 1. All legislative Powers herein granted shall be vested in a Congress of the United States, which shall consist of a Senate and House of Representatives.

SECTION. 2. The House of Representatives shall be composed of Members chosen every second Year by the People of the several States, and the Electors in each State shall have the Qualifications requisite for Electors of the most numerous Branch of the State Legislature.

No Person shall be a Representative who shall not have attained to the Age of twenty five Years, and been seven Years a Citizen of the United States, and who shall not, when elected, be an Inhabitant of that State in which he shall be chosen.

[Representatives and direct Taxes shall be apportioned among the several States which may be included within this Union, according to their respective Numbers, which shall be determined by adding to the whole Number of free Persons, including those bound to Service for a Term of Years, and excluding Indians not taxed, three fifths of all other Persons.][1] The actual Enumeration shall be made within three Years after the first Meeting of the Congress of the United States, and within every subsequent Term of ten Years, in such Manner as they shall by Law direct. The Number of Representatives shall not exceed one for every thirty Thousand, but each State shall have at Least one Representative; and until such enumeration shall be made, the State of New Hampshire shall be entitled to choose three, Massachusetts eight, Rhode-Island and Providence Plantations one, Connecticut five, New-York six, New Jersey four, Pennsylvania eight, Delaware one, Maryland six, Virginia ten, North Carolina five, South Carolina five, and Georgia three.

When vacancies happen in the Representation from any State, the Executive Authority thereof shall issue Writs of Election to fill such Vacancies.

The House of Representatives shall choose their Speaker and other Officers; and shall have the sole Power of Impeachment.

SECTION. 3. The Senate of the United States shall be composed of two Senators from each State, [chosen by the Legislature][2] thereof for six Years; and each Senator shall have one Vote.

Immediately after they shall be assembled in Consequence of the first Election, they shall be divided as equally as may be into three Classes. The Seats of the Senators of the first Class shall be vacated at the Expiration of the second Year, of the second Class at the Expiration of the fourth Year, and of the third Class at the Expiration of the sixth Year, so that one third may be chosen every second Year; [and if Vacancies happen by Resignation, or otherwise, during the Recess of the Legislature of any State, the Executive thereof may make temporary Appointments until the next Meeting of the Legislature, which shall then fill such Vacancies.][3]

No Person shall be a Senator who shall not have attained to the Age of thirty Years, and been nine Years a Citizen of the United States, and who shall not, when elected, be an Inhabitant of that State for which he shall be chosen.

The Vice President of the United States shall be President of the Senate, but shall have no Vote, unless they be equally divided.

The Senate shall choose their other Officers, and also a President pro tempore, in the Absence of the Vice President, or when he shall exercise the Office of President of the United States.

The Senate shall have the sole Power to try all Impeachments. When sitting for that Purpose, they shall be on Oath or Affirmation. When the President of the United States is tried, the Chief Justice shall preside: And no Person shall be convicted without the Concurrence of two thirds of the Members present.

Judgment in Cases of Impeachment shall not extend further than to removal from Office, and disqualification to hold and enjoy any Office of honor, Trust or Profit under the United States: but the Party convicted shall nevertheless be liable and subject to Indictment, Trial, Judgment and Punishment, according to Law.

SECTION. 4. The Times, Places and Manner of holding Elections for Senators and Representatives, shall be prescribed in each State by the Legislature thereof; but the Congress may at any time by Law make or alter such Regulations, except as to the Places of choosing Senators.

The Congress shall assemble at least once in every Year, and such Meeting shall [be on the first Monday in December,][4] unless they shall by Law appoint a different Day.

SECTION. 5. Each House shall be the Judge of the Elections, Returns and Qualifications of its own Members, and a Majority of each shall constitute a Quorum to do Business; but a smaller Number may adjourn from day to day, and may be authorized to compel the Attendance of absent Members, in such Manner, and under such Penalties as each House may provide.

Each House may determine the Rules of its Proceedings, punish its Members for disorderly Behaviour, and, with the Concurrence of two thirds, expel a Member.

Each House shall keep a Journal of its Proceedings, and from time to time publish the same, excepting such Parts as may in their Judgment require Secrecy; and the Yeas and Nays of the Members of either House on any question shall, at the Desire of one fifth of those Present, be entered on the Journal.

Neither House, during the Session of Congress, shall, without the Consent of the other, adjourn for more than three days, nor to any other Place than that in which the two Houses shall be sitting.

SECTION. 6. The Senators and Representatives shall receive a Compensation for their Services, to be ascertained by Law, and paid out of the Treasury of the United States. They shall in all Cases, except Treason, Felony and Breach of the Peace, be privileged from Arrest during their Attendance at the Session of their respective Houses, and in going to and returning from the same; and for any Speech or Debate in either House, they shall not be questioned in any other Place.

No Senator or Representative shall, during the Time for which he was elected, be appointed to any civil Office under the Authority of the United States, which shall have been created, or the Emoluments whereof shall have been increased during such time; and no Person holding any Office under the United States, shall be a Member of either House during his Continuance in Office.

SECTION. 7. All Bills for raising Revenue shall originate in the House of Representatives; but the Senate may propose or concur with Amendments as on other Bills.

Every Bill which shall have passed the House of Representatives and the Senate, shall, before it becomes a Law, be presented to the President of the United States: If he approves he shall sign it, but if not he shall return it, with his Objections to that House in which it shall have originated, who shall enter the Objections at large on their Journal, and proceed to reconsider it. If after such Reconsideration two thirds of that House shall agree to pass the Bill, it shall be sent, together with the Objections, to the other House, by which it shall likewise be reconsidered, and if approved by two thirds of that House, it shall become a Law. But in all such Cases the Votes of both Houses shall be determined by yeas and Nays, and the Names of the Persons voting for and against the Bill shall be entered on the Journal of each House respectively. If any Bill shall not be returned by the President within ten Days (Sundays excepted) after it shall have been presented to him, the Same shall be a Law, in like Manner as if he had signed it, unless the Congress by their Adjournment prevent its Return, in which Case it shall not be a Law.

Every Order, Resolution, or Vote to which the Concurrence of the Senate and House of Representatives may be necessary (except on a question of Adjournment) shall be presented to the President of the United States; and before the Same shall take Effect, shall be approved by him, or being disapproved by him, shall be repassed by two thirds of the Senate and House of Representatives, according to the Rules and Limitations prescribed in the Case of a Bill.

SECTION. 8. The Congress shall have Power To lay and collect Taxes, Duties, Imposts and Excises, to pay the Debts and provide for the common Defence and general Welfare of the United States; but all Duties, Imposts and Excises shall be uniform throughout the United States;

To borrow Money on the credit of the United States;

To regulate Commerce with foreign Nations, and among the several States, and with the Indian Tribes;

To establish an uniform Rule of Naturalization, and uniform Laws on the subject of Bankruptcies throughout the United States;

To coin Money, regulate the Value thereof, and of foreign Coin, and fix the Standard of Weights and Measures;

To provide for the Punishment of counterfeiting the Securities and current Coin of the United States;

To establish Post Offices and post Roads;

To promote the Progress of Science and useful Arts, by securing for limited Times to Authors and Inventors the exclusive Right to their respective Writings and Discoveries;

To constitute Tribunals inferior to the supreme Court;

To define and punish Piracies and Felonies committed on the high Seas, and Offences against the Law of Nations;

To declare War, grant Letters of Marque and Reprisal, and make Rules concerning Captures on Land and Water;

To raise and support Armies, but no Appropriation of Money to that Use shall be for a longer Term than two Years;

To provide and maintain a Navy;

To make Rules for the Government and Regulation of the land and naval Forces;

To provide for calling forth the Militia to execute the Laws of the Union, suppress Insurrections and repel Invasions;

To provide for organizing, arming, and disciplining, the Militia, and for governing such Part of them as may be employed in the Service of the United States, reserving to the States respectively, the Appointment of the Officers, and the Authority of training the Militia according to the discipline prescribed by Congress;

To exercise exclusive Legislation in all Cases whatsoever, over such District (not exceeding ten Miles square) as may, by Cession of particular States, and the Acceptance of Congress, become the Seat of the Government of the United States, and to exercise like Authority over all Places purchased by the Consent of the Legislature of the State in which the Same shall be, for the Erection of Forts, Magazines, Arsenals, dock-Yards and other needful Buildings;—And

To make all Laws which shall be necessary and proper for carrying into Execution the foregoing Powers, and all other Powers vested by this Constitution in the Government of the United States, or in any Department or Officer thereof.

SECTION. 9.   The Migration or Importation of such Persons as any of the States now existing shall think proper to admit, shall not be prohibited by the Congress prior to the Year one thousand eight hundred and eight, but a Tax or duty may be imposed on such Importation, not exceeding ten dollars for each Person.

The Privilege of the Writ of Habeas Corpus shall not be suspended, unless when in Cases of Rebellion or Invasion the public Safety may require it.

No Bill of Attainder or ex post facto Law shall be passed.

No Capitation, or other direct, Tax shall be laid, [unless in Proportion to the Census or Enumeration herein before directed to be taken.][5]

No Tax or Duty shall be laid on Articles exported from any State.

No Preference shall be given by any Regulation of Commerce or Revenue to the Ports of one State over those of another; nor shall Vessels bound to, or from, one State, be obliged to enter, clear, or pay Duties in another.

No Money shall be drawn from the Treasury, but in Consequence of Appropriations made by Law; and a regular Statement and Account of the Receipts and Expenditures of all public Money shall be published from time to time.

No Title of Nobility shall be granted by the United States: And no Person holding any Office of Profit or Trust under them, shall, without the Consent of the Congress, accept of any present, Emolument, Office, or Title, of any kind whatever, from any King, Prince, or foreign State.

SECTION. 10.   No State shall enter into any Treaty, Alliance, or Confederation; grant Letters of Marque and Reprisal; coin Money; emit Bills of Credit; make any Thing but gold and silver Coin a Tender in Payment of Debts; pass any Bill of Attainder, ex post facto Law, or Law impairing the Obligation of Contracts, or grant any Title of Nobility.

No State shall, without the Consent of the Congress, lay any Imposts or Duties on Imports or Exports, except what may be absolutely necessary for executing it's inspection Laws: and the net Produce of all Duties and Imposts, laid by any State on Imports or Exports, shall be for the Use of the Treasury of the United States; and all such Laws shall be subject to the Revision and Control of the Congress.

No State shall, without the Consent of Congress, lay any Duty of Tonnage, keep Troops, or Ships of War in time of Peace, enter into any Agreement or Compact with another State, or with a foreign Power, or engage in War, unless actually invaded, or in such imminent Danger as will not admit of delay.

Article. II

SECTION. 1.   The executive Power shall be vested in a President of the United States of America. He shall hold his Office during the Term of four Years, and, together with the Vice President, chosen for the same Term, be elected, as follows:

Each State shall appoint, in such Manner as the Legislature thereof may direct, a Number of Electors, equal to the whole Number of Senators and Representatives to which the State may be entitled in the Congress: but no Senator or Representative, or Person holding an Office of Trust or Profit under the United States, shall be appointed an Elector.

[Sections on electoral college and amendments omitted.]

The Congress may determine the Time of choosing the Electors, and the Day on which they shall give their Votes; which Day shall be the same throughout the United States.

No Person except a natural born Citizen, or a Citizen of the United States, at the time of the Adoption of this Constitution, shall be eligible to the Office of President; neither shall any person be eligible to that Office who shall not have attained to the Age of thirty five Years, and been fourteen Years a Resident within the United States.

[In Case of the Removal of the President from Office, or of his Death, Resignation, or Inability to discharge the Powers and Duties of the said Office, the Same shall devolve on the Vice President, and the Congress may by Law provide for the Case of Removal, Death, Resignation or Inability, both of the President and Vice President, declaring what Officer shall then act as President, and such Officer shall act accordingly, until the Disability be removed, or a President shall be elected.][6]

The President shall, at stated Times, receive for his Services, a Compensation, which shall neither be increased nor diminished during the Period for which he shall have been elected, and he shall not receive within that Period any other Emolument from the United States, or any of them.

Before he enters on the Execution of his Office, he shall take the following Oath or Affirmation:—"I do solemnly swear (or affirm) that I will faithfully execute the Office of President of the United States, and will to the best of my Ability, preserve, protect and defend the Constitution of the United States."

SECTION. 2.   The President shall be Commander in Chief of the Army and Navy of the United States, and of the Militia of the several States, when called into the actual Service of the United States; he may require the Opinion, in writing, of the principal Officer in each of the executive Departments, upon any Subject relating to the Duties of their respective Offices, and he shall have Power to grant Reprieves and Pardons for Offenses against the United States, except in Cases of Impeachment.

He shall have Power, by and with the Advice and Consent of the Senate, to make Treaties, provided two thirds of the Senators present concur; and he shall nominate, and by and with the Advice and Consent of the Senate, shall appoint Ambassadors, other public Ministers and Consuls, Judges of the supreme Court, and all other Officers of the United States, whose Appointments are not herein otherwise provided for, and which shall be established by Law: but the Congress may by Law vest the Appointment of such inferior Officers, as they think proper, in the President alone, in the Courts of Law, or in the Heads of Departments.

The President shall have Power to fill up all Vacancies that may happen during the Recess of the Senate, by granting Commissions which shall expire at the End of their next Session.

SECTION. 3.   He shall from time to time give to the Congress Information of the State of the Union, and recommend to their Consideration such Measures as he shall judge necessary and expedient; he may, on extraordinary Occasions, convene both Houses, or either of them, and in Case of Disagreement between them, with Respect to the Time of Adjournment, he may adjourn them to such Time as he shall think proper; he shall receive Ambassadors and other public Ministers; he shall take Care that the Laws be faithfully executed, and shall Commission all the Officers of the United States.

SECTION. 4.   The President, Vice President and all civil Officers of the United States, shall be removed from Office on Impeachment for, and Conviction of, Treason, Bribery, or other high Crimes and Misdemeanors.

Article. III

SECTION. 1.   The judicial Power of the United States shall be vested in one supreme Court, and in such inferior Courts as the Congress may from time to time ordain and establish. The Judges, both of the supreme and inferior Courts, shall hold their Offices during good Behaviour, and shall, at stated Times, receive for their Services a Compensation, which shall not be diminished during their Continuance in Office.

SECTION. 2.   The judicial Power shall extend to all Cases, in Law and Equity, arising under this Constitution, the Laws of the United States, and Treaties made, or which shall be made, under their Authority;—to all Cases affecting Ambassadors, other public Ministers and Consuls;—to all Cases of admiralty and maritime Jurisdiction;—to Controversies to which the United States shall be a Party;—to Controversies between two or more States;—[between a State and Citizens of another State;—] between Citizens of different States;— between Citizens of the same State claiming Lands under Grants of different States, [and between a State, or the Citizens thereof, and foreign States, Citizens or Subjects.][7]

In all Cases affecting Ambassadors, other public Ministers and Consuls, and those in which a State shall be Party, the supreme Court shall have original Jurisdiction. In all the other Cases before mentioned, the supreme Court shall have appellate Jurisdiction, both as to Law and Fact, with such Exceptions, and under such Regulations as the Congress shall make.

The Trial of all Crimes, except in Cases of Impeachment, shall be by Jury; and such Trial shall be held in the State where the said Crimes shall have been committed; but when not committed within any State, the Trial shall be at such Place or Places as the Congress may by Law have directed.

SECTION. 3.   Treason against the United States, shall consist only in levying War against them, or in adhering to their Enemies, giving them Aid and Comfort. No Person shall be convicted of Treason unless on the Testimony of two Witnesses to the same overt Act, or on Confession in open Court.

The Congress shall have Power to declare the Punishment of Treason, but no Attainder of Treason shall work Corruption of Blood, or Forfeiture except during the Life of the Person attainted.

Article. IV

SECTION. 1.   Full Faith and Credit shall be given in each State to the public Acts, Records, and judicial Proceedings of every other State. And the Congress may by general Laws prescribe the Manner in which such Acts, Records and Proceedings shall be proved, and the Effect thereof.

SECTION. 2.   The Citizens of each State shall be entitled to all Privileges and Immunities of Citizens in the several States.

A Person charged in any State with Treason, Felony, or other Crime, who shall flee from Justice, and be found in another State, shall on Demand of the executive Authority of the State from which he fled, be delivered up, to be removed to the State having Jurisdiction of the Crime.

[No Person held to Service or Labour in one State, under the Laws thereof, escaping into another, shall, in Consequence of any Law or Regulation therein, be discharged from such Service or Labour, but shall be delivered up on Claim of the Party to whom such Service or Labour may be due.][8]

SECTION. 3.   New States may be admitted by the Congress into this Union; but no new State shall be formed or erected within the Jurisdiction of any other State; nor any State be formed by the Junction of two or more States, or Parts of States, without the Consent of the Legislatures of the States concerned as well as of the Congress.

The Congress shall have Power to dispose of and make all needful Rules and Regulations respecting the Territory or other Property belonging to the United States; and nothing in this Constitution shall be so construed as to Prejudice any Claims of the United States, or of any particular State.

SECTION. 4.   The United States shall guarantee to every State in this Union a Republican Form of Government, and shall protect each of them against Invasion; and on Application of the Legislature, or of the Executive (when the Legislature cannot be convened), against domestic Violence.

Article. V

The Congress, whenever two thirds of both Houses shall deem it necessary, shall propose Amendments to this Constitution, or, on the Application of the Legislatures of two thirds of the several States, shall call a Convention for proposing Amendments, which, in either Case, shall be valid to all Intents and Purposes, as Part of this Constitution, when ratified by the Legislatures of three fourths of the several States, or by Conventions in three fourths thereof, as the one or the other Mode of Ratification may be proposed by the Congress; Provided that no Amendment which may be made prior to the Year One thousand eight hundred and eight shall in any Manner affect the first and fourth Clauses in the Ninth Section of the first Article; and that no State, without its Consent, shall be deprived of its equal Suffrage in the Senate.

Article. VI

All Debts contracted and Engagements entered into, before the Adoption of this Constitution, shall be as valid against the United States under this Constitution, as under the Confederation.

This Constitution, and the Laws of the United States which shall be made in Pursuance thereof; and all Treaties made, or which shall be made, under the Authority of the United States, shall be the supreme Law of the Land; and the Judges in every State shall be bound thereby, any Thing in the Constitution or Laws of any State to the Contrary notwithstanding.

The Senators and Representatives before mentioned, and the Members of the several State Legislatures and all executive and judicial Officers, both of the United States and of the several States, shall be bound by Oath or Affirmation, to support this Constitution; but no religious Test shall ever be required as a Qualification to any Office or public Trust under the United States.

Article. VII

The Ratification of the Conventions of nine States, shall be sufficient for the Establishment of this Constitution between the States so ratifying the Same.

Done in Convention by the Unanimous Consent of the States present the Seventeenth Day of September in the Year of our Lord one thousand seven hundred and Eighty seven and of the Independence of the United States of America the Twelfth In Witness whereof We have hereunto subscribed our Names, [Signers omitted.]

AMENDMENTS TO THE CONSTITUTION OF THE UNITED STATES OF AMERICA

Amendment I[9]

Congress shall make no law respecting an establishment of religion, or prohibiting the free exercise thereof; or abridging the freedom of speech, or of the press; or the right of the people peaceably to assemble, and to petition the Government for a redress of grievances.

Amendment II

A well regulated Militia, being necessary to the security of a free State, the right of the people to keep and bear Arms, shall not be infringed.

Amendment III

No Soldier shall, in time of peace be quartered in any house, without the consent of the Owner, nor in time of war, but in a manner to be prescribed by law.

Amendment IV

The right of the people to be secure in their persons, houses, papers, and effects, against unreasonable searches and seizures, shall not be violated, and no Warrants shall issue, but upon probable cause, supported by Oath or affirmation, and particularly describing the place to be searched, and the persons or things to be seized.

Amendment V

No person shall be held to answer for a capital, or otherwise infamous crime, unless on a presentment or indictment of a Grand Jury, except in cases arising in the land or naval forces, or in the Militia, when in actual service in time of War or public danger; nor shall any person be subject for the same offense to be twice put in jeopardy of life or limb; nor shall be compelled in any criminal case to be a witness against himself, nor be deprived of life, liberty, or property, without due process of law; nor shall private property be taken for public use, without just compensation.

Amendment VI

In all criminal prosecutions, the accused shall enjoy the right to a speedy and public trial, by an impartial jury of the State and district wherein the crime shall have been committed, which district shall have been previously ascertained by law, and to be informed of the nature and cause of the accusation; to be confronted with the witnesses against him; to have compulsory process for obtaining witnesses in his favor, and to have the Assistance of Counsel for his defence.

Amendment VII

In Suits at common law, where the value in controversy shall exceed twenty dollars, the right of trial by jury shall be preserved, and no fact tried by a jury, shall be otherwise re-examined in any Court of the United States, than according to the rules of the common law.

Amendment VIII

Excessive bail shall not be required, nor excessive fines imposed, nor cruel and unusual punishments inflicted.

Amendment IX

The enumeration in the Constitution, of certain rights, shall not be construed to deny or disparage others retained by the people.

Amendment X

The powers not delegated to the United States by the Constitution, nor prohibited by it to the States, are reserved to the States respectively, or to the people.

Amendment XI[10]

The Judicial power of the United States shall not be construed to extend to any suit in law or equity, commenced or prosecuted against one of the United States by Citizens of another State, or by Citizens or Subjects of any Foreign State.

Amendment XII

[Amends procedures for selection of the president; superseded by the Twentieth Amendment.]

Amendment XIII[11]

SECTION. 1. Neither slavery nor involuntary servitude, except as a punishment for crime whereof the party shall have been duly convicted, shall exist within the United States, or any place subject to their jurisdiction.

SECTION. 2. Congress shall have power to enforce this article by appropriate legislation.

Amendment XIV[12]

SECTION. 1. All persons born or naturalized in the United States, and subject to the jurisdiction thereof, are citizens of the United States and of the State wherein they reside. No State shall make or enforce any law which shall abridge the privileges or immunities of citizens of the United States; nor shall any State deprive any person of life, liberty, or property, without due process of law; nor deny to any person within its jurisdiction the equal protection of the laws.

SECTION. 2. Representatives shall be apportioned among the several States according to their respective numbers, counting the whole number of persons in each State, excluding Indians not taxed. But when the right to vote at any election for the choice of electors for President and Vice President of the United States, Representatives in Congress, the Executive and Judicial officers of a State, or the members of the Legislature thereof, is denied to any of the male inhabitants of such State, being twenty-one years of age, and citizens of the United States, or in any way abridged, except for participation in rebellion, or other crime, the basis of representation therein shall be reduced in the proportion which the number of such male citizens shall bear to the whole number of male citizens twenty-one years of age in such State.

SECTION. 3. No person shall be a Senator or Representative in Congress, or elector of President and Vice-President, or hold any office, civil or military, under the United States, or under any State, who, having previously taken an oath, as a member of Congress, or as an officer of the United States, or as a member of any State legislature, or as an executive or judicial officer of any State, to support the Constitution of the United States, shall have engaged in insurrection or rebellion against the same, or given aid or comfort to the enemies thereof. But Congress may by a vote of two-thirds of each House, remove such disability.

SECTION. 4. The validity of the public debt of the United States, authorized by law, including debts incurred for payment of pensions and bounties for services in suppressing insurrection or rebellion, shall not be questioned. But neither the United States nor any State shall assume or pay any debt or obligation incurred in aid of insurrection or rebellion against the United States, or any claim for the loss or emancipation of any slave; but all such debts, obligations and claims shall be held illegal and void.

SECTION. 5. The Congress shall have power to enforce, by appropriate legislation, the provisions of this article.

Amendment XV[13]

SECTION. 1. The right of citizens of the United States to vote shall not be denied or abridged by the United States or by any State on account of race, color, or previous condition of servitude—

SECTION. 2. The Congress shall have power to enforce this article by appropriate legislation.
[Amendments 16 to 27 omitted.]

End Notes

1. Changed by section 2 of the Fourteenth Amendment.
2. Changed by the Seventeenth Amendment to allow popular election of senators.
3. Changed by the Seventeenth Amendment.
4. Changed by section 2 of the Twentieth Amendment.
5. Changed by the Sixteenth Amendment to allow for an income tax.
6. Changed by the Twenty-fifth Amendment.
7. Changed by the Eleventh Amendment to prohibit suits against state governments without their consent.

8. Changed by the Thirteenth Amendment.
9. The first ten amendments (the Bill of Rights) were ratified effective December 15, 1791.
10. The Eleventh Amendment was ratified February 7, 1795.
11. The Thirteenth Amendment was ratified December 6, 1865.
12. The Fourteenth Amendment was ratified July 9, 1868.
13. The Fifteenth Amendment was ratified February 3, 1870.

APPENDIX B
SELECTED JUSTICES OF THE SUPREME COURT

SUMMARY INFORMATION ABOUT SELECTED SUPREME COURT JUSTICES

Justice	President Appointing	Years of Service	Political Party	Positions and Noted Action in Criminal Procedure
John M. Harlan (I)	Hayes	1877–1911	Rep.	Championed total incorporation of Bill of Rights to apply to the states.
Oliver W. Holmes	T. Roosevelt	1902–1932	Rep.	*Moore v. Dempsey* (1923)—apply due process to state errors; *Olmstead v. U.S.* (1928) dissent.
Louis Brandeis	Wilson	1916–1939	Rep.	*Olmstead v. U.S.* (1928) dissent—classic statement of Rule of Law.
William H. Taft, CJ	Harding	1921–1930	Rep.	Conservative. *Olmstead v. U.S.* (1928)—wiretapping not covered by Fourth Amendment.
George Sutherland	Harding	1922–1938	Rep.	*Powell v. Alabama* (1932; Scottsboro case)—due process violated by lack of counsel.
Edward Sanford	Harding	1923–1930	Rep.	Wrote opinions incorporating First Amendment rights; advanced incorporation.
Harlan Fiske Stone	Coolidge	1925–1941	Rep.	Moderate. *U.S. v. Carolene Products Co.* (1938)—footnote 4 pointed to a civil rights agenda.
Benjamin Cardozo	Hoover	1932–1938	Dem.	Blocked advance of incorporation in *Palko v. Connecticut* (1937).
Hugo Black	F. Roosevelt	1937–1971	Dem.	Championed incorporation; dissent in *Adamson v. California* (1947); *Gideon v. Wainwright* (1963)—right to counsel.
Stanley Reed	F. Roosevelt	1938–1957	Dem.	Opposed incorporation; majority opinion in *Adamson v. California* (1947).
Felix Frankfurter	F. Roosevelt	1939–1962	Ind.	Conservative-moderate. Opposed incorporation; favored due process approach.
William Douglas	F. Roosevelt	1939–1975	Dem.	Liberal. Favored incorporation.
Frank Murphy	F. Roosevelt	1940–1949	Dem.	Liberal. Favored incorporation.
Harlan Fiske Stone, CJ	F. Roosevelt	1941–1946	Rep.	Moderate-liberal. Championed freedom of belief in flag-salute cases.
Robert Jackson	F. Roosevelt	1941–1954	Dem.	New Deal liberal. Close to Frankfurter in criminal procedure cases.
Wiley Rutledge	F. Roosevelt	1943–1949	Dem.	Liberal. Favored incorporation; classic definition of probable cause in *Brinegar v. U.S.* (1949).
Harold Burton	Truman	1945–1958	Rep.	Stalwart conservative.
Fred Vinson, CJ	Truman	1946–1953	Dem.	Stalwart conservative.
Tom Clark	Truman	1949–1967	Dem.	Conservative-moderate. Wrote majority opinion in *Mapp v. Ohio* (1961).
Sherman Minton	Truman	1949–1956	Dem.	Stalwart conservative.
Earl Warren, CJ	Eisenhower	1953–1969	Rep.	Liberal. Deep belief in fairness; authored *Miranda v. Arizona* (1966), *Terry v. Ohio* (1968).
John Harlan (II)	Eisenhower	1955–1971	Rep.	Conservative-moderate. Opposed incorporation; authored *Spinelli v. U.S.* (1969).
William Brennan	Eisenhower	1956–1990	Dem.	Liberal. Wrote many liberal dissents in Burger and Rehnquist Court eras.
Charles Whittaker	Eisenhower	1957–1962	Rep.	Stalwart conservative.
Potter Stewart	Eisenhower	1958–1981	Rep.	Moderate-conservative. Wrote many criminal procedure opinions.
Byron White	Kennedy	1962–1993	Dem.	Mixed. Wrote many criminal procedure opinions.

Justice	President Appointing	Years of Service	Political Party	Positions and Noted Action in Criminal Procedure
Arthur Goldberg	Kennedy	1962–1965	Dem.	Liberal. *U.S. v. Ventresca* (1965)—preference for search warrant.
Abe Fortas	L. Johnson	1965–1969	Dem.	Liberal. Major opinions for juvenile rights: *In re Gault* (1967).
Thurgood Marshall	L. Johnson	1967–1991	Dem.	Liberal. Wrote many liberal dissents in Burger and Rehnquist Court eras.
Warren Burger, CJ	Nixon	1969–1986	Rep.	Conservative. Initially opposed the exclusionary rule.
Harry Blackmun	Nixon	1970–1994	Rep.	Changed from conservative to liberal over time.
Lewis Powell	Nixon	1972–1987	Dem.	Conservative. Opinions limited access to courts on Fourth Amendment issues.
William Rehnquist	Nixon	1972–1986	Rep.	Conservative. Wrote many criminal procedure opinions.
John Paul Stevens	Ford	1975–	Rep.	Moderate. Has swung to liberal in criminal procedure.
Sandra Day O'Connor	Reagan	1981–2006	Rep.	Conservative. Joined some moderate, pro-defendant decisions.
Antonin Scalia	Reagan	1986–	Rep.	Conservative; originalist. Favors defendant regarding Confrontation Clause.
William Rehnquist, CJ	Reagan	1986–2005	Rep.	Conservative. Upheld *Miranda* rule after a career undermining it.
Anthony Kennedy	Reagan	1988–	Rep.	Conservative-moderate. Can join moderate, pro-defendant decisions.
William Souter	G. H. W. Bush	1990–2009	Rep.	Moderate-liberal. Moved from conservative to more liberal in criminal cases.
Clarence Thomas	G. H. W. Bush	1991–	Rep.	Ultra-conservative; originalist.
Ruth Bader Ginsburg	Clinton	1993–	Dem.	Moderate-liberal; pragmatic. Seeks fewer jurisdictional barriers for defendants.
Steven Breyer	Clinton	1994–	Dem.	Moderate-liberal. Takes conservative position in some cases.
John Roberts Jr., CJ	G. W. Bush	2005–	Rep.	Conservative. Dissent in *Georgia v. Randolph* (2006).
Samuel Alito	G. W. Bush	2006–	Rep.	Ultra-conservative; upholds *Batson* protection for minorities.
Sonia Sotomayor	B. H. Obama	2009–	Dem.	No cases at time of publication; likely to be moderate liberal.

GLOSSARY

Absolute immunity Rule that a party need not answer in law to civil claim or wrongdoing, based on the function the party has performed; applies to witnesses in regard to their testimony, judges performing judicial duties, and prosecutors performing essential prosecutorial duties. Immunity is claimed before trial in a motion for summary judgment.

Abuse of discretion A high standard for an appellate court to reverse the decision of a lower court where the trial court was lawfully invested with discretion. It does not imply an intentional wrong or act of bad faith, just that the exercise of discretion was clearly against logic.

Accusatorial trial The type of trial that is at the heart of the Anglo-American or common law system of adjudication. Key elements: the judge is an impartial referee; lawyers control the presentation of evidence; witnesses are cross-examined; innocence is presumed; the prosecutor must prove guilt beyond a reasonable doubt; the privilege against self-incrimination protects the defendant from testifying; facts are conclusively determined by a citizen jury.

Actual border For purposes of border search cases, stops that are made at or very near to the actual border between the United States and a neighboring nation. Border searches may also take place further inland, either at fixed checkpoints or by roving patrols.

Actual imprisonment rule Counsel is an absolute Sixth Amendment requirement for the trial of a misdemeanor only if the defendant has been actually imprisoned after conviction.

Actual mobility The automobile exception to the search warrant requirement applies to vehicles that are actually capable of being driven.

Ad hoc Literally, "for this." For a special purpose without application to a general purpose. For example, an *ad hoc* rule is intended to apply to only the particular circumstances at hand and is not intended to be a general rule.

Adequate and independent state grounds A state court ruling concerning the rights of a suspect that is based exclusively on state constitutional grounds cannot be disturbed by a federal court as long as the state constitutional ruling does not fall below the minimum standards of the Fourteenth Amendment Due Process Clause. To determine whether a state ruling is based on state or federal grounds, where the ruling discussed both federal and state law, the Supreme Court examines it to determine if the holding is based on adequate and independent state grounds. See also *judicial federalism.*

Adjudicate To judge a case; to resolve an issue in the exercise of judicial authority.

Administrative search The entry and search of a premises by a government officer who is enforcing a government regulation regarding public health or safety rather than a police search for people or items in relation to the enforcement of the criminal law.

Admission Statements made by a party that acknowledge the existence of certain facts. Compare *confession.*

Adversarial trial See *accusatorial trial.*

Adverse comment A comment by the judge or prosecutor to a jury in a criminal case, pointing out that the defendant did not take the witness stand.

Advisory opinion An opinion issued by a court at the request of the government or a party indicating how it would rule on an issue were it to arise in litigation. Some state supreme courts issue advisory opinions. The U.S. Supreme Court does not issue such opinions because its jurisdiction is limited by Article III, Section 2, of the Constitution to "cases and controversies."

Affiant The person who makes and subscribes an affidavit.

Affidavit A written declaration or statement of facts made voluntarily and confirmed by oath before a person with the authority to take such an oath.

Affirm To uphold the ruling of a lower court.

Agent provocateur Police undercover agent who infiltrates a criminal or a legitimate organization with the intention of stimulating members of the organization to commit illegal or violent acts.

Anticipatory warrant A search warrant authorized by the Federal Rules of Criminal Procedure that may be issued on probable cause that evidence will be located in a particular place on the date of execution. See also *controlled delivery.*

Antifederalists Those opposed to the ratification of the Constitution in 1788 on the grounds that it created too much central power.

Appearance bond See *bail bond.*

Appellate decision The outcome of an appellate court trial; an appellate court may affirm, modify, reverse, and remand the decisions of a lower court.

Appellate opinion See *opinion.*

Appointed counsel A lawyer for an indigent defendant, appointed by the court on an informal basis through organized lists established by a local bar association or by the court. The lawyer is paid by the county according to a fee schedule for work performed. Also called "assigned counsel."

Arraignment The procedure whereby a defendant is brought before a court to plead to a criminal charge.

Arrest To deprive a person of liberty by legal authority; an arrest occurs in law when a person is taken into custody by government officers, even if the purpose is for investigation or harassment. It is not necessary for a booking to occur for an arrest to be made. An arrest may be made with or without a warrant.

Arrest warrant Judicial warrant concluding that probable cause exists supporting the belief that a crime has been committed, and that the named person has committed it, and authorizing law enforcement to take the suspect into custody. An arrest warrant is required, except for an exigency, if officers must enter the home of the person to be arrested.

Asset forfeiture Laws that authorize the forfeiture of noncontraband assets used in and money derived from the commission of certain crimes. The assets may be seized as of the time the crime was committed and thus be denied to lawyers representing defendants whose assets are forfeited.

Assigned counsel See *appointed counsel.*

Assizes General trial courts in England and France.

Attenuation An exception to the "fruits of the poisonous tree" doctrine. It comes into play when the link between the initial illegality and the evidence sought to be introduced has become so weak or tenuous that the "fruits" have become "untainted."

Authorized imprisonment rule A position that counsel should be absolutely guaranteed by the Sixth Amendment in all misdemeanor trials where the statutory penalty allows for imprisonment. This rule was rejected by the Supreme Court.

Automobile search An exception to the requirement that a search of an effect be authorized in advance by a judicial search warrant, based on the exigency of a mobile vehicle and on the lower expectation of privacy accorded to automobiles. The officer must have probable cause to believe there is contraband in the automobile. Also called the "vehicle exception."

Bail To procure the release of a person charged with a crime by ensuring his or her further attendance in court; this is done by having the person pledge or deposit something of value that will be returned when he or she appears in court and/or by having a third party agree to be responsible for the return of the person.

Bail bond A bond (an "instrument" or written promise to pay money) that is executed by a third party promising to forfeit money to the court if the defendant who is released on bail does not appear for further criminal proceedings. Also called an "appearance bond."

Bail bondsman A businessperson who receives a portion of the bail amount from a defendant, usually 10 percent, and posts a bail bond with the court promising to pay the full bail amount if the defendant does not return to court as required. The bail bondsman is responsible for ensuring the appearance of the defendant in court.

Balancing of interests See *balancing test.*

Balancing test A widely used phrase in criminal procedure, especially in Fourth Amendment adjudication, referring to the attempt of appellate courts to balance the needs of effective law enforcement against the privacy rights of individuals.

Beeper An electronic device that emits a signal indicating its location. It may be used by agents to track the movement of a vehicle or object.

Bench In law, a term for the court or the judge. For an appellate court, the bench consists of all the judges on the court or who are sitting on a panel of the court.

Bench trial A trial without a jury. The judge (who sits on the "bench") is the trier of both the facts and the law. In a jury trial, on the other hand, the judge is the finder only of legal issues, and the jury is the finder of the facts. Also called "waiver trial."

Bill of attainder A special act of a legislature passing the death penalty or other penalty on a person without recourse to standard judicial proceedings. In England, attainder led to the entire estate of a person convicted of a felony or treason being forfeited to the Crown. The U.S. Constitution (Art. I, §§ 9 and 10) forbids the federal government and the states from passing bills of attainder.

Bill of particulars A form of discovery in which the prosecution sets forth the time, place, manner, and means of the commission of the crime as alleged in the complaint or indictment.

Bill of Rights A designation for the first ten amendments to the U.S. Constitution.

Bind-over decision The decision of the judge, at the conclusion of the preliminary examination, as to whether there is sufficient evidence to establish probable cause that the defendant committed the crime and to "bind the defendant over,"—that is, to require him or her to go to trial.

***Bivens* suit** A federal tort suit by a person against federal officers alleged to have violated the person's Fourth Amendment rights; created in *Bivens v. Six Unknown Named Agents* (1971).

Body cavity search Procedure whereby authorized law enforcement or correctional personnel conduct a visual inspection of oral, genital, or anal areas for contraband. Also called "strip search."

Booking An administrative process conducted by police officials that typically follows an arrest and includes recording the suspect's name and identifying information; photographing, fingerprinting, and searching the suspect; and inventorying the suspect's personal property.

Border The international boundary of a nation. For purposes of law, immigration, and customs searches, the border includes international airports, inland ports, and fixed checkpoints remote from the actual boundary.

Border search A search at the national border by immigration officers for illegal immigrants and by customs officers for contraband, criminals, fugitives, and terrorists.

Brevity requirement A rule under *Terry v. Ohio* (1968) that a "stop and frisk" be concluded quickly, or in just enough time for an officer to confirm or dispel whether the officer's reasonable suspicion constitutes probable cause. The brevity requirement has been strictly interpreted by the Supreme Court.

Brief A written argument presented to a trial or appellate court by a lawyer to support the attorney's position on legal issues. Briefs can be as long as fifty to one hundred pages. Appellate briefs are accompanied with the record on appeal and may include the trial transcript.

Briefing a case Taking notes that abstract the essential points of an opinion, especially the facts, legal issues, holding, and reasons for the holding.

Bright-line rule A clear-cut and easy-to-apply standard established by a court to distinguish legal categories.

Bug An electronic listening device that is placed surreptitiously to overhear conversations.

Burger Court The Supreme Court during the period that Warren Burger was chief justice of the United States (1969 to 1986); a moderately conservative period in criminal procedure.

Capital crime In common law, a crime punishable with death. Today, in some states, it includes crimes punishable with life imprisonment. Under the laws of some states, bail may be denied to defendants charged with capital crimes.

Case law See *common law.*

Case of first impression A law case in which the issue to be decided has never been resolved by an appellate court.

Caveat A warning to be careful.

Certiorari, writ of A writ used by the U.S. Supreme Court to determine in its discretion which filed cases it will hear and decide.

Challenge for cause In the voir dire, the ability of one of the sides to request the judge to dismiss a prospective juror because the juror has indicated a bias. The number of challenges for cause are unlimited.

Chancery English court established under the king's chancellor to do equity or to decide cases according to rules of justice rather than under formal writs of common law courts of Common Pleas and King's Bench. Over time, chancery courts became part of the common law court system. Common law courts render money judgments as legal remedies, whereas equity or chancery courts grant "equitable relief,"—that is, orders requiring that a party perform or cease some activity. Most American states merged courts of law and equity; a few still have separate chancery or equity courts. Also called "equity."

Character witness A witness whose testimony in a trial vouches for the defendant's good moral character, based on the witness's personal knowledge and the defendant's reputation in the community. Such testimony usually does not add any substantial facts of the case.

Charging The process by which the prosecutor decides which offenses to formally prefer, or "charge," against a suspect in either a prosecutor's information or an indictment.

Checks and balances A political and constitutional doctrine for maintaining balanced government by giving different branches of government the power to limit the authority of other branches in specified ways. This doctrine is closely related to the separation of powers doctrine.

Citizen's arrest An arrest made by a person who is not a law enforcement officer. If the arrest is in error (i.e., no crime was committed or the wrong person was arrested), the citizen who made the arrest is subject to a civil suit for false arrest, even if probable cause existed.

Civil law system The legal system of the nations of Europe, Latin America, Africa, and Asia (except for England and former British colonies). The civil law system is found primarily in codes, and trials follow the inquisitorial model. It is contrasted to the common law system.

Civil rights function One of two broad functions of criminal procedure law: to protect the civil rights of suspects and defendants. Compare *facilitating function*.

Civil War amendments The Thirteenth, Fourteenth, and Fifteenth Amendments to the Constitution, ratified in 1866, 1868, and 1870, respectively. Also called the "Reconstruction amendments."

Class action A lawsuit filed by one or more persons on behalf of a group of individuals all having the same grievance. Also called a representative action.

Collateral proceeding Not a direct appeal from a conviction on a point of law, but instead a second "appeal," not of right. Habeas corpus proceedings are collateral proceedings.

Common law In England, America, and other common law countries (e.g., Australia, Canada, and India), law is created by judges through appellate court opinions. Also called "case law" or "precedent" because the rule established in one case becomes a binding precedent on later courts. The term arose because the law created by royal judges was common to all of England. Common law is subordinate to legislation.

Common law trial system See *accusatorial trial*.

Companion case A case decided along with another case. Companion cases may be consolidated into one case.

Compulsion A person is protected by the Fifth Amendment against being "compelled in any criminal case to be a witness against himself." The Fifth Amendment applies only if evidence is obtained by compulsion, as by a court order or a grand jury subpoena. Fifth Amendment compulsion in the law of confessions, under *Miranda*, is supplied by in-custody police interrogation, which is inherently compelling. See also *self-incrimination rule*.

Compulsory process A subpoena to produce witnesses or real evidence. The compulsory process is a right guaranteed to defendants by the Sixth Amendment.

Confession A statement made by one person to another, admitting guilt of an offense and disclosing facts about the crime and the person's role in it. A confession may include inculpatory or exculpatory statements. Compare *admission*.

Conflict of interest In regard to the right to counsel, a conflict of interest most typically arises when, as a result of multiple representation, an attorney must sacrifice a defense strategy for one defendant to better defend another defendant. See also *multiple representation*.

Confrontation Clause The provision of the Sixth Amendment that, in all criminal prosecutions, "the accused shall enjoy the right ... to be confronted with the witnesses against him."

Consent The voluntary agreement of one person who has the capacity to make an agreement of free will to do an act proposed by another. In the administration of criminal justice, a suspect or defendant can consent to cooperate with police or prosecutors. More specifically, a person can consent to a search or seizure of an area over which the person has an expectation of privacy. See also *waiver*.

Consent search A search made by a police officer after a person has given consent to the search. Consent to search validates a warrantless search or a search made without probable cause.

Constitutionalism A political theory of balanced government. Modern constitutionalism includes the concepts of civil rights and the Rule of Law.

Constitutionally protected area Obsolete test to determine if the Fourth Amendment applies to protect a person whose privacy has been invaded by government officers; replaced by the "expectation of privacy" doctrine announced in *Katz v. United States* (1968).

Contempt of court An act calculated to embarrass, hinder, or obstruct a court in the administration of justice. A judge may punish contempt of court with a fine or imprisonment.

Continuance A delay in legal proceedings granted by the judge.

Contraband Any property that is illegal either to produce or to possess, such as controlled substances or untaxed, smuggled goods.

Controlled delivery A law enforcement technique by which contraband is intercepted and then delivered to the suspected criminal party under police surveillance. "Anticipatory warrants" may be issued in cases where controlled deliveries are set up.

Counsel Lawyer. The term is used interchangeably with *lawyer, attorney,* and *attorney-at-law*.

Court of general jurisdiction A trial court with jurisdiction to try all matters, including felonies; typically called a "superior" or "circuit court."

Court of limited jurisdiction A trial court whose jurisdiction is limited by statute to certain matters—usually to civil cases where the amount in dispute is below a certain amount (e.g., $10,000), to the dispositions of misdemeanors, and to conducting the preliminary phases of a felony case before binding over the case to a court of general jurisdiction for trial.

Covert facilitation See *encouragement*.

Crime Control Model A theory developed by Herbert Packer that suggests that within a constitutional system of criminal justice, there are two general attitudes. The Crime Control Model stresses crime control, efficiency, a presumption of guilt, and finality. Compare *Due Process Model*.

Crime scene investigation exception A Fourth Amendment exception, which the Supreme Court has refused to create, to allow police, without warrant, to remain beyond the time of the exigency, on the premises where a crime has been committed, for purposes of conducting an investigation of the premises.

Criminal law approach In the law of entrapment, the majority rule, known also as the "subjective test." It is based on the legal fiction that the legislature did not intend the statute to apply to those who were not predisposed to commit the crime but were induced to do so by the police.

Criminal procedure approach In regard to the law of entrapment, another term for the objective test, which is the minority rule of entrapment.

Critical stage The point in criminal proceedings when counsel is constitutionally required because, at that point, rights may be lost, defenses waived, or privileges claimed or waived that can affect the outcome of the case.

Cross-examination The examination of a witness at a trial or hearing by the party opposed to the side that produced the witness. Cross-examination occurs after direct examination and is used to test the truth of the witness, to further develop the evidence, or for other purposes.

Cruel trilemma Three negative consequences faced by a witness who is asked a question that may prove to be incriminating: self-accusation, perjury, or the risk of being held in contempt of court for refusing to testify.

Curtilage The area around a house protected by the Fourth Amendment. The curtilage includes the area under the eaves of the main house; within the fenced-in area around the house; and various small structures that are near the main house, such as a garage, shed, or smokehouse. Compare *open fields*.

Custodial arrest When a police officer arrests a person for a crime that authorizes the officer to take the suspect into custody, the officer may perform a complete search incident to arrest.

Custody The keeping, guarding, care, watch, inspection, preservation, or security of a thing or person. The custody of a person is a prerequisite for a Fourth Amendment seizure under *California v. Hodari D.* (1991).

Damages Monetary compensation awarded by a court in a civil case to compensate a party for losses.

Decoy In entrapment law, an officer who poses as a potential victim (usually of a crime of violence such as a street robbery) and waits to be attacked in order to arrest the perpetrator.

Deficient performance The first prong of the rule that the ineffective assistance of counsel in a criminal trial violates the Sixth Amendment rights of the defendant. The deficient performance of an attorney is an objective standard determined by what constitutes reasonably effective assistance according to prevailing norms of legal practice.

De minimis Shorthand for *de minimis non curat lex*: The law does not take notice of very small or trifling matters. In other words, a technical violation of a law that results in trifling or purely theoretical injury may not be recognized by a court.

Democracy A political philosophy that emphasizes the participation of all citizens in government decisions on an equal basis, either directly or by representation. It is a value that underlies constitutional criminal procedure.

De novo review A rehearing of an issue that does not take into consideration findings made at an earlier hearing.

De novo trial See *trial de novo*.

Deposit bond A bail bond that is executed by the defendant. Under the laws of several states, the defendant puts up 10 percent of the bail amount, which is returned, except for a 1 percent fee, when the defendant returns to court for the trial.

Derivative evidence In the Fourth and Fifth Amendment context, evidence that police obtain on the basis of illegally seized evidence. Under the "fruits of the poisonous tree" doctrine, derivative evidence must be excluded from trial and cannot be used to prove the guilt of the defendant.

Dictum An abbreviated form of *obiter dictum*: a "remark by the way"—that is, a remark by a judge in an opinion, commenting on the legal rule of the case, that is not essential to the determination of the holding or decision and therefore does not have weight as precedent.

Direct examination In a trial or case-in-chief, the first stage in the process of obtaining evidence from a witness, by questioning by the party or attorney for the party who has called the witness. Its purpose is to establish facts that will support the prosecution's or defendant's contentions. It is usually improper to ask a witness leading questions on direct examination, unless the witness's testimony turns against the party and permission is obtained from the judge to treat the witness as a hostile witness.

Discovery A set of practices in both civil and criminal trial procedure that allows both sides to obtain factual evidence in the possession of the other side. Discovery is designed to encourage settlements or to prevent surprises at the trial so as to avoid delays. There is no constitutional right to discovery in criminal cases.

Disgorgement A theory of jurisprudence stating that a person who has wrongfully obtained goods should be made to give them up.

Disseised In English and medieval land law, to be dispossessed of one's land. See also *novel disseisin*.

Diversity of citizenship jurisdiction Article III of the Constitution allows federal courts to hear cases between "citizens" of different states.

Domestic tranquility A phrase in the Preamble to the Constitution of the United States. It recognizes that maintaining public safety is a fundamental purpose of government.

Dossier French for "a bundle of papers"; a report on an individual.

Drug courier profile A set of behavioral characteristics developed by the Drug Enforcement Agency to identify people who are likely to be surreptitiously transporting illegal drugs. The profile itself, even if it consists entirely of innocent actions, constitutes a basis for finding that reasonable suspicion exists.

Due process approach In constitutional criminal procedure, a philosophy on the part of Supreme Court justices that errors in state criminal procedure that constitute grossly unfair and unjust proceedings can be reviewed by the federal courts under the Due Process Clause of the Fourteenth Amendment. The term also conveys the idea that a decision made under this approach does not necessarily produce bright-line rules because every case is decided on the totality of its facts and circumstances.

Due Process Clause A clause found in the Fifth and Fourteenth Amendments saying that no person shall be deprived of life, liberty, or property without due process of law. The Fifth Amendment clause applies against the federal government, and the Fourteenth Amendment clause against state governments.

Due process defense In entrapment law, the theory that entrapment may be established by police conduct that was so outrageous as to violate the Due Process Clause.

Due Process Model One of two general attitudes within a constitutional system of criminal justice, as identified in a theory by Herbert Packer. The Due Process Model stresses formal, adjudicative, adversary fact-finding, the prevention and elimination of mistakes, legal (as opposed to actual) guilt, and viewing the presumption of innocence to mean that every suspect must be treated as if he or she were innocent. Compare *Crime Control Model*.

Due process revolution The period from 1961 to 1969 when most of the criminal provisions of the Bill of Rights were incorporated. See also *incorporation doctrine*.

Dying declaration In the law of evidence, an exception to the hearsay rule that allows a witness to testify to the statement of a dying person on the theory that a person who believes that he or she is about to die will not lie.

Egalitarianism A political theory that supports the eradication of legal and social distinctions between citizens. Egalitarianism is an ideal of American republicanism and has been a force behind the expansion of rights, such as the right of all citizens to serve on juries; it is a value that underlies constitutional criminal procedure. Also called "equality."

Emergency aid doctrine An exigency that authorizes a police officer to enter a home without a search warrant where the officer reasonably believes that persons in the house are in imminent danger to life or limb. The officer may seize contraband in plain view but is not authorized to conduct a search beyond what is necessary to come to the aid of persons at risk.

En banc An appellate case heard and decided by the entire appellate bench rather than by a panel of judges drawn from the entire bench.

Encouragement A police investigatory activity designed to create a criminal opportunity for offenders who commit crimes that are difficult to detect, but without inducing them to commit the crime. Compare *entrapment*.

Enhancement device A mechanism that is used to enhance the natural senses of a law enforcement officer to detect contraband. Enhancement devices may include flashlights, binoculars, and sophisticated electronic listening and thermal detection devices.

Entrapment An act of police officers or government agents inducing a person to commit a crime for the purpose of arresting and prosecuting the person. Also, a criminal defense. Compare *encouragement*.

Equality See *egalitarianism*.

Equal Protection Clause The guarantee in Section 1 of the Fourteenth Amendment that "[n]o state shall … deny to any person within its jurisdiction the equal protection of the laws." This right can be enforced by federal courts and by congressional legislation.

Equity See *chancery*.

Exclusionary rule A legal rule stating that illegally obtained evidence may not be used in legal proceedings. The exclusionary rule may be created by common law (e.g., to the exclusionary rule for coerced confessions), constitutional adjudication (e.g., the Fourth Amendment exclusionary rule established in *Weeks v. United States* [1914]), or by statute (e.g., the exclusionary rule for illegal electronic eavesdropping).

Exculpatory Tending to justify, excuse, or clear the defendant from alleged fault or guilt. Compare *inculpatory*.

Exigency Generally, an emergency requiring immediate action; something that is pressing or urgent. In Fourth Amendment law, an exigency is an emergency that gives rise to an exception to the warrant requirement.

Exigency exception In search and seizure law, police can intrude on areas and things normally protected by the expectation of privacy without a warrant when an emergency exists and the police intrusion or action is a reasonable response to the emergency.

Exoneration Unlike a not guilty verdict, which establishes that the prosecution has not proved its case beyond a reasonable doubt and may leave the lingering doubt that the legally innocent person may have been "factually guilty," an exoneration means that the defendant or a convicted person is factually innocent. Official exonerations of prisoners occur when a governor's pardon, a post-appeal dismissal of charges by a prosecutor, a post-appeal dismissal of charges by a court based on a defense motion (often joined by the prosecution), or a posthumous exoneration is declared explicitly on the grounds of factual innocence. Many preciously convicted prisoners who have been released (for example, after acquittal in a second trial) and are considered to have been wrongfully convicted are not officially exonerated.

Ex parte On one side only. A judicial hearing is *ex parte* when it occurs at the request of one party in the absence of the other party.

Expectation of privacy The basis for determining the existence of Fourth Amendment rights under *Katz v. United States* (1967).

Expert witness A witness who, by reason of specialized education or experience, possesses superior knowledge regarding a subject about which people having no particular training are incapable of forming an accurate opinion. A witness who is qualified as an expert is allowed to assist the jury in understanding complicated or technical subjects and may be allowed to answer hypothetical questions.

Ex post facto law A criminal law passed after the occurrence of an act that retrospectively changes the legal consequences by making an innocent act criminal, by increasing the penalty for the act, or by changing rules of evidence, making it easier to obtain a conviction. Article I, §§ 9 and 10, of the U.S. Constitution prohibits the federal and state governments from creating such laws.

Extraterritorial Beyond the physical and juridical boundaries of a particular state or nation. Laws may have extraterritorial effect.

Eyewitness A person who saw the act, fact, or transaction to which he or she testifies. An eyewitness may be distinguished from an earwitness (*auritus*), but for purposes of the law of identification, similar rules apply.

Facial attack A legal challenge to the constitutionality of a statute "on its face," or in every way in which the statute may be applied. Statutes may also be challenged "as applied," a narrower attack claiming that the statute is unconstitutional only if applied in a certain way.

Facilitating function One of two broad functions of criminal procedure law: to facilitate prosecution. Compare *civil rights function*.

Fair cross section See *representative cross section*.

False arrest An arrest that is not based upon probable cause. Evidence seized as the result of a false arrest is inadmissible. A false arrest is a basis for a civil action against a peace officer who made the arrest.

Federalism The division and relationship of power between the state and federal governments.

Federalists Those favoring the ratification of the Constitution in 1788; those favoring a strong federal government. This group emerged as the political party of Presidents George Washington and John Adams; Chief Justice John Marshall was a prominent Federalist.

Field interrogation The police practice of ordering people to briefly stop and answer questions in regard to suspicious behavior.

Fixed checkpoint In border search law, a search of vehicles for illegal aliens at a fixed checkpoint on a road within one hundred air miles of the U.S. border. An investigative stop of a car slowed at such a point must be based on reasonable suspicion.

"Fleeing felon" rule A common law rule that allows a police officer to shoot to kill any fleeing felon, whether or not the felon had used deadly force. The rule was brought under the Fourth Amendment by *Tennessee v. Garner* (1985): An officer may now lawfully shoot at a fleeing felon only if the suspect is reasonably believed to be armed and dangerous.

Formal charge rule A rule stating that the right to counsel at a lineup or showup attaches only after the defendant has been formally charged with a crime. In these procedures, the Supreme Court has not applied the critical stage rule.

Formal charges The charges upon which the state intends to prosecute the defendant. A suspect is informally charged with an offense by a police officer's report or arrest warrant or other initial charging document issued by the magistrate after an initial appearance. Formal charges typically are found in a prosecutor's information that has been found by a magistrate to establish probable cause in a bind-over proceeding or in an indictment that has been voted on by a grand jury. Formal charges can only be amended with the approval of a court.

Formal rights In the history of the incorporation doctrine, prior to 1961 the designation of rights located in the Bill of Rights as "formal" (as opposed to "fundamental") meant that they were not incorporated into the Fourteenth Amendment Due Process Clause.

Framers The men involved in the drafting of the U.S. Constitution and the Bill of Rights. It is a narrower term than *founders*, which refers to the individuals who led the rebellion from England and helped to found the federal republic of the United States.

Frisk A colloquial term used to describe a police search of a person who is stopped. A frisk consists of a pat-down of the outer clothing to determine whether the person stopped has a weapon.

"Fruits of the poisonous tree" doctrine A Fourth Amendment doctrine stating that evidence derived from illegally seized evidence cannot be used by the prosecution. The doctrine applies to confessions if an otherwise valid confession is obtained from a suspect who is illegally detained.

Fundamental fairness A meaning attached to due process—that is, a procedure violates due process if the procedure is deemed by a court to be fundamentally unfair. It is another way of stating the "due process approach," so that for a court to decide if a procedure is fundamentally unfair, it must examine the totality of the circumstances.

Fundamental rights test The test by which it is decided whether a right located in the Bill of Rights is to be incorporated into the Due Process Clause of the Fourteenth Amendment by a process of selective incorporation and made applicable to the states. A right that is "fundamental" must be incorporated, but one deemed "formal" need not.

Fusion center A terrorism prevention and response center. Fusion centers gather and combine data on individuals from official crime and homeland security data bases, and also from private sector data banks. More than seventy exist and are used by police departments. They were initiated by the Homeland Security and Justice departments in the early 2000s.

General-reasonableness construction In Fourth Amendment jurisprudence, a conservative doctrine that emphasized the idea that the constitutionality of a search and seizure is to be decided by whether it is reasonable.

General warrant A search warrant without a limit. A general warrant violates the particularity requirement of the Fourth Amendment. The term was used at the time of the Revolution by Americans to describe the writs of assistance issued by colonial governors.

Grand jury A jury summoned to hear charges against those accused of crime to determine whether there is enough evidence for the accused to stand trial. The common law grand jury (i.e., the "large" jury) consists of twenty-three people and decides whether to indict by a majority vote.

Habeas corpus, writ of A judicial writ requiring that a person claiming illegal detention be brought to court forthwith to determine the legality of the detention.

Hearsay evidence A statement, other than one made by the declarant while testifying at the trial or hearing, offered in evidence to prove the truth of the matter asserted. In ordinary affairs, hearsay evidence may be reliable, but a hearsay statement cannot be subject to cross-examination. The general rule of evidence is that hearsay statements are not admissible, but there are numerous exceptions to the hearsay evidence rule.

Hierarchy of constitutional rights The Burger Court's rulings in criminal procedure have tended to be more supportive of Fifth and Sixth Amendment rights in comparison to the Fourth Amendment, especially the Fourth Amendment exclusionary rule, which is treated as a right of lesser status.

Hierarchy of courts Courts may be ranked by their authority to declare precedent, with a supreme court establishing common law rules that must be followed by all courts "below" it, and an intermediate appellate court having such authority over trial courts.

Hierarchy of law The relative authority of law derives from the body that creates it; thus constitutional law is superior to legislation, which may in turn abolish or modify court-made common law.

Holding The legal principle to be drawn from the opinion or decision. In an appellate case, the holding includes the rule and the facts on which the decision rests.

Hot pursuit A common law right of a police officer to follow a felon across jurisdictional lines or to enter a house or other area protected by a Fourth Amendment expectation of privacy to make an arrest if the officer is in hot pursuit—that is, closely following the felon.

Human rights A special class of rights held by a person simply by virtue of being human; moral rights grounded in the equal moral dignity of each person that can and should be made legally binding in national, regional, or international law.

Hung jury A hung jury is one that cannot reach a verdict of guilty or not guilty in a trial. The judge usually will exhort a jury to continue to deliberate. If the jury is hopelessly deadlocked, the judge declares a mistrial, allowing the prosecutor, in his or her discretion, to retry the defendant.

Hypothetical person test In entrapment law, an element of the "objective test," where the inducement offered by the government agent is so great as to persuade people other than those who are ready and willing to commit the crime.

Identification parade British term for a lineup.

Illegal arrest An arrest that is made by an officer who has no legal authority or jurisdiction to make such an arrest—for example, where an officer arrests a person in a foreign state. Where a suspect is brought into the jurisdiction of a court on the basis of an illegal arrest, the court does not thereby lose jurisdiction to try the case.

Immunity In criminal law, a binding promise by the government, allowed by statute, to not prosecute a person in return for the person's testimony in another prosecution. Immunity is granted to override the person's privilege against self-incrimination. See also *transactional immunity* and *use immunity*.

Impaneling a jury A process whereby the clerk of court makes up a list of the jurors selected for a particular trial.

Impeach To challenge the truthfulness of a witness by presenting evidence that tends to contradict the testimony or to show that for some other reason the witness might have lied.

Impound To seize and take an item, such as an automobile, into the lawful custody of a court or law enforcement agency. An impoundment is a prelude to an inventory search, and the rules of many police departments require an inventory search following an impoundment.

In camera Hearings held in the judge's chamber, away from the public and the jury.

Incompetent evidence Evidence that is relevant to prove an issue but is not allowed to be used in the trial because of other policy considerations; generally, inadmissible evidence. Examples are hearsay or unconstitutionally seized evidence.

Incorporation by reference The method of making one document of any kind become a part of a separate document by referring to the former in the latter.

Incorporation doctrine The constitutional doctrine by which provisions of the Bill of Rights become "incorporated" (in a rough analogy to the legal concept of incorporation by reference) into the Fourteenth Amendment and thus are made applicable to the states. See selective incorporation; total incorporation.

Incorporation plus The incorporation doctrine plus the ability of courts to apply the due process approach where a specific right in the Bill of Rights does not apply.

Inculpatory Tending to establish guilt or to incriminate. Compare *exculpatory*.

Independent source An exception to the "fruits of the poisonous tree" doctrine. It comes into play when the evidence in question also was obtained in a lawful manner via an independent source.

Index crime One of eight felonies counted by the FBI to construct a "crime index." The index crimes are murder or nonnegligent manslaughter, rape, robbery, aggravated assault, burglary, automobile theft, larceny, and arson.

Indictment A formal, written criminal accusation voted on by a grand jury, setting out the charges (crimes) for which the defendant must stand trial.

Indigent Needy; poor. An indigent defendant is a person without funds to hire a lawyer for his or her defense and is entitled to appointed counsel by operation of the Sixth and Fourteenth Amendments.

Inducement In entrapment law, the benefits offered by an undercover agent to commit a crime.

Industrial curtilage The privacy protection of the curtilage rule under search and seizure law applies not only to private homes but also to commercial property.

Inevitable discovery A Fourth Amendment doctrine that overlooks unconstitutional police acts so as not to exclude evidence if the evidence would have been discovered in any event.

Inferior courts Lower courts; for example, trial courts, which are "below" appellate courts in the judicial hierarchy.

Information A formal, written, criminal accusation drawn up by a prosecutor, setting out the charges (crimes) for which the defendant must stand trial. An information replaces the indictment in many states and often follows the bind-over decision.

Initial appearance The hearing before a magistrate that occurs typically within twenty-four hours after a defendant's arrest. The purposes of the hearing are to inform the defendant of the charges, take an initial plea, set bail, and determine whether a defendant has an attorney. The initial appearance is known as the "arraignment on the [arrest] warrant" in some states.

Injunction A court order requiring that a party perform some act or refrain from some act; a remedy in an action in a court of equity or in a court with equitable powers.

In loco parentis The doctrine that a schoolteacher stands in the place of a parent and may exercise parental authority. The Supreme Court has ruled that this is *not* a basis for a search of a public school student under the Fourth Amendment.

In personam **jurisdiction** The jurisdiction a court has over a person in its custody. A court does not lose *in personam* jurisdiction if a defendant was brought into the court's custody as the result of an illegal arrest.

In-presence rule In the law of arrest, the general common law rule is that a police officer can arrest a person for a misdemeanor only if the crime was committed in the officer's presence. Exceptions for traffic violations and domestic violence have been created by statute.

Inquisitorial trial The mode of trial in Europe and most countries, except England and former English colonies, based on Roman law in civil law countries. Distinguishing features include cases are developed by civil service prosecutors operating under judicial instruction; defendants are under a general obligation to answer some questions in the preliminary stages but need not answer at trial; defendants' silence may be used against them; the judge plays an active role in the trial by questioning witnesses; and there is no independent jury, although jurors may advise the professional judges.

Internal passport Official personal identification. In some countries, residents must carry personal identification at all times; in the United States, under the Fourth Amendment, there can be no general obligation to carry an internal passport or to provide identification without an arrest or stop.

Interrogation Generally, to question. In criminal procedure, the term refers more specifically to the series of questions posed by the police to a suspect or a witness in an effort to solve a crime. Interrogation may also include the functional equivalent of questioning whereby actions by the police are designed to elicit incriminating statements from a suspect.

Inventory and return A sworn document prepared by law enforcement officers who have been issued and have executed a search warrant, indicating the execution of the warrant and itemizing the items seized.

Inventory search A search made for the purpose of making an inventory—that is, a detailed list of articles of property.

Investigative stop The forceful stopping of a person for field questioning when reasonable suspicion exists to believe that the person is involved in criminal activity. Also called a "*Terry* stop."

Invidious discrimination The kind of distinction based on race, gender, or other irrational factor that allows a court to determine that a distinction caused by law violates the rights of a person to the "equal protection of the laws" under the Fourteenth Amendment. Not every legal distinction between people is invidious.

Involuntary confession A confession is involuntary if it was induced by interrogation that included coercion, threats of coercion, or promises of lenient treatment. An involuntary confession is not admissible in court.

Ipse dixit "He himself said it"; a bare assertion resting on the authority of the individual.

Irrelevant evidence Evidence that does not logically pertain to the issue to be decided.

Judicial craftsmanship The quality of a judge's opinions, based on the intensity of the judge's legal scholarship, the judge's understanding of issues, and the caliber of the judge's writing style.

Judicial federalism In constitutional criminal procedure, the interaction between federal and state constitutional rights. The Fourteenth Amendment establishes a "constitutional floor" of minimum standards of rights that cannot be violated by a state; above this "floor" a state may grant additional rights under its own constitution or statutes. See also *adequate and independent state grounds*.

Judicial independence The right and the actual ability of a court to decide cases on the basis of the facts and its interpretation of law without interference from other branches of the government; a vital aspect of the rule of law. Judicial independence is made more certain by the appointment of judges for good behavior and by the provision of Article III that the compensation of federal judges shall not be diminished.

Judicial philosophy An aspect of judicial statesmanship—whether a judge favors judicial restraint or judicial activism.

Judicial policy An aspect of judicial statesmanship—what particular policy views a judge may hold on any issue. For example, in criminal procedure, some justices are identified by their voting patterns as being "pro-prosecution," others as "pro-defense," and others as "middle of the road."

Judicial restraint A philosophy of the judicial function holding that judges should not make broad rulings that have legislative effect.

Judicial review The authority of a court to review a statute and declare it null and void if the statute is in conflict with a provision of the state or federal constitution.

Judicial statesmanship The ability of Supreme Court justices to write opinions that properly guide the nation.

Jurisdiction Legal power or authority.

Jurisprudence The philosophy of law; also, a body of rules in a subfield of law—for example, "criminal jurisprudence."

Jury deliberation In deciding on a verdict, a jury is supposed to discuss the evidence, and not simply take a vote.

Jury independence The right of a jury to determine the facts of a case independently without judicial interference. This right was held to be a part of the common law jury process in *Bushell's* case (1670).

Jury nullification The idea that a jury may disregard the legal instruction of the judge and render a verdict purely on the basis of conscience or feelings. Although this happens, it is not usually authorized by legal doctrine.

Jury pool The group of prospective jurors called to the courthouse from which juries are chosen.

Jury trial The trial of a matter before a jury. Jury trials are guaranteed by the U.S. Constitution (Art. III, § 2) and by the Sixth and Seventh Amendments. Compare *bench trial*.

Jury wheel A physical device or electronic system for the storage and random selection of the names or identifying numbers of prospective jurors.

Just Compensation Clause A clause in the Fifth Amendment stating that "private property [shall not] be taken for public use without just compensation." This provision was in effect incorporated as a due process right that federal courts applied against state takings (*Chicago, Burlington and Quincy Railroad Co. v. Chicago*, 1897) in an era when personal rights were not incorporated, thus creating a double standard.

Justice A judge of the Supreme Court.

"Key man" method A method of selecting members of petit or grand juries whereby a judge picks a small number of jury commissioners known to him personally, and the commissioners in turn select people known to them for the grand jury. This method, which dates back to the nineteenth century and tends to perpetuate established power relationships in county government while keeping minorities or new residents from jury service, is no longer used.

"Knock and announce" rule The common law rule that before an officer may open or break in the door to a premises to execute a search warrant, the officer must announce the presence of police and demand entry. It was declared to be a constitutional rule in *Wilson v. Arkansas* (1995). Compare *no-knock warrant*.

Law A body of written rules issued by legitimate sources of order in a state (e.g., the legislature or the appellate courts) and designed to guide and control the actions of citizens. Law also derives from the text of a written constitution and, in common law jurisdictions, from the opinions of appellate judges.

Law of the land A phrase in Magna Carta, indicating that no peer could be punished except by "the law of the land," believed to express the concept of due process.

Least intrusive means When a constitutional liberty collides with a state action required to maintain order, courts at times require that the state's intrusion be done in a manner that intrudes the least on individual privacy. Such a rule has not been applied to arrest or stop under the Fourth Amendment.

Legal doctrine The common law process of case interpretation results in the development of rules that arise from the decisions of numerous similar, but not identical, cases. The rules in a related body of law are formed into legal doctrines. Over time, the rationales for such doctrines often change or erode. Thus many legal doctrines of the common law often have a life cycle of birth, a period of growth and utility, change, and decline.

Legal fiction A legal doctrine or assumption that may not be true but that is adopted in order to achieve a beneficial end. For example, the idea that entrapment is a criminal defense that is inferred by the legislature is a legal fiction adopted by judges who first announced the doctrine.

Legal reasoning The mental process of ratiocination by a judge, by which the rules of an earlier case are discerned and applied to a case at hand. Legal reasoning is not a mechanical process and is considered a branch of jurisprudence or legal philosophy. See also *precedent*.

Legislative history The background and events, including committee reports, hearings, and floor debates, leading up to the enactment of a law (including constitutional provisions). Such history is important to courts when they are required to determine the legislative intent of a particular statute.

Liberty A political theory that undergirds criminal procedure. It connotes that the purpose of government is to allow individuals maximum freedom to pursue their individual and collective goals within the Rule of Law.

Lineup A police identification procedure by which the suspect in a crime is exhibited before the victim or witness to determine if the suspect committed the offense. In a lineup, the suspect is lined up with other individuals for purposes of identification.

Magistrate An inferior (i.e., lower) judicial officer; any judge; or any public civil officer with executive or judicial authority.

Magna Carta (1215) A charter of liberties sworn by King John of England to his barons. Its "law of the land" clause is believed to be the forerunner of due process.

Mandamus, writ of A judicial writ ordering a government officer to perform some "ministerial act"—that is, an act required by law over which the officer has no discretion to not carry out.

Master jury list The master list compiled by a county or district jury commission from the most widely available lists of eligible voters, including voting registration lists, driver's license and state identification lists, and city directories. Jury venires are drawn from the master jury list. Also called a "jury wheel."

Material witness A person who can give testimony that no one else, or very few other people, can give. A material witness may be held by the state against his or her will to ensure testimony.

Media ride-along A practice of some police departments to invite news reporters, photographers, and broadcast journalists to accompany officers during the execution of warrants. Media ride-alongs were held to violate the Fourth Amendment rights of householders in *Wilson v. Layne* (1999).

Merchant's privilege A statutory right enacted in most states that allows security personnel to conduct brief investigatory detentions of suspected shoppers—an act that would be tortious or criminal if carried out by ordinary citizens.

Missouri Compromise A compromise measure adopted by Congress in 1820 declaring that slavery could not be introduced into new states north of the southern boundary of Missouri. The compromise paired the admission of new free and slave states into the Union as a way of maintaining parity between the North and the South. It was designed to preserve the Union and to prevent sectional conflicts from erupting into disunion or civil war. An 1850 extension was declared unconstitutional in *Scott v. Sandford* (1857), hastening the Civil War.

Mistaken arrest An arrest that is based on probable cause but results in the arrest of a person who is not, in fact, the suspect. A police officer who makes such an arrest is protected against civil liability; a private person who makes a mistaken citizen's arrest is subject to a tort action for false imprisonment. A statutory exception exists; see *merchant's privilege*.

Mixed question of law and fact A question depending for solution on questions of both law and fact, but really a question of either law or fact to be decided by either judge or jury.

Motion An application made to a court to obtain an order requiring some act to be done in the favor of the applicant.

Multiple-district prosecution A practice of federal prosecutors whereby an enterprise is simultaneously prosecuted in several districts in which the enterprise does business. This is generally viewed as an unfair prosecution tactic.

Multiple representation A situation in which one attorney represents two or more defendants in the same matter. The defendants may be tried in the same or in different (severed) trials. See also *conflict of interest*.

Neutral and detached magistrate A phrase from *Johnson v. United States* (1948) explaining the rationale for Fourth Amendment search warrants: that a judicial officer is less partisan than a police officer in deciding whether probable cause exists on the basis of the institutional role and traditions of the judicial officer.

No-knock warrant A warrant that explicitly authorizes police officers to enter a premises without knocking and announcing their presence, based on probable cause to believe that the occupants are likely to immediately destroy contraband or pose a threat of deadly violence to officers executing the warrant. Compare *"knock and announce" rule*.

Nonincorporation era A period designated in this text as falling between the ratification of the Bill of Rights in 1791 and the ratification of the Civil War amendments in 1870, when it was clear doctrine that the Bill of Rights was not intended to be applied to the states. Thereafter, the issue became contested.

Notice The due process requirement that a defendant be informed in writing of the precise crimes charged and the facts on which those charges are based. The defendant can be tried only on those charges.

Novel disseisin A medieval English writ that set up an efficient procedure to determine the rightful possession of land taken by force. It utilized a precursor to the modern jury to determine facts.

Nulla poena sine lege "No punishment without law."

Nullum crimen sine lege "No crime without law."

Objective test In entrapment law, the view held by a minority of Supreme Court justices and a minority of the states that entrapment should be based on whether the conduct of the police reached such a level as would induce a hypothetical person to engage in the criminal behavior.

Open fields Private land not protected against police trespass under the Fourth Amendment. Compare *curtilage*.

Opinion The essay written by the majority in an appellate court trial, expounding the law that applies to the case and giving the reasons for its decision. A signed majority opinion is primarily written by the named judge, but the judges in the majority may have suggested that certain points be included or excluded. Individual judges may write concurring or dissenting opinions. Compare *per curiam opinion*.

Order The lawful limits placed on the freedom of individuals to maintain the "domestic tranquility" that is a necessary function of government. The contrast to liberty cannot be absolute because public order is necessary for individuals and groups to enjoy their liberty.

Ordered liberty A resonant phrase found in *Palko v. Connecticut* (1937) and other cases that encapsulates the tension between two fundamental aspects of American governance: liberty and order.

Originalism A theory of constitutional interpretation that holds that judges must apply the Constitution in accordance with the true intent of the Framers. The theory is based on the principle of separation of powers and the idea that judges should not "make" law. Opponents argue that the true intent of the Framers cannot be known with certainty in regard to broad constitutional rights (e.g., due process) and that changing conditions require justices to interpret provisions to meet contemporary needs.

Outrageous conduct test See *due process defense*.

Overrule To replace with a different ruling. When an appellate court finds that one of its prior decisions was incorrect or unsound, it may overrule the prior case and replace it with a different ruling. Thus, strictly speaking, an appellate court is not bound by its own precedent. See also *reverse*.

Parallel right Prior to the incorporation of the Bill of Rights, the Supreme Court established certain rights under the Due Process Clause that were parallel to rights found in the Bill of Rights but were not applied with the same level of certainty. An example is the Sixth Amendment rule stating that counsel was automatically required in every federal felony trial, unless waived, whereas due process required states to provide counsel for indigents only if special circumstances existed.

Parliamentary supremacy The English system in which the statute (a declaration of the legislature) is superior to any written or unwritten constitutional provision or custom.

Particularity requirement The requirement, drawn from the Fourth Amendment, that search warrants "particularly describ[e] the place to be searched, and the persons or things to be seized." The opposite is a general warrant, which the Fourth Amendment was designed to abolish.

Pattern and practice suit A review of a local police department by the U.S. Justice Department for discriminatory patterns and practices. Under the law passed in 1994, a special master can be appointed to oversee modifications in the training and supervision provided by the local police department.

Peer In England, a member of the nobility. Originally, "jury of peers" meant that non-nobles could not sit on juries to judge the guilt of peers. In modern usage, the term refers to equals. A "jury of peers" in America is composed of fellow citizens, without regard to class, gender, race or ethnicity, economic status, or other irrelevant attributes.

Pen register A device that electronically registers the telephone numbers with which a particular telephone connects, without recording the contents of the conversations.

Per curiam opinion An unsigned opinion written by the entire appellate court.

Peremptory challenge In the voir dire, each side has a limited number of challenges that may be used to excuse a prospective juror even though the person has not exhibited any clear bias. Recently, the Supreme Court has limited the ability of parties to exercise peremptory challenges in ways that are based primarily on race or gender. See also *voir dire*.

Persuasive authority When an appellate court follows the reasoning of another court, even though the other court has no power to set binding precedent for the appellate court, the opinion followed is called "persuasive authority."

Pervasively regulated industry In the law of administrative searches, an administrative warrant is not required to search the place of a "pervasively regulated" industry.

Petit jury The common law, twelve-person trial jury that has the authority to determine the facts and to render a verdict in criminal trials. *Petit* is the French word for "small" and refers to the size of the jury in contrast to the twenty-three-person grand jury.

Petty crime A crime that may be tried without a jury.

Plain feel rule The concept that evidence seized in plain view includes evidence lawfully felt by police and that is immediately apparent as contraband.

Plain statement The U.S. Supreme Court will not disturb a state court criminal procedure ruling if the state opinion includes a plain statement that the ruling is based on adequate and independent state grounds.

Plain view Contraband that is located in a public place or in a private place where an officer has a right to be present may be seized "in plain view" without a search warrant.

Plurality opinion A decision of the Supreme Court (or any appellate court) that is based on a vote of less than a majority. A plurality opinion occurs when there are concurring opinions but fewer than five justices (if nine justices participate) agree on the reason for a rule. Plurality opinions represent the law but do not have the same authority as majority opinions, and they are more easily subject to being overruled.

Police officer expertise In *Terry v. Ohio* (1968), the traditional rule that a Fourth Amendment seizure of a person may be based only on probable cause was eased to allow a temporary stop on the basis of reasonable suspicion based in part on the fact that the on-the-street situation was evaluated by a police officer applying his or her special expertise. This element of *Terry* was dropped when the Court decided that reasonable suspicion could be based on the hearsay statement of an informant.

Police power A concept of constitutional law that state governments have plenary or general authority to pass laws for the health, safety, morals, general welfare, and good ordering of the people.

Police state A state in which the government exercises rigid and repressive controls over the social, economic, and political life of the population. It typically exhibits elements of totalitarianism and social control, and there is usually little or no distinction between the law and the exercise of political power by the executive.

Precedent In law, an adjudged case or decision of a court that furnishes authority for an identical or similar case that arises afterward on a similar question of law. See also *legal reasoning*.

Predisposition In entrapment law, a defendant's state of mind that is inclined toward the commission of the crime in question prior to the police "encouragement" activity.

Prejudice In appellate procedure, an error that occurred at the trial or pretrial stage that was the likely cause of the guilty verdict. In some instances, a conviction will not be overturned unless the appellate court finds prejudice in this sense.

Prejudice the case The second prong of the rule stating that the ineffective assistance of counsel in a criminal trial violates the Sixth Amendment rights of the defendant. Prejudice in this sense is made out by a reasonable probability that, absent the errors, the fact-finder would have had a reasonable doubt respecting guilt.

Preliminary examination A hearing before a magistrate to determine whether the prosecution can present sufficient evidence to establish probable cause to show that the defendant committed a crime. If so, the judge binds the defendant over for trial.

Presentment Instead of an indictment, a formal accusation based on the personal knowledge of the grand jurors themselves. This is rare or nonexistent today. Also, an accusation initiated by the grand jury; an instruction to the prosecutor to prepare an indictment.

Presumption of innocence A feature of the common law trial that is guaranteed by the Due Process Clause. It requires that the burden of proof of guilt of every element of a crime be placed on the prosecution and that the burden be proof beyond a reasonable doubt.

Pretext search A search of an automobile made by an officer who stops the car on the objectively correct basis of a traffic violation even though the traffic stop is made for the real purpose of searching the automobile for drugs. Pretext searches were found to be valid in *Whren v. United States* (1996).

Preventive detention The confinement of a defendant before trial; the formal denial of bail on the grounds that the defendant is likely to commit a crime while awaiting trial.

Prima facie case Sufficient evidence to require a criminal defendant to proceed with his or her case; evidence to sustain an indictment; if uncontradicted, evidence sufficient to establish a guilty verdict.

Private law Law involving the rights and disputes of private individuals, groups, and corporations. Subject matter areas include contracts, property, torts (the law of injuries), commercial law, and civil procedure. Compare *public law*.

Privilege In law, a particular benefit or a right or immunity against or beyond the course of law. Thus the privilege against self-incrimination allows a person to refuse to testify despite the general legal obligation that a person has to testify when summoned to a court.

Privileges or Immunities Clause A clause in Section 1 of the Fourteenth Amendment stating that "[n]o state shall make or enforce any law which shall abridge the privileges or immunities of citizens of the United States." This clause was thought to be the basis of the idea of "total incorporation." The clause was interpreted in such a manner as to render it a virtual nullity by the *Slaughterhouse Cases* (1873).

Probable cause A standard to determine whether sufficient evidence exists that allows a prudent person to conclude that other facts exist; also, the standard for the validity of an arrest, a lawful search, and the holding of a person for trial.

Pro bono publico For the good of the public. Attorneys take a certain number of cases without fee to represent indigents *pro bono*.

Procedural law Law that prescribes the methods of enforcing rights that are breached and includes rules of jurisdiction and the serving of legal process (e.g., a summons) and rules that guide the conduct of a trial.

Pro forma "As a matter of form." A decision made *pro forma* is made not because it is right, but merely to facilitate further proceedings.

Property theory The concept that Fourth Amendment rights are based on an individual's legal claims over private property. This theory has been superseded by the "expectation of privacy" concept.

Prosecutor's information A formal document charging a defendant with crimes on which the defendant must stand trial. The prosecutor's information replaces the grand jury indictment in some states; it is used in jurisdictions with grand juries in cases in which the defendant waives the right to a grand jury.

Pro se **defense** Latin for "for himself"; self-representation.

Protective sweep "A quick and limited search of a premises, incident to an arrest and conducted to protect the safety of police officers or others. It is narrowly confined to a cursory visual inspection of those places in which a person might be hiding" (*Maryland v. Buie,* 1990).

Public defender A full-time paid position as a defense attorney for indigent defendants. Caseloads of public defenders tend to be high.

Public duty doctrine The idea that, under ordinary circumstances, a municipality or other government unit is not liable to an individual for tortious failure to provide adequate police protection because the duty to provide such protection is owed to the public generally rather than to specific individuals.

Public law Law that concerns the powers of government bodies and involves disputes between government departments or between private individuals and government. Public law includes such subjects as constitutional law, administrative law, tax law, substantive criminal law, and criminal procedure. Compare *private law.*

Qualified immunity Rule that government agents need not answer in law to civil claims for wrongful conduct when their conduct does not violate clearly established statutory or constitutional rights of which a reasonable person would have known. Immunity is claimed before trial in a motion for summary judgment.

Quash To annul or make void—for example, to quash an indictment.

Radio bulletin Information transmitted by radio from one police department to others, notifying them that a specified individual is wanted for a crime. Evidence seized in a search incident to an arrest made on the basis of such a report is admissible, even if there was no probable cause for the initial report; it has the effect of a mistaken arrest.

Real evidence Physical evidence.

Reasonable doubt The standard of evidence sufficiency for a verdict of guilt in a criminal case; a doubt that would cause a prudent person to hesitate before acting in a matter of personal importance; not a fanciful doubt.

Reasonable force Police may use reasonable force to make an arrest, as determined by all the facts and circumstances.

Reasonableness Clause The first part of the Fourth Amendment, which prohibits "unreasonable searches and seizures." It is the basis of the *general-reasonableness construction.*

Reasonable suspicion The standard of evidence sufficiency that allows a police officer to temporarily stop a person in order to ask questions to either dispel the suspicion or gather probable cause to arrest; defined as articulable facts that would lead an experienced police officer to believe that a crime has been, is, or is about to be committed.

Reconstruction amendments See *Civil War amendments.*

Recoupment The process by which the state or unit of local government later recovers the cost of providing assistance of counsel to a formerly indigent defendant.

Rehnquist Court The Supreme Court during the period that William Rehnquist was chief justice of the United States (1986–2005); a conservative period in criminal procedure.

Release on recognizance Pretrial release of a defendant without the posting of a bail bond or other security, but only on the promise of the defendant to return to court for trial or further proceedings.

Remand An action of an appellate court sending all or part of a case back to the lower court without overturning the lower court's ruling but with instructions for further proceedings that may range from conducting a new trial to entering a proper judgment.

Remedial law Law that determines the actual benefits or remedies that a successful party to a lawsuit will receive. In criminal law, the "remedy" is the punishment meted out. In constitutional criminal procedure, the exclusion of evidence after a court has decided that evidence has been seized in violation of a person's constitutional protections is deemed a "remedy."

Reparation Repayment; a remedy designed to restore the injured party to his or her position before the injury occurred.

Representative cross section In jury selection, the larger groups of prospective jurors on the jury master list or jury wheel, or the venire, must be selected in a manner to be most likely to statistically represent the larger community under federal law and constitutional standards of equal protection. The particular jury panel (or venire) from which the petit jury is selected, and the jury itself, need not be a representative sample. Also called "fair cross section."

Republicanism The political theory that government is instituted for the benefit of all the people. Formal classes, nobility, and monarchy are inconsistent with republicanism. As a result, for example, "jury of peers" means a jury of citizens.

Retained counsel A lawyer hired by and paid for by the defendant.

Reverse To disagree with the decision of a lower court and order it to change the decision to conform to the appellate court ruling. See also *overrule.*

Roadblock An automobile that crashes into a police roadblock effectively arrests the driver; injuries that result from such a crash may be the basis of police liability for effecting the arrest with excessive force if the placement of the roadblock was unreasonable.

Roving patrol The stop of a vehicle being driven on the highway by border patrol agents within one hundred air miles of the U.S. border. Compare *fixed checkpoint stop.*

Rule application A major function of trial courts: to decide cases in accordance with the law. Compare *rule making.*

Rule making A process of interpretation of prior cases, statutes, or constitutional provisions by appellate courts by which rules of common law are developed. See also *legal reasoning* and *precedent.*

Rule of Law The political and legal principle that the government must act in accordance with established law and that government officers must not exceed their authority. Also known as the "principle of legality."

Scope of a search incident to arrest The area that the police may search within an arrested person's immediate control to ensure officer safety and to secure evidence from destruction. The scope may include an area to which the arrested person may reach, but does not authorize the search of an entire premises.

Screening The preliminary hearing and grand jury are pretrial screening devices. They screen out cases where probable cause cannot be established in order to prevent hasty or oppressive prosecutions.

Search incident to arrest The search of an individual and the person's immediate surroundings that takes place immediately upon or after the person's arrest. The search, a part of the arrest process, is for weapons (to protect the arresting officer and others) and for incriminating evidence.

Secret informant A person who supplies evidence of probable cause to obtain a search warrant but whose identity is not divulged to the magistrate in order to maintain the security of an investigation; may be an undercover police agent or a paid "snitch."

Section 1983 suit A civil lawsuit in federal court against a state officer, or a municipality, who has violated the federal or constitutional rights of an individual; established under 42 U.S.C. § 1983 and enacted in 1871 as a civil rights act designed to curb the terrorism of the Ku Klux Klan. Also called a "constitutional tort suit."

Sectional conflict Political, economic, or social friction between different sections of the nation; specifically, the conflict between the North and the South before the Civil War.

Seditious libel A writing intended to incite the people to overthrow the government by force. Seditious libel was long a political crime in Great Britain.

Seizure of the person Under the Fourth Amendment, an arrest or stop.

Selective incorporation The concept that individual provisions of the Bill of Rights may become incorporated into the Fourteenth Amendment due process doctrine if the Supreme Court finds that such provisions are fundamental to our system of ordered liberty. Compare *total incorporation*.

Selective prosecution The prosecution of a defendant singled out for charging on impermissible grounds, such as race, religion, or political beliefs or for exercising constitutional rights.

Self-representation A situation in which the defendant waives the right to appointed counsel and conducts his or her own defense.

Separation of powers A political and constitutional doctrine that states that the essential functions of one branch of government are not to be exercised by another.

Sequester a jury To require a jury to be removed from the community during the period of a trial to avoid the contaminating influences of news accounts or discussions with friends, relatives, and strangers about a crime. Sequestered juries were required in the early common law but are now rare.

"Shocks the conscience" test A formula for the due process test to determine when police action is so egregious during arrest and/or search activity so as to violate the Due Process Clause. The test excludes the notions of the application of the Fourth Amendment and its exclusionary rule.

Showup A one-to-one confrontation between the suspect and a witness to the crime. It is a form of pretrial identification procedure in which the suspect is confronted by or exposed to the victim or witness to a crime.

"Silver platter" doctrine Rules established by the U.S. Supreme Court under its supervisory power prior to *Mapp v. Ohio* (1961) that forbade federal officers from supplying state officers with illegally seized evidence and then testifying as to the evidence in state court, and from receiving illegally seized evidence from state officers.

"Sneak and peak" warrant Under the USA PATRIOT Act, a judge issuing a search warrant may allow a delay in notifying the owner of a premises that a warrant was executed if the court finds that immediate notification may endanger a person's life or safety, or cause a suspect to flee from prosecution, tamper with evidence, or intimidate witnesses. Such warrant may be issued in any kind of case, not just terrorism investigations.

Sobriety checklane A roadblock set up by police to determine whether drivers are under the influence of intoxicants. A detention at a sobriety checklane is not considered a stop for criminal investigation, and therefore such temporary detentions without individualized suspicion do not violate the Fourth Amendment.

Source city An element of the drug courier profile is that the place from which the stopped person has traveled from is a "source city" for drugs.

Source of law The specific institution that created the law: Courts develop rules of common law; legislatures and governors fashion legislation, and constitutions are made by "the people" in special constitutional conventions or by special rules for amending constitutions.

Sovereign immunity The legal doctrine that prevents a party from suing a government unless the government by law allows itself to be sued.

Special circumstances rule The rule of *Powell v. Alabama* (1932) that due process requires a state to pay for a lawyer for an indigent defendant only if special circumstances exist.

Special needs doctrine A doctrine developed by Supreme Court constitutional adjudication that allows government agents to search without a warrant, and possibly without individualized suspicion, when searches are conducted for "special needs beyond the normal need for law enforcement," such as the search of the bags of public school students suspected of carrying items banned under school rules.

Standby counsel Counsel appointed at the discretion of the trial judge to advise a *pro se* defendant and to ensure that the defendant's rights are not undermined.

Standing The ability to sue in court. A plaintiff has standing to sue in a court when there is an actual case or controversy between the plaintiff and a defendant that a court may hear and decide; the party must have a real stake in the outcome of the case. In Fourth Amendment cases, a defendant's standing is based on the violation of his or her reasonable expectation of privacy.

Stare decisis The doctrine of precedent.

Status quo ante The existing state of things before a given time.

Stop The temporary restraint of a person's mobility by a police officer where the officer has reasonable suspicion to believe that the person stopped has just committed, is committing, or is about to commit a crime. The practice was declared constitutional in *Terry v. Ohio* (1968).

Stop and frisk The colloquial term for a *Terry* stop. See *investigative stop*.

Strip search See *body cavity search*.

Sub rosa Confidential, secret.

Subjective test The majority rule of entrapment law; the theory that entrapment occurs when police activity plants the idea of the crime in a person who is otherwise not predisposed to commit it.

Subpoena The command of a court to a witness to appear at a certain time and place to give testimony. A grand jury also has subpoena power. If the subpoena is not obeyed, the person refusing to appear may be held in contempt of court and fined or jailed until he or she agrees to cooperate with the legal process. The word derives from the Latin, meaning under (*sub*) the penalty (*poena*) of law.

Subpoena *ad testificandum* A subpoena to testify.

Subpoena *duces tecum* A subpoena to produce documents, books, papers, and other materials for inspection.

Subpoena power The power of a court, or the authority granted by statute to a grand jury or other body, to compel a person or organization to testify or to produce documents or things under a threat of being cited for contempt of court.

Substantive due process The concept that the Due Process Clause includes substantive rights that limit the power of government to legislate. The concept was applied to property rights by the Supreme Court before the New Deal. The right to privacy that supports the abortion rights case, *Roe v. Wade* (1973), is a substantive due process concept.

Substantive law Establishes, defines, and governs rights, powers, obligations, and freedoms. Rules of substantive law, for example, establish contractual obligations, property rights, or the right to recovery for personal injuries (torts). Substantive criminal law defines crimes such as homicide and theft and defenses such as insanity.

Suggestibility The human process by which the subtle reactions of one person can influence the thinking of another. In *U.S. v. Wade* (1967), suggestibility was the legal basis for the Supreme Court to determine that state action existed as the basis for its holding.

Sui generis Of its own kind or class; unique; the only one of its kind.

Supervisory authority The power of higher courts to require lower courts to act within their jurisdiction. The power is sometimes used by the U.S. Supreme Court as a way of enforcing appropriate standards on federal law enforcement agencies.

Supremacy Clause Article VI, paragraph 2, of the U.S. Constitution, which declares that the Constitution, laws, and treaties of the federal government are the "Supreme Law of the Land"—that is, that they supersede state laws when there is a conflict between state and federal law.

Target theory The idea that when the prosecution seeks to introduce evidence against a defendant, the defendant has an automatic right to challenge the legality of the seizure. The target theory would eliminate the need for "standing" in Fourth Amendment cases.

Telephonic warrant A search warrant, allowed by the Federal Rules of Criminal Procedure and the laws of some states, that allows a magistrate to receive an affidavit from an officer by telephonic means.

***Terry* stop** See *stop* and *stop and frisk*.

Testimonial evidence Evidence elicited from a witness to prove a fact, as opposed to documentary evidence or real (i.e., tangible) evidence.

Thermal imaging An advanced technology used by law enforcement to detect whether an unusually high amount of heat is emanating from a premises, suggesting the commercial cultivation of marijuana indoors.

Third degree The process of securing a confession or information from a suspect or a prisoner by prolonged questioning, the use of threats, or actual violence.

Tort A private or civil wrong or injury, other than a breach of contract, for which the court will provide a remedy in the form of an action for damages.

Total incorporation The concept that the Privileges and Immunities Clause or the Due Process Clause of the Fourteenth Amendment was intended to make the first eight amendments of the Bill of Rights applicable to the states upon ratification in 1868. Compare *selective incorporation*.

Totality of circumstances See *due process approach*.

Transactional immunity A blanket immunity against prosecution for the crimes about which the immunized witness is testifying. Transactional immunity offers broader protection than use immunity.

Treason Clause Provisions of U.S. Constitution (Art. 3, § 3) that limit the definition and punishment of treason against the United States. Such limitation implies that the republican government intended to be liberal and restrained and to operate within the rule of law.

Trespass A common law tort; the wrongful interference with property rights.

Trial *de novo* A second or new trial that is held as if no decision had been previously rendered. A trial *de novo* is not an appeal because the facts are relitigated. Also called "*de novo* trial."

True bill An indictment that has not yet been signed by the prosecuting attorney. When the grand jury votes to indict an accused person, it issues a "true bill"; when it votes against indicting an accused, it votes a "no bill."

Two-pronged test In Fourth Amendment law, a test to be applied by a magistrate on whether or not to issue a warrant where information has been supplied by a secret informant. The test requires that the affidavit indicate the basis of the informant's knowledge and a basis for accepting the informant's veracity. The test has been supplanted by a "totality of the circumstances" test.

Undercover agent A police officer who lies about his or her identity in order to pose as a victim or criminal for the purposes of law enforcement investigation.

Unenumerated Rights Clause The Ninth Amendment to the constitution: "The enumeration in the Constitution, of certain rights, shall not be construed to deny or disparage others retained by the people." The Supreme Court has yet to decide a case that declares an unenumerated right to be protected by the Court.

Unindicted co-conspirator A person, named by a grand jury, against whom there may be a prima facie case of guilt but who for some reason is not indicted.

Universal Declaration of Human Rights A formal document promulgated by the United Nations in 1948 that attempts to codify all human rights. Many provisions are borrowed from or parallel to provisions of the Bill of Rights.

Use immunity A form of immunity that prohibits the witness's compelled testimony or its fruits from being used in any way to prosecute the witness. However, the witness may be prosecuted on the basis of independently obtained evidence. Use immunity offers a narrower protection than transactional immunity.

Vagrancy statute A law making it a crime to loiter. Older vagrancy statutes prior to *Papachristou v. City of Jacksonville* (1972) were quite vague and gave police discretion to arrest whom they would; modern vagrancy statutes are closely tailored to describe particular types of vagrancy, such as house prowling or streetwalking prostitution.

Venire In jury practice, the list of jurors summoned to serve during a particular court term; from the Latin word meaning "to come"; to appear in court.

Venue The locality or place where a trial is to be held. The usual rule is that it is to be held in the locality (often the county) in which the crime was committed. The venue may be changed if there is so much publicity in the locality that it becomes impossible to select an unbiased jury.

Verdict The decision of a jury or judge as finder of fact in a criminal case; guilty or not guilty of the charges.

Vindictive prosecution The bringing of new and more serious charges against the defendant simply because he or she has exercised statutory or constitutional rights.

Voir dire The process of jury selection involving the questioning of prospective jurors in order to determine biases. After questioning, the juror is either selected or dismissed for cause or for no reason under the peremptory challenge. See also *challenge for cause* and *peremptory challenge*.

Voluntariness test A common law rule developed in the eighteenth and nineteenth centuries claiming that any confession obtained by violence, threats, or promises is involuntary and is excluded from evidence. The rule was adopted as a due process rule that the Supreme Court applied to state cases. The rule still exists as a backup to the *Miranda* rule.

Waiver The waiver of a Fifth or Sixth Amendment right must be an "intelligent relinquishment or abandonment of a known right or privilege." See also *consent*.

Waiver of counsel A defendant can waive the right to the assistance of counsel if the decision is made with full knowledge of the right. A trial judge cannot require that a defendant be represented by counsel if the defendant can do a minimally competent job of defending himself or herself.

Waiver trial A trial that occurs when the defendant waives the right to a jury and opts to be tried by a sole judge. Also called "bench trial."

Warrant Generally, the command of an authority; in criminal procedure, a written order issued by a judge or magistrate. A search warrant authorizes police officers to search a premises where there is probable cause to believe that contraband is hidden. An arrest warrant authorizes officers to arrest a named person where there is probable cause to believe that the person committed a crime.

Warrant Clause The second clause of the Fourth Amendment specifying rules concerning a search warrant.

Warrantless search A search conducted by an officer without having obtained a search or arrest warrant.

Warrant-preference construction A liberal construction of Fourth Amendment rights that holds that a search is presumptively unreasonable if it is not accompanied by a search warrant unless there exists a narrowly drawn exception to the warrant requirement.

Warren Court The Supreme Court during the period that Earl Warren was chief justice of the United States (1953–1969); a liberal period in criminal procedure.

Whig party A political party in the United States in the first half of the nineteenth century. It was absorbed by the Republican Party in the 1850s.

Wiretap A means of listening in on telephone conversations by electronically intercepting the conversations at some point outside the place where the telephone is located. Also called a "tap."

Work product rule An exception to discovery that exempts materials prepared specifically for litigation, including writings, notes, memoranda, reports on conversations with the defendant or witnesses, research, and confidential materials that an attorney has developed in preparation for trial.

Writ of assistance General search warrants issued by British colonial governors in America to enforce the hated Stamp Act. These writs and their enforcement became political issues that helped to ignite the American Revolution.

Wrongful conviction Technically this can refer to the conviction of a factually guilty defendant obtained by means that violate due process. Today, this term more typically refers to the conviction of a factually innocent person where another person committed the crime, no crime ever occured, or a jury was in error regarding a defense such as self-defense.

TABLE OF CASES

SUBJECT INDEX